Augsburg College
WITHDRAWN
George Sverdrup Library
Minneapolis, Minnesota 55404

The American
Immigration Collection

Immigration: Select Documents and Case Records

EDITH ABBOTT

Arno Press and The New York Times
NEW YORK 1969

Copyright © 1969 by Arno Press, Inc.

All rights reserved

*

Library of Congress Catalog Card No. 69-18754

*

Reprinted from a copy in the
Howard College Library

*

Manufactured in the United States of America

IMMIGRATION
SELECT DOCUMENTS
AND CASE RECORDS

THE UNIVERSITY OF CHICAGO PRESS
CHICAGO, ILLINOIS

THE BAKER & TAYLOR COMPANY
NEW YORK

THE CAMBRIDGE UNIVERSITY PRESS
LONDON

THE MARUZEN-KABUSHIKI-KAISHA
TOKYO, OSAKA, KYOTO, FUKUOKA, SENDAI

THE MISSION BOOK COMPANY
SHANGHAI

IMMIGRATION
SELECT DOCUMENTS
AND CASE RECORDS

By

EDITH ABBOTT

*Dean of the Graduate School of Social Service Administration
in The University of Chicago*

THE UNIVERSITY OF CHICAGO PRESS
CHICAGO · ILLINOIS

COPYRIGHT 1924 BY
THE UNIVERSITY OF CHICAGO

All Rights Reserved

Published March 1924
Second Impression September 1924

Composed and Printed By
The University of Chicago Press
Chicago, Illinois, U.S.A.

PREFACE

This is not a book of "readings." It is a source book, compiled to make available for students of immigration a collection of published documents and hitherto unpublished case records that will throw light on some of the historical, legal, and social aspects of the subject. Like "source books" and "case books" in other fields, it may be more difficult for the teacher to use than a simpler textbook; but, if the work is harder, it is also more rewarding both for the teacher and for the student. Although prepared for the use of classes in graduate schools of social service, it is not, of course, designed as a single "text," for neither this nor any other one volume will meet the needs of mature students. It is hoped, however, that this collection of material will make it possible for large numbers of students to use conveniently an important series of documents heretofore accessible to very few, and will place at the disposal of students and others interested in immigration problems a body of case records hitherto not available in any form.

A few words of explanation are needed about the selection both of the documents and of the case records. The documents have been selected largely from official sources, and represent, for the most part, reports that are now out of print, and, therefore, not conveniently available for the use of large classes. In the controversial field of modern immigration policies an attempt has been made to present documents on more than one side of a question on which public opinion has been or is clearly divided. This is notably the case, for example, with regard to the "literacy test" and the "per centum" or "quota" act. Comments are, of course, withheld since it is the purpose of the book to present carefully selected source material and to leave the conclusions to others. Finally, it should be explained that no documents relating to Asiatic immigration are presented. The study of European immigration should not be complicated for the student by confusing it with the very different problems of Chinese and Japanese immigration.

The adaptation of the case records of social agencies for study purposes is in the experimental stage. Many of the records in this book have, however, been used in mimeographed form in the classroom, and their value tested. Perhaps a few comments are needed on the editing of the records. The original form of the record has been followed as closely as possible; that is, instead of a summary of the record in "story" form, an attempt has been made to follow the record as literally as possible in order that the actual methods of procedure may appear. Certain changes have been found necessary, however, for the sake of clarity and brevity. Thus, the language of the foreign visitors has at times necessarily been changed, spelling corrected, and punctuation altered whenever the meaning was not clear. The "face card" of the record is omitted to save space, but the essential facts on the face card usually appear in one of the first interviews. Certain other condensations and omissions have also been necessary.

The records that are used were not chosen on the theory that the work was always as well done or as promptly done as it ought to have been. But it is believed that bona fide case records will be interesting and helpful to students and to those interested in work for immigrants, whether the method of treatment is approved or not. A record of work actually done is always useful as a basis for criticism and discussion.

Case records have another use. They throw light, as do few other documents, on the administration of social legislation. It is believed that the case records dealing with the admission, exclusion, and deportation of immigrants (Part II, Section IV) will be of special interest to those studying the administration of our federal immigration laws, and some of the records in the last section (Part III, Section II) will be interesting to students of local administrative problems.

Social workers and investigators have long recognized the great value of the material that our social agencies have been storing away in the files of their case records during the last thirty years since the "case-paper" system has been more and more widely adopted. The system was designed primarily, if not solely, to make it possible for the social worker to assist those families and individuals who have come for help, but the problem has been to make these records available for more general and perhaps permanent uses. Especially exigent, since the growth of professional schools in the social-service field, has been the demand for collections of case records for teaching purposes.

The records in this volume have been selected from the files of the Immigrants' Protective League of Chicago and the Immigrants' Commission of Illinois, and cover approximately the last ten years. An attempt was made at first to include also records from other cities, but this was given up because it was difficult to find nonsectarian agencies working with immigrants that used the case-record system, and it seemed important to use a series of records in which the standard method of case recording had been used. Moreover, the local records seemed to be varied enough and sufficiently typical of conditions found in many other communities to make it practicable to use a single series of records that were in standardized form.

In conclusion, I wish to express my deep obligations to my sister, Grace Abbott, who was from 1908 to 1921, except for an occasional leave of absence, in charge of the work of the Immigrants' Protective League and the Immigrants' Commission. Many of the social case records I have used were selected for me by my sister, and I have also had the benefit of her suggestions and criticisms. I am also greatly indebted to my long-time friend and colleague, Miss S. P. Breckinridge, for help at many points, and to Miss Marian Schibsby, the director of the Immigrants' Protective League since 1921. I wish also to express my indebtedness to Dean L. C. Marshall for a stimulating and helpful interest in the preparation of a source book in this field. Finally, my thanks are due to Miss M. E. Lavery for the preparation of the Index, for assistance in proofreading, and other laborious tasks.

EDITH ABBOTT

UNIVERSITY OF CHICAGO
January 15, 1924

THE UNIVERSITY OF CHICAGO SOCIAL SERVICE SERIES

PREFATORY NOTE

The present volume is the first in a series which will include both source books and treatises in the social-science field. The series has been planned primarily to provide adequate scientific material heretofore not available for the use of students in the Graduate School of Social Service Administration of the University of Chicago and other institutions of the same kind. In a recent report on the work of such schools (James H. Tufts, *Education and Training for Social Work*, 1923), attention was called to the "general complaint of the lack of sufficient source material in form which is most desirable for critical teaching and which can be placed in the hands of all students." The report went further and expressed confidence that ultimately the schools themselves would meet this need and added: "Publication of such material is an illustration of what has been previously referred to as one of the two great functions of the professional school; namely, raising the standard of the profession through research and publication."

This volume and the others that are nearing completion represent an attempt on the part of the members of the Faculty of one of these schools to help to meet this need. It is believed, however, that the different volumes in the series will be useful, not only to those interested in social service, but to others whose interests lie in other departments of the wide field of the social sciences.

TABLE OF CONTENTS

PART ONE

THE JOURNEY OF THE IMMIGRANT

	PAGE
INTRODUCTORY NOTE	3

SECTION I. THE EARLY EMIGRANT SHIPS AND ATTEMPTED REGULATION OF STEERAGE CONDITIONS, 1751–1882

1. A Colonial Steerage Act. *Acts of the Province of Massachusetts Bay* . . . 6
2. The Ocean Voyage in the Eighteenth Century. *Gottlieb Mittelberger* . . . 7
3. Condition of Arriving Immigrants, 1789. *Phineas Bond* . 9
4. Condition of German Redemptioners on the American Ship "General Wayne," April 27, 1805. *German Society of Philadelphia* . . . 11
5. Incidents of the Ocean Voyage for Immigrants, 1817–18. *Niles' Weekly Register* . . . 13
6. Exploitation of Emigrants by Passenger Brokers, 1822. *Report of the American Chamber of Commerce in Liverpool* . 15
7. Disastrous Effects of the Steerage Voyage, 1827. *Niles' Weekly Register* . . . 16
8. Attitude of the House of Commons to Proposed Revival of Passenger Regulations, 1828. *Hansard's Parliamentary Debates* 17
9. An Emigrant Ship from Londonderry to Montreal, 1834. *Montreal Advertiser* . . . 20
10. The Failure of the British Passenger Act of 1835. *Earl of Durham* . . . 21
11. A British Economist on "The Policy of the Passenger Acts." *John Ramsay McCulloch* . . . 24
12. Transport Conditions and Activities of Steamship Agents in Europe, 1840–45. *A. van der Straten-Ponthoz* . . . 26
13. Complaints of the Almshouse Commissioner of New York City, 1846 . . . 27
14. Resolution of the New York Legislature on the Regulation of Emigrant Ships, 1847 . . . 28
15. The Irish "Fever-Ships," 1840–50. *John Francis Maguire* 29
16. The British Passenger Bill in the House of Commons, 1848. *Hansard's Parliamentary Debates* . . . 33
17. The British Emigrant-carrying Trade, 1850. *Edward Everett Hale* . . . 37

TABLE OF CONTENTS

	PAGE
18. Some Problems of Steerage Regulation in 1854. *U.S. Senate Reports*	40
19. Protest of the New York Legislature against Sufferings of Emigrant Passengers, 1854	42
20. The Fever Ship "Leibnitz," 1868. *N.Y. Commissioners of Emigration*	42
21. American Cholera Epidemics and Emigrant Ships, 1832–73. *Dr. Elisha Harris*	47
22. Steerage Conditions in 1873. *Senate Executive Documents*	48
23. The Close of the Old Period, 1882. *Congressional Record*	53

SECTION II. THE JOURNEY IN THE TWENTIETH CENTURY

1. Emigration Regulations of European Countries. *International Labour Office*	59
2. The Protection of Emigrants before Departure. *International Labour Office*	63
3. Land Transport of Emigrants. *International Emigration Commission*	69
4. Inspection of Emigrants Abroad. *U.S. Immigration Commission*	71
5. Care of Emigrants by Steamship Companies before Embarkation at Liverpool. *U.S. Immigration Commission*	76
6. The Steerage Problem in 1921. *International Emigration Commission*	79
7. The Italian Method of Enforcing Regulations for Protecting Emigrants on the Voyage. *Bollettino della Emigrazione*	82
8. Experiences of an Investigator in the Steerage. *U.S. Immigration Commission*	82
9. A German-Russian Frontier Control Station and a Journey in the Steerage. *U.S. Immigration Commission*	86
10. Recommendations of the United States Immigration Commission, 1911	92

PART TWO

THE ADMISSION, EXCLUSION, AND EXPULSION OF ALIENS

INTRODUCTORY NOTE 97

SECTION I. ADMISSION OF IMMIGRANTS UNDER STATE LAWS, 1788–1882

1. Legislation Relating to the Landing of Foreign Convicts, 1788–89
  A. Pennsylvania. *Pennsylvania Statutes at Large* . . . 102
  B. South Carolina. *Laws of South Carolina* 103

TABLE OF CONTENTS

	PAGE
2. Treatment of Foreign Paupers under State Poor Laws	
A. New York. *Laws of New York*	104
B. Massachusetts. *Laws of Massachusetts*	105
3. Admission of Immigrants under State Legislation, 1820–33	
A. New York. *Laws of New York*	106
B. Massachusetts. *Laws of Massachusetts*	108
C. Maryland. *Laws of Maryland*	108
4. Comments on the Admission of Foreign Paupers, 1830–35. *Niles' Weekly Register*	110
5. The Burden of Foreign Pauperism in Massachusetts, 1836. *U.S. House Documents*	112
6. Deportation of Paupers from Europe: Letters from United States Consuls. *U.S. Senate Documents*	114
7. The First United States Supreme Court Decision Relating to the State Passenger Acts, 1837. *U.S. Supreme Court Reports*	118
8. Evasion of the State Immigration Laws, 1837. *Aaron Clark*	122
9. Friedrich List's Proposed Method of Preventing Emigration of Foreign Convicts, 1837. *U.S. House Reports*	127
10. Consular Reports on Importation of Foreign Criminals and Paupers, 1845–46. *U.S. Senate Documents*	128
11. Frauds upon Immigrants after Arrival at the Port of New York	
A. Testimony of the Secretary of a Protective Society, 1846. *New York Assembly Documents*	130
B. A Legislative Committee's Report, 1848. *New York Assembly Documents*	131
12. The Abuses of the Bonding System under the New York State Passenger Acts before 1847	
A. Neglect of Poor Immigrants. *George H. Purser*	134
B. Necessity of Public Care for Destitute Immigrants. *New York Board of Aldermen*	136
C. Demand for a Head Tax System by a Citizens' Mass Meeting in New York	139
13. An Act for the Protection of Emigrants, 1848. *Laws of New York*	140
14. Emigration of German Paupers, 1847. *U.S. House Documents*	142
15. Activities of the German Society of New York, 1848. *New York Assembly Documents*	144
16. A Defense of the State Head Tax System, 1849. *U.S. Supreme Court Reports*	147
17. State Head Taxes Declared Unconstitutional, 1849. *U.S. Supreme Court Reports*	151
18. Undesirable Immigrants: "Who Shall Remedy the Evil?" *U.S. House Documents*	157

19. Some Early Cases of Deportation
   A. "An Infamous Case of Extradition," 1855. *Boston Daily Advertiser* 160
   B. "Another Shame for Massachusetts," 1855. *The Citizen* 161
20. "Retransportation" of Foreign Paupers Proposed, 1856. *New York Assembly Documents* 162
21. An Argument against Federal Control of Immigration. *Friedrich Kapp* 164
22. New York Commutation System Declared Unconstitutional, 1875. *U.S. Supreme Court Reports* 168
23. The Institutions Established by the New York Commissioners of Emigration. *Friedrich Kapp*
   A. The State Emigrant Refuge and Hospital, Ward's Island 172
   B. The Castle Garden Landing Depot 174
24. National Legislation for the Protection of Immigrants Recommended. *Frank B. Sanborn* 176

SECTION II. THE FEDERAL IMMIGRATION LAWS: PROVISIONS, ADMINISTRATION, AND REASONS FOR ENACTMENT
   1. The Beginning of Modern Immigration Legislation, 1882. *U.S. Statutes at Large* 181
   2. The Enforcement of the Federal Immigration Laws, 1882–91. *"Ford Committee" Report* 182
   3. Early Difficulties with Contract Labor Legislation. *U.S. Industrial Commission* 186
   4. The Contract Labor Law: Typical Cases. *U.S. Commissioner-General of Immigration* 188
   5. An Early Advocate of a Literacy Test to Restrict Immigration. *Henry Cabot Lodge* 192
   6. The First Presidential Veto of a Literacy Test Act. *Grover Cleveland* 198
   7. Recommendations for Changes in the Federal Immigration Laws, 1911. *U.S. Immigration Commission* 201
   8. The Later Veto Messages Dealing with the Literacy Test
      A. Criticisms of the Literacy Test. *Secretary Nagel* . . . 211
      B. President Wilson's First Veto Message of 1915 . . . 213
   9. The Comprehensive Immigration Act of 1917. *U.S. Statutes at Large* 215
   10. The Alien Anarchist Act of 1918–20. *U.S. Statutes at Large* 231
   11. Emergency Immigration Legislation: The Quota System Recommended. *U.S. Senate Reports* 232
   12. The "Quota" Act, 1921–22. *U.S. Statutes at Large* . . . 240
   13. Criticism of the "Quota" Law. *Minority Report U.S. House Committee* 242
   14. Line Inspection at Ellis Island. *E. H. Mullan* 244

TABLE OF CONTENTS

SECTION III. SELECTED IMMIGRATION CASES: COURT DECISIONS

PAGE

1. "Persons Likely to Become a Public Charge" Defined. (*Wallis* v. *U.S. ex rel. Mannara*) 252
2. "Ability to Earn a Living" and Economic Conditions in the United States. (*Gegiow* v. *Uhl*) 254
3. Surgeon's Certificate of Physical Defect. (*Canfora* v. *Williams*) 256
4. Finality of Decision by Immigration Authorities; Certificate of Physical Defect. (*Barlin* v. *Rodgers*) 258
5. Crime Involving Moral Turpitude Defined. (*Prentis* v. *Stathakos*) 261
6. Interpretation of the Contract Labor Law. (*Church of the Holy Trinity* v. *United States*) 262
7. The Spirit and Purpose of the Contract Labor Statutes. (*Botis* v. *Davies*) 264
8. Contract Labor: "Implied Offer of Employment." (*U.S.* v. *International Silver Co.*) 268
9. Domiciled Alien Subject to Exclusion. (*Lewis* v. *Frick*) . . 270
10. Detention When Deportation Is Impossible. (*Ex parte Matthews*) 273
11. Expulsion: What Constitutes a "Fair Hearing." (*Whitfield* v. *Hanges*) 275
12. Status of a "Philosophic Anarchist" Defined. (*Turner* v. *Williams*) 280
13. Advocacy of Assassination and of Unlawful Destruction of Property during a Strike. (*Diamond* v. *Uhl*) 284
14. Expulsion: "Controlling Legal Principles." (*Colyer* v. *Skeffington*) 288

SECTION IV. SOCIAL CASE RECORDS: DETENTION, EXCLUSION, DEPORTATION, EXPULSION, BRINGING OVER RELATIVES

1. Mary Baranowski. (*Temporary Detention*) 298
2. Joseph and Rachel Rosenbaum. (*Exclusion—Feeble-minded*) 299
3. Karolina Klimek. (*Exclusion—Contagious Disease*) . . . 300
4. The Family of Nicholas Kapalo. (*Sick Child—Curable Disease*) 303
5. Nicolo and Francesca Archieri. (*Contagious Disease—Hospital Treatment*) 307
6. Josef Roeder. (*Contagious Disease—Hospital Treatment*) . 309
7. Katerina Kosice. (*Excluded—Contagious Disease*) . . . 310
8. Carl and Johanna Peterson and Their Children. (*Sick Child—Possible Permanent Disability*) 313
9. Rachel and Kazia Aronoff. (*Attempted Deportation—Hospital Treatment—Contagious Disease*) 319

		PAGE
10.	Wife and Children of Michael Kubelik. (*Excluded—Contagious Disease*)	332
11.	Andrew Cesky. (*Detention—Citizenship Claimed*)	339
12.	Bozena Jozka. (*Excluded—Fugitive from Justice*)	340
13.	Henry Pahl. (*Excluded—Criminal Record*)	341
14.	Max Rothstein. (*Stowaway*)	342
15.	Rozalia Slovienski. (*Misstatement to Inspector*)	344
16.	Maryana Rosozki. (*Young Woman Manifested to Unsatisfactory Address*)	345
17.	Rosa Markewicz. (*Exclusion—Young Woman Manifested to Male Relatives*)	346
18.	Three Polish Girls: Maryanna Czarnecowska, Maryanna Kruza, Maryanna Vraza. (*Exclusion—Unsatisfactory Conditions in Chicago*)	347
19.	Axenia Balik. (*Exclusion—Girl Manifested to Uncle*)	348
20.	Greta Schmidt. (*Exclusion—Young Woman Assisted by "Cousin"*)	350
21.	Rachel Badad. (*Girl Coming to Fiancé—Admission on Bond*)	352
22.	Esther Litski. (*Illegal Entry*)	355
23.	Riva Leah Zimber. (*Detention of Deformed Alien Abroad*)	363
24.	Mary Zabern. (*Arrival without Passport*)	365
25.	Jacob Joseph. (*Illiteracy—Temporary Admission*)	367
26.	Rosa Livitzki. (*Illiteracy—Difficulties of Temporary Admission*)	368
27.	Marie Tabescu. (*Temporary Admission—Illiteracy*)	372
28.	Marie Boreija. (*Detention of Mother of an Illegitimate Child*)	375
29.	Marya and Anastasia Bazanoff. (*Temporary Admission without Bond*)	377
30.	Margaret Heckert and Leopold Koenig. (*Unmarried Man and Woman Traveling Together*)	382
31.	Lida and Marie Stirbei. (*A "Common-Law" Wife and Illegitimate Child*)	384
32.	The Family of Steve Jassy. (*Detention of Domiciled Alien, Contagious Disease*)	386
33.	The Family of Joseph Revesz. (*Quota—Exclusion of Wife and Children*)	392
34.	Annie and Katherine Szoeke. (*Operation of the Quota Law*)	395
35.	Carmella Fiori. (*Temporary Detention—Excess Quota*)	397
36.	The Wife and Child of Solomon Stein. (*Detention Abroad—Contagious Diseases—Exhausted Quota*)	399
37.	Elena Petrovna. (*Attempted Expulsion—Charges of Immorality*)	400
38.	Peter Johann Simann. (*Deportation after Landing—Public Charge within One Year*)	402

TABLE OF CONTENTS xix

39. Patrick O'Brien. (*Request for Deportation after Landing*) . 404
40. Michael Stefan. (*Expulsion Recommended*) 405
41. Demetrius Spiros. (*Deportation after Temporary Admission—Certified Physical Defect*) 406
42. Stephanie Woloski. (*Expulsion Prevented by the War*) . . 408
43. Katie Schultz. (*Expulsion—Feeble-minded*) 420
44. Hedwig Kallen. (*Bringing over Relatives—Physical Defects*) 427
45. Mary Kizis. (*Bringing over Relatives—Passport Visa*) . . 444
46. Maryana Batuchkin. (*Inquiry about Detention Abroad*) . . 447
47. Sophia Joseph. (*Passport Visa*) 451
48. The Mother of Isadore Sukloff. (*Passport Visa—Trachoma—Hospital Treatment—Deportation*) 452
49. The Wife of Paul Benjamin. (*Difficulties with the "Near East" Quota*) 454

PART THREE

DOMESTIC IMMIGRATION PROBLEMS

INTRODUCTORY NOTE 463

SECTION I. SOCIAL CONDITIONS AND PROBLEMS IN RELATION TO IMMIGRATION

1. The End of the Immigrant's Journey
   A. Conditions at Immigration Stations. *Advisory Committee U.S. Bureau of Immigration* 466
   B. Protection of Immigrant Girls on Arrival at Interior Points. *Immigrants' Protective League* 468
2. Finding Employment
   A. Methods of Securing Immigrant Labor. *U.S. Immigration Commission* 474
   B. Private Employment Agencies. *New Jersey Commission of Immigration* 478
   C. The Unskilled Immigrant in Chicago. *Immigrants' Protective League* 481
3. Labor Camps and Labor-Camp Inspection
   A. Labor Camps in New York. *New York Commission of Immigration* 485
   B. Labor-Camp Inspection in California. *California Commission of Immigration* 489
4. Peonage in Relation to Immigration. *U.S. Immigration Commission* 492
5. Immigrant Banks. *U.S. Immigration Commission* . . . 498
6. Transmission of Savings to Europe. *U.S. Immigration Commission* 510

TABLE OF CONTENTS

	PAGE
7. The Immigrant and the Notary Public. *New Jersey Commission of Immigration*	514
8. The Immigrant in the Courts. *Massachusetts Commission on Immigration*	521
9. The Immigrant Lodger. *Massachusetts Commission on Immigration*	526
10. Land Purchasing by Immigrants	
A. The Immigrant and Agriculture in New Jersey. *New Jersey Commission of Immigration*	532
B. Typical Land Fraud Cases in California. *California Commission of Immigration*	536
11. A Review of the Pre-War Immigration Situation. *U.S. Immigration Commission*	539
12. Educational Needs of Immigrants	
A. Lack of Provision for Alien Education in Illinois. *Illinois Immigrants' Commission*	549
B. The Problem of Adult Education in Passaic, N.J. *U.S. Bureau of Education*	556
C. Financing Immigrant Education. *U.S. Bureau of Education*	560
D. Need of State Supervision of Private Schools. *Massachusetts Commission on Immigration*	563
13. State Aid for Immigrant Education	
A. Massachusetts. *Massachusetts Department of Education*	566
B. New York. *New York University Bulletin*	572
14. Protection for Immigrants through a State Bureau	
A. Massachusetts. *Massachusetts Bureau of Immigration*	580
B. California. *California Commission of Immigration*	587

SECTION II. SOCIAL CASE RECORDS: PROTECTIVE WORK

   Difficulties in Reaching Final Destination

1. Anna Oleson. (*The Train Journey from Ellis Island*)	597
2. Allegra Salvatore. (*Wrong Destination*)	602
3. Take Jonika. (*Stranded en Route*)	604
4. Raisa and Maria Pavlik. (*Lost Tickets and Refund*)	604
5. Paul Swanson. (*Arrival at Wrong Station*)	606
6. Maria Kowal. (*A Ruthenian Woman Ill en Route to Oregon*)	606

   Immigrant Girls Traveling Alone Who Failed to Reach Destination

7. Emelia Anderson	609
8. Maryana Pajakiewicz and Theresa Olshefski	609
9. Rozalia Kazewski	610
10. Maryana Kucynski	610
11. Rozalia Michaelis and Marya Kopek	611
12. Marya Piotowski. (*Tracing a "Lost" Polish Girl*)	611
13. Mathild "Moreik." (*Tracing a "Lost" Magyar Girl*)	613

Lost-Baggage Cases
- 14. Sofia Zichi 617
- 15. Valeria Rezka 618
- 16. Domenica Levitzka 618
- 17. The Grunbergs' Baggage Case 619

Finding Employment
- 18. Steve Blaha, Tony Arnescu, and Jan Ombroz. (*A "Harvesting Laborers" Advertisement*) 621
- 19. Ivan Orliniecky. (*Employment-Agency Refund*) ... 622
- 20. Peter Ganos, Seven Other Greek Men, and an Employment Agency 623
- 21. Andrew Michaliuk. (*Buying Jobs for Friends*) ... 624
- 22. The Employment-Agency Case of Alexander Mercu and Eight Other Roumanians 627

Other Employment Cases
- 23. The Wage Claim of Frank Capek and Seven Other Bohemian Immigrant Workers 633
- 24. Twenty-five Bulgarian Laborers in Mississippi ... 646
- 25. Joseph Toney. (*Difficulties of a Chicago Laborer Sent to a Wisconsin "Job"*) 650

Recent Immigrants on Farms
- 26. Vlas Deniches. (*A Russian on a Wisconsin Farm*) . 652
- 27. Vincent and Lucija Kleinaitis. (*A Lithuanian Family in the Beetfields*) 655
- 28. Andrei Ivanov. (*A Russian Immigrant on a Kansas Farm*) 664
- 29. Choma Lutnicki. (*A Russian Laborer in Tennessee*) . 673

"Lawyers" and Notaries
- 30. Domenica Mareska. (*Industrial Insurance: Incompetent Legal Advice*) 676
- 31. Martzen and Vassey Rubnik. (*Complaint against a "Lawyer"*) 685
- 32. Jan Piotowski and Others. (*Notary-Public Complaint*) 690

Purchase of Steamship Tickets and Foreign Exchange
- 33. Kasimir Pulaski. (*A Returned Immigrant's Non-receipt of Money*) 695
- 34. Paul Nicholayev. (*Purchase of Steamship Tickets*) . . 698
- 35. Ignace Prystalski and Others. (*Issue of Worthless Steamship Tickets*) 699
- 36. Michael Dobinski. (*Transmitting Money*) 707
- 37. Jan Witkowski. (*Attempted Purchase of Steamship Tickets*) 708
- 38. Filiat Halaban. (*Steamship-Ticket Refund*) 712
- 39. Strophin Trepoff. (*Steamship-Ticket Complaint*) . . 715

Immigrant Girls in Chicago

 40. Lucja Krajulis. (*An Unmarried Lithuanian Mother*) . 718
 41. Anastazia Pastrozna. (*A Russian Rooming-House Case*) 719
 42. Nina Talpiniuk. (*Assisting a Croatian Girl*) . . . 722

Industrial Accidents and Workingmen's Compensation

 43. John Jalchow. (*Settlement without Controversy, Indiana Law*) 723
 44. Andrey Valeskii. (*Workmen's Compensation under the Wisconsin Law*) 725
 45. Bozena Jez. (*Injury in Box Factory—Legal Aid*) . . 744
 46. Nicolai Naumoff. (*Hand Injured—Compensation by Agreement*). 745
 47. Marie Macek and Three Children. (*Mysterious Homicide—Illinois Industrial Board—Supreme Court*) . . 752
 48. Katherine Saurisaitis and Her Two Children. (*Murder by Fellow-Workman—Illinois Industrial Board—Supreme Court*) 760
 49. Maryana Rusteika and Four Children. (*Fraudulent Insurance—Workmen's Compensation*) 765

Miscellaneous

 50. Marciana Stender. (*Unnecessary Arrest*) 780
 51. Christina Hensinger. (*Unnecessary Commitment to Bridewell*) 780
 52. Marciana Ripalis. (*Non-enforcement of Compulsory Education Law*) 787
 53. Josef and Marya Novak. (*A Croatian Family in Trouble*) 789
 54. Stefan Trimaitis. (*Co-operative Assistance*) 797

SUBJECT INDEX 803

PART I
THE JOURNEY OF THE IMMIGRANT

INTRODUCTORY NOTE

The journey in the steerage should be one of the first subjects of study for American students of immigration. The first immigration laws passed by Congress were laws dealing with the transportation of immigrant passengers; and, at an earlier date, even the colonies passed laws regulating the immigrant passenger traffic. The purpose of the early, as of the modern, laws was of course twofold: to protect the immigrant from disease and death on shipboard and to protect our own communities from the dangers of epidemics brought by the victims of the insanitary ships.

The history of the attempts to regulate the transportation of immigrants is essential to a proper understanding of the steerage laws and steerage problems of the present day; and the documents in Section I were selected to illustrate the condition of the "emigrant ships" at different periods and the effect of the steps taken by various legislative bodies to improve those conditions. An early colonial statute has been selected as Document 1. The horrors of the eighteenth-century ships are described in Documents 2 and 3, and Document 4 shows the terrible sufferings of the "redemptioners" even in the early nineteenth century.

The protection of the immigrant on his journey is a matter of importance to the country that he leaves, that is, to the country of emigration, as well as to the country that receives him, the country of immigration. The first law passed by any emigrating country to protect the immigrant on shipboard was an act of the British Parliament in 1803. Between that date and the period of our Civil War, a long series of so-called "passenger acts" was passed by Parliament; and, later, some of the continental countries passed similar laws. In the United States, Congress also undertook at an early date to regulate steerage conditions and to prevent the landing at American ports of ships that did not meet the requirements of our "passenger acts." The first of these acts of Congress was passed in 1819; and between that date and the Civil War, five later acts or amendments were passed, two in 1847, and the others in 1848, 1855, and 1860. Documents 5 to 12 indicate the problems involved and, in general, the failure of the attempts at regulation. The terrible mortality rates of the "emigrant ships" continued while one law after another was passed by Parliament or Congress, and new regulations were adopted on the Continent. New York, burdened with the care of the sick from the insanitary ships, petitioned Congress for relief, and the new American law of 1847 was largely due to the conditions in New York (Document 13) and the appeal of the state legislature for Congressional action (Document 14).

The famine year of 1847 is forever memorable as the year of the great exodus of the starving and fever-stricken Irish, and the conditions on the "coffin ships" of that year are described in Document 15. In the parliamentary debates of 1848 the mortality among Irish steerage passengers was discussed, and the facts given in Document 16 bear witness to the futility of the legislative restrictions that had been established. How tolerant public opinion often was of the evils in the steerage and how hopeful of each halfway measure of reform is indicated in Edward Everett Hale's account of the immigrant's voyage in 1850 (Document 17).

The report of a Senate investigating committee of 1853-54 (Document 18), a protest from the New York legislature in 1854 (Document 19), a report to the New York Emigration Commissioners in 1868 (Document 20), a physician's account of the relation between immigration and cholera epidemics (Document 21), and the extracts from the report of the Senate investigating committee of 1873 (Document 22) show that the insanitary conditions of the steerage continued decade after decade, in spite of new laws and new ships. The year 1882 marks the beginning of the modern steerage period in the United States, and the law of that year is the basis of steerage regulation by the United States at the present day. In Document 23 will be found extracts from the Congressional debate of 1882, which marked the close of the old period.

There is no period in the nineteenth century that is free from steerage "horrors."[1] Looking back for more than a hundred years at the misery entailed by the failure of all attempts to regulate the steerage problem, the question that presents itself to the student is, Why did these attempts fail? Was it impossible for Parliament and Congress to discover what ought to be done, or was there a lack of courage to take the steps shown by experience to be necessary?

[1] For a valuable account of the history of the transportation of immigrants see Thomas W. Page, "The Transportation of Immigrants before 1870," *Journal of Political Economy*, XIX, 732. See also *Reports of United States Immigration Commission*, XXXIX, 336-485. See also S. C. Johnson, *A History of Emigration from the United Kingdom* (London: Routledge, 1913), chap. v.

The documents in Section II deal with the immigrant's journey in the twentieth century. Documents 1 and 2 describe the restrictions on emigration that still survive in many European states, the regulations for departure prescribed by various countries of emigration, and, in general, the attempts made to exercise official supervision over the departure of would-be immigrants. Immigrants leaving Central and Eastern Europe have a long journey before they reach the ports of embarkation, and the present conditions of land transport for intending immigrants are described in Document 3. In view of our restrictions upon the admission of diseased, defective, or otherwise undesirable aliens, the whole subject of the examination of immigrants before embarkation is one of great importance. An extract from the pre-war report on this subject by the United States Immigration Commission is presented in Document 4, and an account of the actual procedure of caring for immigrants at a great port of departure is given in Document 5. The present-day steerage regulations of various countries are described in the extract from a recent report of the International Labour Office (Document 6.) The Italian method of protecting immigrants on the voyage is worthy of special attention and is prescribed in the Italian law of 1919 (Document 7). There has been no Congressional inquiry into steerage conditions since the investigators of the United States Immigration Commission made their reports in 1908.[1] Documents 8 and 9 describe the steerage conditions found by these investigators.

The report of the Commission (Document 10) called attention to the fact that the enforcement of steerage legislation is a matter of great difficulty, and recommended that our government should make compulsory the adoption of the Italian plan of carrying inspectors on all ships bringing immigrants to our ports. This sole recommendation made by the Commission for the improvement of steerage conditions has never been adopted by Congress.

[1] See, however, *Annual Report, United States Commissioner-General of Immigration, 1914,* Appendix IV, pp. 359–87, for special report on "Dangers of Steerage Voyage for Women and Girls."

SECTION I

THE EARLY EMIGRANT SHIPS AND ATTEMPTED REGULATION OF STEERAGE CONDITIONS, 1751–1882

1. A Colonial Steerage Act, 1751[1]

WHEREAS, Germans and other persons may be imported in so great numbers in one vessel, that through want of necessary room and accommodations, they may often contract mortal and contagious distempers, and thereby occasion not only the death of great numbers of them in their passage, but also by such means on their arrival in this province, those who may survive, may be so infected as to spread the contagion, and be the cause of the death of many others; to the end, therefore, that such an evil practice may be prevented, and inconveniences thence arising avoided as much as may be—

Be it enacted by the Lieutenant-Governor, Council and House of Representatives:

SECTION 1. That from and after the publication of this act, no master or commander of any ship, or other vessel whatsoever, bound to the port of Boston, or elsewhere within this province, shall import into said port of Boston, or into any other port within this province, any greater number of passengers, in any one ship or other vessel, than such only as shall be well provided with good and wholesome meat, drink and other necessaries for passengers and others, during the whole voyage; and shall have room therein to contain, for single freight or passengers of the age of fourteen years or upwards, at least six feet in length, and one foot and six inches in breadth, and if under the age aforesaid, to contain the same length and breadth for every two such passengers.

SEC. 2. And if any master or commander of any ship or other vessel, against the tenor of this act, shall import into this province any one or greater number of passengers not accommodated or provided during his voyage with good and wholesome meat, drink, room and other necessaries as aforesaid, such master or commander shall forfeit and pay, for every passenger so imported into this province, the sum of five pounds. . . . .

Be it further enacted:

SEC. 3. That the commissioner of impost for the time being, or his lawful deputies, in going on board any ship or other vessel importing pas-

[1] Extract from "An Act to Regulate the Importation of Germans and Other Passengers Coming to Settle in This Province, February 6, 1751," *Acts and Resolves of the Province of Massachusetts Bay*, Vol. III (1742–56), chap. xii, pp. 536–37.

sengers, either by his or their view, or otherwise, shall, and is hereby required to, inform himself of the condition and circumstances of the passengers on board, and whether they have been provided for, and accommodated with the provisions, room and other necessaries herein directed; and where at any time a deficiency shall appear to him or any of them, he or they shall forthwith give notice of the same to some one or more of the justices of the peace for the county where the offence is committed, to the end the person or persons delinquent may be sent for, or bound over, to the next court of general sessions of the peace, then and there to answer for such offence.

And be it further enacted:

SEC. 4. That every master or commander of any ship or other vessel importing any passenger or passengers to be landed within this province, who, in their passage hither, or soon after their arrival, may happen to die, leaving goods, chattels, money or other effects on board such ship or other vessel, or in the hands or custody of any such master or commander, every such master or commander within the space of twenty days next after his arrival, or after the decease of every such passenger, shall exhibit to the register of the judge of probate of wills and granting administration, for the county where such goods and effects shall be, a true and perfect inventory, upon oath, of all such goods, chattels, money or other effects, to the end that after payment of all just demands which shall be due to the said master or commander, or to his or their owner or owners, the remainder of such goods and effects may be committed to the custody of some proper person or persons for the benefit of the wife and children, or other kindred, or creditors of the deceased, as the case may require, and the law in such case shall direct.

And be it further enacted:

SEC. 5. That if any such master or commander of any such ship or other vessel shall neglect or refuse to exhibit such an inventory of the goods and effects of any such passenger or passengers so dying as aforesaid, every such master or commander shall forfeit and pay the sum of two hundred pounds, to be recovered and applied as aforesaid.

Passed February 6, 1750–51.

2. The Ocean Voyage in the Eighteenth Century[1]

This journey lasts from the beginning of May to the end of October, fully half a year, amid such hardships as no one is able to describe adequately with their misery.

The cause is because the Rhine-boats from Heilbronn to Holland have to pass by 36 custom-houses, at all of which the ships are examined, which

---

[1] Extract taken by permission from Gottlieb Mittelberger's *Journey to Pennsylvania in the Year 1750 and Return to Germany in the Year 1754*, pp. 18–25; translated by Carl T. Eben. Philadelphia: John Jos. McVey, 1898.

is done when it suits the convenience of the custom-house officials. In the meantime the ships with the people are detained long, so that the passengers have to spend much money. The trip down the Rhine alone lasts therefore 4, 5, and even 6 weeks.

When the ships with the people come to Holland, they are detained there likewise 5 or 6 weeks. . . . .

Both in Rotterdam and in Amsterdam the people are packed densely, like herrings so to say, in the large sea-vessels. One person receives a place of scarcely 2 feet width and 6 feet length in the bedstead, while many a ship carries four to six hundred souls; not to mention the innumerable implements, tools, provisions, water-barrels and other things which likewise occupy much space.

On account of contrary winds it takes the ships sometimes 2, 3, and 4 weeks to make the trip from Holland to Kaupp (Cowes) in England. But when the wind is good, they get there in 8 days or even sooner. . . . . Many suffer want already on the water between Holland and Old England.

When the ships have for the last time weighed their anchors near the city of Kaupp (Cowes) in Old England, the real misery begins with the long voyage. For from there the ships, unless they have good wind, must often sail 8, 9, 10 to 12 weeks before they reach Philadelphia. But even with the best wind the voyage lasts 7 weeks.

But during the voyage there is on board these ships terrible misery, stench, fumes, horror, vomiting, many kinds of seasickness, fever, dysentery, headache, heat, constipation, boils, scurvy, cancer, mouth-rot, and the like, all of which come from old and sharply salted food and meat, also from very bad and foul water, so that many die miserably.

Add to this want of provisions, hunger, thirst, frost, heat, dampness, anxiety, want, afflictions and lamentations, together with other trouble, as c.v. the lice abound so frightfully, especially on sick people, that they can be scraped off the body. The misery reaches the climax when a gale rages for 2 or 3 nights and days, so that everyone believes that the ship will go to the bottom with all human beings on board. In such a visitation the people cry and pray most piteously.

When in such a gale the sea rages and surges, so that the waves rise often like high mountains one above the other, and often tumble over the ship, so that one fears to go down with the ship; when the ship is constantly tossed from side to side by the storm and waves, so that no one can either walk, or sit, or lie, and the closely packed people in the berths are thereby tumbled over each other, both the sick and the well—it will be readily understood that many of these people, none of whom had been prepared for hardships, suffer so terribly from them that they do not survive it. . . . .

Among the healthy, impatience sometimes grows so great and cruel that one curses the other, or himself and the day of his birth, and sometimes come near killing each other. Misery and malice join each other, so that they cheat and rob one another. One always reproaches the other with having persuaded him to undertake the journey. Frequently children cry out against their parents, husbands against their wives and wives against their husbands, brothers and sisters, friends and acquaintances against each other. But most against the soul traffickers.

Many sigh and cry: "Oh, that I were at home again, and if I had to lie in my pig-sty!" Or they say: "O God, if I only had a piece of good bread, or a good fresh drop of water." Many people whimper, sigh and cry piteously for their homes; most of them get homesick. Many hundred people necessarily die and perish in such misery, and must be cast into the sea, which drives their relatives, or those who persuaded them to undertake the journey, to such despair that it is almost impossible to pacify and console them. In a word, the sighing and crying and lamenting on board the ship continues night and day, so as to cause the hearts even of the most hardened to bleed when they hear it. . . . .

At length, when, after a long and tedious voyage, the ships come in sight of land, so that the promontories can be seen, which the people were so eager and anxious to see, all creep from below on deck to see the land from afar, and they weep for joy, and pray and sing, thanking and praising God. The sight of the land makes the people on board the ship, especially the sick and half dead, alive again, so that their hearts leap within them; they shout and rejoice, and are content to bear their misery in patience, in the hope that they may soon reach the land in safety. But alas!

When the ships have landed at Philadelphia after their long voyage, no one is permitted to leave them except those who pay for their passage or can give good security; the others, who cannot pay, must remain on board the ships till they are purchased, and are released from the ships by their purchasers. The sick always fare the worst, for the healthy are naturally preferred and purchased first; and so the sick and wretched must often remain on board in front of the city for two or three weeks, and frequently die, whereas many a one, if he could pay his debt and were permitted to leave the ship immediately, might recover and remain alive. . . . .

3. Condition of Arriving Immigrants, 1789[1]

As to the condition and treatment of the passengers, my Lord,[2] the legislature of Pennsylvania well aware of the consequence of encouraging migrations hither from Europe as the most speedy and effectual mode of contributing to the settlement and of increasing the strength of the country

---

[1] Extract from a letter of Phineas Bond, British consul at Philadelphia, to the British Foreign Office, in the *Annual Report of the American Historical Association, 1896*, I, 643-45.

[2] [The letter is addressed to Lord Carmarthen, afterward Duke of Leeds, secretary for foreign affairs.]

from time to time passed very salutary laws to regulate this trade and to secure the good treatment of the passengers; but these laws were formerly too often evaded—numbers were crowded in small vessels destitute of proper room and accommodations and abridged of the necessary allowance of proper food; by which means the unfortunate emigrants not only suffered greatly but contagious diseases were often introduced into the province—the terms too of paying the passage money were frequently departed from— passengers who embarked as redemptioners were hurried from on shipboard before the limited time for their redemption was expired, and before their friends could have notice of their arrival to interpose their relief and rescue them from servitude. Perhaps, my Lord, no stronger proof can be offered of the wretched situation of these unhappy people than the lists of the different importations would afford. In the list of German passengers which I have carefully perused I observe several instances of upwards of 500 passengers imported in one vessel, this list as I have already remarked was confined prior to the war to *male* passengers of full age who were required to take the oaths of allegiance—so that allowing an additional third for women and children, there have been several instances of between 7 and 800 German passengers crowded in one vessel, and I should presume few of the vessels employed in this trade exceeded 250 or 300 tons burden. The Irish vessels were exceedingly crowded before the War but lately the numbers in each vessel have been less, *only* because fewer passengers have offered.

Formerly, my Lord, a large portion of the passengers from Ireland were redemptioners or indented servants, those who could not redeem themselves by paying their passage money within a limited time were then indented for a term of years to any master who would advance the price of their passages—those who came out as servants were indented in Ireland for so many years to the master or owner of the vessel and the original indenture was either assigned or a new one given upon their arrival in America to the first person who would pay the price demanded for their time. The laws of Pennsylvania require certain freedom dues to be allowed by the master to the servant upon the expiration of the term of servitude. Lately, my Lord, few redemptioners or servants have arrived here from Ireland, the passengers from thence have been chiefly such as have paid their passage before they embarked; in this sort of trade there is very little risk and great profit, the passengers who have arrived in the Delaware this year from Ireland have been for the most part people in tolerable good plight with some property beforehand and who have come to settle as farmers or to engage as artificers in some branch of manufacture. A large embarkation of this description of passengers as well as of redemptioners and servants is expected in the course of next year.

It has been very common of late to publish testimonials from the passengers of the good treatment they have experienced on the voyage from the master.

The practice of bringing passengers hither, my Lord, independent of every consideration as to their personal convenience or inconvenience is detrimental in many respects to Great Britain and profitable to America—as an essential means of extending the population of America it adds to her strength and it diminishes ours by abridging us of so many industrious subjects of the benefit of their increase and of their useful labor—but above all, my Lord, it facilitates the improvement of manufactures by the introduction of various sorts of useful and ingenious artificers. . . . .

4. Condition of German Redemptioners on the American Ship "General Wayne," April 27, 1805[1]

SIR: Having just returned from the errand sent upon by you and the other officers of the German Society, relative to the German redemptioners lately arrived at Perth Amboy, New Jersey, I have thought proper without loss of time to communicate to you in writing, for your and their information, how far I proceeded with the business entrusted me, respecting the said German redemptioners.

Immediately on our arrival at Amboy we went to the river with an intention of going on board the ship "General Wayne," or with an expectation of seeing some of the redemptioners on shore. However, we saw none of them at the time, and the ship was weighing anchor, and soon after set sail fo. New York. By enquiry we found the passengers were deposited in the Jail of Amboy, however not closely confined, having permission granted them by the agent to walk about the place or town. From what I could learn, the captain began to be uneasy, as some of the inhabitants had spoken to him with respect to the malconduct exercised by him toward those unhappy beings, and resolved to leave Amboy and go to New York.

I went to visit those unfortunate people, and in truth they may be called unfortunate. And I must confess I have seen a number of vessels at Philadelphia with redemptioners, but never did I see such a set of miserable beings in my life. Death, to make use of the expression, appeared to be staring them in the face. The complaints were numerous which they made against the captain respecting the bad treatment they received from him on and during the passage. The complaints which I conceive are of the greatest importance I shall briefly state. My intention was to have had them confirmed with their oaths, but as they are made by every one of the passengers I thought it unnecessary. They are that they left Hamburg some time in November last, and arrived at Tönningen, where lay the ship "General Wayne," John Conklin, Master, bound for New York, with whom they entered into a certain agreement, on condition that he, the said Conklin,

[1] Extract from a report to the president of the German Society of Philadelphia taken from the *Records of the Society*, Appendix, Friedrich Kapp, "Immigration and the Commissioners of Emigration of the State of New York," pp. 183–86. New York: The National Press, 1870.

would take them to New York, that during the passage they should be allowed a certain quantity of bread, meat, peas, fish, vinegar, butter, potatoes, tobacco, etc., as also a dram in the morning, as will appear by a reference to the agreement itself, each passenger having one. About fourteen days after they left Tönningen they put into an English port near Portsmouth, where they remained about four weeks; that during that time a British recruiting officer came on board the ship, when the captain informed them that they now had an opportunity of enlisting, that those who so chose to do might, as the recruiting officer was on board the ship. Ten men consented, and entered their names, giving to the other passengers their reasons for so doing, namely, that, having been already put on allowance by the captain, they were apprehensive that, should they stay on board the ship, they should be starved before they arrived in America. Amongst those that enlisted was a man who had a wife and child on board the ship; that eight days after they had thus entered their names they were taken from the ship by the recruiting officer, although some of them wished to withdraw their names, but to no effect; go they must. The woman and her child are now at Amboy, lamenting the loss of the husband and father.

On the last day of their remaining in this British port, the same recruiting officer came the third time on board the ship, when the mate called four or five of the passengers by name, and told them, in the presence of the captain, they must be soldiers and go with the officer. They replied they had no intention of being soldiers, they wished to go to America. . . . . The captain was highly dissatisfied with these men for refusing to go, and declared that they should not have anything to eat on board the ship, that they might starve, and ordered one of them to be flogged for refusing, which was performed, too, in a cruel manner. That the whole of the passengers, when at this British port, complained to the captain that the treatment they received was not such as was agreed to between them at Tönningen. He replied they were not then in Tönningen, neither were they in America, but in England. They then set sail, and after fourteen days had elapsed the captain informed them that they would get nothing to eat except two biscuits, one pint of water, and the eighth part of a pound of meat per day. This regulation continued for two or three weeks, when they one and all declared they could not any longer exist on the small allowance they received; that they must, without doubt, perish. The hunger and thirst being at this time so great, and the children continually crying out for bread and drink, some of the men resolved, at all events, to procure bread, broke open the apartment wherein it was kept, and took some. This was discovered by the captain, as were also those who did the same, when each of them was ordered to, and actually did, receive, after being first tied, a number of lashes on their bare backs well laid on. The whole of the passengers were also punished for this offence. The men received no bread, the women but one biscuit. This continued for nine days, when the men were again allowed one biscuit per day; however, the captain would at least make or proclaim a fast day. In this situation their condition became dreadful, so much so that five and twenty men, women, and children actually perished for the want of bread. . . . . The hunger was so great on board that all the bones about the ship were hunted up by them, pounded with a hammer and eaten; and what is more lamentable, some of the deceased persons, not many hours before their death, crawled on their hands and feet to the captain, and begged him, for God's sake, to give them a mouthful of bread or a drop of water to keep them from perishing, but their supplications were in vain; he most obstinately refused, and thus did they perish. The cry of the children for bread was, as I am informed, so great that it would be impossible for man to describe it, nor can the passengers believe that any other person excepting Captain Conklin would be found whose heart would not have melted with compassion to hear those little inoffensive ones cry for bread. The number of passengers, when the ship arrived at Amboy, amounted to one hundred and thirty-two. Fifty-one remained there still; the others have been disposed of.

The passengers further state that they did not receive the tobacco, the fish, nor the potatoes, as they ought to have received, and which they were entitled to as by their contract with the captain, neither did they receive their dram but four or five times during their passage, and no butter after they left the British port until within three or four days ago.

The foregoing are the principal causes of complaint, and indeed they appear very serious ones too to me. However, I having heard those complaints, and understanding that the captain's intention was to take the ship to New York, ... I determined to push on for New York, and there inform the German Society of his conduct. I did so, and on Sunday I found the President of the society. To him I communicated the whole of this disagreeable affair. His feelings can be more easily conceived than described. He, however, gave directions to have the officers of the society summoned to meet the next day, which was done, ... and, after hearing the circumstances relative to those unfortunate people, they appointed three of their members officers, to act in such way as they should, after taking legal advice, think best to bring the captain to that punishment which his conduct should merit.

5. Incidents of the Ocean Voyage for Immigrants, 1817–18[1]

October 25, 1817.—The British ship "Mary Ann" has arrived at Boston in 50 days from London, with two hundred and four passengers. The "Mary Ann" was bound to St. John (N.B.), but the passengers, not wishing to go there, rose upon the crew and brought the vessel into Boston.

[1] Extracts from *Niles' Weekly Register*, XIII, 143, 157, 378; XIV, 117, 392.

November 1, 1817.—We have very distressing accounts of the state of the German emigrants attempting to reach the United States through the ports of the Netherlands. One ship with 500 on board, after being a considerable time at sea, was forced back—60 had died on board her while she was out. In another prepared to sail, a destructive epidemic had broken out, and carried off many persons. There were 700 at the Texel engaged to go to Philadelphia, but prevented by the want of means, and in great distress, etc. Two vessels, *crammed* with these unfortunate people, touched at St. Michael's, one of the Azores, for supplies—one of them, a Dutch brig, had been out *ninety-one* days—during which she had lost 40 passengers—the other had 400 on board, but they were tolerably healthy.

January 31, 1818.—It is asserted in the *Delaware Gazette*, that of about *eleven hundred* passengers, who embarked on board the ship "April," captain, DeGroot, at Amsterdam, which vessel is now lying at New Castle, about *five hundred* died, many of them before they departed from Europe. Such as were unable to advance the money for their passage, who survive, are still detained on board in the most deplorable condition, several of whom are children who have lost their parents on the voyage.

April 11, 1818.—The heart is sickened with accounts of the sufferings to emigrants from Germany, making their way to the United States, through the cold-blooded cruelty and infernal avarice of the masters and owners of passenger ships. We are glad that very few of those guilty of such deeds are our countrymen—the actors are chiefly Dutch. Cargoes of emigrants, who had wholly or partially paid their passage to the United States, after suffering almost starvation on shipboard, have, on various pretexts, been landed at Lisbon, or the western islands, etc., and left to perish in strange countries, unless saved by the already over-burthened demands on the few that are able to assist them.

Some hundreds of Swiss and Germans have also arrived at New Orleans, who have been wretchedly treated. Their case considerably excited the feelings of the citizens of that place.

August 1, 1818.[1]—The "Royal Edward," of Liverpool, and the brig "Jessey," of Ayr, bound to North America, sailed a short time ago from Belfast, with 467 emigrant passengers on board. Both vessels were, a few hours afterwards, detained and sent into the above port, by his majesty's ship "Mutine." The detention of these ships was in consequence of their having a greater number of passengers on board than allowed by act of parliament, and not having twelve weeks' provision on board for each passenger, which renders the masters and owners liable to penalties amounting to £5000.

[1] Extract from a letter from London dated June 5.

6. Exploitation of Emigrants by Passenger Brokers[1]

The attention of the merchants composing the American Chamber of Commerce, and of others interested in foreign trade, has been drawn of late to the iniquitous practices of a number of persons styling themselves passenger brokers, or men who make it their business to procure accommodations for individuals emigrating to the United States, British America, etc., and which practices are in their effects so opposed to the advantage of the emigrant, and of the merchant and shipowner, as well as at variance with the principles of common honesty, as to call for prompt exertion to counteract their operation, and to substitute, so far as it may be practicable, some other mode of an equitable nature for all the parties concerned.

The practices alluded to, and their consequences, though generally notorious, may be illustrated by the following examples:

Some time since, an American vessel, the "Caledonia," was about to proceed from this port to New York, and the captain was induced to enter into an agreement with two passenger brokers, that they should find, and he would receive, as many steerage passengers as the law allowed his vessel to take, at a certain fixed rate, they being free to make their own terms with the passengers. At the time the "Caledonia" was ready for sea, the tide surveyor, in the discharge of his duty, compared the muster roll with the passengers on board, when there appeared many more than the law allowed the ship to carry, of which the surplus number, from the statute being imperative, were turned on shore, although the whole had paid the brokers, the stipulated price for their passage, in many instances with the last of their small pittance. The unhappy individuals applied to the consignee for redress, and he to the brokers, who it appeared had, with a view to a profitable speculation, and in defiance of the laws, engaged this excess of numbers for the "Caledonia," without the knowledge of the captain, giving the most distinct assurances to each person of the security of his passage, with the hope that the vessel might quit the port previous to discovery. The application for a return of passage money was refused by the brokers, and the consignee, pursuing the only alternative, arrested them. In the issue, after much expense, only a part of the money was recovered, and the consignee remained a considerable loser, as he had returned the passage money immediately to the parties, to enable them to provide other means of proceeding on their voyage.

In another instance, some passenger brokers had, by false and interested representations, induced a party of husbandmen to engage their passages by a ship bound to Virginia, their real destination being the neighbourhood of Boston. . . . .

---

[1] Extract from "A Report of a Committee of the American Chamber of Commerce in Liverpool, 1822," reprinted in Appendix to *Report from Select Committee on Emigration from the United Kingdom* (1826), pp. 296-97.

Indeed it might be shown that emigrants have been actually induced to proceed to parts distant from that of their destination, by one or two thousand miles, under a belief that they were in the most direct road to the places of their intended settlements; nor does the evil stop here, for the emigrant is exposed to extortion on every hand, in the shape of charges for making out entries, taking charge of luggage, passing his name at the custom-house, frequently under the statement that he is of a trade which, by the existing laws, disqualifies him from going abroad, and that the broker has to provide another person to pass the examination for him (a practice not of unfrequent occurrence, though requiring a false oath), and for which service, whether real or imaginary, a high compensation is required, and thus the emigrant in reality often pays more for his passage than he would, were he to make his arrangements with the merchant, independent of these men. . . . .

It may not be out of place to mention here, that the legislature watches this branch of trade with a jealous eye, and that during the last session of parliament, a bill was under preparation, having in view such restrictions on the carrying of passengers as would, if enforced, almost have put an end to that part of the business of this port, so far at least as regards any profit (already very small) to the shipowner, or a moderate rate of conveyance to the emigrant; and it is to be feared, that that bill is rather postponed than abandoned, so that if any cases of cruelty or injustice to passengers should be brought before the legislature, it may be revived, and, with the view of humane interference, passed into a law.

It remains to be seen if any suitable remedy for the abuses adverted to can be provided, which will not compromise the interest of either the emigrant or the shipowner, whilst it may render that particular business more amenable to the laws of integrity and justice.

The plan suggested, as most likely to promote those ends, is the establishment of an office, under the sanction of the merchants generally interested in the trade, at which all persons seeking a passage across the Atlantic, may, without expense, receive the requisite information on their arrival in the town; the appointment of a competent agent for its management, whose remuneration will be derived from such a percentage on the amount of passage money as may appear fair and reasonable; the publication of the existence of such an establishment throughout the country as universally as possible, and the support obtained of all the shipowners, merchants and captains, engaged in the American trade.

7. Disastrous Effects of the Steerage Voyage, 1827[1]

The distress of the emigrants landed in Halifax during the season is represented as being melancholy in the extreme. There are at present about 500 persons dependent upon the public charity, some of whom are

[1] From *Niles' Weekly Register*, XXXII, 387–88.

suffering from disease, and others confined in the poorhouse. Death is daily thinning their numbers. Nearly forty have died since their landing. Even those who are free from sickness are so enfeebled and emaciated from the effects of the voyage across the Atlantic that they are totally unable to work, and unless charity should hold out to them her benevolent meed, the consequences might in many instances be fatal.

The same is said of those emigrants who have been landed in large numbers in St. John's, Miramichi, and P. Edward's Island. Numerous instances of suffering among them are sufficient to touch the most obdurate heart. Whole families have travelled across the country from Miramichi to Fredericton in search of work, with nothing to subsist upon, save the scanty contents of a knapsack, and the charity of the settlers among whom they passed.

The season in the British provinces of Nova Scotia, New Brunswick, etc., is said to be in the highest degree favorable to the hopes of the husbandman. No prospect for ten years has equalled the present.

The typhus fever and measles prevail in a most distressing degree among the Irish emigrants at New Foundland. A letter describes the mortality as truly appalling. The contagion was brought to the country by several vessels with Irish passengers, on board of which it was engendered by the filth and pestilential exhalations arising from the crowded state of their holds. The restrictions for regulating the number of passengers to be taken by each ship being now removed,[1] they seemed to have been crowded on board literally as thick as they could stow, men, women, and children, promiscuously. Since their arrival, not a day was passed without witnessing the deaths of numbers of these wretched beings, of diseases contracted on the passage. One morning thirty were lying dead at once.

8. Attitude of the House of Commons to Proposed Revival of Passenger Regulations, 1828[2]

Mr. Stanley said some restrictions were necessary to restrain the excessive cupidity of the adventurers who speculated in passage vessels. . . . . The ships selected for this purpose were old vessels, specially taken up for the occasion, and never used again. They were crammed with human beings, badly provided with necessaries, and the consequences were disease and death. The persons who carried on this system were left to play the game over and over again, with new victims. . . . .

Mr. Robinson said however desirable it might be to encourage emigration from Ireland and Scotland, he was convinced that the act of last session[3]

---

[1] [The British passenger regulations were all repealed in 1827 (7–8 George IV, c. 19) but new regulations were passed in the following year. Document 8, which follows, contains extracts from the debate which dealt with the revival of these regulations.]

[2] Hansard's *Parliamentary Debates*, Vol. XVIII (2d series, 1828), cols. 963–1217.

[3] [That is, 7–8 George IV, c. 19. See n. 1 above.]

was productive of consequences appalling to humanity, and mischievous to the people amongst whom the emigrants went to settle. He would read an extract from a colonial paper, containing a case of a very distressing nature. The paper was published at St. John's, Newfoundland, on the 30th of August last: "We happened, on Wednesday last, to go on board a vessel with emigrants from the west of Ireland, bound to Halifax; it contained one hundred and sixty-four passengers. The captain stated, that they had had no sickness on board but what arose from hunger and the peculiar situation of one or two of the people. The passengers found provisions for themselves, and by the time they had half finished the voyage, their stock was nearly exhausted. It then became necessary to draw on the stores of the ship, and indications followed of a very alarming character. A short time before the ship made land, such was the desperation to which these wretched people were driven, that they absolutely insisted upon having bread or blood." Now, was there any black slavery equal to this? . . . . He could vouch for it, that such was the ignorance of those unfortunate individuals who were stimulated to leave their native country, in consequence of that heartrending distress, of which the House had heard so much, that they knew not how, when going out, to provide for themselves; and they were left at the mercy, and subjected to the cupidity of the owners of vessels, who extorted the largest freight they possibly could from those wretched creatures. He, therefore, implored the House to give their support to the measure recommended to them. . . . .

Mr. V. Stuart said it appeared to him that this bill merely consisted of regulations which secured sufficient space for the passengers during the voyage; he could not, therefore, understand by what party, or on what ground, so useful a measure was to be opposed. As to the Irish shipowners, if they meant to do what was right, they could have no objection to do it under an act of parliament, and if they did not, then the sooner they were made to do it the better. In his opinion the bill encouraged rather than retarded emigration, and he therefore should support it.

Mr. Robinson said the present state of the Passengers' law was, in his opinion, monstrous, and a disgrace to the country. . . . .

Mr. J. Grattan considered the present measure to be one designed more for the benefit of the colonies, than for the advantage either of England or Ireland. In his opinion it was calculated to impede emigration rather than to promote it. He was desirous of affording every facility to the purposes of free emigration. The inspection of the vessels was a measure to which he had no objection, but he did not think it necessary to sanction a bill imposing such restrictions as the present. . . . .

Mr. Huskisson said he could not consent to speak of these people—the most helpless and uninformed of the community—as a mere commodity which was the subject of export from one locality to another. . . . . Honourable gentlemen spoke of the Passengers' act, as being calculated to check the flow of voluntary emigration; but he was certain that nothing could be more likely to prevent voluntary emigration than the accounts which parties now received of the miserable fate of those who had gone before them. He agreed entirely that it was the duty of government towards emigrants to see that they were not shipped in any case without a competent supply of food and water. The food might be of the very commonest description, but a proper quantity of it they should have. And the water should be of a drinkable quality, shipped in a condition fit for human creatures; and not in old casks which had recently contained molasses or salt hides, which had been the case in more than one instance. It was too much to talk of there being no necessity for these regulations. Even in the time of the slave-trade there had been a law regulating the number of slaves by the tonnage upon the middle passage; and that which we had thought it right to do for the negroes of Africa ought we to refuse to do for our own countrymen? Honourable gentlemen talked of its being hard that ships should be put to the trouble of furnishing an account of every passenger that they carried out. Why, they were compelled to furnish an account of the smallest parcel that they took out, and that which they did for a bale of goods, they might surely well make shift to do for a living man. He wished to throw as little difficulty in the way of the shipping trade as possible; but he would insist upon having such a quantity of provision and water always on board, as should guarantee the emigrants from famine in case of a protracted passage; and the state of the vessels as to numbers should be such as was conducive to the health and common safety of the human beings who were on board of them. . . . .

Mr. Hume said the whole of the provisions of the Passengers' acts had been calculated to do nothing but mischief, and the trade of carrying emigrants must have stopped if they had not been evaded. The stores required to be put on board were perfectly unsuited to the habits of the persons who were to use them. The Irish were made sick by the diet of beef and pudding; and the right honourable gentleman talked of providing biscuit on board. Who wanted biscuit? For the Scotch he would answer that oatmeal and water was all that was necessary. The business of emigration had gone on very well without any restrictions until the year 1817, and then, because one or two cases of abuse arose, the trade was cramped with laws which, if they had not been evaded, would have put an end to it entirely. . . . . For himself, he was against the bill altogether. He would have no interference whatever with the Irish who might wish to emigrate. . . . .

Mr. Wilmot Horton said he begged to deny that the regulations contained in the present bill were any infraction of the principles of free trade. What did those regulations propose? They made it imperative on the master of a ship, taking out emigrant passengers, to provide a sufficient quantity of water and proper food for the voyage. Were not these called for by the common dictates of humanity? Could any thing be more reasonable or humane, than that some such regulations should be enforced, for the benefit of those who, from their situation, could not be aware of the privations to which they might be exposed in a long voyage? He was astonished that honourable gentlemen were not ashamed to come down to that House, and object to regulations such as those proposed by the bill, on the ground that they were in violation of the principles of free trade. .... Was no attention to be paid to the official statements of such men as the governors of Nova Scotia, New Brunswick, or Newfoundland? Yet all these had concurred in their communications to government, as to the evils produced by large masses of emigrants going out without any preparation or provision. .... The whole of the colonies cried out against the system as it has been recently carried on; and there was scarcely a private letter which reached this country, which was not full of such representations, and which did not call for relief from the pressure of emigration so conducted.

9. An Emigrant Ship from Londonderry to Montreal, 1834[1]

We have frequently heard the character of emigrant ships from Ireland declared to be worse than that of those concerned in the slave trade of Africa; the account given by the passengers of the "Thomas Gelston," from Londonderry, substantiates the opinion.

The passengers by this vessel state the number, including children, to have been somewhere from 450 to 517. They were nine weeks on the passage, and suffered much from want of water and provisions. Besides two tiers of berths on the sides, the vessel was filled with a row of berths down the center, between which and the side berths there was only a passage of about three feet. The passengers were thus obliged to eat in their berths, each of which contained a great many persons, say five and upwards. In one were a man, his wife, his sister and five children; in another were six full-grown young women, while that above them contained five men, and the next one eight men.

These statements are given upon the concurrent testimony of several of the passengers. Fortunately a succession of fine weather enabled them to keep the hatches open; in a storm they would have smothered.

Although these people landed safely at Grosse Isle, a great deal of sickness has broke out among them since. A part of them came up by the "Canadian Eagle" on Wednesday, from which about a dozen persons were taken to the cholera hospital soon after their arrival.

[1] Extract from the *Montreal Advertiser*, reprinted in *Niles' Weekly Register*, XLVII (September 27, 1834), 55–56.

10. The Failure of the British Passenger Act of 1835[1]

[As to the present operation of the Passengers' Act, the report of the Agent General of Emigration claims that the officers enforcing it serve in every port as the] poor man's friend. They take notice whether the ship offered for his conveyance is safe, and fit for its purpose; they see to the sufficiency of the provisions on board; they prohibit overcrowding; and they make every effort to avert or to frustrate those numerous and heartless frauds which are but too constantly attempted at the moment of departure upon the humbler classes of emigrants. "Every effort," adds the reporter, speaking of emigrants to North America, "is made for the ease and safety of their transit."

At Quebec, at least, where are landed the great majority of emigrants to the North American Colonies, an opinion prevails which is greatly at variance with the above representation. Nobody in the Colony denies that the Passengers' Act, and the appointment of agents to superintend its execution, is a considerable improvement upon the utterly lawless and unobserved practices of former times; . . . . but that there is still great room for further improvement, as respects emigration to the Colonies in North America, is, I think, established by . . . . the following evidence of Dr. Poole [inspecting physician of the quarantine station at Grosse Isle, Quebec].

. . . . He was summoned to give evidence before the Commissioners of Inquiry on Crown Lands and Emigration; and it was in answer to questions put to him that he said, "I have been attached to the station at Grosse Isle for the last six years. My description applies down to the present year. We had last year upwards of 22,000 emigrants. The poorer class of Irish, and the English paupers sent by parishes, were, on the arrival of vessels, in many instances, entirely without provisions, so much so that it was necessary immediately to supply them with food from shore; and some of these ships had already received food and water from other vessels with which they had fallen in. Other vessels with the same class of emigrants were not entirely destitute, but had suffered much privation from having been placed on short allowance. This destitution, or shortness of provisions, combined with dirt and bad ventilation, had invariably produced fevers of a contagious character, and occasioned some deaths on the passage; and from such vessels numbers, varying from 20 to 90 each vessel, had been admitted to hospital with contagious fevers immediately on their arrival. I attribute the whole evil to defective arrangements; for instance, parish emigrants from England receive rations of biscuit and beef, or pork, often of bad quality (of this I

[1] Extract from the *Report of the Earl of Durham, Her Majesty's High Commissioner and Governor General of British North America, January 31, 1839* (reprinted London, 1902), pp. 181–86.

am aware from personal inspection); they are incapable from seasickness of using this solid food at the beginning of the passage, when, for want of small stores, such as tea, sugar, coffee, oatmeal, and flour, they fall into a state of debility and low spirits, by which they are incapacitated from the exertions required for cleanliness and exercise, and also indisposed to solid food, more particularly the women and children; and, on their arrival here, I find many cases of typhus fever among them. . . . . I also wish to mention, as loudly calling for remedy, a system of extortion carried on by masters of vessels, chiefly from Ireland, whence come the bulk of our emigrants. The captain tells emigrants the passage will be made in three weeks or a month, and they need not lay in provisions for any longer period, well knowing that the average passage is six weeks, and that it often extends to eight or nine weeks. When the emigrants' stores are exhausted, the captain who has laid in a stock for the purpose, obliges them to pay often as much as 400 per cent, on the cost price for the means of subsistence, and thus robs the poor emigrant of his last shilling. Such cases are of frequent occurrence, even down to the present year. . . . . Parish emigrants are generally at the mercy of the captain or mate, who serve out the provisions, and who frequently put emigrants on short allowance soon after their departure. Complaints of short weight and bad quality in the provisions are frequently made. . . . . The captains have, in many instances, told me that the agents only muster the passengers on deck, inquire into the quantity of provisions, and, in some cases, require them to be produced, when, occasionally, the same bag of meal or other provisions was shown as belonging to several persons in succession. This the captain discovered after sailing. The mere mustering of the passengers on deck, without going below where the provisions are kept, is really no inspection at all; and it frequently happens that passengers are smuggled on board without any provisions. . . . . Very few of these vessels have on board a sufficient quantity of water, the casks being insufficient in number, and very many of them old oak casks, made up with pine heads, which therefore leak, if they do not fall to pieces, which often happens. I have had many similar cases from Liverpool. . . . . That part of the law which regulates the height between decks of emigrant ships is frequently evaded in the smaller class of vessels, by means of a false deck some distance below the beams, bringing the passengers nearly in contact with the damp ballast, pressing them into the narrow part of the ship, and the beams taking an important part of the room allotted to them by law. It is quite impossible that such fittings should escape observation in the port of departure, if that part of the vessel intended for emigrants be visited. . . . . There is another evil which might be readily obviated by a proper selection of vessels at home, that of employing as emigrant-ships vessels that are scarcely seaworthy; and which, consequently, being unable to carry sail, make very long passages. As the tonnage of the best class of vessels coming to Canada is more than sufficient to bring all the emigrants in any year, the employment of these bad ships ought not to be permitted. . . . . The report made to me by the class of captains and surgeon-superintendents now bringing passengers are seldom to be relied upon. In illustration, I beg leave to mention a case that occurred last year. It was a vessel with about 150 passengers on board, from an Irish port. The captain assured me that they had no sickness on board; and the surgeon produced a list, which he had signed, of certain slight ailments, such as bowel complaints and catarrhs, which had occurred during the passage, and which appeared on the list with the remark 'cured' to all of them. On making my usual personal inspection, I found and sent to hospital upwards of forty cases of typhus fever, of which nine were below in bed. These nine they had not been able to get out of bed. Many of the others were placed against the bulwarks, to make a show of being in health, with pieces of bread and hot potatoes in their hands. As there are many respectable captains in the lumber trade, a proper selection by the emigrant agents at home would prevent this abuse. . . . . The medical superintendence on board vessels obliged by the Passengers' Act to carry a surgeon is very defective. The majority of such persons called surgeons are unlicensed students and apprentices, or apothecaries' shopmen, without sufficient medical knowledge to be of any service to the emigrants, either for the prevention or cure of diseases. On board a ship the knowledge of the means of preventing disease in such a situation is the first requisite in a medical man, and in this the medical superintendents are lamentably deficient. It is not much better as to the cure of diseases. I boarded a ship last year, of which the captain and three passengers, who had met with accidents, had their limbs bandaged for supposed fractures, which, upon examination, I found were only simple strains or bruises. On examining the captain's arm, I said that there had been no fracture. The surgeon, so called, replied: 'I assure you the *tibia* and *fibula* are both broken.' It happens that the *tibia* and *fibula* are bones of the leg. This is an extreme case, apparently; but it is not an unfair illustration of the ignorance and presumption of the class of men appointed to comply with that part of the Act which is intended to provide for the medical care of emigrants during the voyage."

The Agent General's *Report*, which was laid before Parliament last year, does not even allude to another feature of our system of emigration, on which I have yet to offer some remarks. However defective the present arrangements for the passage of emigrants, they are not more so than the means employed to provide for the comfort and prosperity of this class after their arrival in the Colonies. Indeed, it may be said that no such means are in existence. . . . . Nearly all that is done for the advantage of poor emigrants, after they have passed the Lazaretto, is performed by the Quebec and Montreal Emigrants' Societies, benevolent associations of which I am bound to speak in the highest terms of commendation; to which, indeed, we owe whatever improvement has taken place in the yet unhealthy mid-passage, but which, as they were instituted for the main purpose of relieving the inhabitants of the two cities from the miserable spectacle of crowds of unemployed and starving emigrants, so have their efforts produced little other good than that of facilitating the progress of poor emigrants to the United States, where the industrious of every class are always sure of employment at good wages. In the *Report on Emigration*, to which I have alluded before, I find favourable mention of the principle of entrusting some parts of the conduct of emigration rather to "charitable committees" than to "an ordinary department of Government." From this doctrine I feel bound to express my entire dissent. I can scarcely imagine any obligation which is more incumbent on Government to fulfil, than that of guarding against an improper selection of emigrants, and to securing to poor persons disposed to emigrate every possible facility and assistance, from the moment of their intending to leave this country to that of their comfortable establishment in the Colony. . . . .

11. A British Economist on "The Policy of the Passenger Acts," 1835[1]

. . . . During 1833, 1834, and 1835, no fewer than 183,237 voluntary emigrants left the United Kingdom; 173,344 being destined for America, and 9,893 for the Australian colonies and the Cape of Good Hope. Such being the extent to which emigration is carried, the propriety, or rather necessity, of enacting some general regulations, with respect to the conveyance of emigrants to their destination, must be obvious to every one at all acquainted with the subject. The great number of emigrants are in humble life; few among them know anything of ships, or of the precautions necessary to insure a safe and comfortable voyage; they are, also, for the most part poor, and exceedingly anxious to economise, so that they seldom hesitate to embark in any ship, however unfit for the conveyance of passengers, or inadequately supplied with provisions, provided it be *cheap*. Unprincipled masters and owners have not been slow to take advantage of this, and in order to prevent the frauds that have been, and that would be, practised on the unwary, it has been found indispensable to lay down some general regulations as to the number of passengers to be taken on board ships as compared with their tonnage, the quantity of water and provisions as compared with the passengers, etc. But this is no very easy task. If the limitations be too strict, that is, if comparatively few passengers may be carried, or if the stock of provisions to be put on board be either unnecessarily large or expensive, the cost of emigration is proportionally enhanced; and an artificial and serious impediment is thrown in the way of what ought to be made

[1] Extract from John Ramsay McCulloch, *A Dictionary, Practical, Theoretical, and Historical, of Commerce and Commercial Navigation*, I (new ed.; Philadelphia, 1847), 652–53

as easy as possible, consistent with security. But, on the other hand, if too many passengers be allowed, their health is liable to suffer; and should the supply of provisions be inadequate, or the quality bad, the most serious consequences may ensue. The Passage Act[1] (6 G. 4. c. 116) obliged too great a quantity of expensive provisions to be put on board, and was, in consequence, objected to by emigrants as well as shippers. The act 9 G. 4. c. 21 (1828) avoided this error; but it, too, was defective, inasmuch as it made no provision with respect to the sufficiency of the ship, the having a surgeon or other properly qualified medical person on board ships carrying a certain number of passengers, and in other particulars.

These deficiencies have been in part supplied by the act of 1835 (5 and 6 W. 4. c. 53). . . . . But we doubt whether even it will completely answer the end in view. During 1834 no fewer than 17 ships, with passengers on board, bound for Quebec, were wrecked on the passage; 731 emigrants losing their lives in consequence, while many more lost most part of their property, and were reduced to the greatest difficulties. These losses principally took place in the gulf and river of St. Lawrence; but we should err if we ascribed them entirely, or principally even, to the difficulty of the navigation. Emigrants to Quebec are mostly taken out in ships engaged in the timber trade; and it is well known that, speaking generally, these are a very inferior class; it being the usual practice to turn worn-out ships, unfit to carry dry cargoes, into this department. Most part of the catastrophes alluded to may, we are assured, be ascribed to this circumstance, and to the misconduct of the masters and crews. We doubt whether the clause in the present act as to the seaworthiness of the ship will be sufficient to obviate the disasters arising from the use of improper vessels. . . . . There can be no question as to its being the bounden duty of government to take every reasonable precaution for obviating shipwreck. And, even if higher considerations did not make an effectual interference imperative, it is pretty certain that the check given to emigration to Canada, by the shipwrecks and destruction of life that have recently taken place, is much greater than any that could be given by the trifling addition that the adoption of some such plan as has now been suggested would make to its cost. . . . .

The new act does not make it imperative on ships conveying passengers to America to have a surgeon on board; and, perhaps, when bound for New York, he may not be required. But the voyage to Quebec is often very tedious; and much suffering and loss of life have frequently arisen from no medical officer being on board emigrant ships destined for that port.

It has been said, that if we lay constrictions on the conveyance of emigrants to Quebec, it will make New York the great landing port, and

---

[1] [This was the Act of July 5, 1825, "An Act for Regulating Vessels Carrying Passengers to Foreign Ports," which was repealed in 1827 (7–8 George IV, c. 19), see p. 17, n. 1.]

throw the business of their conveyance entirely into the hands of the Americans. But the regulations enforced in the subjoined act, and those we have suggested, apply equally to both parties. And it is, besides, true that a continuance of the old system, attended as it, no doubt, would have been by a repetition of the most appalling disasters, would have had the very effect falsely ascribed to judicious regulations. It would have prevented anyone not compelled by necessity—who was not, in fact, a beggar—from sailing in a vessel bound for Quebec.

12. Transport Conditions and Activities of Steamship Agents in Europe, 1840-45[1]

The transportation of emigrants is organized as a commercial undertaking. Companies have been formed that agree to take them from any of the ports of Europe and to conduct them to their destination even to the very extremities of the territory of the United States. These transport companies have agents who scour the countries from which emigration is taking place. They recruit all those who have means to pay for their passage without concerning themselves as to what will become of the emigrant after he is landed.

The emigrants are sent by the agents to the ports of embarkation, and, once they reach this point, it is impossible for them to turn back. They are in the power of the captain or the brokers. Frequently the captain refuses to be bound by the promises made by the travelling agents and refuses to honor the certificate of passage that has been issued, although these promises and these certificates have led the unfortunate peasants to leave their homes and to submit to the most severe privations. The transportation of emigrants has become a kind of slave trade among white people. These abuses call for the establishment of some companies whose interest it would be to treat their passengers with humanity. . . . .

As a general rule, the inhabitants who wish to go to the United States ought to make their contracts only at the port of embarkation and after having seen the ship. . . . . The sufferings of emigrants at the time of debarkation on foreign territory have made necessary the formation of philanthropic protective societies. Charitable associations are equally necessary to protect these inexperienced people at the time of embarkation.

When the emigrant is on shipboard, he continues to suffer whether from the bad condition of the ship or the quality of the food and the water. If he has undertaken to provide his own food, he is likely to have an insufficient supply and to have no place to prepare his meals.

In England an act of Parliament has established certain rules of maritime police in order to protect passengers. At Bremen, at Hamburg, in

---

[1] Extract translated from Baron A. van der Straten-Ponthoz, *Recherches sur la situation des émigrants aux États-Unis de l'Amérique du Nord* (Bruxelles, 1846), pp. 35-37.

Belgium, and in the United States similar steps have been taken with the same end in view. But the shipmasters elude surveillance, and the complaints of the abuses suffered during the crossing are without results. At the port of arrival the consuls are without jurisdiction, and the courts incompetent to apply a law of a foreign country. The complaint made on the deposition of the passenger cannot serve as a basis for punishment in the country of embarkation.

13. Complaints of the Almshouse Commissioner of New York City, 1846[1]

ALMSHOUSE COMMISSIONER'S OFFICE, NEW YORK
January 20, 1847

Your communication of the 9th instant, asking the department for a "statement of the number of emigrants received into the almshouse, from September, 1846, to the present time; the ship in which they arrived; the condition when received into the almshouse," etc., has been duly attended to; and I herewith cheerfully furnish you with the substance of the information in my possession.

My present observations will be confined to the "condition" in which the arriving emigrants appear upon their arrival on our shores.

Large numbers of these unfortunate emigrants, as soon as they quit the decks of the vessels, having no home to which to direct their movements, wander through the streets in a state of utter desolation, until some benevolent hand, appalled by the misery and wretchedness before him, guides their prostrated frames and tottering gait to the Park almshouse board; and here is exhibited so sickening a picture of human destitution and suffering as no pen, however eloquent in the sad gloom of misfortune's description, could well paint in illustration of the dark and solemn truth. The deplorable infirmity of their desolate unhappiness must be *seen and felt*, to be appreciated; and then, to often find amid the motley groups some with the last gasp of expiration issuing from their cold and blanched lips, forms a scene of dismay and distress too agonizing to look upon with any other than feelings of horror and overwhelming sympathy.

It is perhaps natural for you to inquire in the cause of such a state of misery consequent upon *emigration.* You ask, no doubt, were the emigrants' condition so dilapidated in their own country? . . . .

"Leaving their homes," they say, "with the brightest prospects," alluring representations presented to them of the blessed state of American life, a few scanty coins in their pockets, though feeling in the enjoyment of rugged health, and surrounded by their young and innocent offspring, little

[1] Extract from a report to a committee of the Common Council of the City of New York, reprinted in United States 29th Congress, 2d session, *House Document No. 54,* pp. 8–9.

did they imagine the trials to which they would be exposed, but at length they discover to their sorrow, and very natural discontent, that the foul steerage of some ocean-tossed ship is to form the filthy receptacle of their persons, crowded too with hordes of human beings, with scarcely space enough to contain the half of them—certainly not more than the *quarter* of them *comfortably;* and thus huddled together *en masse*, they become the "*emigrant passengers*" destined to this country.

Nor is this alone the full picture of this heartless *enterprise.* Untutored in the ways of travelling, and led astray by the cupidity of their almost criminal advisers, who promise them that in a few days they will happily land on the shores of America, they provide—indeed, their means are too limited to do otherwise—a very economical supply of food to serve them during their passage; and ere they half complete their voyage, they are destitute of a mouthful of sustenance to save them from the horrors of starvation. The water tanks, too, of the vessel have also nearly become exhausted; and this, with the near approach of *famine*, and the foul atmosphere of their narrow and contracted apartments, induce the *fever and dysentery* of camps and crowded ships.

Numbers of them, unprovided with medical assistance—though even that essential aid could be but transient and temporary—fall victims to the destroying contagion, and the ocean wave becomes their silent tomb; and when at length our shores are reached, many of them had far better have been cast into the "deep sea," than linger in the pangs of hunger, sickness, and pain, to draw their last agonizing breath in the streets of New York. They come, however, in rags and tatters, pale and ghastly shadows, shrouding their pinched and haggard features, scarcely able to utter the sound of complaint, and staggering with the feebleness of dire prostration to the doors of an institution.

14. Resolution of the New York Legislature on the Regulation of Emigrant Ships, 1847[1]

WHEREAS, The regulation of commerce between foreign countries and the United States belongs, by virtue of the Constitution, to the Congress of the latter; and

WHEREAS, From the increase of emigration within the last few years the transportation of steerage passengers from the nations of Europe to this country has become a large and lucrative branch of commerce, profitable in proportion to the number of persons who can be induced to take passage on board of each vessel employed in this trade; and

WHEREAS, Many inhumane persons, careless of the wants, the health, and comfort of their passengers and eager only for gain, are now engaged in such transportation; and

[1] "Concurrent Resolution, February 5, 1847," *New York State Laws* (1847), p. 379.

WHEREAS, Almost weekly some such vessel, swarming with human beings, arrives at our port, and the details of their sufferings arising from the crowded state of such vessel, the neglect of the master to see secured a sufficiency of provisions and water for the voyage, and the conveniences for preparing food, the inattention of such master to the cleanliness of the steerage and the comfort and health of the passengers, are shocking to our sense of humanity and disgraceful to any country possessing the power to prevent the recurrence of such enormities: Therefore

Resolved, That our Senators in Congress be instructed, and our Representatives requested, to use their best efforts to obtain the passage of a law limiting and defining the number of passengers for each vessel engaged in the transportation of passengers from any foreign country to the United States, according to her burthen, determining the quantity of provisions and water for each passenger on the voyage, securing the presence of a physician on shipboard, and prohibiting the stowing of merchandise or other freight between decks when occupied by emigrant passengers, and containing such other regulations as may be thought necessary or proper to prevent the great and crying evils which at present so often occur, and which are so contrary to the controlling and benevolent spirit of the age.

15. The Irish "Fever-Ships," 1840–50[1]

The emigrant seemed marked out, as it were, as the legitimate object of plunder and oppression; and were not the frauds of which these helpless people were made the constant victims matters of public record, and against which Legislatures at both sides of the ocean struggled, and for a time ineffectually, one could scarcely credit the lengths to which those who lived upon plunder carried their audacity. Little did the intending emigrants know of the difficulties and dangers that lay in their path in every stage of their momentous journey by land and water, by city and by sea. . . . .

The ships, of which such glowing accounts were read on Sunday by the Irish peasant, on the flaming placards posted near the chapel gate, were but too often old and unseaworthy, insufficient in accommodation, without the means of maintaining the most ordinary decency, with bad or scanty provisions, not having even an adequate supply of water for a long voyage; and to render matters worse, they, as a rule rather than as the exception, were shamefully underhanded. True, the provisions and the crew passed muster in Liverpool—for, twenty years since, and long after, it was from that port the greater number of the emigrants to America sailed; but there were tenders and lighters to follow the vessel out to sea; and over the sides of that vessel several of the mustered men would pass, and casks, and boxes,

[1] Extract from John Francis Maguire, *The Irish in America*, pp. 179–83, 134–45. London: Longmans, Green & Co., 1868.

and sacks would be expeditiously hoisted, to the amazement of the simple people, who looked on at the strange, and to them unaccountable, operation. And thus the great ship with its living freight would turn her prow towards the West, depending on her male passengers, as upon so many impressed seamen, to handle her ropes, or to work her pumps in case of accident, which was only too common under such circumstances. What with bad or scanty provisions, scarcity of water, severe hardship, and long confinement in a foul den, ship-fever reaped a glorious harvest between decks, as frequent ominous splashes of shot-weighted corpses into the deep but too terribly testified. Whatever the cause, the deaths on board the British ships enormously exceeded the mortality on board the ships of any other country. . . . . It was no unusual occurrence for the survivor of a family of ten or twelve to land alone, bewildered and broken-hearted, on the wharf at New York; the rest—the family—parents and children, had been swallowed in the sea, their bodies marking the course of the ship to the New World.

But there were worse dangers than sickness, greater calamities than death and a grave in the ocean, with the chance of becoming food for the hungry shark. There was no protection against lawless violence on the one hand, or physical helplessness and moral prostration on the other. To the clergyman, the physician, and the magistrate are known many a sad tale of human wreck and dishonour, having their origin in the emigrant sailing ship of not many years since. Even so late as 1860, an Act was passed by Congress "to regulate the carriage of passengers in steamships and other vessels, for the better protection of female passengers"; and a single clause of this Act is a conclusive proof of the constant and daily existence of the most fearful danger to the safety of the poor emigrant girl. . . . .

A notion of the manner in which emigrants were treated in some vessels, the dishonesty of whose owners or charterers was only equalled by the ruffianism of their officers and crews, is shown in a letter published in 1851 by order of the House of Commons; but facts similar to those described by Mr. Foster have been frequently complained of since then. The ship in question had 900 passengers on board, and this is a sample of the manner in which the luckless people were supplied with a great necessary of life:

"The serving out of the water was twice capriciously stopped by the mates of the ship, who, during the whole time, without any provocation, cursed and abused, and cuffed and kicked, the passengers and their tin cans, and, having served out water to about 30 persons, at two separate times, said they would give no more water out till the next morning, and kept their word."

A very simple mode was adopted of economising the ship's stores—namely, that of not issuing provisions of any kind for four days; and had it not been for the following remonstrance, it is probable that as many more days would have passed without their being issued:

RESPECTED SIR: We, the undersigned passengers on board the ship . . . . paid for and secured our passages in her in the confident expectation that the allowance of provisions promised in our contract tickets would be faithfully delivered to us. Four entire days having expired since the day on which (some of us having been on board from that day, and most of us from before that day) the ship was appointed to sail, and three entire days since she actually sailed from the port of Liverpool, without our having received one particle of the stipulated provisions excepting water, and many of us having made no provision to meet such an emergency, we request that you will inform us when we may expect to commence receiving the allowance which is our due. . . . .

I have more than once referred to the unfavourable circumstances under which the vast majority of the Irish arrived in America, and the difficulties with which, in a special degree, they had to contend; but the picture would be most imperfect were not some reference made to the disastrous emigration of the years 1847 and 1848—to that blind and desperate rush across the Atlantic known and described, and to be recognized for time to come, as the Irish Exodus. We shall confine our present reference to the emigration to Canada, and track its course up the waters of the St. Lawrence. A glance even at a single quarantine—that of Grosse Isle, in the St. Lawrence, about thirty miles below Quebec—while affording a faint idea of the horrors crowded into a few months, may enable the reader to understand with what alarm the advent of the Irish was regarded by the well-to-do colonists of British America; and how the natural terror they inspired, through the terrible disease brought with them across the ocean, deepened the prejudice against them, notwithstanding that their sufferings and misery appealed to the best sympathies of the human heart.

On the 8th of May, 1847, the "Urania," from Cork, with several hundred immigrants on board, a large proportion of them sick and dying of the ship-fever, was put into quarantine at Grosse Isle. This was the first of the plague-smitten ships from Ireland which that year sailed up the St. Lawrence. But before the first week of June as many as eighty-four ships of various tonnage were driven in by an easterly wind; and of that enormous number of vessels there was not one free from the taint of malignant typhus, the offspring of famine and of the foul ship-hold. This fleet of vessels literally reeked with pestilence. [For] all sailing vessels . . . . a tolerably quick passage occupied from six to eight weeks; while passages of ten or twelve weeks, and even a longer time, were not considered at all extraordinary at a period when craft of every kind, the most unsuited as well as the least seaworthy, were pressed into the service of human deportation.

Who can imagine the horrors of even the shortest passage in an emigrant ship crowded beyond the utmost capability of stowage with unhappy beings of all ages, with fever raging in their midst? Under the most favourable circumstances it is impossible to maintain perfect purity of atmosphere between decks, even when ports are open, and every device is adopted to secure the greatest amount of ventilation. But a crowded emigrant sailing ship with fever on board!—the crew sullen or brutal from very desperation, or paralysed with terror of the plague—the miserable passengers unable to help themselves, or afford the least relief to each other; one-fourth, or one-third, or one-half of the entire number in different stages of the disease; many dying, some dead; the fatal poison intensified by the indescribable foulness of the air. . . . . Of the eighty-four emigrant ships that anchored at Grosse Isle in the summer of 1847, there was not a single one to which this description might not rightly apply.

The authorities were taken by surprise, owing to the sudden arrival of this plague-smitten fleet, and, save the sheds that remained since 1832, there was no accommodation of any kind on the island. These sheds were rapidly filled with the miserable people, the sick and the dying, and round their walls lay groups of half-naked men, women, and children, in the same condition—sick or dying. Hundreds were literally flung on the beach, left amid the mud and stones, to crawl on the dry land how they could. "I have seen," says the priest who was then chaplain of the quarantine, and who had been but one year on the mission, "I have one day seen thirty-seven people lying on the beach, crawling on the mud, and dying like fish out of water." Many of these, and many more besides, gasped out their last breath on that fatal shore, not able to drag themselves from the slime in which they lay. Death was doing its work everywhere—in the sheds, around the sheds, where the victims lay in hundreds, and in the poisonous holds of the plague-ships, all of which were declared to be, and treated as, hospitals. . . . .

When the authorities were enabled to erect sheds sufficient for the reception of the sick, and provide a staff of physicians and nurses, ... there was of course more order and regularity; but the mortality was for a time scarcely diminished. The deaths were as many as 100, and 150, and even 200 a day, and this for a considerable period during the summer. The masters of the quarantine-bound ships were naturally desirous of getting rid as speedily as possible of their dangerous and unprofitable freight; and the manner in which the helpless people were landed, or thrown on the island, aggravated their sufferings, and in a vast number of instances precipitated their fate. Then the hunger and thirst from which they suffered in the badly-found ships, between whose crowded and stifling decks they had been so long pent up, had so far destroyed their vital energy that they had but little chance of life when once struck down. . . . .

It was not until the 1st of November that the quarantine of Grosse Isle was closed. Upon that barren isle as many as 10,000 of the Irish race were consigned to the grave-pit. By some the estimate is made much higher, and 12,000 is considered nearer the actual number. A register was kept, and is still in existence, but does not commence earlier than June 16, when the mortality was nearly at its height. According to this death-roll, there were buried, between the 16th and 30th of June, 487 Irish immigrants "whose names could not be ascertained." In July, 941 were thrown into nameless graves; and in August, 918 were entered in the register under the comprehensive description—"unknown." There were interred, from the 16th of June to the closing of the quarantine for *that* year, 2,905 of a Christian people, whose names could not be discovered amidst the confusion and carnage of that fatal summer. In the following year, 2,000 additional victims were entered in the same register, without name or trace of any kind, to tell who they were, or whence they had come. Thus 5,000 out of the total number of victims were simply described as "unknown."

This deplorable havoc of human life left hundreds of orphans dependent on the compassion of the public. . . . .

The horrors of Grosse Isle had their counterpart in Montreal. As in Quebec, the mortality was greater in 1847 than in the year following; but it was not till the close of 1848 that the plague might be said to be extinguished, not without fearful sacrifice of life. During the months of June, July, August, and September, as many as eleven hundred of "the faithful Irish," were lying at one time in the fever-sheds at Point St. Charles, in which rough wooden beds were placed in rows, and so close as scarcely to admit of room to pass. In these miserable cribs the patients lay, sometimes two together, looking as a Sister of Charity since wrote, "as if they were in their coffins," from the boxlike appearance of their wretched beds. Throughout those months, hundreds of the poor Irish were dying daily, in the fever-sheds.

16. The British Passenger Bill in the House of Commons, 1848[1]

Mr. Hume considered it absolutely imperative on the House to adopt some such measure as this for the prevention, in future, of the sufferings to which emigrants to Canada and other countries had hitherto been exposed in the crowded and badly-arranged emigrant ships. He found that during the last emigration season to the Canadas, the mortality on the whole number of emigrants had amounted to between 17 and 18 per cent—

[1] Extract from *Hansard's Parliamentary Debates* (3d series), Vol. XCVI, cols. 1024–33. This debate occurred in the House of Commons on the second reading of the so-called "Passenger Bill." In introducing the bill Mr. Labouchere had said: "The House was aware of the dreadful abuses which prevailed last year in consequence of the crowded state of the vessels which conveyed the emigrants from Ireland to our North American colonies. There was a prospect of a large emigration taking place this year also from Ireland, and the Government wished the House to legislate against the recurrence of the evils complained of during the past year. Out of 106,000 emigrants, who during the last twelve months crossed the Atlantic for Canada and New Brunswick, 6,100 perished on the voyage, 4,100 on their arrival, 5,200 in the hospitals, and 1,900 in the towns to which they repaired. The total mortality was no less than 17 per cent upon the aggregate number emigrating, the number of emigrants being 106,000, and the number of deaths 17,300" [cols. 540–41].

death in most cases being attributable to fever brought on while on board ship; and it was a well-known fact that the mass of those who were landed were left in a state of utter destitution, and that through them the seeds of disease were spread through the whole colony. The evils which were thus occasioned arose entirely from the want of proper regulation in the emigrant ships, and he was glad that means were now proposed to be taken to remedy such a state of things henceforward. . . . . Every precaution ought to be taken to secure the necessary comforts and conveniences to the unfortunate people who were driven by poverty from our own shores, and compelled to seek a livelihood in other countries; and no vessel ought to be allowed to clear from harbour here until it was proved on inspection that she was safe, properly fitted up, and in her cabin accommodation well ventilated. The hon. Member referred to letters from the Members of Council at Canada, describing the condition of the emigrants on arrival out from Ireland last year. It was disgraceful to this country that she had ever permitted such evils to continue unnoticed. We had by our neglect inflicted serious injury on the inhabitants of our own colonies in introducing annually among them fever and disease; and if the House had any regard to humanity or to the sufferings entailed in this way on helpless fellow-creatures, it would at once take the matter into consideration.

Mr. Labouchere said . . . . that it was the bounden duty of that House and of the Government to apply themselves most earnestly to prevent if possible a recurrence of the dreadful calamities which the system of emigration to North America, especially from Ireland, was accompanied by during the last year, both to the emigrants themselves and the colonists. . . . . He would beg leave to remind the shipowners that it was impossible for this country to prevent the North American Colonies to take what steps they might find necessary to protect themselves, if Parliament here neglected to adopt measures for saving the colonists from a recurrence of such dangers. In order to show the necessity of legislating on the matter, he need only state the one fact, that in former years the average mortality among emigrants to Canada was not more than $\frac{1}{2}$ per cent, whereas last year it amounted to the frightful rate of 17 per cent. It was true that that proportion did not perish in the vessels, but they died either on the voyage or in quarantine, or in the hospitals immediately after arriving. Such a state of things deserved the most serious consideration of Parliament; and he should deeply regret if the emigration of the coming season—which, he might remark, promised to be quite as large from Ireland as it was last year—was allowed to go on without the House doing what it could to prevent a recurrence of evils so shocking to humanity, and so destructive to all sound policy in matters of the kind. He was aware that a great cause—perhaps the principal cause—of the sufferings of last year, was one against which it was impossible for them to guard by legislation, namely, the prevalence of fever in Ireland during the last season. The emigrants brought the seeds of fever out with them, which it was impossible to discover until after the ship had put to sea; but if any hon. Gentleman would look to the evidence that had been laid on the table of the House, he would see that that cause had been infinitely aggravated by the course of mismanagement which had been pursued, and by the want of any proper regulations or control in the vessels into which these unfortunate creatures entered. In this state of things the Colonial Office, and more especially the Commissioners of Emigration, had applied themselves seriously to consider what alterations in the law had been best to recommend for the adoption of the House. The result was the Bill which he had the honour to submit to the House. The main alterations which it proposed in the existing law were—In the first place it proposed to increase the space allotted to the emigrants on board from ten feet for each person to twelve feet; but even then the British law would be less restrictive than the American law, which provided that a vessel should carry only one for every fourteen feet. Another point on which he thought it right to introduce an alteration in the law was that which provided that a certain quantity of food should be carried for each emigrant. The quantity was by no means sufficient for the support of an emigrant during the voyage, as it was expected that the emigrants would always bring some food for themselves. During last year, however, it was found that in the unfortunate position of Ireland whole crowds threw themselves almost without any food into the vessels, relying entirely upon what they might get on board. This alone was sufficient to account for the dreadful state of things that had been reported to the House in the papers lately presented. One very important alteration was proposed to be made in this respect: it was that emigrant ships to America, like those to Australia, should be provided with a sufficient quantity of food to sustain the lives of the passengers. He came now to the provision which had excited the greatest alarm among the parties interested in emigrant vessels, namely, that each ship should carry a respectable Government officer to protect the emigrants by seeing that the regulations for the voyage were properly enforced, and if necessary to complain of the conduct of those who had violated them upon the arrival of the vessel at its destination. Many of the emigrants who had arrived bore most abundant proof that no care was taken on board to observe the law; they were afraid to make complaints, and he feared that whatever laws might be made, the emigrants had no redress. The Government officer and superintendent, however, would attend to these complaints— he would attend to the proper ventilation of the ship, and provide for decent habits of cleanliness and some moral restraint among the emigrants—both of which had been sadly wanting in some instances that had come under his notice. A proposal had been strongly urged upon the attention of the Government, which was most deserving of consideration. It was that every emigrant ship should be obliged to take out a surgeon. . . . . But, after the fullest inquiry, ... the Emigration Commissioners had come to the conclusion that it would not be possible to find surgeons for so great a number of emigrant ships as were expected to sail this year. With these opinions, expressed by competent medical authority, the Government had reluctantly abstained from proposing that every emigrant ship should be obliged to carry a surgeon. . . . . Before he sat down he would read an account of what had actually taken place last year on board one of the emigrant ships for America—an account contained in a private letter, but which the Colonial Office thought of so much importance that it would be made a public document and presented to the House. The letter was written by an Irish gentleman of station and family, Mr. Stephen De Vere, brother of Sir Aubrey De Vere, who, having occasion to go to British North America, and knowing that some emigrants from his own part of Ireland were going out, actuated by the most honourable and humane motives, determined to go himself in the condition of a steerage passenger, that he might make himself personally acquainted with the condition of the steerage passengers when crossing the Atlantic. The picture drawn by this gentleman of what had actually taken place afforded the strongest evidence of the absolute necessity of some more stringent regulations than those which now existed:

No moral restraint is attempted; the voice of prayer is never heard; drunkenness, with its consequent train of ruffianly debasement, is not discouraged, because it is profitable to the captain, who traffics in grog. In the ship which brought me out from London last April, the passengers were found in provisions by the owners, according to a contract, and a furnished scale of dietary. The meat was of the worst quality. The supply of water shipped on board was abundant; but the quantity served out to the passengers was so scanty that they were frequently obliged to throw overboard their salt provisions, and rice (a most important article of their food), because they had not water enough both for the necessary cooking and the satisfying of their raging thirst afterwards. They could only afford water for washing by withdrawing it from all the cooking of their food. I have known persons to remain for four days together in their dark close berths because they suffered less from hunger, though compelled at the same time by want of water to heave overboard their salt provisions and rice. No cleanliness was enforced, the beds never aired, the master during the whole voyage never entered the steerage, and would listen to no complaints; the dietary contracted for was, with some exceptions, nominally supplied, though at irregular periods, but false measures were used (in which the water and several articles of dry food were served), the gallon measure containing but three quarts, which fact I proved in Quebec, and had the captain fined for. Once or twice a week ardent spirits were sold indiscriminately to the passengers, producing scenes of unchecked blackguardism beyond description; and lights were prohibited, because the ship with her open firegrates upon deck, with lucifer matches and lighted pipes used secretly in the sleeping berths, was freighted with Government powder for the garrison of Quebec. The case of this ship was not one of peculiar misconduct; on the contrary, I have the strongest reason to know, from information which I have received from very many emigrants, well known to me, who came over this year in different vessels, that this ship was better regulated and more comfortable than many.

It was fortunate that the House was able to have the testimony of so competent a witness as this gentleman. He (Mr. Labouchere) believed what was here said was true, and by no means a single instance. It showed that any legal provisions, without a Government officer to see them carried into effect, would be nugatory and ineffective. . . . .

Mr. Wakley thought the present system of emigration was highly discreditable to the Government and to the Legislature. It had been officially stated . . . . that deaths had occurred in emigrant ships to the extent of seventeen per cent. . . . . The persons who chartered emigrant ships did so as a pecuniary speculation, their object was to get everything done at the lowest possible cost; and he considered that the Government ought to step in and to insist that proper measures should be taken to insure the comfort of the miserable beings who were compelled to leave this country to seek a subsistence in a foreign land. The Government, however, had not struck at the root of the evil; and he was satisfied that without placing in every emigrant ship a competent medical practitioner, it was impossible to remedy many of those evils which had been deplored.

17. The British Emigrant-carrying Trade, 1850[1]

The competition between different lines of packets and different shipping houses has been enough to scatter through the most barbarous parts of Ireland full information as to the means of passage to America. The most remote villages receive the advertisements of different lines, just as we find in our most remote villages the inducements which the same lines scatter to Irishmen to send out remittances and passage tickets for their friends.

The correspondence from this country carries a great deal of detailed information, and at present it is the principal means of supply for the expenses of the voyage. An emigrant who has succeeded here sends out for his friends, and sends money enough to bring them. Or, which amounts to the same thing, he buys here passage tickets which he sends to them.

It is impossible to tell the amount of such remittances, of course, with precision. But the last *Report of the British Land and Emigration Commissioners* shows that they had ascertained that, in 1850, as large an amount as £957,008 had been remitted thus in small sums. A very considerable amount must have escaped their observation. The facilities for making such remittances increase yearly.

The average passenger money for an adult may be called twenty dollars; for a child fifteen. . . . .

The importance of this business to shipowners will readily be seen. Ships of large accommodations for freighting, which carry out our bulky

[1] Extract from Edward Everett Hale, *Letters on Irish Emigration* (Boston, 1852), pp. 6–16.

raw produce, and bring back the more condensed manufactures of England, have just the room to spare, which is made into accommodations for these passengers. In Mr. Robert B. Minturn's testimony before the "Lords' Committee" June 20, 1848, he says that the amounts paid for the passage of emigrants go very far towards paying the expense of voyages of ships from America to Europe and back.

By far the larger number of these emigrants collect at Liverpool therefore—the large commerce of that port offering all the facilities for the cheapest passage. Of 223,078 who sailed from the United Kingdom to the United States in 1850, 165,828 were from Liverpool, 31,297 were from Irish ports, and 11,448 from Scotch ports. The ease of passage from Ireland to Liverpool carries most of the Irish emigration that way. The English Commissioners suppose that almost all the Liverpool emigration is Irish; certainly much more than nine-tenths of it. Our own returns at New York confirm this supposition.

Vessels engaged in this trade are now subject to a double inspection. In Great Britain they are examined by English officers, that it may be known that they comply with the British statute—and here, that they may comply with ours. The experience of the awful suffering of emigrants in 1847, when, of 90,000 who embarked for Canada in British vessels, 15,000 died on the way, or after arrival, called the attention of the English Government to the necessity of a more stringent law for passenger vessels. Our laws, amending former statutes, had passed February 22, and March 2, 1847, and no such terrible suffering took place on American vessels. The English law of March, 1848, covered the ground with care, though it was not yet so stringent as our statute. In the session of Parliament of 1849, after hearing full testimony on the subject, from one of our own shipowners among others, their present effective law was passed. Additions were made to it in 1850. That statute applies to all vessels sailing from British ports. Their previous statute applied to British vessels only. It is prepared with careful reference to the comfort of the emigrant, and to secure him against fraud. . . . .

Emigrants do not themselves usually make their bargains with the masters or owners of ships, but are brought together and put on board by some "passenger broker" with whom they have contracted, and who furnishes their stores. Instances of fraud and cruelty on the part of these men sometimes take place, but, on the whole, they are not so many as in so immense a business one might have feared. The English Government has taken what pains it could, by a system of licensing, to keep in order the passenger brokers; but the great competition leads to frauds, practiced by their runners, if not by them. . . . .

. . . . The general health of passengers in these vessels has been better than could have been anticipated. Suffering, in cases where it has been made public, has more often come from the emigrant's negligence to supply his own stores sufficiently, than from other mismanagement. . . . .

THE EARLY EMIGRANT SHIPS 39

A family of settlers, in the charge of a shipping agent, are put by him on board the first of the vessels of his lines which is ready. People sometimes cross and land here without knowing what is the name of the vessel in which they come. On board, they meet for the first time with their fellow passengers, constituting a party of all numbers, up to 1,100 or 1,200. If the vessel sails from Liverpool, there will be among them all a few Germans perhaps, for there are arrangements in London for receiving German emigrants by steampacket and forwarding them; there will be a few English families from the manufacturing towns—a few Scotch; but the great company of those who are swarming over will be Irish adventurers. . . . .

Every inducement which interest or statute can bring to bear, rests, under the present legislation, on the captains to bring their living freight over in good health. Generally speaking, in our packets, the men in command understand their business, and undertake with real spirit this humane responsibility. It is the general agreement, I believe, that the real difficulty in carrying it out is in the dullness of the poor sea-tossed emigrants themselves. But an effort is made, and generally with success, to have the berths cleaned daily—to have the decks as well ventilated as possible, and kept clean. Even these provisions require a good deal of sternness on the part of the officers who carry them out. A sea-sick person will not hear to reason more than to any other voice, if he can help it.

Besides the ship's rations, the emigrant ought to have some stores of his own. Before the late British statute, this was necessary to a larger amount than now. Cooking places are provided for them, and they organize themselves at pleasure into messes, each of which has its cook, who takes the charge of preparing the meals. Arrangements more precise than this are, as I have said, now proposed. The ship's supplies are served out twice a week. For, as two governments regulate the matter, the more severe requisitions of each must be complied with. A description of the suffering from starvation on the ship "Speed," of St. John, which had twelve weeks' passage to New York, in the autumn and winter of 1848, as I received it from some of those who shared them, was one of the most terrific accounts of lingering distress. But it was a case which belongs of course rather to the general hazards of the sea than to this particular emigration.

After all—the comfort or discomfort, the health or the sickness in a particular passage—depends upon the weather—the winds—the previous condition of the passengers—and a world of other unmanageable circumstances. I have known some of the finest vessels, under careful captains, bring in, after a short run, a sickly and suffering freight of passengers, on the same day when a heavy built, carelessly arrayed ship, with a commander unused to the trade, came in with a good bill of health. The reason for such difference is sometimes that the passengers of the first have been at sea in another ship, and have put back—so as to sail already exhausted—or they have been long waiting passage at the port they sailed from, or from some other reason, were not in good condition for the restriction and other hardships of the voyage. The provision for detained passengers, humane enough in its intention, of the British passage act, aggravates danger of such passengers' sailing unprepared. It provides, that "in case a failure of the voyage arises from wreck or any other accident or default after the voyage has actually begun, the passengers are entitled, within six weeks at farthest, to a passage in some eligible vessel, and in the meantime to be maintained by the master."

In the winter of 1849–50 some ships were obliged to put back, after having been out 70 days; their passengers were, of course, transferred as soon as possible, to other vessels, by the masters, who were responsible. It is not surprising that among such passengers, thus reduced, ship-fever should break out, whatever the vessel's accommodations. I hardly need mention to intelligent readers that the ship-fever, commonly so-called, is a severe form of Irish typhus.

18. Some Problems of Steerage Regulation in 1854[1]

.... The great difficulty of preparing a general law which shall embrace in its operation all of the minute points involved in the management of passenger ships, and effectively place the passenger and shipowner on the best possible footing, must present itself to every mind. In the first place, our country being the general receptacle of emigrants from almost every country of Europe, it becomes necessary so to legislate as to avoid coming into conflict with the legislation of the countries whence these people come, and at the same time protect their interests and the interests of American citizens at home and abroad. Great Britain,[2] France, the various nations of Germany, the Hanseatic cities, have all of them their passenger laws, in which they prescribe the terms upon which those who emigrate from among them shall be conveyed across the ocean. These laws or regulations include not only the equipment and nautical management of the ships engaged in this trade, but also prescribe such dietary provisions as to their makers respectively appear essential to the health and comforts of passengers. To legislate in this country, therefore, so as not to come in conflict with these foreign enactments on some of the many minute points which present themselves in the treatment of such a subject requires an extent and accuracy of information on details difficult to attain, and would involve a minuteness and variety of legislative enactment suited to the local require-

[1] Extract from "Report of the Select Committee of the Senate of the United States on the Sickness and Mortality on Board Emigrant Ships, August 2, 1854" (U.S. 33d Congress, 1st session, *Senate Committee Report No. 386*), pp. 17–18.

[2] The emigrant passenger act of Great Britain was communicated to the Senate of the United States, with a message of the President of the United States, at the present session, and was printed. (See *Ex. Doc. No. 58*, 1st session, 33d Congress, Senate.)

ments of each country whence emigrants seek a home on our shores, and liable to become oppressive whenever a change of policy suggests a change in those foreign enactments. It is, of course, the intention of every lawmaker that the laws passed by him shall be enforced; and to place enactments on the statute books which cannot be carried into effect, without subjecting those who are governed by them to difficulty and annoyance from foreign countries, is worse than useless. That such a state of things at present exists, under the passenger laws now in force, has been proved by experience; and those engaged in the transportation of passengers do not hesitate to say that the laws under which they are acting are in many respects impracticable, unless at great expense and loss to the American shipowner. It is only necessary to allude to one case of the kind by way of illustration. The acts of Congress require that every passenger ship shall be furnished with provisions of a certain description to a given amount. An American ship goes to Bremen or Hamburg and there takes on board a cargo of passengers. The laws of those cities require that all passenger ships sailing from them with passengers shall be supplied with a prescribed amount of certain provisions, which are specified. Now, in order to comply with the regulation of the port whence he sails for America, the American captain must provide a supply of the articles required by the local law, and, at the same time, to comply with the law of his own country, he must be provided with the food called for by the act of Congress. This single case involves a double expense in the provisions made for the subsistence of passengers. To obviate this difficulty, it has been the desire of the committee to present a law which shall, in its general operation, provide for the safety and comfort of passengers, and, at the same time, leave the management of minute details in the hands of those whose interest as well as business it is to be thoroughly acquainted with them. It is utterly impossible for Congress to know what is required in each case to make a ship comfortable and healthy. One ship may be ventilated and made perfectly wholesome for passengers by a process which in another vessel, and under different circumstances, would be totally inadequate. It would, therefore, be best, in the opinion of the committee, to leave the means by which ships are made safe and comfortable mainly at the disposal of their owners, and, at the same time, to make them responsible for any untoward results that may attend the administration of their own affairs.[1]

[1] [The Committee proposed to make unsanitary ships unprofitable by fining the shipowner a proper sum for the death of every passenger.]

19. Protest of the New York Legislature against Sufferings of Emigrant Passengers, 1854[1]

WHEREAS, During the last twelve months great and increasing mortality has occurred on board of vessels engaged in the business of carrying emigrants to various ports of the United States, and undoubted evidence exists that such suffering and death results from insufficient ventilation; and

WHEREAS, The existing laws are inadequate to secure the emigrants from these calamities: Therefore

Resolved, That we respectfully ask the Congress of the United States to investigate this important subject and enact such laws as may be necessary to secure the health of passengers on emigrant vessels.

20. The Fever Ship "Leibnitz," 1868[2]

.... The undersigned deemed it their duty to go on board the ill-fated ship "Leibnitz," and to inquire into the condition of her passengers transferred to the hospital-ship "Illinois," in the lower bay. ....

We were informed that her last trip was her second with emigrants on board. Last summer she went to Quebec with about seven hundred passengers, of whom she lost only a few on her passage; this time, she left Hamburg, November 2, 1867, lay at Cuxhaven, on account of head-winds, until the 11th, whereupon she took the southern course to New York. She went by way of Madeira, down to the Tropics, 20th degree, and arrived in the lower bay on January 11, 1868, after a passage of 61 days, or rather 70 days—at least, as far as the passengers are concerned, who were confined to the densely crowded steerage for that length of time.

The heat, for the period that they were in the lower latitudes, very often reached 94 degrees of Fahrenheit. Her passengers, 544 in all—of whom 395 were adults, 103 children, and 46 infants—came principally from Mecklenburg, and proposed to settle as farmers and laborers in Illinois and Wisconsin; besides them, there were about 40 Prussians from Pomerania and Posen, and a few Saxons and Thuringians.

It is not proven by any fact that the cholera (as has been alleged) raged or had reached in or near their homes, when or before they left them. This statement appears to have been made by or on behalf of those who have an interest in throwing the origin of the sickness on its poor victims. Of these 544 German passengers, 105 died on the voyage, and 3 in port, making in all 108 deaths—leaving 436 surviving.

---

[1] Joint resolution of the New York Assembly and Senate, passed January 6, 1854, from the *New York State Laws* (1854), p. 1105.

[2] Extract from *Annual Report of the Commissioners of Emigration, State of New York* (January 21, 1868), pp. 124–32. The document is a report signed by two of the emigration commissioners.

The first death occurred on November 25th. On some days, as for instance on December 1st, nine passengers died, and on December 17th, eight. The sickness did not abate until toward the end of December, and no new cases happened when the ship had again reached the northern latitudes; .... during the voyage some families had died out entirely; of others, the fathers or mothers are gone; here, a husband had left a poor widow, with small children; and there, a husband had lost his wife. ....

Prior to our arrival on board, the ship had been cleansed and fumigated several times, but not sufficiently so to remove the dirt, which, in some places, covered the walls. Dr. Frederick Kassner, our able and experienced boarding officer, reports that he found the ship and the passengers in a most filthy condition, and that when boarding the "Leibnitz" he hardly discovered a clean spot on the ladder, or on the ropes, where he could put his hands and feet. He does not remember to have seen anything like it within the last five years. Captain True, who likewise boarded the ship immediately after her arrival, corroborates the statement of Dr. Kassner.

As to the interior of the vessel, the upper steerage is high and wide All the spars, beams, and planks which were used for the construction of temporary berths had been removed. Except through two hatchways and two very small ventilators, it had no ventilation, and not a single window or bull's-eye was open during the voyage. In general, however, it was not worse than the average of the steerages of other emigrant ships; but the lower steerage, the so-called orlop-deck, is a perfect pest-hole, calculated to kill the healthiest man. It had been made a temporary room for the voyage by laying a tier of planks over the lower beams of the vessel, and they were so little supported that they shook when walking on them. The little light this orlop-deck received came through one of the hatchways of the upper-deck. Although the latter was open when we were on board, and although the ship was lying in the open sea, free from all sides, it was impossible to see anything at a distance of two or three feet. On our inquiring how this hole had been lighted during the voyage, we were told that some lanterns had been up there, but that on account of the foulness of the air, they could scarcely burn. .... And in this place about 150 passengers were crowded for seventy days. ....

When the ship "Lord Brougham," belonging to the same line, arrived on the 6th of December last, from Hamburg, and had lost 75 out of 383 passengers, we personally examined the majority of the survivors, and found them not only healthy and in good spirits, but, at the same time, in every respect, satisfied with the treatment they had received on board.

The present case, however, is different. There was not a single emigrant who did not complain of the captain, as well as of the short allowance of provisions and water on board. As we know, from a long experience, that the passengers of emigrant ships, with a very few exceptions, are in the habit of claiming more than they are entitled to, we are far from putting implicit faith in all their statements. There is as much falsehood and exaggeration among this class of people as among any other body of uneducated men. We have, therefore, taken their complaints with due allowance, and report only so much thereof as we believe to be well founded.

All the passengers concur in the complaint that their provisions were short, partly rotten, and that, especially, the supply of water was insufficient, until they were approaching port. We examined the provisions on board, and found that the water was clear and pure. If the whole supply during the voyage was such as the samples handed to us, there was no reason for complaint as to quality. But, in quantity, the complaints of the passengers are too well founded; for they unanimously state, and are not effectually contradicted by the captain, that they never received more than half a pint of drinkable water per day, while by the laws of the United States they were entitled to receive three quarts. Some of the biscuits handed to us were rotten and old, and hardly eatable; other pieces were better. We ordered the stewart to open a cask of corn-beef, and found it of ordinary good quality. The butter, however, was rancid. Once a week, herrings were cooked instead of meat. The beans and sourkrout were often badly cooked, and, in spite of hunger, thrown overboard.

The treatment of the passengers was heartless in the extreme. The sick passengers received the same food with the healthy, and high prices were exacted for all extras and comforts. A regular traffic in wine, beer, and liquors was carried on between the passengers on the one side and the steward and crew on the other. . . . .

There was no physician on board. Although we found a large medicine chest, it was not large enough for the many cases of sickness, and was, in fact, emptied after the first two weeks of the voyage.

. . . . Of the whole crew, the cook alone fell sick and died, as he slept in the steerage. Three passenger girls who were employed in the kitchen, and lived on deck, enjoyed excellent health, during the whole voyage.

The physicians above-mentioned, to whose report we refer for particulars, most positively declare that it was not the Asiatic cholera, but intestinal and stomach catarrh, and contagious typhus, which killed the passengers. From what we saw and learned from the passengers, we likewise arrive at the conclusion that the shocking mortality on board the "Leibnitz" arose from want of good ventilation, cleanliness, suitable medical care, sufficient water, and wholesome food.

The present case is another instance of the mortality on board the Hamburg sailing-vessels, and increases their bad reputation. Of 917 passengers on board of two ships of the Sloman line, not less than 183 died within one month! As often as complaint has been made here, it has not induced them to make any improvement. It appears that the Hamburg authorities either did not care to examine the merits of the charges brought against their ships, or that they were imposed upon by their officials. On the other hand, local interests, friendly feelings, family connections, and other personal considerations, usually prevailing in small political communities, seem to stand in the way of energetic administration of the police of emigrant ships, and of the removal of the several grievances. . . . .

Thus, of 11,264 steerage-passengers who arrived in 1865 in our port, from Hamburg, 128 died on the passage; of 14,335 who arrived in 1866, 387; and of 8,788, in 1867, not less than 199.

In our opinion, it is of great importance for the interest of humanity, in which both Europe and this country are concerned, and as a question of political economy, that the transportation of emigrants across the Atlantic to this port, should be confined to steam-vessels, as they not only convey the passengers more comfortably and land them in better health, but, in consequence of the regularity and rapidity of the passage, save an immense amount of labor for their own benefit and that of this country.

We are sorry to say that our laws afford very inadequate relief for the punishment of these crimes against humanity, and that, in the majority of cases, the institution of legal proceedings for redress, and the prosecution of the guilty parties, is almost an impossibility.

Much of the suffering, disease, and death on board of emigrant ships could have been prevented, and a recurrence of such abhorrent scenes might hereafter be avoided, by proper enactments of Congress, enforced by suitable penalties.

We would therefore propose to petition Congress for an amendment of the Emigrant Passengers' Act, of March 3, 1855, incorporating into the same the following provisions:

I. The appointment of a physician or surgeon on board of all emigrant vessels with more than fifty passengers. . . . .

II. The doing away with the orlop-deck on board of emigrant ships. . . . .

III. A more stringent rule for enforcing the payment of the penalty for the dead passengers. With a view to protecting emigrants against the rapacity of shipowners, the fourteenth section of the present law requires the payment of $10, as a penalty, for every passenger, other than cabin passengers, and over the age of eight years, who shall have died on the voyage from natural disease; for the non-payment of which penalty within twenty-four hours after arrival, a further penalty of $50 is imposed, to be recovered by the United States in any Circuit or District Court. Under this wording of the law, no particular officer of the United States appears to be authorized to prosecute or enforce the collection, and consequently many of the penalties are not paid, and the law, to some extent, becomes a dead letter. . . . .

IV. The power of obtaining redress to be lodged in the hands of the parties injured—the emigrants themselves.

V. Summary proceedings for the recovery of damages.

As to the two latter provisions, we would state that the efforts which have been made by legislation at Washington and at Albany to protect the lives and health of emigrant passengers from the rapacity of shipowners have been attended with but a very limited share of success. . . . .

The Act of 1855 provides that, if some of its provisions are violated, the master shall be guilty of a misdemeanor; and that, if others of its directions are not complied with, the master or the owners, or both, shall forfeit money penalties against the ship by the *authorities of the United States.*

It is found that indictments are not feared, and that suits for the recovery of penalties are never instituted.

To make the law effective, the power of obtaining redress must be lodged in the hands of the emigrants themselves.

The law gives them an action against the ship for marine *torts* and for breaches of marine contracts; but this action must be prosecuted through the dilatory form of admiralty practice. The ship is bonded, and goes on her way. The emigrant, poor, friendless, and often emaciated by disease, is kept loitering in a crowded city, dancing attendance on the delays of litigation, while the Western fields, which he came to till, lie fallow. The loss falls immediately on himself, but indirectly likewise on the entire country, which receives and detains a languishing pauper, when it needs industrious and able-bodied laborers.

It is absolutely necessary to authorize a summary proceeding, simple and expeditious, such as the case of the emigrant requires. . . . .

It will also be necessary to establish certain principles of remedial law, not now considered established.

The owner of a ship should be made responsible in damages to the natural representatives of persons dying in the course of a voyage from causes produced by misconduct of such owner, or his agent. Such claims must be declared liens on the ship, recoverable by action *in rem* in the admiralty form. . . . .

The shipowner must be prevented from pleading that the emigrants, having seen the ship when they came on board, had assumed their own risks, and precluded themselves against bringing suits for damages occasioned by its imperfections. . . . .

Under the present system, the emigrants are treated more like beasts of burden than like human beings, starved and crowded together in ill-ventilated, ill-fitted, ill-supplied, and ill-manned vessels.

The arrival of an emigrant ship in our ports, if it does not bring disease and pestilence among us, often occasions great apprehension and alarm, disturbing the regular business of our city, and creating an indefinable prejudice against the worthy emigrant, instead of extending to him, as he truly deserves, a kind and hearty welcome. . . . .

21. American Cholera Epidemics and Emigrant Ships, 1832–73[1]

.... From the beginning of June until the succeeding autumn, in the year 1832, ships freighted with emigrants sick with cholera continued to arrive in the ports of New York and Quebec, and as they speedily dispersed upon every line of travel throughout the states, the cholera attended them, and in their wake it followed as an epidemic. Whether by the canal barges, crowded with these emigrants, which left the port of New York for the western canals, or by the boats from Quebec for Champlain or the western lakes, the immediate following of cholera and the creation of vast numbers of new foci for the epidemic became the very first line in the history of the epidemic in America. Again in 1848–49, beginning at New Orleans immediately upon the arrival of cholera-infected emigrants from Havre, in December, 1848, the epidemic took its course up the Mississippi and its great tributaries, and in a single fortnight, at dates which in each river port correspond with the first week after the arrival of steamboats with the first cholera patients on board, the disease made its outbreak. In river towns a thousand miles distant from each other, the epidemic made its appearance at the same time in those instances in which the first cholera patients arrived by the steamboats in the respective localities at about the same date. Surviving the winter, the .... great epidemic continued its ravages during the years 1849 and 1850. But from the ports of New York and Quebec no extension of cholera was propagated until the succeeding month of May, when the events of 1832 were repeated.

The events of 1854 repeated the historical and epidemical facts of 1848–49. The numbers of infected ships and cholera-sick emigrants were scarcely less than those of the latter period. .... It was less virulent as a pestilence in 1854. .... It spread to Central America and up and down the Pacific coast, and was repeatedly re-imported from Central America (by way of the port of Aspinwall) to the quarantine grounds on Staten Island, and there renewed its locally epidemic phenomena by extending its destructive power throughout the greater portion of that area of thirty acres, but chiefly in the hospital buildings occupied by convalescents from fever and by the sick or convalescents from small-pox. ....

The events of 1865–66 are fresh in memory, and their historical record is remarkably clear and instructive. .... The local factors of epidemic cholera, the environment which insured the fatal sweep of the pestilence in 1832, 1848–49, 1854, and 1866, have been everywhere correctly described. .... The one great and determining factor in regard to the epidemic or the non-epidemic following in the fifteen years in which persons sick and dying with Asiatic cholera were brought into our port is this, namely, that

[1] Extract from a paper by Dr. Elisha Harris in *Reports and Papers of the American Public Health Association*, I (1873), 345–47.

in the epidemic years the number of such sick and dying emigrants arriving in port was enormously larger, and the number of persons infected with cholera who failed to be detained and prevented from travel beyond the harbor of New York admits of no estimation, because the condition of dangerous infectedness admits of no positive definition within the limits which must, in the travel and business of the world, be overpassed, by multitudes of travellers, as respects any external restrictions in the chief ports and commercial towns.

The prevalence of cholera throughout a vast extent of the great River Valley of the West in the year 1873 has confirmed the belief that the direct connection between a great epidemic of this pestilence and any exotic source at a particular port or place to which it was introduced may not in every epidemic be ascertained. . . . .

The epidemic of 1873 has differed chiefly from those last mentioned (1832 and 1852) by the vastly greater extent of its prevalence. Already its ravages have been definitely reported in more than two hundred places in no less than thirteen States of the Union. . . . .

22. Steerage Conditions in 1873[1]

A. REPORT BY DR. JOHN M. WOODWORTH[2]

With the gradual supplanting of sailing-vessels by steamers have come shorter voyages, increased space, improved accommodations, more light, better ventilation, more abundant supplies of more wholesome food and water, and superior *morale* of officers and crews; though in this latter respect there is still much to be desired.

As a direct result of these changes the mortality among steerage-passengers has been reduced over 50 per cent, in five years, the respective per millages for the two periods and for each class of vessels being—

	1867	1872
On sailing-vessels	11.67	5.42
On steamships	1.03	.45

This reduction is due, undoubtedly, to the improved administration of the immigrant service, an improvement for which, it must be confessed, the United States is entitled to little if any credit. For while, in the language of ex-Secretary Boutwell, "the interest of the United States lies in the character and health of the emigrants this country receives, and, therefore, ... it is deemed of the utmost importance to hold foreign vessels to such regulations as will give greatest security to the life and health of the emigrants,"

[1] Extracts from "Reports to the Secretary of the Treasury by Special Investigators," United States 43d Congress, 1st session, *Senate Ex. Document No. 23*, pp. 12–13, 52–85, 145–49.

[2] Supervising surgeon, United States Marine Hospital Service.

the fact is that, owing to the interpretation of existing emigration laws, with the single exception of collecting a penalty of $10 for every immigrant-passenger over eight years of age who dies on the voyage, we do not hold foreign vessels to any regulation at all; and the examinations of such vessels by our inspectors of customs to ascertain "whether the requirements of law have been complied with,"[1] are made as a matter of form only, so far as the exaction of any penalties for non-compliance with the requirements of law is concerned.

While this improvement in the immigration service has thus reduced the general mortality, the effect of the competition of steamships in driving sailing-vessels out of the service has also had much to do with lessening the death-rate. This is shown by the fact that where the service is to any great extent still performed by sailing-vessels, the mortality rises in direct ratio to the proportion of passengers carried by them. Thus, during the five years above quoted, while the mortality on sailing-vessels was reduced over 50 per cent, only about 8 per cent of the total number of immigrants was carried on them in 1872, while nearly 25 per cent was so carried in 1867.

A striking proof of the connection between these two facts, as cause and effect, was found in the statistics at the port of Baltimore, during the spring of 1873. At this port for the quarter ending March 31 there arrived 1,602 steerage-immigrants, of whom 711 were brought by sail and 954 by steam. Of the former, 32 died on the voyage, and only two of the latter, being in the ratios of one death to every 477 steam-passengers and one to every 22.2 sail-passengers.

The usual mode of stating mortality on shipboard misleads the general reader who is not careful to distinguish between per annum mortality and the mortality per voyage. Through this oversight a mortality of 261 in 228,722 passengers is quoted in a recent report to the Secretary of the Treasury as "a most favorable showing," and, inferentially, as indicating little room for improvement in the immigration service.

As a matter of fact, this mortality represented an *annual* death-rate of over 35 per thousand, or very nearly three times as great as the annual death-rate in the United States according to the last census. The real discrepancy is even greater than this, since immigrants are, generally, in the prime of life, the most enterprising and the most viable of the class to which they belong, and, before being allowed to go aboard, are inspected by a medical officer to prevent those unlikely to stand the voyage from embarking; so that they represent "selected lives" in a measure, while the census returns include all ages and conditions, and, during the last decade, covered the mortality of the war. During the last six months of 1872, however, the per annum mortality of steam-passengers was, as it should be, from the causes above enumerated, a little less than the United States per annum mortality, and may be justly cited as a "most favorable showing" for steam-

---

[1] Section 9, act March 3, 1855, 10 Stat., 718.

ships when compared with the mortality on sailing-vessels for the same period—a mortality which equaled a per millage of 44.8 per annum.

With the exception of certain measures looking to protecting passengers from contact with the crew, there would seem, from the general testimony, little to be desired in the treatment of immigrants on steamships, while as to sailing-vessels it is believed that competition is driving them out of the passenger-carrying trade so rapidly as to render it unnecessary to recommend any specific action with regard to them.

B. REPORT BY THOMAS B. SANDERS

Immigration is a *vast* subject of inquiry and of the greatest importance to the country. If by wise legislation its character can be improved, and the condition of immigrants during their transit ameliorated and their morals protected; if, instead of being landed with the seeds of enfeebling disease sown in their systems, and with minds debauched on the voyage, they can reach our shores as strong and virtuous as when they embarked, it appears to me that the end warrants the efforts of the highest statesmanship and the purest philanthropy for its attainment.

No one will fail to recognize the vast difference, as it affects our country, between the influx of a great population of healthy and virtuous people and the introduction of a people disabled by disease and corrupted by vicious habits; yet, that difference may depend in a greater degree than is commonly supposed upon the regulations under which immigrants are transported across the ocean.

The ship "Leibnitz" a few years ago started from Hamburg on a voyage across the Atlantic with five hundred and forty-four steerage-passengers. The passengers received but a half pint of drinkable water per day. The investigating committee reported that the lower steerage was a perfect pesthole, calculated to kill the healthiest man. . . . .

No change in our laws has taken place since then; and similar cases may occur again. In either of those cases the loss of life and health, and the probable moral degradation, need not have occurred had there been proper laws properly enforced.

Carriage in fast steamships is in favor of the emigrant. The competition of rival companies has done much for him, and legislation more. But there is an opportunity for improvement, and we who are chiefly concerned, but whose legislation upon the subject has been the sport of the parties interested, should seize that opportunity to provide a code containing such reasonable provisions in favor of the emigrant as, while it will *not unjustly* burden the shippers, will enable him to be conveyed without undue risk to his *health or morals.* . . . .

A new statute upon the subject is necessary. Since the passage of the act of 1855 the condition of things has altered, and provisions then applicable are no longer so. It may, perhaps, be well to group together briefly the acts relating to emigration: March 2, 1819 (3 Stat., 488), Congress passed a law allowing a space of five tons for each two passengers in the steerage, but did not provide upon what decks such passengers should be carried. In 1830 another act was passed requiring that the space assigned to passengers should be 5 feet high, and have a comfortable and easily-accessible place for cooking.

Other acts affecting the subject were passed, as follows: Act of February 22, 1847 (9 Stat., 127); act of March 2, 1847, chap. 34 (9 Stat., 210); act of May 17, 1848 (9 Stat., 220); act of March 3, 1849 (9 Stat., 399); act of July 4, 1864, sec. 1 (13 Stat., 385) (repealed). These acts, among other things, regulated the number of passengers which might be lawfully carried on board of vessels; the space to be appropriated to each passenger; the means of ventilation, and the penalties for a violation of their provisions. But they, perhaps unfortunately, were repealed, and the act of March 3, 1855 (10 Stat., 715), "to regulate the carriage of passengers in steamships and other vessels," took their place. Today that statute is almost inoperative. At the port of New York and elsewhere hundreds of cases of violation of the provisions of the statute have been reported to the district attorney for prosecution, but without result, so remarkably defective are the provisions themselves and the phraseology of the statute. . . . .

A district attorney of the United States writes officially that "it is to be regretted that statutes upon a subject of such importance to the public as those regulating the carriage of passengers on sailing-vessels, as well as those propelled by steam, should not have been framed with such care and accuracy as to leave little doubt as to the true intent of all the provisions."

C. REPORT BY HELEN M. BARNARD

Upon the observations and investigations made, I have the honor to report that the treatment of steerage-passengers on the responsible and respectable English and German lines is generally good, judged by the popular standard of what is due the poor and ignorant classes in return for value given by them. . . . .

I observed that among the superior officers there was far greater kindness extended to the passengers than among the subordinates who have charge of the administration of affairs. With the latter class, the fundamental principle of action seems to be that an emigrant is an unpleasant fact with which he has to deal, and as an individual he has no rights they are bound to respect. The result of this feeling renders them coarse, and often brutal, in speech and manner toward them. This would soon be corrected if the passengers themselves understood their rights, but subordination to authority has so long been the habit of their thought and life, they never question it, and are often, in consequence, subjected to arbitrary rule when unauthorized. Another fact, that the sentimental humanitarian, in his efforts at reformation, often loses sight of, or does not know, is that the large majority of this people are of the lowest order of humanity. They are filthy in their habits, coarse in manner, and often low in their instincts. There are frequently petty thievings, discords, and treachery practiced among themselves, and their ignorance is in many instances appalling, and the women are ofttimes worse than the men. . . . .

A great amount of discomfort among these emigrants arises from their own ignorance and life-long habits. Many of them have lived in hovels to which the steerage of the steamship, in comparison, is a palace. I visited some of these homes, while in Europe, which seemed to be too comfortless for human beings to occupy. One especially which I examined while in Scotland consisted of one room, so dark that at first, on entering, I could not see across it. The furniture embraced one bedstead, a few old blankets, a broken stool, and one chair, a table with a number of broken dishes, and a clock in one corner of the room. On the hearth a peat-fire filled the room with smoke and blackened the wall with its clouds. There was no place for light or air to penetrate into this abode save through a small pane of glass which filled an aperture in the wall, but was so begrimed that it had long ceased to serve either purpose. In this room lived a family consisting of three adults and four children. It is from this class that a large portion of our emigrant army is yearly recruited. . . . .

The profit of the immigrant traffic is greater to the steamship companies than any other portion of their traffic, and if the emigrants themselves knew the value of it, and were sufficiently informed to understand the fact, the abuses would soon correct themselves. Six guineas, the price of a steerage-ticket, is nearly half the cost of a cabin-passage; but in this, as in all the wants of the poor and ignorant, they pay much larger prices in proportion to what they get than the rich.[1] For the price paid for a steerage-passage not one-twentieth part of the value is given as the cabin-passenger receives for his outlay. They are obliged to furnish their own bed to sleep upon; a plate, cup, knife and fork to eat with, and also to keep clean for use. They are furnished with the plainest and most inexpensive food, and hundreds are crowded into space that twenties occupy in the cabin.

While there are no such abuses and outrages as once disgraced this traffic, there is still room for advance upon the present. For the price paid, tables should be furnished by all the companies, as is now done by some of them, upon which their meals should be served. Dishes necessary to eat

---

[1] [This point was also discussed in the *Report* (p. 159) of Mr. J. Fred. Meyers, who said: "Considering the fact that the passenger in the first cabin pays $120, in the second cabin $72, and in the steerage $40, the steerage-passenger pays four times more in proportion to that of the two other classes. The passenger of the first class has at least eight times the room of the steerage-passenger, with five meals per day of the most expensive character, the absolute worth of which cannot be less than $3, while the food of the emigrant is at best of the most simple character, the cost of which cannot exceed 25 cents per day."]

their food should also be furnished and kept for their use, as is done in the cabin. The very limited room allowed each person, and often the scarcity of water to wash them with, renders the care of these utensils a great burden, and in case of sickness almost an impossibility. Especially to women who have children clinging to them for care and attention, themselves sick, in a strange place, terrified by the motion of the ship and the state of confusion the first few days of the voyage, it is found to be a great tax. The outlay to the company would be trifling; the comfort to the passengers very great.

23. The Close of the Old Period, 1882[1]

MR. GUENTHER:

The purpose of the bill is to pass a law for the protection of emigrants on the high seas in transit to this country, which will apply not only to sailing vessels, but also to steamships. In view of the unprecedented large emigration from Europe this year, which in all probability will run up to more than one million, it becomes the imperative duty of this Congress, demanded alike by reasons of hygiene as well as by sentiments of charity, morality, and humanity, that the gross abuses that have so long been practiced unpunished upon the helpless immigrant by the cupidity of soulless transportation companies, and the brutality and utter disregard for decency by officers and crew of many emigrant steamers, be checked and punished. . . . .

The bill under consideration, which has so generously been given the unanimous recommendation of the Committee on Commerce for its adoption by this House, marks an important epoch in our naval legislation. It replaces all former defective and insufficient enactments upon the subject of sanitary provisions and other protective measures for the benefit of those who must face the "perils of the deep" in trying to better their condition in life, and who must always, at best, battle with some disadvantages which no humane legislation can remove. In a word, the bill aims at the protection of the immigrant at sea, and upon its passage by this Congress will stand upon our statute-books as the "passenger act of 1882." . . . .

The bill under discussion is similar to the one pending before the Forty-sixth Congress, and the necessity of its passage has in the meantime only become all the more apparent. In a letter dated February 10, 1882, Mr. Graham [surveyor of the port of New York] concludes as follows:

"The passenger act of 1855 for the protection of immigrants has never been and cannot be enforced. . . . . There have been during the last two years one hundred complaints of overcrowding on board of immigrant passenger steamships, some to the number of 250 (aggregating 8,000) in excess of their capacity. The agents of the companies ignore the law.

[1] Extract from the debate in Congress, April 18, 1882, on "A Bill to Regulate the Carriage of Passengers by Sea," *Congressional Record*, 47th Congress, 1st session, pp. 3013–22.

"The immigration the coming year will doubtless exceed all former years, and some action on this bill seems absolutely necessary."

This act will of course repeal the act of 1855, and mark our progress in nautical sanitation; indeed, it will be an index of a general sanitary advance of the country, because, apart from the dangers to public health that may occur from the introduction of contagious or infectious diseases, it is a matter of serious interest to the prosperity of the country that the health and lives of immigrants should be protected during their transportation by sea. . . . .

In his excellent treatise on "the hygiene of emigrant ships," read in December, 1880, before the American Public Health Association, the author, Dr. Thomas J. Turner, medical director, United States Navy, truthfully and pointedly says:

One of the methods of determining the passenger capacity is constantly in use at the present time, and is based on the avarice of owners of vessels and steamship companies. This method recognizes nothing else but to carry as many as can be put on board. It has no regard for the health or comfort of the emigrant, views him only as supplying so many dollars to the bank account, and is a marine inheritance from the slave trade, with the horrors of the "middle passage." Although carrying an excess of passengers over that allowed by law renders a vessel liable to a penalty, official reports do not show that any prosecution has resulted in the recovery of such penalty from vessels reported as violating the provisions of any act to secure the emigrant from the evils of overcrowding. . . . .

In September, 1880, the British steamship "Hecla," 2,421 tons, superficial area 5,320 square feet, ... carried 370 passengers, of which number 159 were females, during a trip of twelve days. There were no compartments for the separation of the sexes on the steerage deck, and the steerage passengers were indiscriminately berthed without regard to sex. Five hundred and seventy-five vessels arrived during these nine months, with 172 deaths, as previously mentioned. Thirty-four of the vessels were overcrowded, with 37 deaths. The mean duration of the passage across the Atlantic was 12.7+ days.

Although most of the immigrants to our shores are carried in vessels under foreign flags and not directly amenable to our laws, yet it is within the province of the Government, if not its duty, to provide for the health of its citizens; and as these emigrants become its future citizens it certainly has the right to demand that they shall be protected by legislation in life and health in their transit of the ocean to their homes in the New World.

The steamship "Ohio," of the Bremen line, arrived on Friday with 1,342 passengers crowded into the steerage.[1] There were 272 children under ten years of age, 156 being infants less than a year old. There was much sickness among them; 13 died during the passage, and one at Castle Garden after the immigrants landed. All the deaths were sudden, and were not caused by the outbreak of any contagious disease. There were no cabin passengers aboard. Complaints were promptly made to Superintendent Jackson, charging ill-ventilation, overcrowding, and bad management generally. . . . .

[1] [The number of passengers allowed by law for this ship was only 857.]

The most fitting commentary upon the deplorable state of affairs are the same author's observations at the close of his treatise, when he says:

And yet these owners of large steamship lines, boasting of their superior accommodations and discipline, admitting the demonstrated facts of increased disease and death rates, of the disease-producing effects of overcrowding, of all the violations of the law, etc., in their vessels, recognizing at the same time the preventive measures proposed by the sanitarian as efficient safeguards to the health of this mass of the population, with a sublimity than to which impudence can rise no higher, suggest a rise in the rates of fare for the emigrant in their floating stockyards.

The execution of the existing statutes for the protection of the immigrant is a sorry travesty upon even a feeble enforcement. The laws stand on the statute-books ignored, and so long as they remain so will they be bright and shining examples of ponderous wordiness,

"Full of sound and fury, signifying nothing."

The remedy for all this is in the hands of the legislator. Enforce the law or make a law that can be enforced. Prevent all landing on our shores of emigrants rather than subject them to the present degradations of the steerage permitted by laws now in existence, which are no more regarded than the bleating of a sheep.

There is no argument for overcrowding at the price paid for lives save

"The accursed greed of gain."

The condition of the emigrant vessels arriving on our shores would be a disgrace to barbarism. How much more so are they to our sham enlightenment? . . . .

It would be Utopian to hope for any reform to come from these greedy ship-owners. On the other hand, every interest conceivable should prompt us to afford prompt relief by the passage of this bill.

The emigrants who leave European countries nowadays belong mostly to the agricultural classes. They come here and buy and settle our lands; they convert the wilderness into green pastures and productive fields, and thereby add so vastly to our national wealth.

As to the superior character of the emigrants now leaving Germany, Consul Grinnell, of Bremen, writes to the Department at Washington under date of April 1, 1881:

The emigrants this year are, without exception, of the best agricultural and industrial classes, taking money with them, the savings of years, the proceeds of their little tenements sold here, etc. My own inquiry and observation confirm the truth of the statement of the German journals, that Germany has never before lost such numbers of worthy and industrious people as are this year emigrating to the United States, and that the loss to the German Empire can scarcely be overestimated. . . . .

The countries of Europe look upon this emigration with jealous eyes. It is the marrow-bone that leaves them. It is not to be presumed that the law-making powers of these countries will exert themselves to any great extent in favor of these people. On the contrary, they look upon the privations which the emigrants have to undergo with a sort of grim satisfaction.

But we, the representatives of the American people, who receive the benefits of this immigration, a people which is ever ready to stand by those who need our help, always willing to correct all abuses of human beings, should not now hesitate to pass a law which is so urgently required. . . . .

I could say nothing more appropriate in this respect than to repeat the closing passage of the report made to the Legislature of my State this year, by the Board of Immigration of the State of Wisconsin:

In conclusion, this board would call again the attention of your honorable body to the fact that Congress has made no provision yet for the regulation of immigration and to protect immigrants while coming to this country.

It seems strange that Congress should remain indifferent to the protection of a class of people who not only add a valuable and important element to our population, but whose capital, labor, energy, and enterprise help in developing the resources of the country and in increasing the aggregate wealth. For sundry reasons, also, it is the duty of Congress to so control the transportation of such large bodies of people as to insure their arrival in this country in sound health. There can be no doubt that the want of proper ventilation, the insufficient supply of water, and the inferior quality of the food supplied to emigrants on their way across the ocean, operates in developing and spreading contagious diseases among them, which are brought into this country and carried wherever they may go; and this without any fault or means of prevention on their part. We do not speak of the suffering and loss of life which is incident to this condition of things. Surely it would be as humane as it would be prudent for this Government to take such steps as shall secure good treatment to them, while protecting ourselves against harm.

The immigration of such large numbers of people to this country is a matter of so much importance that it seems difficult to understand why the central government should not assume the responsibility of caring for them in every way that concerns their welfare and our own interest. There can be no question as to the need of some higher and stronger authority than now regulates the matter, to prevent the ill-treatment which is so often meted out to emigrants upon the high seas, and the wrongs inflicted upon them when they have reached our shores.

If your honorable body can in any way assist in directing the attention of Congress to these facts, and securing such legislation as is needful, you will be conferring a boon upon every foreigner who sets his face toward this country, and promoting every region of the land which is waiting for industrious men and women to help build up its prosperity and happiness. . . . .

MR. COX:

[The Passenger Act of 1882] will be a lasting monument of the humane thoughts of the gentlemen from Wisconsin [Mr. Deuster and Mr. Guenther] who have reported it. . . . . In the winter or spring of 1880 the complaints were numerous and grievous as to the violation of the passenger laws. These laws were inefficient and inapplicable to steamships. Complaints as to the ill ventilation and overcrowding of vessels, lack of room and comfort, were rife in the public press. United States officials were harshly criticised for failure to convict. It would seem that the old laws were so imperfect that a new code was needed. I suggested to the officers of the law in the customhouse that they prepare a bill to remedy the wrongs. This is the bill before us; it draws from the Revised Statutes and the British laws the best provisions to secure the desired object.

One of the great troubles in the execution of the existing law was the transitory nature of the testimony required to convict. Immigrants could not be detained, and witnesses were wanting on the final trial. No convictions resulted. Outrages had no punishment. The decks of the vessels continued to be crowded. "Outrages worse than death" were more than hinted at. The bill also undertakes to guard against the introduction of contagious diseases. It would lessen the risk from this source. . . . .

It is to the credit of the great lines which run into New York that they are growing more vigilant to prevent and correct abuses, but there are lines not so responsible and heedful. This the testimony shows. True, these vessels are under foreign flags, but we have a right nevertheless to see to it that the health, morals, and lives of our future citizens shall be protected. Not alone diphtheria, pneumonia, catarrh, and other diseases are generated by foul air, and bad ventilation, and overcrowding on shipboard; not alone is the death list of old and young increased by the avarice of owners of vessels, but the seeds of disease are sown which have their baleful and contagious fruit during subsequent life. . . . .

MR. DEUSTER:

. . . . This bill is identical with the one before the Forty-sixth Congress, in which it received the unanimous indorsement of the Committee on Commerce, as it again has been indorsed by the same committee of the present Congress. The purports of the bill have been stated; but too much cannot be said in behalf of the urgency and necessity of the measure. It supplants defective and inoperative provisions heretofore made at various times and and in an insufficient manner for so vital an interest to the whole country. Briefly reviewed, the bill contains the following important provisions and changes:

The first section changes the method of determining the amount of space allowed each passenger from superficial to cubic measurement, in order to conform to the universal method of admeasurement of vessels for their tonnage. It allots to each steamship passenger carried on the first deck, next below the uppermost deck, or in a poop or deck-house on main deck, one hundred cubic feet of space, and on the second deck, below the uppermost deck, one hundred and twenty feet; it forbids the carrying of passengers on any other decks, and regulates the height between decks at not less than seven feet. In sailing-vessels passengers shall be carried on a deck not being an orlop deck, that is, next below the uppermost deck, or in a poop- or deck-house built on the main deck, and shall be allotted one hundred and twenty cubic feet of space.

This section applies all legislation for the protection of steerage passengers to steamships as well as sailing-vessels, and thereby removes the barrier which, under the rulings of our courts, had made it impossible heretofore to afford relief upon complaints made by steerage passengers against steamship companies, because under these rulings the present laws did not apply to steamships, but only to sailing-vessels. The courts thereby virtually declared steamship passengers, although they constitute at the present time 99 per cent of all immigrants now crossing the sea, to be at the mercy of these companies. . . . .

SECTION II

THE JOURNEY IN THE TWENTIETH CENTURY

1. Emigration Regulations of European Countries[1]

The right to emigrate follows logically from the principle of personal freedom. This right is recognized, with a few reservations, by almost all writers on the subject, Grotius, Vattel, Kluber, G. F. de Martens, Heffter, Pradier-Fédéré, F. de Martens, Pasquale Fiore, etc. . . . .

In no country is the principle of the right to emigrate recognized without exception. The interests of justice, national defence, and sometimes even of intending emigrants themselves, frequently bring about limitations.

National laws generally specify the classes of persons who are forbidden to emigrate and the reasons for any general prohibition. These reasons may be tabulated as follows: (1) military service; (2) legal proceedings; (3) minors; (4) special regulations concerning women; (5) old age and permanent incapacity; (6) sickness and infirmity; (7) cases in which it is probable that the emigrant will be refused admission into the country to which he is travelling; (8) absence of identity papers or other documents; (9) obligations undischarged by the emigrant; (10) occupation of emigrant workers; (11) lack of resources either on arrival or on departure; (12) collective emigration; (13) receipt of an advance for the expenses of the journey; (14) the obligation to embark at certain ports; (15) emigrants previously repatriated at the expense of the State; (16) reasons of a general nature.

MILITARY SERVICE

1. The Austrian Bill of 1913 refers to the Act and regulations under the Act dealing with Military Service.

2. Czechoslovakia restricts emigration for military reasons only; Sec. 51 of the National Defence Act of 19 March, 1920, states that all male subjects of the country from the time they complete their 17th year until they complete their 40th year, who desire to leave the country with the intention of becoming subjects of a foreign country, must obtain the permission of the Minister of National Defence. Passports for men of 17 to 40 years are granted for a limited period only, and in view of the possibility of war a list of persons living abroad is kept in the Ministry. Sec. 2 of the Emigration Bill provides similarly that "the restrictions laid on emigration for purposes of national defence shall be regulated by the Army Act."

[1] Extract from International Labour Office, *Emigration and Immigration: Legislation and Treaties* (Geneva, 1922), pp. 13–24.

3. The German Act of 1897 forbids the emigration of individuals between 17 and 25 years of age, unless they have been duly granted leave or freed from military service, or have left a substitute in the army. Since the date of the Treaty of Versailles, however, this practice has been modified, and a communication of the German Migration Office states that it is no longer necessary for emigrants to show any papers relating to their military service.

4. In Greece "every citizen having no military duty at present or previously unfulfilled has the right to emigrate, but all who are included under Sec. 63 of the Recruiting Act must obtain an authorization, in accordance with that Act, the amount of the fine which may be imposed for failure to do this varying from 500 to 10,000 drachmas."

5. In Hungary, according to the Act of 1909 no man may emigrate from 1 January in the year he reaches his 17th year until he has completely fulfilled his military duties, unless he has obtained special authority from the Minister of the Interior or the Minister of National Defence. This authority can be granted only if the applicant deposits a sum of from 100 to 1,000 crowns in Hungarian money with the Minister of the Interior. This deposit is forfeited if the depositor does not return at the end of the period for which his passport is granted. In the event of the emigration of persons subject to military service assuming large proportions, the law allows a total prohibition, for one year, of the emigration of men coming under this heading. This prohibition must be communicated to Parliament.

6. Italy does not allow the emigration of persons liable for military service who have completed their 18th year of age, or who will complete it within the calendar year, or of those liable for naval service or as soldiers in the Royal Marines unless they have obtained permission from the competent authority. Soldiers included in the first and second classes who have not completed their 28th year of age may emigrate only if they obtain permission from the commanding officer of the district. Emigration is freely allowed in the case of soldiers and sailors of the third class, and also to those in the first and second classes who have completed their 28th year, but until they have completed their 32nd year they must notify their departure to the commanding officer of the district. The right to emigrate so far as soldiers and sailors of all classes are concerned may be temporarily suspended in exceptional circumstances on the proposal of the Ministers for War and the Navy.

Authority to emigrate may be refused if there is a presumption that the person concerned is trying to escape the fulfilment of his military duties. The intending emigrant may in that case appeal from this decision to the Minister of War.

7. The legislation of Norway subjects to military service all fit young men who have reached their 20th year. These men are not allowed to emigrate unless they are in possession of the requisite authority, which can

be obtained only after an examination of their position as regards military service. In addition to the Act of 19 July, 1910, Norway has adopted measures dealing with the military service of emigrants by the conclusion of a number of treaties, with the Republic of Hawaii (1852), Italy (1862), the United States (1869), the Argentine (1885), Mexico (1885), and Japan (1911). . . . .

9. In the Kingdom of the Serbs, Croats and Slovenes a passport is not delivered to an emigrant unless he can prove that he has carried out all his military service obligations.

10. In the Swedish law the obligation for military service is included among the reasons for the limitation of the right to emigrate. . . . .

. . . .
MINORS

6. The Greek Act of 1920 forbids the emigration of children of either sex, less than 16 years of age, unless they go with older relations or brothers of full age, or are going to join relations living abroad, or in exceptional circumstances at the discretion of the Minister of the Interior. In the cases referred to above, and generally speaking, whenever there is any question of a minor less than 21 years of age going to another country, either the father or the guardian must put in an application, giving the name of the person who is to accompany the minor.

This provision has been rendered executive by a Royal Decree of 24 September, 1920, which, amended by a second Decree of 17 February, 1921, lays down that "the emigration of minors of the male sex of 16 years of age or less is generally prohibited, whatever the class on the ship or railway in which they propose to travel. The certificate issued by the Mayor or President of the Commune of the person concerned, stating that the latter has been inscribed on the matriculation register, will be considered sufficient proof of the year of birth."

7. According to the Hungarian Act (1909), minors who are under parental authority may emigrate without their father only if they have authority in writing, stamped with the official visa. Those who are under the care of a guardian must have the formal permission of their guardian and of the guardian's authorities. In either case they are not allowed to emigrate unless it can be shown that their support is provided for at the place to which they are going.

Women who are not yet of age and boys less than 16 years of age may emigrate without their parents only if it can be shown, apart from the conditions mentioned above, that they are travelling to their destination with an adult person absolutely worthy of confidence.

8. The Italian law states that any person who procures to go, takes, or sends abroad, a young person below the age of 15 years for purposes of work, unless such young person has been presented for medical inspection

and has received from the municipal authority the book provided for in Arts. 4 *et seq.* of the regulations respecting child labour, shall be liable to a fine. Any person who procures or takes charge of one or more young persons below the age of 15 years, for purposes of employment abroad in occupations detrimental to health, shall be liable to imprisonment, etc., and the same applies to any person who deserts in a foreign country a young person below the age of 17 years who was entrusted to him within the kingdom for the purpose of employment. . . . .

SPECIAL REGULATIONS CONCERNING WOMEN

1. In Great Britain, the London County Council obtained special powers from Parliament in 1910 (London County Council General Powers Act, 1910) for the strict supervision of employment agencies, including those for recruiting women and children for abroad. Every agency must obtain a license from the County Council, which may refuse to renew or to grant a license if it considers that the holder or the offices of the agency are unsuitable or that the agency is or has been a suspect. No agent may recruit women for abroad unless in possession of information obtained from a responsible person or society or from other sources worthy of confidence, indicating the satisfactory nature of the proposed work. No agent may make proposals or conclude arrangements for employing abroad women under 16 years of age unless he has previously obtained the written consent of their parents or guardians and unless he has himself ascertained that suitable steps have been taken for the well-being of such persons during their engagement and, after the latter has terminated, for return to their own country, and that the recruitment is allowed by the law of the country where the work is to be performed.

The Foreign Office also takes special precautions in the case of women and young girls who desire to emigrate. Every application has to be personally supported by a responsible person, and all applications are the subject of very careful scrutiny. Except in the case of a passport required for a short holiday abroad, it is necessary to provide a certificate of the relatives living abroad or, in the case of a person recruited, a certificate of the employers. For young girls of under 18 years of age, the passport is only issued on the receipt of the written agreement of her parents or guardians.

2. In Greece according to the Royal Decree of 24 September, 1920, as amended by that of 17 February, 1921, the emigration of women and minors of the female sex over 16 years of age is not allowed unless accompanied by a husband, father or mother, elder brother, uncle, son-in-law, brother-in-law, or other near relation; or unless they are invited by such persons or by their prospective husbands living in the country where they wish to go, who will expressly guarantee their protection by declaration made either before the local authorities and legalised by the Greek Consul, or directly

before the Greek Consular authorities. The emigration of an adult woman may be authorised without previous declaration if, in the view of the Minister of the Interior, there are exceptional reasons for so doing.

3. In Hungary, in addition to the general provisions of the Emigration Act of 1909, the instruction issued to all municipalities by the Minister of the Interior in 1869 requires them to prevent the journey of young girls or women to the East for immoral purposes. . . . .

CASES IN WHICH IT IS PROBABLE THAT THE EMIGRANT WILL BE REFUSED ADMISSION IN THE COUNTRY TO WHICH HE IS TRAVELLING

1. According to the Austrian Bill of 1913, emigration is forbidden to all persons who would be refused permission to land in the country to which they are going.

2. The Czechoslovak Bill would prohibit the emigration of persons who would be refused admission to the countries where they intend to go.

3. In Hungary, persons who do not satisfy the conditions imposed on immigrants in the country to which they wish to go are not allowed to emigrate.

4. In the Kingdom of the Serbs, Croats and Slovenes, a passport is not granted to an emigrant unless he complies with the immigration conditions laid down in the country to which he is going. Further information on this subject will be given by the Minister for Social Affairs.

5. Under the terms of the Swiss Federal Act, emigration agents must not arrange for the departure of persons who, in accordance with the laws of the country to which they are going, would be refused admission.

Other countries (Greece, Italy, Spain) confine themselves to making clear the obligation of shipping companies to repatriate at their own cost any emigrant who is refused permission to land at the port of disembarkation for a reason which existed before embarkation, or to compensate such emigrant for all losses sustained by him in consequence. . . . .

2. **The Protection of Emigrants before Departure**[1]

Protecting the emigrant and giving him exact information constitute, one might say, the underlying principles of the legislation of most countries concerning emigration.

This protection can be most effectively provided before the departure of the emigrant. If emigration is to be carried out methodically and with the greatest possible advantage, both to the emigrant and to the countries of emigration and immigration, the persons concerned must above all be able to obtain, without difficulty, precise information on the questions which

[1] Extract from International Labour Office, *Emigration and Immigration: Legislation and Treaties* (Geneva, 1922), pp. 46-59.

affect them, particularly with regard to transport, and the conditions prevailing in the country to which they are going.

Several Governments have a National Information Office for emigrants. Generally, this office forms part of the governmental machinery which is set up for dealing with all emigration matters. In addition, there are in many countries private information offices, or other institutions or associations which make it easy for future emigrants to obtain useful information.

Apart from this, legislation aims at preventing illegal propaganda, regulating recruiting, and intervening in the matter of labour contracts in foreign countries. Supervision is exercised over the action of agencies, transport contracts, and the embarkation of emigrants, even the price of the tickets for the journey being determined.

In Austria an Information Office for Emigrants (*Oesterreichische Auskunftsstelle für Auswanderer*), established at Vienna, was founded by the Government in 1920, and is placed under the immediate control of the Minister of the Interior. Its sole object is to give all who desire to emigrate gratuitous information on emigration, particularly on the economic and health conditions of different countries, on the travelling formalities, etc.

The Austrian organisation is intended—on the assumption that the right to emigrate is recognised by law—to protect the emigrant against all forms of injury and exploitation, to prevent illegal propaganda, and to safeguard the home country against an abnormal emigration of workers. . . . .

The Czechoslovak Republic, in view of the emigration from districts formerly belonging to Hungary, the population of which has at all times been attracted to America, has established, at Bratislava, under the Minister Plenipotentiary charged with the administration of Slovakia, and at Uzhorod (Ungwar), under the Administration for the Carpathians and Ruthenia, a special section, whose duty it is to give information to emigrants and to dissipate the erroneous ideas which the inhabitants of those districts may hold with regard to the conditions in America.

Wage earners who desire to emigrate in order to obtain work abroad can apply for this purpose to the public employment exchanges.

Illicit propaganda carried on by emigration agencies is forbidden by the law of 21 April, 1897 (No. 27 of the *Bulletin of Imperial Laws*). All the regulations now in force with regard to emigration aim at the protection of emigrants against exploitation and dishonest practices.

The Emigration Bill would lay upon the Minister of Social Welfare the duty of watching over the accuracy of the information given to emigrants as to the prospects of emigration. Such information cannot be given unless authorised by the Ministry of Social Welfare. Special permission for giving information would not be needed by an undertaking authorised by law to carry on emigration business for the purpose of engaging emigrants and for performing its ordinary duties. Nor would permission be needed for publishing official information nor for publishing occasional information without a view to profit. Authorisations might always be restricted or cancelled. The Bill adds that a council would be created at the Ministry of Social Welfare for the study of all questions relating to emigration. . . . .

In Germany, the *Reichswanderungsamt* has to examine and to make extracts from communications addressed by official organisations in different countries and German representatives abroad on the conditions affecting emigration, immigration, and repatriation in each place, to obtain information on the situation from German emigrants in foreign countries, to register particulars of persons who desire to emigrate, immigrate, or be repatriated, to give information to future emigrants to any particular country, to prevent illegal recruiting of emigrants, to supervise colonisation companies or societies, to oppose in every possible way the activities of persons who attempt to draw profit from the present depression by way of recruiting, to give encouragement to all plans for the protection of emigrants, to supervise and improve the working of institutions concerned with emigration and immigration, and to ensure the regulation of repatriation, the reception of the repatriated, and the settlement of their affairs.

The information is frequently given orally to the persons interested. The activity of the office embraces the whole of Germany, and it is assisted in this by a number of subordinate offices, of which there are at present 25, and which help the central office in collecting information and in giving it to those who need it. In addition, the central office recognizes a large number of private institutions as being of benefit to the public, and it maintains official relations with them.

With a view to distributing its information more effectively, the office publishes a journal twice a month, which is available for everybody to see. It also publishes pamphlets on conditions of emigration and on the state of affairs in foreign countries, as well as leaflets (*Merkblätter*) with reference either to particular classes of emigrants or to emigrants in general. The office frequently publishes articles in the press and organises popular lectures.

Finally, the office is in communication with institutions, professional associations and trade unions, which may be able to co-operate with it, and with the Evangelical Society for Emigrants and the Catholic Association of Saint-Raphael.

The office is kept informed of the issue of passports, so that it may be able to give future emigrants all the information that may be of use to them.

The public employment exchanges are available for the use of all those who desire to emigrate. Special arrangements have been made with regard to this matter between the Federal Migration Office and the Federal Employment Board. . . . .

In Greece, the supervision and administration of the services dealing with emigration and departure for foreign countries are placed under the direction of the Minister of the Interior and entrusted to a department of this Ministry under the Director of Public Aid and Public Health.

At the Piraeus, at Patras, and in other towns determined by Royal Decree, there are emigration offices, including as a rule a section dealing with departure for foreign countries. The offices are attached to the Prefectures at emigration ports, with the exception of the emigration office at the Piraeus which is directly under the Emigration Department of the Ministry of the Interior. The work relating to emigration and to departure for foreign countries and that of the Prefecture may, on the advice of the prefect and with the approval of the Home Secretary, be concentrated in the above-mentioned offices.

There are at present no offices in Greece, either official or private, giving information on conditions of emigration and colonisation, nor are there any institutions or associations which assist emigrants to obtain information concerning the journey.

In Hungary, the Emigration Department supplies the necessary information and publications of general interest to emigrants. The Emigration Commissioners are charged with the supervision of all work concerning the protection of the emigrant.

An Emigration Council has been established at Budapest, and the Ministry of the Interior must be advised by this Council before granting a license to a transport agent, or before cancelling a license already granted. Similarly, the Council has a voice in all questions concerning emigration. . . . .

In Italy, the General Emigration Office is the central authority dealing with everything concerning emigration affairs. The Office, placed under the Ministry for Foreign Affairs, is composed of a Commissioner-General and three Commissioners. A central office is maintained, and, apart from that, officials are placed in different parts of the kingdom and in foreign countries. The Office, under the direction and political responsibility of the Ministry of Foreign Affairs, organises the emigration services of the kingdom for the grant of licenses to transport agents, fixing the price of journey tickets, maintaining organisation in the ports of embarkation, the grant of permits to recruit workers for European countries, etc.; ensures the protection of emigrants on board ship; prepares international agreements on emigration and labour; is responsible for giving aid and protection to emigrants in foreign countries; and supervises aid institutions, both public and private.

Apart from the General Emigration Office and the auxiliary services dependent upon it, there are other offices and societies, both public and private, which give emigrants the information and assistance of which they stand in need. The municipal and communal emigration committees (*comitati mandamentali e communali dell'emigrazione*), appointed by the Emigration Office and subject to its supervision, and provincial and communal labour offices (*uffici provinciali e communali del lavoro*) are official organisations.

All these institutions give information which may be useful to emigrants, either by replying to verbal or written questions or by publishing information on the conditions of emigration by means of the press or by any other means, or by distributing, sometimes gratuitously and sometimes at a small charge, guides, handbills, bulletins, etc., published by special institutions or by the Emigration Office. There are a number of weekly and monthly publications in Italy devoted entirely to emigration questions. Some of these institutions organise special instruction and evening classes in order to prepare the emigrants for the new conditions under which they will be placed. The curriculum of these classes varies according to the place to which emigrants are going, the trade or profession in which they will be engaged, the economic and social conditions of the different countries of immigration, and the intellectual standard of the intending emigrants.

Before starting, emigrants have to undergo a medical examination and are vaccinated, and their luggage is disinfected. At Naples, the principal port of emigration in Italy, there is a hostel where emigrants receive medical attention and where they are vaccinated, where they undergo a period of isolation (if necessary), are submitted to a bacteriological examination, and other medical precautions that may be found necessary are taken. Arrangements are being made for similar hostels in other Italian ports, always under the control of the Emigration Office.

At the time of departure, a committee visits and inspects the ship, and has to satisfy itself with regard to the medical condition of the passengers and the crew and the sanitary arrangements on board.

Finally, propaganda in favour of emigration by means of handbills, guides or publications of any kind is punished under the Italian Penal Code. . . . .

In Poland, the Emigration Office, established on 22 April, 1920, at the Ministry of Labour and Social Welfare, deals with all questions concerning emigration, repatriation, and the giving of assistance to emigrants. It deals particularly, in agreement with the Minister for Foreign Affairs, with the preparation of conventions and all international agreements relating to emigration, immigration, and repatriation; with the control of the recruiting of workers for foreign countries; with the action to be taken against harmful propaganda in favour of emigration and the illegal recruiting of emigrants; with gathering and supplying information as to conditions of immigration in foreign countries; the transport of emigrants and persons repatriated; assisting emigrants and persons repatriated during the voyage; the protection of the interests and rights of emigrants when at work; assisting those who have been repatriated immediately after their return; collaboration with the Finance Ministry with regard to the transfer of emigrants' savings; the encouragement of economic and social societies and institutions in Poland and abroad, whose objects are to give assistance to emigrants and repatriated persons; and the control of these associations from the point of view of the official regulations; it makes recommendations with regard to granting permission to shipping companies to sell third-class and steerage tickets; it deals, in agreement with the Superior Statistical Department, with the statistics of emigration.

The bodies through which the Emigration Office works are (*a*) the Emigration Commissioner, appointed by the Minister of Labour and the Minister of Foreign Affairs, (*b*) the offices for employment and the protection of emigrants, so far as emigration affairs are concerned, in accordance with the Decree of 27 January, 1919.

The offices for employment and the protection of emigrants, instituted by the Decree of the President of 27 January, 1919, have the duty, apart from finding employment for workers at home and abroad, of giving emigrants information as to the conditions and duration of the journey, and the work abroad, to supervise the contracts concluded by foreign recruiting agents with temporary workers, to act as intermediaries in procuring advances for the workers, to assist them in exchanging their money into the required foreign currency, and, generally, to give every possible assistance to emigrants on the outward and homeward journeys. The consular attachés . . . . are the officials who have to carry out the Polish emigration policy.

The Decree of 22 April, 1920, provided for the establishment of an advisory council or committee in connection with the Emigration Office.[1]

This committee was established by an Order of the Council of Ministers of 9 June, 1921. Its duties are to give advice on all questions of emigration and immigration, assistance to foreigners, international Draft Conventions, and the applications of steamship companies for permits authorising them to sell third-class and steerage tickets. . . . .

In the Kingdom of the Serbs, Croats and Slovenes, an emigration and immigration section has been formed in the Ministry for Social Affairs and

---

[1] With regard to social institutions for the assistance of emigrants the Polish Emigration Society at Cracow and the Emigrants' Aid Society at Warsaw were both closed at the outbreak of war. Societies which were formed during the war—such as, for example, the society for assisting the victims of the war—are philanthropic institutions having as their object a rather more general assistance of a social nature. Only occasionally has assistance been granted to emigrants by the Polish Philanthropic Society at Paris. The Polish branch of the Red Cross at Paris, the Franco-Polish Society, and the Young Men's Christian Association are developing a service of help of an intellectual nature to Polish emigrants in France. Of far greater importance is the Emigrants' Refuge at New York, kept up by the National Polish Union. Recently a Polish branch of the Hebrew-American Immigration Society has been founded; the aim of this branch is to facilitate the emigration of the Jewish population from Poland to America.

is to deal with all questions relating to emigration and to supervise all emigration and immigration services. It appoints in the principal ports of the country emigration and immigration commissioners whose duty it is to inform the police and port authorities of all contraventions of the law. All questions relating to the emigration of Jugo-Slav subjects are dealt with by the Ministry for Social Affairs, which has to publish a complete annual report of the work of the emigration section. The Minister for Social Affairs has an unlimited right of supervision over all licensed shipping companies and over their representatives, their offices, and their ships. . . . .

Swedish legislation on this subject aims primarily at protecting the emigrant against the abuses of emigration agents. This official protection is assisted by the action of certain emigrants' protective societies, such as the National Anti-Emigration Society, which has its central office at Stockholm, with subsidiary offices at the two principal ports of embarkation, Gothenburg and Malmoe. . . . .

3. Land Transport of Emigrants[1]

Emigrants travelling by rail are subject to conditions which are no better than those which prevail at sea.

Everyone has seen troops of continental emigrants travelling in old carriages, in which young and old, men, women, and children are crowded together, with their luggage, clothing and tools of all kinds.

They travel slowly, from station to station, and from country to country, in filth and misery; frozen in winter, and suffocated in summer, without proper nourishment, medical attendance, or guidance.

After a long journey, they arrive at the port of embarkation, or at their destination, in a deplorable condition. They then have to submit to long and wearisome formalities before they can sail, and they must undergo the fatigue of the sea voyage before they can reach their employment.

Such was the situation before the war. Since then it has become still worse. The trains are slower, and the carriages more dilapidated than ever. Food is even more difficult to obtain, and the customs formalities take still longer.

The German Emigration Office issued several communiqués at the beginning of 1921, drawing attention to the deplorable conditions which at present prevail in the land transport of emigrants, and to the fact that young children had died on the journey, owing to insufficient feeding, or the severity of the weather.

This situation ought to be remedied. In 1913 the 4th International Congress on Hygiene in Housing, which met at Antwerp, passed a resolution stating that the points which should be regulated were as follows:

[1] Extract from *Report of the International Emigration Commission* (International Labour Office, Geneva, Switzerland, August 21, 1921), p. 123. See also the first part of Doc. 9, p. 86, for a further incident of the land journey.

arrangement of carriages, lighting, ventilation, lavatories, drinking water, speed of trains, disinfection of carriages after use, and organisation of special disinfecting stations at various junctions and stopping places. To these should be added medical attention and feeding on the way, disinfection of persons and luggage, measures for getting rid of vermin, quarantine conditions, and various other questions.

The legislation relating to the transit of emigrants, and to continental emigration has been given in another report.[1] Some of these measures deal with the sanitary inspection of emigrants, but their aim is rather to protect the native population against epidemics introduced by emigrants than to safeguard the emigrants themselves, who are nearly always regarded as foreigners by the laws in question.

In the labour treaties which have been concluded between France and Italy and various other countries, more attention has been paid to these questions from a humanitarian point of view. Even in these treaties, however, questions relating to the transport of emigrants are generally treated superficially, or referred to special arrangements to be made by the competent administration. These arrangements have not yet been published as appendices to the treaties themselves.

[1] [*Ibid.*, pp. 86–89, and see also the report issued by the International Labour Office in 1922 on *Emigration and Immigration*, which contains the following statement regarding the transportation of emigrants by land (p. 123): "Although very numerous regulations deal with the transport of emigrants by sea, there are very few relating to their transport by land. Very few countries have adopted special measures concerning the transport of emigrants by rail, but the International Conference on Passports, Customs Formalities, and Through Tickets, which was held in Paris in October, 1920, under the auspices of the Provisional Committee on Communications and Transit of the League of Nations and charged with the study of the methods necessary to facilitate international passenger traffic by rail, considered the special situation of emigrants during their journey by land. This Conference passed the following resolution:

"That the most efficient measures should be taken to ensure that the transport of emigrants be carried out in the conditions most favourable to public health; that corridor-trains should be used, as far as possible, for the transportation of emigrants; that prolonged stoppages at frontier or other stations for the purpose of passports, customs, or sanitary formalities in connection with the transport of emigrants, should take place where material facilities exist which permit of this being done without danger to the public health; that authorities issuing passports to emigrants should, at the same time, furnish them with particulars of the sanitary and other conditions to which they will be subject, and the expenses which they will incur en route until arrival in the country of destination.

"This decision was communicated to the different Governments by the League of Nations and, although the measures indicated have not yet been adopted, several Governments have declared themselves in favour of the recommendation (Austria, Czechoslovakia, Finland, Great Britain, Germany, Greece, Hungary, Luxemburg, Netherlands, Norway, Poland, Siam, and Switzerland)."]

4. Inspection of Emigrants Abroad[1]

The practice of examining into the physical condition of emigrants at the time of embarkation is one of long standing at some European ports. In the earlier days, and in fact until quite recently, the purpose of the inspection was merely to protect the health of steerage passengers during the ocean voyage. The Belgian law of 1843 provided that in case the presence of infectious disease among passengers was suspected there should be an examination by a naval surgeon, in order to prevent the embarkation of afflicted persons. The British steerage law of 1848, the enactment of which followed the experiences of 1847, when thousands of emigrants driven from Ireland by the famine died of ship fever, provided that passengers should be examined by a physician, and those whose condition was likely to endanger the health of other passengers should not be permitted to proceed. Similar laws or regulations became general among the maritime nations and are still in effect.

The situation is also affected somewhat by provisions of the United States quarantine law, which require American consular officers to satisfy themselves of the sanitary condition of ships and passengers sailing for United States ports. The laws above referred to are intended to prevent the embarkation of persons afflicted with diseases of a quarantinable nature, and the only real and effective protection this country has against the coming of the otherwise physically or mentally defective is the United States emigration law, which, through rejections and penalties at United States ports, has made the transportation of diseased emigrants unprofitable to the steamship companies. This law is responsible for the elaborate system of examination which prevails at ports of embarkation and elsewhere in Europe at the present time.

EFFECT OF UNITED STATES IMMIGRATION LAWS

The selection of immigrants by means of national laws denying entrance to the United States to persons of certain classes began in 1875. . . . . The first really comprehensive immigration law, however, was enacted in 1891. . . . . This legislation marked the real beginning of the systematic examination of immigrants at United States ports, and the number of rejections which resulted soon compelled steamship companies to exercise some degree of care in the selection of steerage passengers at foreign ports.

The necessity of an examination abroad, however, was greatly increased by two subsequent events. The first of these occurred in 1897, when trachoma was classed by the United States Public Health and Marine-Hospital Service as a "dangerous contagious" disease within the meaning of the immigration law of 1891, and the second in 1903, when Congress, by

[1] Extract from "Emigration Conditions in Europe," *Reports of the U.S. Immigration Commission*, IV (1911), 69–80.

the immigration act of that year, provided that a fine of $100 should be imposed on steamship companies for bringing to a United States port an alien afflicted with a loathsome or dangerous contagious disease, when the existence of such disease might have been detected by a competent medical examination at the foreign port of embarkation.

As already noted, previous to this enactment the law merely provided that steamship companies should return rejected aliens at their own expense, a requirement obviously difficult of enforcement, and, in any event, not very expensive to the carrier. The fine of $100 in each case of a loathsome or dangerous contagious disease that might have been detected at a foreign port, however, made the elimination of such cases a business necessity, and it was not long until a much more thorough and effective examination abroad was instituted by the steamship companies. . . . .

THE UNITED STATES QUARANTINE LAW

Mention has been made of the United States quarantine law as a partial safeguard against the embarkation of diseased emigrants for the United States. It is this law which authorizes American consular officials, acting as quarantine officers, to participate with more or less effectiveness, according to circumstances, in the inspection of emigrants abroad. . . . .

. . . . Consular officers are required to satisfy themselves that ships sailing to United States ports, as well as the cargo, passengers, and crew of such ships, are in good sanitary condition. This is the basis for such consular examinations of emigrants as are in force at European ports.

An important provision of the law is that which authorizes the President to detail medical officers to serve in the office of the consul at any port for the purpose of making the quarantine law effective. . . . .

INSPECTION OF EMIGRANTS IN EUROPE

How to prevent the embarkation at foreign ports of emigrants who, under the immigration law, cannot be admitted at United States ports, is a serious problem, in which the welfare of the emigrant is the chief consideration. In a purely practical sense, except for the danger of contagion on shipboard, the United States is not seriously affected by the arrival of diseased persons at ports of entry, because the law does not permit them to enter the country.

From a humanitarian standpoint, however, it is obviously of the greatest importance that emigrants of the classes debarred by law from entering the United States be not allowed to embark at foreign ports. This is accomplished in a large measure under the present system of inspection aboard, for in ordinary years at least five intending emigrants are turned back at European ports to one debarred at United States ports of arrival.

In view of the importance of the subject, the Commission made a careful investigation of examination systems prevailing at the ports of Amsterdam, Antwerp, Bremen, Cherbourg, Christiania, Copenhagen, Fiume, Genoa, Glasgow, Hamburg, Havre, Libau, Liverpool, Londonderry, Marseille, Messina, Naples, Palermo, Patras, Piraeus, Queenstown, Rotterdam, and Southampton, from which ports practically all emigrants for the United States embark.

There is little uniformity in the systems of examination in force at these ports. At Naples, Palermo, and Messina, under authority of the United States quarantine law, and by agreement with the Italian Government and the steamship companies, the medical examination of steerage passengers is made by officers of the United States Public Health and Marine-Hospital Service, who exercise practically absolute control in this regard. These officers examine for defects contemplated by the United States immigration law every intended emigrant holding a steerage ticket and advise the rejection of those whose physical condition would make their admission to the United States improbable. While acting unofficially these officers have the support of both government and steamship officials, and their suggestions relative to rejections are always complied with.

The other extreme, so far as United States control is concerned, exists at Antwerp, where the Belgian Government is unwilling to yield even partial control of the situation, this attitude being due in part to a former disagreement incidental to the administration of the United States quarantine law at that port.[1] At this port not even American consular officers are permitted to interfere in the examination of emigrants. Between these extremes there exists a variety of systems in which, for the most part, American consular officials perform more or less important functions, as outlined in the United States quarantine law previously referred to.

The examination of intending emigrants, however, is not confined entirely to ports of embarkation, but in several instances is required when application for a steamship ticket is made or before the emigrant has proceeded to a port of embarkation. The most conspicuous example of such preliminary examination is the control-station system which the German Government compels the steamship companies to maintain on the German-Russian and German-Austrian frontiers. There are 13 of these stations on the frontier and 1 near Berlin. Germany, as a matter of self-protection, requires that all emigrants from eastern Europe intending to cross German territory to ports of embarkation be examined at such stations, and such as do not comply with the German law governing the emigrant traffic through the Empire or who obviously would be debarred at United States ports are rejected. . . . .

[1] [Conditions at this and certain other ports have, of course, changed in various ways since the war. There still exist, however, wide differences in procedure at the ports of different countries as regards conditions of embarkation and examination.]

In some countries an effort is made to prevent intending emigrants from leaving home unless it is evident that they will meet the requirements of examinations at control stations, ports of embarkation, or of the United States immigration laws. This is particularly true of Hungary, where at several points there is local supervision of the departure of emigrants for seaports. While this supervision is largely due to Hungary's purpose of controlling emigration, particularly where emigrants are liable to military service, the system prevents many from leaving home who would be rejected at ports of embarkation on account of disease. Members of the Commission witnessed an examination of this nature at Budapest and at Kassa, the northern terminus of the Hungarian state railway, where a government control station had recently been established. Formerly the examination at Kassa was controlled by the city police, but at the time of the committee's visit it was under the supervision of the frontier state police. It was the duty of the officer in charge at Kassa to examine all intended emigrants on their arrival at the railway station and to see that their departure was in accordance with both the Hungarian and the United States law. There was no medical examination, but the officer advised those whose physical condition was obviously defective that they would probably be rejected at the port of embarkation or at the United States port of arrival. Such emigrants, however, were allowed to proceed if they were disposed to do so. A case of this nature was observed by members of the Commission at the police-control station at Budapest, where a youthful emigrant who met the requirements of the Hungarian law was allowed to proceed to Fiume with a warning that he would be rejected there.

The numbers of rejections at the police-control stations in Hungary is not inconsiderable. According to the police records, 9,489 emigrants arrived in Kassa during the calendar year 1906 and 262 were rejected, while during the first five months of 1907, 6,526 emigrants arrived and 207 were rejected.

Medical examinations, with a view to determining the admissibility of emigrants under the United States law, are not uncommon in connection with the sale of steamship tickets. A member of the Commission found this to be the practice in Warsaw, where the ticket business is carried on secretly. At Gothenburg it was stated that steamship agents were particular not to sell tickets to emigrants whom they suspected of being diseased until the applicant had passed a private medical examination. The most conspicuous example of examinations in connection with the purchase of United States tickets was found in Greece, and this resulted from a most forcible illustration of the rigidity of the United States law.

In 1906 the Austro-Americano Company, which was then new in the emigrant carrying business, had over 300 emigrants refused admission to the United States and returned on a single voyage. On arrival at Trieste these returned emigrants mobbed the steamship company's office, and the experience resulted in the establishment by the Austro-Americano Company of a systematic scheme of examining intended emigrants in Greece. Agents of the company in that country sent their head physician to study the medical examination of immigrants at United States ports, and physicians were provided for the forty subagencies of the company in different parts of Greece. Under the system in force in Greece, before any document is given to an intended emigrant he is examined by the physician attached to the subagency. If that physician accepts him he receives a medical certificate, makes a deposit towards the price of his ticket, and space is reserved for him on a steamer. When he goes to the port of embarkation, the emigrant is examined by the company's head physician, and if accepted is permitted to complete his purchase of a ticket. On the day of sailing all emigrants are again examined at the company's office. Following the inauguration of this system of examinations there was a great and immediate reduction in the number of rejections at United States ports of immigrants brought from Greece by the Austro-Americano Line.

In Italy it is the policy of the Government to examine the records of intended emigrants at the time application is made for a passport, and unless the applicant can comply with the Italian and the United States laws the passport is refused. But this refers particularly to the cases of criminals and convicts rather than to the physically defective, and usually Italian and many other emigrants are given their first medical examination at ports of embarkation. . . . .

The large number of rejections at United States ports is not essentially an unfavorable reflection on the medical examinations conducted in Europe for the reason that the latter are in the main confined to the physical condition of emigrants, while at United States ports the examination is much broader, as may be illustrated by the fact that more are rejected there as paupers and persons likely to become public charges than on account of physical defects. It is, of course, in the interest of the steamship companies that persons likely to be rejected at United States ports be denied the privilege of crossing the ocean, for rejected persons must be returned at the expense of the company bringing them, and besides there is the likelihood of a fine being imposed for bringing diseased persons. But this is not all, for, in addition to the requirements of the United States law relative to the return of rejected immigrants to ports of embarkation, European laws, as a rule, require that steamship companies forward those returned to their homes, or home countries, which in many cases are at a considerable distance from the ports at which the rejected ones embarked. The Italian law relative to emigrants returned from foreign ports imposes even greater burdens on the carriers. Under that law the returned emigrant is entitled to damages from the carrier if he can prove that the carrier was aware, before his departure from Italy, that he could not be admitted under the law of the country to which he emigrated. A tribunal known as the arbitration commission has been established in each province of Italy to examine cases of this nature, and the emigrant who has been returned may make a claim before that commission without expense to him. In many cases, besides returning the passage money, the carrier is compelled to pay the returned emigrant for loss of wages incurred by reason of his journey across the sea. For these reasons the transportation of emigrants who cannot be admitted to the United States is usually unprofitable, but notwithstanding this fact some companies are willing to assume considerable risk for the sake of increasing their steerage business. In the main, however, the examinations conducted at the various ports are good and effective, so far as concerns the physical condition of emigrants, and as a safeguard against the transportation of the diseased, who are certain to be rejected at United States ports, they are of the greatest importance, a fact which the Commission believes is not always fully realized by students of the immigration problem in the United States.

5. Care of Emigrants by Steamship Companies before Embarkation at Liverpool[1]

Emigrants from all parts of northern and eastern Europe pass through the port. The majority of the people from the Continent land at Hull or Grimsby, where they are taken in charge by representatives of the Liverpool lines and directed to their port of embarkation. Several agents of the Commission employed in the investigation of steerage conditions on trans-Atlantic ships passed through the port of Liverpool in the guise of emigrants. One of these agents describes his experiences there as follows:

On arrival at Liverpool we were separated into groups. Those destined for the White Star Line and the Dominion Line were met by the agents of those companies; we were met by an agent of the Cunard Line. Large busses with a seating capacity ranging from 6 to 25 awaited us right at the depot. Our hand baggage was put on top and off we went to the hotel. On our way we were divided again as to nationality, for the companies named try as far as possible to keep each nationality under one roof, or at least in one part of the hotel, thus avoiding unnecessary difficulties. I was sent to the Scandinavian Hotel because they took me for a Scandinavian. The Cunard Hotel system is a village by itself in the center of Liverpool, and consists of several buildings, holding over 2,000 guests if need be. In those hotels second as well as third class passengers may remain until their steamer departs, entirely free of charge. At the Hotel Cunard, where we stayed, we were welcomed by a matron and a hotel keeper in the uniform of the Cunard Steamship Company. We were asked most kindly to eat something before we retired. I said I did not care for anything, but they insisted that I should eat something or at least drink a glass of milk. Then my room was shown to me. It held 10 beds and was well ventilated and provided with steam heat and electric lights. Both beds and floor were clean. I did not

[1] Extract from "Emigration Conditions in Europe," *Reports of the U.S. Immigration Commission*, IV (1911), 85–102. This *Report* also contains interesting accounts of the care of emigrants at the German ports of Bremen and Hamburg during the pre-war period.

see any room in this hotel with more than 15 beds in it. Women were strictly separated from the men in the sleeping rooms.

There are two dining rooms, one with a seating capacity of about 500, one with 200. The meals are wholesome. A printed menu was found in several conspicuous places. The Hebrews who stay in a separate hotel get kosher cooked meals.

The toilet and bathrooms were strictly sanitary and every part of them is marble and tiled lined. The water-closets have running water. The hotel provided towels and soap. Mostly all the hotel employees were Britonized foreigners, so as to be able to understand the foreign-speaking guests. In our Scandinavian Hotel, for instance, nearly all the employees were Swedes.

The hotel or emigrant boarding-house system above described is similar to those maintained by the other steamship lines carrying passengers from Liverpool. On the arrival of emigrants at the steamship boarding houses they are examined by resident physicians of the steamship companies who visit the houses daily. In cases or suspected cases of infectious or contagious disease the emigrants are either rejected or held for further observation.

While the majority of rejections at Liverpool are made at the boarding houses, a considerable number are turned back at the steamer on the day of sailing. Emigrants are required to board the ship several hours before sailing, and there the final examination is made. At this time emigrants are examined by one of the resident physicians of the steamship company, by the ship's doctor, and finally by a medical officer representing the British Board of Trade. Under the British law one or more Board of Trade physicians are stationed at every port from which emigrants sail, and at the time of the committee's visit the services of four such medical officers were required in connection with the embarkation of emigrants at Liverpool. When the examination is concluded a representative of the American consulate stamps with the consular seal the inspection cards of those passed. As previously explained, the British Board of Trade doctors do not inspect emigrants for defects contemplated by the United States immigration law, and do not regard trachoma as a dangerous disease within the meaning of the British merchant shipping act. Consequently steamship companies are forced to exercise every precaution to prevent the embarkation of persons likely to be rejected at United States ports. As usual, particular attention is paid to trachoma, and eye specialists are employed by the various lines to examine for this disease.

The various steamship companies at Liverpool endeavor to have their agents on the Continent require a medical examination of intended emigrants in connection with the sale of tickets, and it was stated that some of the companies allow a fixed sum to cover the cost of such examination. Cabin passengers are not medically examined at Liverpool.

When cholera, plague, or other infectious or contagious diseases prevail in continental countries from which emigrants come such emigrants are detained at Liverpool for at least five days, and are examined daily by the steamship company's resident physician, who, after the completion of the observation, certifies to the American consul that he has made a daily inspection of the detained persons, that they are free from disease, and that they will sail on the ship specified. Until this certificate is presented the consular bill of health is not issued. On the arrival of passengers from infected districts arrangements are made for the disinfection of their effects under the supervision of the American consulate. This baggage is disinfected in accordance with the United States quarantine laws and regulations. A representative of the American consulate is always present while the disinfecting process is in progress and does not leave the premises until it is completed. The committee was informed that the various steamship companies are always ready to carry out the requirements and suggestions of the consulate.

Hon. John L. Griffiths, American consul at Liverpool, at the time of the Commission's inspection, made the following statement relative to the situation at that port:

I have given a great deal of attention to the matter of the examination of third-class passengers sailing from this port to America and think that the examinations by the medical representatives of the Government and by the ships' surgeons are in the main satisfactory. I have had recently an illustration at this consulate of the rigid character of these medical examinations. An Armenian girl has been detained in Liverpool for over six months on account of trachoma, and has been pronounced cured by the physician attending her, and after such announcement has been twice rejected, the first time by the White Star Line, and the second time by the Cunard Company. The fact that the steamship companies are required to bring back all rejected passengers and are penalized for taking them over to America is of course, as you recognize, a most efficient safeguard.

I have talked frequently with the medical officers who conduct the examinations for the Government and for the steamship companies, and have been impressed with their sincere desire to do everything they possibly can to prevent the sailing of any persons who are tainted with a contagious or infectious disease. Each third-class passenger is required to submit to at least three medical examinations before being finally accepted or rejected. I required an affidavit from the ship's doctor as to all rejected passengers and the cause of rejection, so that evidence may be preserved of these facts. There is a representative from the consulate present at the final examination of third-class passengers sailing from Liverpool to American ports, and while he is not a medical expert and does not in any way control the medical examination, he does not stamp the "inspection card" until after the passenger has been medically examined and approved. In addition to this the vice-consul or myself is present from time to time at these examinations. During the three years and more that I have been at the Liverpool consulate there has been no complaint as to ill-treatment of any sort on the part of third-class passengers, or of inadequate accommodations, or inefficient or unpalatable food at the boarding houses in Liverpool which are maintained by the steamship companies.

It is the practice of steamship companies at Liverpool to detain in that city all rejected steerage passengers whose physical disabilities, in the opinion of the company's physician, would be likely to yield to medical treatment within a reasonable time. But this is only done when the company is assured by reliable persons or societies that the emigrant will be produced when demanded by the steamship company or the inspector appointed under the British aliens act. This act permits the transmigration through England of diseased or otherwise undesirable aliens who would not be permitted to remain in that country, and emigrants other than British finally rejected at British ports are deported to the country whence they came. The British inspector is advised when emigrants are detained for treatment, as above explained, and is also informed as to the final disposition of the case. The cost of the detention of diseased emigrants held for treatment is defrayed in various ways. In the case of Hebrews it is sometimes borne by the Jewish Board of Guardians, and sometimes by other charitable organizations, and in some cases the steamship companies meet the expense.

6. The Steerage Problem in 1921[1]

NATIONAL LEGISLATION

.... It is generally agreed that before the war transport conditions for emigrants were gradually improving. At the present time, however, owing to the decrease of passenger tonnage, due to destruction and to the stoppage of building during the war, they seem to have deteriorated again, especially from a sanitary point of view.

There has, nevertheless, been a certain amount of legislation on this subject, a number of laws and regulations having been passed and issued by countries of emigration.

Vessels which are intended for the transport of emigrants are usually subjected to a general preliminary inspection, in order to see whether satisfactory sanitary conditions are provided. A special classification is made in consequence of this inspection (first, second, and third-class vessels); and in some countries different rates are fixed for transport by the different classes of vessels.

The vessels have to be re-inspected before each voyage, in order to discover whether they fulfil the special conditions necessary for that particular voyage. The following points in particular are investigated: (1) food to be supplied to the emigrants and the stocks on board; (2) accommodation, air space, separation of men's and women's quarters, arrangement of bunks; (3) the hygienic arrangements, organisation of medical, sanitary, and pharmaceutical services, organization of sick bays, etc.; (4) security of vessels and passengers, life-saving apparatus, life-boats, cargo; (5) the supervision and protection of emigrants, especially women and children, against abuses and dangers to which they are exposed.

[1] Extract from *Report of the International Emigration Commission* (International Labour Office, Geneva, Switzerland, August 21, 1921), pp. 120–22.

In nearly all ports of embarkation the emigrants are also subjected to personal medical examination with a view to eliminating those who may be a source of danger to themselves or their companions on the voyage.

The countries of immigration which desire to receive healthy and vigorous immigrants also take measures in many cases to see that the travelling conditions are good. The Government of the Argentine Republic has every emigrant ship inspected on arrival, in order to see whether the sanitary conditions and safety apparatus are satisfactory; what food supply and medical attention have been provided for the passengers; whether the ship has been overcrowded; the size of the decks, the steerage and the bunks; whether any illnesses or epidemics have prevailed on board, and what is the composition of the cargo.

The legislation of the United States also contains a number of provisions concerning travelling conditions for emigrants, which are inspired by the same spirit and pursue the same object as those of the countries of emigration.

INADEQUACY AND CONTRADICTIONS OF NATIONAL LAWS

The question arises in the first place whether the situation can be regarded as satisfactory from the point of view of the emigrants. Evidence is so abundant as to make selection difficult. It will be sufficient to quote from a report of the Dutch public welfare association *Landverhuizing*, which was forwarded to the Commission by the Government of the Netherlands. This report possesses all the greater interest as it comes from a country through which a number of emigrants pass in transit, and where sanitary and hygienic conditions are generally considered to be satisfactory.

The accommodation on board emigrant vessels is seldom in accordance with modern ideas concerning the transport of passengers. Only too often the emigrants are transported as if they were human packages.

Large numbers of emigrants are crowded together in a comparatively small space, part of which is in the lower part of the vessel. Bunks to the number of 32 and more are placed close together, forming a compact mass with narrow passages between.

As regards ventilation, the port-holes—if any exist—have to be shut at least on one side when there is the slightest sea running; while the lighting is so insufficient that it is sometimes necessary to use artificial light in the middle of the day.

Communication with the deck where the boats are kept is often defective; it consists of one or two ladders which are generally steep and narrow, so that if there is any danger or panic, especially at night, when most of the passengers are in their quarters, accidents are inevitable.

Part of the accommodation is often used as a dining room, and this makes conditions still worse on account of the bad ventilation. In bad weather, when the passengers are seasick, the position becomes intolerable. It ought to be forbidden to serve meals in the sleeping quarters. The feeding of young children, and particularly infants, is often unsatisfactory.

Insufficient care is often taken from the moral point of view in providing accommodation for married couples women travelling alone, and young girls. The amount of lavatory accommodation, as well as its cleanliness, often leaves much to be desired.

It may also be asked whether the present system is satisfactory from the point of view of the shipping companies themselves.

Emigrant ships generally embark their passengers at several ports in succession—such as Hamburg, Rotterdam, Antwerp, Southampton, and Cherbourg—and also land them in different ports—e.g., Halifax and New York. They often call at half-a-dozen different countries where they are subject to different legal regulations as regards inspection and conditions of all kinds concerning the hygiene and security of the emigrants.

It should be possible to send emigrant ships to different countries, according to the season, economic conditions, and changes in legislation concerning the admission of emigrants. This, however, may be made difficult by the wide divergence between the regulations in different countries.

Up to a certain point, a shipping company may make alterations in its vessels as regards the hygienic and safety conditions of its passengers. It can allow the embarkation of doctors and increase the amount of lifesaving apparatus, but the fundamental structure of the ship cannot be changed.

At present, however, a shipowner may find very different regulations in force in different countries even on these points. . . . .

The Immigration Commission of the United States in its *Report on Steerage Conditions in 1909*, stated the amount of (cubic) air space required by the laws of the United States, the United Kingdom, Germany and Italy, both for emigrants on the lower deck and for emigrants on the passenger deck:

[AIR SPACE REQUIRED PER PERSON]

[CUBIC FEET WHEN VERTICAL SPACE BETWEEN DECKS IS SIX FEET]

On the Lower Deck				On the Passenger Deck			
U.S. Law of 1908	British Law	German Law	Italian Law	U.S. Law of 1908	British Law	German Law	Italian Law
180	150	100.6	105.9	126	108	100.6	97.1

* [The original table also gives the cubic air space requirements for each country when the height between decks is 6½, 7, 7½, 8, and 8½ feet.]

These examples show how much the legislation of various countries differs as regards sanitary conditions for emigrants on board ship. The co-ordination of the regulations would not only facilitate the application of laws on the transport of emigrants, both for the Governments and the shipping companies, but would also secure better conditions for the emigrants by the enforcement of uniform legislative, in place of the present contradictory regulations, which can never be satisfactorily applied.

7. The Italian Method of Enforcing Regulations for Protecting Emigrants on the Voyage[1]

SECTION 7. A royal commissary shall travel on every vessel carrying emigrants to overseas destinations, and shall supervise the sanitary services and the carrying out of laws and regulations respecting emigration in such manner as shall be determined in the regulations.

Royal commissaries shall as a rule be chosen from among the medical officers on active service in the Royal Navy. The medical officers of the Royal Navy who are appointed to the emigration service shall be under the control of the Commission, but shall remain on the naval list.

The royal commissaries shall be paid out of the Emigration Fund, to which the carrier shall pay the amount of the salary due to them, and they shall be entitled on both outward and return journeys, at the expense of the carrier, to accommodation of the highest class available on board the vessel.

The appointment of royal commissaries for steamships in the emigration service shall be dealt with as prescribed in the regulations.

The royal commissaries shall exercise their functions also during the return journey from the overseas port, if the vessel is going to a European port with Italian passengers travelling third class or with accommodation corresponding thereto who are returning home. When the duties of a royal commissary come to an end at a place outside the kingdom, owing to the arrangements made by the carrier, the said carrier shall furnish him with means for returning to Italy, in manner to be determined by the regulations.

8. Experiences of an Investigator in the Steerage[2]

The statements in this report, unless otherwise indicated, are based on actual experiences and observations made during a twelve days' voyage in the steerage of the ———:

I arrived in ——— as a "single woman" in the disguise of a Bohemian peasant, under an assumed name, and with passage engaged in the steerage on the ———. I called out the name of the agent from whom my ticket was purchased, ———, as directed in the circular sent me, and was approached by a porter, who carried my baggage and led me to ——— office. From here we were directed to a lodging house at which Bohemians and Moravians are usually lodged. Here I remained until my vessel sailed. . . . .

---

[1] Extract from "Act to Co-ordinate the Provisions Respecting Emigration and the Legal Protection of Emigrants, 13 November, 1919," *Bollettino della Emigrazione*, XIX, 85. Translated and published by International Labor Office, Geneva, Switzerland, Legislative Series, 1920, It. 1. For an excellent account of the Italian legislation relating to emigration, see R. F. Foerster, *The Italian Emigration of Our Times* (Cambridge, 1919), pp. 477 ff.

[2] Extract from "Steerage Conditions," *Reports of U.S. Immigration Commission*, XXXVII (1911), 13-23. The ship on which this woman investigator traveled was one having the older type of steerage.

THE JOURNEY TODAY 83

During the day it was necessary to present myself at the agent's office, pay the balance of my passage money, and give certain information about myself. This consisted of my name, age, occupation, name and address of people to whom I was going, name and address of nearest relative left behind, amount of money in my possession, nationality, last residence, whether married or single, and whether ever before in America.

Beyond this no inquiries or investigation were made as to my literacy, my past, the source of my passage money, my morals, or mental condition. My "work book"[1] which was to serve as my passport out of Austria, a counterfeit with a false and completely blurred seal, was closely examined, but no unfavorable criticism was offered.

On the day just prior to sailing all the steerage passengers who were not American citizens were vaccinated by the physician from the ——— and one other. . . . . The skin was not even pierced in any one of the three spots on my arm, and I later found this to be true in the case of many of the other passengers. The eyes were casually examined by the same physicians. Each "inspection card" was stamped by the United States consulate and also marked "vaccinated."

July 30 we went by train from ——— to ———, where in the waiting room we were classed as "families," "single women"—that is, women traveling alone—and "single men" or men traveling alone. Thus subdivided we went on board, each class into a compartment especially assigned to it.

The compartment provided for single women was in some respects superior to the quarters occupied by the other steerage passengers. It was likewise in the stern of the vessel, but was located on the main deck and had formerly been the second cabin. The others were on the first deck below the main deck.

All the steerage berths were of iron, the framework forming two tiers and having but a low partition between the individual berths. Each bunk contained a mattress filled with straw and covered with a slip made of coarse white canvas, apparently cleaned for the voyage. There were no pillows. Instead, a life-preserver was placed under the mattress at the head of each berth. A short and light-weight white blanket was the only covering provided. This each passenger might take with him on leaving. It was practically impossible to undress properly for retiring because of insufficient covering and lack of privacy. Many women had pillows from home and used shawls and other clothing for coverings.

Other conditions in our compartment were unusually good, owing to the small number of passengers, 36 instead of 194 in this particular section. We were not crowded and there was better air and fewer odors. The vacant berths could be used as clothes racks and storage space for hand baggage.

Our compartment was subdivided into three sections—one for the German women, which was completely boarded off from the rest; one for Hebrews; and one for all other creeds and nationalities together. The partition between these last two was merely a fence, consisting of four horizontal 6-inch boards. This neither kept out odors nor cut off the view.

The single men had their sleeping quarters directly below ours, and adjoining was the compartment for families and partial families—that is, women and children. In this last section, every one of the 60 beds was occupied and each passenger had only the 100 cubic feet of space required

[1] A small record book showing past employment, common among working classes in many sections of Europe. The "work book" also serves as a local passport.

by law. The Hebrews were here likewise separated from the others by the same ineffectual fence, consisting of four horizontal boards and the intervening spaces. During the first six days the entire 60 berths were separated from the rest of the room by a similar fence. Outside the fence was the so-called dining room, getting all the bedroom smells from these 60 crowded berths. Later the spaces in, above, and below the fence were entirely boarded up.

The floors in all these compartments were of wood. They were swept every morning and the aisles sprinkled lightly with sand. None of them was washed during the twelve days' voyage nor was there any indication that a disinfectant was being used on them. The beds received only such attention as each occupant gave to his own. When the steerage is full, each passenger's space is limited to his berth, which then serves as bed, clothes and towel rack, cupboard, and baggage space. There are no accommodations to encourage the steerage passenger to be clean and orderly. There was no hook on which to hang a garment, no receptacle for refuse, no cuspidor, no cans for use in case of seasickness.

Two wash rooms were provided for the use of the steerage. The first morning out I took special care to inquire for the women's wash room. One of the crew directed me to a door bearing the sign "Wash room for men." Within were both men and women. Thinking I had been misdirected, I proceeded to the other wash room. This bore no label and was likewise being used by both sexes. Repeating my inquiry another of the crew directed me just as the first had done. Evidently there was no distinction between the men's and women's wash rooms. These were on the main deck and not convenient to any of the sleeping quarters.

The one wash room, about 7 by 9 feet, contained 10 faucets of cold salt water, 5 along either of its two walls, and as many basins. These resembled in size and shape the usual stationary laundry tubs. Ten persons could scarcely have used this room at one time. The basins were seldom used on account of their great inconvenience and because of the various other services to which they must be put. To wash out of a laundry tub with only a little water on the bottom is quite difficult, and where so many persons must use so few basins one can not take the time to draw so large a basin full of water. This same basin served as a dishpan for greasy tins, as a laundry tub for soiled handkerchiefs and clothing, and as a basin for shampoos, and without receiving any special cleaning. It was the only receptacle to be found for use in the case of seasickness. . . . .

Steerage passengers may be filthy, as is often alleged, but considering the total absence of conveniences for keeping clean, this uncleanliness seems but a natural consequence. Some may really be filthy in their habits, but many make heroic efforts to keep clean. No woman with the smallest degree of modesty, and with no other conveniences than a wash room, used jointly with men, and a faucet of cold salt water can keep clean amidst such surroundings for a period of twelve days and more. It was forbidden to bring water for washing purposes into the sleeping compartments, nor was there anything in which to bring it. On different occasions some of the women rose early, brought drinking water in their soup pails and thus tried to wash themselves effectively, but were driven out when detected by a steward. . . . .

The day of landing, when inspection was made by the customs official who came on board, the toilets were clean, the floors in both toilets and wash rooms were dry, and the odor of a disinfectant was noticeable. All these were conditions that did not obtain during the voyage, or at any one time.

Each steerage passenger is to be furnished "all the eating utensils necessary." These he finds in his berth, and like the blanket they become his possession and his care. They consist of a fork, a large spoon, and a combination workingman's tin lunch pail. The bottom or pail part is used for soup and frequently as a wash basin; a small tin dish that fits into the top of the pail is used for meat and potatoes; a cylindrical projection on the lid is a dish for vegetables or stewed fruits; a tin cup that fits onto this projection is for drinks. These must serve the passenger throughout the voyage and so are generally hidden away in his berth for safe-keeping, there being no other place provided. Each washed his own dishes, and if he wished to use soap and a towel, he must provide his own.

Dish washing is not easy as there is only one faucet of warm water, and when there is no chance to use this, he has no other choice than to try to get the grease off of his tins with cold salt water. As the ordinary man doesn't carry soap and dish towels with him, he has not these aids to proper dish washing. He uses his hand towel, if he happens to have one, or his handkerchief, or must let the dishes dry in the sun. The quality of the tin and this method of washing is responsible for the fact that the dishes are soon rusty, and not fit to eat from. Here, as in the toilet and wash rooms, it would require persons of very superior intelligence, skill, and ingenuity to maintain order with the given accommodations.

The steamship company clearly complies with the requirement that tables for eating be supplied in the steerage, and in spite of efforts can not make the steerage passengers use these tables. Apparently it is true that the immigrants did not make use of the conveniences provided. But where are these tables and how convenient is it to eat at them? The main steerage dining room was a part of a compartment on the first deck below the main deck. It contained seven long tables, each with two benches, and seating at most 12 persons. The remainder of the compartment contained 60 berths closely crowded together, the sleeping quarters for families. During the first few days the partition between these crowded sleeping quarters and the dining room was but a fence made of four 6-inch boards running horizontally. Only later was this partition made a solid wall. Most people preferred the open deck to this dining room and its disagreeable odors.

A table without appointment and service means nothing. The food was brought into the dining room in large galvanized tin cans. The meat and vegetables were placed on the tables in tins resembling smaller-sized dishpans. There were no serving plates, no knives, or no spoons. Each passenger had only his combination dinner pail, which is more convenient away from the table than at it. This he had to bring himself and wash when he had finished. . . . .

The daily medical inspection of the steerage was carried on as follows: The second day out we all passed in single file before the doctor as he leisurely conversed with another officer, casting an occasional glance at the passing line. The chief steerage steward punched six holes in each passenger's inspection card, indicating that the inspection for six days was complete. One steward told me this was done to save the passengers from going through this formality every day. The fourth day out we were again reviewed. The doctor stood by. Another officer holding a cablegram blank in his hand compared each passenger's card to some writing on it. There was another inspection on the seventh day, when we were required to bare our arms and show the vaccinations. Again our cards were punched six times and this completed the medical examination. Just before landing we were reviewed by some officer who came on board and checked us off on a counting machine operated by a ship's officer.

In the women's sleeping compartment, in an inconspicuous place, there hung a small copy of section 7, passenger act of 1882, in German and English. A similar copy hung in the so-called dining room. Few of the women could read either of these languages. From the time we boarded the steamer until we landed, no woman in the steerage had a moment's privacy. One steward was always on duty in our compartment, and others of the crew came and went continually. Nor was this room a passageway to another part of the vessel. The entrance was also the only exit. The men who came may or may not have been sent there on some errand. This I could not ascertain, but I do know that, regularly, during the hour or so preceding the breakfast bell and while we were rising and dressing, several men usually passed through and returned for no ostensible reason. If it were necessary for them to pass so often, another passageway should have been provided or a more opportune time chosen. . . . .

To sum up, let me make some general statements that will give an idea of the awfulness of steerage conditions on the steamer in question. During these twelve days in the steerage I lived in a disorder and in surroundings that offended every sense. Only the fresh breeze from the sea overcame the sickening odors. The vile language of the men, the screams of the women defending themselves, the crying of children, wretched because of their surroundings, and practically every sound that reached the ear irritated beyond endurance. There was no sight before which the eye did not prefer to close. Everything was dirty, sticky, and disagreeable to the touch. Every impression was offensive. Worse than this was the general air of immorality. For fifteen hours each day I witnessed all around me this improper, indecent, and forced mingling of men and women who were total strangers and often did not understand one word of the same language. People can not live in such surroundings and not be influenced. . . . .

9. A German-Russian Frontier Control Station and a Journey in the Steerage[1]

In order to pass through the control station[2] Myslowitz, at the junction of the three countries, Germany, Austria, and Russia, it was necessary to come from some eastern point in Austria. Because of my familiarity with

[1] Extract from a report of a woman investigator who was disguised as an immigrant. "Steerage Conditions," *Reports of the United States Immigration Commission*, XXXVII (1911), 29–39.

[2] [The following account of the German "control stations" as they existed before the war is given in the *Reports of the U.S. Immigration Commission*, IV (1911), 93–94.

"One of the most interesting instances of emigrant inspection in Europe is the control-station system on the German-Russian and German-Austrian frontier. There are thirteen of these stations located at railway points along the border, and through them passes a great tide of eastern European emigration which embarks at British, French, Dutch, Belgium, and German ports. At these stations emigrants are required by a law of Germany to submit to a medical inspection, and those not meeting the requirements of that country or who obviously cannot comply with the physical tests applied to immigrants at United States ports are not allowed

it and the consequent convenience, I chose to come from Krakow. Unfornately, there was no agent for the ——— Line in that city. A partial payment on my passage brought me a ticket from the main office. The steamer ——— was to sail November 3. From Krakow to ——— is less than a twenty-four hour ride with even an ordinary train. Thinking to give myself ample time, I left Krakow Saturday, October 31, about noon, with a through ticket to ——— on fast trains. Late in the afternoon we arrived in Myslowitz. The immigrants to America were led through a narrow hall before a desk at which stood three men, one apparently an agent of the steamship companies, the other, judging by their uniforms, a Russian gendarme and a German officer. To the agent we gave up our tickets both for steamer and railroad. Then with our baggage we were led into a large hall; we from Galicia into one, immigrants from Russia into another.

These halls have tiled floors, painted walls, high ceilings, and colored-glass windows. They are steam heated and electric lighted and equipped with means of ventilation. Around the entire hall are wide wooden shelves or benches. The baggage is placed under these and on them the immigrants sleep—as many as find space. The rest sleep either on their baggage or on

---

to pass over German soil, and every year thousands are turned back to the country whence they came.

"The system has its origin in the cholera epidemic of 1892, when the port of Hamburg was badly infected, the disease presumably being introduced by Russian emigrants bound for the United States. Immediately following this outbreak it was decreed that such emigrants should not be allowed to pass through German territory and soldiers were stationed along the frontier to enforce the decree. This regulation was in effect for several months and resulted in a great loss to the steamship companies, for by that time the emigration movement from Russia to the United States had become large. The Hamburg-American and North German Lloyd lines were finally able to effect a compromise with the Government whereby the steamship companies were to erect and maintain control stations at frontier railway towns where all emigrants should undergo a thorough examination before being allowed to pass through Germany. . . . .

"At these stations all emigrants are subjected to an examination as to their health, and such persons as do not seem liable to be refused admission by the American authorities and whose transportation to America is undertaken by a representative of the above-named steamship companies will be permitted to continue their journey. . . . ."

During the year ending June 30, 1907, when the U.S. Immigration Commission obtained certain data about these stations, 455,916 "intended emigrants" were inspected at these stations and 11,814 were rejected. During the same period only 13,064 aliens were rejected or debarred at all of our American ports or only 1,250 more than were rejected at the "control stations" on the German frontier. The most important causes of rejection were trachoma for which 5,090 persons were turned back, and "granulosis," which caused the rejection of 3,779 persons.]

the floor. No other sleeping accommodations are at hand. Men, women, and children from one country are all in one hall. Poor and insufficient toilet and washrooms are situated in the small yard. Nothing is charged for accommodations during this enforced stay at Myslowitz, nor can they rightly be called accommodations.

The walls in the two halls were alive with vermin. When I noticed this and learned that I must remain until the evening of the following day, I sought to escape the threatening danger. There was no responsible person in charge to whom to apply. Finally one watchman allowed himself to be convinced that my baggage might become infected and permitted its removal to an adjoining hall, where I also insisted upon being allowed to remain. Two Polish girls who arrived on a later train were lodged with me and the three of us slept on the bench along the wall. A watchman made his bed in the other end of the room.

When once the emigrant has entered this hall or control station, and he is conducted there immediately on descending from his train, he is not allowed to leave the building except to enter the train that is to bear him from there. Food and provisions are to be had only at the canteen. The keeper was intoxicated the evening of our arrival, as were the watchman and porters during the entire time. Though the price lists on the walls contained fruits and other desirable foods, the stock at the canteen consisted mostly of drinks, beer and various wines and whiskies in small bottles. There were also tobaccos, some bread and sausage. The travelers ate such provisions as they still had from home. Sunday morning we tried to get either some coffee or tea. The canteen keeper was either still or again drunk and there was nothing to be had of him but liquors, and, moreover, his manner was most objectionable. The officers who again appeared to relieve newly arrived emigrants of their tickets declined to release us to go to the adjoining depot for some breakfast. Their reply was that there was a canteen to supply all an emigrant's needs. Finally, after 9 o'clock, the wife of the canteen keeper appeared and she consented to get us some coffee. By ordering it immediately we were able to have some dinner at noon. This consisted of soup, boiled beef, potato salad, and bread. The price charged us was 25 cents. Later a higher price was asked of others. This, of course, was exorbitant and far beyond the means of the average emigrant. Besides, not less than the full meal could be had, and this must be ordered a half day in advance. Prices, too, were constantly wavering, and getting correct change was all mere luck. German, Russian, and Polish were all spoken in the canteen, and German, Russian, and Austrian money all accepted. Ignorance of some one of these languages or coins was continually affected in order to defraud. A Russian laid a half mark on the counter and ordered a glass of beer. He drank it and waited for change. Receiving none, he asked for it. The waiter pretended he had been given only the price of the beer. In other instances he argued that the coin given him had not the supposed value, or returned too little change. More often he insisted on explaining in a language unknown to the emigrant. There was constant argument at the bar about overcharges, and watching the transactions there for some three hours I saw that most of the complaints were well founded. In a few instances where the emigrant insisted and was about to prove his point beyond dispute he was turned over to the drunken canteen keeper, who talked so loudly and so without reason that no argument availed.

It was not only difficult, but practically impossible to get any food, while beer and whiskey tempted the hungry and the thirsty. Needless to say many of the emigrants drank more or less, not only in Myslowitz but later in the train. Liquor was the one thing with which a person could supply himself for the journey.

About 2 o'clock the doctor came and the examination, for which some were detained twenty-four hours, some longer, was to take place. All were driven into one room and passed single file before the doctor. He examined each one's eyes and the ordeal was over. The clothing and baggage of some of the Russian Jews was disinfected, our tickets were returned, and we were sorted and packed into the train. . . . .

The coaches were the regular third-class kind, supplied with wooden seats, and divided into coupés. They were filled to the utmost capacity and the numerous and bulky baggage filled the racks overhead and the floor. Some coupés were so filled that the occupants took turns standing. . . . . After twenty hours' ride we gladly piled out of the train at ———.

We were first led into a room for examination. A physician looked into each one's eyes. Another officer measured each one, noted his description and birthplace. Another officer put the usual questions as to age, kind of employment, address of friends in America and Europe, and amount of money at hand. To him were also given such papers as each had to indicate that his passage was paid or partly paid. . . . .

When the officers returned, the names of all those having passage engaged in the steerage of the ——— were called off and an interpreter was told to inform us that the steerage passengers had gone on board just before noon; that we had either to wait ten days for the steamer ——— or pay the difference, 30 marks, and go third class on the ———. This news caused great dismay to all. Waiting meant not only weariness and loss of time, but considerable expense for board and lodging. The payment of an additional 30 marks was impossible for some, for others it meant the paying out of their last coin, and how was one to get to his destination? What could he show in money in America, or how telegraph his friends there? And there was no longer time to get money from home by telegraph. Many of those from eastern Galicia and Slavonia had already had to make unexpected additional payments along the way after thinking that their transportation to New York had all been paid to the agent at home. Serious consultations took place. . . . . The agent in Prague had been most unwilling to sell a ticket for passage in the steerage, saying that practically none but Russian and Polish Jews of the filthiest habits traveled thus. Now, all my fellow-travelers from Myslowitz were to go third class and no doubt many others who were lodged elsewhere. . . . . There was more consulting, counting, borrowing, and lending. At last all had decided to pay and go and take the chances of being admitted on the other side because of lack of money. My lot was cast with the rest. . . . .

The third class on the ——— proved to be an idealized steerage. The passengers were treated with care and consideration. There was every attempt to give satisfaction. Where cabins were for any reason unsatisfactory, a new arrangement was attempted and made wherever possible. All actual human needs were supplied, with cleanliness, order, and decency. The third class was confined to the stern of the vessel.

The sleeping quarters were situated on the second deck, below the main deck. A large space extending the width of the ship was subdivided into cabins containing two, four, and six berths. Families and friends were lodged together. Men had cabins on one side, women on the other. The beds were arranged in two tiers and consisted of an iron framework, very simple but clean. Each bed was supplied with a mattress, white sheet, and a blanket and pillow having a colored gingham covering. These were clean at the outset, but were not changed during the voyage. Each cabin was furnished with a wash-basin, drinking glasses, towels, sick cans, and was cleaned every day and supplied with fresh water. . . . .

Meals were served in a large dining room seating 300 persons and situated on the first deck below the main deck. The tables accommodated 14 persons each for the most part and each was the special charge of one steward. There were red covers, white napkins (which were changed once during the journey), heavy white porcelain dishes, and good cutlery. There was a double supervision and a thorough one by two higher officers of the dining room, as well as of the sleeping quarters and promenade deck. In consequence of this the stewards performed their duties carefully and thoughtfully, and so gave splendid service. The food, though it offered practically only actual necessities, was sufficient in quantity and properly prepared and decently served. . . . .

The stewards cleaned and scrubbed all day and everything was kept clean. The floor in the dining room, the decks, and all the passage ways between the cabins were washed every day. The floors in the cabins were swept as often and washed when necessary.

There was a separate entrance to the steward's quarters, and except when taking the air on deck they did not mingle with the passengers. Sailors and others of the crew came into the third-class quarters only to perform definite duties. . . . .

During daily visits to the steerage I made the acquaintance of a Bohemian girl there. She, though somewhat surprised at the generous offer, gladly changed places on the steamer with me. Our arrangement occasioned no serious inquiries.

The steerage was located in the bow of the vessel. The first entirely inclosed deck extending the entire length and width of the steamer was termed the main deck. On this there were three large compartments. The foremost of these was assigned to the use of families or women with children. The next, not being required for sleeping quarters on this trip, had its beds piled in one corner and was supplied with long wooden tables, having benches attached on either side. This was the dining room, also the general lounging place in stormy weather. The third room was the sleeping quarters of women traveling alone. On the deck below were three similar compartments. The men slept in the middle one of these. The other two were not used on this trip. The beds were the usual iron frames used in the steerage built in two tiers and of the required dimensions. Each was supplied with a mattress and pillow of seagrass and covered with a colored slip, a pair of gray blankets and a life-preserver acting as a second pillow. These beds received no attention from the stewards throughout the entire voyage. Besides being a sleeping place, each bed also served as a repository for all hand baggage, additional clothing, and food, and as a rack for towels. Whatever belongings the steerage passenger had with him must be tucked away in his bed. Each berth, littered as it necessarily was by every possession that the passenger could not wear or carry continually on his person, was nevertheless his one and only place of refuge or withdrawal. Here, amid bags and baskets, outer wraps and better garments saved for disembarking, towels, and private drinking cups and teapots, each of us undressed for the night and combed and dressed in the morning. Nor could there be proper or even decent preparation for retiring owing both to lack of privacy and to the lack of space for the disposal of clothes. These must remain in the berth, and so it made little difference whether they were about or merely over the person. If the pipes running overhead sprung leaks, as they did on several occasions, garments were safer under the blankets than on top of them. As for privacy, that is left entirely out of consideration in the steerage, where people are housed together in such large numbers and must spend every hour of the twenty-four, and this for many days, in the presence of so many others. . . . .

The sleeping quarters were always a dismal, damp, dirty, and most unwholesome place. The air was heavy, foul, and deadening to the spirit and the mind. Those confined to these beds by reason of sickness soon lost all energy, spirit, and ambition. . . . . Such surroundings could not produce the frame of mind with which it is desirable that newcomers approach our land and receive their first impressions of it. . . . .

The steerage passenger certainly gets but very little besides his passage. Practically no consideration is had for him as regards either space, food, service, or conveniences. One of ten rules on the walls announces that the passengers are responsible for the order and cleanliness of the steerage. The difference in cost between passage in the third class and the steerage is about $7.50; the difference between accommodations is everything, and the third class does no more than provide decently for the simplest human physical needs. The white napkins are the only nonessential that might be omitted. Every other provision is essential to decency, propriety, health, and the preservation of self-respect. To travel in anything worse than what is offered in the third class is to arrive at the journey's end with a mind unfit for healthy, wholesome impressions and with a body weakened and unfit for the hardships that are involved in the beginning of life in a new land. . . . .

Observing everything closely and considering it very carefully I could not see how conditions could be improved without changing the entire general arrangement of the steerage. The undesirable features of the large sleeping compartments will continue as long as the use of the large compartments themselves continues. And so with many of the other evils; they are the inevitable accompaniments of the system itself. The total abolition of the present steerage and the substitution for it of the third class would seem the complete solution of the many evils of the steerage. . . . .

There were 450 passengers in the steerage and almost 300 in the third class. They differed very little in kind. Nevertheless it was possible to maintain cleanliness and order in the third class. The blame for the filth of the steerage can not then be placed entirely on the passengers. The third class is proof that if given an opportunity the poorer passengers do keep clean.

10. Recommendations of the United States Immigration Commission, 1911[1]

While the conditions under which immigrants are transported by sea are immeasurably better than in the days of sailing vessels or even in the early days of steam navigation, bad conditions are still found in the steerage of many transatlantic ships. Agents of the Commission traveled as immigrants in the steerage of 14 ships, representing practically all the more important transatlantic lines. These agents found that some of the lines had entirely abolished the proverbial steerage and substituted so-called third-class accommodations which were in every way comfortable and satisfactory, while on the ships of some lines the old-time steerage still prevailed. These bad conditions are at the present time entirely avoidable; and as the conditions under which immigrants are brought to the United States and the treatment they receive on shipboard are matters of concern to this country, not only from a humanitarian but from a practical standpoint, measures should be taken to insure the improvement of the immigrants' accommodations, where such improvement is needed. . . . .

[1] Extract from *Reports of the U.S. Immigration Commission*, I (1911), 30 and 46.

As the new statute relative to steerage conditions took effect so recently as January 1, 1909, and as the most modern steerage fully complies with all that is demanded under the law, the Commission's only recommendation in this connection is that a statute be immediately enacted providing for the placing of Government officials, both men and women, on vessels carrying third-class or steerage passengers for the enforcement of the law and the protection of the immigrant. The system inaugurated by the Commission of sending investigators in the steerage in the guise of immigrants should be continued at intervals by the Bureau of Immigration.

PART II

THE ADMISSION, EXCLUSION, AND EXPULSION OF ALIENS

INTRODUCTORY NOTE

The modern period of federal control over the admission of immigrants does not begin until 1882. Long before that date, however, the seaboard states, in the absence of national regulation, enacted a variety of laws dealing with the landing of alien passengers. The documents in Section I deal with these state laws and illustrate their provisions as well as certain problems of enforcement and constitutionality. In general these state laws may be classified as follows: (1) the laws relating to the landing of foreign convicts (illustrated in Document 1), of which a considerable number were passed during the closing years of the eighteenth century; (2) the poor laws (illustrated in Document 2), in which sections dealing with the importation of paupers, of the insane, and of other persons likely to become a burden to the taxpayers are found; (3) the quarantine or public-health laws, which in New York provided for a tax on alien passengers in support of the Marine Hospital—a tax which was invalidated by the decision of the United States Supreme Court in *Turner* v. *New York* (an extract from which will be found in the first part of Document 17); and, finally (4) the so-called "passenger acts" (Document 3), which may more properly be called immigration laws and which served as precedents for the later United States exclusion acts. These state passenger acts should be carefully distinguished from the so-called "passenger acts" of the United States which have already been discussed. The United States acts dealt with the carrying of passengers, and the state laws, although called passenger acts, dealt only with the admission of passengers to the respective states. The state passenger acts were the direct outgrowth of the poor laws, and in a few states, notably New York and Massachusetts, were certainly only a later substitute for those sections of the poor laws that had established a bonding system to protect the taxpayers in the port cities and states by providing for the support of the pauper, diseased, lunatic, and other immigrants who became chargeable. It should be noted that the Supreme Court of the United States in discussing the New York Passenger Act spoke of it as a police measure designed to protect the state against pauper and convict immigrants (*New York* v. *Miln*, Document 7). Similarly, in the "Passenger Cases," counsel for the city of Boston (Document 16) defended the Massachusetts Passenger Act as manifestly a pauper law growing out of a pressing emergency.

The state laws, however, proved quite ineffective to prevent the influx of undesirable immigrants. Complaints in the press (Document 4); in the Massachusetts House of Representatives (Document 5); letters from our consuls in Great Britain, Germany, and other places in Europe (Document 6); the message of Aaron Clark, Native-American mayor of New York City (Document 8); the letter of Friedrich List, our United States consul in Leipsic (Document 9); and a later series of consular letters of 1845–46 (Document 10), as well as the later complaint from the city of New York (Document 14), and the *Congressional Report of 1856* (Document 18) are typical of the numerous documents dealing with this subject.

In New York a new passenger act became necessary to prevent the gross frauds practiced on immigrants (Document 11), and to protect the destitute, whose sufferings in the private poorhouses maintained by the shipping companies or their representatives are dealt with in Document 12. The establishment in 1847 of the board known as the Commissioners of Emigration of the State of New York, which was probably the first public-welfare commission in this country, resulted in the setting-up of some very useful protective machinery at the port of New York (Documents 13 and 23). The large number of immigrants who were assisted by the commission is indicated in the "Memorial" of the German Society (Document 15).

In spite of the arrival of vast numbers of destitute immigrants and in spite of all the complaints about "undesirable immigrants," the state laws were concerned with the protection rather than the exclusion of immigrants. Deportations did occasionally take place under state laws (Document 19); but the modern drastic remedy of deportation or "retransportation" of all criminals and paupers, although discussed (Document 20), was never adopted by the states.

The decision of the United States Supreme Court in the famous passenger cases (Documents 16 and 17) did not destroy the state passenger acts since a method of getting around the decision by providing for "commutation money" (paid in lieu of bonding) was devised as a substitute for the unconstitutional head taxes. By the later decision in the case of *Henderson* v. *The Mayor* (Document 22) the commutation system was also declared unconstitutional; and the state of New York was obliged to carry on the protective work at Castle Garden and Ward's Island (Document 23) at the expense of its taxpayers, while for seven years, from 1875 to 1882, the federal government delayed the passage of an effective immigration act imposing a federal head tax, although the necessity for such legislation was vigorously urged upon Congress, especially by those connected with public charitable boards (Document 24).

The period of federal control over the admission of immigrants is dealt with in Sections II, III, and IV. The documents in Section II relate to the development of our present immigration law and the present method of enforcement. The first general immigration act of 1882,[1] entitled "An Act to Regulate Immigration," is presented as Document 1. Other acts dealing with the admission of immigrants were passed by Congress in 1885, 1887, 1888, 1891, 1893, 1903, 1907, 1910, 1917, 1918, 1919, 1921, and 1922. Extracts are given only from the law of 1882 (Document 1) and the acts of 1917–22 (Documents 9, 10, and 12), under which immigration is now regulated. Instead of extracts from the other laws, certain other documents have been selected to illustrate the problems of administration at different times and the reasons for amending the older statutes. The early exclusionist provisions were not effectively enforced; and before a decade had passed, a more vigorous policy of debarment was considered by Congress (Document 2). There were difficulties with the early attempts to exclude contract laborers (Document 3), but an extract from a more recent report of the commissioner-general of immigration (Document 4) illustrates the modern methods of preventing contract labor.

Among the methods proposed at an early date for excluding a larger number of immigrants was the adoption of the so-called "literacy test." Senator Lodge, of Massachusetts, was not only one of the earliest, but one of the most influential of the literacy-test advocates, and in Document 5 will be found extracts from one of his Congressional speeches in support of this measure. After a controversy continuing approximately for a quarter of a century, the principle of the "literacy test" was finally adopted in 1917. During this period of controversy three presidents of the United States in four different veto messages refused to sign the various bills that had been passed by Congress providing for the exclusion of illiterate immigrants, and extracts from some of these messages are reprinted in Documents 6 and 8. The literacy test was also recommended by the United States Immigra-

[1] The federal immigration act of 1875 is not considered important since it was never enforced. For a convenient topical synopsis of all the federal acts before 1910 see *U.S. Immigration Commission*, XXXIX, 85 ff.

tion Commission of 1908–11, and in Document 7 will be found the reasons on which this recommendation was based, together with other conclusions and recommendations of this important federal commission.

The Act of 1917 is important as the general law under which immigration is regulated at the present time. So important are the provisions of this Act that a considerable number of sections from it will be found in Document 9, together with certain of the rules drawn up by the Department of Labor for its administration. Extracts are also given in Documents 10 and 12 from the more recent alien anarchist and "quota" acts. The reason for the enactment of the post-war "percentum" or "quota" legislation will be found in the report of the Senate Committee on Immigration (Document 11), which recommended emergency immigration legislation; and a minority report drawn up by some opponents of the quota act in Congress is given in Document 13. Finally, the present methods of admitting or debarring immigrants at Ellis Island are described by a representative of the United States Public Health Service in Document 14.

In Section III are presented some extracts from a few of the long series of decisions of the various United States courts relating to the immigration laws and their administration. No comment on the cases selected is needed, but the importance of these cases should be emphasized since they show, as other published documents do not, the interpretation of the law by its administrators. These cases have been selected not to illustrate points of "ruling case law" nor subjects of interest to students of constitutional or administrative law. They have been chosen instead rather because of the information they give as to the problems raised from time to time in the enforcement of the immigration laws and the attitude of the courts to administrative policies. Old cases as well as "ruling cases" are valuable to the student of immigration problems.

Finally Section IV contains a series of social case records[1] taken from the files of the Immigrants' Protective League and the Immigrants' Commission of Illinois.[2] These records show the problems of admission, exclusion, and expulsion, as they arise in the cases of families

[1] In no case are the real names in the case records used. See below, p. 298, n. 1.

[2] These two organizations are really one and the same. During the years 1919–21 the League was a part of the organization of the State Commission, and after 1921, when the appropriation for the Commission was vetoed, the work was again carried on with private funds and on a smaller scale.

and individuals. They show also the methods of assisting immigrants who do not understand the terms of the law, nor the rights secured under the law to their relatives and friends who are seeking admission. Again no comment on the selection of cases is necessary, but a word as to their general significance is needed.

One of the first problems about which the immigrant needs assistance is the making of arrangements to bring over the relatives he has left behind, the wife and children, the brother and sister, the aged parents. There is every reason for encouraging the immigrant to do this and to do it promptly, and the way should be made as easy as possible. The most fundamental obligation that the good citizen feels is the duty of helping "his own," those who are dependent on him and who have a claim on him as members of the same family group. The men who are here will not live normal lives if they are long separated from their wives and children; nor will those who forget their aged parents or other relatives left behind in poverty and distress develop the strength of character and generosity of spirit that we respect. The immigrant should therefore be encouraged by public as well as private agencies to undertake the responsibilities involved in bringing over his relatives and to make the sacrifices necessary to assist them whenever there is reasonable hope of admission for those who are coming. It is hoped that the cases presented will show some of the difficulties to be faced by the immigrant who is willing to share his hard-won savings with the members of his family, the contingencies that arise in connection with the problem of admission, and the methods adopted by the government and by private welfare agencies of meeting some of these contingencies.

SECTION I

ADMISSION OF IMMIGRANTS UNDER STATE LAWS, 1788–1882

1. Legislation Relating to the Landing of Foreign Convicts, 1788–89

A. PENNSYLVANIA[1]

WHEREAS, It hath been represented to this house by the United States in Congress assembled that a practice prevails of importing felons convict into this state, under various pretences which said felons convict so imported have been sold and dispersed among the people of this state whereby much injury hath arisen to the morals of some and others have been greatly endangered in their lives and property:

Be it enacted:

.... No captain or master of any vessel or any other person or persons shall knowingly or willingly import, bring or send or cause or procure to be imported, brought or sent or be aiding or assisting therein into this commonwealth by land or water any felon convict or person under sentence of death or any other legal disability incurred by a criminal prosecution or who shall be delivered or sent to him or her from any prison or place of confinement in any place out of the United States.

And be it further enacted by the authority aforesaid:

That every captain or master of a vessel or any other person who shall so as aforesaid, import bring or send or cause or procure to be imported, brought or sent or be aiding and assisting therein, into this commonwealth by land or water or who shall as factor or agent of the person or persons so offending or as consignee sell or offer for sale any such person as above described knowing him or her so to be, shall suffer three months' imprisonment without bail or mainprize, and shall forfeit and pay over and beyond the costs of prosecution for every such person so brought, imported or sent or caused or procured so to be or sold or offered for sale, fifty pounds lawful money of Pennsylvania, one half thereof to the commonwealth and the other half to him or her who shall sue or prosecute for the same, which said penalty shall be recovered by action of debt or information in any court of record, and the defendant or person sued or impleaded therefor shall be ruled to give special bail in like manner and under the same rules as is usual in actions of debt founded on contract.

[1] "An Act to Prevent the Importation of Convicts into This Commonwealth, March 27, 1789," *Pennsylvania Statutes at Large from 1682 to 1801*, XIII, 261–62.

And be it further enacted by the authority aforesaid:

That every person who shall offend against this act or anything herein contained shall on conviction thereof be adjudged and ordered to enter into a recognizance with sufficient sureties to convey and transport within such reasonable time as shall be ordered and directed by the court to some place or places without the bounds, limits and jurisdiction of the United States every such felon convict. . . . .

B. SOUTH CAROLINA[1]

WHEREAS, The honorable the Congress of the United States by their resolve of the 16th of September last, did recommend to the several states to pass proper laws for preventing the transportation of convicted malefactors from foreign countries into the United States, and the Legislature of this State have judged it expedient to comply therewith, to prevent a practice so injurious and affrontive to the American nation;

Be it therefore enacted:

That every master or person having charge of any ship or other vessel, who shall hereafter bring into this State any convicted malefactor or person ordered for transportation for any crime or offense whatever from any foreign country, state or dominion, the ship or vessel bringing such persons shall be obliged to leave the port in which she shall arrive within 10 days after her arrival, and shall not be permitted to take or receive on board any lading whatsoever, on pain of forfeiture of such ship or vessel; and if any master shall land, or suffer to be landed, or dispose of the time or service of such person, for the payment of his passage, or any other claim or demand, such master of vessel or other person having the charge thereof, shall forfeit and pay for every convicted malefactor or person ordered for transportation, which such master shall bring into this State and offer to dispose of on indenture or other contract for service, the sum of £500 sterling.

II. And every master of any vessel, or person having charge thereof, who shall bring into this State any passenger or passengers, with intent to dispose of the time of service of such passenger or passengers for payment of his or their passage money, or any other claim, such master of vessel shall and he is thereby obliged to deliver, at the time of entering his vessel, to the collector of the port where he shall enter, a list of all such persons whom he intends to dispose for service, and a particular description of each, and the collector shall administer the following oath or affirmation, viz.—

"I A. B. do swear (or affirm) in the presence of Almighty God, that the passenger or passengers whom I have brought in my ship or vessel to be disposed of on service for his, her, or their passage, is not or are not any of

---

[1] "An Act for Preventing the Transportation of Convicted Malefactors from Foreign Countries into This State, November 4, 1788," *Public Laws of the State of South Carolina, from Its Establishment as a British Providence down to the Year 1790, Inclusive*, p. 464.

them convicted malefactors, or persons ordered for transportation for any crime or offense whatever, but on the contrary, are to the best of my information, belief and knowledge, of good fame, character and reputation, nor have I brought in my ship or vessel, with intent to be landed in this State, any person or persons who I have reason to expect is a convicted malefactor, or has been ordered for transportation for any crime or offense whatever. So help me God."

III. And if any master of any ship or other vessel shall dispose of any person for service in this State, or shall land and put on shore any passenger suspected to be a convicted malefactor before such captain or master had made oath as aforesaid, every such captain or master of such vessel shall forfeit and pay the sum of £500 for every person who shall be disposed of or put on shore contrary to the meaning and intention of this act. . . . .

2. Treatment of Foreign Paupers under State Poor Laws

A. NEW YORK[1]

And be it further enacted:

That every master of any ship or other vessel, who shall enter his ship or other vessel in the custom house of this State in the city of New York, shall, within twenty-four hours after his arrival, make a report in writing, on oath, to the mayor of the said city, or in case of his sickness or absence to the recorder of the said city for the time being, of the names and occupations of every person who shall be brought into port, in his said ship or other vessel; and in case of neglect the master of such ship or other vessel shall forfeit the sum of twenty pounds for every person so neglected to be reported. *And further:* That if any person so neglected to be reported to the mayor or recorder of the said city as aforesaid shall be a foreigner, the master of such ship or other vessel, so neglecting to make report as aforesaid, shall forfeit the sum of thirty pounds, for every foreigner so neglected to be reported. *And further:* That if any householder shall entertain in his or her house or family any such foreigner, and not report the same to the mayor, or in case of his absence or sickness, to the recorder of the said city for the time being, within twenty-four hours after he or she shall receive such foreigner into his or her house or family, he or she shall forfeit the sum of five pounds; which said respective forfeitures, shall and may be recovered by action of debt, with costs of suit, in any court within this State, having cognizance thereof, by any person or persons who shall sue and prosecute for the same to effect; the one-half of which forfeitures, when recovered, to be paid to the treasurer or chamberlain of the said city, for the use of the poor thereof, and the other half to the person or persons who shall sue and prosecute for the same to effect as aforesaid.

[1] Extract from "An Act for the Better Settlement and Relief of the Poor, March 7, 1788," *Laws of the State of New York, 1785 to 1788, Inclusive*, pp. 742–43.

And be it further enacted by the authority aforesaid:

That if any master of any ship or other vessel shall bring or land within this State, any person who cannot give a good account of himself or herself to the mayor or the recorder of the said city, for the time being as aforesaid, or who is like to be a charge to the said city, such master shall within one month, carry or send the person so imported by him, back again to the place from whence he or she came, and shall for that purpose, enter into bond to the mayor, alderman and commonalty of the city of New York, with one or more surety or sureties, to be approved of by such mayor or recorder, in the sum of one hundred pounds, conditioned for the purposes aforesaid, or shall enter into bond to the said mayor, alderman and commonalty of the said city, with one or more sufficient surety or sureties, to be approved by such mayor or recorder as aforesaid, in the sum of one hundred pounds, conditioned that the person so imported shall not be or become a charge to the said city as aforesaid or any other city or town in this State; and in case such master of any ship or other vessel, shall refuse to become bound as aforesaid, it shall and may be lawful for such mayor or recorder, by warrant under his hand and seal, directed to any constable of the said city, to cause such person so refusing, to be committed to the common gaol of the said city, there to remain until he shall consent to become bound as aforesaid; and such bond shall not be avoided by plea of duress.

B. MASSACHUSETTS[1]

[Removal or deportation upon complaint of overseers] . . . . any justice of the peace may, by warrant directed to, and which may be executed by any constable of their town or district, or any particular person by name, cause such pauper to be sent and conveyed, by land or water, to any other State, or to any place beyond sea, where he belongs, if the justice thinks proper, if he may be conveniently removed, at the expense of the Commonwealth; but if he cannot be so removed, he may be sent to and relieved, and employed in the house of correction, or work-house, at the public expense. . . . .

And be it further enacted:

That if any master or other person, having charge of any vessel, shall therein bring into, and land, or suffer to be landed in any place within this Commonwealth, any person, before that time convicted in any other State, or in any foreign country, of any infamous crime, or any for which he hath been sentenced to transportation, knowing of such conviction, or having reason to suspect it, or any person of a notoriously dissolute, infamous and abandoned life and character, knowing him or her to be such, shall, for every such offence, forfeit the sum of One Hundred Pounds, one-half

[1] Extract from "An Act Providing for the Relief and Support, Employment and Removal of the Poor, February 26, 1794," *Laws of Massachusetts, 1780 to 1800,* II, 628–29, secs. 12, 16, 17.

thereof to the use of the Commonwealth, and the other half to the use of any person being a citizen of, and residing in this Commonwealth, who shall prosecute and sue for the same, by action of debt, as aforesaid.

And in order to prevent charge to the Commonwealth, or any towns or districts therein, by the importation of such convicts, or of infirm and vicious persons,

Be it further enacted:

That the master, or any other person having charge of any vessel arriving at any place within this Commonwealth with any passengers on board, from any foreign dominion or country without the United States of America, shall, within forty-eight hours after such arrival, make a report, in writing, under his hand, of all such passengers, their names, nation, age, character and condition, so far as hath come to his knowledge, to the overseers of the poor of the town or district, at or nearest to which such vessel shall arrive, who shall record the same in a book kept for that purpose in their office. And every such master or other person, that shall neglect to make such report, or that shall wittingly and willingly make a false one, shall for each of those offences forfeit the sum of *Fifty Pounds*, to be sued for and recovered by action of debt, as aforesaid, by and to the use of such town or district.

3. Admission of Immigrants under State Legislation, 1820–33

A. NEW YORK[1]

SECTION I. *Be it enacted by the People of the State of New York, represented in Senate and Assembly,* That every master or commander of any ship or other vessel arriving at the port of New York from any country out of the United States, or from any other of the United States than this state, shall within twenty-four hours after the arrival of such ship or vessel in the said port, make a report in writing, on oath or affirmation, to the mayor of the city of New York, or in case of his sickness or absence, to the recorder of the said city, of the name, place of birth, and last legal settlement, age and occupation of every person who shall have been brought as a passenger in such ship or vessel on her last voyage from any country out of the United States, into the port of New York, or any of the United States, and from any of the United States, other than this state, to the city of New York, and of all passengers who shall have landed, or been suffered or permitted to land from such ship or vessel, at any place during such her last voyage, or have been put on board, or suffered or permitted to go on board of any other ship or vessel, with the intention of proceeding to the said city, under the penalty, on such master or commander, and the owner or owners, consignee or consignees of such ship or vessel, severally and respectively, of seventy-five dollars for every person neglected to be reported as aforesaid, and for

[1] "An Act concerning Passengers in Vessels Coming to the Port of New York, February 11, 1824," *New York Laws, 1824,* chap. 37.

every person whose name, place of birth, and last legal settlement, age and occupation, or either or any of such particulars, shall be falsely reported as aforesaid, to be sued for and recovered as hereinafter provided.

SEC. II. *And be it further enacted*, That it shall be lawful for the said mayor, or in case of his sickness or absence, for the said recorder, to require by a short endorsement on the aforesaid report, every such master or commander of any such ship or vessel to be bound with two sufficient sureties (to be approved of by the said mayor or recorder) to the mayor, alderman and commonalty of the city of New York, in such sum as the said mayor, or recorder may think proper, not exceeding three hundred dollars for each passenger not being a citizen of the United States, to idemnify and save harmless the said mayor, alderman and commonalty, and the overseers of the poor of the said city, and their successors, from all and every expense and charge which shall or may be incurred by them for the maintenance and support of every such person, and for the maintenance and support of the child or children of any such person, which may be born after such importation, in case such person or any such child or children shall at any time within two years from the date of such bond, become chargeable to the said city; and that if any such master or commander shall neglect or refuse to give such bond within three days after such vessel shall have so arrived at the said port of New York, every such master or commander, and the owner or owners, consignee or consignees of such ship or vessel, severally and respectively, shall be subject to a penalty of five hundred dollars, for each and every person not being a citizen of the United States, for whom the mayor or recorder shall determine that bonds should have been given as aforesaid, to be sued for and recovered as hereinafter provided.

SEC. III. *And be it further enacted*, That whenever any person brought in any such ship or vessel, and being a citizen of the United States, shall by the said mayor or recorder be deemed likely to become chargeable to the said city, the master or commander, owner or owners of such ship or vessel shall, upon an order for that purpose, under the hand of the said mayor, or the said recorder, remove every such person without delay to the place of his last settlement, and in default thereof shall severally and respectively be bound to pay all such charges and expenses as the said city shall or may sustain, or be put unto, in and about the maintenance and removal of such person, to be sued for and recovered as hereinafter provided.

SEC. IV. *And be it further enacted*, That every person not being a citizen of the United States, who shall enter the said city with the intention of residing therein, shall within twenty-four hours thereafter make a report of himself in writing, on oath or affirmation, to the mayor, or in case of his sickness or absence, to the recorder of the said city, stating his name, age, and occupation, the name of the ship or vessel in which he arrived, the time and place when and where he landed, and the name of the commander of such ships or vessel, under the penalty of one hundred dollars.

SEC. V. *And it be further enacted*, That all and singular the aforesaid penalties and forfeitures shall and may be sued for and recovered, with full costs of suit, by action of debt, in any court having cognizance thereof, in the name of the said mayor, alderman and commonalty, and when recovered by them shall be applied towards the support of the poor of the said city, and the defendant or defendants in every such suit shall be held to special bail, and the said *supreme* court may direct the trial thereof by a jury of any county that may be judged proper; and that it shall be lawful for the said mayor, alderman and commonalty to compound for the said penalties and forfeitures, or any of them, either before or after suing for the same, upon such terms as they may think proper. . . . .

B. MASSACHUSETTS[1]

Be it enacted by the Senate and House of Representatives:

That when any ship or vessel, having any passengers on board, who have no settlement within this Commonwealth, shall arrive at any port or harbor within the Commonwealth, the master of such ship or vessel shall, before such passengers come on shore, leave a list of their names and places of residence, with the Selectmen or Overseers of the Poor of the town where such passengers shall be landed; and if, in the opinion of said Selectmen or Overseers of the Poor, any such passengers may be liable to become chargeable for their support to the Commonwealth, the master of such ship or vessel shall, within five days after his arrival, as aforesaid, and on being notified by the Selectmen to that effect, enter into bonds, with sufficient sureties, to the satisfaction of said Selectmen, in a sum not exceeding five hundred dollars for each passenger, to indemnify and save harmless such town, as well as the Commonwealth, from all manner of charge and expense, which may arise from such passengers, for and during the term of three years; and if the master of such ship or vessel shall land any such passengers, without entering their names and giving bonds as aforesaid, he shall forfeit and pay the sum of two hundred dollars for each passenger so landed, to be recovered by action of debt, by any person who shall sue for the same; one moiety thereof to the use of the Commonwealth, and the other moiety to the prosecutor; *provided*, this act shall not take effect until the first day of May next, and that nothing in this act shall be construed to extend to the master of any ship or vessel, in any voyage on which such ship or vessel may now be employed.

C. MARYLAND[2]

WHEREAS, The frequent arrivals of passengers at the port of Baltimore have introduced into that city a great number of paupers who have become

[1] "An Act to Prevent the Introduction of Paupers from Foreign Ports or Places, February 25, 1820," *Massachusetts Laws, 1820*, chap. 290.

[2] "An Act Relating to the Importation of Passengers, March 22, 1833," *Maryland State Laws, 1833*, chap. 303.

charges upon the city and county and upon the several associations in said city, incorporated by the State, for the relief of foreign emigrants to the United States; and WHEREAS, A large proportion of the passengers in the various ships are paupers, and are, as such paupers, embarked, it is believed, under the direction of public authorities of foreign countries; and WHEREAS, It is right that the evil in question should be remedied or alleviated as far as practicable: Therefore

SECTION 1. *Be it enacted by the general assembly of Maryland*, That from and after the 1st day of September next, every master or commander of every vessel arriving from a foreign country or from any other of the United States, who shall enter said vessel at the custom-house in the city of Baltimore shall, within twenty-four hours after such entry, make a report in writing on oath to the mayor or register of said city of the name, age, and occupation of every alien who shall have been brought or carried as passenger in such vessel on the voyage whence said vessel shall have, as aforesaid, arrived, upon pain of forfeiture for every neglect or omission to make such report, of the sum of twenty dollars for every such passenger neglected or omitted to be so reported.

SEC. 2. *And be it enacted*, That said master or commander shall within forty-eight hours after the entry of said vessel pay in respect of each and every passenger aforesaid who shall be above the age of five years the sum of one dollar and fifty cents to the said mayor or register, or, at the option of said master or commander, he may, in lieu of such payment as to all or any of said passengers, become bound by specialty to the mayor and city council of Baltimore, with two sufficient sureties, to be approved by the mayor or register, in such sum not exceeding one hundred and fifty dollars for each passenger as aforesaid, as the mayor or register shall fix to indemnify and save harmless the mayor and city council of Baltimore and the trustees of the poor for Baltimore city and county from all and every expense and charge which shall or may be incurred at any time within two years from said entry for the maintenance and support of any such passenger as aforesaid so imported; and if any alien passenger brought by such vessel shall be permitted or suffered to land within said city before payment made or bond given as aforesaid, in respect of any such passenger, and before or after entry as aforesaid, the master or commander of any such vessel shall forfeit and pay the sum of one hundred dollars for every person so suffered and permitted to land as aforesaid.

SEC. 3. *And be it enacted*, That if any person, an alien passenger as aforesaid in such vessel, shall be suffered to land from such vessel at any place within a distance of fifty miles from said city with the intent to proceed to said city otherwise than in said ship or vessel, the master or commander thereof shall forfeit and pay for every such person so suffered to land the sum of one hundred dollars unless within forty-eight hours after entry as aforesaid he shall pay said sum of one dollar and fifty cents in respect of such person or persons so landed or shall become bound as aforesaid.

SEC. 4. *And be it enacted*, That all and singular the said forfeitures and penalties shall and may be sued for in the name of the mayor and city council of Baltimore before any justice of the peace, and when recovered shall be paid over to the trustees of the poor for Baltimore city and county, or in part or to such extent and in such proportion as to the mayor and city council of Baltimore shall seem fit to the German Society of Maryland and to the Hibernian Society of Baltimore, and either party in such suits shall have the right and remedy of appeal as provided in case of recovery of small debts. . . . .

SEC. 7. *And be it enacted*, That each and every master or commander of any vessel coming from a foreign country, or from any other of the United States, shall prior to her landing any alien passenger at any place in any county in this State, pay in respect of each and every passenger aforesaid. who shall be above the age of five years, the sum of one dollar and fifty cents to the clerk of the county in which such alien is landed, or at the option of said master or commander, he may prior to such landing in lieu of such payment as to all or any of said passengers become bound to the clerk of such county with two sufficient sureties to be approved by such clerk in such sum not exceeding one hundred and fifty dollars for each passenger as aforesaid, as the clerk shall fix to indemnify and save harmless such county and the trustees of the poor for such county from all and every expense or charge which shall or may be incurred at any time within two years from such landing for the maintenance and support of any such passenger as aforesaid so imported, and if any alien passenger brought by such vessel shall be permitted or suffered to land within any county in this State before payment made or bond given as aforesaid, in respect of any such passenger, the master or commander of any such vessel shall forfeit and pay the sum of one hundred dollars for every person so suffered or permitted to land as aforesaid, one-half to the use of the State, and the other to the use of the informer, to be recovered in an action of debt or indictment in any county court of any county in this State, where such master or commander shall be arrested: *Provided*, That nothing in this section shall be construed to extend to any such passenger landed in the city of Baltimore.

4. Comments on the Admission of Foreign Paupers, 1830–35

A. JULY 3, 1830[1]

Infamous conduct!—The ship "Anacreon" arrived at Norfolk last week from Liverpool, with 168 passengers, *three-fourths of whom were transported English paupers*, cast on our shores, at about four pounds, ten shillings a head, to get rid of the cost of maintaining them! And a great part of these

[1] Extract from *Niles' Weekly Register*, XXXVIII (July 3, 1830), 335.

are from 50 to 60 years of age—some older! Charity will give some of these a passage to Baltimore, and we undertake to say that we shall support at least *thirty* of this cargo of live stock in our poor house, next winter, to relieve British *agriculturalists* of the burthen of keeping them. If there was *barbarity* enough in the United States to ship off our old worn-out negroes to England, by *cargoes*, would their landing be permitted? We would not be cruel—but must resist, to the utmost possible point, such infamous *speculations* on our pockets. John Bull has "squeezed his orange," but insolently casts the skins in *our* faces.

It seems that many parishes in England have adopted this plan for relieving themselves of their old and decayed paupers. The landing of such must be prevented; and we trust that the general assembly of Maryland will adopt some strong regulations on the subject, and prevent the taxation of the good people of this state for *the support of the British government*. It will not accept our flour to feed Englishmen at home, though offered at one-half less price than their own, in exchange even for calicoes; and we must forbid the eating of it here by English paupers, at our expense.

We have a large proportion of these *miserables* from England and Ireland. Measures must be taken to shut the doors of the asylums, for our own unfortunate poor, against all such inhuman impositions. Let them be piled up in the halls of the houses of the *British* consuls, and *British* humanity take charge of them—*pay their passages back again or feed them.*

B. AUGUST 14, 1830[1]

Smuggling.—A new kind of smuggling has lately been set on foot by the British, namely, sending their perishing paupers to this country. Several cases of the kind have been noticed during the summer, in the seaboard papers; and the *Albany Daily Advertiser* contains another—witness the annexed affidavit:

Albany County, ss.—John Warren being duly sworn, says that he was born in Frazenfield, in Suffolk, England—that he is 24 years of age; that he landed in the city of New York about seven weeks ago; that he came to this country in the ship "Brunswick," and sailed from London. That his passage was paid by the parish officers of the parish to which he belonged, viz.: the parish of Shelfanger, Norfolk. He has a wife and one child, and received from the parish officers ten shillings sterling for each of his family, in addition to his passage—that a number of people from the same parish to which he belonged were sent over in the same ship. There were about 200 passengers on board of the ship, the greater part of whose passages were paid by the parish officers. That he remained in the city of New York two or three days, and then came to this city, and paid his own passage out of the money given him as above stated. That he is sick and unable to labor, and all

---

[1] *Ibid.* (August 14, 1830), p. 433.

his money is expended, and he has no means to support himself and family, and prays for relief.

C. AUGUST 21, 1830[1]

It is said that from 7,000 to 8,000 paupers have arrived in Canada during the present season, to be dropped into the United States. How much are we indebted to John Bull for such acts of kindness—such reliance on our charity!

D. OCTOBER 3, 1835[2]

The *Baltimore American* says:

A principal subject of self-congratulation to Americans, in comparing their country with those of Europe, is the exemption we enjoy from the burden of a large pauper population—a burden oppressive from the moral evils attending it, as from the tax it inflicts on a community. By the unexampled facility which all foreigners, without distinction in character, enjoy in settling among us, we are in a fair way of being deprived of this cause of congratulation. In the almshouses of the four principal American cities, the foreign paupers exceed in number the native, and the same proportion exists in many other places.

The city government of Boston lately appointed an agent, Mr. Simonds, to visit the houses of industry, correction, and reformation in various parts of the northern and middle states. One of the results of his inquiries is that in the four almshouses of New York, Philadelphia, Baltimore, and Boston, there are 4,786 Americans and 5,303 foreigners. *Would there not be a saving of expense if these five thousand and odd should be shipped back to their respective homes?* This calculation is worth making. In the same report of Mr. Simonds it is stated that of 187 persons admitted in 1833 into the poor house in Clinton county (on Lake Champlain) 152 were foreigners. This startling abuse of hospitality, as it may be called, is moreover increasing. In Niagara county, New York, the foreign poor were, in 1830, 33; in 1831, 61; and in 1833, 111. An overseer of the poor in Rochester says that seven-eighths of those who apply for relief are foreigners. Poor house officers concur in the opinion that the poor tax is paid for the support of persons, at least three-fourths of whom have fallen into poverty through intemperance.

The paupers *ought* to be sent "home"—*as they are in Great Britain.* The amount of paupers in Clinton, Niagara, etc., are on account of *invasions* by wretched beings *via Canada.* These fly direct to the poor houses of the "states," as a sure place of refuge. We have seen herds of them on the way.—*Ed. Reg.*

5. The Burden of Foreign Pauperism in Massachusetts[3]

COMMONWEALTH OF MASSACHUSETTS, HOUSE OF REPRESENTATIVES

April 9, 1836

The Committee appointed by this House, on the 25th ultimo, "to consider the expediency of instructing the Senators and requesting the Repre-

[1] Extract from *Niles' Weekly Register*, XXXVIII (August 21, 1830), 449.

[2] *Ibid.*, XLIX (October 3, 1835), 69.

[3] Extract from a report of a committee, Massachusetts House of Representatives, on "The Introduction into the United States of Paupers from Foreign Countries, April 18, 1836," U.S. 24th Congress, 1st session, *House Doc. No. 219*, pp. 1–3.

sentatives of this Commonwealth in the Congress of the United States, to use their endeavors to obtain the passage of a law by Congress to prevent the introduction of foreign paupers into this country, or to favor any other measures which Congress may be disposed to adopt to effect the object," have attended to the duty assigned them, and respectfully ask leave to report:

That, at this late period in the session of this Legislature, they have not thought it advisable to go into the minute details of this most interesting, not to say *alarming*, subject, especially as it has occupied so much of the attention of this House for several of the last years, and so much valuable information relating to it has heretofore been communicated. They have preferred to come directly to the point referred to their consideration, adverting only to such circumstances as seemed to have a direct bearing upon it.

The immense, insupportable, and by us almost inconceivable, burden of pauperism in England, which originated at first in a well intended but ill judged and most disastrous provision of law, would most naturally occupy the attention of her statesmen and philanthropists, and induce them to look in every direction for some efficient mode of relief. And it is not at all surprising that the peculiar facilities and inducements for the emigration of paupers to this country, in our immediate contiguity to the British provinces, in our extended seacoast, and more than all perhaps, in the comfortable provision here made for the poor, and "our open philanthropy and freedom in giving strangers a hearty welcome to our shores," have decided them to fix upon emigration hither as the most available measure. Former Committees of this House have perceived and pointed out the gradual developments of a plan to this effect. They have also perceived the insufficiency of any State enactments "effectually" to prevent the rapid ingress of paupers to this country, under the operations of such a plan. An appeal to Congress has been considered the only adequate remedy of the evil. But, so far as your Committee have been informed, no such appeal has yet been made. They are solemnly of the opinion, however, that it cannot safely be any longer delayed. They have ascertained that the plan of His Majesty's poor law commissioners, recommending the emigration of their poor, has not only reached its maturity in positive enactments of law, but has actually gone into operation. . . . .

Your committee find that . . . . 320 paupers, from nineteen parishes,' in eleven different counties, are reported to have emigrated during the last year. Of these 320, the cost of whose transportation was £2,473, or about £7 15s. 6d. per head, 9 went to Prince Edward's Island, 261 to Upper Canada, and the remaining 50 to the United States, notwithstanding the regulation restricting them "to some British colony."

Now let it be considered that England contains 15,635 parishes [and that if] they should all conclude, this year to follow the example of the 19 reported, so "signally beneficial" in its results, our proportion of them would be about 41,145. But, alarming as this simple calculation may seem, it is but a trifle to what we have every reason to fear. When we consider that these paupers have no claim whatever upon the provinces, how easy is the passage from the British North American provinces to the United States; and the fact, so many times communicated to this Legislature, that nearly all of the host of foreign paupers, with which we are already infested, have come in by land through the provinces; is there not reason enough to fear that we shall soon be inundated with population of this kind, if it cannot, by some means, be speedily prevented? No comment, surely, is necessary upon the fact that 261 of the 320 above-mentioned emigrants came to Upper Canada. Can it be for a moment supposed that England intends thus to burden her colonies, or that her colonies will quietly receive and provide for such accessions to their population?

As the result of their inquiries, therefore, your committee will only add the appended resolve. . . . .

Resolved, That it is expedient to instruct the Senators and request the Representatives of this Commonwealth, in the Congress of the United States, to use their endeavors to obtain the passage of a law by Congress to prevent the introduction of foreign paupers into this country; or to favor any other measures which Congress may be disposed to adopt to effect the object.

6. Deportation of Paupers from Europe: Letters from United States Consuls[1]

[On July 4, 1836, the United States Senate passed a resolution directing the secretary of the treasury to collect such facts as could be obtained respecting the deportation of paupers from Great Britain and other places "ascertaining, as nearly as possible, to what countries such persons are sent, where landed and what provision, if any, is made for their future support." Inquiries were at once addressed by the State Department to the United States consuls and commercial agents abroad. Among the replies received were the following:]

From the United States Consulate at Bremen (letter of September 5, 1836):

. . . . I am sorry that the information desired is not to be procured from authentic sources; for, properly speaking, it cannot be said that paupers are deported from Germany, though it may sometimes (but very rarely) be the case that families, almoners, and civil authorities, in order to get rid of a burdensome fellow or troublesome subject, pay what is necessary for such a person to cross the Atlantic. But, among the German emigrants, a great number of which annually embark at this port, and who nearly all

---

[1] Extract from "Report from the Secretary of the Treasury, Relative to the Deportation of Paupers from Great Britain, etc., in Obedience to the Resolution of the Senate of the 4th of July, 1836," U.S. 24th Congress, 2d session, *Senate Doc. No. 5*.

go to the United States, there are many persons and families who, when they have paid for the passage, have little or no money left, and probably many of them, on arriving in the United States, are quite destitute of all. The different Governments of Germany are, in general, not much pleased with the spirit of emigration since several years predominant in Germany, and, as is said, try by all means to keep their subjects at home. The emigrants very often loudly and bitterly complain that the said Governments, before they give to people the permission to depart, put as many obstacles as possible in the way of persons who intend to emigrate. Such emigrants, as I hear, must usually prove to their Governments that they have money enough to pay for their travelling expenses and for their passage, the said Governments being afraid that the emigrants may, by travelling uselessly, spend their little fortune, and then return and come on the charge of the community; and the emigrants are therefore obliged to renounce and give up all their rights as natives of the country. After the emigrants have got the permission to emigrate, and set out, then their former Governments do not further care for them. . . . .

From the United States Consulate at Hesse Cassel (letter of September 8, 1836):

. . . . As far as I have been able to ascertain, none of the German Governments have caused, or even indirectly sanctioned, any deportation of their paupers; on the contrary, their laws and finances forbid such operation.

The only forced deportation which has come to my knowledge, is from the free Hanseatic town of Hamburg, the Government of which deports, from time to time, those criminals which have been either condemned for life or a long period; they give them the choice either to endure their time or to emigrate; in which case the Government pays their passage. A number of them have been sent to New York, and this year to Brazil.

The great number of German paupers in the United States arises from the low rate of passage-money which of late had existed. Steerage passengers were taken last spring from Bremen, and found with good provisions, at $16 each grown person. This price the Bremen shipowners could only afford by carrying always a large number, to obtain which they had their agents all over in the interior of Germany, and induced the lower class, which live in a very impoverished state, to emigrate, by making them believe that labor was so much demanded in the United States that any able-bodied man could earn, as soon as landed, $2 a day. Young and old, healthy and sickly, thought now of nothing but to emigrate; every sacrifice was made, even their clothes were sold, and if this did not suffice, the balance begged; and all those who could scrape together enough to pay their passage went to the United States, where the majority landed penniless, and a great number of them, consisting of old people, women, and children, unable to work, as the German Government does not allow their young men to emigrate until they have fulfilled their military obligation. This traffic on the part of the Bremen shipowners will continue as long as the laws of the United States do not make their masters liable for the support of the passengers which they bring to the United States, and our shores will be filled so long with paupers of all kinds. . . . .

From the United States Consulate at Rotterdam (letter of September 13, 1836):

. . . . No deportation of paupers has taken place from this country. The passengers from hence to the United States are chiefly Germans, who emigrate voluntarily, and at their own expense; although many of them have but just the means to defray the expenses of the voyage, and are destitute on their arrival in the United States. . . . .

From the United States Consulate at Dublin (letter of September 1, 1836):

. . . . If the word "pauper" is intended to refer to that description of persons so termed in England as being entitled to relief from the parish, having no poor laws in this country, we are, of course, without any such persons in Ireland.

Our poor, in this country, are very poor indeed—so poor as to be altogether without the means of support, even for a few days, and, consequently, totally unable to provide the cost of transport to a foreign country.

The population of Ireland being very great, and rapidly increasing, and the wages of labour being very low, emigration has prevailed to much greater extent than in England or Scotland.

After having made strict inquiry on the subject, I cannot ascertain that any fund has been established by Government, or any public body, or body of individuals, for the deportation of emigrants, and I am of opinion that none such exists; but it is by no means an uncommon occurrence for individuals possessed of large landed properties in this country, being desirous to thin or lessen the population on their estates, and to increase the size of their farms by throwing several small holdings into one, to agree with such tenants to pay the expense of their passage to America. The number so deported, however, is not considerable, and has not, at this port, exceeded five or six hundred in the last five or six years, and they have been provided, I understand, with a few pounds each, with a view to their support until they could procure labor, after their arrival.

Of those who emigrate to America from this country, I should think nineteen-twentieths embark for Canada, whatever their ultimate destination may be. This is attributable, in a great measure, to the low charge for passage from hence to Quebec, compared with that from the United States, the former being twenty-five to thirty shillings for adults, the latter about five pounds. . . . .

From the United States Consulate at Belfast (letter of September 1, 1836):

. . . . There are no paupers deported by the public authorities from within my consular district. I however may remark that a considerable number of the emigrants who leave here for the United States, Canada, etc., are supposed to do so with little or no property beyond their sea-stock, and consequently land abroad nearly or wholly destitute. . . . .

From the United States Consulate at Londonderry (letter of September 19, 1836):

. . . . There has been for many years past, and still continues, a large emigration from this port to different parts of the United States, and also to the British settlements in North America; and, from my knowledge on the subject, I have no hesitation in stating that the description of persons who generally embark for the United States from this port are of good character, in comfortable circumstances, and certainly many degrees removed from paupers.

On the contrary, the greater number of the persons who embark for the British settlements, on account of the cheap conveyance, are the evil and ill-disposed, who will not do well in their own cóuntry, and the landed proprietors are glad to get rid of them, which they do by paying their passages, and laying in sufficient provisions for the voyage, totally regardless of how they are to make out life on their arrival.

The reason why North America is preferred is on account of the cheapness of the passage. . . . .

From the United States Consulate at Liverpool (letter of September 15, 1836):

. . . . I find it has been the practice with many parishes, for some years past, to send abroad such of their superabundant population as would consent to go, and although there has never been a restriction as to the place, they have invariably preferred the United States, and ninety out of a hundred, New York. Regular contracts are made by the different parishes with passenger-brokers at this place to ship them; the extent of this deportation, however, always limited in comparison with the general emigration, has recently been much diminished, in consequence, probably, of the increased demand for labor and the general prosperity of the country. The following facts are obtained from authentic sources and may be relied on. In all instances the emigration is voluntary, and the parish is not relieved by it from its obligation of support should the individual ever return. Convicts are never sent, nor the inmates of work-houses, nor those who, from age or decrepitude, are unable to support themselves. Not one person out of fifty is over fifty years old; they are generally young people who have made improvident marriages, and, without ostensible means of support, with increasing families are likely to become chargeable to their parish. Reputed poachers are a class of people frequently sent from agricultural districts, and out of at least a thousand, of various descriptions, shipped off by one of my informants, he is quite sure not more that twenty have ever returned. Some provision is always made for their immediate support, on landing at their place of destination. From five to ten pounds is paid by the shipping agent

118   IMMIGRATION: DOCUMENTS AND CASE RECORDS

to each individual on the vessel's leaving port, besides their passages being paid for, and their provisions found for the voyage.

In the year 1830, the emigration from this port to the United States is estimated at sixteen thousand; out of which about six hundred were sent by different parishes. In 1832 there were about five hundred sent at parish expense; since when, not more than three hundred have gone in a similar way in any one year; and during the last, although the general emigration was greater than at any former period, out of twenty-four or twenty-five thousand there were but about one hundred and fifty paupers. . . . .

From United States Consulate Kingston-upon-Hull (letter of August 30, 1836):

. . . . No list that can be relied on, of passengers sailing from Hull, is kept at the custom-house, which distinguishes the paupers from those of a better class; regular muster-rolls are kept, but the parties are merely described by their names, ages, and from whence they come and occupation.

The officers of the customs are well aware that paupers do proceed, both to the United States and Canada, and it has been admitted by the owners of several vessels sailing there, that their passages are paid by the overseers of the parishes to which they belong. The mode of doing this varies according to the trustworthiness of the pauper; if good, he is trusted to make his own bargain, and generally has a trifle of money advanced to him for use when he quits the vessel, to enable him to get up the country. If the man is a bad character, he is generally the best off, as the overseers pay his passage-money and procure for him the necessaries for his voyage. The man then turns restive, and oftentimes refuses to go unless more money is given him, generally £5 or £10 more than was first agreed on. So that the worse the character the better able the pauper is to make his way when he quits the vessel.

7. The First United States Supreme Court Decision Relating to the State Passenger Acts, 1837[1]

MR. JUSTICE BARBOUR:

We shall not enter into any examination of the question whether the power to regulate commerce, be or be not exclusive of the states, because the opinion which we have formed renders it unnecessary; in other words, we are of opinion that the act is not a regulation of commerce, but of police; and that being thus considered, it was passed in the exercise of a power which rightfully belonged to the states.

[1] Extract from *City of New York* v. *Miln* (36 U.S. 102), pp. 132–42, 148–51.

The constitutionality of the New York Passenger Act of 1824 was tested in the Supreme Court of the United States. This extract from the decision of the court explains the scope and purpose of the Act, which was held to be constitutional by the court. The decision was rendered in the January term, 1837, but the case was begun in 1829.

That the state of New York possessed power to pass this law before the adoption of the Constitution of the United States, might probably be taken as a truism, without the necessity of proof. But as it may tend to present it in a clearer point of view, we will quote a few passages from a standard writer upon public law, showing the origin and character of this power.

Vattel, book 2d, chap. 7, sec. 94: "The sovereign may forbid the entrance of his territory, either to foreigners in general, or in particular cases, or to certain persons, or for certain particular purposes, according as he may think it advantageous to the state."

Ibid., chap. 8, sec. 100: "Since the lord of the territory may, whenever he thinks proper, forbid its being entered, he has, no doubt, a power to annex what conditions he pleases, to the permission to enter."

The power then of New York to pass this law having undeniably existed at the formation of the constitution, the simple inquiry is, whether by that instrument it was taken from the states, and granted, to Congress; for if it were not, it yet remains with them.

If, as we think, it be a regulation, not of commerce, but police; then it is not taken from the states. To decide this, let us examine its purpose, the end to be attained, and the means of its attainment.

It is apparent, from the whole scope of the law, that the object of the legislature was, to prevent New York from being burdened by an influx of persons brought thither in ships, either from foreign countries, or from any other of the states, and for that purpose a report was required of the names, places of birth, etc., of all passengers, that the necessary steps might be taken by the city authorities to prevent them from becoming chargeable as paupers. . . . .

It has been contended, at the bar, that there is that collision [between a law of the State and a law of Congress]; and in proof of it we have been referred to the Revenue Act of 1799, and to the act of 1819, relating to passengers. The whole amount of the provision in relation to this subject, in the first of these acts, is to require, in the manifest of a cargo of goods, a statement of the names of the passengers, with their baggage, specifying the number and description of packages belonging to each respectively; now it is apparent, as well from the language of this provision as from the context, that the purpose was to prevent goods being imported without paying the duties required by law, under the pretext of being the baggage of passengers.

The Act of 1819 contains regulations obviously designed for the comfort of the passengers themselves; for this purpose it prohibits the bringing more than a certain number proportioned to the tonnage of the vessel, and prescribes the kind and quality of provisions, or sea stores, and their quality, in a certain proportion to the number of the passengers.

Another section requires the master to report to the collector a list of all passengers, designating the age, sex, occupation, the country to which they belong, etc.; which list is required to be delivered to the Secretary of State, and which he is directed to lay before Congress.

The object of this clause, in all probability, was to enable the government of the United States, to form an accurate estimate of the increase of population by emigration; but whatsoever may have been its purpose, it is obvious, that these laws only affect, through the power over navigation, the passengers whilst on their voyage, and until they shall have landed. After that, and when they have ceased to have any connexion with the ship, and when, therefore, they have ceased to be *passengers;* we are satisfied, that acts of Congress, applying to them as such, and only professing to legislate in relation to them *as such*, have then performed their office, and can, with no propriety of language, be said to come into conflict with the law of a state, whose operation only begins when that of the laws of Congress ends; whose operation is not even on the same subject, because although the person on whom it operates is the same, yet having ceased to be a *passenger*, he no longer stands in the only relation in which the laws of Congress either professed or intended to act upon him.

There is, then, no collision between the law in question and the acts of Congress just commented on; . . . .

Now in relation to the section in the act immediately before us, that is obviously passed with a view to prevent her citizens from being oppressed by the support of multitudes of poor persons, who come from foreign countries without possessing the means of supporting themselves. There can be no mode in which the power to regulate internal police could be more appropriately exercised. New York, from her particular situation, is, perhaps more than any other city in the Union, exposed to the evil of thousands of foreign emigrants arriving there, and the consequent danger of her citizens being subjected to heavy charge in the maintenance of those who are poor. It is the duty of the state to protect its citizens from this evil; they have endeavoured to do so, by passing, amongst other things, the section of the law in question. We should, upon principle, say that it had a right to do so. . . . .

Again, the power to pass quarantine laws operates on the ship which arrives, the goods which it brings, and all persons in it, whether the officers and crew, or the passengers; now the officers and crew are the agents of navigation; the ship is an instrument of it, and the cargo on board is the subject of commerce, and yet it is not only admitted, that this power remains with the states, but the laws of the United States expressly sanction the quarantines, and other restraints which shall be *required and established by the health laws of any state;* and declare that they shall be duly observed by the collectors and all other revenue officers of the United States.

We consider it unnecessary to pursue this comparison further; because we think, that if the stronger powers under the necessity of the case, by inspection laws and quarantine laws to delay the landing of a ship and cargo, which are the subjects of commerce and navigation, and to remove or even to destroy unsound and infectious articles, also the subject of commerce, can be rightfully exercised; then, that it must follow as a consequence, that powers less strong, such as the one in question, which operates upon no subject either of commerce or navigation, but which operates alone within the limits and jurisdiction of New York upon a person, at the time not even engaged in navigation, is still more clearly embraced within the general power of the states to regulate their own internal police, and to take care that no detriment come to the commonwealth.

We think it as competent and as necessary for a state to provide precautionary measures against the moral pestilence of paupers, vagabonds, and possibly convicts, as it is to guard against the physical pestilence, which may arise from unsound and infectious articles imported, or from a ship, the crew of which may be labouring under an infectious disease.

As to any supposed conflict between this provision and certain treaties of the United States, by which reciprocity as to trade and intercourse is granted to the citizens of the governments, with which those treaties were made; it is obvious to remark, that the record does not show that any person in this case was a subject or citizen of a country to which treaty stipulation applies: but, moreover, those which we have examined, stipulate that the citizens and subjects of the contracting parties shall submit themselves to the laws, decrees, and usages to which native citizens and subjects are subjected.

We are therefore of opinion, and do direct it to be certified to the circuit court for the southern district of New York, that so much of the section of the act of the legislature of New York, as applies to the breaches assigned in the declaration, does not assume to regulate commerce between the port of New York and foreign ports; and that so much of said section is constitutional. . . . .

Mr. Justice Thompson:

Can any thing fall more directly within the police power and internal regulation of a state, than that which concerns the care and management of paupers or convicts or any other class or description of persons that may be thrown into the country, and likely to endanger its safety, or become chargeable for their maintenance? It is not intended by this remark to cast any reproach upon foreigners who may arrive in this country. But if all power to guard against these mischiefs is taken away, the safety and welfare of the community may be very much endangered.

A resolution of the old Congress passed on the 16th of September, 1788, has an important bearing on this subject; 13 vol., *Journals of Congress*, 142. It is as follows: "*Resolved*, That it be and it is hereby recommended to the several states to pass proper laws for preventing the transportation of convicted malefactors from foreign countries into the United States."

Although this resolution is confined to a certain description of persons, the principle involved in it must embrace every description which may be thought to endanger the safety and security of the country. But the more important bearing which this resolution has upon the question now before the Court relates to the source of the power which is to interpose this protection. It was passed after adoption of the constitution by the convention, which was on the 17th of September, 1787. It was moved by Mr. Baldwin, and seconded by Mr. Williamson, both distinguished members of the convention, which formed the constitution; and is a strong contemporaneous expression, not only of their opinion, but that of Congress, that this was a power resting with the states; and not only not relinquished by the states, or embraced in any powers granted to the general government, but still remains exclusively in the states. . . . .

Whether, therefore, the law of New York, so far as it is drawn in question in this case, be considered as relating purely to the police and internal government of the state, and as part of the system of poor laws in the city of New York, and in this view belonging exclusively to the legislation of the state; or whether the subject-matter of the law be considered as belonging concurrently to the state and to Congress, but never having been exercised by the latter; no constitutional objection can be made to it. Although the law, as set out in the record, appears to have been recently passed, 11th February, 1824, yet a similar law has been in force in that state for nearly forty years, 1 *Rev. Laws of 1801*, p. 556; and from the references at the argument to the legislation of other states, especially those bordering on the Atlantic, similar laws exist in those states. To pronounce all such laws unconstitutional would be productive of the most serious and alarming consequences; and ought not to be done, unless demanded by the most clear and unquestioned construction of the constitution.

8. Evasion of the State Immigration Laws[1]

MAYOR'S OFFICE, NEW YORK
June 5, 1837

GENTLEMEN OF THE COMMON COUNCIL:

On the 18th of May last past, I received information that the masters or commanders of certain ships, for the manifest purpose of evading the salutary provisions of our laws, had lately landed passengers in our vicinity, with the intent that they should forthwith proceed to this city. . . . .

On the 30th of May, a letter from Dr. Rockwell, the health officer at Staten Island, was placed in my possession, as president of the board of health, in which it is stated that on the day previous there arrived at quar-

[1] Extract from "The Message of Aaron Clark, Mayor of New York, to the Common Council" (reprinted in *Niles' Weekly Register*, LII [June 17, 1837], 250–51). Aaron Clark was a member of the "Native-American" Party, and even his official messages must be read with the Native-American prejudices in mind.

antine the British ship "Lockwoods," William Lawton, master, 46 days from Liverpool, with thirty officers and seamen, two cabin passengers, and three hundred and fifty steerage passengers; that it was stated by the captain that two children were born on the passage; that the passengers were consigned to Rawson & McMurray, and the vessel to Messrs. Thomas Irvin & Company, of this city.

The health officer gave orders that the passengers should wash and clean their clothes and bedding—be landed there, and afterwards have the ship cleansed. But by the direction of the consignees, and aided by the steamboat "Statesman," and a New York pilot, all acting in gross violation of our laws, and against the best interests of our suffering city, this vessel was taken by the captain to Amboy, where the two American lighters, previously hired by him for the purpose, took the 350 steerage passengers and brought them to Jersey City. Having been early apprised of the predetermined fraud and intended insult to our rights, I despatched during the night several officers to the mayor of Jersey City, informing him of all the circumstances, and respectfully requesting his co-operation to prevent such criminal evasion of our laws. His honor at once seconded my wishes in a generous and spirited manner. The consequence was, those passengers were not landed there, but were finally put ashore in our city from the lighters, after having promised one of the commissioners of health to return to quarantine. . . . .

On the 2nd inst. I received a further notice from Dr. Rockwell, informing me that the British ships "Phoebe" with 325, "Sherbrooke" with 202, and "Harriet" with 246 steerage passengers are now on their way here, with orders to land their passengers at Amboy—all to be sent into our city.

I have also received from the commissioners of the alms house a document, of which the following is a copy, viz.:

"OFFICE OF COMMISSIONERS OF ALMS HOUSE, NEW YORK
"June 2, 1837

"At a meeting of the board, the following preamble and resolutions were adopted:

"'WHEREAS, Several vessels from foreign countries have recently entered the port of Amboy in the state of New Jersey, with passengers, have landed the same at that place, and caused them to be conveyed to the city with the view of evading the laws of this state, as existing in regard to alien passengers, and WHEREAS, Many of said passengers are liable to become a burden to this city and county by reason of poverty, and some of said passengers so introduced have already made application for admission into the alms house—

"'*Therefore, resolved,* That the mayor of this city be requested to bring the subject of such illegal introduction of passengers before the common council as speedily as possible, that such measures may be taken in the case as may be deemed appropriate and necessary. . . . .'"

The opinion is entertained that there is a settled arrangement in some parts of Europe, to send their famishing hordes to our city. The operations of certain companies have been noticed. But contractors are becoming so covetous that they afflict this country with a pauper population in consideration of receiving from steerage passengers more than $2 per head extra, for agreeing to land them in New York; instead of which, these traders in foreign paupers secretly clear their vessels for Amboy, in New Jersey, there to land the said passengers, and thereafter send them to New York by other conveyance, or leave them there to provide for themselves. Our city is generally the place to which they contract to be carried, on leaving Liverpool.

This business is likely to be fiercely driven throughout the ensuing year. Hundreds of thousands of the population of portions of Europe are in a state of poverty, excitement and wretchedness—the prospect before them very discouraging. The old country has more people than it is convenient to support. And although many of them feel no particular anxiety to leave their native land, they see others depart—they read the mixture of truth and fiction, published by those employed to obtain passengers—they are assured they can easily return if they are not suited with the country—that certain employment, enormously high wages, and almost sure wealth, await them. The times being more unpromising in other countries than in our own, they imagine they cannot change for the worse; and hither they come. They cannot fail to be an intolerable burthen to us. As soon as they arrive within our limits, many of them begin to suffer, and to beg. Some of those by the "Lockwoods" commenced as mendicants on the first day they saw our city, and some of them on the first night thereafter sought the watch house for a shelter; others solicited aid at the commissioner's office, and not a few at the mayor's residence. Nearly 2,000 arrive each week, and it is not likely that many months will elapse before the number per week will be 3,000. In the "Boreas," which came in on Saturday, there were about 150 steerage passengers. They were landed from a lighter, near the foot of Rector street, at 10 A.M. on Sunday. Some of them declared they had not means to obtain one day's storage for a chest.

Our streets are filled with the wandering crowds of these passengers— clustering in our city—unaccustomed to our climate—without money— without employment—without friends—many not speaking our language—and without any dependence for food, or raiment, or fireside— certain of nothing but hardship and a grave; and to be viewed, of course, with no very ardent sympathy by those native citizens whose immediate ancestors were the saviours of the country in its greatest peril. Besides, many of them seem not to hold opinions in harmony with the true spirit of our government. They drive our native workmen into exile, where they must war again with the savage of the wilderness—encounter again the tomahawk and scalping knife—and meet death beyond the regions of civilization and of home. It is apprehended they will bring disease among us; and if they have it not with them on arrival, they may generate a plague by collecting in crowds within small tenements and foul hovels. What is to become of them is a question of serious import. Our whole alms-house department is so full that no more can be received there without manifest hazard to the health of every inmate. Petitions signed by hundreds, asking for work, are presented in vain. Private associations for relief are almost wholly without funds. Thousands must therefore wander to and fro on the face of the earth—filling every part of our once happy land with squalid poverty and with profligacy.

It is mercy to them to keep them where they are, at their own fireside, be it ever so humble—where they will be among their relatives, and under governments that are bound to take care of them at all hazards.

The immortal patriots who declared our national independence were willing this country should form an asylum for the oppressed of all nations. And while they stood boldly forth on behalf of the several states, and counselled them to "assume among the powers of the earth, the separate and equal station to which the laws of nature and of nature's God entitled them," and while they insisted "that governments were instituted among men to *secure* the inalienable rights of life, liberty and the pursuit of happiness"— they stated as one of the causes of separation from England that the king "had sent hither swarms of officers, to harass our people and eat out their substance." Our city now complains of a similar grievance, of no less magnitude. I cannot doubt that all our citizens, both native and those we have adopted, must abhor to see this blood-bought land of liberty and hope, forcibly made the common resort, and finally the general residence, of the drones, lazzaroni, conspirators, agrarians, revolutionary incendiaries and fugitives from justice, of various parts of the old world. . . . .

The exertions to evade our laws arise, it is said, from the circumstance that the expenses and responsibilities of landing alien passengers at Amboy are merely nominal. It is, therefore, greatly desirable that the Common Council of this city should solicit the co-operation of the government of this state in an application to the proper authorities of the state of New Jersey, for the enactment of such laws there, as will make it no longer profitable for shippers, in Europe, to leave their passengers, intended for this city, at any port in that state. Justice and propriety ask this at our hands. Amboy is not the choice of the passengers, but sought by those who gather them in Europe. They soon arrive among us, with disease upon many of them; and bringing with them their miserable remains of ragged, uncleansed clothes and bedding.

Another arrangement is very desirable. At present, the vessel arrives, and the passengers very frequently, and indeed generally, come into, and become scattered throughout, the city, before they are bonded or commuted for. I am inclined to the opinion that no passengers should leave the vessel before such arrangements are first satisfactorily completed.

By chap. 56, sec. 16, of the laws and ordinances of the city of New York, it is enacted, that in all cases where the mayor shall deem it expedient to commute for alien passengers arriving at this port, instead of requiring indemnity bonds, he is authorised to receive such sum, in lieu of such bonds, as he shall deem adequate, not less than one dollar, and not more than ten dollars, for each passenger. I deem it my duty to inform the Common Council, that it is my intention, hereafter, in all cases where it would be not unreasonable, to require and demand ten dollars for such commutation, from each alien passenger. And on advising with the commissioners of the alms house as to this intention, I am authorised to say that they approve and unite with me in it. And I am bound to believe that it will receive the sanction of the public. Our city should not, whenever it can be avoided, receive more persons likely to become chargeable. It will be a herculean task to employ and take care of those who are already within our jurisdiction. Our fund appropriated for charitable purposes promises no overplus. Provisions, fuel and clothing for the alms house are still very expensive.

Laborers are not sought after; and while we pity the griefs and sorrows of all our fellow creatures, we cannot deny that a preference, in the distribution of charities as well as place and employment, is due to the descendants of the soldiers of the Revolution, and to the heroes and sufferers of the second war for independence. It was asked by the fathers of American liberty. It has been promised to their sons. It cannot be conceded to aliens without great indignity to our native and adopted citizens; and if foreign paupers and vagrants come here for political purposes, it is proof irresistible "that our naturalization laws ought to be immediately revised," and the term of residence greatly extended to qualify them to vote or hold office. Many are, I admit, orderly, well disposed men—but many of them are of the opposite character. It is believed the action of the Common Council in the premises is particularly desirable.

Our citizens had no serious turnouts—no riotous parades—no conspiracies against the business and families of quiet, industrious and honest American operatives, until after officious interference by mischievous strangers; and it is melancholy to observe, that, in the mad career of some of these foreigners to destroy our happy system, they have lately recommended to a large meeting of our citizens that they should carry with them deadly weapons, of various kinds, to all our future public assemblages. These wild strangers should learn that to do so is not "peaceably" to assemble, as provided for by the Constitution. Indeed a reason for taking proper measures to diminish the number of arrivals is drawn from the fact, that, in addition to the great and grievous expense they would add to the city, should they continue to be numerously thrown upon us, the Common

Council will be called upon to provide an armed and a mounted police for both the day and the night time. Peace cannot be otherwise expected. Many of them come from places where nothing less secures tranquillity.

9. Friedrich List's Proposed Method of Preventing Emigration of Foreign Convicts[1]

CONSULATE OF THE UNITED STATES OF AMERICA
LEIPSIC, March 8, 1837

SIR:

On your circular letter of July 7, 1836, I have made inquiries in respect to the transport of paupers from this country to the United States; but state that affairs being in this country not so openly conducted as might be desired, I have not been successful, until of late, when, by confidential communications, I have learned things which will require energetic measures upon the part of the United States to be counteracted.

Not only paupers, but even criminals, are transported from the interior of this country to the seaports, in order to be embarked there for the United States.

A Mr. De Stein, formerly an officer in the service of the Duke of Saxe Gotha, has lately made propositions to the smaller States of Saxony for transporting their criminals to the port of Bremen, and embarking them there for the United States, at $75 a head; which offer has been accepted by several of them. The first transport of criminals, who, for the greater part, have been condemned to hard labor for life (among them two notorious robbers, Pfeifer, and Albrecht), will leave Gotha on the 15th of this month; and it is intended to empty, by and by, all the workhouses and jails of that country in this manner. There is little doubt that several other states will imitate that nefarious practice. In order to stop it, I have sent an article in to the *General Gazette*, of Augsburg, wherein I have attempted to demonstrate that this behavior was contrary to all laws of nations, and that it was a shameful behavior towards a country which offers the best market to German manufacturers.

It has of late also become the general practice in the towns and boroughs of Germany, to get rid of their paupers and vicious members, by collecting the means for effectuating their passage to the United States among the inhabitants, and by supporting them from the public funds.

This practice is not only highly injurious to the United States, as it burdens them with a host of paupers and criminals, but it deters also the better and wealthier class of the inhabitants of this country from emigrating to the United States. The property the latter class has of late exported

[1] Extract from "Report from Select Committee on Foreign Paupers and Naturalization Laws, July 2, 1838," U.S. 25th Congress, 2d session, *House Report No. 1040*, pp. 54–55.

annually to the United States, has been calculated at a value of from two to four millions of dollars; and it is to be expected that this very profitable emigration would increase from year to year, in case the honest people of this country would not have to fear to be associated in the new country with the worst class of their countrymen. This, indeed, seems to be the secret motive of the above-mentioned measure. It is intended to stigmatize thereby that country which the wealthier class of the farmers and mechanics commence to consider as the land of promise.

To remedy that evil, I would propose the following measures:

1. That all persons intending to emigrate to the United States would have to produce to the Consul of the United States in the seaport a testimonial from the magistrate of their residence, purporting that they have not been punished for a crime (political punishments excepted) for the last three years; that they have not been in a jail or workhouse during that period; and that they are able to maintain themselves by their labor or capital.

2. That the Consul of the United States in the seaport should have to certify these testimonials; and that the masters of ships who would take a passenger without such a testimonial should have to pay a considerable fine on landing him in the United States.

3. That the Consul of the United States in the seaport should have power to refuse his certificate to all those emigrants who, in his opinion, would become a burden to the community on their arrival in the United States.

I am, sir, with high consideration, your most obedient and humble servant,

(Signed) F. List

Hon. Levi Woodbury
Secretary of the Treasury

10. Consular Reports on Importation of Foreign Criminals and Paupers, 1845–46[1]

From a communication of George H. Goundie, United States consul, Basle, Switzerland, to the secretary of state, dated March 27, 1846:

"It has come to my knowledge, of late, that the custom of congregations or town authorities sending their paupers to the United States still prevails, and is again practised to a serious extent this spring. I have seen people thus sent passing through this place on their way to Havre, and from their own lips have ascertained the fact. Contracts are made with emigrant agents (who swarm in these parts) in order to ship them in the cheapest possible manner to New York or New Orleans; landing them, and in many cases old and infirm, without a cent of money in their possession. In order to put a stop to this business, I had published, in Swiss and German papers, the late act passed by the legislature of the State of New York, and which

[1] Extract from U.S. 29th Congress, 2d session, *Senate Doc. No. 161*.

I obtained from the *New York Herald* of the 17th January, 1846, which makes owners, captains, and agents of vessels landing emigrants at New York, liable that they shall not become a charge to the city or State for a term of two years after their arrival. This, of course, will make captains, etc., more particular. I have already seen the beneficial effects of these publications. It has not entirely put a stop to sending paupers to the United States; but in every instance since its publication have they been provided with sufficient means to carry them into the interior after their landing, and also for providing themselves with the most necessary articles after arriving at their place of destination. The emigrant business is entirely in the hands of foreigners, who are in the habit of misleading these poor people in the most shameful manner, merely for the sake of getting their 5 per cent, for forwarding them to the seaport. This commission is then paid by the brokers or agents residing at the place of shipment, who draw their commissions from the owners or captains of the vessels, or have the benefit of supplying the emigrant with provisions for the voyage. Papers in this section of the country are filled with such emigrant advertisements—one underbidding the other, in order to induce the emigrant to apply to them for passage. I have had instances where they were promised a passage of ten days to New York, and three more to Milwaukee!

"One man in Bremen advertises that he takes passengers in large 3-mast frigates to the United States!"

From a communication of the same to the same, October 10, 1846:
"I also enclose a slip taken from the Frankfort-on-the-Main *Journal* of the 21st September, headed "Berlin," by which you will find that the charge made against certain German governments of sending their convicts to the United States, and which has been contradicted by certain German representatives in the United States, appears to be only too true. It had formerly been practised in Switzerland and Baden, also; but shortly after my arrival I remonstrated against the practice, and I believe I have been successful in completely putting a stop to it in these parts. I think it is enough if we take their paupers, and should resist the introduction of their criminals with determination. If thousands of paupers have been sent to the United States (the funds having been raised by contribution in the towns and villages), next year will bring tens of thousands, if they can be saved from starvation during this winter. It is a matter of serious consideration."

From a communication of John Cuthbert, United States consul at Hamburg, to the secretary of state, October 27, 1846:
"I had the honor to address you on the 13th instant; and after my letter was sealed, I received information of the arrival of ten convicts from Mecklenburg, to be transported to Galveston, per brig "Albatross." I called immediately at the police, and warned the officers not to permit their

being sent on board, and that in the morning I would hand them a protest against those, or any other convicts, being sent to the United States; copy of which I enclose. I have since learned that those ten were to be followed by three or four hundred in the spring, the prisons in Germany being full."

11. Frauds upon Immigrants after Arrival at the Port of New York

A. TESTIMONY OF THE SECRETARY OF A PROTECTIVE SOCIETY, 1846[1]

William L. Roy, of the city of Brooklyn, being duly sworn, deposes and says, that he is over forty-five years of age, that he has been secretary of the United States Immigrant Society for the protection of English and Scotch immigrants, for the last three years. That these societies were formed principally to protect the English or Scotch immigrants from the frauds practiced upon them on their arrival in this country. That the resident English and Scotch were made conversant with so many evils and frauds committed upon their countrymen that they deemed it an act of humanity to protect them on their arrival; and in saving their own countrymen from these evils, they ascertained that other immigrants also suffered from similar causes, and their efforts have also been directed to relieve the Irishman, German, and indeed, all who sought the free institutions and liberal views of this country, and a freedom from the oppressions of the old world; and for similar purposes, other societies have been formed in the city, and all done more or less for the relief of the ignorant and oppressed, the sick and the poor, as they come to our shores. This examination has enabled the benevolent to discover evils incident to the present quarantine laws, and the citizens who have associated themselves for the benevolent purpose of aiding their friends or strangers find that the law is now, in many respects, oppressive, and might be remedied with safety to the health of the city, and at the same time add to the happiness of many objects of humanity, and keep the stranger from the ills incident to the operation of the law as it now exists. The property of these individuals is often unjustly taken, their morals injured, their health destroyed, and they not unfrequently prevented from becoming good citizens by being driven from the correct channels of citizenship, to the waywardness and crime of dissipation, poverty and despair.

That on arrival of vessels from Europe with steerage passengers, during the summer months, they are required to remain at quarantine, land their passengers, and they be brought to the city by lighters. That this subjects the immigrants to be sent to the quarantine dock immediately, and the bunks for the sleeping of the passengers are immediately broken up, and the passengers to be taken from the dock in open and uncovered lighters to the city

[1] Extract from testimony given by William L. Roy in 1846 before a committee of the New York State Assembly (*New York Assembly Doc. No. 60* [1846], pp. 303–4).

or interior. That in the crowding of great numbers at a time, and the necessity of having their baggage examined in great haste, often baggage is lost, the passengers out without a shade in a hot sun for a long time, or exposed to the night air, rains and storms, without any comfortable places for rest, and without food; and landed at a wharf in a strange city, at all hours, which creates the necessity of engaging lodgings without any judgment, or passages west, and paying for them without knowing to whom the money is going, or whether they will be justly credited therewith, or if credited with what is paid; whether the price paid is not exorbitant. These ills, necessary to a just performance of duty, are very great; but when enhanced by those which the cupidity of man devises, they become so severe that Heaven calls for relief.

Persons are allowed to go on shipboard, the lighters, and on the wharves in the city, who make representations which prove to be false; lead the immigrant into houses in the city unfit for man to live in and they require exorbitant pay; or take money for the transporting of the immigrant west, and give worthless tickets for a passage, or charge a very much larger price than the actual charge by respectable and responsible lines of steam or canal boats. Cases, which come under the evils above enumerated, are very frequent and very grievous, and the fact that some vessels arrive with from three to five hundred passengers each, and together bring to our port from 60,000 to 80,000 immigrants annually, and they principally in the summer months, make the evils not only great in individual cases, but enormous when looked at in the aggregate.

B. A LEGISLATIVE COMMITTEE'S REPORT[1]

. . . . The reports and rumors which have, from time to time, appeared in the public newspapers, within the last year, of the frauds and impositions practiced upon these strangers in our land, have fallen vastly short of the reality. It . . . . appears that this is no new invention, but that these frauds have been carried on for several years to a more limited extent, without attracting much notice, or seeming to excite much interest among those who should be the first to protect and the last to prey upon this class of their fellow beings. But it has been left to the present year, when the increase of emigration, owing to causes well known to exist in the old world, has been not only beyond all former precedent, but beyond all calculation, for those who make it their business to subsist by defrauding and plundering these people, to realize a golden harvest.

Your committee must confess, that they had no conception of, nor would they have believed the extent to which these frauds and outrages have been practiced, until they came to investigate them.

[1] Extract from "Report of the Select Committee to Investigate Frauds upon Emigrant Passengers," *New York Assembly Doc. No. 46* (1848), pp. 4–8.

As soon as a ship loaded with these emigrants reaches our shores, it is boarded by a class of men called runners, either in the employment of boarding house keepers or forwarding establishments, soliciting custom for their employers. In order the more successfully to enable the latter to gain the confidence of the emigrant, they usually employ those who can speak the same language as the emigrant. If they cannot succeed in any other way in getting possession and control over the object of their prey, they proceed to take charge of their luggage, and take it to some boarding house for safe-keeping, and generally under the assurance that they will charge nothing for carriage hire or storage. In this way, they are induced to go to some emigrant boarding house, of which there are a great many in the city, and then too often under a pretence that they will charge but a small sum for meals or board, the keepers of these houses induce these people to stay a few days, and when they come to leave usually charge them three or four times as much as they agreed or expected to pay, and exorbitant prices for storing their luggage, and in case of their inability to pay, their luggage is detained as security.

Some of these runners are employed by the month, and some work upon commission. Where they are in the employment of the forwarding establishments or passenger officers, and receive a commission for each passenger they bring in, they are in many cases allowed by their employers to charge all they can get over a certain sum for transporting the passenger to a particular place. This, it will be seen, stimulates the runners to great exertions, not only to get as many passengers as possible, but to get them at the highest possible prices. To enable them to carry out their designs, all sorts of falsehoods are resorted to, to mislead and deceive the emigrant as to the prices of fare and the modes of conveyance.

Your committee have been shocked to find that a large portion of the frauds committed upon these innocent and in many cases ignorant foreigners are committed by their own countrymen who have come here before them; for we find the German preying upon the German—the Irish upon the Irish—the English upon the English, etc.; but at the same time we cannot hold our own countrymen entirely guiltless, for many of them it is to be regretted are engaged in this nefarious business.

Amongst the numerous frauds practised by these runners and forwarding houses, there is perhaps none greater than that which exists in the sale of passage tickets.

The emigrant is shown a neatly printed ticket, with a picture of a steamboat, railroad cars, and canal packet with three horses attached to it, and is given to understand that such a ticket will take him to a given place beyond Albany in a specified manner, and for a price to be agreed upon, and after disposing of the ticket for an exorbitant price, the emigrant is furnished with a steamboat ticket to take him to Albany, where he is to present his passage ticket to some person or company upon which it is drawn, where it is often either protested, or objections taken to the mode of conveyance, and the passenger, instead of going upon the railroad or packet boat, as agreed upon, is thrust into the steerage or hold of a line boat. . . . .

. . . . In the course of the investigation by your committee in the city of New York, they felt themselves called upon to make some inquiry into the conduct of the commissioners of emigration, who, under the act of last winter, have been clothed with high powers, and charged with the most responsible duties. In furtherance of this object, they took occasion to visit Staten Island, and examine the temporary buildings erected by them for the accommodation of the unexpected number of sick and destitute emigrants arriving at quarantine, during the last summer; and they feel called upon to state that they found said buildings in as good order and as comfortable as could be expected under the circumstances attending their erection. They also embraced that opportunity to visit the hospitals under control of the commissioners of health, and feel a just pride in bearing testimony to the good order, neatness and comfort, which they found to exist in all the various branches of that department.

Your committee also visited the establishment upon Ward's Island, under the control of the commissioners of emigration, and where they had leased a large building which had not been occupied for many years, and which they have fitted up as a retreat for the sick and destitute emigrants, which could not be accommodated elsewhere. Your committee also feel that it is due to these commissioners to say, that, in their judgment, they are entitled to great credit for the energy and perseverance displayed by them in procuring and fitting up said buildings and grounds upon that island under the most adverse and trying circumstances, where the whole country for miles around was alarmed by the fears created by the ship fever, and when they had hundreds of sick and destitute emigrants upon their hands without shelter or food. . . . .

Whilst your committee are compelled to acknowledge that they have been very much aided in their investigations by the kindness and courtesy extended to them by the officers of various emigrant societies, yet a sense of duty compels them to declare that in their judgment some of these societies do not afford that substantial aid to their brethren upon their arrival in a strange land, which they have reason to expect, and your committee fear that there may be cases where the officers or agents of some of these societies have a more tender regard for the *money* of the emigrant than for their safety and comfort, but they do not intend to give this remark a general application, for they believe that many of them have too much respect for the places they occupy, if not for their kindred, to abuse the high trust reposed in them.

In conclusion, your committee cannot too strongly recommend to the favorable consideration of the House, the important subject which has engaged their anxious attention. If there is anything of which we, as

Americans, ought to be proud, it is our noble and free institutions; and the fact that our country is now becoming so generally the resort and resting place of the down trodden and oppressed of the old world should serve but to increase that pride. Whilst we have millions of acres of unsettled and uncultivated lands which are constantly holding out encouragement to the hardy and industrious laboring classes of other less favored portions of the globe to come amongst us, and whilst we are drawing a large sum by way of commutation money from them, although in a small amount from each, we owe it to them, as well as to the character of our State and the cause of humanity, to see them protected after they reach our shores. Although this may be regarded as an extraordinary year for emigration, yet from causes that are operating in Europe, other than those which have existed the present year, we may safely calculate that this tide of emigration will continue to set in upon us in a manner that will require our constant care and vigilance.

12. The Abuses of the Bonding System under the New York State Passenger Act

A. NEGLECT OF POOR IMMIGRANTS BY SHIPOWNERS AND PASSENGER BROKERS[1]

.... The bonding system, repealed in 1847, in effect threw the entire responsibility of maintaining the emigrant in sickness or destitution on shipowners and passenger agents, who preferred bonding to commuting, from the profit it afforded. Some of the passenger agents maintained establishments for the reception of those who might become chargeable under their individual bonds, but usually like the shipowners and merchants, transferred all the destitute and sick to a description of persons, who made a living by what were denominated emigrant hospitals and poor houses, and who either made a contract at so much per head to sustain all the passengers in a particular ship, that might become chargeable, or received inmates at $2.00, $1.50, and even $1.25 per week. With the gradual but vast increase of emigration from 1843 to 1846, the competition in this business increased, while it was conducted naturally with less humanity. In 1845, 78,788 emigrant passengers arrived at the port of New York, of which 71,068 were bonded, and in 1846 about 110,000 arrived, of which 100,000 were bonded, the aggregate bonds taken amounting to $56,636,400. In 1846, within seven months, one passenger agent gave bonds to the extent of $3,360,600, who afterwards failed and absconded, and was very recently a prisoner in England. The proprietors of these establishments were always

[1] Extract from testimony of Alderman George H. Purser, of New York City, before a state legislative committee appointed to investigate the work of the New York commissioners of emigration. Alderman Purser described conditions under the old system which the commissioners had changed (*New York Assembly Doc. No. 34* [1852], pp. 170–72).

interested in giving insufficient and indifferent food and accommodation. In all cases their profits were measured by this economy, and in some instances when they had made a bad speculation in relation to a ship's entire passengers, cruelty, evasion, and neglect were resorted to as the only means by which they could escape bankruptcy. Under this system, the emigrant was utterly without protection of the law, the hopeless victim of private rapacity.

If a woman and helpless children in a starving condition applied to the alms house, and they appeared to be bonded passengers, all aid was refused. If they turned their weary steps to the counting house of the merchant who had actually bonded them, they were unceremoniously referred to some passenger agent, or the office of the proprietor of some emigrant hospital or poor house, where they almost universally received abuse, and too frequently denial as well as insult.

The merchants who had driven good bargains with these men, were thus inclined to protect them; and the interests of both these classes were in constant conflict with the rights of the unfortunate emigrant, and the dictates of humanity.

When famine spread over Ireland, and provisions became high throughout Europe, the ship-fever manifested itself among the emigrants, and the utter inefficiency, cruelty, and even danger of the system became apparent. The provision made for the sick in these miscalled hospitals was wholly inadequate. The buildings employed were usually selected in the suburbs of the city, rather for economy than for adaptation, and almost necessarily deficient in ventilation. In a two-story dwelling house at Bloomingdale, 46 by 40 feet, the proprietors admitted that 120 patients had been crowded, though several of the rooms were exclusively occupied by the officers and servants. The food, clothing and attendance, insufficient; the sick and convalescent, the old and young huddled together, and police arrangements, so essential in such establishments to maintain health and morals, utterly disregarded. So odious did these places become that hundreds of sick and destitute quitted them in terror and disgust, and attempted to obtain admittance in the alms house, or the hospital at Bellevue, frequently representing themselves as citizens, or pretending that they had been in the country for a period that rendered the municipal authorities responsible for their support. When bonded emigrants, ascertained to be such, were admitted into the institutions of the alms house department, the bondsmen were notified of the fact, and became liable for the expense, and almost invariably attempted by their emissaries to induce the parties to withdraw, and while chairman of the committee of that department, I frequently had occasion to forbid their interference with the sick. . . . .

One peculiar and deplorable result was the neglect of the children in these establishments; they were permitted to wander where they pleased; they were placed under no special government; never in any instance received the elements of education, but were exposed to influences and language calculated to corrupt and degrade them. Frequently so scantily provided with food that they were constrained to go out begging with their parents, and the neighbors informed me that they often furnished them with meals; on many occasions they were separated from their parents and handed over to employers from distant locations with the probability of never seeing their friends again.

Another evil was the want of reliability in the information given in relation to labor, the object was to get rid of them and they were often induced to accept cheap conveyances to distant States with the expectation of employment where none could be obtained. In one instance 500 Germans, chiefly aged paupers and young children, were shipped by subscription from their homes and arrived in a fearful condition of suffering and destitution; the passenger agents engaged lighters to take them to Albany, but being alderman of the ward in which the ship landed them, I interfered, and they were removed in wagons to the alms house where many died. The city eventually received 4 or 5 dollars per head from the shipping merchants as a commutation fee.

One important benefit resulting from having all the sick and destitute emigrants under one local and responsible government is the facility which it affords of communicating with and receiving intelligence from their friends and relations without the danger of their letters being intercepted or the inquiries instituted proving abortive.

If the emigrant dies it can be easily ascertained and his unfortunate children traced and recovered. Thousands are now temporarily supported till they can communicate with and receive aid and counsel from their connections and friends, and they are protected from the temptations and impositions to which they would otherwise be exposed. . . . .

B. NECESSITY OF PUBLIC CARE FOR DESTITUTE IMMIGRANTS[1]

Your Committee conceive that the evidence before them is sufficient to convince the Common Council and the Legislature that poor houses and hospitals should not be continued by passenger carriers. The proprietors are certainly not likely to provide liberally for the necessities, much less the comforts, of a household which is a constant source of individual trouble and expense. The same selfishness that would induce them to evade relieving the applicants would dictate the reduction of their fare, when admitted to the work house, to the lowest standard, both of quality and quantity.

[1] Extract from "Report of a Committee of the Board of Assistant Aldermen of the City of New York Relating to the Treatment of Poor Emigrants at the Tapscott Poor House and Hospital, February, 1846" (an institution in North Sixth Street, Williamsburg, established by W. and J. T. Tapscott, passenger brokers in South Street, New York). The Committee's "Report" is reprinted in Friedrich Kapp, *Immigration*, pp. 55–58.

Neither the Common Council nor the Legislature could feel disposed to permit these irresponsible establishments to multiply, a result which must occur, however, unless the law is amended. The unwholesome nature of the food, and the treatment of the helpless infants, is in evidence before you. No wearing apparel appears to have been distributed among the sick or well, with some trifling unimportant exceptions; and Margaret Bertram, an inmate nearly a year, and very destitute, acknowledged that she never received, with the exception of a order for a pair of shoes, any clothing whatever. Even on the confinement of any of the women, the other women have to provide the requisite articles of clothing for the infants. No attention is paid to the education of children who become chargeable to these brokers, and the only boy at Tapscott's workhouse, the superintendent, Mr. Miller, stated, was held back from school for want of clothing, and the proprietor himself acknowledged that he did not know whether he went to school or not.

The accommodation and arrangements of the house preclude the proper separation of the sexes, and the moral habits of the unfortunate inmates must deteriorate. The sick and destitute, the vicious and the innocent, are gathered together promiscuously, without any of the ordinary restraints to which, perhaps, in a distant country, they have been subjected, while they are denied the salutary influence of even police regulations.

These facts, which rest upon sworn testimony, must command attention. It cannot be disputed that the heavy responsibilities connected with a poor house and hospital should be transferred to the municipal authorities. The health and character of our city, and humanity to the alien stranger, are involved in this measure.

The great acknowledged inferiority of such an establishment to Bellevue is a strong incentive to the destitute to obtain admission to our almshouse by deception. Aware that their reception and continuance in the almshouse depends on suppressing the fact of being chargeable to any particular passenger broker, they manufacture facts to secure better fare and treatment. Indeed, it is not improbable, though no direct evidence exists before the Committee, that they have co-operated with the pauper in the practice of these frauds. It is unquestionably true that thousands are annually relieved from the city treasury, which are properly chargeable to the bondsmen. Intentional inaccuracies frequently appear on the passenger list regarding the ages, occupations, and names of the passengers, with the view of transferring legal responsibility from the carriers. In the event of establishing the system of commutation, the duty of examining the emigrant passengers will require the exercise of vigilance and honesty. To deceive the quarantine officers, and obtain permission to proceed immediately to the city, the captains of vessels dress up their sick, and similar artifice will be employed to evade the provisions of the proposed law.

The German and other emigrants not familiar with our language are liable to even more than ordinary imposition and suffering. To secure the assistance from the bondsmen, without which in the winter months they would perish, constantly requires the co-operation of the officers of their national benevolent institutions, and many remarkable instances of deception and cruelty have become known to your Committee.

Agents are sent to the principal cities and ports of Germany with the view of securing passengers from some particular line of vessels, and from three to six dollars is imposed as "head" or commutation money, though, even if the law we commended was adopted, $1.25 (25 cents for hospital fee) would be the actual outlay.

It is maintained among some, if not all, of the passenger brokers that they are released from the obligation of sustaining the persons bonded whenever convicted of an offence and sentenced to imprisonment. Though we must dissent from this opinion, it appears to have been formerly acquiesced in by the authorities, or to have escaped their examination. The commission of crime, committals for misdemeanor or vagrancy, serve the selfish interests of passenger agents, though we are unwilling to believe that the practice is resorted to ordinarily. Occasionally, however, the inmates of these private work houses and hospitals are unwarrantably consigned to the Penitentiary on Blackwell's Island. Hugh Graham, who was a sick man, was sent with eight others to be disgraced and contaminated in one of our worst prisons for insubordination. He, with his companions, purchased bread, and even ate it, without permission of the officials. He was taken before a magistrate, and committed without even being made acquainted with his crime or called upon for defence.

Another illustration of the feelings governing some of the passenger carriers is to be found in the following anecdote, communicated by the President of the Irish Emigrant Society: A man named O'Connor, with his wife and three children, arrived in this country, and, having contracted a fever on board the vessel, was detained in the city till his money was exhausted, and the bondsmen were applied to for relief. Recovering sooner than the other members of the family, he set out for St. Louis, where his father was comfortably settled, and, securing the necessary funds, returned with the fond expectation of accompanying his wife and children to their new home. He found, however, on reaching New York that his wife was dead and his children shipped to Liverpool, where they had neither friends nor relatives. One of the children died on the passage, and of the others no tidings have been obtained, though diligent enquiries have been instituted. Messrs. Tapscott were the agents and bondsmen in this case.

With the gradual but certain increase of immigration, these evils must extend. The cupidity of the proprietors of these private establishments threatens even the health of our city, not only from uncleanliness, but the introduction of cases of ship-fever.

With these views, your Committee respectfully submit the following resolution for adoption:

Resolved, That the condition of Tapscott's Poor House and Hospital, and the evidence relative to the general treatment of the inmates, strongly demand a change in the present system of bonding and commuting alien passengers.

C. RESOLUTION PASSED AT A CITIZENS' MASS MEETING IN NEW YORK CITY DEMANDING A HEAD TAX SYSTEM[1]

WHEREAS, The law of this State relative to passengers arriving at the port of New York, as at present administered, has failed alike to afford indemnity to the city and protection to the emigrant, causing a traffic in their sufferings which is abhorrent to humanity, creating private hospitals and poor-houses, which give to the emigrant neither the food nor care proper to their situation, and they deny to their dying hours even the consolation of religion; and, WHEREAS, a bill has passed the House of Assembly, which tends in some measure to remedy these evils, and is now before the Senate of the State, awaiting its action;

Resolved, That, in the opinion of this meeting, any and all legislation on this subject should be directed in that course which, while it but advances the interests of the emigrant, will have reference to the complete indemnity of the city and State from their support, and will not, at the same time, by imposing unnecessary burdens on the honest shipowner, tend to enhance the price of passage and retard immigration from lands of starvation to lands of plenty.

Resolved, That the enactment of a law requiring, from the master or consignee of any vessel arriving at this port with foreign emigrants, the sum of one dollar for each and every passenger, with the privilege of exacting instead thereof, in cases of mental or physical incapacity for self-support, where, from the total want of relatives and friends, such persons are liable to become charges to the city or State, bonds which will secure the city or State for their support, will create a fund which, properly administered, will not only relieve the city and State from a heavy burden, but will greatly benefit the emigrant.

Resolved, That, in the opinion of this meeting, it would be advisable to separate the receipt and disbursement of the fund so to be created from the rest of the city revenue, and place the same in the hands of commissioners, whose high character and moral integrity would, apart from all political considerations, be the guarantee for the proper administration of their duties.

Resolved, That a committee of five be appointed to proceed to Albany, and urge upon the Legislature the passage of a law comformable to the policy of the preceding resolutions.

[1] At the Tabernacle in Broadway, March 22, 1847. Reprinted in Friedrich Kapp, *Immigration*, pp. 92–93.

13. An Act for the Protection of Emigrants, 1848[1]

The People of the State of New York, represented in Senate and Assembly, do enact as follows:

SECTION 1. The commissioners of emigration[2] are hereby authorized and empowered to lease or purchase suitable docks or piers in the city of New York, and to erect necessary enclosures thereon, and such docks and piers to be appropriated and set apart for the exclusive use of landing emigrants, alien passengers.

SEC. 2. It shall be the duty of every ship-master, owner or consignee bringing to the port of New York any alien emigrants, steerage or second cabin passengers, in vessels not subject to quarantine, to cause the same with their baggage to be landed on the emigrant piers aforesaid, either directly from the vessel or by means of some steamboats or lighters licensed as aforesaid; and the landing of them upon any other pier or wharf shall be punished by a fine not less than one hundred dollars, which fine may be recovered of the master, owner or consignee of such ship or vessel. The commissioners of emigration are hereby empowered to make all necessary regulations for the preservation of order, and the admission to or exclusion from said dock of any person or persons excepting such as are duly licensed, and any person violating any of such regulations shall be liable to a penalty of one hundred dollars for each and every offence, to be recovered by the said commissioners of emigration.

SEC. 3. All persons keeping houses in any of the cities of this state for the purpose of boarding emigrant passengers, shall be required to have a license for said purpose from the mayor of the city in which such houses are located, and each person so licensed shall pay to said city the sum of ten dollars per annum, and shall give bonds satisfactory to said mayor, with one or more sureties, in the penal sum of five hundred dollars for their good behavior, and said mayor is hereby authorized to revoke said license for cause. Every keeper of such boarding house shall, under a penalty of fifty dollars, cause to be kept conspicuously posted in the public rooms of such house in the English, German, Dutch, French, and Welsh languages, a list of the rates of prices which will be charged emigrants per day and week for boarding and lodging, and also the rates for separate meals. The keeper of such house shall also file a copy of said list in the city of New York, in the office of the commissioners of emigration, and in each of the other cities of this state, with the mayor of said city. . . . .

SEC. 4. No keeper of any emigrant boarding house shall have any lien upon the baggage or effects of any emigrant for boarding, lodging, storage

---

[1] *Laws of New York, 1848*, chap. 219 (passed April 11, 1848).

[2] [The New York state commissioners of emigration had been created by act of the preceding legislature. See "An Act concerning Passengers in Vessels Coming to the City of New York," *ibid.*, *1847*, chap. 195.]

or on any other account whatever, and upon complaint being made upon oath before the mayor or any police magistrate of the city in which such boarding house is located, that the luggage or effects of any emigrant are detained by the keeper of any emigrant boarding house under pretence of any lien upon such luggage or effects . . . . it shall be the duty of the officer before whom such complaint is made, immediately to issue his warrant. . . . .

SEC. 5. No person shall, in any city in this state, solicit emigrant passengers or their luggage for emigrant boarding houses, passenger offices, forwarding or transportation lines, without the license of the mayor of such city, for which he shall pay the sum of twenty dollars per annum, and give satisfactory bonds to said mayor in the penal sum of three hundred dollars as security for his good behavior. Every person so licensed shall wear in a conspicuous place about his person a badge or plate of such character and in such manner as said mayor shall prescribe, with the words "licensed emigrant runner," inscribed thereon, with his name and the number of his license; no person who is not of approved good moral character, shall be licensed as such runner. . . . .

SEC. 6. The commissioners of emigration may, when in their opinion it shall seem necessary, appoint a proper person or persons, to board vessels from foreign ports at the quarantine ground or elsewhere in the port of New York, having on board emigrant passengers, for the purpose of advising such emigrants, and putting them on their guard against fraud and imposition. . . . .

SEC. 7. No person or persons shall exercise the vocation of booking emigrant passengers or taking money for their inland fare, or for the transportation of the luggage of such passengers, without keeping a public office for the transaction of such business, nor without the license of the mayor . . . . for which shall be paid the sum of twenty-five dollars per annum. and give satisfactory bonds in the penal sum of one thousand dollars. . . .

SEC. 8. No person holding office under the government of the United States, or of this state, or of any of its cities, or who shall be in the employment of the commissioners of emigration, shall solicit custom for any transportation line, or shall be interested in any way, directly or indirectly, in the forwarding of emigrants, under a penalty of not less than one hundred dollars, and not exceeding three hundred dollars, to be sued for in the name of the people of this state, and which money, when collected, shall be paid into the county treasury, for the use of the poor of said county. . . . .

14. Emigration of German Paupers, 1847[1]

Your memorialists further represent, that large numbers of paupers are sent every year to this country from the poor-houses of Europe, and for the sole reason that it is much cheaper to pay their passage to this country than to support them at home. Those sent are the diseased, infirm, and helpless portion of the community, who, when they arrive, can be of no benefit to our country, and remain inmates of our alms-house. Within the last year, two vessels—the ships "Sardinia" and "Atlas," from Liverpool—arrived in this port, one with 294, and the other with 314, steerage passengers, all of whom were paupers, sent by the parish of Grosszimmern, in Hesse Darmstadt, to which they belonged, and the expenses of which were paid by said parish.

Your memorialists cannot consider the paupers sent here from the poorhouses of Europe as emigrants, or worthy of that name, and would suggest that a representation of the facts be made through our ministers and consuls to the foreign governments from which paupers are sent; and your memorialists call the special attention of Congress to the copies of letters from the parishes of Hall and Grosszimmern, hereto annexed. . . . .

The Overseers of the Hospital and the Poor at Hall to the Local Authorities of Grosszimmern, in Darmstadt [May 5]: . . . .

"We learn that a considerable number of emigrants will, within a few weeks, proceed from the neighboring parish of Grosszimmern, on their voyage to America. It is an emigration of the poorer class, who are without the means of gaining a livelihood, as already has been partially done in Ireland at the public expense. In this case, the parish of Grosszimmern defrays the charges, and besides providing for these rather numerous paupers on their passage across the ocean, places at their disposition the means of supplying the wants of the moment, on their arrival at the North American coast.

"In the parish here, is also unfortunately a number of paupers, by no means inconsiderable, of both the male and female sex; and we are not disinclined to adopt similar means to those which you found suited to your design; for which reason, information is respectfully requested on the following points: First, how the thing was managed; second, with whom the bargain for transportation was made; third, how many persons were sent off; fourth, how much was paid; and, fifth, how much was appropriated for their first wants on the other side of the sea. Persuaded of your friendly disposition, the undersigned believe they have made no vain request; and offering to reciprocate the service, look respectfully for the desired communication."

[1] Extract from "Memorial to Congress from the Corporation of the City of New York Relative to the Exportation from Abroad of Paupers and Criminals," U.S. 29th Congress, 2d session, *House Doc. No. 54* (January 25, 1847), pp. 2–8.

The answer of the burgomaster of Grosszimmern followed on the first of September, 1846, and reads thus:

"The Board of Overseers of the Hospital and the Poor will not misconstrue the circumstance that their esteemed letter of the eleventh of last month did not receive an earlier reply. Now, however, that the many labors which became necessary on account of the emigrants in question are in some degree lightened, I hasten to impart the following explanations concerning the questions put to me. To the first question: This parish, which numbers four thousand inhabitants, comprehends so many who have not the least property, that it was no longer possible for them to support themselves and their families.

"In consequence of letters received last year from emigrants from this place, in which it was said that in North America, on account of the cheapness of the means of subsistence, laborers, and especially such as were able to assist in field labors, made good earnings, the wish arose in many of our inhabitants of the poorer class to be aided in reaching North America by the funds of the parish. The local authorities availed themselves of this opportunity, and issued a public invitation to all such poor persons as of their own free motion desired to emigrate to America, to apply to the burgomaster. Hereupon a list was made out, arranged under the following titles, to wit: 1st, number of the emigrant; 2d, his name; 3d, statement of the members of his family and parents; 4th, amount of his property; 5th, his wants, both for the expenses of the journey and clothing; 6th, remarks.

"To question second: For the passage, a bargain was made with Mr. Gansenberg, at Darmstadt, and Mr. Grülen, Gernsheim, by whom it was executed to our full satisfaction.

"To question third: There were 674 persons sent off at the expense of the parish, besides more than a hundred who emigrated with them at their own charge.

"To question fourth: For each person over twelve years old, 71 florins were paid for passage and board; but for each person under twelve, 56 florins from Gernsheim to New York, including the capitation and poor tax there to be paid, which amounts to about two florins and 24 kreutzers.

"To the fifth question: Each family that was large received a bill of exchange of from 15 to 25 florins, drawn upon the house of Speyer, in New York. This was handed to the emigrants in London by one of the local authorities who accompanied them thither.

"The parish had to take up a sum amounting nearly to 50,000 florins, for which, it is true, that the titles of the emigrants to the undivided lands of the parishes were made over. It may be asked whether the parish has lost or gained. Aside from the considerable sum of ready money which in this manner is withdrawn from us, the parish has at all events gained, for the yearly expense of 2,500 florins for the support of the poor is done away with, and the possessions of the parish not only remain undiminished, but the share of those who remain is even become larger."

15. Activities of the German Society of New York, 1848[1]

The memorial of the undersigned officers of the German Society of the city of New York respectfully showeth:

That the immigration from Germany at this port during the last year, was greater than that from any other country, while the expenditures arising therefrom, which had to be borne by the Commissioners of Emigration, were trifling in comparison with the great burden thrown upon said Commissioners by the immigration from other countries.

According to the report of said Commissioners, submitted to the Honorable the Legislature of the State of New York, there arrived at this port from the 5th of May to the 31st of December, 1847, 129,069 immigrant passengers, of whom 53,180 were natives of Germany, 52,946 were natives of Ireland and 22,943 were natives of other countries.

The number of those who became chargeable to the Commissioners was 10,422, and the amount expended for their support was, from the commutation fund, $65,317.44; from the hospital fund, $82,829.87; in all, $148,147.31. Which sum, divided by the above number of those for whose sake it was expended, say 10,422, shows the average cost of each to have been $14.21½.

The report of the Commissioners does not state distinctly how many of said 10,422 persons whom they had to support were Germans, inasmuch as it includes 3,416 persons admitted into the marine hospital from ship board, without mentioning places of nativity; but your memorialists believe the Germans among said 3,416 persons were proportionately not *more* numerous than among those sent to the hospital from the city. The number thus sent was 2,802, of whom 196 were Germans; hence, of the 3,416 admitted from ship board, 238 were Germans. Adding these 238 to the number enumerated as natives of Germany, in Table B, appended to the *Report of the Commissioners of Emigration*, it appears that the total number of Germans, who became chargeable to the Commissioners, out of an immigration of 53,180, was 872.

Your memorialists feel confident that this estimate is quite large enough and that they may safely refer to the Commissioners of Emigration themselves for the correctness of this view. In fact the latter will readily admit that the patients sent to the marine hospital from ship board were almost exclusively natives of Ireland, and assuming 238 to have been Germans, is a larger number than should fairly be allowed. But your memorialists desire

[1] Extract from "Memorial of the Officers of the German Society of the City of New York to the New York State Legislature, Demanding a Share of the Head Tax Receipts," *New York Assembly Doc. No. 165* (1848), pp. 1–6.

to be on the safe side, and prefer, if err they must, to do so to their own disadvantage.

Your Honorable Body is aware that the tax collected from emigrant passengers is one dollar from each, commutation money, and fifty cents from each, hospital money. Hence the money collected from 53,180 Germans, at $1.50 each, is $79,770.00. The expenditures for the support of 872 Germans, who became chargeable, at $14.21½ each, is $12,395.48. And thus the surplus of receipts over expenditures of the German immigration at this port, is $67,374.52.

The number of immigrants, other than Germans was 75,889, and the hospital and commutation money collected from them, at $1.50 each, was $113,833.50. Of these 75,889 immigrants, 9,550 became chargeable to the Commissioners, at a cost of $14.21½ each, amounting in the aggregate to $135,753.25, showing an excess of expenditures over receipts of $21,919.75.

Thus then it is shown by the *Report of the Commissioners of Emigration* that the receipts from immigrant passengers, natives of Germany, overran the expenditure caused by the same, $67,374.52, while on the other hand the receipts from the immigrants from other countries fall short of the expenditures occasioned by the same, $21,919.75; in other words, the German immigration shows a net *gain* of $67,374.52, and the immigration from other countries a *loss* of $21,919.75.

This result is no doubt principally owing to the fact that the immigrants from Germany arrived in better condition than the great mass of those from other countries, but it would be incorrect to take this fact as a full and satisfactory explanation of the remarkable disparity. Your memorialists feel convinced, and beg leave to show, that in a great degree it is brought about by the working of the German Society.

The German immigrant, on his arrival here, if he requires assistance, does not call on the Commissioners of Emigration, but at the place where his native language is spoken, he calls on the German Society; and the German Society does not send him to the office of the Commissioners (except in extraordinary cases) because the Commissioners have made it a rule to grant relief only in their own institutions. But ample proof is daily furnished by the visitors of our Society, that it is next to impossible to induce the German immigrant voluntarily to become an inmate of those institutions; he will rather submit to actual suffering, and thus, ignorance of the language of the country, and the dread of the alms-house, which the German looks upon as a sort of penitentiary, throw the chief burden of the indigent German immigration on the German Society, and the latter, by the force of circumstances, is compelled to perform a part of the duties, and to defray a portion of the expenses, which, by the act of May 5, 1847, "concerning passengers in vessels coming to the city of New York," are intended to fall on the Commissioners of Emigration. For the truth of this, your memorialists may confidently refer to the Commissioners themselves.

The enormous immigration at this port from Germany, which, during the year of 1847, according to the books kept at the office of the German Society, amounted to 70,735 persons, proves a serious burden to the citizens of German origin. It will be readily admitted that among such a mass of people there must be many having neither friends nor relatives among the resident Germans, but requiring medical as well as pecuniary assistance. As already stated, the suffering and needy will in the first place apply to the German Society, but failing to receive all the aid they require, they will throw themselves, not on the Commissioners of Emigration, but on the sympathy of their countrymen, and these cannot possibly resist the appeal. Hence it is that the indigent and suffering German immigration proves a constant and daily increasing tax upon all the resident Germans, and this explains the circumstance, that out of 10,000 German voters, only about 500 are members of the German Society. It is not an unfriendly feeling towards the society which prevents so many from joining the same, but the consciousness of doing enough without contributing towards its funds. On the other hand, the society feels keenly the absence of that general co-operation which it would enjoy, but for the reasonable objection urged by so many of its well wishers.

There are now 58 persons actively engaged in carrying on the business of the society, viz.: 15 members of the executive council, 17 physicians, 24 district visitors and 2 employees in the agency office. The services of all are gratuitous, with the exception of the agent and his clerk, who receive salaries. The total expenditures during the last twelve months was $7,823.10, which sufficed to afford substantial and adequate relief to 3,721 deserving applicants, while the agency procured employment to 4,743 persons. Your memorialists would say that it would be impossible to accomplish a greater amount of good with equally limited means.

There is one channel through which the German Society is constantly endeavoring to extend the sphere of its benevolent action, which your memorialists take leave to notice more particularly. This is an arrangement with the regular German physicians of New York and Brooklyn, now numbering about twenty, by which the latter are represented in the board of officers of the society, and take charge of all the sick German poor, attending them gratuitously, the society paying for medicines, nurses, etc. According to the last annual report of the society, its physicians, during the last twelve months, prescribed medicines in 2,808 cases, and had under treatment, for account of the society, 714 patients. Considering that the inmates of the hospitals under the control of the Commissioners of Emigration cost $14.21½ each, it will not be deemed extravagant on the part of your memorialists to say that the medical department of the German Society has saved the city and the Commissioners of Emigration *many thousand dollars.*

But the extraordinary exertions made by the society during the last twelve months have exhausted its means and it is now threatened with the prospect of having to suspend its usefulness. Your memorialists, therefore, compelled by the embarrassing condition of the society, and in consideration of its being so efficient an auxiliary to the Commissioners of Emigration, venture to ask your honorable body for aid, and they also venture to hope their prayer will be satisfactorily responded to on the ground that the German immigrant, as shown in the beginning of this "Memorial," has not derived the same amount of benefit from the operation of the act of May 5, 1847, as the emigrant from other countries, having in fact furnished the means by which not his own wants but those of others have been relieved.

It is not the intention of your memorialists, nor the object of their prayer, to relieve the members of the German Society from the claims on them of their poor countrymen; on the contrary, your memorialists wish to keep alive, and if possible, to enlarge the springs of private charity; and the prayer of your memorialists is this:

That an act be passed requiring the Commissioners of Emigration to pay to the treasurer of the German Society for its use, the sum of ——— dollars, and further authorizing said commissioners to pay annually to said treasurer on or before the 1st of March of every year an amount equal to one-half the sum of voluntary contributions, collected during the preceding twelve months from the members of said society, so long as said commissioners can satisfy themselves that the German Society has a fair claim to such support, and provided, also, that such annual payment shall not exceed the sum of $3,000; these payments to be made out of the Commutation Fund.

16. A Defense of the State Head Tax System[1]

. . . . The law of Massachusetts[2] was not made for the purpose of regulating foreign commerce, although it affects it so far as is necessary in providing for the regulation of a class of persons connected with it, but it is in fact an act modifying the pauper laws of the State, and designed to mitigate, in some degree, the burdens attempted to be thrown upon us in subjecting us to support the alien poor.

This can be made manifest by tracing the history of our legislation upon this subject, and the causes which have led to it. It will appear that the Colony, Province, and State, each in turn, exercised a free, unrestrained authority over paupers and pauperism. I shall do little more than refer the court to some of the laws, and state in the briefest way their provisions.

---

[1] Extract from argument of counsel representing the city of Boston in the so-called "Passenger Cases," 48 U.S. 282, pp. 316–37.

[2] [The Massachusetts law in question was the so-called "Passenger Act" of 1837, which provided for a head tax on alien passengers.]

In 1639, there is an act of the colony providing for the poor, which evidently alludes to still earlier laws (*Ancient Charters and Colony Laws*, 173). This act made it the duty of towns, not only to provide for the poor, but for all alike, whether native inhabitants, alien sojourners, or transient persons.

In 1692, provision was made compelling the relatives of poor persons to contribute, when able, to their support (*ibid.*, 252).

In 1693, provisions was made for the forcible removal of paupers, not only from one town to another, but out of the Colony; and further provision of the like kind was made in 1767 (*ibid.*, 252, 662).

In 1720, the overseers of the poor were authorized and required to bind out as apprentices the children of paupers (*ibid.*, 429).

By the statute of 1793, c. 59, Secs. 15 and 17, felons, convicts, and infamous persons are denied the right of landing in the Commonwealth, and shipmasters forbidden under penalties to bring in such.

By the statute of 1819, c. 165, masters of vessels, if required by the overseers of the poor in any town, are obliged to give bonds to indemnify the town for three years against any cost or charge from persons brought in who might become paupers.

By the statute of 1830, c. 150, masters of vessels are required to give bonds to indemnify the towns where they may land alien passengers against liability for their support as paupers, unless excused from so doing by the overseers of the poor. And there is a further provision, that, by paying five dollars for any passenger, the claim for a bond should be commuted.

These various provisions were carried substantially into the Revised Statutes in 1836.

Thus stood the law at the end of nearly two hundred years from the first legislation now on record, by which it appears that the Colony, Province, and State had in succession asserted an unlimited power over paupers and pauperism. They asserted not only the right to compel the body politic to provide for the poor but they made the relatives within certain degrees contribute, if able; they bound out poor children, expelled from their territory paupers who belonged elsewhere, denied to such the right to come in, and also shut out convicts, felons and infamous persons. . . . .

[The Royal Commission on the Poor Laws of Great Britain which reported in 1834] found that several of the parishes had already adopted emigration as the most sure and effectual method of obtaining certain relief They had, therefore, raised money to pay the charges of shipping paupers to foreign lands. The commission gave it as their opinion, that this mode of disposing of paupers promised much, and ought to be encouraged. The fruits of this policy were soon visible among us. Indeed, such a fraudulent conspiracy to relieve themselves, not only of the obligation of humanity, but of the expense of supporting their own helpless population, could not remain long concealed. Idiots, lunatics, the lame, the aged and infirm, women and children, were thrown upon our shore destitute of every thing, and our poor-houses were filled with foreigners in this hopeless and helpless condition.

The same plan of relief was also adopted at a later day on the Continent, and we seemed in a fair way to become the poor-house of Europe. The evil has gone on increasing, until not only the poor-houses and hospitals are full, but in Boston and New York immense sums have been expended in mitigating the sufferings of the alien poor and destitute.

The proof of these coming events was unmistakable farther back than 1837, when the act of Massachusetts now in question became a law. The State saw, not only parishes which were insensible to the dictates of humanity and capable of transporting their poor and destitute to unknown lands, there to leave them to the mercy of strangers, but relatives and kindred regardless of the ties of blood, who were willing to thrust from them the aged, the infirm, the insane, and the helpless, and to place them beyond the possibility of a return.

These were the circumstances which, in 1837, demanded legislation, and the act, in our view, met the exigency, and nothing more. It secures two things: first, a bond to indemnify against the liability for the support of those wholly incapable of providing for themselves; and, secondly, two dollars for each and every other alien passenger. This bond and money must be furnished before the passengers are permitted to land. . . . .

The act is in every feature manifestly a pauper law, growing out of a pressing emergency, and although as lenient as the circumstances would allow, yet our right to make and enforce it is denied. We have seen that the State has exercised for two hundred years the right to make pauper laws. Can she do it now? I contend that this power is one of her attributes of sovereignty, which she has never surrendered, and now has the right to enjoy.

[Was the charge upon the owner, master, or consignee for bringing in alien passengers unconstitutional because it was a duty on imports levied by the state of Massachusetts without the consent of Congress? Counsel asked, "What are imports?"]

. . . . Men are not imports, or articles of trade or traffic. If they are, I would ask, Who is the importer? Who trades in them? Who claims the right to sell? . . . .

. . . . I have maintained that the law of Massachusetts is a police law, and although I have argued the two-dollar assessment as a revenue measure, yet I maintain that the police power carries with it a right to provide for the expense of executing any law which the public exigency demands. . . . .

The law of Massachusetts has no reference whatever to foreign commerce, except as the instrument employed to inflict an injury upon the State. It is the avenue through which these persons are introduced, and is controlled just so far as is necessary to mitigate the evil and make it endurable, but no farther. Can we not do this? Is our right doubted and denied? . . . . Have we no right to control the mercenary shippers, who, stimulated by the hope of gain, are struggling to empty both the prisons and poorhouses of Europe upon us? I have read the language of this bench, in which they concede the right and declare it to be our duty, to exercise our police power by protective and preventive measures. We are warned that it is as much our duty to provide against the moral pestilence of pauperism as against infection. We have not overstepped this boundary a hair's breadth; on the contrary, we have not come fully up to the advice, for we do not shut out the pestilence.

What kind of measures are we authorized to adopt? We may, under the authority and sanction of this court, determine who shall reside with us; we may shut out or expel vagabonds and paupers; we may guard against moral and physical pestilence; we may protect life, health, and property; we may stop the approach of that foreign commerce which brings contagion; we may say to a ship-master, "You shall take a pilot—you shall anchor here, and deposit your ballast there." In a word, we may give as much direction to commerce as is necessary to accomplish these objects.

This is what we may do—it is what is conceded to us by the highest authority. When we exact bonds of indemnity for lunatics, paupers, aged and infirm persons, and those incapable of supporting themselves, is it doing more than to protect ourselves by very reasonable measures? When we exact of masters two dollars for each alien brought in, to be expended in relieving these alien paupers, whom, if we receive, we must support, is this a measure outside of what is recommended?

How are we met when we attempt to exercise the power conceded to us? If we attempt to meet pauperism in the great highway of its introduction, we are rebuked for regulating foreign commerce, although everybody can see that, if this privilege be denied to us, we can take no effective measures to prevent its introduction; for we must see the persons and know their condition before we can decide what is expedient. Moreover, nothing can be effectual that is not felt by those who are chiefly instrumental in the introduction of such persons.

We may protect ourselves, says the court; but when, how, where? These are pregnant inquiries. Can we deal with paupers and pauperism as with contagion or infection? Can we hold those who bring the calamity upon us accountable? Can we protect ourselves as we do against the dangers of gunpowder and explosive articles, which put in peril life and property? We lay the burden of protective measures upon those who bring in such merchandise or such diseases.

What can a State do to avert or prevent, after the paupers and vagabonds are landed and mixed with the population? Such an exercise of the power conceded to us would be barren and useless. We must meet it on shipboard, as we do disease and dangerous merchandise. There we can put our hands upon the lunatics, idiots, aged and infirm paupers, etc. There we can learn what the shipowner, the master, and the agents for emigration are about. There we can detect their conspiracy with the parishes of Europe to transfer their poor and their culprits to this country, to poison our morals and increase our burdens. There is the place, and the only place, to apply the corrective, where the evidence can lead to no mistake.

If we cannot meet the evil here, and regulate it here, the power to expel and the power to prevent are empty and worthless. The result will be, that ship-masters and traffickers in emigration can and will force upon us paupers, vagabonds, felons, and infamous persons, though we have an admitted power to expel them.

. . . . [Counsel say] we cannot meet and correct the evil of pauperism. England, Ireland, and Germany may empty their poor-houses upon us, and compel us to assume their burdens and to perform their duties to humanity because we are passive, powerless instruments in their hands.

We do not believe that the States are thus shorn of their authority. . . . .

17. State Head Taxes Declared Unconstitutional[1]

MR. JUSTICE MCLEAN:[2]

Under the general denomination of health laws in New York, and by the seventh section of an act relating to the marine hospital, it is provided that "the health-commissioner shall demand and be entitled to receive, and in case of neglect or refusal to pay shall sue for and recover, in his name of office, the following sums from the master of every vessel that shall arrive in the port of New York, viz.:

1. From the master of every vessel from a foreign port, for himself and each cabin passenger, one dollar and fifty cents; for each steerage passenger, mate, sailor, or mariner, one dollar.

2. From the master of each coasting-vessel, for each person on board, twenty-five cents; but no coasting-vessel from the States of New Jersey, Connecticut, and Rhode Island shall pay for more than one voyage in each month, computing from the first voyage in each year.

The eighth section provides that the money so received shall be denominated "hospital moneys." And the ninth section gives "each master paying hospital moneys a right to demand and recover from each person the sum paid on his account." The tenth section declares any master, who shall fail to make the above payments within twenty-four hours after the arrival of his vessel in the port, shall forfeit the sum of one hundred dollars. By

---

[1] Extract from decision of the United States Supreme Court in the so-called "Passenger Cases," *Smith* v. *Turner, Health Commissioner of Port of New York* and *Norris* v. *City of Boston* (1849), 48 U.S. 282.

[2] In *Smith* v. *Turner*, p. 391.

the eleventh section, the commissioners of health are required to account annually to the Comptroller of the State for all moneys received by them for the use of the marine hospital "and if such moneys shall, in any one year, exceed the sum necessary to defray the expenses of their trust, including their own salaries, and exclusive of such expenses as are to be borne and paid as a part of the contingent charges of the city of New York, they shall pay over such surplus to the treasurer of the Society for the Reformation of Juvenile Delinquents in the city of New York, for the use of the society. . . . ."

To encourage foreign emigration was a cherished policy of this country at the time the Constitution was adopted. As a branch of commerce the transportation of passengers has always given a profitable employment to our ships, and within a few years past has required an amount of tonnage nearly equal to that of imported merchandise. . . . .

The act of New York now under consideration is called a health law. It imposes a tax on the master and every cabin passenger of a vessel from a foreign port of one dollar and fifty cents; and of one dollar on the mate, each steerage passenger, sailor, or mariner. And the master is made responsible for the tax, he having a right to exact it of the others. The funds so collected are denominated hospital moneys, and are applied to the use of the marine hospital, the surplus to be paid to the treasurer of the Society for the Reformation of Juvenile Delinquents in the city of New York, for the use of that society.

To call this a health law would seem to be a misapplication of the term. It is difficult to perceive how a health law can be extended to the reformation of juvenile offenders. On the same principle, it may be made to embrace all offenders, so as to pay the expenses incident to an administration of the criminal law. And with the same propriety it may include the expenditures of any branch of the civil administration of the city of New York, or of the State. In fact, I can see no principle on which the fund can be limited, if it may be used as authorized by the act. The amount of the tax is as much within the discretion of the legislature of New York as the objects to which it may be applied.

It is insisted that if the act, as regards the hospital fund, be within the power of the State, the application of a part of the fund to other objects, as provided in the act, cannot make it unconstitutional. This argument is unsustainable. If the State has power to impose a tax to defray the necessary expenses of a health regulation, and this power being exerted, can the tax be increased so as to defray the expenses of the State government? This is within the principle asserted.

The case of *The City of New York* v. *Miln*,[1] 11 Pet., 102, is relied on with great confidence as sustaining the act in question. As I assented to the points ruled in that case, consistency, unless convinced of having erred, will

[1] [See Doc. 7, p. 118.]

compel me to support the law now before us, if it be the same in principle. The law in Miln's case required that "the master or commander of any ship or other vessel arriving at the port of New York shall, within twenty-four hours after his arrival, make a report, in writing, on oath or affirmation, to the Mayor of the city of New York, of the name, place of birth and last legal settlement, age, and occupation of every person brought as a passenger; and of all persons permitted to land at any place during the voyage, or go on board of some other vessel, with the intention of proceeding to said city; under the penalty on such master or commander, and the owner or owners, consignee or consignees, of such ship or vessel, severally and respectively, of seventy-five dollars for each individual not so reported." And the suit was brought against Miln as consignee of the ship "Emily," for the failure of the master to make report of the passenger on board of his vessel.

In their opinion this court says, "The law operated on the territory of New York over which that State possesses an acknowledged and undisputed jurisdiction for every purpose of internal regulation"; and "on persons whose rights and duties are rightfully prescribed and controlled by the laws of the respective States, within whose territorial limits they are found." This law was considered as an internal police regulation, and as not interfering with commerce.

A duty was not laid upon the vessel or the passengers, but the report only was required from the master, as above stated. Now, every State has an unquestionable right to require a register of the names of the persons who come within it to reside temporarily or permanently. This was a precautionary measure to ascertain the rights of the individuals, and the obligations of the public, under any contingency which might occur. It opposed no obstruction to commerce, imposed no tax nor delay, but acted upon the master, owner, or consignee of the vessel, after the termination of the voyage, and when he was within the territory of the State, mingling with its citizens, and subject to its laws.

But the health law, as it is called, under consideration, is altogether different in its objects and means. It imposes a tax or duty on the passengers, officers and sailors, holding the master responsible for the amount at the immediate termination of the voyage, and necessarily before the passengers have set their feet on land. The tax on each passenger, in the discretion of the legislature, might have been five or ten dollars, or any other sum, amounting even to a prohibition of the transportation of passengers; and the professed object of the tax is as well for the benefit of juvenile offenders as for the marine hospital. And it is not denied that a considerable sum thus received has been applied to the former object. The amount and application of this tax are only important to show the consequences of the exercise of this power by the States. The principle involved is vital to the commercial power of the Union. . . . .

Mr. Justice McLean:[1]

This is a writ of error, which brings before the court the judgment of the Supreme Court of the State of Massachusetts.

"An act relating to alien passengers," passed the 20th of April, 1837, by the legislature of Massachusetts, contains the following provisions:

Section 1. When any vessel shall arrive at any port or harbour within this State from any port or place without the same, with alien passengers on board, the officers whom the mayor and aldermen of the city, or the selectmen of the town, where it is proposed to land such passengers, are hereby authorized and required to appoint, shall go on board such vessels and examine into the condition of said passengers.

Sec. 2. If, on such examination, there shall be found among said passengers any lunatic, idiot, maimed, aged, or infirm person, incompetent, in the opinion of the officer so examining, to maintain themselves, or who have been paupers in any other country, no such alien passenger shall be permitted to land, until the master, owner, consignee, or agent of such vessel shall have given to such city or town a bond in the sum of one thousand dollars, with good and sufficient security, that no such lunatic or indigent passenger shall become a city, town, or State charge within ten years from the date of said bond.

Sec. 3. No alien passenger, other than those spoken of in the preceding section shall be permitted to land, until the master, owner, consignee, or agent of such vessel shall pay to the regularly appointed boarding officer the sum of two dollars for each passenger so landing; and the money so collected shall be paid into the treasury of the city or town, to be appropriated as the city or town directs for the support of foreign paupers.

The plaintiff . . . . [arrived] in the port of Boston, ... in command of a schooner which had on board nineteen alien passengers, for each of which two dollars was demanded of the plaintiff, and paid by him, on protest that the exaction was illegal. . . . .

Under the first and second sections of the above act, the persons appointed may go on board of a ship from a foreign port, which arrives at the port of Boston with alien passengers on board, and examine whether any of them are lunatics, idiots, maimed, aged, or infirm, incompetent to maintain themselves, or have been paupers in any other country, and not permit such persons to be put on shore, unless security shall be given that they shall not become a city, town, or State charge. This is the exercise of an unquestionable power in the State to protect itself from foreign paupers and other persons who would be a public charge; but the nineteen alien passengers for whom the tax was paid did not come, nor any one of them, within the second section. The tax of two dollars was paid by the master for each of these passengers before they were permitted to land. This, according to the view taken in the above case of *Smith* v. *Turner*, was a regulation of commerce, and not being within the power of the State, the act imposing the tax is void.

[1] In *Norris* v. *City of Boston*, p. 408.

The fund thus raised was no doubt faithfully applied for the support of foreign paupers, but the question is one of power, and not of policy. . . . .

JUSTICE GRIER:[1]

Before proceeding to examine the more prominent and plausible arguments which have been urged in support of the power now claimed by the State of Massachusetts, it may be proper to notice some assumptions of fact which have been used for the purpose of showing the necessity of such a power, from the hardships which it is supposed would otherwise be inflicted on those States which claim the right to exercise it.

It was assumed as a fact, that all the foreigners who arrived at the ports of Boston and New York, and afterwards became paupers, remained in those cities, and there became a public charge; and that, therefore, this tax was for their own benefit, or that of their class. But is this the fact? Of the many ten thousands who yearly arrive at those ports, how small a proportion select their residence there? Hundreds are almost daily transferred from the vessels in which they arrive to the railroad-car and steamboat, and proceed immediately on their journey to the Western States. Are Boston, New York, and New Orleans, through which they are compelled to pass, the only cities of the Union which have to bear the burden of supporting such immigrants as afterwards become chargeable as paupers? It may well be questioned whether their proportion of this burden exceeds the ratio of their great wealth and population. But it appears by the second section of the act now before us that all persons whose poverty, age, or infirmities render them incompetent to maintain themselves are not permitted to land until a bond has been given, in the sum of one thousand dollars, with sufficient security, that they will not become a city, town, or State charge within ten years. By the stringency of these bonds, the poor, the aged, and the infirm are compelled to continue their journey and migrate to other States; and yet, after having thus driven off all persons of this class, and obtained an indemnity against loss by them if they remain, it is complained of as a hardship that the State should not be allowed to tax those who, on examination, are found *not* to be within this description—who are *not* paupers, nor likely to become such; and that this exaction should be demanded, not for a license to remain and become domiciled in the State, but for leave to pass through it. But admitting the hardship of not permitting these States to raise revenue by taxing the citizens of other States, or immigrants seeking to become such, the answer still remains, that the question before the court is not one of feeling or discretion, but of power. . . . .

It is true, that if a State has such an absolute and uncontrolled right to exclude, the inference that she may prescribe the conditions of entrance, in the shape of a license or a tax, must necessarily follow. The conclusion can-

[1] *Ibid.*, p. 458.

not be evaded if the premises be proved. A right to exclude is a power to tax; and the converse of the proposition is also true, that a power to tax is a power to exclude; and it follows, as a necessary result, from this doctrine, that those States in which are situated the great ports or gates of commerce have a right to exclude, if they see fit, all immigrants from access to the interior States, and to prescribe the conditions on which they shall be allowed to proceed on their journey, whether it be the payment of two or of two hundred dollars. Twelve States of this Union are without a seaport. The United States have, within and beyond the limits of these States, many millions of acres of vacant lands. It is the cherished policy of the general government to encourage and invite Christian foreigners of our own race to seek an asylum within our borders, and to convert these waste lands into productive farms, and thus add to the wealth, population, and power of the nation. Is it possible that the framers of our Constitution have committed such an oversight, as to leave it to the discretion of some two or three States to thwart the policy of the Union, and dictate the terms upon which foreigners shall be permitted to gain access to the other States? Moreover, if persons migrating to the Western States may be compelled to contribute to the revenue of Massachusetts, or New York, or Louisiana, whether for the support of paupers or penitentiaries, they may with equal justice be subjected to the same exactions in every other city or State through which they are compelled to pass; and thus the unfortunate immigrant, before he arrives at his destined home, be made a pauper by oppressive duties on his transit. Besides, if a State may exercise this right of taxation or exclusion on a foreigner, on the pretext that he may become a pauper, the same doctrine will apply to citizens of other States of this Union; and thus the citizens of the interior States, who have no ports on the ocean, may be made tributary to those who hold the gates of exit and entrance to commerce. If the bays and harbours in the United States are so exclusively the property of the States within whose boundaries they lie, that, the moment a ship comes within them, she and all her passengers become the subjects of unlimited taxation before they can be permitted to touch the shore, the assertion, that this is a question with which the citizens of other States have no concern, may well be doubted. If these States still retain all the rights of sovereignty, as this argument assumes, one of the chief objects for which this Union was formed has totally failed, and "we may again witness the scene of conflicting commercial regulations and exactions which were once so destructive to the harmony of the States, and fatal to their commercial interests abroad."

To guard against the recurrence of the evils, the Constitution has conferred on Congress the power to regulate commerce with foreign nations, and among the States [in order that], as regards our intercourse with other nations and with one another, we might be one people—not a mere confederacy of sovereign States for the purpose of defence or aggression.

18. Undesirable Immigrants: "Who Shall Remedy the Evil?"[1]

It is not alone, however, in the effects following the influx of vicious foreigners that we have the evidence of the evil consequences resulting from it. We are left in no doubt as to the fact that a large number of them are paupers and convicts, whose passage across the Atlantic is paid for them, and who come here without character, morality, religion, industry, or anything else to commend them to our favor. . . . .

In January, 1855, the evil became so manifest, and assumed such a magnitude in the city of New York, as to induce Mayor Wood to address the President of the United States a letter, in which he asked the interference of the general government to protect our country against these foreign aggressions. About the same time resolutions of inquiry on the subject were introduced in the Senate, by Senator Cooper, of Pennsylvania, who made a speech showing the enormous extent of the evil. Mayor Wood also addressed our ministers, consuls, and other representatives in Europe, invoking their aid and co-operation to put an end to the evil. . . . .

RIGHT OF RELIEVING OURSELVES DENIED

So emboldened have foreign powers become in making our country the receptacle for the dregs and off-scourings of their population, and thus relieving themselves of the burden of pauperism and crime, that some of them even now have the audacity to deny our right to prevent them from so doing. It will be perceived by the following preamble and resolution, adopted by the government of Würtemberg, and a copy of which was transmitted to the German Emigration Society of New York, in 1855, that that government has the effrontery to claim the right to impose its paupers and convicts upon us, and impudently denies our right to relieve ourselves by returning from whence they came their wretched outcasts. The preamble, it will be seen, fully admits that these vagabonds are transported at the public expense.

WHEREAS, It has repeatedly occurred that German emigrants to America, and among them natives of Würtemberg, who desired to return home on account of sickness, or incapacity to labor, have been forwarded to this country by the German Emigration Society, of New York, and

WHEREAS, It is desirable that those who have once emigrated to America, *and especially those who have been transported thither at the expense of the State, or the communes,* and are unable, whether or not it be from any fault of their own, to earn their subsistence, should not return here, to be a burden to the State or the commune (*which in that case will have defrayed the expense of their journey in vain*): and

WHEREAS, The American authorities *are scarcely authorized* to send back those who, having once been admitted to the country, cannot earn their subsistence in America, and

[1] Extract from "Report of the Committee on Foreign Affairs of the House of Representatives on 'Foreign Criminals and Paupers,' August 16, 1856," U.S. 34th Congress, 1st session, *House Doc. No. 359*, pp. 19–26.

WHEREAS, It is much less the business of the German Emigration Society of New York to promote the return of such individuals; therefore,

Resolved, That necessary steps are to be taken to prevent their transportation back to this country.

The Würtemberg denial of our rights to protect ourselves against their criminals and paupers is, in itself, strong evidence of the necessity which exists for so doing. It is undoubtedly true, as Vattel, in his work on international law, states, that "it belongs to the nation and its rulers to fulfill the duties of *humanity* toward strangers"; but it is equally true, as he also states, that "it belongs exclusively to each nation to form her own judgment of what her conscience prescribes to her—of what she can or cannot do—of what it is proper or improper for her to do; and, of course, it rests solely with her to examine and determine whether she can perform any office for any other nation, without neglecting the duty which she owes to herself." The duty we owe to our own country, and its free institutions, is the highest imposed on us next to that we owe to our God. Hence the legislation to protect society against the gigantic evils growing out of the introduction into this country of foreign criminals and paupers commenced with the settlement of the first colonists. . . . .

DUTY TO OUR COUNTRY

Adopting the sentiment expressed by Mayor Wood, in his letter to the President of the United States, "that the inherent right of every community to protect itself from dangers arising from such immigration cannot be questioned," so it must be conceded by every one fully sensible of the enormity of the evil, that it is the duty of the community, so threatened with danger, to guard and protect itself against it. If it be the duty of government to protect us from foreign aggression with ball and cannon, it surely must also be . . . . its duty to protect us from an enemy more insidious and destructive, though coming in another form. The evil is upon us, and it is our imperative duty to relieve the country from it as far as possible. As now administered, our institutions seem almost to be alone for the use of foreign paupers and criminals, while we who have established and support them have comparatively very little use for them. Ours has been a policy which has substantially rather invited than repelled the refuse of Europe to our shores, that we might support them, or suffer from their idleness and crime. Facts abundantly show to what a ruinous extent our misguided philanthropy and ridiculous sentiments of philanthropy have been carried. "Behold, therefore, I will bring strangers upon thee, the terrible of the nations; and they shall draw their swords against the beauty of thy wisdom and they shall defile thy brightness" was the prophetical language of one of the inspired writers, which may with force be just now applied to us. Can it be possible that with the experience we have, there are any among us who do not feel it a duty to put an end to the evil under which the country now labors? It is sincerely to be hoped there are none such. Our duty is a plain one. Let us manfully and faithfully perform it. How can that be best done?

HAS CONGRESS POWER OVER IMMIGRATION?

It is the inherent right of every community to protect itself against all public evils; and why has it not also the power to close our ports against convicts and paupers, sent here by foreign governments, and whose corrupt public morality disseminates and popularizes infidelity, disturbs the public peace, degrades our character as a nation, fills our prisons and almshouses, and seriously impairs the stability of our free institutions? The power exists somewhere either in the states, or in the general government, or in both of them. . . . .

POWER OF THE STATES ON THE SUBJECT

Whatever difference of opinion may be entertained as to the power of Congress over immigration, there can be none as to the internal police power of the States being sufficiently extensive to enable them, *if they deem it necessary* to exercise it, to exclude entire classes of persons. They have reserved that power which relates to the public morals, and even in that limited view would embrace pauperism and crime, whilst in law it includes all legislation for the internal policy of a State. In the case of *New York* v. *Miln*, Justice Barbour in delivering the opinion of the court, 11 *Peters*, made use of this emphatic language: "We think it as competent and as necessary for a State to provide precautionary measures against the moral pestilence of paupers, vagabonds and possibly convicts, as it is to guard against the physical pestilence which may arise from unsound and infectious articles imported, or from a ship, the crew of which may be laboring under an infection." So Justice Story, in the case of *Prigg* v. *Pennsylvania*, expressed himself as follows on the same subject: "We entertain no doubt whatsoever that the States, in virtue of their general police power, possess full jurisdiction to arrest and restrain runaway slaves and remove them from their borders, and otherwise to secure themselves against their depredations and evil example, *as they certainly may do in cases of idlers*, vagabonds and paupers." . . . .

WHO SHALL REMEDY THE EVIL?

Both the general and State governments can do much to stay the tide of immigration of this undesirable population, and to protect society against its pernicious influences, and the injuries it threatens, not only to the prosperity and welfare of the country, but the perpetuity of our republican institutions. Each can, within its own sphere and the limits of its constitutional power, not only adopt measures which will contribute greatly to prevent and put an end to the introduction of foreign convicts and paupers, but to save our country from the further increase of the evils resulting from such an accession to our population. . . . .

HOW TO BE REMEDIED

So far as State legislatures are concerned, with a few exceptions, they have been as remiss as Congress in the discharge of their duties on the subject. Though they cannot enact laws that will come in conflict with the power of Congress over commerce, they may enact such as will materially prevent the landing of convicts and paupers upon our shores. Under the reserved internal police power which they all possess, they may throw such safeguards around the community, and such obstacles in the way of disembarking foreign imbeciles and desperadoes, as will soon put an end to their transportation hither. This is, however, not all they may do. They may adopt measures, also, to remedy the evil which those now in the country have brought upon it. Congress has not the power to adopt and carry out such measures of reform. The States have the power to its fullest extent, and should exercise it to restrain and suppress those evil influences, now everywhere felt, and which, if they be not checked, will evidently undermine public and private virtue and public and private liberty. Congress can and ought to exert its authority to prevent the further introduction of those who exercise such influence upon society, but beyond this it can accomplish but little. It cannot reform, though it may materially aid in preventing a further accumulation here of the refuse population of Europe, who, after they come here are only fit to fill our streets as beggars, our almshouses as paupers, or our jails as criminals.

19. Some Early Cases of Deportation

A. "AN INFAMOUS CASE OF EXTRADITION," 1855[1]

Yesterday morning there sailed from this port a splendid packet-ship, bearing the noble name of "Daniel Webster," which fitly belongs to so fine a vessel. Yet so many fine ships sail out of our harbor that the reader may inquire why we make this departure the occasion for such conspicuous notice.

Among the crowd of human beings on board that proud vessel was one poor woman, with an infant daughter. Her passage and that of her child were paid by the rich and powerful commonwealth of Massachusetts. She left our free and happy shores unwilling and reluctant. She went away against her own free will, constrained by force of the civil authorities of the State. Her cries as she begged not to be thus so cruelly banished, were, we are told, most piteous, and such as to cause the accidental witnesses of the scene to burn with indignation.

The offence of this poor woman, for which she was thus violently and ignominiously expelled from Massachusetts, was the fact that she was born in Ireland and is called a pauper. Her infant daughter, who unconsciously shares her mother's sad fate, is a native of the commonwealth of Mas-

[1] From the *Boston Daily Advertiser*, May 16, 1855. Reprinted in the *Citizen*, II (New York City, May 26, 1855), 332.

sachusetts; but she too partakes of that hard lot of poverty which it has been reserved for Massachusetts to make a crime, and a crime which Massachusetts punishes as no other crime is punished in America, by banishment —banishment from one's native land.

The name of this victim to Know-Nothing intolerance was Mary Williams; and her infant, Bridget, is but a few weeks old. About thirty-five paupers, perhaps more, were sent away at the same time, in the same vessel, at the expense of the State. These facts we learn from eye-witnesses of the scene, and from other certain and authentic sources of information.

Our readers are aware that there exists upon our statute book a law which authorizes any Justice of the Peace upon complaint, by a warrant directed to and to be executed by any constable, or any other person there designed, to cause any pauper to be removed out of the State, to any place beyond the sea where he belongs, if the Justice thinks proper, and he may be conveniently removed, and also that, independently of this provision of law, a practice has arisen by which the Commissioner of Alien Passengers undertakes, even without the warrant of a Justice of Peace, to send back paupers in cases in which he sees fit, and pays the expenses from money in his hands belonging to the State Treasury.

On account of the temporary absence of the Commissioner of Alien Passengers, and none of the gentlemen in his office being possessed of the facts, we are unable to state which of these two methods was employed as the pretext of authority for effecting the rendition of the unfortunate creatures who sailed yesterday in the "Daniel Webster"; nor can we state by what Justice of the Peace, if any, the warrant was issued. But the facts that they were sent away and that the State paid their passage, and that the piteous cries of this poor woman with her child were such as to attract the attention of the bystanders as she was led on board the vessel—these facts we have certainly ascertained.

B. "ANOTHER SHAME FOR MASSACHUSETTS"[1]

Every week brings forth some new disgrace for Massachusetts. The extradition of the Irish girl, Mary Williams, and her infant daughter, is fresh in the memory of our readers, but a recent discovery has brought to light a still more atrocious case. The same vessel that bore off this poor, friendless girl, carried also a helpless lunatic, huddled from his cell in the asylum, on board, alone, among strangers, to be conveyed to his native country, where, perhaps, not a solitary relative remains to cheer the dark remnant of his life.

Hugh Carr, a native of Ireland, long resident in this country, an inchoate citizen, who, up to the period when Heaven mysteriously deprived him of reason, faithfully performed all the duties of a good citizen, and contributed his measure of taxation for the support of the State, was, at the time of his

[1] From the *Citizen*, II, 361.

affliction, consigned by his family to the Lunatic Asylum, in the hope of restoration to his senses.

His brother and family are all residents of Massachusetts; capable and willing to support him if the State considered him an unjust burden—which he certainly was not—yet, without consulting them as to his provision, or acquainting them with their intentions, the fanatical officials of this hot-bed of bigotry smuggle the unconscious lunatic on board ship, and pack him off to Ireland, utterly indifferent as to his future fate.

The most hateful of European tyrannies would not be guilty of a more truculent crime than this.

The threat of an action at law by the brother of Mr. Carr has brought the managers of the Asylum to their senses, and they now propose to bring the unfortunate man back again. It is too late for the reputation of the State. His restitution may lessen *his* misery, but it will not lessen *her* crime. Subsequent investigation also has put the case of Mary Williams in a worse form than it was at first represented. The Boston *Atlas* has sifted the matter to the bottom, and declares:

> She was not a pauper abroad, and she never had been a pauper. . . . . She came here with an aunt who is now living in the State, and is not a pauper. This girl—for she is quite young—had been deceived abroad, and she came here to conceal her shame. When near the time of her confinement, she was sent to the alms-house; and when next we hear of her, she is torn from the only being who loves her, and is sent over the sea. Before she could make her wants known, before she could appeal to benevolent men or women for aid, before she could effect any arrangement for supporting herself by her own labor, she is driven by force out of this hospitable Commonwealth—to want, to loneliness, to irreclaimable infamy. And all this cost the State of Massachusetts just $12 passage money! . . . .

20. "Retransportation" of Foreign Paupers Proposed, 1856[1]

The question naturally arises, What is the cause of this constant increase of pauperism in the State, distinguished as it is for wealth and prosperity? . . . . But it will be seen by the report that the chief cause of the increase arises from the unchecked emigration of foreigners. Over 111,000 paupers of foreign birth were relieved last year.

It is the duty of the State to take care of its poor, but it may be questioned, whether New York should be made the poorhouse of Europe or be forced to lighten the taxation of foreign countries. Whole towns and counties in Europe, find it more economical to pay for the transportation of paupers to our shores, than support them at home, and hence deposit them in ship loads in our cities. Our poor records and criminal statistics are used by foreign historians at this day to prove that a republican form

---

[1] Extracts from "Reports of County Superintendents of the Poor, *New York State Assembly Documents*, No. 214 (1856), pp. 8–10.

of government, so far as equalizing the means of subsistence and protecting property and life is concerned, is a failure. It is fearlessly asserted that taxation for the support of the poor is as oppressive in this country as in the monarchies of the old world. We owe it to ourselves and to our institutions to arrest this flood of pauperism and crime that sets so constantly on our shores.

There should be a limit to it. Barriers should be erected and checks furnished by which it should be graduated so as not to oppress the people of the State or endanger the integrity of its free institutions. The suggestion of the Commissioners of Emigration, in their report of last year, deserves the early attention of the Legislature. They say:

During the year the attention of the Commissioners has been repeatedly called, through the vigilance of their officers, to the fact of cargoes of helpless or broken down paupers having been shipped to this port by the local authorities of the cities and villages of Europe, upon which they have been a charge. Occasionally, too, there appeared sufficient evidence that convicts, for crimes dangerous to society, had been sent out by the governments and other authorities abroad. It would be most desirable to return to their own countries all of the latter class, and most of those of the former; but this direct power is not granted by the existing laws of the State, and is perhaps a regulation of the intercourse with foreign nations, not within the competence of the State Legislature.

It is to be hoped that if this evil can be reached by the State Legislature, it will not wait the tardy, uncertain action of Congress, but devise some method by which the Commissioners of Emigration can relieve the commonwealth from so unnecessary and so heavy a burden.

Measures, however, that should secure this result would furnish only a partial remedy to the evils of pauperism. Under our liberal laws the legitimate emigration would still be enormous, and of the hundreds of thousands that annually enter our State the greater part exhaust their means in reaching this continent. Unacquainted with our customs, many of them with our language, ignorant and degraded, they are unfit for most employments, and often unable to obtain those which they might fill. Debased themselves, they educate their children in the same habits, and rear only paupers for the State to support. These mixed races we shall be compelled to receive and incorporate into our body politic, and it is therefore of the highest importance that they should not be merely cared for themselves, but placed in a position to educate their children to a higher life than their own. The State would find it economical in the end to introduce some system of employment for the adult poor, and means of common and religious education for their children. Industrial institutes and model farms have both been demonstrated to be practicable; but it is more than a matter of economy—it is one of the most pressing necessity that some system more extensive than can be carried out by private enterprise should be devised to prevent the frightful increase of pauperism.

The evil, great and embarrassing as it is, must be met, and every postponement only enhances the difficulties which surround it. . . . .

21. An Argument against Federal Control of Immigration[1]

We hear it often said that immigration is to the country, not to a State; that it has a national bearing; and that in more than one respect we stand in absolute need of a national board of emigration. I do not agree with this. Immigration is undoubtedly a matter of national importance, but it is a matter of State concern also. I will endeavor to state the grounds on which this opinion rests.

Ever since immigration has attained greater proportions, legal questions have grown out of the financial interests connected with it, which have turned on the point whether a single State has or has not the right to tax the immigrant on his arrival for sanitary purposes and for his protection. As this tax, or commutation money, of $2.50, which is levied on each immigrant landing at New York, amounts to between one-half and three-quarters of a million per year, it will easily be understood that the magnitude of the amount involved induced a reference of the questions to the highest tribunals of the land. Lately, this same question has again been taken up by Western newspapers, and by some Western members of Congress. They demand that the commutation money which immigrants pay at the several ports of entry be distributed, *pro rata*, among the States where they settle; and to effect this purpose they insist that the United States Government should take the whole business of immigration in its own hands; that the Secretary of the Treasury make all needful rules and regulations, and appoint the proper officers in the same manner in which the Custom House officers are appointed; thus doing away entirely with all State institutions which have been established in the course of years for the protection of immigrants. I believe not only that existing laws authorize the single State to exercise an exclusive control over immigrants, but that the real interest of the country requires this exclusive State control to be continued.

It is a well-known fact that New York is the principal port of entry for immigrants and that more than five-sevenths of them are landed there. Whether directly pointed out or not, it is the port and State of New York against which the attacks of those who wish to give to the General Government the exclusive power of dealing with immigration are directed. Now, the State of New York, is, as far as my knowledge extends, the only one which heretofore has organized a proper system for the protection of immigrants. As has been stated, it took years to effect a wholesome reform in the former management of immigration, and to create the Board of the Commissioners of Emigration of the State of New York.

[1] Extract from F. Kapp, *Immigration* (1870), pp. 153–61. Friedrich Kapp was one of the New York state emigration commissioners.

All that can be admitted in regard to the question of State or national control is, that the Congress of the United States has not only the right, but is absolutely bound, in the interests of humanity, to protect the immigrant on the high seas, in his transit from foreign countries, and to make for that purpose international treaties, which Congress alone can do. But the authority of the federal legislative power extends no further in the premises, and completely ceases after the immigrant has landed and put himself under the operation and protection of the State laws. For Congress to attempt, then, to collect from him any tax, or to assume his support, would be not less absurd than if it were to undertake to license the boarding-house where he puts up, to appoint the policeman who protects him, or to provide him with transportation to his railway depot. The care of the immigrant, after he lands, is purely a police regulation in which the people of the State where he lands are so exclusively interested as to have, beyond a doubt, the best right to provide for him. The harbor of the city of New York, while of national importance, is still of State concern, and so it is with foreign immigration.

But granting, for the sake of argument, that immigration is a matter of national concern, it is doubtful if anything but evil would result from abandoning a system which has fully realized its purpose—which has been tried and perfected by the experience of nearly a quarter of a century; whose operations are greatly facilitated by being concentrated upon a comparatively small area, and the agents under which are few, practised, and under the immediate supervision of a Board of unsalaried and non-partisan Commissioners, located and laboring on the spot. To replace such a system by the clumsy machinery of a central board, or by a single Commissioner, stationed at an inland city, remote from the chief objective points of foreign immigration, with an unwieldy multitude of subordinates scattered over the land, whose irresponsibility would inevitably increase in the direct ratio of their distance from the seat of authority, would be worse than unreasonable. The transfer to the National Government of the control of the immigrant would lead to quarrels, heart-burnings, and jealousies among the States, as the controlling officers would certainly be required to use their power to influence the current of immigration. The effect would undoubtedly be to so increase the cost of supporting the immigrant as either to quadruple the present tax, and then make it virtually a prohibitory one, or to impose the burden on the national treasury, and thus make the immigrant the nation's pauper. . . . .

While New York has to endure nearly all of its evils, the other States reap most of the benefits of immigration. New York protects and shields the immigrant in his health and property, and the rising communities of the West flourish upon the fruits of her vigilant care. Our State acts, so to speak, as a filter in which the stream of immigration is purified; what is good passes beyond; what is evil, for the most part, remains behind.

Experience shows that it is the hardy, self-reliant, industrious, wealthy immigrant who takes his capital, his intelligence, and his labor to enrich the Western or Southern States. As near as a calculation can be made, it has been ascertained that out of one hundred continental immigrants, seventy-five go West, and twenty-five remain in the great cities of the East, while of the Irish and English, twenty-five settle in the country, and seventy-five remain in the cities of the East. Thus, about fifty per cent of all newcomers go to the country, and of these again about seventy-five per cent to what is now called the West. In 1867, of 242,731 immigrants, only 91,610 declared New York State and City to be the place of their destination; in 1868, out of 213,686, only 65,734 proposed to remain in our city and State; and in 1869, out of 258,989, the total who stated they would remain in New York was 85,810.

A large proportion of those who remain here is made up of the idle, the sickly, the destitute, the worthless, who would become a burden instead of a help to our people, were it not for the wise institution of that fund which, at the least possible cost to the immigrant, yet still at a cost that relieves him from the degradation of eleemosynary aid, provides him with shelter and support. It is this feature of our State emigrant laws which is so admirable, and which, at the same time, for reasons aready indicated, it would be most difficult for the General Government to imitate.

The same trifling sum which the immigrant pays to secure himself against the danger of possible sickness or destitution for five years after his arrival, and which is, as it were, the insignificant premium on a policy of health insurance for that time, supports the establishment which takes care of him without burden to the people of the State. It is this feature which invalidates the Western claim for division of the commutation money *pro rata* among the States in which the immigrant settles. For the commutation fund is the consideration of a contract between the immigrant and the State of New York, by which the latter binds herself to protect him on his arrival, and for the period of five years thereafter provide him with shelter if destitute, and with medical and other aid if sick.

Contrary to the arguments of those who favor the distribution of the commutation money among the several States to which immigrants go to settle, it is susceptible of proof that such a distribution would eventually result in injury rather than in benefit to the State in question. For, in that event, the share of New York would not be sufficient to meet the expense of caring for the disproportionately large number of sick and destitute who remain within her limits. Our State could not then, as she does now, act in the interest of the whole Union, by efficiently protecting all the immigrants on their arrival, and by preventing the spread of the diseases imported by them over the country at large, and this while deriving far less advantage from immigration than the Western States. Let those who compare the exaction of the commutation money by the Commissioners of Emigration of this State to the "Sound dues" formerly levied by Denmark, consider whether it would not be a far greater disadvantage for the Western States to have ship-fever, cholera, and other pestilential diseases carried among their people, than it is for them to do without the share of the commutation money which they claim. In 1846-47, more than twenty thousand immigrants died on the sea-voyage and immediately after landing, and thousands of others carried the germs of disease to the remotest corner of the land. It is the Commissioners of Emigration who have since prevented the spread of contagious diseases beyond their hospitals, and the East as well as the West ought to thank them for their disinterested care of the immigrants, and for the protection of the whole country from pestilential scourges.

It seems to me that those who wish to put an end to this beneficent work estimate the value of the immigrant by dollars and cents instead of by his productive power, and forget entirely that what the West wants is healthy men, capable of assisting actively in the development of her resources. This want is certainly better supplied under the present system than it would be were a change made. The same persons also seem to overlook entirely the beneficial influence exercised upon the immigrant by the protection against fraud and imposition of every kind afforded to him by the Commissioners. It is in this that benevolence and sympathy find their true sphere of action. The pecuniary losses of the immigrant from his own ignorance and inexperience, and from the rapacity of others, are to be deplored as much, and even more, on account of the community than on his own account. For, whenever the poor immigrant is fleeced by rogues, his judgment is impaired, his energy is diminished, and in general that moral elasticity lost which he needs more than ever to start well in a strange land; and thus a heavy injury is inflicted on his adopted country, which, instead of self-relying, independent men, receives individuals who are broken in spirit, and, at least for a time, useless, who are burdensome to themselves and to others. From this point of view, every one who has the interest of his fellow-being and of his country at heart, has the strongest interest in having the immigrant efficiently protected, and in co-operating with those who are officially called upon to provide for this protection.

If the same people who engage our attention on their landing here crossed our path in their native country while in their old accustomed track of life, the task would be comparatively easy, for in that case they would much more readily understand their interest and advantage; they would not be confused by a hundred new impressions; and the majority of them would distinguish the honest man from the scoundrel. Upon emigrating, however, the masses enter into entirely new relations, into a new world; two-thirds of them do not know the language of the country, and all receive in one single hour more new notions and ideas than formerly in years. Thus, they find themselves without proper guidance, and fall the easier into the hands of impudent impostors, perhaps for the very reason that they have been warned against them. This sudden transition from one country into another, this change of old homelike surroundings, with new conditions of life, all of which, strange and some offensive to the immigrants, often stuns them temporarily, and creates a general bewilderment, which even makes an intelligent man appear awkward and stupid.

Whatever we may do, we cannot absolutely protect the immigrant against the practices of sharpers as long as we cannot obstruct the sources from which credulity and ignorance flow. We can take some precautionary measures, we can point out the right way, but it is just as impossible entirely to cure the evil as it is to put an end to human depravity in general. The Commissioners cannot be expected to accomplish an impossibility. In New York, a special detective would have to be assigned to each immigrant in order to render him absolutely secure against all attempts to swindle him. What a board like that of the Commissioners can do is to give the immigrant the best possible protection, and this duty they are certainly discharging.

22. New York Commutation System Declared Unconstitutional[1]

MR. JUSTICE MILLER:

Immediately after this decision [in the Passenger Cases],[2] the State of New York modified her statute on that subject, with a view, no doubt, to avoid the constitutional objection; and amendments and alterations have continued to be made up to the present time.

As the law now stands, the master or owner of every vessel landing passengers from a foreign port is bound to make a report similar to the one recited in the statute held to be valid in the case of *New York* v. *Miln;* and on this report the mayor is to indorse a demand upon the master or owner that he give a bond for every passenger landed in the city, in the penal sum of $300, conditioned to indemnify the commissioners of emigration, and every county, city, and town in the State, against any expense for the relief or support of the person named in the bond for four years thereafter; but the owner or consignee may commute for such bond, and be released from giving it, by paying, within twenty-four hours after the landing of the passengers, the sum of one dollar and fifty cents for each one of them. If neither the bond be given nor the sum paid within the twenty-four hours, a penalty of $500 for each pauper is incurred, which is made a lien on the vessel, collectible by attachment at the suit of the Commissioner of Emigration.

[1] Extract from United States Supreme Court decision in *Henderson et al.* v. *Mayor of New York et al.* (1875), 92 U.S. 259.

Another attempt to find a constitutional method of collecting "head money" was made by the New York legislature in 1881, which provided for the collection of money for inspection purposes. This act was also declared unconstitutional in *People* v. *Compagnie Générale Transatlantique*, 107 U.S. 59.

[2] See above, pp. 147–56.

Conceding the authority of the Passenger Cases, which will be more fully considered hereafter, it is argued that the change in the statute now relied upon requiring primarily a bond for each passenger landed, as an indemnity against his becoming a future charge to the state or county, leaving it optional with the shipowner to avoid this by paying a fixed sum for each passenger, takes it out of the principle of the case of *Smith* v. *Turner*— the Passenger Case from New York. It is said that the statute in that case was a direct tax on the passenger, since the act authorized the shipmaster to collect it of him, and that on that ground alone was it held void; while in the present case the requirement of a bond is but a suitable regulation under the power of the State to protect its cities and towns from the expense of supporting persons who are paupers or diseased, or helpless women and children, coming from foreign countries.

In whatever language a statute may be framed, its purpose must be determined by its natural and reasonable effect; and if it is apparent that the object of this statute, as judged by that criterion, is to compel the owners of the vessels to pay a sum of money for every passenger brought by them from a foreign shore, and landed at the port of New York, it is as much a tax on passengers if collected from them, or a tax on the vessel or owners . . . . as was the statute held void in the Passenger Cases.

To require a heavy and almost impossible condition to the exercise of this right with the alternative of payment of a small sum of money is, in effect, to demand payment of that sum. To suppose that a vessel, which once a month lands from three hundred to one thousand passengers, or from three thousand to twelve thousand per annum, will give that many bonds of $300 with good sureties, with a covenant for four years, against accident, disease, or poverty of the passenger named in such bond, is absurd, when this can be avoided by the payment of one dollar and fifty cents collected of the passenger before he embarks on the vessel.

Such bonds would amount in many instances, for every voyage, to more than the value of the vessel. The liability on the bond would be, through a long lapse of time, contingent on circumstances which the bondsman could neither foresee nor control. The cost of preparing the bond and approving sureties, with the troubles incident to it in each case, is greater than the sum required to be paid as commutation. It is inevitable, under such a law, that the money would be paid for each passenger, or the statute resisted or evaded. It is a law in its purpose and effect imposing a tax on the owner of the vessel for the privilege of landing in New York passengers transported from foreign countries.

It is said that the purpose of the act is to protect the State, against the consequences of the flood of pauperism immigrating from Europe, and first landing in that city.

But it is a strange mode of doing this to tax every passenger alike who comes from abroad.

The man who brings with him important additions to the wealth of the country, and the man who is perfectly free from disease, and brings to aid the industry of the country a stout heart and a strong arm, are as much the subjects of the tax as the diseased pauper who may become the object of the charity of the city the day after he lands from the vessel.

No just rule can make the citizen of France landing from an English vessel on our shore liable for the support of an English or Irish pauper who lands at the same time from the same vessel. . . . .

As already indicated, the provisions of the Constitution of the United States, on which the principal reliance is placed to make void the statute of New York, is that which gives to Congress the power "to regulate commerce with foreign nations."

. . . . The transportation of passengers from European ports to those of the United States . . . . has become a part of our commerce with foreign nations, of vast interest to this country, as well as to the immigrants who come among us to find a welcome and a home within our borders. In addition to the wealth which some of them bring, they bring still more largely the labor which we need to till our soil, build our railroads, and develop the latent resources of the country in its minerals, its manufactures, and its agriculture. Is the regulation of this great system a regulation of commerce? Can it be doubted that a law which prescribes the terms on which vessels shall engage in it is a law regulating this branch of commerce?

The transportation of a passenger from Liverpool to the city of New York is one voyage. It is not completed until the passenger is disembarked at the pier in the latter city. A law or a rule emanating from any lawful authority, which prescribes terms or conditions on which alone the vessel can discharge its passengers, is a regulation of commerce; and, in case of vessels and passengers coming from foreign ports, is a regulation of commerce with foreign nations.

. . . . A regulation which imposes onerous, perhaps impossible, conditions on those engaged in active commerce with foreign nations, must of necessity be national in its character. It is more than this; for it may properly be called *international*. It belongs to that class of laws which concern the exterior relation of this whole nation with other nations and governments. . . . .

It is equally clear that the matter of these statutes may be, and ought to be, the subject of a uniform system or plan. The laws which govern the right to land passengers in the United States from other countries ought to be the same in New York, Boston, New Orleans, and San Francisco. A striking evidence of the truth of this proposition is to be found in the similarity, we might almost say in the identity, of the statutes of New York, of Louisiana, and California, now before us for consideration in these three cases.

It is apparent, therefore, that, if there be a class of laws which may be valid when passed by the States until the same ground is occupied by a treaty or an act of Congress, this statute is not of that class.

The argument has been pressed with some earnestness that inasmuch as this statute does not come into operation until twenty-four hours after the passenger has landed, and has mingled with, or has the right to mingle with, the mass of the population, he is withdrawn from the influence of any laws which Congress might pass on the subject, and remitted to the laws of the State as its own citizens are. It might be a sufficient answer to say that this is a mere evasion of the protection which the foreigner has a right to expect from the Federal government when he lands here a stranger, owing allegiance to another government, and looking to it for such protection as grows out of his relation to that government.

But the branch of the statute which we are considering is directed to and operates directly on the shipowner. It holds him responsible for what he has done before the twenty-four hours commence. He is to give the bond or pay the money because he *has* landed the passenger, and he is given twenty-four hours' time to do this before the penalty attaches. When he is sued for this penalty it is not because the man has been here twenty-four hours, but because he brought him here, and failed to give the bond or pay one dollar and fifty cents.

The effective operation of this law commences at the other end of the voyage. The master requires of the passenger, before he is admitted on board, as a part of the passage-money the sum which he knows he must pay for the privilege of landing him in New York. It is, as we have already said, in effect a tax on the passenger, which he pays for the right to make the voyage—a voyage only completed when he lands on the American shore. The case does not even require us to consider at what period after his arrival the passenger himself passes from the sole protection of the Constitution, laws, and treaties of the United States, and becomes subject to such laws as the State may rightfully pass. . . . .

It is too clear for argument that this demand of the owner of the vessel for a bond or money on account of every passenger landed by him from a foreign shore is, if valid, an obligation which he incurs by bringing the passenger here, and which is perfect the moment he leaves the vessel.

We are of opinion that this whole subject has been confided to Congress by the Constitution; that Congress can more appropriately and with more acceptance exercise it than any other body known to our law, state or national; that by providing a system of laws in these matters, applicable to all ports and to all vessels, a serious question, which has long been a matter of contest and complaint, may be effectually and satisfactorily settled.

23. The Institutions Established by the New York Commissioners of Emigration

A. THE STATE EMIGRANT REFUGE AND HOSPITAL AT WARD'S ISLAND[1]

Previous to the year 1847, the Quarantine law provided for the care of the sick emigrant. A general tax, levied under State authority on all passengers arriving at the port of New York, was applied to the support of the Marine Hospital at Quarantine. Aliens as well as others arriving here, suffering under contagious or infectious diseases, such as yellow-fever, ship-fever, etc., were there received and gratuitously treated for one year. But no further provision was made at that period for the relief of emigrants not afflicted with any contagious disease, and they had to apply to the Almshouse authorities for admission to their medical institutions.

The whole government and property of the Quarantine hospitals was transferred to the Commissioners of Emigration immediately after the constitution of the Board. But, owing to the want of other buildings, they were at first obliged to send all their patients to [these hospitals]. In consequence of this, the hospitals were filled to excess, while, in spite of every precaution, crowds of sick, suffering under milder or non-contagious diseases, or requiring only surgical aid, were exposed to ship-fever, small-pox, yellow-fever, or cholera. These difficulties continued until April 11, 1849, when the Marine Hospital was formally restricted to the reception of contagious diseases. After this step, the Commissioners considered it their first duty to provide for and furnish hospital accommodations for those who suffered from other contagious diseases, and a refuge for those who were destitute.

In 1847, the pressure for increased accommodations became very great. Thousands of sick emigrants arrived in the summer of that year, the greater portion of whom were the victims of the Irish famine, and had to be provided for at once, and as well as possible. Several hundreds of them were sent to private hospitals, such as Dr. Williams's and Dr. Wilson's, others to the New York City hospitals, and still others to the Almshouse. . . . . Others, as, for instance, the passengers of the cholera-ship, the "New York," from Havre, were, by permission of the Secretary of War, sent to Bedloe's Island, where temporary hospitals had been erected for their accommodation. These temporary measures, however, were wholly inadequate to the many wants and necessities of the emigrant; and the Commissioners speedily came to the conclusion that, in order to save expenses and provide sufficient accommodation for all their sick, they would have to build their own hospitals and places of refuge.

Ward's Island (which consists of about 200 acres) was the spot which they selected for the location of these establishments. . . . . Its proximity to the city, and its accessibility at all seasons of the year [were among the

[1] Extract from F. Kapp, *Immigration* (1870), pp. 125-29.

advantages which] induced that selection. The Commissioners have not been disappointed in the result, now that the demands upon the island have reached to a magnitude much beyond their anticipation. . . . . On July 14, 1847, the Commissioners resolved to erect a two-story shed, 200 feet long and 22 feet wide, for the accommodation of those who could not find employment and had not the strength to work. Early in 1848, they determined to build a hospital, within a short distance of the building used as a refuge. On November 1, 1848, it was finished and occupied. The structure was of wood, filled in with brick, having a frontage of 119 feet, and two wings, running east and west, of 40 feet long by 25 feet wide. It contained, besides apartments for physicians, apothecary, and nurses, and the apothecary's shop, eleven large rooms for patients, each of the dimensions of 40 feet by 25, and affording accommodations for 250 beds.

While this hospital was in the course of construction, the Board became satisfied that still more ample accommodations would soon be needed, and that more especially a proper establishment for children was imperatively demanded. They, therefore, determined to erect a nursery building, to contain, besides dormitories and play-room, a school-room and chapel. By the end of 1848 this building was finished and partly occupied.

As it became essential to have more ground than, under the lease, was in the possession of the Commissioners, and as several lots or parcels of land on Ward's Island happened to be for sale, it was resolved to take advantage of the opportunity. Accordingly, in the month of July, 1848, 12 acres . . . . were purchased. . . . .

When the Commission was organized in 1847, it had no lands, nor buildings, nor means. Hence it was a wise policy to commit to its charge the Quarantine grounds and hospitals, even saddled with the condition that the Commissioners of Emigration had to receive and gratuitously nurse nonemigrants, such as sailors and sick citizens. In this way, the indispensable means were at once provided for receiving and caring for arriving immigrants, who were affected with various contagious and infectious diseases, among which cholera, small-pox, and ship-fever were widely prevalent. The number of sick was appalling. In the first eight years of the Commission, nearly 50,000 were treated within these hospitals. Since that time, large hospitals on Ward's Island have been erected, owing to which the sanitary condition of the immigrants has greatly improved. Accommodations for all emigrants not affected with infectious diseases being afforded on Ward's Island, the reason for placing the Marine Hospital in the charge of the Commissioners ceased to exist. There was, in addition, other strong and positive ground for a change; it was unjust to those from whom the emigrant fund is collected to make that fund contribute towards the support of the Quarantine and the maintenance of the health laws. In years in which the means of the Commissioners were seriously diminished by a decrease of immigration, it was hardly possible for them to maintain those who paid the commutation money. Nevertheless, the Commissioners were expected to bear the cost of supporting all who suffered from infectious diseases. This injustice was only repaired by the act of April 29, 1863, which created a Board of Quarantine Commissioners.

B. THE CASTLE GARDEN LANDING DEPOT[1]

The Commissioners [of Emigration created by the Law of 1847] were not long in discovering that the benevolent intentions of the law creating their Board could not be realized as long as they had not the absolute control of the emigrant, and as long as they were thus prevented from protecting him against the frauds practised on him by forwarders, boarding-house keepers, agents, and runners. They therefore, in the first year of their existence, applied to the Legislature for an act authorizing them to lease a dock or pier, where all the emigrants should be landed; where no outsiders would be allowed to enter without permission of the Commissioners; and where the emigrant could be cautioned and admonished against all the wiles of those who lay waiting for him on his arrival. The law of April 11, 1848, authorized the Commissioners to purchase or to lease such a pier or dock, and by virtue of this act, on May 8, 1848, they leased from the Common Council, for a term of five years, the large and commodious pier at the foot of Hubert Street, at an annual rent of $3,000.

It was anticipated that this pier would be in proper order for use by the middle of July; but, to the surprise of the Commissioners, they were, immediately after the execution of the lease, served with an injunction, obtained by some of the residents in the neighborhood. This injunction was granted and sustained against the appeal of the Commissioners on the ground that the landing of emigrants at the foot of Hubert Street, in the vicinity of St. John's Park, would bring into a quiet part of the city a noisy population, without cleanliness or sobriety; would endanger the health and good morals of the ward, and seriously affect the value of real-estate.

The Commissioners now endeavored to get some other landing-place in the lower part of the city, where the nuisance, if such it could be called, already existed, and where the emigrants for a number of years had been landed. But, though the Common Council, whom they considered bound, in a measure, to furnish a pier, seemed favorably disposed, yet none could be procured and rendered suitable for the purpose. Consequently the Commissioners could not reach the emigrant before he fell into the hands of the plunderers who stood ready to deceive him; frauds which had formerly excited so much indignation and sympathy were practised with as much boldness and impunity as ever, and all the exertions of the Commissioners, though beneficial in many cases, were quite insufficient to put an end to these abuses.

[1] Extract from F. Kapp, *op. cit.*, pp. 106–10.

In spite of repeated petitions to the Legislature to provide efficient remedies by giving to the Commissioners exclusive possession and occupation of a pier for the landing of newly arrived emigrants, it took just eight years before that body, by the Act of April 13, 1855, complied with that wish. This act was as important as the one creating the Board of the Commissioners, for it first gave the power to afford really efficient protection to the emigrant. It . . . . authorized the Commissioners of Emigration "to designate some one place in the city of New York, as they should deem proper, for the landing of emigrant passengers"; providing further that "it should be lawful for such passengers to be landed at such place so designated; and likewise (meaning the Commissioners) to purchase, lease, construct, and occupy such wharves, piers, and other accommodations, in the city of New York, as may be necessary for the accommodation of emigrant passengers."

This important act finally enabled the Commissioners fully to carry out the benevolent objects of their trust. From that time only the Board could be said to be clothed with the necessary powers and to have become responsible for the well-being and protection of the emigrant. The Commissioners, on May 5, 1855, leased the old fort at the foot of Manhattan Island, known as Castle Garden, and immediately proceeded with the fitting up of the premises in a manner suitable to the designed purpose.

Owing, however [says the *Commissioners' Report* for 1855] to the extensive repairs required, and the obstructions thrown in the way by those who, on different grounds, apprehended injury to their private interests, the place was not in readiness for use until the first of August, when it was formally opened as the *Emigrant Landing Depot*.

It is not deemed necessary to allude to the efforts made to obstruct the execution of the law in this instance, further than to state that, where that effort was resorted to with the design of rendering nugatory the power conferred, and for the ejectment of the Commissioners from the occupancy of Castle Garden, the courts have sustained the law in its beneficent objects, and the Commissioners in the possession of the premises for the purpose of carrying the law into effect; and that, where violence threatened with a strong hand to lay waste and destroy, the police authority of the city, by prudent and decisive action, effectually checked the thoughtless and lawless in their course, and preserved a valuable property from destruction or damage, and the reputation of the State from disgrace.

Two hundred and fifty vessels have landed their passengers at the Depot in the five months it has been in operation, bringing, in the aggregate, fifty-one thousand one hundred and fourteen persons, during which period no accident of any kind has occurred. All have been landed safely, without accident to themselves or property. When landed, proper means have been used to secure their comfort and protection. They have been screened from the intrusion of that class of persons who have heretofore abused the confidence of the emigrants, and despoiled them of the means they had provided to convey them to their ultimate destination, and to sustain them after they had reached it—who have long been in the practice of taking possession of the person and property of confiding emigrants, and seldom permitting them to pass out of their hands without damage; in many cases reducing them from comparative affluence to destitution, and making them subjects for relief by the funds of the Commission; but in a larger proportion crippling their means to an extent which has affected their after life.

Every facility is provided at the Depot, for those whose destination is to the interior, to proceed without unnecessary delay; and without need or pretext for intercourse with the class of persons in the city before mentioned. By this arrangement, much for the benefit of the emigrant, the shipper, the Commission, and the community at large, has been accomplished. Among these benefits may be mentioned:

First.—To the emigrants. In a more safe and speedy landing of their person and effects: In the greater safety of their effects after having been put on shore, depredators being limited to fellow-passengers, and but slight opportunity existing for successful pillage by them. In relief from the importunities and deceptions of runners and brokers. In being enabled to continue their journey without delay from the same wharf where they had just landed. In relief from all charges and exactions for landing, "baggage smashing," and porterage; and, where they are proceeding to the interior, from cartages. In being enabled to obtain passage tickets at the lowest rates directly from the various transporting companies. In having their baggage accurately weighed; and in being relieved from excessive charges for that which is extra. In obtaining reliable information relative to the various routes of travel throughout the country. In being relieved from the necessity of transporting their baggage to boarding houses when exigencies require a temporary sojourn in the city of New York. And thus in being enabled to depart for their future homes without having their means impaired, their morals corrupted, and probably their persons diseased. . . . .

24. National Legislation for the Protection of Immigrants Recommended[1]

A bill introduced into Congress at its last session, and favorably considered by the committee on commerce . . . . seeks to extend to all immigrants arriving in any port of the United States, the same protection, in substance, that has been given for nearly thirty years by the state of New York, to those immigrants who have landed since 1847, at the great commercial center of this country. Out of something more than 8,000,000 immigrants reported as arriving in the United States since May 5, 1847, nearly 6,000,000, or about two-thirds of the whole number, have landed in the city of New York, where, under a well-devised but imperfectly administered system of care and protection, they have been forwarded to their places of destination in near or remote parts of the country, have been aided in distress, relieved in sickness, supported in poverty, and sometimes sent back to the land from which they came. The number of poor immi-

[1] Report by Frank B. Sanborn, secretary of the Massachusetts State Board of Charities, to the National Conference of Charities and Correction (*Proceedings* [1876], pp. 163–69). Unfortunately this bill to which Mr. Sanborn referred did not pass. Federal legislation was delayed until 1882, and the law that was then passed (see Doc. 1 in Sec. II, below, p. 181), was quite unlike the bill recommended in this report.

grants thus assisted has been very large, something more than 1,500,000, I believe, though of course the greater part of these received very slight pecuniary aid from the state of New York through the Commissioners of Emigration, a board which, since 1847, has had the oversight of all the immigrants arriving at the port of New York. The expenses necessary for the care and relief of all these poor persons have been paid out of a common fund created by requiring every immigrant to pay a small sum varying from $1.50 to $2.50 *per capita*, upon landing in New York. . . . . No simpler and more practicable mode having been found, of assessing upon all the countries sending immigrants the cost of supporting and relieving such paupers as they send us, the same impost or tax has been levied in the bill before Congress, and will become a part of the new national policy in regard to immigrants, in case the bill passes.

We call this a *new* policy, only because it has never been adopted by the national government. In fact, it is an old policy in the seaboard states, having been commenced in Massachusetts as early as 1701, in New York and Pennsylvania before the revolution, and adopted almost in its present form in Massachusetts and New York before the great wave of European emigration had brought to their shores the millions that Ireland, Germany, England, Scandinavia and France have sent us since the Irish famine of 1846, and the years of revolution that succeeded it on the continent of Europe. . . . . The immigrants were taxed, and, so far as they were concerned, the tax was cheerfully paid. But the shipowners and steamship corporations, through whose hands the immigrant's capitation money passed on its way to the public treasury, sought to divert it to their own profit, and at last refused to pay it over, alleging that the state laws exacting it were unconstitutional. This question which had been several times before the United States Supreme Court, in one form or another, during the past fifty years, finally came up for decision last year, and the opinion of the court rendered last March by Justice Miller was to the effect that the state laws, being regulations of commerce, *were* unconstitutional. . . . .[1]

Acting upon the suggestion contained in this decision of the highest court in the land, the official boards in the seaboard states which have had, under state laws, the supervision of immigration, and of the support of the foreign-born poor, at once took counsel with each other in regard to framing a system of laws such as had become necessary. After much consultation and correspondence, in which the Boards of Charities of New York, Massachusetts, Pennsylvania, Rhode Island, Michigan, Wisconsin and Illinois, have taken part, and in which the New York State Commission of Emigration has had an important share, the bill which we now lay before you was agreed upon as satisfactory in substance, though open to modification in some of its details. It provides for a capitation tax of two dollars

---

[1] See *Henderson* v. *The Mayor*, Doc. 22, above, p. 168.

on each immigrant, to be collected by United States authority, and to form in the aggregate a fund which, like the funds formerly accruing from the same source in New York and other states, is to be applied for the protection of the immigrants in general at the ports where they land, and for the care of the sick, the relief of the poor, and the support of the insane and infirm among the recent immigrants, in whatever part of the country they may be. In short (as before said) it is an extension to the whole nation and under the authority of national law, of the old state system of dealing with immigration.

This system has been found by long experience to check and prevent pauperism among the newly arrived immigrants, not absolutely, of course, but in a considerable degree, when well administered, and to some extent even when its administration is faulty. It checks pauperism in two ways, directly and indirectly. It does so *directly* by furnishing to the industrious immigrant that temporary aid in sickness or pecuniary distress, without which he might become a permanent pauper; by bringing together the members of separated families, by placing the immigrant who needs the help of friends among his friends, and by maintaining in many other ways an effective supervision of those who become permanent residents of the United States. It checks pauperism *indirectly*, by maintaining such a supervision also that those paupers who are sent over here by persons in their own country in order to escape the burden of supporting them, are in many instances discovered and sent back; while others, who could only be paupers if they remained here, but who could be provided for in their native land, are also returned to the places they came from. This policy of detaining and returning paupers (and criminals also, if they can be discovered), when persevered in for a period of years, has the effect to raise very much the standard of immigration, by making it more and more difficult for the unworthy and undesirable elements of the European populations to flow this way and mingle in the ocean-stream of our own industrious, self-reliant people. Time is required for this effect to be produced, and there will be many instances where the supervision is quite ineffectual to prevent the influx of foreign pauperism, and still more, of foreign criminality. But the experience of nearly thirty years in New York and of twenty-five years in Massachusetts proves that much good can thus be done. It is a fact that since this strict examination and watchful protection of immigrants began, the quality of immigration has much improved, and its quantity has increased. For this there are other causes, but one useful auxiliary has been this very supervision of which we have spoken.

We have not proposed to enter here upon the important but difficult question of how to exclude from our immigration that considerable infusion of criminals and convicts which has long been noticed by those who have observed the growth of a criminal class in America. . . . . Our own subject deals only with immigration and pauperism, but since many of these imported criminals are, at intervals in their career, paupers also, the two topics are intimately connected. And this may be said—that one of the best means of detecting and turning back the flow of criminals towards this country from older lands is to keep up such an organization for the prevention of pauperism as has just been described.

It used to be objected to such legislation as this now proposed in Congress, that it was unconstitutional, because enacted by the State governments. This objection, of course, falls to the ground the moment Congress takes the matter up, now that the Supreme Court has decided in favor of the constitutional power of Congress to pass such laws as may be deemed wisest to regulate immigration. Let us then consider some other objections that have been raised from time to time, against the *policy* of regulating immigration, the *right* to do so being fully conceded to the general government, and certain incidental rights and powers remaining undisputed in the state governments. In this policy, several things are to be considered, the good of the immigrant being one of these, the security and prosperity of the community to which he comes being another, and his relations to the community *from* which he comes being a third, and by no means unimportant consideration.

It has been said by some persons that a tax levied on each immigrant, to be expended for the common good of all, is an oppressive exaction, having a tendency to check immigration and to impoverish the immigrant. But when we consider that he generally comes from a country where he has been more heavily taxed, that this "head money" (amounting, let us suppose, to two dollars), is the only direct tax that he is called upon to pay for some years, and that it is no greater than the common poll-tax of New England, which each resident voter must pay, there seems to be nothing oppressive in the capitation tax at the port of landing. If now we compare the small sum paid with the great benefit that may be and often is derived from it to the immigrant himself, it will appear to be anything but oppressive. It is in fact a sort of insurance premium which he pays to secure himself the right to relief and support should he need it within five years after landing. If he is prosperous and does not need aid, so much the better can he afford to pay it; if he falls into distress, then it is much more than repaid to him in the care which he receives and has a right to claim from the authorities to which his capitation tax was paid. Thousands of instances might be cited to show how this beneficent system works, but I will only give one. There landed in Boston some eight years ago, a simple and honest young Irish woman, who, under a contract of marriage, had followed her lover to Massachusetts. By some mistake she had lost his address, and he had not been informed when she would arrive. Consequently, upon landing, she found herself alone amid strangers, with little money and in no condition to earn any. She had paid her "head money" and therefore became a charge to the State of Massachusetts, which received her into one of its charitable establishments, maintained her there for six months or more, found out the residence of her lover, brought them together and saw them happily married and established in life. For all this it is probable that Massachusetts expended $100, in return for the two dollars which poor Bessie Dempsey had paid as head money. We maintain, therefore, that the good of the immigrant is not only promoted by this system of taxation and protection, but actually demands such a system.

The good of the country which receives the immigrant is quite as much to be considered as the good of the individual alien who, for one reason or another, comes to our shores. Immigration is by no means an unmixed blessing, and even in cases where it appears so in the end, it is often a blessing in disguise, to the country receiving an indiscriminate and unregulated immigration. It introduces youth, vigor, poverty and industry, but it also introduces disease, ignorance, crime, pauperism and idleness. There was a time when convicts and the sweepings of London streets were shipped over to the American colonies, just as they were afterward sent to Botany Bay. That was long ago, but even now we receive a great many persons of the same class—

> True patriots they, for be it understood
> They left their country for their country's good.

We will not enlarge upon this disagreeable phase of immigration. . . . .

SECTION II

THE FEDERAL IMMIGRATION LAWS: PROVISIONS, ADMINISTRATION, AND REASONS FOR ENACTMENT

1. The Beginning of Modern Immigration Legislation[1]

SECTION 1. Be it enacted by the Senate and House of Representatives of the United States of America in Congress assembled, That there shall be levied, collected, and paid a duty of fifty cents for each and every passenger not a citizen of the United States who shall come by steam or sail vessel from a foreign port to any port within the United States. The said duty shall be paid to the collector of customs of the port to which such passenger shall come, or if there be no collector at such port, then to the collector of customs nearest thereto, by the master, owner, agent, or consignee of every such vessel, within twenty-four hours after the entry thereof into such port. The money thus collected shall be paid into the United States Treasury, and shall constitute a fund to be called the immigrant fund, and shall be used, under the direction of the Secretary of the Treasury, to defray the expense of regulating immigration under this act, and for the care of immigrants arriving in the United States, for the relief of such as are in distress, and for the general purposes and expenses of carrying this act into effect. The duty imposed by this section shall be a lien upon the vessels which shall bring such passengers into the United States, and shall be a debt in favor of the United States against the owner or owners of such vessels; and the payment of such duty may be enforced by any legal or equitable remedy. *Provided*, That no greater sum shall be expended for the purposes hereinbefore mentioned, at any port, than shall have been collected at such port.

SEC. 2. That the Secretary of the Treasury is hereby charged with the duty of executing the provisions of this act and with supervision over the business of immigration to the United States, and for that purpose he shall have power to enter into contracts with such State commission, board, or officers as may be designated for that purpose by the governor of any State to take charge of the local affairs of immigration in the ports within said State, and to provide for the support and relief of such immigrants therein landing as may fall into distress or need public aid, under the rules and regulations to be prescribed by said Secretary; and it shall be the duty of such State commission, board, or officers so designated to examine into the

[1] Extract from "An Act to Regulate Immigration (1882)," chap. 376, 22 *U.S. Statutes at Large* 214 (47th Congress, 1st session).

condition of passengers arriving at the ports within such State in any ship or vessel, and for that purpose all or any of such commissioners or officers, or such other person or persons as they shall appoint, shall be authorized to go on board of and through any such ship or vessel; and if on such examination there shall be found among such passengers any convict, lunatic, idiot, or any person unable to take care of himself or herself without becoming a public charge, they shall report the same in writing to the collector of such port, and such persons shall not be permitted to land.

SEC. 3. That the Secretary of the Treasury shall establish such regulations and rules and issue from time to time such instructions not inconsistent with law as he shall deem best calculated to protect the United States and immigrants into the United States from fraud and loss, and for carrying out the provisions of this act and the immigration laws of the United States; and he shall prescribe all forms of bonds, entries, and other papers to be used under and in the enforcement of the various provisions of this act.

SEC. 4. That all foreign convicts except those convicted of political offenses, upon arrival, shall be sent back to the nations to which they belong and from whence they came. The Secretary of the Treasury may designate the State board of charities of any State in which such board shall exist by law, or any commission in any State, or any person or persons in any State whose duty it shall be to execute the provisions of this section without compensation. The Secretary of the Treasury shall prescribe regulations for the return of the aforesaid persons to the countries from whence they came, and shall furnish instructions to the board, commission, or persons charged with the execution of the provisions of this section as to the mode of procedure in respect thereto, and may change such instructions from time to time. The expense of such return of the aforesaid persons not permitted to land shall be borne by the owners of the vessels in which they came.

2. The Enforcement of the Federal Immigration Laws, 1882–91[1]

PAUPERS AND OTHER UNDESIRABLES

The great majority of immigrants landing in the United States are received at the port of New York; therefore the investigation of the committee was more extended in that city than at any other place. The local affairs of immigration at New York are in charge of the commissioners of immigration of the State of New York, by virtue of a contract entered into with the Secretary of the Treasury on the 27th day of September, 1883. During the fiscal year 1888 the number of immigrants landing at the different seaports of the United States was 546,889. Of this number, 418,423 (or about 76 per cent) came via the port of New York, and the greater portion of them arrived between the months of April and September; and

[1] Extract from "Report of the 'Ford Committee,' the Select Committee to Inquire into the Importation of Contract Laborers, Convicts, Paupers, etc., January, 1889," 50th Congress, 2d session, *House Report No. 3792*.

during this period the daily arrival of immigrants is exceedingly large, sometimes amounting to as many as 9,000.

When the vessel containing them has been moored to her dock, the immigrants are transferred to barges, which are towed to Castle Garden. There they disembark, and are required to pass in single file through narrow passage-ways, separated from each other by wooden railings. In about the center of each of these passage-ways there is a desk at which sits a registry clerk, who interrogates the immigrant as to his nationality, occupation, destination, etc.—questions calculated to elicit whether or not he is disqualified by law from landing.

Owing to the large number of immigrants received each day during the spring and summer months these questions must be asked rapidly, and the inspection is necessarily done in a very hurried manner, in order that there may be no undue delay in landing them.

The committee visited Castle Garden on several occasions and witnessed the arrival and inspection of immigrants, and it was very obvious to them that it was almost impossible to properly inspect the large number of persons who arrive daily during the immigrant season with the facilities afforded; and the testimony taken puts it beyond question that large numbers of persons not lawfully entitled to land in the United States are annually received at this port. In fact, one of the commissioners of immigration himself testified that the local administration of affairs at Castle Garden, by the method and system now followed, was a perfect farce.

Upon this subject the committee invite attention to the testimony of Dr. Hoyt, for twenty years connected with the board of charities and corrections, who testified that every charitable institution in the State of New York is now not only filled with occupants, but overflowing, and that the State annually expends in taking care of paupers, insane persons, etc., $20,000,000, and that this condition of affairs is largely due to improper immigration.

The investigation at Pittsburgh, Pennsylvania, elicited the fact that over 500 immigrant paupers and insane persons were received at that city within the last six years, the great majority of whom were admitted through the port of New York, and that many of these pauper immigrants bore upon their clothing the branded name of the work-house of which they had recently been inmates in Ireland.

The investigation at Boston disclosed that a few years ago an organized effort was made by the officials of Great Britain and Ireland, through and by means of an association known as the "Tuke Society," to assist poor persons, paupers, etc., to immigrate to this country, by furnishing them with tickets for the necessary transportation, and that the number of such assisted immigrants who were landed in Boston between April 3, 1882, and July 8, 1888, was 4,922, a great many of whom subsequently became inmates of charitable institutions in this country.

And by certain English statutes guardians of the poor are authorized to appropriate funds at their disposal for the purpose of exporting to other lands persons who have become public charges; that the English authorities have made liberal use of these laws is absolutely attested by the number of aliens who are inmates of charitable institutions in this country. In fact, the testimony upon the subject of pauper immigration conclusively shows that there are thousands of alien paupers, insane persons, and idiots annually landed in this country, who become a burden and a charge upon the States where they happen to gain a settlement, many of whom are aided and assisted to emigrate by the officials of the country from whence they come.

IMMIGRATION ALONG THE CANADIAN BORDER

Along the border between Canada and the United States no inspection whatever is made of immigrants; and alien paupers, insane persons, etc., may land at Quebec and at once proceed to this country without any let or hindrance. The number of persons not lawfully entitled to land in the United States who thus arrive in this country by way of the Canadian frontier is rapidly assuming large proportions, and has become a matter of serious contemplation. The testimony shows that in many instances immigrants coming by steamer to Quebec have within forty-eight hours after the arrival there been applicants for shelter in the almshouses of the State of New York. . . . .

CONVICTS

It was also shown that many persons belonging to the criminal class have been sent to the United States by officials of the European Governments. In Germany there exists an association whose object is the exportation of their incorrigible convicts, and their vicious and lawless members of society. Quite a number of this class of persons have been assisted by this society to immigrate here, and they have succeeded in effecting a landing. According to the testimony, this practice has also been carried on by officials of Great Britain and of the Swiss Republic, and in this manner this country has been made the refuge for a great many criminals whose character was such that they were deemed to be irreclaimable; and therefore the officials of the Governments from whence they came have purchased tickets for them, opened the prison doors, conducted them on board a steamer, and shipped them to the United States, some of them being sent as cabin passengers, in order thereby to render detection more difficult. And they have persisted in this course even after having been requested by officials of our Government to discontinue it.

The result of the investigation into the enforcement of the law of 1882 demonstrates beyond a doubt that it has been and is being repeatedly violated, and to such an extent, in fact, that it has become a matter of grave concern and demands immediate remedial legislation.

CONTRACT LABORERS

By the act of February 26, 1885, it is made unlawful to prepay the transportation or in anywise assist or encourage the importation of aliens into the United States under a contract to perform labor or service of any kind, except skilled workmen in a new industry when such workmen can not be otherwise obtained. The Secretary of the Treasury is given the same power in this act as is conferred by the act of 1882, to contract with such State commission or board as may be designated by the governor to examine passengers arriving at ports within such State, in reference to detecting violations of this law.

The enforcement of this act is not easily accomplished. Evasions of the law are much more numerous than convictions, for the reason that it is a difficult matter to prove in court a violation of it. The committee have discovered some cases of actual transgression of the act, but still the instances of failure to obey the letter of the law have been, comparatively speaking, few, yet the proof disclosed that the spirit of the law has been violated with impunity. A reference to the testimony will show that it is constantly evaded to a large extent, and also the manner in which it is done.

In the opinion of the committee the non-enforcement of these acts of 1882 and 1885 is not so much due to a want of diligence on the part of the officials having their administration in charge as it is to a lack of proper machinery to carry them into effect. The committee believe that the enforcement of all acts designed to regulate immigration should be intrusted to the Federal Government and not to the States. The regulation of immigration is a matter affecting the whole Union, and is pre-eminently a proper subject for Federal control. . . . .

MINORITY REPORT

The undersigned member [Richard Guenther] of the Select Committee to Inquire into the Importation of Contract Laborers, Convicts, Paupers, etc., agrees with the majority of the committee in reaching the conclusion that some law should be enacted which would, more effectually than the present laws, restrict and if possible stop entirely the influx into the United States of all such persons who, instead of benefiting our country, as the large majority of immigrants undoubtedly do, are a direct source of evil in many ways.

The undersigned thinks that a large number of people who now fill our poor-houses, insane asylums, hospitals, and other charitable institutions, ... should never have been admitted to land in the United States. He is, however, of the opinion that no law should be passed to lessen the immigration of industrious, law-abiding people, who come here in good faith with the intention of making this country their permanent home, who bring their families with them, and who in due course of time become useful and valuable citizens of the Republic, especially when every unprejudiced mind must admit that that class of immigrants for the last fifty years has been one of the main causes of our unexampled progress in every field of industry and enterprise.

The undersigned opposes any measure that would unnecessarily annoy the desirable immigrant, but he is in favor of all such measures as would most likely result in excluding all such foreign elements whose coming is not a benefit to our country, but rather the opposite. . . . .

3. Early Difficulties with Contract Labor Legislation[1]

It is impossible to understand the weakness of the contract-labor law without understanding first that at the basis of the immigration laws there lies a curious contradiction. The earlier laws enacted by Congress—those of 1875 and 1882—were designed to exclude the vicious, the criminal, and the pauper, those who would not or could not support themselves. The next laws, the anti-contract labor laws of 1885, 1887, and 1888, practically sought to exclude those who had the forethought to provide that on landing here they would find a sure means of supporting themselves. The earlier laws exclude the worst, the later laws exclude the best. The consequence is that the immigrant must summon all his ingenuity and subterfuge to dodge the two extremes. He strives to show that he can support himself, and he strives to show that he does not know of any job by which he can support himself. If he cannot support himself he is sent back as liable to become a public charge. If he has provided beforehand for self-support he is sent back as liable to displace American workmen. The immigration inspectors are therefore reduced to a queer predicament. They must discover, first, whether the immigrant is sound in body and mind—that is, whether he can compete successfully for a living with American workmen. If so, they admit him. They must discover, secondly, whether he really has a prospect of finding work, and thereby of competing with American workmen. If so, they exclude him. They exclude him if he cannot or will not compete with American workmen, and they exclude him if he gives the best of all evidence that he will compete successfully with American workmen. On the face of the law the contradiction seems inexplicable. But if we look into its history and the conditions surrounding its adoption, we can see a sane explanation. The alien contract-labor law was enacted almost solely at the demand of organized labor. Organized labor meets its test at the critical point of a strike or a lockout. At such a crisis the issue turns solely on the ability of the employer to find workmen who will take the places of his former employees. While the unions may have fortified themselves by controlling the American labor market, they often saw themselves attacked in the rear and utterly routed by a block of immigrants suddenly

[1] Extract from "Immigration," *Reports of the U.S. Industrial Commission*, XV (1901), 647–48.

imported by the employer from abroad or by his agent from Ellis Island. With wages in Europe only one-half or one-third of the corresponding grades in America a foreign solicitor would be overrun by applicants on the promise of prepaid transportation and immediate employment. To meet this unfair competition the labor unions, and especially the Knights of Labor, secured through Congress specific legislation known as the alien contract-labor law of 1885, with the amendments of 1887 and 1888. There had already been established by the Chinese exclusion act of 1882 a precedent for the exclusion of immigrants whose amazingly low standard of living and equally amazing industriousness had enabled them wholly to displace American workmen whenever they entered in competition. But in the case of the Chinese there were other considerations not found in dealing with European immigrants. The Chinese were of a distinct race and religion, unacquainted with representative institutions, not bringing their families, expecting to return to their native land, and while temporarily here resorting to low practices and filthy abodes. The excitement and determination of practically the entire population of the Pacific coast left no alternative except absolute exclusion. The case of the Europeans was not so unmitigated. The great majority at that time were coming from countries closely related to our own in ancestry, language, literature, religion, and representative government. Those countries were indeed the fatherland of America. It could not for a moment be considered that, against our own races coming from the lands of our origin, any sweeping exclusion could be adopted. Any restriction which could hope for adoption must be a specific protection against a definite recognized evil. This evil existed and came prominently to view. It was the artificial immigration induced by employers for the purpose of breaking labor organizations. Immigrants of our own race who came here on their own motive or on the representation of friends and relatives were especially exempted from the operation of the law. The first law, that of 1885, applied only to those American employers who induced alien immigration. . . . .

The law as enacted in 1885 was seriously defective. In the first place, it applied only to the importer of contract laborers and not to the immigrant. This defect was attempted to be amended in 1887 by a clause which, liberally interpreted, strikes also at contract laborers, and commanded that they should "be sent back to the nation to which they belong and from whence they came."

In so far as the law has been effective it has been due to this clause which gives power to deport the immigrants. Owing to the strict construction of the law there have been very few cases in which the importer was fined. But there have been over 8,000 deemed contract laborers sent back by the immigrant inspectors. The reasons for the difference are plain. The prosecution and conviction of the importer depends upon district attorneys and judges, who must necessarily follow the strict rules of evidence and must hold themselves to exact definitions of a contract. But the deportation of an immigrant turns upon the circumstantial evidence presented to administrative authorities and the inferences which may be drawn therefrom.

4. The Contract Labor Law: Typical Cases[1]

As illustrative of the good work done in enforcing the alien contract-labor feature of the immigration law, the Bureau cites the following typical cases in which action has been taken against the aliens, and prosecutions brought, with the co-operation of the United States attorneys and the Department of Justice wherever it was possible to develop the necessary evidence, and punishment meted out to the importers—the most effective way of preventing future violations. Other cases have arisen, but these are given as the most important and typical.

The Allis-Chalmers Company, a large corporation of Chicago, having direct business connections with concerns bearing similar names in England and Canada, brought to the United States four English iron molders, who were apprehended and deported after being used as witnesses in the prosecution of the company. The plan followed by this concern was to engage men in England to come to a plant in Montreal allied with their American house, and in making such importations to bring more men than they needed in Canada. Upon arrival there the men would be advised that work could not be furnished them, but if they would proceed to the United States employment would be given at better wages than those offered in Canada at the time their immigration from England was induced. The corporation employed able counsel, and resorted to every possible effort to avoid the penalty of the law, but the United States Attorney at Chicago finally secured a conviction and the assessment of a fine of $4,000, and the decision of the district court to that effect was sustained when the case was taken to the higher court on appeal.

The Duquesne Mining and Reduction Company, a large mining corporation of Tucson, Arizona, imported from Mexico 29 miners, who were subsequently taken into custody by the immigration officers and deported on departmental warrant. Prosecution was instituted, after the men had been carefully examined, their evidence showing that the company had instructed one of its employees, a Mexican, to proceed to his native country and secure a stated number of miners, and that under these instructions he brought the 29 aliens into the United States. After considerable delay and careful consideration of the evidence that it would be possible to produce in court against the company, a compromise of the case was effected, the

[1] Extract from *Annual Report of the Commissioner-General of Immigration for 1908*, pp. 130–33. See Sec. III below, pp. 262–70, for court decisions in contract-labor cases. And see also *Annual Report of Commissioner-General of Immigration for 1914*, p. 9, for an account of some contract-labor cases with larger fines assessed.

corporation pleading guilty to one of the counts of the complaint and paying a fine of $1,000, and in addition costs to the amount of $1,500.

The Arizona Copper Company case arose in the same section of the country as that last above mentioned, but the violation of the law was arranged in quite a different manner. The company is a branch of a concern organized in Edinburgh, Scotland, and the violations consisted in bringing from Scotland employees for the mines located in Arizona, and the stores and other enterprises connected therewith. Two of the aliens were deported; and a compromise of the suit against the company was eventually effected, after careful consideration of the evidence available, the conditions of the compromise being the payment by the company of $2,000 on account of the two aliens who were deported.

The Grasselli Chemical Company, a corporation with factories located in the vicinity of Clarksburg, West Virginia, is shown by the evidence collected to have been in the habit of encouraging certain classes of foreigners to take employment in their works, the main object apparently being to obtain several quite distinct races, and thus prevent a general organization of the men into unions which might give the company more or less trouble. Unfortunately, it was not possible to develop from the testimony taken indicating this state of facts sufficient evidence, in a technically legal sense, to justify the institution of proceedings against the offending corporation. The Department did, however, issue warrants for the deportation of 15 Spaniards found at the works after having recently entered, and also took measures which prevented another party of Spaniards destined to the same place from entering at the port of Boston.

On February 25, 1908, there arrived at the port of New York 15 Belgian glassworkers, who were held for examination by a board of special inquiry because it was found that they were destined to western Pennsylvania, and a report had been received by the immigration inspector in Pittsburgh to the effect that, because of a controversy between several glassworkers' unions, one of the local unions would endeavor to import foreign glassworkers, so as to compel its competitors to agree to a wage rate upon which it had seen fit to fix. A most careful investigation was conducted, which resulted in the deportation of 14 of the 15 applicants, the evidence showing that the remaining man had become attached to the party through a misunderstanding. While not sufficient evidence to justify proceedings in court was developed, it was shown to a reasonable certainty that the report of the inspector to the effect that one of the unions was attempting to import labor was substantially correct; and, strange as it may seem, this peculiar case has arisen among one of the skilled trades which was most persistent before Congress in securing the passage of the alien contract-labor law to protect the union men of this country.

The two Tsokas brothers, Bulgarians (in conjunction with their father, located in Turkey), brought to this country, under a most outrageous system of exploitation and violation of law, a large number of Bulgarians, Turks, and Macedonians. As many as 87 of the men were apprehended in New York, Pennsylvania, and Virginia, and eventually deported on the ground that they had entered the United States in violation of law, their passages having been prepaid and their immigration induced by promises of employment. The plan followed by the Tsokas brothers was to have their subagents in Turkey loan money to peasants induced to migrate by glowing promises of employment at high wages, mortgages on real and personal property being taken as security and exorbitant rates of interest charged. The men would come to the United States, destined to addresses of a fictitious character so as to avoid suspicion, and would be met at the port of arrival and taken to central points from which they were distributed to employers, the brothers combining with their enterprises in Turkey a regular employment agency in this country. Both men were apprehended and brought to trial in New York City, and the one really responsible for the transactions (the other being merely a tool in his hands) was convicted, the United States attorney very adroitly availing himself of a slight change in the wording of section 4 of the new law, making a violation thereof a misdemeanor to draw the indictment for conspiracy under section 5440 of the Revised Statutes, and Tsokas was sentenced to eight months' imprisonment.

In the Steelton case 177 aliens were apprehended, and, after hearing, ordered deported by the Department because it appeared that their migration had been induced by offers and promises of employment, that they had come to this country under a system of exploitation similar to that adopted by the Tsokas brothers, and that they had by stress of circumstances become destitute and practically a charge upon the public at Steelton, Pennsylvania. Unfortunately it was not possible, although a most diligent investigation was conducted, to secure sufficient evidence to justify prosecuting any one or more persons responsible for the aliens' presence in this country.

Nelson H. Marsden, an employee of the Utica Cotton Mills, induced 10 operatives located in Canada to enter the United States under promises of employment. The aliens were apprehended and deported. Prosecution was brought but was not completed, a compromise being effected on Marsden's paying a fine of $500.

In the case of the Simonds Manufacturing Company, of Fitchburg, Massachusetts, complaint was made by the secretary-treasurer of the Sawsmiths' International Union of North America that the company had been importing saw smiths from England. An exhausting investigation was conducted, resulting in the ascertainment of the fact that a number of saw smiths had been imported by the company. The company was able to show, however, to the Department's entire satisfaction, that at the time the importations were made it was impossible to obtain in this country at regular wages skilled labor of like kind unemployed. It was also ascertained that the president of the union had known of the intention of the company to import foreign laborers, and had practically given his consent to said importation. The strange part of the case is that neither the corporation nor the union seemed to consider for an instant that there was any necessity, or even propriety, of approaching the Department charged with the enforcement of the alien contract-labor laws with respect to such a matter. The only action that it was possible to take was to advise both the corporation and the president of the union of the Department's unqualified disapproval of the course pursued, directing attention to the provisions of the law, and advising that in future when an importation of foreigners was contemplated by the one, or agreed to by the other, the Department should first be allowed opportunity to determine whether labor of like kind unemployed could be secured in the United States.

The Washburn Lignite Coal Company, located in Wilton, North Dakota, was accused of having sent an employee into Canada to induce miners to migrate. Three of the miners were apprehended and deported, and an effort was made to show the agency of the employee who had imported them, said employee not being situated financially so as to make it worth while to bring a prosecution against him. The evidence was not considered by the United States attorney as sufficient to secure the indictment of the company, and the proposal to institute suit was therefore abandoned.

The Hecker Cereal Mills, of Milwaukee, induced an alien to come to the United States from Canada, to accept employment as an oatmeal miller, and in connection therewith still another alien proceeded to the same place, he having received assurances from the firm that he also would be given employment. The peculiar feature of the case was that the first-mentioned alien was apprehended at the border and turned back into Canada, being advised that he was a contract laborer, and could not enter the United States for a year. He wrote the company of this misfortune, and the company replied that they could not now give him any assurances of employment, but if he came to Milwaukee they thought they could arrange the matter to his satisfaction, thus endeavoring to observe the letter of the law and violate its spirit. Suit was instituted by a private individual on his own behalf, in view of which it was not deemed by the district attorney advisable to proceed on account of the Government.

The Tile-Makers' case arose at Mobile, Alabama. The National Mosaic Floor Company, a concern originally organized in Cuba, constructed a plant at Mobile and endeavored to bring to the United States a number of operatives for employment in what they claimed was a new system of manufacturing tiles. The operatives were rejected at the port of entry, and, not understanding the law, failed to take an appeal to permit the company to make any showing with respect to the claim that it was impossible to secure in this country the operatives required for the new industry.

Later the same men were brought to the port of Mobile, and a full investigation was made of the entire matter, which resulted in a decision by the Department that the company, engaged in establishing a new industry, was entitled to the benefit of the exception to the law.

It will be noted from the foregoing that the Bureau is always quite as anxious to extend to those legally entitled thereto the benefit of the exception to the contract-labor law, permitting of the importation of skilled labor if labor of like kind unemployed can not be found in this country, as it is to rigidly enforce the general provisions of the statute.

One respect in which the law does not even yet work satisfactorily is with reference to the exceptions made in favor of States and Territories advertising the facilities and inducements they offer to immigrants. Some of the States, particularly in the South and West, are vitally interested in securing settlers. Yet the new law, like the old, does not, in terms and according to the literal letter, contemplate in the exception more than that the said States should be allowed to place in foreign newspapers and magazines advertisements describing in general terms the opportunity for settlers and wage-earners within their limits. Moreover, the Attorney-General has held (26 Op. At. Gen. 410, advance sheets) that, if a representative of a State or Territory induces an alien to immigrate by holding out to him individually a promise of employment, such alien is inadmissible. . . . .

5. An Early Advocate of a Literacy Test to Restrict Immigration[1]

SENATOR LODGE:

Mr. President, this bill is intended to amend the existing law so as to restrict still further immigration to the United States. Paupers, diseased persons, convicts, and contract laborers are now excluded. By this bill it is proposed to make a new class of excluded immigrants and add to those which have just been named the totally ignorant. The bill is of the simplest kind. The first section excludes from the country all immigrants who cannot read and write either their own or some other language. The second section merely provides a simple test for determining whether the immigrant can read or write, and is added to the bill so as to define the duties of the immigrant inspectors, and to assure to all immigrants alike perfect justice and a fair test of their knowledge.

Two questions arise in connection with this bill. The first is as to the merits of this particular form of restriction; the second as to the general policy of restricting immigration at all. I desire to discuss briefly these two questions in the order in which I have stated them. The smaller question as to the merits of this particular bill comes first. The existing laws of

---

[1] Extract from speech of Senator Lodge in *Congressional Record* (March 16, 1896), 54th Congress, 1st session, pp. 2817–20. For a history of the literacy test, see H. P. Fairchild, *Quarterly Journal of Economics*, XXXI, 447.

the United States now exclude, as I have said, certain classes of immigrants who, it is universally agreed, would be most undesirable additions to our population. These exclusions have been enforced and the results have been beneficial, but the excluded classes are extremely limited and do not by any means cover all or even any considerable part of the immigrants whose presence here is undesirable or injurious, nor do they have any adequate effect in properly reducing the great body of immigration to this country. There can be no doubt that there is a very earnest desire on the part of the American people to restrict further and much more extensively than has yet been done foreign immigration to the United States. The question before the committee was how this could best be done; that is, by what method the largest number of undesirable immigrants and the smallest possible number of desirable immigrants could be shut out. Three methods of obtaining this further restriction have been widely discussed of late years and in various forms have been brought to the attention of Congress. The first was the imposition of a capitation tax on all immigrants. There can be no doubt as to the effectiveness of this method if the tax is made sufficiently heavy. But although exclusion by a tax would be thorough, it would be undiscriminating, and your committee did not feel that the time had yet come for its application. The second scheme was to restrict immigration by requiring consular certification of immigrants. The plan has been much advocated, and if it were possible to carry it out thoroughly and to add very largely to the number of our consuls in order to do so, it would no doubt be effective and beneficial. But the committee was satisfied that consular certification was, under existing circumstances, impractical; that the necessary machinery could not be provided; that it would lead to many serious questions with foreign governments, and that it could not be properly and justly enforced. It is not necessary to go farther into the details which brought the committee to this conclusion. It is sufficient to say here that the opinion of the committee is shared, they believe, by all expert judges who have given the most careful attention to the question.

The third method was to exclude all immigrants who could neither read nor write, and this is the plan which was adopted by the committee and which is embodied in this bill. . . . .

The illiteracy test will bear most heavily upon the Italians, Russians, Poles, Hungarians, Greeks, and Asiatics, and very lightly, or not at all, upon English-speaking emigrants or Germans, Scandinavians, and French. In other words, the races most affected by the illiteracy test are those whose emigration to this country has begun within the last twenty years and swelled rapidly to enormous proportions, races with which the English-speaking people have never hitherto assimilated, and who are most alien to the great body of the people of the United States. On the other hand, immigrants from the United Kingdom and of those races which are most closely related to the English-speaking people, and who with the English-speaking people themselves founded the American colonies and built up the United States, are affected but little by the proposed test. These races would not be prevented by this law from coming to this country in practically undiminished numbers. These kindred races also are those who alone go to the Western and Southern States, where immigrants are desired, and take up our unoccupied lands. The races which would suffer most seriously by exclusion under the proposed bill furnish the immigrants who do not go to the West or South, where immigration is needed, but who remain on the Atlantic Seaboard, where immigration is not needed and where their presence is most injurious and undesirable.

The statistics prepared by the committee show further that the immigrants excluded by the illiteracy test are those who remain for the most part in congested masses in our great cities. They furnish, as other tables show, a large proportion of the population of the slums. The committee's report proves that illiteracy runs parallel with the slum population, with criminals, paupers, and juvenile delinquents of foreign birth or parentage, whose percentage is out of all proportion to their share of the total population when compared with the percentage of the same classes among the native born. It also appears from investigations which have been made that the immigrants who would be shut out by the illiteracy test are those who bring least money to the country and come most quickly upon public or private charity for support. The replies of the governors of twenty-six States to the Immigration Restriction League show that in only two cases are immigrants of the classes affected by the illiteracy test desired, and those are of a single race. All the other immigrants mentioned by the governors as desirable belong to the races which are but slightly affected by the provisions of this bill. It is also proved that the classes now excluded by law, the criminals, the diseased, the paupers, and the contract laborers, are furnished chiefly by the same races as those most affected by the test of illiteracy. The same is true as to those immigrants who come to this country for a brief season and return to their native land, taking with them the money they have earned in the United States. There is no more hurtful and undesirable class of immigrants from every point of view than these "birds of passage," and the tables show that the races furnishing the largest number of "birds of passage" have also the greatest proportion of illiterates.

These facts prove to demonstration that the exclusion of immigrants unable to read or write, as proposed by this bill, will operate against the most undesirable and harmful part of our present immigration and shut out elements which no thoughtful or patriotic man can wish to see multiplied among the people of the United States. The report of the committee also proves that this bill meets the great requirement of all legislation of this character in excluding the greatest proportion possible of thoroughly undesirable and dangerous immigrants and the smallest proportion of immigrants who are unobjectionable.

THE FEDERAL IMMIGRATION LAWS

I have said enough to show what the effects of this bill would be, and that if enacted into law it would be fair in its operation and highly beneficial in its results. It now remains for me to discuss the second and larger question, as to the advisability of restricting immigration at all. This is a subject of the greatest magnitude and the most far-reaching importance. It has two sides, the economic and the social. As to the former, but few words are necessary. There is no one thing which does so much to bring about a reduction of wages and to injure the American wage earner as the unlimited introduction of cheap foreign labor through unrestricted immigration. Statistics show that the change in the race character of our immigration has been accompanied by a corresponding decline in its quality. The number of skilled mechanics and of persons trained to some occupation or pursuit has fallen off, while the number of those without occupation or training, that is, who are totally unskilled, has risen in our recent immigration to enormous proportions. This low, unskilled labor is the most deadly enemy of the American wage earner, and does more than anything else toward lowering his wages and forcing down his standard of living. An attempt was made, with the general assent of both political parties, to meet this crying evil some years ago by the passage of what are known as the contract-labor laws. That legislation was excellent in intention, but has proved of but little value in practice. It has checked to a certain extent the introduction of cheap, low-class labor in large masses into the United States. It has made it a little more difficult for such labor to come here, but the labor of this class continues to come, even if not in the same way, and the total amount of it has not been materially reduced. Even if the contract-labor laws were enforced intelligently and thoroughly, there is no reason to suppose that they would have any adequate effect in checking the evil which they were designed to stop. It is perfectly clear after the experience of several years that the only relief which can come to the American wage earner from the competition of low-class immigrant labor must be by general laws restricting the total amount of immigration and framed in such a way as to affect most strongly those elements of the immigration which furnish the low, unskilled, and ignorant foreign labor.

It is not necessary to enter further into a discussion of the economic side of the general policy of restricting immigration. In this direction the argument is unanswerable. If we have any regard for the welfare, the wages, or the standard of life of American workingmen, we should take immediate steps to restrict foreign immigration. There is no danger, at present at all events, to our workingmen from the coming of skilled mechanics or of trained and educated men with a settled occupation or pursuit, for immigrants of this class will never seek to lower the American standard of life and wages. On the contrary, they desire the same standard for themselves. But there is an appalling danger to the American wage earner from the flood of low, unskilled, ignorant, foreign labor which has poured into the country for some years past, and which not only takes lower wages, but accepts a standard of life and living so low that the American workingman can not compete with it.

I now come to the aspect of this question which is graver and more serious than any other. The injury of unrestricted immigration to American wages and American standards of living is sufficiently plain and is bad enough, but the danger which this immigration threatens to the quality of our citizenship is far worse. That which it concerns us to know and that which is more vital to us as a people than all possible questions of tariff or currency is whether the quality of our citizenship is endangered by the present course and character of immigration to the United States. To determine this question intelligently we must look into the history of our race. . . . .

During the present century, down to 1875, there have been three large migrations to this country in addition to the always steady stream from Great Britain: one came from Ireland about the middle of the century, and a somewhat later one from Germany, and one from Scandinavia, in which is included Sweden, Denmark, and Norway. The Irish, although of a different race stock originally, have been closely associated with the English-speaking people for nearly a thousand years. They speak the same language, and during that long period the two races have lived side by side, and to some extent intermarried. The Germans and Scandinavians are again people of the same race stock as the English who founded and built up the colonies. During this century, down to 1875, then, as in the two which preceded it, there had been scarcely any immigration to this country, except from kindred or allied races, and no other, which was sufficiently numerous to have produced any effect on the national characteristics, or to be taken into account here. Since 1875, however, there has been a great change. While the people who for two hundred and fifty years have been migrating to America have continued to furnish large numbers of immigrants to the United States, other races of totally different race origin, with whom the English-speaking people have never hitherto been assimilated or brought in contact, have suddenly begun to immigrate to the United States in large numbers. Russians, Hungarians, Poles, Bohemians, Italians, Greeks, and even Asiatics, whose immigration to America was almost unknown twenty years ago, have during the last twenty years poured in, in steadily increasing numbers, until now they nearly equal the immigration of those races kindred in blood or speech, or both, by whom the United States has hitherto been built up and the American people formed.

This momentous fact is the one which confronts us today, and if continued, it carries with it future consequences far deeper than any other event of our times. It involves, in a word, nothing less than the possibility of a great and perilous change in the very fabric of our race.[1] The English-speaking race, as I have shown, has been made slowly during the centuries. Nothing has happened thus far to radically change it here. In the United States, after allowing for the variations produced by new climatic influences and changed conditions of life and of political institutions, it is still in the great essentials fundamentally the same race. The additions to this country until the present time have been from kindred people or from those with whom we have been long allied and who speak the same language. By those who look at this question superficially we hear it often said that the English-speaking people, especially in America, are a mixture of races. Analysis shows that the actual mixture of blood in the English-speaking race is very small, and that while the English-speaking people are derived through different channels, no doubt, there is among them none the less an overwhelming preponderance of the same race stock, that of the great Germanic tribes who reached from Norway to the Alps. They have been welded together by more than a thousand years of wars, conquests, migra-

[1] [For other views of the "new immigration" see, e.g., I. A. Hourwich, *Immigration and Labor* (new ed.; New York, 1922); W. Z. Ripley, "The European Population of the United States," *Journal of the Royal Anthropological Institute*, XXXVIII (1908), 221, and same article in *Atlantic Monthly*, CII (1908), 745, and "Race Progress and Immigration," *Annals of the American Academy of Political and Social Science*, XXXIV (1909), 130; A. P. Andrew, "Crux of the Immigration Question," *North American Review*, CXCIX (1914), 866. See also Franz Boas, *The Mind of Primitive Man* (New York, 1911), chap. x. For books dealing with the newer immigrant groups, see E. G. Balch, *Our Slavic Fellow-Citizens* (New York, 1910); H. P. Fairchild, *Greek Immigration to the United States* (New Haven, 1911); R. F. Foerster, *Italian Emigration of Our Times* (Cambridge, 1919); W. I. Thomas and F. Znaniecki, *The Polish Peasant in Europe and America* (Boston, 1918–20); Samuel Joseph, *Jewish Immigration* ("Columbia University Studies," LIX [1914], No. 4); E. J. James (editor), *The Immigrant Jew in America* (New York: Liberal Immigration League, 1907); Jerome Davis, *The Russian Immigrant* (New York, 1922); Thomas Čapek, *The Čechs (Bohemians) in America* (Boston, 1920); Antonio Mangano, *Sons of Italy* (New York, 1917); the "New Americans Series" including K. D. Miller, *The Czecho-Slovaks in America* (1922); J. P. Xenides, *The Greeks in America* (1922); Paul Fox, *The Poles in America* (1922); Jerome Davis, *The Russians and Ruthenians in America* (1922); P. M. Rose, *Italians in America* (1922); and D. A. Souders, *Magyars in America* (1922). See also books by Peter Roberts and Edward A. Steiner. For another point of view see Madison Grant, *The Passing of the Great Race* (4th ed.; New York, 1921); S. K. Humphrey, *Mankind* (New York, 1917); William McDougall, *Is America Safe for Democracy?* (New York, 1921); C. S. Burr, *America's Race Heritage* (New York, 1922); T. L. Stoddard, *The Rising Tide of Color against White World Supremacy* (New York, 1920); H. H. Laughlin in a recent House report, "Analysis of America's Modern Melting Pot," Hearings, House Committee on Immigration (67th Congress, 3d session, November 21, 1922, Ser. 7C).]

tions, and struggles, both at home and abroad, and in so doing they have attained a fixity and definiteness of national character unknown to any other people. . . . .

Mr. President, more precious even than forms of government are the mental and moral qualities which make what we call our race. While those stand unimpaired all is safe. When those decline all is imperiled. They are exposed to but a single danger, and that is by changing the quality of our race and citizenship through the wholesale infusion of races whose traditions and inheritances, whose thoughts and whose beliefs are wholly alien to ours and with whom we have never assimilated or even been associated in the past. The danger has begun. It is small as yet, comparatively speaking, but it is large enough to warn us to act while there is yet time and while it can be done easily and efficiently. There lies the peril at the portals of our land; there is pressing in the tide of unrestricted immigration. The time has certainly come, if not to stop, at least to check, to sift, and to restrict those immigrants. In careless strength, with generous hand, we have kept our gates wide open to all the world. If we do not close them, we should at least place sentinels beside them to challenge those who would pass through. The gates which admit men to the United States and to citizenship in the great Republic should no longer be left unguarded.

6. The First Presidential Veto of a Literacy Test Act[1]

To the House of Representatives:

I herewith return, without approval, House bill numbered 7864, entitled "An Act to Amend the Immigration Laws of the United States. . . . ."

A radical departure from our national policy relating to immigration is here presented. Heretofore we have welcomed all who came to us from other lands, except those whose moral or physical condition or history threatened danger to our national welfare and safety. Relying upon the jealous watchfulness of our people to prevent injury to our political and social fabric, we have encouraged those coming from foreign countries to cast their lot with us and join in the development of our vast domain, securing in return a share in the blessings of American citizenship.

A century's stupendous growth, largely due to the assimilation and thrift of millions of sturdy and patriotic adopted citizens, attests the success of this generous and free-handed policy, which, while guarding the people's interests, exacts from our immigrants only physical and moral soundness and a willingness and ability to work.

---

[1] Extract from message of President Grover Cleveland, returning to the House of Representatives, without approval, the Immigration Bill of 1897, which provided a literacy test for the admission of aliens (U.S. 54th Congress, 2d session, *Senate Doc. No. 185*).

THE FEDERAL IMMIGRATION LAWS 199

A contemplation of the grand results of this policy can not fail to arouse a sentiment in its defense; for however it might have been regarded as an original proposition and viewed as an experiment, its accomplishments are such that if it is to be uprooted at this late day its disadvantages should be plainly apparent and the substitute adopted should be just and adequate, free from uncertainties, and guarded against difficult or oppressive administration.

It is not claimed, I believe, that the time has come for the further restriction of immigration on the ground that an excess of population overcrowds our land.

It is said, however, that the quality of recent immigration is undesirable. The time is quite within recent memory when the same thing was said of immigrants who, with their descendants, are now numbered among our best citizens.

It is said that too many immigrants settle in our cities, thus dangerously increasing their idle and vicious population. This is certainly a disadvantage. It can not be shown, however, that it affects all our cities, nor that it is permanent; nor does it appear that this condition, where it exists, demands as its remedy the reversal of our present immigration policy.

The claim is also made that the influx of foreign laborers deprives of the opportunity to work those who are better entitled than they to the privilege of earning their livelihood by daily toil. An unfortunate condition is certainly presented when any who are willing to labor are unemployed. But so far as this condition now exists among our people, it must be conceded to be a result of phenomenal business depression and the stagnation of all enterprises in which labor is a factor. With the advent of settled and wholesome financial and economic governmental policies and consequent encouragement to the activity of capital, the misfortunes of unemployed labor should, to a great extent at least, be remedied. If it continues, its natural consequences must be to check the further immigration to our cities of foreign laborers and to deplete the ranks of those already there. In the meantime, those most willing and best entitled ought to be able to secure the advantages of such work as there is to do.

It is proposed by the bill under consideration to meet the alleged difficulties of the situation by establishing an educational test by which the right of a foreigner to make his home with us shall be determined. Its general scheme is to prohibit from admission to our country all immigrants "physically capable and over 16 years of age who can not read and write the English language or some other language"; and it is provided that this test shall be applied by requiring immigrants seeking admission to read and afterwards to write not less than twenty nor more than twenty-five words of the Constitution of the United States in some language, and that any immigrant failing in this shall not be admitted, but shall be returned to the country from whence he came at the expense of the steamship or railroad company which brought him.

The best reason that could be given for this radical restriction of immigration is the necessity of protecting our population against degeneration and saving our national peace and quiet from imported turbulence and disorder.

I can not believe that we would be protected against these evils by limiting immigration to those who can read and write in any language twenty-five words of our Constitution. In my opinion it is infinitely more safe to admit a hundred thousand immigrants who, though unable to read and write, seek among us only a home and opportunity to work, than to admit one of those unruly agitators and enemies of governmental control, who can not only read and write but delights in arousing by inflammatory speech the illiterate and peacefully inclined to discontent and tumult. Violence and disorder do not originate with illiterate laborers. They are rather the victims of the educated agitator. The ability to read and write as required in this bill, in and of itself, affords, in my opinion, a misleading test of contented industry and supplies unsatisfactory evidence of desirable citizenship or a proper apprehension of the benefits of our institutions. If any particular element of our illiterate immigration is to be feared for other causes than illiteracy, these causes should be dealt with directly instead of making illiteracy the pretext for exclusion to the detriment of other illiterate immigrants against whom the real cause of complaint can not be alleged.

The provisions intended to rid that part of the proposed legislation already referred to from obvious hardship appear to me to be indefinite and inadequate.

A parent, grandparent, wife, or minor child of a qualified immigrant, though unable to read and write, may accompany the immigrant or be sent for to join his family provided the immigrant is capable of supporting such relative. These exceptions to the general rule of exclusion contained in the bill were made to prevent the separation of families, and yet neither brothers nor sisters are provided for. In order that relatives who are provided for may be reunited, those still in foreign lands must be sent for to join the immigrant here. What formality is necessary to constitute this prerequisite, and how are the facts of relationship and that the relative is sent for to be established? Are the illiterate relatives of immigrants who have come here under prior laws entitled to the advantage of these exceptions? A husband who can read and write and who determines to abandon his illiterate wife abroad will find here under this law an absolutely safe retreat. The illiterate relatives mentioned must not only be sent for, but such immigrant must be capable of supporting them when they arrive. This requirement proceeds upon the assumption that the foreign relatives coming here are in every case by reason of poverty liable to become a public charge unless the immigrant is capable of their support. The contrary is very often true. And yet if unable to read and write, though quite able and willing to support themselves and their relatives here besides, they could not be admitted under the provisions of this bill if the immigrant was impoverished, though the aid of his fortunate but illiterate relative might be the means of saving him from pauperism. . . . .

GROVER CLEVELAND

EXECUTIVE MANSION
March 2, 1897

7. Recommendations for Changes in the Federal Immigration Laws, 1911[1]

CAUSES OF IMMIGRATION

While social conditions affect the situation in some countries, the present emigration from Europe to the United States is in the largest measure due to economic causes. It should be stated, however, that emigration from Europe is not now an absolute economic necessity, and as a rule those who emigrate to the United States are impelled by a desire for betterment rather than by the necessity of escaping intolerable conditions. This fact should largely modify the natural incentive to treat the immigration movement from the standpoint of sentiment and permit its consideration primarily as an economic problem. In other words, the economic and social welfare of the United States should now ordinarily be the determining factor in the immigration policy of the Government.

Unlike Canada, Argentina, Brazil, Australia, and other immigrant-receiving countries, the United States Government makes no effort to induce immigration. A law for the encouragement of immigration by guaranteeing in this country labor contracts made abroad was enacted in 1864 but repealed in 1868. Later legislation has tended to prevent the introduction of contract laborers and assisted or induced immigration, the purpose of the Government being that the movement should be a natural one. The law respecting assisted immigration, however, does not deny the right of a person already in this country to send for an otherwise admissible relative or friend, and a large part of the present movement, especially from southern and eastern Europe, is made possible through such assistance. The immediate incentive of the great bulk of present-day immigration is the letters of persons in this country to relatives or friends at home. Comparatively few immigrants come without some reasonable definite assurance that employment awaits them, and it is probable that as a rule they know the nature of that employment and the rate of wages. A large number of immigrants are induced to come by quasi labor agents in this country, who combine the business of supplying laborers to large employers and contractors with the so-called immigrant banking business and the selling of steamship tickets.

[1] Extract from "Brief Statement of the Investigations of the Immigration Commission, with Conclusions and Recommendations and Views of the Minority," *Reports of the U.S. Immigration Commission*, I (1911), 25–49.

Another important agency in promoting emigration from Europe to the United States are the many thousands of steamship-ticket agents and subagents operating in the emigrant-furnishing districts of southern and eastern Europe. Under the terms of the United States immigration law, as well as the laws of most European countries, the promotion of emigration is forbidden, but nevertheless the steamship-agent propaganda flourishes everywhere. It does not appear that the steamship lines as a rule openly direct the operations of these agents, but the existence of the propaganda is a matter of common knowledge in the emigrant-furnishing countries and, it is fair to assume, is acquiesced in, if not stimulated, by the steamship lines as well. With the steamship lines the transportation of steerage passengers is purely a commercial matter; moreover, the steerage business which originates in southern and eastern Europe is peculiarly attractive to the companies, as many of the immigrants travel back and forth, thus insuring east-bound as well as west-bound traffic.

IMMIGRATION OF DISEASED ALIENS

Prior to 1882, when the Federal Government first assumed control of immigration, the movement was practically unregulated. No process of selection was exercised among the immigrants who came between 1819 and 1882, and as a result the diseased, defective, delinquent, and dependent entered the country practically at will. With the development of federal immigration laws the situation in this respect has entirely changed, and while, unfortunately, the present law, from the difficulty in securing proof, is largely ineffectual in preventing the coming of criminals and other moral delinquents, it does effectively debar paupers and the physically unsound and generally the mentally unsound. The law provides that debarred aliens must be returned at the expense of the steamship companies, and also that companies bringing diseased persons of certain classes whose condition might have been detected at ports of embarkation shall be subjected to a fine of $100 in each case. Consequently the transportation of diseased aliens has become so unprofitable that steamship companies have inaugurated at foreign ports of embarkation a medical inspection of intending emigrants similar to that made at United States ports. As a result of the foreign inspection, in an ordinary year about four times as many intending emigrants are refused transportation for medical reasons alone as are debarred here for all causes, and about ten times as many as are debarred for medical reasons only. In the fiscal year 1907, 1,285,349 aliens were admitted to the United States, and only 4,040 were debarred because of physical and mental diseases. When it is considered that the great majority of all immigrants now come from countries where trachoma and other contagious diseases are prevalent among the emigrating classes, the relatively small number of rejections at United States ports is good evidence of the effectiveness of the steamship-company inspections abroad.

It is highly desirable both for humanitarian and medical reasons that aliens who are not admissible to the United States should be turned back at foreign ports of embarkation, or better still, that they should not leave their homes for such ports only to be returned. It has been strongly urged by immigration officials and other students of the question that the embarkations at foreign ports of persons not admissible to the United States because of their physical condition would be more effectually prevented by a medical inspection by American officers at such ports. This plan was so strongly urged that this Government a few years ago made official inquiry respecting the probable attitude of European Governments toward it. At that time one or two Governments expressed a willingness to permit such an inspection by American officials; others made indefinite replies to the inquiry, while others were positively opposed. No attempt was thereafter made to further the plan. After an investigation by the Commission of the situation at all the principal ports of Europe it is clear that even were its consummation possible, such an arrangement would not materially improve conditions. As a matter of fact American medical officers, in an advisory capacity, have conducted a medical inspection of emigrants at Italian ports for the past ten years and their recommendations invariably have been respected by the steamship companies. A comparison of results at United States ports, however, shows that the proportion of aliens rejected here for medical reasons was somewhat larger among persons embarking at Italian ports than among those from several other European ports where the medical inspection was made solely by physicians employed by steamship companies. This is not a reflection on the work of American surgeons at Italian ports, which is highly efficient, but rather an illustration of the impossibility of making an absolutely effective medical inspection at foreign ports of embarkation. Considering the time that elapses between embarkation at European ports and arrival in the United States and the opportunities for surreptitiously avoiding inspection which frequently exist at European ports, it is clear that no medical inspection abroad, however thorough it might be, would obviate the necessity of a rigid inspection at United States ports.

It has been suggested that some system ought to be devised by which intending emigrants could be physically examined as to their admissibility to the United States before leaving their homes for ports of embarkation. While an effective arrangement of that nature would be of great benefit to the many thousands annually who are turned back at foreign ports of embarkation, it is a matter over which our Government has no jurisdiction.

Steamship companies should be held responsible for the transportation to the United States ports of physically and mentally diseased aliens. That policy has been pursued since the first federal immigration law was enacted and it has increased in effectiveness accordingly as the bringing of such aliens became more unprofitable to the companies. The present law operates to secure a reasonably careful medical inspection by steamship companies at foreign ports of embarkation, but as circumstances vary materially in different cases, the law should be amended so as to retain the present fine as a minimum but permit the imposition of a fine not exceeding $500.

IMMIGRATION OF CRIMINALS

While control of the immigration movement so far as physical and mental defectives are concerned has reached a high degree of efficiency, no adequate means have been adopted for preventing the immigration of criminals, prostitutes, and other morally undesirable aliens. The control of the latter classes is a much more difficult matter. In spite of the stringent law, criminals or moral defectives of any class, provided they pass the medical inspection, can usually embark at European ports and enter the United States without much danger of detection. A considerable number of criminals or aliens with criminal records are debarred annually at United States ports, but this results from the vigilance of immigrant inspectors or from chance information rather than from our system of regulation.

While it does not appear from available statistics that criminality among the foreign-born increases the volume of crime in proportion to the total population, nevertheless the coming of criminals and persons of criminal tendencies constitutes one of the serious social effects of the immigration movement. The present immigration law is not adequate to prevent the immigration of criminals, nor is it sufficiently effective as regards the deportation of alien criminals who are in this country. The effective exclusion of criminals merely by means of inspection at United States ports of entry is obviously impossible, and the movement can not be satisfactorily controlled in the absence of definite knowledge respecting the alien's criminal record in the country from which he comes.

Several years ago the Italian Government decided to assist in enforcing the provisions of our law by refusing to issue passports to criminals subject to exclusion here. Subsequently this was enacted as a part of the Italian emigration law. As passports are not demanded at our ports,[1] the benefit of this act of comity has not been great, as, while Italian criminals can not embark at Italian ports, they can and do come through the ports of other countries. No apparent attempt has been made on the part of our Government to treat this attitude on the part of the Italian Government as a basis for negotiations to secure an agreement which might have produced more practical results.

While in Italy the Commission investigated the operation of this Italian statute and found that in the main it was enforced, though in some instances acts of minor officials resulted in giving passports to criminals.

Members of the Commission found an apparent willingness on the part not only of the Italian, but of other Governments, to cooperate with us, by

[1] [Passports are demanded now (1923) as a result of war conditions, but proposals for their abolition are reported to be under consideration in Washington.]

governmental action, in the enforcement of our immigration laws. The best place to bar alien criminals is in their own countries, and the best way is through the utilization of the police records of such countries. Aliens from countries where adequate records are kept should be admitted only upon the production of proper certificates showing an absence of convictions for excludable crimes. If this is done, the alien criminal can be largely barred. Under the immigration act of 1907 the President is authorized to send commissioners to foreign countries for the purpose of entering into agreements with such countries to prevent the evasion of the laws governing immigration to the United States. Such agreement with the principal countries from which immigration comes is the best method through which to secure the desired result.

IMMIGRATION OF THE MENTALLY DEFECTIVE

The immigration of the mentally defective aliens is reasonably well controlled under the existing immigration law. The law provides for the exclusion of "insane persons, persons who have been insane within five years, and persons who have had two attacks of insanity at any time previously." Owing to the nature of mental diseases, they are not easily detected through such necessarily limited inspection as can be made at ports of arrival. When the least evidence of mental disease is exhibited by an arriving alien, such alien is invariably held for observation until his mental condition is determined. It is entirely possible, however, that persons may exhibit no evidence of insanity and yet that they may become insane within a short time after their admission. Such cases have occurred and the matter has given rise to considerable apprehension. Until some means can be devised of informing the immigration authorities as to the previous mental history of arriving aliens, the present safeguards are practically all that can be afforded, unless all arriving aliens are detained for observation as to their mental condition, a plan which is impracticable.

CONTRACT LABOR AND ASSISTED OR INDUCED IMMIGRATION

Since 1884 aliens brought to the United States in pursuance of contracts to perform labor in this country have, with certain exceptions, been debarred by law. This provision does not apply to skilled laborers where labor of a like kind unemployed can not be found in this country. The law has been made more rigid from time to time until under its terms almost any semblance of a contract or agreement is now sufficient to include immigrants within the contract-labor clause. Owing to the rigidity of the law and the fact that special provision is made for its enforcement there are probably at the present time relatively few actual contract laborers admitted. There are annually admitted, however, a very large number who come in response to indirect assurance that employment awaits them. In the main these assurances are contained in letters from persons already in this country who advise their relatives or friends at home that if they will come to the United States they will find work awaiting them. On the other hand, it is clear that there is a large induced immigration due to labor agents in this country who, independently or in cooperation with agents in Europe, operate practically without restriction. As a rule only unskilled laborers are induced to come to the United States by this means.

It is impossible to estimate what part of the present immigration movement to the United States is assisted to come either by friends in this country or by persons here and abroad who advance transportation contingent on the immigrants repaying the same from wages received after admission to the United States.

In earlier times a good many immigrants were enabled to come to this country through public assistance, and, in fact, it is recorded that many paupers and even criminals who had become a burden upon the public in Great Britain and some of the German States were practically deported to this country. So far as the Commission is able to learn, however, no part of the present immigration movement direct to the United States is thus publicly assisted. . . . .

BOARDS OF SPECIAL INQUIRY

Boards of special inquiry are one of the most, if not the most, important factor in the administration of the immigration law. To them are referred for decision all cases held by the examining surgeon because of disease or mental or physical defects, and also every alien who may not appear to the examining immigrant inspector to be clearly and beyond doubt entitled to land. In the case of aliens certified by the examining surgeon as being afflicted with a loathsome or dangerous contagious disease, tuberculosis, or pronounced mental defects, the board has no alternative but to exclude, and from its decision in such cases there is no appeal. In the case of persons held as contract laborers or because of the likelihood that they may become a public charge, and in other cases, the board exercises discretionary power as to the admission or rejection of the alien, in which cases, however, there lies the right of appeal to the Secretary of Commerce and Labor. The boards exercise a power which if not properly used may result in injustice to the immigrant or, through the admission of undesirable aliens, in harm to the country. It is important, therefore, that these boards should be composed of unprejudiced men of ability, training, and good judgment. Under the present law these boards are appointed by the commissioners of immigration at the various ports, from such of the immigrant officials in the service as the Commissioner-General of Immigration, with the approval of the Secretary of Commerce and Labor, shall from time to time designate as qualified to serve. At ports where there are fewer than three immigrant inspectors other United States officials may be designated for service on such boards.

All hearings before boards are required to be separate and apart from the public, but a complete permanent record of the proceedings, including all testimony produced, is kept. The decision of any two members of the board shall prevail, but either the alien, or any dissenting member of the board, may take an appeal to the Secretary of Commerce and Labor, and the taking of such appeal shall operate to stay any action in regard to final disposal of the case until it has been decided upon by the Secretary. At all the important ports the boards of special inquiry are composed of immigrant inspectors, who are generally without judicial or legal training. This, together with the fact that they are selected by the commissioners of immigration at the ports where they serve, tends to impair the judicial character of the board and to influence its members in a greater or less degree to reflect in their decisions the attitude of the commissioner in determining the cases. The character of their decisions is indicated somewhat by the fact that nearly 50 per cent of the cases appealed are reversed by the Secretary of Commerce and Labor, whose decision, under the law, must be based solely upon the evidence adduced before the board. This record of reversals on appeal suggests that their decisions which are not reviewed may be equally wrong.

In justice to the immigrant, and to the country as well, the character of these boards should be improved. They should be composed of men whose ability and training fit them for the judicial functions performed, and the provision compelling their hearings to be separate and apart from the public should be repealed. . . . .

RECOMMENDATIONS[1]

As a result of the investigation the Commission is unanimously of the opinion that in framing legislation emphasis should be laid upon the following principles:

1. While the American people, as in the past, welcome the oppressed of other lands, care should be taken that immigration be such both in quality and quantity as not to make too difficult the process of assimilation.

2. Since the existing law and further special legislation recommended in this report deal with the physically and morally unfit, further general legislation concerning the admission of aliens should be based primarily upon economic or business considerations touching the prosperity and economic well-being of our people.

3. The measure of the rational, healthy development of a country is not the extent of its investment of capital, its output of products, or its

---

[1] [Reference to the Act of 1917, below, p. 215, will show that some of these recommendations were followed by Congress. Attention should be called to the fact that the conclusions and recommendations of the Commission have been vigorously criticized. See, especially, I. A. Hourwich, *Immigration and Labor* (new ed.; New York, 1922).]

exports and imports, unless there is a corresponding economic opportunity afforded to the citizen dependent upon employment for his material, mental, and moral development.

4. The development of business may be brought about by means which lower the standard of living of the wage earners. A slow expansion of industry which would permit the adaptation and assimilation of the incoming labor supply is preferable to a very rapid industrial expansion which results in the immigration of laborers of low standards and efficiency, who imperil the American standard of wages and conditions of employment.

The Commission agrees that:

1. To protect the United States more effectively against the immigration of criminal and certain other debarred classes—

a) Aliens convicted of serious crimes within a period of five years after admission should be deported in accordance with the provisions of House bill 20980, Sixty-first Congress, second session.

b) Under the provision of section 39 of the immigration act of February 20, 1907, the President should appoint commissioners to make arrangements with such countries as have adequate police records to supply emigrants with copies of such records, and that thereafter immigrants from such countries should be admitted to the United States only upon the production of proper certificates showing an absence of convictions for excludable crimes.

c) So far as practicable the immigration laws should be so amended as to be made applicable to alien seamen.

d) Any alien who becomes a public charge within three years after his arrival in this country should be subject to deportation in the discretion of the Secretary of Commerce and Labor.

2. Sufficient appropriation should be regularly made to enforce vigorously the provision of the laws previously recommended by the Commission and enacted by Congress regarding the importation of women for immoral purposes.

3. As the new statute relative to steerage conditions took effect so recently as January 1, 1909, ... the Commission's only recommendation in this connection is that a statute be immediately enacted providing for the placing of Government officials . . . . on vessels carrying third-class or steerage passengers for the enforcement of the law and the protection of the immigrant.[1]

4. To strengthen the certainty of just and humane decisions of doubtful cases at ports of entry it is recommended—

[1] [A more complete statement on this point from the Commission's conclusions and recommendations will be found above, pp. 92–93, Doc. 10.]

That section 25 of the immigration act of 1907 be amended to provide that boards of special inquiry should be appointed by the Secretary of Commerce and Labor, and that they should be composed of men whose ability and training qualify them for the performance of judicial functions; that the provisions compelling their hearings to be separate and apart from the public should be repealed, and that the office of an additional Assistant Secretary of Commerce and Labor to assist in reviewing such appeals be created.

5. To protect the immigrant against exploitation; to discourage sending savings abroad; to encourage permanent residence and naturalization; and to secure better distribution of alien immigrants throughout the country—

a) The States should enact laws strictly regulating immigrant banks.

b) Proper State legislation should be enacted for the regulation of employment agencies.

c) Since numerous aliens make it their business to keep immigrants from influences that may tend toward their assimilation and naturalization as American citizens with the purpose of using their funds, of encouraging investment of their savings abroad, and their return to their home land, aliens who attempt to persuade immigrants not to become American citizens should be made subject to deportation.

d) Since the distribution of the thrifty immigrant to sections of the country where he may secure a permanent residence to the best advantage, and especially where he may invest his savings in farms or engage in agricultural pursuits, is most desirable, the division of information should be so conducted as to cooperate with States desiring immigrant settlers; and information concerning the opportunities for settlement should be brought to the attention of immigrants in industrial centers who have been here for some time and who might be thus induced to invest their savings in this country and become permanent agricultural settlers. The division might also secure and furnish to all laborers alike information showing opportunities for permanent employment in various sections of the country, together with the economic conditions in such places.

6. One of the provisions of section 2 of the act of 1907 reads as follows:

And provided further, That skilled labor may be imported if labor of like kind unemployed can not be found in this country.

Instances occasionally arise, especially in the establishment of new industries in the United States, where labor of the kind desired, unemployed, can not be found in this country and it becomes necessary to import such labor. Under the law the Secretary of Commerce and Labor has no authority to determine the question of the necessity for importing such labor in advance of the importation, and it is recommended that an amendment to the law be adopted by adding to the clause cited above a provision to the effect that the question of the necessity of importing such skilled labor in any particular instance may be determined by the Secretary of Commerce and Labor upon the application of any person interested prior to any action in that direction by such person; such determination by the Secretary of Commerce and Labor to be reached after a full hearing and an investigation into the facts of the case. . . . .

8. The investigations of the Commission show an oversupply of unskilled labor in basic industries to an extent which indicates an oversupply of unskilled labor in the industries of the country as a whole, and therefore demand legislation which will at the present time restrict the further admission of such unskilled labor.

It is desirable in making the restriction that—

a) A sufficient number be debarred to produce a marked effect upon the present supply of unskilled labor.

b) As far as possible, the aliens excluded should be those who come to this country with no intention to become American citizens or even to maintain a permanent residence here, but merely to save enough, by the adoption, if necessary, of low standards of living, to return permanently to their home country. Such persons are usually men unaccompanied by wives or children.

c) As far as possible the aliens excluded should also be those who, by reason of their personal qualities or habits, would least readily be assimilated or would make the least desirable citizens.

The following methods of restricting immigration have been suggested:

a) The exclusion of those unable to read or write in some language.

b) The limitation of the number of each race arriving each year to a certain percentage of the average of that race arriving during a given period of years.

c) The exclusion of unskilled laborers unaccompanied by wives or families.

d) The limitation of the number of immigrants arriving annually at any port.

e) The material increase in the amount of money required to be in the possession of the immigrant at the port of arrival.

f) The material increase of the head tax.

g) The levy of the head tax so as to make a marked discrimination in favor of men with families.

All these methods would be effective in one way or another in securing restrictions in a greater or less degree. A majority of the Commission favor the reading and writing test as the most feasible single method of restricting undesirable immigration.

The Commission as a whole recommends restriction as demanded by economic, moral, and social considerations, furnishes in its report reasons for such restriction, and points out methods by which Congress can attain the desired result if its judgment coincides with that of the Commission.[1]

8. The Later Veto Messages Dealing with the Literacy Test

A. CRITICISMS OF THE LITERACY TEST[2]

. . . . The [literacy test] provision as it now appears will require careful reading. In some measure the group system is adopted—that is, one qualified immigrant may bring in certain members of his family—but the effect seems to be that a qualified alien may bring in members of his family who may themselves be disqualified, whereas a disqualified member would exclude all dependent members of his family, no matter how well qualified they might otherwise be. In other words, a father who can read a dialect might bring in an entire family of absolutely illiterate people, barring his sons over 16 years of age, whereas a father who can not read a dialect would bring about the exclusion of his entire family, although every one of them can read and write. . . . .

[1] [A minority report submitted by one member of the Commission, Congressman William S. Bennet, contained the following: "I recognize the great value of the work of the Immigration Commission and unite in the conclusions, so far as they are based on the reports, whether they coincide with my personal and previously formed opinions or not.

"A slowing down of the present rate of the immigration of unskilled labor is justified by the report, and, according to the report, restriction should be limited to unmarried male aliens or married aliens unaccompanied by their wives and families. The reports show that in the main the present immigrants are not criminal, pauper, insane, or seekers of charity in so great a degree as their predecessors. The educational test proposed is a selective test for which no logical argument can be based on the report. As the report of the Commission is finally adopted, within a half hour of the time when, under the law, it must be filed, there is no time for the preparation of an elaborate dissent. I sincerely regret that I can not fully agree with the remainder of the Commission, and if time permitted I would point out the many excellent provisions contained in the report, some of my own suggestion. My main ground of dissent is the specific recommendation by the majority of the educational test, though there are other instances in which it has not my full approval."]

[2] Extract from a letter from the Secretary of Commerce and Labor to the President of the United States, which was transmitted to the United States Senate with President Taft's message accompanying his veto of the Immigration Bill of 1913. President Taft said: "I can not make up my mind to sign a bill which in its chief provision violates a principle that ought, in my opinion, to be upheld in dealing with our immigration. I refer to the literacy test. For the reasons stated in Secretary Nagel's letter to me, I can not approve that test. The Secretary's letter accompanies this" (U.S. 62d Congress, 3d session, *Senate Doc. No. 1087*, pp. 1–4).

Apart from these considerations, I am of the opinion that this provision can not be defended upon its merits. It was originally urged as a selective test. For some time recommendations in its support upon that ground have been brought to our attention. The matter has been considered from that point of view, and I became completely satisfied that upon that ground the test could not be sustained. The older argument is now abandoned, and in the later conferences, at least, the ground is taken that the provision is to be defended as a practical measure to exclude a large proportion of undesirable immigrants from certain countries. The measure proposes to reach its result by indirection and is defended purely upon the ground of practical policy, the final purpose being to reduce the quantity of cheap labor in this country. I can not accept this argument. No doubt the law would exclude a considerable percentage of immigration from southern Italy, among the Poles, the Mexicans, and the Greeks. This exclusion would embrace probably in large part undesirable but also a great many desirable people, and the embarrassment, expense, and distress to those who seek to enter would be out of all proportion to any good that can possibly be promised for this measure.

My observation leads me to the conclusion that, so far as the merits of the individual immigrant are concerned, the test is altogether overestimated. The people who come from the countries named are frequently illiterate because opportunities have been denied them. The oppression with which these people have to contend in modern times is not religious, but it consists of a denial of the opportunity to acquire reading and writing. Frequently the attempt to learn to read and write the language of the particular people is discouraged by the Government, and these immigrants in coming to our shores are really striving to free themselves from the conditions under which they have been compelled to live.

So far as the industrial conditions are concerned, I think the question has been superficially considered. We need labor in this country, and the natives are unwilling to do the work which the aliens come over to do. It is perfectly true that in a few cities and localities there are congested conditions. It is equally true that in very much larger areas we are practically without help. In my judgment, no sufficiently earnest and intelligent effort has been made to bring our wants and our supply together, and so far the same forces that give the chief support to this provision of the new bill have stubbornly resisted any effort looking to an intelligent distribution of new immigration to meet the needs of our vast country. In my judgment no such drastic measure, based upon a ground which is untrue and urged for a reason which we are unwilling to assert, should be adopted until we have at least exhausted the possibilities of a rational distribution of these new forces.

Furthermore, there is a misapprehension as to the character of the people who come over here to remain. It is true that in certain localities newly arrived aliens live under deplorable conditions. Just as much may be said of certain localities that have been inhabited for a hundred years by natives of this country. These are not the general conditions, but they are the exceptions. It is true that a very considerable portion of immigrants do not come to remain, but return after they have acquired some means, or because they find themselves unable to cope with the conditions of a new and aggressive country. Those who return for the latter reason relieve us of their own volition of a burden. Those who return after they have acquired some means certainly must be admitted to have left with us a consideration for the advantage which they have enjoyed. A careful examination of the character of the people who come to stay and of the employment in which a large part of the new immigration is engaged will, in my judgment, dispel the apprehension which many of our people entertain. The census will disclose that with rapid strides the foreign-born citizen is acquiring the farm lands of this country. Even if the foreign-born alone is considered, the percentage of his ownership is assuming a proportion that ought to attract the attention of the native citizens. If the second generation is included it is safe to say that in the Middle West and West a majority of the farms are today owned by foreign-born people or they are descendants of the first generation. This does not embrace only the Germans and the Scandinavians, but is true in large measure, for illustration, of the Bohemians and the Poles. It is true in surprising measure of the Italians; not only of the northern Italians, but of the southern.

B. PRESIDENT WILSON'S FIRST VETO MESSAGE OF 1915[1]

To the House of Representatives:

It is with unaffected regret that I find myself constrained by clear conviction to return this bill (H.R. 6060, "An act to Regulate the Immigration of Aliens to and the Residence of Aliens in the United States") without my signature. Not only do I feel it to be a very serious matter to exercise the power of veto in any case, because it involves opposing the single judgment of the President to the judgment of a majority of both the Houses of the Congress, a step which no man who realizes his own liability to error

[1] United States 63d Congress, 3d session, *House Doc. No. 1527*, pp. 3–4. President Wilson vetoed another immigration act in 1917, but it was passed over his veto and became the comprehensive immigration act of 1917. In this second veto message he said: "I can not rid myself of the conviction that the literacy test constitutes a radical change in the policy of the Nation which is not justified in principle. It is not a test of character, of quality, or of personal fitness, but would operate in most cases merely as a penalty for lack of opportunity in the country from which the alien seeking admission came. The opportunity to gain an education is in many cases one of the chief opportunities sought by the immigrant in coming to the United States, and our experience in the past has not been that the illiterate immigrant is as such an undesirable immigrant. Tests of quality and of purpose can not be objected to on principle, but tests of opportunity surely may be."

can take without great hesitation, but also because this particular bill is in so many important respects admirable, well conceived, and desirable. Its enactment into law would undoubtedly enhance the efficiency and improve the methods of handling the important branch of the public service to which it relates. But candor and a sense of duty with regard to the responsibility so clearly imposed upon me by the Constitution in matters of legislation leave me no choice but to dissent.

In two[1] particulars of vital consequence this bill embodies a radical departure from the traditional and long-established policy of this country, a policy in which our people have conceived the very character of their Government to be expressed, the very mission and spirit of the Nation in respect of its relations to the peoples of the world outside their borders. It seeks to all but close entirely the gates of asylum which have always been open to those who could find nowhere else the right and opportunity of constitutional agitation for what they conceived to be the natural and inalienable rights of men; and it excludes those to whom the opportunities of elementary education have been denied, without regard to their character, their purposes, or their natural capacity.

Restrictions like these, adopted earlier in our history as a Nation, would very materially have altered the course and cooled the humane ardors of our politics. The right of political asylum has brought to this country many a man of noble character and elevated purpose who was marked as an outlaw in his own less fortunate land, and who has yet become an ornament to our citizenship and to our public councils. The children and the compatriots of these illustrious Americans must stand amazed to see the representatives of their Nation now resolved, in the fullness of our national strength and at the maturity of our great institutions, to risk turning such men back from our shores without test of quality or purpose. It is difficult for me to believe that the full effect of this feature of the bill was realized when it was framed and adopted, and it is impossible for me to assent to it in the form in which it is here cast.

The literacy test and the tests and restrictions which accompany it constitute an even more radical change in the policy of the Nation. Hitherto we have generously kept our doors open to all who were not unfitted by reason of disease or incapacity for self-support or such personal records and antecedents as were likely to make them a menace to our peace and order or to the wholesome and essential relationships of life. In this bill it is pro-

[1] [It will be noted that the presidential veto is based on objections not only to the literacy test but to an extension of the definition of anarchist. The old 1907 statute had excluded only "anarchists, or persons who believe in or advocate the overthrow by force or violence of the Government of the United States or of all government, or of all forms of law, or the assassination of public officials." The act vetoed contained the provisions to be found in the present act, see p. 216 (sec. 3), which was finally passed over President Wilson's veto in 1917.]

posed to turn away from tests of character and of quality and impose tests which exclude and restrict; for the new tests here embodied are not tests of quality or of character or of personal fitness, but tests of opportunity. Those who come seeking opportunity are not to be admitted unless they have already had one of the chief of the opportunities they seek, the opportunity of education. The object of such provisions is restriction, not selection.

If the people of this country have made up their minds to limit the number of immigrants by arbitrary tests and so reverse the policy of all the generations of Americans that have gone before them, it is their right to do so. I am their servant and have no license to stand in their way. But I do not believe that they have. I respectfully submit that no one can quote their mandate to that effect. Has any political party ever avowed a policy of restriction in this fundamental matter, gone to the country on it, and been commissioned to control its legislation? Does this bill rest upon the conscious and universal assent and desire of the American people? I doubt it. It is because I doubt it that I make bold to dissent from it. I am willing to abide by the verdict, but not until it has been rendered. Let the platforms of parties speak out upon this policy and the people pronounce their wish. The matter is too fundamental to be settled otherwise.

I have no pride of opinion in this question. I am not foolish enough to pretend to know the wishes and ideals of America better than the body of her chosen representatives know them. I only want instruction direct from those whose fortunes, with ours and all men's, are involved.

Woodrow Wilson

The White House
January 28, 1915

9. The Comprehensive Immigration Act of 1917[1]

SECTION 1. That the word "alien" wherever used in this act shall include any person not a native-born or naturalized citizen of the United States; . . . .

SEC. 2. That there shall be levied, collected, and paid a tax of $8 for every alien, including alien seamen regularly admitted as provided in this act, entering the United States: *Provided*, That children under sixteen years of age who accompany their father or their mother shall not be subject to said tax. . . . .[2]

[1] Extract from "An Act to Regulate the Immigration of Aliens to, and the Residence of Aliens in, the United States," chap. 29, 39 *U.S. Statutes at Large* 874 (64th Congress, 2d session).

[2] [Various classes are exempt from payment of head tax, the most important being aliens in transit through the United States, aliens legally domiciled for a period of one year in Canada, Newfoundland, Cuba or Mexico who are entering the United States for a temporary visit of not more than six months, and diplomatic and consular officers.]

SEC. 3. That the following classes of aliens shall be excluded from admission into the United States:[1] All idiots, imbeciles, feeble-minded persons, epileptics, insane persons; persons who have had one or more attacks of insanity at any time previously; persons of constitutional psychopathic inferiority; persons with chronic alcoholism; paupers; professional beggars; vagrants; persons afflicted with tuberculosis in any form or with a loathsome or dangerous contagious disease; persons not comprehended within any of the foregoing excluded classes who are found to be and are certified by the examining surgeon as being mentally or physically defective, such physical defect being of a nature which may affect the ability of such alien to earn a living; persons who have been convicted of or admit having committed a felony or other crime or misdemeanor involving moral turpitude; polygamists, or persons who practice polygamy or believe in or advocate the practice of polygamy; anarchists, or persons who believe in or advocate the overthrow by force or violence of the Government of the United States, or of all forms of law, or who disbelieve in or are opposed to organized government, or who advocate the assassination of public officials, or who advocate or teach the unlawful destruction of property; persons who are members of or affiliated with any organization entertaining and teaching disbelief in or opposition to organized government, or who advocate or teach the duty, necessity, or propriety of the unlawful assaulting or killing of any officer or officers, either of specific individuals or of officers generally, of the Government of the United States or of any other organized government, because of his or their official character, or who advocate or teach the unlawful destruction of property; prostitutes, or persons coming into the United States for the purpose of prostitution or for any other immoral purpose; persons who directly or indirectly procure or attempt to procure or import prostitutes or persons for the purpose of prostitution or for any other immoral purpose; persons who are supported by or receive in whole or in part the proceeds of prostitution; persons hereinafter called contract laborers, who have been induced, assisted, encouraged, or solicited to migrate to this country by offers or promises of employment, whether such offers or promises are true or false, or in consequence of agreements, oral, written or printed, express or implied, to perform labor in this country of any kind, skilled or unskilled; persons who have come in consequence of advertisements for laborers printed, published, or distributed in a foreign country; persons likely to become a public charge;[2] persons who have been deported

[1] [This section is very important since all but two of the excluded classes are enumerated here. A description of these two remaining classes may be found in secs. 18 (last proviso) and 23 (last proviso).]

[2] [This clause excluding aliens on the ground "likely to become a public charge" was shifted to its present position in order to indicate the intention of Congress that aliens should be excluded upon this ground for economic reasons and in order to overcome the effect of the decision of the Supreme Court in *Gegiow* v. *Uhl*, 239 U.S. 3, see below, p. 254.]

under any of the provisions of this act, and who may again seek admission within one year from the date of such deportation, unless prior to their reembarkation at a foreign port or their attempt to be admitted from foreign contiguous territory the Secretary of Labor shall have consented to their reapplying for admission; persons whose tickets or passage is paid for with the money of another, or who are assisted by others to come, unless it is affirmatively and satisfactorily shown that such persons do not belong to one of the foregoing excluded classes; persons whose ticket or passage is paid for by any corporation, association, society, municipality, or foreign government, either directly or indirectly; stowaways, except that any such stowaway, if otherwise admissible, may be admitted in the discretion of the Secretary of Labor; all children under sixteen years of age, unaccompanied by or not coming to one or both of their parents, except that any such children may, in the discretion of the Secretary of Labor, be admitted if in his opinion they are not likely to become a public charge and are otherwise eligible; unless otherwise provided for by existing treaties, persons who are natives of islands not possessed by the United States adjacent to the continent of Asia, situate south of the twentieth parallel latitude north, west of the one hundred and sixtieth meridian of longitude east from Greenwich, and north of the tenth parallel of latitude south, or who are natives of any country, province, or dependency situate on the continent of Asia west of the one hundred and tenth meridian of longitude east from Greenwich and east of the fiftieth meridian of longitude east from Greenwich and south of the fiftieth parallel of latitude north, except that portion of said territory situate between the fiftieth and the sixty-fourth meridians of longitude east from Greenwich and the twenty-fourth and thirty-eighth parallels of latitude north, and no alien now in any way excluded from, or prevented from, entering the United States shall be admitted to the United States. The provision next foregoing, however, shall not apply to persons of the following status or occupations: Government officers, ministers or religious teachers, missionaries, lawyers, physicians, chemists, civil engineers, teachers, students, authors, artists, merchants, and travelers for curiosity or pleasure, nor to their legal wives or their children under sixteen years of age who shall accompany them or who subsequently may apply for admission to the United States, but such persons or their legal wives or foreign-born children who fail to maintain in the United States a status or occupation placing them within the excepted classes shall be deemed to be in the United States contrary to law, and shall be subject to deportation as provided in section nineteen of this act.

That after three months from the passage of this act, in addition to the aliens who are by law now excluded from admission into the United States, the following persons shall also be excluded from admission thereto, to wit:

All aliens over sixteen years of age, physically capable of reading, who can not read the English language, or some other language or dialect, including Hebrew or Yiddish: *Provided,* That any admissible alien, or any alien heretofore or hereafter legally admitted, or any citizen of the United States, may bring in or send for his father or grandfather over fifty-five years of age, his wife, his mother, his grandmother, or his unmarried or widowed daughter, if otherwise admissible, whether such relative can read or not; and such relative shall be permitted to enter. That for the purpose of ascertaining whether aliens can read the immigrant inspectors shall be furnished with slips of uniform size, prepared under the direction of the Secretary of Labor, each containing not less than thirty nor more than forty words in ordinary use, printed in plainly legible type in some one of the various languages or dialects of immigrants. Each alien may designate the particular language or dialect in which he desires the examination to be made, and shall be required to read the words printed on the slip in such language or dialect. That the following classes of persons shall be exempt from the operation of the illiteracy test, to wit: All aliens who shall prove to the satisfaction of the proper immigration officer or to the Secretary of Labor that they are seeking admission to the United States to avoid religious persecution in the country of their last permanent residence, whether such persecution be evidenced by overt acts or by laws or governmental regulations that discriminate against the alien or the race to which he belongs because of his religious faith; all aliens who have been lawfully admitted to the United States and who have resided therein continuously for five years and who return to the United States within six months from the date of their departure therefrom; all aliens in transit through the United States; all aliens who have been lawfully admitted to the United States and who later shall go in transit from one part of the United States to another through foreign contiguous territory: *Provided,* That nothing in this act shall exclude, if otherwise admissible, persons convicted, or who admit the commission, or who teach or advocate the commission, of an offense purely political: *Provided further,* That the provisions of this act, relating to the payments for tickets or passage by any corporation, association, society, municipality, or foreign Government shall not apply to the tickets or passage of aliens in immediate and continuous transit through the United States to foreign contiguous territory: *Provided further,* That skilled labor, if otherwise admissible, may be imported if labor of like kind unemployed can not be found in this country, and the question of the necessity of importing such skilled labor in any particular instance may be determined by the Secretary of Labor upon the application of any person interested, such application to be made before such importation, and such determination by the Secretary of Labor to be reached after a full hearing and an investigation into the facts of the case: *Provided further,* That the provisions of this law applicable to contract labor shall not be held to exclude professional actors, artists, lecturers, singers, nurses, ministers of any religious denomination, professors for colleges or seminaries, persons belonging to any recognized learned profession, or persons employed as domestic servants: *Provided further*, That whenever the President shall be satisfied that passports issued by any foreign Government to its citizens or subjects to go to any country other than the United States, or to any insular possession of the United States or to the Canal Zone, are being used for the purpose of enabling the holder to come to the continental territory of the United States to the detriment of labor conditions therein, the President shall refuse to permit such citizens or subjects of the country issuing such passports to enter the continental territory of the United States from such other country or from such insular possession or from the Canal Zone: *Provided further*, That aliens returning after a temporary absence to an unrelinquished United States domicile of seven consecutive years may be admitted in the discretion of the Secretary of Labor, and under such conditions as he may prescribe: *Provided further*, That nothing in the contract-labor or reading-test provisions of this act shall be construed to prevent, hinder, or restrict any alien exhibitor, or holder of concession or privilege for any fair or exposition authorized by act of Congress, from bringing into the United States, under contract, such otherwise admissible alien mechanics, artisans, agents, or other employees, natives of his country as may be necessary for installing or conducting his exhibit or for preparing for installing or conducting any business authorized or permitted under any concession or privilege which may have been or may be granted by any such fair or exposition in connection therewith, under such rules and regulations as the Commissioner General of Immigration, with the approval of the Secretary of Labor, may prescribe both as to the admission and return of such persons: *Provided further*, That the Commissioner General of Immigration with the approval of the Secretary of Labor shall issue rules and prescribe conditions, including exaction of such bonds as may be necessary, to control and regulate the admission and return of otherwise inadmissible aliens applying for temporary admission:[1] *Provided further*, That nothing in this act shall be construed to apply to accredited officials of foreign Governments, nor to their suites, families, or guests.

[1] [The administrative *Rules of the United States Bureau of Immigration* contain the following provision regarding the temporary admission of otherwise inadmissible aliens as subdivision 2 of Rule 16: "The ninth proviso to section 3 authorizes the bureau and the department to issue rules and prescribe conditions to control and regulate the admission and return of otherwise inadmissible aliens applying for temporary admission. In cases in which aliens who are mandatorily excluded from permanent entry apply for the privilege of entering the United States temporarily, they shall be required to show that their temporary entry is an urgent necessity or that unusual and grave hardship would result from a denial of their request. A bond, a cash deposit, or other equally satisfactory assurance that such alien will depart in due course from the United States will be exacted by the department in every instance. . . . ." (See *Immigration Laws and Rules* [7th ed., August, 1922], pp. 71–72.)]

SEC. 4. That the importation into the United States of any alien for the purpose of prostitution, or for any other immoral purpose, is hereby forbidden; and whoever shall, directly or indirectly, import, or attempt to import into the United States any alien for the purpose of prostitution or for any other immoral purpose, or shall hold or attempt to hold any alien for any such purpose in pursuance of such illegal importation, or shall keep, maintain, control, support, employ, or harbor in any house or other place, for the purpose of prostitution or for any other immoral purpose, any alien, in pursuance of such illegal importation, shall in every such case be deemed guilty of a felony, and on conviction thereof shall be punished by imprisonment for a term of not more than ten years and by a fine of not more than $5,000. . . . .

SEC. 9. That it shall be unlawful for any person, including any transportation company other than railway lines entering the United States from foreign contiguous territory, or the owner, master, agent, or consignee of any vessel to bring to the United States either from a foreign country or any insular possession of the United States any alien afflicted with idiocy, insanity, imbecility, feeble-mindedness, epilepsy, constitutional psychopathic inferiority, chronic alcoholism, tuberculosis in any form, or a loathsome or dangerous contagious disease, and if it shall appear to the satisfaction of the Secretary of Labor that any alien so brought to the United States was afflicted with any of the said diseases or disabilities at the time of foreign embarkation, and that the existence of such disease or disability might have been detected by means of a competent medical examination at such time, such person or transportation company, or the master, agent, owner, or consignee of any such vessel shall pay to the collector of customs of the customs district in which the port of arrival is located the sum of $200, and in addition a sum equal to that paid by such alien for his transportation from the initial point of departure, indicated in his ticket, to the port of arrival for each and every violation of the provisions of this section, such latter sum to be delivered by the collector of customs to the alien on whose account assessed. It shall also be unlawful for any such persons to bring to any port of the United States any alien afflicted with any mental defect other than those above specifically named, or physical defect of a nature which may affect his ability to earn a living, as contemplated in section three of this act, and if it shall appear to the satisfaction of the Secretary of Labor that any alien so brought to the United States was so afflicted at the time of foreign embarkation, and that the existence of such mental or physical defect might have been detected by means of a competent medical examination at such time, such person shall pay to the collector of customs of the customs district in which the port of arrival is located the sum of $25, and in addition a sum equal to that paid by such alien for his transportation from the initial point of departure, indicated in his ticket, to the port of arrival, for each and every violation of this provision, such latter sum to be delivered by the collector of customs to the alien for whose account assessed. It shall also be unlawful for any such person to bring to any port of the United States any alien who is excluded by the provisions of section three of this act because unable to read, or who is excluded by the terms of section three of this act as a native of that portion of the continent of Asia and the islands adjacent thereto described in said section, and if it shall appear to the satisfaction of the Secretary of Labor that these disabilities might have been detected by the exercise of reasonable precaution prior to the departure of such aliens from a foreign port, such persons shall pay to the collector of customs of the customs district in which the port of arrival is located the sum of $200, and in addition a sum equal to that paid by such alien for his transportation from the initial point of departure, indicated in his ticket, to the port of arrival, for each and every violation of this provision, such latter sum to be delivered by the collector of customs to the alien on whose account assessed. And no vessel shall be granted clearance papers pending the determination of the question of the liability to the payment of such fines, or while the fines remain unpaid, nor shall such fines be remitted or refunded: *Provided*, That clearance may be granted prior to the determination of such questions upon the deposit of a sum sufficient to cover such fines: *Provided further*, That nothing contained in this section shall be construed to subject transportation companies to a fine for bringing to ports of the United States aliens who are by any of the provisos or exceptions to section three hereof exempted from the excluding provisions of said section. . . . .

SEC. 12. That upon the arrival of any alien by water at any port within the United States it shall be the duty of the master or commanding officers, owners, or consignees of the steamer, sailing, or other vessel having said alien on board to deliver to the immigration officers at the port of arrival typewritten or printed lists or manifests made at the time and place of embarkation of such alien on board such steamer or vessel, which shall, in answer to questions at the top of said list, contain full and accurate information as to each alien as follows: Full name, age, and sex; whether married or single; calling or occupation; personal description (including height, complexion, color of hair and eyes, and marks of identification); whether able to read or write; nationality; country of birth; race; country of last permanent residence; name and address of the nearest relative in the country from which the alien came; seaport for landing in the United States; final destination, if any, beyond the port of landing; whether having a ticket through to such final destination; by whom passage was paid; whether in possession of $50, and if less, how much; whether going to join a relative or friend, and, if so, what relative or friend, and his or her name and complete address; whether ever before in the United States, and if so, when and where; whether ever in prison or almshouse or an institution or hospital for the care and treatment of the insane; whether ever supported by charity; whether a polygamist; whether an anarchist; whether a person who believes in or advocates the overthrow by force or violence of the Government of the United States or of all forms of law, or who disbelieves in or is opposed to organized government, or who advocates the assassination of public officials, or who advocates or teaches the unlawful destruction of property, or is a member of or affiliated with any organization entertaining and teaching disbelief in or opposition to organized government, or which teaches the unlawful destruction of property, or who advocates or teaches the duty, necessity, or propriety of the unlawful assaulting or killing of any officer or officers, either of specific individuals or of officers generally, of the Government of the United States or of any other organized government because of his or their official character; whether coming by reason of any offer, solicitation, promise, or agreement, express or implied, to perform labor in the United States; the alien's condition of health, mental and physical; whether deformed or crippled, and if so, for how long and from what cause; whether coming with the intent to return to the country whence such alien comes after temporarily engaging in laboring pursuits in the United States; and such other items of information as will aid in determining whether any such alien belongs to any of the excluded classes enumerated in section three hereof; and such master or commanding officer, owners, or consignees shall also furnish information in relation to the sex, age, class of travel and the foreign port of embarkation of arriving passengers who are United States citizens. . . . .

SEC 15. That upon the arrival at a port of the United States of any vessel bringing aliens it shall be the duty of the proper immigration officials to go or to send competent assistants to the vessel and there inspect all such aliens, or said immigration officials may order a temporary removal of such aliens for examination at a designated time and place, but such temporary removal shall not be considered a landing, nor shall it relieve vessels, the transportation lines, masters, agents, owners, or consignees of the vessel upon which said aliens are brought to any port of the United States from any of the obligations which, in case such aliens remain on board, would under the provisions of this act bind the said vessels, transportation lines, masters, agents, owners, or consignees: *Provided,* That where removal is made to premises owned or controlled by the United States, said vessels, transportation lines, masters, agents, owners, or consignees, and each of them, shall, so long as detention there lasts, be relieved of responsibility for the safekeeping of such aliens. Whenever a temporary removal of aliens is made the vessels or transportation lines which brought them and the masters, owners, agents, and consignees of the vessel upon which they arrive shall pay all expenses of such removal and all expenses arising during subsequent detention, pending decision on the aliens' eligibility to enter the United States and until they are either allowed to land or returned to the care of the line or to the vessel which brought them, such expenses to include those of maintenance, medical treatment in hospital or elsewhere, burial in the event of death, and transfer to the vessel in the event of deportation. . . . .

Sec. 16. That the physical and mental examination of all arriving aliens shall be made by medical officers of the United States Public Health Service who shall have had at least two years' experience in the practice of their profession since receiving the degree of doctor of medicine, and who shall conduct all medical examinations and shall certify, for the information of the immigration officers and the boards of special inquiry hereinafter provided for, any and all physical and mental defects or diseases observed by said medical officers in any such alien; or, should medical officers of the United States Public Health Service be not available, civil surgeons of not less than four years' professional experience may be employed in such emergency for such service upon such terms as may be prescribed by the Commissioner General of Immigration, under the direction or with the approval of the Secretary of Labor. All aliens arriving at ports of the United States shall be examined by not less than two such medical officers at the discretion of the Secretary of Labor, and under such administrative regulations as he may prescribe and under medical regulations prepared by the Surgeon General of the United States Public Health Service. Medical officers of the United States Public Health Service who have had especial training in the diagnosis of insanity and mental defects shall be detailed for duty or employed at all ports of entry designated by the Secretary of Labor, and such medical officers shall be provided with suitable facilities for the detention and examination of all arriving aliens in whom insanity or mental defect is suspected, and the services of interpreters shall be provided for such examination. Any alien certified for insanity or mental defect may appeal to the board of medical officers of the United States Public Health Service, which shall be convened by the Surgeon General of the United States Public Health Service, and said alien may introduce before such board one expert medical witness at his own cost and expense. That the inspection, other than the physical and mental examination, of aliens, including those seeking admission or readmission to or the privilege of passing through or residing in the United States, and the examination of aliens arrested within the United States under this act, shall be conducted by immigrant inspectors, except as hereinafter provided in regard to boards of special inquiry. All aliens arriving at ports of the United States shall be examined by at least two immigrant inspectors at the discretion of the Secretary of Labor and under such regulations as he may prescribe. . . . . Every alien who may not appear to the examining immigrant inspector at the port of arrival to be clearly and beyond a doubt entitled to land shall be detained for examination in relation thereto by a board of special inquiry. In the event of rejection by the board of special inquiry, in all cases where an appeal to the Secretary of Labor is permitted by this act, the alien shall be so informed and shall have the right to be represented by counsel or other adviser on such appeal. The decision of an immigrant inspector, if favorable to the admission of any alien, shall be subject to challenge by any other immigrant inspector, and such challenge shall operate to take the alien whose right to land is so challenged before a board of special inquiry for its investigation.

SEC. 17. That boards of special inquiry shall be appointed by the commissioner of immigration or inspector in charge at the various ports of arrival as may be necessary for the prompt determination of all cases of immigrants detained at such ports under the provisions of the law. Each board shall consist of three members, who shall be selected from such of the immigrant officials in the service as the Commissioner General of Immigration, with the approval of the Secretary of Labor, shall from time to time designate as qualified to serve on such boards. When in the opinion of the Secretary of Labor the maintenance of a permanent board of special inquiry for service at any sea or land border port is not warranted, regularly constituted boards may be detailed from other stations for temporary service at such port, or, if that be impracticable, the Secretary of Labor shall authorize the creation of boards of special inquiry by the immigration officials in charge at such ports, and shall determine what Government officials or other persons shall be eligible for service on such boards. Such boards shall have authority to determine whether an alien who has been duly held shall be allowed to land or shall be deported. All hearings before such boards shall be separate and apart from the public, but the immigrant may have one friend or relative present under such regulations as may be prescribed by the Secretary of Labor. Such boards shall keep a complete permanent record of their proceedings and of all such testimony as may be produced before them; and the decisions of any two members of the board shall prevail, but either the alien or any dissenting member of the said board may appeal through the commissioner of immigration at the port of arrival and the Commissioner General of Immigration to the Secretary of Labor, and the taking of such appeal shall operate to stay any action in regard to the final disposal of any alien whose case is so appealed until the receipt by the commissioner of immigration at the port of arrival of such decision which shall be rendered solely upon the evidence adduced before the board of special inquiry. In every case where an alien is excluded from admission into the United States, under any law or treaty now existing or hereafter made, the decision of a board of special inquiry adverse to the admission of such alien shall be final, unless reversed on appeal to the Secretary of Labor: *Provided*, That the decision of a board of special inquiry shall be based upon the certificate of the examining medical officer and, except as provided in section twenty-one hereof, shall be final as to the rejection of aliens affected with tuberculosis in any form or with a loathsome or dangerous contagious disease, or with any mental or physical disability which would bring such aliens within any of the classes excluded from admission to the United States under section three of this act.¹

Sec. 18. That all aliens brought to this country in violation of law shall be immediately sent back, in accommodations of the same class in which they arrived, to the country whence they respectively came, on the vessels bringing them, unless in the opinion of the Secretary of Labor immediate deportation is not practicable or proper. The cost of their maintenance while on land, as well as the expense of the return of such aliens, shall be borne by the owner or owners of the vessels on which they respectively came. That it shall be unlawful for any master, purser, person in charge, agent, owner, or consignee of any such vessel to refuse to receive back on board thereof, or on board of any other vessel owned or operated by the same interests, such aliens; or to fail to detain them thereon; or to refuse or fail to return them in the manner aforesaid to the foreign port from which they came; or to fail to pay the cost of their maintenance, while on land; or to make any charge for the return of any such alien, or to take any security for the payment of such charge; or to take any consideration to be returned in case the alien is landed; or knowingly to bring to the United States at any time within one year from the date of deportation any alien rejected or arrested and deported under any provision of this act, unless prior to reembarkation the Secretary of Labor has consented that such alien shall reapply for admission, as required by section three hereof. . . . . No alien certified, as provided in section sixteen of this act, to be suffering from tuberculosis in any form, or from a loathsome or dangerous contagious disease other than one of quarantinable nature, shall be permitted to land for medical treatment thereof in any hospital in the United States, unless the Secretary of Labor is satisfied that to refuse treatment would be inhumane or cause unusual hardship or suffering, in which case the alien shall be treated in the hospital under the supervision of the immigration officials

---

¹ [Rule 17 of the administrative *Rules of the United States Bureau of Immigration* contains (pp. 72–73) the following:

"Subd. 4. *Where no appeal lies.*—No appeal lies where the decision of a board of special inquiry, based upon the certificate of the examining medical officer, as required by section 17, rejects an alien because (*a*) he is afflicted with tuberculosis in any form or a loathsome contagious or dangerous contagious disease, or (*b*) he is an idiot or an imbecile, or an epileptic or is insane or feeble-minded, or (*c*) he is afflicted with constitutional psychopathic inferiority or has any mental defect or is a chronic alcoholic.

"Subd. 5. *Where appeal lies despite certificate.*—When an alien is certified for a physical defect other than tuberculosis in any form or a loathsome contagious or dangerous contagious disease, the board of special inquiry must decide, on the basis of all the evidence (including the certificate) whether or not such certified defect may affect his ability to earn a living. An alien rejected on said ground is entitled to appeal."]

at the expense of the vessel transporting him: *Provided further,* **That** upon the certificate of an examining medical officer to the effect that the health or safety of an insane alien would be unduly imperiled by immediate deportation, such alien may, at the expense of the appropriation for the enforcement of this act, be held for treatment until such time as such alien may, in the opinion of such medical officer, be safely deported: *Provided further,* That upon the certificate of an examining medical officer to the effect that a rejected alien is helpless from sickness, mental or physical disability, or infancy, if such alien is accompanied by another alien whose protection or guardianship is required by such rejected alien, such accompanying alien may also be excluded, and the master, agent, owner, or consignee of the vessel in which such alien and accompanying alien are brought shall be required to return said alien and accompanying alien in the same manner as vessels are required to return other rejected aliens.

SEC. 19. That at any time within five years after entry, any alien who at the time of entry was a member of one or more of the classes excluded by law; any alien who shall have entered or who shall be found in the United States in violation of this act, or in violation of any other law of the United States;[1] any alien who at any time after entry shall be found advocating or

[1] The latter part of this provision relates to Chinese entering or found in the United States in violation of the Chinese-exclusion laws (S. Rept. 352, 64th Congress, 1st session).

[This section is important because all cases in which aliens may be expelled (i.e., arrested and deported after landing) are mentioned here. The following extracts from Rule 22 of the administrative *Rules of the Bureau of Immigration* show the methods adopted by the Bureau for administering these deportation clauses.

"RULE 22. SUBDIVISION 2. *Investigation and report of cases.*—Officers shall make a thorough investigation of all cases when they are credibly informed or have reason to believe that a specified alien in the United States is subject to arrest and deportation on warrant. All such cases, by whomsoever discovered, shall be reported to the immigration officer stationed nearest the place where the alien is found to be.

"SUBD. 3. *Application for warrant of arrest.*—The application must state facts showing prima facie that the alien comes within one or more of the classes subject to deportation after entry, and, except in cases in which the burden of proof is upon the alien (Chinese) involved, should be accompanied by some substantial supporting evidence. If the facts stated are within the personal knowledge of the inspector reporting the case, they need not be in affidavit form. But if based upon statements of persons not sworn officers of the Government (except in cases of public charges covered by subdivision 4 hereof), the application should be accompanied by the affidavit of the person giving the information or by a transcript of a sworn statement taken from that person by an inspector. In all cases shown in subdivision 1 to be subject to a time limitation the application must be accompanied by a certificate of landing (to be obtained from the immigration officer in charge of the port where landing occurred, unless entry without inspection within such

teaching the unlawful destruction of property, or advocating or teaching anarchy, or the overthrow by force or violence of the Government of the United States or of all forms of law or the assassination of public officials; any alien who within five years after entry becomes a public charge from causes not affirmatively shown to have arisen subsequent to landing; except as hereinafter provided, any alien who is hereafter sentenced to imprisonment for a term of one year or more because of conviction in this country of a crime involving moral turpitude, committed within five years after the entry of the alien to the United States, or who is hereafter sentenced more than once to such a term of imprisonment because of conviction in this country of any crime involving moral turpitude, committed at any time after entry; any alien who shall be found an inmate of or connected with the management of a house of prostitution or practicing prostitution after such alien shall have entered the United States, or who shall receive, share in, or derive benefit from any part of the earnings of any prostitute; any alien who manages or is employed by, in, or in connection with any house

---

limitation is confessed, or a reason given for its absence. In the absence of such certificate, effort should be made to supply the principal items of information mentioned in the blank form provided for such certificate. Telegraphic application may be resorted to only in case of necessity, or when some substantial interest of the Government would be subserved thereby, and must state (*a*) that the usual written application is being forwarded by mail, and (*b*) the substance of the facts and proof therein contained. The code supplied by the department should be used whenever practicable.

"SUBD. 4. *Proof in cases of aliens who have become public charges.*—The application in such cases must be accompanied by a certificate of the official in charge of the institution in which the alien is confined, or other responsible public official if the alien is not confined, showing that the alien is being maintained at public expense. There should be submitted also, whenever readily available, evidence (such as certificates from attending physicians, etc.) tending to show that the causes for the alien's being a public charge existed prior to entry.

"SUBD. 5. *Execution of warrant of arrest and hearing thereon.*—(*a*) Upon receipt of a telegraphic or written warrant of arrest the alien shall be taken before the person or persons therein named or described and granted a hearing to enable him to show cause, if any there be, why he should not be deported. (If the alien is unable to speak or understand English, an interpreter should be employed where practicable. If the alien is physically or mentally incapable of testifying, some relative or friend, if any, should be questioned.) Pending determination of the case, in the discretion of the immigration officer in charge, he may be taken into custody or allowed to remain in some place deemed by such officer secure and proper, except that in the absence of special instructions an alien confined in an institution shall not be removed therefrom until a warrant of deportation has been issued and is about to be served.

"*b*) At the beginning of the hearing under the warrant of arrest the alien shall be allowed to inspect the warrant of arrest and all the evidence on which it was issued, and shall be apprised that he may be represented by counsel. The alien

of prostitution or music or dance hall or other place of amusement or resort habitually frequented by prostitutes, or where prostitutes gather, or who in any way assists any prostitute or protects or promises to protect from arrest any prostitute; any alien who shall import or attempt to import any person for the purpose of prostitution or for any other immoral purpose; any alien who, after being excluded and deported or arrested and deported as a prostitute, or as a procurer, or as having been connected with the business of prostitution or importation for prostitution or other immoral purposes in any of the ways hereinbefore specified, shall return to and enter the United States; any alien convicted and imprisoned for a violation of any of the provisions of section four hereof; any alien who was convicted, or who admits

---

shall be required then and there to state whether he desires counsel or waives the same, and his reply shall be entered on the record. If counsel be selected, he shall be permitted to be present during the conduct of the hearing, and to offer evidence to meet any evidence presented or adduced by the Government. Objections and exceptions of counsel shall not be entered on the record, but may be presented by him in accompanying brief. If during the hearing it shall appear to the examining inspector that there exists a reason additional to those stated in the warrant of arrest why the alien is in the country in violation of law, the alien's attention shall be directed to the facts which constitute such reason, and he shall be given an opportunity to show cause why he should not be deported therefor.

"*c*) At the close of the hearing the full record shall be forwarded to the bureau, together with any written argument submitted by counsel and the recommendations of the examining officer and the officer in charge, for determination as to whether or not a deportation warrant shall issue.

"*d*) The record of the hearing accorded an alien who is suffering from any physical or mental disability shall be supplemented by a medical certificate showing (1) whether such alien is in condition to be deported without danger to life; (2) whether he will require special care and attention on the ocean voyage. . . . .

"SUBD. 7. *Warrant for deportation and deportation thereon.*—Upon receipt of the department's decision, or as soon thereafter as the circumstances of the case may require, the alien shall be taken into the custody of the immigration officials (if this has not occurred already) for deportation. Thereafter he shall be deported, previous notice of deportation having been given the steamship company concerned, together with a brief description of the alien and any other appropriate data, including the cause of deportation, physical and mental condition, and destination. . . . .

"SUBD. 11. *Deportation by consent.*—Any alien who is a lawful resident of the United States and who has become a public charge from physical disability arising subsequent to landing may be deported, with his consent and approval of the bureau, within three years from date of landing, at Government expense, provided he is delivered to the immigration officers at a designed port free of charge. If the alien's deportation is directed, the charges incurred for his care and treatment in any public or charitable institution from the date of notification to an immigration official until the expiration of one year after landing may be paid by the bureau at such rates as it shall accept as reasonable."]

the commission, prior to entry, of a felony or other crime or misdemeanor involving moral turpitude; at any time within three years after entry, any alien who shall have entered the United States by water at any time or place other than as designated by immigration officials, or by land at any place other than one designated as a port of entry for aliens by the Commissioner General of Immigration, or at any time not designated by immigration officials, or who enters without inspection, shall, upon the warrant of the Secretary of Labor, be taken into custody and deported: *Provided*, That the marriage to an American citizen of a female of the sexually immoral classes the exclusion or deportation of which is prescribed by this act shall not invest such female with United States citizenship if the marriage of such alien female shall be solemnized after her arrest or after the commission of acts which make her liable to deportation under this act: *Provided further*, That the provision of this section respecting the deportation of aliens convicted of a crime involving moral turpitude shall not apply to one who has been pardoned, nor shall such deportation be made or directed if the court, or judge thereof, sentencing such alien for such crime shall, at the time of imposing judgment or passing sentence or within thirty days thereafter, due notice having first been given to representatives of the State, make a recommendation to the Secretary of Labor that such alien shall not be deported in pursuance of this act; nor shall any alien convicted as aforesaid be deported until after the termination of his imprisonment. . . . .

SEC. 21. That any alien liable to be excluded because likely to become a public charge or because of physical disability other than tuberculosis in any form or a loathsome or dangerous contagious disease may, if otherwise admissible, nevertheless be admitted in the discretion of the Secretary of Labor upon the giving of a suitable and proper bond or undertaking, approved by said Secretary, in such amount and containing such conditions as he may prescribe, to the United States and to all States, Territories, counties, towns, municipalities, and districts thereof, holding the United States and all States, Territories, counties, towns, municipalities, and districts thereof harmless against such alien becoming a public charge. In lieu of such bond, such alien may deposit in cash with the Secretary of Labor such amount as the Secretary of Labor may require, which amount shall be deposited by said Secretary in the United States Postal Savings Bank, a receipt therefor to be given the person furnishing said sum showing the fact and object of its receipt and such other information as said Secretary may deem advisable. All accruing interest on said deposit during the time same shall be held in the United States Postal Savings Bank shall be paid to the person furnishing the sum for deposit. In the event of such alien becoming a public charge, the Secretary of Labor shall dispose of said deposit in the same manner as if same had been collected under a bond as provided in this section. In the event of the permanent departure from the United States, the naturalization, or the death of such alien, the said sum shall be returned to the person by whom furnished, or to his legal representatives. The admission of such alien shall be a consideration for the giving of such bond, undertaking, or cash deposit. Suit may be brought thereon in the name and by the proper law officers either of the United States Government or of any State, Territory, District, county, town, or municipality in which such alien becomes a public charge.

SEC. 22. That whenever an alien shall have been naturalized or shall have taken up his permanent residence in this country, and thereafter shall send for his wife or minor children to join him, and said wife or any of said minor children shall be found to be affected with any contagious disorders, such wife or minor children shall be held, under such regulations as the Secretary of Labor shall prescribe, until it shall be determined whether the disorder will be easily curable or whether they can be permitted to land without danger to other persons; and they shall not be either admitted or deported until such facts have been ascertained; and if it shall be determined that the disorder is easily curable and the husband or father or other responsible person is willing to bear the expense of the treatment, they may be accorded treatment in hospital until cured and then be admitted, or if it shall be determined that they can be permitted to land without danger to other persons, they may, if otherwise admissible, thereupon be admitted:[1] *Provided*, That if the person sending for wife or minor children is naturalized, a wife to whom married or a minor child born subsequent to such husband or father's naturalization shall be admitted without detention for treatment in hospital, and with respect to a wife to whom married or a minor child born prior to such husband or father's naturalization the provisions of this section shall be observed, even though such person is unable to pay the expense of treatment, in which case the expense shall be paid from the appropriation for the enforcement of this act.

[1] [The *Rules* issued by the Bureau include under Rule 19, "Hospital Treatment," certain rules of procedure for staying deportation of wives and children of naturalized citizens and permanently resident aliens. This rule provides, however, that "Deportation shall occur promptly with respect to such wives and minor children if and when it is ascertained that the disorder is not easily curable or that the alien can not be landed without danger to others; and with respect to all others if and when it is ascertained that the alien is diseased; unless, in behalf of either, application for treatment is made promptly in accordance with the terms of subdivisions 2 and 3 hereof. To expedite the handling of cases under this rule, examining surgeons should include, so far as possible, in their certificates for tuberculosis in any form or loathsome contagious or dangerous contagious diseases a statement as to whether or not the disorder will be easily curable and whether or not the person certified can be permitted to land without danger to other persons."]

10. The Alien Anarchist Act of 1918–20[1]

That the following aliens shall be excluded from admission into the United States:

a) Aliens who are anarchists;

b) Aliens who advise, advocate, or teach, or who are members of or affiliated with any organization, association, society, or group, that advises, advocates, or teaches, opposition to all organized government;

c) Aliens who believe in, advise, advocate, or teach, or who are members of or affiliated with any organization, association, society, or group, that believes in, advises, advocates, or teaches: (1) the overthrow by force or violence of the Government of the United States or of all forms of law, or (2) the duty, necessity, or propriety of the unlawful assaulting or killing of any officer or officers (either of specific individuals or of officers generally) of the Government of the United States or of any other organized government, because of his or their official character, or (3) the unlawful damage, injury, or destruction of property, or (4) sabotage;

d) Aliens who write, publish, or cause to be written or published, or who knowingly circulate, distribute, print, or display, or knowingly cause to be circulated, distributed, printed, published, or displayed, or who knowingly have in their possession for the purpose of circulation, distribution, publication, or display, any written or printed matter, advising, advocating, or teaching opposition to all organized government, or advising, advocating, or teaching: (1) the overthrow by force or violence of the Government of the United States or of all forms of law, or (2) the duty, necessity or propriety of the unlawful assaulting or killing of any officer or officers (either of specific individuals or of officers generally) of the Government of the United States or of any other organized government, or (3) the unlawful damage, injury, or destruction of property, or (4) sabotage;

e) Aliens who are members of or affiliated with any organization, association, society, or group, that writes, circulates, distributes, prints, publishes, or displays, or causes to be written, circulated, distributed, printed, published, or displayed, or that has in its possession for the purpose of circulation, distribution, publication, issue, or display, any written or printed matter of the character described in subdivision (*d*).

For the purpose of this section: (1) the giving, loaning, or promising of money or anything of value to be used for the advising, advocacy, or teaching of any doctrine above enumerated shall constitute the advising, advocacy, or teaching of such doctrine; and (2) the giving, loaning, or promising of money or anything of value to any organization, association,

[1] Extract from act entitled "An Act to Exclude and Expel from the United States Aliens Who Are Members of the Anarchistic and Similar Classes," approved October 16, 1918, as amended by the act approved June 5, 1920, chap. 251, 41 *U.S. Statutes at Large* 1008 (66th Congress, 2d session).

society, or group of the character above described shall constitute affiliation therewith; but nothing in this paragraph shall be taken as an exclusive definition of advising, advocacy, teaching, or affiliation.

SEC. 2. That any alien who, at any time after entering the United States, is found to have been at the time of entry, or to have become thereafter, a member of any one of the classes of aliens enumerated in section one of this act, shall, upon the warrant of the Secretary of Labor, be taken into custody and deported in the manner provided in the immigration act of February fifth, nineteen hundred and seventeen. The provisions of this section shall be applicable to the classes of aliens mentioned in this act irrespective of the time of their entry into the United States.

11. Emergency Immigration Legislation: The Quota System Recommended[1]

The present conditions can not be understood without a brief review of the causes which have led up to the great immigration movement from Europe to the United States during the years immediately preceding the World War.

It must be remembered that the national expansion in agriculture, in industries, and in transportation systems has occurred since the close of the war between the States. What is known as the old immigration—that coming from northern and western Europe—began early in our history, gradually increased after the war of 1861–1865 until 1882, when it reached its height. This immigration consisted almost wholly of families who came to this country with the full intention of making it their home and of becoming American citizens. It was this immigration that aided so much in the development of agriculture in the great Central West and in the construction of our incomparable transportation system.

It was during this period also that the manufacturing industries of the country had their marvelous growth. As early as 1880 the products of our manufacturers equaled in amount and value those of Great Britain. The development of these industries created a large demand for common labor, and it was then that the so-called new immigration, coming mainly from eastern and southern Europe, began to arrive in large numbers. In the year 1900 the manufactured products of the United States were greater than those of Great Britain, France, and Germany combined, and between that time and 1910 the value of such products increased from $11,000,000,000 to $20,000,000,000 annually. This increase alone was greater than the whole product of 1890. Without a comparison of this character it is impossible to comprehend the demand that has been created in the United States for European labor, and this expansion in our manufacturing and mining

[1] Extract from "Report of Mr. Dillingham, from the Committee on Immigration, April 28, 1921," U.S. 67th Congress, 1st session, *Senate Report No. 17*, pp. 3–8.

THE FEDERAL IMMIGRATION LAWS

industries explains the vast increase in the immigration from eastern and southern Europe.

The following table pictures the old immigration as well as the new immigration and shows the gradual decrease of the old and the rapid increase of the new immigration:

[IMMIGRANTS FROM EUROPE, 1882–1914]

8 YEARS (1882–1889)

Old immigration	3,019,696
New immigration	708,357
	3,728,053

7 YEARS (1890–1896)

Old immigration	1,562,797
New immigration	1,194,189
	2,756,986

18 YEARS (1897–1914)

Old immigration	2,983,548
New immigration	10,057,576
	13,041,124

Total old immigration for the whole three periods, 33 years (1882–1914)	7,566,041
Total new immigration for the whole three periods, 33 years (1882–1914)	11,960,122
Total immigration from Europe, old and new (1882–1914)	19,526,163

This new immigration coming almost wholly from eastern and southern Europe differed in character from the old immigration in that substantially 70 per cent of it, as a whole, consisted of males and substantially 86 per cent of the males were living single lives, being unmarried or having left their wives in Europe. They came to the United States not so much for the purpose of remaining here and making homes as to seek profitable employment at the seats of our great basic industries. As a class they were strong, healthy, able-bodied men, industrious and frugal in their habits. Substantially 95 per cent were under 45 years of age. The investigation of the Immigration Commission showed that a great majority of the employees in the great industries in the United States, investigated by that commission, were of this class.

During the period of the World War the European and home orders for munitions and other war material created an abnormal demand upon the manufacturing industries of the United States, but during the same period European immigration was almost wholly cut off. During the five years previous to the war we had admitted over 5,000,000 immigrants, a large proportion of whom proceeded directly to our cities or to the seats of our greater industries. During the war period, 1915-1919, inclusive, we admitted no immigrants from Europe. Thus it will be seen that although our industries had so largely increased they were conducted without the 4,000,000 immigrants who would undoubtedly otherwise have been admitted and given employment.

An unusual demand for American labor in the industries was so created Unusual and unprecedented prices were offered to the available young manhood of the country which had not been called to the ranks. They responded in such numbers that the agricultural and the rural communities of our country were left substantially without common labor. Although a depression now exists among the manufacturing industries these young men have not returned to the farms nor to the rural communities, and there is no indication of a desire on their part to do so.

It is apparent that on the 1st day of July, 1920, the opening of the present fiscal year, the ordinary supply of common and farm labor in the country was much lower than at any time in the past. Competent writers have estimated such shortage at no less than 4,000,000.

Conditions were little changed during the fiscal year 1920; the number of aliens admitted during that year were 430,001 but only 57 per cent of such aliens came from Europe, while approximately 90 per cent of the immigration prior to the World War was derived from that source.

The present alarm in the country arises in part from the fact that during the months of July, August, September, October, November, and December, 1920, we received immigrants to the number of, approximately, 412,000. When it is considered that the industrial systems of the United States have absorbed such a large proportion of the common labor of the country, the committee fails to see why the admission of this number of immigrants can of itself work injury in a nation containing 105,000,000 souls.

In this connection it may be mentioned that during the same six months aliens have departed from this country for Europe in numbers aggregating about 40 per cent of the number admitted.

In connection with alien departures, it should be noted that the number of departures of the new group of aliens comprising southern and eastern Europe far exceeds that of the old group comprising northern and western Europe. For example, in the year ending June 30, 1920, there were 226,560 departures of the new group as compared with 41,532 of the old group; in other words, there were 122 departures of the new group to every 100 admitted, while of the old group there were only 25 departures to every 100 admitted. In the month of July, 1920, of the new group there were 22,534 departures and there were 34,228 admitted, while of the old group there were only 3,451 departures and 19,869 were admitted. These figures forcibly illustrate the temporary character of the emigration from southern and eastern Europe.

As bearing on the question of the present emergency, it should also be mentioned that on January 3, 1921, the Secretary of State notified this committee that "The Italian Government has suspended the issuance of passports to subjects emigrating to the United States, and will refrain from issuing such passports until informed as to the classes of immigrants desired in this country." In a further communication from the Secretary of State, dated January 31, 1921, this committee was informed that the emigration committee at Valetto, Malta, had issued the following notice:

Information having been received that there may be a slackness in the demand for labor during the winter months, intending emigrants to America are warned that no passports to the United States of America will be issued until further notice.

Exception will be made in the case of families who wish to join their heads in America, and also of domiciled persons and former residents. Passports may be issued to such persons at the discretion of and after careful investigation by the emigration office.

This notice only emphasized the well-known fact that the determining factor in emigration is economic; in other words, that the flow of immigration to America depends upon economic conditions here, and when we are passing through a period of business depression immigration automatically is largely checked. In the year following the panic of 1907 immigration fell off more than half a million. In the years following the business reaction of 1893 immigration declined one-half, while the effect of the business depression of 1873 and 1875 was to reduce immigration to one-third the normal numbers. And it is undoubtedly true that the tendency toward a decrease in immigration during the past two months, and especially in January, is due to the immediate economic conditions in the United States. Should the present business conditions continue, we need have little fear of an impending "flood" of immigration.

For reasons stated and for others which will further appear in this report the committee are of the opinion that no emergency exists at the present time which warrants a general prohibition of European immigration into the United States, although it has been advocated by some.

A prohibition measure of this character has never been resorted to by the United States and should only be adopted under the most extraordinary circumstances.

The committee does not look upon normal immigration from northern and western Europe as in any sense a problem. Such immigration has from the beginning been to a large extent one of families; they have come to the United States with the intention of remaining and making homes; they have distributed themselves throughout the United States, have become property owners, are interested in all local and national problems, and are also readily assimilated into the body of American citizenship. As has already been stated, this old immigration, so called, which has proved so valuable to us as a Nation, reached its highest point in 1882, but from that time it diminished gradually to a normal status, which normal status has maintained for 25 or 30 years.

Does an emergency of another character now exist? Or may an emergency arise in the near future which must be met by marked restriction in immigration until the changes wrought by the war, both in the United States and in European nations, can be deliberately ascertained and considered and a system of legislation adapted to such changed conditions be framed to meet the exigency?

The committee are of the opinion that such an emergency is at hand. There never has been a time during the last 40 years when there has not been a general desire upon the part of the younger and more enterprising men in the nations of eastern and southern Europe to better their conditions by coming to the United States. The extent to which this desire has been gratified has been shown by the table already inserted in this report. This is further shown by an examination of the following table, covering the general movement of immigration between the years of 1908–1920, inclusive:

[ALIENS ADMITTED AND DEPARTED, 1908–1920]

Net Increase of Population by Arrival and Departure of Aliens, Fiscal Years Ended June 30, 1908, to 1920*

	Admitted			Departed			Increase
	Immigrant	Nonimmigrant	Total	Emigrant	Nonemigrant	Total	
1908	782,870	141,825	924,695	395,073	319,755	714,828	209,867
1909	751,786	192,449	944,235	225,802	174,590	400,392	543,843
1910	1,041,570	156,467	1,198,037	202,436	177,982	380,418	817,619
1911	878,587	151,713	1,030,300	295,666	222,549	518,215	512,085
1912	838,172	178,983	1,017,155	333,262	282,030	615,292	401,863
1913	1,197,892	229,335	1,427,227	308,190	303,734	611,924	815,303
1914	1,218,480	184,601	1,403,081	303,338	330,467	633,805	769,276
1915	326,700	107,544	434,244	204,074	180,100	384,174	50,070
1916	298,826	67,922	366,748	129,765	111,042	240,807	125,941
1917	295,403	67,474	362,877	66,277	80,102	146,379	216,498
1918	110,618	101,235	211,853	94,585	98,683	193,268	18,585
1919	141,132	95,889	237,021	123,522	92,709	216,231	20,790
1920	430,001	191,575	621,576	288,315	139,747	428,062	193,514
Total	8,312,037	1,867,012	10,179,049	2,970,305	2,513,490	5,483,795	4,695,254

*[The classes in this table are defined as follows in the *Report of the Commissioner-General of Immigration:* "In the classification of aliens the terms (1) immigrant and emigrant and (2) nonimmigrant and nonemigrant, respectively, relate (1) to permanent arrivals and departures and (2) to temporary arrivals and departures. In compiling the statistics under this classification the following rule is observed: Arriving aliens whose permanent domicile has been outside the United States who intend to reside permanently in the United States are classed as immigrant aliens; departing aliens whose permanent residence has been in the United States who intend to reside permanently abroad are classed as emigrant aliens; all alien residents of the United States making a temporary trip abroad and all aliens residing abroad making a temporary trip to the United States are classed as nonemigrant aliens on the outward journey and nonimmigrant aliens on the inward."]

It also appears that during the 10 years, 1905–1914, that we admitted 10,121,940 immigrants; that the number admitted during the five years, 1915–1919, was almost negligible, while that in the fiscal year 1920 was 430,001, or less than one-half the normal flow before the war.

That the general movement of immigrants toward the United States is increasing is evidenced by the fact that during the first six months of the present fiscal year there were admitted 411,901 immigrants. Evidence taken by the committee indicates that the general desire among the people of many nations of Europe to emigrate to the United States has been quickened as a result of the war. While it is not probable that undue numbers will seek admittance to the United States during the present existing depression in our manufacturing industries, it is probable that when such industrial activities revive the number seeking admittance will increase accordingly, and it is possible that it will equal in number the immigration during the last years preceding the World War, when the average number admitted, 1910–1914, was more than 1,000,000 annually. . . . .

The immigration of the present year has very largely come from southern and eastern Europe and in the opinion of the committee the largest immigration of the immediate future will also come from that section of the world.

This opinion is borne out by the fact that during the 18 years, 1897–1914, we received of the old immigration only 2,838,548, while during the same period we received of the new immigration 10,570,576. It was the new immigration coming in unprecedented numbers which created our prewar problem and, as already indicated, it is the impending return of this movement to its prewar status which in the opinion of the committee constitutes the present emergency. Unlike the older immigration, which distributed itself to every part of the country, entered every branch of activity and was, as a rule, quickly and thoroughly assimilated, the new immigration has consisted largely of single men, it has gone directly to the cities and to the manufacturing centers, and has remained there. It has moved in racial groups and to a large extent has maintained them, and compared with the older immigration it, as a rule, shows a slighter tendency to become American citizens and the number who have gone to the land have been negligible.

The committee are of the opinion that in the present emergency a restriction should be applied to the type last described and are convinced that such restriction should be accomplished through some measure that will insure definite effectiveness.

A percentage plan was suggested by the United States Immigration Commission in 1910 as a possible means of immigration control, but the proposal made at that time was a limitation to a certain percentage of the average immigration from such country for a given period of years. The publication of the census returns for 1910, however, afforded a new and more equitable basis for the purpose, and the plan was accordingly revised so as to limit immigration to a fixed percentage of the foreign born of each nationality resident in the United States. A bill limiting the number from any country in any fiscal year to 10 per cent of the natives of such country resident in the United States was introduced in the Senate as early as June 2, 1913, but as the period of the war immediately followed and the flow of immigration almost ceased, the proposition was not pushed to a decision. . . . .

The Senate bill, which the committee now recommends . . . . provides that until June 30, 1922, the number of immigrants who may be admitted to the United States from any country, in any fiscal year, shall be limited to 3 per cent of the number of natives of that class resident in the United States in 1910. Immigration from countries on the American continent and from adjacent islands and from China, Japan, and the so-called Asiatic barred zone is not subject to the provisions of the proposed measure, so that, in effect, it is applicable only to European countries, Turkey in Asia, Africa, and Australasia.

The approximate number of immigrants who would be admissible from each of the various countries which come within the scope of the measure, compared with the average annual immigration from such countries in 1910–1914, is shown in the following table:

[IMMIGRANTS ADMISSIBLE: QUOTA ESTIMATES]

NUMBER OF NATIVES OF COUNTRIES SPECIFIED WHO WERE RESIDENT IN THE UNITED STATES IN 1910; AVERAGE NUMBER OF IMMIGRANT ALIENS WHO WERE ADMITTED FROM SUCH COUNTRIES DURING 1910–1914; AND THE NUMBER WHO WOULD BE ADMISSIBLE ANNUALLY UNDER THE 3 PER CENT PLAN

COUNTRIES	POPULATION IN UNITED STATES 1910	AVERAGE ANNUAL IMMIGRATION 1910–1914	APPROXIMATE NUMBER WHO WOULD BE ADMISSIBLE ANNUALLY UNDER SPECIFIED PER CENT LIMIT		
			5 Per Cent	4 Per Cent	3 Per Cent
Belgium	49,400	5,690	2,470	1,976	1,482
Denmark	181,649	6,694	9,082	7,266	5,449
France	117,418	8,601	5,871	4,697	3,523
Germany	2,501,333	32,239	125,066	100,053	75,040
Netherlands	123,134	7,147	6,157	4,925	3,694
Norway	403,877	11,416	20,194	16,155	12,116
Sweden	665,207	17,843	33,260	26,608	19,956
Switzerland	124,848	3,762	6,232	4,994	3,745
United Kingdom	2,573,534	89,188	128,677	102,941	77,206
Total northwestern Europe	6,740,400	182,580	337,009	269,615	202,211
Austro-Hungary	1,670,582	225,931	83,529	66,823	50,117
Bulgaria	11,498		575	460	345
Servia	4,639	4,964	232	186	139
Montenegro	5,374		269	215	161
Greece	101,282	26,442	5,064	4,051	3,038
Italy	1,343,125	220,967	67,156	53,725	40,294
Portugal	59,360	10,380	2,968	2,374	1,781
Rumania	65,923	2,570	3,296	2,637	1,978
Russia	1,732,462	210,922	86,623	69,298	51,974
Spain	22,108	5,722	1,105	884	663
Turkey in Europe	32,230	13,930	1,612	1,289	967
Turkey in Asia	59,729	16,780	2,986	2,389	1,792
Total	5,108,312	738,608	255,415	204,331	153,249

Attention is called to the fact that under the provisions of the proposed measure the number of the older immigration class from northern and western Europe who would be permitted to enter the United States in any fiscal year would be 202,211, when, as a matter of fact, the normal flow of this immigration annually from 1910–1914 was only 182,580. There is no reason to believe that such number would be increased under the provisions of such an amendment.

On the other hand, an examination of the table shows that the provisions of the proposed measure would reduce the number of immigrants of the so-called new class, coming from southern and eastern Europe, to a most remarkable degree. The reduction is indicated by the fact that the average annual immigration of this class in 1910–1914 was 738,608, while under the provisions of the proposed measure it can not exceed 153,249 annually. In other words, the numbers admissible annually from southern and eastern Europe would be substantially one-fifth of the average number who were annually admitted by the United States during the years 1910–1914. The committee are of the opinion that the admission to the United States during the next fiscal year of less than one-fifth of the number of immigrants (of the class named) that were admitted annually for three years prior to the opening of the World War will meet every requirement dictated by prudence and will, at the same time, obviate the many objections which have been offered to a system absolutely prohibiting general immigration.

The present immigration laws of the United States are admirable for the protection of the United States against those who are physically and mentally defective as well as against all objectionable classes and conditions. Those who have not studied existing laws know but little regarding their breadth and character.

New problems have been presented as the result of changed conditions in the United States resulting from our peculiar and excessive industrial development and from the changed conditions which have been caused and accentuated as the result of the World War.

Marked improvements are demanded in the administration of existing laws. Our national condition demands the adoption of new policies regarding the selection of immigrants who shall in the future be admitted to the United States and some strong policy must be adopted whereby a better selection and distribution of arriving immigrants shall be secured. The situation in the agricultural and rural sections of the country so far as common and agricultural labor is concerned is distinctly bad, and means must be adopted by which future immigration shall to a certain extent at least be deflected from industrial centers and find employment upon the land.

To study this problem and to frame adequate legislation is impossible during the present short session of Congress.

For the reasons stated the committee favor temporary legislation which, while it will protect the United States during the next fiscal year, will not operate to the great injury or disadvantage of sections and classes nor prevent the admission of such a reasonable number of immigrants as will meet present conditions in the United States.

12. The "Quota" Act, 1921–22[1]

SEC. 2. (*a*) That the number of aliens of any nationality who may be admitted under the immigration laws to the United States in any fiscal year shall be limited to 3 per centum of the number of foreign-born persons of such nationality resident in the United States as determined by the United States census of 1910. . . . .[2]

b) For the purposes of this Act nationality shall be determined by country of birth, treating as separate countries the colonies or dependencies for which separate enumeration was made in the United States census of 1910.

c) The Secretary of State, the Secretary of Commerce, and the Secretary of Labor, jointly, shall, as soon as feasible after the enactment of this Act, prepare a statement showing the number of persons of the various nationalities resident in the United States as determined by the United States census of 1910, which statement shall be the population basis for the purposes of this Act. In case of changes in political boundaries in foreign countries occurring subsequent to 1910 and resulting (1) in the creation of new countries, the Governments of which are recognized by the United States, or (2) in the transfer of territory from one country to another, such transfer being recognized by the United States, such officials, jointly, shall estimate the number of persons resident in the United States in 1910 who were born within the area included in such new countries or in such territory so transferred, and revise the population basis as to each country involved in such change of political boundary. For the purpose of such revision and for the purposes of this Act generally aliens born in the area included in any such new country shall be considered as having been born in such country, and aliens born in any territory so transferred shall be considered as having been born in the country to which such territory was transferred.

d) When the maximum number of aliens of any nationality who may be admitted in any fiscal year under this Act shall have been admitted all other aliens of such nationality, except as otherwise provided in this Act, who may apply for admission during the same fiscal year shall be excluded:

[1] Extract from "An Act to Limit the Immigration of Aliens into the United States," approved May 19, 1921, and amended May 11, 1922, chap. 187, 42 *U.S. Statutes at Large* 540 (67th Congress, 2d session).

[2] [Certain classes of aliens are not counted against the quotas, e.g., government officials, aliens in continuous transit, alien tourists, aliens who have resided continuously for at least five years immediately preceding the time of their application for admission to the United States in Canada, Cuba, or Central and South America, and aliens under eighteen who are the children of American citizens.]

Provided, That the number of aliens of any nationality who may be admitted in any month shall not exceed 20 per centum of the total number of aliens of such nationality who are admissible in that fiscal year: *Provided further*, That aliens returning from a temporary visit abroad, aliens who are professional actors, artists, lecturers, singers, nurses, ministers of any religious denomination, professors for colleges or seminaries, aliens belonging to any recognized learned profession, or aliens employed as domestic servants, may, if otherwise admissible, be admitted notwithstanding the maximum number of aliens of the same nationality admissible in the same month or fiscal year, as the case may be, shall have entered the United States; but aliens of the classes included in this proviso who enter the United States before such maximum number shall have entered shall (unless excluded by subdivision [a] from being counted) be counted in reckoning the percentage limits provided in this Act: *Provided further*, That in the enforcement of this Act preference shall be given so far as possible to the wives, parents, brothers, sisters, children under eighteen years of age, and fiancées, (1) of citizens of the United States, (2) of aliens now in the United States who have applied for citizenship in the manner provided by law, or (3) of persons eligible to United States citizenship who served in the military or naval forces of the United States at any time between April 6, 1917, and November 11, 1918, both dates inclusive, and have been separated from such forces under honorable conditions.

SEC. 3. That the Commissioner General of Immigration, with the approval of the Secretary of Labor, shall, as soon as feasible after the enactment of this Act, and from time to time thereafter, prescribe rules and regulations necessary to carry the provisions of this Act into effect. He shall, as soon as feasible after the enactment of this Act, publish a statement showing the number of aliens of the various nationalities who may be admitted to the United States between the date this Act becomes effective and the end of the current fiscal year, and on June 30 thereafter he shall publish a statement showing the number of aliens of the various nationalities who may be admitted during the ensuing fiscal year. He shall also publish monthly statements during the time this Act remains in force showing the number of aliens of each nationality already admitted during the then current fiscal year and the number who may be admitted under the provisions of this Act during the remainder of such year, but when 75 per centum of the maximum number of any nationality admissible during the fiscal year shall have been admitted such statements shall be issued weekly thereafter. All statements shall be made available for general publication and shall be mailed to all transportation companies bringing aliens to the United States who shall request the same and shall file with the Department of Labor the address to which such statements shall be sent. The Secretary of Labor shall also submit such statements to the Secretary of State, who shall transmit the information contained therein to the proper diplomatic and consular officials of the United States, which officials shall make the same available to persons intending to emigrate to the United States and to others who may apply. . . . .

SEC. 6. That it shall be unlawful for any person, including any transportation company other than railway lines entering the United States from foreign contiguous territory, or the owner, master, agent, or consignee of any vessel, to bring to the United States either from a foreign country or any insular possession of the United States any alien not admissible under the terms of this Act or regulations made thereunder, and if it appears to the satisfaction of the Secretary of Labor that any alien has been so brought, such person or transportation company, or the master, agent, owner, or consignee of any such vessel, shall pay to the collector of customs of the customs district in which the port of arrival is located the sum of $200 for each alien so brought, and in addition a sum equal to that paid by such alien for his transportation from the initial point of departure, indicated in his ticket, to the port of arrival, such latter sum to be delivered by the collector of customs to the alien on whose account assessed. . . . . Such fine shall not be remitted or refunded unless it appears to the satisfaction of the Secretary of Labor that such inadmissibility was not known to, and could not have been ascertained by the exercise of reasonable diligence by, such person, or the owner, master, agent, or consignee of the vessel. . . . .

13. Criticism of the Quota Law[1]

Under the provisions of this resolution the same exceptions which were heretofore made in the 3 per cent quota law in favor of the people of the States contiguous to the Canadian border are again granted. Another exception in favor of the States of Texas, Utah, Arizona, Colorado, New Mexico, and other border States is continued, so as to permit the employment therein of an unlimited number of Mexicans. The cigar manufacturers of Florida are also granted an exception, so that they can import from Cuba and other adjacent islands such help as is desired by them. The people of the United States who are not fortunate enough to reside in the States just mentioned are unable to obtain any household help, but no exception in their behalf has been made.

From July 1, 1921, up to December 31, 1921, inclusive, the number of aliens who have been admitted are 265,408; the number who have left the United States from July 1, 1921, up to December 31, 1921, inclusive, are 224,627, leaving a net gain of 40,781. . . . .

[1] "Report of the Minority of the House Committee on Immigration and Naturalization on House Joint Resolution 268, Recommending the Continuation of the Quota System," U.S. 67th Congress, 2d session, *House Report No. 710*, pp. 9–11. The minority report was signed by Representatives Isaac Siegel, of New York, and Adolph J. Sabath, of Illinois.

THE FEDERAL IMMIGRATION LAWS 243

It is now admitted by all that the finding of the Senate committee that "it is a well recognized fact that the immigration from southern and eastern Europe is to a very considerable extent made up of relatives coming to join relatives who have preceded them" is true. This further affirms what we have consistently contended in our previous reports that practically all who were coming here are doing so in order to join the surviving members of their families.

No previous immigration law enacted by Congress has caused more hardships and sufferings than the so-called quota law which we are asked to extend by this resolution for another year. Practically all of the newspapers at various times have reported cases of the return of members of families who were refused admission because the quota for a particular month had been exhausted. The provisions of this law are inhumane and unjust because immigrants are excluded or accepted solely on the basis of percentage. The mental, moral, and physical qualifications of immigrants are made a secondary consideration.

The 1920 census has been taken and the figures are now available. No logical reason can be urged why, if the principle of the quota law is correct, the 1920 statistics of population in the United States of the nationals of the particular countries should not be adopted as the basis of calculation. Furthermore, we repeat that the adoption as a basis of the 1910 census discriminates against the very people who have demonstrated their worth to the Nation during the late war.

Under the provisions of this resolution the doors of our country for those fleeing from religious or political persecution, whether at the hands of their own Government or otherwise, are closed when the 3 per cent limit has been reached.

Under this resolution, lecturers, singers, actors, and artists are permitted to come regardless of the quota, but parents and children over the age of 17, orphan brothers or sisters of American citizens, can not come in. No one can help but see the unfairness of legislation which permits the Japanese and Chinese students to come in but excludes students of every other nationality.

Creditable evidence was presented to the committee showing that a large number of unfortunate Armenians had their passports viséed many months before the quota law was enacted. Notwithstanding the fact that they suffered most during the war, on arrival here they found themselves barred by the present quota law, which this resolution seeks to extend for another year.

This law has misled many unfortunate immigrants in disposing of all their household effects, and then on arriving here finding themselves not permitted to land solely because the ship which brought them came across later than a faster vessel which had left later. The spectacle off Sandy Hook of ships arriving toward the end of the month waiting until after midnight for the beginning of a new month to enter the port has not been an infrequent one.

We exceedingly deplore that even the discretionary power formerly exercised by the Secretary of Labor has been taken away from him by the quota act.

We are unalterably opposed to the admission of any person into the United States who is not mentally, morally, and physically fit and who does not firmly believe in our institutions and our form of Government.

Above all administration expenses, over $10,000,000 has been put into the Treasury of the United States from visé fees and head taxes collected from immigrants, yet not a single dollar of this money has been used toward the elimination of the indescribable conditions which prevail at various immigration stations.

It is our firm belief that the failure to create a sufficient staff of inspectors to serve along the Canadian and Mexican borders has resulted in extensive smuggling. With approximately 23 examiners to look after 12,000,000 people who are passing to and fro from the United States into Canada, and vice versa, ... conditions against which we have repeatedly protested [must continue].

Those who favor complete restriction of immigration use as their weightiest argument the alleged failure of aliens to naturalize. The evidence of practically all of the naturalization division chiefs showed clearly that it was not the fault of the alien. The fault lies with Congress, as it has refused to provide a sufficient number of judges and clerks for naturalization purposes, and that notwithstanding the fact that over $800,000 above all expenses has come into the Treasury from naturalization fees. The alien desires to become an American citizen. To our minds this matter is one which is vitally important to the Nation. Relief should be promptly granted.

We reiterate that the quota law is inhumane and contrary to the highest American ideals and traditions. It has not met the approval of the American people and should not be continued.

14. Line Inspection at Ellis Island with Special Reference to the Mental Examination of Immigrants[1]

Immigrants, not traveling in the cabin, who enter the United States at the port of New York, are first brought to Ellis Island in order to undergo an examination to determine their fitness for admission.

The average immigrant remains at Ellis Island two or three hours, during which time he undergoes an examination by the Public Health Service

[1] Extract from E. H. Mullan, "Mental Examination of Immigrants, Administration and Line Inspection at Ellis Island" (Reprint No. 398 from the *U.S. Public Health Reports*, May 18, 1917), pp. 3–7, 9–10, 13–16.

in order to determine his mental and physical condition, and by the Immigration Service in order to find out whether he is otherwise admissible.

Immigrants are brought from the various steamships throughout New York Harbor to Ellis Island by means of barges. As soon as they land at Ellis Island they undergo the medical inspection and examination which are conducted by the officers of the Public Health Service.

LINE INSPECTION

Upon entering the examination plant of the Public Health Service, the immigrants are guided by an attendant into the different inspection lines. These lines, separated by iron railings, are four in number at their proximal end and two in number at their distal end. . . . .

Four medical officers who carry on the general inspection are stationed each in one of the four proximal lines, and two medical officers stand at the extreme ends of the two distal lines or just where these lines merge into two common exits.

At this merging point stands an attendant whose duty it is to separate the chalk-marked aliens from those who are not chalk marked. Accordingly, immigrants who have passed the medical inspection are guided into the exit which leads to the upper hall of the Immigration Service, while the chalk-marked ones pass through the exit which leads to the examination department of the Public Health Service. . . . .

Every immigrant in undergoing the medical inspection passes two medical officers. As above stated, the officer who occupies the proximal position carries on the general inspection.

It is the function of this officer to look for all defects, both mental and physical, in the passing immigrant. As the immigrant approaches, the officer gives him a quick glance. Experience enables him in that one glance to take in six details, namely, the scalp, face, neck, hands, gait, and general condition, both mental and physical. Should any of these details not come into view, the alien is halted and the officer satisfies himself that no suspicious sign or symptom exists regarding that particular detail. For instance, if the immigrant is wearing a high collar, the officer opens the collar or unbuttons the upper shirt button and sees whether a goiter, tumor, or other abnormality exists. A face showing harelip, partial or complete, is always stopped in order to see if a cleft palate, a certifiable condition, is present.

It often happens that the alien's hand can not be distinctly seen; it may be covered by his hat, it may be hidden beneath his coat, or it may be deeply embedded in blankets, shawls, or other luggage. Of all the physical details in the medical inspection of immigrants it is perhaps most important to watch the hands. In many cases where the hands can not be plainly seen at a glance further searching has revealed a deformed forearm, mutilated or paralyzed hand, loss of fingers, or favus nails.

Likewise, if the alien approaches the officer with hat on he must be halted, hat removed, and scalp observed in order to exclude the presence of favus, ringworm, or other skin diseases of this region of the body. Pompadours are always a suspicious sign. Beneath such long growths of hair are frequently seen areas of favus. The slightest bit of lameness will show itself in an unevenness of gait or a bobbing up-and-down motion. After constantly observing the passing of thousands of immigrants the experienced eye of an examiner will quickly detect the slightest irregularity in gait. Where the alien carries luggage on his shoulder or back, it may be necessary to make him drop his parcels and to walk 5 or 10 feet in order to exclude suspicious gait or spinal curvature. Immigrants at times carry large parcels in both arms and over their shoulders in order that the gait resulting from a shortened extremity or ankylosed joint may escape notice. In like manner they maneuver in attempting to conceal the gaits of Little's disease, spastic paralysis, and other nervous disorders. All children over 2 years of age are taken from their mothers' arms and are made to walk. As a matter of routine, hats and caps of all children are removed, their scalps are inspected, and in many cases palpated. If care is not exercised in this detail, ringworm and other scalp conditions are apt to escape the attention of the examiner.

Immigrants that are thin and of uncertain physical make-up are stopped while the officer comes to a conclusion as to the advisability of detaining them for further physical examination. A correct judgment is often arrived at in these cases by the officer placing his hands against the back and chest of the alien, so as to obtain an idea of thoracic thickness, and also by feeling the alien's arm. Very often a thin and haggard face will show on palpation a thick thorax and a large, muscular arm.

Many inattentive and stupid-looking aliens are questioned by the medical officer in the various languages as to their age, destination, and nationality. Often simple questions in addition and multiplication are propounded. Should the immigrant appear stupid and inattentive to such an extent that mental defect is suspected, an X is made with chalk on his coat at the anterior aspect of his right shoulder. Should definite signs of mental disease be observed, a circle X would be used instead of the plain X. In like manner a chalk mark is placed on the anterior aspect of the right shoulder in all cases where physical deformity or disease is suspected.

In this connection B would indicate back; C, conjunctivitis; CT, trachoma; E, eyes; F, face; Ft, feet; G, goiter; H, heart; K, hernia; L, lameness; N, neck; P, physical and lungs; Pg, pregnancy; Sc, scalp; S, senility. The words hand, measles, nails, skin, temperature, vision, voice, which are often used, are written out in full.

The alien after passing the scrutiny of the first medical officer passes on to the end of the line, where he is quickly inspected again by the second examiner. This examiner is known in service parlance as "the eye man." He stands at the end of the line with his back to the window and faces the approaching alien. This position affords good light, which is so essential for eye examinations. The approaching alien is scrutinized by the eye man immediately in front of whom the alien comes to a standstill. The officer will frequently ask a question or two so as to ascertain the condition of the immigrant's mentality. He may pick up a symptom, mental or physical, that has been overlooked by the first examiner.

He looks carefully at the eyeball in order to detect signs of defect and disease of that organ and then quickly everts the upper lids in search of conjunctivitis and trachoma. Corneal opacities, nystagmus, squint, bulging eyes, the wearing of eye glasses, clumsiness, and other signs on the part of the alien, will be sufficient cause for him to be chalk-marked with "Vision." He will then be taken out of the line by an attendant and his vision will be carefully examined. If the alien passes through this line without receiving a chalk mark, he has successfully passed the medical inspection and off he goes to the upper hall, there to undergo another examination by officers of the Immigration Service, who take every means to see that he is not an anarchist, bigamist, pauper, criminal, or otherwise unfit.

Roughly speaking, from 15 to 20 per cent of the immigrants are chalk-marked by the medical officers, and it is these chalked individuals who must undergo a second and more thorough examination in the examination rooms of the Public Health Service. Those aliens marked X and circle X are placed in the mental room. All other marked aliens are placed in the two physical rooms, one for men and the other for women.

The physical details in the medical inspection of immigrants have been dwelt on at some length, and necessarily so, because a sizing up of the mentality is not complete without considering them. Speech, pupil symptoms, goiters, palsies, atrophies, scars, skin lesions, gaits, and other physical signs, all have their meaning in mental medicine.

In the medical inspection, which is conducted by the first officer or the one who occupies the proximal position, attention is paid to each passing alien. The alien's manner of entering the line, his conversation, style of dress, any peculiarity or unusual incident in regard to him are all observed. Knowledge of racial characteristics in physique, costume and behavior are important in this primary sifting process.

Every effort is made to detect signs and symptoms of mental disease and defect. Any suggestion, no matter how trivial, that would point to abnormal mentality is sufficient cause to defer the immigrant for a thorough examination. . . . .

WEEDING-OUT PROCESS

The immigrants who are chalk marked with an X or a circle X at the line inspection are taken immediately to the mental room. This is a large room containing two examining desks and 18 benches upon which the detained immigrants sit. The benches are arranged in rows and face the examining desks. This room will seat 108 immigrants and in an emergency can comfortably accommodate double that number.

At the termination of the line inspection, the line officers go to the different examination rooms. Two or three of them usually proceed to the mental room and there conduct the secondary mental inspection, or, as it is sometimes styled, the "weeding-out" process.

In this room the examiner faces the detained passengers who occupy the benches and calls them up, one at a time, to his desk in order to give them another brief inspection.

This secondary inspection consists in observing the X-marked alien as he approaches the desk, takes his seat, and responds to tasks in counting, addition, and Cube Test. The examiner then decides as to whether or not the subject is a suspect of mental abnormality. Should the examiner decide to detain the immigrant as a mental suspect, a yellow "hold card" is issued, and the immigrant is held over night in order to undergo a complete mental examination.

However, if an alien does not present sufficient symptoms to become a mental suspect, the examiner presents him with a small gray card, which either frees him entirely from the medical department or returns him to one of the physical examination rooms.

In the weeding-out process the examiner constantly observes the marked aliens seated in front of him. During such observation insane persons not infrequently show symptoms. It occasionally happens that an X-marked alien while sitting on one of the benches will do some strange thing or exhibit some symptom of psychosis, in which event he immediately becomes a circle X case. The circle X cases are examined by means of an interpreter, after which they are either liberated or held for further mental examination.

At the line inspection about 9 out of 100 immigrants are set aside as mental suspects in order to undergo the secondary or weeding-out process. Out of the 9 immigrants thus put aside 1 or 2 are ordered detained for a thorough mental examination. This last detention lasts anywhere from 24 hours to a week before the case is finally disposed of. Most of the detained circle X cases are sent immediately to the hospital for observation and examination, while the X cases are detained in the detention rooms of the Immigration Service.

The examining officer in sending the suspect to the hospital makes a notation on the alien's "hold card." This notation is either a statement of the principal symptoms which have occurred or a statement as to why the alien is sent to the hospital for observation. . . . .

EXAMINATION

The third stage of the sifting process having been reached, it is found that there are two classes of mental cases to dispose of: namely, the cases which have been sent to the hospital for observation, and those which are

THE FEDERAL IMMIGRATION LAWS   249

held in the detention rooms for further examination. What becomes of the first class of cases, and how they differ from the ordinary run of insane persons, will not be touched on here. The disposition of the latter class of cases will now be described.

The examination proper of the detained mental suspects occurs on days or at times when the line inspection is not in operation. Twenty-four hours, however, always intervene between the time of arrival and the first regular examination.

The regular mental examinations are conducted in a number of rooms, each of which is provided with chairs, benches, and an examining desk which contains suitable blanks and psychological apparatus. In each examination room is a medical officer who examines with the aid of an interpreter the detained immigrants one at a time.

The following hypothetical explanation, which corresponds closely with the facts, is given in order to show how the third stage in the mental examination of aliens takes place.

Suppose three large and two small immigrant ships arrive at the port of New York on September 1 and 2. Suppose also that they bring 2,500 steerage passengers and that 40 of them are presented with "hold cards" and are detained in the detention rooms for further mental examination. We shall now see what becomes of these 40 detained persons.

The line inspection does not take place on September 3, hence the day is spent largely in the mental examination of the detained cases. Early on this day the 10 detained Italians are sent to room A to be examined by doctor A. Ten Greeks go to room B to be examined by doctor B. Ten Irish are examined in room C by doctor C, while the 10 miscellaneous cases are examined in room D by doctor D.

The first examination on September 3 is comparatively brief, the main purpose being to weed out the normals who have recovered from a physiological upset arising from various causes incident to landing. The first examination of an alien is performed in the presence of all the aliens of the same group. In many instances each alien is put through the same tests and questions. This is done in order that the normals, who observe and learn from what the others are doing, may be more readily separated from the stupid or subnormal cases. On the afternoon of September 3, we find that out of the 40 immigrants that have been examined, 24 have given evidence of normality and have been liberated while 16 are still held for further examination. On the morning of September 4 there are no immigrants to land. Consequently the examination of the detained cases is resumed. This morning the remaining five Italians are examined in room B by doctor B, the five Greeks in room C by doctor C, the three Irish in room D by doctor D, while doctor A examines the three miscellaneous cases (West India negro, Englishman, Scandinavian) in room A. In other words, a shift has taken place and each detained immigrant now meets a different examiner who puts him through a more searching examination than he encountered on September 3.

The second examination of each immigrant consumes anywhere from 20 to 60 minutes. It may comprise an inquiry into the home life, customs, schooling, occupation, voyage, and intentions of the subject. When necessary, questions are put in order to bring to light the whys and wherefores regarding the immigrant's attitude, emotional states, habits, interests, and health. In addition to the psychological tests and questions a neurological examination and test of vision are occasionally made. An endeavor is made at this examination to size up the immigrant from all angles. At the second examination it will be found that the more intelligent immigrants have improved in their execution of the various tests and can still be classed among the normals. They are consequently liberated, and only those who still show symptoms of mental deficiency or mental abnormality are detained. During the second examination one of the detained aliens is found to be markedly inattentive and exhibits a facial mannerism. Consequently he is considered an insane suspect and is sent to the hospital for observation. Therefore at noon on September 4, when the line inspection again begins, only 6 of the original 40 immigrants remain for further examination. They are distributed as follows: Italians 3, Greek 1, Irish 2.

On September 5 at 11 A.M., during a temporary recess in the line inspection, a third examination of the 6 detained immigrants takes place. This time the three Italians are examined in room C by doctor C, the Greek in room D by doctor D, while the two Irish are examined by doctor A. This is the third regular examination, at which time the most obvious cases of mental deficiency are certified. This examination is thorough and in all respects resembles the second examination. During the third examination one of the Italians, although stupid, showed a definite improvement in responding to questions and in performing the tests. While a border-line case, there was a doubt in the mind of doctor C as to how the immigrant should be classified. He was consequently liberated by doctor C. At 4 P.M., September 5, we find that a Greek, an Italian, and an Irishman have been certified as being feeble-minded, while an Irishman and an Italian are still held for further mental examination.

On September 6, the line inspection is in operation all day and the mental cases can not be taken up. On September 7, the two detained cases are again examined which results in certifying the Italian as "Feeble-minded" and in detaining the Irishman for further examination. On September 8, this Irishman is again carefully examined and certified as "Feeble-minded." Thus it is seen that 5 immigrants out of the original 40 are certified as "Feeble-minded."

While the above description of the examination and certifying process is hypothetical, it is believed that it is a fair presentation of what actually happens. It is the rule that no immigrant is certified as being feeble-minded until he has had 3 regular examinations. In some cases 4 and even 5 examinations are given before such a certificate is rendered.

It is certain that the experience gained in the careful examination of subnormal immigrants is of much assistance to medical officers when conducting the primary line inspection.

No attempt is here made to explain the various mental abilities in normal and defective immigrants. It may be said, however, that certificates of feeble-mindedness are not rendered because an alien failed on this test or that test or because he is at a certain mental age according to a certain standard. The immigrant is certified "Feeble-minded" because his common knowledge, retentiveness of memory, reasoning power, learning capacity, and general reaction are severally and distinctly below normal. The feeble-minded alien learns with difficulty, his attention may be at fault, he may exhibit peculiar and subnormal mental traits, all of which point to an awkward mentality, which is beyond hope of much improvement. His appearance, stigmata, and physical signs may confirm such diagnosis. It is further believed by the certifying officer that his mental condition will decidedly handicap him among his fellows in the struggle for existence. The following table is inserted in order to show what was accomplished in the mental examination of aliens in the line department at Ellis Island during the months of June, July, and August, 1916.

[EXAMINATION OF ALIENS AT ELLIS ISLAND, SUMMER, 1916]

	Number of Steerage Passengers Inspected on the Line	Chalk Marked with X or a Circle X at Line Inspection	Liberated in Weeding-out Room on Day of Arrival	Given "Hold Cards" and Detained	Certified on Line		
					Feeble-minded	Imbecile	Epileptic
June.........	11,465	1,219	974	245	35	1	....
July..........	8,282	936	737	199	15	....	1
August.......	10,964	895	729	166	20	....	.....
Total....	30,711	3,050*	2,440	610*	70	1	1

* Some of these aliens were sent to the hospital and there certified as insane and feeble-minded. The total number of mental certificates at Ellis Island for the months of June, July, and August was 108.

There is individuality in each officer's method of conducting a mental examination. There is also a great deal in common about the various examination methods. Some tests and questions are used by all, while individual preference obtains in regard to other tests. As time goes on, new tests and methods are tried, and the ones that are found to be of value are adopted by all. Other tests are tried, found to be useless, and are given up.

SECTION III

SELECTED IMMIGRATION CASES: COURT DECISIONS[1]

1. "Person Likely to Become a Public Charge" Defined

Wallis v. U.S. ex rel. Mannara[2]

CIRCUIT JUDGE MANTON:

The appellees sued out a writ of habeas corpus, asking a review of an order of deportation made by the Commissioner of Immigration and subsequently approved on appeal by the Secretary of Labor. Both appellees, subjects of the kingdom of Italy, arrived in the United States on the steamship "Madonna" on September 7, 1920. Salvatore Mannara was 54 years of age and Rosaria Mannara was his daughter. They were accompanied by a son and brother, Antonio. While at Ellis Island, Salvatore and Rosaria were examined by the medical examiner and were found physically defective. The medical certificate in the case of Salvatore especially specified senility, which may affect ability to earn a living, and in the case of Rosaria, grave valvular disease, chronic and cardiac, which may affect ability to earn a living.

On September 8, 1920, Salvatore was given a hearing and testified that, in addition to the son and daughter accompanying him, he had a wife and three children in Italy; that he and his son were laborers, and his daughter was a dressmaker. He stated he had $100 and was coming to his two brothers. Both brothers testified to the same effect, and said they were

---

[1] It has already been pointed out (p. 100) that the extracts from court decisions in this section have been chosen, not because of their importance as "ruling cases" from the lawyer's point of view, but because of the social interest that attaches to the court's interpretation and discussion of the immigration law and its administration. Legal points are in general omitted. Omissions are, however, indicated in the customary method except where the references cited in the court's opinion have been simplified. In the references to statutes, only the first reference to the statutes at large is given, and additional references, for example, to the annotated statutes are omitted. Duplicate references to cases are also omitted.

For citations to other cases and a discussion of legal problems of the immigration law, the law encyclopediae should be consulted, especially *Corpus Juris*, Vol. II, article on "Aliens," Section VI, "Exclusion and Expulsion"; *Ruling Case Law*, Vol. I, article on "Aliens," Section V, "Immigration"; *American and English Encyclopedia of Law* (2d ed.), Vol. XV, article on "Immigration." See also Clement L. Bouvé, *Laws Governing the Exclusion and Expulsion of Aliens* (Washington, D.C., 1912).

[2] From 273 Federal Reporter 509 (1921).

fully able to support Salvatore and his two children, and declared their intention to do so. The Board of Special Inquiry excluded Salvatore and his two children, and advised them of their right to appeal from its decision to the Secretary of Labor in Washington for a review of the case. Their finding is found in the following language:

It is the unanimous opinion of the Board that the aliens are likely to become a public charge, for the following, among other reasons: They arrive here with a small amount of money, insufficient to provide for their necessary wants any reasonable length of time; they have no one in the United States who could be held legally liable for their maintenance; the father is 54 years of age, certified for senility, and would not be capable of continued self-support; we further find that the certified condition of the father and daughter is of such a nature as will affect their ability to earn a living.

The order of deportation was approved by the Acting Secretary of Labor "after carefully considering the evidence presented in the record," and deportation was directed.

1, 2. The order below directed the discharge. The decision on the writ provided:

"Relators released upon giving a bond for $1,000 for each relator; condition, none will become a public charge."

We know of no provision of law which warrants a release upon bond. If the appellees were entitled to enter the country, and therefore to their discharge, they were entitled to enter free from the condition of a bond. Immigration Act 1917, Section 3, provides (39 Stat. 874 [Comp. St. 1918, Comp. St. Ann. Supp. 1919, section 4289$\frac{1}{4}$b]):

SEC. 3. That the following classes of aliens shall be excluded from admission into the United States: . . . . Persons not comprehended within any of the foregoing excluded classes who are found to be and are certified by the examining surgeon as being mentally or physically defective, such physical defect being of a nature which may affect the ability of such alien to earn a living . . . . persons likely to become a public charge. . . . .

There is a finding by the Board of Special Inquiry, which is approved by the Department of Labor, certifying to a physical condition of both of the relators, which may affect their ability to earn a livelihood. There is evidence to support this finding that the relators were likely to become public charges. The court's jurisdiction, when the remedy of a writ of habeas corpus is invoked in immigration cases, is to inquire whether the ground of exclusion given by the administrative authorities is without any evidence to support it. Unless there is no evidence at all proving or tending to prove that an alien is within one of the excluded classes, the decision of the immigration authorities is conclusive upon the court, even though the evidence to the contrary be very strong. . . . .

3. A person likely to become a public charge is one whom it may be necessary to support at public expense by reason of poverty, insanity and poverty, disease and poverty, idiocy and poverty. *Ex parte Mitchell*

(D.C.) 256 Fed. 229. We think that the finding by the administrative authorities, showing a physical defect of a nature that may affect the ability of the relator and appellee to earn a living, is sufficient ground for exclusion. His physical condition, together with his financial condition, having but $100 with him, justified the conclusion of the administrative authorities in finding that he and his children were aliens likely to become public charges. Howe v. *United States*, 247 Fed. 292.

The order sustaining the writ is reversed, with directions to dismiss the writ, and that the appellees be remanded to the custody of the appellant, to be deported to the country from whence they came in conformity with the law.

2. "Ability to Earn a Living" and Economic Conditions in the United States

Gegiow v. Uhl, Acting Commissioner[1]

MR. JUSTICE HOLMES:

The petitioners are Russians seeking to enter the United States. They have been detained for deportation by the Acting Commissioner of Immigration and have sued out a writ of *habeas corpus*. The writ was dismissed by the District Court and the Circuit Court of Appeals. . . . . By the return it appears that they are a part of a group of illiterate laborers, only one of whom, it seems, Gegiow, speaks even the ordinary Russian tongue, and in view of that fact it was suggested in a letter from the Acting Commissioner to the Commissioner General that their ignorance tended to make them form a clique to the detriment of the community; but that is a trouble incident to the immigration of foreigners generally which it is for legislators not for commissioners to consider, and may be laid on one side. The objection relied upon in the return is that the petitioners were "likely to become public charges for the following, among other reasons: That they arrived here with very little money ($40 and $25, respectively), and are bound for Portland, Oregon, where the reports of industrial conditions show that it would be impossible for these aliens to obtain employment; that they have no one legally obligated here to assist them; and upon all the facts, the said aliens were upon the said grounds duly excluded," etc. We assume the report to be candid, and, if so, it shows that the only ground for the order was the state of the labor market at Portland at that time; the amount of money possessed and ignorance of our language being thrown in only as make-weights. It is true that the return says for that "among other reasons." But the state of the labor market is the only one disclosed in the evidence or the facts that were noticed at the hearing, and the only one that was before the Secretary of Labor on Appeal; and as the order was general

[1] From 239 United States Reports 8 (1915).

for a group of twenty it cannot fairly be interpreted to stand upon reasons undisclosed. Therefore it is unnecessary to consider whether to have the reasons disclosed is one of the alien's rights. The only matter that we have to deal with is the construction of the statute with reference to the present case.

The courts are not forbidden by the statute to consider whether the reasons, when they are given, agree with the requirements of the act. The statute by enumerating the conditions upon which the allowance to land may be denied, prohibits the denial in other cases. And when the record shows that a commissioner of immigration is exceeding his power, the alien may demand his release upon *habeas corpus*. The conclusiveness of the decisions of immigration officers under section 25 is conclusiveness upon matters of fact. This was implied in *Nishimura Ekiu* v. *United States*, 142 U.S. 651, relied on by the Government. As was said in *Gonzales* v. *Williams*, 192 U.S. 1, 15, "as Gonzales did not come within the act of 1891, the Commissioner had no jurisdiction to detain and deport her by deciding the mere question of law to the contrary." Such a case stands no better than a decision without a fair hearing, which has been held to be bad. *Chin Yow* v. *United States*, 208 U.S. 8. . . . .

The single question on this record is whether an alien can be declared likely to become a public charge on the ground that the labor market in the city of his immediate destination is overstocked. In the act of February 20, 1907, c. 1134, section 2; 34 Stat. 898; as amended by the act of March 26, 1910, c. 128, section 1; 36 Stat. 263, determining who shall be excluded. "Persons likely to become a public charge" are mentioned between paupers and professional beggars and along with idiots, persons dangerously diseased, persons certified by the examining surgeon to have a mental or physical defect of a nature to affect their ability to earn a living, convicted felons, prostitutes and so forth. The persons enumerated in short are to be excluded on the ground of permanent personal objections accompanying them irrespective of local conditions unless the one phrase before us is directed to different considerations than any other of those with which it is associated. Presumably it is to be read as generically similar to the others mentioned before and after.

The statute deals with admission to the United States, not to Portland, and in section 40 contemplates a distribution of immigrants after they arrive. It would be an amazing claim of power if commissioners decided not to admit aliens because the labor market of the United States was overstocked. Yet, as officers of the General Government, they would seem to be more concerned with that than with the conditions of any particular city or State. Detriment to labor conditions is allowed to be considered in section 1, but it is confined to those in the continental territory of the United States and the matter is to be determined by the President. We cannot suppose that so much greater a power was entrusted by implication in the same act to every commissioner of immigration, even though subject to appeal, or that the result was intended to be effected in the guise of a decision that the aliens were likely to become a public charge. *Order reversed.*

3. Surgeon's Certificate of Physical Defect

Canfora v. Williams, Immigration Commissioner[1]

DISTRICT JUDGE HOLT:

This is a rehearing on a writ of habeas corpus granted to test the legality of the detention of Vincenzo Canfora, who is held under an order for his deportation. Canfora is an Italian 60 years old. He came to this country with his family in 1895, 16 years ago. He was early in life an engraver, and later a book binder, both of which are arts which usually require artistic skill and intelligence. He has a wife and six children, all of whom but one are now adults. About six years ago gangrene developed in his foot, which ultimately made necessary the amputation of his leg. Last summer he went to Italy to visit his mother. Shortly before his return, the commissioner of immigration received the following letter:

Dec. 16/10

Honorable Commissary of Emigration
Ellis Island, N.Y.

SIR: I beg to inform you that on the S.S. "Cincinnati" due from Naples next Monday will arrive in New York, as a passenger of second class cabin, the Italian Vincenzo Canfora, 60 years old.

The same, when in New York, was recovered, on public charge, at the Bellevue Hospital, where a foot was amputated to him. He was deported nine months ago by the Italian Consulate as a destitute.

He has no relatives here who can support him, while at Naples Canfora has brothers and sisters with means and can take good care of him.

Very respectfully,

JOSEPH RUGGIO

Upon his arrival, therefore, he was detained, the usual proceedings for an investigation followed, and an order for his deportation was issued on the ground that he was liable to become a public charge. He has about $200 deposited in the bank. Most of his children are adults, earning good wages. They are able and willing to support him, and they offer to give a surety company bond, in any amount required, to indemnify against his becoming a public charge. The facts in regard to the charge in Ruggio's letter that he was a charity patient at Bellevue Hospital when his foot was amputated, to which much weight was given by the inspector who reported in favor of deportation, were these: About seven months passed after the gangrene developed in his foot before the amputation. During that period he had expended about $1,500 for medical services in an effort to be cured.

[1] From 186 Federal Reporter 354 (1911).

Most of his children at that time were not self-supporting. The doctor advised that he should go to a hospital for the amputation. He went to Bellevue Hospital, and felt that under the circumstances he was justified in asking them to perform the amputation without compensation. The hospital authorities did so, and have never asked for compensation, or complained that it was not paid. The facts in regard to the charge in Ruggio's letter that he was deported by the Italian consul as a destitute are these: Canfora had an old friend who was an assistant in the Italian consul's office. Canfora had frequently made him presents of books which he had bound. When the friend learned that he was about to go to Italy, he offered to get him transportation. Canfora at first refused, stated that he could purchase his ticket. But his friend urged him to accept it as a gift to a friend, and in recognition of Canfora's previous gifts to him. Canfora thereupon accepted the ticket, and went to Italy on it.

The alien's counsel urges that the fact that the alien had established a residence and lived for 16 years in this country makes the law inapplicable to him, and cites rule 4 of the rules relating to the exclusion of aliens, prescribed by the Department of Commerce and Labor, which states that the provisions of the immigration act do not apply to aliens who have once been duly admitted to the United States. That rule was adopted under the earlier immigration acts. Those acts described the persons who are liable to deportation as immigrants, and the courts in construing those acts held that the term "immigrants" only applied to aliens on their first arrival in this country, and did not apply to aliens who had been duly admitted to the country and had established a residence here, and who had left the country for a temporary absence. In 1903 Congress amended the immigration acts (Act March 3, 1903, c. 1012, 32 Stat. 1213), and substituted the term "aliens" for the term "immigrants." The courts thereupon held that under such amendments the law applied to all aliens whether they had previously entered this country or not. . . . . The provisions of rule 4 have remained unchanged, but the rules, of course, are subordinate to the acts of Congress, and the provision of that rule which is relied on has been superseded by the later immigration acts.

I consider that, if this order of deportation is carried out, it will be an act of cruel injustice. If this alien had remained in this country, he probably never would have been molested. If he had not lost his leg, he probably would not have been detained on his return. No offense is charged against him. It is proposed to deport him because he has suffered a pitiable misfortune, and notwithstanding a proposition to give a satisfactory bond, which would appear to be a complete protection to the government from his becoming a public charge. But the immigration acts confer exclusive power upon the immigration officials to determine such questions, and the courts, so long as the procedure prescribed by the immigration acts and the rules established for their administration is substantially followed, have under the decisions of the United States Supreme Court no jurisdiction to interfere. I am therefore compelled to dismiss this writ. But I desire to express the hope that the immigration authorities will reconsider this case. I cannot believe that on a candid reconsideration of this record this man, who is charged with no offense, will be sent away, because he has suffered a grievous calamity and has been denounced by a malicious enemy, to pass his last years and to die in a distant land, far from his wife and children, and from the home in this country in which he has lived a blameless life for so many years.

4. Finality of Decision by Immigration Authorities; Certificate of Physical Defect

U.S. ex rel. Barlin v. Rodgers[1]

CIRCUIT JUDGE GRAY:

A careful examination of the records in each of the cases before us fails to convince us that any of the relators had other than a fair hearing before the inspectors and the special boards of inquiry, with full notice of their right of appeal to the Commissioner of Immigration and the Secretary of Commerce and Labor in Washington, of which rights the relators availed themselves. At the hearings, the aliens were present, testified in their own behalf, and it does not appear that the testimony of any witness offered by or on behalf of such aliens was refused. No criticism is made as to the fairness of the hearings, or as to the opportunity given to the aliens to testify and produce witnesses in their behalf. The objection urged is, either that there was no testimony, or insufficient testimony to warrant the findings of the inspectors. The records disclose the fact that in every case beside the examination of the alien, the testimony of witnesses summoned in his behalf was heard by the inspectors, and in some of the cases the certificates of the official surgeon, in regard to the physical disability, were produced. But more than all, the alien himself was present and subjected to personal examination by the inspectors. It is obvious that the printed record of the answers made by the alien and witnesses to the questions propounded by the inspectors, does not fairly present the case to us that was actually before the inspectors. The important factor of the impression made upon the inspectors by the personal appearance of, and the conversations had with, the aliens, is necessarily absent from the record. We can well conceive that such an impression would have a most important bearing upon the determination by the inspectors in those cases in which the alien was debarred from entry, on the ground that he was likely to become a public charge, or as having been certified by the examining surgeon as mentally or physically defective in such a way as to affect his ability to earn a living.

[1] From 191 Federal Reporter 973 (1911).

We are not at liberty to set aside such determination, because on the record we think we might or would have reached a different conclusion. . . . .

Taking up the cases separately, we turn to that of Michael Barlin. It is disclosed by the record in his case that he arrived at the port of Philadelphia on the 25th day of September, 1910; that upon his arrival, he was given a physical and mental examination by medical officers of the United States Public Health and Marine Hospital Service; that he was given a hearing before a board of special inquiry, as provided for by the act of 1907, at which hearing he was examined at length, as were also the witnesses who were called in his behalf; that the medical officer who made the examination certified that Michael Barlin "had a rudimentary right hand, congenital, affecting his ability to earn a living." This certificate does not appear in the printed record. The original thereof, however, has been produced at the hearing, and by consent of counsel for the respondent has been incorporated therein. At the conclusion of the hearing, there is the following entry:

This alien has a certificate against him of a nature which may affect his ability to earn a living and render him likely to become a public charge, but as the relatives have signified their ability to furnish bond, the board is unanimous to withhold the final decision, in order that the case may be submitted to the Bureau for consideration as to whether or not the bonding privilege should prevail.

This application to the Bureau was accordingly made and refused by the Acting Secretary of Commerce and Labor. Thereupon, we find the following entry in the record:

September 31, 1910.—Telegram receipt from the Bureau this day to effect that the Secretary denied the bond application in the case of Michael Barlin.
The case was further considered by the board, and it was the unanimous decision to exclude, as likely to become a public charge, for the reason that he is certified as having a rudimentary right hand, affecting his ability to earn a living.
Excluded by original board.
Alien advised of right of appeal.

While it is true that the record produced in the court below on habeas corpus proceedings must show a regular procedure by the ministerial officers of the government, in accordance with the requirements of the law, to justify an order of deportation, it is only a substantial conformity of the procedure to such requirements that is demanded and a technical precision in the exemplification of the record is not to be looked for.

If the surgeon's certificate, by reason of its failure to certify that the defect would affect the alien's ability to earn a living, was not to be considered as final under the rules of the Bureau, it seems to us that it was clearly within the power of the board to take the finding of the physical defect into consideration with the examination and the other evidence in excluding, on the ground that the respondent was likely to become a public charge, and that this was the ground of the exclusion is emphasized by the fact that the alien is advised of the right of appeal. We find nothing in the record, therefore, indicating that in any respect the alien was deprived of any right accorded to him by law or regulation, nor do we find anything in the conduct of the case from which this court would have jurisdiction to review the findings of facts made by the board.

In the case of the appellant, Zozie Popek, we find the same situation as in the Barlin Case. There is no contention that the board acted beyond the scope of their authority, but only the suggestion that they acted upon insufficient evidence. The alien in this case was subjected to a personal examination, and two witnesses named by him were called in his behalf. The order entered by the board was as follows:

In view of the appearance of this alien, and the fact that he stammers to such an extent that he can scarcely make himself understood, and has a wife and four small children in Russia dependent upon him for support, this board unanimously votes to exclude him as a person likely to become a public charge.

Notified of his right of appeal.

To assert the right to review the findings of the board in this regard would be to open the door for a review of every case in which it is suggested that the findings of fact are not in accord with the weight of the evidence.

In the case of Attanasio Parebianco, the record shows that the alien was sworn and personally examined by the board of special inquiry. At such examination, he declared that he was 17 years of age. His cousin, residing in Philadelphia, was examined in his behalf and the board made the following entry:

The unanimous opinion of the board is that the alien, Attanasio Parebianco, is a person likely to become a public charge, because of the fact that he has very little money, is only 17 years of age and is very small for his age, which would prevent his earning his own living, and has no one in the United States who would be responsible for him except his cousin.

Notified of his right of appeal.

Appeal was made and record transmitted to the Commissioner General of Immigration. Five days thereafter, the Acting Secretary notified the Immigration Service in Philadelphia that the excluding decision of the board had been affirmed.

We cannot say that in this case there was no evidence upon which the board was authorized to act, and especially we cannot ignore the weight that the personal inspection of the alien may have had upon the minds of the inspectors. No ground is presented by which the finality of the decision by the immigration authorities can be avoided. . . . .

5. Crime Involving Moral Turpitude Defined

Prentis, Immigration Inspector v. Stathakos[1]

CIRCUIT JUDGE GROSSCUP:

The appeal is on behalf of the government, and from an order releasing appellee on a writ of habeas corpus from the custody of the appellant, who had him in charge, as immigrant inspector, to return to Greece under the immigration laws. . . . . The arrest and proposed deportation is under that section of the statute relating to aliens who have been convicted in their own country of crimes involving moral turpitude, or who have admitted the commission of such crimes—the evidence before the Secretary of Commerce and Labor consisting of a statement by affidavit of the petitioner admitting that he was convicted of the crime of murder, accompanied by his statement in detail of the circumstances that attended the commission of the crime. . . . .

Congress has chosen to exclude from our soil aliens who admit that in their own country they had been convicted of crimes involving moral turpitude; Congress has provided that such exclusion shall extend to those who have succeeded in getting through the port of entry but have, within three years, been apprehended by the authorities—the arrest and deportation of such persons being only a continuation of the exercise of the same power at the port; a supplemental proceeding provided in case the immigrant escapes the department at the port; and Congress has chosen that not only shall the deportation be conducted by the Department of Commerce and Labor, but the question whether the person involved is an alien upon whom such exclusion acts shall be a question also for the Department of Commerce and Labor. Under these provisions appellee has been adjudged by the Secretary of Commerce and Labor to be an alien within the deportation provisions of the act. Congress having this power, the court below was without jurisdiction to issue the writ, unless the record shows that the appellee did not come within the power conferred on the Secretary of Commerce and Labor.

Appellee admits the shooting; admits the conviction in the courts of Greece; and admits that a sentence of seven years was imposed upon him, which he served. These circumstances carry a strong conviction that the crime was a serious one and that the necessity of a severe disciplinary punishment was recognized. We have no authority to say that the courts of Greece are cruel, or unjust, or inhuman, or anything but fair; and such a sentence implies that, if the court be not unjust, nor cruel, nor inhuman, nor unfair, the crime for which it was inflicted was more than the result of accident or self-defense. Instead, therefore, of the record failing to show any case falling within the power conferred upon the Secretary of Commerce

[1] From 192 Federal Reporter 469 (1911).

and Labor, it shows a case that circumstantially supports the finding of the Secretary of Commerce and Labor.

True, the crime was committed when the appellee was but fourteen years old. He came to this country immediately upon the sentence being served and lived here ten or fifteen years, acquiring property. Unfortunately for him, he then returned to Greece, and thereby, by coming back, laid the foundation for his deportation, notwithstanding his long residence and good record. These circumstances undoubtedly lay the foundation for the exercise of a broader discretion in cases like this than the mere plain enforcement of the act. But whatever discretion shall be exercised is for the Secretary of Commerce and Labor, and not for the courts.

The order appealed from is reversed and the case remanded with instructions to deny the petition and remand the petitioner to the custody of the appellant.

6. Interpretation of the Contract Labor Law
Church of the Holy Trinity v. *United States*[1]

MR. JUSTICE BREWER:

Plaintiff in error is a corporation, duly organized and incorporated as a religious society under the laws of the State of New York. E. Walpole Warren was, prior to September, 1887, an alien residing in England. In that month the plaintiff in error made a contract with him, by which he was to remove to the city of New York and enter into its service as rector and pastor; and in pursuance of such contract, Warren did so remove and enter upon such service. It is claimed by the United States that this contract on the part of the plaintiff in error was forbidden by the act of February 26, 1885, 23 Stat. 332, c. 164, and an action was commenced to recover the penalty prescribed by that act. The Circuit Court held that the contract was within the prohibition of the statute, and rendered judgment accordingly (36 Fed. Rep. 303); and the single question presented for our determination is whether it erred in that conclusion. . . . .

We cannot think Congress intended to denounce with penalties a transaction like that in the present case. It is a familiar rule, that a thing may be within the letter of the statute and yet not within the statute, because not within its spirit, nor within the intention of its makers. This has been often asserted, and the reports are full of cases illustrating its application. This is not the substitution of the will of the judge for that of the legislator, for frequently words of general meaning are used in a statute, words broad enough to include an act in question, and yet a consideration of the whole legislation, or of the circumstances surrounding its enactment, or of the absurd results which follow from giving such broad meaning to the words, makes it unreasonable to believe that the legislator intended to include the particular act. . . . .

[1] From 143 United States Reports 457 (1892).

.... Now, the title of this act is, "An Act to Prohibit the Importation and Migration of Foreigners and Aliens under Contract or Agreement to Perform Labor in the United States, Its Territories and the District of Columbia." Obviously the thought expressed in this reaches only to the work of the manual laborer, as distinguished from that of the professional man. No one reading such a title would suppose that Congress had in its mind any purpose of staying the coming into this country of ministers of the gospel, or, indeed, of any class whose toil is that of the brain. The common understanding of the terms labor and laborers does not include preaching and preachers; and it is to be assumed that words and phrases are used in their ordinary meaning. So whatever of light is thrown upon the statute by the language of the title indicates an exclusion from its penal provisions of all contracts for the employment of ministers, rectors, and pastors.

Again, another guide to the meaning of a statute is found in the evil which it is designed to remedy; and for this the court properly looks at contemporaneous events, the situation as it existed, and as it was pressed upon the attention of the legislative body (*United States* v. *Union Pacific Railroad*, 91 U.S. 72, 79). The situation which called for this statute was briefly but fully stated by Mr. Justice Brown when, as District Judge, he decided the case of *United States* v. *Craig* (28 Fed. Rep. 795, 798):

The motives and history of the act are matters of common knowledge. It had become the practice for large capitalists in this country to contract with their agents abroad for the shipment of great numbers of an ignorant and servile class of foreign laborers, under contracts, by which the employer agreed, upon the one hand, to prepay their passage, while, upon the other hand, the laborers agreed to work after their arrival for a certain time at a low rate of wages. The effect of this was to break down the labor market, and to reduce other laborers engaged in like occupations to the level of the assisted immigrant. The evil finally became so flagrant that an appeal was made to the Congress for relief by the passage of the act in question, the design of which was to raise the standard of foreign immigrants, and to discountenance the migration of those who had not sufficient means in their own hands, or those of their friends, to pay their passage.

It appears, also, from the petitions, and in the testimony presented before the committees of Congress, that it was this cheap unskilled labor which was making the trouble, and the influx of which Congress sought to prevent. It was never suggested that we had in this country a surplus of brain toilers, and, least of all, that the market for the services of Christian ministers was depressed by foreign competition. Those were matters to which the attention of Congress, or of the people, was not directed. So far, then, as the evil which was sought to be remedied interprets the statute, it also guides to an exclusion of this contract from the penalties of the act.

A singular circumstance, throwing light upon the intent of Congress, is found in this extract from the *Report of the Senate Committee on Education and Labor*, recommending the passage of the bill:

The general facts and considerations which induce the committee to recommend the passage of this bill are set forth in the *Report of the Committee of the House.* The committee report the bill back without amendment, although there are certain features thereof which might well be changed or modified, in the hope that the bill may not fail of passage during the present session. Especially would the committee have otherwise recommended amendments, substituting for the expression "labor and service," whenever it occurs in the body of the bill, the words "manual labor" or "manual service," as sufficiently broad to accomplish the purposes of the bill, and that such amendments would remove objections which a sharp and perhaps unfriendly criticism may urge to the proposed legislation. The committee, however, believing that the bill in its present form will be construed as including only those whose labor or service is manual in character, and being very desirous that the bill become a law before the adjournment, have reported the bill without change [6059, *Congressional Record,* 48th Congress.]

And, referring back to the report of the Committee of the House, there appears this language:

It seeks to restrain and prohibit the immigration or importation of laborers who would have never seen our shores but for the inducements and allurements of men whose only object is to obtain labor at the lowest possible rate, regardless of the social and material well-being of our own citizens and regardless of the evil consequences which result to American laborers from such immigration. This class of immigrants care nothing about our institutions, and in many instances never even heard of them; they are men whose passage is paid by the importers; they come here under contract to labor for a certain number of years; they are ignorant of our social condition, and that they may remain so they are isolated and prevented from coming into contact with Americans. They are generally from the lowest social stratum, and live upon the coarsest food and in hovels of a character before unknown to American workmen. They, as a rule, do not become citizens, and are certainly not a desirable acquisition to the body politic. The inevitable tendency of their presence among us is to degrade American labor, and to reduce it to the level of the imported pauper labor [*Congressional Record,* 48th Congress, p. 5359].

We find, therefore, that the title of the act, the evil which was intended to be remedied, the circumstances surrounding the appeal to Congress, the reports of the committee of each house, all concur in affirming that the intent of Congress was simply to stay the influx of this cheap unskilled labor. . . . .

7. The Spirit and Purpose of the Contract Labor Statutes

Botis v. Davies et al., Immigration Inspectors[1]

DISTRICT JUDGE SANBORN:

The return to the writ of habeas corpus shows the reason for the detention complained of, and the evidence upon which an order for the deportation of petitioner was based. He is a Greek, 18 years of age, held for depor-

[1] From 173 Federal Reporter 996 (1909).

tation under the contract labor statutes. He came to this country April 3, 1907, when Immigration Act March 3, 1903, c. 1012, 32 Stat. 1213, was in force. On November 11, 1908, a warrant for his arrest was issued to the respondent Seraphic [an immigration inspector] setting forth that Botis was a contract laborer and a member of the excluded classes, in that he migrated to this country pursuant to an offer, solicitation, promise or agreement, made previous to such migration, to perform labor herein, and directing the inspector to take the alien into custody and enable him to show cause why he should not be deported. He was arrested, and a hearing had; a copy of the evidence being attached to the return. The evidence was submitted to the Secretary of Commerce and Labor, and, being satisfied that Botis was a member of the excluded classes in that he is a contract laborer, the Secretary used his warrant directing his return to his native country. He then sued out habeas corpus, and the case was heard on the petition and return.

The evidence taken by the inspector is clear and undisputed, and consists of an affidavit and sworn testimony of petitioner. It shows that before emigration he wrote to one Alexios Delyannis, of Chicago, whose wife and petitioner's mother are second cousins, asking whether he could receive him and give him work in his place of business if he came to the United States. Delyannis answered by letter, saying he could do so. Petitioner's father mortgaged some property owned by him in Greece in order to pay the passage money. If Delyannis had written him that he could not give him a job, but that he might stay at his house until he could get one, he would have come just the same. When young Botis got to Chicago, Delyannis received him at his house, and gave him work in a bootblacking establishment conducted by him at $180 a year and his board. He worked at this for fourteen months, saving all his wages, and then left the work and Delyannis' house, bought a horse and wagon, and went into the business of peddling fruit. At the time of giving his testimony he was earning at this business $3 to $4 a day, and had his horse and wagon and about $100 held for him by his uncle, George Malliris.

Upon the evidence the Department of Labor has reached the conclusion that Botis is a contract laborer, subject to deportation, and is in this country in violation of the acts of Congress of March 3, 1903, and February 20, 1907 (34 Stat. 898, c. 1134). Turning to those statutes it is found that neither one of them seems to apply to the case. The statute of 1903 makes no provision for the exclusion of contract laborers. It describes 11 classes of undesirables who are to be excluded, but entirely omits all mention of contract laborers. This act was in force in April, 1907, when Botis was admitted to this country; but, as it does not cover the case of contract laborers, it need not be further noticed on this point (32 Stat. 1214). The other statute, relied on by the immigrant inspectors, and cited by the Secretary of Commerce and Labor as authorizing the deportation, does, indeed, cover contract laborers, including those who have been induced or solicited to emigrate by offers or promises of employment (34 Stat. 898). But it contains a section making it entirely inapplicable to this case, reading as follows:

Nothing contained in this act shall be construed to affect any prosecution, suit, action or proceedings brought, or any act, thing or matter, civil or criminal, done or existing at the time of the taking effect of this act; but as to all such prosecutions, suits, actions, proceedings, acts, things, or matters, the laws or parts of laws repealed or amended by this act are hereby continued in force and effect [Act Feb. 20, 1907, c. 1134, sec. 28, 34 Stat. 907].

The act of 1907, therefore, is wholly prospective in its operation. The language used in the quoted section could hardly be made more comprehensive or explicit. All acts, things, and matters done or existing when the statute took effect are governed by earlier laws. The date of taking effect was July 1, 1907, several months after Botis landed. So there can be no question that the act of 1907 has no bearing or effect on Botis' status, which is governed entirely by pre-existing laws. The act of 1903, as has been seen, has no application, and prior legislation must be examined. It may be said, however, that a warrant of exclusion based entirely on inapplicable laws does not commend itself to the judgment, or occupy a very favorable position, in a case involving personal liberty. A proceeding so preemptory and harsh as deportation, savoring so much of punishment, should have a better basis than statutes which are applicable wholly to different conditions of immigration.

Looking, then, to the earlier laws, it is found that the only one which may apply is Act Feb. 26, 1885, c. 164, 23 Stat. 332, and upon examination of its provisions it is also found inapplicable. It is a penal statute, and denounces the prepayment by any person or corporation of the transportation of an emigrant under contract to perform labor in the United States, as well as the assisting or encouraging of his importation or migration. It also makes such a contract void. It falls far short of reaching the facts of this case. Botis emigrated on his own initiative, without being solicited to do so by Delyannis, and also without being induced to come by the promise of employment. Nor was there any contract or agreement to perform labor in this country; no wages being agreed on, nor definite time, and Botis being under age. What Botis and Delyannis did was most usual and proper. The boy wished to come, so he simply wrote to a distant relative about it, and was promised work and a temporary home. Neither could have understood that he was doing anything unlawful or improper. If Delyannis in any way assisted or encouraged Botis to come, pursuant to any offer, solicitation, promise, or agreement, he was liable to a penalty of $1,000.
. . . . It is clear that the act of Delyannis,.in answering Botis' letter, and saying he would receive him and give him employment, had nothing intentionally criminal in it. On the contrary, it was a worthy and laudable act. He was not trying to hurt the labor market, reduce American labor to the

level of assisted emigrants, or lower the character of foreign immigration, but was simply responding to a reasonable and proper appeal to considerations of country and relationship. The immigration officers have inadvertently extended the statute so as to cover a case neither within the letter nor spirit of the law, and have done so without even mentioning the only statute which can possibly apply to the case. They have applied a rigorous rule to a worthy alien, industrious, prudent, and self-supporting, who has every prospect of becoming a good and desirable citizen; and they now insist that their finding of facts, that Botis was a contract laborer under the acts of 1903 and 1907, although those laws are most clearly inapplicable, is final and conclusive, and must be accepted in this proceeding without question.

Before examining this question, a word in regard to the object of the exclusion statute may not be out of place. In several cases persons plainly within the letter of the contract labor statutes, but not within their spirit or purpose, have been held not to be within such statutes. It had been the practice for capitalists to import in large numbers an ignorant and servile class of foreign laborers, under contracts by which the employer agreed, on the one hand, to prepay their passage, while, on the other, the laborers agreed to work after their arrival for a certain time at a low rate of wages. The effect was to break down the labor market, and reduce other laborers in like occupations to the level of the assisted emigrants.

The evil finally became so flagrant that an appeal was made to Congress for relief by the passage of the act in question, the design of which was to raise the standard of foreign immigrants, and to discountenance the migration of those who had not sufficient means in their own hands, or those of their friends, to pay their passage [*U.S.* v. *Laws*, 163 U.S. 258, 263].

We find, therefore, that the title of the act, the evil which was intended to be remedied, the circumstances surrounding the appeal to Congress, the reports of the committee of each house, all concur in affirming that the intent of Congress was simply to stay the influx of this cheap, unskilled labor [*Church of the Holy Trinity* v. *U.S.*, 143 U.S. 457].

It seems needless to say that $15 a month and board for a 16-year-old boy is not cheap labor, nor calculated to injure the domestic supply. Botis was neither solicited nor induced to migrate. He had made no contract. He expected to obtain no cheap labor. He is in business for himself, earning his own living and more, and is fully within that liberal and enlightened policy which has always dominated our naturalization laws, and accomplished so much for our own nation and for those accepting its benefits. America means something to the emigrant, whether he is from England or Sweden, Little Russia or Armenia. Many a man now representing the best American manhood was, when he came to this country, though then perhaps of full age and stature, utterly unable to read or write. No industrious or self-supporting emigrant should be cast out because of a technical infraction only of a loosely drawn statute, which has often been interpreted not to mean what it says. Botis has long ceased to be in a position where he could by any possibility be classed as a contract laborer; much less should he be excluded when he does not come within the statute at all. Banishment, as Justice Brewer has well said, is a punishment of the severest sort, and should not be inflicted in a case like this, unless the law positively and unequivocally demands it.

But it is said that these questions are wholly reserved to the political department, with which the courts have nothing to do; and this is often a question of considerable difficulty. There is nothing in the law which expressly makes the decisions of those officers conclusive. Sections 25 of the acts of 1903 and 1907 both provide that, when an alien is refused admission (never being allowed to land, or only pending further examination) "the decision of the appropriate immigration officers, if adverse to the admission of such alien, shall be final, unless reversed on appeal to the Secretary of Commerce and Labor." Such appeal is provided for in the same section. But in case of aliens who have been permitted to land, and have become in all respects subject to our jurisdiction and part of our population, but who are found within a limited time to fall within an excluded class, there is no express provision that the decisions of the department shall be final. No appeal is provided, but simply a warrant of deportation of the Secretary of Commerce and Labor, when he shall be satisfied that the alien is here in violation of law. The effect of such decisions by immigration officers has been often discussed by the courts, with a general disposition to hold them final within certain limits. Many of these cases are those involving the right to land, not to stay after landing. In such cases the statute expressly gives an appeal, and makes the decision conclusive. By such express provision a presumption arises that the official decisions in other cases was not to be a finality. . . . .

I am convinced that in this case the officers have unwittingly gone outside the law, that great injustice would result from carrying out their decision, and that the court is not bound thereby. No criticism of immigration officers as a class is intended, or would be justified. They have been "loyal to the interests of their country," and have on the whole discharged their onerous and difficult duties "humanely, justly, and without prejudice, with men of every kindred and tongue and people and nation."

The petitioner should be discharged.

8. Contract Labor: "Implied Offer of Employment"

United States v. *International Silver Company*[1]

CIRCUIT JUDGE WARD:

This is an action by the government to collect the penalty provided in section 5 for violation of section 4 of the Immigration Act of 1907 (34 Stat. 898).

[1] From 271 Federal Reporter 925 (1921).

The complaint contained two counts. The first alleged that Mrs. George C. Pearson, a citizen of Great Britain, residing in Nova Scotia, on or about February 29, 1916, wrote to the defendant which operated a factory at Meriden, Connecticut, seeking employment for herself as a hand burnisher, and also inquiring whether the defendant had positions open for men, as her husband and son likewise wished employment. March 9, 1916, the defendant answered this letter as follows:

DEAR MADAM:

Referring to yours of the 29th ult., we are in need of hand burnishers that have had experience on the general line of hollow ware, such as tea ware, waiters, meat dishes, cake baskets, sandwich trays, nut bowls, etc., made of German or nickel silver, also white enamel. We are also looking for unskilled men. Our female help in the burnishing line average from $12\frac{1}{2}$ cents per hour to 20 cents per hour; unskilled labor $17\frac{1}{2}$ cents to 25 cents per hour. The girl's minimum wage is $12\frac{1}{2}$ cents per hour. If you were in the States, and applied to us for a position, we could place you.

March 15, George C. Pearson answered the defendant's letter to the effect that his wife was unable to accept employment, but that he and his son were ready to start at once, if assured of employment by the defendant. March 20, 1916, the defendant replied as follows:

DEAR SIR:

Referring to yours of the 15th, will say that conditions stated in your letter are satisfactory and we will keep a place open for Mrs. Pearson. Kindly advise when you will report for duty.

The complaint went on to allege that on or about April 4, 1916, George C. Pearson migrated from Nova Scotia to Meriden; that by means of the aforesaid express and implied promise of employment the defendant knowingly assisted, encouraged, and solicited the immigration of the aforesaid alien into the United States, he not being exempt under the last two provisions of section 2 of the act. The second count set up the same allegations as to George C. Pearson, Jr. Each count prays judgment against the defendant in the sum of $1,000. . . . .

1, 2. It seems to us quite plain that the defendant's answer of March 9, 1916, to Mrs. Pearson's letter of February 29 was an implied offer of employment to both Mrs. Pearson and her husband and son and a solicitation to them to migrate to this country to perform labor here. They were consequently contract laborers within section 2 of the act. Furthermore, the defendant's reply of March 20, 1916, to George C. Pearson's letter of March 15 was an encouragement to both Pearson and his son to migrate to the United States within section 4 of the act. That section is not limited to encouragement by prepaying transportation of contract laborers but extends to encouragement "in any way." Asking contract laborers, who said they were ready to start at once if assured of employment by the defendant, when they will report for duty is a manifest encouragement. Both these contract laborers did migrate to the United States after receiving the letter.

3. Counsel argued that these replies of the defendant to the letters of the aliens were mere courtesies and as such did not violate either the letter or the spirit of the statute. They rely for this on the case of *Botis* v. *Davies* (D.C.) 173 Fed. 996, which arose under the Act of March 3, 1903, 32 Stat. 1213, containing an entirely different provision. It excluded aliens—

. . . . Whose ticket or passage is paid for with the money of another, or who is assisted by others to come, unless it is affirmatively and satisfactorily shown that such person does not belong to one of the foregoing excluded classes; but this section shall not be held to prevent persons living in the United States from sending for a relative or friend who is not of the foregoing excluded classes [sec. 2].

It was no doubt to correct the liberality of the act in this respect that the provision was repealed by section 43 of the act of 1907 and the much stricter provision enacted in its place. We are quite clear that the defendant violated the act as charged in each count both in letter and in spirit.

The judgment is therefore reversed.

9. Domiciled Alien Subject to Immigration Act

Lewis v. *Frick, United States Immigration Inspector*[1]

MR. JUSTICE PITNEY:

. . . . The alien had an established domicile and residence in the United States dating from September 20, 1904, having obtained his admission into the country legally, and maintained a domicile here continuously from the date of his entry until the time of his arrest; and it is insisted that the fact of his having crossed the river into Canada, even though it was done with the object of bringing a woman into this country for the purpose of prostitution, did not bring him within the reach of the Immigration Act or subject him to the summary procedure therein prescribed.

This question is settled adversely to the contention of petitioner by our recent decision in *Lapina* v. *Williams*, 232 U.S. 78. That case arose under the act of February 20, 1907, while this arises under the same act as amended March 26, 1910. But the changes are not such as to affect the authority of that decision upon the present point.

In *Lapina* v. *Williams* it did appear that the alien had practiced prostitution for many years before her temporary departure from the country, and that she not only returned with the intent to continue the practice but did almost immediately engage in it, and continued it until her arrest under the provisions of the Immigration Act. But the real ground of decision was that Congress in the act of 1903 sufficiently expressed, and in the act of

[1] From 233 United States Reports 291 (1914).

1907 reiterated, the purpose of extending the prohibition against the admission of aliens of certain classes, and the mandate of their deportation, to all aliens within the descriptive terms of the excluding clause, irrespective of any qualification arising out of a previous residence or domicile in this country. This view was based (*a*) upon the legislative history of the act of 1903 (from which the material provisions of the 1907 act were taken), ... (*b*) upon the clear language of the excluding clause of section 2 of the act of 1907 (quoted in full, 232 U.S. 91); (*c*) upon the fact that none of the excluded classes (with the possible exception of contract-laborers) would be any less undesirable if previously domiciled in the United States; and (*d*) upon the fact that the section contains its own specific provisos and limitations, which, upon familiar principles, tend to negative any other and implied exception.

We hold, therefore, that the fact that the petitioner, Lewis, had been domiciled for six years or more in this country, he remaining still an alien, did not change his status so as to exempt him from the operation of the Immigration Act; and that if he departed from the country, even for a brief space of time, and on reentering brought into the country a woman for the purpose of prostitution or other immoral purpose, he subjected himself to the operation of the clauses of the Act that relate to the exclusion and deportation of aliens, the same as if he had had no previous residence or domicile in this country. In short, the period of three years from entry, prescribed by sections 20 and 21, runs not from the date when the alien first entered the country, but from the time of the prohibited entry; that is to say, in the present case, the entry made by the alien when bringing in the woman.

The next question is whether there was sufficient evidence to fairly sustain the finding of the Secretary of Commerce and Labor to the effect that petitioner did on November 17, 1910, import and bring into the United States a woman for an immoral purpose. Upon this question, petitioner's contention was and is, that the woman is in fact his wife. He testified that he married her in Warsaw shortly before he came from Russia to this country, and that when he brought her across the river from Windsor he intended that he and she should live together in Detroit as husband and wife. The contention of respondent was and is, that the story of the marriage was a pure fabrication, resorted to in the effort to conceal the fact that the woman was a prostitute and imported by petitioner for immoral purposes. There is much in the evidence to support this view. . . . .

This being so, and there being no contention that the hearing was not fairly conducted, the finding of the Secretary upon the question of fact is binding upon the courts. *Low Wah Suey* v. *Backus*, 225 U.S. 460, 468; *Zakonaite* v. *Wolf*, 226 U.S. 272, 275. . . . .

The final contention is that petitioner should have been deported to Canada, whence he came upon the occasion of his unlawful entry into this country, rather than to Russia, the land of his birth, from which he came six years earlier. By Section 20, the alien is to be "deported to the country whence he came at any time within three years after the date of his entry into the United States"; by section 21, the Secretary of Commerce and Labor, upon being satisfied that an alien is subject to deportation, "shall cause such alien within the period of three years after landing or entry therein (within the United States) to be taken into custody and returned to the country whence he came, as provided by section 20 of this Act"; by section 3, an alien convicted thereunder is at the expiration of his sentence to be "returned to the country whence he came, or of which he is a subject or a citizen in the manner provided in sections 20 and 21 of this Act"; and by section 35, "The deportation of aliens arrested within the United States after entry and found to be illegally therein, provided for in this act, shall be to the trans-Atlantic or trans-Pacific ports from which said aliens embarked for the United States; or, if such embarkation was for foreign contiguous territory, to the foreign port at which said aliens embarked for such territory."

Petitioner not having been convicted under section 3, his destination is to be determined rather in the light of sections 20, 21, and 35. And first, we take it to be clear (notwithstanding the peculiar phraseology of section 20) that the three-year period limits only the authority to deport, and does not affect the determination of the country to which an alien is to be deported. Respecting this matter, the sections are somewhat lacking in clearness. But, at least, section 35 indicates a legislative intent that aliens subject to deportation shall be taken to trans-Atlantic or trans-Pacific ports, if they came thence, rather than to foreign territory on this continent, although it may have been crossed on the way to this country. This was recognized by Rule 38 of the Immigration Regulations, in force December 12, 1910.

It is to be noted that the classes of aliens who are subject to deportation are not wholly made up of those who enter in violation of the law; in some cases cause for deportation may arise after a lawful entry. And in many cases the unlawfulness of the entry may not be discovered until afterwards. The theory of the Act, as expressed in section 2, is that the undesirables ought to be excluded at the seaport or at the frontier; but sections 20, 21, and 35, recognize that this is not always practicable. Of course, if petitioner's attempt to bring a woman into the country for an immoral purpose had been discovered in time, he might have been physically excluded from entry at Detroit upon his return from Windsor. In that event he would naturally have remained upon Canadian soil. But since his offense was not discovered in time to permit of his physical exclusion, so that he becomes subject to the provisions for deportation, his destination ought not to be controlled by the factitious circumstance that he went into Canada to procure the prostitute. And, upon the whole, it seems to us that the Act reasonably admits of his being returned to the land of his nativity, that being in fact "the country whence he came" when he first entered the United States. See *Lavin* v. *LeFevre*, 125 Fed. 693, 696; *Ex parte Hamaguchi*, 161 Fed. 185, 190; *Ex parte Wong You*, 176 Fed. 933, 940; *United States* v. *Ruiz*, 203 Fed. 441, 444. We need go no farther, and may therefore leave undecided the question whether the Act leaves any room for discretion on the part of the Secretary of Commerce and Labor.

10. Detention When Deportation Is Impossible

Ex parte Matthews[1]

DISTRICT JUDGE NETERER:

1. The petitioner under oath charges that:

"Under the provisions of the United States immigration statute on the 19th day of February, 1921, after a due hearing, it was determined by said Secretary of Labor for the United States that your petitioner had been born in and was a citizen of Ukrania[2] aforesaid, and should be deported thence under the provisions of the immigration statute above referred to; that ever since said date your petitioner has been and still is unlawfully and unreasonably restrained of his liberty in the county jail . . . . under the pretended authority of said warrant or order of deportation; and that said restraint is unreasonable and unlawful in this: That the government of the United States, as your deponent is informed and believes, has no diplomatic relations with the government of Ukrania, and is unable to execute its order or warrant of deportation aforesaid, and is unable to deport your petitioner to said Ukrania, and is making no attempt to do so, and has no intention of so doing, and that, unless the said Henry M. White, Commissioner of Immigration aforesaid, is prevented from so doing he will continue unlawfully and unreasonably to restrain your petitioner of his liberty, and confine him as a prisoner in the county jail of King county aforesaid, all in violation of your petitioner's right under the Constitution and laws of the United States,"

—and prays a writ. A writ was issued, and a return and supplemental return made, in which the record taken before the Commissioner of Immigration is set out, from which it appears that the department is unable to secure a "Polish passport" for the petitioner, for the reason "that no satisfactory information has been furnished as to alien's place of birth." The order is to deport the petitioner "to his home in Ukrania." This was entered on the 19th day of February, 1921.

2. A supplemental return is presented, stating that the warrant of deportation has been amended, directing the deportation of petitioner to

[1] From 277 Federal Reporter 858 (1921).

[2] [The spelling of "Galacia" and "Ukrania" is necessarily retained as in the text of the decision.]

"Eastern Galacia," to which is attached a telegram from the Assistant Secretary of Labor as follows:

"Ukrania and Eastern Galacia two separate countries with separate and distinct governments of their own. Not recognized by the United States. Town of which Jack Matthews is native is now in Eastern Galacia and passport had to be secured from Eastern Galacian representative before deportation could take place. Warrant of deportation is hereby amended directing deportation of alien to Eastern Galacia."

The testimony shows that the Bureau of Immigration had determined as a fact that the petitioner was a native of Ukrania. A party may not be deported to any country other than of his nativity or of his allegiance. There is no established fact in the record, and none has been presented before the court, upon which to predicate an order of deportation to Eastern Galacia. It appears that Ukrania, Galacia, and Eastern Galacia are distinct sovereignties; that—

"The Galacian Republic is now temporarily in exile outside the boundaries of its country because Galacia in 1919 . . . . was militarily occupied by Poland, and that Eastern Galacia is a separate state."

The Eastern Galacian government it appears in the record is contending against the occupation by Poland. It further appears that Eastern Galacia is regarded as a distinct entity, whose political status has not yet been determined.

"The Supreme Council, by its decisions of December 8, 1919, defined the so-called Curzon-Pope line as the extreme eastern *temporary* boundary of Poland" [italics mine].

This boundary line excludes all of Eastern Galacia, together with Lemberg, capital of that country. There is no evidence as to the location of this line, and it is admitted that Poland is the de facto military occupant of Eastern Galacia, and the Galacian government, so-called, is in exile. It is stated that the petitioner was born in Kaminetz, Podolska province, Ukrania; that he left his place of birth when 15 years of age, and came to Ontario, Canada, with his parents, where he resided until his entry into the United States in 1917. There is no testimony (the telegram is not evidence) in the record or produced upon this hearing which would warrant the deportation of the petitioner to "Eastern Galacia."

It appearing that the petitioner cannot be deported to Ukrania, he will be discharged, unless within 10 days an appeal is prosecuted, pending which he may be released on his recognizance in the sum of $1,000, with sufficient sureties and the usual conditions.

11. Expulsion: What Constitutes a "Fair Hearing"

Whitfield, Immigrant Inspector, et. al. v. *Hanges et. al.*[1]

CIRCUIT JUDGE SANBORN:

George Hanges, Demetrios Lamper, Steve Pantza, and Peter Francas, citizens of Greece, were resident aliens who had been admitted to the United States pursuant to its acts of Congress prior to 1907. Two of them owned and operated the Main Café in Mason City, Iowa, where they had lived for years, and two of them were employed in the café. They were arrested by the immigrant inspector on October 24, 1913, and such proceedings were had that he found them guilty, recommended their deportation, and held them in confinement in the charge of the sheriff when, on their petition, the court below issued a writ of habeas corpus and, after a return thereto, and answer to the petition, and a full hearing, ordered their discharge. The inspector has appealed from this order on the grounds that the hearing of the appellees was full and fair, and that he committed no abuse of discretion or arbitrary action.

The deportation of the appellees was recommended by the inspector, and they were held in confinement under his finding that they were guilty of the charge that they were aliens employed by or in connection with a music or dance hall, or other place of amusement, habitually frequented by prostitutes, or where prostitutes gather, that they were aliens connected with the management of a house of prostitution, and that they were aliens found receiving, sharing or deriving benefit from a part or the whole of the earnings of prostitutes. . . . . It is well to call to mind the rules and principles which govern proceedings in cases of this nature.

1. A full and fair hearing on the charges which threaten his deportation and an absence of all abuse of discretion and arbitrary action by the inspector or other executive officer, are indispensable to the lawful deportation of an alien. Where, by the abuse of the discretion or the arbitrary action of the inspector, or other executive officer, or without a full and fair hearing, an alien is deprived of his liberty, or is about to be deported, the power is conferred and the duty is imposed upon the courts of the United States to issue a writ of habeas corpus and relieve him. . . . .

2. An alien, as well as a citizen, is protected by the prohibition of deprivation of life, liberty, or property without due process and the equal protection of the law. This principle is universal. It applies "to all persons within the territorial jurisdiction of the United States without regard to any differences of race, or color, or of nationality." . . .

An alien is entitled to a hearing upon and a decision of the charge that he has violated the acts of Congress and is therefore liable to deprivation of his liberty and deportation, according to "the fundamental principles

[1] From 222 Federal Reporter 745 (1915). See also Doc. 14, p. 288.

that inhere in due process of law." It is not competent for an inspector, or the Secretary of Labor, or any executive officer

.... Arbitrarily to cause an alien who has entered this country and has become subject in all respects to its jurisdiction and a part of its population, although alleged to be illegally here, to be taken into custody and deported without giving him an opportunity to be heard upon the questions involved, his right to be and remain in the United States. No such arbitrary power can exist where the principles involved in due process of law are recognized [Japanese Immigrant Case, 189 U.S. 86, 100, 101].

3. Indispensable requisites of a fair hearing according to these fundamental principles are that the course of proceeding shall be appropriate to the case and just to the party affected; that the accused shall be notified of the nature of the charge against him in time to meet it; that he shall have such an opportunity to be heard that he may, if he chooses, cross-examine the witnesses against him; that he may have time and opportunity, after all the evidence against him is produced and known to him, to produce evidence and witnesses to refute it; that the decision shall be governed by and based upon the evidence at the hearing, and that only; and that the decision shall not be without substantial evidence taken at the hearing to support it. .... That is not a fair hearing in which the inspector chooses or controls the witnesses, or prevents the accused from procuring the witnesses or evidence or counsel he desires. ....

4. The Secretary of Labor is authorized to make or approve such rules "not inconsistent with law" for the enforcement of the immigration laws as he deems desirable. .... Rule 22 of the Department of Labor provided in effect that the inspector prior to any arrest might procure the best proof that could be obtained to the effect that the aliens belonged to one or more of the classes subject to deportation after entry; that he might state the facts evidenced by this proof and apply for a warrant of arrest; that telegraphic application for such a warrant might "be resorted to only in case of necessity"; and that it must state that the usual written application had been made and mailed and the substance of the facts and proof contained therein. The inspector had no authority to administer an oath in the cases in hand. His power so to do is limited to administering oaths touching the right of any aliens to enter the United States. .... Nevertheless, between October 7 and October 23, 1913, the inspector gathered, mainly by the use of police officers of Mason City, a large number of prostitutes in the grand jury room in that city, and in the presence of the captain of police, or some other police officer, there questioned them, wrote down in narrative form purported statements made by them, went through the form of administering oaths to them, and on these statements applied for and obtained a telegraphic warrant for the arrest of the appellees, although they were permanent residents, two of them property owners and business men of Mason City, and there seems to have been no necessity whatever for desperate haste. ....

Rule 22, subd. 4 (a) provides that upon receipt of the warrant of arrest the alien shall be taken before the person or persons therein described and granted a hearing to enable him to show cause, if any there be, why he should not be deported, and that in the discretion of the immigration officer in charge, he may, pending determination of his case, be taken into custody or allowed to remain in some place deemed by such officer secure and proper, and that—

b) during the course of the hearing the alien shall be allowed to inspect the warrant of arrest, and all the evidence on which it was issued, and at such stage thereof as the officer before whom the hearing is held shall deem proper, he shall be apprised that he may thereafter be represented by counsel. . . . . If counsel be selected he shall be permitted to be present during the further conduct of the hearing, to inspect and make a copy of the minutes of the hearing, so far as it has proceeded, and to offer evidence to meet any evidence theretofore or thereafter presented by the government. . . . . (c) At the close of the hearing the full record shall be forwarded to the Bureau, together with any written argument submitted by counsel and the recommendations of the examining officer and the officer in charge as to whether or not a warrant for deportation shall issue.

The appellant received a telegraphic warrant of arrest, caused the appellees to be arrested, and was examining one of them and with his employés, Captain Campbell and another police officer, was holding them in confinement and preventing them from seeing or consulting with any other person, when their counsel appeared and demanded to see and consult with them and to take part in the examination. The inspector refused this request, permitted no one to see and consult with them until after he had examined each of them in secret. After their examination was completed he permitted them for the first time to see anyone but himself and the police officers and to have counsel and to introduce the testimony of witnesses. It will be noticed that the rule gives the inspector no authority secretly, in the presence of no one but himself and his police officers, whose presence and power unavoidably places the defenseless alien under fear and restraint, to examine or question him. It is limited to giving authority to the inspector to give the alien a hearing to enable him to show cause why he should not be deported, and by its terms it excludes a secret examination of the alien to extort a confession or evidence unfavorable to him. The provisions of the rule that the inspector shall grant the alien a hearing, that during the hearing he shall be permitted to inspect the warrant, and that at such stage thereof as the officer deems proper he shall be permitted to have counsel were made for the benefit of the alien for the purpose of giving him a fair trial. The liberty, and the property also, for if he is imprisoned and deported he must lose his business and sacrifice his property, of a permanent resident alien, like the appellees, as well as their deportation, are involved in the issue, and these provisions of the rule should be liberally construed to accomplish their plain purpose. To the same end the discretion of the inspector in determining when the alien shall inspect the warrant and when he shall have counsel should be exercised, so that his hearing shall be full and fair. A denial of permission to him to see the warrant and to have counsel[1] until within five minutes of the close of the hearing would be a clear abuse of discretion, and would render the provisions of the rule as administered "inconsistent with law" and void. Although a law or rule be fair and just in appearance, yet if it is applied and administered by public authority with an evil eye and an oppressive hand, so as to deprive a person of his fundamental rights, it cannot be sustained. . . . .

One of the objects of this rule was to give, not to deprive, the alien of the benefit of counsel. The time when an alien, who is ordinarily ignorant of the law, of legal procedure and of his rights, may derive the most benefit of counsel is when he is arrested and his hearing begins. It would have been no abuse of the discretion of the inspector to have permitted the appellees to have counsel to advise them immediately upon their arrest, and to have permitted them and their counsel to inspect the warrant of arrest, to be present and to take part in the proceedings at and after the first stage of the examination and hearing of the aliens. Such a course would have been in accord with the fundamental principles of English and American jurisprudence consistent with the law, and it should have been pursued. The refusal of the inspection of the warrant of arrest and the refusal to permit the aliens to see and consult their counsel before, and to permit them to participate in the proceedings at, their examination directly tended to prevent a fair hearing upon the charges against them.

5. Whether or not the weight of the evidence, in substantial conflict at the hearing, sustained the charges against the appellees is a question of fact within the exclusive jurisdiction of the officers of the Department of Labor, and the courts, in the absence of fraud or mistake, are without jurisdiction to review or reverse their finding thereon.

But whether or not there was any substantial evidence at the hearing in support of those charges and of the finding of the inspector that they were proved, and of his recommendation that the aliens be deported, under which the appellees were being deprived of their liberty, is a question of law, the power and duty to determine which are vested in the courts, and any injurious error in deciding that question by any executive or quasi-judicial officer or tribunal is reviewable and remediable by them. Administrative orders and findings quasi-judicial in character are void if the finding is contrary to the "indisputable character of the evidence." . . . .

[1] [The old rule was changed after this decision so that the inspector was obliged to tell the alien at the beginning of the proceedings that he was entitled to counsel. For a discussion of this point and the change of the rule, temporarily, during the anarchist raids of 1919–20, see U.S. Congress, House Committee on Rules, *Investigation of Administration of Louis F. Post; Hearings on H. Res. 522* (66th Congress, 2d session, April-May, 1920), pp. 224–26. See below, Doc. 14, pp. 294–96.]

For the purpose of determining the question of law whether there was any substantial evidence to support the finding and recommendation of the inspector the evidence in this case has been carefully read and examined, and the irresistible conclusion is that there was no such evidence at the hearing, and that the undisputed evidence was that the charges against the appellees were baseless. This state of things resulted from the fact that the government introduced no evidence whatever at the hearing in support of the charges, the appellees under oaths administered by the inspector introduced their own testimony on which they were cross-examined by the inspector, and the testimony of 15 other witnesses on which they were cross-examined by the inspector, all of which tended to show that the charges were not true. Business men of Mason City and boarders at the Main Café of the appellees came to say that their restaurant was orderly and respectable, was patronized by all classes of people, business men, professional men, clerks, and that they never saw any evidence of the truth of the charges against the aliens. For example, J. C. Buchanan testified that he was 41 years of age; that he had been either a deputy sheriff or a police officer in Mason City most of the time from 1907 to 1913; that from February 13 to May 20, 1913, he was police officer; that during these three months he passed appellees' Main Café two or three times each night; that during March his beat extended past it; that its reputation was good; that it was patronized by the general run of people; that he had eaten there; that he had taken his wife to midnight lunches there several times; that at these times there were other people in the restaurant; that he certainly would not have taken his wife there if he had thought the place disreputable or disorderly. . . . .

6. That was not a fair hearing in which the inspector after the hearing imported into the case and based his finding and recommendation of deportation on hearsay and rumors of alleged facts which there was no evidence to support, and which the accused had no notice of and no opportunity to refute at the hearing. . . . .

And because the inspector arbitrarily prevented the aliens from consulting their counsel and arbitrarily prevented their counsel from being present and participating in the hearing until after the inspector had examined the aliens in secret, while he and the police officers held them in confinement; because there was no substantial evidence at the hearing in support of the charges against them; because the inspector prevented the accused from procuring testimony of important witnesses; because the inspector based his findings and recommendation of deportation on hearsay that was not in evidence at the hearing, and much of which the accused had no notice of and no opportunity to refute at the hearing- the conclusion is that the court below fell into no error and committed no mistake in its finding that the hearing of the accused was unfair and unjust and entitled the appellees to the relief of the court. . . . .

12. Status of a "Philosophic Anarchist" Defined

U.S. ex rel. John Turner v. Williams[1]

EXTRACT FROM STATEMENT OF THE CASE

The return stated:

"That the above named John Turner is an alien, a subject of the Kingdom of Great Britain and Ireland; that said alien came to the United States from England on or about ten days prior to October 24, 1903, as deponent is informed and believes.

"Said John Turner was arrested in the city of New York on or about October 23, 1903, under a warrant issued by the Secretary of the Department of Labor of the United States, and was taken to the Ellis Island immigration station, where he was examined by a board of special inquiry, duly constituted according to law, upon his right to remain in this country, and that said alien was by said board found to be an alien anarchist, and was by unanimous decision of said board ordered to be deported to the country from whence he came as a person within the United States in violation of law. That on October 26, 1903, said alien appealed from the said decision of the board of special inquiry to the Secretary of Commerce and Labor, who dismissed the appeal and directed that said alien be deported to the country from whence he came upon the ground that said alien is an anarchist and a person who disbelieves in and who is opposed to all organized government and was found to be in the United States in violation of the law.

"That annexed hereto is a copy of the above-mentioned warrant for the arrest and deportation of said John Turner, and copies of the minutes of said hearing before the board of special inquiry, and a copy of the order or decision of the Secretary of Commerce and Labor dismissing said appeal and again directing deportation. That said John Turner is now held in deponent's custody at the Ellis Island immigrant station pending deportation to the country from whence he came in accordance with the above-mentioned decision or order of the Secretary of Commerce and Labor."

The warrant issued by the Secretary was addressed to certain United States immigrant inspectors, and recited that from the proofs submitted the Secretary was satisfied that Turner, an alien anarchist, came into this country contrary to the prohibition of the act of Congress of March 3, 1903, and commanded them to take him into custody and return him to the country from whence he came at the expense of the United States. On appeal to the Secretary the record of proceedings before the board of inquiry was transmitted, and the Secretary held:

"The evidence shows that the appellant declined to give exact information as to the manner in which he secured admission to this country, although he swears that he arrived here about ten days ago. He admits that he is an anarchist and an advocate of anarchistic principles, which brings him

[1] From 194 United States Reports 279 (1903).

within the class defined by section 38 of the act approved March 3, 1903. In view of these facts, the appeal is dismissed and you are directed to deport the said John Turner in conformity with warrant now in your hands for execution."

The hearing before the Board of Inquiry was had October 24, 1903, and it appeared from the minutes thereof that Turner testified that he was an Englishman; that he had been in the United States ten days, and that he did not come through New York, but declined to either affirm or deny that he arrived *via* Canada; that he would not undertake to deny that he had in the lecture delivered in New York, October 23, declared himself to be an anarchist, which, he said, was a statement that he would make; and that the testimony of the inspectors was about correct. That evidence gave extracts from the address referred to including these: "Just imagine what a universal tie-up would mean. What would it mean in New York city alone if this idea of solidarity were spread through the city? If no work was being done, if it were Sunday for a week or a fortnight, life in New York would be impossible, and the workers, gaining audacity, would refuse to recognize the authority of their employers and eventually take to themselves the handling of the industries. . . . . All over Europe they are preparing for a general strike, which will spread over the entire industrial world. Everywhere the employers are organizing, and to me, at any rate, as an anarchist, as one who believes that the people should emancipate themselves, I look forward to this struggle as an opportunity for the workers to assert the power that is really theirs."

Certain papers were found on Turner, one of them being a list of his proposed series of lectures (which, when the warrant was in execution, he rolled up and threw away), the subjects including: "The legal murder of 1887," and "The essentials of anarchism"; notices of meetings, one of a mass-meeting November 9, at which "Speeches will be delivered by John Turner in English, John Most in German, and several other speakers. Don't miss this opportunity to hear the truth expressed about the great Chicago tragedy on the eleventh of November, 1887"; and another, stating: "It may be interesting to all that Turner has recently refused to accept a candidacy to Parliament because of his anarchistic principles. . . . ."

DECISION OF THE COURT

MR. CHIEF JUSTICE FULLER:

. . . . Repeated decisions of this court have determined that Congress has the power to exclude aliens from the United States; to prescribe the terms and conditions on which they may come in; to establish regulations for sending out of the country such aliens as have entered in violation of law, and to commit the enforcement of such conditions and regulations to executive officers; that the deportation of an alien who is found to be here in violation of law is not a deprivation of liberty without due process of law, and that the provisions of the Constitution securing the right of trial by jury have no application. . . . .

Whether rested on the accepted principle of international law that every sovereign nation has the power, as inherent in sovereignty and essential to self-preservation, to forbid the entrance of foreigners within its dominions, or to admit them only in such cases and upon such conditions as it may see fit to prescribe; or on the power to regulate commerce with foreign nations, which includes the entrance of ships, the importation of goods, and the bringing of persons into the ports of the United States, the act before us is not open to constitutional objection. . . . .

. . . . But it is said that the act violates the First Amendment, which prohibits the passage of any law "respecting an establishment of religion, or prohibiting the free exercise thereof; or abridging the freedom of speech, or of the press; or the right of the people peaceably to assemble, and to petition the government for a redress of grievances."

We are at a loss to understand in what way the act is obnoxious to this objection. It has no reference to an establishment of religion nor does it prohibit the free exercise thereof; nor abridge the freedom of speech or the press; nor the right of the people to assemble and petition the government for a redress of grievances. It is, of course, true that if an alien is not permitted to enter this country, or, having entered contrary to law, is expelled, he is in fact cut off from worshipping or speaking or publishing or petitioning in the country, but that is merely because of his exclusion therefrom. He does not become one of the people to whom these things are secured by our Constitution by an attempt to enter forbidden by law. To appeal to the Constitution is to concede that this is a land governed by that supreme law, and as under it the power to exclude has been determined to exist, those who are excluded cannot assert the rights in general obtaining in a land to which they do not belong as citizens or otherwise.

Appellant's contention really comes to this, that the act is unconstitutional so far as it provides for the exclusion of an alien because he is an anarchist.

The argument seems to be that, conceding that Congress has the power to shut out any alien, the power nevertheless does not extend to some aliens, and that if the act includes all alien anarchists, it is unconstitutional, because some anarchists are merely political philosophers, whose teachings are beneficial rather than otherwise.

Counsel give these definitions from the *Century Dictionary:*

Anarchy.—1. Absence or insufficiency of government; a state of society in which there is no capable supreme power, and in which the several functions of the state are performed badly or not at all; social and political confusion. Specifically.—2. A social theory which regards the union of order with the absence of all direct government of man by man as the political ideal; absolute individual liberty. 3. Confusion in general.

Anarchist.—1. Properly, one who advocates anarchy or the absence of government as a political ideal; a believer in an anarchic theory of society; especially an adherent of the social theory of Proudhon. (See *Anarchy*, 2.) 2. In popular use, one who seeks to overturn by violence all constituted forms and institutions of society and government, all law and order, and all rights of property, with no purpose of establishing any other system of order in the place of that destroyed; especially, such a person when actuated by mere lust of plunder. 3. Any person who promotes disorder or excites revolt against an established rule, law, or custom.

And Huxley is quoted as saying:

Anarchy, as a term of political philosophy, must be taken only in its proper sense, which has nothing to do with disorder or with crime, but denotes a state of society in which the rule of each individual by himself is the only government the legitimacy of which is recognized.

The language of the act is "anarchists, or persons who believe in or advocate the overthrow by force or violence of the Government of the United States or of all government or of all forms of law, or the assassination of public officials." If this should be construed as defining the word "anarchists" by the words which follow, or as used in the popular sense above given, it would seem that when an alien arrives in this country, who avows himself to be an anarchist, without more, he accepts the definition. And we suppose counsel does not deny that this Government has the power to exclude an alien who believes in or advocates the overthrow of the Government or of all governments by force or the assassination of officials. To put that question is to answer it.

And if the judgment of the board and the Secretary was that Turner came within the act as thus construed, we cannot hold as matter of law that there was no evidence on which that conclusion could be rested. Even if Turner, though he did not so state to the board, only regarded the absence of government as a political ideal, yet when he sought to attain it by advocating, not simply for the benefit of workingmen, who are justly entitled to repel the charge of desiring the destruction of law and order, but "at any rate, as an anarchist," the universal strike to which he referred, and by discourses on what he called "The legal murder of 1887," *Spies* v. *People*, 122 Illinois, 1, and by addressing mass meetings on that subject in association with Most, *Reg.* v. *Most*, 7 Q.B. Div. 244; *People* v. *Most*, 171 N.Y. 423, we cannot say that the inference was unjustifiable either that he contemplated the ultimate realization of his ideal by the use of force, or that his speeches were incitements to that end.

If the word "anarchists" should be interpreted as including aliens whose anarchistic views are professed as those of political philosophers innocent of evil intent, it would follow that Congress was of opinion that the tendency of the general exploitation of such views is so dangerous to the public weal that aliens who hold and advocate them would be undesirable additions to our population, whether permanently or temporarily, whether many or few, and, in light of previous decisions, the act, even in this aspect, would not be unconstitutional, or as applicable to any alien who is opposed to all organized government.

We are not to be understood as depreciating the vital importance of freedom of speech and of the press, or as suggesting limitations on the spirit of liberty, in itself unconquerable, but this case does not involve those considerations. The flaming brand which guards the realm where no human government is needed still bars the entrance; and as long as human governments endure they cannot be denied the power of self-preservation. . . . .

13. Advocacy of Assassination and of Unlawful Destruction of Property during a Strike

United States ex rel. Diamond v. Uhl[1]

CIRCUIT JUDGE ROGERS:

The petitioner applied for a writ of habeas corpus and alleged that he was being unlawfully detained at the immigration station at Ellis Island, New York, and was about to be deported to Italy. A hearing was had before the District Court for the Southern District of New York, and the writ of habeas corpus has been dismissed, and the petitioner remanded to the custody of the acting commissioner of immigration at the port of New York.

It appears that the relator is an alien, a native of Italy, born in 1876, and that he came to the United States in 1901, and declared his intention to become a citizen in 1917. It also appears that he was arrested on July 18, 1919, under a warrant of arrest issued by the Department of Labor which charged "that he advocates the assassination of public officials, and that he advocates the unlawful destruction of property." His arrest was followed by hearings, one on July 23, 1919, and another on September 16, 1919, before the United States immigrant inspector. The inspector at the close of the hearings found the following facts:

"(1) That the said Rocco Di Blasis is an alien, namely, a subject of Italy. (2) That he is in the United States in violation of law in that he is an anarchist, that he believes in or advocates the overthrow by force or violence, of the government of the United States, and that he advocates the unlawful destruction of property. It is recommended that the said Rocco Di Blasis be deported."

The report of the hearings and the findings were submitted to the Department of Labor.

The relator being unable to speak and understand the English language satisfactorily, an interpreter in Italian was sworn, who interpreted all questions asked and answers given at the hearings. The relator was

[1] From 266 Federal Reporter 35 (1920).

informed at the time that the purpose of the hearings was to afford him an opportunity to show cause why he should not be deported to the country whence he came. He was represented throughout the hearings by counsel, and witnesses called by him were heard.

The arrest of the relator was due to a riot in the city of Rome, New York, on July 14, 1919. In June and July there was a strike on among the operatives at certain mills in that city. The petitioner was a restaurant keeper, and apparently not connected with any of the mills. He appears, however, to have been active in the strike, and to have taken part in an attack made on one Spargo, the president and manager of one of the mills, who was assaulted and stabbed while in his automobile. The result was that relator was placed under arrest by the state authorities, charged with two offenses, and was released on bail; $3,000 on one charge and $5,000 on the other charge. An affidavit made by Spargo is in the record, which is as follows:

"James A. Spargo, being duly sworn, says that he is president of the Spargo Wire Company, of Rome, New York; that on July 14, 1919, as he was going down East Dominick street, in the city of Rome, New York, in his automobile about 8 o'clock in the morning, a large crowd of people led by Rocco Di Blasis attacked deponent, stopping his automobile and breaking same; that the said Rocco Di Blasis jumped on the running board of said car and stabbed deponent on the arm; that after deponent was stabbed he grabbed his gun, but deponent was overpowered, stabbed, bruised, clubbed, and beaten about the head and body and by the crowd led by Di Blasis; that deponent had been told that he was a marked man and would be killed; that deponent had been told that his house would be blown up, and that the houses and plants of the various manufacturers of the city of Rome would be destroyed, and that the manufacturers themselves would be gotten."

This affidavit was read to relator, and he was asked whether it was true. He denied that it was, and denied that he was leading the crowd, but admitted that he was present. The following is an excerpt from the record:

"*Question.* Were you present? *Answer.* I was.

"*Q.* Tell me what happened. *A.* I was present and saw Mr. Spargo with a revolver in his hand, and he shot three times; then for don't let somebody killed I jumped upon his automobile; in meantime he started to shoot me; I give him a punch on the arm and let the revolver knock down. I took the revolver in my hands and I give it away to first man, then I come out of automobile. Mr. Spargo claims I had a knife in my hand, but I did not have anything. If I wanted to hurt Mr. Spargo, I could use his gun on him. I think I save his life."

There is in the record an affidavit from a policeman which is as follows:

"Joseph M. Nero, being duly sworn, says that he was on duty as patrolman on East Dominick street, in the city of Rome, New York, on the morning of July 14, 1919, at the time of the riot when Spargo was stabbed; that Di Blasis was the leader of the mob, and opened the door of Spargo's automobile, and jumped in on Spargo; that deponent saw Di Blasis in the car and pulled him out; that the same morning, previous to the Spargo incident, deponent saw Di Blasis in a trolley car putting people off and insisting that no one could ride on the trolley; that deponent argued with Di Blasis that he had no right to put people off the car, but Di Blasis insisted no one should ride; that deponent arrested Di Blasis, and in searching his residence found I.W.W. literature, consisting of paper, 'Il Nuovo Proletario,' pictures of Rosa Luxemburg and Liebknecht, the speech of Debs at Atlanta prison gates, 'La Russia Socialists,' preamble and constitution and due books of the I.W.W., application blanks for membership, etc.; that deponent has been informed and believes that said Di Blasis has been advocating violence during the strike in the city of Rome during the last two months, and advocating destruction of persons and property, and has been the leader of agitation, and has known of said Di Blasis addressing crowds; that deponent found revolver in the kitchen of Di Blasis residence; that Officer Uhl saw Di Blasis at 3 o'clock one morning during the strike with a baseball bat walking the street; that June 30th, during a riot in the city, Di Blasis was urging and inciting the crowd, by hollering, 'Get um! Get um!' A large quantity of literature was found."

The relator's attention was called to this affidavit and he was asked:

"*Q.* Is any or all of that true? *A.* Some is all right. I went up to the street car, I was last one to go in and last one to go out; Nero told me I had no right to ask people if they had a book of the Union. I did not force them; I merely asked for their union card."

"*Q.* Did you lead that crowd? *A.* No; I was with the people, but I was not leading them.

"*Q.* Are you a member of the I.W.W.? *A.* I was a member, but not now. Now I am a member of the A.F. of L." . . . .

The relator's counsel asked him whether he believed in and supported the government of the United States. He replied in the affirmative. He was asked whether he desired to become a citizen of the United States, and answered that he did. He stated that he could read and write in Italian and in English.

At the conclusion of the first hearing relator was remanded to the custody of the sheriff of Oneida county, Rome, New York. The evidence taken having been submitted to the Department of Labor, the Acting Secretary of Labor issued his warrant directing that the relator be taken into custody and granted a hearing, to enable him to show cause why he should not be deported.

At the second hearing there was considerable testimony as to the radical class literature found in the relator's possession and admittedly distributed by him. The I.W.W. newspaper, "Il Nuovo Proletario," was regularly received by him and distributed. . . . .

1. The testimony in the record certainly does not disclose that the relator is a desirable personage to have within the limits of the United States. But the government has not given authority to the Department of Labor to cause to be deported aliens who may be regarded as undesirable. The act of Congress under which this deportation proceeding is instituted is the Act of October 16, 1918, 40 Stat., Part 1, p. 1012. Under that act aliens may be taken into custody and deported who advocate or teach the unlawful destruction of property, as may those who advocate or teach the assassination of public officials. Other classes of aliens may also be deported, but with them we are not concerned at this time. The relator is charged in the warrant for his arrest with being unlawfully in the United States, because he advocated the assassination of public officials and the unlawful destruction of property; and the warrant of deportation simply directs the relator's deportation upon the ground that he advocated the unlawful destruction of property. We are therefore alone concerned with the question whether there is evidence in the record from which the Acting Secretary of Labor could find that the relator did advocate the unlawful destruction of property. In his affidavit Capozzoli[1] swears that the relator told him that he and his associates would blow up the shops of the manufacturers if the strike was not settled. That statement is sufficient evidence to sustain the finding. We have nothing to do with its weight.

2. It is, however, assigned for error:

"That the court erred in holding that the relator was not given a fair hearing because of the admission of certain hearsay affidavits by one Capozzoli without permitting relator to cross-examine affiant."

The ordinary rules of evidence do not apply to such proceedings as those now under consideration (*Sibray* v. *United States*, 227 Fed. 1, 7). The hearsay affidavit of Capozzoli was admissible in the proceedings (*Choy Gum* v. *Backus*, 223 Fed. 487, 493; *Healy* v. *Backus*, 221 Fed. 358, 364).

3. It is true that there was no cross-examination of Capozzoli and that he was not produced at the hearing. The defendant, however, did not ask to have him produced, and made no demand for his cross-examination, although represented at the hearing by counsel; and no request was made for any extension of time in which to produce testimony in refutation of the statements in Capozzoli's affidavit. The affidavit was, however, presented at the hearing on July 23, 1919. There was a subsequent hearing, as already stated, on September 16, 1919, when witnesses were called on behalf of the relator; but no attempt was made to discredit the statement quoted from the Capozzoli affidavit, beyond the relator's denial of its truth.

[1] [Capozzoli was a private detective acting for the city.]

The affidavit of the immigrant inspector submitted to the department as respects the second hearing on September 16th was in part as follows:

Pursuant to your instructions of September 13th, and referring to the above-mentioned files I respectfully report that I gave said Rocco Di Blasis a further hearing on September 16th. I allowed him to obtain witnesses, and I also gave the attorney for said alien the privilege of cross-examination of two of the affiants, Mr. Spargo and Mr. Nero. Mr. Capozzoli, who was a private detective hired by the city of Rome, was not in the city, and I was unable to learn where he was at present. Mr. Searle, the alien's attorney, however, made no request to examine him.

We think that, if possible, Capozzoli should have been present for cross-examination, and his absence is certainly regrettable. But we do not believe that the failure to have him present is sufficient ground for setting these proceedings aside, especially in view of the fact that no demand for his presence and cross-examination was made. The relator knew the contents of the affidavit, and was fully apprised of the evidence against him, and was given an opportunity to call witnesses in his defense, and to offer evidence in explanation or rebuttal. If Capozzoli could not be produced on the day set for the hearing, and relator deemed it important to cross-examine him, he should have made his desire known, and requested that he be produced on some subsequent day. The failure to make the request may, we think, be regarded as a waiver of the right. The fact that the rules of the Bureau of Immigration provide in respect to such hearings that "objections and exceptions of counsel shall not be entered on the record, but may be presented by him in accompanying brief,"[1] does not excuse the failure of counsel to insist that a witness whose affidavit is presented shall himself be produced with a view to his cross-examination. We do not agree with counsel that, because of the rule above referred to, the situation as respects the cross-examination "is exactly the same as if the request had been made and denied"; and we do not agree that the court below should have found that the hearing was unfair.

The order is affirmed.

14. Expulsion: "Controlling Legal Principles"

Colyer v. Skeffington[2]

CIRCUIT JUDGE ANDERSON:

These are petitions for habeas corpus brought by or in behalf of 20 aliens against the Commissioner of Immigration at Boston. They were heard together; they fall into two classes: William T. Colyer, Amy Colyer, Frank Mack, Lew Bonder, Frank Matchian, Tehon Lanovoy, Trofim Yarmoluk, Anton Harbatuk, Anton Gessewich, Fred Chaika, Koly Honchereoff, Adam Musky, and Sedar Serachuk have, after appeal to the

[1] Rule 22, subd. 5*b*, Immigration Law, 1917.

[2] From 265 Federal Reporter 20 (1920).

COURT DECISIONS 289

Secretary of Labor, been ordered by him to be deported. Seven of the aliens were at the time of the filing of the petitions held at Deer Island by the respondent in default of bail, fixed, on recommendation of Assistant Commissioner of Immigration Sullivan, as follows:

Ivan T. Hyrnchuk	$10,000
Theodore Pashukoff	5,000
William Maches	5,000
William Chriupko	5,000
Joe Sinkus	5,000
Wladimir Serachuk	5,000
Samuel Drakewich	5,000

Near the end of the long hearing, in which it clearly appeared that none of the aliens were in any way involved, by the use of bombs, guns, or other weapons, in plans of injuring persons, or property, and that the cases could not for many months be finally disposed of, the writs were ordered issued, and all the petitioners admitted by this court to bail in the sum of $500 each. No such responsibility would have been taken by the court if there had been a scintilla of evidence that any alien thus set at liberty was committed in any way to acts of force or violence against person or property.

At the opening of the trial the cases were said by counsel on both sides to be, in many important aspects, test cases of the legality of an undertaking of the government to deport several thousand aliens[1] alleged to be proscribed by a portion of section 1 of the Act of October 16, 1918, as follows:

That .... aliens who are members of or affiliated with any organization that entertains a belief in, teaches, or advocates the overthrow by force or violence of the government of the United States .... shall be excluded from admission into the United States.

Section 2 (section $4289\frac{1}{4}b$ [2]) provides for the deportation of such aliens, irrespective of the time of their entry.

The sole charge against these aliens is membership in the Communist Party or the Communist Labor Party. The proposition of the Department of Justice, adopted by the Commissioner General of Immigration, as hereafter set forth, is that membership in one of these parties is, alone, enough to bring the aliens within the purview of this provision; that both parties are

[1] [For a discussion of the "anarchist" deportations of 1919–20 see Z. Chafee, Jr., *Freedom of Speech* (New York, 1920); C. M. Panunzio, *The Deportation Cases of 1919–1920* (New York, 1921); National Popular Government League, *Report upon the Illegal Practices of the United States Department of Justice*, a report by a committee of American lawyers on the deportation proceedings in the cases of suspected anarchists in 1919–20 (Washington, D.C., 1920); U.S. Congress, House Committee on Rules, *Investigation of Administration of Louis F. Post, Assistant Secretary of Labor, in the Matter of Deportation of Aliens; Hearings on H. Res. 522* (Washington, D.C., 1920); K. H. Claghorn, *The Immigrant's Day in Court* (New York, 1923); Louis F. Post, *The Deportations Delirium of Nineteen-Twenty* (Chicago, 1923).]

committed to a scheme to overthrow our government by force or violence. In both classes of cases the petitioners attack, on grounds fatal if sustained, the validity of the proceedings, instituted by the government on January 2, 1920, for their deportation. . . . .

CONTROLLING LEGAL PRINCIPLES

A preliminary statement of the well-settled and familiar principles of law on which all of these habeas corpus cases involving the exclusion or deportation of aliens depend will bring into clearer perspective the field of facts in which this court must perform its most important duties.

1. It has been repeatedly held that "the right to exclude or to expel all aliens, or any class of aliens, absolutely or upon certain conditions, in war or in peace," is "an inherent and inalienable right of every sovereign and independent nation, essential to its safety, its independence, and its welfare"; that this "power to exclude and to expel aliens, being a power affecting international relations, is vested in the political departments of the government, and is to be regulated by treaty or by act of Congress, and to be executed by the executive authority according to the regulations so established, except so far as the judicial department has been authorized by treaty or by statute, or is required by the paramount law of the Constitution, to intervene."

Otherwise stated, there is no constitutional limit to the power of Congress to exclude or expel aliens. An invitation once extended to the alien to come within our borders may be withdrawn. He has no vested right to remain. This was expressly adjudicated in the Chinese Exclusion Cases, 130 U.S. 581, in which the Supreme Court unanimously held that the fact that a Chinese laborer had legally entered the United States conferred upon him no right of which he could not be deprived by a subsequent act of Congress.

2. It is also familiar and perfectly well-settled law that the courts have no jurisdiction, on habeas corpus proceedings, to interfere with the proceedings in the Department of Labor concerning the exclusion or the expulsion of aliens, unless and until there is some error of law in that department. Unless the proceedings in that department are unfair, thus lacking some of the essential elements of due process of law, or are based upon some misconstruction of the statute or disregard of the rules made pursuant thereto, or on other vitiating error of law, the courts have no jurisdiction. In these habeas corpus cases, therefore, it may be said that the primary function of the court is to try, not the right of the alien to enter or to remain in the United States, but to try the trial of the alien in the Department of Labor; if that trial was fair and legal, even though the result was, in the opinion of the court, erroneous on the facts, the court has no right to interfere; it may not, in habeas corpus proceedings, usurp the function that Congress has delegated by statute to the Department of Labor.

COURT DECISIONS 291

3. But, while the courts have no jurisdiction on habeas corpus to substitute their judgment on pure questions of fact for that of the Secretary of Labor, it is equally well settled that if the proceedings in the Department of Labor are shown to be unfair or otherwise lacking in the essential elements of due process of law, then the courts must review.

4. While deportation proceedings are not criminal proceedings, aliens who are thereby deprived of their liberty may have their legal right to liberty tested on habeas corpus proceedings. . . . .

Aliens have constitutional rights. The Fourth, Fifth, Sixth, and Fourteenth Amendments are not limited in their application to citizens. They apply generally to all persons within the jurisdiction of the United States. See *Yick Wo* v. *Hopkins*, 118 U.S. 356. . . . .

ADMINISTRATION OF IMMIGRATION LAWS VESTED BY CONGRESS IN DEPARTMENT OF LABOR

6. The administration of the immigration laws has been intrusted by Congress to the Department of Labor—not to the Department of Justice. The latter department has no more legal right or power to deal with the exclusion or the expulsion of aliens than has the Department of the Interior. The Department of Justice prosecutes for crime. But deportation proceedings are not criminal proceedings (*Pang Sho Yin* v. *United States*, 154 Fed. 660).

There are obvious reasons why Congress delegated the important and delicate functions of excluding and expelling aliens to the Labor Department. This department is charged with certain functions pertaining peculiarly to human welfare; it exercises large powers over millions of persons, many of them poor, comparatively helpless, and unacquainted with our language and institutions. As the functions of the Department of Justice and the Department of Labor are radically different, the official personnel of the two departments would naturally have different methods of procedure. But, without elaborating reasons, the mandate of Congress, intrusting immigration matters to the Labor Department, is binding upon all government departments, including the courts. The Commissioner General of Immigration is a subordinate in the Department of Labor. . . . .

8, 9. From the foregoing it is apparent that the records upon which the decisions of the Secretary of Labor are based are under the provisions of these rules intended to be made in summary, but fair and adequate, fashion by real trials before immigration inspectors. Due process of law requires that these trials should be fair, unbiased, dispassionate. They may be summary, lacking in formalities of judicial procedure; but they must be conducted in an honest and reasonably intelligent attempt to ascertain and report the truth; otherwise the alien is deprived of the rights which the statutes of Congress contemplate that he shall have, including the right to have his appeal passed on by the Secretary of Labor with an adequate and truthful record before him. Moreover, an unfair or otherwise misleading record is as much a fraud upon the law and upon the Secretary of Labor as upon the alien. It is as much the duty of the Department of Labor to admit aliens impliedly invited by Congress into this country as it is to exclude or expel those proscribed by Congress. The general policy of the United States towards immigrants has been to admit and to welcome all, except specifically described and limited undesirables. No executive department has any right by strained construction to substitute its theories for those adopted by the national Legislature.

One important inquiry in this case is as to whether the records in the case of 13 of the aliens who have been ordered deported, were made by labor inspectors acting soberly, conscientiously, and with an unbiased and uncontrolled attempt to find and report the facts on which the rights of these aliens depend. The petitioners urge that in the proceedings here brought in question the Department of Labor abdicated its functions; that those functions were usurped by the Department of Justice, through its Bureau of Investigations, and that the proceedings are therefore void *ab initio;* that if not absolutely void, at any rate the trials by the inspectors were under such circumstances as to prevent a fair, impartial, conscientious attempt to find and report the facts upon which the rights of many of the aliens must depend. The methods adopted are contended to have deprived the petitioners, many of whom have but a meager knowledge of English and scant education, of any fair opportunity to have their real status determined. This contention makes it necessary to set forth in considerable detail the facts under which the petitioners, and hundreds of other aliens, were arrested and held for trial.

INITIATION AND CONDUCT OF THE RAID IN NEW ENGLAND

. . . . Thus equipped with explicit written instructions from the Department of Justice in Washington, the local Bureau of Investigation made arrangements with the police forces in the cities and towns in which the alleged Communists were for the arrests on the night of January 2, 1920. The officials, both of the Department of Justice and of the Department of Labor, described these proceedings, properly enough, as a "raid" and as "catching the Communists in the net." The word "raid" seems appropriate, and will hereafter be used in this report.

It was arranged to have at what were called "concentration points"—generally a police station—an inspector of the Labor Department; in some cases, apparently having possession of the warrants intended for service in that neighborhood; in other cases, apparently not. It is difficult from the evidence to ascertain what function, if any, was actually performed by these inspectors of the Labor Department. The arrests were in fact made by the representatives of the Department of Justice, assisted by the local police authorities, all of whom acted under the direction of the agents of the Department of Justice. The raids were made on the evening of January 2, 1920, in the following cities and towns: Boston, Chelsea, Brockton, Bridgewater, Norwood, Worcester, Springfield, Chicopee, Holyoke, Gardner, Fitchburg, Lowell, Lawrence, Haverhill, all in Massachusetts; Nashua, Manchester, Derry, Portsmouth, Claremont, Lincoln, all in New Hampshire. In some cities several halls were raided. In most communities, homes were invaded.

Kelleher[1] says that he had operating, practically under his control, for this raid, from 300 to 500 men. This may fairly be assumed to be a moderate estimate. Most of these were agents of the Department of Justice and policemen of the various cities and towns. The plan was to make up a list of the persons intended to be arrested in a particular community; for the police and Department of Justice agents thereupon, generally without warrants, to go about to the halls or homes where these people were, arrest them, and bring them to the concentration point—commonly a police station. When halls were raided, the occupants were, as required by the instructions, lined up against the wall and searched. Many citizens were gathered into the net in this fashion, and brought to the various police stations. At the concentration points the sifting process went on during the night. . . . .

Assistant Superintendent West of the Boston Bureau of Investigation estimates that the total number of persons actually arrested on this raid was approximately 600. This also must be taken to be a moderate estimate. The circumstances under which the raid was carried on make it impossible for him or any other person to know with any approximate accuracy the number of persons arrested. Weighing this evidence in connection with the other testimony adduced before me, I am convinced that a much larger number of people was arrested—probably from 800 to 1,200.

Much credible evidence, as, for instance, that from the witness Liberman, bears out this estimate. Liberman testified that, at the close of a publicly advertised mass meeting held at the Finnish Hall in Mulberry Street, Worcester, plain clothes agents held up the entire audience of about 200 and asked each one whether he was a citizen or not; that they held those who answered that they were not citizens, taking about 100 to the jail; later during the night all but 16 were released after being booked and answering the typical questionnaire. Steiner's and Ryder's evidence, *post*, points to the same conclusion.

The evidence as to the exact number of warrants then in the possession of the agents of the Department of Justice or the inspectors of the Bureau of Labor is somewhat confusing. Apparently, however, 463 warrants had been received in Boston, dated December 29, 1919. But, assuming that this number of warrants was in Boston, over 100 of them could not have been served; for the evidence is explicit that out of the 440 persons arrested

[1] [Head of the local Bureau of Investigation, Department of Justice, in Boston.]

and taken to Deer Island warrants for about 100 were not at that time outstanding. For persons thus taken and held, telegraphic warrants were applied for and in most cases subsequently received. These people (100 or thereabouts) were seized on the theory that, although warrants had not then been received, there was evidence that they were alien members of the Communist or Communist Labor party, and were therefore, under the instructions, to be held and warrants thereafter obtained.

After the sifting process at the various concentration points, at which at least one-third to one-half of the total number of persons arrested were discharged after various periods of detention in cells (from a few hours to two or three days), about 440 persons were transported to Deer Island and there locked in cells. . . . .

WERE THE HEARINGS FAIR OR UNFAIR?

By the methods thus briefly described, the Department of Justice had gathered at Deer Island, nominally in the custody of the Department of Labor, some 440 aliens. In order to carry out the plans of wholesale deportation, it was then necessary that these aliens be given hearings before inspectors of the Labor Department. It was recognized that legal hearings could not be conducted, in form at any rate, by agents of the Department of Justice. Burke's[1] long letter of December 29, 1919, to Kelleher, expressly enjoined the agent of the Department of Justice that—

At the hearings before the immigration inspector you will render all reasonable assistance to the immigration authorities both in the way of offering your services to them and the services of any of your stenographic forces.

This was construed as requiring the Department of Justice agents to be present at the hearings of the aliens before the immigration inspector, practically in many instances undertaking to participate or even give direction to those hearings. These Department of Justice agents were particularly active in producing and putting before the trial tribunal documents and publications claimed to have been obtained under such circumstances as to be evidence against the particular alien. Many of the records show that, after the hearings were practically closed, the Department of Justice agents were given opportunities to present further evidence and to express their opinions as to the conclusion that ought to be reached by the trial inspector.

11. In dealing with these hearings, it is necessary to consider with care the extraordinary circumstances surrounding the change of rule 22, subd. 5 (b), as quoted above. Just prior to the initiation of this raid, this rule read:

At the beginning of the hearing under the warrant of arrest *the alien shall be allowed to inspect* the warrant of arrest and all the evidence on which it was issued, and *shall be apprised that he may be represented by counsel.*

[1] [Chief of the Bureau of Investigation of the Department of Justice in Washington.]

Under date of December 31, 1919, Commissioner General Caminetti, two days after the date of his confidential letter of instructions to the Boston Commissioner of Immigration setting forth the plan of the proposed raid, issued a circular letter modifying this rule. The pertinent part of this circular letter is as follows:

December 31, 1919

COMMISSIONER OF IMMIGRATION AND INSPECTORS IN CHARGE:

By direction of the *Acting* Secretary, paragraph (*b*) of subdivision 5, rule 22, Immigration Rules, is hereby amended, effective immediately, to read as follows:

"Preferably at the beginning of the hearing under the warrant of arrest or *at any rate as soon as such hearing has proceeded sufficiently in the development of the facts to protect the Government's interests*, the alien shall be allowed to inspect the warrant of arrest and all the evidence on which it was issued and shall be apprised that *thereafter* he may be represented by counsel."

The practical result of this changed rule, it is to be observed, was to cut the alien off from any representation by counsel, until the inspector, cooperating with or advised by the agent of the Department of Justice, was of the opinion that the hearing had proceeded "sufficiently in the development of the facts to protect the government's interests." This left these aliens, many of them uneducated and seriously hampered by their inability to understand English, or even the interpreters, many of whom were but meagerly equipped with knowledge of the language and dialects used by these aliens, entirely unprotected from the zealous attempts of the Department of Justice agents to get from them some sort of apparent admission of membership in the Communist or Communist Labor Party. . . . .

The modification of the rule by the authority of the Acting Secretary of Labor, continued in force about a month, during which substantially all the hearings at Deer Island were practically completed. But on January 28, 1920, the Secretary of Labor, who is stated to have been absent on account of illness on December 31, 1919, when the change in the rule was made cutting off the right of the alien to have any real assistance from counsel, by telegram (copy below) ordered the old rule restored:

"January 28

"IMMIGRATION SERVICE, BOSTON, MASS.:

"By direction of secretary paragraph B subdivision five rule twenty-two restored to form in which it existed previous to amendment December thirtieth nineteen nineteen. In other words amendment of December thirtieth nineteen nineteen should be disregarded from and after receipt of this telegram.

ABERCROMBIE"

. . . . Deliberately to plan to cut these aliens off from the advice and assistance of counsel until they were involved in apparent admissions that they were members of or affiliated with an organization teaching the overthrow of this government by force and violence, the practical equivalent of a charge of treason if against citizens, is utterly inconsistent with every notion involved in the conception of "due process of law."

I hear from the government no convincing answer to Mr. Frankfurter's[1] proposition that these petitioners had a right to the—"Protection that rule 22 afforded them as it stood before the *ad hoc* repeal of that rule for the purpose of these cases. Now, if there is one thing that is established in the law of administration, I take it that it is that a rule cannot be repealed specifically to affect a case under consideration by the administrative authorities; that is, if there is an existing rule which protects certain rights, it violates every sense of decency, which is the very heart of due process, to repeal that protection, just for the purpose of accomplishing the ends of the case which come before the administrative authority. . . . . And there was a sudden, calculated, and surreptitious deprivation of that safeguard which was sought to protect the rights of all, and particularly protect those who were innocent."

As the hearings before the immigration inspectors progressed, it became evident that the preliminary investigations made before arrests, not, as contemplated by the rules of the Department of Labor, by the experienced inspectors of that Department, but by agents of the Bureau of Investigation of the Department of Justice, were wholly inadequate and unreliable. . . . .

I note again that with the inspector at the hearing was an agent of the Department of Justice that had initiated and carried on this great raid, and that the alien had no counsel to represent him until the hearing was practically closed. Under such circumstances, it is not to my mind conceivable that these immigration inspectors could do justice to these ignorant non-English-speaking, bewildered aliens.

It is not necessary to attack the purposes or character of the immigration inspectors. I would say of them nothing unjust or harsh. They were in a most uncomfortable position. Weighing fairly the conditions, perhaps they could not be expected adequately to resist the pressure put upon them to find evidence of membership in the Communist Party when there was no real evidence. At any rate, after a careful consideration of their testimony and of the records they made, in the light of their appearance before me, I am satisfied that they did not extend to a large share of the aliens a fair and impartial trial. The conditions under which these aliens were tried for their right to live in America were, in my view, inconsistent with due process of law conditions. . . . .

16, 17. I turn, now, to deal with the statute. What is its fair interpretation? At the outset I note that it is not to be extended by construction. The traditional policy of the United States is to admit all aliens except specifically designated classes. It is for Congress, not for the Department of Labor, the Department of Justice, or the courts, to determine this impor-

[1] [Professor Frankfurter, of the Harvard Law School, acted as *amicus curiae*.]

tant part of our national policy towards other nations and other peoples. And statutory restrictions on immigration, like all other statutes, are, if possible, to be construed in accordance with the spirit as well as within the letter of our Constitution, including the First Amendment and its declaration for freedom of speech, press, and assemblage.

Nor should it be overlooked that the words "overthrow the government of the United States by force or violence" are found in a context which indicates that Congress had in mind military insurrections of the ordinary kind, and bombing and assassination attacks on the government. . . . .

It is perhaps true that if the records which went to the Secretary of Labor could be regarded as accurate, adequate, and reliable, there may be in them some evidence warranting the Secretary's conclusion that the aliens are members of the Communist Party. But the difficulties are that these records originated in hearings conducted by the inspectors, in an atmosphere and under conditions which I have already outlined, and which I am constrained to believe prevented the aliens from having a fair, legal, due process of law consideration of their real status.

Bringing the functions of the court strictly within the limits laid down by the authorities cited above, and trying, not the merits of the aliens' cases, but the *trial* of the aliens, I am compelled to hold that the Secretary of Labor has in these cases, of necessity, grounded his decisions upon records misrepresenting or omitting facts of controlling importance.

I find on all the evidence that the records in these cases are not reliable, and that they originated in proceedings which were unfair and therefore lacking in due process of law. . . . .

SECTION IV

SOCIAL CASE RECORDS: DETENTION, EXCLUSION, DEPORTATION, EXPULSION, BRINGING OVER RELATIVES[1]

1. Mary Baranowski
(Temporary Detention)

November 5, 1920.—Nicholas Kralski in the office [Immigrants' Commission] asking help in locating his young sister-in-law, Mary Baranowski. She arrived October 10 on "New Amsterdam" and cannot be located at Ellis Island. Man has already wired Ellis Island but she is not there. Telegram sent to Miss Freeman [New York representative of Commission] as follows: "Please ascertain cause detention Mary Baranowski steamer New Amsterdam detained three weeks. Commissioner wired no record.—LYDIA GARDNER, *Secretary, Immigrants' Commission of Illinois*." *Later.*—Reply from Elsa Freeman: "Mary Baranowski admitted October 26, proceeded Chicago via N.Y. Central and Michigan Central destined to Nicholas Kralski, 2232 Henry Street. If she has not arrived telegraph me immediately for further investigation. Girl was temporarily detained for money." *Later.*—Visited to see if girl had arrived. Family have heard nothing. Sister much worried and frightened. Another girl who came on same boat and travelled with Mary arrived two weeks ago. *Later.*—Telegram to Miss Freeman as follows: "Mary Baranowski destined Nicholas Kralski not arrived Chicago. Investigate further.—LYDIA GARDNER." *Later.*—Mrs. Kralski telephoned she has had a letter from Mary saying she has no money. Woman will come to office this afternoon. *Later.*—Telegram from Miss Freeman as follows: "Mary Baranowski placed detention room instead of railroad room after discharge. I found her and advanced five dollars as money had been returned to Chicago. Girl leaves six-seventeen tonight arriving Lehigh Valley nine-thirty Sunday evening." *Later.*—Mr. Kralski in office. Gave him copy of telegram.

[1] In these case records fictitious names have been substituted for real names in order to make it impossible to identify either the immigrants or any other persons mentioned in the records. Not only the names of private individuals, but also the names of public officials, social workers, and employers as well as street names have been quite uniformly changed. The names of social agencies and institutions and the names of towns, steamships, railroads, etc., have in general been changed only when necessary to prevent identification. The cases are all from the files of the Immigrants' Protective League of Chicago except in cases indicated from the Immigrants' Commission of Illinois. The two organizations, however, were really the same. See p. 100.

November 8, 1920.—Neighbor telephoned. Mary has arrived at last. Family wish to thank the Commission and Miss Freeman.

November 9, 1920.—Letter from Miss Freeman containing the following:

Upon receipt of your telegram inquiring for cause of detention of Mary Baranowski yesterday, I investigated immediately and found that the girl had been temporarily detained pending receipt of money from Chicago. The temporary detention sheet gave the time and day of the girl's discharge and the address to which she was proceeding. I then found the detention card of the immigrant filed away with the completed record cards, and the information entered on the card agreed with that on the detention list sheet. I made inquiry at the railroad room and learned that immigrants destined to Chicago on October 26, the date of the girl's discharge according to the records, travelled via N.Y. Central and Michigan Central. I telegraphed you on November 5 the information I had received as above. Early today I went to Ellis Island in response to your later telegram of yesterday. Upon further investigation I found that Mary Baranowski had a prepaid ticket through to Chicago and that she was detained for extra travelling money and that same had been received from Chicago and girl then discharged to the railroad room. There are no records in the railroad room of any tickets except those bought there for cash. The agents therefore could not trace the ticket on which Mary Baranowski travelled. As a last resort I succeeded in getting an inspector to go into the detention room where hundreds were crowded in, and call out the name of the immigrant I was trying to trace. She responded and told me that she had never been in any room but the New York detention room; that she had been called out and questioned but never given the money she needed. It seems that she was discharged, but before the money was actually placed in her hands, she was, in some unexplained manner, returned to the detention room, and the record was completed and filed away. Meanwhile, the case having been completed, the $25 remaining at the treasurer's and not called for, was returned to Chicago. This meant another detention of a few days and I objected. Upon my assurance that the immigrant's relatives would return to me the money advanced, I was permitted to lend the girl five dollars so that she might proceed today. Mary Baranowski leaves today by Grand Trunk Railroad at 6:17 P.M. and should arrive via Lehigh Valley Railroad at about 9:30 tomorrow, Sunday evening. I telegraphed you fully. Out of the five dollars advanced to Mary Baranowski she spent before leaving, eighty-one cents, which is the charge for transportation from Ellis Island to the train, and one dollar and fifty cents for a carton with food for meals while enroute. She therefore left with a balance of only $2.69.

[The record also contains account of follow-up visit to family, sending money to Miss Freeman, receipts, etc. The family were prosperous and very nice Polish people. Man had a steady job, earning $35.00 to $40.00 a week.]

2. Joseph and Rachel Rosenbaum
(Exclusion—Feeble-minded)

March 10, 1921.—Isaac Berg, a Jewish man, born in the United States, in the office [Immigrants' Commission]. He wants help for his relatives, Joseph and Rachel Rosenbaum, his wife's brother and sister-in-law, who are at Ellis Island ex S.S. "Petrograd." He has telegram from Commissioner: "Joseph Rosenbaum dangerously ill." Council of Jewish Women in New York have the case. Man says Rachel is reported feeble-minded. Told man the Council would do everything that could be done. Man urged that we make inquiry. *Later.*—Telegram finally sent to Council as follows: "Please wire status case Joseph and Rachel Rosenbaum steamship Petrograd and what can be done for them."

March 11, 1921.—Telegram from Council Jewish Women: "Re Rosenbaum case steamship Petrograd man died Thursday of pneumonia. Appeal made to Washington for woman. Result doubtful." Telephoned Mrs. Berg. Her husband will come to the office. *Later.*—Mr. Berg in office. He is a post-office clerk, earning $150 a month. He owns $500 in Liberty Bonds and has $2,000 in first mortgage bonds. He says sister-in-law has a brother, Joseph Cohen, who has $6,000 worth of property. Man has telegram from nephew in New York. Telegram said he was expecting to hear from Washington today. Mr. Klein [Congressman] is working on case. Russian-American Bureau prepared affidavits for man. L. G. [Secretary of Commission] talked with man. Told him that with Council, Congressman, etc., working on case, it was useless for us to come in. Evidently also the case is almost settled or New York relatives would not be expecting Washington decision today.

March 18, 1921.—Mr. Berg in office. He has been to Mr. Klein's office and his nephew has been in Washington. The case has been appealed. Man says his sister-in-law will commit suicide if she is taken back. She has no one over there now that her husband is dead. Her sisters and brothers are all in the United States. He thinks her condition is result of anxiety and grief over husband's death. Told Mr. Berg we are very sorry but we can not do anything.

March 25, 1921.—Telegram from Council as follows: "Rachel Rosenbaum was deported Thursday, steamship Petrograd." *Later.*—Telephoned Mr. Berg, Canal 90, and told him of telegram. Man said he had also had telegram; the family feel very bad about it.

3. Karolina Klimek
(Exclusion—Contagious Disease)

November 7, 1921.—Stanislaw Horan, a Polish man, in office, asking help in a detention case. Man has four stepchildren detained at Ellis Island—three sisters and a nine-year-old brother. M. J. made out affidavit and sent telegram. [Both are given below.]

Telegram sent to Commissioner of Immigration at Ellis Island: "Official affidavits Karolina Klimek and party steamship Potomac sent today. If excluded hereby appeal.—STANISLAW HORAN, *Stepfather*, 2229 Cooley Avenue."

Affidavit[1] as follows:

I, Stanislaw Horan, hereby petition that Karolina Klimek (age eighteen, stepdaughter); Kunegunda (age sixteen, stepdaughter); Marianna (age eleven, stepdaughter); Valdyslaw (age nine, stepson), who arrived on the S.S. "Potomac" at New York on November 2, 1921, be permitted to enter the United States. I promise to hold harmless the United States . . . . against these persons ever becoming a public charge. . . . . I was born on the third day of May, 1886, in the town of Falkow, country of Poland. I emigrated to the United States in 1910. I also state that I am a resident of Chicago and live at 2229 Cooley Avenue, in a four-room apartment with my wife. I further state that I am not yet a citizen of the United States. I have my first papers . . . . secured in the Circuit Court of Cook County on December 27, 1920. I am a laborer employed by the Falstaff works at 600 Elerton Avenue. My average weekly earnings are $35; my approximate net savings since arrival in the United States are $3,200. I have $2,000 in bank; personal property valued at $1,200 as follows: Furniture, $1,000; Liberty Bonds, $200. If necessary, I will furnish bond.

November 21, 1921.—Man in office with steamship agent Petovsky. He had a telegram from one of the children urging him to come to Ellis Island. The children are delayed because the oldest one is under observation for eyes. Sent telegram to Mrs. Lee, Y.W.C.A. representative at Ellis Island, asking her assistance.

November 23, 1921.—Telegram delivered after office hours. Read as follows: "Ellis Island, November 23, 1921. To Immigrants' Protective League. Karolina Klimek steamship Potomac excluded. Certified trachoma. Other children held pending appearance of parent.—K. F. LEE."

November 25, 1921.—Telephoned Petovsky's Ticket Office. Mr. Petovsky will have Mr. Horan go to Ellis Island for other children. Explained to agent procedure for obtaining medical treatment at Ellis Island for Karolina.

December 30, 1921.—Telegram from Y.W.C.A. to Immigrants' Protective League, Chicago: "Karolina Klimek ordered deported, probably leaving tomorrow steamship Potomac.—YOUNG WOMEN'S CHRISTIAN ASSOCIATION."

January 3, 1922.—Frank Lukovic, son-in-law of Mr. Horan, in office. Mr Lukovic is a chauffeur, earning $32 a week, and he has savings amounting to $1,700. He is an ex-service man and an American citizen. Steamship agent tried to handle case at first. Then Mr. Horan took it to a lawyer, a relative of Herbert Kurtz, Congressman. Mr. Kurtz asked $400 for his services. The Congressman in Washington helped him on the case. Mr. Horan paid $165 for medical treatment on or about November 28. The family cannot understand what has happened. *Later.*—M. J. prepared a special affidavit for Mr. Lukovic and sent it to Washington to the Secretary of Labor with appeal. Telegram sent to Commissioner of Immigration as

---

[1] [This is the usual form of "public charge" affidavit furnished by relatives in the United States for persons whom they wish to assist.]

follows: "Please wire collect present status Karolina Klimek steamship Potomac. Reported she is to be deported. She was certified trachoma. Stepfather requested medical treatment at Ellis Island. Sent through his lawyer $165 for treatment about December first.—IMMIGRANTS' PROTECTIVE LEAGUE."

January 5, 1922.—Telegram received from Ellis Island: "Petition for hospital treatment, Karolina Klimek refused by Secretary of Labor and deportation directed. ———, *Assistant Commissioner*."

[The two letters that follow give the further facts in the case:]

January 7, 1922

The Secretary of Labor, Washington, D.C.

DEAR SIR: At the request of the relatives of Karolina Klimek, S.S. "Potomac," we forward the inclosed affidavit which, we believe, contains information not previously submitted. We have been informed that she is to be deported from New York on the fourteenth or seventeenth. As the affidavit shows, her brother-in-law is an American by birth. He is also an ex-service man. He is willing to guarantee prompt payments if you will permit the girl to receive medical treatment in this country. Sending this girl back to Poland will cause great sorrow to her and her family. She has, in this country, her mother, stepfather, three sisters and a brother, as well as the brother-in-law at whose request we write. On the other hand, she has in Poland not one single relative who can give her a home or even the guidance and supervision which any girl of her age, eighteen, needs. There is only one uncle, her mother's brother, an elderly and helpless man, who has to be helped by the relatives here. For years the mother has looked forward to having her children with her again. She is in great distress at the prospect of another long period of separation. We feel very strongly that this is a case of rather unusual circumstances and appeal. For that reason, we trust you will pardon us for asking you to reopen it for further consideration.

Yours very sincerely,

ALICE MARION

January 11, 1922

[Letter to the Immigrants' Protective League from the office of the United States Secretary of Labor:]

DEAR MADAM: Your letter of January 7th has been received, with its enclosures in behalf of Karolina Klimek, who was excluded at Ellis Island because of being afflicted with a dangerous and contagious disease, trachoma. Because of the long period required successfully to treat this disease, the lack of facilities at Ellis Island for any considerable number of patients, and the fact that this disease may relapse even after a cure is thought to have been effected, the Department is very much averse to granting hospital treatment in cases of this kind. The United States Public Health Service, moreover, is not willing that such patients be permitted to leave the port of arrival for treatment at hospitals elsewhere, as past experience has shown this to be, far too often, to the disadvantage of the Government. I believe that the representations made in your letter and those accompanying it are all in good faith, but I do wish to impress upon you that this case does not materially differ from a very large number of others, continually arriving, and that to make an exception in the favor of the one in which you are interested would lay the Department open to a bombardment of criticism should it not extend the same facilities to all. Instructions have been sent to the Commissioner of Immigration at Ellis Island to deport this alien, and I cannot see my way clear to reversing those orders.

Very sincerely yours,

[Remaining portion of record relates to return of money ($165) sent to Ellis Island and to a refund of $200 secured from the lawyer.]

4. The Family of Nicholas Kapalo
(Sick Child—Curable Disease)

September 15, 1920.—Nicholas Kapalo in office [Immigrants' Commission] to ask assistance in securing the release of his family from Ellis Island. He is a Jugo-Slav from the village of Arkres, Croatia, age thirty-six. He came to the United States in September, 1912. He is literate, had twelve years' schooling, worked in a restaurant in Croatia. He has been employed for the last three years as a meat grinder in the stockyards and now earns $36 a week. He left in Europe his wife, Rozalia, now aged thirty-two; two sons, Anton now twelve, and Peter now ten; and a little daughter, Mary, now eight. Owing to the war he could not send for his family all these years. At last all arrangements were completed, and they arrived in New York on the S.S. "Cracow." Now he has a telegram that the whole family are detained at Ellis Island and not allowed to proceed to Chicago. He can be reached by telephone through the Croatian Bank, N Street. Man has $600 in the Croatian Bank and has furnished a flat for his family. Value of personal property $500. Man is not yet a citizen, but he took out first papers January, 1917. *Later.*—Affidavit prepared and telegram sent to Ellis Island.

September 24, 1920.—Mr. Kapalo in office, family not yet arrived. He has had a letter from his wife that she has not received money sent to "Cracow" and Ellis Island. *Later.*—A. M. sent telegram to Miss Freeman [New York representative of Immigrants' Commission].

September 25, 1920.—Telegram from Miss Freeman: "Mary Kapalo has measles. Family temporarily detained." *Later.*—Mr. Kapalo in office. He received a letter from his wife today. She claims no money arrived for her. She asked him to send some immediately. Telegram sent to Ellis Island and $20 wired to wife.

September 29, 1920.—Mr. Kapalo in office. He is worried about family. Explained that family will be sent on as soon as Mary recovers. Told him to return if there are any more difficulties.

November 26, 1920.—Mr. Kapalo in office; his wife and children have not yet arrived. *Later.*—Following telegram sent to Miss Freeman at Ellis Island: "Rozalia Kapalo and children steamship Cracow September 15 still detained. One child measles. Please wire present condition. Does she need money?"

November 27, 1920.—Letter sent to Miss Freeman as follows:

You may remember that about September 23 we sent you a telegram asking you to find out about Rozalia Kapalo and her three children, who arrived on the "Cracow" about September 15, and who are being detained at Ellis Island. At that time you wired back to us that Mary (eight years old) was in the hospital with measles. Mr. Kapalo was in our office today and told us that his family has not yet arrived in Chicago. He seems to have heard very little from them, or with regard to them. He is much worried and much wrought up to think that he should have spent all this money to bring his family to him, and that then they should be kept for weeks at Ellis Island, running up, he fears, all sorts of bills which he will be unable to pay. We tried to explain to him the necessity of the detention and to reassure him with regard to the expenses, but it was difficult to make any impression on him. He is really—and, of course, it is only natural—very much excited and worried. Would you please once more look them up and let us know what the present situation is, and when they are likely to be released? Does Mrs. Kapalo need money? He feels he has sent a great deal, but we could not get a very satisfactory report from him about the matter. He seems to think that none of the money he sends gets into her hands. . . . .

December 2, 1920.—Letter received from Miss Freeman:

I am very sorry that Mr. Kapalo did not come to you much sooner, so that I might have kept him informed about his family at Ellis Island. Having no word from you since the little girl was placed in the hospital with measles, I assumed that the family had long ago been discharged from the Island.

Upon inquiry today I learned that Mary Kapalo recovered from the measles but that there remained an acute nephritis which will take a long time to cure. The little girl is improving slowly as is usually the case with nephritis. She may remain in hospital a very long time. The main cure in such cases is quiet and an exceedingly careful diet, any deviation from which may cause a very serious relapse. Long after the child is able to travel and arrives in Chicago, it is essential that she be kept upon a rigidly careful diet under a doctor's care. Mrs. Kapalo has received the various remittances that Mr. Kapalo has sent her. She now has on deposit with the treasurer at Ellis Island $90. I shall advise her that she may call upon any of this money at any time, in case she is not aware of that fact. Under the circumstances I do not believe the child would recover so quickly if taken to Chicago as soon as she can be moved, and therefore suggest that no attempt be made in this direction. We can, however, try to secure the admission of Mrs. Kapalo and the healthy children, upon deposit of $150. This would mean that Mr. Kapalo would have to deposit at least an additional $100 at Ellis Island. This sum would be returned to him upon the child's admission. Since, however, an eight-year old child would have to be accompanied to Chicago, it would be necessary for one of the parents to call for her upon her discharge. This would entail a considerable additional expense, the cost of an extra round trip from Chicago. Will you kindly explain the circumstances to Mr. Kapalo and especially that it may be possible to secure the admission of his wife and well children upon deposit of $150, this sum to be returned when Mary has recovered and one of her parents calls for her personally.

Later.—Letter sent to Mr. Kapalo giving facts about his family.

December 3, 1920.—Mr. Kapalo in office to say he wishes his wife and little boys admitted as soon as possible. He will wire deposit $150, etc. *Later.*—The following telegram sent to Miss Freeman: "Nick Kapalo wants wife and two boys steamship Cracow admitted as soon as possible. He will deposit $150 for Mary and will go New York for her when she is well. Is money to be deposited with Chicago Federal Immigration Inspector?"

December 6, 1920.—Miss Freeman telegraphed, "Send Kapalo money deposit in wife's name care of me my address." *Later.*—Called Croatian Bank and asked them to tell Mr. Kapalo to come to the office with money. *Later.*—Mr. Kapalo in office. He will send money this afternoon.

December 7, 1920.—Telegram received from Miss Freeman, "Mr. Kapalo should send me immediately affidavit offering public charge bond and guaranteeing to call for Mary when admitted if wife and healthy children are admitted. Will take case before board when I receive affidavit. Remittance received." *Later.*—Telephoned Croatian Bank that Mr. Kapalo must come to the office to make out affidavit.

December 10, 1920.—Mr. Kapalo in office. Showed receipt from Western Union that he had sent $150 to Rozalia Kapalo care of Elsa Freeman December 6. A. M. prepared and sent new affidavit.

December 13, 1920.—Telegram from Miss Freeman, "Received affidavit and secured admission today of Rozalia Kapalo and two boys. They leave by Lehigh Valley and Grand Trunk Railway and should arrive in Chicago Monday night about nine o'clock. Am writing fully." *Later.*—Telephoned Croatian Bank, asking them to let Mr. Kapalo know his family is arriving. Mr. Kapalo had already heard from Ellis Island and knew line of route, etc. *Later.*—Letter received from Miss Freeman, dated December 7, saying:

I received the $150 for the release of Mrs. Kapalo. I could take no action because Mary just then was quite seriously ill. I therefore placed the money on deposit at Ellis Island. I took the matter up with Mr. A— who ordered that the case be placed before the Board of Special Inquiry so that the Kapalo family, with the exception of Mary might either be admitted or, if excluded, given an opportunity to be admitted on bond. I had the case held up to give me time to secure Mr. Kapalo's affidavit offering to give bond and stating that he had telegraphed money for deposit to guarantee that he would call for Mary as soon as she is discharged or would see that his wife would accompany her in case of deportation. As soon as I have the affidavit the case will come before the Board for decision.

December 17, 1920.—Letter from Miss Freeman, dated December 13:

Yesterday I received the affidavit of Mr. Kapalo. I had Mrs. Kapalo taken before the Board at once and appeared on her behalf. Fortunately the chairman of the Board knew me well from my work during war times and admitted Mrs. Kapalo and her two boys on the deposit of the $150 sent by Mr. Kapalo for the purpose. Unfortunately I did not know that, since the increase in traveling rates, especially across the Atlantic, the deposit required has been set at $250. The chairman of the Board of Special Inquiry admitted Mrs. Kapalo on my word, not insisting upon the additional $100. I, however, had much difficulty in making the deposit as the Treasurer did not want to accept less than the usual $250. Finally, I have secured the receipt for Mr. Kapalo's $150. Your organization, per myself, is entered as depositor. Shall I hold receipt until money is to be returned? Mary Kapalo is now out of danger, but her illness is of such a nature that there is a slight possibility of relapse. As the amount on deposit is not sufficient to pay the expenses of a guardian in case of deportation (though there is only the remotest possibility of such a contingency), I would suggest that Mr. Kapalo deposit with you $100 so as to make sure that all government requirements will be met in any contingency. This is merely a suggestion as a safeguard and in no wise alters the fact that there is every reason to believe that Mary will soon be well enough to proceed to Chicago. I shall know a few days in advance of the child's discharge from the hospital in order to give the father a chance to take her home as soon as admitted. *Any* detention in general detention quarters would mean regular meals as served to all. This might cause a relapse. The child ought to travel in a regular train where her guardian could purchase special diet food for her. This would not be possible on the immigrant train.

December 20, 1920.—Mr. Kapalo in office. He is willing to deposit additional $100, but we told him it was not necessary. He wishes League to send telegram, at his expense, to Miss Freeman, thanking her and asking her to send semi-weekly telegrams to him about Mary. The boys and Mrs. Kapalo are well. They complain of the lack of sleeping accommodations at Ellis Island and of the crowds. Otherwise they were well cared for. They are all very happy to be together again after their long years of separation.

December 24.—Letter received from Miss Freeman. [Extract from letter.]

According to your telegraphic request of the twentieth, I telegraphed Mr. Kapalo that Mary is sitting up and feeling much better. I shall try to telegraph Mr. Kapalo twice weekly about his little girl but, owing to the holiday this week, I may be unable to secure authentic medical information concerning her condition toward the end of this week.

January 18, 1921.—Mr. Kapalo in office; worried because he has heard nothing from Miss Freeman for two weeks. He brought Mrs. Kapalo with him, a pleasant, motherly looking woman, who wished to thank all of us for helping her. She is full of happiness to be in America. The boys are very well and are both attending school. Telegram sent to Miss Freeman:

"January 18, Mr. Kapalo worried about Mary. Please wire him, 836 South M Street."

January 21.—Extract from letter from Miss Freeman:

Yesterday I telegraphed Mr. Kapalo that his child is getting along well at the Ellis Island Hospital. Today I learned that she runs a low fever occasionally and that this seems now to be due to a running ear. The ear trouble is not at all serious. Should there be any serious developments, I shall telegraph Mr. Kapalo. The nephritic condition improves exceedingly slowly.

[The remaining portion of the record is omitted except the following, which indicates the outcome of the case.]

March 14, 1921.—Mr. Kapalo in office. He brought Mary from Ellis Island March 7. Says she is well now and "healthy looking." Mr. Kapalo wants us to write with regard to the $150 deposit.

5. Nicolo and Francesca Archieri and Lina Arcolini
(Contagious Disease—Hospital Treatment)

October 29, 1920.—John Archieri in office [Immigrants' Commission]. His father, Nicolo Archieri, age sixty-five, is detained at Ellis Island, reported to be "under observation." With his father are his mother, Francesca Archieri, age sixty-one, and his sister-in-law, Lina, age twenty-four. They all arrived together on the S.S. "Pesaro." He wishes us to write to Ellis Island to find cause of detention. Man is a full citizen (1917), has been in the United States since 1908, is married, and has two children, and is thirty-seven years old. He is a musician, earning $60 a week. He owns real estate valued $6,000 and personal property valued $3,000. He is not certain of the name of steamship on which they finally came. They may have come on "Dante Alighieri." Prepared and sent affidavit. Gave man telegram to send as follows: "*Commissioner of Immigration, Ellis Island, New York:* Affidavits sent today Nicolo Archieri and wife and Lina Arcolini steamship Pesaro. Wire reason detained. If excluded hereby appeal.—JOHN ARCHIERI, 9 Ashland Street."

November 2, 1920.—Mr. Archieri in office with telegram from Commissioner of Immigration as follows: "Nicolo Archieri and wife and Lina Arcolini detained hospital under observation." Mr. Archieri has learned that his family came on S.S. "Corsica," October 25. He wishes us to write Ellis Island to learn cause of detention, will refund money for telegrams. *Later.*—Telegram sent as follows: "*Commissioner of Immigration, Ellis Island, New York:* Nicolo and Francesca Archieri, Lina Arcolini steamship Corsica detained Ellis Island Hospital. Wire cause detention. If excluded hereby appeal.—JOHN ARCHIERI, 9 Ashland Street." *Later.*—The following letter sent to the Italian Immigrants' Society, New York:

GENTLEMEN:

John Archieri, 9 Ashland Street, tells us that his old father, Nicolo, his old mother Francesca and his sister-in-law, Lina Arcolini, are being detained at Ellis Island Hospital. They arrived on the "Corsica," October 25. Mr. Archieri has sent official affidavits of support. He has likewise today wired the Immigration Commissioner that if they are excluded he hereby appeals. Will you be good enough to look up these people and assist them if they need help?

Very truly yours,

LYDIA GARDNER

November 4, 1920.—Mr. Archieri in office. He is very anxious about his parents.

November 5, 1920.—Telegram received from New York as follows: "Nicolo Archieri certified ringworm of nails contagious disease not appealable. Francesca and Lina Arcolini detained. Doing all possible to have petition accepted.—SOCIETY FOR ITALIAN IMMIGRANTS." *Later.*—Mr. Archieri in office. Explained telegram. He will leave at five o'clock this afternoon for New York.

November 9, 1920.—Telegram from Mr. Archieri as follows: "Nicolo Archieri petition filed and appeal for my mother Francesca made through the Italian Immigrant Society. Can you help in having Washington accept petition and appeal.—JOHN ARCHIERI." *Later.*—Letter written to Mr. Archieri expressing regret that Commission cannot go any farther but suggesting that he get a specialist and ask to have his father treated at hospital at his own expense.

December 9, 1920.—Mr. Archieri in office. He is very happy and wishes to express thanks to the Commission for assistance. His father was operated on at Ellis Island for the trouble with his nails and got on nicely. Both parents finally admitted and are here in Chicago. They are all very happy and everything is going well. He would like to have Mrs. L— [Italian visitor] come to see his parents.

December 17, 1920.—V. L. [Italian visitor] visited. Father is well now. Family live in comfortable, nicely furnished house. All very happy to be together again.

January 15, 1921.—Mr. Archieri in office. He has not yet had returned to him Liberty Bonds deposited at Ellis Island, November 26. He deposited $1,000 in Liberty Bonds for his father. On December 4, when he left, he was told these were to be returned to him in about ten days. He has not received them yet. He has receipt File No. 9878–69, second issue Liberty Bond of $1,000, serial No. DO 112963. He wishes us to write to Ellis Island. Promised to write.

[The remaining portion of the record deals wholly with the return of the bond, which was finally sent to Mr. Archieri through the Immigrants' Commission on March 3, 1921.]

6. Josef Roeder
(Contagious Disease—Hospital Treatment)

August 29, 1923.—August Becker in office with telegram from Mrs. Lee [Y.W.C.A. representative, Ellis Island] about Josef Roeder, his wife's cousin, forty years old, who arrived S.S. "Berlin," August 15, and is certified to have favus of the nails. Telegram advised Mr. Becker to send $165 for treatment. Mr. Becker has been in the United States twenty years and was naturalized January of this year. He and his wife keep a large rooming-house and earn about $50 a week. He has property valued at $3,600 and is willing to furnish bonds or to pay for treatment. Advised him to telegraph the $165 to Mrs. Lee. Prepared affidavit and sent it to Ellis Island and also sent copy to Mrs. Lee. Telegram sent to Commissioner of Immigration, Ellis Island, as follows: "Official affidavits Josef Roeder steamship Berlin sent today. If excluded hereby appeal.—AUGUST BECKER, *Cousin.*"

August 30, 1923.—Mr. Becker in office with telegram from Assistant Commissioner, Ellis Island: "Josef Roeder mandatorily excludable account loathsome contagious disease nails. No appeal lies in this case." Mr. Becker says Josef Roeder was wounded in left arm during the war but has never been ill since. He has had a black spot on one of his nails for a long time.

September 1, 1923.—Letter written to Secretary of Labor, Washington:

MY DEAR MR. SECRETARY:

I am writing you in behalf of Josef Roeder, S.S. "Berlin." He has been excluded because of favus of the nail. His cousin in Chicago, August Becker, has telegraphed $165 to the Commissioner of Immigration at Ellis Island with a request that the man be allowed to have an operation on the nails and be kept at Ellis Island till cured. We understand that only a slight operation is necessary. The relatives in Chicago are perfectly willing to bear the expenses involved.

Josef Roeder is a tailor. In his own country he seems to have had a small shop of his own. Before leaving for the United States he sold the materials he had in stock at a sacrifice, hoping to get enough money for his transportation and for his family. He has had his machine sent on from Austria. When his cousin, August Becker, came to our office to make affidavits, he stated that the machine had already arrived in Chicago and was at his house. If this man has to go back and has to resume work over there, it will mean much financial loss; in fact, he could not possibly at the prices prevailing there now replace the stock and tools and so forth which he disposed of.

We would not petition in this man's behalf if this were a serious case of favus involving long treatment; we know how crowded the Ellis Island hospitals are. But we have been assured that this particular case would in all probability take only a short while to cure. And the consequences to this man of deportation are so very serious. That you may know something about the Chicago relatives and their standing in this community, we inclose two letters of reference. Mr. Becker is an American citizen.

Very truly yours,
ALICE MARION
Superintendent, Immigrants' Protective League

310   IMMIGRATION: DOCUMENTS AND CASE RECORDS

September 15, 1923.—Letter received from Assistant Secretary of Labor:

MADAM:

Referring to your interest in the case of Josef Roeder, it gives me pleasure to inform you that the Department has granted the application of this alien for hospital treatment, and has directed that he be admitted if and when cured.

September 17, 1923.—Letter written to Mr. Becker:

MY DEAR MR. BECKER:

We are happy to send you a copy of a letter just received from the Assistant Secretary of Labor.

The $165.00 which you wired on August 29th will pay for your cousin's medical treatment and other expenses for two months. Undoubtedly, he will be cured by that time. However, if he should not then be cured, be sure you pay promptly in advance $82.50, the cost of a third month's treatment, and so on till he is cured. We will hope that it will not be necessary, however. Be sure you let us know what news you hear from him.

Very truly yours,

ALICE MARION, *Superintendent*

[The record shows further that the man was cured and admitted within the two months.]

7. Katerina Kosice
(Excluded—Contagious Disease)

July 25, 1923.—Mrs. Elizabeth Kosice, a Slovak woman, in office. Her husband's sister, Katerina Kosice, a Slovak girl, age twenty-one, was coming to this country. Mrs. Kosice sent Katerina through the Mala Steamship Ticket Agency [a West Side agency in Chicago] a prepaid ticket on the Bohemian-American Line, July 15, 1922, third class, $102.50; in addition she paid $8 head tax, $25 landing money, and $30.70 for railroad fare. Katerina secured her visa from the American Consul and was ready to leave but was detained at Libau, probably for some trouble with eyes. The doctor said it was not important and she would soon be cured. The people she was travelling with arrived in Chicago weeks ago. They said Katerina was coming soon, but her brother has not heard from her. He is worried and wants to know if there is any way to find out whether she is really sailing and when. Advised Mrs. Kosice to go to the steamship agency and ask if they have heard anything.

July 28, 1923.—Mrs. Kosice in office. Katerina is already at Ellis Island. Agent did not notify family until Mr. Kosice went to Mala's yesterday to make inquiries. Mr. Kosice thinks the girl will arrive any day. Mr. Kosice has been in the United States twelve years and is an American citizen and an ex-service man. He is a shoemaker, earning

$36.50 a week. They have one child, two years old. Gave Mrs. Kosice affidavits for her husband to have signed tonight; prepared telegram for him to send: "*Commissioner of Immigration, Ellis Island, New York:* Official affidavits Katerina Kosice steamship Masyryk sent today. If excluded hereby appeal.—STEFAN KOSICE, *Brother*, 4700 West Street."

August 4, 1923.—Mr. and Mrs. Kosice in office. They have a telegram from Ellis Island. Katerina has been excluded for trachoma. Her brother said she had taken a long cure in Czecho-Slovakia for trachoma, for which he paid 3,000 crowns. The doctor in Prague certified her as cured. Brother does not believe Ellis Island diagnosis is correct and wishes to pay for another examination. He also has friends who know Senator X., and those friends are going to wire the Senator to get the deportation stayed. Mr. Kosice said his sister has had a very hard time. First she went to the city of Y. in July, 1922, but the steamship company examination showed that she had trachoma and she had to go back home again for treatment. She was under doctor's care until October, when he said she was cured. Then she went to Prague for American Consul's visa in October, 1922; but when she got there she was sent home again because the Czecho-Slovak quota was filled. Then she was called again and got her visa in June, 1923. He feels very much discouraged that she may be sent back again. He will pay anything necessary for treatment here. *Later.*—Telegram sent to Mrs. Lee [Y.W.C.A. worker at Ellis Island]: "Relatives Katerina Kosice convinced diagnosis trachoma wrong, certified cured by European doctor. Brother wishes come Ellis Island with specialist for consultation. Wire when her boat sails.—IMMIGRANTS' PROTECTIVE LEAGUE." *Later.*—Telegram received from Mrs. Lee: "*Stefan Kosice, 4700 West Street, Chicago:* Trachoma diagnosis of doctors final. Katerina will be put on board steamship Masyryk Monday afternoon. If you so desire she might stay in Prague under our care to get more treatment and full healing. Nothing else can be done. She sails Tuesday ten A.M.—K. F. LEE, *Y.W.C.A. Worker.*"

August 6, 1923.—Telegram received from Mrs. Lee: "Katerina Kosice heartbroken over deportation. Please urge brother to have girl treated in Prague, have given her address of our worker in Prague if he decided to have her treated there. Please communicate directly with our office, 600 Lexington Avenue. Am reporting deportation there to follow up.—K. F. LEE."

August 7, 1923.—Mr. and Mrs. Kosice in office. He has a telegram from Assistant Commissioner's Office, Ellis Island, as follows: "Katerina Kosice will be deported today on steamship Masyryk. This office has no authority to grant her treatment."

September 11, 1923.—Mrs. Kosice in office. She brought a note sent by Katerina signed by Dr. Jan Val Klobouky, January 11, 1923, written in French and German, stating "Miss Katerina Kosice of Z—, Slovakia, is not suffering from trachoma or from any other contagious disease; she is in good health." She is now probably in Prague. The Mala Company has refunded railroad fare $30.70 but refused to refund landing money, $25, and head tax. Mr. Kosice wants to change ticket to a second-class one. Mrs. Kosice said Katerina wrote that on July 26 the doctors at Ellis Island offered to operate on her if she had $70. Katerina sent two telegrams that the Kosices did not receive. She could find nobody who understood her.

September 21, 1923.—Mr. Kosice in office. He is very anxious to have his sister here. He will pay any medical care she needs and will send her a second ticket. He has had $30.70 refunded and agent is going to refund $25 landing money. He will also ask for head tax. He said Katerina was given $40 on ship the day before she landed. He does not know how that happened. She has a mother in Czecho-Slovakia, who owns a farm there. Mr. Kosice is her only brother. She writes that she feels so humiliated that she will not go home to live. Everybody knows that she has left three times already to come to the United States and each time she had to go home again. Everybody will make fun of her. If she cannot come to the United States, she is going to take service somewhere.

September 24, 1923.—Mrs. Kosice brought letter from steamship company, stating that refund of head tax and passage money depends on whether a fine has been imposed on company. If so, sum would be deposited with Collector of Customs, who in turn sends it through the nearest American Consul to passenger. Proceeding takes six to eight months. Mrs. Kosice says that Mr. Mala refuses to refund the $25 landing money. He claims the money was used for hospital expenses at Ellis Island.

September 25, 1923.—Letter received from the National Board of the Young Women's Christian Association, inclosing copy of letter from their worker in Prague:

I am writing to you in the case of Katerina Kosice, twenty years old, deported on account of trachoma. This girl has arrived in Prague and came to our office. The next day we went with her to the Prague hospital, where her eyes have been examined. The physician told us it is not necessary that she have regular treatment; he has given her some medicine and said that she can go home. Also he has advised her not to go back to the United States, saying that she has scars in her eyelids which always remain after trachoma and which show that the person has suffered from it. Therefore the American physicians will never grant her permission to enter America. But her only idea is to go back to her brother, and she thinks as soon as her brother will send her the necessary papers that she will start on. We did not succeed in making her understand the reasons why she cannot do so. We think that it would be better for her if her brother would give up the idea of having his sister with him, especially when there would be the possibility of being deported again. We would be very glad if you could give us your opinion on this.

[The League in reply sent the name of a well-known eye specialist in Prague, and advised that the girl see him and follow his advice.]

8. Carl and Johanna Peterson and Their Two Children
(Sick Child—Possible Permanent Disability)

November 5, 1920.—Mrs. O'Brien in office [Immigrants' Commission], asking advice about her sister, who is detained at Ellis Island. Mrs. O'Brien says she herself is "an American." Her sister, Mrs. Johanna Peterson, with her husband, Carl Peterson, and two little boys arrived in New York last week on the S.S. "Sweden." The whole family are detained at Ellis Island; one child is in hospital. He injured his leg on board ship. The doctor attended to it, but evidently some infection has set in. Mrs. O'Brien is anxious to have her sister and other child sent on to Chicago. She says conditions at Ellis Island are frightfully unpleasant, no blankets, etc.

Mrs. O'Brien is apparently well-to-do, says she was born in Denmark but married an American, who earns $125 per month and often more than that. They own real estate to the value of $6,000 and have some other property. She wishes to do what is necessary to help her sister. Her sister is twenty-six years old, her sister's husband thirty, the little boy Carl Heinrich, who is in the hospital, is six, and the other child, Hans, is five. She will pay for telegrams.

M. S. explained the probable complications in the situation and the reason for keeping family together. Telegraphed Miss Freeman [social worker at Ellis Island]: "Carl and Johanna Peterson and two children, steamship Sweden, detained Ellis Island. Child in hospital. Wire nature illness and probable duration. Must family remain Ellis Island?"

November 6, 1920.—Reply telegram from Miss Freeman. Child has acute osteomyelitis. She will try to arrange discharge of Mr. Peterson and other child. *Later.*—Telephoned Mrs. O'Brien the contents of Miss Freeman's telegram. Mrs. O'Brien will telegraph money to her relatives, care Immigration Commissioner, Ellis Island.

November 8, 1920.—Letter from Miss Freeman, with following details:

In the telegram today, I advised you that Carl Heinrich Peterson was suffering with acute osteomyelitis of the left leg. This seems to be due to a fall shortly before the family sailed on the "Sweden." On November first an operation was successfully performed. I went over the hospital record with the doctor in charge today. He says he is willing to give an official diagnosis that would permit the admission of the rest of the family. He also says that the boy may recover soon, but that occasionally these cases drag along as practically chronic. The boy is doing very well. Mr. and Mrs. Peterson and the younger child are temporarily detained pending the recovery of Carl. The family has $210 and in Danish crowns approximately $30. It would be necessary for the immigrants to deposit $150 for the sick child before the officials would consider whether or not the healthy members of the family might be admitted. Mr. Peterson says he wishes to make such deposit and is willing that his wife should remain at Ellis Island until the patient has recovered, if this should be the condition of his admission with the younger child. I shall make every effort on

Monday to arrange for the release of Mr. Peterson and younger child, and if possible, I shall have Mrs. Peterson paroled to the Swedish Immigrant Home here until the sick boy is discharged from the hospital. Within a few days I shall be able to send you definite information in this matter.

November 10, 1920.—Wire received from Miss Freeman: "Am delaying action Peterson family until sure saving boy's leg. Boy doing well. Will write fully."

November 12, 1920.—Mr. and Mrs. O'Brien in office. Filled out affidavits. Sent telegram to Commissioner of Immigration, Ellis Island, New York: "Affidavits sent today Carl Peterson, Johanna, Carl and Hans, steamship Sweden. If excluded hereby appeal." *Later.*—Telegram sent to Miss Freeman, Ellis Island, New York: "Official affidavits sent today Peterson family, also Carl steamship Sweden. Is it possible to get release of Carl for medical attention here? Family desirous this action be taken. Wire further information."

November 13, 1920.—Letter from Miss Freeman:

Referring to the Peterson family about which you telegraphed me on the fifth inst., I wish to advise you that I have deferred acting in the matter of securing the release of all but the sick boy. The facts are as follows: The family is temporarily detained because the boy, Carl Heinrich, is in the hospital suffering with acute osteomyelitis. As this diagnosis does not involve any medical certification that might exclude the family, I secured from the doctors in charge a memorandum giving the diagnosis and prognosis. This is necessary to secure the admission of aliens accompanying a sick immigrant. The memorandum read as follows: "The above-described alien child is afflicted with osteomyelitis, acute, left leg, for which condition he was operated on October 31, 1920. Further hospitalization in this case is indicated for perhaps an extended period of time. Prognosis in the case is doubtful as regards the saving of the affected limb."

The inspector in the Discharge Division was unwilling to act in the case as a question of public charge would be involved if the patient were to lose his leg. The inspector therefore wanted to send the family before the Board of Special Inquiry to decide whether or not the family might be admitted pending the recovery of the child, Carl Heinrich Peterson. I asked the inspector to take no action until I could secure affidavits from Chicago guaranteeing the Government against the boy becoming a public charge— that I might have this evidence for the Board of Special Inquiry. I believe it quite possible that a Board of Special Inquiry would either defer action pending the recovery of the patient, or exclude the family in order to have the question decided by appeal to Washington. Either action would involve a very long delay, and the admission of the family would become doubtful. I have kept the doctor's memorandum in my possession and decided to wait some days until there can be some assurance that the patient will not lose his leg. In that case I may be able to secure from the physicians a more favorable statement with which to ask for the release of the healthy members of the Peterson family. It seems too bad to keep the family in detention quarters, but it seems to me to be the best we can do under the circumstances. The Peterson family has about $250 or a little less. One hundred and fifty dollars would have to be deposited for the sick child as a guarantee that he will be called for and taken to Chicago upon his recovery. The balance of $100 will be more than enough to pay the railroad fares of the entire family because the children would require only half-fare tickets; they are six and five years old.

I do not know anything about the relatives in Chicago, but if they are in a position to make affidavit, assuming responsibility for the boy, Carl Heinrich, or for the whole family, including a specific statement on behalf of the boy, I should like to receive such affidavit to be used in case of need. If you can suggest any other action on my part, will you kindly let me know? If you believe the family should not be detained but taken before the Board of Special Inquiry, despite the risk involved, please advise me. The latest report from the Ellis Island Hospital is to the effect that Carl Heinrich is not improving.

November 15, 1920.—Telegram received from Commissioner of Immigration, Ellis Island: "Carl Peterson detained hospital under observation."

November 18, 1920.—Letter received from Miss Freeman as follows:

Referring to your telegram of the 12th inst., in which you say that the relatives of Carl Peterson are eager to have the boy Carl transferred to the care of private physicians in Chicago, I did not reply at once as I was awaiting some change in the boy's condition that would indicate some possible line of procedure. Until today his condition showed no improvement and the possibility of his travelling safely was out of the question and I could therefore not take the matter up with the Ellis Island doctor—the first necessary step. Today Carl Peterson showed considerable improvement. In two or three days I hope the physicians will be able to say that the boy is no longer in danger of losing his left leg. As soon as this occurs I will ask that the family be taken before a Board of Special Inquiry, which will have the power to admit Mr. Peterson and the healthy child and either to detain Mrs. Peterson until Carl has recovered, or to admit her and require a cash deposit of $150 as a guarantee for the sick child. After that it may be possible to secure permission from Washington for the transfer of Carl to Chicago for treatment under bond bending his recovery. Please assure the relatives of the Peterson family that I will watch developments carefully and take the first favorable opportunity to try to secure the admission to Chicago of all members of the Peterson family. The affidavit they sent (and which I have had no opportunity to read) will be essential for the hearing before the Board.

December 1, 1920.—Telegram received from Miss Freeman: "Leg improving but has contracted measles. That will delay action." *Later.*—Telephoned Mrs. O'Brien contents of telegram. Mrs. O'Brien is no longer very much worried. Mrs. Peterson has written in praise of Ellis Island Hospital, where boy is getting excellent care. She thinks doctor is especially fine.

December 2, 1920.—Letter received from Miss Freeman:

Carl Heinrich Peterson has been improving considerably the last few days. I therefore hope to secure a favorable written prognosis from the doctor in charge. In that case I shall at once ask to have the family taken before the Board of Special Inquiry to decide the question of the admission of the healthy members of the family and the possible admission of Carl for treatment in Chicago. As the affidavit sent by the relatives is not yet made part of the record, and will not be until the case comes before the Board, I have been unable to see the affidavit. It would enable me to judge more correctly of the probable outcome of a hearing before the Board, if I could see the affidavit. I do not know what it contains with reference to possible medical care for the child in Chicago and what guarantees it offers. Would it be possible for you to send me at once a copy of the affidavit as I may be able to take action in a very few days? The doctor will probably give me a favorable prognosis in a day or two.

December 6, 1920.—Mrs. O'Brien telephoned that her sister writes the boy is now well enough to be out of bed and he is able to stand on the troublesome leg. The Peterson family have been trying to see the doctor to learn when they can travel but they cannot get access to him. Mrs. O'Brien wants Immigrants' Commission to wire Miss Freeman about the matter. Mrs. O'Brien had told the Peterson family that $150 was to pay for child's medical care. Explained to her once more the nature of a bond and the necessity for it in this case. She will write to her family at once and reassure them. *Later.*—Wrote Miss Freeman, enclosing copy of official affidavit as follows:

I am enclosing a copy of the official affidavits for the Peterson family. I notice with regret that it is not very strong as regards medical care, etc., for Carl Peterson. However, it may be adequate; if it is not, let us know and we will get additional affidavits from the family.

December 8, 1920.—Telegram received from Miss Freeman: "Second child, Hans Peterson, is now in hospital, not serious—will be admitted with father when discharged from hospital."

December 18, 1920.—Telegram from Miss Freeman: "Please send me directly affidavit nearest relatives Peterson family giving financial standing offering deposit or bond for Carl Heinrich and offering assume full responsibility for child Hans in case mother is detained with Carl and asking discharge of all but Carl on $250 guarantee deposit." Called up Mrs. O'Brien. She was very much upset. She said she would speak to her husband and come in Monday with him. *Later.*—Mr. O'Brien called up. Read telegram to him and tried to explain. Man was very indignant. Tried to explain to him why $250 was necessary, but he said he does not want Miss Freeman to do anything more about the case. They have politicians in Washington, he said, who would take care of the case. I told him that we would write Miss Freeman to withdraw at once.

December 22, 1920.—Letter written to Miss Freeman, containing the following:

On the receipt of your telegram we telephoned the Peterson relatives. Although they have on a number of occasions declared their willingness to help their family with money and to deposit bonds if necessary, they took your communication about the $250 deposit very badly. They refuse absolutely to do this and have asked us not to do anything further in the matter. We are very sorry that this should have occurred after you have done so much and were just on the point of helping them out of their difficulties. It is also pretty hard on the Peterson family. There is, however, nothing further we can do in the matter.

December 24, 1920.—Letter from Miss Freeman:

On December 17, when Hans Peterson was discharged from the Ellis Island Hospital, I tried to secure his admission with his father but the Division Inspector refused to take responsibility for admitting Hans Peterson because he claimed he might become a public charge in case the mother were deported with Carl Peterson. . . . . Carl Heinrich Peterson is a diphtheria carrier. He will probably be cured of this trouble by the time his leg is healed. His condition is improving, but I fear he will have to remain in the hospital for some time longer. For this reason I believe that we ought now to try to secure admission of all but Carl. It will be necessary to place their case before the Board of Special Inquiry. To secure a favorable decision it will be necessary to be prepared to deposit at Ellis Island a guarantee of $250 to assure the Government that a responsible adult will accompany the patient in case he is deported. Mr. Peterson, I believe, arrived with about $250 some of which he has no doubt spent at Ellis Island. He might possibly make the deposit but would not then have enough to cover travelling expenses for himself, wife and one child. It would, however, make a better impression if the relatives in Chicago were to send the $250. They should also send directly to me their affidavit expressing their desire to assume full responsibility for the child Hans, if admitted before the mother. The affidavit should of course contain the usual items in public charge affidavits, together with a statement that the relatives are ready to offer bonds if required for the admission of the Peterson family. If the relatives do not wish to assume as much responsibility as I suggest, please advise me so that I can either refer the matter of securing the admission of the two of the immigrants to the Commissioner again, or take it before the Board without the affidavits.

December 29, 1920.—Mrs. O'Brien telephoned. They have had a telegram from Mr. Peterson, asking them to deposit $250. They wanted to know if Immigrants' Commission would transmit the money. Advised Mrs. O'Brien to wire money to Mr. Peterson himself, care of Ellis Island.

January 4, 1921.—Letter received from Miss Freeman. The Peterson family, except sick child, admitted. The $250 has been deposited. The sick child now has scarlet fever. [Extract from Miss Freeman's letter follows:]

Upon receipt of your letter of December 22, I explained the whole matter to Mr. Peterson and told him that if he wished to try to secure his admission, he should write his relatives that he could not leave Ellis Island unless they sent him the necessary deposit money for the sick child at Ellis Island. Mr. Peterson had only about $105 left in his possession. He needs this for railroad fares and travelling expenses. Mr. Peterson wrote his brother-in-law immediately. On December 30, Mr. Peterson received a telegram from his relatives telling him that they were telegraphing him $250 and urging him to be careful of it and to demand a receipt. Whether the relatives sent the deposit money after thinking over what you had told them, or whether they sent it in response to Mr. Peterson's personal request, I do not know. At any rate, I had the Peterson family taken before the Board of Special Inquiry, explained the case and testified as to the medical facts I secured verbally from the hospital doctors. I am very glad to say that I was able to secure the release of all but the sick child. Mr. Peterson made the deposit of the requisite $250 personally and holds the receipt for same. He understands the facts perfectly and will explain them to the Chicago relatives to whom I saw that Mr. Peterson telegraphed his departure.

Carl Heinrich has recovered from both measles and diphtheria, but has now had scarlet fever for two weeks. The doctors hope that this disease, as well as the osteomyelitis, will have disappeared within the next two weeks.

January 7, 1921.—Wrote letter to Miss Freeman:

The Peterson family arrived safely and are well and very happy to be here. They feel deeply grateful to you. Mrs. Peterson's sister, Mrs. O'Brien, who was most unpleasant last month, called up this morning to thank us. She expects to go to New York to get Carl Heinrich, when he is ready for release, and she threatens to see you then to express her gratitude in person. She tells us that Mrs. Peterson is very much worried about Carl Heinrich. She says when she last saw him there was a window wide open by his bedside; she is convinced that he will have pneumonia next. She begs that you will speak to the nurses about the matter. We tried to make it clear to her that the nurses undoubtedly know their business and would resent being interfered with, but she seems to think that a word from you would be very efficacious. She also begs that when you write to us you will include some little message about the child. We are infinitely obliged to you.

January 10, 1921.—Mrs. O'Brien called, wanted news; told her about message just received in letter about another case. "Carl Peterson convalescing nicely." She wants to know if she will need letter from us when she goes to new York.

January 11, 1921.—Mrs. O'Brien telephoned. Mr. Peterson has had letter from Carl's doctor that Carl will be discharged from hospital probably January 14. Mrs. O'Brien would like us to telegraph that it would be more convenient for her to get to New York City on the 18th. When told we could not dictate in such a matter, she said the Government was inconsiderate. Advised her to have written authorization from Mr. Peterson to get child and collect deposit, also ample identification material; advised her to get in touch with Miss Freeman. Gave her Miss Freeman's address and telephone number.

[The remaining portion of the record is not important except for the following entry:]

January 20, 1921.—Extract from letter written by Miss Freeman, January 17, 1921, to Immigrants' Protective League:

Carl was discharged from the hospital on January 15. I have been unable to get the detention sheets to learn whether or not the boy was admitted the same day. I assume that Mrs. O'Brien called on that date, and the doctor, in accordance with his promise, discharged the child. It might have been well for the boy to remain in hospital a while longer because an X-ray picture taken a day earlier showed that the leg required another operation. No doubt the doctor explained this to Mrs. O'Brien but it might be well to make sure of this.

9. Rachel and Kazia Aronoff
(Attempted Deportation—Hospital Treatment—Contagious Disease)

April 25, 1912.—Joseph Aronoff in office; asks help for his son Nathan, aged eighteen, and his daughter Rosa, aged sixteen, detained at St. John, New Brunswick. Mr. Aronoff has been in the United States for a year and a half and is earning from $10 to $12 a week. He is boarding with a married cousin. His wife and five children are still in Russia. The two older children came on prepaid steamship tickets. Mr. Aronoff also sent them $50 after they arrived at St. John. Told Mr. Aronoff we will write to Commissioner of Immigration. *Later.*—Letter sent to the Immigration Commissioner at St. John and also to the Secretary of Labor at Washington as follows:

DEAR SIR:

I am writing in behalf of Nathan and Rosa Aronoff who are detained at St. John. I judge that their detention is due to the fact that the father has not yet provided a home but is, instead, boarding with a cousin. If this is the only objection I should be glad to assure the department that the son and daughter will be properly cared for. There is a very good boarding-club for Jewish girls to which the girl can be admitted, or we will undertake to inspect any place to which they come if they are admitted.

Sincerely yours,

LYDIA GARDNER

May 4, 1912.—Letter received from the Department of Labor. The boy and girl have been admitted. [Record of follow-up visits omitted.]

July 14, 1914.—Mr. Aronoff in office with the following letter from the Commissioner of Immigration at Baltimore:

SIR:

On the North German Lloyd S.S. "Koenigin Luise," reaching here July 8th, 1914, there arrived your wife, Esther Aronoff, with four children, Rachel, ten years, Kazla, eight years, Isaac, four years, and Anton, three years, and all have been excluded. The Public Health Surgeon has certified Rachel and Kazia for *tinea tonsurans* (ringworm of scalp), a loathsome, contagious disease, not easily cured, and requiring an indefinite period to effect a cure.

Upon receipt of this letter you are requested to advise this office at once whether or not you have taken out your declaration of intention to become a citizen (if so send copy thereof here); state your occupation, average weekly earnings, money on hand or in bank, and whether or not you are in a position to pay for hospital treatment here in Baltimore for the afflicted children should the Secretary of Labor grant the necessary permission therefor, and provided you can induce any of the hospitals in Baltimore to accept the children for treatment. I might say for your information that heretofore the hospitals of this city have been disinclined to receive patients suffering from ringworm of scalp. The usual cost of treatment is $1.00 per day for each child plus the charge of X-ray applications (generally $2.00 per application); two or three X-ray applications may be given each week, and as under the rules (if permission is granted to allow the children to receive treatment here, and a hospital found to take them) payment for hospital charges sixty days in advance is required, you should be prepared to forward at least $200.00, i.e.:

Sixty days' treatment (exclusive of X-ray) at $1.00 per day for each child...	$120.00
X-ray applications for same period (estimated at $5.00 per week for 8 weeks for each child)...	80.00
	$200.00

Give this matter your prompt attention.

Respectfully,

———, *Commissioner*

Later.—Telegraphed Hebrew Immigrant Aid Society of Baltimore as follows: "Advise seriousness Aronoff case Koenigin Luise. Is treatment advisable?" *Later.*—Reply from Hebrew Immigrant Aid Society of Baltimore: "Surgeon reports indefinite period cure Aronoff children. We have Hebrew Hospital which will take children provided relatives able to meet hospital charges dollar day each child. If satisfactory take up matter in Chicago direct with Commissioner of Immigration."

July 15, 1914.—Letter received from Secretary of the Baltimore Hebrew Immigrant Aid Society:

GENTLEMEN:

I beg to confirm my telegram sent today in reference to the Aronoff children who are excluded for ringworm of scalp. I am sure you realize that it will mean an unlimited expenditure, for in addition to the regular treatment there will be an additional charge for X-ray. The Hebrew Hospital is willing to accept the children, provided the money for treatment is sent regularly. The Abramson children who were eventually sent to Chicago about a year ago, were at the hospital fourteen months, and only recently three children were sent to Atlanta, Georgia, having been at the hospital seven months at a cost of $1,000. I am writing this, so that the relatives may know what they are up against, if the Bureau gives its consent to have the children treated. They may be prepared to have them stay at the hospital for a year or longer, at an expense of $100 a month. Let me know what the family intends doing.

Yours truly,

MARY STEINMETZ

[Reports of a general investigation into the situation of the father and two children already here is omitted since it is summarized in the letter of July 17.]

July 17, 1914.—Letter written to Mr. X., a friend of the League, asking assistance:

MY DEAR MR. X.:

Mrs. Esther Aronoff is detained at Baltimore with four children aged ten, eight, four, and three years. The two oldest ones have ringworm of the scalp and must go back unless hospital treatment can be secured. The family in Chicago earn as follows: The father, Joseph, forty-two years, presser, wages $12 per week, a son, Nathan, customer peddler (on borrowed capital) $10 per week; a daughter, Rosa, finisher on ladies' waists, $7 per week; a daughter, Katya, tailoring, $6 per week.

They owe $200 which they are repaying at the rate of $4 per week; $175 of this amount was sent to the mother in Bremen for five weeks' treatment of the two girls and for the board of the others while they were detained there. They supposed the children were cured, but the marine surgeon has found they are not. The family paid cash for the steamship tickets and for their furniture, so they have no money and, owing to the slack season in the sewing trades, are earning less at present than the amounts given, but hope that by September it will again amount to this. They are an unusually attractive family. The father has been here four years, the son and one daughter two years, and the third daughter one year. The boy and girls are bright, have had some education at home, and have made remarkable progress in English since they arrived. They will eventually earn considerably more.

I inclose a copy of a letter from Miss Steinmetz of the Hebrew Immigrant Aid Society of Baltimore and from the Commissioner with regard to admission under bond guaranteeing treatment. If permission could be secured, this is a very heavy expenditure to undertake. If this cannot be arranged for, the boy thinks the best plan would be for him to return to Germany or Belgium with the two older children for treatment, and have his mother come to Chicago with the two younger children. He is confident that he can earn his living in any place, and I am sure he can; but I think he should arrange for X-ray treatment for the two children, and, for this, help will be necessary in providing for the immediate expenses of the boy and in arranging for treatment. We can, of course, send him to the Jüden Hilfsverein in Bremen or Antwerp for help but they will insist that payments must be made regularly from this side. Do you feel that help could be guaranteed? I am sure you would be impressed with the family if you could see them.

Sincerely yours,
LYDIA GARDNER

Later.—Telegraphed Hebrew Immigrant Aid Society of Baltimore: "If unable to arrange for hospital treatment here for the Aronoff children father desires son to return with them and have mother and two younger children come to Chicago at once." [Other telegrams, etc., omitted here.]

July 19, 1914.—Telephone inquiry from Mr. X. Letter to Mr. X.:

The expense, if the Aronoff children return to Europe with their brother, can only be estimated. It will cost $44 for him to go from Chicago to Bremen third class. What the treatment and board will cost, I cannot say definitely—certainly less than one-half of what it will cost in Baltimore as *residence* in the *hospital* during treatment will not be required there and through the societies in Antwerp or Bremen treatment can be arranged for at very much less cost than here. There is not time to write and get a reply on this. If we submitted the case to them before returning the children, they would, I am sure, insist on treatment here because there is always the danger of disagreement between doctors. After they are pronounced cured by a doctor in Europe the Marine hospital doctors may reverse the decision and re-exclude them. The Commissioner at Baltimore refuses to allow the mother to enter and the boy to return with his sisters because the "mother is the natural guardian." Because immediate action was necessary, I have appealed to the Secretary of Labor asking that he permit the children to land under guarantee of hospital treatment and if he refuses this, to allow the son to return with his sisters. He may refuse both requests. If he grants the first and the return seems to you advisable, we can ask for that on Monday.

[Some letters and other entries on the case record are omitted here.]

July 20, 1914.—Mr. Aronoff in office. He has had a letter from Congressman Stein, saying that the children will be allowed to have hospital treatment and that the mother and younger children may proceed to Chicago. *Later.*—Letter received from Mr. X., guaranteeing payment not to exceed $100 per month.

[Correspondence with Baltimore regarding forwarding of money omitted.]

July 27, 1914.—Telegram from Hebrew Immigrant Aid Society of Baltimore: "Commissioner received instructions from Washington Aronoff mother and two children to be admitted. Two certified children to be deported accompanied by older brother in Chicago. Steamer leaves Wednesday noon. Have guardian leave immediately. Will return check."

July 28, 1914.—Telegraphed H.I.A.S. of Baltimore: "Aronoff boy left Monday evening. If he is required to pay steamship fare will you advance the money, and we will remit as soon as we hear from you."

July 20, 1914.—Telegram from H.I.A.S.: "Nathan Aronoff arrived Baltimore in time to accompany two children to Bremen. Mrs. Aronoff and two children leave tonight, B. & O. road, arrive seven Thursday night. Notify husband. Letter follows." *Later.*—Following letter written to H.I.A.S. of Baltimore:

MY DEAR MISS STEINMETZ:

Thank you very much for all your trouble in connection with the Aronoff case. How the misinformation from the Department of Labor was sent here, I do not understand. The news was sent to Congressmen Stein's office that the children would be admitted under bond guaranteeing hospital treatment. In the appeal I made both to Baltimore and to Washington, I asked for this first and also if this was refused that the boy be allowed to return with the children. At any rate the case is closed for the present. The check was received.

Sincerely yours,

LYDIA GARDNER

Later.—Letter written to Commissioner of Immigration at Baltimore explaining forwarding of check. [Extract from letter:]

I have been much confused in this case because Congressman Stein, who was working independently on it, stated that he had received word that the children would be admitted under bond guaranteeing treatment and so, as I wrote you, I forwarded the money at once, thinking that the payments were to be made.

Later.—Letter to Mr. X. as follows:

I regret very much to say that the decision in the Aronoff case was changed and the two children afflicted with ringworm were ordered excluded, but the son was allowed to return in place of the mother, so that she and the two younger children arrive in Chicago this evening. The news came to us on Monday afternoon, and the boy had to leave at once for Baltimore as the children were to be returned on Wednesday morning. Our visitor found that the family had only ten dollars that they could give the boy; and so with my approval, she advanced him twenty-five dollars, which would be enough for the trip and enough to enable him to get into connection with some organization on the other side. They went out on the "Friedrich der Grosse."

As this payment had not in any sense been authorized by you, I am sending a voucher through so that the check for the full amount which I received from Baltimore today will be returned to you.

We shall hear from the Aronoff boy as soon as he has arrived in Bremen and I hope that he will have been able to make some arrangement for treatment there. I have not yet learned what was the cause of this change in plans of the Department.

August 1, 1914.—Letter from H.I.A.S. as follows:

I beg to confirm my night letter in reference to the final disposition of the Aronoff family. I am glad to say there was no further delay, for the boy arrived in time to have a long talk with his mother before the steamer sailed. I have written to the Hilfs-Verein in Bremen, asking that organization to extend all possible help to the young man in obtaining treatment for the two children, which can be obtained there at about one-half the amount which would have been paid here. I also arranged to have the steamship company take the boy without charge, as a substitute guardian in place of the mother, which they agreed to do. As he only had about $15 with him, I advanced $5. . . . .

[Some other letters omitted here.]

August 6, 1914.—Mr. Joseph Aronoff in office. He is greatly excited on account of the war. The "Friedrich der Grosse" could not go to Bremen but turned around and returned to New York. He has a letter from Nathan, saying that the boy and his two sisters who were being deported are now being held on the boat and are not even allowed to land at Ellis Island.

[The letter written by Nathan Aronoff to his father is given below. Ellis Island gradually accumulated a large number of persons who could not be deported because of the war.]

[Translation from the Yiddish:]

NEW YORK, August 3, 1914

TO MY LOVING AND DEAR PARENTS:

As to our health, thanks to God. Be it known to you that the 29th of July we left Baltimore—this was the last Wednesday—and we traveled until Saturday night. Saturday night a telegram was received from the steamship company to the captain of our ship that the ship shall come back to America because England or France or others will take the German ships on the sea. So we sailed to New York Sunday at eight o'clock in the evening. We arrived not far from the harbor and the steamer stopped amidst the waters until Monday at 12 A.M. Then came a little boat, took all passengers who were going to Europe and carried them to New York. And I think from there they will be sent each to the place where he came from, because the steamer will not sail now any more to Europe. We, in the name of the Blessed God, I and Rachel and Kazia and a few others, who were deported, remained in the ship. And our ship still remains amidst the waters. How long it will remain I do not know and when it will sail and where it will sail I do not know either, but I think it will move to Castle Garden[1] in New York, but I cannot tell you anything for certain. I write this letter while the ship is on the waters. I send this letter to you as soon as I will get an opportunity. The name of my ship is "Friedrich der Grosse." I beg my dear parents do not worry or grieve. I am not the only one here, there are many with me. What will happen to us when we shall leave this place, I do not know. Perhaps you could better find out what will happen to us when you will inquire. Dear father, maybe you will find a way if you will apply for advice to somebody. Maybe the children could remain in New York. Your son, NATHAN. I beg once more do not worry and do not grieve. God will help us. The children send regards. I discovered a way to send my letter to you. I will stand on the deck and will wait until maybe a boat will pass not far away. I will wrap the letter with something heavy and will throw it into the boat and ask them to mail my letter.

Later.—Letter written to Senator Graves as follows:

MY DEAR SENATOR GRAVES:

On July 18, I applied to you in behalf of the Aronoff family, the wife and four children being detained at Baltimore, because two of the girls were certified for ringworm. At that time we requested that the Department allow the two children to land on bonds guaranteeing hospital treatment; and if this was refused, that the son, who was here in Chicago, be allowed to return with the afflicted sisters and that the mother and the two younger children be allowed to proceed to Chicago. This last request, as you were kind enough to notify us, was granted; and the boy started with his sisters on the S.S. "Friedrich der Grosse." Today the parents have received word that the "Friedrich der Grosse" returned to New York and is outside the harbor. The passengers were allowed to disembark, but the deported immigrants are detained. As these children are in need of treatment and

---

[1] [It is interesting that this boy speaks of the Immigrant Landing Depot as "Castle Garden." So well known was the old name that, after twenty years of Ellis Island, Castle Garden still was better known than the new depot.]

as the possibility of cure is made more expensive by delay, it seems to me that the Department might very well rule that they should be admitted for hospital treatment at Ellis Island, as their period of detention on the boat may be indefinitely prolonged. I shall be very grateful to you if you will endeavor to arrange for this.

Sincerely yours,
LYDIA GARDNER

Later.—Letter [in English] received from Nathan Aronoff as follows:

DEAR FRIEND, MISS GARDNER:

Pleas be kindly and do something for me if you can. I am now in a big trouble. God knows how long our boat will stay here. I can't pronounce everything in english all the knews about me. If you want know more ask my parents. The name of my boat is Friedrich d. Grosse. Your truly, N. ARONOFF. I thank you.

August 8, 1914.—Telegram from Hebrew Society of New York: "Rachel and Kazia Aronoff detained. Ordered deported account ringworm. Brother here desires you to communicate with relatives on our suggestion to apply for hospital treatment which costs seventy-five cents day each child until cured. Must deposit ninety dollars two months advance treatment. If satisfactory have them send to us that amount at once. Mail also proper affidavit."

August 10, 1914.—Letter received from Nathan Aronoff. [The letter is written in Yiddish to Miss Bourtseff, the Russian visitor of the League.]

[Translation from the Yiddish:]

MY HONORABLE FRIEND MISS BOURTSEFF:

I come to inform you that I and my two sisters left Baltimore Wednesday the 29th of July. We were sailing until Saturday night the first of August. Saturday night the steamer received a telegram, saying it should turn back to America because in Europe is declared war. The 2d of August at eight o'clock in the night we arrived in the harbor of New York, but our ship did not come to the land but stood far from the shore and all the passengers stayed on the ship. Monday at four o'clock came a little boat and took all passengers to New York; and I, my sisters, and three other persons[1] remained on the ship. I went to the captain of the ship and asked him how long I will remain on the ship so he answered: "We will remain here very long until the war in Europe will be over and the ships will be able to sail again." As I hear the ship can remain here for months. I cannot describe my grief. Before, we had more than twenty Jewish passengers, so we had "Kosher"[2] meals, but since all passengers were sent away we are the only Jews. And the two children, though I try to tell them that they must eat the food, they don't do it, and it is really impossible to eat this food.

[1] [These were all persons who were being deported and hence were not "passengers," but persons under detention.]

[2] [Prepared according to Jewish ritual.]

I have been some time ago a few weeks in Castle Garden, and then I said that it is like the Russian jails; but now I am on board of ship not far from New York and nevertheless so far from human beings—to be so near and yet unable to reach them is too sad and too horrible. The men employed on the ship for long hours go on little boats to the city; and I and my sisters, we can only stand on the deck and look from far off at the city of New York. I will not be able to bear it. Days go by, and there is nobody to whom to talk. The food is not good; they give us only cooked potatoes and tea. I would have considered myself happy if I could better be in New York in Castle Garden, at least I would have come in contact with people.

Thus I ask you, maybe you can do something for me. Maybe you could go to the Immigrants' Office, at least to see if they could take my sisters to the Hospital in New York. Do what you think best and whatever you can, and if you will want to let me know about it write me at the following address—care of the "Friedrich der Grosse." Please do not give this letter to my parents because I wrote two letters to them and wrote that I feel fine here, they are very much worried already, they have had enough of it. But if you want to take the trouble, you can send this letter to my relatives Berkavitch, who live at 111 West Street, Chicago, and ask them that my parents should not know anything about this letter. Once more I ask you to do for me as much as you can. Thanking you in advance, Nathan Aronoff and the children. P.S.—Give my regards to Miss Gardner. I would like to write her all about my trouble, but I cannot express myself in English.

NATHAN

August 11, 1914.—Letter received from Mr. X. He will provide the same medical attention for the Aronoff children at Ellis Island that he had agreed to provide at the hospital in Baltimore.

Telegram received from New York that the Department of Labor had admitted the Aronoff children to hospital treatment at New York. Nathan released. *Later.*—Ninety dollars sent to Commissioner of Immigration at New York. *Later.*—Letter to Hebrew Immigrant Aid Society of New York as follows:

DEAR SIR:

We are in receipt of your telegram with regard to the Aronoff case. On last Thursday we applied for treatment guaranteeing hospital treatment and have, today, received word, that the children were admitted, and have sent the money direct to the Commissioner. I do not know whether this payment of $0.75 a day includes X-ray treatment. I feel very strongly, from our experience with cases of this sort, that recovery is very slow without the X-ray treatment and that it should be arranged for if that is possible. I do not speak of this in the letter to the Commissioner, but should be very glad if you would take the matter up.

Sincerely yours,
LYDIA GARDNER

August 15, 1914.—Letter received from the Hebrew Immigrant Aid Society:

We do not know whether the medical authorities here contemplate using X-ray treatment or not, but if they do, the charge will remain the same. We do not feel that it is within our province to suggest to the doctors a method of treatment, for we are laymen and they are physicians and they ought to know how to proceed. If you feel that you can ask for a certain mode of treatment, I should suggest your writing to the Commissioner.

Later.—Notification received from Commissioner of Immigration at New York that bonds had been forwarded to the father, Mr. Joseph Aronoff.

August 26, 1914.—Letter written to the Commissioner of Immigration at Ellis Island:

DEAR SIR:

The family of Rachel and Kazia Aronoff, who are in the hospital undergoing treatment for favus, are in receipt of a letter, asking for permission that their hair be cut. The parents are anxious to have this done if it is desirable. What is the policy in the hospital with regard to X-ray treatments? Are they ever given, what is the additional expense, and would it seem to be desirable in this case?

Sincerely yours,

LYDIA GARDNER

September 2, 1914.—Letter received from the Acting Commissioner at Ellis Island:

In reference to your inquiry concerning X-ray treatment, I quote the following statement made by the Acting Chief Medical Officer: "In regard to the question of X-ray treatment I have to say that its use is followed by permanent baldness. There is a certain element of danger, even in the most careful hands, of X-ray burns. There is no additional expense attached to this treatment, and the hospital is prepared to administer the same; but in view of the possible baldness and possible danger from burns, it never has been the policy to make use of this treatment without permission from responsible individuals with a full knowledge of the possibilities. If the parents of the Aronoff children will give permission under their own signature for this treatment to be employed, it will then be given due consideration."

[Various items are omitted here regarding the furnishing of bonds (which were finally demanded by the authorities), the sending of money for hospital treatment, receipts, etc. From August 11, 1914, to June 1, 1915, regular payments were made for treatment through the League. Periodically a request was made for a report regarding the condition of the children, and the following replies were received from time to time:]

October 21, 1914.—"The doctors report that their condition is the same and that much more treatment is necessary."

November 17, 1914.—"The doctors state (as to both children) that this condition is very hard to cure and improvement is slow."

December 17, 1914.—"The doctors report that there is no apparent change in the condition of the scalps during the past month."

February 9, 1915.—"The doctors have reported today that Rachel Aronoff is much improved. Her sister Kazia is also improved. It is impossible to state at this time, however, just when they will be in a condition to be discharged from the hospital."

March 16, 1915.—"The doctors report that their condition remains about the same."

March 31, 1915.—"As this disease is practically incurable by medical treatment, we are unable to report that they have made any perceptible progress towards recovery and I think that their relatives and friends should be informed of the hopelessness of their condition."

May 18, 1915.—"In the case of Rachel there may be some improvement, but there is no perceptible change in the case of Kazia since the last report."

June 1, 1915.—Letter received from the Hebrew Immigrant Aid Society of New York:

I understand that you are interested in Rachel and Kazia Aronoff, detained on Ellis Island for treatment of favus and ringworm of the scalp and that payments therefor are made through your office. Because of the fact that the treatment for favus and ringworm at this station is so slow and ineffective that a cure could not be obtained for several years, if at all, I took the matter up with the Department of Labor and after numerous conferences with the Secretary in Washington, we finally obtained a ruling from the Department that it would consent to the transfer of such patients to private hospitals in New York City where the X-ray treatment can be given, providing that bonds guaranteeing the payment of the hospital bills to such private hospitals and for detention until admission or deportation are furnished. The hospitals must be located in New York City and not outside thereof. That provision is made for the purpose of preventing possible spread of the disease while in transit. We are reliably informed by the New York hospitals that with the X-ray treatment, a cure can be effected within eight months.

If you are desirous of taking advantage of this privilege for the benefit of the Aronoff children and are willing to furnish such a bond and pay for their treatment at the rate of seven dollars per week, for each, please advise me and I will endeavor to secure their transfer too. I believe that you will see the advisability of following the course suggested as in that way only will a speedy cure and discharge follow.

June 11, 1915.—Letter written to Hebrew Immigrant Aid Society:

MY DEAR MR. SCHWARTZ:

I am very glad indeed that you have succeeded in making arrangements for the removal of the Aronoff children from the Ellis Island hospital to a New York hospital where X-ray treatment can be given. Will you let us know the name of the hospital at which the treatment that you suggest has been offered?

I take it that the bonds to which you refer will be sent to the United States Immigration Office here to be signed. This is usually a slow process, we have found, and I hope that removal can be made at once. Payments could be made promptly so that there would be no difficulty in that connection. I should like, however, to know the name of the hospital so that I may suggest it in connection with the plan.

Sincerely yours,
LYDIA GARDNER

[Some letters omitted here.]

June 16, 1915.—Family visited. Mr. Aronoff and Nathan bought a newspaper route seven months ago. They borrowed $300 from a loan association and have been paying $6 a week on the debt. They clear only about $10 a week. The girls together earn $14 a week. The family is large, and they hardly have enough to make both ends meet. They believe it will take six months to pay off the debt. Then they will begin to help pay hospital expenses.

June 17, 1915.—Letter written to Mr. X. [Extract from letter follows:]

We have all been very much disappointed with the lack of progress made by the Aronoff children. When I was in New York recently, I talked over this matter and the case of a Magyar child who has been there eighteen months under treatment for trachoma, with the Commissioner. He thought that perhaps both might be removed to Chicago under bonds guaranteeing hospital treatment. Later he apparently decided that this could not be arranged, but permission has now been given for the removal of the Aronoff children to a New York hospital. The Hebrew Immigrant Aid Society have arranged for X-ray treatment at the New Hospital, New York, at $7 per week, payable bi-weekly in advance. This seems the only way in which progress can be made. Will you be willing to have this arrangement completed?

Sincerely yours,

LYDIA GARDNER

June 18–July 13, 1915.—[Various entries may be summarized here. Mr. X. guaranteed to continue payments for treatment if the children were moved to a private hospital, and the children were moved from Ellis Island Hospital to New Hospital, New York, on July 2. On July 13, fifty dollars were received from Nathan Aronoff (the children's brother) toward payment for their treatment. He promised to pay $3.50 per week, the difference between the cost of their treatment at Ellis Island and that at the New Hospital.]

November 5, 1915.—Letter written to the H.I.A.S. of New York:

MY DEAR MR. SCHWARTZ:

Would you be kind enough to talk with the doctor who is treating the Aronoff children at the New Hospital for ringworm, and will you let us know how the children are getting along and what the prospects of cure are? We have inquired as to their condition several times when sending the checks for board, but have had no reply. The parents are very anxious to know something about their condition. We shall be very grateful for a report from you.

Very truly yours,

LYDIA GARDNER

November 25, 1915.—The following letter was received from the H.I.A.S.:

DEAR MADAM:

Your letter of the 5th inst. with reference to the Aronoff children was not answered until now because I had considerable difficulty in getting a report. The report I finally did get is very discouraging. Dr. Y., who until now was in charge of this case, tells me that these children are as far away from a cure now as they were when they were originally transferred. He tells me that for the last two weeks they have been applying a new serum for which wonderful claims are made. He thinks that it ought to show results within three months, as in many cases where that serum was used the patients were cured within that time. If, however, at the end of the three months no cure will be noticed, he will have no recourse but to apply the X-ray treatment, which we understood was to have been applied upon their admission to the New Hospital. Dr. Y. tells me that the reason why the X-ray was not used and why he did not care to use it is because usually it removes the hair, a condition not desired, especially in the case of girls.

Very truly yours,

HENRY SCHWARTZ

December 6, 1915.—Letter from Mr. X. asking what would happen if monthly payments for these children were stopped.

December 7, 1915.—Letter to Mr. X.:

MY DEAR MR. X.:

If the payments for the treatment of the Aronoff children were discontinued, the children would have to be returned to Ellis Island to remain without treatment until the end of the war when they would be sent back to Russia and some member of the family here would be required to go with them. At least this is what the law requires. Of course, a good many exceptions are made and it might be worth while trying again to see if we could not get permission for removal to Chicago for treatment. A payment of $28 is due now for the current two weeks.

Sincerely yours,

LYDIA GARDNER

February 26, 1916.—Letter to New Hospital requesting report on the progress of the cure and a statement of their condition. *Later.*—Letter to Hebrew Immigrant Aid Society asking them to investigate again.

March 2, 1916.—Letter from New Hospital: "The Doctor reports that the condition is still present but improving slowly. X-ray treatments are being used now."

March 3, 1916.—Letter received from H.I.A.S.:

DEAR MADAM:

Answering yours of the 26th inst. concerning the Aronoff children, I beg to advise you that the serum treatment did not come up to expectations and the hospital physicians have therefore decided to put them on the X-ray treatment. They have so far only received one treatment under the X-ray. It is a little too early to tell just now as to the progress of these cases. I believe, however, that there should be some results shown within a reasonably short time.

Very truly yours,

HENRY SCHWARTZ

[The following letters summarize remaining portion of record.]
April 23, 1916.—Letter from H.I.A.S. as follows:

DEAR MADAM:

Replying to yours of the 17th inst. for information concerning the Aronoff children, I beg to state that the last report shows considerable improvement. An examination of their scalp by the officers of the Public Health Service a week ago verified that report. Those officials have promised to make another examination in about two weeks from now at which time they will be in a better position to express an opinion on the case.

Very truly yours,

HENRY SCHWARTZ

May 11, 1916.—Letter to H.I.A.S. asking report:

It is now nearly two years since the children were put in the Ellis Island Hospital for treatment. It will be difficult to secure the expenses of hospital treatment should this continue to be necessary much longer.

May 15, 1916.—Reply received from H.I.A.S.:

DEAR MADAM:

Replying to yours of the 11th inst., I beg to advise you that an examination by the officers of the Public Health Service last Saturday discloses the following facts: These patients were treated by means of the X-ray process and all of the hair has been removed. It is now believed that they are cured but the physicians prefer to wait until the hair will come back and if the hair will show that it is free from the disease they will be immediately admitted. According to the doctors it will take another three or four weeks.

Very truly yours,

HENRY SCHWARTZ

June 15, 1916.—Letter from H.I.A.S.:

MY DEAR MISS GARDNER:

Replying to yours of the 8th inst. concerning the Aronoff children, I beg to advise you that both have been certified by the Attending Physician of the New Hospital, as no longer suffering with favus. Upon that certificate they were brought to Ellis Island for examination by the officers of the Public Health Service. The result of that examination was that whereas they concurred as to the diagnosis in the case of Rachel, they failed to do so in the case of Kazia, and remanded Kazia back to the New Hospital for further treatment. In the case of Rachel, the Public Health Service Physicians submitted a statement to the immigration authorities to the effect that although they do not find any favus germs, yet they fear that there may be a recurrence within a very short time, and in order to avoid it, they believe that Rachel ought to be held on Ellis Island under observation for a period of fourteen days, and accordingly recommended the same. The Commissioner of Immigration sent a communication on to the Department of Labor at Washington and is waiting for instructions before taking any further action. In the meantime Rachel will remain in our Home.

Rachel tells me that the prepaid tickets to Chicago were taken along with her mother when she was admitted. I would suggest that you see her and have the same sent to me. Rachel has no money at all and it would be also wise if some money be sent for her use while waiting in New York.

Will you please inform me whether it is the parents' wish for Rachel to remain in New York until Kazia is also discharged or do they want her to proceed to Chicago immediately?

Very truly yours,

HENRY SCHWARTZ

June 23, 1916.—Letter from H.I.A.S. as follows:

DEAR MADAM:

With further reference to the case of Rachel Aronoff, I beg to advise you that the Department of Labor has directed her to be returned to Ellis Island for observation. She is to be held here for a period of fourteen days at the expense of the relatives. She has been this day returned to the Ellis Island Hospital. I will advise you as soon as a final decision is rendered.

Very truly yours,

HENRY SCHWARTZ

June 25, 1916.—Letter from New Hospital reporting that Kazia had been discharged.

[Various entries are omitted dealing with the transportation of the children (for which Nathan Aronoff paid), their arrival and enrolment at school (they were soon "promoted to third grade"). For several years nothing was heard of the family, except a card of Christmas greetings to the League Superintendent sent each year by Nathan Aronoff. Early in 1921 a visitor who was in the neighborhood "dropped in" to see how they were all getting on, and the following new entry was made:]

January 10, 1921.—Family visited. Live in a rather large, comfortably furnished flat. Rachel and Kazia are both very well and have an abundance of hair. They will graduate from grammar school in February. Rachel will take a business course. Kazia is anxious to go through high school, but Nathan thinks it impossible. Their father's health is precarious, and the girls must help take care of the four younger children. *Later.*—Telephoned the Vocational Guidance Bureau of the Jewish Charities about Kazia Aronoff. It may be possible to arrange for her to go on to high school. The Bureau will visit.

10. The Wife and Children of Michael Kubelik
(Excluded—Contagious Disease)

[Michael Kubelik's case first came to the attention of the Immigrants' Protective League, June 20, 1923, when the superintendent of the League received the following telegram from the Ellis Island representative of the Y.W.C.A.: "Please urge Michael Kubelik, 900 Lyman Street, to communicate with us. Wife Antonina, daughter Domicilla, steamship

Pulaski, held under observation for eyes. Had no response from him to communications. Better have him make affidavit which send to me in case of trachoma certification for one or both."

A visitor of the League was sent at once to Lyman Street but found that Mr. Kubelik had moved some months earlier and no one knew where he was living. After a great deal of trouble he was finally located at 2900 Broad Street, but he was not at home. Word was left for him to come to the office in the evening and, when he came, he gave the following facts:] He came to the United States from Poland in 1913, leaving his wife, Antonina, and two small children, Domicilla, now aged eleven, and Anton, now aged thirteen. He has been employed in the Western Glue Works for several years and was earning about $29 a week. He said he had been making every effort since the war to bring over his family and had savings amounting to $1,650. He has furnished a nice three-room flat and has everything ready for his wife and children. He had only his first papers and said he could not get his second papers until his wife arrived.[1] He brought with him various letters from a steamship agent on the West Side from whom he had purchased the three prepaid tickets. These letters were all written by the general manager of the Chicago office of the Polish American Steamship Line to the West Side agent and contained the following:

January 26, 1923

In further reference to prepaid XY 23 Kubelik. Kindly note we are today in receipt of a letter from our New York Office dated the 26th instant, reading: "*Prepaid XY 23 Kubelik.* Our Antwerp Office, under date of January 6th, write us that, according to information received from the Warsaw Office, the passengers booked on the above prepaid are registered to sail in the course of this month. One of the party, Domicilla, is afflicted with trachoma, and in case the Warsaw doctor does not find her, after a second examination, fit to be transported, she may be prevented from sailing."

May 9, 1923

In reference to prepaid XY 23. Kindly note we are today in receipt of a letter from our New York Office dated the 3d instant, reading: "*Prepaid XY 23 Antonina Kubelik et al.* Referring to our letter of March 9th, regarding the above passengers, we beg to advise that, according to letter which Antwerp received in the meantime from Warsaw, the children booked under this prepaid, viz.: Anton and Domicilla, were rejected by the doctor on account of their being afflicted with sore eyes. The mother of these children called on our Mr. Berg on March 20th and told that they are now undergoing a thorough cure, and with the opening of the Polish quota, they will be able to proceed. We also beg to advise you that these two children are now over ten years of age, and in order to make the prepaid

[1] [Although the naturalization law does not provide for refusing naturalization papers to a man with a wife in Europe, in the administration of the law this has come to be the usual procedure. The immigrants who have been making every effort to bring over their families feel that this procedure is unduly harsh.]

available for three full passages, we would thank you to kindly communicate with the purchaser and endeavor to collect the difference in the fares of the two children. Please advise us to this effect as soon as possible."

From the above you will note that the children on this ticket now require full fares and we will ask you to kindly make the additional payment as promptly as possible, and oblige.

A later letter of May 17, 1923, noted that "the purchaser of the tickets had called at the office and remitted the additional amount." The wife and children finally sailed May 30 on the S.S. "Pulaski" and arrived at Ellis Island June 8. A telegram was received by the Chicago agent of the steamship company on that date as follows: "Anton Kubelik Steamship Pulaski temporarily detained awaiting release mother and sister placed hospital observation eyes."

Mr. Kubelik said his wife and little girl had been treated for trachoma in Poland and they had had two doctors' certificates, one certificate from a doctor in Mirsky (their native village) and one from Posen, saying that they were cured. The steamship company had the affidavits, and they were sent to Warsaw. The man had sent $100 to his wife at New York through the steamship company, so that she had "landing money." *Later.*—An affidavit was prepared for the man and sent to New York.

[Further extracts from the case record follow.]

June 25, 1923.—Extract from a letter with inclosure received from Mrs. Lee (Ellis Island):

I am inclosing a carbon of a letter to Mr. Kubelik, who also sent $100 through the Polish-American Line. The affidavits came. The family is temporarily detained only, waiting for the discharge of Domicilla. They have railroad tickets. . . . .

The "inclosure" was a letter from Mrs. Lee to Mr. Kubelik as follows:

ELLIS ISLAND, NEW YORK

DEAR SIR:

You will be glad to know that your wife has been discharged from the hospital cured and that she is waiting now for your daughter Domicilla, who like her mother, is also suffering with conjuntivitis, which ought to yield to treatment in a few days. Your wife was very troubled when no word came to her from you during her stay in the hospital. She was happy to hear that you had been found at your new address, and we hope that you will wait for her and the children at the railroad station when the train from New York arrives.

Yours very truly,

K. F. LEE, *Y.W.C.A. Worker*

June 28, 1923.—Mr. Kubelik and Mr. Joseph [West Side steamship ticket agent] in the office. The father had a letter from Anton Kubelik, saying the whole family were to be deported because the sister has trachoma. The letter begs the father to come to New York with bonds to save them.

Mr. Joseph has already seen Congressman X. and showed a letter from the Commissioner of Immigration to Congressman X., saying the case is not yet under appeal, but he will be glad to give it consideration when it is.

Mr. Kubelik is very wretched and looks exhausted. He says he is so worried he cannot eat, he cannot sleep, he cannot work. *Later.*—Telegram sent to Mrs. Lee, Ellis Island, as follows: "Letter from Anton Kubelik states preparations being made to deport family, also that girl has trachoma. He urges father come Ellis Island to furnish bond. What is present status? Is case appealed to Washington? Please wire immediately so we can write Washington if necessary. If girl has trachoma, could you arrange escort for her so mother and son might be admitted?"

June 29, 1923.—Mr. Kubelik in office. He brought a telegram he had just received from Mrs. Lee (Ellis Island): "Take this telegram to Immigrants' Protective League, eight hundred South Halsted Street. Your family excluded because daughter Domicilla has trachoma. It is useless to petition for you are charged two dollars seventy-five cents each day from time petition is filed even when permission to treat is not granted." *Later.*— Telegram sent to Congressman X.: "Domicilla Kubelik certified trachoma. If possible secure permission she receive medical treatment at Ellis Island. If that is impossible, please get permission she return under escort and mother and brother be admitted this country.—ALICE MARION, *Superintendent, Immigrants' Protective League.*"

June 30, 1923.—Letter received from Mrs. Lee (Ellis Island):

DEAR MISS MARION:

To our sorrow we discovered that little Domicilla is afflicted with trachoma and was excluded on the 26th. I wired to the father, asking him to see you, but I felt that the telegram needed to be explained.

Before asking Mr. Kubelik to send money for treatment, I consulted the authorities here on the probability of the Bureau of Immigration granting treatment. Their answer was that no permission for treatment has been granted these past three months and that while they are willing to put the papers through to Washington, they think that the petition will be dismissed and that the two dollars and seventy-five cents ($2.75) per day which Mr. Kubelik will have to pay from the day on which the petition was filed will be an utter loss to him.

To deport Mrs. Kubelik seems exceptionally cruel to me. Mr. Kubelik has more than sixteen hundred dollars ($1,600) saved and may be willing and able to meet the expense of eighty-two dollars and a half ($82.50) per month and then a bond of one thousand dollars ($1,000). If Mr. Kubelik is willing to face the difficulties please communicate directly with Washington on the case. I was told that one reason why the Bureau of Immigration refuses to give permission for treatment is that they have no guarantee that the bills will be paid, for the simple reason that bonds given as security are worthless and that the government must bring suit to recover sums like eight and nine hundred dollars.

Yours sincerely,
K. F. LEE

Later.—Telegram received from Mrs. Lee (Ellis Island): "Have filed petition to-day for permission to substitute person for mother to accompany Domicilla Kubelik. Am seeking reliable person through Polish Emigration Home. Father should send to my name one hundred twenty-five dollars for passage of such person. Will arrange for medical treatment, maintenance, social care of child in Warsaw. Petition sent Washington today."

Later.—Letter written to Assistant Secretary of Labor, Washington:

My dear Sir:

Re Antonina Kubelik and children Domicilla and Anton, S.S. "Pulaski." We are writing you at the request of Michael Kubelik, the husband and father of the above immigrants. We understand that the papers in their case have been forwarded to you for decision. Domicilla, the eleven-year-old daughter, has been certified as having trachoma. Mr. Kubelik asks that the child may be permitted to receive treatment at Ellis Island. He will furnish bond as guarantee of prompt payment of all costs involved in such treatment. We have, however, explained to Mr. Kubelik that he will be unusually fortunate if such a favor is granted him and that his daughter will probably have to return to Poland or some other European country for medical care.

Perhaps, however, the following arrangement would be possible: Mr. Kubelik would be willing to pay some reliable Polish woman to take his daughter Domicilla back to her native country. In Warsaw, the Young Women's Christian Association could arrange for the child's care and treatment and could keep her under supervision until she is cured and ready to return to this country. If this were done, would it not be possible for the mother and the son to be admitted?

Mr. Kubelik is all ready to secure American citizenship. He has taken the necessary examination and he holds petition card No. 51,000 issued to him in the Cook County Circuit Court, October 22, 1922. The judge of the court has told him that as soon as his wife and children arrive in this country he will be given his certificate. Of course, unless his wife is here, he cannot obtain naturalization.[1] Probably by the time the little girl is ready to return to this country, the Polish quota will be exhausted or at least assigned. If her father is a citizen, she would not be bound by quota restrictions.

We shall greatly appreciate your help in this case.

Very truly yours,

Alice Marion, *Superintendent*

July 5, 1923.—Telegram received from Mrs. Lee, Ellis Island: "Kubelik family ordered deported. Petition denied. Mrs. Kubelik begs husband come here. Family to be put on board steamship Pulaski July tenth. Am informing you that you advise Mr. Kubelik this decision is final. Nothing can be done. Ask him to bring his wife money. He should arrange with us for family in Warsaw." *Later.*—Telephoned Mr. Joseph (steamship agent). He seemed to think that Mr. Kubelik would not go

[1] [See p. 333, n. 1.]

to Ellis Island. Mr. Joseph also does not yet believe the decision is final. He expects another telegram from Congressman X. Congressman Y. is also working on case.

July 7, 1923.—Mr. Kubelik in office. He will leave for New York today. Gave him instructions and a letter to Mrs. Lee.

July 11, 1923.—Letter received from Department of Labor as follows:

Referring to your interest in the case of Antonina Kubelik and children, Anton and Domicilla, I regret to advise you that the Department has found it necessary to affirm the excluding decision as to these aliens, and to deny the request for the substitution of an attendant for the child, Domicilla. The record shows that Domicilla has been certified for trachoma, a dangerous, contagious disease, and excluded on said certification without right of appeal; the mother excluded as an accompanying alien, and the son, Anton, as likely to become a public charge, predicated on the exclusion of the mother.

July 13, 1923.—Letter received from Mrs. Lee:

MY DEAR MISS MARION:

They went out on the "Pulaski." I was able to help Mr. Kubelik get several visits with his family. He is a kind and sensible person, who acted upon my suggestions so nicely that when he bade his wife and children goodbye, they left for Poland reassured that all would be well and that eventually they would all come back and then enter the United States without any trouble. He gave his wife $250, which she tucked away carefully on her person. I have given Mrs. Kubelik a letter to Miss M— in Warsaw. This seemed all that was necessary for the time being, until all the money in Mrs. Kubelik's possession should be used up. Of course, we are cabling to have the family met in Antwerp, and we will also notify the Polish Secretary to look out for this family.

Yours sincerely,

K. F. LEE

[The following letters relate to the reopening of the case in September:]

September 5, 1923.—Letter to Polish American Line, New York Office, as follows:

GENTLEMEN:

Re Prepaid XY 23. On December 2, 1920, Michael Kubelik bought, through one of your Chicago agents, Mr. Paul Joseph, Prepaid XY 23 for his wife and two children. This ticket was not used until June 8, when Mrs. Kubelik and her children arrived on the S.S. "Pulaski." The son and daughter, who were under ten when Mr. Kubelik bought the ticket, were, by the time the family was ready to sail, of an age requiring full fare. Consequently, your Chicago agent collected $57.84 from Michael Kubelik on May 17, 1923. It seems, however, that about the same time your Warsaw office collected a sum from Mrs. Kubelik for the same purpose.

Mrs. Kubelik and her children were deported because the child Domicilla was certified to have trachoma. As you know, one of the reasons why the family did not come sooner was because the little girl was undergoing treatment for trachoma in Europe. We understand from Mr. Kubelik that he has not yet been notified whether it was decided by the immigration authorities that your Company must refund the steamship passage to these immigrants. However, we suppose there is no question that Mr. Kubelik is entitled to a refund of the $57.84 paid by him May 17. He has asked the agent for this money and also for refund of the unused railroad fares. We understand that he has been told that the railroad fares will be refunded, but that, in all probability, your Warsaw office will refund to Mrs. Kubelik the money she advanced for increase in the children's fare.

Neither Mr. Kubelik nor Mrs. Kubelik desires such a procedure. The reason for this is obvious; it is certainly to their advantage to have the refund in American dollars rather than to have Mrs. Kubelik receive the same amount in Polish marks which she paid your Company in Warsaw early this spring. This family has been through a very unhappy and very costly experience. We hope you will agree with us in thinking they should not be called upon to bear any further loss than is absolutely unavoidable.

September 17, 1923.—Letter received from the Y.W.C.A. International Migration Service Bureau, New York:

In July Mrs. Lee at Ellis Island sent you a report on the case of Antonina Kubelik, wife of Michael Kubelik, 2900 Broad Street, Chicago, Illinois, who was deported on the S.S. "Pulaski," together with their two children Anton and Domicilla. Domicilla was afflicted with trachoma.

Our Warsaw representative writes us that the family arrived safe in Poland and that they have found a doctor to treat Domicilla. He hopes that she will be cured in a month or so. The case was apparently light as it was not detected by the medical examiner at the port of embarkation. Our representative is doing all in her power to assist Mrs. Kubelik in obtaining passage. She has deposited one hundred and ninety-five dollars in the Warsaw office to be drawn at need.

As there is a possibility of Domicilla's being detained longer, the migration secretary would like to know if Mr. Kubelik would be willing to have his wife and son come in advance of the little girl, who could be sent later in care of fellow-travellers. Since we do not know under what conditions or with whom the Kubeliks are living in Poland, we cannot express an opinion on the advisability of such a plan. Our record states that Mr. Kubelik will receive his naturalization papers as soon as his family arrives. Does this mean that citizenship is being withheld from him because his family is still abroad?

September 19, 1923.—Letter received from Polish American Line, New York:

GENTLEMEN:

Re Prepaid XY 23. Referring to your communication of September 5th, we have received letters from our friends on the other side in reference to Mrs. Kubelik and child who, we understand, now decided to come out and have written them for authority to refund to the purchaser of the prepaid ticket the additional fare collected on the other side. The child afflicted with trachoma will remain with her on the other side. It is quite possible to bring out the mother and the child even though they were deported less than a year ago, inasmuch as the Immigration Law applies only to the deportee and not to those accompanying them. Just as soon as we receive the necessary authority from the other side we will promptly arrange refund to our Chicago Office.

[The remaining portion of the record contains further details of the arrangements for bringing back the mother and one child and leaving the child with trachoma under care in Europe. The mother and child, however, had not yet arrived (November, 1923).]

11. Andrew Cesky
(Detention—Citizenship Claimed)

January 15, 1921.—Michael Maly, a Czecho-Slovak, in office [of Immigrants' Commission]. He wishes to help his friend Andrew Cesky, who was returning to his home in the United States from Czecho-Slovakia and has been detained for special inquiry at Ellis Island because he is unable to read. Mr. Maly says Andrew Cesky is a full citizen. He went back to Czecho-Slovakia for a visit just before the war. He was not able to get back to the United States during the war and now that he has returned he is not allowed to land. Maly does not know name of steamer on which Cesky arrived but can probably find out and let us know. *Later.*—Mr. Maly in office at 2 P.M. Andrew Cesky arrived on S.S. "Vaterland." Maly learned name from Wanda's Bank and Steamship Agency. Mr. Maly wishes to pay for telegrams. Telegram sent to Miss Freeman [representative of Commission in New York] as follows: "Andrew Cesky steamship Vaterland detained probably illiteracy. He is citizen has second papers. Please investigate." Telegram sent to Commissioner of Immigration at Ellis Island as follows: "Andrew Cesky steamship Vaterland is American citizen if excluded hereby appeal.—MICHAEL MALY, 2000 W. 48th St."

January 17, 1921.—Reply from Miss Freeman as follows: "Andrew Cesky excluded because illiterate. Travelling Czecho-Slovak passport not renewing American passport since leaving United States in 1914. Will interview and read minutes[1] when available and advise regarding appeal."

January 18, 1921.—Letter to Mr. Maly containing the following:

We have today a telegram from Ellis Island with regard to your friend Andrew Cesky. We are very much afraid that in his case the American citizenship papers will be useless. It seems he was travelling under a Czecho-Slovak passport. Furthermore, he has not renewed his American passport since leaving the United States in 1914. As you undoubtedly know, such passports should be renewed every two years, and his failure to do this would be taken as a sign that he had renounced his American citizenship and renewed his allegiance to Czecho-Slovakia. We are extremely sorry not to be able to help him, but we are afraid there is nothing to be done in his case.

[1] [Minutes of Board of Special Inquiry, Ellis Island, containing excluding decisions.]

January 24, 1921.—Letter from Miss Freeman containing the following:

I have written a special appeal for Andrew Cesky, who was excluded as an illiterate alien on the supposition that he had expatriated himself by living outside of the United States for over six years, never appealing during that time for a renewal of his passport, and returning here on a Czecho-Slovak passport. The man's story sounded quite true to me, and the circumstances that made him apparently expatriate himself seemed to me to be the unhappy accompaniment of the war.

Later.—Telephoned Wanda's bank and asked them to tell Mr. Maly what is being done.

January 31, 1921.—Letter received from Miss Freeman containing the following:

No reply to my appeal for Andrew Cesky had been received at Ellis Island yesterday. I waited with the appeal until the day before deportation as I was unable to get hold of the minutes of the Board hearing. I found that the immigrant was to be placed on board ship the afternoon before the sailing and immediately tried to file notice of appeal. This notice was refused on one pretext or another at various offices, either because it would be troublesome to rearrange records if deportation did not take place or because most appeals of illiterates are dismissed and the officials do not want to have detentions prolonged uselessly. However that may be, I had to see the commissioner to get a stay of deportation and acceptance of my notice of appeal on behalf of Andrew Cesky. It was my first experience of this kind. Andrew Cesky was manifested as Andrew Lesci, hence my difficulty in finding his record. The papers now have been corrected to read Cesky.

Later.—Mr. Maly in office with telegram from Congressman X. saying that Andrew Cesky was admitted under bond. Told Mr. Maly to await official notification from Ellis Island about the bond and then go to the Chicago Immigration Department about the matter.

February 10, 1921.—Telephoned Mr. Maly. He reports that Andrew Cesky arrived in Chicago last week.

March 29, 1921.—Visited. Andrew Cesky has a job and is working at the Steel Mills. Mr. Maly does not understand how his friend got in. Two days after his telegram from Congressman X. the man arrived, and the bond was never asked for.

12. Bozena Jozka
(Excluded—Fugitive from Justice)

August 8, 1914.—Joseph Jozka, Bohemian, 714 East Avenue, in office. Man was very much excited. He spoke with B. P. [Bohemian visitor] about his sister. His sister, Bozena, is about to be deported from Ellis Island. Mr. X., editor of Bohemian newspaper, sent him to us. Mr. Jozka has letter from brother in Trieste about what happened. Bozena was a cashier at the "Cas" *Daily* in Prague. She was engaged to be married to a young man who was not able to find any permanent work in Bohemia and left for America. Bozena promised to come after him as soon as she saved enough money for passage. It was very slow, because wages were small. She took some of her employer's money and sailed for the United States. "Cas" sent a cablegram to New York, where she was detained and will be deported. Her brother Joseph is desperate about it and asks the League to save the girl from the shame and disgrace which affects the whole respectable family in Prague.

B. P. [Bohemian visitor] explained to man that girl will have to be deported if she has taken the money. Man wanted to speak also with Miss Gardner [Superintendent]. Miss Gardner told him we are very sorry but there is nothing to do. Bozena will have to be deported. If man wishes to go to New York to see his sister, we could give him a letter. Man does not want to go, if she must be deported. He says it will kill his mother. Told him we could do nothing.

13. Henry Pahl
(Excluded—Criminal Record)

April 25, 1923.—Otto Pahl (German) in office with his wife, asking advice about how to help their son at Ellis Island. The boy has been at Ellis Island a week, but father has had no word from him or about him. Steamship agent (Mr. Nieman) from whom the father bought prepaid ticket has referred case to Congressman X. Mr. Pahl has following telegram sent to Mr. Nieman by Congressman X.: "Have taken appeal in case of Henry Pahl will advise." Family have sent no affidavits; whole thing has been handled by ticket agent, and man is getting frightened. He says his son is twenty-three years old and was in the German army but is perfectly well. Mr. Pahl (the father) came to the United States in 1913 and was naturalized in 1920. He is a fireman, earning about $20 a week. Another son, George (Henry's brother), is here and lives with his father and mother. He earns $25 a week. Mr. Pahl has property valued at $1,600 and he wishes to furnish bonds if his son is sick or anything. Affidavits sent to Commissioner, Ellis Island, and also to Mrs. Lee, Y.W.C.A. worker at Ellis Island. Gave Mr. Pahl telegram to send as follows: "Official affidavits Henry Pahl steamship Denmark sent today. If excluded hereby appeal.—OTTO PAHL, *Father*." *Later.*—Letter written to Mrs. Lee (Y.W.C.A.) as follows:

DEAR MRS. LEE:

We inclose affidavit (copy) made in our office by the father of Henry Pahl, ex S.S. "Denmark." Mr. Pahl does not know the reason for his son's exclusion. Congressman X. has appealed in the boy's behalf to Washington. Please keep us informed as to the status.

Sincerely yours,
ALICE MARION

May 7, 1923.—Mr. and Mrs. Pahl in office with telegram from Assistant Commissioner's office as follows: "Henry Pahl excluded likely to become public charge and admits commission crime involving moral turpitude. Appeal forwarded Washington yesterday." Mr. Pahl says that Henry and some other boys stole a cow some time during the war in Germany and they were all punished for it. Henry was three months in a reformatory. Mr. Pahl has had a letter from Henry saying he is going to be deported. Mr. Nieman (ticket agent) has had word that Henry is being deported on S.S. "Copenhagen" May 5, but Henry's last letter, written May 4, does not mention it and he surely did not know he was going out the next day. *Later.*—Telegram sent Mrs. Lee as follows: "Please wire whether Henry Pahl steamship Denmark still there. Boy excluded. Case appealed April twenty-fifth. Parents worried. Fear deportation May fifth."

[The two following documents in reply to the telegram summarize the remaining portion of the record. Further interviews with parents omitted.]

May 8, 1923.—Telegram received from Mrs. Lee as follows: "Pahl deported steamship Copenhagen May fifth moral turpitude. Am writing.—K. F. LEE."

May 10, 1923.—Letter received from Mrs. Lee as follows:

MY DEAR MISS MARION:

Re Henry Pahl I asked permission to read the record in this case and found the following: He has a wife in Furselnwalde, Germany, who is living with his mother. He is a wood-carver, aged twenty-three. Code number 2 on visa from American consul. Father in United States ten years; has a brother with father; mother divorced; father remarried. Otto married one year. Convicted of the crime of selling stolen goods; sentenced to prison for three months; sentence served fully; consul had copy of his police record. When asked whether he was warned that he would be excluded and deported, he said that he had not been warned, but had been admonished "keep straight."

I believe that it was impossible to procure his release, but I am sorry that we did not notify the father of the young man's fate before he embarked for his return voyage.

Yours sincerely,

K. F. LEE

14. Max Rothstein
(Stowaway)

August 4, 1920.—Emil Rothstein, a Russian-Jewish man, wishes to know how he can help his brother, who is coming soon to the United States from Holland. Man is a barber, works at Stockyards, earns $50-$60 a week, age twenty-six, unmarried, not a citizen. He has been in the United States since April 2, 1919; has just taken out first papers. Brother is twenty-two years old and in good health. Prepared affidavit and explained to him about sending it to Ellis Island to wait for his brother

September 27, 1920.—Emil Rothstein in office. His brother Max Rothstein served in the Russian Army and was a prisoner of war in Germany. He escaped from Germany and got to Rotterdam and from there got on S.S. "Rotterdam" and came to the United States as a stowaway. He had, of course, no passport. Emil Rothstein received on Saturday, September 25, a telegram from Jacob Sternberg, attorney at 80 Broadway, asking him to come at once to New York and appear personally in behalf of his brother, at the latest, Monday. Man said he received the telegram late on Saturday, and it was not possible for him to go on at once. He has friend who will also sign his brother's affidavit. Man went to Mr. Roberts (congressman) this morning, and Mr. Roberts sent a telegram for him. He thinks congressman stopped the deportation temporarily.

October 4, 1920.—Man in office. Received a telegram from a friend asking him to come to New York and give a bond of $500–$1,000. Man states that Congressman Roberts has sent several telegrams. Man also has sent and received telegrams.

October 5, 1920.—Letter written to Hebrew Immigrant Aid Society of New York City:

Gentlemen:

Emil Rothstein, residing at 531 Bridge Street, this city, has been in to see us about his brother Max Rothstein, twenty-two, who arrived on the steamship "Rotterdam" as a stowaway and is now detained at Ellis Island. Mr. Rothstein tells us that he has received a telegram from an attorney in New York, Jacob Sternberg, at 80 Broadway, asking him to come to New York. He has also received a telegram from a relative in New York by the name of Berlin asking him to come to New York. We are in doubt as to what to advise the man to do. There seems already to be a number of other persons interested and active in the matter. A congressman here has done some work on the case, and according to Mr. Rothstein stopped the deportation. We did, however, advise him to have Mr. Berlin call at your office and feel confident that you will do everything possible to have Max Rothstein admitted. We shall be glad to communicate any information you can get on this case to the brother or you may communicate directly with him at the address given above.

Yours very truly,

Lydia Gardner

October 15, 1920.—Telegram from Hebrew Immigrant Aid Society as follows: "Max Rothstein Rotterdam stowaway still detained Ellis Island little chance of admission." *Later.*—Called Emil Rothstein on telephone. Man has moved from there. New address 633 Harlem Avenue. Letter written giving him information.

November 16, 1920.—A. F. called at 633 Harlem Avenue. Man lives with a family by name of Jacob Dick. Mr. Dick said that Mr. Rothstein's brother was deported three weeks ago. Man felt very bad about it and was ill from it. Rothstein works downtown in a barber shop.

January 25, 1921.—Man in office. Brother was deported from Ellis Island to Rotterdam. From there he returned to Canada, where he is now working and satisfied. He wants to bring another brother, Israel Rothstein, Czentochowa, Poland. Filled out affidavit of support.

15. Rozalia Slovienski
(Misstatement to Inspector)

April 4, 1914.—A post card received from Miss Fromirski [a representative of a Polish organization working at Ellis Island] read:

My dear Protective League:

Rozalia Slovienski, of S.S. "Rotterdam," to her intended husband, Nicholas Cirua, 4332 N. Street, Chicago, Illinois, needs affidavit for immigrant inspector. Telegram was sent, but there was a wrong number and so he might not have received it.

Sincerely yours,

Teresa Fromirski

Later.—A. F. [the Polish visitor] called at 4332 N. Street. Nicholas lives with Polish people from same village, Mr. and Mrs. Y. Nicholas also has brother, who lives on next street. A. F. spoke with Nicholas who said he did not know what Rozalia meant by saying she was going to marry him; that Rozalia was his first cousin; she was age 19; that they started together from the old country but when they came to Ellis Island she was kept two weeks for her eyes and he was let to go on and so he arrived here three weeks earlier. Nicolas said that he did not know what happened to Rozalia and he did not get any telegram from her. A man will bring him to the League to make affidavit. *Later.*—Nicholas Cirua was brought to the League by Mr. S., but it was too late to take him to the Immigration Office to make affidavit.

April 7, 1914.—Sylvester Cirua, brother of Nicholas and cousin of Rozalia, came to the office and will make affidavit. Sylvester Cirua has a barber shop at 4408 K. Street. He was taken to the Immigration Office, where the Inspector-in-Charge told him to come back again and to bring Nicolas and the wife of another brother with whom they expect the girl to live.

April 26, 1914.—Mrs. Cirua in office. She is the wife of Sylvester Cirua and asks for information about what happened to Rozalia. Letter of inquiry written to the Commissioner of Immigration, Ellis Island, as follows:

We are writing to ask the result of the detention of Rozalia Slovienski S.S. "Rotterdam," who arrived the latter part of March or the first of April. The Chicago relatives have not heard from the girl since they received notice of her detention. They went to see the Inspector of Immigration in Chicago and are anxious to know whether or not she was deported.

April 30, 1914.—Letter received from the office of the Commissioner, Ellis Island:

SIRS:

Replying to your letter of the 26 inst., I have to advise you that Rozalia Slovienski, ex S.S. "Rotterdam," March 27, was admitted on April 5, to the custody of the Polish National Alliance, 180 Second Avenue, New York City.

16. Maryana Rosozki
(Young Woman Manifested to Unsatisfactory Address)

February 1, 1914.—Mr. Roberts, Inspector-in-Charge, United States Immigration Service, telephoned to ask co-operation in connection with the detention case of Maryana Rosozki, a Polish girl, eighteen years old. He wishes to know if the League will find a place for her at housework if she is admitted. The girl is at present in Canada, detained at St. John pending the inspector's report of living conditions of uncles in Chicago to whom she is manifested. They are Stanislaw Olshefsky and Vladimir Woloski, 518 Marble Avenue. Mr. Roberts investigated personally and sent an unfavorable report, house insanitary, too many boarders, etc. He received a telegram from St. John, saying girl would be admitted if she could be placed in good home. She wants to do housework. Relatives will send on $25. Told Mr. Roberts that a Polish visitor could meet Maryana and would find a good place for her. He will let us know time of girl's arrival in Chicago.

[Various entries are omitted. The following letter from the League to the Immigration Officer closes the record:]

MY DEAR MR. ROBERTS:

We beg to make the following report in the case of the Polish girl admitted from St. John. Our Polish visitor met the girl last Wednesday at 12:37 P.M., at the Wabash, and placed the girl the same day in the family of Mrs. Laski, 763 Russell Avenue. She is employed at general housework there at $4 a week. Both the girl and Mrs. Laski, our visitor learned on a subsequent visit, are pleased with the arrangement. Our visitor called also upon the relatives of the girl at 518 Marble Avenue. She reports a state of affairs which appears to be an improvement over conditions as they were when you investigated. The woman had cleaned and scrubbed and appeared altogether very respectable. She was planning to visit Maryana and take the girl some clothes. She said she had planned to place her cousin with a dressmaker upon her arrival. She hopes that at some future date the Immigration Inspector will allow the girl to live with her, but she is satisfied for the present.

Very sincerely yours,

LYDIA GARDNER

17. Rosa Markewicz
(Exclusion—Young Woman Manifested to Male Relatives)

June 24, 1914.—Two Russian men, Michel Markewicz and Michel Dombrowski, in office. They wish the League to help in obtaining admission for a Russian girl, a relative, Rosa Markewicz, who had been detained in Quebec after landing. They gave the following facts: Rosa Markewicz, age twenty-one years, arrived on S.S. "Hesperian" at Quebec, June 15. Rosa Markewicz is the cousin of Michel Markewicz, who is nephew of Michel Dombrowski. The nephew and the uncle are both living at 1140 West Lincoln Street. Uncle and nephew are janitors in a large bank building. The nephew who earns $50 a month has been in the United States nine months. He already has sent $100 home and has $40 in the bank. The uncle has been here six years and has been continuously at work for his present employer. He brought bank books with him showing that he had $520 in one large downtown bank and $1,005 in another. They had already sent on public charge affidavits to Washington through the local branch of the United States Immigration Department and have taken an appeal from the ruling that the girl was to be deported. An ex-Congressman, Mr. Z., has been assisting them. They have been told that immigration authorities objected to place where they were living, said girl could not be admitted to live there. They came to League to find place for girl. Telephoned United States Immigration Office. Inspector-in-Charge said only reason for unfavorable report was that these relatives to whom the girl was manifested were living in a non-family group of men. Nine Russians were living together. Telephoned ex-Congressman Z. He said he had sent the telegram to Washington asking for stay of deportation order. He knows the girl's relatives well as they have been janitors in his building for some time, and he is willing to recommend them highly. L. G. [Superintendent] spoke with men. They will be glad to have League take charge of Rosa and find her good place to work. *Later.*—The following telegram sent to Washington: "*Secretary of Labor, Washington, D.C.*: Regarding Rosa Markewicz, steamer Hesperian, Quebec. Immigrants' Protective League herewith offers to take charge of girl if admitted and find suitable home for her. Letter follows.—IMMIGRANTS' PROTECTIVE LEAGUE."

June 25, 1914.—Letter to the Secretary of Labor at Washington:

We telegraphed last night regarding Rosa Markewicz, a Russian girl who is now detained at Quebec, having arrived on the steamer "Hesperian" June 15th. Her relatives here are afraid that the fact that they are living in a non-family group of men may jeopardize her chances of admission, and they have come to us, asking us to assume responsibility for the girl when she arrives, and find her a place to live and work, etc. Unless there is some other reason for refusing her admission, we wish to urge that she be allowed to proceed to Chicago, and we offer to look after her. Her relatives here, Michel Markewicz and Michel Dombrowski, seem to us very well able financially to provide for her in case any such need should arise. One of them has shown us his bank book indicating that he has savings amounting to over $1,500. I believe all the assurances of the financial ability have been sent forward to you in the affidavit.

July 5, 1914.—Telegram received from Washington as follows: "*Immigrants' Protective League:* Department has ordered Rosa Markewicz deported.—F. H. LARNED, *Acting Commissioner-General of Immigration.*" *Later.*—Called ex-Congressman Z. and reported receipt of telegram. He will notify men.

18. Three Polish Girls: Maryanna Czarnecowska, Maryanna Kruza, Maryanna Vraza
(*Exclusion—Unsatisfactory Conditions in Chicago*)

May 26, 1914.—Michael Antak, Polish, in office. A. F. [Polish visitor] spoke with man. He says he is brother-in-law of Maryanna Czarnecowska and was sent to the League office by the United States Immigration Inspector. Maryanna, a sister-in-law, is detained in Quebec with two other Polish girls. He says he had purchased tickets for his wife, her sister, and three children, but there arrived only his wife's sister in company with two other Polish girls, Maryanna Kruza and Maryanna Vraza. All three were detained for special inquiry. Maryanna Czarnecowska, who according to Michael's statement was his wife's sister, upon being questioned by the Immigration Inspector at Quebec answered that Michael had parted with his wife and that she, Maryanna, was therefore coming instead. The man, Michael Antak, told the Chicago Immigration Inspector that the children took sick so that his wife must stay over and sent her sister on to America. He said he had a Polish letter from his wife, and she asks him to take care of the girl. Telephoned Mr. Roberts [Immigration Inspector], who said he would like to have a Polish visitor tell him the contents of the letter. (A. F. read the letter and the contents were as Michael Antak had described --the wife and children cannot come but her sister, Maryanna, is coming and will Michael please take care of her.) The Immigration Inspector said he had also investigated home and found conditions unfavorable and had so reported. He will be glad to have any help the League can given in the matter. *Later.*—Sent Immigration Inspector certificate from the Russian Steamship Company, showing that five tickets'had been purchased by Michael Antak as he said. *Later.*—Sent affidavit from Henry Antak, brother of Michael, who is a citizen, owns property, is a carpenter in the railroad shops at X., earning $3 a day. Affidavit also sent for George Vladja, who claims to be the affianced husband of Maryanna Kruza; he works for the X. Foundry, earning $12 a week, and has $120 in the bank.

May 28, 1914.—Letter to Mr. Roberts, United States Immigration Inspector, as follows:

My dear Mr. Roberts:

Michael Antak, 823 South Avenue, was in our office, explaining the case of the three Polish girls, Maryanna Czarnecowska, Maryanna Kruza, and Maryanna Vraza, concerning whom our visitor had a telephone conversation with you on Monday. We shall be very glad to take the girls, concerning whose release you are doubtful on account of the boarding conditions, and guarantee to release them only if they go to decent conditions. We would have no difficulty in placing them in house work at once.

Yours very sincerely,

LYDIA GARDNER

June 8, 1914.—Telegram of inquiry sent to Immigration Commissioner at Quebec.

June 9, 1914.—Telegram received from Quebec as follows: "Maryanna Kruza, Maryanna Vraza, and Maryanna Czarnecowska case pending before Secretary of Labor, Washington."

June 15, 1914.—Letter received from Washington as follows:

In response to your letter of May 30th, addressed to the Secretary of Labor, concerning the aliens Maryanna Czarnecowska, Maryanna Vraza, and Maryanna Kruza, who have been excluded at Quebec, I beg to advise you that the Assistant Secretary of Labor has affirmed the excluding decision of the immigration officers and directed the aliens' deportation after careful consideration of the case.

June 16, 1914.—Letter to Michael Antak, sending report from Washington.

June 21, 1914.—Michael Antak telephoned, he does not understand letter, does not understand disposition of case. Decision and deportation explained to him. Explained that girls are already on way back to Europe and nothing can be done about it.

19. Axenia Balik
(Exclusion—Girl Manifested to Uncle)

February 9, 1914.—Michael Balik, 194 Hoyne Avenue, in office to ask about his niece, aged nineteen, detained in Quebec. She arrived on S.S. "Montgomery," February 7. He sent ticket for girl. Man's wife is dead, and he wanted niece to keep house for him. Telegram to Quebec sent signed by man: "Wire collect cause detention Axenia Balik, steamship Montgomery, February 7, 1914. Uncle in Chicago.—MICHAEL BALIK, 194 Hoyne Avenue." Told man that girl will probably not be allowed to come to him if he has not a good home. Told him we will visit later. *Later.*— Telephoned United States Immigration Office. They have already had case. Girl said her uncle was married, and his wife in old country. Man said his wife was dead. Inspector visited and found man occupying two rooms with another man.

February 10, 1914.—Man in office again. He said yes it was true that he had a wife at home, but she is his second wife and drinks and he left her. She has money of her own. He has three children by his first wife, and the children stay with the man's parents. When he sent the steamship ticket to girl he also sent a ticket for one of his children, a little boy. He thought boy would go to school and Axenia would look after him and the house; and later he would send for the other children. In Russia there was some kind of misunderstanding about the ticket, and the boy who was to come was not sent. The man is a carpenter by trade and earns $5 per day. He says the girl is his brother's child, the brother is dead, and the mother married again. The stepfather did not treat the girl right, so the uncle decided to bring her to this country. He says there is nothing for the girl to do in Russia. Since his child did not come along, he did not intend to have girl stay with him. He was going to have her live with married friends. R. B. [Russian visitor] asked Mr. Balik if he would let girl live where League placed her, let us find work for her. He is glad to do this. *Later.*—Telegram appealing case sent for man.

February 17, 1914.—Man in office with telegram received from United States Immigration Service, Quebec, as follows: "Xenia Balik age twenty-four steamer Montgomery seventh inst. excluded by our board special inquiry as likely to become a public charge on account of the conditions existing at your home as per report of investigation by Chicago Immigration Office. Case being forwarded on appeal today to Secretary Department of Labor, Washington, D.C." Mr. Balik wants League to help him.

February 18, 1914.—R. B. visited to see the home; man lives in basement, front door locked. The landlord lives in rear of basement, locked also. The first-floor people say they do not know anything about man, as they just moved in.

February 20, 1914.—Man came in with landlord. Latter says he has known Balik for last three years as he was working on the house, being a carpenter. He always knew him as a respectable man, would like the League to take care of girl if she be permitted to land, and also try to get permission for the girl to land.

February 22, 1914.—Man came in with woman who seemed very nice and said she would be willing to take girl and board her. She has been seventeen years in this country; they own their own home. Telegram sent, explaining status of case to Commissioner, Quebec.

February 23, 1914.—Telegram received from Commissioner as follows: "Papers on appeal case Axenia Balik forwarded Secretary Labor, Washington, February seventeenth."

February 28, 1914.—Mr. Balik in office, wants to know what became of girl. He wishes to send another telegram. Telegram sent for him to Quebec.

March 1, 1914.—Mr. Balik came in with telegram from Commissioner, Quebec, as follows: "Xenia Balik still detained here. Case on appeal before Secretary of Labor, Washington, D.C., with whom you should communicate if you have anything further to say in her behalf."

March 9, 1914.—Letter written to Secretary of Labor as follows:

May I ask you about the status of Axenia Balik, a Russian girl, who has been detained at Quebec since February seventh? The case is on file before the Secretary.

March 15, 1914.—Reply from Assistant Secretary as follows:

Answering your letter of the 9th instant, asking for the status of the case of Xenia Balik, I beg to quote as follows from the memorandum, dated February 29, with which the appeal of said alien was submitted to me by the Commissioner-General of Immigration: "The record in this case shows that the uncle is not so situated that he should receive this young woman. He and a brother live together, the families of both being abroad. He informed the inspector that he intended this girl should keep house for them. Alien stated she did not know she was expected to perform this labor. On a second visit to the relative the inspector found a number of empty beer bottles about the rooms. There is also a disagreement between the testimony of alien and the relative regarding the whereabouts of his wife. There is no other relative to whom alien can go, and, apparently, no intimate friends." On this showing I did not feel that I could properly do anything else than approve the recommendation for deportation. A telegram was sent to the Quebec office on March 1, directing deportation, and presumably the alien has been returned to the port of foreign embarkation, as a sailing was scheduled to occur on March 2.

20. Greta Schmidt

(Exclusion—Young Woman Assisted by "Cousin")

[The first interviews with relatives are omitted in this case since the essential facts are all given in the following letters except some details regarding a controversy with the steamship company. The relatives in Chicago felt that the steamship company was largely responsible for the fact that the girl was not admitted and were insisting on a reduced fare if and when she returned to this country.]

August 28, 1923.—Letter written to Mrs. Lee [Ellis Island representative of the Y.W.C.A.]:

Can you procure, as early as possible, the following information for us? Greta Schmidt, a young German woman, twenty years old, who arrived on the S.S. "Steuben" about the tenth of May, was coming to join two elderly second cousins, Henry Mayer and his sister, Mrs. Mary Peterson, Oakdale, Illinois. The girl was deported after she had spent about a month at Ellis Island. The reason given in the Ellis Island telegram received by the steamship company was that she was "likely to become a public charge" and was "an assisted alien" (which, by the way, seems to be a blanket term covering many situations).

The cousin assures us that he had no official telegram and no request for any references or any information from Ellis Island. He handled everything through the steamship company's office here, where they assured him constantly that everything would be all right and that the delay was due to pressure of business, etc. In consequence, he was not worried and did not especially bestir himself, and the girl was deported. He has done so, however, since the girl was sent back, with the result that now he says he has obtained from the Bureau of Immigration or the Secretary of Labor official permission for the girl to return at any time it is convenient. Before he sends for her again, however, he would very much like to know what there was about the girl, or what there was in the case, that made the Board of Special Inquiry refuse her admission. If there is reason to think that she will be an undesirable person, or a difficult person to manage, he does not wish to run the risk of bringing her into this country.

September 14, 1923.—Letter received from Mrs. Lee:

I remember seeing this girl once or twice in the detention room just before she was deported. She did not seem to know why she was excluded, and I did not follow up the matter, because she went out the day after my first interview with her.

She did not establish clearly her relationship to Mr. Mayer, and she seemed to know very little about him.

From the following digest of the Special Inquiry hearing you will be able to judge for yourself what impression she made before the Board:

"Mother Katie in Holpen, Germany; Mayer fifty years old; he paid passage because he invited her to visit here; never saw him; invited her because she corresponded with him a long time and he always asked her to come over and pay him a visit, became acquainted with him through father, who lived in Chicago twelve years; father died March 9th; Mayer a widower; she has no relatives in United States; expects to be supported by him; will stay about six months; she is engaged to Georg Nieman, who is in Panama; he has been there two and a half years; does not know when she is to be married; Mayer knows she is to be married; Mayer thinks she is seventeen; at end of visit with Mayer she will go to South America; fiancé will pay passage; Board think it strange that a young girl should permit a man to pay expense of coming here for six months and let him support her. She says Mayer has female cousin Mary Peterson, with whom she has been corresponding; hasn't her address; had affidavit from Mayer, a pharmacist, earning fifty ($50) dollars per week; has two thousand five hundred ($2,500) dollars saved."

The Board excluded her as an assisted alien and a person likely to become a public charge. They did not ask how she was related to Mayer; they believed there was no relationship. If the girl is really related to Mrs. Mary Peterson and this lady is willing to assume responsibility for the girl, she had better make her plans known through an emphatically worded affidavit, and the girl had better say nothing about coming for a visit.

September 18, 1923.—Letter written to Mr. Mayer:

We have a letter from Ellis Island regarding Greta Schmidt. If you care to come to our office, we shall be glad to let you know its contents. If it is more convenient for you to come in the evening, our office is open Wednesday evenings between seven and nine-thirty.

September 21, 1923.--Mr. Mayer in office. Told him about report. He believes Greta so nervous and worried that she did not know what she was being asked. He will bring her back probably in November. Steamship company seems inclined to compromise the matter of fare. He has a meeting with the steamship agent this evening.

21. Rachel Badad
(Girl Coming to Fiancé—Admission on Bond)

[The following letters have been selected from a case record involving the admission of a Syrian girl, eighteen years of age. No extracts from the case record are given since the letters indicate the problems involved.]

1. Copy of a letter from the Superintendent of the Immigrants' Protective League to the Secretary of the Near East Relief, New York, dated August 27, 1923:

MY DEAR MISS X.:

We telegraphed you for your assistance on Friday for a Syrian girl by the name of Rachel Badad. She arrived on August 1, S.S. "Nineveh," and is still detained at Ellis Island. She came to this country with the intention of marrying a second cousin, David Solomon, living at 10 East Street, Chicago. He is of Syrian descent but was born in Chicago. He is an ex-service man. His father, Andrew Solomon, who is Rachel's great-uncle, arranged with her parents for the match. He was very anxious that his son should marry a Syrian girl, and David was willing to follow his wishes. The relationship in the family is quite patriarchal still. The girl sent over some photographs. We inclose one of them, as you may need it for purpose of identification.

David Solomon went on to New York and to Ellis Island in person to claim the girl. He seems to have incurred the suspicion or ill-will of the Board of Special Inquiry. Part of this was due to an error in his affidavits; through carelessness the affidavits were made in the name of Andrew Solomon instead of David. The inspectors at the Island kept asking about his brother Andrew and refused to believe that he was the affiant. He showed them his "Army Discharge," on which his character was listed as excellent, but he was told that that meant nothing and was told also to return to Chicago to get character references.

He went first to the United States Immigration Office here to ask them to investigate. He says they referred him to our office. We asked a Greek Orthodox priest to make an affidavit as to the family's respectability, especially the father's and David's. The Solomons belong to the Greek Orthodox Church, and one of the priests has known them well for about eighteen years. He spoke of them in high terms. Another letter of reference was sent with that affidavit. Nothing further was heard from Ellis Island for a week or so. Then we had a telegram from one of the officials, saying that the girl was excluded as "likely to become a public charge" and an "assisted alien," both reasons that we cannot accept without protest. David Solomon and his father had paid for the girl's ticket, but if that constitutes being an assisted alien then most of the immigrants coming over belong in the same class. David Solomon is a chauffeur and has been making about $50 a week. His father owns the property in which they live and has net savings of about $12,000. The girl is in good health and only eighteen. Why she should become a public charge is not clear. We inclose an additional affidavit made by a great-aunt, Mrs. Mary Matlas. The girl has a number of other relatives here in Chicago. We have investigated the home conditions and found them above the average of the homes to which immigrants come. We have spoken to the Syrian priest about the family. Though they are not members of his congregation (he is Catholic), he knows them and speaks of them in favorable terms. We have also sent a letter from Hull-House. The Solomon family used to live near Hull-House and are known to some of the older residents.

We shall very much appreciate your help or advice. We cannot feel that it is just or right that this girl should be sent all the way back to the Near East, and we believe if the true situation can be properly presented to the authorities, this may be prevented.

Sincerely yours,

ALICE MARION, *Superintendent*

2. Letter from the Superintendent of the Immigrants' Protective League to the Secretary of the Near East Relief, dated August 30, 1923:

MY DEAR MISS X.:

The bearer of this letter is Mrs. Mary Matlas, of Chicago, a great-aunt of Rachel Badad. She is going to New York to see if the United States immigration authorities will release the girl to her.

David Solomon may be with her, but at the present writing the family has not decided. It might be very much better if she was admitted to her aunt, and if the proposed marriage with David was postponed till the young people know each other better.

To us the family has always maintained that Rachel came to this country for the purpose of marrying David. The oldest son, Andrew, whom we saw for the first time today, is responsible for a statement made at the United States Immigration Office here in Chicago, to the effect that she is brought over here to marry one of the three sons of Joseph Solomon, not David, unless she prefers him to the others. If one did not know the family, had not seen the family in its own home, and spoken with people of good standing in the community who hold them in high esteem, one might be rather shocked at the situation and inclined to think it dangerous. We think it is unfortunate they should have made these conflicting statements.

Sincerely yours,

ALICE MARION, *Superintendent*

3. Extract from a letter from the Superintendent of the Immigrants' Protective League to the Secretary of the Near East Relief, dated September 1, 1923:

MY DEAR MISS X.:

. . . . It is true that one reason for bringing Rachel Badad over is so that there may be a housekeeper in the Solomon family. Mr. Solomon has an unmarried daughter who lives at home, but being an American-born girl she is not satisfied to stay at home to look after her father and three brothers but wishes to earn her own living. Bringing a Syrian girl from the old country to marry David was Joseph Solomon's solution of the difficulty. If you are willing to allow Syrians, Armenians, Greeks, and, for that matter, French parents to arrange the marriages for their children in their own way, instead of in our way, the above does not constitute a very serious offense. It was the original intention of the Solomons that Rachel Badad should marry David. When they learned what a shocking thing such a project seemed to us in this country, they were willing to be very American and to allow her a choice. . . . .

Old Mrs. Mary Matlas, the great aunt, was intending to go to New York to get the girl; we understood she was leaving on Thursday or Friday. If she has not changed her plans you have probably seen her by now, as we gave her a letter of introduction to you.

Sincerely yours,

ALICE MARION, *Superintendent*

4. Extract from a letter from the Near East Relief to the Superintendent of the Immigrants' Protective League, dated September 5, 1923:

MY DEAR MISS MARION:

Your letter of September 1 has just come to us, and we have also had word that Mrs. Matlas has come on, hoping to help in the matter of Rachel Badad. . . . . It would be necessary in the eyes of the immigration people to have a definite home for the girl, and I believe their objection to turning her over was that it was not definitely decided which of several people she was finally to marry.

Yours very sincerely,

Personal Service Division

5. Letter from the Near East Relief to the Superintendent of the Immigrants' Protective League, dated September 14, 1923:

MY DEAR MISS MARION:

Mrs. Matlas started today for Chicago with her niece, Rachel Badad, and I hope their troubles are ended for a while. She was admitted on $500 permanent bond, which a friend of Mrs. Matlas, Mr. Benjamin, covered for her.

Before Rachel marries, the immigration officials should be notified, as that would alter the character of her bond, which I understand would either be annulled or transferred to her husband.

Sincerely yours,

Personal Service Division

6. Extract from a letter from the United States Bureau of Immigration to the Superintendent of the Immigrants' Protective League:

Referring to your interest in the case of Rachel Badad it gives me pleasure to inform you that the Department has authorized the admission of this alien upon the filing of a public-charge bond in the sum of $500.

22. Esther Litski
(Illegal Entry)

January 4, 1921.—Harry Litski and Joe Litski, his son, Polish-Jewish, address 244 Ruth Street, in office [Immigrants' Commission] asking help about Esther Litski, detained in Montreal. Esther is the daughter of Harry Litski and is twenty-two years old. The father (Harry Litski) is sixty-six years old; he came to the United States in May, 1912, and took out first papers April, 1918. He has five other children, four of them married and in Chicago and the fifth working in New York. The father (Harry Litski) is a junk peddler, earning about $50 a week. Esther was brought to Canada by Mr. Fritz, a Canadian subject, who went to Europe to bring his wife over. He was to bring Esther with him when he returned. The father has received a telegram from Mr. Fritz from Montreal, asking for $500. He does not know date of girl's arrival or steamship but has telegraphed for information. He will come in when he receives answer. *Later.*—Father (Harry Litski) in office again. He received another telegram from his daughter from Montreal asking for $500 to show inspector. He said he was going to send it.

January 6, 1921.—Father in office again. He has another telegram from his daughter. She arrived on S.S. "Grampian." He has sent her $500, care of United States Commissioner of Immigration, Montreal. *Later.*—Prepared and sent official affidavit; also sent telegram as follows: "*Commissioner of Montreal:* Official affidavit sent today Esther Litski steamship Grampian. If excluded hereby appeal. Please wire reason detention and advise if not detained by American authorities.—HARRY LITSKI, 244 Ruth Street."

January 7, 1921.—Harry Litski in office with letter received from United States Commissioner of Immigration, Montreal:

DEAR SIR:

Receipt is acknowledged of your telegram of the 6th instant, concerning affidavit which you state you have mailed in behalf of Esther Litski, ex S.S. "Grampian." We have no record of this passenger at our Montreal office. The S.S. "Grampian's" last voyage disembarked its passengers at St. John West, N.B., and I am communicating with our Inspector-in-Charge at that port with a view to ascertaining whether Esther Litski was among the United States detained passengers. You will be communicated with further as soon as report is received from our St. John West, N.B., Office.

January 11, 1921.—Mr. Litski in office. Affidavit and $500 were returned from Montreal, saying girl is not detained there. Man also received telegram from Mr. Fritz, 14 Avenue A, Montreal, saying daughter is sick and that he should come to Montreal. He went to Canada but was turned back at border as he is not a citizen. *Later.*—Letter written to Jewish Immigrant Aid Society as follows:

Secretary, Jewish Immigrant Aid Society
725 Notre Dame Street, W.
Montreal, Canada

MY DEAR SIR: Would you be good enough to investigate and send us the facts with reference to this case? Harry Litski, residing at 244 Ruth Street, this city, believes that his daughter, Esther Litski, twenty-two years of age, is detained in Montreal. She is supposed to have arrived on the steamship "Grampian" and all telegrams he has had have been from Montreal. The United States Commissioner of Immigration, however, says that the steamship "Grampian" disembarked its passengers on its last voyage at St. John. He has received a telegram from Mr. I. Fritz, 14 Avenue A, Montreal, saying that his daughter is seriously ill and urging him to come at once. In response to this he started for Canada but was stopped at the border as he has only his first citizenship papers. He sent $500 to the United States Immigration Inspector but the money was returned because the girl was not held there. He then sent the $500 to I. Fritz, 14 Avenue A, and it was not returned. The father is naturally very anxious as to what is the situation.

Yours very truly,
ALICE MARION

January 12, 1921.—Mr. Litski in office. He has been to Western Union and received the $500, which was again returned. He also sent $150 to St. John. He received following letter from the United States Commissioner of Immigration at Montreal:

DEAR SIR:

Supplementing my letter to you of the 7th instant, concerning the case of Esther Litski, ex S.S. "Grampian," it is now ascertained that this passenger is detained at St. John West, N.B., by the Canadian authorities, she having been manifested to Canada. It is understood that the passenger named has been refused admission to Canada, and that she has taken an appeal from such decision. All records on appeal must be presented to the Dominion Government authorities at Ottawa, Ont., for consideration and final decision. Should an adverse decision be given in the case of Esther Litski, our Inspector-in-Charge at St. John West, N.B., understands that the passenger is to be permitted to make application for admission to the United States, but this step cannot be taken until the Canadian authorities have rendered final decision in the case. You will be kept informed of further proceedings in connection with the above.

Later.—Wrote United States Inspector-in-Charge, St. John West, N.B., as follows:

I am writing in behalf of Harry Litski, residing at 244 Ruth Street, this city, with reference to Esther Litski, S.S. "Grampian," now detained at St. John, N.B., by the Canadian authorities. she having been manifested to Canada. Mr. Litski is the father of Esther Litski, and it was his intention that she should come to the United States. The person with whom she travelled from Europe must have made a mistake in applying for admission to Canada. The girl's family here are willing and ready to furnish such money as is necessary for her journey to the United States. They are very anxious to have the case transferred from the Canadian to the American authorities.

January 14, 1921.—Mr. Litski in office. He received another telegram from Mr. Fritz, saying girl is better and asking him to send $500. If girl has been admitted and is in Montreal he does not understand why he should send $500. He says he has already paid all possible travelling expenses. Money the man sent to St. John was returned to him.

January 19, 1921.—Letter received from Jewish Immigrant Aid Society containing the following:

Your letter of January 11 regarding Esther Litski received. **In reply** I can inform you that this lady arrived in Montreal from St. John this morning. She is at present stopping at 153 Avenue A and she could be communicated with at that address. The reason for her coming to Montreal not earlier than today is because she contracted a slight cold in St. John and she was forced to stay there for two weeks. Now, however, she has fully recovered and her friends in Chicago can be quite at rest about her. On being questioned by one of our representatives whether she received the $500 which Mr. Harry Litski of your city claims to have sent to Montreal for her, she answered that no such amount reached her. Mr. Fritz to whom the money is supposed to have been addressed also claims never to have received same. If you will inform me of how Mr. Litski sent the money, that is, whether by wire or mail or otherwise, we will try to help him trace it. Assuring you of our wish to co-operate with you in any way that we can, I remain,
Yours very sincerely,
JEWISH IMMIGRANT SOCIETY OF CANADA

Later.—Letter written to Jewish Immigrant Society as follows:

We are in receipt of your letter of January 17, for which we thank you. Mr. Litski apparently made some mistake in the address when he sent the money to Mr. Fritz, for he has had all money which he sent returned to him unclaimed. He is, however, still receiving letters from Mr. I. Fritz, 14 Avenue A, Montreal, asking for $500. He hesitates to send this amount as he does not understand for what purpose it will be used. Would it be possible for you to investigate this case further and to ascertain why the money is wanted; whether Esther Litski was admitted only to Montreal and if so would it be possible to get her to the United States? Her father is very anxious to have her come here as soon as possible and would appreciate anything you can do in her behalf.

Later.—Mr. Litski called up. He received letter from Mr. Fritz again asking for $500, which he sent.

January 27, 1921.—Letter received from Jewish Society:

Your letter dated January 19 *re* Esther Litski received. In reply I can inform you that we have discovered that Miss Litski is not in Montreal. She left this city last week. We had Mr. Fritz of 14 Avenue A call on us this afternoon for explanation why he wrote to Mr. Litski for $500. Mr. Fritz claims that he has spent some money on the girl and would like to have that amount returned. He says he has written to Mr. Litski all the details connected with the case. Assuring you of our further co-operation in the future, I am,
Yours very truly,
JEWISH IMMIGRANT SOCIETY OF CANADA

Later.—Telephoned Mr. Litski. He received letter from Mr. Fritz that his daughter is coming, and they expect her tomorrow. Mr. Litski said that as soon as Mr. Fritz received the money he began to make arrangements for girl to come to Chicago. Asked Mr. Litski to let us know when girl arrives.

February 14, 1921.—Telephoned Mr. Litski. Esther arrived last Thursday.

March 1, 1921.—Visited 244 Ruth Street. Esther Litski came two weeks ago. Her brother met her at the station. Mr. Litski said that his daughter is working in a tailor shop and that everything is all right. Family have a comfortable flat.

March 18, 1921.—Mr. Litski in office. Girl's baggage is held by Mr. Fritz in Montreal and Mr. Litski wishes to get it. He says Mr. Fritz agreed to bring Esther and her mother to this country. In July, 1920, Mr. Litski paid him $200. Meanwhile the mother died. After girl got to Canada Mr. Fritz demanded another $500 which Mr. Litski sent. Out of the $700 Mr. Fritz paid travelling expenses for the girl from Warsaw to Chicago, paid $15 for a dress, $20 for a coat, $5 for shoes. He holds her baggage, largely things valuable to her because they were her mother's and refuses to turn them over unless he is paid $100 more.

March 22, 1921.—Letter written to the Secretary of the Federation of Jewish Philanthropies of Montreal:

We are writing to you in spite of the fact that this is a case in which we have already had some assistance from the Jewish Immigrant Aid Society. Our reason for asking your help is that that Society devotes itself so exclusively to immigration problems. Harry Litski, 244 Ruth Street, Chicago, made arrangements last spring with a Montreal man, Mr. I. Fritz, 14 Avenue A, to bring his wife and daughter from Warsaw to Chicago. In June he made an initial payment to Mr. Fritz of $200. Before Mrs. Litski and her daughter could start out, Mrs. Litski died. The daughter, Esther, arrived in St. John on the steamship "Grampian" about the last of this year. She was detained by the Canadian authorities, having been manifested to Canada. As Mr. Fritz knew the girl was to join her father in Chicago, it is hard to understand why he should have made such an arrangement. At the request of Mr. Fritz, Mr. Litski sent him $500 about the middle of January. Mr. Litski has never had any real accounting from Mr. Fritz as to how this money was spent, and he feels very much dissatisfied. Furthermore, Mr. Fritz is still holding the girl's luggage—especially valuable to her because a number of the things belonged to her dead mother—and he refuses to give up this baggage unless he is paid $100 more. Mr. Litski's story is that out of the $700 Mr. Fritz has paid the girl's passage from Warsaw to Chicago, which would amount to $176.69—$158.69 for her ticket, $8 head tax, and $10 for the passport. He bought the girl a dress, a coat, and a pair of shoes when she arrived in Montreal, and paid for same $42. Mr. Litski would like to know how the rest of the money was used. Would it be possible for you to see Mr. Fritz and get from him his list of expenditures? Will you also find out from him why he considers himself entitled to an additional hundred dollars, and considers himself justified in withholding the girl's baggage? We shall greatly appreciate your co-operation in this **matter.**

April 22, 1921.—Letter received from Federation of Jewish Philanthropies of Montreal:

I am in receipt of your letter of inquiry of the 22d ultimo, with reference to obtaining a statement of expenditures from Mr. Fritz. Enclosed please find a copy of the statement Mr. Fritz handed me today, demanding payment of the balance of $82.84. Kindly advise Mr. Litski and his daughter to examine the statement carefully and advise me whether or not it is correct. With reference to the belongings left with Mr. Fritz, he informed me he had obtained some forms from the Custom House some time ago, which were to have been filled out by Miss Litski before a notary, to the effect that these clothes belong to her and are for her personal use. Kindly have Miss Litski do so and send the forms to us. I will then demand from Mr. Fritz and he will then deliver the goods to an express company and have them shipped direct to Chicago. The express charges will have to be paid in advance, as it cannot go C.O.D., and the American Consul will also have to be paid in Montreal. I shall be pleased to give you any further information you may desire. Trusting this information is satisfactory, I am,

Very truly yours,

A. L. K., *Superintendent, Legal Aid Department*

[Copy of statement inclosed:]

Mr. Litski
Chicago, Illinois

DEAR SIR: Inclosed please find a full statement of all I have spent on your daughter from beginning to end. I received on account $700, which leaves a balance of $82.84.

- $ 54.00 I spent to obtain an affidavit, and other papers which were necessary to get her here.
- 17.85 Ticket to Detroit
- 90.00 Return ticket from Detroit
- 25.00 Polish passport
- 65.00 Fare from Lockorfitz to Lemberg
- 10.00 Spending money
- 10.00 Spending money
- 160.00 Ticket to Montreal
- 50.00 Spent on her in Slalchoff, Poland, when we were arrested
- 10.00 Spending money
- 2.00 Spending money
- 4.00 Spending money
- 2.00 Spending money
- 6.00 Spending money
- 150.00 Spending money in Warsaw, including board and ticket to Antwerp. We were five weeks in Warsaw
- 15.00 Spending money
- 84.00 Spent to bring her from St. John, N.B., to Montreal. I had to go there to get her out
- 18.00 Two weeks' board in Montreal
- 9.34 Telegrams

April 27, 1921.—United States Immigration Office telephoned, asking for a Yiddish-speaking visitor to interpret in this case. Esther Litski has been arrested. A. M. [Jewish visitor] went to Immigration Office. Girl is now under arrest at Clark Street Police Station Annex—was taken there by order of United States Immigration Bureau as having come to the United States without passport, also as being illiterate. Visited the Annex with inspector (Mr. Henry). Brother who came to see girl was told to bring $500 Liberty Bonds as bail until case is settled as to whether she is to remain or be sent back. According to Esther Litski a United States Immigration Inspector came to the tailor shop where she is working and took her to the Immigration Bureau. She was not notified previously that she was under arrest, neither was she told why they were taking her from her work. This happened yesterday afternoon. Shortly after I came in the brother arrived. He was notified by someone (does not know who) to go to the United States Immigration Office. He did not know why the girl had been taken there. At the hearing which was about 3:50 P.M. I told Mr. Henry, the United States inspector, that the file we had in our office would throw some light on the case especially as to how the girl was brought here from Poland but I was told it wasn't needed and I was also told that I was only acting in the capacity of an interpreter. At the close of the hearing about 4:25 Mr. Henry said the girl was to be taken to Clark Street Detention Station and he told the brother to bring $500 Liberty Bonds as bonds for the girl and she could then be released. The man could not understand what the money was needed for and upon my asking Mr. Henry he explained it was to serve as a bond for the girl until they determined whether or not she will be sent back. I asked if there was anything we could do to prevent her from being taken to the Police Station but was told it was too late to do anything as the office was closing. Mr. Henry immediately walked away after telling the switchboard operator to take care of girl—I also asked switchboard operator if there wasn't any other place girl could be kept until bond was furnished but she replied: "That is the place where all government girls are taken—everything will be all right and her meals will be ordered for her." I also tried to explain to Mr. Henry how it came about that girl knew nothing about passport; I doubted whether she had been questioned by any United States immigration authorities in Canada as Mr. Fritz had taken care of all that; but was told that it had nothing to do with the hearing. *Later.*—Sent telegram to Montreal to Superintendent of Federation of Jewish Philanthropies as follows:

"Esther Litski, 244 Ruth Street, placed under arrest by Immigration Department as having come to United States without proper passport. Will you see Mr. I. Fritz, 14 Avenue A, who brought girl to Detroit. According to his bill he paid $25 for Polish passport and $54 for affidavit and other necessary papers. Wire collect result of investigation. Have him send passport.—ILLINOIS IMMIGRANTS' COMMISSION."

April 28, 1921.—Man, his son, and son-in-law in office. Did not deposit $500 Liberty Bonds as they did not understand what bonds were for.

Explained it to them. Also showed them itemized list of expenditures Mr. Fritz sent. They also received lists which do not tally with ours. They will try to locate their lists and bring them to office. Brother-in-law has brother here who traveled with Mr. Fritz and girl. His expenses were not half so large. He will come to office to make sworn affidavit as to what he had to spend on same items. The custom house blanks were not filled out. Told them to bring girl to office with blanks and we would help them to fill them out. Man also claims that he filled out affidavits at Silver & Co. (West Street bankers), for which he paid $10, which were sent to Washington in April of 1920. They were returned with other papers from Washington and were sent to the girl on May 3 before Mr. Fritz started for Poland. Mr. Fritz is a Canadian citizen and a cousin of Mr. Litski's daughter-in-law. About the same time the affidavits were sent to the girl, $107 (15,000 marks) were also sent her which she says she received.

May 3, 1921.—Telegram received from Federation of Jewish Philanthropies: "*Re* Esther Litski. Sending passports today's mail." *Later.*— Telephoned Mr. Litski. He said the bonds were deposited and his sister is home and working again.

May 4, 1921.—Mr. Litski in office. Asked our advice about engaging an attorney. Told him not necessary for the present. If we think so later we will tell them.

May 5, 1921.—Brother in office. He says girl is almost sick from worry. She is very much afraid she will be deported. He asked again about an attorney. They do not care to spend more money but will do anything not to have girl deported. The girl's mother is dead and she has no one but an aunt in Poland. Family are all greatly distressed. *Later.* —Received letter and passport from Federation of Jewish Philanthropies:

Your telegram of April 27th received. I immediately communicated with Mr. Fritz, who called at my office, but could not get a satisfactory reply from him. He stated that he does not care anything about all that has occurred, that he did not take the girl over to Detroit but that someone came for her. However, I obtained from him Polish passport No. 29417–920, ser. A, No. 174584, for Miss Esther Litski, which I am enclosing. Kindly acknowledge receipt of same. I hope this will settle the case satisfactorily.

Very truly yours,

A. L. K., *Superintendent, Legal Aid Department*

Later.—Letter written to Federation of Jewish Philanthropies acknowledging receipt of passport.

May 6, 1921.—L. G. talked the matter over with Mr. X. [a Chicago citizen interested in welfare of Jewish immigrants]. He will write Congressman or Senator if sent form for letter. *Later.*—Sent form for letter as follows:

Would you be good enough to find out from the Secretary of Labor what can be done for Esther Litski, an immigrant girl now under arrest for being illegally in this country? The facts of the case are as follows. Her mother is dead, and all her immediate family, her father, three brothers, and two sisters are all here. They have been trying to bring her here ever since travel from Poland became possible. They finally arranged with a man named Fritz, who is a cousin of one of the girl's sisters-in-law, who is himself a Canadian citizen and was returning to Poland for some relatives of his, to bring Esther back with him. Every effort was made to have the proceeding regular. About a year ago in accordance with the procedure then used, application was made to the State Department for authorization of her passport, etc. In January of this year she arrived at St. John, Canada, and was apparently admitted to Canada. She came to the United States the first part of February and was at work when she was arrested last week. She is, I take it, technically illegally in the country—a passport irregularity being at the bottom of the difficulty. When arrested she did not have her passport. That has been secured through the Federation of Jewish Philanthropies of Montreal. It and some of her personal belongings had been held by Mr. Fritz, the man who went to Poland and was supposed to help her, because of some dispute about further payments due him for money he had advanced. The Immigrants' Commission was endeavoring with the help of the Federation in Montreal to untangle this before her arrest occurred. I am enclosing the passport which you will note has not been visaed by the United States—visas for Canada are, I understand, unnecessary. Will it be possible for you to straighten out this matter so that she may be regularly admitted to the United States and the warrant for her arrest cancelled?

June 1, 1921.—Called up Mr. Litski. He had not heard anything more about the case.

July 14, 1921.—Letter from Mr. X., inclosing letter received by Senator Y. from United States Department of Labor, Bureau of Immigration:

United States Senator Y.
Washington, D.C.

SIR: Referring to your letter of May 10, inclosing one dated May 7, from Mr. X., of Chicago, in behalf of Esther Litski, I have to advise the Department has decided to order the removal of this alien to her native country on account of the following facts: The father of this girl resides in the United States, and he paid one Fritz, a resident of Canada, to bring her to this country. After arrival at St. John they proceeded to Windsor, Ontario, and effected surreptitious entry into the United States, leaving their baggage on the Canadian side to avoid questioning. The alien's passport was not visaed by any United States Consul, and it is unlikely the State Department would waive the passport requirements. Accordingly, there is no other course open but to effect deportation.

Respectfully,

July 15, 1921.—Letter sent to Harry Litski as follows:

We have today received news from Washington to the effect that your daughter is to be deported as she is in this country illegally, having entered without the proper passport visa and without the proper inspection at the Canadian border. She will be sent back to Canada, we suppose. We feel extremely sorry, but unfortunately, there is nothing further we can do for you in the matter. The decision of the Department of Labor is final.

July 18, 1921.—Joseph Litski in office. He has not yet been notified by United States Immigration Bureau that sister is to be deported. He is fearfully worried lest she be sent back to Poland. Wishes to know what they can do to prevent this.

July 22, 1921.—Mr. Litski, girl, and stepmother in office. They had received letter from Immigration Bureau that she is to be deported, August 2. They wish to know that she will surely be sent to Canada and not to Poland. Called up Immigration Office, spoke with Mr. Roberts. He said order reads "to be deported to country she originally started from."

[The remaining portion of the record deals with some difficulties about the girl's passport, which was needed for her return journey to Poland. She was finally deported August 6.]

23. Riva Leah Zimber
(Detention of Deformed Alien Abroad)

September 14, 1921.—Mrs. Miriam Schmidt, address 1000 North Street, in office with her mother, for advice about bringing over a Roumanian Jewish girl, aged twenty.

[The facts in this case, gathered chiefly from the sister, Mrs. Schmidt, are contained in the following letter, which was written at once to the Commissioner-General of Immigration, Washington, D.C.:]

We are writing you at the request of the relatives of Riva Leah Zimber, a twenty-year-old Jewish girl who is at present at Havre, and is refused passage to this country by the Compagnie Générale Transatlantique, though she has the passport and visa that are required. The letter which we inclose, written by Dr. Fletcher of the United States Public Health Service, Havre, will make clear why the Company refuses, but will also show how little reason there is for their action. All the other members of her family are in this country. The father came in 1911. Several sons and a daughter came a few years later. Last June the mother and four younger children arrived; she had been compelled to leave the daughter at Havre. The father and two older brothers are quite well-to-do business men; their net earnings are at least $12,000. Feeling that this girl is somewhat handicapped, the father has left her the bulk of his property in his will. He and the mother are insured for her for $1,500. The separation of this girl from her family is a source of great anxiety and unhappiness to them all and especially to the mother. Will you be good enough to let us know what it is possible to do under such circumstances? We shall greatly appreciate such assistance.

[The letter from Dr. Fletcher (written on the letter head of the American Consular service, Havre, France, dated August 4, 1921) was as follows:]

This is to certify that I have this day examined Riva Leah Zimber, who desires to join her parents in America, and I have found her in good physical condition except for a congenital deformity of the right leg. There is a lack of development below the knee, resulting in a shortness of this limb of some six or eight inches. By means of a mechanical extension which she is now wearing, she is able to move about from place to place at almost normal gait, accompanied with only a moderate limp.

September 26, 1921.—Letter received from Washington, signed by Assistant Commissioner-General, Immigration Bureau, United States Department of Labor, Washington, D.C.:

In reply to your letter of September 14, inclosing a certificate signed by Dr. Fletcher, of the United States Public Health Service at Havre, France, relative to the physical condition of one Riva Leah Zimber, I have to advise that there is nothing in the information in hand which indicates that the alien would be excluded upon her arrival, nor that a vessel bringing her would be subjected to a fine for so doing. The admissibility of an alien cannot be determined in advance of arrival at a port of entry in this country. But should the case come before the Department at a later date, on an appeal from an excluding decision by a Board of Special Inquiry, I am confident that the Secretary would authorize the admission of the alien in question, and would refuse to assess a fine against the vessel bringing her here, if the facts developed at that time agree with the information now in hand.

Later.—Letter written to Mr. Zimber, the girl's father:

We have today had a reply from the Immigration Bureau to the letter which we wrote some time ago to the Commissioner-General with regard to your daughter, Riva Leah Zimber, and her detention at Havre. We inclose a copy of the letter. We also inclose a copy of the letter which we wrote the Commissioner-General. Our letter was based on information furnished by your daughter, Mrs. Schmidt, and we trust it is accurate in all points. We should advise you to show these letters to the Chicago representative of the Compagnie Générale Transatlantique. Possibly they may be able to adjust the matter here, or, if not, they may be willing to take it up with the main office, which, we suppose, is in France. In view of the Bureau's letter, we do not believe that there will be any further difficulty. Be sure to take with you the notaried copy you have of Dr. Fletcher's diagnosis. The one we sent to Washington was not returned to us. We return the other two papers left here by you [letters from attorneys]. We decided it was not necessary to send them to Washington.

September 28, 1921.—Mrs. Schmidt in office. She took the letters to Compagnie Générale Transatlantique. They told her they were just the sort wanted and advised her to send them to her sister at once. She is very grateful to League.

[The remaining portion of the record deals with the sending of affidavits to New York and arrangements for meeting the girl, who arrived October 24, and was admitted without any difficulty.]

24. Mary Zabern
(Arrival without Passport)

August 5, 1920.—Samuel Zabern, a Polish Jew, in office [Immigrants' Commission], wishes help for his daughter Mary, twenty years old, who arrived in New York August second, on the S.S. "La Savoie" and is detained at Ellis Island. The father says he and his wife have five other children with them here. They left Mary with relatives long ago when they first came over and would have brought her over in 1914 except for the war. Telegram taking appeal sent. Affidavit made out for man.

August 20, 1920.—Mr. Zabern called at office to say he had a telegram from Ellis Island that his daughter is detained because of quarantine.

August 24, 1920.—Mr. Zabern in office—has telegram from Ellis Island saying Mary admitted August 19. He is worried because she has not arrived. *Later.*—The following telegram sent to Miss Freeman, representing the Commission in New York: "Telegram says, Mary Zabern steamship La Savoie admitted August 19th. Not arrived. Please wire cause."

August 25, 1920.—Mr. Zabern in office to say he has not heard yet. He wants to go to New York. Told him to wait until tomorrow. *Later.*—Telegram from Miss Freeman: "Mary Zabern excluded August 17th, illiterate and has no passport, appealed to Washington."

August 26, 1920.—Mr. Zabern in office. Told him about telegram. He got very much excited and said he must do something for he could not let his daughter be deported. Sent him to Mr. Roberts, Inspector-in-Charge, United States Immigration Station. *Later.*—Mr. Zabern in office again. He brought a letter from the Inspector addressed to the Assistant Commissioner in Washington. Mr. Zabern wants to go to Washington tonight. He says he must do something. Advised him not to go. He says his wife is almost insane from anxiety.

August 27, 1920.—Mr. Zabern in office. He says he went to Congressman X., who sent a telegram to Washington.

August 30, 1920.—Mr. Zabern in office. The man seems desperate. He says Congressman X. has heard nothing yet. He sent another telegram this morning. Mr. Zabern got letter from Mr. Goldberg, a friend in New York City, telling him about the awful situation at Ellis Island and about his daughter's suffering. Mr. Zabern wants us to send another telegram. Wired to Miss Freeman: "Father of Mary Zabern steamer La Savoie anxious. Please wire collect status of case."

August 31, 1920.—Night letter from Miss Freeman:

Mary Zabern, special inquiry case, eighteen, La Savoie, arrived without passport. Makes affidavit that passport, money, ticket, other papers, were stolen from her on steamer. Case has been appealed to Washington asking authorities waive passport regulations. Am writing Washington friends to expedite matters. Letter follows. Counsel father to be patient.

Telephoned Mr. Zabern—not at home. *Later.*—Mr. Zabern in office. Gave him night letter to read. He was satisfied and says now he will be more patient.

September 1, 1920.—Letter from Miss Freeman:

This is to acknowledge receipt of your telegram of today regarding Mary Zabern, Special Inquiry No. 18, S.S. "La Savoie." This girl who was excluded by the Board of Special Inquiry as likely to become a public charge, having no passport, arrived without papers although she does hold an official receipt for $2.00 signed by the American Consul at Warsaw in payment of fee for visa. The affidavit submitted by her father was considered by the Board and found satisfactory. The case was appealed to Washington on August 24th. We set forth the facts as we learned them from the girl and submitted that in view of the circumstances we requested a waiver of the passport regulations. I am today writing some friends who happen to be in Washington, D.C., asking them to press the matter so that the girl may be admitted as quickly as possible. I do not think that there is anything further for the father to do. What do you think of sending a letter yourself to the authorities and putting the case before them? I think such a letter would carry weight. I am sorry that we can do nothing further about the case at this time.

Mr. Zabern in office. Showed him the letter from Miss Freeman. Wants to write Miss Freeman a letter and send $25 to his daughter in Miss Freeman's care.

Later.—Letter written to the Assistant Secretary of Labor as follows:

MY DEAR SIR:

I am informed that the case of Mary Zabern who arrived on the "La Savoie" on August 2d and has been excluded because she is without a passport has been appealed to Washington. The anxiety of Mr. and Mrs. Zabern here seem to me to leave no doubt as to the relationship of the girl, and I hope that the passport regulations may be waived in view of all the facts, which I understand are before you.

Very sincerely yours,

LYDIA GARDNER

September 2, 1920.—Wrote Miss Freeman:

Many thanks for your telegram and letter regarding Mary Zabern. I have written the Assistant Secretary, and the father has also been to see Congressman X. I hope very much the girl may be admitted.

September 3, 1920.—Mr. Zabern in office. He wanted to know if we had heard anything. He says he is desperate. *Later.*—Man called up. Received letter from daughter begging him to come and see her and take her home. Man wants to go either to Washington or Ellis Island.

September 5, 1920.—Letter received from Miss Freeman:

This is to thank you for the letter which you wrote me regarding Mary Zabern. I have cashed the money order today and have turned it over to the Treasurer at Mary's request, as this, together with the $25 already deposited with the Treasurer at Ellis Island, will suffice for a ticket to Chicago as soon as word comes from Washington that she may be admitted. I am hoping that the matter will be adjusted at a very early date.

September 7, 1920.—Mr. Zabern in office. He wants to know if we have heard about his daughter.

September 10, 1920.—Mr. Zabern in office. He received letter from Miss Freeman and says that he probably will go to Washington tomorrow and then to Ellis Island, although letter received says she is doing all that can be done on the case.

September 20, 1920.—Letter from Miss Freeman that Mary Zabern was put on train for Chicago September 17. Called family. Daughter at last with them. All very happy.

September 26, 1920.—Visited. Mary works in a tailor shop, but Mrs. Zabern could not tell the address or name of shop. Mary makes $15 a week. She attends evening school. Mr. Zabern finally went to New York to get Mary but found her gone two hours before he got there.

25. Jacob Joseph
(Illiteracy—Temporary Admission)

June 30, 1921.—Jacob Joseph, a Persian Jew, brought to office [Immigrants' Commission] by Miss White [teacher of English in a Chicago Settlement]. Man is about to be deported for illiteracy. He was born in Nennia, Persia, and is Jewish, age twenty-three. He filed first papers September 30, 1920. He has been working in a lunchroom, Third and Central, earning $20 a week. [Other facts obtained in this interview are indicated in the following letter written to the Commissioner of Immigration, Ellis Island:]

We are writing at the request of Jacob Joseph, 113 South Street, Chicago. This man was admitted under bond July 13, 1920. The bond was apparently required because of his illiteracy. Since his arrival in Chicago he has been studying with Miss White, who has classes for adult foreigners at the Y. Settlement. Six months ago, she took this man to the local United States Immigration Office for examination. At the time he did not do well enough to be passed, nor did he do well enough so that the Inspector in Charge felt justified in asking for an extension of his stay. This extension was, however, procured by Congressman X. A few days ago, Miss White went once more with him to the local office to have him take a second examination. He was refused the opportunity, and was told that the files in that office show he was admitted on a public-charge bond. As he is twenty-three years of age, is apparently in very good health, and has been working almost ever since his arrival (he has saved almost $200), this seems rather strange, and we think there must be some clerical error. The Ellis Island file number is 9877-52. The date for his deportation is set for July 13, 1921. Will you not be good enough to look into this matter, and let us have a report on it at your earliest convenience.

July 29, 1921.—Miss Moore [Supervisor in the Public Schools] telephoned. Evidently the Ellis Island inquiry was taken up with the local

Immigration Office. Man was re-examined a few days ago, failed in test, though he has been working hard and doing excellent work. Miss Moore thinks the test much harder than was justifiable. *Later.*—Letter written to United States Commissioner of Immigration, Washington:

I am writing to call your attention to the following case. A Persian Jew, Jacob Joseph, arrived in this country in June, 1920. He was illiterate and was admitted on a $500 bond for six months. At the end of the first six months he was not able to pass the examination, but through the effort of friends he was permitted to stay six months longer. A few days ago he was re-examined at the local Immigration Office. He again failed to pass the test. Miss White, who has been his teacher, and Miss Moore, who has supervision of the English classes for adult foreigners in the public school system of Chicago, are both very much interested in the man. They say he is unusually intelligent, and both feel sure he could pass any reasonable test. As I understand it, Miss Moore was present at the hearing. She gives it as her opinion that the passages which the man was asked to read are more difficult than was justifiable.

October 18, 1921.—Miss White in office. Mr. Joseph was allowed to take a third test and passed. Everything is all right, and deportation warrant cancelled.

26. Rosa Livitzki
(Illiteracy—Some Difficulties of Temporary Admission)

June 2, 1920.—A Russian-Jewish man, H. Livitzki, in the office [Immigrants' Commission] to ask help in getting aid to his sister. [The following telegram sent to the Hebrew Immigrant Aid Society in New York City explains his problem:]

Hebrew Sheltering and Immigrant Aid Society, New York City:

Rosa Livitzki now at Danzig awaiting sailing via Copenhagen detained account strike. Cable from Herr Kaplan to brother asked for forty dollars for new ticket. Sent this May third. Letter today asks for fifty dollars and does not acknowledge receipt of other. Brother would like to have you make arrangements. Will pay expenses. Wire instructions to H. Livitzki, 1237 North West Street, Chicago.

June 3, 1920.—Mr. Livitzki called to know if there is a reply to telegram.

June 4, 1920.—Mr. Livitzki called again to know if there is a reply to telegram. He insisted on having another telegram sent. The office refused to send one, but the man finally sent one on his own initiative as follows: "Cable seventy-five dollars to your Danzig representatives for Rosa Livitzki and have them make arrangements for her. Five dollars for your cable expenses. Wire reply to H. Livitzki, 1237 North West Street, Chicago."

June 9, 1920.—Letter sent to the Hebrew Immigrant Aid Society as follows:

Mr. H. Livitzki of 1237 North West Street, Chicago, has called on us with reference to his sister Rosa Livitzki, who is detained at Danzig on account of the strike. On June 2, we advised him to send a telegram, a copy of which we inclose. On June 4, on his own initiative he telegraphed you $80 and asked that you remit $75 to your representative in Danzig for Rosa Livitzki, and have them make arrangements for her. The remaining $5.00 were for your cabling expenses. Mr. Livitzki has not yet received any reply. He is very anxious to know whether the money he previously sent reached his sister, and whether your society will undertake to help him by advising what he must next do. We shall appreciate your advice on this matter.

June 22, 1920.—Reply received from the Hebrew Immigrant Aid Society as follows:

Replying to your letter dated June ninth concerning the above named, we beg to advise you that we have instructed our Danzig representative to locate and investigate the family of Mr. Livitzki now in Danzig. Our representative advised us to the effect that since the matter was taken up by Herr Kaplan we cannot intervene. Also that Mr. Livitzki must act through him in all matters. We are therefore returning herewith the check of $80 which you will kindly forward to Mr. Livitzki, and advise him what steps he must take in this case.

June 26, 1920.—Letter sent to Mr. Livitzki, returning check and explaining reply of the Society.

June 28, 1920.—Mr. Livitzki came in for further explanations. He will leave matter as he originally planned with the Herr Kaplan.

July 8, 1920.—Mr. Livitzki in office to have official affidavits filled out for his sister Rosa, who is detained at Ellis Island because not able to read. He says Hebrew Immigrant Aid Society is handling the case.

July 17, 1920.—Mr. Livitzki in office. *Jewish Courier* sent a telegram to Congressman X., who replied, asking to have affidavits sent showing ability to support and also to teach girl to read. Hebrew Immigrant Aid Society in New York received affidavits from brother also. Told Mr. Livitzki to come in on Monday, when Miss Gardner [Secretary of Commission] will be there.

July 20, 1920.—Mr. Livitzki in office to ask about his sister. He gave these facts. His sister arrived on S.S. "Philadelphia." She has been a servant since she was thirteen years old. Father died when she was a baby; mother and one sister were also servants. When she was twenty-four years old she married; but her husband deserted her a few weeks later, and she never heard from him again. Mother died during the war in Warsaw. Sister is in this country. Girl was alone there, and her brother, Mr. H. Livitzki, has been trying to get her over. Money never reached her for transportation, until January, 1920. Brother promises to see that she learns to read and write within six months. Mr. Livitzki received message through *Jewish Courier* from Congressman X. that everything possible is being done.

July 21, 1920.—Letter written to the Assistant Secretary of Labor, Washington:

MY DEAR SIR:

A Russian Jew by name of H. Livitzki, who resides at 1237 North West Street, Chicago, sent for his sister Rosa Livitzki, who was in Poland and who after many delays arrived on the steamship "Philadelphia" at Ellis Island. She has been excluded on the ground of illiteracy, and her brother has filed an appeal for temporary admission under bond. The circumstances surrounding her return seem to me to merit consideration. Her father died when she was a baby. Her mother and her older sister worked as servants, and she became a servant herself when she was only thirteen years old, so that she had no opportunity for an education. When she was twenty-four years old she married, but her husband deserted her a few weeks later. The mother died during the war. Her brother and sister are both in this country. Her brother is able and very eager to give necessary assistance to his sister. He feels sure that he can teach her to read and write Yiddish in a period of six months if she were admitted for that time. The man has been to see us a number of times during the period of her detention at Warsaw and Danzig, and I know of the expenses which he has met and the anxiety which he has suffered. I therefore hope very much that it will be possible for the Secretary to grant this request.

Very truly yours,
LYDIA GARDNER

July 24, 1920.—Mr. Livitzki telephoned he has sent telegrams and letter to sister and has had no answer. He wants Immigrants' Commission to send telegram to Hebrew Immigrant Aid Society and inquire why sister does not answer telegram. Told him to wait a few days.

July 26, 1920.—Sent night letter to Hebrew Immigrant Aid Society, New York: "Rosa Livitzki, steamer Philadelphia, detained illiterate. Her brother H. Livitzki much worried. Sent telegram letters to her, no answer. Please see her and wire state of health also status case.—LYDIA GARDNER."

July 27, 1920.—Mr. Livitzki telephoned that the *Jewish Courier* has notified him that his sister is coming to Chicago. *Later.*—Telegram from Hebrew Immigrant Aid Society: "Appeal for Rosa Livitzki is now pending in Washington. She is well. Will wire as soon as we have definite information."

July 28, 1920.— Letter from United States Bureau of Immigration:

In response to your letter of the 21st inst., addressed to the Assistant Secretary, the Bureau has to advise you that the admission of Rosa Livitzki has been directed for a period of six months provided a bond is filed.

Mr. Livitzki in office asking what to do next. Telephoned the United States Immigration Office, asking whether they have received instruction for bonds. They have not received any, but they will notify us when they do. Explained the situation to Mr. Livitzki. He thought his sister was already on her way to Chicago.

July 30, 1920.—Mr. Livitzki in office with letter from Washington, instructing him to go to United States Immigration Bureau and furnish two bondsmen, $1,000 each (real estate). He brought two friends with him to give bond. M. J. [Russian visitor] took them to Inspector-in-Charge. One of the men was not satisfactory. Mr. Livitski telephoned to another friend who is a property-owner. Left Mr. Livitzki waiting at Immigration Office.

August 2, 1920.—Mr. Livitzki in office with second bondsman. Explained to him importance of sister's learning to read Yiddish and told him someone in office would help if he had any difficulties arranging for lessons. He thinks he will take her to Neighborhood Settlement.

August 18, 1920.—Mr. Livitzki telephoned that his sister Rosa has arrived. Wants to know in what language she must learn to read. Told him again she must learn Yiddish because it will be so much easier for her than English. Explained to him that she must learn to read some language in six months or she will be deported.

October 5, 1920.—Called on Rosa Livitzki. On account of the holiday she is staying with her sister. Mr. Livitzki said that she was attending the evening school at Neighborhood Settlement and learning English upon the advice of the teacher there.

January 4, 1921.—Mr. Livitzki in office. The teacher told him his sister cannot pass examination; she will have to stay in school six months longer. Man wants sister to go to work and says some ladies on South Side want her to work for them. Explained to him that this is impossible, that she must learn to read or she cannot stay here.

January 5, 1921.—Telephoned Mr. Braun, head of Settlement. Rosa Livitzki is attending their day school for two hours each morning. Mr. Braun thinks they will be able to get time extended as he has written to the Secretary of Labor, to their Congressman, and also to a New York Society. He also thinks a place may be found for the girl to do housework in return for room and board with someone who will allow her to go to school in morning and evening if necessary and give her time to study. The teacher had spoken to the brother and asked him to be patient with her and give her time to learn so she can pass examination, should the time be extended; otherwise, she will be deported. Asked whether she would not better attend public school, suggested adult classes in Haven School. Mr. Braun said he thought their school better as teacher takes particular interest in each individual, which Miss Livitzki especially needs and does not think she will make more progress at Haven School.

January 6, 1921.—M. J. visited Neighborhood Settlement and talked with Rosa's teacher, Miss Davis. She seems very much interested and is working very hard to get Rosa so she can pass. However, she and Rosa have both got very nervous about it. Rosa went to the Haven School for a short time and then returned to the Settlement.

Telephoned Miss Moore, of the Board of Education. She thinks Rosa should have been taught Yiddish rather than English.

March 3, 1921.—Mr. Livitzki has letter, saying sister must sail by March 15. Letters have been written to bondsmen. He says he is going to see the Congressman through a "political friend." *Later.*—Telephoned Rosa's teacher. She says that Rosa has not been to school since January. The teacher blames Mr. Livitzki. He has wanted her to go to work and has been sure she could not learn. The teacher has visited the family and explained importance of Rosa's returning to class. Later she also telephoned the brother and made this even more emphatic.

March 5, 1921.—Telephoned Mr. Livitzki. He says the Congressman and his secretary are out of town. Tried to explain to him what the teacher reported, and he promised to come to the office Monday.

March 7, 1921.—Mr. Livitzki in office. Told him in view of report from the teacher at the Settlement we have nothing we can write to the department. He says that his sister always went to school except when she was sick, that she could not learn if she went three years, etc., etc. Evidently relies on sympathy preventing fulfilment of bonds. He will see the teacher and still expects to be saved by the Congressman.

March 8, 1921.—Mr. Livitzki in office again. Told him Immigrants' Commission could not do anything for him in the matter. He declared sister had never been absent from school except when she was ill, had never held a job but merely looked for one, etc. He insisted the Immigrants' Commission must do something for her. She would "be killed" if she returned to Poland. We advised him we could do nothing about it.

[Although the Commission had no further connection with this case, they learned that the brother had secured another stay of deportation for his sister, and still claimed he was trying to have her learn English.]

27. Marie Tabescu
(Temporary Admission—Illiteracy)

April 1, 1921.—Miss Henry, Social Service Society, Gary, Indiana, telephoned. They are sending Andrew Banir, a Roumanian, to Immigrants' Commission for advice and help. He got his illiterate sister-in-law admitted on bond June, 1920. She has made no effort to learn to read, has given him a great deal of trouble, and brought quarrels between him and his wife. He is willing that the Immigration Department should send her back and at first she wanted to go. Now, however, she says she is going to Canada instead of to Europe. He is afraid he will lose his bond ($500).

April 7, 1921.—Mr. Banir in office with letter to the Immigrants' Commission from the Gary Society:

The bearer of this letter is Mr. Andrew Banir, of whom Miss Henry telephoned you the other day. Mr. Banir gave a bond of $500 when his sister-in-law, Marie Tabescu, an illiterate, came to the United States from Roumania. Mr. Banir, when he thought there was a probability of his sister-in-law going to her brother in Canada, gave his bond to Mr. Roberts of the Immigrants' Labor Bureau[1] to see if he could be released from the obligation. Mr. Banir does not necessarily wish to take this out of Mr. Roberts' hands, but he wants advice as to whether he must leave it there until Mr. Roberts looks into it or whether he could go to Mr. Roberts with the same problem that he is coming to you with. The brother-in-law in Canada has written that in order to bring this sister-in-law into Canada, according to immigration information, he must take out a bond of $600 and must have two witnesses, each taking out a bond to verify the relationship. A difficulty is that an immigration inspector came to Gary about a month ago with a warrant against Marie Tabescu as a prostitute. When he came down here with this information, he also found, at least so he believed, that Mrs. Banir is a prostitute. We are not so sure of this; feeling that perhaps Mrs. Banir with her bad English implicated herself when she was trying to explain that her sister had caused so much trouble since coming into their family. Mr. Banir will appreciate any advice you may be able to give him.

A. M. spoke with Mr. Banir. His own statement is that his sister-in-law, Mrs. Tabescu, arrived in June, 1920, that she was found illiterate, detained at Ellis Island and later was admitted on bond for six months, that she appeared before Mr. Roberts, United States Immigration Inspector, to try to pass the literacy test again in December, 1920; did not pass the examination and was told she must work harder; her stay was prolonged for another six months. Lately she has been trying to study—at first she wouldn't—but she simply cannot learn. She is now anxious to remain in the United States, and he is willing she should. Apparently there has been a reconciliation. If she cannot stay in the United States she would like to go to Canada, where she has two brothers, John and Wassil Tabescu. Both have large farms. Both are married. They are willing she should come. She is quite unwilling to be sent back to Roumania, but the United States Immigration Office has threatened to deport her for immorality. Someone told Mrs. Tabescu that if she married an American citizen, she could stay in spite of being illiterate. She met a Roumanian in Gary who claimed he was a citizen. She agreed to marry him and let him take out a license. Then she found he was not a citizen, and she refused to marry him. This man is vindictive, and he has written Department of Labor, accusing her of immorality and wants her deported. United States Inspector Roberts has decided to have a hearing on April 28. Mr. Banir is then to produce witnesses testifying to his sister-in-law's character, conduct, etc. Mr. Banir thinks she will be permitted to remain until June.

Mr. Banir is chiefly worried about his $500. Assured him his money was safe enough but that he could not get it back until his sister-in-law had left United States or else had been declared admissible.

[1] [United States Immigration Office in Chicago.]

April 12, 1921.—Telephoned Mr. Roberts, United States Inspector. He says man's money is safe enough but the woman must not leave the United States till she is deported. She will be deported in all probability on the illiteracy charge by June 1. She may be deported before that on immorality charge if the hearing indicates that she is guilty.

April 15, 1921.—Letter written to Mrs. Kelly, Social Service Society at Gary:

MY DEAR MRS. KELLY:

We have spoken with Mr. Roberts, the Immigration Commissioner, about Mr. Banir and his sister-in-law, Marie Tabescu. Mr. Roberts states that the following is the status of the case. Mrs. Tabescu will undoubtedly be deported on the charge of illiteracy sometime after June 1. She may be deported on the charge of immorality, and in that case may possibly be sent away before June 1. There is to be a hearing sometime this month at the immigration office, at which time Mr. Banir and other people concerned will have the chance to present her side of the case. She must under no circumstances leave the United States till she is notified by the Immigration Department. If she were to go to Canada and succeed in getting across the border it would probably mean that Mr. Banir's bond would be forfeited. Mr. Banir told us when he was here that Mrs. Tabescu really seemed to be studying. Perhaps by June 1 it will be possible for her to secure another extension.

Very truly yours,

ALICE MARION

Later.—Miss Doseff, Bulgarian worker from Gary Society, in office. She thinks Mrs. Tabescu has undoubtedly been leading an immoral life in Gary. There is probably no doubt of her being found guilty at special hearing. Mrs. Banir is also implicated, but Miss Doseff thinks she will probably be exonerated. However, Mrs. Tabescu has found another man—an American citizen—who is willing to marry her, and she thinks that in this way she may avoid deportation. Explained that such a subterfuge would not help Mrs. Tabescu.

April 17, 1921.—Spoke to United States Inspector. Mrs. Banir is under warrant, too. Charge immorality. Evidence against her is strong. Her house has been raided twice by the police because of immoral conditions there. Inspector was very unfavorably impressed by her. He said, "She looked the part."

Against Mrs. Tabescu the charges are illiteracy and possible "public charge." The immorality evidence is not strong and will probably not be introduced. If she marries an American citizen she still will be deported. She will be deported to Europe and not to Canada, and if she succeeds in escaping to Canada, she will be considered a fugitive from justice. At the hearing, if Mr. Banir can prove that her brothers have secured permission to have her admitted to Canada, it may be possible for the local Immigration

Department to make some such recommendation. Mr. Roberts does not think that even if Mrs. Banir be proved immoral she will be deported since she has four children born in this country.

April 20, 1921.—Mr. Banir in office. Explained to him concerning sending Mrs. Tabescu to Canada. He has letter (Roumanian) from brother in Canada saying bond has already been deposited and that the matter of admission to Canada is arranged. Sent night letter to brother in Canada as follows: "Send at once affidavit showing your relationship to Marie Tabescu, your ability and willingness to keep her from becoming a public charge and giving information with regard to the six hundred dollar bond you have deposited with Canadian Immigration Office.—ANDREW BANIR, 204 Smith Street, Gary, Indiana."

April 21, 1921.—Telephoned Immigration Inspector. Hearing was held and minutes forwarded to Immigration Bureau. Inspector-in-Charge thinks she will be permitted to go to brother in Canada. Concerning Mrs. Banir there is really no evidence indicating immorality.

28. Marie Boreija
(Detention of Mother of an Illegitimate Child—Father Admitted)

[The first interview and report of home visit are omitted here since the facts are summarized in the letter below:]

November 10, 1914.—Letter to United States Inspector at Winnipeg:

DEAR SIR:

We write in behalf of Marie Boreija, a Lithuanian woman, who together with her child is detained at Winnipeg. The father of the child is Gregory Suleika, 22 North Street. He has been in the United States four months and has expected from the beginning to bring the woman here. We have talked with the man at some length on two occasions and are convinced that he is eager to marry the woman and to take care of his child. If you will release the woman to us, we will guarantee to keep her in our charge until the marriage ceremony is performed. If the woman has been excluded, we should like to give notice of an appeal to Secretary Wilson. You can, of course, see at once the injustice of allowing a man to come in under these circumstances and then excluding the woman. As the man is not deportable, the only way to bring about justice in the case is to admit the woman.

Sincerely yours,

LYDIA GARDNER, *Superintendent*

November 13, 1914.—The following reply received from Winnipeg:

Miss Lydia Gardner
Immigrants' Protective League
Chicago, Ill.

DEAR MADAM: I have your communication of November 10, 1914, with regard to the case of Marie Boreija and child. You are advised that in view of your statements, as contained in this letter, the Board of Special Inquiry in Winnipeg today ordered the admission of the aliens in question, they being booked to leave Winnipeg on the "Soo Line" train leaving here at five o'clock in the afternoon Saturday, November 14, destined to your offices. It is expected that arrangements will be made by you to have a representative of your League meet them on their arrival in Chicago, see that the marriage ceremony is duly performed and that our Chicago Office is informed, they to be requested to inform this Office accordingly. Thanking you for your kindness and consideration in this matter, I am,

Respectfully,

————, *Inspector-in-Charge*

November 14, 1914.—Man in office with telegram from the woman in Winnipeg: "Will arrive Central Station, Chicago, Sunday night at 10:30." He wants to know what he should do as he cannot be married until Monday. Told him our visitor would meet her at train and keep her overnight. Man will be at train and will come in Monday for advice concerning marriage ceremony.

November 16, 1914.—Marie Boreija and her child arrived last night, Sunday, at 10 P.M. Mr. Suleika and Mrs. J— [visitor of the League] met her. She spent Sunday night at Plymouth House [League boardinghouse]. Mrs J— took them to City Hall this morning. Judge White, who married them, gave the marriage certificate free.

May 31, 1916.—Mr. Suleika called to see if the League could help him find work. He has been two weeks without work. He has been working during the last two years in different printing shops (gave names) and has also sold sewing machines. Miss E.— [employment department of the League] gave him several addresses.

[Following this is a series of items in the record dealing with visits to the family, securing doctor and nurse for child, who is sick. Man seems to try hard to find work. Woman had boarders, but they left. Later, Mr. Suleika starts with three other men to publish a Polish casualty list of the war. He furnished the work, and the others the "production expenses," but this does not go well. Later he finds himself a printing job.]

September 30, 1917.—Mr. Suleika called at office to say he had been working in a printing shop at 100 West Street and was arrested with many other employees in an I.W.W. "raid." He was released but must report every day. He was much distressed, said he can not speak enough English to be with I.W.W. Advised man to write out an absolutely truthful statement in Polish, which could be translated at hearing. Man released after hearing and got work in a printing shop himself.

September 22, 1920.—Mr. Suleika came to office, wants "advices how to secure second papers." He says everything "is fine" with them. He has good job in a Polish printing shop.

February 11, 1921.—Man called on way to Naturalization Bureau for second papers. Mrs. J— [League visitor] went with him as witness. Hearing set for June 10.

29. Marya and Anastasia Bazanoff
(Temporary Admission without Bond)

August 15, 1914.—Demeter Bazanoff, Russian, in office. He wants to get information about his sisters, Marya, age nineteen, and Anastasia, age seventeen, who arrived at Ellis Island on S.S. "Vaterland" August 4. Man had telegram saying sisters were detained. Demeter is twenty-three years old, married, and has one child, and has been in United States nearly a year. Has had steady work except for one month. The following telegram sent: "*Commissioner of Immigration, Ellis Island:* Wire cause detention Marya and Anastasia Bazanoff steamship Vaterland. If excluded hereby appeal.—DEMETER BAZANOFF, 122 Fourteenth Street."

August 17, 1914.—Brother came in with following telegram: "Marya Bazanoff admitted today temporarily admission Anastasia authorized under bond letter follows. ———, *Acting Commissioner*, Ellis Island."

August 19, 1914.—Man in office with letter from Ellis Island. He thinks his sister Anastasia may be tubercular. He cannot get bondsmen; he has no money, or friends. [His letter from Commissioner read as follows:]

Confirming my telegram of even date, I have to advise you that your sister, Marya Bazanoff, has been admitted today, and that the temporary admission of Anastasia Bazanoff has been authorized provided a bond is filed guaranteeing that she will depart from the United States within one year, or sooner if so ordered by the Department of Labor, and that she will not become a public charge in this country. Blank forms for the bond have been sent to the United States Immigration Inspector-in-Charge, 845 Wabash Avenue, Chicago, to whose office you should send two bondsmen each of whose equity in real estate is at least $1,000. Bondsmen must take with them deeds and tax receipts showing the value and location of their property. A married woman will not be accepted as surety.

Later.—Letter written to Mr. A. B. Adamonis, of Slavonic Immigrant Society, New York City, containing the following:

We should be very grateful if you would visit Anastasia Bazanoff, a Russian girl, who arrived on S.S. "Vaterland," August 4, and is detained at Ellis Island. The Commissioner has written the brother here that Anastasia may be admitted for a year or less provided he furnish bond guaranteeing that she will depart from the country at any time the Government should order. She travelled together with an older sister, who was admitted. The brother thinks the girl may be tubercular. We shall be glad if you will write us what you are able to learn about her.

August 22, 1914.—Demeter Bazanoff in office. His sister Marya has already arrived. Mr. Bazanoff brought in the following letter which he had received from Chicago office, United States Immigration Service:

Sir:

I am in receipt of a letter from the Commissioner of Immigration, Ellis Island, N.Y., stating that you have been requested to send the necessary sureties to this office to sign a bond in the case of Anastasia Bazanoff, who is detained at Ellis Island. In order to shorten the detention of this alien you should take action in this matter immediately.

Respectfully,

J. R. ROBERTS
Inspector-in-Charge

IMMIGRATION SERVICE
CHICAGO OFFICE

Telephoned Mr. Roberts. He knows nothing about the case except facts in Commissioner's letter to Demeter Bazanoff. Mr. Bazanoff will return to our office in a few days to learn what we hear from Slavonic Society.

August 26, 1914.—The following letter received from the Slavonic Immigrant Society:

Immigrants' Protective League
Chicago, Ill.

DEAR FRIENDS: Referring to your inquiry regarding Anastasia Bazanoff, a Russian girl who arrived on S.S. "Vaterland" and is detained at Ellis Island, I beg to state that she is not tubercular but pregnant. That is at least the opinion of the doctors here, although she denies this to be a fact. Unless her brother furnishes the affidavit required from him, she will have to wait at Ellis Island until conditions in Europe make it possible for her to be returned to her home in Russia.

Very respectfully yours,

A. B. ADAMONIS

August 31, 1914.—Demeter and Marya Bazanoff in office. Told them of Mr. Adamonis' letter. They believe their sister, and think the doctors are wrong. Demeter is janitor in a saloon, 179 Blue Island Avenue, earns $25, room, and board. Marya has no job yet, will take place as servant if we can find her one, wants to work where she can learn English. Nice-appearing young people, very fond of their sister, very anxious to help her, and unhappy that they cannot bring her here.

[Arrangements about a position for Marya are omitted here.]

September 18, 1914.—Letter written to Marya in Russian, asking if she has heard anything more from her sister.

September 20, 1914.—The following letter received from Marya.

[Translation from the Russian:]

DEAR PROTECTORS:

You placed me somewhere to work with American people. My brother and I, we were happy that I will have a chance to learn English. I did not care for the wages. A Jew came and told me that I will work for him. We went there with the car. The man's wife spoke to me Russian and Polish, and told me that she likes everything should be done nice and clean. The house was very dirty. I could not stay there because I never would learn English. Now I am working in a shop. I would like to work for *American* people to learn the language. My brother is still visiting different agents. He has no work. If my sister could not come to Chicago, if they would not free her from Ellis Island, I will not live long. I am thinking all the time about her, and I am crying. I can't eat, I can't sleep. My sister will die there, and I here. I can't live without her. My brother did not call at your office, because he has not work. As soon as we will live better, we will call at your office.

Marya Bazanoff

October 17, 1914.—Demeter Bazanoff in office. He is now working at United States Cold Storage Company, Chicago Avenue, at $9 a week. Told him visitor who speaks Russian will prepare affidavits and go with him October 19 to Immigration Office. Sister is working at 2100 X Street.

October 19, 1914.—Demeter Bazanoff in office. Affidavits prepared. He went with R. B. [Russian visitor] to Immigration Office. Mr. Roberts [Inspector-in-Charge] said report from Ellis Island not final as to girl's pregnancy and asked if the brother and sister could furnish bonds. Told Mr. Roberts this was impossible and asked if release on personal bonds could not be arranged. Mr. Roberts will write Ellis Island.

[The remaining portion of the record is omitted since it is summarized in the following letters:]

November 4, 1914.—Letter from Demeter Bazanoff to Immigrants' Protective League [translation from Russian]:

I beg you, my dear protectors, to let me know what happened with my sister. Two weeks ago we made out some papers asking to free my sister Anastasia. You told me in two weeks you will probably know something about her. What do they want from me? I am not idle or drinking. I am working and I want to help my poor sister but the wind is blowing against every poor man's face.

Later.—Letter from Immigrants' Protective League to Commissioner of Immigration, Ellis Island, New York:

My dear Sir:

In August of this year Marya Bazanoff, ex S.S. "Vaterland," August 4, was admitted to her brother, Demeter Bazanoff, 122 14th Street, and the other sister, Anastasia, was detained at Ellis Island, but her admission was conditional under bonds guaranteeing that she would depart from the United States within one year or sooner if so ordered and that she would not become a public charge. The brother has been here only a comparatively short time and the sister only since August. Both are at work and earning wages and very eager to help their sister. It would be absolutely impossible, however, for them to furnish bonds as they have no acquaintances among people who could act as bondsmen. Would it not be possible for her to be admitted on a personal bond or on the affidavit that the brother sent? The brother and sister who are here are very nice-appearing young people and were absolutely unaware, until we told them, that the sister had been detained because she was thought to be pregnant. They will, I am sure, help her. Although work is as hard to find in Chicago as in other places, we can doubtless place her in some kind of domestic service. If you think that the girl might be admitted, I should be glad to undertake to take care of her and inform the Department if there should be anything wrong.

Sincerely yours,
LYDIA GARDNER

November 11, 1914.—Letter from Acting Commissioner of Immigration, Ellis Island, to Immigrants' Protective League:

This is in reply to your letter of November 4, relative to Anastasia Bazanoff. The doctors stated on November 7 that while the absolutely positive signs of pregnancy have not been found, the signs present strongly support the diagnosis of pregnancy. She has been taken to the hospital in hope that a positive certificate can be issued without unnecessary delay. When such certificate is received, it will be necessary to refer the matter to the Secretary of Labor, since at present her admission can only occur upon the filing of the bond authorized, blanks for which were returned by the Immigrant Inspector-in-Charge at Chicago with the statement that her relatives were unable to secure bondsmen.

December 1, 1914.—Letter from Commissioner at Ellis Island to Immigrants' Protective League containing the following:

Referring further to your communications as to Anastasia Bazanoff, I have to advise you that the medical officers have now issued a definite certificate to the effect that she is pregnant, and the Department has stated that "she cannot be landed even temporarily without bond." Unless the persons interested in her are able to furnish the required bond it will be necessary to detain her here until deportation can be effected.

January 13, 1915.—Letter from Demeter Bazanoff to Immigrants' Protective League [translation from the Russian:]

I beg you most earnestly to intercede for my sister Anastasia. I cannot come to see you personally, for I have been working thirteen hours a day and even Sundays. I get paid for ten hours' work $10.50 a week, and with the extra work $13–$14 per week. My sister Marya is also working and does not spend her money on trifles.

Yours respectfully,
DEMETER BAZANOFF

January 15, 1915.—Letter to Commissioner of Immigration, Ellis Island, New York:

MY DEAR SIR:

The brother and sister of Anastasia Bazanoff have requested us again to take up with you the matter of their sister, who is detained at Ellis Island awaiting deportation. Both the brother and sister are, as I have written you before, very nice sort of people and are very anxious to have their sister with them in order that they may take care of her. They are living with a very nice family who are also interested in helping the girl, and I wish very much that an investigation could be made by the Department with a view to granting permission for her admission to the United States. I think it would be possible to secure a bond guaranteeing that she would not become a public charge, but bonds for temporary landing could not be secured.

Sincerely yours,
LYDIA GARDNER

January 31, 1915.—Reply received from Ellis Island containing the following:

Upon receipt of your communication of the 15th instant the attention of the Department was again called to the case of Anastasia Bazanoff and a copy of your letter submitted. The Bureau of Immigration has advised me that what you say does not materially change the situation and that no further action can be taken at this time.

April 14, 1915.—Letter from the Commissioner of Immigration, Ellis Island:

Under date of November 4 you wrote this office in behalf of the immigrant girl, Anastasia Bazanoff, who arrived on the S.S. "Vaterland," August 4, 1914. At that time the medical officers stated "that while the absolutely positive signs of pregnancy have not been found, the present signs strongly support the diagnosis of pregnancy." I now write to inform you that a female infant was born to her in the Ellis Island Hospital on January 22. If you are still interested in this case and will secure from the brother and sister in Chicago an affidavit to the effect that they are willing to receive the girl and care for her infant child such affidavit will, upon its receipt here (it should be submitted in duplicate) be forwarded to the Secretary of Labor in Washington with a view to having the young woman admitted without the necessity of a bond being filed in her behalf.

April 25, 1915.—Letter with inclosure received from Acting Commissioner, Ellis Island:

Referring to the Commissioner's letter of April 12th, concerning the case of Anastasia Bazanoff, who arrived on the S.S. "Vaterland," August 4, 1914, I have to advise you that the Secretary of Labor now directs that she be admitted. She leaves here today for Chicago and will be taken by railroad officials to the immigration office in that city, where she may be called for by her brother. For your information I enclose a copy of a letter which I have directed the girl to present to the immigration officials in Chicago upon her arrival.

[Inclosure:]

United States Immigrant Inspector-in-Charge
Chicago, Illinois

DEAR SIR: This letter will be presented to you by Anastasia Bazanoff, a 19-year-old Russian girl who arrived here on the S.S. "Vaterland," August 4, 1914. She wishes to go to her brother, Demeter Bazanoff, whose address appears on our records as 122 Fourteenth Street, Chicago, Illinois. Miss Lydia Gardner, Director, Immigrants' Protective League, Chicago, is interested in this case, and I shall be very glad if you would advise her upon arrival of the girl and her infant child.

JOSEPH HENRY, *Acting Commissioner*

April 28, 1915.—The following letter sent to the Inspector-in-Charge, United States Immigration Service, Chicago:

MY DEAR MR. ROBERTS:

I am writing in further reference to the case of Anastasia Bazanoff, the Russian girl, whose brother made an affidavit in your office last week and who has now been released from Ellis Island and is in Chicago with her baby. As you suggested, we made an investigation of the home where the brother boards and find conditions there unusually good. He is living with a family named Batik, 1416 Maxwell Avenue, where they have five rooms very nicely furnished. These people came from the same village in Russia and are very fond of the girl and the baby. We shall keep in touch with them, and we feel certain that things will come out very nicely.

Very truly yours,
LYDIA GARDNER

30. Margaret Heckert and Leopold Koenig
(Unmarried Man and Woman Traveling Together)

April 18, 1914.—Leopold Koenig, a German, brought to League by E. D. [Russian man employed by League to protect immigrants from expressmen at railroad stations]. Man arrived on Michigan Central ticketed from Ellis Island, ex S.S. "Lapland." He did not want to leave the station, said he must go back to Ellis Island, was much excited, almost wild because girl who came with him is kept at Ellis Island. The girl is Margaret (or Margretta) Heckert (also German). The man is engaged to marry her and says he could not marry her at home because he has not completed his military service. Girl is pregnant, and man fears she will be deported. They came together but were separated at Ellis Island. Now he does not know what to do. He expected to find her where they were put on the train but some others who were with them on board saw girl taken out of line and detained. Man has money, seems honest, says he has a friend in Chicago, George Henhke, 22 North Street. *Later.*—Telephoned George Henhke. His wife will get word to him to come to League office at once. *Later.*—George Henhke in office. He explained that yesterday a telegram came to his house from Margaret Heckert to Leopold Koenig. Mr. Henhke replied to telegram that Koenig was in Germany. Telegram said that he should send affidavit at once. Mr. Henhke knew Margretta when she was a little girl in Germany; says he knows her parents, all are nice people. He feels very bad about all the trouble and wants to help the girl. Affidavits for both men prepared and sent.

Telegram sent to Secretary of Labor appealing case. Telephoned local office of United States Immigration Service, spoke with Mr. Roberts, Inspector-in-Charge. He would like to interview both men. Sent men to Mr. Roberts. Koenig will then go home with Mr. Henhke. Man is terribly upset; was crying. *Later.*—R.B. visited 22 North Street. Spoke with both Mr. and Mrs. Henhke, very good home, everything very clean, nice furniture. They have been living in same house for two years and in neighborhood for more than six years. Mrs Henhke has three children by her first husband.

April 19, 1914.—Letter to United States Secretary of Labor as follows:

I am writing in behalf of Margretta Heckert, ex S.S. "Lapland," who is detained at Ellis Island and debarred as pregnant. She was accompanied to this country by Leopold Koenig, who is the father of her child. The man, who was admitted and is here in Chicago, has told us that he could not marry Margretta at home because he had not completed his military service. To save her from disgrace he decided to leave home and bring her to this country and marry her here. Those of us who have talked with the man are convinced that he wishes to marry the girl and take care of her and that he is able to do this. He has a friend here, Mr. George Henhke, who is an American citizen, has a good home and who has furnished a public charge affidavit which has been forwarded to the Commissioner at Ellis Island. I cannot protest too strongly against a policy which excludes a helpless and friendless girl and admits a man who is responsible for her condition and for bringing her to this country. The man cannot be deported, and it would seem to be an act of simple justice to admit the woman under these circumstances. We shall be glad to take charge of the girl upon her arrival and until her marriage if you wish this to be done, but our visitor who has spoken with Mrs. Henhke, the wife of the man's friend, does not think this necessary as they are very nice, respectable people with a good home and are willing and eager to take care of the girl and help the man get a start here.

April 25, 1914.—Letter from Assistant Secretary of Labor as follows:

Miss Lydia Gardner
Immigrants' Protective League
Chicago, Ill.

My dear Miss Gardner: In response to your letter of April 19, I beg to advise you that the record in the case of Margretta (Margaret) Heckert, who has been detained at Ellis Island, reached me yesterday. After careful consideration thereof, I have directed that the alien be admitted. This is upon the assumption that she will be married to the man with whom she came to this country. I have been influenced in reaching this conclusion by the assurances contained in your letter and shall expect you to advise me within thirty days that the marriage ceremony has been performed.

Telephoned Mr. Henhke. They have had telegram from Margretta. She will arrive this afternoon. They will be married at St. Michael's Church, Elm and First streets, tomorrow morning between ten and eleven o'clock. Told him Miss B— [League visitor] will attend wedding.

April 29, 1914.—Marriage occurred as arranged. Man has work at his trade, bookbinder, to start work this morning. Report sent to Assistant Secretary of Labor.

31. Lida and Marie Stirbei
(*A "Common-Law" Wife and Illegitimate Child*)

[The following documents state the case of the detention of the "common-law" wife and daughter of George Sturdza.]

1. Copy of affidavit forwarded to Ellis Island, January 5, 1923:

I hereby petition that Lida Stirbei, age thirty-three, my "common-law" wife, and Marie Stirbei, age thirteen, my daughter, who arrived on S.S. "Russia" at New York on January 2 be permitted to enter the United States. I promise to hold harmless the United States and each State, Territory, County and Municipality against these persons ever becoming a public charge and agree to send the child who is under 16 to school until at least 16 years of age. I, George Sturdza, being duly sworn, depose and state that I was born on the 16th day of December, 1888, in the town of Toruntal, Country of Roumania. I emigrated to the United States in 1914. I further state that I am a resident of Chicago and live at 2000 Green Street in a three-room flat alone. I have furnished this flat for Lida and our child. I further state that I am not yet a citizen of the United States. I have first citizen papers No. 124700 secured in the Superior Court of Cook County on November 10, 1920. I further state that I am employed by Lloyd and Company Tannery as a laborer (Canal and Halsted streets). I further state that my average weekly earnings are $27.50; I have $1,300 in bank; personal property valued at $300, as follows: furniture, $300. I further state that Marie Stirbei is my child. I have supported her and her mother since the child's birth. I wished to marry her before I came to the United States, but I was not yet the age when I could secure a license. I intend to marry her as soon as she arrives in Chicago.

2. Telegram sent to the Commissioner of Immigration, Ellis Island, New York, January 5: "Official affidavits Lida and Marie Stirbei steamship Russia sent today. If excluded hereby appeal. Marie is my daughter. I will marry Lida on arrival.—GEORGE STURDZA, *Father*, 2000 Green Street."

3. Letter from the Immigrants' Protective League to the Secretary of Labor, Washington, January 8, 1923:

DEAR SIR:

Re Lida and Marie Stirbei, S.S. "Russia." George Sturdza, 2000 Green Street, a Roumanian, has asked us to write you in his behalf and that of the above-mentioned immigrants. Lida Stirbei is his common-law wife and Marie, who is thirteen, is their daughter. Lida has been excluded because of illiteracy.

George Sturdza tells us that he and Lida wanted to be married when he was nineteen and she eighteen. He insists that it was impossible, because of the regulations of his government—his village then belonged to Austria-Hungary—for him to marry Lida on account of his age, and as a result they lived together without legal ceremony, and Marie, also detained, is their daughter. He supported mother and child until he came to the United States in 1914, and he has been sending money for their support since then. It was his intention to bring them over shortly after his own arrival in this country, but the war made that impossible. He looks upon

Lida as his wife, and he has every intention of marrying her legally as soon as he can.

He has gone on to Ellis Island today where he hopes to be able to induce the Commissioner to let him marry Lida and bring her in as his wife. We understand that the case is on appeal before you. George Sturdza impresses us very favorably; we believe him to be a hard-working resident of this country. He is taking with him two strong letters of recommendation; one is from the bank in which he has net savings of $1,300; the other is from a former employer for whom he has worked for three years and whose employ he has left only temporarily because there was nothing for him to do these winter months. We also wish to say that George Sturdza has already rented a small flat for his wife and daughter and furnished it in anticipation of their coming.

We hope very much that you may be willing to permit this man to marry Lida and to provide for the daughter. It seems to be clear that deportation will mean only a further prolongation of their very unsatisfactory status.

Very truly yours,

ALICE MARION

4. Letter received from an Assistant Secretary of Labor, January 23, 1923:

Miss Alice Marion, Superintendent
Immigrants' Protective League
Chicago, Ill.

DEAR MADAM: Receipt is acknowledged of your letter of January ninth relative to the aliens Lida Stirbei and daughter, Marie, excluded at Ellis Island on January 2 on the ground that they were persons likely to become a public charge and the woman on the additional ground that she is unable to read. I am pleased to inform you that, after careful consideration of the evidence presented on appeal, the Second Assistant Secretary has authorized aliens' temporary admission for three months under public charge and departure bonds of $500 each, the bond for the child to contain the school clause,[1] and that in the event the marriage of the woman and her intended husband is consummated before the expiration of aliens' temporary admission, consideration will be given the possiblity of cancelling the bonds.

Very truly yours,

————, *Assistant Secretary*

5. Letter to the Assistant Secretary of Labor, February 8, 1923:

DEAR SIR:

Re Lida Stirbei. Thank you very much for your letter of January 23, with regard to the above-named woman. We are very glad that she and her daughter were admitted.

George Sturdza brought Lida Stirbei to our office on the morning after her arrival. One of our workers went with them to the City Hall, where a license was secured and the marriage ceremony performed by Judge X. We inclose a certified statement as to this.

[1] [That is, a promise to send the child to school until she has reached the age of sixteen.]

In your letter you say that in the event of the marriage of the woman and her intended husband before the expiration of her period of temporary admission there is a possibility that the bonds may be cancelled. We hope very much that this may be possible.

Very truly yours,

ALICE MARION

6. Letter from the Assistant Secretary of Labor, February 27, 1923:

Miss Alice Marion, Superintendent
Immigrants' Protective League
Chicago, Ill.

DEAR MADAM: In reply to your letter of February 8, it gives me pleasure to advise you that the Department has ordered that the temporary admission of Lida Stirbei and daughter, Marie, be made permanent, and that bonds given in their behalf be canceled.

Very truly yours,

————, *Assistant Secretary*

32. The Family of Steve Jassy
(Detention of Domiciled Alien with Contagious Disease)

April 24, 1921.—Steve Jassy, 700 Center Avenue, in office [Immigrants' Commission] to ask help and advice about his family. His wife, Clara, age twenty-six, and three children, Mary age seven, Edward age five, and Fabian age three are all detained at Ellis Island, having arrived on the S.S. "Belgrade," April 1, from Jugo-Slavia. Mr. Jassy has been to New York and says they are all sick, and he is afraid they will be deported. The three children were all born in Chicago. The man himself arrived in the United States, December 16, 1909, on the S.S. "Atlantic." He is a cabinet-maker by trade, employed by the Wright Boat Company. His average weekly earnings are about $35. He filed his declaration of intention [first citizenship papers], June 16, 1917, in the Circuit Court of Cook County. Mr. Jassy will send the children's birth certificates to his wife at Ellis Island.

[Further facts regarding the family's detention are included in a letter written the next day to the New York Y.W.C.A.:]

May we ask your assistance in the following detention case? Mrs. Clara Jassy and three little children (the oldest seven) arrived at Ellis Island on April 1, on the S.S. "Belgrade." They had been in Jugo-Slavia for a year's visit to her people. They are still in detention on the Island. One child had measles on their arrival, and we believe that the mother and another child have been taken ill since. The father went on to New York. He was permitted to see the family but not to take them away. Likewise, it was impossible for him to obtain any information as to when they would be released, how serious the illness was, etc. He is very much worried. He says the children are separated from the mother, and that they are not looked after well. He also says that several articles of the children's clothing have been stolen. All these children were born in this country. We have asked him to get the birth certificates and, when he does, to send them to his wife. Will you then see what the present situation is, and what possibility there is of having the family released, or at least the mother and the well children?

April 30, 1921.—Mr. Jassy in office. Wife writes that she is well and so are the children. He has already sent their birth certificates to Ellis Island, and his wife has written that they have arrived.

May 2, 1921.—Letter received from Miss Mann, Y.W.C.A.:

Marie was discharged from the hospital on the 20th and Edward on the 27th. These children are now in the detention room. The mother is still in the hospital with Fabian. Fabian has the measles, and the mother has been certified for syphilis. The Jassy family had a first hearing on April 16th. When the doctor's report reaches the office, they will probably have another hearing at which time they will undoubtedly be excluded.

May 5, 1921.—Report received from Miss Mann as follows:

Report further on the Jassy family, they had another hearing on April 30th, at which time a doctor's certificate was presented, also the birth certificates of the children. The children were admitted, and the mother was excluded *with no right of appeal*.

May 6, 1921.—Telegram sent to Mr. Steve Jassy, 700 Center Avenue, Chicago: "Come at once to our office. Your wife excluded. Necessary to take immediate action.—IMMIGRANTS' COMMISSION."

May 7, 1921.—Mr. Jassy in office. Talked over the situation with him. He seems to speak English well but could not or would not understand what the trouble was. Explained that the children could come in but not the mother. Asked if he wanted the children to come on to him here or to go back with the mother. Man could not understand, kept saying, "I want all to come." Telephoned Jugo-Slav Consulate. The Consul will try to make him understand the situation. L. G. gave man letter to the Consul:

Following our telephone conversation, I am sending this man, Mr. Steve Jassy, to you for counsel and explanation in his present difficulty. About a year ago his wife, Clara Jassy, returned from the United States to Jugo-Slavia for a visit, taking with her her three American-born children. They returned on the "Belgrade," arriving in New York about the first of April. One child had measles on its arrival, and another one had been sick, so that the whole family was detained. During the period of detention it was discovered that the mother had syphilis. This is one of the contagious diseases for which people are denied admission to the United States. We have therefore just received word that the mother and wife has been denied admission. The children can, of course, come in, as they are American citizens and it is impossible to exclude them. It is sometimes possible to secure treatment for contagious diseases at Ellis Island. The Government, however, requires payments in advance, and an initial deposit of $165. The length of time required for the cure of the disease is, of course, uncertain. If Mr. Jassy undertakes to make this request for treatment here, he assumes heavy financial responsibilities. On the other hand, if the woman goes back, arrangement ought to be made for her treatment in Jugo-Slavia so that the next time she comes she could be admitted. While the man speaks a good deal of English, he does not seem to understand this situation at all. I should be very glad if you would explain it to him, and if there is anything we can do, we shall be very glad to do it.

Later.—Mr. Jassy came back, saying they had advised him at the Consulate to pay for her treatment, but he says he cannot afford to. He has sent her $700 already. He says $500 will "buy everything in Jugo-Slavia." He thinks she will have to go back. He does not seem to believe she really has the disease, but says that if she has, she caught it on the boat. He still hopes to get her in and says he cannot take care of the children without her.

May 16, 1921.—Mr. Jassy has changed his mind and wants his family treated here. His wife writes she will jump from the ship if sent back, and he believes she will. He also wants to send shoes for children. His wife asked for them. He brought $165 (in two post-office money orders) to be sent to the Commissioner of Immigration. Made special affidavit, which was sent with money orders and a letter to the Commissioner of Immigration, Ellis Island, New York, as follows:

We are inclosing two money-orders for $165. Mr. Steve Jassy, husband of Clara Jassy, S.S. "Belgrade," is, as you will see from the inclosed affidavit, very anxious to secure medical treatment for his wife, who has been excluded because of venereal disease. As you will see, it is a difficult case. The children were born in this country and are, therefore, entitled to admission. Mr. Jassy is of course anxious to have his children with him, and his wife also. If, however, she has to go back to Jugo-Slavia, it will be necessary to send the children also, as there is no one here who can give them adequate care, and they are too young (seven, five, and three years old) to be separated from their mother. We hope that it may be possible to prevent the breaking up of this family. As you will note from the affidavit, Mr. Jassy is prepared to send more money for the medical treatments. In case it is impossible for you to grant his request, will you let us know as soon as possible and will you return the money-orders to him in our care?

Telegram also sent to Commissioner of Immigration, Ellis Island: "Are sending special affidavit for Clara Jassy and $165 for her medical treatment. Letter follows.—ILLINOIS IMMIGRANTS' COMMISSION."

May 21, 1921.—Mr. Jassy in office. He has letter from Commissioner of Immigration, acknowledging receipt of money for treatment. He also received letter from wife. Mrs. Jassy claims she is well and needs no treatment. She asked husband to decide immediately about her stay in Ellis Island. She does not care now what happens, but she will not stand this situation longer. Children are hungry, and she wants the third separated child to stay with her. She is not satisfied with the treatment at the hospital or with anything at Ellis Island.

June 10, 1921.—Mr. Jassy in office. He has had telegram from Slavonic Society. Children are to be sent to him as soon as suitable escort can be found. Mrs. Jassy still needs treatment. Slavonic Society asks for $20 for expenses. Mr. Jassy reluctant but finally agreed to send it as requested.

June 11, 1921.—Letter written to Miss Mann:

Mr. Steve Jassy about whom we wrote you before, received a telegram from the Slavonic Immigrant Society yesterday, asking him to wire them $20 for traveling expenses for the children, and saying that as soon as a suitable escort could be found, the children would be sent on to him. He came to us to ask our advice. He is very much afraid that they will send the children on here, and then deport his wife afterwards. He evidently does not want the children unless he has someone to take care of them. We told him that undoubtedly there was no such intention on the part of the immigration authorities. He therefore decided to send the money, and he will make arrangements to get someone to take care of the children temporarily.[1]

Letter written to Slavonic Immigrant Society, New York City:

Mr. Steve Jassy, 700 Center avenue, Chicago, was in our office yesterday to show us a telegram he had just received from you, in which you ask him to send $20 for the children's traveling expenses, and state that his children

[1] [The remainder of the letter is reproduced below, not because it has any bearing upon the case of Mrs. Jassy and her children, but because the story of the other woman's family illustrates some of the reasons for immigration from Europe since the war, and some of the difficulties of the relatives in this country.

"There is another case in which we should very much like your assistance. A Roumanian woman, Mrs. Leonora Rittman, 4800 Ada street, has two sons, Leon sixteen, and Victor fourteen, at Ellis Island. They and a fifteen-year-old cousin, Leopold Boranka, arrived on the 'Rochambeau,' June 11. Leopold has a father here who is an American citizen, and who has net savings amounting to $1,950; so there probably will be no difficulty about his entry. We are, however, very much afraid that Mrs. Rittman will have trouble getting her children in. She is a widow, her husband having died in December, 1919. She has two children born in this country with her in Chicago. She receives a mother's pension from the State of Illinois, $25 per month for the two native-born children. She is able to earn about $45 a month herself. Of course, the financial outlook is not satisfactory. Leopold Boranka's father, and another cousin, Arthur Rittman, are both willing to help her with bonds if they are required. Mrs. Rittman came to us first in May, 1920. She asked our help in locating her four children whom she had left behind her in 1913 when she came to this country. Through the help of the Joint Distribution Committee we found out that Mrs. Rittman's sister, with whom she had left the children, had died in 1917, leaving the children homeless; that the youngest, a seven-year-old boy, had been picked up by the Russians and taken no one knew just where; and that the other three children were scattered, one in Suchawa, another in Plavalar, and a sixteen-year-old girl 'in all probability in Constanza.' Finally, the older of the two boys who are coming, Leon, has some physical defect which may make him liable to exclusion. Mrs. Rittman is not able to state just the extent of the physical handicap. She tells us that during the war he was homeless for a while, and forced to sleep out-of-doors, and that his arm was frozen in consequence. We shall be ever so much obliged if you will do what you can for these children. If you will let us know what further papers or what further information is necessary, we shall forward them to you as soon as possible. Official affidavits have been sent today."]

will leave for Chicago as soon as a suitable escort can be furnished. Mr. Jassy was rather reluctant to do so, for he fears the children will be sent on to him, and later on his wife will be deported. We reassured him on this point, as we feel convinced that nothing of the sort could possibly happen. Consequently he promised us to comply with your request.

June 14, 1921.—Mr. Jassy in office with letter from immigration authorities, Ellis Island, that he must deposit bond. [Copy of letter follows:]

I have to advise you that the Department of Labor has directed that the alien Clara Jassy be accorded hospital treatment in the Ellis Island Hospital, provided a bond in the sum of $1,000 is furnished. You can either file a surety bond in the sum of $1,000 or you can file liberty bonds in like sum (any loan except the Victory loan), or you can file a real estate bond. If the latter is desired, you should bring two real estate owners, each of whose equity in real estate is at least $2,000, to the office of the Inspector in Charge of Immigration, Chicago, Illinois. They should bring their deeds and last tax receipts with them. No married woman will be accepted as surety on a bond. Forms for the bonds have been sent to the Inspector's Office, Chicago, Illinois.

Mr. Jassy is greatly upset and says he cannot possibly raise $1,000, and does not think any friends with real estate will go bond. He is inclined now to send children back to New York and let them and wife be deported. Explained nature of bond to him, but he thinks it a cloak under which the United States will get a lot of money from him for further treatments. Children are well. He has had them examined. Refused to give the name of doctor and would not agree to have Immigrants' Commission telephone the doctor for a report. He says the children do not remember him and cry for their mother constantly. He has not been able to find a woman to look after them. He is very unhappy. Sent him to United States Immigration Office to see if signing bonds could wait until Saturday, by which date a message regarding his wife's condition may be received from Ellis Island. (He reported later that there is no hurry.) *Later.*—Mr. Jassy telephoned. He has tried all day to find friends who will help him with bonds but without success. *Later.*—Telephoned Father Ressinot, St. Gauden's Church. He knows the Jassy family, feels sorry for Mr. Jassy. He will try to get bondsmen but does not feel optimistic of success.

June 25, 1921.—Mr. Jassy in office. He is very miserable, discouraged, and also angry. He says he cannot find anybody who will sign bond for him. He is determined to send the children back and says he cannot support them without the mother. He says his wife is not sick and that the Government wants to make money out of him.

July 8, 1921.—Wrote Commissioner-General of Immigration, Washington, D.C.:

We are writing to you with regard to the case of Clara Jassy, S.S. "Belgrade," at Ellis Island. Mrs. Jassy had been in the United States for a number of years and had gone back to Jugo-Slavia for a visit in March,

1920. She and her three American-born children, aged seven, five, and three years, arrived on the 1st of April. She was found to be suffering from venereal disease. Permission for treatment was given and Mr. Jassy on May 16 sent $165 to the Commissioner for the two months' medical treatment. His three children were sent to Chicago about June 10, though Mr. Jassy was very reluctant to have them come without their mother. Immediately after the arrival of the children in Chicago, Mr. Jassy was notified that he would have to deposit $1,000 bond if Mrs. Jassy was to be accorded treatment. Mr. Jassy has tried hard to secure the necessary money but cannot comply with this demand. As he puts it, it would be easy for him to get bail if he were a criminal, but everyone thinks he wants to desert his wife and children. His difficulty seems to us to be due to the widespread unemployment. Mr. Jassy has not been laid off, and does not expect to be, but jobs are uncertain these days. He can, however, pay for the hospital treatments. His sister-in-law is temporarily taking care of the children, but Mr. Jassy has been unable to make permanent arrangements for their care and is convinced that if his wife is excluded the children must go back with her. Mr. Jassy is not yet a citizen but he filed his petition for final papers about June 15, and has had every intention of remaining in this country. And from what we have seen of him and have learned from his church we believe that he is a steady worker and that he means to do what he can for his wife and children. Whether Mrs. Jassy was infected before she left the country we have been unable to learn. At any rate since the man cannot be deported and since he is to remain in the country, we believe he will be a better man and a better citizen if his family are allowed to join him.

July 12, 1921.—Mr. Jassy in office. He has not heard from New York. Money sent for medical care will be exhausted by July 15.

July 15, 1921.—Letter from Department of Labor, Washington, D.C.:

The receipt of your letter of the 8th inst., with reference to the case of Mrs. Clara Jassy is acknowledged. In reply, you are advised that this alien woman was granted hospital treatment by the Department's order; and $165 having been deposited, treatment was begun without waiting for the filing of the bond which is always required in such cases. The Ellis Island Office, under the date of June 28, reported that the man was unable to file a bond; and at the same time transmitted a medical certificate reading, in part, as follows: "Because of intensive treatment, is no longer in need of hospitalization. However, further treatment extending over a long period of time is indicated before a cure could be expected." This is understood to mean that the alien can be released without danger to others, and if treatment is continued, the public welfare will not be endangered by such action. It has therefore been ordered that the woman be released to proceed to her husband, with the requirement that treatment be continued until cure is effected under the supervision of the Chicago Office of the Immigration Service and the Public Health Service there. It is believed that you will agree that the case has had the consideration you desire.

[The remaining portion of case covers a period of follow-up work, efforts to get the man and the children examined and to have treatments for Mrs. Jassy continued, etc.]

33. The Family of Joseph Revesz
(Quota—Exclusion of Wife and Two Children)

November 23, 1921.—[The facts about Joseph Revesz and his family are stated in the following affidavit and telegram, which were sent by the Immigrants' Protective League to Ellis Island:]

I hereby petition that Teresa Revesz, age 37, wife; Adam Revesz, age 16, son, and Joseph Revesz, age 12, son, who arrived on S.S. "France" at New York on November 19, 1921, be permitted to enter the United States. I promise to hold harmless the United States and each State, Territory, County and Municipality against these persons ever becoming a public charge and agree to send any who are under sixteen to school until at least sixteen years of age.

I, Joseph Revesz, being duly sworn, depose and state that I was born on the 7th day of September, 1882, in the town of Eula, country of Jugo-Slavia. I emigrated to the United States in 1914. I also state that I am a resident of Chicago and live at 500 Siegel Street, in a five-room flat, alone. The flat is prepared for my family. I further state that I am not a citizen of the United States. I have first papers . . . . secured in the Circuit Court of Cook County on September 1, 1921. My present occupation is that of a teamster. I am employed by the Southwestern Ice Company, 1200 Peoria Street. My average weekly earnings are $45; my approximate net savings since arrival in the United States are $600. I have personal property valued at $600, as follows: furniture $400, cash $200.

The telegram received from Ellis Island states that my family is "excess quota." I respectfully ask that they be allowed to make me a visit at least.—JOSEPH REVESZ.

Telegram sent to Commissioner of Immigration, Ellis Island, New York: "Official affidavits Teresa Revesz and sons steamship France sent today. If excluded hereby appeal.—*Husband*, JOSEPH REVESZ, 500 Siegel Street."

November 25, 1921.—Mr. Lawson, a brother-in-law of Mrs. Revesz, called at the office. He is worried about Mrs. Revesz. He is worried about the effect of her possible deportation on her husband. For several years Mr. Revesz did not hear from his wife, and he took to drink. After the war, when he finally got word from them and knew they were alive and there was hope of bringing them here he braced up and is almost pitifully anxious to have his family with him. He is sure his wife will die of grief and humiliation, if deported. Mr. Lawson will get Congressman McMillan to work on case. Mr. Lawson says he cabled $641 to his sister-in-law to Havre. She had written that she had money enough from sales of property, etc., for the journey. However, she cabled from Havre for $600. He spent about $50 for cables. Mr. Lawson also made public-charge affidavit. Mr. Lawson is a salesman and has been employed by a bicycle supply company for four years, earning approximately $2,500 a year. He has net savings of at least $3,500. He is a citizen, and so is his father, who is also quite well to do.

December 5, 1921.—Letter from an Assistant Commissioner of Immigration, Ellis Island:

DEAR MADAM:

I beg to acknowledge receipt of affidavit and special letters in the case of Mrs. Teresa Revesz and children, and have to advise that the same have been forwarded to the Immigration Bureau in Washington for consideration in passing on the case. Record of appeal went forward yesterday, and no decision has as yet been received.

———, *Assistant Commissioner*

December 7, 1921.—Mr. Lawson telephoned. They have been notified from Ellis Island that Mrs. Revesz and children were deported on December 3. Mr. Lawson wanted information about possible refund. Explained that aliens who are deported solely on the ground of excess quota are taken back at the expense of the steamship company, but are not entitled to a refund of the passage money paid in coming over.[1]

December 23, 1921.—Mr. Lawson in office. He brought letters received from a Congressman and an Assistant Secretary in Washington. [That from the Congressman read as follows:]

MY DEAR MR. LAWSON:

I beg to call your attention to the inclosed letter from the Assistant Secretary of Labor, which is self-explanatory. I had this case up with him and went over it carefully with him. He said there were a hundred cases from Jugo-Slavia asking for temporary admission and that after carefully considering the matter and going over it with the Secretary of Labor they had decided not to admit any of these cases temporarily. I have done everything that can be done in the matter. It is a question of asking the Department to break the law, and they do not appreciate our urging such matters, although in this case I did beg him to make it special and urged that his wife and two children be allowed to go to see their husband and father and the home he had prepared for them, even for a short time. Regretting my inability to aid in this matter, and with kind personal regards, I beg to remain,

Yours very truly,

M. A. McMILLAN

[Inclosed with the Congressman's letter was the following letter from the Department of Labor:]

I note your keen interest in the case of Teresa Revesz and her two children, who were excluded at Ellis Island for the reason that the quota allotted to Jugo-Slavia, of which country they are natives, had been exhausted for the entire year. It was impossible to grant them permanent admission, and their appeal was, therefore, dismissed. It had been found inadvisable to grant them temporary admission.

These aliens were destined to husband and father, a resident of Chicago who has obtained his declaration of intention papers and who is, apparently, fully capable of providing for them properly. This latter question did not receive much attention for reason that these aliens are not members of any of the classes exempt from the application of the Act of May 19, 1921, and

[1] [The amended quota act of 1922 (see Doc. 12, p. 242) provided for a refund.]

their exclusion was mandatory. They do come within the classes to whom special preference is to be shown, but this is predicated upon there being a quota balance to which their admission may be charged, and there being no balance, this feature of this case does not apply.

The Department has consistently extended every consideration to aliens coming to visit their children in the United States, or coming to make their homes with such children, and also to children who are coming to their parents in this country, even where the quota has been exhausted for the entire year. Such aliens are often admitted temporarily for the purpose of visiting their relatives, it being felt that the hardship of deportation which must take place in any event will be somewhat lessened by such visit. But that particular hardship does not exist in the present case, as Mrs. Revesz has her parents abroad, the children are with their mother, and the hardship of deportation is considered no greater at this time than it would be, say, two or three months hence.

Then, further, much pressure is brought upon the Department to extend the temporary admission of such aliens, oftentimes expressly with a view to delaying deportation until after the incoming of a new fiscal year with its new quota or an alleviation of the present restrictions, and the Department feels that it cannot become a party to this subterfuge as a means of evading the direct commands of Congress. You will readily conceive that each and every case is an "individual" one in the minds of those interested or affected, and that the Department must take, as a basis of its actions, the letter and spirit of the law, rather than its interpretation by those who are, for the moment, directly affected by its operation.

Mr. Lawson is convinced that Mrs. Revesz has been deported in spite of our letter of the fifth from Ellis Island, as he asked steamship company to find out and they reported her gone. They say she received $75 landing money which he had deposited for her in their care. He hopes so, as otherwise she would be penniless on her arrival in Havre. He criticizes sharply the fact that at no time has Mr. Revesz been notified by the immigration authorities as to what was being done with his family. Mr. Revesz and he spent more than $1,000, to bring them—a clear loss except for what will be refunded for railroad tickets to Chicago and head tax. Furthermore, Mr. Revesz has flat rent to pay, and now storage for furniture. He had hoped to rent the flat furnished in the hope that his wife would be able to come next July but he has not been able to do so. It is doubtful anyway whether they will have money enough to bring her then. As it was, Mr. Revesz had to borrow $650 from Mr. Lawson.

Mr. Revesz broke down completely when he was told his family had been deported. At first Mr. Lawson was afraid he would not be able to keep him at work. Now he feels more hopeful. Mr. Revesz is practically illiterate. He is going to enrol in night school. He wishes to fit himself for citizenship papers as soon as the two-year period is up.

Mr. Lawson has sent a letter to Mrs. Revesz in Jugo-Slavia, telling her what was done to get her released. They were not able to communicate with her after her arrival at Ellis Island. A letter they wrote was returned from the Island, so they fear she thinks nothing was done for her.

[Further developments in the case of the family of Joseph Revesz are indicated in the following letter, written by the Superintendent, September, 1922, to a friend of the Immigrants' Protective League:]

I thought you might like to know that Adam Revesz, the eldest of the two Revesz boys who were deported with their mother last year, has been taken for military service in Jugo-Slavia. All his mother's efforts to secure his release have been in vain, and consequently she now has decided she will not come to the United States and leave him behind. She has returned the new steamship tickets which were sent her this spring. Mr. Revesz means to remain in the United States. His earning capacity and his opportunities are so much less in Jugo-Slavia. He is very unhappy about the whole situation. He expects to send monthly allowances to his wife and hopes to bring her over after the son has finished his military service.

34. Annie and Katherine Szoeke
(Operation of the Quota Law)

August 31, 1921.—Mr. George Tabor in office. He has had telegrams from Ellis Island, asking official affidavits and also domestic-service affidavits for two sisters-in-law, Annie and Katherine Szoeke, now detained. Mr. Tabor had a long and distressing story about the two girls. They left home with their mother early in July, passports visaed in Belgrade July 7, were detained at Cherbourg, waiting for a boat; finally the steamship company (Blue Line) took on the mother with some other country people, but girls were detained for next boat. When they arrived they were excluded at Ellis Island as excess quota. Mr. Tabor says his wife and mother-in-law, especially the latter, are so unhappy and anxious for fear girls will be deported they are miserable all the time. Mrs. Szoeke cries night and day; the girls have been her sole care since the younger was two, when the father died. She has never been separated from them before this summer. She wants to go back to them if they cannot be admitted. Prepared affidavit and sent telegram to Commissioner of Immigration, Ellis Island, New York: "Official affidavits Annie and Katherine Szoeke, steamship Washington, and affidavits from prospective employers will be sent September first. If excluded, hereby appeal.—GEORGE TABOR, *Brother-in-Law*, 2300 Eighteenth Street."

Mr. Tabor already has places for the two girls in domestic service and will bring in the two prospective employers to make affidavits tomorrow.

September 1, 1921.—Mr Tabor in office; prospective employers (Mr. Rachman and Mr. Packer) are too busy to come to make affidavits. Telephoned Mr. Rachman; he will make affidavit before notary public and have it ready in one hour. Mr. Tabor will explain to Mrs. Parker, and he thinks she will have affidavit sent also.

September 9, 1921.—Telegram from Y.W.C.A. representative at Ellis Island to Immigrants' Protective League, Chicago: "Please find brother-in-law of Anna and Katherine Szoeke on steamship Washington excluded because exceeding quota for Jugo-Slavia, his address George Tabor, 2300 Eighteenth Street. Girls need affidavit. They have appealed."

September 19, 1921.—Mrs. Tabor in office with new telephone number. They have heard nothing from girls. The mother is terribly unhappy. Sent telegram to Assistant Commissioner of Immigration, Ellis Island, asking him to wire present status.

October 1, 1921.—Mr. Joseph Schubert in office. The Szoeke girls came on ship with him. They were deported but will probably be brought back some time in October. Mr. Tabor sent $40 on August 28; money returned September 3, "People not there." Rachman, neighborhood steamship agent and banker, advised that girls should stay in England until they could come in on a later quota. He thinks they will return this month. He brought with him a letter sent to Mr. Rachman by the steamship company:

As requested by you in telephone conversation today, we give you hereunder contents of a communication received from New York:
"In accordance with your telegram of September 22, we have cabled to Liverpool to detain Annie and K. Szoeke at the port of landing, pending further instructions. The sanction of reapplication will doubtless be forthcoming presently and we await your advice as to cabling transportation. Please collect $5.00 cable tolls."

Today Mr. Tabor was notified by Mr. Rachman that girls are held in London, waiting permission from Washington to reapply for admittance. Family find it very hard to buy new tickets for them. People think they ought not to pay over again. Explained that the law does not require refund of passage money for quota exclusion. He will explain to family.

October 12, 1921.—Mr. Tabor in office, asking if we can get official permission for girls to come in again. The girls are in London, working in a good hotel. They are not going back to Jugo-Slavia whatever happens but will stay in England until they can be admitted to the United States. Advised Mr. Tabor to have steamship company bring them over again on another month's quota.

November 1, 1921.—Mr. Tabor and mother-in-law in office to file new affidavits for girls, who are back on S.S. "Lincoln." Sent telegram as follows: "*Commissioner of Immigration, Ellis Island:* Official affidavits Anna and Katherine Szoeke, steamship Lincoln, sent today. If excluded hereby appeal.—KATIE SZOEKE, *Mother*, 2300 Eighteenth Street."

Mr. Tabor is unemployed at present; but his wife and daughter are working. Their average weekly earnings are $14 and $11.

November 7, 1921.—Mr. Tabor in office with the two girls. They are very nice, healthy-looking girls. All are most happy to be together again. The girls are to take positions at housework at once.

December 23, 1921.—Visited family again. Mother is extremely happy that girls are here with her. She has improved in her health very much since I last saw her. Girls are now employed in domestic service with American families; Annie on the South Side at $10, Katherine on the North Side at $9 a week. Girls very well satisfied with their places. Mr. Tabor had to pay an additional $116.66 to Aliens' Bank, $50 of which was for the lawyer, who did not help any but took the money. Mr. Acker, the lawyer, is connected with the Aliens' Bank, and it was on the suggestion of Mr. Rachman, the banker, that Mr. Tabor took the lawyer. The girls stayed in London at the Atlantic Hotel, helping in the kitchen, and so they had the best meals served. Girls also said they had been very well treated on the second trip to America and had no complaints.

35. Carmella Fiori
(Temporary Detention—Excess Quota)

March 7, 1923.—Mr. Joseph de Rosa in office. He sent affidavit two months ago to his wife's second cousin, Carmella Fiori, an Italian girl, age twenty-two. He says she sent him back the affidavit, saying the steamship agent in Italy claimed she needed a permit from Washington. He wrote Washington (Bureau of Immigration) and also Ellis Island and sent affidavit to Ellis Island. No answer has ever come back, but he was sent pamphlet on quota law from Washington. Now he has had another letter from Carmella reporting that the Italian steamship agent says he made a mistake, the affidavit was all right. Told him to come in and make a new affidavit a few days before girl arrives. He does not expect her before last of May.

June 2, 1923.—Mr. de Rosa in office for new affidavits. Carmella is arriving June 5. [The affidavit showed that Mr. de Rosa had been fifteen years in the United States, that he was an American citizen, that he owned and managed a confectionery store, that his yearly income was approximately $2,000, that he owned property valued at $9,100, and that he had a wife and one child. The affidavit also explained that though Carmella Fiori was a relative she was really coming to the United States to be a servant in his home. He had returned to Italy for a visit of six months in 1921; and, while he was there, Carmella had done the housework in the home of his sister where he had stayed.] *Later.*—Copy of affidavit sent Society for Italian Emigrants, New York. Telegram sent to Commissioner of Immigration, Ellis Island, as follows: "Official affdavit Carmella Fiori, steamship Roma, sent June second. If excluded, hereby appeal.—JOSEPH DE ROSA, 2000 Central Street."

June 8, 1923.—Mr. de Rosa telephoned. He has had a telegram from Ellis Island, saying girl is excess quota.

June 13, 1923.—Letter received from Mr. de Rosa with inclosure:

DEAR MADAM:

I just received this letter, which I include, from Carmella Fiori. I made a translation on the back sheet so you can read it. She says they will not let her out unless I go and get her. I do not think it can be possible.

Maybe she is little excited, and she thinks they are going to keep her in there forever. You will understand that it would be very hard for me to leave my wife in the store and go to New York and spend another additional hundred dollars. In fact I do not think that my presence in New York would change very much the procedure of the burocracy [sic]. If I am not too exigent, I would appreciate it very much, if you would write me or call me advising me about this matter. Hoping you will excuse me, I thank you.

Very respectfully yours,

JOSEPH DE ROSA

The following translation of a letter from Carmella at Ellis Island was inclosed:

SIGNOR GIUSEPPI:

I hope you received my telegrams; one from the S.S. "Roma" and the other from where I am now, from the "Battery." Please be kind enough to come and get me, for otherwise they never let me out from here. It looks to me as if I am in jail, so please, come as soon as you possibly can.

June 15, 1923.—Letter received from Mr. de Rosa:

DEAR MADAM:

Just now received a telegram from Ellis Island which I transmit to you for your kind guidance: "Carmella Fiori case on appeal will be forwarded to Secretary of Labor within a few days." The telegram it is signed by the assistant immigration commissioner. Thanking you for your insuperable kindness and expressing my deep admiration for your philanthropic work, I am

Very respectfully yours,

JOSEPH DE ROSA

June 16, 1923.—Letter received, with inclosure, from Mr. de Rosa:

DEAR MADAM:

Some time past I received the enclosed affidavit made by Carmella's former employers previous to date employed by me, testifying to that effect. If you think proper to intercede to the Secretary of Labor, I send to you, I mean, so that you may use the way you think best. Thanking you very much,

Very respectfully,

JOSEPH DE ROSA

Later.—Telegram sent to Society for Italian Emigrants in New York.
Later.—Letter sent to Italian Society:

GENTLEMEN:

We have just wired you for Joseph de Rosa in behalf of Carmella Fiori, ex S.S. "Roma." We sent you a copy of the affidavit he made toward the end of May. Mr. de Rosa had a telegram from Ellis Island stating that the girl was held for special inquiry, being excess quota. A more recent telegram stated that the case was on appeal at Washington. Will you please do what you can for the girl.

Mr. de Rosa is willing to furnish bonds to secure her admission. She was formerly employed as domestic in his home when he was in Italy in 1921.

We inclose a document made in Villa Rosa, Italy, by Giuseppi and Elide Montessori, former employers; perhaps this will be of use to you.

Yours very sincerely,

ALICE MARION, *Superintendent*

June 25, 1923.—Telegram received from Society for Italian Emigrants, New York, as follows: "Take pleasure informing Carmella Fiori ordered admitted."

June 30, 1923.—Letter received from Mr. de Rosa:

DEAR MADAM:

This morning Carmella arrived well and safe. She was very glad. I could not close the present without expressing my deepest admiration and gratitude for all the work you have done regarding this case. Thanking you very much,

Very respectfully yours,

JOSEPH DE ROSA

36. The Wife and Child of Solomon Stein
(*Detention Abroad—Contagious Diseases—Exhausted Quota*)

[The following letters state the case of Solomon Stein:]

1. Letter written December 31, 1921, to the Commissioner-General of Immigration, Washington:

DEAR SIR:

Would it be possible for you to come to the assistance of the following family? The husband, Solomon Stein, 1816 Allen Street, came to Chicago in 1912 from Warsaw, Poland. In 1914, before the war broke out, he bought tickets on the Canadian Pacific for his wife and children. Owing, however, to war conditions, they could not come over then. In December, 1914, he heard from his wife. Then there was a long period during which he could get no news from her and during which he was very anxious and unhappy as to what might have happened. As the letter which we inclose shows, his family was finally located through the efforts of the American Red Cross in 1919. Since then, Mr. Stein has bent all his energies to getting his wife and children to the United States. In June, 1920, a Chicago man who was in Warsaw for some reason or other promised to bring them over. They went from Lodz to Warsaw to join this man; but, when they arrived they learned that he had left the city in haste, because of some threatened Bolshevik uprising. That attempt cost Mr. Stein a good deal of money and brought only disappointment. Then last spring he was able to make what promised to be a successful arrangement. His wife and three little boys, twelve, ten, and nine, were granted passport visas by the American Consul and started for this country. At Antwerp one of the boys was found to have a contagious disease, apparently favus. Two of the boys came on to the father in September, but the mother and the youngest boy were detained. Now the child has been certified as cured but the Polish quota being exhausted they are refused passage by the steamship company. In view of the fact that this family secured visas in June, and because of the anxiety and worry Mr. Stein has undergone for several years because of his family, is it not possible to do something in their case? Certainly her young sons need the mother's care here. We shall greatly appreciate any information you can give us as to what may be done for this family.

Yours very sincerely,
ALICE MARION

2. Letter from United States Department of Labor, Bureau of Immigration, Washington, January 7, 1922, to Superintendent of Immigrants' Protective League:

DEAR MADAM:

In reply to your letter of December 31, relative to the desire of Mr. Solomon Stein to bring his wife and child from Poland to the United States, the Bureau is inclosing a copy of its circular form 14 and invites your attention to paragraphs 1, 2, 3, 9, and 17. As the quota allotted to Poland is wholly exhausted for the balance of the fiscal year ending June 30, 1922, the aliens cannot be admitted unless they come within the exemptions enumerated in paragraph 17.[1] The fact that visas were granted last June does not affect their status under the immigration law.

Very truly yours,

37. Elena Petrovna

(Attempted Expulsion—Charges of Immorality)

[The following letters summarize the case of Elena Petrovna, who was maliciously reported for deportation as a prostitute two months after landing.]

1. Letter to Inspector-in-Charge, United States Immigration Service, Chicago, from the Superintendent, Immigrant's Protective League:

Mr. J. R. Roberts, Immigrant Inspector-in-Charge
United States Immigration Service
Chicago, Illinois

MY DEAR MR. ROBERTS: I am writing you in behalf of a Russian girl, Elena Petrovna, now married to Jan Ivanov. On July 11 she came to the office of the League to ask our advice. She said that a man by the name of George Grouble had sent $140 to his father in Russia to send him a wife. He had then arranged with her father, and she had come about a month ago. She did not, however, like Grouble and refused to marry him and wanted to marry another man from the same village, Jan Ivanov. Grouble had however frightened her by threatening to do her all kinds of harm if she did not marry him and she was afraid she would have to marry him. Miss Farbi, a Polish visitor for the League, went to see everyone concerned. Grouble said the girl had not lived with him as his wife since coming or before and that he had no claim on her beyond the fact that he had paid

[These exemptions are referred to above, p. 240, n. 2.]

for her passage. Jan Ivanov said he would gladly repay this, and payment was made in Miss Farbi's presence. Mr. Grouble then agreed not to annoy the girl any more and she was to be married the following week to Ivanov. On July 21, the girl's friends came to our office and said she had just been arrested by an immigration inspector. Going to your office we found the girl had been arrested on the complaint of Grouble on the charge that she was a prostitute and had come to America to live as such. We found that a marriage license had been obtained by Ivanov on July 15, that they were to be married on Sunday evening, July 23, that the hall, music, and food had been paid for and the girl's dress and veil were ready, that they both had been living with a friend in the new flat since the license had been secured because they considered it entirely proper and she wanted to get their flat ready for the wedding. The wedding had to be postponed of course. The hearing was held July 23 before Inspector Thompson, who had made some investigation of the case. Grouble and one other man appeared against her, and thirteen neighbors and people from her home village in her behalf. Grouble testified that he had lived with the girl, contradicting what he had told Miss Farbi. He said that she bore a bad name in Russia. There was no other evidence against the girl beyond the fact that she had lived in the same boarding house with a group of men, as a great many virtuous Polish and Russian girls do when they first come to Chicago. Had an American girl lived in such a way the conclusion that she was immoral might well be drawn, but it would not be warranted in the case of these girls. I am inclosing a page from my annual report of February last which indicates how common such living conditions are.

Evidence showed that Grouble, who is a widower forty-eight years old, had a bad name at home and was not trusted by the Russians in Chicago.

The girl was released on bail and was married to Ivanov, July 26, in the Greek Orthodox church. The man is at work and has furnished the small flat where he and his wife are living.

The hearing brought out absolutely no evidence of prostitution. For evidence of immoral relations between Grouble and the girl there is only his word against hers. The motive of the man easily explains his testimony. As to the general character of the two the evidence is all in her favor. She is a simple peasant girl, but the news of all this has already gone to her village; and if she is deported as a prostitute, her future will be ruined. The United States government will have condemned a girl against whom there is only a case such as a malicious man could make against almost any Russian or Polish girl in the city.

This is, as I see it, the whole case against the girl. There is no proof that she was ever a prostitute and no evidence against her general character except that of Grouble. His motive seems clear. The girl is now married and living under conditions which would be entirely sanctioned by American standards. To send her back as a prostitute would mean that her life would be ruined—there would be nothing open for her but to become one.

I am leaving town for a few days and am sorry not to have seen and discussed the case with you. I hope that you will feel that you can recommend to the department that the girl should not be deported.

Sincerely yours,

LYDIA GARDNER

2. A similar letter was sent to the Secretary of Commerce and Labor, Washington.

3. Letter dated August 8, 1914, from Inspector-in-Charge, United States Immigration Service, Chicago:

Miss Lydia Gardner, Director
Immigrants' Protective League

MY DEAR MISS GARDNER: I beg to acknowledge receipt of your letter of the fourth instant in behalf of the Russian girl Elena Petrovna. I shall be pleased to accompany my report to the Commissioner-General with a copy of your letter.

Respectfully,
J. R. ROBERTS,
Inspector-in-Charge

4. Letter dated August 11, 1914, from Office of Assistant Secretary, Department of Commerce and Labor, Washington:

MY DEAR MISS GARDNER:

I have given instructions to cancel the warrant in the case of Elena Petrovna, about whom you wrote me. I am frank to say that the record does not speak very well for her. In view of the fact that she is now married and evidently leading a respectable life as far as I know, no immediate steps will be taken. . . . .

5. Letter dated March 8, 1915, to Inspector-in-Charge, United States Immigration Service, Chicago:

MY DEAR MR. ROBERTS:

In accordance with your telephone request, I am reporting on Elena Petrovna, who lives at 84 West Street, and the question of whose deportation was up last July. She was visited on December 12 by Miss Farbi, who found her living very happily with her husband and bearing a good name in the neighborhood. The husband has regular work and seems to be a very respectable hard-working man.

Sincerely yours,
LYDIA GARDNER

38. Peter Johann Simann
(Deportation after Landing—Public Charge within One Year)

February 6, 1914.—Man brought to office by the Parmalee Transfer Agent at seven in the morning. Man speaks no English. He arrived at the Northwestern Station with no money and no place to go. *Later.*— [Interviewed by N. R.] The man's name is Peter Simann, born in Germany. He is thirty-four years old. He is sick and wishes to go home to Europe. He has in Europe a wife, Emilie, and two children, Marie aged ten and Hans aged nine. He cannot read and write. He will stay in office until we find out what to do with him. *Later.*—N. R. spoke with Miss Kenneth [Assistant Director] and then spoke with man again. He came to the United States on May 3, 1913, with his countryman, Heinrich Mayer. He went first to Riverdale, Illinois, where for three months he worked on the streets. Then he got work in a brewery in Menominee, Michigan, but he worked there only one month and became sick from the hard work which he was doing in this place. He was taken to a hospital in Menominee, Michigan, but after three weeks in the hospital was sent to the County Almshouse. He was there one month. He was taken from there and put on a train to come to Chicago. The man arrived February 6 in the morning at seven o'clock and was sent here, i.e., to League office, from the passenger station with Parmalee. He has no money and no friends; he wants to be sent home. *Later.*—N. R. telephoned Mr. Roberts [the United States Immigration Inspector-in-Charge in Chicago]. He says the man is not deportable but if he is sick and only one year in this country and willing to go back, United States government will pay his passage on steamer but not his railroad fare to the port. Telephoned the County Agent's Office and spoke with Mr. Smith, who has charge of deportations. He says they will furnish transportation to New York if they have to; wants to have letter with information.

February 7, 1914.—Telephoned to United States Immigration Inspector, who said they must verify his landing. Told him man has inspection card from the S.S. "Kaiser Wilhelm." Told him we will send card over.

February 9, 1914.—N. R. took the inspection card to Mr. Roberts, United States Inspector-in-Charge. They also want a statement from man that he is willing to go back, a statement from a physician that he is unable to work, also a statement that he can travel without injury to himself, and a statement from whoever will furnish the railroad fare that it will be furnished. A United States Inspector will come to see the man. *Later.*— Mr. Jones, Immigration Inspector, came to office and interviewed man.

February 10, 1914.—The following letter was sent to Mr. Smith, County Deportation Agent:

My dear Mr. Smith:

In confirmation of our telephone conversation of the other day relative to Peter Simann, the Russian-German man who wishes to return to Europe, we wish to report the following: The man still has a steamship inspection card which shows that he came to the United States in May, 1913. He lived first in Riverdale, Illinois, where he worked on the streets for some time. He then went to Menominee, Michigan, and found work in a brewery. The work there was too hard for him, and after a month he became sick and was taken to a hospital where he remained for three weeks, after which he was taken to the poorhouse. He reports that he was put on a Northwestern train for Chicago, without money or resources. He arrived here February 6, and was brought to our office. The man is very anxious to return to Russia and we have taken the matter up with Mr. Roberts of the United States Immigration Service and he thinks that the man can be returned if he signs a statement to the effect that he is willing to return. The United States, under these conditions, will pay for the steamship passage but not his railroad fare to the port. As soon as we have secured the verification of his landing and the statement from the doctor as to his inability to work, we will notify you and send you duplicate copies as these must be in Mr. Roberts' office. Will you be kind enough to let us know if you are willing to pay his transportation to New York?

Sincerely yours,

Lydia Gardner

February 13, 1914.—Received letter from Mr. Smith, Cook County Deportation Agent:

I am in receipt of letter dated February 10th, relative to one Peter Simann, who wishes to return to Europe. In reply, beg to say that as soon as you have secured the verification of his landing and statement from the doctor as to his inability to work, would request that you send us duplicate copy of his landing, as well as a copy of the statement from the doctor, when he will take up the question of his transportation to New York, provided the United States Immigration Bureau decide to deport him.

Later.—Telephoned to Dr. Brin. He will come in to see man in a few days.

February 17, 1914.—Dr. Brin examined man, said his general mental and physical condition is very poor. Wrote out two certificates. *Later.*—N. R. took certificates to Mr. Roberts. He says now that the man had been reported for deportation some time ago by Menominee poorhouse; that the verification of landing was written for and obtained and a warrant has been issued by the department. On October 6, when Mr. Ransom, the Inspector, went out to Menominee to serve the warrant, he found the man gone. The people in Menominee told the Inspector that they could not wait so long and so they had sent the man on to Chicago. The reason that the Immigration Bureau did not recognize the man was that his name was spelled a little different way by the Menominee people. The man will be deported in the regular way, probably with the next party, February 24. The government will pay for man's maintenance from February 17 until day of deportation, 50 cents each day.

February 24, 1914.—Peter Simann left for New York to be deported.

39. Patrick O'Brien
(Request for Deportation after Landing)

[The following letters summarize the case of an Irish immigrant:]

CHICAGO, February 28, 1915

Inspector-in-Charge
United States Immigration Service
Chicago, Illinois

DEAR MR. ROBERTS: An Irish man named Patrick O'Brien, 300 Arthur Street, has asked us whether he is deportable. He arrived in the United States about February first, 1913, on the steamer "Celtic." After he had been here six months he became paralyzed and has since been living in various hospitals and on the charity of his friends. He has brothers in Waterford, Ireland. He has only one sister here, and she is doing housework at 3000 Lakeside Avenue. I could not discover whether he has become a public charge on account of causes existing prior to his arrival in this country, but your investigation will, of course, show this.

Very truly yours,

LYDIA GARDNER
(For the Immigrants' Protective League)

CHICAGO, March 2, 1915

Miss Lydia Gardner, Director
Immigrants' Protective League
Chicago, Illinois

MADAM: Referring to your letter of the 21st ultimo, in the matter of Patrick O'Brien, I beg to advise you that under date of February 29th, the Public Health and Marine Hospital Surgeon in Command at the port of Chicago reports that the alien has been found suffering from paralysis of both lower limbs, which condition is due to an attack of Acute Anterior Poliomyelitis with which the alien was afflicted some six months after his arrival in this country and concerning which it is impossible that the cause of the disease existed prior to landing.

In view of the surgeon's certificate there appear to be no grounds upon which to institute deportation proceedings.

Respectfully,
J. R. ROBERTS
Inspector-in-Charge

40. Michael Stefan
(Expulsion Recommended)

[The following letters summarize the case of a Croatian immigrant:]

CHICAGO, February 28, 1914

Inspector-in-Charge
United States Immigration Service
Chicago, Illinois

MY DEAR MR. ROBERTS: A Croatian by the name of Michael Stefan, who lives at Gary, is at present in Chicago for treatment at the Illinois Eye and Ear Infirmary for trachoma. The man came to the United States, he says, in April of 1912, and he thinks that he has at Gary papers showing on what boat he came. He is unable to work and came into the office to see if we could not help him to collect the money or benefit that he believes to be due him from a Croatian Society to which he belongs. As he is a menace to the people with whom he is living, as there seems no possibility of his cure, and as the advanced condition of his case leads one to think that he must have had the disease before coming to the United States, it seems to me desirable that he should be deported. If you will let me know when he can be taken for examination I will be glad to send him to you.

Sincerely yours,
LYDIA GARDNER
(For the Immigrants' Protective League)

CHICAGO, March 5, 1914

Miss Lydia Gardner, Director
Immigrants' Protective League
Chicago, Illinois

MADAM: As per our conversation over the telephone today, in *re* Michael Stefan, I find that this office wrote you under date of the 2d instant as follows:

"Referring to your letter of the 28th ultimo concerning the case of Michael Stefan, I beg to state that the Public Health and Marine Hospital

Surgeon in Command at Chicago has written this office under date of February the 29th that it was impossible to state that the eye disease (trachoma) with which this alien is suffering, existed prior to landing.

"It appears therefore that there exist no statutory grounds upon which deportation proceedings may be instituted."

Respectfully,

J. R. ROBERTS
Inspector-in-Charge

41. Demetrius Spiros
(Deportation after Temporary Admission—Certified Physical Defect)

November 21, 1914.—A Greek man, Peter Fortios, in the office. He brought a telegram from the United States Department of Labor informing him that an alien by the name of Demetrius Spiros, who had been temporarily admitted under bonds and who was to be deported, must leave on November 30, when the S.S. "Thessalonica" would sail from New York for Piraeus. Mr. Spiros failed to pass the physical examination at Ellis Island; had been excluded because of a slight physical defect; would have been deported but for the war. Mr. Fortios, a friend, had signed a bond securing the temporary release of Spiros from Ellis Island, but guaranteeing his departure from the United States within a year if requested to go by the Department of Labor. Told man to come in Monday to see Miss Gardner [the Superintendent].

November 25, 1914.—Mr. Fortios called at office again. He could not come in on Monday. Reports that Mr. Spiros went to Davenport, Iowa, on Monday. He promised to return Wednesday night, but as he does not wish to return to Greece, Mr. Fortios is afraid he will not come. Advised him to go to Davenport for Mr. Spiros if he did not come Wednesday night. Told him to take the man to Hull-House Thursday if he returned, where the Greek visitor would explain the situation. Telephoned Mr. Roberts, United States Immigration Inspector-in-Charge. He says that the United States assumed absolutely no responsibility about getting the man to his destination and that if he did not appear ready to sail Monday, suit would be automatically started against Fortios for recovery of bond. Mr. Fortios says that Spiros was excluded on account of hernia, but has worked for him (Fortios) steadily since his arrival, loading and unloading vegetable wagons, and his hernia has not bothered him at all. Congressman X. has already obtained one stay from November 10 to November 30. *Later.*—Telephoned Congressman X.; he said his secretary in Washington knew all about it.

Letter written to Chief of Police, Davenport, Iowa:

We are interested in the case of the bearer of this note, Peter Fortios, who has come to Davenport for Demetrius Spiros who has been ordered deported by the Department of Labor and must be in New York by the morning of November 30. His presence in Chicago at the earliest possible moment, however, is necessary before any action toward appealing the case can be taken. We are therefore asking you to give him whatever assistance is within your power in getting the man to Chicago.

November 27, 1921.—Mr. Fortios brought Demetrius Spiros to Hull-House last night. Man returned from Davenport after Mr. Fortios had started there to bring him back. Greek visitor arranged to have him come back to Hull-House at 9:00 o'clock Friday to see about a medical examination. *Later.*—Telegraphed Assistant Secretary of Labor as follows: "Is it possible to secure stay of deportation pending medical examination in the case of Demetrius Spiros directed to leave the United States by Department of Labor according to terms of bond on or before November 30? Please wire answer."

November 28, 1914.—Mr. Fortios in office. Report from physician: "Hernia slight, easily curable. Immediate operation not necessary but can be done any time." *Later.*—The following telegram received from an assistant secretary, Department of Labor: "Not possible to stay deportation Demetrius Spiros for purposes assigned. Full explanation by letter." *Later.*—Telegraphed United States Department of Labor again as follows: "Demetrius Spiros has worked steadily since arrival. Doctor certified hernia slight and easily corrected. Is it possible to stay deportation for re-examination by physician of Marine Hospital Service, Chicago, so case can be considered on present status rather than status at time of arrival? Alien willing to undergo operation. Please reply immediately. Steamer sails Monday." *Later.*—Telegram also sent to Ellis Island: "Demetrus Spiros will arrive New York Monday, 6 A.M., for deportation unless Secretary of Labor grants stay.—PETER FORTIOS." *Later.*—Telegram from Ellis Island: "Will Demetrius Spiros be provided with transportation Greek Line Steamer Thessalonica sailing thirtieth? Necessary that he or bondsman do this." *Later.*—Mr. Fortios in office again. Told him contents. He did not know that he was required to pay man's return passage to Greece. He had arranged to leave Saturday night, if stay was not granted. *Later.*—Telegram from United States Department of Labor: "Careful reconsideration case Demetrius Spiros discloses no reason for interference with department's previous decision."

November 29, 1914.—Letter received from Assistant Secretary, United States Department of Labor:

Referring to your telegram of the 26th inst., I beg to state that I have wired you today that it is not possible to stay deportation of the alien Demetrius Spiros for the purpose stated by you. This man upon his arrival at the port of New York in August last was certified by the medical examiners for "hernia, right, which affects ability to earn a living." He left his wife and three children in Greece, and came here to join a cousin in New York City. As you are no doubt aware, section 2 of the act of February 20, 1907, excludes from this country aliens who upon arrival "are found to be and are certified by the examining surgeons as being . . . . physically defective, such . . . . physical defect being of a nature which may affect the ability of such alien to earn a living." While the same act vests the Department with discretion to admit an alien so certified under bond, it is the well-established practice not to allow the entry of physically defective aliens upon such conditions where it is shown that they have in their native country a family dependent upon them for support, as is the case here. At the time the appeal was considered this alien was regarded as clearly excludable and would have been deported were it not for the fact that disturbed conditions abroad prevented that course of action. In order, therefore, to avoid undue detention at the port, authority was granted for the man's release under a bond guaranteeing his departure at the expiration of one year, or prior thereto if so directed. The alien is a native of a neutral country, and deportation on a neutral vessel can now be accomplished with safety. Acting under the Department's general instructions in the premises, the Commissioner of Immigration at Ellis Island has accordingly called for the man's departure under the terms of the bond filed in the case.

November 30, 1914.—A second letter received from Assistant Secretary. [The letter contained the following:]

Unless the Department could have concluded, notwithstanding the findings of the doctors and the members of the board of special inquiry, that his affliction did not interfere with his earning ability, he could not have been permitted to land without actually violating the law, unless a bond had been exacted; and, there being no peculiar hardship involved in deportation, the man's wife and children being in his native country to which it was proposed to return him, there would have been no occasion, under the well-established practice, to accept a bond. Of course it is realized that individual cases of this kind when viewed alone take on an aspect of hardship; but in administering the law the Department has to consider, not only the individual case, but the general policy that must be pursued if the law is to be effective of its purpose. There are now pending many cases in which aliens, who would have been returned promptly but for war conditions, have been granted special consideration and permitted to remain temporarily in the country; and you can readily appreciate that it would not do to establish a precedent in connection with the handling of these cases that would result in leaving here aliens who under the law are not admissible.

42. Stephanie Woloski
(*Expulsion Prevented by the War*)

June 12, 1914.—The following letter of inquiry received:

GERMANVALE, WISCONSIN

Miss Lydia Gardner, Director
Immigrants' Protective League

DEAR MISS GARDNER: The case of an Austrian woman by the name of Stephanie Gurdalisch (as near as we can get it), twenty-two years old, said to have married a man by the name of Walter Woloski, Austrian, twenty-three years old, at the Randolph Police Station, Chicago, on February 15, this year, has been given to me for investigation by the City Poor Department here. She has one child, a baby two weeks old. This woman came to Germanvale some two months ago with a Greek by the name of Sam Granos, who she says was running a Greek hotel at 800 East Halsted Street, Chicago, where she worked for three months before she married Woloski.

This Greek, it would seem, was the one who had Woloski arrested when he was forced to marry her. Afterwards Woloski abused her and failed to provide for her, and she had to leave him, tried to find work but could not, and was going to drown herself when she met the Greek, who told her he had sold his hotel and was going up into Wisconsin to find another hotel, and he told her to go with him and she could keep house for him and he would take care of her and the baby, and afterwards she could go to work and repay him. He is said to have a wife and two children in Greece. She said Woloski did work for a while, before he married, at a laundry on Kenzie Street. About two weeks ago the Greek took the woman to the Germanvale Poor Department for care (was told to by another Greek living here) and the city sent them to the Home for the Friendless. She was refused admittance until the city would investigate. The Poor superintendent then placed her with another woman on the city poor list and the baby was born 11 days ago. The superintendent now informs me he expects to ship her back to Chicago as soon as he can. If you can verify any of the statements she has made to above, perhaps you can give me some advice what to do with her and where to have her sent in Chicago. Anything you can do in the case will be greatly appreciated.

Yours very truly,
MARY H. AMERY, *Secretary*
Associated Charities

June 15, 1914.—Letter to Germanvale, saying, "Mrs. Woloski's connections will be investigated at once and reported to you."

June 22, 1914.—[Account of inquiries made omitted.] Letter to Germanvale Associated Charities reporting the results of the investigation as follows:

MY DEAR MISS AMERY:

Regarding the Polish woman Stephanie Woloski, of whom you wrote us on June 12, we wish to report the following: We have interviewed her former husband, Mr. Walter Woloski, 20 Polk Street, who states that he was married to the woman, December 15, 1913, and that he was divorced two months later. Our visitor saw the divorce papers. At the time of the marriage, the girl stated that she would leave in thirteen days with the Greek, which she did. Mr. Woloski maintains that he is not the father of the child. He states that the girl has led an immoral life since her arrival in this country, and the neighbors and landlady corroborate this. They understand that she was immoral in Europe. Her former husband will have nothing more to do with her. He states that she has relatives here, whose addresses he will furnish our visitor. We called also at 800 East Halsted Street. Very little, however, was learned concerning the Greek, Sam Granos. The present proprietor states that he knows only that the man left two months ago. Mr. Granos has a daughter in this city, Mrs. John Demepolis, 2430 West Street. She also states that she has not heard from her father for two months. We shall communicate with you again at once when our visitor has again interviewed Mr. Woloski, whom she expects to call upon her tomorrow evening. Should the relatives here be unable to care for the woman and should it develop that she has relatives who might care for her in Europe, it might seem best that she be deported. Trusting the information will be of service, I remain,

Sincerely yours,
LYDIA GARDNER

July 2, 1914.—Reply received from the Germanvale Associated Charities:

I would advise that immediately upon receipt of your letter the Greek man and Polish woman were arrested here by the District Attorney, and the case placed in the hands of the United States authorities, the man to answer for bringing the woman here under the Mann Act, and the woman to be deported. A United States Agent, from Chicago, J. G. Brown, took her evidence day before yesterday. The woman is now an inmate of the Home for the Friendless. She has a nice little baby boy but cares nothing for it. I do not know how far the United States agents will go with the case, but if you can see any of the relatives I thought perhaps they would take the baby. They could ascertain from Mr. Brown, the United States Agent, when the woman will be taken to Chicago.

July 3, 1914.—Telephoned Mr. Brown, Inspector, United States Immigration Service. He would be glad to have such facts as we can get about the girl. Her name on their record is Stephanie Gursdatoc.

July 13, 1914.—The following letter was written to the Inspector-in-Charge of the United States Immigration Service in Chicago:

I am sorry not to have reported sooner with regard to Stephanie Woloski, as we have her, or Gursdatoc as I believe you have her on your record. Our Polish visitor called on June 18 at 20 Polk Street and interviewed Mr. Woloski, the man whom the girl married, and his landlady; both of them gave indirect stories about the girl and said that she had a generally bad reputation. The man reported that he had secured a divorce two months after his marriage, the woman having left thirteen days after her marriage. At the place where the Greek formerly lived, 800 East Halsted Street, nothing could be learned of the girl. Mr. Woloski insisted that the girl has a brother and a sister here and promised to secure their address for us. This he did not do, and on July 2 we called on him again, asking him to let us know where her relatives were living, and he again promised to secure the address, but he has not done it. Our Polish visitor says that Mr. Woloski is no longer living at 20 Polk Street, as he contemplated moving at the time of her last visit and said he would let us know where he was going.

Sincerely yours,

LYDIA GARDNER

[Some entries on the case record and letters omitted here.]

August 1, 1914.—Letter from Germanvale inclosing a statement of the case:

DEAR MISS GARDNER:

Wishing to follow your suggestion to make further inquiry of the United States Attorney General in the case of the Greek man and the Polish woman, trial not having been tried in this district by the United States Attorney, I am writing you again. I inclose a statement of the case, and as I do not have the name of the United States Attorney General, will you kindly have inquiry made from your office—if you think best. As certain officials are fighting me hard at this point because of my "meddling," it will be better for me to have the inquiry made through another source, if possible. If this man had not been a Greek I doubt very much if the jury would have given a verdict of guilty here. As the Greeks are not American citizens and have no vote, the controlling side here has no use for them. But had he been most anything else and a good patron of the saloon he would have gotten off—at least that is quite general in similar cases. Where a young girl is the victim, she will always be sent to the Industrial School at M—, while the man is either let off entirely, or given a fine or court costs. I would state that in the deportation of this Polish woman she was taken from this point by the County Sheriff, and I know she was sent on to New York on tickets allowed by the United States immigration authorities.

Yours very truly,

MARY H. AMERY

[Statement inclosed:]

Greek—Sam Granos. Man of about 45 years, had been running a Greek rooming house at 800 East Halsted Street, Chicago, Illinois. Sold place about March 1st and came to Germanvale, Wisconsin, bringing with him a Polish woman he had had working for him according to his statement, but court evidence proved her immorality. When the woman became pregnant, a marriage was forced to a young Pole, Walter Woloski, in the Randolph Police Station, February 15, 1914 (date given by woman). This man within two months obtained a divorce proving her immorality.

About March 1st the Greek came to Germanvale, living at 504 North Avenue (a Greek rooming house) with the Polish woman as housekeeper. When within a week of birth of child his associates told him to put her on the City for support. The City Poor Department accepted the case without investigation. The child was born May 29, during which time the Greek visited her regularly, buying her clothing and taking liquor to the house where she had been placed.

An investigation started by the Associated Charities June 6 resulted in the arrest of both parties by the District Attorney at this point, who stated that the case would be tried under the Mann Act by the United States District Attorney in Milwaukee. This was not done, however, but tried in the Police Court here, the man found guilty by a jury trial, and given $80 fine by the Judge, or a 6 months' jail sentence. He took the jail sentence and is serving time.

The Polish woman, Stephanie Woloski, was proved by the United States Immigration Service of Chicago to be an immoral character and deported.

This Greek, Sam Granos, has a wife with children in Greece. A jail sentence means very little here, and as work is scarce, he is the gainer by living in jail and saving his $80.

[The case of Stephanie Woloski was supposedly closed with this notice of her deportation, August 1, 1914.]

May 19, 1915.—The following card was received by one of the foreign visitors of the League from Miss Sobieski, Slavonic Church missionary at Ellis Island:

DEAR FRIEND:

Excuse me for using this card and a bad pen. Zefanie Guedala, a Polish, may be you already heard about her, needs an affidavit, money for transportation and hand money from her sister Kata Guedala, 1300 Corner Street, or from her cousin John Berlak. You do not need to hurry as she is better off here than any place else, but she does not realize it now and therefore she gets angry and cries and is noisy. But it would be better if she would go. . . . .

May 21, 1915.—Called at 1300 Corner Street. Mrs. Kudzala (landlady) states that Katie Guedala and a cousin (both single girls) moved about ten months ago. Woman took me to a home on Augusta Street, but girls were not there; we also inquired in a few other buildings but could not find any trace of the girls.

May 22, 1915.—The following notice inserted in Chicago Polish newspapers:

Katarzyna Guedala, who lived not long ago somewhere on Corner Street, is asked to call immediately at the office of the Immigrants' Protective League at 920 South Michigan Avenue, because her sister and her sister's son are detained at Ellis Island for lack of funds.

May 26, 1915.—The following letter was sent to Miss Sobieski, Ellis Island, New York:

MY DEAR MADAM:

In accordance with your request, one of our visitors attempted to locate the sister of Zefanie Guedala at 1300 Corner Street but found that she had moved. Inquiry was made in the building, but no address could be found. A notice was inserted in the Polish daily paper in Chicago, but we have as yet had no response. As soon as we hear from her, we shall communicate with you.

Very truly yours,

LYDIA GARDNER

May 28, 1915.—Sister and cousin in office. They reported that the girl was in the United States about a year ago and she was married at the Chicago Avenue Station. A little later they heard that man was going to get a divorce, but they do not know whether or not he did get it. They said they could not guarantee to take care of her. If she would be able to work she could come out to Chicago and board her baby and go to work, but if she cannot work, they cannot guarantee to take care of her as the cousin has wife and three children to support and the sister has been out of work for a very long time.

May 29, 1915.—Letter to Miss Sobieski, Ellis Island, New York:

DEAR MADAM:

In further reference to Zefanie Guedala, we wish to say that her cousin and her sister Katie called at our office yesterday. It seems that they have not known the whereabouts of Stephanie for about a year. Just before that she was married and they heard that the man was going to get a divorce, but do not know whether or not he got it. The sister and the cousin who called at the office do not either of them feel that they can can take care of both Stephanie and the baby. We gave them, at their request, the address by which she may be reached at Ellis Island, so that they will probably write to her at once. It may be that when they hear from her, they may be more willing to have her come on. We shall be very grateful for more details concerning the woman.

Very truly yours,
Lydia Gardner

June 16, 1915.—A letter from Miss Sobieski saying:

My dear League:

Stephanie Gurdalisch needs now only an affidavit of support from her sister. Thanking you in advance for your assistance, I remain,

Sincerely yours,
T. Sobieski

June 29, 1915.—Another letter received from Miss Sobieski as follows:

My dear League:

I spoke to Stephanie right after receiving your letter and she promises to work for her and her son's support and to be good to her sister. It looks that there is gratitude toward the sister in her heart. Also she promises to keep honest in behalf of relations with men. "What I was, I am not any more!" The matrons and other employees who are staying with immigrants, the nurses in both hospitals where she spent several months of her detention and all missionaries think that she is a good woman. She knows too that she would be deported again when she does not keep right, and she purposes to do all to help her sister and live in peace with her. That is what I have to report to you and I expect that you will use your great experience to do the right thing. Thanking you for your great help, I remain,

Very sincerely yours,
T. Sobieski

June 30, 1915.—Katie Guedala called at office with following letter:

Miss Katie Guedala
520 Harrison Street
Chicago, Illinois

Go as soon as possible to the Immigrants' Protective League, 920 South Michigan Avenue. They will tell you what your sister needs to be helped.

Sincerely yours,
T. Sobieski

Katie said that she did not understand previously and is willing to make out affidavit. Her sister came with her to Chicago two years ago, was taken ill, went to a hospital, and was confined, then deported, but war interfered. Katie heard that sister has married a Russian but does not know. Will come in Saturday noon.

July 1, 1915.—Visited office of United States Immigration Inspector and saw record. Has various spellings: Gursdota, Gurzato, Gurzdatoc, Gurdalisch, Guedala. Girl arrived February 18, 1913, and baby born June 4, 1914. Girl came from Libava. Married Walter Woloski, February 15. [Case identified with former League record of Stephanie Woloski.]

Letter sent to Miss Sobieski as follows:

DEAR MADAM:

We write again with regard to Stephanie Guedala, who is held at Ellis Island with her infant son. We have just found that we have a record in connection with her deportation under a very different name. We have never actually known her because she was deported from Germanvale, Wisconsin, but our record shows that she is a very difficult person, and we do not wish to advise her sister to make out the affidavit and assume any responsibility for her until we have gone into the matter thoroughly. Could you tell us from your observation of Stephanie there in New York whether you think she will be likely to behave herself if released and whether she is likely to be self-supporting? Her sister Katie is a very nice girl, and is working now, but is absolutely unable to support her sister if she should prove to be unemployable or unwilling to work. We realize, however, the hardship of her indefinite detention at Ellis Island and will be glad to help in gaining her release if it seems best.

Very truly yours,

LYDIA GARDNER

July 2, 1915.—Letter to the Secretary of the Germanvale Associated Charities:

We had a lengthy correspondence with you last summer during June and July concerning a Polish woman, Stephanie Gurzdatoc or Gurdalisch, whose case you investigated in connection with her deportation. You will remember that the woman was ordered deported and taken to New York from Germanvale. It has just come to our attention that the outbreak of the war prevented her departure and that she has been at Ellis Island all these months. A society in New York has asked us to help to secure her release and have her put in care of her sister here in Chicago. In view of the extraordinary situation with regard to those subjects of belligerent nations who are detained at Ellis Island, the government is granting temporary releases and will probably do so in this case. We, however, hesitate to recommend this until we have gone into the matter more thoroughly. The sister is only nineteen and is an exceptionally nice girl, is working but averages only $7.00 a week. We think it would be a great pity to have her assume the responsibility of her very difficult sister if the latter is likely to be unemployable or unwilling to be self-supporting. We have no actual knowledge of Stephanie and wonder if you will be good enough to give us your impression of her. Do you think it would be wise to ask to have her released? Do you know anything further about the Greek, Sam Granos, who received a jail sentence in this case? Is he still in Germanvale? We shall greatly appreciate your co-operation. I am,

Very truly yours,

LYDIA GARDNER

July 3, 1915.—Katie in office. She is sure that she wants her sister to come. She says that she has had much trouble with her, but she does not want her to stay at Ellis Island. She will go to see M. K. [League's Polish visitor] Tuesday night at her office hour at Northwestern Settlement to find out what letter from New York says.

July 6, 1915.—Talked to Mr. Brown, United States Immigration Service, who held hearing. He remembers the woman and says she is very much below the average in intelligence. He thinks she will not lead a good life if admitted.

Letter received from Germanvale containing following statement:

Replying to your inquiry of the second, relative to deportation case Stephanie Gurdalisch and baby from Germanvale. During the time we had this woman in the Home for the Friendless it was found she was dishonest and tricky and only admitted the facts as to her life when she knew she was cornered. She steadily maintained her innocence until she heard his testimony in court and then turned on him and called him a liar. From your correspondence June 22, 1914, you will see that your investigator proved her an immoral character. I do not believe her a type ever to reform, particularly considering her relations with the type of Greek as the man Sam Granos. It would, in my judgment, be very unfair to the sister to have to associate with such a woman and very dangerous considering her age. Trusting this answers your inquiry, I am,

Yours very truly,

MARY H. AMERY

(*For the Associated Charities*)

July 7, 1915.—Katie Gurdalisch visited R. B. in Settlement office last night; she begged me to bring her sister to Chicago, thinks woman will behave now after having all this trouble. Katie also is willing to support Stephanie's baby.

July 13, 1915.—Letter written to Dr. Alexis Winitzki, Superintendent of Slavonic Society in New York, as follows:

MY DEAR SIR:

We are interested in the case of Stephanie Gurdalisch, who is detained at Ellis Island with her infant son Rudolph, having been ordered deported the last of July, 1914, just before the war broke out. We are interested because of the sister Katie, since Miss Sobieski has written to us that it will be possible to have Stephanie released. From what we knew of the woman at the time of her deportation and from what we have since learned by corresponding with people who had her in charge just before her deportation, and the Inspector who examined her, we feel that it is extremely doubtful that it is the wise thing to bring her in. The Immigration Inspector remembers the woman well and says that she is very much below the average intelligence, in his opinion. He thinks that if admitted she would be an extremely difficult person to keep in touch with and help. Her sister is a very nice girl and is only nineteen and we hesitate to have her take this responsibility without due consideration. Would it be possible for us to have your opinion of the woman as well as Miss Sobieski's, and could you arrange to have a mental examination made at Ellis Island so that we may know just what her mentality is? We are trying to get as accurate an opinion as possible about her before deciding. We shall greatly appreciate your co-operation.

Very truly yours,
LYDIA GARDNER

July 26, 1915.—Reply received from Dr. Winitzki as follows:

Your letter arrived while I was on my vacation, and so only today I have been able to find out that Stephanie Gurdalisch was discharged to the Polish Immigrant Home, Second Avenue, last Monday, July 19. Her discharge, I understand, is only temporary and conditional on her good behavior.

July 26–August 5, 1915.—[During this period the record shows two further interviews with Katie, who called on the Polish visitor during the evenings when she kept an evening office hour in a settlement in a Polish neighborhood. Katie was uneasy about her sister and felt unhappy because she was not helping her. She had sent Stephanie $25.00 at one time and wanted to send her some more as soon as she could save a little. She was anxious to have her sister's new address.]

August 5, 1915.—Letter written to Dr. Winitzki as follows:

MY DEAR DR. WINITZKI:

We received your letter of July 26 with regard to Stephanie Gurdalisch and note that she has been discharged to the Polish Immigrant Home, Second Avenue. We hope very much that, if it is possible for her to be placed at work in New York, she will not be allowed to come on to Chicago, since her sister here is very young and we feel that Stephanie might be influenced again by some of the people that she got into trouble with while she was here, before her deportation. Will you be good enough to let us know if the conditions of her discharge would permit her coming to Chicago, since if such is not the case her sister here would be very much more contented about her remaining in New York.

Very truly yours,
LYDIA GARDNER

August 21, 1915.—Reply received from Dr. Winitzki containing the following:

Referring to your letter regarding Stephanie Gurdalisch, I ascertained that she has been placed in domestic service not far from New York. The Polish Society, who took out the woman on parole and who are expected to return her whenever the immigration authorities may order so, are just as anxious as you to keep her where they can easily reach her. There is therefore no immediate danger of Stephanie's coming to Chicago. In fact, I understand that she is quite content to stay here and has no desire to go to Chicago.

August 22, 1915.—Letter written to Katie that her sister is under parole in New York.

November 4, 1915.—Katie called on R. B. [Polish visitor] during office hour at Settlement. Reports she moved to 210 Grand Street. Would also like to know if sister Stephanie is still at the same address. She wrote two letters and did not get any reply. Told her Polish Society would look after her sister, and we thought she was better in New York.

November 5, 1919.—Katie Gurdalisch in office to see if she can get in touch with her sister. Katie is now married. Her name is Mrs. Koukol. Address, 316 Blank Court. She would like to have her sister know she has had a letter all about their family in Europe and what happened to them in the war. Promised to write to New York. *Later.*—Letter written to Slavonic Immigrant Society, New York City, as follows:

GENTLEMEN: On August 21, 1915, we had a letter from you regarding Stephanie Gurdalisch, a Polish woman, and her son, Rudolph. Will you kindly let me know if you have the present address of this woman and give us any information as to how she is getting along? Her sister is very anxious to hear of her, and any information which you can give will be much appreciated. She was also known to Miss T. Sobieski, the Slavonic missionary on Ellis Island.

Yours very truly,

LYDIA GARDNER

November 24, 1919.—Letter received from Slavonic Immigrant Society:

DEAR FRIENDS:

Your letter regarding Stephanie Gurdalisch was received some time ago but through an oversight was misplaced, and only today I happened to come across it. This woman was paroled to the Polish Immigrant Home, Second Avenue, and inquiry at that institution brought the information that her whereabouts are unknown. She disappeared about two years ago, leaving her child with a woman who was to board it. Stephanie, however, failed to pay the board, and the child was placed in a public institution. The manager of the Polish Home also informs me that Stephanie did not behave as a respectable woman should even while she was under their care.

Very truly yours,

ALEXIS WINITZKI

Later.—Letter written to Mrs. Koukol about her sister.

December 6, 1919.—Mrs. Koukol in office, is very anxious about her sister. Explained to Mrs. Koukol about letter received from Slavonic Society. She felt quite bad about it, would like to know just where the child is. Told Mrs. Koukol to go to Settlement any Friday evening, where she could see Polish visitor.

December 19, 1919.—Mrs. Koukol at Settlement. She would like the League to write to Polish Immigrant Home and ask if they will give address of Stephanie's baby's home. She wishes to ask for a picture of the baby. She thinks her sister committed suicide from grief.

December 20, 1919.—Letter to Slavonic Immigrant Society:

DEAR DR. WINITZKI:

Many thanks for your letter of November 21 in answer to our inquiries regarding Stephanie Gurdalisch. The sister of Stephanie has had letters from the old country telling about the family and has been much worried over her sister's fate and the fate of the child. She has asked us to try to find out the name of the institution in which the child is placed and whether she can write to those who have charge of the child. She also asked about a picture of the baby. She feels that her sister must have committed suicide, as she does not think that she would otherwise have deserted the child. We have known this sister since 1915 and she appears to be a respectable and sensible woman. She says that she could not afford to adopt Stephanie's child but that she is much interested in his future and would like to keep up some kind of communication with him. If you feel that it is wise to give her this information will you be good enough to write us? We shall be glad to let her know.

Yours very truly,

LYDIA GARDNER

January 24, 1920.—Mrs. Koukol called at office to know if reply has been received to letter about baby's picture.

February 3, 1920.—Another letter to Slavonic Society as follows:

DEAR DR. WINITZKI:

We wrote you on January 2 asking if you could ascertain for the sister of Stephanie Gurdalisch the name of the institution in which Stephanie's baby was placed, whether or not the sister could write to that institution and whether she could obtain a photograph of the baby. If any word has been received from Stephanie, it would be great relief to her if she could be given such information. We should be glad if you would write us as soon as possible.

Yours very truly,

LYDIA GARDNER

February 17, 1920.—Reply from Superintendent of Polish Home:

GENTLEMEN:

Stephanie Gurdalisch's son was under care of Mrs. X., Main Street College Point, L.I., New York. About three years ago Stephanie abandoned the child, and local charities department took charge of the boy. From that time we lost all trace of Stephanie Gurdalisch and her child.

Yours very truly,

————, *Superintendent*

February 18, 1920.—Letter written to Mrs. Koukol.

February 27, 1920.—Mrs. Koukol at Settlement last night to see R. B. [Polish visitor] about letter of the seventeenth from the Polish Home.

March 1, 1920.—Letter written State Board of Charities, Albany, New York, as follows:

GENTLEMEN:

We are interested in trying to locate the child Rudolph, about six years of age, of a woman by the name of Stephanie Gurdalisch. She was ordered deported from this district in 1914 and was held for a considerable period of time in Ellis Island, New York, because of the war situation. She was finally released to the Polish Immigrant Home, Second Avenue, New York City. We understand that the Polish Society placed the woman in domestic service and made arrangements for her to pay the board of her child. Stephanie eventually disappeared and the Society is unable to furnish her present address. They write that when last known the child was with Mrs. X., Main Street, College Point, L.I., New York, and that when Stephanie gave up paying the child's board he was taken charge of by the local charities. The sister, Katie, is very anxious for some news of what has become of her sister's child. Stephanie Gurdalisch was thoroughly demoralized, but her sister Katie feels great responsibility for both her and her child and is quite unwilling to give up that she will have no further word regarding her sister's child. If the child is well placed and cared for, so that we can assure the sister of that fact, I think she will be content not to know exactly where he is if it seems better for her not to.

Yours very truly,

LYDIA GARDNER

March 13, 1920.—Letter received from State Board of Charities. Albany, New York:

Miss Lydia Gardner
Immigrants' Protective League
Chicago, Illinois

DEAR MADAM: Replying to your letter of inquiry regarding the boy Rudolph Gurdalisch, we would say that this child was taken in charge by a children's agency in New York City. We have referred your letter to this agency and assume that you will hear directly from its officials.

Yours very truly,

CHARLES H. JOHNSON, *Secretary*

March 18, 1920.—Letter received from the Catholic Home Bureau for Dependent Children, New York City:

DEAR MADAM:

Mr. Charles H. Johnson, the secretary of our State Board of Charities, has forwarded to me for attention your letter addressed to him, inquiring as to the present whereabouts of Rudolph Gurdalisch. Due to the fact that this child was abandoned by its mother and that nothing was known concerning its father, he was placed in a family home and later legally adopted by the family. The home is a most desirable one in every respect, and the foster parents are people of education and refinement and in good circumstances and the child is well placed and likely to receive careful training and development. I note that you state in your letter that the sister of the child's mother does not insist upon learning of the child's whereabouts, but desires only to be assured that he is well located. I think if the facts as above stated were furnished to her, she would feel satisfied.

In any event, it would be impossible for us to disclose the present whereabouts of the child, as it might be responsible for creating results detrimental to his interests. Hoping the foregoing may prove satisfactory, I am,

Very truly yours,

EDMOND J. BUTLER, *Executive Secretary*

Later.—Letter written to Mrs. Koukol.

March 19, 1920.—Mrs. Koukol called at Settlement. R.B. [Polish visitor] explained letter of March 15 from Catholic Home Bureau. Mrs. Koukol was very happy to know Stephanie's baby has such a good home and is well cared for. She will write about it to the family in Europe. She still wishes she could have a picture of the baby.

April 7, 1920.—Letter to Catholic Home Bureau:

Mr. Edmond J. Butler, Secretary
Catholic Home Bureau for Dependent Children

DEAR SIR: We duly received your report regarding the welfare of Rudolph Gurdalisch and have passed on the facts to the child's aunt who seemed very much pleased and entirely satisfied to know that the child was in such good hands. Thanking you for your kind co-operation, I remain,

Yours very truly,

LYDIA GARDNER

43. Katie Schultz

(*Expulsion—Feeble-minded*)

[The record in the case of Katie Schultz is a very long one. The following letters, however, contain the most essential facts:]

1. Letter to the Inspector-in-Charge, United States Immigration Service, Chicago, from the Director of the Immigrants' Protective League, dated May 13, 1913:

MY DEAR MR. ROBERTS:

I should like to report Katie Schultz, a German-Hungarian girl, eighteen years old, who says she arrived the first part of August, 1912, on the S.S. "Bordeaux." Our attention was called to her by the social service worker at the County Hospital in November, and since that time we have been in constant touch with her. We arranged for her to go to the Elizabeth Hospital for an appendicitis operation and later sent her to the Convalescent Home in Evanston. Since then we have tried her in several different positions.

We finally became convinced that the girl was not moral and took her to Dr. X., of the Psychopathic Clinic, for an examination. He pronounced her feeble-minded to such a degree that she would be unable to protect herself; and as she is a pretty girl, it seems extremely dangerous for her to be at large. I had a chance to place her with a woman I could trust and did this in the hope of hearing from her people in Hungary something about her. I have had a reply to the first letter we wrote, saying that she ran away and that her people are extremely poor.[1]

She is now at the Detention Home of the Juvenile Court on the charge of stealing from the people with whom I placed her, and she will remain there until your Department is able to take some action. I have written Dr. X. that you will send him a statement to be filled out and signed by him as to the girl's mental condition, but I thought that in the meantime you would be able to "verify her landing."

Yours very sincerely,

LYDIA GARDNER

2. A letter to Dr. X., of the Psychopathic Clinic, from the Director of the Immigrants' Protective League, dated May 13, 1913:

MY DEAR DOCTOR X.:

I have just asked Mr. Roberts, the Immigration Inspector, to send you the blanks to fill out in the case of Katie Schultz. I had placed Katie in a home where I thought she would be safe until we should have replies from the letters written to Hungary. I had one letter, saying that the girl had

[1] [At this time the League had learned very little about the relatives of Katie Schultz in Hungary. The girl, however, left at the League at different times a letter she had received and copies of two letters she had written home. She enjoyed writing and receiving letters and wished the League superintendent to know that she could write and that she had friends at home. The three letters are of some interest and are given below.]

Letter to Katie Schulz from a friend in Hungary, Justina Reis [translation from the German]:

January 26, 1913

BEST FRIEND, GOOD BEST OF ALL FRIENDS:

With joy in my heart I am taking the pen in my right hand and write to you in an unknown country. I have to thank you in short and I think you will always remain my best friend.

Dear friend, I cannot express strongly enough how much I enjoyed your writing, and I have to write you that I would be glad to come to you but I have no money. I would be glad to go with you for walks as we used to do at home. Dear friend, I was glad to hear that you are going to send me something and I am curious to know what you are going to send.

Maybe you will send me a little money in remembrance, because I think you have very much money now, and it would make me much joy if you could put a few dollar bills in a letter, then I would buy something for myself and always think of you. If you will do it, put the dollar in the center of the letter so that it shall be hidden and nobody shall see it. Best Katie, I some day will come and see you and will not forget how good you have been to me. Dear friend, I would have been glad if you were here on "fasching" day [German holiday with carnival], you could have danced a great deal and all the boys that know you and my brother would have been glad too. Just wait, maybe I will be soon able to come to you, we will then be jolly. If I only had money I would come right now, and then we could together come home from work.

Dear comrade, at home it is very cold and also very jolly, and I am lonesome for you and constantly thinking if I could only once more see Katie.

Dear friend, how are you? I hope better than I am. Therefore I would be glad if you would send me a few dollars, when I will come to you I will repay it. Whatever you do, I will always remain your truest friend and will never forget

run away, that her parents had no knowledge of where she was going, but I am waiting to hear more of the girl's and her mother's history. However, the woman with whom I placed her had trouble with Katie and refuses to keep her so that I have placed her in the Detention Home and asked Mr. Roberts to proceed with the matter of deportation.

Yours very sincerely,
LYDIA GARDNER

3. Letter, not dated, from Katie Schultz, awaiting deportation at Ellis Island, to the Director of the Immigrants' Protective League, received June 16, 1913 [translation]:

DEAR MISS LYDIA GARDNER:

In the beginning of my letter I send you my regards. Then I come to inform you that I am still not on the steamer. I don't even know how long I will have to remain here, I think a week more. I have been so sick on the train I think I shall be sick on the ship too, but may God help me, that I shall be well, this is the best I can hope in the world since I left Chicago. Finally with regards I close my letter, while from my eyes are running the tears. Please answer me immediately. I am in Ellis Island's House. Good night,

KATIE SCHULTZ

---

you. My mother, brother, and sister were very glad that you thought of me and they send their regards.

Now I have to close my poor letter because tears are dropping from my eyes. I close my letter with many thousand hearty regards and kisses and remain your true friend until death.

[The following lines are written in verse:]

Dear letter, do not fly too high or too low and bring me soon an answer; and again do not fly too high or too deep so that you should not forget your way. Look who signed the letter.—JUSTINA REIS.

When in Rossidisch the bell is ringing and in the air a bird is singing, then my heart is burdened and I wish I were near you.

Write to me at once and I will answer you also at once. Many hearty thanks from your true friend,

JUSTINA·REIS

Letter from Katie Schultz in Chicago to Justina Reis in Hungary, dated March 21, 1913 [translation]:

DEAR FRIEND:

With a joyful heart I take the pen in my right hand and write to you right back. Dear friend, did you receive my letter or not, I wrote to you two letters and did not receive from you any. Dear friend, how is it at home? It is very cold. Here it is very cold. Dear Justina, I like this place and I wish you a happy Easter. Dear friend, this letter I am writing to you on Palm Sunday. It is very cold here. I cannot go out at all, I am always at home.

Dear friend, how is Theresa Erhelyi, is she the same as she was? I do not write any more to her. She was the reason that I have to work. I cannot forget how she acted toward me. I cannot forget this, but God shall help me I shall be good. Dear friend, you know it from Maria how she was to me. I shiver in my dreams.

Dear friend, you cannot even imagine how life is here. When I come from work I have to take the car. Sometimes I walk and then such men (robbers) are

4. A second letter from Katie Schultz at Ellis Island to the Director of the Immigrants' Protective League; letter received June 20, 1913 [translation]:

DEAR MISS GARDNER:

With sadness in my heart I take the pen to write you a few lines, because I have to inform you that I have to wait so long for the steamer. Because I have been so long sick on the train I did not eat anything. I think I will be sick on the ship too. Besides this I cannot write anything more. I will write you on the water. I will close my letter. Good night from

KATIE

5. Letter dated June 20, 1913, from a foreign-speaking social worker at Ellis Island to the Director of the Immigrants' Protective League [the League had asked the social worker to look after Katie]:

MY DEAR LEAGUE PROTECTIVE:

To Katie Schultz I gave the whole dollar because when I asked her what she wants me to buy for her, she said that she does not need anything. I wonder if she was a bad character as they kept her locked up with such.

Respectfully yours,

MARIA Z.

---

standing and when the girls pass by they say, "Money or your life," and so they have to give up their money. And once, it was seven o'clock and I was passing by and five men were standing and they said, "Money or your life." But there was a policeman, and he heard me scream.

Dear friend, I do not go out at all. Where shall I go? It is very cold. And now I will finish my poor letter this time and I remain your best friend until death. My address is 70 Ewing Street, Chicago. Send me right away an answer if you received my letter or not.

Letter from Katie Schultz to her mother in Hungary, dated March 21, 1913 [translation]:

DEAR MOTHER:

At the beginning of my writing I am sending my regards and letting you know that I did not have any time to write to you sooner, but now I have the time to write to you.

Dear mother, I wrote to grandfather and grandmother and Maria also at the same time as I wrote to you. Don't be vexed with me that I did not write for so long for I did not have any time. I have to sew dresses all the time. All together I have eight dollars this week. This makes it nice for me. Every week I pay in 25 cents and in a year I will have 200 dollars and in case I die you will get the money and this is the reason why it is good for you also.

Dear Mother, how are you and how is everybody at home? Is Maria better? How is Juliana? Is she still with you? I hope she is. Answer me at once, dear Mother, if you did receive my letter or not. I wrote already twice and you never answer. I do not know what happens that you do not answer. I do not know what to think about it; maybe you are sick. Write me at once what is going on at home. I hope everything is all right.

Dear Mother, I have such a good position at the house of a German lady. She is so good to me. She has two daughters. Her husband died. She has one daughter a year and four months old and the other is eight months old. The lady does the cooking the sewing and she has no friends here just like me. Now I will close my letter and please answer soon. My address is Katie Schultz, 70 Ewing Street, Chicago. I remain your daughter,

KATIE

6. Letter to the Inspector-in-Charge, United States Immigration Service, Chicago, dated June 23, 1913, from the Director of the Immigrants' Protective League:

MY DEAR MR. ROBERTS:

I have just received word that Katie Schultz was confined while at Ellis Island with the prostitutes. As this, of course, was the worst possible thing that could happen to the girl, and there was no occasion for it, I wonder if you could not investigate it.

Yours very sincerely,

LYDIA GARDNER

7. Letter, dated June 27, 1913, from the Inspector-in-Charge, United States Immigration Service, Chicago, to the Director of the Immigrants' Protective League:

Referring to your letter of the 23d instant, the Commissioner of Immigration at Ellis Island states that Katie Schultz was not confined with any prostitutes.

8. Letter, not dated, but received June 29, 1913, from Madame Klomser, a correspondent of the League, in Budapest, Hungary:

MY DEAR MISS GARDNER:

I have been trying all I could to get a home for your poor feeble-minded girl, but it is hard because she is no child, eighteen years old, and not a complete idiot. Now I shall hear from two places on Monday if they will take her but please let me know when she comes for I must know exactly with which boat she arrives. I hope that Baron Villani in Fiume will take care of her for a few days, till I can get her to a place where she is well taken care of. Is she Roman Catholic or Protestant? This is a question of importance. I asked Judge M— to come to see me, he may be able to help. I wrote to Mr. B— if he could take her to Tolna, for such easy work in the silk factory she could easily do. I am waiting for his answer since yesterday and shall let you know what he thinks about it.

With hearty greetings, dear Miss Gardner, believe me,

Yours sincerely,

CHARLOTTE KLOMSER

9. Letter from Madame Charlotte Klomser, of Budapest, dated June 24, 1913:

MY DEAR MISS GARDNER:

I received this minute your letter of June 12 and would be so glad if I could do something for Katie Schultz, but it is doubtful if we can help much since she is returning by way of a French port. Havre is so far, and I do not know how to reach the poor girl. We have been expecting her in Fiume and Baron Villani wrote to me just yesterday about her. He said that everything is arranged to receive her in Fiume and to have her sent to a home if necessary and if she is fit for the place of Mr. B— he will take her to Tolna, he wrote me this also yesterday. Now you tell me that she is sailing for Havre and arrives there day after tomorrow. I cannot possibly be there at such very short notice; it is now evening and so we only have tomorrow at our disposal. I wonder who will send her to Hungary and where she will be sent to. How shall I know? If they could only have sent her to a southeastern port! How shall she find her way and will she not be lost in France where she does not know the language? It is a great pity that this was done in this way. . . . .

CHARLOTTE KLOMSER

10. Letter from Madame Klomser written from Villa Rosenhof, Bavaria, and dated July 25, 1913:

MY DEAR MISS GARDNER:

I am waiting many days for an answer from Budapest and Paris, to let you know more about poor Katie Schultz. As I received your letter just now, I hasten to tell you all I know about the poor girl. We had telegraphed to Paris to have someone meet her at the boat in Havre, and it was good that we did so, as the poor girl arrived sick with convulsions and delirious and had to be taken to some home or asylum. After a few days she was sent on to Paris, from where they will send her on to Hungary as soon as it is possible. His Excellency told me that he is ready to pay her trip to Tolna, if she is able to be in his place. I am waiting most anxiously for news from her but cannot do anything till she is in Hungary. I understand from your letter that your government sent her to Havre because she originally sailed on a French boat. I wonder only how Katie ever got to Havre from her little village and where she got the money for her journey. . . . .

CHARLOTTE KLOMSER

11. Letter from a Hungarian local officer, dated October 28, 1913, to the Immigrants' Protective League, replying to inquiries about Katie Schultz [translated from the Magyar]:

DEAR SIR:

We received your nice letter and have the pleasure to notify your office that Katie Schultz arrived safe from the United States to her birthplace and is still staying there. We have already made arrangements for supporting the girl; she will be taken in a short time to the Working Woman's Home in the town of Szegexard. We hope that she will be better in this home. With special and best regards,

Yours truly,
X. Y.

12. Letter from Madame Klomser, undated, received November 14, 1913:

MY DEAR MISS GARDNER:

At last I can give you news about poor Katie Schultz. At last they answered one of my letters and told me that she had arrived in her native village and was well but without work, the same as her very poor mother. I wrote at once to his Excellency, and he promised to take her to Tolna and pay her there if she was able to do the work there. I have not had any news yet if she is settled in Tolna but hope to hear soon. When I come to Budapest I shall try to find out how she could get to America without money and from Havre. . . . .

CHARLOTTE KLOMSER

426 IMMIGRATION: DOCUMENTS AND CASE RECORDS

13. Letter from Madame Klomser, dated November 16, 1913, Budapest, to the Immigrants' Protective League:

MY DEAR MISS GARDNER:

Katie Schultz has just left me; she is well and will be in Tolna under his Excellency's charge! As I cannot leave my room, his Excellency was kind enough to send me the girl here accompanied by her uncle and the director of the factory of Tolna. Katie Schultz was sick on her way back on the steamship. She was spitting blood and seems not to remember about the brain trouble she had. She was in Havre only a few days till she was taken to Paris, where she was with a saloonkeeper's wife, a good woman. The next day she was taken by a matron to Basel, and from there a man took her to Vienna, from here the agent brought her back to Serosszik. Her mother gave her 400 kronen for her trip and with two other girls and a married woman whose husband lives in America she started for Vienna. A countryman waited for her at the station in Vienna and took her to the French line. There they were sent to Havre without papers. It seems that all the people from that part of the country go all by the French line and do not need any papers or are supplied there with some kind of documents. Katie seems to be quite cheerful and is proud that she can speak a little English. She began to cry when I mentioned your name; she says you were always good to her and she wants to write to you some day. I am glad we got the girl at last and have her at Tolna, where she will be happy and have a healthy home.

With warm greetings, I remain,

Yours faithfully,

CHARLOTTE KLOMSER

14. Extract of a letter from Madame Klomser, of Budapest, dated December 9, 1913, to Miss Lydia Gardner:

I had several letters from his Excellency. He is so kind to write to me all about Katie Schultz. The first days she cried quite a bit, because she can't talk to her companions, who do not speak German. She could only speak to the foreman and the matron. His Excellency found out some one who knows German and made them work together. Now Katie is as happy as a bird, she learns Hungarian so quickly that she will be able to speak it quite well in two or three months. She likes her work, is very diligent. The first to begin and the last to stop with the work. She is so clever that they are going to put her in a part of the factory where it is more difficult, but where she earns more money. His Excellency says that neither he nor anyone else could find why one would call her feeble-minded, she is quite bright and all are fond of her. Nor could I find her feeble-minded, she must have been shy and as she did not speak sufficient English I dare say they said so. It is a great blessing you found the poor girl and took so much interest in her, else she would have been lost entirely. I think it is more than hard for your government to send back such a poor girl, without any proper reason. She has been operated on in Chicago and perhaps one thought she would not be able to earn her living. The poor mother had given her all her money, 400 crowns, to have her go to America to earn much money. Now the girl was sent back and would have been lost in France not speaking the language, if one could not have had some one meet her at the boat. Well I hope all will be for her best and she will be quite happy in her new home. I shall send her something for Xmas in your name.

When she came to see me in the hotel she was so shy and would not speak until I gave her your parcel with the little present which I said you had sent from Chicago. She began to cry and said how good you and "the other ladies" had been to her. . . . .

CHARLOTTE KLOMSER

44. Hedwig Kallen
(Bringing over Relatives—Physical Defects)

July 28, 1913.—Joseph Kallen, address 500 Maxwell Street, in the office. He wishes to bring over his two sisters, Hedwig and Raisa. Hedwig is totally blind. She was engaged to a man by the name of Jacob Lasky[1] and broke her engagement, whereupon he threw a bottle of vitriol in her face, which disfigured her and left her blind. The brother's account of the situation is this: The mother of the two girls and two brothers and two other sisters are all in the United States living at 800 Maxwell Street and are very unhappy about the girls' being left alone in Russia and are willing to make any sacrifice to bring them in. The family tried to bring the girls over when the mother came and a steamship ticket was bought for Hedwig as well as for Raisa, but steamship company refused to let Hedwig go on board after examination. Raisa, a sister aged sixteen, was therefore left behind with the blind Hedwig. Relatives here include, in addition to the mother, the following persons: Brother, Joseph Kallen, a printer in the firm of Henry & Co., earning $24 per week regularly. He is married, lives at 500 Maxwell Street, and will become a full citizen in October. He is buying a $700 lot at State and 73d Street. Brother, Jake Kallen, sixteen years old, printer in the firm of Rosen and Matz, 1007 S. Johnson, earning $9 per week. Sister, Jennie Kallen, nineteen years old, who is a milliner, earning $15 a week. Sister, Mrs. Bertha Sachs, husband Harry Sachs, a tailor, earning $35 per week. He is buying an $800 lot at Greenwood and 91st Avenue. Uncle, Jake Albright, 120 Twelfth Street, who is a carpenter, earning $28. He owns in partnership with his brother, Morris Albright, a house and lot where he lives, which he values at $4,000. Uncle, Morris Albright, who is also a carpenter, earning $28 per week, and owning in partnership with his brother Jake the house and lot at 120 Twelfth Street. Uncle, Harry Beeman, 6 Hill Street. He owns a delicatessen store worth $2,000 and also real estate at 30 Oakwood Street and in New Chicago which he values at $3,000.

Brother (Joseph) says he recently went to see Mr. Roberts, the Inspector-in-Charge, United States Immigration Service, and Mr. Roberts thought Hedwig might be admitted and gave him affidavits to fill out, but family

[1] [There is a cross-reference to the case of Jacob Lasky, who migrated to the United States. The relatives of Hedwig Kallen, however, had reported his conduct to the Immigrants' Protective League, and the League helped to secure his deportation. The man refused to return to Poland after his deportation and remained in Paris.]

do not wish to repeat the former experience of getting her to port of departure and of having her refused admission before the boat sails and when they explain circumstances to steamship companies to try to obtain assurances that she will be allowed on board, the companies will not sell a ticket. If girl could be got to Ellis Island, family think they could give bonds to prevent deportation. Told Mr. Kallen that League will write to Commissioner-General of Immigration and also will interview some steamship officials and will let him know what we think can be done.

September 2, 1913.—The following letter written to the Commissioner-General of Immigration:

I am writing to ask your advice about a girl named Hedwig Kallen, now in Russia, who wishes to come to the United States. This girl broke her engagement with a man named Jacob Lasky, whereupon he threw a bottle of vitriol in her face, which blinded her. The man tried to escape to the United States, but her relatives and the Immigrants' Protective League assisted in having him deported when he reached Ellis Island. The girls' mother, two brothers, and two sisters are in this country and are fairly well-to-do. One brother will become a citizen in October, and several relatives are property-owners. However, no steamship company will sell a ticket for this girl.

I know that, as a general policy, your department will not state in advance what the probabilities of admission may be for any particular alien. I wonder, however, whether an exception may be made in this case. We would be glad to know whether she would have any chance of admission, providing there were no other complications not stated herein. The girl is blind but otherwise in good health. She would travel with her sister. The relatives are willing to deposit with any company money to cover the expense of her deportation, but we have advised them that such an arrangement is contrary to a provision of the Immigration Law. Assuring you that we shall be very grateful for a reply with regard to this, I am,

Very truly yours,

LYDIA GARDNER

September 9, 1913.—The following reply received from the Commissioner-General:

Miss Lydia Gardner
Immigrants' Protective League
Chicago, Illinois

DEAR MADAM: The Bureau is in receipt of your letter dated September 2d, requesting information as to whether an exception will be made in the case of the alien Hedwig Kallen, who has been refused passage to this country on account of blindness caused by acid thrown by Jacob Lasky, who was deported by the Department March 7, 1911. You desire to know whether Miss Kallen would have any chance of admission, provided there were no other complications.

In reply I beg to state that no decision can be rendered in advance and no assurance given whatsoever. The question of admissibility has been vested, by law, in the inspection officers at the port of entry, and the right of this Department limited to those cases which come before it on appeal from an excluding decision of the Board of Special Inquiry. It is suggested that in the event the said alien secures passage, the inclosed affidavit form be filed by the relatives in accordance with instructions printed thereon, but it is understood that this is in no sense a guaranty of landing. It is offered as a means of placing before the examining officers such facts as will enable them to dispose promptly of the case.

Very truly yours,

September 10, 1913.—Telephoned North German Lloyd and White Star lines. Both companies say that no steamship company will sell a ticket for the girl. *Later.*—Letter written to Joseph Kallen. [Letter notifies him of the decision of the Commissioner-General and tells him that the League will take up the matter again in October after he gets his citizenship papers.]

October 14, 1913.—Letter to Joseph Kallen. [Letter asks if he has become a citizen and if he still wishes help about his sister.]

November 11, 1913.—The following letter received:

I received your kind letters for which I am much obliged to you for your remembrance. I did not answer you in the first letter you sent me because that was a week before I could go for my second papers but now I wish to tell you that I have not taken them out because one of my witnesses was sick that day and I could not go with one witness so I don't know when I could go again to ask for my papers. I wrote a letter this week to the chief of naturalization to inform me when my time will be to come again so the first thing I'll hear from him, I will come up to see you. We are very thankful to you for your favors.

Respectfully yours,

JOSEPH KALLEN

November 25, 1913.—Joseph Kallen telephoned that he has his citizenship papers and family wish League to do whatever can be done about the sister.

December 6, 1913.—Spoke with Miss Green, who is a daughter of the local manager of the Royal Blue Line. She will talk with her father and let us know what he thinks of the situation.

December 17, 1913.—Mrs. Kallen, mother of girl, in office. She is heartbroken and cried when she tried to talk about Hedwig. She cannot bear to think of the two girls left behind in Russia. She thinks she ought to return to Russia if they cannot come here.

January 6, 1914.—Report from Miss Green. Her father thinks the case hopeless. Nothing can be done.

February 21, 1914.—Joseph Kallen in office. He has moved to 473 Fairview Avenue, telephone Rockwell 6550. If the League finds any way to help him, he asks us to send him word.

April 11, 1914.—Joseph Kallen in office to ask advice about returning to Russia. He spoke with N. R. [Russian visitor]. He says if the case is hopeless, he thinks probably it will be advisable for him to go back to Russia with the mother. They simply cannot live here without the girls. Told Mr. Kallen that League was not hopeless about case though as yet we had no plan to propose. Advised him not to go back since the family are all doing well now but to wait and see if we cannot find some plan to bring Hedwig in under bond. He said he would talk it over with his mother. Told him that Miss Gardner [Superintendent] has been away from the League for some months and when she returns probably next month she may have some new plan to suggest.

April 20, 1914.—N. R. interviewed local head of Russian Trade Line. He thinks his company might sell the ticket if League thinks girl would be admitted. He asked if family would deposit $100 to cover steamship company fine in case of deportation. Explained to him that this was probably not legal, and we could not advise this plan. Told him family could pay for bond and if girl got to Ellis Island we felt sure she could be admitted on bond. He wishes to refer the matter to the general office in New York before definitely promising to carry passenger and would like to have a letter containing all the facts. *Later.*—Telephoned Joseph Kallen to come to office tomorrow.

April 21, 1914.—Mr. Kallen in office to give present occupation and wages of all members of family. [These facts are omitted since they do not differ materially except as to addresses, and Joseph Kallen's citizenship, from the statement already given.]

Gave Mr. Kallen letter to Russian Trade Line. [This letter contains detailed statement about circumstances of family and also states that family are quite willing to buy second-class tickets for both girls.]

May 4, 1914.—Mr. Kallen in office. He says Russian Trade Line will carry the two passengers if round-trip tickets are purchased. Fare will be as follows, second-class per passage: Alexandroff to Chicago via Halifax $57.95, via New York $62.45. From Alexandroff to Chicago via New York, and return from New York $96.90, for both $193.80. The company will refund return fare if girls are admitted, probably without deducting commission. Mr. Kallen says family are willing to pledge (deposit) $100 to pay fine in case of deportation. N. R. explained that company was probably not allowed to do this, and League would not wish to have anything to do about it.

October 9, 1914.—Joseph Kallen in office. He says all arrangements had been completed about his sister's coming over when the war started. Now his mother cries all the time. The family are terribly depressed about the situation. Everything is hopeless. Man says "the poor are used to suffer, but this is killing my mother." Told him we would try to send a letter and some money to the girls through the American Consul. He left sealed envelope for League to send.

October 19, 1914.—The following letter sent:

The United States Consul
Warsaw, Russia

MY DEAR SIR: Joseph Kallen, an American citizen, the brother of Hedwig Kallen, to whom the inclosed is addressed, is very anxious about his sister. He has requested that you convey to her, if possible, the inclosed envelope. He would appreciate very much any information that you might be able to send to us regarding the girl.

Very truly yours,

LYDIA GARDNER
(For the Immigrants' Protective League)

December 14, 1914.—The following reply received·

AMERICAN CONSULAR SERVICE
WARSAW, RUSSIA
November 8, 1914

Immigrants' Protective League
Chicago, Illinois

DEAR SIRS: In reply to your letter of the 19th ult. regarding Miss Kallen and enclosing a letter to her, I have to inform you that the town of Alexandrowo is the boundary station between Russia and Germany, and communication with that point which controls the main railroad line into Germany was interrupted on the day war was declared, on August 1st, and has been occupied by the Germans ever since. It has been ascertained that many miles of track running from Alexandrowo into Russia are destroyed, while on the other hand it is not unlikely that the German side is still intact. The only way, therefore, to reach Miss Kallen, at least at present, would be via Germany through the American Consul at Stettin. Of course, should communication be restored with Alexandrowo, I will immediately attempt to reach Miss Kallen.

Very respectfully yours,

HENRY CHARLES, *American Consul*

December 15, 1914.—Letter written to Stettin as follows:

The American Consul
Stettin, Germany

MY DEAR SIR: Joseph Kallen, an American citizen, whose sister Hedwig Kallen is at Alexandroff, Russia, is very much concerned about her. The girl, who is twenty-one years old, is blind and has only a younger sister in Russia with her. We wrote the American Consul at Warsaw, inclosing a letter which Mr. Kallen was anxious to get to his sister, but we have just had a reply stating that up to date it had been impossible for him to communicate with her and suggesting that we write you. We shall be very grateful if you will try to find her and advise us.

Yours very sincerely,

LYDIA GARDNER
(For the Immigrants' Protective League)

February 12, 1915.—Letter received from Stettin, Germany, dated January 18, 1915:

Immigrants' Protective League
Chicago, Illinois

In answer to your inquiry regarding Hedwig Kallen, said to be in Alexandroff, Russia, I beg to say, that the American Consul at Warsaw probably referred you to me because the town Alexandroff is located in western Poland, in territory now occupied by the German army. I shall be glad to do all I can to communicate with the girl, but am not certain whether I shall be successful.

Very respectfully yours,

Robert Johnson, *American Consul*

Later.—Letter written to Joseph Kallen:

My dear Mr. Kallen:

The inclosed letter we received yesterday from the American Consul at Stettin, Germany. So far as we can see there is nothing to do but wait for a further communication from him. We believe that he will do whatever is possible.

Very truly yours,

Immigrants' Protective League

Later.—The following letter sent to Stettin:

Dear Sir:

We are very grateful for your letter of January 18th relating to Hedwig Kallen who is thought to be in Alexandroff. We are inclosing herewith a letter which her relatives wish to have forwarded to her. We hope very much that you may be successful in reaching the girl.

Very truly yours,

Immigrants' Protective League

March 2, 1915.—Mr. Kallen in office. Present address 1020 Linden Avenue. He wishes the League to ask the Russian Trade Line about the tickets purchased in spring of 1914. The Kallens paid $124.90 for two tickets second class prepaid passage contract, No. 8205, to be sent May 4, 1914, to the sister in Alexandroff. The Kallens say that tickets had been received and that the sisters had applied for passports before the war.

[The record here contains some correspondence with the Russian Trade Line regarding the possible cancellation of the tickets. Mr. Kallen finally decided that he did not want to have the tickets cancelled but wished to let them stand as they were so that his sister might come on as soon as conditions were favorable.]

SOCIAL CASE RECORDS 433

April 10, 1915.—The following letter and inclosure received:

FILE No. 703, AMERICAN CONSULAR SERVICE
STETTIN, GERMANY
March 13, 1915

Immigrants' Protective League
Chicago, Illinois

SIR: In reply to your letter dated February 12 last, I beg to state that I have forwarded to the authorities at Alexandrowo the letter you sent me for Hedwig Kallen and I hope that she will receive it. I also did receive a letter from the Mayor of Alexandrowo addressed to the "Kaiserl. Deutschen Civil Commissar" at Alexandrowo. A copy of that letter you find enclosed, which is self-explanatory.

Very respectfully yours,
EMIL SCHMIDT
American Vice-Consul in Charge

[Inclosure; translation from the German:]

To the German Imperial "Civil Commissar":

The following reply is respectfully submitted: That Hedwig Kallen has lived here many years and has had no other resource during the whole time except the material assistance given by her relatives now resident in Chicago. Since the outbreak of the war, that is, for more than seven months, there has been no possibility of her receiving any help whatever from America, and for this reason she finds herself in a very painful situation. The parish in which she lives can not help her much, for it has very small means at its disposal. If there should be any possibility now of permitting Hewdig Kallen to receive money from America this would be very desirable. It is indeed true that Hedwig Kallen is totally blind and that she has remained here under the protection of her younger sister, who is seventeen years old. Shortly before the outbreak of the war the sisters received steamship tickets from America with instructions to proceed via Libau. Since this is no longer possible, the undersigned respectfully inquires whether the sisters could not in the future undertake the journey to America through Germany. In this case the steamship tickets must be exchanged.

B. BODOWIG, *Burgomaster*

April 12, 1915.—N. R. [Russian visitor] called on Joseph Kallen, 1020 S. Linden Avenue. Left with him the letter and inclosure received from Stettin. Advised him to send money to Hedwig through the Chicago Jewish Relief, of which Mr. W. J. Kohn is secretary. He proposed sending some through a steamship agent as others are doing. Advised against this plan.

April 20, 1915.—Mr. Kallen called. He sent $15 to Hedwig through Jewish Relief Committee.

July 7, 1915.—Mr. Kallen telephoned that he has had a card from his sister in Alexandrowo, mailed sometime in May. They have not had a letter from America for a year, they need money and had, of course, not yet received the $15 sent through Jewish Relief Committee. He sent some money through postoffice on Saturday; it was accepted all right.

August 26, 1915.—Mr. Kallen in office. The money sent through Jewish Relief Committee and also through postoffice was not received, wanted to know whether League would send money to American Consul and have him forward it to Alexandrowo. Promised to consult Miss Gardner and notify him soon.

August 30, 1915.—Telephoned Mr. Kallen and informed him that League would be glad to send money to consul, advised him to send about $20. He will bring money to office this week.

September 4, 1915.—Mr. Kallen in office with money, $15. Telephoned Jewish Relief Committee. They said they had just had word from European Committee that money was delivered to Hedwig. Sent Mr. Kallen back to Jewish Relief Committee and advised him to send money through them again.

September 10, 1915.—Mr. Kallen in office, says he sent the $15 through Jewish Relief Committee as advised but of course has heard nothing yet. Family very anxious.

October 2, 1915.—Mr. Kallen in office. He has a letter from girl written in German saying she had received the money sent through Jewish Relief Committee. He also had letter from American Consul saying money could now be forwarded to her through American Express Company. Advised him to reply in German as this might avoid delay. He cannot write German. Told him to dictate and we will write for him. Letter in German sent. He will send money through Jewish Relief Committee unless they advise changing to American Express Company.

January 28, 1916.—Letter received from American Ambassador at Berlin, inclosing copy of letter from Consul at Warsaw:

WARSAW, RUSSIA
January 6, 1916

Hon. James W. Gerard, American Ambassador
Berlin, Germany

SIR: I have the honor respectfully to request the Embassy kindly to notify the Immigrants' Protective League, 743 Plymouth Court, Chicago, Illinois, that referring to the League's letter of October 10, 1914, and other correspondence as to the well-being of Hedwig and Raisa Kallen, this Consulate has to report, that, so soon as the postal service with Alexandrowo, Province of Warsaw, was open from this side, an inquiry was sent to the authorities there, who now state that the ladies are not to be found in that place. Thanking the Embassy for its courtesy, I have the honor to be, Sir,
Your obedient servant,

HENRY CHARLES, *American Consul*

N.B.—The letter for Miss Hedwig from her brother is being retained here in the event of her being located later.—C.

February 1, 1916.—Saw Mr. W. J. Kohn, Secretary, Jewish Relief Committee. He said there was a Jewish Relief Society in Hamburg, Germany, and he thinks it is still in existence. He says that Mr. Abraham Stein has a friend who was a very active member of that organization and advised us to take matter up with Mr. Stein. *Later.*—Telephoned Mr. Kallen, told him of letter from Ambassador Gerard.

February 11, 1916.—Letter written to Mr. Abraham Stein, containing the following:

Do you think it would be possible for you to get someone in Berlin interested in the case of Hedwig Kallen, a Russian-Jewish girl whose relatives wish to bring her to the United States. She is twenty-two years old and is in Alexandrowo near Warsaw with a younger sister. A rejected suitor threw vitriol at Hedwig and destroyed her sight. A brother, Joseph, a United States citizen, a married sister, and three uncles are in Chicago. They have supported the girls for many years. After much difficulty they arranged for them to come to the United States on the Russian Trade Line, but the war broke out just at the time when their tickets reached them. The brother is afraid, and I share his fear, that after the war is over it will be increasingly difficult to secure the admission of a blind person. It seemed to me it might be possible for someone in Berlin to persuade some steamship company to take the girls. The brother wants to have them come second class and will be very glad to send the necessary money at any time.

We have had some correspondence in regard to them with the American Consul at Stettin and the Imperial German "Civil Commissar" in Alexandrowo—the latter suggested the possibility of their now coming to America through Germany. In the cases of other Russian subjects we have found there was much delay in getting permits to get out of Germany. A Polish family, for example, has been kept in Berlin some weeks although the American Consul has been interested in them and assures us the permit will be forthcoming. It would, therefore, be necessary to have someone look after these girls in Berlin.

Sincerely yours,

Lydia Gardner

February 18, 1916.—Letter from Mr. Stein inclosing a letter from Mr. Isaacs, of the American Jewish Relief Committee for Sufferers from the War, New York City:

Dear Mr. Stein:

We have a letter from Washington under date of February 16 as follows: "The matter of securing the admission into this country of Hedwig Kallen presents serious difficulties. The girl is, of course, clearly inadmissible under our immigration laws, and I believe it would be worse than useless to endeavor to secure any assurances from the Department of Labor that she would be admitted, presupposing that it would be possible to bring her here. In view of Secretary Wilson's statement at the relief meeting here that no deportations were being made to any of the countries at war, the thought occurred to me that if this girl could be gotten to the United States there might be a very good chance of having her admitted under bond to secure against any likelihood of her becoming a public charge. Although I could not ask the State Department to interpose officially in the matter, Mr. X. is willing to make a personal request to our Consul-General in Warsaw, that he do everything within his power to facilitate the departure of Miss Kallen. With the active assistance of the Consul-General it might not be so difficult to get the girl started to this country as it would be to secure her admission after she got here.

The Mr. X. mentioned is an official in the Consular Service. Might I suggest that the relatives of the girl may be communicated with and if they are willing to have her brought to this country on the chance of securing admission, after she gets here, I will immediately have Mr. X. communicate with the Consul-General in Warsaw that he facilitate her departure from Warsaw.

Very truly yours,
J. L. Isaacs

February 19, 1916.—Mr. Kallen called up saying that he wrote Hedwig asking her to return the ticket orders. He wants to know whether it would be best to cancel tickets upon receipt of orders. Mr. Kallen fears that after the war it will be more difficult to secure Hedwig's admission into the United States. Informed him of letter from Mr. Isaacs and advised him to have $250 ready to send whenever notified. He said he could get money in a week.

March 4, 1916.—The following letter sent to Mr. Isaacs:

J. L. Isaacs, Esq.
The American Jewish Relief Committee
New York City

My dear Mr. Isaacs: Mr. Stein has suggested that I write you with regard to Hedwig Kallen, the blind Jewish girl, who together with her sister is in Alexandrowo near Warsaw. Her relatives here are very eager to have her brought to this country on the chance of securing her admission. Inasmuch as the members of the family here do not ever expect to return to Europe, they are, of course, very anxious to have the two sisters with them. They want to have them come second class, and I suppose the money had better be sent directly to you so that the tickets can be bought by your correspondent in Europe; or we can send the money directly to the girl through your Committee, whichever you suggest. With appreciation of your assistance in the matter, I am,

Sincerely yours,
Lydia Gardner

March 12, 1916.—Letter from Mr. Isaacs advising that money for tickets be sent directly to Hedwig Kallen and that she be told to see the American Consul-General at Warsaw, who has been notified about her.

March 14, 1916.—Mr. Kallen in office. He has received a card from Hedwig saying that she has moved to 22 Garden Street and that she and the sister are in good health. Mr. Kallen also said that he had the money ready to send. Advised him to send money to Hedwig through American Express Company.

March 17, 1916.—Letter sent to Mr. Isaacs containing the following:

We are arranging to have Hedwig Kallen's brother transmit the letter to her at once and also to inform her about going to the Consul-General at Warsaw. I am sure, however, that the real difficulty will be in purchasing a ticket to come to this country, and I hope very much that you will be able to connect with some one in Berlin who will help her in persuading a steamship company to sell her a second-class ticket.

April 23, 1916.—Mr. Kallen telephoned. He wishes to know if he can bring his mother to the office so she can dictate a letter to be written in German and sent to Hedwig and Raisa. Would like to come in evening. Appointment made for April 24.

April 24, 1916.—Mrs. Kallen and Joseph Kallen in office. The following letter written in German for Mrs. Kallen:

DEARLY BELOVED CHILDREN:

I inform you that in a few days we shall be sending $275 to your address. As soon as you shall receive this money, go with this letter to the American Consul in Warsaw where the Consul will read this and will tell you what you are to do with the money. The Immigrants' Protective League in Chicago (*Einwanderungs Schutz Gesellschaft*) has already been corresponding with the Hebrew Immigrant Aid Society of New York about your situation and it has been arranged that the American Consulate will help you to leave. When the money comes be careful to give it to no one except to the American Consul himself or put it in a bank which he recommends to you. Do not fail to go immediately to the Consul when the money arrives and ask for his advice.

We hope you are well and that we shall see you soon. With most loving greetings and embracing you both,

MIRIAM KALLEN

103 LOGAN AVENUE
CHICAGO, ILLINOIS

[The record from June 24–27 contains entries relating to the sending of $10 on June 24, by Mrs. Kallen, who came in to report what she had heard from the Jewish Committee, and again to send another $10, and again to write another letter to her daughters.]

September 6, 1916.—Following letter written for the Kallens in German:

DEAR CHILDREN:

On the 24th of April we wrote you a long letter in German but we have not yet had any reply from you. We also sent money to you but we have had no word about it. Please let us know what is happening to you and how you are. Are you well? We are all well but we think of you constantly and hope before long to bring you here out of your sad condition. We greet you a thousand times and hope soon to see you.

YOUR MOTHER AND BROTHERS AND SISTERS

[Entries from January 1, 1917, to June, 1917, relate chiefly to the attempt, finally successful, to collect back from the Russian Trade Line the refund on the tickets and the deposit. On June 11, 1917, Mrs. Kallen begs the League to help her send some money to her girls but is told no money can be sent now. From June, 1917, to January, 1918, efforts are made to send letters and money to Hedwig through the assistance of the Spanish Embassy,

Washington, D.C. February 4, 1918, the League is notified by the Spanish Ambassador to communicate with the "War Trade Board," Washington, D.C., who have been vested with power to grant licenses to send money or communications to the Central Powers.]

July 18, 1917.—The following letter was written in German for Mrs. Kallen:

Hedwig and Raisa Kallen
Schul Strasse 6
Alexandrowo, Russ. Polen.

My dear Children: For many months I have been expecting a letter from you, and I am very unhappy about your situation. I can do nothing at all about sending you money or tickets. I beg that you write us only a single post card. Perhaps that will reach me. We are all well, but we have a heavy care that we do not know that you remain well. This letter I am sending you in German through the Spanish consul in Washington and if this letter should reach you will you not try to find someone who will help you write to us in the same way? We are praying that you are well, we greet you and embrace you.

Your devoted mother,
MIRIAM KALLEN

103 LOGAN AVENUE
CHICAGO, ILLINOIS

February 7, 1918.—The following letter was sent to the War Trade Board, Washington, D.C.:

We write to ask if it will be possible to send money to a Jewish girl named Hedwig Kallen now living in Alexandroff, Russia. Her brother is Joseph Kallen, 103 Logan Avenue, Chicago. Miss Kallen is blind, and her possible sufferings are a cause of anxiety to her family. We also wish to know if money can be sent to the family of Samuel Leven, 2519 Cortez Street, Chicago. His wife and daughter Rachel were at Pinsk, Minsk Gubernia, Russia. If it is possible to send the money these men will forward it as soon as we get exact directions from you.

[Efforts to get word from the girls through the War Trade Board were unsuccessful.]

November 4, 1918.—M. C. visited Mrs. Kallen. She has had no word from her daughters. Explained that we could now write through the Red Cross. She will be glad to try this. Left blank to be filled out for Red Cross.

December 18, 1918.—Mr. Joseph Kallen called. Paid five dollars as contribution to League. Suggested he make this a membership. He is very grateful to the League. Family are doing well in business.

[From January 1 to June 1, 1919, the record shows that Mrs. Kallen comes to the office several times to write letters to her children. Letters are now written in Polish. In June, 1919, an attempt is made to communicate through the Hebrew Immigrant Aid Society. September 11, 1919, she came in with a card from Raisa, and the mother wrote again to her.]

January 20, 1920.—Mr. Kallen in the office. His mother died on January 16. He also wishes to tell the Immigrants' Commission [formerly Immigrants' Protective League] that he has heard rumors that Jacob Lasky, who blinded his sister, is again in New York. He has already reported case to Federal Immigration Office and left there the man's photograph and name and address of man's sister in New York. He had been sending money to his sisters through American Express and Western Union and every way he can hear of but Raisa writes they do not get any money. Today he called at the Western Union and was told that it will be possibly two months before they can tell whether the money was delivered. He wishes League to let him know when anything can be done.

March 11, 1920.—Joseph Kallen in office. He wishes to try again to bring over his sisters. Prepared a new affidavit for him as follows:

I, Joseph Kallen, being duly sworn, depose and state that I have been a citizen of the United States since 1913. I am a resident of Chicago and am living at 1617 Northern Avenue.

I respectfully ask that my sisters, Hedwig, 26 years old, and Raisa, 21 years old, be allowed to come to this country. They are now living at Ogvadova, Number 20, Warsaw Gubernia, Poland.

I further state I own the Victor Printing Company at 1617 Northern Avenue, which is valued at $5,000, have household furniture valued at $1,000 and own lot at State and 93rd Streets valued at $1,000. I further state that my sisters Hedwig and Raisa have $3,500 in insurance and savings left them by our mother, lately deceased. I ask that they be allowed to join me in the United States and guarantee that if admitted they will not become a public charge.

Letter written to American Ambassador in Warsaw, Poland. [Letter introduces Hedwig and her sister to the ambassador, contains brief statement about their conditions and adds:]

Except for these two girls all the family is in the United States. They are all responsible, hard-working people, who have made good in this country. There is no question about their being able to give satisfactory bonds guaranteeing support of the afflicted sister. The continued separation is such a cruel one that I hope very much that every possible assistance will be given to enable them to come to this country.

Yours very truly,

L. GARDNER

(*For the Immigrants' Commission of Illinois*)

September 7, 1920.—Mr. Kallen in office. He has received cable from Danzig representative of Hebrew Immigrant Aid Society as follows: "Consul advises that we go to America. Arrange State Department instruct Consul Danzig visa passport blind sister. Cable ticket Cunard. Instruct agent Danzig take sister aboard. Cable through HIAS 229 East Broadway, New York City, two hundred fifty dollars for expenses.—RAISA KALLEN, Troyl Danzig."

Last week he went to United States Commissioner Green, who made out affidavits and wrote letter to Consul Harry A. McBride, Warsaw, Poland, saying he requests "if consistent with your rules," that passport be visaed. Joseph Kallen has naturalization certificate No. 4088, Superior Court of Cook County, November 21, 1913. He thinks it will be necessary to take question up with the State Department.

September 8, 1920.—Letter to State Department. [Letter contains facts already stated about family and concludes as follows:]

The family have tried to get a visa for a Polish passport from the American Consul and have recently received a cable saying that our Consul at Danzig advises arrangements with the State Department for visa. I am inclosing affidavit, letter, and recommendations prepared by Commissioner Green to be forwarded to the American Consul at Warsaw. In view of the cable received and the fact that the girl has a physical defect affecting her ability to earn a livelihood, we are referring this to you. Personally, I have such confidence in the Kallens and sympathize so thoroughly with their desire to give their sister the affection and care which she can only have here that I hope very much it will be possible to visa the passport.

Yours very truly,
LYDIA GARDNER

September 9, 1920.—Wrote Hebrew Immigrant Aid Society. [Letter contains copy of cable received from the Hebrew Society, Danzig office, recites facts already known and concludes as follows:]

I have personally known the Kallens since 1913, and they have almost lived from year to year in the hope of getting this sister to the United States. The old mother died recently, leaving about $3,500 in insurance and savings for Hedwig, and the family here—two brothers, two sisters, and three uncles—are abundantly able and most eager to care for her. I have forwarded the papers and requests for authorization of visa to the State Department. If you have a local representative in Washington, I wish very much he might call and push the matter. Hedwig Kallen will be accompanied by her sister Raisa, aged 21 years. The Cunard Steamship Company informs Mr. Kallen that it will be necessary for the arrangements for steamship tickets to be made at their general offices in New York. Can you undertake to do this? Mr. Kallen will be glad to forward money at any time you may suggest.

Yours very truly,
LYDIA GARDNER

September 17, 1920.—Letter received from Hebrew Immigrant Aid Society containing the following:

In compliance with your request we are also writing to our Washington representative, to do whatever possible in order to expedite the obtaining of the visa. Concerning the steamship ticket, we wish to ask you to kindly advise Mr. Kallen that he should personally correspond with the Main Office of the Cunard Steamship Company, 24 State Street, New York City. We further suggest that instead of sending a steamship ticket, it would be more advisable to send funds as requested in the cablegram received by him from Danzig.

Very truly yours,
JACOB NATHAN, *General Manager*

October 4, 1920.—Brother in office. Showed him letter and explained that there is nothing to do until we hear from Washington or Hebrew Immigrant Aid Society.

October 14, 1920.—Man in office. Received letter from Hebrew Immigrant Aid Society that authorization has been cabled by State Department to Danzig for Commissioner to visa passport of sisters. Said he was going to communicate himself with Hebrew Society as to cabling money for tickets.

October 22, 1920.—Brother in office with the following letter from Hebrew Immigrant Aid Society:

DEAR MR. KALLEN:

We acknowledge herewith your remittance of $405.04. Our receipt No. E-771 therefor is inclosed herein. Please be advised that we promptly cabled $400, as requested, to our Danzig Branch to be handed over to your sisters, Raisa and Hedwig Kallen.

Very sincerely yours,

BUREAU FOR WORK IN FOREIGN COUNTRIES

[The record contains frequent entries from October to December merely noting that Mr. Kallen called at the office to inquire whether the Immigrants' Commission had "heard anything."]

December 1, 1920.—Letter written to Hebrew Immigrant Aid Society, New York, as follows:

We are writing at the request of Joseph Kallen, 1600 Stewart Avenue, who, with your valued assistance, is bringing to this country his sisters, Raisa and Hedwig. He realizes, of course, that you are making every effort and that the girls will arrive safely and as quickly as possible. However, as is perhaps natural under the circumstances, he is nervous and anxious, and would be very glad to be assured by you that everything is moving along smoothly. We shall appreciate it very much if you will take time to let us know what stage the proceedings have reached and if you can give him and us any idea when he may expect his sisters.

December 8, 1920.—Letter received from Hebrew Immigrant Aid Society as follows:

Replying to your letter of December 1, 1920, concerning Hedwig Kallen we wish to advise you that we have cabled to our Danzig Branch to inform us whether or not Raisa and Hedwig Kallen have already left for the United States. Kindly assure Mr. Joseph Kallen that we will communicate with him as soon as we are advised regarding the matter. Appreciating your interest in this case, we are,

Very sincerely yours,

JACOB NATHAN, *General Manager*

Later.—Called up man. Was not home; told wife about it.

January 20, 1921.—Wrote letter to Mr. Kallen as follows:

In December at your request we wrote to the Hebrew Immigrant Aid Society of New York, asking them how soon you could expect your sisters,

Raisa and Hedwig, who were to come to America under the care of the above-named society. Their reply to us of December 8 stated that they could as yet give no definite information, but that everything was being done that was possible and that they would let you know as soon as they could. We have heard nothing from them since. Are your sisters in Chicago by now? If not, do you know when you may expect them? We should be glad to have you let us know at your earliest convenience just what has happened.

February 16, 1921.—Mr. Kallen called up. He has heard nothing from Hebrew Immigrant Aid Society since six weeks ago, when he sent money to New York Office to be transmitted to Danzig. Asked us to write. Told him to allow more time. Told him we are sure that the Hebrew Immigrant Aid Society are doing all they can.

March 29, 1921.—Mr. Kallen at Hull-House last evening to see L. Gardner. He has had a letter from sisters. The letter said that in accordance with instructions received by them from the Danzig office of the Hebrew Immigrant Aid Society the sisters went to Warsaw and reported at the Warsaw H.I.A.S. office. They were told there office knew nothing about the case. At their request a telegram was sent to Danzig office and Warsaw office was authorized to pay them $400, which they did. Knew nothing about authorization for visa. Sisters unable to purchase tickets or get visa so have returned home. Brother does not know what to do. Said I would write to New York Hebrew Immigrant Aid Society.

March 30, 1921.—Letter to Hebrew Immigrant Aid Society (containing facts given above).

April 5, 1921.—Mr. Kallen called up. He received postal card yesterday from sisters. Said they went to American Consul at Warsaw for visa, which he refused to give. He told them, however, to come back May 25, and he would see what he could do. Mr. Kallen has also read in Jewish papers that that is the regular procedure of the American Consul at Warsaw now, that is, they are only issuing visas for wives and children. Man is very anxious. Told him we had written to Hebrew Immigrant Aid Society. Did not see what they could do since apparently the State Department had not authorized the Warsaw Consul to visa girls' passports.

April 6, 1921.—Wrote letter to Hebrew Immigrant Aid Society containing facts given by Mr. Kallen.

April 9, 1921.—Letter from Hebrew Immigrant Aid Society as follows:

In reply to your letter dated March 30 with reference to the Kallen sisters, we wish to advise you that we shall be pleased to cable our European Offices to advise the Kallen sisters to the effect that the American Consul was authorized to visa their passports and that they should apply to him for same.

April 16, 1921.—Letter received from Hebrew Immigrant Aid Society, advising that man write to State Department himself. *Later.*—Mr. Kallen called, told him of letter. He wished to have us write State Department. Will pay for cabling. *Later.*—Wrote Department of State as follows:

We have been requested to write you by Joseph Kallen, residing at 1600 Stewart Avenue, this city, who is eager to have his two sisters, Raisa and Hedwig Kallen, come to this country. We wrote you about this matter on September 8, 1920, and understand from the brother that he paid you for a cable to be sent to the American Consul at Warsaw authorizing him to visa their passports as soon as they presented them. Mr. Kallen tells us he received a letter from his sisters recently in which they state that they were refused a visa by the American Consul at Warsaw; that the Consul had not received authorization from the State Department, Washington, and that they were told to come back to the Consul on May 25 at which time he would see what he could do. Mr. Kallen is very anxious about his sisters and would be extremely grateful if the State Department could cable again to the American Consul at Warsaw, authorizing him to visa the passports of his sisters as soon as possible. He would also be glad to pay for the cost of cabling.

April 30, 1921.—Mr. Kallen telephoned and read a letter he has had from the State Department to the effect that State Department has cabled Consul General at Warsaw authorizing visa and that sisters should go to Warsaw. Told him to send the letter registered to his sisters and tell them to take the letter to the Consul.

June 25, 1921.—Mr. Kallen in office. He has letter from sisters. They went to the Consul General with the letter of introduction furnished by the Commission. They said they were "treated very nice" and were told passport would be visaed when they bought steamship ticket. They went to one steamship company, and this company would not sell ticket, would not consider it. They went to another steamship company, and this company said they would sell ticket if girls bought return tickets and made a deposit to cover possible steamship fine. The sisters thought they were being cheated and refused to do this. Told Mr. Kallen we could not advise him to do this. He must make his own arrangements with steamship company over there either through Hebrew Immigrant Aid Society or through his sisters. Gave him letter of introduction to Mr. Z. (a well-known Jewish man who had just returned from a visit of investigation in Poland). *Later.*—Mr. Kallen in office again. Mr. Z. has given him a letter to send to his sisters, and Mr. Z. will also write himself to the Warsaw Hebrew organization.

[The "Kallen case" continued to drag on for months. Finally, however, the family moved to California, and the League has had no word from them since. The case record has been given somewhat in detail because it so well illustrates the discouraging way in which cases sometimes drag on for years.]

45. Mary Kizis
(Bringing over Relatives—Passport Visa)

March 8, 1920.—Vladas Kizis in office, wishes Immigrants' Commission to help him bring his mother to this country. He is thirty years old, was born in Kaunas, Lithuania, where his mother is still living. He has three married sisters in the United States. His father, who came over just before the war, died in 1916, after a long illness at Oak Forest (County Infirmary). His mother, Mary Kizis, fifty-two years old, residing at Ragoro, Province Kaunas, Lithuania, is now all alone. Son has money to bring her to United States. Told son we will make application to State Department for passport. [Other facts given are omitted here since they appear in the letter below.]

Affidavit prepared and letter sent to the State Department:

Secretary of State
Washington, D.C.

MY DEAR SIR: Vladas Kizis, a naturalized Lithuanian, who came to this country in 1908 and served in the United States Army Company B, 24th Engineers, and was in France over one year desires to bring his mother to this country. He is living with his sister at 2490 28th Street, and also has three married sisters. He is employed at the Smith Saw Company, earning $30 a week and has about $200 saved. The name of Mr. Kizis' mother is Mary Kizis. She is fifty-two years old and is at present residing at Ragoro, Province Kaunas, Lithuania. We shall be very grateful if permission can be granted him to allow him to bring his mother to this country.

Yours very truly,

LYDIA GARDNER

March 18, 1920.—Mr. Kizis in office. He had a paper with the name Ellis, 5700 Green Avenue, 1st floor. He said a man came to his house yesterday morning and wrote his name and told his sister to tell Vladas Kizis to come to his house this evening to fill out an application of some sort. Mr. Kizis does not know who man is. Telephoned Mr. Ellis, Oakwood 3801. His son said his father must have left the paper. Father can be reached at the Department of Justice, Federal Building. Telephoned Department of Justice. Mr. Ellis said he had letter from Washington regarding passport for mother of Vladas Kizis. Vladas must fill out a blank giving information about his mother before he can get visa. He did not want the man to stay home from work so asked him to call in evening at his home. Explained to Mr. Kizis, who said he would like to get back to work and will go to Mr. Ellis this evening. Will come to our office again Saturday afternoon.

March 20, 1920.—Mr. Kizis in office. He saw Mr. Ellis who asked where he worked and all about what he had done. Mr. Ellis said everything would be all right.

March 29, 1920.—Letter received from an assistant secretary in the State Department, Washington, as follows:

Miss Lydia Gardner
Immigrants' Commission
Chicago, Illinois

MADAM: The Department acknowledges receipt of your letter of March 8, written in behalf of Mr. Vladas Kizis, who desires to have his mother, Mary Kizis, come to this country from Lithuania. The Department is prepared to authorize the American Consul at Riga to grant Mrs. Kizis a visa for the journey to the United States, if no reason is found why such action should not be taken. Such authorization may be sent by telegraph at the expense of Mr. Kizis or by mail, without expense to him. Will you kindly state whether telegraphic authorization is desired? I am, Madam,

Your obedient servant,

H. A. JONES

March 31, 1920.—Letter written to Mr. Kizis explaining letter from the Department of State.

April 6, 1920.—Mr. Kizis in office. He has not sent any money to his mother so far for steamship ticket. He was waiting to hear if permission would be given. Explained to him letter of March 29. He would like to know which way is best to bring mother here, by sending ticket or sending money. Talked with American Express Company. They can send a draft to Königsberg, Germany. Draft would have to be changed for German marks. That is the nearest bank to Lithuania they could send money to. (1,000 marks for $17.50.) Mr. Kizis would have to send draft through United States mail; it would probably take about 3 to 4 weeks to get there. Mr. Kizis thought that he would rather send steamship ticket as his mother would not know how to go about getting one. M. J. called at Blue Star Steamship Agency with him. They can only book man's mother from Antwerp or Paris for second class. This would cost $160 for ticket, and $8 for head tax. This would be fare to New York. From New York to Chicago the railroad fare would be $29.40 more. If woman could come third class they can book her from Danzig to Chicago for $154.40, including tax. Man said his mother lives quite a distance from both places. He will go to *Naujienos* (Lithuanian newspaper) to see if he can get information there as to just how she must come. If he can get a ticket from Libau for his mother, she could get here without any trouble. He would like her to come second class. He wishes Miss Gardner to write to Washington to notify them to send authorization by mail.

April 7, 1920.—Letter sent to Washington saying:

Referring to your letter of March 29, Mr. Vladas Kizis requests that authorization for visa for his mother to come to the United States be mailed to the American Consul at Riga.

April 17, 1920.—Mr. Kizis in office. He bought steamship ticket through Green Line, C 8890, prepaid April 10, 1920, third class, $154.42 from Danzig to Chicago.

April 19, 1920.—The following letter received from Washington:

Miss Lydia Gardner
Immigrants' Commission
Chicago, Illinois

MADAM: In reply to your letter of April 7, concerning the desire of Mrs. Mary Kizis to come to this country from Lithuania, you are informed that instructions are being sent by mail to the American Consul at Riga, authorizing him to grant a visa to Mrs. Kizis for the journey to the United States, when she applies, if no reason is found why such action should not be taken. I am, Madam,

Your obedient servant,

H. A. JONES

Later.—Copy of letter sent to Vladas Kizis. *Later.*—Telephoned steamship company. Ticket for Mrs. Kizis was forwarded to New York office April 16 to be sent to the other side.

November 29, 1920.—John Vileisis, brother-in-law of Vladas Kizis, in office, address 913 Minnesota Avenue, Berwyn, Illinois. The mother, Mary Kizis, arrived S.S. "Imperator" November 14, and on November 22 they received telegram that she was detained at Ellis Island. He sent official affidavit from Berwyn, November 22. Mr. Vileisis owns property in Berwyn. *Later.*—The following telegram sent to Miss Freeman [Commission's representative in New York City]: "Official affidavits sent November 22 Mary Kizis, steamship Imperator arrived November 14. Wire cause detention.—LYDIA GARDNER."

December 1, 1920.—Telegram from Miss Freeman that Mrs. Kizis is waiting for fifty dollars. Telegram forwarded to Mr. John Vileisis, Berwyn.

December 3, 1920.—Telegram from Miss Freeman. Mrs. Kizis will probably arrive in Chicago Sunday A.M. Erie Railroad. Telegram forwarded to Vladas Kizis.

December 9, 1920.—Mr. Kizis in office. His mother is here. She arrived Monday about 2 P.M. She did not come on the Erie; her daughter was waiting at the station for her Sunday and Monday. They do not know by what line she came, and she can't tell. She was transferred to Union Station and sent on Burlington train to Berwyn. Here she just went out from the station to find her way as best she could. She wandered about for quite a while and then sat down on the curbstone. The children came upon her there, a few blocks from their home. The train on which Mrs. Kizis came from New York was wrecked. Many immigrants were badly injured; she thought some were killed. She herself was bruised and cut around the mouth and chin. The train was on fire as a result of the accident. They were delayed a whole night by it. She left New York on Saturday A.M.

but did not get to Chicago till Monday P.M. She has no fault to find with the treatment at Ellis Island. It was rather hard to obtain bed at night. She greatly enjoyed the music and theatrical performances furnished to the immigrants there. She finally came second class on "Imperator" and was well cared for in every way. She had much difficulty getting her passport visaed. She spent probably 1,000 rubles having it done. She had to go to Kovno, Vilna, Danzig, Berlin and Riga before she could get the visa. She finally obtained it in Riga. She cries because she is so glad to be here. The son and the brother-in-law are both very thankful to the Immigrants' Commission.

46. Maryana Batuchkin
(Inquiry about Detention Abroad)

December 23, 1912.—Sergei Batuchkin, Russian, address 19 West Street, in office. Speaks only Russian. Interviewed by A. F. [Russian visitor]. Sergei Batuchkin sent four steamship tickets, Blue Anchor Line, through Abraham Stein, steamship agent, to Russia for his wife and three daughters. His wife Antonina and two daughters, Barbara (eleven years old) and Eva (sixteen years old), arrived, but the third, Maryana (eighteen years old), was detained in Germany by the steamship company because she had some trouble with one eye. Later a cablegram arrived from Tilsit stating that Maryana needed money. They sent out the first time through the same agent $15 and next time they sent $30 by cable. They have had no letters from Maryana, and they do not know where she is or what became of her. They would like to know whether she will be allowed to come here and where she is now. If she is not to be allowed to come here, they would like to have her sent to her former home, and they will support her. She will be able to work there also. Their first address in Chicago was 45 Justice Street.

December 24, 1912.—Letter written to Commissioner of Immigration, Tilsit, Germany:

DEAR SIR:

We are writing to ask the cause of detention of a Russian girl, Maryana Batuchkin, eighteen years of age. Her mother, Antonina Batuchkin, and two sisters, Barbara and Eva, arrived in the United States some time ago via the Blue Anchor Line. Maryana was detained in Tilsit. The parents have sent the girl $45, $30 of which was sent by cable. They have heard nothing from the girl herself and are very anxious to know where she is at present. Did she receive the money? Is she still detained? Or has she been sent back to Russia? She held a ticket to America bought here in Chicago. Thanking you for information at your earliest convenience, I am,

Sincerely yours,

EMMA KENNETH
(For the Immigrants' Protective League)

January 25, 1913.—German letter received from Tilsit [translation from the German]:

AUSWANDERER KONTROLLSTATION, TILSIT
January 1, 1913

The Immigrants' Protective League
Chicago, Illinois

In reply to your letter of December 24, 1912, concerning Maryana Batuchkin, I herewith inform you that this person is having her eyes cured in Tilsit and informs me that as yet she has received no money from America. She has deposited her steamship ticket here with me. She informs me that a week ago she sent a letter to Sergei Batuchkin, 45 Justice Street, Chicago, Illinois.

With highest respect,

H. GROSS

January 28, 1913.—A. F. visited Mrs. Batuchkin, 19 West Street. Mother is Antonina, forty years old; father, Sergei, thirty-five. Man reads Russian; woman is illiterate. They have three-room flat, $6.50 per month rent. Man earns $6 to $10 per week. Eva, age sixteen, earns $6 per week at Schnal and Company. Mother showed receipts for money sent to Maryana in Tilsit. They sent $30 to Tilsit through Western Union, November 18 (charges $4.53); sent $15.95 through Abraham Stein's Bank, November 1; sent $10 through same agent, January 18. They received letter from girl second week of January. She did not mention receiving any money. Told Mrs. Batuchkin Barbara must go to school. I took Barbara to H— school, and principal Mrs. X. will look after her attendance.

January 29, 1913.—Telephoned Abraham Stein. He said first remittance of $15.95 had been received November 16 in Tilsit, was sent November 1, No. 2564. Second remittance sent through agent was sent January 18. No reply about it as yet. Steamship agent says money was probably used for treatment of girl's eyes.

January 30, 1913.—Letter to Tilsit as follows:

Commissioner of Immigration
Tilsit, Germany

DEAR SIR: We wrote you December 24 regarding a Russian girl, Maryana Batuchkin, who has been detained for some weeks at Tilsit, her mother and sisters having proceeded from there to Chicago. We received on January 25 a letter from Mr. H. Gross, of the Auswanderer Kontroll Station in Tilsit, telling us that the girl had been having treatment for a disease of the eyes, which are now cured. He says also that the girl received no money from America. The girl herself writes and does not mention having received money. Her parents have sent her $55.95, $30 having been sent by cable November 18, $15.95 through Abraham Stein, a private banker, on November 1, and on January 18, $10 through the same banker. The banker received notice that the first amount, $15.95, was received in Tilsit, November 16. Can you tell us whether or not the money was received and for what it was spent? The family here in America are hard-working people who spend their money carefully. They are anxious to learn the items of expense while the girl has been detained. When will she be able to proceed to America? We shall be grateful for a reply as soon as possible. We are,

Very truly yours,

LYDIA GARDNER

[*For the Immigrants' Protective League*]

February 14, 1913.—Mrs. Batuchkin came to the settlement [where A. F. (Russian visitor) kept evening office hours], asking if the League had heard about her daughter. They do not know to this time anything about Maryana.

February 20, 1913.—Telephoned the banker (Mr. Stein). He has no further information concerning girl than that she is boarding with some one in Tilsit. Mr. Stein wrote his foreign representative to send the girl on as soon as doctors have given their permission.

February 21, 1913.—Another letter written to Tilsit [in German].

March 8, 1913.—Spoke to Mr. Stein. He says he can do no more than he has done. He said that Maryana Batuchkin lives with some Lithuanian friend by the name of Slezynger, 57 Statbecker St., Tilsit, Germany. He thinks that perhaps Mr. Slezynger got money and does not want to tell the girl, but agent cannot do anything else.

March 27, 1913.—A. F. visited Mrs. Batuchkin. She said that they do not know anything about their daughter and what happened to her. They have not had any letter for some time. Mrs. Batuchkin was told that letter was written twice to the government (i.e., Immigration Commissioner at Tilsit) and probably an answer will come soon. About the ship card (i.e., steamship ticket) she was told that it would be valuable for whole year.

March 28, 1913.—Letter from Tilsit received as follows [translation from German]:

AUSWANDERER KONTROLLSTATION
TILSIT, GERMANY
March 10, 1913

The Immigrants' Protective League:

In reply to your letter of February 21, I refer you to my letter of January 6 and inform you herewith that Maryana Batuchkin will be able to travel in perhaps three weeks, but she is without money and about thirty rubles must be sent to her.

With highest respect,

H. GROSS

Later.—A. F. visited Mrs. Batuchkin. Told her that letter was received from Germany, saying Maryana Batuchkin will be ready to leave Germany for America in about three weeks; she needs only thirty rubles more. Mrs. Batuchkin promised to send her husband to the Immigrants' Protective League Monday morning with money.

March 31, 1913.—Man came. Money sent by postal money order. *Later* —Letter written to Auswanderer Kontrollstation, Tilsit, saying that money has been sent.

April 19, 1913.—Mother has letter from girl saying she left Tilsit March 11; letter was written on March 13. Girl writes she left because doctor wanted to perform operation on her eyes. Girl has gone back to Russia.

April 22, 1913.—Letter written [in German] to Auswanderer Kontrollstation, Tilsit, as follows:

H. Gross, Esq.
Auswanderer Kontrollstation
Tilsit, Germany

MY DEAR MR. GROSS: We write to inquire concerning the Russian girl, Maryana Batuchkin, who has been detained some months in Tilsit. She has been sent back to Russia, we understand from her parents. They wish to know the details of her stay in Tilsit and ask also an itemized account of the expenditures made in her behalf. They fear that the last thirty rubles, sent in response to your letter of March 10, did not reach the girl, as she left Tilsit March 11. They inquire also concerning the doctor's statement of the girl's physical health. We should appreciate a reply at your earliest opportunity.

Sincerely yours,

LYDIA GARDNER
[*For the Immigrants' Protective League*]

May 20, 1913.—Letter received from Auswanderer Kontrollstation. They have no information regarding girl. At Tilsit she lived with Herr Slezynger, 57 Statbecker Street, Tilsit. Address further inquiries to her at that address.

June 5, 1913.—Letter of inquiry [in German] written to Herr Slezynger.

August 7, 1913.—Another letter [in German] written to Herr Slezynger.

August 26, 1913.—A. F. visited and spoke to Mr. Batuchkin. Told him that League wrote two letters to Mr. Slezynger of Tilsit, but letters were not answered. Mr. Batuchkin said that the $15 which was sent March 31 he received back as his daughter already was sent back to Russia. A week later he received a letter from Maryana, saying that she was sent back to Russia because her eyes were sore. The doctor wanted to perform an operation, but she would not let him, so that she was sent back. Mrs. Batuchkin feels very bad about her daughter that she will be all alone in Russia. She will try to earn some money so she can go back to visit Maryana and see if she is all right.

47. Sophia Joseph
(Passport Visa)

[On September 30, 1922, Mr. Samuel Jacob, Assyrian by birth and a naturalized American citizen, asked for advice and help about bringing over his fiancée, Sophia Joseph, then in Mesopotamia. Mr. Jacob reported that he had been ten years in Chicago, that he had worked for various building contractors, that he was a good carpenter, earning on the average about $50 a week. The plan decided on was to have his fiancée go to Marseilles and then for Mr. Jacob to go there to marry her. He was given two telegrams to send to the assistant secretary of labor and the Passport Control Division of the State Department, asking if under the "Cable Law"[1] a naturalized citizen could bring in his wife, married since the passage of the act, on an emergency American passport. The following telegrams and the circular received in reply illustrate some of the present passport difficulties.]

1. Telegram from an official in the United States Department of Labor to Mr. Samuel Jacob: "As alien women married to citizens subsequent to passage Cable Act do not acquire American citizenship impractical definitely pass upon their status as applicants for admission to United States until they arrive port of entry and make application."

2. Telegram from an official in the Division of Passport Control, State Department, to Mr. Samuel Jacob: "Your intended wife cannot be included your American passport. She should secure passport from Government of which she is citizen and have it visaed by American Consular officer in France."

3. Circular of information:

INFORMATION FOR PERSONS DESIROUS OF HAVING ALIEN RELATIVES OR FRIENDS PROCEED TO THE UNITED STATES

Attention is called to the regulations in effect concerning the visaing of passports of aliens desirous of proceeding to the United States from foreign countries. In order to avoid lengthy delays, the following procedure should be carefully followed:

Many aliens, now living abroad and desirous of coming to the United States, have friends and relatives in this country who are anxious that they should come to America. The friends and relatives in the United

[1] [The so-called "Cable Act" is the act of September 22, 1922, chap. 411, 42 Stat. L. 1021, "An Act Relative to the Naturalization and Citizenship of Married Women," which provides *inter alia* that marriage to a citizen of the United States does not confer citizenship upon an alien woman. In general terms, this act is said to confer the right of independent citizenship and naturalization upon women. It has, however, created a group of women who are literally "women without a country," since by the laws of many foreign countries a married woman takes the citizenship of her husband. By marriage to an American citizen she no longer remains a British subject, for example, according to British law, but under the Cable Act she does not become an American citizen.]

States should write the aliens informing them of these regulations and advising them to follow explicitly the following instructions:

1. The aliens abroad should obtain passports from the foreign government to which they owe allegiance.

2. They should present these passports in person to the American Commissioner or Consular Officer in the district abroad where they now reside. At the office of the Commissioner or Consular Officer they should make application for a visa permitting them to proceed to the United States. They should take with them three small photographs and present letters or affidavits from friends or relatives in this country setting forth details as to the latter's citizenship status, length of residence in this country, relationship to applicants, age and citizenship of applicants, reason the applicants desire to come to the United States, whether the applicants are self-supporting and the ability and willingness of the relatives to care for them properly upon arrival.

The fee for preparing the alien's declaration or application is one dollar and the fee for the visa is nine dollars. These fees must be paid by the alien to the American Commissioner or Consular Officer abroad.

The present regulations provide that no alien whose passport does not bear the visa stamped thereon by an American Commissioner or Consular Officer abroad will be allowed entry into the United States. Visas should be obtained from the American Commissioner or Consular Officer nearest the alien's place of residence.

Under the regulations, the American Commissioners and Consular Officers in all foreign countries have been instructed in detail as to those applicants to whom visas are to be granted and those applicants to whom visas are to be refused.

It is important to note that cases should not be taken up with the Department of State by persons in this country, but the aliens themselves should make the application direct to the American Commissioner or Consular Officer abroad.

[After the receipt of the telegrams and circular Mr. Jacob was advised by the superintendent of the League to postpone his marriage until the late spring so that his wife could come in on the new July quota. The fiancée went to Marseilles, and Mr. Jacob went over in May and was married there. However, he learned that she could not obtain a passport visa until she had made a year's residence in France. Mr. Jacob then took his wife to a South American country, where she secured a visa under which she was able to enter on the September quota. When visited by a representative of the League early in October, Mrs. Jacob was already enrolled in a public-school English class which she was attending four evenings a week.]

48. The Mother of Isadore Sukloff
(Passport Visa—Trachoma—Hospital Treatment—Deportation)

September 18, 1922.—Isadore Sukloff (Russian-Jewish) in the office. He wishes advice about bringing over his mother, who is now in Constantinople. His mother suffered terribly during the Russian famine, but she survived and was brought out of Odessa with about seventy-five other people by a Mr. Leib, who acted as agent for the Odessa Relief Society. Mr. Leib got them all to Constantinople safely; then he came on to the United States himself. Arrangements were made for the Chicago contingent, about fifty people, to sail on the S.S. "Dardanelles." All sorts of plans were made for giving them a grand welcome when they arrived, but none came on that boat. Then it was learned that all were held up in Constantinople, waiting for passport visas. Consul refuses to visa more than ten a week. Now it is said they will arrive on boats leaving September 9 and September 24, and Mr. Sukloff wishes to send affidavits. Mr. Sukloff is thirty years old, was born in Vilna, emigrated in 1907, was naturalized in 1915. He is a foreman in a tailor shop and earns about $3,000 a year. He has $500 in the bank and will use it for bond or for anything his mother needs. He also has some Liberty bonds. He has a wife and five children. The mother has also another son here, Abe Sukloff, who is a presser in a tailor shop and earns $40 a week and a daughter whose husband is "rich," a cigar manufacturer. Affidavits prepared stating these facts and sent to Commissioner, Ellis Island, and also to Mr. Schwartz, Secretary, Hebrew Immigrant Aid Society, New York. Gave Mr. Sukloff telegram to send to Commissioner, Ellis Island, as follows: "Official affidavits Miriam Sukloff steamship Dardenelles sent August twenty-ninth. If excluded hereby appeal.—Isadore Sukloff, *Son*."

December 1, 1922.—Mr. Sukloff in office. His mother did not arrive. She was kept back by a physician in Constantinople because of her eyes. But she has had treatment, and now she is coming on the S.S. "Crimea," Roumanian Line. Prepared new affidavits and sent to Commissioner, Ellis Island, and also to Mr. Schwartz, Hebrew Immigrant Aid Society, New York.

December 6, 1922.—Mr. Sukloff in office. He is worried because he has not heard from his mother. Told him we will write to Mr. Schwartz. *Later.*—Letter sent to Mr. Schwartz as follows:

My dear Mr. Schwartz:

When we sent you the affidavit for Miriam Sukloff, we did not know that she had been detained in Constantinople for several weeks because of eye trouble. Her son, Isadore Sukloff, has just been in our office; he is worried about his mother, and in the course of conversation we found out about the possible trachoma. We are passing the information on to you as you may need it in handling the case.

Very truly yours,
Alice Marion

December 8, 1922.—Telegram received from H.I.A.S. as follows: "Miriam Sukloff held hospital observation eyes. We will wire you developments.—H.I.A.S., Ellis Island Bureau." *Later.*—Telephoned to Mr. Sukloff. He is going to appeal to the Secretary of Labor.

December 11, 1922.—Mr. Sukloff in office with his sister's husband, Benjamin Morris. They brought a telegram from Hebrew Immigrant Aid Society. Mrs. Sukloff has been certified for trachoma. Mr. Sukloff asked help in writing appeal to the Assistant Secretary of Labor. [Extract from letter follows. First paragraph containing facts already given is omitted.]

. . . . I would not trouble you in this matter were it not for the fact that if she is deported, her condition will be very pitiful. She has been a resident of Odessa for the past fifteen years. If she is sent back there we fear a repetition of last year's famine, when, in spite of all we could do and in spite of all the food checks and parcels we sent, she almost starved. Also, we learn that there is cholera in Odessa. She sailed from Constantinople; I do not need to tell you why we dread to have her return there.

My mother is about fifty-five years old; she has no one in Russia who can contribute to her support. She has no near relatives anywhere but in the United States. Here in Chicago, she has two sons—one of them a citizen, the other a declarant, and both able to support her. I am amply able to guarantee against her ever becoming a public charge, and I am likewise amply able to guarantee that all medical treatment which she may require shall be promptly paid for. I will furnish bond to that effect. If you can be of any assistance to us in this great trouble of ours, we shall indeed be grateful to you.

Very truly yours,
Isadore Sukloff

[The remaining portion of this case is omitted. Mrs. Sukloff was allowed to be admitted for hospital treatment at Ellis Island; but after four months there seemed to be no improvement in her condition, and she was finally deported. In July, 1923, Mr. Isadore Sukloff again came to the League office for further advice. His mother was then in Constantinople, and she was receiving medical treatment from a doctor there, who insisted that her case of trachoma was curable. Mr. Sukloff, however, wished advice about having her go to Germany or some other place where he might be more certain that she was getting the best medical care. He said that "they worried always about her over there alone and always while he lived he would try to bring her where he could take care of her."]

49. The Wife of Paul Benjamin
(Difficulties with the "Near East" Quota)

[The case of the wife of Paul Benjamin and a group of Assyrian immigrants is set forth briefly in the five letters selected from the Benjamin case record. Paul Benjamin first applied to the League for assistance in September, 1922. At that time his wife was in Naples. Mr. Benjamin, who had himself immigrated in 1916, was a skilled workman (bricklayer), earning, according to his own statement, about $65 a week. He had been attending evening school, had learned to read and speak English, and had taken out his first citizenship papers not long after his arrival here. This case record and several others belonging to other members of the same party contain numerous letters, copies of affidavits, interviews, etc., which are omitted here. The difficulties encountered by the "Near Eastern" immigrants who are trying to bring over relatives are indicated in the letters that are here presented.]

1. Letter from the Superintendent of the Immigrants' Protective League to the Commissioner-General of Immigration, May 17, 1923:

MY DEAR SIR:

There is at present in Mexico City a group of Assyrians (Persians) who are most desirous of being allowed to enter the United States and to join their relatives in Chicago. We are frequently consulted by these relatives as to how this can be effected, and we shall be grateful if you will let us know what solution you see for them in their difficulties.

First of all we wish to make it clear that our account is based on what we have been told at different times by the Chicago relatives of this group and also by an Assyrian who till recently was with the group but is now in Chicago. These people have impressed us as being intelligent and truthful, and we believe our account to be accurate in the essentials.

It will be necessary to give a résumé of the previous wanderings of these people. They were given passport visas by our Consul in Bagdad sometime in May, 1921. On the twenty-eighth of that month they left for Bombay, where they expected to take ship. While waiting to sail, they were notified by cable from the Near East Relief that they would not arrive in the United States until after the year's quota for their nationality was exhausted, and they were urged to remain in Bombay. Most of the party disregarded this advice and went on to New York, and they were fortunate enough to be admitted in August, 1921, even though they did arrive as "excess quota." Those who were more law abiding remained in Bombay till, because of the bad effect of that city and its climate upon the health of the group, they decided to go where conditions were better. About nineteen of them went to Naples.

Here they were told that first-class passengers were not subject to quota restrictions and were advised to buy tickets for the December sailing of the steamship "Mesopotamia," Persian-American Steamship Company. But the "Mesopotamia" was seized that month by the Turkish government. As their money was tied up in these tickets and it was impossible to secure refunds, they had to make up their minds to wait for the next year's quota. Possibly had the "Mesopotamia" sailed as per schedule, they would have been among the fortunate immigrants admitted on the special Christmas order, 1921.[1]

They were persuaded to exchange their tickets for similar tickets on the steamship "Anaconda" and were to sail on July 16, 1922. They had secured fresh passport visas from our Consul at Naples. However, the "Anaconda," after taking passengers on board, did not sail; it was seized while still in the harbor of Naples by its creditors—we understand by order of the Italian government. Before the party could make arrangements to come to the United States by another ship, the quota for the year was again exhausted.

[1] [An order of the United States secretary of labor admitting approximately eleven hundred immigrants who were being held for deportation at Ellis Island because they had been debarred as "excess quota."]

These Assyrian immigrants settled down once more to wait for a new immigration year, their third year. Then a member of the party, a man who had lived in this country for many years and was an American citizen and could have returned here at any time, but because of his relationship to this group of Assyrians elected to remain with them, conceived the unfortunate idea of taking them to Mexico. This man is now in Chicago and is the chief source of our information about these people; we have, however, known the relatives of some of the members of the party ever since this group arrived in Naples. This informant tells us that he consulted the Mexican Consul, who told him that work was plentiful in that country. He consulted various other people who, he thought, should know conditions there, and he was told that probably they could come at once to the United States but that, if such were not the case, they could surely come after July 1, 1923.

As a result there are some fifteen Assyrians in Mexico City since January 1923. They write their Chicago relatives, pleading with them to do something for them. Among these people is the wife of a man who has lived in Chicago for six years; the fiancée of another; the minor son of a third. None of the Chicago relatives known to us are yet citizens, but all are declarants and some have applied for certificates of arrival. Recently, some persons in Mexico City—they say an American company but we do not yet know the name—have been advising them to exchange Mexico for Cuba, claiming that they can come from the latter place without difficulty. We have explained the situation to the relatives on that point.

But what can these people do? They have passport visas which do not expire till July 15, or thereabouts. Is there any way in which they can use them? If they remain in Mexico, it is our understanding that they will not be able to enter this country until after two years' residence there.

We shall greatly appreciate your advice in this matter.

Very truly yours,

ALICE MARION, *Superintendent*

2. Letter from United States Bureau of Immigration to the Superintendent of the Immigrants' Protective League:

DEAR MADAM:

I have read with care your letter of May 17, relative to the unfortunate situation of the fifteen Assyrians now in Mexico City. You are entirely right in the belief that under the immigration law these people will not be entitled to enter the United States from Mexico until after a two years' residence in that country. This provision is in the general immigration law and has no reference to the quota limit act, which has accounted for the inability of these Assyrians to come to the United States direct. If they go to Cuba, as your letter suggests, the two years' bar would not apply as the provision of law referred to concerns foreign contiguous territory only. They might, however, have a repetition of the former quota difficulties in any attempt they might make to come from Cuba to the United States.

The quota of "Other Asia," to which these people would be charged, is only 81 for the present fiscal year, and presumably that will be the permissible number for the next fiscal year also and under the law only 16 would be admissible in any one month. This number would, of course, take in the entire group, but the question would be whether they could arrive at a

United States port before the monthly quota for July was entirely exhausted. The experience in the past, as you know, has been that the smaller monthly quotas have usually been exhausted a few minutes after midnight on the first of each month by trans-Atlantic steamers bringing aliens to New York.

I fully realize that the information I have given you may be of no practical value, but I am sure you will understand why it is not possible for me to make any very definite suggestions as to what course these people might pursue.

Sincerely yours,

3. Letter from the Passport Division of the State Department to the Superintendent of the Immigrants' Protective League:

MADAM:

The Department has received your letter of May 17, 1923, concerning the desire of a number of Assyrians, who are now in Mexico, to come to this country. You state that they have visas which do not expire until July 15, or thereabouts, and request to be advised whether there is any way in which they can use them. You inquire whether they will be able to enter this country prior to their completion of a two years' residence in Mexico.

In reply you were informed that the Department of State has no objections to the admission into the United States of any alien who is in possession of a properly visaed passport, and, should the aliens in question be in possession of visas which are valid until July 15, interposes no objections to their admission prior to that time.

It is pertinent to add that Section 23 of the Immigration Act of February 5, 1917, provides that aliens desirous of entering the United States from Mexico must have resided in that country for at least two years before they were admissible. However, if they should proceed to Cuba, it is not believed that they would experience any difficulty in obtaining entry into the United States from that country. For further information on this phase of the case, it is suggested that you communicate with the Bureau of Immigration, Department of Labor. I am, Madam,

Your obedient servant,

VISA OFFICE

4. Letter from the Superintendent of the Immigrants' Protective League to Mr. Paul Benjamin, an Assyrian resident of Chicago, dated June 1, 1923:

MY DEAR MR. BENJAMIN:

Since you told us about your wife and your niece, who are at present in Mexico City and who wish very much to be permitted to join you in this country, we have made numerous inquiries as to how it can be managed. We have come to the conclusion that it is going to be very difficult though not impossible, and we do not wish to give you any advice in the matter.

We will, however, put the facts before you and let you judge for yourself as to whether you wish to take the chance.

The Assyrian quota opens on July 1. Your relatives, if we have been informed correctly, have visas from the American Consul in Naples which are good until July 15 or 16. These visas cannot be used from Mexico because there is a special two-year regulation with regard to that country which makes it impossible. They can, however, be used if your relatives arrive from other ports where these restrictions are not in force. Cuba would be such a port, as would the other islands in the Atlantic.

This sounds as though it might not be difficult for them to enter. However, this is where the trouble comes in. Unless they can make arrangements to sail from Cuba on a ship that arrives in New York or Key West or some other United States immigration port, very shortly after midnight of July 1, they probably have little chance of being admitted. We think, but we do not know for sure, that they may find it very difficult to find a steamship which meets with these requirements. But unless they can succeed in reaching the United States before the steamships bring the Assyrians to New York harbor after the opening of the year's quota, they stand no chance of entering because either they or the Assyrians coming from Marseilles and other European ports will be excess quota. As you probably know, the Assyrian monthly quota is only 16, and this number is usually filled before the first day of July is over.

You probably realize that, unless they use their visas before July 15, they cannot use them at all. At least, we do not see how they could prove to the United States immigration officers that their visas expired while they were on the ocean and yet they failed to reach the American port till August first. As you see, that would imply an ocean voyage of sixteen to seventeen days, which is of course much longer than is required for making the trip from any port that they may choose.

We hope we have made the situation clear to you. If not, we shall be glad to explain to you if you come to our office. Of course you understand that if your relatives succeed in entering the United States, it means that other Assyrians will be excluded. You perhaps feel that no one has had a more difficult time than your people and that they are entitled to preference in the matter. As to that we are unable to judge; we know that most Assyrians have had a pretty hard time.

We wish to impress upon you once more that if you decide to have your relatives try to enter the country in the manner suggested, you are running the risk that they will be excess quota and that they will have had the trouble for nothing and will have wasted their money. On the other hand, they have, of course, a fighting chance and may be able to win through. However, as we said before, we are unable to advise you in the matter.

Very truly yours,

ALICE MARION, *Superintendent*

5. Letter to Mrs. J. R., living in Havana and well known for her philanthropic activities there, dated July 27, 1923:

MY DEAR MRS. R.:

Through friends who have visited in Havana, we have learned of you and of your interest in the helpless and the unfortunate, and we write in the hope that you may perhaps be willing to help a group of Assyrians of whom we know and who are stranded in Cuba. There are fifteen members in the party. They are at present living at the Hotel Gomez in Havana, but they hope soon to move to new lodgings. Apparently they are very uncomfortable; they describe the hotel as a most uncomfortable place, crowded and dirty, and yet they have been paying very high rates.

The wanderings and troubles of these people read like a second *Odyssey*. We will not here go into detail; some of the members speak English and can tell you about them; we will merely say that they secured their passport visas from our Consul in Bagdad in May, 1921, and that they have been all this time trying to join their relatives in Chicago. They had to wait months in Bombay and then months in Naples, where they twice bought steamship tickets to New York on ships that were seized by creditors just as they were on the point of sailing. Then, due to misinformation and poor advice, they came to Mexico last January. They finally went to Cuba some time in June, hoping to reach the United States on July first, somehow or other, when the new quota opened. They were, however, unable to secure transportation. Furthermore, ten of the people were placed in a hospital under observation for possible eye trouble. It is impossible for the relatives here to tell us whether this was done by order of our United States Public Health Service or our Consul, or by Cuban authorities. They were all ten finally discharged; but they claim that they had to pay $50 each for the treatment or expenses of detention or whatever it was.

Their passport visas—the second they have had to get—expired July 16; that is why it was so important they should reach this country on July 1. Now they write that the American Consul in Havana is willing to extend their passport visas. We hope he is, but they have so often acted through misinformation or because they themselves misunderstood what was told them, that we fear they may again be mistaken. Could you, I wonder, find out from the American Consul what he really is willing to do in the matter, if anything? If it should happen to be true that he will extend their visa period, could you help them make arrangements in the matter of securing transportation on some steamer that reaches New York on September first—it is undoubtedly too late now to try for an August first boat. Unless they come by a steamer that reaches harbor very early on September first, they have no chance of admission; the quota under which they come is only 16 for the month, and it is usually filled before noon of the first day.

We realize that your other activities and interests may make it impossible for you to undertake this. In that case, could you not find some other philanthropic person in Havana who would be willing to assist these people, that is, to prevent their exploitation while they are in Havana and to help in making the necessary arrangements for them to come to this country?

One thing more. They write in their letters that the cost of living in Cuba is so frightfully high and they ask if it would not be better for them, if they cannot come to the United States, to go back to Mexico, where they could live much more cheaply. It is inadvisable to have them go to Mexico, as our Immigration Law requires that aliens must live there two years before they can be admitted to the United States, but could you suggest some other place near Cuba where the cost is not so great? The Virgin Islands, for instance, or some such place? Or if they were to stay in Cuba, do you think there is any possibility of their securing employment?

We shall be deeply grateful to you for your assistance with these people, and we trust you will pardon us for troubling you in the matter. We have not been able to hear of anyone else in Havana to whom we could refer the case.

Very truly yours,
ALICE MARION, *Superintendent*

[No satisfactory method of helping these people was found. With an Assyrian quota so small, no steamship company was willing to attempt to bring them on, and on October first the Assyrian quota for the entire year was exhausted, so there is no hope of their coming in before July 1, 1924. In the meantime, they may be tempted to follow the example of other similarly unfortunate migrants and attempt to come into Florida illegally. The League has sternly warned all immigrants against such methods of entry. In such cases the relatives in America pay a large price to have their people smuggled in, in spite of the fact that they will almost certainly be discovered and be deported back to the country from which they originally came. If they are not discovered on landing in Florida, they are usually discovered shortly after they reach their place of final destination. Sooner or later they will be reported to the United States inspector-in charge, who is then, under the law, required to arrest and expel them for being illegally in the country.]

PART III
DOMESTIC IMMIGRATION PROBLEMS

INTRODUCTORY NOTE

The problems of immigration within the United States are dealt with in the following sections. We are not concerned here with the question of whether or not immigration should be free or to what extent it should be limited. More than 14,000,000 immigrants are already residents of the United States, and large numbers are still arriving annually. It is a matter of public concern that these foreign-born residents of our country should be able to live decent, self-supporting, self-respecting lives. The documents in Section I and the social case records in Section II have been selected to illustrate the difficulties faced by the immigrant who is trying to adjust himself to the new conditions of American life and who is frequently defeated and exploited because of his ignorance of our language, our social resources, our customs, and our laws.

The documents in Section I have been selected, not to give a general account of conditions under which immigrants are living in this country, but to state the definite problems they are likely to face after arrival, and to present also some of the remedies that have been suggested in public reports for dealing with these problems. In Document 1, which describes the conditions at the port of entry and the immigrant's journey to the point of final destination, the importance of having a federal distributing station at an important inland center like Chicago is clearly indicated. Released from the supervision of the federal authorities when he leaves Ellis Island, the immigrant is often in need of help before he reaches his new home; and, indeed, for the lack of such help, he sometimes fails to reach that new home.

The immigrant also needs to be protected from exploitation in his search for employment (Document 2), in the provision of decent living conditions in the labor camp to which he is sent (Document 3), and in securing fair treatment and fair conditions of work (Document 4). He also needs protection or, more concretely, he needs advice and at times legal assistance in safeguarding his savings (Document 5), and in the transmission of his savings to his relatives at home (Document 6). He needs to be protected from dishonest or incompetent notaries (Document 7), and from the unscrupulous or ignorant interpreter in the courts (Document 8). He needs a decent place to live (Document 9), an opportunity to purchase a farm without falling into the hands of "land sharks" (Document 10), and most of all he needs an education, not only for himself and his children, but also for the mother of his children (Documents 11 and 12). It is a commonplace to say that all of the discussions of "Americanization" and "assimilation" center about a single point—the importance of making it possible for every immigrant to learn our language as soon as possible after his arrival. In very few communities have adequate facilities for adult education been provided; but note should be taken of the new method of state assistance to local authorities (Document 12). In Document 13 a general review of the situation of the new immigrants is presented.

A remedy for some of the difficulties illustrated has been sought in the creation of state immigration commissions. These commissions have been of two kinds:

1. Temporary investigating commissions that have made reports dealing with existing conditions and possible remedies. Such commissions made reports to the state legislature of New York in 1909; to the New Jersey legislature in 1913; and to the Massachusetts legislature in 1914.

2. Permanent commissions or bureaus created to deal with various questions affecting the foreign-born. Such state bureaus, recommended by the earlier investigating commissions, were created in New York in 1911 and in Massachusetts in 1917. Other state commissions were created in California in 1913, and in Illinois[1] in 1919, without a preliminary investigation having been made. Documents 14 and 15 indicate the kind of work undertaken by these state organizations.

Section II contains a series of social case records selected from the files of the Immigrants' Protective League of Chicago and the Immigrants' Commission of Illinois. These cases illustrate certain problems of immigration with which the social worker is frequently called upon to deal. In general, the social conditions from which the immigrant suffers in this country and about which he needs assistance and advice are of several kinds. There are, in the first place, the difficulties that belong exclusively to the immigrant and do not affect the native-born at all. Thus the difficulties of admission and exclusion, expulsion and deportation, of the bringing over of relatives, the purchase of

[1] Unfortunately this Commission is no longer actively at work. See above, p. 100.

steamship tickets, the transmission of savings to Europe, and of the process of naturalization are difficulties that the native-born do not share. In another group are such questions as the provision of free evening schools, or the establishment of properly administered free employment agencies, or postal savings banks. The native-born as well as the immigrant suffers from the lack of such facilities, but the immigrant obviously suffers much more frequently and more acutely. Finally, there are still other questions that are in no sense special problems of the immigrant but problems in which foreign-born and native-born need much the same help or protection in kind and degree. Thus the immigrant and the native American alike need the same services when they are destitute, sick or physically infirm, or orphaned; and the vast majority of social agencies, both public and private, are quite properly organized to deal with those who seek assistance on the basis of the specific need that is to be met rather than along lines of nationality or race. A relief society in a large city, for example, or a juvenile court, a mental hygiene association, or a vocational guidance bureau offers assistance to all who come for help or advice, whether foreign or native. All these agencies are agencies dealing with immigrants, but they deal with them not as immigrants but as persons who are destitute or sick or otherwise handicapped, or in need of counsel. In Section II an attempt has been made to present only cases[1] that arise out of the fact that the person dealt with is an immigrant and the problem confronted is peculiarly an immigrant's problem.

[1] In no case are real names used. In the case records selected the names have all been changed to make it impossible to identify either the "cases" or any individuals mentioned in the record (see p. 298, n. 1).

SECTION I
SOCIAL CONDITIONS AND PROBLEMS IN RELATION TO IMMIGRATION

1. The End of the Immigrant's Journey

A. CONDITIONS AT ELLIS ISLAND AND OTHER IMMIGRATION STATIONS[1]

The Advisory Committee on the Welfare of Immigrants held hearings in the fall of 1921 with representatives of various welfare agencies working at the New York port of entry, carefully investigated the Ellis Island station, and early in January, 1922, made the following recommendations:

An official director of information should be appointed to take entire charge of the welfare work at Ellis Island, such official to be under the immediate direction of the commissioner of immigration of New York.

That interpreters speaking several languages and trained in social work be appointed to serve immigrants pending their inspection and during such time as they are not permitted direct communication with their friends.

That a plan be developed for the systematic exchange of allowed information between immigrants who are detained and their waiting friends.

That women and young children be provided with separate and considerably improved night quarters and that a trained dietitian be placed in charge of the feeding of the children.

That detained immigrants be provided with better laundry facilities.

That the representatives of private welfare organizations who are authorized to carry on work at the station be allowed, under the direction and supervision of the Federal director of information, to aid in general welfare service for immigrants after they have been duly examined.

That three separate religious services, Protestant, Jewish, and Catholic, be held on Sundays "with occasional services for other groups when needed."

That when aliens are excluded and deported an explanation of the reason for such action should be given to them and also, when practicable, to their interested relatives and friends.

That there shall be some welfare workers on duty at all hours.

That official interpreters meet arriving immigrants when embarking on the barges taking such aliens from the vessel to Ellis Island and that an information service be made available to them while they are detained at the Island. Heretofore immigrants have been without service of this

---

[1] Recommendations of the Advisory Committee of the U.S. Bureau of Immigration. Extract from "Immigrant Aid: Legislative Safeguards, and Activities of Bureau of Immigration," U.S. Bureau of Labor Statistics, *Monthly Labor Review*, XVI (February, 1923), 256–59. This Advisory Committee was appointed by the Commissioner-General of Immigration in June, 1921. The investigations of the Committee were largely confined to Ellis Island, but some of the other stations were also visited. The full report of the Committee has never been published. Cf. an account of conditions of arrival in Boston in 1914, *Report of the Massachusetts Commission on Immigration*, pp. 163–74.

kind until their examination was completed, and frequently they have been held apart from the public for several weeks pending their examination by a special board of inquiry.

That pending medical examination immigrants be taken to large and comfortable reception rooms in the main immigration building instead of being held on the barges.

That milk and crackers be served to all women and children at meals in the dining room and between meals and at bedtime in the detention quarters. Previously only the small children had been provided with such food.

That the large room on the ground floor of the main building which is being used as a money exchange and railway ticket office be converted into a day room for detained women with children, such room to be provided with conveniences for the care of the children and to have easy access to an outdoor recreation place fitted up as a playground. That other commodious outside rooms near large porches with a view of the bay be made available as day rooms for other detained immigrants. That a large outside room be made into a dormitory for women and children, so that they will not have to occupy the general dormitories. . . . .

Boston.—The Advisory Committee found the East Boston station (1) lacking in facilities for taking care of the sick; (2) without any recreational facilities; (3) with overcrowded offices for the officials and employees; (4) without provision for the care of mothers with very young babies.

It had been hoped to move the station to the Boston side of the harbor to piers which were constructed during the war by other governmental agencies, but it was found that the law would require the United States Immigration Service to rent the pier space at a sum greatly exceeding any available funds under present appropriations. The Secretary of Labor has recommended "consideration of the suggestion that proper legislation be had which will make possible the use of otherwise unemployed Government buildings for the immigration service in Boston."

San Francisco.—The Secretary of Labor recommends that "steps be taken for the erection of a suitable immigrant station in the city of San Francisco with a view of abandoning the station at Angel Island." Both the island and the station are unsuitable for the purpose for which they are being used. The buildings are of wood, without adequate fire protection, and nearly all the fresh water for the island has to be brought there in scows. The cost of putting the station in repair would, the Secretary of Labor states, "go a long way toward constructing a new station on the mainland." The new buildings would cost approximately $600,000. It has been estimated that this change in location would save from $75,000 to $100,000 annually in overhead charges.

Seattle.—The Government pays a very high rent for the Seattle immigration station, which is not half large enough for its purpose. The need for a new station at this port which would be commensurate with the volume of immigration handled there has been emphatically pointed out by the Secretary of Labor.

Chicago.—The activities of the Chicago immigration station are confined chiefly to enforcing the deportation provisions of the law and the meeting of arriving immigrants, their direction and protection being left largely to welfare organizations. The acting inspector in charge, under date of October 25, 1921, wrote to headquarters in Washington, D.C., as follows: "In my opinion the organizations engaged in this class of work in this city are able to handle the situation adequately. . . . . I do not believe that official aid is necessary. In fact these organizations, which are engaged solely in aiding the immigrants, can work advantageously without connection with or aid from any official agency which is engaged in enforcing deportation provisions of the law." He also suggested that the methods of communication between detained immigrants at Ellis Island and relatives at points of destination should be improved. In many cases these relatives go from depot to depot, meeting train after train, because of having no definite knowledge as to when or where the expected immigrants will arrive.

According to the chairman of the Advisory Committee, a large crowd of newly arrived aliens going to Chicago is sometimes put on a train which "has no real accommodations," and the immigrants arrive in that city in a "deplorable condition." . . . .

B. PROTECTION OF IMMIGRANT GIRLS ON ARRIVAL AT INTERIOR POINTS[1]

Much improvement in the methods of the inspection, detention, and release of immigrants at the various ports of arrival has been made in recent years. Because of more efficient organization of the service, immigrants are now treated with humane consideration by government officials; moreover, runners from cheap hotels, expressmen, employment agents, and all those who might profit by their ignorance and dependence are denied access to them. The moral exploitation of the girl is guarded against by a careful examination of the person to whom she is released.

Journey to Chicago.—But in contrast to these improvements made at the ports, there is, for the girl destined to Chicago, no corresponding protective machinery. She is carefully guarded by the federal authorities until she is placed on the train, but the government then considers that its responsibility is at an end. She may be approached by anyone *en route*. Through her own mistake or intention or the carelessness of railroad officials she may never reach Chicago. As a result of an arrangement with the federal immigration authorities the Immigrants' Protective League has been receiving from the various ports of arrival the names and addresses of the girls and women destined for Chicago.[2] All these newly arrived

[1] Extract from first and fifth *Annual Reports of the Immigrants' Protective League of Chicago.*

[2] [The Immigration Law requires arriving immigrants to state their final destination in the United States and the names and addresses of friends or relatives to whom they are coming.]

girls and women have been visited by representatives of the League able to speak the language of the immigrant.

At present it is practically impossible to trace the girls who leave New York, but who never reach their friends in this city. Sometimes it is possible to reach some conclusions as to what became of them, but these conclusions only point to the necessity for some safeguarding of the journey. For example, two Polish girls, seventeen and twenty-two years of age, whose experience before they started for America had been bounded by the limits of a small farm in Galicia, were coming to their cousin, who lived back of the Yards in Chicago. Her name and address had been sent to us on one of our regular lists; and, when one of the visitors of the League called at the house, she found the cousin and the entire household much alarmed because the girls had not arrived. Inquiring of others who came on the same boat we found that the girls had become acquainted with a man from Rochester on the way over, and he was "looking out for them." The only information the Commissioner at Ellis Island could give was that the girls had left there and that one ticket on that date had been sold to Rochester and two Chicago tickets had been used as far as Rochester. The girls had completely disappeared, and no one was responsible for their failure to arrive in Chicago.

Usually the girls we find are the ones to whom nothing did happen, although they may have been for a time in an extremely dangerous position. One seventeen-year-old girl was put off the train at South Chicago by mistake and wandered about for several hours at night. Finally a man offered to take her to her friends. He proved worthy of her confidence, and she was conducted safely to the northwest side. Another girl, nineteen years old, who came in by way of Quebec became separated from her sister and friends at Detroit. She was taken to the police station for the night and in the morning continued her journey. She arrived at South Chicago without money or the address of her relatives. She spent a night in the South Chicago police station and another at the Annex of the Harrison Street police station. The police regarded it as impossible to find the girl's friends and so the matron of the Annex found her work in a down-town hotel. A visitor for the League returning from South Chicago reported great excitement in one neighborhood over the fact that an immigrant girl had been lost at Detroit. This report was connected with the story of the matron at the Harrison Street Annex, and a visit to the hotel proved the identity of the girl. Except for this she would have been alone in Chicago, ignorant of our language and the dangers of the city, with no one to turn to in case of sickness or unemployment.

Several girls have told of being approached on the trains and invited by strange men to get off at "some big city and see the town," but they wisely concluded to continue their journey without these gay excursions into the unknown.

National and even international attention has been drawn to the work of the United States District Attorney in prosecuting so-called "white slavers" in Chicago. Important as this work is it should not be the only remedy attempted. For in prosecutions, we must, of necessity, wait until the girl has been ruined, and no fine or penitentiary sentence inflicted upon the man or woman responsible for her downfall can undo for her or for society the damage that has been wrought. Some constructive preventive measures should be undertaken as well. First among these perhaps should be the guarantee to every immigrant girl of a safe arrival at her destination, even if it can be done only by making inland cities like Chicago ports of arrival for immigrants just as they are ports of entry for imported merchandise.

Any woman can understand the nervous apprehension which the immigrant girl must feel as she comes into one of Chicago's bewildering railroad stations, but very few realize how well grounded her fears are. Friends and relatives of those who come find it impossible to meet them because immigrant trains are sidetracked for all other kinds of traffic so that no one can determine just when they will reach Chicago.

Several hundred immigrants get off the train. Many of them are very young, and one feels their disappointment as they peer eagerly and anxiously about for the father or sister or friend they hope to see. On one occasion a Polish girl of seventeen was taken at three o'clock in the morning to the place where her sister was supposed to live. But the address was incorrect, and the woman who lived there angrily refused to let her stay until morning. The girl had no money and wept disconsolately, when the expressman told her "nobody could find her sister if nobody knew her address and that he wasn't going to take her back for nothing." The saloon keeper next door finally offered her a refuge, and she lived with his family behind the saloon three days before her sister, who was making daily trips to the depot, was found.

The station master and police officers at the Grand Central Station feel a certain responsibility for the immigrants who come in at that station and have been eager to help us in our work. They require the expressman to bring back to the depot all those whose friends or relatives are not found, and from there they are referred to the League. Not long ago a twelve-year-old German boy was brought to the office in this way. The policeman assured him that we would take good care of him, but he found it very hard to be brave when he faced the fact that he was hungry amd without money and that the older brother who had sent him his ticket and was going to look out for him could not be found. While the boy was being cared for, a visitor for the League started out on the trail of the brother. He was found before night, although he had moved three times since he left the address in Oak Park which his little brother had brought. The steamship agent had promised to notify him when the boy would arrive, and he had carefully kept the agent informed of his changes of address.

A wide acquaintance in the various foreign colonies often enables the League's visitors to find the missing friends or relatives. A Russian boy who was on the "Volturno" was brought to us. He had an Ashland Avenue address but no one at the number given knew the boy. On talking with him the Russian visitor discovered that he had started with a brother, the two had become separated before they reached the port of embarkation, and the boy had sailed without the address of his Chicago relative, and ignorant of what had become of his brother. The address on Ashland Avenue which he had shown us, had been given him by a passenger on the boat, who told the boy he would never be admitted if he had no address. He hoped that on Ashland Avenue he would find this chance acquaintance and so would be spared the necessity of revealing his plight and, as he supposed, lay himself liable to immediate deportation. On Clybourn Avenue where there is a colony of Russians who came from the same district as the boy, his brother was found.

Because of a lack of adequate supervision at the stations, such cases are not always discovered. A Polish girl, for example, who had only the address "South Chicago," was put off the train at that station and wandered about for some time. She was finally picked up by the police and brought to the League. The next day her aunt was found at 87th Street and Superior by one of the League's visitors. Under federal supervision of all those who arrive, such girls and men would be held until a private agency could render the assistance of which they are so much in need.

Sometimes the grocery stores, saloons, steamship agents and other neighborhood sources of information fail us. Not long ago a girl was brought to the office who had arrived in the city on Sunday afternoon and because her friends could not be found had been taken to the Annex of the Harrison Street police station and so had received her first initiation into Chicago life. She had the name and address of the girl friend who lived in Chicago and who had promised to get her work, written in the front of her prayer-book and could not understand its incorrectness. She tearfully insisted on accompanying the visitor on the search for her friend and grew more discouraged as one clue after another was tried and failed. Finally the girl said that her friend worked in a bed spring factory. Starting out on this clue the visitor found her in the third bed spring factory they visited. The friend explained that her address was not as the prayer-book showed, 110 Canal Street, but 1110 Canal Street.

If the United States Immigration Department would establish a protective bureau under the Department of Information and Distribution, this situation might be greatly improved. It is true that the railroad companies could by agreement put the business of delivering immigrants on the same responsible and efficient basis that the transfer business is now. But more than this is needed. There should be a central place in Chicago to which those who are expecting friends or relatives from Europe might go and learn whether they had come and to whom they had been released.[1]

Girls not located.—During the year and a half since the League began this work, we have received from the various ports the names of 734 women and girls who gave as their Chicago addresses, streets and numbers so incorrect that it was useless even to attempt to find the girls, while 1,203 other girls whose addresses were apparently possible we were unable to locate. Two hundred and thirty-one of these 1,203 we found some trace of—the neighbors knew the people, they were expecting a sister or a cousin, but they had "moved away to 18th street or the town of Lake." Of the 972 others nothing so definite as this could be learned. In 66 cases we found that the person named on the manifest as the one to whom the girl was destined lived at the address given, but knew nothing at all about the girl and said no immigrant had come to that address. In each of the cases the people seemed quite baffled by the use of their names, and inquiry among the neighbors showed that the people were well known and that no one had heard of any Polish, Bohemian or Irish girl, as the case might be, coming to that neighborhood. The conclusion reached in all these cases was that there had been a fraudulent use of the names of these people.

Sometimes these facts are almost reversed. One girl nineteen years old was coming, she said, to a brother-in-law on North Avenue. When a visitor for the League called at the number given, the woman who lived there told how an expressman had brought an immigrant girl to the house

[1] [A law was finally passed by Congress in February, 1913, largely as a result of the efforts of the League, which provided for the establishment in Chicago of a federal immigration station which should take charge of all arriving immigrants, assist them to find their relatives, and keep them over night if necessary. Concerning this new feature of the federal immigration service the Secretary of Labor made the following comment in this *Report* for 1913: "An improvement in the care by the Federal Government of aliens about to be admitted into this country is contemplated by the act of Congress providing for immigration stations at interior places. Stations have been maintained heretofore only at ports or places of entry. From those points the immigrant, after being admitted, has been left by the government to shift for himself; but under the interior-station act immigrants will have government protection until they are discharged from the interior station nearest their destination. . . . . Further arrangements are now in progress for the safe conduct of admissible immigrants destined to points beyond Chicago from their port or place of entry to the station at Chicago, and thereafter until they are properly routed thence to their respective destinations. On their way to Chicago they will be in charge of immigrant official-inspectors for men and matrons for women."

The later history of what might have been the first federal station for the protection of arriving immigrants at interior points is of some interest. The location

a few days before, but as no one was expecting her, she suggested to the expressman that the "7" in the address the girl had looked like a "1" and he had better try that. So he had gone off with her saying he would try the suggestion made. But at this number there was a blacksmith shop and no one there could help with any information about the girl. An Irish girl, twenty-two years old, was coming to a sister on 51st Street. Here we learned that a girl had come looking for her sister, but the people who lived at the address the girl had knew nothing about the person she described. The girl was accompanied by a young man who, she said, was a stranger to her, but was going to help her find her sister, and they went off together. Three German girls, fifteen, sixteen and seventeen years old, gave an address on South Clark Street. Here the visitor found a business house and learned that the man whose name had been given had formerly been a member of the firm, but had been dead ten years and that no one knew anything about the girls. A Polish girl gave an address on Ashland Avenue. This proved to be a saloon; and, although we often find that the foreigner whose place of residence is uncertain uses the saloon as his permanent address and is well known to the proprietor, no one here knew anything about the girl or the man to whom she was coming. In this case the saloon keeper could not remember anything about this particular girl as he said that the expressman often left a load of them at his saloon and someone always finally called for them. A good many give the addresses of neighborhood steamship agents. This is especially true of the Italians for whom the agent often serves as a banker, notary public, and official letter-writer. Very often these agents assist us in locating the girl, but in forty-two cases they did not know anything about the person whose name was given and said the girl's ticket had not been purchased from them.

---

of the new federal station was decided on in November, 1913, and the receiving-room, dormitories, bathrooms, and laundry were furnished and ready for use in January, 1914. In the following summer, certain additional officers were assigned to the Chicago station, it was believed, to undertake the new work of assisting arriving immigrants, but they were later withdrawn.

Administrative officials in Washington refused to issue orders for the opening or use of the station, and this administrative hostility to a new policy, in effect, nullified the law.

The large receiving-room, after being entirely unused for a year, was taken over for other departmental work. But the dormitories, bathrooms, laundry-rooms, etc., which were furnished ready for use, were not used for any purpose whatever during a period of two years and four months while the government was paying rent for the space. That is, the opposition of administrative officials in Washington who apparently did not approve the establishment of the new interior station was successful in preventing the law from going into operation. The Chicago station still exists on the statute books, but only on the statute books. (See Grace Abbott, *The Immigrant and the Community*, pp. 21–22.)]

2. Finding Employment

A. METHODS OF SECURING IMMIGRANT LABOR[1]

The chief methods of securing immigrants in the Middle West and Northwest involve the use of labor agencies. Especially is this true of races other than the Italian, who are secured through the padrone system. The agencies generally have contracts with the railroads and send out the labor in an intelligent, systematic way, but it often happens that a number of small agencies having no contract with the railroads or contractors will hear of work and all rush men to the place, with the result that many of the men are left on their own resources to get back to the cities, where they can again apply to the agencies.

Early in the season the men present themselves to the agencies for registration, for which they are usually charged $2, the maximum legal fee. In the order they have registered they are shipped off in gangs when the demands come in from the railroads. Before a month has passed some of the first gangs may begin returning and are then shoved through the machinery again. Sometimes they are not returned all the way to the city from which they originally started but are transported from where they were discharged, or gave up their places on account of various hardships or because the work ceased, to other points where they may be reemployed. This circulation is encouraged, for at each shift the men pay the agencies. When the supply of men runs low, toward the end of the season, the agencies sometimes cooperate. One may have an order for a large gang which it cannot fill on short notice. It solicits help from other agencies and the two divide the profits. Some do this continually. One agency that handles Bulgarians exclusively has not been able to get large contracts from the railroads. It must therefore divide its gains with some larger agency which has succeeded in getting contracts. On the other hand, there is every reason to believe that the large agency in its turn pays heavily for its contracts, so that the secondary agencies lose not so much as at first seems. As has already been indicated, there are two distinct movements during the year; in the spring the gangs move westward, especially northwestward, to points beginning in Chicago suburbs and extending up into Minnesota, the two Dakotas, Iowa, and Montana. In August and September a lull in the labor-agency business occurs. In October the men begin swarming back into Chicago, those who can afford it to winter in the colonies. The Bulgarians return to Granite City, Illinois, although there is also a colony of them in Chicago. Then the agencies are busy again, sending gangs southward into Kansas, Missouri, Mississippi, and Louisiana. One agency, as an instance, has a permanent contract with three different railroads. The Southwest movement is not so heavy, partly because many of the

[1] Extract from "Immigrants in Industries," *Reports of the United States Immigration Commission*, XVIII (1911), 425–31.

immigrants prefer wintering in the cities, because the constructional work in the South is not so seasonal in its nature, and also because there are large cities nearer than Chicago from which immigrant labor can also be drawn. . . . .

Kind of work done.—The occupations filled by the immigrants in construction work are for the most part those of unskilled workmen. Much of the work herein referred to is repair and maintenance work on railroads, rather than the initial construction. The principal occupations are carrying cross-ties, shoveling ballast under the track, shifting the track with bars, digging ditches, and picking the sloping sides of the cuts. Most of the work in this region, especially in the Northwest, is seasonal, since the railroads do most of the track raising and general repair work between spring and fall. The term of employment is very short for each job, which keeps the men on the move. This feature debars women from accompanying their husbands, and for this reason it is little sought except by unmarried men or else those whose wives are abroad. Being in the open air this is much more healthful than most other work, and this strongly appeals to the Italian.

Housing.—Housing and living conditions vary little, or not at all, even among the various companies. Freight cars, fitted up inside with from eight to ten bunks, are used as sleeping quarters. Separate cars are used as kitchens and as dining rooms. The bunks in the sleeping cars have been roughly put together, four in either end of each car, leaving ample space in the middle even when two extra bunks are crowded in. There is usually a table in this clear space where the men play cards and sometimes eat instead of in the regular mess car. Even with ten men in one car, they could never be described as crowded. The kitchen car is fitted with a range, tables, an ice chest, and numerous lockers in which the provisions are kept. The cook or cooks sleep here in one end of the car, and sometimes an interpreter is with them. The mess car is always next to the kitchen. Through its entire length, in the middle, runs a plain board table, a bench of equal length on either side, with lockers on the walls where the tableware is kept. Usually these cars were found to be neatly kept for this is the business of the cooks (about 1 to each 30 men) for they have no work other than this and their cooking. There was always drinking water in plenty, supplied in buckets by the water boys, iced when spring water was not available. The Greeks and Italians seemed the most unclean in their living arrangements. The Italians are fond of decorative effects, hanging out flags and gaily colored rags and sometimes the outsides of their cars are lined with growing plants in boxes. These camps are strung on sidings, ladders being raised to the open doorways. So long as the work is within several miles of the camp, the car is not moved, the men travelling to and fro on hand cars; but when necessary a switch engine appears and hauls the entire camp to the next siding, or switch, causing the men no other inconvenience than, in the case of those who bake their own bread, the building of a new bake oven—a small cave in an embankment or hillside. . . . .

Systems of living.—Everywhere the men must pay their own living expenses. The companies pay the wages of the cooks, equal to those of the laborers. Fuel, sometimes old ties, sometimes coal, sometimes both, is supplied free. The cooking ranges and the kitchen utensils are bought by the men. Theoretically, the men may buy their provisions from whom they please, and wherever they insist on this right no doubt they do. It is always the interpreter, the chief of the gang, who finances the living fund, made up from contributions from the men, collected by the interpreter on each pay day. In the beginning, the provisions are usually had on credit from some local store, guaranteed by the roadmaster or the boss, the interpreter settling the bills fortnightly after each pay day. Those gangs which were near enough to a city usually bought their bread in the city, but otherwise the bread was baked in the camps, holes being hollowed in an embankment, filled with burning embers, emptied when well heated, and then filled with the loaves, the entrance being sealed with stones and mud. The management of the oven is left to volunteers, the cook mixing and forming the dough only. . . . .

Exploitation.—The different phases of exploitation practiced in the West may be separated under the following heads: (I) charging exorbitant fees and commissions; (II) discharging the men from their work that they must pay for reinstatement, or that the labor agents may collect more fees for finding them other work, or being obliged to "square" themselves with foremen; (III) sending men to places where jobs do not exist; (IV) interpreters' dishonesty; (V) the furnishing of poor food at a high price by contracting supply companies; (VI) transportation dishonesty; the charging of fares where men are entitled to ride free.

There are state laws in the Middle West forbidding labor agents to charge more than $2 registration fee; but it has no significance, for by giving it another name they may charge so much as they please, or so much as the laborers can pay, meaning that the right of private contract is unlimited. Registering is only done at the beginning of the season. The fees that are really charged are from $2 to $15, according to the statement of a reliable labor agent, and there have been cases where $20 has been paid for places. . . . .

. . . . Dishonesty in transportation seems not to have attracted so much attention as other forms of exploitation, among persons interested in the welfare of the laborers, perhaps because it is apparently aimed at the stockholders of the railroad companies rather than at the laborers. But it cuts both ways and seems to be even harder upon the laborers than are the other forms of exploitation. It is true that men never pay more for their railroad tickets than the regular rates. But if the railroad companies recognize the theory that the labor they employ should be transported at their cost, and do transport it free of charge, and still the men pay their own transportation, the money extorted from the men under this pretext must be clear exploitation. Private individuals are taking money from them for service which the companies intend to give them free of charge.

The difficulty in defining the limits of this practice is in learning just how much free transportation the railroads allow. Sometimes the laborers, in going to their work, pass over roads not connected with the company for which they are to work. In that case fare may be charged, but at a rebate. What that rebate is nobody but the labor agent and certain railroad officials know. It must be more than the mere party rates, otherwise some of the labor agencies could not flourish as they do and still offer cut-rate tickets. The two railroad offices visited would tell nothing definite on this point, nor could it be ascertained whether the men must pay fare in passing over the road of a company consolidated with, but still distinct from, the company for which they were to work. When the engineer of maintenance of way, the official of a railroad who hires the construction gangs for that company, was called on, he flatly stated that they would give no information on that subject. In the office of the assistant manager of another railroad, officers were courteous but evasive, though they did make the definite statement that the laborers whom they employed passed over its roads free. The indications of private dishonesty in granting contracts are strong.

As has been stated in the foregoing pages, many railroads, as well as contractors, have regular boarding and lodging trains. In constructing new lines of railroad grading, bridging, tunneling, etc., the work is always in a more or less sparsely inhabited section, and in this case houses for the accommodation of the men have to be built. A prevalent custom in the Middle West and Northwest is to have a fixed charge for board and lodging, rather than to have the men do their individual cooking. It has been found that all laborers of European nativity, except the Italian, will readily accept this form of accommodation. This is another reason why the Italians are not so much desired as the other races in this section.

Without reference to fraud, labor agents' fees in the West and Northwest are sometimes unreasonably high, varying with the relative proportion of supply and demand. The season (1909) in the Northwest has seen a scarcity of men, obvious from the rise in wages as the season advanced and the decrease of agents' fees in the same time. The various gangs investigated had paid as follows:

Sixty-five Bulgarians in Hastings, Minnesota, paid $3.50 each; 27 Roumanians in Red Wing, Minnesota, paid $12 each; 73 Bulgarians in Red Wing, Minnesota, paid $12 each; 27 Bulgarians in Frontenac, Minnesota, paid $3 each; 50 Italians in Frontenac, Minnesota, paid $4 each; 70 Bulgarians in Savage, Minnesota, paid $15 each; 42 Bulgarians in St. Louis Park, Minnesota, paid $3 each; 40 Italians in Roscoe, South

Dakota, paid $11 each; 53 Croatians in Bowdle, South Dakota, paid $10 each; 40 Italians in Selby, South Dakota, paid $3 each; 15 Greeks in Selby, South Dakota, paid $3.50 each; 24 Greeks in Sitka, South Dakota, paid $7 each; Croatians in Pontus, South Dakota, paid $9 each; Italians in Pontus, South Dakota, paid $4 each; 32 Bulgarians in Aberdeen, South Dakota, paid $7 each; 30 Roumanians in Aberdeen, South Dakota, paid $10 each; and 61 Italians in Aberdeen, South Dakota, paid $11 each.

Those paying the higher fees came early in the season, in March and April. In some cases, as will presently be explained, the fees were increased by falsification. Some of those most heavily charged came from Minneapolis, and some lightly charged from Chicago, so that transportation could not have been included. In fact all had traveled on their identification tags.

B. PRIVATE EMPLOYMENT AGENCIES[1]

In 1907 the Legislature enacted a law regulating employment agencies which requires all agencies which charge a fee or receive compensation for their service, to be licensed. . . . . [The law] definitely places upon the governing body of a municipality the responsibility for fixing a license fee. Notwithstanding this, in only fifteen out of the twenty localities investigated, had the common council or governing board enacted an ordinance for this purpose. In the fifteen cities and towns where such an ordinance had been passed, there were found to be, in addition to one hundred and fifteen agencies properly licensed by the authorities to conduct their business, at least fifty-one others which were operating without licenses, some of which were even advertising in the local newspapers. In the five other cities where no fee was fixed, seventeen agencies were in existence. Where the fee is fixed, it varies from $3 in some localities to $25 in others. In the majority of the cities, however, $5 is the usual amount charged for a license. In a number of cities it is collected for revenue only and is not used to provide for a fund for the enforcement of the law.

Taking all the agencies considered, without regard to whether they do business in a municipality which has fixed a fee or not, it was found that sixty-nine, or 37 per cent, are operating without a license and are, therefore, doing so without the knowledge of the authorities and consequently without proper supervision. At least thirty-two of these agencies are located in cities which have fixed a license fee. No attempt is made by them to conceal their existence, and only the indifference of the police or their ignorance that the law places any responsibility upon them can account for these conditions. . . . .

[The law also provides that] "No such agency shall be located in rooms used for living purposes or where boarders or lodgers are kept, ... or in

[1] Extract from *Report of the Commission of Immigration of the State of New Jersey* (1914), pp. 57–65.

connection with a building or on the premises where intoxicating liquors are sold to be consumed upon the premises."

Notwithstanding this section of the law, in thirty-four of the fifty-one licensed agencies visited, the offices were found to be located in living rooms. In addition to these, a number of offices were found in connection with rooms let out to lodgers or boarders, and at least three were found to be operated in saloons. In other words, 72 per cent of the licensed agencies investigated were not complying with this provision of the law. Among the unlicensed agencies, twelve were found conducting their business in living rooms. These agencies which were conducted in living rooms were found to be located in kitchens of tenement houses, in dining rooms and in bedrooms, in total disregard, not only of the law, but also of adequate or efficient methods for dealing with applicants. . . . .

Of the fifty-one licensed agencies, only twenty were found keeping proper books. Nine others kept records of some kind, though in every case they were very inadequate. Names of applicants were often entered without addresses and without any further information with regard to fees and such data as would be of assistance either to the agent or the applicant in cases of disagreement. Only one of the twenty-one unlicensed agencies kept a book of any description. . . . .

In fifteen of the fifty-one licensed agencies it was found that adequate receipts were issued. In seven others receipts of a very inadequate character were issued, some of them being merely a slip of paper with the amount of fee written upon it and the agent's name signed. In the remaining twenty-nine agencies no receipt whatever was given. In only four of the twenty-one unlicensed agencies did agents give receipts. . . . .

It was found that of the fifty-one licensed agencies investigated, twenty-eight were regularly inspected by the responsible authorities; all these twenty-eight agencies were in one city. In no other city were employment agencies found to be regularly inspected by the police or by an inspector of any kind. The law definitely places the responsibility upon the chief of police in municipalities where no license inspector has been appointed. The chief of police of one of the largest cities in the State testified that they never attempted to enforce the act in his city. The police, he said, usually granted the license if it was found after investigation that the character of the applicant warranted it. After that no further investigations were undertaken unless complaints were made. He stated later, however, that he had knowledge of only one complaint during his term of office.

In this very city a short time later an employment agent who was regularly licensed by the police attempted to exploit two Austrian laborers who applied for work at the agency in answer to the following advertisement which they found in a New York newspaper:

> Men 150—railroad work for Chicago. $1.75 and $2.00 per day —free transportation—no strike . . . . [name and address].

The agent told them that he could obtain work for them on the Indiana Division of the Erie Railroad and charged them each a fee of $3. Having paid the $3 and having received a receipt, written on the agent's business card, they were taken to the Erie Railroad Station, where they were handed over to a representative of a New York Employment Agency, who was sending five Italians, presumably to the same work. This representative gave them all a transportation pass and put them on the train.

The conductor on taking up the tickets told them that their passes were no good and put them off at Goshen, New York. They appealed to the ticket agent there, who handed them over to the local police and they had to remain in the station house for a night and a day. At the end of that period the ticket agent advised them to take a train to New York and explain the situation to the conductor. This they did, but the conductor refused to accept their story and put them off at Tuxedo. Here they again appealed to the ticket agent and were given the same advice—to take the next train to New York, which they promptly did, and this time were put off at Paterson, where they were compelled to buy tickets for Jersey City. Arriving at Jersey City they endeavored to take the matter up with the superintendent, but were arrested for stealing rides from Goshen to Paterson and were locked up in the Jersey City police station over night. After losing five or six days' time and having the added humiliation of being arrested twice and having been put off trains at three different places they were discharged. Fortunately the two Austrians, on the arrest of the agent, against whom they complained, received back their $6 while the agent was paroled pending trial.

If the police in the beginning had taken steps to find out the former business of the agent they would have learned that he was not a fit person to run an employment agency. He had formerly been in the same business in New York City and for certain illegal transactions had been refused a license by the New York authorities.

In another city the license inspector said that he does all in his power to investigate the employment agencies and enforce the law in the city, but that it is impossible for him to do it efficiently with the small force which he has at his disposal.

As long as agencies are allowed to conduct their business with so little supervision from the municipal authorities and with so little regard for the law, ... just so long are applicants in constant danger of overcharges and other mistreatment.

The Commission believes that the present employment agency law in New Jersey is sufficiently comprehensive, as it stands, and that if it were properly enforced, the exploitation of foreign or native-born men and women seeking work could be ended. . . . .

C. THE UNSKILLED IMMIGRANT IN CHICAGO[1]

The immigrant man finds himself much handicapped when he tries to obtain work in the country in which he has been led to believe work is most abundant. In the first place, because of his ignorance of English and consequent inability to give or receive directions he cannot work without an interpreter. Interpreters can be profitably employed only when large groups of immigrants work together. Such groups are employed by the foundries, at the stock yards, in mines, on railroad, car-line and building construction, in the harvest fields, in ice and lumber camps, and other similar kinds of work. Much of this work is seasonal and is located at a great distance from the city. A large number of men are needed for a few months or weeks to harvest Dakota crops, to build a railroad in Wyoming or Arkansas, to harvest ice in Minnesota, to pick Michigan berries, and to work in the oyster beds of Maryland. This work is most undesirable. The pay is not good, board is expensive and poor in quality, and the work lasts usually only a very short time. Worse than this, the men must come back to Chicago to get their next work, so return railroad fare must be counted on. Such work, because of its undesirability, can usually be obtained. The American workman does not want it because it places him at the mercy of contractors and employment agencies and makes of him a homeless wanderer. It is work the immigrant can do and, because in most cases he must have work immediately, he takes it gladly. This means that whatever his training or experience may be he must serve an apprenticeship in the ranks of the unskilled seasonal laborers. . . . .

It is most significant that the only kind of work offered by two-thirds of the agencies handling immigrants is "gang work" at a distance of from about a hundred to a thousand miles from Chicago and is work which from its very nature is sure to be of short duration. Chicago is apparently a clearing-house for the seasonal laborers of the country and the proper handling of them is a problem which needs much attention. This is not a question that concerns the immigrants alone. Because of their return to Chicago to secure their next work there are always large numbers of unskilled laborers in the city who in prosperous times keep down the price paid this class of workers in and around Chicago and in times of distress and unemployment become a great burden to Chicago's charitable organizations.

Men are employed for this kind of work not as individuals, but in groups of thirty or more, and are sent to parts of the country of which they are entirely ignorant. If the employment agent were honest, philanthropic, and intelligently interested in the men, the situation would be difficult and discouraging enough for those who are anxious to see the immigrant adjusted

[1] Extract from Grace Abbott, "The Chicago Employment Agency and the Immigrant Worker," report to the Immigrants' Protective League, published in *American Journal of Sociology*, XIV (November, 1908), 292–300.

to his work with the least possible loss to himself and the community. The state of Illinois maintains free employment agencies. There are three in the city of Chicago.[1] But these are of little or no help to the immigrant. The superintendent of the south-side office, who also has charge of the inspection of private agencies, says the state agencies cannot place these groups of seasonal workers because they have no fees to divide with contractors and because the funds at their disposal are inadequate. To handle this kind of work successfully, interpreters are required, someone must accompany the men to the place of work, and often the railroad fare must be advanced. For this, the free employment agencies have no funds. . . . .

Forced to obtain work through the private employment agent the immigrant usually suffers in one of three ways: (1) he is overcharged for the services rendered; (2) the work obtained is not as represented by the agent either in character, permanency, or remuneration; (3) he fails to get work or the work lasts only a few days, leaving him often at an enormous distance from the city labor markets.

The maximum "registration fee" which the employment agent may charge is fixed by statute at two dollars. This term is not defined by the law but it is interpreted by the Attorney-General, as it would undoubtedly be by the courts, as in no way limiting the right of private contract. This means an agent may charge any amount for a particular job and as the registration system is practically never used by agents supplying unskilled workers the statutory provision is no protection to the immigrant. An investigator who represented himself to be a man who collected "gangs" was told frankly, "We charge all we can get."

Fees are higher when the applicant is unable to speak English. In several cases the investigator was offered the same job for two or three dollars less than was demanded of the man who was ignorant of our language. . . . .

The agent usually promises a "steady job" even when he is speaking of work which from its very nature cannot last more than a few weeks or a month or two. The wage promised in nearly every case was less than two dollars a day. All things considered then, it seems very clear that the service rendered is not worth the price paid, and yet it is the only way by which the men can get work. In many cases the fee includes railroad fare. What this amounts to is difficult to determine. The agent always gets reduced rates or, when the work is in connection with a railroad, the men are shipped free. How much is railroad fare and how much the agent's fee never appears on the receipt the men receive. In many cases it is divided between the agent and the contractor. Fourteen agents said they had arrangements of this sort with contractors. An agent who sent fifty Bulgarians to work near Springfield claimed that one-half of the six-dollar

[1] [After the publication of this study, the three state agencies were combined into one.]

fee was railroad fare. The men failed to get work and in a hearing before the Commissioner of Labor the fact was brought out that one hundred and fifty dollars had gone, not to the company, but to the company's contractors. We have said the fee was too large even if work which lasts a few weeks or months is secured on the terms promised, but too often this is not the case. Several concrete cases which have come to the attention of the League since its very recent formation will illustrate this. During the past year a railroad has been building from Searcey in north-central Arkansas to Leslie, about ninety miles farther west. Great numbers of men were sent from Chicago to Leslie to work on this road. We found two groups who had been there. One of these was made up of Hungarians. There were fifty-three men and two women—one of these had a baby—who expected to act as cooks for the gang. They were shipped April 14, by a Chicago agent, through a St. Louis agent. They paid the Chicago agent fourteen dollars apiece and were promised steady work at $1.40 a day. When they reached Leslie this is what happened, according to the story told by the men. They were told that the work was twenty-five miles from there. They walked to this place but the foreman only laughed at them and said he had no work for any such number. He finally put to work fifteen men and the woman who was unencumbered with the baby. The rest were told there would be work for them later on but they were without money or food and so could not stay. They started to walk back to Chicago where more such jobs are always to be had! At the end of the third day the woman gave out and the men pooled their money and sent her home on the railroad. Then they scattered so as to find work on the way. Two of them were shot by the police in St. Louis and when last heard from were in a hospital there. The rest of them eventually reached Chicago.

This is the story one of the men told an investigator in answer to a question as to whether the agency which shipped them was not the best place to get jobs. The story was told not with any hope of getting back their money but to warn a fellow-workman. It seemed to be true so an effort was made to have the fees paid the agent refunded. The agent denied that the men could not get work and in attempting to learn the facts, we came to appreciate how helpless the immigrant is who has risked all his money to get work and is sent to a remote and isolated part of the country where no one understands his language or cares about his difficulties. We wrote to various people about these Hungarians but were unable to learn anything definite. The contractor assured us that though the men were moved on from one place to another they were all eventually offered work but refused because they objected to being separated. This the men denied, but at such a distance from Searcey they were unable to prove their story.

We found, however, that another agent had shipped about five hundred men to Searcey during the winter, but said, "You cannot get men to go there now because other agents sent too many men and they did not get jobs." A third agent offered, in July after the contractor in a letter written July 21 had assured us that all the men who came had been "put to work and kept to work as long as they would stay, or *until the work was finished a few weeks ago,*" to send thirty men a week to Leslie for fifteen dollars apiece. Eighteen Bulgarians were sent there early in the spring, ten were given work and the others walked back to Chicago. These were the ones we learned about. How many of the hundreds of men sent down there during the winter and spring "walked back" one cannot say.

Ten Polish laborers from one house on the west side went to Wyoming last winter expecting to work in a lumber camp. They paid an agent ten dollars apiece. When they were put off the train in Wyoming they found no work of the character described but were given work for a short time on the railroad. Then they started to walk back. One of the men, a bright young fellow of twenty-two, froze his foot. With no money to pay to a doctor for treatment and compelled to walk on, when he finally reached Chicago blood poisoning had set in and it was necessary to amputate the foot. Although crippled for life, he feels not so much resentment against the agent who sent him as shame that he should have been so ignorant of the climate of Wyoming and humiliation that he should have proved such an easy victim. This is one of the most pathetic things in connection with the work. The men are ashamed to tell their story. "Everyone cheats a greenhorn," they say, and they want to hide, even from those who are anxious to help them, what they consider a reflection on their intelligence.

We had other cases of the same sort. Fifty Bulgarians, already referred to, failed to get work and walked back from near Springfield, and fourteen Macedonians had the same experience at Winchester, Illinois. A Jewish carpenter was sent to Nebraska expecting to work at his trade. When he reached his destination he found that the work was digging trenches, that he had to stand in water all day long, and that the wages were $2.00 instead of $2.75 a day. He left his wife and children in Chicago and does not know whether to walk back or continue to do work which will eventually leave him sick and stranded at a distance from his relatives and friends.

For any of these men to get work without first returning to Chicago, is practically impossible. There probably is work near where they are left in Wyoming, Arkansas, or Nebraska, but they have no means of knowing where it is to be found. Unable to speak English and with no funds to live on temporarily, they are afraid to go farther in search of work. It is little to be wondered at that they are homesick and discouraged and anxious to get back to their friends in the city. The law provides redress for such breaches of contract, but the civil courts are not available for men who are without money or friends. The risks anyone would run in dealing with such men as most of the employment agents are would be great enough, but for men who know nothing of our language, who cannot give accurate accounts of where they have been because of their ignorance of the country, who do not understand what is told them when they reach their place of destination, the risks are enormous. The agent, on the other hand, takes few chances when he sends men out to jobs that do not exist because the men are so defenseless. . . . .

3. Labor Camps and Labor-Camp Inspection

A. LABOR CAMPS IN NEW YORK[1]

To accommodate alien and other contract laborers installed temporarily in a given place, labor camps have been established in various parts of the State. These camps house laborers on public works, such as the barge canal, State roads and the Ashokan Dam, or on private work such as lumber camps, brick yards and canneries.

For these works the labor camp is a necessary institution in the present development of the United States. Work has often to be carried on where there are no permanent accommodations for boarding and lodging the workmen. For this reason a well-equipped boarding camp, with kitchens, dining-rooms and bunk houses, and assistants, equipments and supplies is as much a necessity for a contracting company as the picks, shovels, and machinery for doing the work.

In these labor camps the various races mix together and in this crude form get their first contact with American institutions and ways of living. The Italians, unlike other races, live or herd by themselves in boarding houses under the management of the padrone. The padrone encourages the boarding house method of living on account of the profits he realizes from the sale of food, and because, through this system, he is continually in touch with his countrymen and can control their movements and employment. When work ceases with one employer, he can transfer them to another and make a profit on the fee for each man. It is said that the Italian laborer himself insists upon this system, because in this way he can live more cheaply even if he must buy of the most unscrupulous padrone, and can have the food to which he is accustomed at home. Nearly every agency friendly to the Italian also encourages him in this method of living. The Italian societies themselves, which aim to protect him from the misconduct of the padrone and others, insist upon the establishment at labor camps of the commissary or store, and of his own methods of cooking, they as well as the padrone making it one of the conditions of employment. This is disproved, however, by the fact that in emergency cases, when a

[1] Extract from *Report of the Commission of Immigration of the State of New York* (1909), pp. 124–28. Cf. the *First Annual Report of the Bureau of Industries and Immigration, New York State Department of Labor* (1911), pp. 70–72. "Of all the wretched living conditions in this great State today these in the railroad camps surpass anything investigated by this Bureau. Nowhere else has been found such an absolute disregard for comfort, health, morality, and justice."

railroad finds it necessary to assemble a body of Italian and other laborers quickly at some given point, the Italians not only use the company's boarding cars, but accept without question the free meals of soups and roasted and boiled meats prepared in the usual American style.

Mr. Sheridan [of the federal Bureau of Labor], in concluding his discussion of labor camps, says:

So long as the commissary system, good or bad, exists, just so long will the Italian remain a stranger in a strange land. The difficulty is not one, merely, of reforming the padrone system. Compelling honest dealing will not remedy the evil. The action of some railroads has brought about reforms, and there will continue to be at normal prices a big profit to the padrone in the sale of supplies to 4,000 or 5,000 men. The honest, independent labor camp, where employment is furnished without cost, is just as bad a thing for the purpose of American citizenship as is the padrone camp, if the commissary system of segregation is in operation at both camps.

The labor camps investigated differed greatly as to nationality of workmen, conditions of life, methods of securing employment, sanitary arrangements, charges and hours of labor. The lumber camps appear to be better in many respects than the other camps investigated, constituted, as they are, largely of French Canadians who are skilled men in receipt of higher wages than the Italians and other unskilled workers in other camps.

Reports from eight camps give returns largely for Italian labor, but include Polish, Russian, Spanish, and other laborers. In these camps the storekeeper is usually a commissary agent who has secured the privilege of selling goods to the men. Misrepresentations as to work, non-payment of wages, overcharges at the commissary, and brutality on the part of overseers, of foremen or of bosses, are the principal complaints of the men.

The twenty-one camps investigated were located from one-quarter of a mile to as many as $24\frac{1}{2}$ miles from the nearest railroad station. The nearest justice of the peace in any case was one-half mile distant, while in one case this officer of the law was so far as $15\frac{1}{2}$ miles. The smallest number of employees in any one camp was 14, the largest 2,000. Seven were lumber camps employing a total of 229 men, practically all of whom were skilled workers. Four were State road camps, and in three others 178 men were employed, thirty being teamsters, or skilled workers, and 148 unskilled laborers. One camp was located near a quarry, where the 350 laborers were principally engaged in stone quarrying and crushing, the remaining seven were camps, the population of which was engaged on the barge canal, or on dam and like construction work. The number of laborers in each of these construction camps ranged from eighty to 2,000.

Accidents in the lumber camps visited by investigators of the Commission average in each about one a month, and are largely due to the laborer being caught by falling trees and to being cut by the axe slipping on knots. These camps do not report accidents to any State authority. There is no accident insurance on the part of the men, nor does there exist among the laborers or employers any mutual relief or insurance society. Quite frequently however, the camp employees voluntarily make up a purse out of their wages to care for a fellow-worker seriously injured. The employer seldom, if ever, insures in any casualty company against the liability of accidents to his men. These statements apply with equal force to the State road labor camps. Some railroad construction companies provide for casualty insurance against accidents to employees.

The shanties furnished for lodgings in many camps are rough and inadequately supplied with the ordinary necessities for decent and cleanly living. Such conditions are particularly objectionable in camps where women and children form an element. The standard charge for bunking in these camps is $1 a month per man. There is much overcrowding, and the shanties and wooden shacks are almost uniformly dirty, the air being frequently stifling and malodorous. Sanitary conditions in and about these shanties are usually bad, as illustrated by the following reports of the investigators of the Commission:

Camp No. 15.—The quarters consist of one room shanties, accommodating from twenty to fifty laborers. No attempt is made to clean them, and they have an unwholesome odor. They are covered with tar paper and have no windows.

Camp No. 16.—One shanty is an old family house arranged to accommodate fifty laborers. The roofs are covered with tar paper, and the ceilings of clay are broken and falling. Around the shanty the water thrown from the kitchen forms a muddy belt, giving an unpleasant odor. There was no cleaning of the floors, bed stalls or the mattresses. No provision is made for a toilet. There are no provisions for washing, and no dining-room. Tables are arranged by nailing boards on poles stuck in the ground outside under the cooking place.

Camp No. 17.—The shanty consists of one room about 25×75. The bed stalls are arranged around the walls in three stories. Access to each row is obtained by a single movable step-ladder used in turn by the climbers. The floor is the bare ground, and has not been cleaned, and dirt is massed all over the disagreeably odorous place. The shanty accommodates about 120 men. No provisions are made for toilet or washing, the neighborhood of the shanty being used for the former. There was no standing water; no dining-room. The laborers eat mostly on flat stones arranged like tables on poles stuck into the ground.

Camp No. 18.—This was an old brick house, two stories high. Piles of dirt were accumulated on the floor as the room was being swept, and flying dust covered every object. On the first floor were Polish and Russian laborers, and on the second, Italian. The beds consisted of folding bed frames with a mattress of straw. The mattresses were in no case clean. There is a stove in the house, around which refuse water forms a belt, emitting a disagreeable odor. There is only one room on each floor, with no partitions, and beds are arranged to touch one another.

Strikingly in contrast with these filthy and uncomfortable conditions are the neat shanties, some of them having attractive gardens, at the Ashokan Dam. The bachelor quarters have running water and shower baths, and there is a well-arranged dining-room in the center of the quarters. Filth is not allowed to accumulate near the shanties, and forethought was exercised in building the accommodations on the hillside so that standing water could not stagnate. The entire camp gave an impression of cleanliness, which cannot fail to influence the habits and character of the workers.

The living conditions at the canneries, in which many aliens work, is similar to that of the labor camps, and they are equally in need of public supervision. From notes of agents of the State Department of Labor are quoted the following observations, showing injurious physical and moral conditions.

In one cannery the sanitary conditions are "quite good, with the exception that floors are kept unclean in many rooms." In another, "cleanliness and drainage good; several of the rooms contained two to five beds, and it appears that overcrowding exists here." "Company owns two buildings in which Italians live packed in like sardines." "Two buildings contain 32 rooms, each having a small window about $1\frac{1}{2} \times 2$ feet. The rooms are kept very filthy and congestion is obvious. The rooms are not fit to live in in their present unsanitary condition."

Of sleeping quarters in various canneries it is said: "Large room, concrete construction, three small windows, six women, seven children, one married man, one stove, six beds, two females nursing babies." "One room upstairs (stairway weak); two windows 20×18 inches; three beds, one cot; five women, five children, one man."

"Large room, six women, two men (one with his wife and one with his mother), two children." "One room 12×20 feet, six women, one man, three children."

Such conditions are injurious not only to the workers and their families, but to the community and to the State, which suffers from the physical and moral degeneration caused by herding human beings like cattle. Some of the high records of criminality among immigrants might be explained by the conditions of living tolerated in the labor camps and similar places.

Summer camps must necessarily be built as cheaply as possible, but the health and decency of the workers should be considered, and if contractors do not regard these considerations as important to their own interest, they certainly are to the public interest. In view of the number of these camps and their probable continuance, it seems wise to urge that the supervision of sanitary conditions be placed under some proper State authority.

As to the amelioration of the sanitary conditions in labor camps and canneries, it is of interest to note that while the present Labor Law of the State of New York (Articles 6 and 7) enforces the laws of hygiene in factories, it leaves laborers not working in factories unprotected, and hence result the deplorable conditions existing in the shanties and camps used as living quarters. The overcrowding and bad ventilation in these places are sources of danger, and tuberculosis frequently develops in these surroundings, where, under normal conditions, it should not be encountered.

The Commission believes that the present uncontrolled operations of the padrone entail grave evils upon the State and upon the aliens. It, therefore, recommends that the present supervision of canneries by the Department of Labor be extended so as to include regulation of sanitary and housing conditions, and that all labor camps be placed either under the supervision and regulation of the Department of Labor, or under that of the Bureau or Department of Industries and Immigration, for which provision [should be] made.

B. LABOR-CAMP INSPECTION IN CALIFORNIA[1]

Under section 7 of the act [creating the California Commission of Immigration and Housing] "with the object in view of rendering to the immigrant that protection to which he is entitled," the Commission was given authority to "inspect all labor camps within the state." Although it had been planned to examine into labor camp conditions, the Commission was almost unwittingly drawn into what proved to be one of its most important works when this examination was actually begun.

The Wheatland case.—There had occurred on August 3, 1913, on the Durst hop ranch near Wheatland, Yuba County, a riot among the hop pickers employed on the ranch, resulting in the killing of two police officials and two pickers. It was the claim of the pickers that one of the primary causes of the discontent in their ranks, leading to riot and bloodshed, was the insanitary condition of the camp in which they were segregated on the ranch. Brief investigations and reports of state officials had partially substantiated these claims. Before the trial of Richard Ford and Hermann Suhr, charged with having caused the murder of one of the state officials by inciting the crowd of pickers to riot, was begun, it was announced that evidence concerning the sanitary and living conditions in the camp would be introduced. Consequently the Commission decided to avail itself of this opportunity to conduct a careful investigation into the economic and social causes leading up to the riot. This investigation was decidedly pertinent, as a preliminary survey disclosed the fact that, at the time of the riot, approximately one half of the pickers on the Durst ranch were immigrants.

[1] Extract from the *First Annual Report of the Commission of Immigration and Housing of California* (1914), pp. 15–30.

During the trial of the accused pickers, which was begun on January 12, 1914, the Commission had present at times four and at other times two investigators, besides its executive secretary and attorney. The investigation was directed by the Commission's attorney along legal lines. All hearsay was excluded and only direct evidence from persons who had actually been present in the camp on the Durst ranch and who spoke from actual knowledge was considered. From the witnesses at the trial the names and addresses of other persons who had been employed on the Durst ranch in 1913 were obtained, and investigators were sent to the homes of these people throughout central and northern California to get their direct testimony. This testimony was of particular value, because it was entirely free from the possible influence of the prejudice which might have governed the feelings of some of the witnesses in the murder trial. Besides the evidence bearing on the living conditions recorded during the progress of the trial, 67 affidavits were secured and interviews with 30 witnesses recorded. The results of this investigation are here merely summarized.

In previous years there had often been a lack of pickers when the hops were ripe, but in the season of 1913, by means of coastwide advertising, the Durst brothers succeeded in assembling an army of nearly 3,000 persons, and at the time of the riot there were probably 2,800 workers in the camps, about half of them women and children. Of this number, fully 1,000 were foreign born males, including Syrians, Mexicans, Italians, Porto Ricans, Poles, Hindus and Japanese. The American element was made up of wandering casual workers, poor persons from near-by towns, owners of small ranches in the foothills of the Sierras, roving hoboes and a few families of the better laboring class from towns and cities, who often go to the hop fields for their summer "outing."

When this motley horde arrived at the Durst ranch, they found a desolate, sunbaked field, without shelter from the burning California sun. There were a few tents to be rented at 75 cents a week, but the majority had to construct rude shelters of poles and gunny sacks, called "bull pens," while many were compelled to sleep in the open on piles of vines or straw. . . . .

There was a scarcity of drinking water, some of the wells were pumped dry, while others became infected from the surface water that drained back from stagnant pools, which formed in close proximity to the toilets and garbage piles. Under such shocking insanitary conditions sickness followed as a matter of course. There were cases of typhoid and malaria, caused probably by these germ laden waters.

While the wage scale and other factors contributed to the feeling of discontent, the real cause of the protest of the pickers seemed to come from the inadequate housing and the insanitary conditions under which the hop pickers were compelled to live.

Statewide labor camp inspection.—The Commission decided that these conditions constituted an aggravation of industrial warfare, and that they could and should be changed. It was ascertained that the Durst camp was no exception; similar conditions existed in other labor camps throughout California and it was evident that a statewide "clean-up" campaign was necessary. This task really came under the jurisdiction of the State Board of Health, but that body was without funds to do the work of inspection and of correction. Consequently, the Commission, with the consent of the State Board of Health, decided to enter upon the undertaking itself, particularly because over one half of the population of the labor camps of the state is made up of immigrants.

The existing state law pertaining to the housing and sanitation of labor camps was found to be indefinite and inadequate. It merely states in general terms that tents, sleeping quarters, and the ground about the camp must be kept clean. No way is provided for ascertaining the conditions of the camps, except through the occasional complaint of a laborer fearless enough to risk incurring the displeasure of his employer. Nor does the statute attempt to set forth a minimum standard of housing and sanitation. Owing to these weaknesses in the existing law, the Commission had first to work out a minimum standard of living conditions in labor camps. This minimum standard must be sufficiently high to insure results, but not so expensive and so impracticable as to deter employers of labor from adopting it, since employers had to be persuaded, rather than compelled by law, to make the improvements suggested.

It was not until after eight months of experience in camp sanitation work that the Commission drafted a detailed law to govern labor camp sanitation. This law does not deal in generalities but makes specific regulations for every feature of the camp.

In order that it might be sure of its ground in the beginning, the Commission decided to take over a camp and make it sanitary, thus putting theories to actual test. This first experiment in camp sanitation was made at Shingle Springs, El Dorado County, where 129 men were employed by the state on the state highway. The sanitary engineer of the Commission was sent to the camp, where he installed sanitary camp latrines, shower baths, fly-screened cooking and dining tents, model sleeping quarters, garbage incinerators and other modern improvements at a minimum cost. The results were very satisfactory and a set of sanitation rules was accordingly drawn up. These rules and the practical suggestions for carrying them out were incorporated in a small pamphlet of seven pages, which met with the approval of the State Board of Health.

These pamphlets were distributed among camp operators, and two inspectors, under the direction of a sanitary engineer, were put in the field. Although most of the camps were below the minimum standard, the inspectors found that employers or operators were willing to co-operate in the effort to improve the conditions of the men, but they did not know *how* to go about the work. Consequently, a larger and more comprehensive pamphlet, containing detailed plans and instructions, was prepared for general distribution. . . . .[1]

During the months of June, July, August and September, when the largest number of labor camps are in existence, from five to seven inspectors were kept in the field. The inspectors found little, if any, antagonism, some procrastination, and a great deal of good feeling and hearty cooperation. They reported their findings to the office of the Commission on blanks prepared for the purpose, which gave every detail of the camp inspected, including the number and nationality of men employed, permanent or transient, skilled or unskilled labor, living conditions, sanitary conditions, toilets, bathing facilities, etc. A letter of instructions and a pamphlet were then promptly mailed from the main office to each owner or superintendent, calling attention to the special needs of his camp, and inviting correspondence with the office of the Commission if his difficulty arose in trying to make his camp conform to the requirements. . . . .

The statistics gathered from 876 of these camps have been tabulated. These 876 camps housed 36,846 persons on the date of inspection and had an ultimate capacity of 60,813. By "ultimate capacity" is meant the number the camp is arranged to accommodate and those figures represent the true population of the camps, because many hop, berry and fruit camps, etc., were empty when inspected, as the season had not begun.

Camps were classed as "good," "fair" and "bad," according to a rating established in connection with the minimum standard; 297 of the 876 camps were "good" and housed 21,577 persons; 316, housing 22,382, were "fair"; 263, housing 16,854, were "bad."

4. Peonage in Relation to Immigration[2]

The Immigration Commission was already planning an investigation of alleged peonage cases in which immigrants were concerned, when, on

[1] "Advisory Pamphlet on Camp Sanitation and Housing," 56 pages. Mailed free upon request, by Commission of Immigration and Housing, 525 Market Street, San Francisco. ["In this booklet it was pointed out that a sanitary camp meant an increase in the willingness and efficiency of the laborer, and that it was in the employers' own pecuniary interest, as well as that of humanity, to have a sanitary and livable camp. Every phase of camp housing and sanitation was dealt with, costs in different parts of the state were quoted, and building specifications were given. Blue prints were furnished when desired. The suggestions covered the site of camp, with advice as to choosing high ground; layout of camp, giving proper distances from chicken houses, pig pens, toilets, garbage receptacles, etc., from sleeping, eating and cook houses; water supply, how polluted; construction of tents, buildings, and bunks, etc." (p. 22).]

[2] Extract from *Reports of the United States Immigration Commission*, II (1911), 443–49. The report quotes the following definition of peonage: "Peonage is a

March 2, 1908, the following resolution was passed by the House of Representatives:

That the Immigration Commission be requested to make an investigation into the treatment and conditions of work of immigrants on the cotton plantations of the Mississippi Delta, in the States of Mississippi and Arkansas, and upon the turpentine farms, lumber camps, and railway camps in the States of Florida, Mississippi, Louisiana, and other States, and to report them at as early a date as possible. . . . .

The word "peonage" does not appear in the House resolution, the Commission having been requested "to make an investigation into the treatment and conditions of work of immigrants." It was evidently intended, however, that an examination should be made of complaints and cases in which peonage had been alleged, and the peonage committee has confined its work chiefly to such matters. . . . .

Because of the public interest in connection with the allegations of peonage in the southern States, the Commission commenced its investigations there, and because of the resolution passed by the House the investigation was undertaken personally by a subcommittee of the Commission. This committee found and reports that instances of peonage had occurred in 1906 and 1907 in some of the southern States, but these were only sporadic instances and the Commission found no general system of peonage anywhere. There had been convictions in Florida, including one case in which the defendants resided in Alabama, and the most flagrant case found was in the State of Arkansas. In the Arkansas case the immigrant was arrested as a vagrant, convicted before a justice of the peace, and sentenced to pay a fine of $10 and costs. There was added to his sentence, without authority of law, the expenses and mileage of the constable who came to the town where he was arrested, and the expenses and mileage of the constable and prisoner going from the place of arrest to the convict farm, the lessee of which paid to the county where the arrest took place 25 per cent of the fine only and the justice's costs, but held the prisoner to work out both the legal and illegal expenses at the rate of 75 cents a day. In this case the prisoners were kept in a barn, 80 men being kept in a moderate-sized building with no special arrangements for ventilation or sanitation. On Saturday nights the men were locked in the building and kept there until Monday morning. There was a good deal of sickness among the men, despite the fact that during the week days they were healthfully employed out of doors. While at work the men were guarded by "trusties" armed with shotguns. There were both white and colored men among the trusties. Members of the subcommittee were present in the United States circuit court in Little

---

status or condition of compulsory service based upon the indebtedness of the peon to the master. The basic fact is indebtedness" (Clyatt case, 197 U.S. 207). See also *Report of the Massachusetts Commission on Immigration* (1914), p. 41.

Rock when the proprietor of this particular farm was the unsuccessful defendant in the suit for damages brought by a prisoner who had been so illegally detained and in whose favor the jury gave a substantial verdict. These prisoners, held to work at illegal sums and some of whom were whipped and otherwise ill-treated, illustrate what is commonly accepted as peonage. On the other hand, the following statement of facts also constitutes peonage:

A laborer secures an advance, either in money or by way of payment of transportation expenses, under an agreement to work out the amount. He leaves his employment with or, as frequently happens, without justification before the employer is fully repaid. The employer procures his arrest, either on the ground of obtaining money under false pretenses or under the labor statutes of many of the States, and then enters into a new agreement with the laborer that if he will return to his employment and work out his indebtedness the criminal proceeding will be dropped. A majority of the cases brought to the attention of the Commission approach nearer the latter class than the first.

While in the South the Commission was informed that cases of restraint of foreign laborers, which constituted peonage under the Clyatt decision, existed in many northern States, and consequently an investigator who had been with the committee in the South was directed to investigate these complaints. The result was that in every State except Oklahoma and Connecticut the investigator found evidence of practices between employer and employee which, if substantiated by legal evidence in each case, would constitute peonage as the Supreme Court has described it. In connection with the southern cases it should be noted that in nearly every instance brought to the attention of the Commission the laborers who were held in peonage had been sent south from New York City, the victims of gross misrepresentations by labor agents there as to conditions under which they were to work, and totally unfitted for the work to which they were going. The committe found the local United States district attorneys in the southern States conversant with the statutes and successful in prosecutions. Practically all of the prosecutions for peonage have been had in the South; indictments have been found in Virginia, West Virginia, North Carolina, South Carolina, Georgia, Florida, Alabama, Mississippi, Tennessee, Kentucky, Missouri, Arkansas, and Louisiana, and convictions or pleas of guilty in Virginia, West Virginia, North Carolina, Georgia, Florida, Alabama, Mississippi, Arkansas, and Missouri. In the opinion of the Commission the vigorous prosecutions have broken up whatever tendency there was toward peonage in connection with aliens in the southern States, and the fact that juries in those States will convict even in cases of technical peonage unaccompanied by brutality would seem to indicate that offenses against alien laborers will not be permitted to go unpunished.

Possibly the most widely heralded case of alleged peonage was that connected with the building of the extension of the Florida East Coast

Railway. These allegations were investigated by the Bureau of Labor, by the governor of Florida, and by the Immigration Commission. A member of the Commission went to all of the construction camps in existence in 1909, and was permitted free and untrammelled conversation with the men there employed. Members of the Commission also examined the officers of the road, former employees in the hospital at Miami, and even prisoners in the chain gang on the streets in Miami. All of these investigations indicate that from the beginning the officers of the road issued strict orders against either brutality toward the men or acts in the nature of peonage or illegal restraint. In the beginning, however, of the organization of this large force of 4,000 men the company suffered from the carelessness—to use no harsher term—of the labor agents in New York City, who, in receipt of commissions for each man sent, recruited many men totally unfit for construction work, numbers of whom had no intention of ever even going to Florida, and 25 per cent of whom, as a matter of fact, never did reach any of the construction camps. In some of the camps in the earlier days there was some coercion of this sorry labor; there were attempts to compel individuals to work, and some foremen who indulged in these practices were discharged by the company.

Neither the governor of Florida, the Commission, nor the Department of Justice has been able to find anything in the nature of legal proof that peonage ever existed upon any of this work of the Florida East Coast Railway. Men were found in 1909 who had left the work as many as three times and were in their fourth employment. These men testified that their treatment had been good throughout. In one or two instances men who came in the early days of the work had remained and risen to positions of some responsibility. The cases in which agents of the company were sought to be convicted of peonage in no instance resulted in a conviction.

The peonage cases in the South relating to immigrants have been found to cover almost every industry—farming, lumbering, logging, railroading, mining, factories, and construction work. The chief causes of the abuses have been the systems of making advances to laborers, the operations of contract-labor laws, and the misrepresentations made to laborers by unscrupulous employment agents. The cases of beating and brutal treatment have been exceptional. . . . .

PEONAGE IN NEW ENGLAND

The peonage investigation has developed the fact that involuntary servitude may be found in the East as well as in the South and the West.

Since the evils of involuntary servitude have been largely stamped out in the southern States, there has probably existed in Maine the most complete system of peonage in the entire country. In late years the natives who formerly supplied the labor for the logging concerns in that State have been engaged in the paper mills, and the lumber companies have been compelled to import laborers, largely foreigners, from other States. Boston is the chief labor market for the Maine forests. The employment agents misrepresent conditions in the woods, and frequently tell the laborers that the camps will be but a few miles from some town where they can go from time to time for recreation and enjoyment. Arriving at the outskirts of civilization the laborers are driven in wagons a short distance into the forests and then have to walk sometimes 60 or 70 miles into the interior, the roads being impassable for vehicles. The men will then be kept in the heart of the forest for months throughout the winter, living in a most rugged fashion and with no recreation whatever. A great many of them have rebelled against this treatment, and they have left their employers by the score. The lumbermen having advanced transportation and supplies have appealed to the legislature for protection. In February, 1907, a bill became a law making it a crime for a person to—

Enter into an agreement to labor for any lumbering operation or in driving logs and in consideration thereof receive any advances of goods, money, or transportation, and unreasonably and with intent to defraud, fail to enter into said employment as agreed and labor a sufficient length of time to reimburse his employer for said advances and expenses.

Judges in municipal courts and trial justices were given jurisdiction to try cases under this law, and the act provided that it would take effect immediately upon approval. When this bill was before the legislature, requests were made by citizens interested in factories and other industries that the provisions of the statute be made to protect all employers of labor. The attorney who introduced the bill on behalf of the lumber interests which he represented, has stated that he had refused to accede to these requests, inasmuch as he believed the provision should not be extended. The protection granted by the statute, therefore, was restricted to a favored class, persons interested in "lumbering operations and in driving logs."

There is no provision in the Maine statute that—

the failure or refusal of any employee to perform such labor or render such services in accordance with his contract or to pay in money the amount for such transportation or such advancement shall be prima facie evidence of his intent to defraud;

as appears in the contract-labor law of Minnesota and in the statutes of other States in the West and the South. However, justices of the peace in Maine have decided indiscriminately that, in order to obtain a conviction under the law of that State, it is necessary to show only that the laborer obtained the "advances" and failed "to labor a sufficient length of time to reimburse his employer."

A justice at Houlton, Maine, who is a lawyer by profession, told the attorney representing the peonage committee that he decided in cases brought under the contract-labor law that "the burden of proof is upon the defendant," who must show to the court "beyond a reasonable doubt that he had no intent to defraud." This justice added that once in a while if a laborer has a really good excuse he will let him off, as he believes "every man has some rights, although he may be poor." Another justice of the peace at Patten, Maine, stated that if it was shown that a laborer had obtained the advances and had not worked sufficiently to settle for them he found the defendant guilty without considering the question of intent to defraud. This seems to be the general attitude of the rural justices of Maine toward the contract-labor law.

Considerable peonage has resulted from this statute. The law has been vigorously enforced. Soon after its passage prosecutions were commenced in the lumber regions, and the jail at Dover, the county seat of one of the large lumber counties of Maine, was crowded with laborers convicted of defrauding their employers out of "advances of goods, money, or transportation."

Involuntary servitude results in utilizing this statute to intimidate laborers to work against their will. On account of the vigorous methods pursued in enforcing the above-described law, it soon became known throughout the lumber region of Maine that any laborer was liable to imprisonment who refused to work according to the provisions of his contract until he had settled for all advances, no matter what misrepresentations may have been made to induce him to enter into the agreement. The contract-labor law has become a club which the foremen and superintendents draw upon the laborers who refuse to go to work or to continue at work. If a man leaves his employer before settling for advances, he will be pursued and apprehended, or someone will telephone to the constable, who will arrest the laborer. He will then be brought before the justice, and "sent down the river," to prison; or if he consents to labor until he shall have reimbursed for all advances and the fine and cost of the prosecution, the employer will settle with the court and constable and will take the laborer back into the forest. No doubt many of the laborers never attempt to escape, although they may consider that they have been basely deceived about the conditions of labor.

No indications of peonage have been found in any industries of Maine except those of the lumbering and logging concerns protected by the contract-labor law.

While from time to time sporadic cases of peonage have occurred in nearly all the States, there is no apparent general system of peonage and no sentiment supporting it anywhere. Prosecutions have occurred in several of the southern States, and where conducted by local United States district attorneys have more frequently succeeded than failed. The law as to peonage does not require any amendment and its enforcement is reasonably efficient in the States where prosecutions have occurred. No prosecutions were conducted in any of the northern and western States where cases of technical peonage were found to have occurred.

5. Immigrant Banks[1]

The "immigrant bank" is a nondescript, unchartered institution which flourishes in every part of the United States where immigrants from southern and eastern Europe are gathered in any considerable numbers. . . . .

It should be stated that prior to this investigation the subject of banking as practiced by immigrants had become one for grave consideration in the State of New York, particularly in New York City, where these concerns flourish as they do nowhere else. Careful investigations had been conducted there by both state and federal authorities. The bulk of the time of the present investigation, therefore, was spent in communities outside of New York City, in an effort to determine the nature and extent of the business

[1] Extracts from *Reports of the United States Immigration Commission*, II (1911), 413–24, 431–38. Although not a recent report it remains the most comprehensive discussion of the subject and it is still true in its essential particulars. The most important change affecting the immigrant bank situation since the Commission made its investigation has been the organization of the United States postal savings banks in June, 1910. The extent to which these banks have been used by immigrants is described in a recent text (S. P. Breckinridge, *New Homes for Old*, pp. 111–12) as follows: "The facilities thus provided were immediately taken advantage of by the foreign-born groups, and the postal savings banks became almost banks for the foreign born. That is, in September, 1916, 375,000, or 80 per cent, of the total number of depositors were persons of foreign birth, and they owned 75 per cent of the deposits. In proportion to population the deposits were in 1916 about eleven times as great as those of the native born (due allowance being made for the age of the two population groups). The Greeks, Italians, Russians, and Hungarians, all coming from countries in which there are postal savings arrangements, found it especially easy to make use of them. . . . . In spite of the fact that this system is characterized not only by security, but also by certain democratic and convenient features especially serviceable to many foreign born, there are certain limitations to which Professor Kemmerer (*Postal Savings Banks*, pp. 100–104) has called attention in the following statement: 'As a matter of fact, the interest rate paid is so low that it makes a very weak appeal to the class of people who deposit in the postal savings banks. Their motive is primarily security. The government is now realizing large profits from the postal savings system—for 1916 the estimated profit was $481,816—and this profit is coming from a class of people in the community, the thrifty poor, from whom it is bad social policy to take it. Of course it would be administratively impracticable to pay interest to depositors on average daily balances—no savings banks do that. Would it be expecting too much, however, to ask for our postal savings depositors the allowances of interest on half yearly or even quarterly balances? Moreover, is it unreasonable to ask the Board of Trustees, in view of the nomadic character of our foreign born population which patronizes the postal savings system most, to devise a simple system of transfer by which a depositor who is changing his place of residence may transfer his postal savings account without forfeiting his accumulated but yet undue interest?'"

elsewhere, rather than in the city itself where the methods had been more clearly brought to light. The results of the New York investigations, however, were supplemented and confirmed by additional inquiries.

Investigation has revealed the fact that there are in this country at the present time at least 2,625 concerns doing a so-called immigrant banking business. This total has been arrived at through a partial enumeration by the agents of the Commission, in connection with information received from authoritative sources, such as state bank commissioners and banking houses with which the immigrant concerns correspond, and does not take into consideration the multitude of saloon keepers, etc., who may be holding deposits for safekeeping or even, in a quiet way, receiving money for transmission abroad. . . . .[1]

Of the 110 immigrant banks examined, only one did a pure banking business; 29 were operated as steamship and foreign exchange agencies; 72 as banks in connection with some other business; and 8 were saloons, etc., whose proprietors were sending money abroad without maintaining a steamship agency. The remaining 6 out of the total of 116 establishments visited were steamship agencies without a bank in connection.

Of the 86 bankers and steamship agents—including the 6 above mentioned—carrying on some other business in connection, some have one other business, some two, and some three or four. These other lines of business and employments are represented as follows: 24 real estate, rental, insurance and collecting agencies, 40 notarial offices, 13 labor agencies, 11 postal substations, 12 book, jewelry, and foreign novelty stores; 21 saloon keepers, 14 grocers, butchers, and fruit venders, 9 general merchants, 7 wholesalers and importers, 2 barbers, 8 boarding bosses or room renters, 2 printers, 2 pool-room keepers, 1 furniture dealer, 1 undertaker, and 28 with similar financial interests apart from the place where the banking business was conducted.

ORIGIN OF IMMIGRANT BANKS

The question arises, How have financial functions become confused with other lines of business? The answer is found in the manner in which these banks originate and the character of the men who operate them. Out of the total of 116 establishments examined as representative of existing conditions, 107 were steamship agencies, and of this number all but 6 did an immigrant banking business. In other words, 94 per cent of the concerns engaged in the business of selling steamship tickets were at the same time engaged in the business of immigrant banking. This shows that the relation between the two is so close as to warrant the characterization of them as interdependent. Even the casual observer readily learns to associ-

[1] In certain large cities and their environs immigrant banks are very numerous. In New York City there are known to be as many as 500, in Pittsburgh 50, in Chicago 75, in Buffalo 40, in Cleveland 20, and in St. Louis 30.

ate the term "immigrant bank" with the poster-bedecked office of the immigrant representative of steamship companies. In the mind of the immigrant the two are almost inseparable. To him the steamship agent is the sole connecting link with the fatherland. As the representative of well-known lines, he ascribes to the agent a standing and responsibility such as he has no cause to assign to any American institution. Nothing is more natural than that the immigrant should take his savings to the agent and ask that the agent send them home for him. Having made the start, it is natural that he should continue to leave with the agent for safe-keeping his weekly or monthly surplus, so that he may accumulate a sufficient amount for another remittance or for the purpose of buying a steamship ticket to bring his family to this country or for his own return to Europe. It is not long before the agent has a nucleus for a banking business, and his assumption of banking functions quickly follows. The transition is then complete—the steamship agent has become an immigrant banker.

CHARACTER OF PROPRIETORS

The responsibilities imposed upon those who act as bankers for the immigrants are so light as to make the assumption of that important office dependent upon no other qualifications than the would-be banker's ability to inspire the confidence of his compatriot, which racial ties render comparatively easy. Numerous instances are at hand where strangers have gone into communities and established themselves as steamship agents and foreign-exchange dealers. Their only qualification was that they were Italians among Italians, or Magyars among Magyars. Even a former evil reputation does not appear to injure their ability to attract patronage. In the course of the investigation, knowledge was gained of two fugitive swindlers, two clerks discharged for dishonesty, and several laborers dismissed for dishonesty or incompetency, who have established themselves successfully as bankers. Hundreds of saloon keepers and grocers act as bankers without the least fitness or equipment. Although banking functions are more or less forced upon men of this character, and although they may be exercised in a thoroughly honorable way by many, the fact remains that many hundreds of thousands of dollars belonging to immigrant laborers are handled by ignorant, incompetent, or untrustworthy men.

CHARACTER OF PATRONS

In this connection it is important to bear in mind that the immigrant banker deals almost wholly with the great body of floating alien labor—that is, those of more recent arrival—who constitute a class farthest removed from Americanization, notably unversed in financial matters, easily influenced by racial appeal, and largely dependent upon the leaders of their own nationality. A successful Italian banker, in commenting upon the ignorance and trustfulness of his patrons, pointed out the ease with which he could exploit them should he so desire. According to this informant, it is not uncommon for laborers who have made deposits to lose their receipts, and, forgetting how much is due them, to take without question whatever balance the banker returns. A member of a leading steamship agency in a large city, which acts simply as depositing agent in assisting immigrants to open accounts in responsible banks, testified that should his firm care to solicit or even to receive without solicitation these deposits, it could command at least $200,000, so frequently and insistently are sums tendered for safe-keeping.

The question arises, Why has not the immigrant laborer, disliking or fearing to carry his savings around with him, turned to American institutions to satisfy his banking needs, rather than to the less responsible men of his own race? The causes for his failure to do this are threefold: (1) The ignorance and suspicion of the immigrant, (2) the fact that American institutions have not developed the peculiar facilities necessary in the handling of immigrant business, (3) the ability and willingness of the immigrant proprietor to perform for his countrymen necessary services that it would be impossible for them to obtain otherwise.

The great hindrance in securing immigrant patronage for American banks lies in the alien's ignorance of the English language. Inability to read and write, necessitating the transaction of business through an interpreter, combined with a poor comprehension of the checking system and other banking devices, is apt to cause him to prefer the money belt to the bank, the saloon keeper to the trust company. A natural hesitancy to place confidence in strangers of other races is augmented in many cases by a positive suspicion of American institutions. It was said of the Greeks in a certain locality that they stood somewhat in awe of the magnificent proportions and equipment of the modern city bank. An Italian banker said of his countrymen that their suspicions were aroused by the very richness and, to them, extravagance in the equipment of the average American bank. The Austro-Hungarian races show a similar inclination to look with distrust upon local American institutions. A possible explanation lies in the fact that these races, largely agricultural in character prior to coming to America, are not accustomed to the extended use of banking facilities, or, if so accustomed, confine their relations to the financial institutions operated by the government in their respective countries. They have learned that the banks of this country are not government institutions, and for that reason look with disfavor upon them.

In any event, it is certain that they are usually suspicious of any attempt on the part of Americans to influence the place or manner of their savings. Not possessed of an intelligent grasp of financial questions, the average immigrant is easily excited in money matters. Perhaps he does not differ essentially from some American depositors in this respect, but he is quicker to accept the assurances of irresponsible persons that his money will at all times and under any conditions be available. This assurance he obtains from the immigrant banker. Thus the man of his own race, be he saloon keeper, grocer, boarding boss, or banker, who agrees to pay on demand at any hour, is more likely to become the custodian of the immigrant's savings than are institutions of unquestioned strength and reliability.

The fact that in many localities immigrants of different nationalities maintain accounts with reputable banking firms may not be regarded as exceptional so much as indicative of a gradual establishment of confidence in such firms, arising from the frequent frauds to which the immigrants have been subjected by their countrymen. At the present time, however, this tendency is perhaps confined to those who are permanently located in the United States or have been in the country for a considerable period of time. It is more or less doubtful whether such relations can ever be established with the large class of floating alien labor in this country. It would seem desirable, but its attainment is dependent largely upon the desire of the local banks to attract immigrant business, and upon their ability to offer the peculiar facilities necessary for obtaining it. In justice to the immigrant it must be stated that in the past neither of these factors has been greatly in evidence. It is true that in recent years there has been a tendency among the banks in the financial districts of St. Louis, Pittsburgh, Chicago, Cleveland, and other large cities to establish foreign departments with competent managers and clerks of the various races of recent immigration. In addition to these departments, "neighborhood" and branch banks in sections populated by immigrants have been more or less successful in securing a share of the immigrant business, both as regards remittances abroad and savings accounts. On the whole, however, there has been a decided disposition among American institutions not to solicit the patronage of the alien directly, especially in view of the fact that his deposits are often for temporary safekeeping only, to handle which would require an unwarranted amount of bookkeeping. Ignorance of foreign languages on the part of clerks of the average savings bank, and unwillingness and inability to extend to the immigrant depositor the very necessary accommodation of patient assistance, do not tend to attract immigrant patronage. These conditions, together with the inconvenient hours maintained by local banks, prevent any widespread patronage of them on the part of the immigrant.

The immigrant banker is often called upon to perform many other services. Not infrequently as saloon keeper or licensed labor agent he secures work for his patrons, and as grocer keeps them supplied with provisions. Even when not actually a labor bureau, the banker's place of business is in a number of instances practically a labor headquarters, where the idle men congregate and where agents or contractors in need of laborers come to secure them. In forwarding mail, in writing letters for the illiterate, and in many other ways, the banker performs necessary and efficient service. He cashes pay checks, and acts as interpreter, intermediary, and, in some cases, legal adviser. As notary public he prepares legal documents for his patrons and assists them in the disposition or management of their property.

The immigrant banker does not, of course, extend such accommodations without compensation. Even if there is not immediate remuneration, such services lead to ultimate gain. By the methods described the banker obtains a distinct hold over his "clients," as they are usually termed, and is in a position to turn their needs to his own advantage.

CLASSIFICATION OF IMMIGRANT BANKS

Early in this investigation it became evident that there were radical differences in the character of the immigrant banks themselves. These differences admit of a classification—depending somewhat on the extent to which the banks considered are removed from comparison with American private banks—as regards (1) business methods, (2) authorization, security, and financial responsibility, (3) degree of predominance given the banking business. By these factors are determined three classes of immigrant banks as follows:

I. State and incorporated banks or highly organized private institutions thoroughly responsible and operated in a regular manner almost exclusively as banks. There are comparatively few of these institutions.

II. Privately owned steamship agencies, labor agencies, and real-estate offices which masquerade under the name of bank, but which are not legally authorized as such. To this class should be added groceries and saloons in which the banking functions are clearly defined as apart from other business. The majority of the banks investigated are of this class.

III. Banks which may or may not be known as such, but in which the functions of caring for deposits and receiving money for transmission abroad are extended more as an accommodation or as incidental to the main business of the concern. Saloon keepers, grocers, boarding bosses, barbers, and men engaged in similar occupations usually conduct this class of banks. This is the largest, as it also is the most irresponsible, class. It is undoubtedly the hardest class to regulate, as it is the one about which it is the most difficult to obtain accurate information.

OWNERSHIP AND CAPITALIZATION

It is one of the striking features of immigrant banks that they are almost without exception unincorporated. It is no less noteworthy that, although privately, they are also individually, owned. . . . .

Equally significant with the lack of incorporation and the prevalence of individual ownership is the fact that these concerns seldom represent any investment on the part of the proprietor. It is generally recognized that to embark in such a venture requires no capital. Of the 116 institutions reported upon, only 6 were capitalized, and in 2 of these the ascribed capital was not a sum paid in, but a fund accruing from the profits of the business.[1] In this relation, special attention is called to those grocers, saloon keepers, and other men who fence off a portion of their store and call it a bank, and who advertise themselves extensively as bankers. Among these, as a general thing, there is a very poor conception of the financial responsibility involved in such an undertaking. The proprietor feels free to invest the funds of the bank in his own interests rather than in those of the bank, and the result is that in case of the bank's failure these personal investments constitute substantially the only capital or fund against which levy can be made. As far as its relation to the State is concerned, therefore, the bank loses its identity as an institution in the personal activities of a proprietor, who is, for the most part, legally and financially irresponsible. . . . .

Immigrant bankers everywhere insist that the accommodations which they have extended to their patrons have been their most effective method of securing business. They emphasize the fact that it is their ability, growing out of their knowledge of languages and conditions, and their willingness to perform for the immigrant necessary services which he could not otherwise obtain, that has brought them their patronage. Great importance must be assigned to the fact that proprietors of these banks fix their business hours to suit the convenience of their patrons. A large part of their business is done at night, after working hours, and on Sundays. One Hebrew banker advertises the fact that his office is open Sundays from 9 A.M. to 1 P.M. Another banker, a Slovak in Pennsylvania, receives deposits on the street on Sundays and late at night. An Italian bank in New York City was found crowded with customers on Sunday morning. All emphasize the fact that deposits will be paid on demand at any time.

BANKING BUSINESS

The purely banking functions of immigrant institutions consist of deposits, loans, money exchange, and foreign exchange. Other activities, such as collections, domestic exchange, insurance, and rentals, are carried on by a considerable number of banks, but the first four are the predominant and distinctive banking functions.

DEPOSITS

It is important to bear in mind that these immigrant banks are rarely savings or commercial institutions. Deposits are usually left for temporary safe-keeping rather than as interest-bearing savings accounts. Such deposits are not subject to check, and there is, therefore, seldom need of

[1] The manager of a large immigrant bank in New York City asserted that less than $1,000 was sufficient to start a pretentious bank in that city, but he insisted that at least $1,000 more ought to be converted into foreign currency and placed in the show window, as this was most essential for the purpose of inspiring confidence and attracting business.

clearing arrangements. The receipt of deposits is merely incidental to the main functions of the bank, and is directly contributory to the personal interests of the proprietor. Many so-called bankers do not openly solicit deposits and do not make a practice of receiving them, while others actively seek after deposits as an important part of their business. But whatever the capacity in which the banker receives money, it is essentially a personal one in which he disposes of it. This fact cannot be too forcibly impressed. It is particularly worthy of note in view of the preponderance of testimony among these pseudobankers to the effect that, beyond an understanding that deposits are subject to demand at any time, there is no consideration given nor limitation implied as to their use. So far as his depositors are concerned, the immigrant banker is at liberty to use their funds to suit himself. It is solely a matter of trust throughout. This fact would be neither remarkable nor significant were there effective safeguards or obligations; but it is startlingly significant in view of the lack of security afforded, and when it is considered that the condition still exists in spite of the many ruinous violations of the confidence imposed.

The customary informality with which deposits are tendered and received, the passive attitude of depositors as regards the use to which they may be put, and the want of legal and financial responsibility for their safekeeping, result in a failure to distinguish between the affairs of the bank and those of the banker. Where the latter is the sole owner of the establishment, as was found to be the case in four-fifths of those examined, and finds himself under no restrictions as to the use of funds left with him, he will ordinarily take advantage of that fact to invest them to his own ends without much regard for the solvency of the bank.

The most objectionable use to which deposits are usually put is that of direct investment in the proprietor's own business. Grocers and saloon keepers have admitted that deposits are used freely to meet current bills or are invested outright in the stocks of their concerns.

It is a common practice with immigrant bankers to redeposit the funds with some regular bank. Many bankers are deriving from 2 to 4 per cent interest on thousands of dollars which have been intrusted to them, but on which they make no return.

If deposits are subject to such active demands as to preclude their redeposit by the immigrant banker as a savings account, they may be deposited as a part of his checking account, and in this way may yield a nominal rate of interest. Instances were found where amounts as high as $11,000 were made to yield 2 per cent interest in this way.

The immigrant banker, however, is not, as a rule, satisfied with these methods, nor with the rate of interest paid by other banks, and seeks a more profitable investment for his depositors' funds. In this way deposits come to be used for loans or investments. As regards the tendency among immigrant bankers to invest funds intrusted to them in real estate and stocks, it is only necessary to state here that many of these bankers who receive deposits are property holders to an extent not warranted by the legitimate profits they would derive from their steamship, foreign exchange, or other business. A strong tendency on the part of the bankers to invest outright in real estate is noticeable. Such holdings are almost uniformly the heaviest assets of the banker. . . . .

UNSOUNDNESS OF THE SYSTEM

The danger connected with banking of this character is obvious. Reviewing the leading features as they have been outlined, the following stand out as evidence of insecurity:

1. Immigrant banks are usually unauthorized concerns, privately owned, irresponsibly managed, and seldom subject to any efficient supervision or examination.

2. They deal with a class ignorant of banking methods, distrustful of American institutions, and easily influenced by the immigrant banker.

3. The affairs of the bank and of the proprietor are, as a rule, indistinguishable. As far as legal restrictions or the demands of his patrons are concerned, the proprietor is at liberty to use the funds of the bank for his own purposes. If he is a saloon keeper or grocer, he may make indiscriminate use of the bank deposits in the conduct of the saloon or grocery. The temptation to speculate with or to use for living expenses the funds intrusted to them has also proven the downfall of many of these bankers.

4. In general, the proprietor's investments are the only security afforded the patrons of his bank. The funds of the bank become the proprietor's personal investments, and there is no limitation as to the character or extent of these investments. If the proprietor has no investments the patrons of the bank have no security. Neither capital nor reserve is required, and, as a rule, neither is found.

5. Men who operate these banks, particularly saloon keepers, labor agents, grocers, and boarding bosses, are often ignorant and without any conception of the responsibility imposed. Even recently arrived immigrants find it easier to embark in the banking business than to enter other occupations which, though less responsible, are nevertheless subject to regulation. Methods employed by bankers of this class are often very loose and unbusinesslike. Such records as are kept are usually wholly inadequate and confused. Many of the immigrant bankers, notably steamship agents, advertise in a manner that is at least misleading, if not actually fraudulent and illegal.

6. Immigrant banks are radically different from other financial institutions. They are rarely savings or commercial institutions, and they can not be considered foreign-exchange houses in the true sense of the word. Their chief functions are the safe-keeping of deposits and the transmitting of money abroad, and from the nature of these functions methods have arisen which are open to serious objection.

a) Evidence of the deposit of money for safe-keeping is often inadequate, useless, or entirely lacking. No reserve or other security for the depositor is required. There is absolutely no preventive or check against absconding. The amount of the deposit is usually too small to warrant the bringing of suit in case of refusal to pay. Deposits are very seldom subject to check. As a rule they are left for safe-keeping without any restriction, except that they are subject to withdrawal upon demand, as to the manner in which they shall be kept, or to what purpose and extent they may be used by the person to whom they are intrusted.

b) The purchaser of a money order receives no satisfactory evidence of his cash deposit. His receipt does not bear the name of the remitting house whose money order has been sold, nor is this house advised of the name of the purchaser. The remitting house does not assume any responsibility for its correspondents, and is fully protected in case of loss of fraud through them. But for the purchaser there is no such security. It is very difficult for him or anyone to fix the responsibility in case of loss or fraud. During the period which must elapse before the purchaser can hear from the payee, often as long as six weeks or two months, a dishonest banker has ample time to accumulate and abscond with a large sum of money. . . . .

The close alliance between the steamship agent and the banker has been remarked upon before. The former is usually the medium through which the latter is established. In the words of a prominent immigrant banker—

Thoroughly irresponsible persons secure with apparent ease the agency for some lines, open up a money-order business, advertise themselves as bankers and agents, receive deposits for a time, and, as perhaps planned, abscond with the money intrusted to them.

Another leading immigrant banker, in condemning a system which allowed an alien fugitive from justice, or a clerk dismissed for dishonesty, or any such untrustworthy person to establish himself as banker, complained of the ease with which men of this character procured the agency of certain second-class lines for the purpose of setting themselves up as bankers. The manager of the foreign department of a leading banking house declares:

The steamship and immigrant banking business are almost inseparable. As a matter of fact the sale of foreign exchange follows upon the establishment of a steamship agency and rarely comes before. In view of this important relation it would appear that the steamship companies are entirely too free in the manner in which they establish agencies. A public suggestion to that effect might be a healthy one.

But if the steamship companies are to be blamed for the apparent freedom with which they grant agencies to irresponsible persons whose aim is a banking business, the large foreign-exchange and money-order houses through which the bulk of this business is conducted are even more deserving of censure. The savings which are intrusted to the immigrant banker are customarily accumulated toward the purchase of steamship tickets or for an ultimate transmission abroad, and the facilities for carrying on this business can be readily obtained by the immigrant banker without any requirement whatever as to his own financial qualification, reputation, or business experience. The ease with which arrangements can be made with reputable banking houses—through solicitors or otherwise—for the transmission of money has been described as a potent factor in the development of the immigrant bank. Various bankers of the more responsible type have assigned as a reason for the Italian predominance in immigrant banking the fact that the business requires no capital, no property, no business experience, no education, and no responsibility. The small grocer, clerk, or saloon keeper has sufficient intelligence to appreciate this, and he reasons that he might as well derive some of the profits which the business offers. He knows that he may rely upon the blind confidence which the Italian immigrants place in the leaders and business men of their own race. It is easy for him to secure the agency for a few steamship lines. It is perhaps easier to get the money-order blanks of some well-known banking house. He has nothing more to do but write the word "banca" on his window, bedeck a corner of his store with flaming steamship posters, and open his money-order book and his safe for business. . . . .

DIFFICULTIES OF LEGISLATION

The greatest difficulty surrounding the enactment of legislation looking to the control of immigrant banks is in framing a law which will reach these concerns without injuriously affecting American private banking interests, and which will, at the same time, stand the constitutional test of non-discrimination. This was the chief problem confronting the framers of the New York law. The same troublesome question arose in Ohio, as indicated by a letter from the state bank commissioner, in which he says:

It has seemed impossible to make any laws to cover this class of bankers in this State, as laws must be general in their application here, and those made to affect one private banker would affect all of the State.

This problem presented itself in Pennsylvania where an attempt was made to impose certain restrictions upon immigrant bankers. Yet the State of Massachusetts under similar conditions appears to have solved it successfully.

The matter of private banking in general does not enter into this question. Some States have seen fit to regulate private banking, while others have no laws whatever upon the subject. Where such laws exist their provisions ordinarily affect immigrant banks in an incidental manner only. On the other hand, the legislation that is necessary for the proper regulation of immigrant banks is hardly applicable to American private banks, many of which have existed for years and have always been operated by men of integrity. To bring American private banks of this character under the same jurisdiction with immigrant banks is not at all necessary for the protection of the alien. It is believed that, owing to the wide difference in the character and mode of operation of the two classes of banks, laws can be so devised as to regulate the one without injuring the other.

A very considerable difficulty will likely present itself in making any such law universally effective. In the different States there are hundreds of steamship agents, saloon keepers, barbers, boarding-house keepers, and other irresponsible persons who are not bankers in the true sense of the word, but who, in a purely personal way, receive deposits for safe-keeping and money for transmission to foreign countries. Any law attempting to regulate the business should cover these small dealers. The evidence, testimony, and opinions in the hands of the Commission clearly indicate that this is essential. But, although the wording of the law should be such as to include all these persons, the fact remains that it will probably never be an easy matter to secure sufficient legal proof that they are conducting such a business in violation of the law. Many of those who do a business of this character keep no record of their transactions; at least none that may be readily obtained and submitted as evidence. If the proprietor chooses to deny the receiving of deposits it will be a hard matter to secure proof to the contrary. For one thing he may issue no receipts. For another, the clannishness of the foreigner is a positive stumbling-block in securing testimony and evidence.

The preponderance of opinion among those who are in a position to speak intelligently on the subject of immigrant banks is that some regulation and the introduction of some element of security are absolutely necessary. .... In many localities visited a keen interest was shown in the problem of regulating immigrant banks. Many of the persons interviewed, who had no definite recommendations to make, nevertheless expressed a sincere desire to see these institutions placed under some effective control and supervision. It is significant that many of the bankers themselves stated that they would welcome restrictive measures. Under the present immigrant banking system hundreds of thousands of dollars annually have been lost to depositors. Unless remedies are applied, the same conditions will continue to prevail. The seriousness of the situation may be clearly seen by a consideration of the class of people upon whom this loss falls. It is the savings of the immigrant laborer which are swept away. It is true that these savings are small, but they represent all the fruits of his labor over a long period of time. The failure or abscondence of an immigrant banker brings disaster to the very class of depositors that can least afford to be exploited. His dishonesty means the ruin of a much greater number of persons than would the defalcation of a banker dealing with any other class.

6. Transmission of Savings to Europe[1]

On the whole, it is believed that the business of receiving money for transmission abroad presents graver problems and deserves more careful study than does that of receiving deposits. It must be borne in mind that many immigrants doing a banking business do not make a practice of receiving deposits other than small sums for temporary safe-keeping, whereas the receiving of money for transmission abroad is a highly important part of the business of every immigrant banker. As a matter of fact, there is scarcely an immigrant steamship agent, saloon keeper, or merchant in the country who does not sell what he is pleased to term "foreign exchange." Through these channels a steady stream of money is poured into Europe. The prevalence of the practice, the vast sums involved, and the peculiarities of the system under which transmission is made, attach to the taking of money for this purpose an overshadowing importance such as can not be ascribed to the receiving of deposits. . . . .

It is of advantage to consider the methods by which sums of money are transmitted abroad by immigrant bankers.[2] Although the process

[1] Extract from *Reports of the United States Immigration Commission*, II (1911), 425–31.

[2] [The New York Commission on Immigration of 1909 called attention to the fact that more money was transmitted abroad through the immigrant banks than was sent by the aliens through the post-office. "The official in charge of the registry department in the New York post-office ascribed the comparatively limited use of the post-office facilities by the alien to the following reasons: (1) He is not educated up to the use of the post-office, because he is often illiterate, and cannot fill out the necessary blanks. The post-office does not render assistance because it cannot assume the responsibility of writing names and addresses as pronounced by foreigners, which might lead to errors and complications and liability on the part of the post-office clerks. (2) Salaries paid to post-office employees are not high enough to attract men able to speak foreign languages, and the force is not large enough to enable the department to detail employees for this special work. Where post-office sub-stations are located in drug stores and like places those in charge are not thoroughly acquainted with foreign exchange and post-office technicalities, and are not permitted to issue foreign money orders. (3) Branch offices close at 8 o'clock in the evening. To keep them open for the accommodation of the alien whose working hours prevent him from utilizing the post-office at an earlier hour would require the attendance of the branch superintendent, since the money received would not be entrusted to a minor official who has not given the statutory bond. (4) Post-offices in small towns do not issue foreign money orders, and the alien being ignorant of the fact that he can, nevertheless, through the postmaster at New York transmit his money abroad, does not utilize the privilege" (p. 27). For a discussion of the post-war difficulty as regards rates of exchange and the losses of immigrants due to the rigidity of the post-office system see *The New Republic*, XXIV (Nov. 3, 1920), 230–31, and XXV (Feb. 2, 1921), 272.]

by which these sums are actually exchanged abroad does not differ from the usual manner of exchange, the nature of these remittances is such as to demand special facilities in their collection here and in their ultimate distribution abroad. In the first place, the peculiarly intimate relations existing between the immigrant laborer and certain leaders of his race cause him to bring to such leaders his savings for safe-keeping or for transmission abroad. By virtue of this fact these men become his bankers, although individually they are, in many cases, without financial responsibility or adequate equipment or facilities for carrying out the obligation imposed. In the second place, it is safe to say that a majority of the sums ordered to be transmitted are intended for towns and villages in Europe without banking facilities other than the government postal savings banks. Consequently, the demand of the immigrant banker for means by which he might expedite the transmission of funds left with him without the institution of clearing arrangements for the prompt delivery and correct distribution of these funds abroad, has given rise to a system whereby certain leading American corporations with comprehensive foreign connections have extended to the immigrant banker facilities for the payment of these remittances without necessitating on his part the maintenance abroad of balances or clearing reserves. Figures that have been presented show that at least $125,000,000 of the amount originating among immigrant bankers was sent by means of money orders through certain leading banking houses and steamship and express companies.

Books of these money orders are furnished immigrant bankers upon application. Each order usually consists of a stub to be retained by the correspondent as a record, an advice or direction slip to be returned to the banking house, an advice slip to be sent to the payee, and a receipt for the purchaser, better termed the sender. . . . .

The time which elapses between the forwarding of the advice sheet by the correspondent and the delivery to him of the postal receipt sent by the European bank is seldom less than a month. It may be much more than that between the date on which the customer turns his remittance over to the correspondent and that on which he hears from the payee that the money has or has not been received. This is pointed out as showing that a dishonest banker has from forty days to two months in which to collect money before arousing the suspicions of his patrons.

The method of ultimate distribution of money received by bankers having their own connections abroad is the same. Orders are advised directly to and paid through these European agents without instructions from any American banking house. Payment covering the orders advised is usually made, however, through one of these houses. New York exchange is not purchased directly, but the immigrant banker sends his check to one of the New York houses with which he deals, and directs that house to issue a draft covering the sum to be transmitted. This remittance is most often in even amounts, sometimes less, sometimes greater, than the total of the orders it is intended to cover. Inasmuch as a balance is usually maintained with the European bank through which the distribution of the orders is to be made, payment of the orders does not necessarily depend upon receipt of the New York draft. However, a limit may be imposed upon the amount of orders that will be paid without full remittance to cover them.

The private form used by bankers employing this more direct method consists of a stub for the proprietor, advice for the European bank, and receipt for the purchaser, or, in some cases, simply of stub and receipt.

This form and the one used by immigrant bankers who transmit through American houses are both open to certain objections. In the first place, there is in reality nothing issued which resembles a money order. The receipt given usually states that the specified sum has been received for transmission, and it is signed by the proprietor of the receiving bank. But there is nothing to indicate through what banking house the money has been transmitted; while the name of the house sometimes appears upon the stub retained by the correspondent, and frequently upon the advice to be forwarded to the house, it never appears upon the receipt given by the correspondent to the immigrant "purchaser." Instead this receipt usually contains personal advertising matter which has been added at the request of the correspondent.

Again, the sender has no means of knowing that the money has been paid abroad until notified by the payee or until the banker chooses to send him the postal receipt obtained from the European bank. This is not the receipt of the payee, for such a receipt is obtained only by special arrangement, if desired, in case of payment of debt. Furthermore, the advice slips or sheets sent in to the banking house by the immigrant banker do not contain the name of the individual sender nor the date on which the money was received. Therefore the banking house can not know from whom the money was received nor how long the correspondent has kept the money before sending it. . . . .

RELATION WITH BANKING HOUSES

The relation which exists between the immigrant banker and his transmitting house is not a close one. While these transmitting houses supply their immigrant correspondents with their own money-order books, rate cards, and printed forms, they do not regard them as their agents. Although ostensibly allowing them to sell their paper, they do not hold them under bond, do not require any reserve or balance, and do not guarantee the payment of their orders until remittances sufficient to cover them have been made. They permit immigrant bankers to use their names, standing, and financial integrity as a means of securing business, but they assume no responsibility for them and exercise no supervision over them.[1]

Little discretion is exercised by the banking houses in accepting immigrant bankers as correspondents. The representatives of one or two of these houses testified that in most cases references were required of the immigrant banker. While this may be true in some instances, it is known that money-order blanks are often sent to unknown persons upon mail applications only. The apparently indiscriminate manner in which unregulated and irresponsible steamship agents, real-estate agents, saloon keepers, grocers, and boarding bosses are granted the privilege of transmitting money abroad through reputable firms was a matter of more or less general comment in every community in which this investigation was conducted.

A reason for this lack of care is that the banking house itself is fully protected from any loss which may arise out of the dishonesty of its immigrant correspondents. This protection is assured to the bank by two circumstances: (1) The paper which is issued to the immigrant banker is not in a legal sense the paper of the banking house, and the purchaser of the order has no evidence of the transaction beyond the personal receipt of the proprietor; (2) the payment of an order is never advised abroad until the issuing bank has covered it with an acceptable remittance.

A certain result of the present system is an almost insurmountable difficulty in fixing the responsibility in case of loss or fraud. Payment abroad is practically assured in all cases in which remittance to cover the order is received by the forwarding house, but whether or not such remittance is made rests solely with the immigrant banker. For those desiring to retain the funds, various subterfuges are at hand to explain the delay. The purchaser of the order has no means whatever of fixing the responsibility for its non-delivery, and there is no doubt that advantage is taken of this fact.

[1] [Attention is also called "to the action of the Post-Office Department in allowing immigrants doing a banking business to operate postal substations. It is thought that the connection between the two is calculated to do much harm, inasmuch as there is shown a disposition on the part of certain bankers to use their official position as an asset in attracting patronage for their banks. An Italian banker in New York failed with liabilities of over $275,000. He had operated a postal substation in connection with his bank, and his private 'money-order' receipts bore a legend somewhat as follows: 'Uffici di Postali e Telegraphos' (postal and telegraph office), which, to the average Italian immigrant, conveys an entirely erroneous meaning. He is more than likely to interpret it to mean that the banker is under the control of the Government, since in Italy postal savings banks are under the control of the minister of posts and telegraphs" (p. 422).]

7. The Immigrant and the Notary Public[1]

The office of a notary public is such a common one and the duties so simple that the average American citizen thinks it of little consequence. The average business man, as a matter of convenience, often has a clerk or employee appointed a notary public; lawyers and others, interested in legal affairs, frequently are also notaries public. But the office of notary public in itself offers no inducement from a financial point of view, nor from the point of view of business or social prestige. The services rendered by a notary in this country are of a clerical rather than of an administrative or judicial character, and requirements for appointment in most of the States are very limited. In Europe, however, the office of notary is one of dignity and the incumbent is regarded as a person of real importance. The responsibilities are of a judicial character, while the requirements of a candidate for office and the duties, obligations, fees, rights and privileges accorded to the office are most carefully defined.

An immigrant, therefore, looks upon a notary public as a legal adviser, with almost unlimited legal powers. Notaries public, in immigrant communities, are also steamship ticket agents, money transmitters, justices of the peace or saloonkeepers, and thus come into constant and intimate relations with the immigrant. Among Americans, notaries are not likely to exceed their authority or the powers conferred upon them by law, but among immigrants it is quite different. Notaries have been found to take acknowledgments and draw up documents for which they have no authority, and in numerous ways to take advantage of the immigrant's misconception of their office. . . . .

NUMBER AND OCCUPATION

In the State of New Jersey there are at present approximately eight thousand notaries. The Commission investigated forty-four different notaries public in fifteen different cities, including Italians, Poles, Russians, Bohemians, Germans and Jews. The occupations of these forty-four notaries were as follows: Nineteen were money transmitters and steamship ticket agents only; four were steamship ticket agents; thirteen were steamship ticket agents only; four were steamship ticket agents, money transmitters and justices of the peace; one was a money transmitter, a steamship ticket agent, a justice of the peace and a saloonkeeper; another a steamship ticket agent, money transmitter and saloonkeeper; two clerks; one undertaker; and the occupations of the three others are not known.

PRACTICES OF NOTARIES PUBLIC

Although the chief function of the notary is the taking of affidavits, it has been found that they also take acknowledgments, make out powers

[1] Extract from *Report of the Commission of Immigration of the State of New Jersey* (1914), pp. 93–105.

of attorney, assume legal service and prepare contracts and other important documents, although not admitted to practice as lawyers.

The following advertisement of a notary illustrates the kind of legal service they profess to render to aliens:

The oldest notarial law and military Russian office. Subject to the legislation of the Imperial Russian Consul General, he draws contracts, powers of attorney, bills of sales, promissory notes and other documents. He takes charge of cases in the United States and Russian courts and draws American papers. Sells property and real estate in Russia and collects debts due on notes. Sells steamship tickets at the companies' rates on the best ocean steamers. Transmits money to all parts of the world, quick and cheap, on the guarantee of the United States Express Company, with a capital of $10,000,000. Takes charge of cases for the release or postponement from the military service.

Very many of our countrymen left their native cities in the old country without properly regulating and disposing of their property, real estate, business, etc., because they either forgot or neglected same or for some other reason. After some time it becomes necessary for them to settle their affairs, but they do not know where and to whom to go.

I make out powers of attorney, bills of sale, contracts, donations, wills and testaments. I collect money in the old country for you and undertake to do any business of any kind for you promising good results.

Every document made out by me in my office is legalized through the Consulate and is recognized by the government abroad. All papers are prepared by me personally and are carefully, cheaply and quickly drawn up.

In its investigations the Commission found that many notaries, both through ignorance and willful dishonesty, assume duties and powers not conferred upon them by law. Some were found willing to take acknowledgments of papers either in the form of power of attorney, special power of attorney, general power of attorney, or expatriation act; some were willing to make powers of attorney without having seen the person for whom the power was to be drawn, and to supply two witnesses, though they did not know him, or to draw up powers of attorney without knowing who the applicant was and to certify under their hand and seal that the party who signed these documents was personally known to them. One notary was found willing to issue an expatriation act to a minor, and still another issued an expatriation act and placed the age of the boy at sixteen, although he was in reality fourteen years of age, in order that he might be allowed to land. Although a number of notaries were found to be honest and law-abiding, investigations made by the Commission disclosed the fact that a large proportion of notaries dealing with aliens are not qualified to perform the duties which they assume, but they are willing to originate to participate in cases in which they have no power to act.

The following abuses encountered by the Commission serve as illustrations of the practices of this class of notaries. They also show how notaries public have exceeded their powers and in so doing have been the means of defrauding immigrants. . . . .

The following advertisement was issued by a certain man in which he claims legal, notarial powers, etc.:

EUROPEAN ATTORNEY'S NOTARIAL AND MILITARY OFFICE

DEAR FELLOW-COUNTRYMEN:

There is not even one colony with Polish and Ruthenian population in entire America and Canada, where our office would not be known. Honesty, knowledge of the old country laws, and quickness and punctuality in conducting cases entrusted to us, procured for us a very legion of friends, who, once acquainted with our office, always apply to us in all cases and recommend others, because they know that cases entrusted to us will be carried through with the greatest conscientiousness and skill. As long as our office has been existing there has not been one person who brought claims or showed dissatisfaction and we receive every day letters of thanks. In the years 1909 and 1910 we received many court and registration cases which other attorneys conducted already and could not settle. These cases were so difficult and complicated that no attorney from the old country was willing to undertake the carrying of them through. If these cases were entrusted to somebody else, he would throw them in the waste basket, but we did not do it, we did not leave our friends without assistance and protection. Listen to what we did with these cases. Knowing that no other attorney has knowledge nor is willing to carry them through, in June of the year 1910, the manager himself went to the old country, lost three months, bore considerable expense and fatigue traveling from one court to the other, but he settled all cases successfully, and it is raining again with letters of thanks and the number of our friends doubled. You have, therefore, an example, dear fellow-countrymen, that is for your good and the good of our friends and clients. We do not mind time nor money, only that they do not depart without honest advice or assistance and that they may not fall into the hands of exploiters of strange nationalities, who frivolously squander your hard-earned money. If you have then, any case whatever, remember we are warning you so you shall not regret later. Do not apply to any firm in particular with a non-Polish name. If you have a case, if you need legal or other advice, write us under this address: . . . . because our attorney and notarial office conducts all kinds of civil and criminal law suits in the annexed regions of Austria and Russia; draws up powers of attorney, transfers, contracts of purchases and sales, donation documents, certificates of debt and is recording such in the old country land-registration record; conducts land and registration matters; collects estates and debts, even superannuated; draws up testaments, antenuptial legacies and petitions for estates, probating and inventories and in general conducts all cases entering in the sphere of activity of attorneys and notaries.

MILITARY OFFICE (BUREAU)

Files petitions for admission to medical examinations in America and exemption from exercises and reclamations for exemption from doing military duty; for subjects of Russia, it obtains prorogation of appearances for military levying.

REAL ESTATE OFFICE (BUREAU)

Purchases for cash and sells at accessible prices real estate in the old country, and sells houses, lots and farms in America.

BANKING HOUSE

Purchases stocks, valuable paper, bills of exchange, property claims in the old country, sells steamship tickets, forwards money to all parts of the world at the lowest rate, and issues and pays off travelers' checks.

At a hearing before the Commission it was found that this man had never been a lawyer nor a notary; that he had only worked a year as a clerk in a lawyer's office abroad when he was sixteen years old; that he was a watchman in the customs house service for seven and one-half years and was for two months in the army.

An immigrant woman desiring to transfer her property and real estate in Galicia to her husband, applied with him to this notarial and legal office for legal assistance. After receiving all the necessary information from the man and his wife, the alleged notary agreed to procure an extract from the land record from the district court in the above locality, for which he charged the applicant $6. The alleged notary then drew up a power of attorney for the man and his wife, which he executed in the absence of the deponent and sent to the district court, which was to carry out the transaction of transferring the property from the wife to the husband. The said court, however, refused to act on the document as it did not comply with the requirements of the Austrian law, and the court turned the document over to the Austro-Hungarian consul in New York City. The husband called time and again upon the alleged notary for information as to whether the transaction had been made abroad, but was always met with various excuses. The complainants in the case, besides paying $6 for the first transaction, paid in addition $20 in small installments without obtaining any results.

Of the forty-four investigations made by the Commission, eleven notaries were visited personally and letters were sent to thirty-three. From the eleven notaries visited, two of whom were not themselves authorized to act as such but were working in conjunction with notaries in other offices, twelve documents were obtained, all acknowledged in the Italian, Polish, Bohemian, German and Russian languages, in the form of powers of attorney. From the thirty-three notaries to whom letters were sent, six refused to execute any document by mail; ten did not answer and seventeen were found willing to execute the documents referred to. Out of this number, five were requested to do so and the documents were executed and sent back by them through the mail.

Of the entire number of documents obtained, both by calling and by mail, in thirteen cases witnesses unknown to the grantor were furnished by the notary; in seven cases the notary did not see the grantors at all, which means that these notaries signed seven different documents in which they falsely stated that a man, personally known to them, signed in their presence with his own hand said document. In the case of one document, which was executed by a notary, the grantor neither saw the notary nor the witnesses, and this document still remains unsigned in the office of the Commission. Six of the documents obtained had been duly legalized by consulates.

The following cases of notaries illustrate the type of cases handled by the Commission:

A was appointed after one year's residence in the United States, having been only six months in New Jersey. He did not know the difference between an affidavit and a power of attorney. He furnished witnesses who swore they knew the grantors. When asked to make out an act of expatriation to bring a brother, aged fifteen, from Italy, the notary stated that it would be impossible for the boy to secure a passport on account of his being under age—that a boy must be at least sixteen years of age to obtain a passport to come to this country. When requested to make out a document stating that the boy was sixteen years of age, the notary was willing to do so. He drew up the expatriation act, stating that the age of the brother was sixteen, although he had been told that he was really fifteen years of age.

B testified before the Commission that he would certify to the acknowledgment of any document if he knew the signature of the grantor, even if he did not sign the document in his presence. That the majority of the foreigners seeking his assistance do not know what it means to take an oath, and he merely assures himself that the signature is correct and is then satisfied. He is also a commissioner of deeds, and as such has the power to take acknowledgments, but he always signs himself as a notary public, because it is not generally understood in Italy what a commissioner of deeds is; he advertises as an Italian and American lawyer in civil and criminal cases. The Commission found that he was willing to sign an acknowledgment to a document giving the power of attorney to a man in Italy to sell a house, though he never saw the man who signed the document.

C sent a document duly acknowledged by mail and perjured himself before the Commission by swearing that he knew the man who had signed the document for a year or more. He finally admitted that he did not see the man sign the document, but that he recognized his signature and considered that sufficient.

D executed an acknowledgment to a document sent him by mail and procured two witnesses to sign it. In the testimony before the Commission it developed that the signature of one of these witnesses was written by his daughter who works in the notary's office; that this daughter often signs her father's name as a witness when he does not happen to be available.

E testified before the Commission that he knew it was illegal for a notary public to take acknowledgments, but he took one nevertheless to a document sent to him by mail without the grantor appearing before him. He also furnished witnesses who did not see the grantor. This notary makes out over two hundred documents a year to be sent abroad.

F was not a notary, but advertised that he made powers of attorney, etc. He was requested by mail to execute a power of attorney. This he did in the Russian language, and as he was not himself a notary, he sent the document to a notary whom he knew and this notary certified to the acknowledgment after it had been signed by the grantor and returned by mail. The notary who signed it did not know whether it was an acknowledgment or an affidavit, as he could not read Russian, nor did he know or see either the man who wished the document made out or the witnesses.

G signed the certificate of acknowledgment to an expatriation act in blank and before it had been signed by the party executing it. The Commission has this paper made by the notary but not signed by anyone. He also certified to and sealed a power of attorney without seeing the party for whom it was drawn and admitted that as soon as the Consulate legalized it, it would be considered a legal document and the person to whom it was made out could do nothing with the property of the man whose signature was attached.

H, a saloonkeeper, real estate agent, justice of the peace, and unauthorized banker, testified that in making out acknowledgments he always read them to the grantor and explained them word by word before sending to the Consulate to be legalized, and perjured himself saying that he knew the signer of the document and the witnesses who were present, which was untrue. The notary himself got one witness to sign, who neither knew nor saw the party executing the document.

ILLEGAL DOCUMENTS

Aside from the acts which are intentionally fraudulent the Commission found a large number of notaries willing to make out documents, and in several cases they actually did make out documents, which the notary public law of New Jersey does not give them power to do. All these notaries are registered with the Consulates of their respective country and the papers which they make out are duly legalized by the Consulates and sent abroad to be used in the courts there.

The question of the legality of papers drawn by notaries was taken up with the Consul General of fourteen of the leading countries in Europe. None of these Consuls was aware of the fact that the powers which these notaries assumed were not legally given them by the State of New Jersey.

The Italian, Austro-Hungarian, Russian, German, British, Swedish and Norwegian Consul Generals stated that documents drawn up by notaries public in New Jersey would not be considered legal in their countries if the laws of New Jersey do not empower a notary public to certify acknowledgments to such documents. As approximately ninety per cent of the foreign-born in this State have emigrated from countries represented by the above Consulates, and have had their documents legalized by them, it will be readily seen how much is involved.

The British, Austrian and Italian Consulates have given orders that no acknowledgments certified to by a notary public of New Jersey shall be legalized.

In their testimony before the Commission it was found that these notaries each acknowledged anywhere from a dozen to two hundred documents a year, which are duly legalized by the Consulates and sent abroad. In other words, each year there are sent through the Consulates hundreds of documents drawn up in this manner, which are illegal, because of the standing of a notary public in the State of New Jersey; in a great many of these cases, even though the notary had had the power to take acknowledgments, the documents would still be illegally drawn, as the notaries are willing to certify that they were acknowledged in the presence of the grantors, although the latter were not present and the witnesses did not see the document executed.

To protect the immigrants against the actions of unscrupulous and ignorant notaries public, the Commission recommends that the Civil Service Commission should be authorized to examine applicants for appointment as notaries public, as to the truth of the statements contained in their application blanks, and that the following laws be enacted:

Any person who shall certify falsely by certificate in writing that any deed or other instrument in writing was acknowledged or proved before him by the party thereto, shall be guilty of a misdemeanor.

Any person not authorized by the laws of this State to take acknowledgments or proofs to deed or other instruments in writing, who shall take an acknowledgment or proof to any deed or instrument in writing, and shall sign a certificate thereon certifying that the said deed or instrument in writing is acknowledged before him, shall be guilty of a misdemeanor.[1]

[1] [For a further discussion of this subject see *Report of Massachusetts Commission on Immigration* (1914), pp. 189–92; *Report of New York Commission of Immigration* (1909), pp. 44–54; and see also the *First Report of the New York Bureau of Industries and Immigration* (1911), pp. 102–4. In this *Report*, the statement is made that "In March, 1910, Gov. Hughes had refused to reappoint 66 notaries public against whom complaints had been made, and also revoked the commissions of 10 other notaries public, on charges after a hearing before a commissioner." And the *Report*, made after a careful investigation, also adds: "The present laws are, however, wholly inadequate, and irresponsible persons scarcely able to read or write, with no legal training or financial responsibility, are acknowledging legal documents, drawing up powers of attorney and bills of sale affecting property interests abroad, and are advertising and acting as 'advocates,' with the result that many worthless documents are paid for by resident aliens and sent abroad, and many litigations begun by wholly irresponsible agents here and there. No records of any kind are required, the notary public in many instances, especially among Italians, not even keeping the address of the parties signing a document. He relies on them to come in if all does not go well on the other side. No improvements in conditions can be effected until the executive law of this State is so amended as to raise the requirements for obtaining a commission to act as a notary public, to provide for records, and for inspection upon complaint. Until the law prohibiting others than lawyers from doing legal work is extended to cover notaries public, these irresponsible officers will continue to impose upon their countrymen. Under present conditions it is easy to place the blame for frauds upon the so-called foreign representative of the notary public. The effect of the losses, exploitation, misrepresentation and frauds practiced by some of them falls heaviest on the man with small property in the old country who wishes to remain here and become a citizen."]

8. The Immigrant in the Courts[1]

INTERPRETERS

The municipal or police courts are, to the immigrant, the courts of surpassing importance as object-lessons in American justice or injustice. In many States the police judges and justices of the peace have been accused of the grossest abuse of their power in cases where immigrants are concerned, so that the worst possible lesson has been learned by the immigrant in his first conscious contact with American law. Fortunately, this has been prevented in Massachusetts by the method of appointment and by the traditions surrounding all trial justices.[2] But impartiality and intelligence on the part of the judge are not sufficient.

In these courts the immigrant appears as complainant or defendant, ignorant not only of American law and court procedure but of the language as well. The judge is therefore dependent upon the interpreter for his knowledge of the facts; the intelligence, honesty and impartiality of the interpreter are as important as his own.

In this matter, as in education, the importance of planning to care for the immigrant in accordance with American standards of justice has never been really faced. Instead of responsible interpreters, those provided are too often dangerously incompetent. Recent improvement has been made in the Municipal Court of Boston. In 1912 a law was passed authorizing the justices of this court to employ official interpreters.[3] In the autumn of 1913, when the justices desired to appoint under this statute an interpreter for the Slavic, Lithuanian and Yiddish languages by civil service examination, they found that the Civil Service Commission had no authority to certify interpreters. The commission agreed, however, as a matter of courtesy, to hold the examination. This examination, which was mainly a test of the applicant's ability to translate these languages, brought out the fact that many of the men who had been for years interpreting about the Boston court had a totally inadequate vocabulary both in English and in the foreign language.

[1] Extract from the *Report of the Massachusetts Commission on Immigration* (1914), pp. 107–13. See also below, Doc. 14, pp. 583–85.

[2] Justices of the peace have no authority to try any cases, civil or criminal, receive complaints or issue warrants (Mass. R. L., chap. 161, sec. 5). The Governor may designate a justice of the peace a trial justice only upon the petition of the mayor and aldermen of a city or the selectmen of a town in which neither a justice of the police or district court nor a clerk or assistant clerk of such courts resides. When so designated he may issue warrants returnable to these courts and take bail, but cannot try cases (Mass. R. L., chap. 161, sec. 3). The position of the justice of the peace in Massachusetts is therefore similar to that of the notary public, and in his appointment for those duties sufficient discretion is not exercised.

[3] *Massachusetts Acts and Resolves* (1912), chap. 648.

The Municipal Court of Boston now has two official interpreters who are paid $1,500 a year, and are used for court work and in the probation service. In South Boston and East Boston and in other parts of the city that are not under the jurisdiction of the Municipal Court of Boston, and in the other cities and towns of the State, there are no official interpreters. Men who speak Italian, Polish, Greek and other foreign languages hang about the court in the hope of being called as interpreters. The judge usually calls the same one over and over, and therefore a few, although never really appointed as interpreters, come to do practically all the interpreting of the court. There is no uniformity in the matter of their selection or their pay. Some receive $2 for every case, some $2 for every day they are used, no matter in how many cases; others are paid $3, and some as little as 60 cents for a day's work. Most of these interpreters, although they may have some other business, are practically dependent for support on their employment about the court.

Owing to this method of selection and payment the legitimate earnings of the interpreter are wholly inadequate and, in consequence, he may be tempted to take money from those interested in the outcome of the case, and to arrange for division of fees with some "shyster" lawyer for whom he acts as runner. In every city in which investigations were made by the commission complaints of dishonesty on the part of present or former interpreters were heard. Police officers and clerks of court said that men ignorant of English as well as of the language they were attempting to interpret are constantly accepted as interpreters because no others are available. In order to determine the general truth of this statement, interpreters who are used in four different cities were selected quite at random by the commission and given a very simple test as to their command of the languages that they testified they were interpreting in court. One of the men met the tests given satisfactorily; the others were quite incompetent. For example, one man who regularly interprets Polish and Lithuanian in the South Boston court was asked to translate from a Polish newspaper a paragraph which, translated, reads as follows:

Rochester, N.Y.—Frank Zgodzinoki, sixteen years of age, was arrested for stealing coal from the New York Central Railroad yard. During the hearing of the case it was learned that the boy was sent by his mother to get coal. The boy was discharged, but the judge threatened to send his mother to jail if she taught the boy to steal.

Of this, the interpreter, after reading and rereading, was, according to the stenographic report, able to make out the following:

Rochester, N.Y.—There was arrested 16 March Francis Zgodzinoki for—something about the mother. I understand some the mother was arrested in some affairs. Central President, that is, New York Central.

The man realized his inability to translate it and offered various excuses: that questions are asked in court in a "quite different way entirely"; that "when the man comes upon the stand to testify we know what he is going to say"; and that in important cases the judge allows him to use a dictionary. Another interpreter who claimed to speak and understand Polish but not read it, and who was sure he could translate this same paragraph if it were read to him, translated sentence by sentence as follows:

It was arrested about sixteen years ago a man by the name of Francisco Zgodzinoki. The charge was the larceny of the New York Central. He was tried and acquitted. His mother sent a boy. He was asked the question whether he was going to learn the children to steal.

An Italian interpreter translated a paragraph taken from an Italian newspaper as follows:

Accusing of fraud in damage of certain Siegfrid Maas, collector of electric house. The fellows William Tantoni and Romeo Rinaldi they appeared before Magistrate Tennant. The day of 12 last May in Massachusetts Avenue aggressed and robbed of $9. They were arrested and those present auditor of the fraud further Rinaldi and Tantoni and a certain William King they are confession the crime. They probated and they return to Rahway Reformatory. The Tantoni and Rinaldi so they got out and proved their innocence and they were set free.

It is unnecessary to give the correct translation here. The man's ignorance of English is sufficiently clear to indicate that he was capable neither of properly putting the questions of the court and attorneys nor of interpreting the answers of a witness, yet he has been doing such work about the courts for the last fifteen years. He said he interpreted both the Sicilian and Calabrian dialects also, but when tested he failed even more completely with these. According to his testimony he is often employed by lawyers to help work up the evidence before the trial, and he usually has some lawyer to whom he refers Italians who come to him with their troubles. This man's own statement seemed to confirm the reports which the commission received that he is not only ignorant but dishonest, and is deliberately using his position to exploit his fellow countrymen and defeat justice.

A common complaint is that an Italian undertakes to translate dialects that he does not understand. The Pole who knows Polish is likewise allowed to translate Russian, Bohemian, Slovak and the other Slavic languages. He may perhaps in rare cases have learned all these, but as a general rule he is able to understand something of what is being said only because of the general similarity of the languages. That means, of course, that he is entirely unable to make the accurate translation that is essential in the administration of justice.

Since the judge can know the facts only through the interpreter, the honesty, competence and disinterestedness of the interpreter, as we have said, are as essential as his own. There can be no assurance that these qualities are possessed under the present system, or lack of system. It is important to the State not only that the individual concerned should not be unjustly punished or deprived of his liberty, but that this injustice should not result in the unfortunate belief that the courts are unfair to the foreigners, and that those who are especially charged with the enforcement of the law lend themselves to its defeat.

The only objection that can be made to official interpreters whose qualifications have been tested is on the ground of expense. How much is paid under the present fee system could be learned only with great difficulty. One interpreter who is paid $2 for every case reported that he was paid during November, 1913, $104 by the county and $24 by the clerk of the court. An official interpreter on a yearly salary could certainly be employed in this court. Often, however, the fees amount to from $25 to $50 in a month and, for languages seldom used, to very much less. This fact does not seem, however, to present insurmountable difficulties. The Civil Service Commission could prepare an eligible list, and appointments when made should be from such a list. In many cases an interpreter's time could be filled by assigning him to the probation service, which, because of the language difficulty, is less frequently used with non-English speaking foreigners than with other offenders.

Neither expense nor occasional delay should outweigh the necessity of having for interpreters only those who are salaried officers of the court, appointed only after a thorough test of their competence by the Civil Service Commission.

LAWYERS

Uneducated and often unscrupulous interpreters usually have some lawyer to whom they direct the immigrant and, according to reports made to the commission, the lawyer and the interpreter often conspire together to encourage the filing of complaints. Not infrequently the runner goes to both parties and helps them to work up their cases, receiving fees from both and promising to "look out for" both when the case comes up for trial.

The lawyers who visit the municipal courts and the jails, offering their services to those who are awaiting trial, or who pay these interpreters a commission on cases, are usually of the lowest grade, both in honesty and ability; and yet upon these men the immigrant is dependent.

Ignorant of all his legal rights, unable to talk to police, attorney or judge, he must have some one who will explain the charge to him, notify his friends, find a lawyer for him and then act as interpreter in his dealings with his lawyer and when his case comes up for trial. For this reason the "runner," whose character and practices are so well known, cannot be excluded from the courts until interpreters and attorneys for the defense are provided by the State.

That an innocent man should not be convicted is as important to the State as that a guilty one should not escape. If, as is often charged, we are making rather than reforming criminals under our present prison system, it is even more important. Until the State concerns itself with the protection both of the Americans and of the immigrants who are having their first experience with courts of any sort, they will suffer much at the hands of these lawyers. Because of the greater handicap, the immigrant will suffer more seriously. How he comes out in his first direct contact with the law will do much to influence his future in America. In order, therefore, to prevent crime and teach respect for law, provision for public defenders should be made. Massachusetts will in any case not be the first to experiment with this policy, since Los Angeles already has its public defender as part of its judicial system; but it is to be hoped that in this reform as in so many others she may at least be one of the leaders.

THE CIVIL COURTS

In the civil court, too, the immigrant suffers at the hands of interpreters and lawyers, and the securing of "redress for grievances" is very expensive. Cases dealing with small wage claims, fraud and misrepresentation, trouble with the loan shark or the company that sells on the installment plan, personal injury and damage suits are the occasions when he most frequently finds himself in need of counsel. If he must pay both interpreter and lawyer the door of the court is closed to him. In many cases payment of either is not warranted by the amount involved, and yet the social effects of the prosecution of these cases make the expenditure necessary from the standpoint of the welfare of the community. The payment of the interpreter, whose impartiality is essential, should here, too, be undertaken by the court.

Lawyers' services could be arranged for through a legal aid society which corresponds to the dispensary or clinic in medicine. There is such a society in Boston, but its existence is not known to the immigrant and advertisement presents some difficulties. A State Board of Immigration such as is recommended in this report would assist in applying all the private as well as public resources of the State to the needs of the immigrant, and so would meet this difficulty. In cities where no regularly organized legal aid society exists some arrangement for disinterested advice by the local bar should be possible. This is a matter of much greater importance than is generally realized.

Because of his bitter experiences at the hands of petty exploiters, and because of the misrepresentation on the part of interpreters and "shyster" lawyers through whom he seeks to obtain justice, the immigrant is learning some of the ugliest aspects of our life, and his Americanization along right lines is, for this reason, being prevented or at least rendered more difficult.

9. The Immigrant Lodger[1]

To discuss this and most of the other problems of the immigrant intelligently it must be kept in mind that a very large per cent of the newcomers are young people; also that a very large number are men who either are unmarried or have left their wives behind them when they started out on the American experiment. Many of the young women from Austria, Hungary and Russia come as pioneers, expecting to bring over the other members of their families on their savings. The relatives and friends to whom they come have themselves usually been here only a short time, and have as yet had no chance to "make good." In many cases these relatives or friends expect to assist them in finding a boarding place and a first job, and after that the girls are entirely dependent on their own resources.

These young immigrant men and women constitute the demand which makes the "lodger problem" in our foreign colonies. In the mill town the wife chooses between taking in lodgers or working in the mill as a means of supplementing her husband's insufficient wage. Sometimes, however, the reason for taking lodgers is not stern necessity but the desire to make payments on a house that is being purchased; in some instances it may be to add to the bank balance because of greed; but in many more the reason is that the immigrant sees that the only possible release for himself and his family from their present condition is the accumulation of some money "for a start."

In many cases the lodger is received into an already overcrowded household out of kindliness, because he comes from the same country, and the older people remember how forlorn they were on arrival. But whatever their motive the unattached immigrant has only two alternatives. He must either become a boarder in a household, or, with a group of others, start co-operative housekeeping, forming what housing reports call a "non-family group." The latter is frequently done by the men and will be discussed later.

The housing of the unmarried immigrant woman is a special problem which has received as yet little consideration.

THE IMMIGRANT GIRL

How large a group the immigrant girls constitute is shown by the fact that during the year ended June 30, 1912, 93,267 unmarried girls between the ages of fourteen and twenty-one were admitted to the United States as immigrants. . . . .

Among these girls are many in every nationality who are coming to relatives or friends who can provide the care and protection they need, but many of them come to live with strangers upon whom they have no claim and who in many cases themselves emigrated only a year or two before.

[1] Extract from *Report of the Massachusetts Commission on Immigration* (1914), pp. 58–69.

SOCIAL CONDITIONS AND IMMIGRATION 527

Because more men than women come, those families with whom they live usually have, in addition to the girl, three or four men boarders. These young men and women have come from family life in a rural community in Europe to absolutely new conditions of overcrowding, lack of privacy, and freedom from parental and community restraint. The following typical cases show what some of the conditions are:

In a dilapidated tenement, where the rain comes in through the walls and ceiling, a family of seven have an apartment of four rooms, with two men lodgers and one woman. There is one toilet in the basement for the thirty-two persons who live in the building. This girl is eighteen and speaks very little English, although she has been here two years. She has not been to night school because she has been afraid "of being treated badly by the men"; but she is entirely ignorant of the danger in her living conditions.

A Jewish girl of eighteen, who has been here seven months, works in a button factory, has already learned a little English and boards with a family of seven, which has also two men lodgers.

A Lithuanian girl has lived for four years in a family of three who have four rooms and eight lodgers, five men and three women. This girl works as a stitcher in a tailor shop. She started to go to night school when she first came, but the landlady objected as she wanted her to help with the housework in the evening.

A sixteen-year-old Jewish girl came with her father, but is not living in the same house with him. She is lodging in a house where there are four in the family, three men lodgers and herself, all in five rooms.

A Lithuanian girl, who was eighteen years of age at the time of her arrival, has been in this country four years. She worked for the first two months in a stocking factory for $2 a week, and since then has been in a brush factory earning $7 a week. She has lived in three different places since coming to this country. In the first place, there were five rooms, four in the family, and two men and two women lodgers; in the second place, there were four rooms, three in the family, and two men and two women lodgers. At present she is living in a tenement of five rooms with a family of three, who have three men and one woman lodger.

A Polish girl of eighteen who has been in America four months, having borrowed her passage money from her brother in this country, is lodging with a family of four who live in four rooms with five lodgers, three men and two women. This girl is working seven days a week, washing cars in the railroad yards in Boston.

Although few Italian girls come alone, the following case was taken from the personal history schedules of the commission:

Two cousins, each sixteen years old, have been here two months. They came alone, and are working in a candy factory. Both gave as the reason for their coming the financial condition of their families in Italy. They lodge in an apartment of three rooms with a family of six, with whom also live two men lodgers.

There are certain housing conditions prevalent among the Greeks which are different from those just described, but quite as dangerous. In mill towns where there are large numbers of young Greek people without their families it is not uncommon for a group of young men and women to have an apartment together on a sort of co-operative plan. Sometimes a brother and sister are the basis of the arrangement, or some of the young people may be cousins.

For instance, in a mill town which has one of the largest Greek colonies in Massachusetts, in the downstairs tenement of a two-story house is a group of eight young people living in this way. There are four girls ranging from sixteen to twenty-four years of age, and four men. They have two rooms and a kitchen. The apartment is clean and orderly Two of the girls are sisters and have been here eight years, taking care of themselves quite successfully, though they have no relatives in this country.

In securing personal history schedules in immigrant neighborhoods, the commission found that out of 750 households 378 had boarders and lodgers, and in 124 of these there were both men and women. . . . .

Of the 65 single women who were found by the commission living in the same households with men lodgers, 45, or nearly 70 per cent, were girls under twenty-one years of age. Of these, four were only sixteen, eight were seventeen, and thirteen were eighteen years of age.

Among the immigrant communities there are many "causes" which explain the unmarried mother. Because of her ignorance of English she is less able to protect herself than the American country girl, whose helplessness has been so often emphasized. Near an immigrant neighborhood, if at all, the disreputable saloon, dance hall and hotel are usually tolerated, so that the environment to which the immigrant girl comes has dangers of which she is entirely ignorant. Her recreational needs are less understood than are those of the native-born American, and the break with her old-world traditions has left her with fewer standards of judgment. Altogether she is in many ways an easy victim of the unscrupulous. But in the housing conditions just described the lack of privacy and of the restraints which privacy brings may be, with entire absence of evil intent, the sole cause of her ruin. In the records of the State Reformatory at Sherborn, of the State Infirmary at Tewksbury, of the social service department of the Massachusetts General Hospital, and of other private agencies, abundant evidence of this was found. The following typical cases were selected:

A Finnish girl of twenty-six came to a Massachusetts mill town alone, leaving a mother in Finland dependent on what the girl was able to earn in America, so she has sent money regularly to her mother. The landlady at her lodging house is practically her only friend. The father of her illegitimate child lived in the same lodging house and is from "near home" in Finland. He disappeared when her condition was discovered, although he had promised to marry her, and she was left terrified by her lack of friends and her new responsibilities. Another girl came from Russia with her family four years ago. There are six in the family and they had three lodgers, two men and one girl, in a tenement of three rooms. The congestion made the tragedy for both girls almost inevitable.

This overcrowding does not necessarily lead to disastrous results in the very houses where it exists, but it brings about a certain carelessness and familiarity which make other conditions dangerous as well.

A Polish girl left the old country when she was nineteen and came to a cousin in Lawrence. Her mother is dead and her father is in Russia. The cousin is a married woman and paid the girl's passage to America. She worked in a mill as a spinner, and as long as she lived with her cousin everything went well. During a strike in the mills she went to Boston and lived in a lodging house, where, among other lodgers, lived the man who is the father of her illegitimate child.

A Polish girl of nineteen, who has been in America two years, working in a restaurant in Boston, lodges in an apartment of four rooms, where a Polish man and his wife have four men and nine girl lodgers. She came from Europe alone, expecting to be with her father, but he had gone to Canada, and she was obliged to find a lodging place and begin to work immediately. She has an illegitimate child by a man who was a lodger in the same house, and who came from the same village in Poland.

A Lithuanian girl of eighteen has been here one year and a half, but speaks no English. In her boarding house there were four rooms, three persons in the family, and eight men and eight women lodgers. She has an illegitimate child who was born at the lodging house. Recently the girl went to live with a sister so that she can keep the child with her.

Although the promise of marriage is a factor in cases of betrayal of American girls, it is especially easy to mislead the foreign girls in this way because of their ignorance of American customs.

There are also the cases where under some special strain or excitement, as, for example, after a wedding or dance, when liquor has been freely used, barriers of moral restraint are broken down. This occurs most frequently in the homes that are overcrowded, and where in consequence a spirit of familiarity has developed.

That the housing conditions described in the first part of this section must almost inevitably produce these results in many cases no one would question. The point that should be emphasized is that at present there seems to be no constructive program for the protection of these girls from the very obvious danger in their living conditions. Enforcement of decent housing standards will reduce the overcrowding, but it will still leave the immigrant girl open to a kind of temptation to which we know that no girl should be exposed. Private agencies have long been at work on the problem of providing boarding clubs for the American country girl who invades the city and the industrial town. But these agencies have not entered this field. They have not developed a means of handling the immigrant girl or the larger groups of single immigrant men.

NON-FAMILY GROUPS OF MEN

For the men the only alternative to the lodging house is co-operative housekeeping in non-family groups—an arrangement even more unsatisfactory so far as the health and morals of the young men are concerned.

For this reason the majority of Poles, Lithuanians and Italians in Massachusetts choose to lodge with their married friends. Among certain nationalities of recent immigration, however, the opportunities for lodging with families are rare, owing to the very small percentage of women in this country. This was found to be especially true in Massachusetts of the Armenians, the Greeks and the Turks. . . . .

It is natural that among immigrants who have come from countries where the present emigration is comparatively new the number of males should be far in excess of the number of females. Single men are, of course, the most free to come. Married men come first alone and try the experiment of life in this country before sending for their wives and children. Moreover, wherever the immigration is to some extent temporary, and men come with the idea of returning to their homes in the future, these men are of course unlikely to bring their families with them. The newness of the immigration is in part responsible for the present conditions among the Armenians and the Greeks, and so the preponderance of the men over the women is, more or less, a temporary condition, which, to some extent, will be remedied by time. The Turks, on the other hand, have strong, permanent motives in their religion and in their attitude toward women for not wishing to bring their wives to this country. . . . .

Nearly all the Armenians, many of whom had come to this country to escape persecution or to avoid serving in the Turkish army, expected to remain here. Many now living in non-family groups were planning to send for their wives within a short time, and a considerable number were already naturalized or had declared their intention of becoming citizens. Most of the Greeks living in non-family groups had come to the United States for economic reasons, and were uncertain as to whether or not they would remain here permanently, for loyalty to their home country is strong among them. The Turks had come for the definite purpose of making money to take back home. They are hard-working and economical, but have little interest in learning English or in sharing in our civic life. The great majority of the Turks were married; among the Greeks many more were young single men, scarcely more than boys. Most of the Armenians and Turks living in such groups are unskilled laborers, earning from $8 to $12 a week; a good many are in large machine works. Among the Greeks, the occupations are more varied. Some are in shoe factories, some in restaurants, some in shoe-shine parlors.

The method of living is similar. The men hire an apartment, or sometimes a house, and share the rent, which generally amounts to between $1.50 and $2.50 a month for each. Sometimes one of the men acts as boss, and runs the apartment for the others, cooking the meals himself perhaps. A few instances were found where the boss was married, or where his sister lived with him. In three of the twenty-three Greek groups visited, a woman was living. In the Armenian groups visited, no women lived, while in the whole Turkish colony at Worcester, of 400 or more men, there is probably not one Turkish woman.

Occasionally, the men club together and hire a cook, each paying usually $1 a month. In most of the groups visited, however, the men do their own cooking, either acting each one as his own commissary, or taking turns at buying and cooking the food. Occasionally, especially among the Greeks, the men eat at restaurants or coffee-houses.

As is to be expected under the circumstances, the living and sleeping conditions of these men are far from good. In most cases economy leads them to choose houses for which rents are low, and which consequently are often in a most dilapidated condition. These houses are planned for a family of four or five persons, and are totally unsuited for the purposes to which they are put. The sanitary conditions are far from adequate; the furnishings are often the poorest possible. Moreover, as the rooms receive the minimum of care and attention from the men, the apartments are seldom clean and are sometimes filthy. The sleeping quarters are, of course, crowded. Frequently the floor is covered with mattresses and pillows, and clothes are scattered about the rooms. Among the Turks beds are seldom used.

It is generally impossible to do more than estimate the size of the group, as the men understate the number. Police and health officers testify that day and night shifts are frequently found. In one case an investigator was told that a house of seven rooms was occupied by fourteen Turks, sleeping two in a room. On a visit at five in the afternoon he found eighteen men who apparently lived there, while four others who worked at night were sleeping in an adjoining room. Making a night inspection, he discovered seventeen men occupying the seven rooms. This investigation was made by the commission early in the autumn. In the winter, when the men drift back to the cities of Massachusetts from construction work all over New England, the numbers are greatly augmented.

The solution usually suggested for these conditions is a good housing law properly enforced. This is, of course, necessary, and cannot be too strongly urged, but to meet the social needs of this group of young foreign men and women something more is necessary. With the men in the non-family groups the most serious difficulty is their general forlornness. They do not touch the outside world, they have no normal family or social relationships in their own group, they work long hours for low wages and are open to every temptation. That abnormal vice develops dangerously among them is not surprising.

Most people appreciate the dangers and temptations which American country girls or young men face in the change from rural to city life, and many agencies are at work on the problem of their proper housing and recreation. For these young immigrants the dangers are more serious because the change is even greater, and the crisis they are facing is therefore more difficult. So far as their housing conditions are concerned, the young men, as we have said, must choose the demoralizing non-family groups or a household which can hardly be so equipped as to offer men and women lodgers proper protection.

10. Land Purchasing by Immigrants

A. THE IMMIGRANT AND AGRICULTURE IN NEW JERSEY[1]

There are a number of reasons why immigrants who have been farm laborers in their own country do not go to farming districts upon their arrival in this country. Ninety-four per cent of the immigrants coming into the United States join relatives or friends upon their arrival. The great majority of immigrants in this country are living in congested colonies in industrial centers. This is due to the fact that wages are higher and work is steadier in the industrial centers and in mining, railroad and other labor camps than on farms. The opportunity to earn and to save money is the first consideration with immigrants coming to this country. In farm labor the hours are long, the wages small and work all year around is uncertain.

In New Jersey the immigrant colonies are situated in the industrial centers in Hudson, Essex, Union and Passaic counties. The process by which the newly arrived immigrant obtains work is governed more or less by the kind of work which his friends or relatives are doing. There is no official agency in the State which can supply the alien with information in regard to farm labor opportunities. There is here and there an employment agency which deals with farm laborers, but in most cases they are subagencies of regular employment agencies in New York City. In fact, most of the laborers placed upon farms in New Jersey are obtained from New York City or Philadelphia. The chief of the Federal Division of Information in New York City states that frequently men who have been working on farms in New Jersey apply to him when they have finished the work, and they are again sent into New Jersey to a farm within a short distance of the place where they last worked. The applicants, however, have been obliged to go to New York to get information about new positions. During the year 1911 this Division sent about 950 men as farm laborers into New Jersey. . . . .

Real estate companies.—According to the report of the Secretary of Agriculture, in addition to numerous cultivated farms, there are 1,200,000 acres in southern New Jersey yet to be developed. Not every acre of this land is adapted to agricultural crops, but a large proportion of it is. Experi-

---

[1] *Report of the Commission of Immigration of the State of New Jersey* (1914), pp. 35–36, 40–46. For a general discussion of the subject of the "new immigration" in relation to agriculture see *Reports of the United States Immigration Commission*, Vols. XXI and XXII (1911); see also P. A. Speek, *A Stake in the Land* (New York, 1921), and C. L. Fry, *The New and Old Immigrant on the Land* (New York, 1922).

ments have been made and others are in progress which clearly demonstrate that most of the pine land can be made to produce paying crops. It is a fact that immigrants who have been in this country several years and who have saved a small amount of money become interested in farming investment opportunities. These immigrants become the easy prey of fraudulent land companies. In New Jersey a large number of such companies are operating. These companies control extensive areas in the southeastern part of the State which are unfit for cultivation.

There is no form of exploitation more detrimental to the agricultural interests and to *bona fide* distribution schemes than the frauds now practiced upon aliens in the sale of this land. Thousands of dollars are invested annually by aliens in land schemes, and once they are defrauded it becomes very difficult to interest them again in land for homes or farms.

The Commission has investigated a number of these schemes. In practically every instance the company advertises in foreign newspapers and distributes pamphlets in foreign languages. In most of these advertisements an absurdly simple puzzle is inserted. For the correct solution of this puzzle, a certificate of credit amounting to $100 or $200 is offered, to be applied towards the purchase of a farm.

A circular of one of these land companies states that the land they have for sale is entirely within the limits of ———, a village of more than four thousand population, which is growing from day to day astonishingly. Their price for the land is $290 per half acre, but for the correct solution of one of the puzzles a certificate for $200 is offered, reducing the price to $90 per half acre. An outside valuation of any of this land would be $25 per acre—a fair valuation for most of it would be about $10 per acre. The village mentioned above is situated in a township with a population, according to the 1910 census, of 2,452. In 1900, the population was 2,618, and in 1890, 2,609.

Two investigators who called on this company were told that the population of the village was 8,000 in the winter and 15,000 in the summer.

Four letters were sent to this company, two giving the correct solution of the puzzle, and two that were entirely wrong. In all four cases letters were received stating that the puzzle had been correctly solved, and, therefore, the certificate was enclosed.

The companies also have Sunday excursions to their property. On arriving at the land, immigrants are met by employees of the company, who speak in the native tongue to the people and extol the worth of the land in glowing terms. In some instances people are told that a factory is to be built on the property where men can find employment. To substantiate these promises they show to the prospective buyers excavations, where they claim the company is preparing to lay the foundation for this factory. An investigation of one piece of property in particular revealed three such excavations in different parts of the property, done for the benefit of the prospective buyers of three different excursions. A payment at the time of the sale of a lot is required, and the balance is payable in instalments. Usually the alien makes two or three payments, and then discovers that conditions have been grossly misrepresented; that even if he is able to pay for the land, he would not be able to live on it, as there would be no opportunity of earning a living during the time it would take to develop the property, and that the amount of time and money that would be required to develop it, makes it an impossible proposition for an immigrant with only a few hundred dollars in all.

The result is that after several payments have been made the immigrant gives up the proposition, and the company still holds the property and goes through this process over again with another victim.

A company having its main office in New York City has an option on a tract of land comprising several thousand acres. The property is said to have cost the company about $11,000, or a little over $1.25 per acre. They advertise this property for sale at the rate of $25 a quarter-acre lot, or $100 per acre. While this is the advertised price, when they get the immigrant on the property they demand higher prices—often as much as $640 per acre.

Their advertisements vary, but are always made as alluring as possible. A typical one which appeared in an Italian newspaper runs as follows:

Five hundred people came to visit our farms, Sunday, April 9th, and all were Satisfied and Made Further Purchases. . . . .
Almost all Italians know ——— for its mild climate in the winter and most temperate climate in summer. . . . .
——— has over 1,500 inhabitants, also a school, a church and stores. The ground is guaranteed drained, good for any kind of cultivation. The winners will receive the deed upon payment of only $12.50. . . . .

As a matter of fact the village referred to in the last paragraph of this advertisement, instead of having a population of 1,500 as stated, has not more than eighty people in winter and but few more during the summer.

Another advertisement in a Hungarian newspaper promotes a profit sharing company, as follows:

What is securer on earth than the ground itself? Is there a more secure investment than if you invest your money in lots? Is there a man in this world who would not like to buy lots? Can you sell anything on earth easier than the ground itself? Is there any enterprise which is securer and gives more profit than a real estate business? The ——— Company is the first Hungarian company in the United States which was started with Hungarian capital, and consists of Hungarian shareholders. Its business is so diverse that a failure is almost impossible, because as the Hungarian proverb says: "If it does not come in large volume, it comes in small quantity." We buy a forest which we clear. This is one profit. The wood obtained thus we utilize in our woodmill in ———. This is another profit. The ground we divide into lots. This is the third profit. On this ground we build houses from our own material. This is the fourth profit. The lots and houses we sell or rent. This is the fifth profit. These various profits enable us to sell our property at a very reasonable price, and these manifold profits remain in the pockets of the shareholders. We call attention of the public to our enterprise, and we think that every Hungarian's duty is to support, especially in this foreign country, a thoroughly Hungarian undertaking. In this case everybody supports himself by supporting us, because the few dollars invested now might be worth thousands in a few years. It cannot be lost as nothing is more secure on earth than the ground. Subscriptions for our shares which can be paid, if desired, on the instalment plan, are received by mail or personally.

To prove without a doubt the earning capacity of their little farms, a diagram is inserted, marked off into sections and having depicted upon it the various kinds of vegetables which can be successfully raised.

To the alien who has saved some money and who really desires to buy a farm, develop a little home of his own and earn a comfortable living, the possibilities portrayed on this land are very enticing. Whether the alien can obtain independence in this way without considerable reserve capital or without being subsidized to some degree by a real estate company, is an important question which has an important bearing upon the general scheme of agricultural distribution. An instance of the failure of some Hungarian people to succeed in farming for reasons beyond their control was brought in a very forcible manner to the attention of the Commission.

A certain company, owning a large area of land not far from Atlantic City, advertised small farms for sale. The land was said to be suitable for the cultivation of all kinds of vegetables, which could be easily sold in nearby markets. Whoever bought farms need only pay $5 down and $1 a month thereafter, the price per acre varying from $30 to $40. Prospective buyers were told that they could obtain work either on nearby farms or upon the roads or in various other improvements which the company was making, until they were able to put their own farm in condition for cultivation.

The land for the most part was covered with a forest of small hard wood and soft pines. The company, however, contracted to clear the land for the settlers as soon as one-quarter of the purchase price had been paid.

Fifteen to twenty Hungarians who had been farmers abroad and who had been working in the mining district of Pennsylvania since their arrival in this country paid down their first instalment on farms, and, leaving their homes, brought their families to southern New Jersey. There they built small rough huts on the uncleared land and settled down with the expectation of developing small produce farms and earning a comfortable living.

For a time they were able to work for the company and live on some of their own savings, but the clearing of the land was a much greater task than the representatives of the land company realized and the fall months came before the trees and stumps had been removed from much of the property, consequently there had been no opportunity for the settlers to raise vegetables either to sell or to store away for their own use during the winter months.

The company continued to provide work for some time, but soon found that money was being spent with little or no returns. Work became scarcer and scarcer and it was not long before the settlers were without means of subsistence.

Lack of work and lack of means eventually drove them from their land back to find work, as best they might, in the cities. The money which they sunk in their farms was practically lost; the company will never clear the remainder of the land, and the hardships which the people suffered will discourage them from returning.

At the National Conference of Immigration, Land and Labor Officials, held in Chicago, November, 1912, composed of Federal and State representatives, convened for the purpose of discussing Federal and State problems relating to immigration, land and labor and of recommending to the Federal and State governments needed legislation with regard to those subjects, the following resolutions were passed relating to land. As they cover the recommendations which the Commission desires to make, in reference to this question in New Jersey, they have been incorporated as they stand:

Resolved, That this conference urge upon the Governors and Legislatures of the States having land suitable for agricultural settlement the necessity of adequate measures providing for the definite guidance of prospective settlers in finding land adapted to their needs, and protecting them against exploitation in the purchase of this land, with the following minimum standards:

1. The voluntary registration of land suitable for agricultural settlement with a description of the land accurately setting forth its location, quality, fitness for cultivation, prices and terms upon which it may be obtained.

2. Publication of lists of land dealers so registered, the same to be revised periodically and furnished to all inquirers.

3. The approval of the forms of contract used by registered dealers in the sale or transfer of land to settlers.

4. The inspection of all advertising material by registered land dealers and the cancellation of their registration for failure to comply with the minimum standard of accuracy of statement.

5. The criminal prosecution of any land dealer, whether registered or not, who is guilty of fraud in the sale of land to a settler, and the securing of all possible redress for the settler.

6. The publication of accurate information with respect to the general opportunities for agricultural settlement in the State.

7. The appropriation of funds sufficient to permit the effective performance of these duties.

B. TYPICAL LAND FRAUD CASES IN CALIFORNIA[1]

In order to better visualize the peculiar problems of the immigrant and the ingenious frauds practiced upon him, a few typical cases that have been handled by the Complaint Bureau are here summarized.

[1] Extract from the *First Annual Report of the Commission of Immigration and Housing of California* (1914), pp. 64–66.

I. An ignorant Slavonian, while residing in the State of Washington, received a letter from a real estate company in San Francisco. The letter stated that the company understood that this man was a leader in the Slavonian colony and that, in view of that fact, they were sending an agent to call upon him with an attractive offer of a fine city lot for $27.50. It was explained that this offer was made in order that he, as a famous man, might aid in advertising the company. Later, the agent called as promised and represented to the Slavonian that the lot offered for sale was in a suburb of San Francisco, twenty minutes from the center of the city and on a five-cent car line. It was represented that the streets were laid out and paved. The fare to San Francisco was more than $27.50, so that the Slavonian decided to pay without going to see the land.

Upon investigation, the Commission found that this company had sold lots to nearly one hundred immigrants and to as many American citizens. The prices varied from $27.50 to $250.00. Two agents of the Commission were used as detectives to investigate the case. When they called upon the company and pretended to be hunting jobs as salesmen, the manager frankly stated the scheme was fraudulent; that if the people saw the land they would never buy it. These agents tricked the manager of the company into sending statements of this nature, as well as other fraudulent statements, through the mail.

The land was investigated and found to be an unsurveyed tract in the hills two hours distant from San Francisco; the railroad fare is 75 cents for the round trip. The Commission sent out letters to all purchasers and thus succeeded in obtaining over forty fraudulent letters mailed out by the company to innocent purchasers.

The case was taken up with the federal post office authorities and all the members of the company were arrested, charged with using the mails to defraud. They were held guilty by the committing magistrate and are now awaiting trial.

II. A large company subdivided its properties into small farms and town lots and engaged in elaborate advertising, particularly in immigrant quarters and among laboring people. They employed salesmen who spoke many languages, and were thus able to induce scores of immigrant laborers to invest thousands of dollars in this land. The foreign speaking salesmen promised the immigrants steady work for at least three years at a wage of $2.25 per day; explained that the company would irrigate all the land and furnish many improvements and *further assured them* that these promises were contained in the contracts which the purchasers signed but could not read. Not one of these promises was written in the contracts. The company gave employment to some for a few days, denied it to others altogether, never installed the promised irrigation, finally discharged all laborers, ceased improvements, and practically shut down. Unfortunately, the laws concerning fraud are not broad enough to allow criminal prosecution. As a result, stricter laws have been proposed by the Commission.

In some cases the Immigration Commission induced the company to refund the pitifully small savings deposited by these defrauded purchasers; in other cases the company has made new contracts, waiving interest and giving more time for payments. In most cases the company retained the ill-gotten money and the poor immigrants have gone away in disgust, to hunt another "job," vowing that they would never again attempt to buy land in California. So not only the discouraged immigrant, but also the state loses.

III. In another land case some real estate operators secured options on a large tract of arid, waste land in the northern part of the state. The tract was subdivided for sale, but no effort was made to sell in this state. Instead, the company used several Bohemian newspapers in the east as advertising mediums and ran full page advertisements for several months to the effect that a strictly Bohemian colony was to be established. A few months after this advertising campaign began, a picture of an attractive California town was reproduced in the center of the advertisement; it was stated that many Bohemian settlers had arrived, that streets were laid out, many homes erected, and that the surrounding farms were being cultivated. Immediately, Bohemians from all over the country were lured by these representations and many bought twenty-five and fifty acre tracts through the mail, at prices ranging from $50 to $65 per acre, being warned that they would have to "act at once" if they wished to get in on the big scheme. When these purchasers came to California, after selling their small holdings in other states, they found a barren, rocky tract of land, no settlers, and in place of the thriving village a rain washed sign bearing the inscription "Domov," meaning "Home!"

Several purchasers complained to the Immigration Commission. Agricultural experts, who were called in, stated that the land was full of alkali, fit only for sheep pasturage, and perhaps not even for that, owing to the lack of vegetation in the dry months. The Commission has collected all the fraudulent advertisements and letters of the company and a criminal prosecution is to be begun in the federal courts on the charge of using the mails to defraud. Some of the purchasers, on the advice of the Commission, have instituted civil suits to recover the purchase price.

IV. In a similar case, land near San Francisco was advertised and sold almost exclusively among immigrant laborers in distant construction camps. The men did not leave their work to look at the land, because they would have lost their jobs, so they bought on the installment plan upon the strength of representations made by agents, and by the promoter through the mail. The land was described as "suburban farms and lots" in a beautiful tract with streets and walks laid, on the edge of a thriving town. When one of the defrauded purchasers became suspicious and wrote to the Commission, an investigation was made. It was found that the land was not even surveyed, that it was rough and mountainous, covered with brush and rocks, and miles from any town. The post office authorities prosecuted the promoter for using the mails to defraud, the Commission aiding in collecting the evidence, and he is now serving a sentence of two years in a federal prison. Several Italians and Greeks had paid installments of from $200 to $450 apiece, and the Commission is endeavoring to secure a refund of this money.

V. A Swiss bought lots in the city of Richmond on an installment contract and was five years in completing his payments. The contract provided the seller was to pay taxes on the then assessed value, the buyer those on any increased value. At the end of the period, $20 taxes were demanded before a deed would be given. The Swiss thought this was too much and complained to the Commission. An investigator obtained from the county assessor the assessed values and rates for each of those particular years. Computation showed about 91 cents actually due. When confronted with these facts, the company auditor passed over the deed for $1.50, the complainant being generous enough to allow the few additional cents and the auditor being small enough to demand them.

VI. An illiterate Italian requested information regarding a cooperative land venture which he had been invited to join. Glowing promises had been made to him, the land was represented as extremely valuable, and he was assured that the project had the backing of great financiers. It was not technical information he wanted, but advice as to the financial soundness of the scheme, which he was entirely unable to investigate. The Immigration Commission sent an investigator to interview the chief promoter, followed the clews obtained, and made inquiries at different sources. It was ascertained that the people interested had a poor, wild tract of land, little money, few settlers, and hazy plans, and that furthermore there was much dissension among themselves. The venture was obviously doomed to failure. The Italian was warned of the unstable nature of the scheme and advised to avoid it. He did so and probably avoided losing the savings of many years.

11. A Review of the Pre-War Immigration Situation[1]

CHARACTER OF IMMIGRANTS [BEFORE 1914]

The old immigration movement in recent years has rapidly declined, both numerically and relatively. .... The new immigration, coming in such large numbers, has provoked a widespread feeling of apprehension. .... The old immigration movement was essentially one of permanent settlers. .... From all data that are available it appears that nearly 40 per cent of the new immigration movement returns to Europe and that about two-thirds of those who go remain there. This does not mean that

[1] Extract from "Brief Statement of the Investigations," *Reports of the U.S. Immigration Commission*, I (1911), 24–43. The complete reports on the various subjects reviewed will be found in the series of reports of the Commission.

all of these immigrants have acquired a competence and returned to live on it. Among the immigrants who return permanently are those who have failed, as well as those who have succeeded. Thousands of those returning have, under unusual conditions of climate, work, and food, contracted tuberculosis and other diseases; others are injured in our industries; still others are the widows and children of aliens dying here. These, with the aged and temperamentally unfit, make up a large part of the aliens who return to their former homes to remain.

The old immigration came to the United States during a period of general development and was an important factor in that development, while the new immigration has come during a period of great industrial expansion and has furnished a practically unlimited supply of labor to that expansion. As a class the new immigrants are largely unskilled laborers coming from countries where their highest wage is small compared with the lowest wage in the United States. Nearly 75 per cent of them are males. About 83 per cent are between the ages of 14 and 45 years, and consequently are producers rather than dependents. They bring little money into the country and send or take a considerable part of their earnings out. . . . . Immigration prior to 1882 was practically unregulated, and consequently many were not self-supporting, so that the care of alien paupers in several States was a serious problem. The new immigration has for the most part been carefully regulated so far as health and likelihood of pauperism are concerned, and, although drawn from [the poorer] classes, the new immigrants as a rule are the strongest, the most enterprising, and the best of their class. . . . .

IMMIGRATION AND CRIME

It is impossible from existing data to determine whether the immigrant population in this country is relatively more or less criminal than the native-born population. Statistics show that the proportion of convictions for crime according to the population is greater among the foreign-born than among the native-born. It must be remembered, however, that the proportion of persons of what may be termed the criminal age is greater among the foreign-born than among natives, and when due allowance is made for this fact it appears that criminality, judged by convictions, is about equally prevalent in each class. It is obviously impossible to determine whether the proportion of unpunished criminals is relatively greater among the foreign or among the native-born. It is sometimes stated that the detection and conviction of criminals, especially for higher crimes, is more difficult in the case of the foreign-born. This is probably true of certain localities and perhaps generally true in the case of certain nationalities, but there is no proof that this condition applies to the foreign-born element as a whole in the country at large. It is possible that in some localities prejudice or sympathy for foreigners influences convictions or acquittals. In large cities a part of the apparent criminality of the foreign-born consists merely of violations of ordinances, which are offenses only because the persons who commit them are not naturalized. Prominent in this class of offenses is street peddling without a license in cities where such licenses are granted only to citizens.

The proportion of the more serious crimes of homicide, blackmail, and robbery, as well as the least serious offenses, is greater among the foreign-born. The disproportion in this regard is due principally to the prevalence of homicides and other crimes of personal violence among Italians and to the violation of city ordinances previously mentioned. . . . .

IMMIGRATION AND THE PUBLIC HEALTH

The effective administration of the present immigration law insures the admission to the United States of physically healthy immigrants, so that there is no adequate cause for concern in this regard. While it is true that a large part of the present-day immigration is drawn from countries where certain dangerous and loathsome contagious diseases are prevalent among the immigrating classes, the medical inspection conducted by the steamship companies at foreign ports of embarkation and elsewhere in Europe prevents the coming to this country of great numbers of diseased aliens, and the inspection here by officers of the United States Public Health and Marine-Hospital Service effectively supplements the examination abroad.

It is doubtless true that some cases of contagious or infectious disease are introduced, and to a limited extent spread, in this country because of immigration, but there is no cause for serious alarm in this regard. From investigations of the Commission in industrial localities and from other investigations that have been made it seems probable that a considerable number of persons afflicted with venereal diseases are admitted to this country and that such diseases have been spread in many communities as a result of immigration. It is difficult always to detect the existence of such diseases by means of a medical inspection as it is now conducted at United States ports, and it would seem impracticable to make the medical examination more thorough in this regard than it is at the present time.

The Commission included within the scope of the investigation the study of cases admitted to Bellevue and Allied Hospitals in New York City.[1] These hospitals are public charitable institutions, and a sufficient number of persons are treated there to warrant some conclusions relative to the existence of disease among the poorer classes of the foreign-born. While it appears that a considerable number of immigrants are treated at these hospitals for various causes within a comparatively short time after their admission to the United States, it does not appear that the number is sufficiently large or the diseases for which they are treated are sufficiently serious to warrant the conclusion that diseased persons are

[1] See *Reports of the United States Immigration Commission*, II, 253–90.

being admitted in any considerable numbers. A study of these cases, however, permits an interesting and significant comparison between immigrants of the old and the new class with regard to alcoholism. Of the 23,758 cases treated at Bellevue and Allied Hospitals during the period covered by the Commission's inquiry, 25.5 per cent of the native-born and 18.2 per cent of the foreign-born persons involved were treated for alcoholism. Among the foreign-born this treatment was confined almost entirely to the races of old immigration, such as the Irish, Scotch, English, and Germans, while relatively very few southern and eastern Europeans were treated for that cause. A striking difference between the old and new immigration in this regard was also apparent to a greater or less degree in many industrial communities included in the Commission's general investigation. Some complaint was made that drunkenness interfered with the industrial efficiency of some southern and eastern Europeans, but these cases were comparatively rare.

IMMIGRATION AND PAUPERISM

In the earlier days of unregulated immigration pauperism among newly admitted immigrants was one of the most serious phases of the problem. In New York, Massachusetts, and other States which received immigrants in large numbers the care of those who either were paupers on arrival or became paupers soon afterwards so taxed the public resources that various attempts were made to levy a duty on arriving immigrants for the purpose of supporting the large number of those who became charges upon the public. It is recorded that in some cases a considerable part of the immigrants arriving on a ship would be so destitute of means of support that it was necessary to transport them immediately to almshouses, and the earlier poorhouse records show that there were constantly being cared for large numbers of newly arrived foreign-born. At the present time, however, pauperism among newly admitted immigrants is relatively at a minimum, owing to the fact that the present immigration law provides for the admission only of the able-bodied, or dependents whose support by relatives is assured.

The number of those admitted who receive assistance from organized charity in cities is relatively small. In the Commission's investigation, which covered the activities of the associated charities in 43 cities, including practically all the larger immigrant centers except New York, it was found that a small percentage of the cases represented immigrants who had been in the United States three years or under, while nearly half of all the foreign-born cases were those who had been in the United States twenty years or more. This investigation was conducted during the winter of 1908–9 before industrial activities had been fully resumed following the financial depression of 1907–8, and this inquiry showed that the recent immigrants, even in cities in times of relative industrial inactivity, did not seek charitable assistance in any considerable numbers. Undoubtedly conditions would have been otherwise had it not been for the large outward movement of recent immigrants following the depression, but however that may be, it is certain that those who remained were for the most part self-supporting.

CONGESTION OF IMMIGRANTS IN CITIES

Of late years the general impression that owing to immigration the poorer districts of the large cities are greatly overcrowded and that in consequence the living conditions are insanitary and even degrading has been so prevalent that it seemed desirable to make a very thorough investigation of this question. In consequence, in seven cities—New York, Philadelphia, Chicago, Boston, Cleveland, Buffalo, Milwaukee—a very careful study was made of the conditions prevailing in the poorer quarters of the city inhabited by immigrants of various races. As was to be expected, many extremely pitiful cases of poverty and overcrowding were found, at times six or even more people sleeping in one small room, sometimes without light or direct access by window or door to the open air. On the whole, however, the average conditions were found materially better than had been anticipated. Moreover, a comparison of the conditions in a great city like New York or Chicago with those in some of the smaller industrial centers, such as mining or manufacturing towns, shows that average conditions as respects overcrowding are very materially worse in some of the small industrial towns than in the large cities. For example, the per cent of households having six or more persons per sleeping room of the race which showed the worst conditions in these large cities was only 5.2, whereas in the industrial centers studied in several cases the proportion was higher than this and in the case of one race was as high as 9.5 per cent.

Moreover, in the large cities much more frequently than is generally thought, the population changes. New immigrants are attracted to these poorer residential quarters by the presence of friends or relatives and the necessity of securing living quarters at the lowest possible cost, but as their economic status improves after living in this country for some time, they very generally move to better surroundings. The undesirable districts of the cities that are now inhabited largely by recent immigrants were formerly populated by persons of the earlier immigrant races. Few of these are now found there, and these remnants ordinarily represent the economic failures—the derelicts—among a generation of immigrants which, for the most part, has moved to better surroundings.

In many instances, too, where deplorable conditions were found they were due in part, at any rate, to circumstances over which the inhabitants have little direct control, such as a poor water supply or unsanitary drainage—matters that should be attended to by the city authorities.

While instances of extreme uncleanliness were found, the care of the households as regards cleanliness and an attempt to live under proper conditions was usually found unexpectedly good, about five-sixths of all the families visited in the poorer quarters of these large cities keeping their homes in reasonably good or fair condition.

There seems to be little doubt that the various races, owing presumably to their differing environments in Europe, differ somewhat as regards overcrowding and the care of their apartments, but the differences are less than might have been anticipated. The reports seem to indicate clearly that the chief cause of the overcrowding is a desire of the families to keep well within their income or to save money, even at the expense of serious discomfort for the present, in order that they may better their condition in the future. The worst conditions were found among those who live in boarding groups, largely unmarried men, whose purpose in the main is to save money in order that they may send it back to their home country or return thither themselves as soon as a sufficient amount has been secured.

Although, as has been intimated, the average conditions are distinctly better than had been anticipated, the bad conditions still prevail to such an extent that the city authorities, as well as landlords and philanthropic people, have rich opportunities of improving them. It should not be forgotten that the bad conditions can not be estimated by the number of people that live on a square acre, but rather by the number of people per room and per sleeping room, by the amount of air space, the opportunities for light and ventilation, and the care that is taken of the rooms. Conditions in New York, where the largest number of people live per acre, were found, generally speaking, distinctly better than in some of the other cities where less care had been taken to pass or enforce proper laws and ordinances.

IMMIGRANTS IN MANUFACTURING AND MINING

A large proportion of the southern and eastern European immigration of the past twenty-five years has entered the manufacturing and mining industries of the eastern and middle western States, mostly in the capacity of unskilled laborers. There is no basic industry in which they are not largely represented and in many cases they compose more than 50 per cent of the total number of persons employed in such industries. Coincident with the advent of these millions of unskilled laborers there has been an unprecedented expansion of the industries in which they have been employed. Whether this great immigration movement was caused by the industrial development or whether the fact that a practically unlimited and available supply of cheap labor existed in Europe was taken advantage of for the purpose of expanding the industries, can not well be demonstrated. Whatever may be the truth in this regard it is certain that southern and eastern European immigrants have almost completely monopolized unskilled labor activities in many of the more important industries. This phase of the industrial situation was made the most important and exhaustive feature of the Commission's investigation, and the results show that while the competition of these immigrants has had little, if any, effect on the highly skilled trades, nevertheless, through lack of industrial progress and by reason of large and constant reenforcement from abroad, it has kept conditions in the semiskilled and unskilled occupations from advancing.

Several elements peculiar to the new immigrants contributed to this result. They came from countries where low economic conditions prevailed and where conditions of labor were bad. They were content to accept wages and conditions which the native American and immigrants of the older class had come to regard as unsatisfactory. They were not, as a rule, engaged at lower wages than had been paid to the older workmen for the same class of labor, but their presence in constantly increasing numbers prevented progress among the older wage-earning class, and as a result that class of employees was gradually displaced. . . . .

Like most of the immigration from southern and eastern Europe, those who entered the leading industries were largely single men or married men unaccompanied by their families. There is, of course, in practically all industrial communities a large number of families of the various races, but the majority of the employees are men without families here and whose standard of living is so far below that of the native American or older immigrant workman that it is impossible for the latter to successfully compete with them. They usually live in cooperative groups and crowd together. Consequently, they are able to save a great part of their earnings, much of which is sent or carried abroad. Moreover, there is a strong tendency on the part of these unaccompanied men to return to their native countries after a few years of labor here. These groups have little contact with American life, learn little of American institutions, and aside from the wages earned profit little by their stay in this country. During their early years in the United States they usually rely for assistance and advice on some member of their race, frequently a saloon keeper or grocer, and almost always a steamship ticket agent and "immigrant banker," who, because of superior intelligence and better knowledge of American ways, commands their confidence. Usually after a longer residence they become more self-reliant, but their progress toward assimilation is generally slow. Immigrant families in the industrial centers are more permanent and usually exhibit a stronger tendency toward advancement, although, in most cases, it is a long time before they even approach the ordinary standard of the American or the older immigrant families in the same grade of occupation. This description, of course, is not universally true, but it fairly represents a great part of the recent immigrant population in the United States. Their numbers are so great and the influx is so continuous that even with the remarkable expansion of industry during the past few years there has been created an oversupply of unskilled labor, and in some of the industries this is reflected in a curtailed number of working days and a consequent yearly income among the unskilled workers which is very much less than is indicated by the daily wage rates paid; and while it may not have lowered in a marked degree the American standard of living, it has introduced a lower standard which has become prevalent in the unskilled industry at large.

RECENT IMMIGRANTS IN AGRICULTURE

According to the census of 1900, 21.7 per cent of all foreign-born male breadwinners in the United States were engaged in agricultural pursuits, but the great majority of these were of the old immigration races. Up to that time comparatively few of the immigrants from the south and east of Europe had gone on the land, and, while during the past ten years some of the races have shown a tendency in that direction, the proportion is still small. Among the races of recent immigration which have shown a more or less pronounced tendency toward agriculture in States east of the Rocky Mountains are the Italians and Poles, while several Hebrew agricultural colonies have been established. A considerable number of the Italians are to be found in various parts of the East, the South, and the Southwest, where, as a rule, they have established communities, and on the whole have made good progress. In the East many have engaged in truck gardening in the vicinity of the largest cities, while in the South and Southwest they have entered fruit and berry raising and, to a lesser degree, general farming. The Poles have gone into general agriculture in many parts of the East and Middle West, while the Hebrews are, as a rule, located in the more populous States and usually near large cities. The small number of Hebrews who have engaged in agricultural pursuits have not been conspicuously successful, although in some localities they have made fair progress. The Polish farmers, as a rule, have succeeded, particularly in some of the eastern localities where they have purchased worn-out lands and succeeded in making them productive and profitable. The Italians have been usually successful in general farming and especially so in truck gardening and small farming in the vicinity of large cities.

While encouragement is to be found in the experiences of the past few years, it is clear that the tendency of the new immigration is toward industrial and city pursuits rather than toward agriculture.

ARTIFICIAL DISTRIBUTION OF IMMIGRANTS

In making the larger cities and industrial communities their place of residence, aliens composing the new immigration movement have continued to follow a tendency which originated with the advent of immigrants in any considerable numbers. This may be ascribed to various reasons. A large part of the immigrants were agricultural laborers at home, and their immigration is due to a desire to escape the low economic conditions which attend agricultural pursuits in the countries from which they come. With no knowledge of other conditions it is natural, therefore, that they should seek another line of activity in this country. The destination of these immigrants in the United States on arrival is controlled by the fact that they almost invariably join relatives or friends, and few of these, even among earlier immigrants of the class, are engaged in agricultural pursuits. Remaining in the cities and industrial centers they follow a general tendency of the times. The law of 1907 provided for the establishment of a division of information in the Bureau of Immigration,[1] the intent being that the division should disseminate among admitted immigrants information relative to opportunities for settlers in sections of the country apart from cities and purely industrial centers. It was hoped that the division could devise means of inaugurating a movement among immigrants which would eventually result in their more equitable distribution. The apparent result, however, does not indicate that the purpose of the law is being fulfilled. As conducted, the work of the division appears to be essentially that of an employment agency whose chief function is supplying individuals to meet individual demands for labor in agricultural districts. It does not appear that persons thus distributed have, as a rule, been distributed with the purpose that they would become permanent settlers in the districts to which they went, but rather that a more or less temporary need of the employer and employee was supplied through this agency.

No satisfactory or permanent distribution of immigrants can be effected through any federal employment system, no matter how widespread, because the individual will seek such social and economic conditions as best suit him, no matter where sent. What is needed is a division of information which would cooperate with States desiring immigrant settlers. Information concerning the opportunities for settlement should then be brought to the attention of immigrants in industrial centers who have been here for some period and who might thus be induced to invest their savings in this country and become permanent agricultural settlers. Such a division might also secure and furnish to all laborers alike information showing opportunities for permanent employment in various sections of the country, together with the economic conditions in such places.

ASSIMILATION OF IMMIGRANTS

It is difficult to define and still more difficult to correctly measure the tendency of newer immigrant races toward Americanization, or assimilation into the body of the American people. If, however, the tendency to acquire citizenship, to learn the English language, and to abandon native customs and standards of living may be considered as factors, it is found that many of the more recent immigrants are backward in this regard, while some others have made excellent progress. The absence of family life, which is so conspicuous among many southern and eastern Europeans in the United

[1] [This division of information ceased to exist and was incorporated into the Bureau of Employment of the Department of Labor during the fiscal year 1920–21. Whether because of lack of funds or for other reasons, the division had failed to fulfil the purposes for which it was established.]

States, is undoubtedly the influence which most effectively retards assimilation. The great majority of some of these races are represented in the United States by single men or men whose wives and families are in their native country. It is a common practice for men of this class in industrial communities to live in boarding or rooming groups, and as they are also usually associated with each other in their work they do not come in contact with Americans, and consequently have little or no incentive to learn the English language, become acquainted with American institutions, or adopt American standards. In the case of families, however, the process of assimilation is usually much more rapid. The families as a rule live in much more wholesome surroundings, and are reached by more of the agencies which promote assimilation. The most potent influence in promoting the assimilation of the family is the children, who, through contact with American life in the schools, almost invariably act as the unconscious agents in the uplift of their parents. Moreover, as the children grow older and become wage earners, they usually enter some higher occupation than that of their fathers, and in such cases the Americanizing influence upon their parents continues until frequently the whole family is gradually led away from the old surroundings and old standards into those more nearly American. This influence of the children is potent among immigrants in the great cities, as well as in the smaller industrial centers.

Among the new immigration as a whole the tendency to become naturalized citizens, even among those who have been here five years or more, is not great, although much more pronounced in some races than in others. This result is influenced by language considerations and by the fact that naturalization is accomplished with greater difficulty than formerly, as the requirements are higher and expense greater, and that adequate facilities are not in all cases provided. Another reason is that many do not regard their stay here as permanent. . . . .

CHANGES IN BODILY FORM OF DESCENDANTS OF IMMIGRANTS

The question of the assimilation of immigrants under American conditions has long been looked upon as vital, and it has been much discussed, but heretofore with little accurate information. Speaking from general personal observation, people have thought that under the influence of the existing educational, social, and political conditions the immigrants gradually change their habits of life and their ways of thinking, and thus become Americans. Little or no thought has been given to the possible effect of these conditions on the physical type of the descendants of immigrants. It was suggested to the Commission that if measurements of the bodies of European immigrants and their descendants at different ages and under different circumstances could be made in a careful way by scientific anthropometrists, valuable results might be reached. One of the best experts on this subject, Professor Franz Boas, of Columbia University, was invited to direct the investigation and was put in general charge. Although the investigation has been carried on only in New York City and its immediate vicinity and with only a few races, the results, in the opinion of Professor Boas, are much more far-reaching than was anticipated. It is probably not too much to say that they indicate a discovery in anthropological science that is fundamental in importance. The report indicates that the descendant of the European immigrant changes his type even in the first generation almost entirely, children born not more than a few years after the arrival of the immigrant parents in America developing in such a way that they differ in type essentially from their foreign-born parents. These differences seem to develop during the earliest childhood and persist throughout life. It seems that every part of the body is influenced in this way, and that even the form of the head, which has always been considered one of the most permanent hereditary features, undergoes considerable change.

The importance of this entirely unexpected result lies in the fact that even those characteristics which modern science has led us to consider as most stable seem to be subject to thorough changes under the new environment, which would indicate that even racial physical characteristics do not survive under the new social and climatic environment of America. The investigation has awakened the liveliest interest in scientific circles here and abroad, and as the subject is one of great importance the Commission expresses strongly the hope that by either private or public means the work may be continued.

12. Educational Needs of Immigrants[1]

A. LACK OF PROVISION FOR ALIEN EDUCATION IN ILLINOIS[2]

Approximately half a million non-English-speaking immigrants have come to Illinois since 1910. If these had been evenly distributed among the 4,500,000 native born people of the state, the problem would be simpler.

[1] [For an excellent review of this subject see F. V. Thompson, *The Schooling of the Immigrant* (New York, 1921). See also H. A. Miller, *The School and the Immigrant* (Cleveland, 1916). See also, in addition to documents from which extracts are taken, *U.S. Bureau of Education Bulletin* (1913), No. 51, "Conference on Education of the Immigrant"; *ibid.* (1916), No. 18, by F. E. Farrington; *ibid.* (1918), No. 18, "Americanization as a War Measure"; *ibid.* (1919), Nos. 76 and 77, by F. C. Butler; *ibid.*, "Proceedings Americanization Conference," 1919; *ibid.* (1923), No. 30, "An Americanization Program," by E. J. Irwin. See also *Bulletins of the Massachusetts State Board of Education*, January, 1919; July, 1921; November, 1922. See also *Reports of California Commission of Immigration and Housing* (*Home Teaching Work*).]

[2] Extract from Grace Abbott, *Educational Needs of Immigrants in Illinois* (*Bulletin of the Illinois Immigrants' Commission No. 1*), pp. 5–35. The Illinois Immigrants' Commission, which was created by the Legislature of 1919, was directed by statute to investigate the educational needs of the foreign born in Illinois. A

But they are segregated in districts of the larger cities and the smaller industrial and mining towns of the state. Great groups of these new arrivals have little or no contact with the older immigrants or the native born. Language barriers, differences in customs, in economic conditions and sometimes racial or religious prejudice, separate them geographically and socially from one another and from the native American. Removing the language barriers is perhaps the most concrete beginning which can be made in reducing the complications which result from our complex population. An examination of the number of classes in English and Civics offered immigrants who are above the age of compulsory school attendance shows to what extent Illinois has been doing this.

The report of the State Superintendent of Education for the 1917-1918 school year showed ten cities and towns in Illinois in which evening schools were conducted. Of that number only six had elementary classes for adults —Aurora (East), Chicago, Decatur, Joliet, Peoria and Springfield. The enrolment in these classes was 4,481 in Chicago and 247 in the other five cities. The enrolment of boys and girls of school age in the evening elementary schools was 6,325. Of that number, 5,574 were in the Chicago schools and 751 were in the Aurora (East), Rock Island and Rockford schools. The reports received by the Immigrants' Commission for the next school year (1918-1919) show some increase in the number of towns providing classes in English and Civics. Twenty superintendents reported classes maintained by public funds, and they had an enrolment of 4,408 in the elementary classes for foreigners. Of that number 3,074 were enrolled in the Chicago evening schools. This was an increase in the downstate enrolment but the number in the Chicago evening schools was smaller. Ten other superintendents reported classes conducted by private agencies in public schools over which the superintendent of schools had some supervision. In some of these the free use of the school building was the only public contribution, the teachers contributed their services or were paid by the Young Men's Christian Association, by an industrial plant, by a community center organization, or by the Daughters of the American Revolution. In some of these combination public-private schools a fee was charged the pupils. In Springfield, when the legality of the use of public funds for evening schools for adults was questioned, the classes were supported by private funds. Two or three superintendents reported plans to open evening schools the next year. Princeton reported classes offered

---

questionnaire was therefore sent out to the superintendents of schools in 177 cities and towns having a school attendance of 500 or more. Personal visits were made to many centers; and representatives of the schools, civic organizations and the foreign born themselves were consulted as to the educational situation. In this summary of the findings of the Commission an attempt was made to "measure the needs with what is actually being done and to work out not an ideal but an immediately practical program for Illinois to undertake."

but no enrolment; Ottawa that the Board contemplates erecting a building to serve the purpose of day and night schools and community center. Rock Island reported the evening school had been abandoned in 1918–1919 on account of the "flu." Small as the enrolment figures were, the average attendance reported for these classes was less than one-half the enrolment.[1]

In 1915 Chicago had an enrolment of approximately 18,000 in its evening classes in Elementary English, in 1918–1919 it had fewer than 5,000. The decrease is explained in part by the great decline in immigration during this period. In the past classes have usually been recruited among very recently arrived immigrants. When they first arrive in this country, they all expect to learn English as a matter of course, but they often find this much more difficult than they anticipated, and they discover also that after a fashion they can get along without it.

In addition to its evening classes for adults Chicago has had for a number of years a small but very successful day school for adults. This school is located near the downtown district and students are allowed to attend all day or such part of the day as their work permits. An elementary school course is maintained and each year a class is graduated. Last year the attendance at this school was about 180. The opening of similar schools in other parts of the city would, if properly advertised, undoubtedly greatly increase the adult enrolment.

During the last few years the Chicago public schools have also provided teachers for factory classes in English and Civics and special classes for immigrant women. These are under a supervisor who is giving special attention to the problems of training of teachers, classification of students, and means of reaching men and women who have not attended evening school classes before.

In the industrial and mining towns of the state there is much evidence of sporadic attempts to meet the educational needs of the adult immigrant. For example, in one of the industrial towns near Chicago the Young Men's Christian Association formerly offered English classes to men for a nominal fee. These met two evenings a week for a term of four months. Four years ago the Board of Education took over the classes and opened them to women as well as men. There was an initial enrolment of between two and three hundred. During the winter months the attendance fell off and many of the classes were dropped because the attendance was below ten on three consecutive nights. After two years the evening school was abandoned. Last year one of the industrial companies paid the teacher while the Board of Education furnished the building and the heat and light for the evening

---

[1] The irregularity of attendance is one of the great problems in connection with classes for adults. Overtime work, sickness of some member of the family or of themselves, discouragement over the progress made, the discovery that the sacrifice involved in attendance is greater than was anticipated are some of the reasons for this irregularity.

classes. These were closed during the time of the steel strike but opened in January with an attendance of about fifteen. The Chamber of Commerce made a nationality survey of the town two years ago, which was to be the basis of its Americanization work, but at the time of our investigation nothing had been done. The judge of the Naturalization Court reported that there was some one of every nationality who conducted private classes, where men were coached for the naturalization examination.

In the same city, priests of the Slovenian, Polish and Lithuanian churches have co-operated with the Woman's Club in organizing special classes for the women. The Woman's Club paid some one to organize the classes, the church furnished the meeting place, and the teachers were volunteers.

Figures were difficult to secure, but in all these classes, public and private, there were not more than 150 enrolled, and yet the town has, in addition to a large pre-war non-English-speaking population of Slovenians, Poles, Lithuanians, Italians, Armenians and Finns, a group of Mexicans who have come in since the war.

In a town in the southern part of the state the superintendent of schools reported that they had a flourishing evening school years ago, with an enrolment of about two hundred and an attendance of about one hundred. The school closed because the attendance fell off when the town voted wet. Although this cause for closing is now gone, there have been no classes since that time. Of 52 men from whom schedules were secured in this town, 48 could speak some English, 7 could read English but not write it, while only 6 could both read and write it; of the 49 women interviewed, 27 could speak English, and only 3 could read and write it. Thirty-one of the men had lived in the town for ten years or over.

In many parts of the state the foreign born live outside the industrial or mining town. Many of these towns permit the men to attend the school, although they are outside of the school district. One superintendent, from a town in which there were no classes for adults last year, wrote in reply to the Commission's questionnaire:

I am sorry that our work has not been more extensive. We have had considerable trouble, however, in getting the foreign born peoples of this city and vicinity to come in to school. . . . . They live some miles out of town. Although we interest them through the local Trades and Labor Assembly, they find it difficult to attend because they have to come so far.

Three or four years ago, when we offered a course, and when I taught one of the classes, there were some men in attendance who came to class without supper and walked six or seven miles home after we were through. A hardship of that kind, however, will keep all except the most enthusiastic away.

Several principals reported that after a visit from a representative of the Bureau of Naturalization classes were started. The principal or one of the teachers taught without pay. The classes met usually twice a week at first and then after a time only once. In most of these classes the interest of the foreign born was said to have kept up but the teachers felt that this, like any other school work, should be supported by the public and they were unwilling to continue it indefinitely on a volunteer basis.

These do not sound like the educational methods of America. They read like the stories of Poland, Lithuania and Russia in the days before the war, when in the absence of schools the *intelligentsia* went out as volunteers organizing and teaching groups of illiterate peasants. While such work is an evidence of the good will of those who offered their services, and is valuable to the few who are reached, a state or community cannot be satisfied that a great educational need should be met in this unorganized and thoroughly unscientific manner. Altogether the numbers enrolled, as compared with the number of non-English-speaking residents in the state, indicate that the most important gain resulting from recent Americanization activities has been the new realization of a need. A real solution of the problem still lies in the future.

Present legal status of public school classes for adults in Illinois.—The school law of Illinois fixes the minimum school age for cities of 100,000 population but leaves to the boards of education the power to determine what the upper age limit shall be. It is thus within the power of the Board of Education of Chicago to maintain day and evening classes for adults. But the statutes limit the powers of the directors of school districts to maintaining free schools for the accommodation of all persons in the district over the age of six and under the age of twenty-one. Boards of education in school districts of from 1,000 to 100,000 inhabitants have the powers of school directors subject to this limitation. In most cities and towns of the state the local committees therefore lack the necessary authority to provide in any way for the educational needs of the adult. The state school law was framed prior to the public appreciation of the importance of adult education.

In the cities and towns under 100,000 where classes for adults are maintained, the public right to meet this very serious need has not been challenged. In a few places classes have been abandoned when the issue was raised by some taxpayer.

In this respect Illinois has not kept pace with other industrial states. In many of these the maintenance of classes for adults is not only authorized by law but is mandatory under certain conditions. . . . .

Illiterate minors.—Illinois has recently adopted a compulsory continuation school law under which schools must be maintained by any community in which there are twenty or more minors who come within the provisions of the law. Beginning September 1, 1921, minors over fourteen and under sixteen years of age, September 1, 1922, minors over fourteen and under seventeen, and September 1, 1923, those over fourteen and under eighteen, who are not in regular attendance at an all-day school, must attend the continuation school 8 hours a week for at least 36 weeks. The school hours are to be between 8 A.M. and 5 P.M. on regular business days except Saturday afternoons.[1]

Before they secure work permits, children between fourteen and sixteen years of age must submit evidence that they have completed the fifth grade in the public school or its equivalent, but immigrant minors who are sixteen years of age at the time of their arrival may go to work in Illinois without a work permit. They are not required to meet the fifth grade test. To be admitted to the United States they must be able to read some language or dialect.[2] Only a small percentage of those who have been coming to the United States are able to speak English or have the educational equivalent of our fifth grade. That they are more in need of education than are those who have completed the fifth grade is obvious. They are young enough to learn easily. A real state educational program is very much needed for them.

Since 1887 Massachusetts has required illiterate minors who are above the age of compulsory attendance at day school to attend evening classes. The state has made the definition of literacy correspond with the educational test required for work permits. The employment of illiterate minors is legal only if weekly reports from the school testifying to their regular attendance at night schools, when such are maintained, are kept on file by the employer. New York[3] and California[4] adopted similar laws in 1918 and 1919.

As Illinois has adopted the compulsory part-time school principle for those who are under eighteen and who have already completed the fifth grade in school, it seems time to require the illiterate under twenty-one years of age to become literate. In the questionnaire sent out to the school superintendents by the Commission, the superintendents of 18 towns in which evening classes were maintained reported that they favored compulsory attendance of illiterate minors; one said he considered securing their interest would be better; two were opposed, and five did not reply.

If compulsion meant a reliance upon compelling people to attend and, in consequence, a relaxation of effort to meet the needs of these younger immigrants, there would be every reason for opposing it. This does not, however, represent the alternative. At present the classes for immigrants are not regarded as constituting a real part of the educational program of the state or the community. While their numbers are steadily decreasing,

[1] Employers are subject to a fine for employing minors between 14 and 16 (not 18) who are not in regular attendance upon the continuation school. (Sec. 8, Act of June 28, 1919.) Truant officers of the schools are charged with the enforcement of the law. (Sec. 9.)

[2] An unmarried or widowed daughter is allowed to accompany or join her father although not herself able to read.

[3] *Laws of 1918*, chap. 415.   [4] *Statutes of 1919*, chap. 506.

there are still principals and teachers who look upon the education of the children as their only responsibility. The adoption of compulsory attendance would change their attitude and would also mean that communities would be required to provide schools.

Requiring those between sixteen and twenty-one years of age who have not completed the fifth grade or its equivalent to attend an evening school would probably meet with less initial opposition than requiring attendance at a part-time day school. Educationally, however, the latter is vastly preferable. The eight-hour day is still the exception for both men and women, the twelve-hour day for men and the ten-hour day for women are not unusual for many of those who would be included in such a law. In spite of all the handicaps, some few exceptionally eager and able individuals have made great progress at the evening schools, but the exceptional cannot be accepted as a group standard. If we rely upon evening school work, we cannot expect satisfactory results. If day continuation schools are necessary for working children who have finished the fifth grade, such schools are even more necessary for minors who have never had a fifth grade education. . . . .

Isolation of many immigrant communities in Illinois makes state aid peculiarly needed.—In the course of its investigation of mining communities, the Commission found small camps which were practically foreign born settlements, sometimes of a single nationality, sometimes of several nationalities. Many of these are quite cut off from neighboring settlements by poor roads, and poor train connections. In these camps and in some of the larger mining towns the schools for the children are far below standard. Thus one town reports closing at the end of eight months, another at seven months, because of inadequate funds; another that schools are so crowded that it is impossible to enforce the truancy law. Another reports 91 children for one teacher in the first grade and an eight-month school because of lack of funds.

Although these particular towns and camps are in the richest coal mining section of the state, the taxable property in the towns is very small. The mines are generally outside the school district and the legal tax on the miners' property is inadequate to provide reasonably good school facilities for the children. Classes for adults on the local budget are out of the question. It was not surprising, therefore, that the Commission found that 96.9 per cent of the women and 88.6 per cent of the men interviewed in the course of its investigation of the mining towns of the state were not able both to read and write English, and that 53.5 per cent of the women and 24.2 per cent of the men could not speak English. Those who have already been here many years can probably not be persuaded to learn English now, but they can be brought in touch with the current of American life by moving pictures and by lectures in their own language. For the younger ones and the more recent arrivals much more can be done.

But some plan other than local organization and maintenance of classes for such settlements is necessary. Many of the camps are not large enough to warrant classes every year; for others the small attendance would make a short term practical. The necessary organization should be worked out by experiments financed and directed by the state.

B. THE PROBLEM OF ADULT EDUCATION IN PASSAIC, NEW JERSEY[1]

The Bureau of Education, in conducting the survey of adult education in Passaic, began with a survey of the general social and industrial conditions of the community, in order to determine the need for adult education. Obviously, since the public schools were created by the people for the use of all the people, it is necessary in making an estimate of any educational system to determine in the first place the needs and desires of the people. Important as this is in the matter of day-school education of children, it is doubly so in the study of adult education, for, while elementary-school education is compulsory, the attendance of adults at day or evening school is optional, and the very existence of the classes depends on the effectiveness of the schools in meeting the needs and desires of the people. Adult education is one of the few types of public education which has to meet the test of making good from day to day, or from night to night, with the people who come to the classes. . . . .

. . . . Inasmuch as the foreign born make up the majority of the people of Passaic, the first task of the public school in the matter of adult education is to meet the needs of the foreign-born adults. Let us consider what is already being done in this direction and what is the attitude of the people most concerned in the matter of adult education.

According to the reports of the board of education, 3,116 people attended evening classes for the teaching of English from 1915 to 1919, but the average daily attendance for each of those years was only 249 pupils per year, as shown in the following table:

[EVENING-SCHOOL STATISTICS]

ENROLLMENT AND AVERAGE ATTENDANCE IN PUBLIC EVENING SCHOOLS

Attendance	1915–16	1916–17	1917–18	1918–19	Total
Pupils enrolled............	1,211	582	580	743	3,116
Average attendance.......	468	203	188	137	249

. . . . The bureau, therefore, in making the survey, followed its usual custom of endeavoring to find out from the people themselves, through their different clubs, foreign groups, and labor organizations, why they did not attend the evening schools and what kind of courses they would be interested in taking.

[1] Extract from a report by Mrs. Alice Barrows Fernandez, *United States Bureau of Education Bulletin*, No. 4 (1920), pp. 5–25.

One of the first things revealed by the investigation was that the people, through their different nationality groups, had already started classes for teaching themselves English. This was particularly interesting in view of the fact that a number of public citizens interested in the subject of Americanization had stated as one of the reasons why so few people took courses in English that "the foreigners do not want to learn English." We are convinced that this is an erroneous impression, for in no case was there found any objection to learning English, and in many cases real eagerness to learn. It was found that the labor organization that had by far the largest number of foreign born, the Passaic Local of the Amalgamated Textile Workers of America, was already starting classes in English and citizenship and was planning to have classes in history, economics, etc. Such efforts, of course, are in line with the general movement among workers to start educational courses through trade-union colleges, workers' institutes, etc. Evidently, then, it was true in Passaic, as in other cities, that there was a desire on the part of the people for courses in English, and in a good many instances for more than the elementary courses in English. Why, then, were they not attending the evening schools in greater numbers?

The following are some of the reasons given by the men and women themselves, Poles, Russians, Hungarians, Bohemians, Austrians, as to why they did not attend evening school:

How can I? I work at night.

I work now during the day, but my wife works at night and I have to stay at home to take care of the children.

I tried it; I learned to read and write some, but not to speak English.

It is childish. We keep saying all the time, "This is a desk"; "This is a door." I know it is a desk and a door. What for keep saying it all the time?

My teacher, she was very nice young lady, but very young. She does not understand what I want to talk about or know about.

7:30 P.M. to 9:30 P.M. is too long; you get home too late. You get out of work at 5, then get out of school at 9:30, and it is 10:30 before you get to bed, and that's too late for a spinner. A spinner can't take chances.

They treat you like a child because you don't know English.

Too tired.

In each of the interviews the people were asked if they would be more likely to come if they had teachers of their own nationality to teach them English. The response was immediate; their faces would light up as they replied, "Yes; that is different. Then we will not get discouraged in the beginning."

If these criticisms are carefully studied, it will be found that most of the fundamental reasons for the present failure in evening school instruction are touched upon in them. The criticisms are of three kinds—those that have to do with the method of instruction in the school; the attitude toward the foreign born, and conditions outside the school which make attendance difficult.

In the first place, investigation proved that it was true that the method of instruction did not sufficiently take into consideration the people who were being taught. . . . .

. . . . With few exceptions there was no attempt at individual instruction. The pupils were taught as a class, instead of being divided into small groups and allowed to progress according to their ability. There was little use of the inductive method in determining the needs of each individual in the class and in developing his power of communication.

As it happens, the best teaching of English which was observed was in a class of workers taught by an organizer of one of the labor organizations. The enunciation was not always correct, but the spirit in the class was that of equals working out a problem together. There was the most thorough individual instruction, and an alertness on the part of the teacher in finding out the difficulties of each pupil and helping him to solve them. The men were working hard, even doing home work for each lesson, and there was an atmosphere of mutual helpfulness that was most inspiring.

But even if the instruction was of the best possible type, there is another reason for the present failure to secure large numbers in evening schools for which the school is not responsible in any way, and of which no amount of attraction on the part of the school can offset. We refer to the hours of work in the average industry and the prevalence of night work. Over and over again, as we have pointed out, when the workers were asked why they did not attend evening schools, the answer was a shrug and "How can I? I have night work," or "My wife works at night, I take care of the children." . . . .

It is only the exceptional person who, after a 10-hour day, will come to evening school for 2 hours' hard work on learning a new language. Nor can it be expected that large numbers of those having an 8-hour and 40-minute day will have the energy to attend school in the evening. But even this is not as great a handicap as the intermittent night work which unexpectedly cuts into the attendance in classes throughout the school, taking a dozen workers from one class, half a dozen from another, etc. The pupils in evening school when asked about night work replied, "Any time may work nights," "Last year worked nights 12 weeks straight," "I work two weeks day work, one week night work," or "May go on night shift next week, one week night work," or "Can't tell when we are going to have night work."

That was the point; they couldn't tell when they were going to have night work, and this uncertainty plays havoc with the administration of the school. No factory with a working force, say of 2,000, would undertake to get out production if suddenly 500 left one week and didn't come back for four weeks, and 200 more left just before the 500 came back, and didn't come back for 12 weeks, etc. Administratively, it would be an impossible proposition, and yet that is exactly the administrative proposition that is being put up to the schools at the present time. There is a great deal of agitation for the teaching of English and the extension of adult education, but the schools cannot be expected to function successfully in this matter when industrial conditions undermine the effectiveness of the work of the schools, as is the case at present.

Recognizing this fact the bureau took up with the manufacturers in Passaic the question of releasing the workers during the day without loss of pay to attend classes in English in the public schools. At least two of the largest woolen manufacturers have already agreed to release their workers who wish to learn English at 4:30 in the afternoon with pay from 4:30 to 5 (which is the end of the day shift in the woolen mills) on consideration that the workers will give until 5:30 to the lessons. The proposition was also taken up with the workers, and although not all the nationalities could be seen, those groups who were interviewed stated that they considered the proposition fair and would be glad to attend the public schools to learn English from 4:30 to 5:30 P.M. . . . .

Recommendations.—As a result, then, of the investigation the bureau makes the following recommendations:

I. *A separate department of adult education.*—Up to the present time adult education has been carried on in evening schools as a sort of adjunct to the day school, and the staff has been largely made up of already overworked day-school teachers. This was not a matter of great importance 25 or 50 years ago, but now the problem of adult education has assumed such proportions and is of such vital importance to the welfare of the community that it warrants the creation of a separate department with a separate staff of workers.

Staff: There should be a director and one assistant and clerical assistance.

Hours: The hours of work of the adult education staff should be from 1 P.M. to 10 P.M.

Purposes: The object of creating such a department would be, in the first place, to insure the undivided attention of a group of experts on the problem of adult education. In the second place, the director would be responsible for building up the work through the coopcration of the people. This would necessitate getting into personal contact with all the different nationality groups, labor-union organizations, clubs, etc., speaking at their meetings, explaining the purposes of the adult education department, getting their criticisms and suggestions, and asking each of them to elect a delegate to a central advisory committee.

II. *An advisory council.*—There should be an advisory council made up of representatives elected by the different nationalities, labor organizations, clubs, etc., which should assist the adult education department in developing the schools in accordance with the demands of the people. These representatives on the council would be responsible for making the plans of the adult education department known to the different nationality and labor-union groups, enlisting their interest, getting criticisms and statement of desires in regard to courses, etc., and thus keeping the adult education department in touch with the needs of the people.

.... Whatever may be the arguments from a pedagogical standpoint as to the relative value of a teacher of native birth or foreign birth teaching English, as a matter of fact, there is no question that in Passaic the large number of foreign born would be more likely to attend English classes if they could be taught by people of their own nationality. As they expressed it, they would not get discouraged in the beginning. The difference in the enrollment and attendance numbers shows how important it is to eliminate the various elements which make for that "discouragement in the beginning." It might be possible to follow a plan sometimes employed in universities of having a native teacher and a foreign teacher each teach one group twice a week. Under such a plan the foreign teacher explains the idiomatic phrases in terms that the foreign group would know, and the native-born American could teach the grammatical construction, etc. In order to make it possible for these specially trained teachers to teach in the evening schools, it would be necessary to take up with the State commissioner the question of changing the regulations in regard to the requirements for teaching in evening school. . . . .

In conclusion, it should be emphasized again that education is a social process. The adult education problem is a social problem. If it is to be worked out successfully, it must be developed through the intelligent understanding and cooperative responsibility of all the people. . . . .

C. FINANCING IMMIGRANT EDUCATION[1]

As yet no Federal aid has been forthcoming. Lacking it, States and local communities have borne the burden as best they could. A comparison of some of the financial provisions obtaining in different places is enlightening.

Massachusetts was one of the first States to provide by legislation for financial returns to cities and towns conducting immigrant education under State auspices. Reimbursement is on the basis of a dollar contributed for every dollar expended, with no limit fixed to the State appropriation; that is, the State pays half the cost. In 1922 the State's share under this arrangement was $140,000. In addition, an amount approximating $15,000 is appropriated annually for the activities of the director of adult alien education and his assistants. Other States that have adopted this "50-50" plan are Minnesota, North Carolina, North Dakota, New Jersey, South Dakota, and Maine (State pays two-thirds). It is to be noted, however, that in these others various limitations are prescribed. South Dakota, for

[1] Extract from *United States Bureau of Education Bulletin*, No. 31 (1923), "Americanization in the United States," by John J. Mahoney, pp. 15-17.

instance, appropriates $15,000 only. It is also to be noted that, excepting South Dakota and more recently Maine, no State office is set up, as in Massachusetts, to prescribe and carry out plans for immigrant instruction. There is no large guaranty, accordingly, that the money expended secures the greatest possible return.

In striking contrast to the Massachusetts idea is the plan in Ohio, where no State aid whatever is given to local communities. As a result these communities find it impossible to assume the burden of immigrant education. "It is out of the question for them to do so." Ohio, accordingly, resorts to the expedient of charging tuition fees. The following table shows how this is worked out in various localities:

IMMIGRANT EDUCATION IN OHIO—TUITION, LENGTH OF TERM

Cities	Tuition	Length of Term	Cities	Tuition	Length of Term
Cleveland	$2.00	12 weeks	East Youngstown	$3.00	3 months
Cincinnati	3.00*		Elyria	2.00†	
Toledo	0		Martins Ferry	2.40	12 weeks
Columbus	.50	Per month	Canton	1.00‡	
Akron	0		West Park	0	
Youngstown	3.00	12 lessons	Lafferty	1.00	Per week
Lorain	5.00	36 lessons	Rhodesdale	1.00	
Alliance	1.00	Per month	Rossford	0	
Barberton	3.00	24 lessons	Dayton	1.00§	

* Refunded in case of 75 per cent attendance.   ‡ Registration fee.
† No refund; includes books.   § Refunded for 85 per cent attendance.

Commenting on this plan, the State director says:

The result of this fee has been that attendance has been greatly stabilized. . . . . To be sure, probably a great number of pupils who need most to come to school are excluded because of their inability to pay. Working conditions are better than last year, however, and more students are able to pay.

Several States may be mentioned together, which, unlike either Massachusetts on the one hand or Ohio on the other, have tried out the expedient of spending money directly in local communities. Delaware bears all costs of immigrant education, and in 1921 appropriated $25,000 therefor. New York, in 1920, expended $100,000 for home and factory teachers, appointed to serve in local communities. Connecticut's original plan provided for the part salaries of certain local directors. Pennsylvania and Utah also pay money direct. It is worth noting in this connection that the experience of both New York and Connecticut seems to prove the unwisdom of attempting to establish a system of immigrant education on this basis. In the case of New York this became very evident when the failure on the part of the State legislature to continue appropriating resulted in a set-back to many activities that had been started in local communities.

The financing in New York during this past year has been practically on a dollar-for-dollar basis,[1] as in Massachusetts; and the Connecticut legislature is this year considering a bill which incorporates, in effect, this same provision.

Another group of States reimburse local communities on an attendance basis. New York applies the idea of the wage grant to teachers. Connecticut at present aids to the extent of $4 for each pupil attending 75 sessions. California, Nevada, New Jersey, Rhode Island, South Carolina, and Washington also apply this idea. Among these it is to be noted that only California and Rhode Island provide likewise State leadership and State machinery.

A careful study of the financing and administration of immigrant education the country over seems to make safe the following conclusions:

1. The education of the adult immigrant in English and citizenship is a public responsibility, and the cost thereof should be borne in proper proportions by the local community, the State, and the Federal Government. As yet, the Federal Government has failed to do its part. This furnishes no excuse for State legislatures to be similarly delinquent. Teaching the adult immigrant costs considerable money—more money than local communities can, unaided, afford to spend.

The failure of New Hampshire, as a State, to accomplish what it gave promise of accomplishing three years ago may be traced directly to the failure on the part of the State legislature to make even reasonably adequate appropriations for carrying into effect the admirable plans adopted. On the other hand, those States where results have been attained—Massachusetts, Rhode Island, Connecticut, New York, South Dakota, Delaware, Ohio, and California—are, except in the case of Ohio, States where financial aid to local communities has been forthcoming. There is much idle talk now, as several years ago, about plans for wiping out illiteracy and non-English-speaking through compulsory registration and through other means. The plain truth is that this is a task that calls for skilled administration, good supervisors, and good teachers—plenty of them. This means money, considerable money, spent under wise direction for a period of years.

Our experience to date is convincing that the imposition of this burden on the immigrant himself, on the local community alone, or on the State alone is not a satisfactory procedure. The State and the local community should between them "foot the bills."

2. The State should create administrative leadership, preferably in the State department of education. State financial support is worth while only in proportion as it is spent to carry out a State plan of immigrant education, wisely conceived and skillfully administered. Reimbursing the

[1] [For an account of the New York plan, see Doc. 13, B, p. 572.]

old-time evening schools will not avail much in the difficult task of eliminating the language barrier. Immigrant education is a specialized type of schooling that needs teachers specially trained. There is even a more crying need for leaders specially trained. State funds are spent judiciously only where these leaders are in charge, both in local communities and over a state-wide area.

3. There should be a minimum of State machinery and activity and a maximum of local responsibility and control. Experience has proved that permanent success in this work demands that we throw the initial responsibility on the local community. The State may easily do too little, by way of promotion, as has New Hampshire for three years past. The State may easily do too much, as New York attempted to do, with its liberal State appropriations in 1920. Once again the immigrant is the ward not of the local community alone, but of the State and the Nation as well. All should share in the cost of the Americanization process. But in accordance with the spirit of American education, the prime responsibility should attach to the community where the immigrant resides.

D. NEED OF STATE SUPERVISION OF PRIVATE SCHOOLS[1]

The school is the civic agency that most directly comes in contact with the immigrant, that most inspires his confidence and that can most effectively accomplish the essential result—assimilation—which makes him an integral part of the community in which he lives.

Therefore, the efforts of those schools endeavoring to fulfill this duty to the State should be stimulated and encouraged, while those schools ignoring, neglecting or indifferent to it should at once be aroused to a thorough realization of their obligation.

Public-school effort to teach the immigrants the English language, and at least a rudimentary knowledge of American and social ideals, has been discussed. Private schools also have an important part in the education of the immigrant children. Of these the most important are the parochial schools. Their development is inspired by a spiritual motive, which, together with the unselfish devotion of the large corps of teachers who voluntarily have consecrated their lives to its advancement, is worthy of the highest respect. . . . .

The large number (over 200) of parochial schools throughout the State may be divided into two groups: first, those in which the teaching is conducted in English exclusively, and second, those in which some of the instruction is conducted in English and some in a foreign language.

Schools of the first group were not investigated by the commission. Like the public schools, many of these enroll children of non-English-speaking parentage, and like the public schools they are affording those children the

---

[1] Extract from *Report of the Massachusetts Commission on Immigration* (1914), pp. 147–51.

associations and all the advantages of instruction that they are affording the native-born.

In the second group, 39 schools in 19 different towns and cities in Massachusetts were visited. The almost universal rule in these schools is to teach in English for half a day, and in Polish, Italian, Portuguese, French or Greek for half a day. These bilingual schools, of which there are over 90 in Massachusetts, present a problem of much difficulty, involving both religious and national motives deeply rooted in the heart and mind of the foreign-speaking peoples, and entitled to sympathetic recognition by the entire community. The problem, moreover, includes highly important social, financial and economic considerations. In some instances it is being successfully solved.

Teachers in all these schools have to deal with a perplexing situation, inasmuch as the pupils when they first enter rarely speak English, and in instruction precedence is given to subjects conducted in their native tongue. The complication is increased by reason of the fact that many of these teachers have but a limited knowledge of the English language; comparatively few speak it fluently, some do not speak it at all. Such lay teachers as are employed are, generally speaking, wholly unqualified. In certain schools of one nationality, conducted wholly by lay teachers, the instruction, discipline and results are a mere travesty of even rudimentary educational methods. Under such conditions proper progress in English or any other study is impossible.

The atmosphere of any one of these schools depends mainly upon the attitude of the pastor of the church with which it is connected. While some of these pastors are thoroughly imbued with American ideals, the majority are of foreign birth, education and training, so intensely devoted to their native land that their patriotism permits no divided allegiance; hence any special emphasis upon the study of English or upon American traditions and ideals, which often the Superior in immediate charge would gladly undertake, does not enlist their sympathy or meet with their approval.

Furthermore, while we have the greatest respect for the exalted character, disinterested service and untiring zeal of the teachers, we must regretfully declare that in very many cases they are not equipped by previous training (often excellent in their own language and literature), by familiarity with American civic or social ideals, or with the stress of modern economic pressure, to impress sympathetically upon the understanding of their pupils the fundamental knowledge which is required alike in the interests of the State and of the future industrial life of the pupils themselves. In some instances the atmosphere is so intensely foreign that progress in acquiring English is deprecated rather than encouraged.

In drawing comparisons between these and other schools the element of time must be considered; for as the system of parochial schools and, particularly, of bilingual schools, is comparatively young, it could hardly be expected that these privately maintained schools should be able to make as rapid progress in the character of their buildings and equipment as those schools maintained by the public purse.

While a large number of the school buildings are of excellent construction in every respect, and many may be rated as reasonably good, some were not originally erected for school purposes; they are distinctly bad in lighting and in ventilation, and are positively injurious to the physical well-being of the children.

The financial resources of these schools—mainly the voluntary offerings of poorly paid wage earners—are utterly inadequate to the magnitude of the work undertaken. This financial handicap may be regarded as the principal cause of the inability of so many of these schools to approach modern educational requirements in housing, in limiting the size of classes to reasonable numbers, in the character of textbooks used, or in the employment of a sufficient number of thoroughly efficient lay teachers to offset the scarcity of teachers of the religious orders.

When we consider the comparatively inelastic character of the wages of the groups who support these schools, and the increasing cost of living, it is difficult to see how the revenues upon which these schools depend can be greatly enlarged.

The beneficent influence of the spiritual training received, and of the constant example of simple dignity and refinement which these teachers afford, is evidenced by the unusual degree of respect and courtesy which marks the conduct of the pupils toward their superiors in age or in authority, and is worthy of special recognition.

That the knowledge of a second language has cultural advantages is beyond dispute, and should be encouraged, for in the history, traditions, literature and art of the various nations there is much that would enrich American life. But it is not in the pursuit of culture that the overwhelming majority of these children are to spend their lives. The far more practical and far more difficult problem of bread-winning is the one to which—day in and day out—they will be forced to devote their unremitting attention. It is therefore of vital importance to them, as well as to the State, that they should be fitted in the best possible manner for this daily bread-and-butter struggle. As they succeed or fail in this they will become an asset or a liability of the State, for, waiving other grave possibilities, there inevitably will be a marked increase in dependence resulting from the premature physical and mental breakdown of those who, from lack of proper training, are forever unable to escape from the most exhausting and the poorest-paid occupations.

It is therefore of importance to the Commonwealth that in the secular instruction in these schools, the study of English should be given first place, and that all studies, except religion and the native language of the children, should be conducted in the English language. The study of the foreign language should be made clearly subordinate to that of English. It should be possible to follow this plan without serious interference with the spiritual or national motive of these schools.

Attendance at public schools or at approved private schools is required by law of the Commonwealth. This law places upon the local school committees the obligation of approving private schools, "when the instruction in all the studies required by law is in the English language, and when they are satisfied that such instruction equals in thoroughness and efficiency, and in progress made therein, the public schools in the same city or town." For obvious reasons, such as local influence, political expediency and in some cases indifference, the school committees make no pretence of fulfilling this obligation and, under existing conditions, there is no prospect that they ever will.

The task of gradually bringing these schools up to the desired standard is one calling for infinite wisdom, tact and patience, as well as for clear comprehension and sympathetic recognition of the aspirations of the people who voluntarily support them. In such a spirit the task should be begun at once, and plans in the best interest of all concerned should be worked out harmoniously. As the local school committees have not even attempted to perform this task, the commission recommends that this responsibility be vested in the State Board of Education, as provided in the bill that is submitted with this report.

13. State Aid for Immigrant Education

A. MASSACHUSETTS[1]

The term "Americanization" is very elastic, and has been stretched, seemingly, to cover all sorts of movements and activities. In its widest significance it means making good American citizens of both native and foreign-born. And this, obviously, is a task that calls for the intelligent effort of many agencies other than the schools. In so far, however, as this task has to do with the foreign-born, it is plain enough that achievement will be delayed as long as millions in our midst are separated from us by a language barrier. The teaching of our common language has accordingly come to be regarded as the first and certainly one of the most important steps in the Americanization process.

This phase of Americanization is most peculiarly the work of the public schools. And it is fortunately a definite work, the results of which can be noted from year to year. There need be no vagueness of thinking with respect to the function of the schools in Americanization. There is nothing mysterious about teaching people how to talk, and read, and write the

[1] Extract from *Massachusetts Department of Education Bulletin No. 50*, November, 1922, *The Massachusetts Problem of Immigrant Education in 1921–22*, report by Charles M. Herlihy, state supervisor of adult alien education.

English language. Nor is there any reason why such work should not be promoted by every intelligent citizen. It is a reasonable certainty that this support will come, in increasing measure, as the public comes to understand just what the schools are trying to do. . . . .

[In Massachusetts] a machine has been set up that works. And in the setting up of that machine several things have been incontrovertibly proved. We know now that the adult immigrant, given the chance, will go to school. We know that he will attend regularly if the teaching is good. We know that good teaching is a highly skilled performance, and makes teacher-training necessary. We know that teachers avail themselves gladly of this training. We know the inestimable importance of the good director in every community and the great need of training directors, too. We know that the rehabilitated evening school reaches many times more immigrants than the school of before-the-war time, when it was thought that any one could teach a foreigner, and when almost any one did. We know that factory classes can be successfully organized and maintained if schools and industries co-operate as they have done in Massachusetts during the past two years. We know that it is possible also to conduct citizenship classes which stress good citizenship, rather than the cramming of inconsequential facts. And finally, we know that the Massachusetts plan of immigrant education will succeed in communities where the people are interested to have it succeed, and will spend the money necessary to this end.

[CLASSES FOR IMMIGRANTS IN MASSACHUSETTS]

DEVELOPMENT OF IMMIGRANT EDUCATION UNDER THE LAW OF 1919*

	1918–1919	1919–1920	1920–1921	1921–1922
a) Total number of adult immigrants belonging in all classes	3,381	9,030	20,475	22,242
b) Number of evening school classes		420	750	855
c) Number of factory classes		131	327	366
d) Number of neighborhood and club classes		92	248	294
e) Total number of classes		643	1,325	1,515

* [See *Acts of 1919*, chap. 295, amended May 27, 1921. Revised form in *General Laws*, chap. 69, secs. 9 and 10. This act provided for state aid for adult immigrant education in Massachusetts. The state contributes one-half the amount expended by every town in the commonwealth for supervision and instruction. The State Department of Education jointly with the local school committee is responsible for the plan of instruction.]

The increase from 3,381 to 22,242[1] [in number of students] as shown in the table above represents a growth of 560 per cent in three years. This is

[1] [The forthcoming report of the Department for the year 1922–23 shows that 27,000 adult men and women attended school voluntarily in Massachusetts last year, an increase of approximately 23,500 since 1918–19.]

significant indeed as tending to answer conclusively two questions often raised:

1. *The adult immigrant given an opportunity will go to school.*—Attendance in all these classes, be it noted, is wholly voluntary, and usually comes at the end of a hard day's work.

2. *Public interest in the education of the immigrant has not waned since the war.*—Massachusetts refuses to regard this phase of Americanization as a war activity. And the cities and towns of Massachusetts, having started the work of removing the language barrier, seem determined to put this task through, and to pay the cost therefor.

Naturally, the largest increase in the number of classes is found in the evening schools. The increase in the number of neighborhood and club classes from 92 to 294 indicates an awakening of the interest of immigrant organizations in the public school opportunities for learning English.

The outstanding development in this work in Massachusetts during the past two years has been the factory class. Despite serious business depression, with accompanying unemployment, short hours, and low industrial morale, the number of public school classes in industry has increased from 131 in 1920 to 336 in 1922. The agreement between the Associated Industries of Massachusetts and the public schools provides a practical working basis for industrial executives and public school officials in the organization and conduct of public school classes in industry. . . . .

Immigrant organizations.—The later Pilgrims to our shores have been eager to take their part in the building of America; and realizing that the first step is the acquiring of the language and history of their new home, have zealously applied themselves to the task.

Clubs of Lithuanians and Greeks in Haverhill, Finns in Quincy, Russians in Peabody, and Italians in Wakefield have all given the use of their club rooms for classes in English and citizenship; while a Portuguese club in Plymouth, a Polish club in Chelsea, Hebrew and Armenian clubs in Lowell, as well as Italian clubs in Belmont, Nahant, Beverly, and Northampton, have taken the initiative by asking for teachers and recruiting the classes. The Poles of Hatfield asked for a speaker from the school department for an open meeting of their club, after which they recruited several large classes. . . . .

Unusual school records.—The eagerness of all nationalities for education and the sacrifices they will make to get it are both inspiring and pathetic. There is a man in Plymouth who rode ten miles after a hard day's work, often without his supper, to attend the evening school. In Pittsfield one class held its members practically intact from October to March, even when the thermometer registered 14 degrees below zero. In Shirley, a group of Poles attended class three nights a week, and stayed at home with the babies so that their wives could attend on the other two nights. At Peabody, in a class of fifty Russian men and women, 93 per cent attended the entire term of forty sessions. A Nahant woman, working in Lynn, left the factory an hour before closing (thereby losing an hour's pay) to get to her afternoon class; while a group of women of Revere, on being refused more sessions after the closing of the regular term by the school committee, hired a private teacher and went on with their education. In Melrose, a French Canadian, who worked nights, cut short his sleep in the daytime to go to school, and a Russian, able to read and write English himself, closed his store three nights a week to take his wife to class. A young man in Cambridge attended factory class two nights a week, the Lowell School two nights and the Hebrew School two nights, a total of six nights a week—and not once missed a session. Three Finnish men in Gardner organized two home classes of Finnish women, twelve in each division.

There is evidently no sex line in the thirst for knowledge, nor does there seem to be an age limit. A great grandmother of sixty-three years, living in Leominster, had spent many hours of her life praying that she might learn to read. Now, thanks to the evening school, she can both read and write—"a gift from God," she says. In Springfield, a Jewish woman, sixty-two years old, has missed only one night at school in three years and now that school is closed she attends an afternoon class. A man in the same city, sixty-five years old, works at an industry six miles from home, yet came to a citizenship class and has missed only one session all winter. In Holyoke, another man of sixty-five has been perfect in attendance throughout the season, and a woman of seventy has joined the citizenship class. A man who came to Webster in 1898, and is now seventy years old, deciding at last that he should never return to the old home, entered the evening school, learned to read and write English, and has passed his citizenship examination with a mark as high as that of the youngest pupil.

The attendance records in many cases have been remarkable. Cambridge reports two hundred and twenty pupils who attended 100 per cent, while Lowell reports one entire evening school and one factory class as having the same record. In all industrial classes in Worcester, over 98 per cent of the men who enrolled at the beginning of the term and are now employed in the plants are still members of their classes. In the Massachusetts Mills at Lowell fourteen Greek women held an attendance of 98 per cent from October to May. Marlboro had two classes and Watertown one, which after fifty night sessions closed with original numbers intact. Twenty-five women in Lynn have attended public school for three consecutive years.

Citizenship class work.—That the newcomers to our shores gladly assume the duties and privileges of citizenship is attested by the large numbers enrolled in naturalization classes. Many, having won their second papers, return to school to improve their English and learn more of our government. In Malden, newly made citizens came back to school to discuss local issues with their teachers. Some citizens who took out papers many years ago in Wakefield have entered classes to get what they had no opportunity to learn before they were naturalized. In Holyoke and Webster, graduates of the public grammar schools, both native and foreign-born, have attended citizenship classes to get a clearer idea of our laws and the functioning of our government. An Italian graduate of a Maynard citizenship class, having passed the Federal examination with honorable mention, formed a club of fifteen of his own race to promote naturalization. An Attleboro man, who recently became a citizen, organized a group of his friends, who under his leadership are studying the things he learned in evening school. Waltham's new citizens of six different races have presented their respective flags to the city to be used on holidays in processions or decorations. The enthusiasm these new Americans display for their adopted country is an inspiration to all who come in contact with them.

Their gratitude for America's gifts to them is illustrated feelingly by a paper written for the graduation exercises in Watertown, and read by the author, a young Armenian:

I was only seventeen years old when I first came to America, the land of heroes and great men. My dream was always to come into this great and free country, to live as a free man, without fear that my life was in danger.

Since I came here I have earned enough money to better myself, and to help my parents come over here.

I was not able to speak English at all, but to-day, with the aid of the night school, I can speak and read and write very well the English language. I love and admire America because she helped me many times and because she is the only unselfish nation in the world.

Here I found liberty, justice, and happiness, and I thank God because I was prosperous enough to become a citizen of this country and enjoy her blessings.

Factory classes.—The manufacturers who employ these men and women are glad of the opportunity to take a part in helping them to citizenship. Many employers give room for classes in their factories, hold foremen's meetings to stimulate the interest of the "little boss," recruit pupils among their employees, and then "follow up" absentees from class. One plant in Worcester pays the pupils for a part or the whole of the time spent in school, while others give time without loss of pay. In a Cambridge plant the foremen make all sorts of shifts and rearrangements that the pupils may have time in the forenoon to go to class; for it is stipulated that no man may be a member of the Shop Committee who cannot speak, read, and write English. Ordinarily, however, factory classes meet at noon or after work. . . . .

Two industries in Springfield have given a dinner to the new citizens in their employ, and in another plant the foreman and employment manager have written a series of industrial themes for texts in their classes. At Ludlow the industrial relations manager has written a set of themes which are used in the hemp business throughout the country. A firm in Palmer gave its men time and free transportation to go to court in Springfield for their citizenship papers, while a mill executive in Holyoke accompanied his men and acted as witness for those of long service.

In Shirley, the management of a large company gave its employees in the English classes a day off and $50 to take a trip to Boston with the teacher to visit the State House. This was a wonderful day for the Poles, for in Warsaw, they said, none but officials were allowed in government buildings. The women of the English classes were given an afternoon at the movies and a restaurant dinner, much to their delight. The three largest textile mills in Lawrence have co-operated with the public schools this year and forty-five industrial classes were organized. Three hundred immigrant mothers "went to school" for the first time in the noon classes held in these woolen mills. Southbridge manufacturers have supported factory classes for the past four years. The attendance this year in the sixteen factory classes was larger than ever before. A large rubber company in Hudson recruited classes from their employees, and co-operated with the schools in helping to maintain regular attendance.

Eight employers in Taunton have shown their faith in the value of factory classes by signing a petition to the school committee for a sufficient appropriation to carry on that work, and in Lynn, one firm employing several thousand men conducts so successful a "follow up" that practically every illiterate in their employ is in class, the average age of the pupils being forty-five. New Bedford has a large foreign-born population and the textile manufacturers have backed the factory-class idea with such whole-hearted support that seventy-one classes in twelve large mills have helped nine hundred employees to learn English. These classes have been held in the mills at noon and after work. The interest of the students has been maintained for over a term of six months. At least thirty classes have been in session over a period of nine months.

All-year-round work.—Gardner[1] continues its adult immigrant classes for ten months (the average term throughout the State is seven months, October 1 to May 1), but Americanization activities do not stop with the closing of classes. Citizenship classes are continued through the summer to prepare for the September court, and mothers' classes are in many cities more successful in summer than in winter. In two places, Springfield and Holyoke, the mothers' classes are held on the playgrounds, and in the latter city, in connection with these classes, the shower-baths in three public schools in foreign sections are open during July and August. The supervisor at Waltham takes groups of foreign women and children on all-day picnics; and Holyoke's classes make visits to the fire stations, libraries, city hall, and other public buildings. Such activities serve to hold the interest of

[1] [A town of 16,000 people that planned to spend approximately $11,000 on immigrant education during the year 1921–22.]

the pupils between spring and fall terms, and have a marked social influence which is an important phase of true Americanization.

B. NEW YORK[1]

As a result of the World War there has developed in the United States a deeper and more widespread interest in the education of the adult immigrant. . . . . For many years, most of the larger communities in this State have maintained night schools for illiterate and non-English-speaking adults, but the State Department of Education took little interest in the problem. In June, 1915, the Department made a brief survey of the situation, and in 1916 it published several bulletins for the use of local public school authorities. In July, 1917, the State Department employed a full-time supervisor to assist local authorities in the improvement of the night schools and in the general extension of the work. During the past 5 years, with the generous support of the Legislature and the earnest efforts of local public school authorities and of the state supervisor and his assistants, an encouraging beginning has been made in immigrant education. Thousands of teachers have been given special training for this work in classes conducted by the State, thus improving the quality of instruction; classes have been established wherever and whenever students would meet for instruction; special citizenship classes have been conducted in many communities and the ceremony of naturalization has been made more dignified and impressive; a better understanding and increased mutual sympathy have been stimulated through organized cooperation between the native and foreign-born. These are tangible results of large value to the State. . . . .

A task for the public school.—Illiterate and non-English-speaking adults are found widely scattered throughout the State. Most of them are in the large centers of population, especially in the industrial centers, but some are employed as servants in residential communities, some as laborers on large estates, and still others are in agricultural sections. . . . .

The education of adult immigrants in the English language and in American citizenship is a public responsibility; the problem is national in scope; the issues at stake are national solidarity and the American standard of living; the only agencies capable of dealing with the problem adequately and on a nationwide basis are trained governmental agencies; and, since the solution is largely one of education, the task is largely one for the public school. Private agencies can and do assist in this educational undertaking; they accomplish much; but it is evident, nevertheless, that their work is but supplemental to that of the public school.

Evening school alone not adequate.—It is evident, also, that the public evening elementary school which has been maintained for a quarter of a

[1] An extract from *University of the State of New York Bulletin* (September 1, 1922), No. 765, "Administration and Organization of Immigrant Education in the State of New York," by John L. Riley, pp. 3–30. The first paragraph is from the Foreword, contributed by Lewis A. Wilson.

century or more in the larger cities of the United States—while it has accomplished much and promises to continue to care for the larger share of these adult students in the future—does not in itself furnish sufficient opportunity to meet the needs, but must be supplemented by classes held at other hours and places if the problem is to be adequately met. An evening school which is open from 7 to 9 o'clock does not provide for people who work nights; it will not attract many who live at too great a distance; its hours are inconvenient for many foreign-born mothers whose families require their attention at these evening hours. The problem can be only partly met by the evening school, however efficient. Wherever and whenever a group sufficiently large can be gathered together for regular instruction—in school, in factory, in hotel, in store, in club room, in home—there the local public school authorities should have a teacher carrying America's language and instilling America's message of individual liberty and responsibility, of justice and equality, of government by law. The public school must do its work in all places and at all hours, for to it more than to any other institution in our country is committed and entrusted the supreme duty of shaping America's citizenship.

Foreign-born mothers neglected.—Perhaps the saddest result of our neglect to extend adequate educational opportunities to the foreign-born adults is the often-observed widening breach between the foreign-born mother and her children. The younger children learn the language of America in the day school; the older children and the father may acquire it in evening school or at their work; the mother alone of the little family group finds no chance to learn English or to study about America.

The foreign-born mother should be induced to come to the school building for instruction, but where her household or other unavoidable duties or conditions prevent, instruction should be given to her in the home, provided the classes so formed are large enough to justify the expenditure of public moneys for this purpose. Experience in many communities in the State has fully demonstrated that these foreign-born mothers are quick to learn and eager for the opportunity; that bonds of affection are quickly established between them and the teachers who work among them; that the children and the father take great interest and pride in the mother's progress; and that the home of such a foreign-born family quickly becomes a school and bulwark of Americanism through the interest and help of the American teacher. . . . .

STATE ASSISTANCE IN IMMIGRANT EDUCATION[1]

The law and its application.—The important laws relating to immigrant education provide, respectively, (*a*) for state reimbursement to local com-

[1] [The New York State Department of Education has a special staff promoting the work of immigrant education throughout the state under the immediate direction of a supervisor of immigrant education. This staff in the State Department "has

munities, (*b*) for compulsory maintenance of night schools in cities and in certain other communities, (*c*) for financial support of immigrant education by giving certain public bodies the authority to make appropriations therefor, and (*d*) for teacher training.

1. *Law providing state reimbursement.*[1]—(*a*) This law directs the Commissioner of Education to apportion to a city or school district in the same manner as teachers' quotas are apportioned, an amount equal to one-half the salary paid to each teacher in immigrant education, the amount not to exceed $1,000 for each teacher so employed.

b) Reimbursement will be made to local communities under the foregoing law: (1) when teachers are properly licensed and are employed by and are under the control and supervision of the local public school authorities; (2) when all instruction is given through the medium of the English language; (3) when classes are of such size as to permit of efficient instruction; (4) when suitable textbooks and instructional material are provided; (5) when the housing facilities and equipment are satisfactory.

c) *Types of classes.*—Under this law, local public school authorities may establish and maintain day or night classes in school buildings, in factories and other places of employment, in neighborhood houses, in homes and in other places they may deem advisable, "for the purpose of giving instruction to foreign-born and native adults and minors over the age of 16 years," thus making it possible to provide instruction at places and hours most convenient to the illiterate and non-English-speaking people for whose benefit the law was primarily enacted.

Classes that are commonly referred to as Americanization classes, English for foreigners classes, and citizenship or naturalization classes are included under this law. Common branch classes in evening schools, where the aim, generally, is to prepare students to meet certain requirements for admission to evening high school, are not considered as coming under the provisions of this law.

---

supervision over all night classes and schools for the elementary instruction of people 16 years of age and over in the English language, in American history, civics, and other subjects tending to promote good citizenship, including naturalization classes, and also all day classes for similar purposes in schools, in places of employment, in community centers or in homes where such instruction is conducted under the direction of the local public school authorities; except that part-time or continuation classes are not under the supervision of this staff." It is said to be the aim of the Department to promote this work throughout the state by "conferences and meetings, to cooperate with local public school authorities in making surveys and in organizing the work, to inspect and supervise it, and to make such provision for the training of teachers for this type of education as the situation may require and the law provide."]

[1] *Education Law*, sec. 94, par. 11-*d*.

d) Qualifications of teachers.—The Commissioner of Education is formulating regulations governing the employment of teachers for whose services state reimbursement is expected under this law.

e) Courses of study prescribed.—The law requires that the course of study shall be prescribed by the Regents of the University and that it shall include instruction in "English, history, civics and other subjects tending to promote good citizenship and to increase vocational efficiency." To meet these requirements, courses of study are being prepared.

2. *Night school law and its applications.*[1]—This law requires that free public night schools shall be maintained three nights each week for 2 hours each night in cities and in certain school districts. The law does not apply to common school districts.

3. *Law authorizing local appropriations.*[2]—This law permits the following public bodies to make appropriations for immigrant education: the board of estimate and apportionment of a city, the council of a city or the common council of a city, the board of supervisors of a county, the board of trustees of an incorporated village, the town board of a town.

The foregoing law gives the power to appropriate money for this type of instruction to bodies other than those which ordinarily exercise the power to make appropriations for the support of the public schools. When local school authorities can not secure adequate appropriations for immigrant education in the usual ways, this law provides additional sources from which funds may be obtained.

4. *Law authorizing state courses for teachers in immigrant education.*— Under the teacher training law, the Legislature has authorized the Commissioner of Education to conduct special courses in colleges, universities and normal schools of the State for the purpose of fitting teachers to give elementary instruction to illiterate and non-English-speaking adults and minors over 16 years of age.

The subjects taught in these courses include special methods of teaching English to illiterate and non-English-speaking adults, immigrant backgrounds, American citizenship and American political foundations and institutions. Outlines of study are in preparation by the State Department of Education and will likely be published for collateral use in teacher training courses and for home study.

It is suggested that superintendents urge all teachers in immigrant education to take advantage of these courses and, other things being equal, to give preference in appointment to those who complete such courses satisfactorily.

GENERAL SUGGESTIONS FOR ORGANIZING IMMIGRANT EDUCATION

Selecting teachers.—Principals, organizers, and teachers of classes in immigrant education should be well educated and professionally trained.

[1] *Ibid.*, sec. 311.   [2] *Ibid.*, sec. 94, par. 11-*c*.

They should know the foreign-born. They should be well informed regarding conditions in the homelands which caused emigration. They should understand the hardships incident to migration, including the struggles of immigrants in America. This will quicken interest, arouse sympathy and humanize teaching. Teachers should be employed who can interpret America adequately and justly and in a spirit of loyalty. Of course, successful workers among the foreign-born should have common sense, good judgment and adaptability.

Principals and assistant principals of day elementary schools undoubtedly make the most successful principals of evening elementary schools and should be selected for these positions wherever possible. If the city or village has only one night school and it comprises both high and elementary school classes with the high school principal in charge, the classes in elementary education for those 16 years of age and over should be organized as a separate department with a person who understands the problem as head and this person should have at least part of each evening free for supervision.

The teacher of English in these classes should know and be able to apply the technic or special method of teaching non-English and illiterate adults. Many of these adult students are well educated in their own tongue; many have had years of experience and have matured minds. They are keenly disappointed with inefficient teaching, but under the trained teacher who is master of the special method of teaching English to adult beginners, they study diligently and make wonderful progress. The greatest care should therefore be exercised in choosing teachers for these adult students. It should be added that the teacher must also be intelligently sympathetic; she must have had sufficient contact with the foreign-born to have discovered that they have their ideals, their refinements and their culture and she must reveal all this in her attitude and behavior. Only through such mutual respect and sympathy, combined with skilful instruction and a pleasing active personality, can these classes be successful.

The teacher of a class in citizenship or naturalization should be a superior student of government and should be able to explain, interpret and justify the fundamental principles of our representative democracy. A teacher of history in a senior or junior high school, especially if he has not neglected the history of the United States, generally handles such a class satisfactorily. Persons without teaching experience should not be placed in charge of these classes if efficient teachers of experience are available. . . . .

Attracting students through a general publicity campaign.—An intensive and persistent publicity campaign should be carried on in the community in order that the schools and classes for adults may hold the attention of the foreign-born. In addition to this kind of a campaign, special methods of approach should be used in organizing classes in places outside of the public schools, such as classes in factories and homes. The general publicity campaign should aim chiefly to secure students for the night schools; in reality, enrolment in all types of classes will be stimulated. The following agencies and means should be used to the fullest extent: (1) illuminating the entrance to the night school to attract attention; providing a transparency over entrance which reads "Free Evening School"; (2) placing large posters in front of night school printed in English and in foreign languages; (3) posting large notices on billboards in foreign section, in store windows, in factories and other places of employment, in immigrant aid offices, in employment offices, in other places where foreign-born people meet; (4) personal solicitation of prospective students by members of adult classes, day teachers in their visits to homes, day school children especially among their relatives, school attendance officers, school and public health nurses, baby welfare workers, immigrant aid workers, employers and foremen, foreign-born leaders, courts, labor leaders, clergy, policemen, postcard invitations sent through mail; (5) oral announcements in meetings of foreign-born in clubs and lodges, in labor meetings, in churches; (6) printed announcements in foreign and native press, in movies, in pay envelopes, in library books.

Maintaining attendance.—The best means of maintaining attendance in these classes are: (1) satisfactory lighting, heating, ventilation, and seating equipment; (2) a teacher—friendly, sympathetic, resourceful and efficient; (3) good classification with frequent regrading; (4) work adapted to the ability and needs of students, including the right kind of textbook; (5) a feeling on part of the student that he is making rapid progress; (6) giving advice and help in personal matters, such as finding employment; giving free legal advice in minor affairs; helping to prevent abuse and exploitation of these foreign-born people; (7) occasional variation in the program including moving pictures, concerts, entertainments, brief talks by local leaders, dancing, club meetings. . . . .

The all-day school for adults.—Some cities now conduct a day school at public expense for the instruction of adults in elementary English and citizenship. The students are mostly those who work nights and those who find it impossible or very inconvenient to attend evening school. It is a great convenience to people who work in such places as restaurants, theaters and shoe-blacking stands. Many women, especially mothers, take advantage of it.

The all-day school has a permanent location and a permanent teaching staff. The classes are held forenoons, afternoons, and evenings at hours most convenient to students. The teacher's program is arranged so that her day is of about the same length as that of the regular day school teacher. A teacher may be assigned for work forenoon and afternoon, forenoon and evening, or afternoon and evening. The teachers are required to visit students at their homes and at their places of employment and to be of help to students in other ways than in that of merely instructing them in English.

Recently arrived immigrants, while waiting to find work, attend the all-day school as well as the evening school. Many of the younger immigrants just over 16 years of age, by thus applying themselves intensively to learning the English language, quickly prepare for entrance to junior or senior high school. The ready adaptation and rapid progress of these younger immigrants and the favorable impression which their success makes upon others of their nationality give this work great importance.

Wherever the all-day school has been established it has tended to become not only a center for varied types of service to the immigrant but a supervisory center for the teachers of scattered day classes for adults which are held in homes and neighborhood houses. Some superintendents predict that the day school for adult immigrants will eventually become the real center of the whole system of night and day elementary classes for adults.

The neighborhood house.—Closely akin to the all-day school for immigrants is the neighborhood house which in some communities has developed into a school for instruction in English and citizenship, a bureau for advice and assistance to immigrants, and a center for the promotion of the happiness and assimilation of the foreign-born through mutual contact in social affairs.

One neighborhood house in New York State in a city of less than 15,000 population conducted, during the first year of its existence, morning and evening classes for men, classes for women, and sewing classes for girls. In addition to reaching 109 adults and 42 children in these classes, the one worker in charge made 309 visits to the homes of these immigrants, besides dealing with many requests for advice and aid. In this particular city, the superintendent of schools found that this neighborhood center attracted students better than the evening school, partly because it was located nearer the homes of the foreign-born but largely because of the closer contacts established by the worker in charge and the wider serviceableness of the center.

In nearly all our cities and industrial centers, the non-English-speaking immigrants suffer because of the lack of information regarding our customs, laws and institutions which affect them vitally. . . . . Large evening schools, as well as the all-day schools for adults, and neighborhood centers are beginning to meet these needs. Some superintendents or directors of immigrant education have taken the leadership in promoting the establishment of such service bureaus in their communities, and have found school boards, other public officials and private organizations sympathetic and cooperative. Neighborhood houses are often supported in part by public funds but in many cases they rely upon private contributions and proceeds from concerts and entertainments.

Organizing a naturalization or citizenship class.—Instruction in citizenship and in preparation for naturalization needs to be much more deeply studied and more broadly and thoroughly organized than has been the case thus far in any of our cities. All the courses for the separate classes organized to prepare for naturalization have been too short; in many classes, the subject of instruction has been the form rather than the function of government; the method has been that of memory cramming, rather than of practice in free discussion of vital issues and of student participation in the solving of social problems. If the educational and intelligence standards for naturalization are raised and the public school given a larger and more definite responsibility in preparing immigrant adults for citizenship, as seems likely in the near future, this type of public school activity will at once assume a position and importance scarcely realized at present.

Who should attend.—All immigrant aliens should be considered as prospective students for classes which prepare for citizenship. They naturally divide into three groups: those who take no step toward naturalization; those who have made the declaration of intention and must wait for 2 years before they may take the next step in the process; and, finally, those who have filed the petition for naturalization and await the expiration of at least 90 days that must elapse before their hearing in court. It is the people in the 90-day group, almost exclusively, who attend the naturalization or citizenship classes and the time is altogether too short to give them the necessary preparation. Generally the course is from 6 to 10 weeks of two sessions each, making a total of from 24 to 40 hours of instruction for those whose attendance is perfect. We should try to reach the declarants as well as the petitioners and we must work out eventually a course which will provide the amount and kind of instruction and training needed to fit these new Americans for their citizenship responsibilities. For several years, however, until higher naturalization standards and a longer course of instruction are established, it will be necessary to continue these shorter courses. . . . .

Organizing special classes for women.[1]—Women students enrolled in classes in immigrant education in New York State are only about one-half as numerous as men students, indicating that our present types of classes do not serve the foreign women so effectively as the foreign men. The non-English speaking home could be more quickly Americanized if the mothers could be reached in larger numbers.

Special classes for women have been conducted for many years in settlement houses and other places by private organizations. During the past 2 or 3 years, many of them have been organized, conducted and financed by local public school authorities. When they are held in places other than school buildings, the school authorities furnish the teacher, the textbooks and supplies and expert supervision, the use of room, heat and light being

[1] [The "home-teacher" as a means of teaching immigrant mothers has been widely used by the California State Commission of Immigration and Housing. See the *Annual Reports* of the Commission, 1914 to date.]

privately donated. School authorities have little trouble in getting active cooperation, assistance and support from women's organizations and from socially-minded people in the work of extending elementary education to the foreign-born mother.

Practical ways of reaching the immigrant woman and getting her into class include, first of all, neighborhood visits to build up confidence and friendly feeling which form the basis of collective classwork. . . . . The names of persons to be visited may be obtained from a foreign-born leader, public school principal, teacher, kindergarten teacher, public school nurse or district nurse, local priest, minister or rabbi, children in public schools, members of mothers' clubs, parent-teacher associations or local foreign clubs, settlements, community centers or libraries. . . . . Classes may be located in any available room in the neighborhood, including school buildings, settlements, day nurseries, libraries and homes. . . . .[1]

The lesson may last 1 hour or more, the best hours are from 9:30 to 11:30 in the morning and from 3 to 5 in the afternoon.

14. Protection for Immigrants through a State Bureau

A. MASSACHUSETTS[2]

The Massachusetts Bureau of Immigration was created by an act of Legislature (*General Acts of 1917*, chap. 321). Its functions are set forth in section 2.

SECTION 2. It shall be the duty of the bureau to employ such methods, subject to existing laws, as, in its judgment, will tend to bring into sympathetic and mutually helpful relations the commonwealth and its residents of foreign origin, to protect immigrants from exploitation and abuse, to stimulate their acquisition and mastery of the English language, to develop their understanding of American government, institutions and ideals, and generally to promote their assimilation and naturalization. For the above purposes, the bureau shall have authority to co-operate with other offices, boards, bureaus, commissions and departments of the commonwealth, and with all public agencies, federal, state or municipal. It shall have authority to investigate the exploitation or abuse of immigrants, and in making any investigation it may require the attendance of witnesses and the production of books and documents relating to the matter under investigation.

SEC. 3. The commission is hereby authorized to expend for the purposes of this act during the current fiscal year a sum not exceeding ten thousand dollars.

[1] Elizabeth A. Woodward, *Educational Opportunities for Women from Other Lands*, 1920 (*University of the State of New York Bulletin 718*).

[2] Extract from *First Annual Report, Massachusetts Bureau of Immigration* (*Massachusetts Public Documents* [1919], No. 121), pp. 7–23. In 1920 the Bureau of Immigration became the Division of Immigration and Americanization in the Department of Education of the State of Massachusetts. In the new Division, however, the work of the old Bureau has been continued and developed. The Division now maintains branch offices in Boston, Lawrence, Springfield, Worcester, New Bedford, and Fall River. See *Annual Report of the Division for 1921–22*.

SEC. 4. This act shall take effect upon its passage. [*Approved May 25, 1917.*]

The Bureau opened its office in the State House, Boston, September, 1917, to which immigrants were invited to come for advice and information. In order to acquaint the immigrant with the existence of the Bureau, railway stations, public buildings, factories, churches, etc., were placarded with the following notice in English and in numerous languages:

MASSACHUSETTS BUREAU OF IMMIGRATION, STATE HOUSE, BOSTON

The Commonwealth has created for the service of its residents of foreign origin, especially those from non-English-speaking countries, a State Bureau of Immigration.

The office of the Bureau is intended to provide contact between the State and its foreign-born residents, so that each may learn more of the other and how each may be helpful to the other, and thus, through mutual co-operation, strengthen the bond of friendship and good will which already exists.

In a strange country, speaking a strange language, meeting strange customs, and with new experiences in every-day life at home and in employment, residents of foreign birth often meet problems for which trustworthy explanation, advice and guidance would be of great advantage.

This service the Massachusetts Bureau of Immigration is created to perform. It earnestly desires and proposes to merit the confidence and friendly co-operation of all those who have come to Massachusetts to find freedom, opportunity and happiness under the laws and institutions of our common country.

Whatever and whenever questions arise affecting these interests you are invited to come to the office of the Bureau in the State House. You will there be given courteous attention, opportunity to state your difficulty, and an honest endeavor will be made to solve it.

The office will be open from 9 A.M. until 5 P.M. every week day, except Saturday, when it will close at noon.

This service department of the Bureau of Immigration quickly proved an effective means of attracting large numbers of immigrants who had problems to solve. Branch offices were opened at New Bedford and Springfield, July 1, 1918. . . . .

Wage claims.—The Bureau has received numerous applications for assistance regarding collection of wages. The Bureau in no sense aims to act as a collection agency, but difficulties due to the migration of the immigrant from place to place, his inability to speak English or write for himself concerning money due him, the uncertain delivery of mail, and the confusion which sometimes arises from the use of check numbers were often eliminated by friendly correspondence with the employer, which cleared up many of the misunderstandings—frequently those of the employee—in the matter of wage contracts. Such cases as could not be settled by friendly intermediation were referred to the State Board of Labor and Industries, if the evidence warranted such reference, or to the Legal Aid Society, both of which have been most cordially co-operative.

The immigrant and money transmission.—Transmission of money by immigrants to their relatives abroad, especially to countries in the war zone, has been extremely difficult. The cases brought to the attention of the Bureau involved not only the banks known as "immigrant banks" but also those of established reputation and reliability. In all cases the transmission has been traced to the larger bank with a foreign office through which the local bank transmitted the money, and the date of transmission has been verified. The bulk of the transmissions concerning which information was sought were those to Russia. The present chaotic condition in that country made it impossible to carry many of these investigations to a satisfactory conclusion. In the cases which involved transmission to Greece or Italy, the usual reason for the money not being received by payee has seemed to be because of lack of accuracy in addressing by the transmitting agency. Where it has been possible to secure proof that money had not been received by payee, refunds have frequently been secured.

In some few cases violations of the seven-day transmission limit of the banking law have been found; in some of these the persons sending money to dependents in their home country stated that grave injustice had been done them by the delay in transmission, claiming that money for the imperative need of their families was illegally retained by the banker until war conditions rendered transmission impossible, and that because of this failure to transmit, their wives and families had suffered unnecessary hardship and privation. While these persons have redress in civil action, no refund of money could change the privation which the delay caused; nor should the immigrant of little means be forced to expend in such civil suit most if not all of the money involved, together with his loss of time. The attention of the Bank Commissioner has been called to these violations.

In many cases where a misunderstanding existed between banker and immigrant an amicable settlement was made. In numerous instances refunds, approximating $2,300, were made through the services of the Bureau, the smallest being $20 and the largest $702.52.

The immigrant patronizes the racial or immigrant bank mainly because his language need is not met by the American banks. In normal times enormous sums, running into the hundreds of millions, are annually sent to foreign countries for saving and investment as well as for support of dependents. The large contributions which the foreign born have made in the different campaigns for the Liberty Loan are conclusive proof that if approached by their own racial leaders, or by Americans in the proper fraternal spirit, they will invest their savings in America rather than in their native country.

There is no advantage, either to the immigrant or to the community, in permitting a multiplicity of "banks" or "bankers" with little capital and little or no knowledge of the banking business. Banking functions are of such vital importance that they should be performed by persons of unquestioned probity, well trained in the technique of banking, with ample capital and of undoubted financial responsibility to the full extent of their obligations, and our banking laws should be so framed as to exclude those not thus qualified. While it is desirable that properly qualified persons of moderate means shall be permitted to conduct a banking business, there is a point beyond which the argument in favor of freedom of personal choice of occupation can be carried to absurdity. Furthermore, it should not be possible for any persons to conduct a deposit, savings and money transmission business unless under State supervision and upon the filing of adequate bonds.

In carrying on investigations in connection with a large number of complaints regarding the transmission or failure to transmit money through various immigrant banks, the importance of further amendments to the banking laws of the Commonwealth, which will increase the protection of the depositors in and senders of money to foreign countries through such banks, has strongly impressed itself upon the Bureau, and to accomplish this purpose it recommends such amendments as it believes to be essential in the public interests.

Exploitation in factories.—An apparently well-founded impression prevails that foreign-speaking workmen in many factories, construction camps, etc., are compelled to make regular payments to foremen and others in order to retain their jobs. The prevailing industrial unrest, together with the difficulty of creating an understanding between employer and employee, can sometimes be traced to the fact that those coming in direct contact with the foreign-born workmen have too often, because of the indifference of the employers, been able to exploit these foreign born in matters of securing and holding their jobs. The elimination of this type of exploitation will do much to convince the foreign worker that he can find in America an opportunity for fair play. Unless Americanization work has this basis of just treatment for one and all in the Commonwealth, no propaganda work can have permanent success.

Many non-English-speaking employees in a shoe factory in Massachusetts testified at a public hearing that for over thirteen years they had constantly paid money to their foreman for their jobs and for increases in pay, or for re-employment after semi-annual stock takings, when, instead of being temporarily laid off, if necessary, they were discharged, and had to buy their job over and over again. The foreman in question was found guilty by the Bureau, resigned his position, and has since been indicted by the Plymouth grand jury.

The immigrant and the courts.—The immigrant often receives his first and most lasting impression of American justice in the courts. In his contact with the law he must frequently use an interpreter, and it is highly important that such interpreters should be directly under the supervision of the court and be competent and reliable. While the municipal court of Boston now has official court interpreters, not all of the courts in the Commonwealth, even in communities with a large immigrant population, are so supplied. The recommendations of the 1914 Commission on Immigration that all interpreters should be salaried officers of the court, appointed after a thorough examination by the Civil Service Commission, still obtains.

A flagrant abuse of the non-English-speaking immigrant has been through the operation of solicitors—"runners"—who securing promptly the name, address and complaint against persons arrested, often on trivial charges, and occasionally on charges apparently deliberately framed to secure the arrest of foreign-speaking peoples, seek them out and undertake to secure bail and counsel for them. Their plan includes the taking of security—usually money or a savings bank book—with signed orders to be held pending disposition of the case, and returned, if at all, indefinitely thereafter, minus outrageous charges for legal or fancied service.

Investigations of the Bureau disclosed the fact that over twenty individuals were found daily in the corridors of the municipal criminal court in Boston soliciting business for attorneys and furnishing bail for persons arrested. Many of these "runners" had criminal records. They dealt mainly with foreign born, ignorant of our customs, our language and legal procedure. They pretended powerful influence with the police, the district attorney and the courts, and they guaranteed to secure the discharge of the person, whether innocent or guilty, for a sum of money to be paid to them or to the attorney in whose interest they were working. They boasted of political influence and of the fact that for over fifteen years they were permitted to do business there, and that not one of them had ever been punished.

Many foreigners who found themselves brought into court for minor offences, such as assault and battery, violation of the sanitary laws, etc., were urged to engage certain attorneys and threatened with a long prison term if they did otherwise. Exorbitant sums of money were extracted as attorneys' fees.

To abate the evil the matter was taken up with the chief justice of the municipal criminal court and the chief probation officer and their active co-operation secured.

The Legislature of 1917 enacted chapter 267 (General), which reads as follows:

It shall be unlawful for any person, not being an attorney at law, to solicit for himself or another from a person accused of crime or his representative, the right to defend the accused person. Violation of the provisions of this act shall be punished by a fine of not more than one hundred dollars, or by imprisonment for not more than six months, for a first offence, and by a fine of not more than five hundred dollars, or by imprisonment for not more than one year, for any subsequent offence.

After conferences with several prominent attorneys and the chief justice of the municipal criminal court it was decided to prosecute these "runners" for violating the above act. Several were arrested, convicted and sentenced to terms ranging from six to ten months' imprisonment, and in some cases heavy fines were imposed. . . . . The Boston police department and the inspectors detailed for this work gave hearty co-operation in the investigation and preparation of these cases.

As a result of these prosecutions, "runners" have practically disappeared from the corridor of the court house. Those who are there do not solicit business, but claim that they are professional bondsmen who are furnishing bail. A sharp watch for their reappearance is being maintained.

Any work undertaken with the view to stimulate the assimilation of the immigrant into the body politic, to awaken in him appreciation of American life and ideals, must necessarily be fruitless unless it be based on a foundation of confidence in American justice. It is of paramount importance that the courts should not be misrepresented to the foreigner as unfair or corrupt. Any movement to rid the courts of those who mislead ignorant foreigners in regard to the working of American justice is a most essential and fundamental step in Americanization. . . . .

ILLUSTRATIVE CASES[1]

Case 3712.—A Lithuanian girl was employed as a scrub woman in an office building. During the influenza epidemic the other scrub women employed were unable to work. The janitor offered to pay this girl $16 per week if she would work double time and do their work. She usually received $8. When her week was finished he gave her only $8, although she had worked not only her usual time, from 8 to 11, but also from 11 to 3. When she demanded what he had promised he told her that he was only joking with her and would give her no more money. The Bureau secured the entire amount for her.

Case 3906.—An Italian laborer, very lame and apparently suffering considerable pain, called at the Bureau of Immigration to ask where he could get financial aid. He had been working in Maryland, and while at his work was injured by a motorcycle. He had been in a Maryland Hospital for four weeks, and his hospital expenses there, together with his doctor's bill, had exhausted his entire savings. He had then returned to Massachusetts and was staying with some friends. He was unable to get medical attention because of lack of funds. The Bureau procured for him hospital attention, which was received just in time to avert an amputation of his foot, also compensation for the time he was disabled, and a refund of the amount paid for medical bills.

[1] These cases illustrating the work of the Massachusetts Bureau of Immigration are taken from the *Second Annual Report of the Bureau* (1920), pp. 38, 39.

Case 3974.—An Italian was arrested for deportation under the anarchist clause of the immigration law. His cousin was told by a person claiming to come from the detained alien that the arrested man could be released from the detention station on the payment of a small bond. The cousin paid $30, and waited some weeks for the release of the detained alien, but heard nothing. On investigation at the United States Immigration Station it was found that the runner did not come from the detained prisoner, that no release under bond was contemplated by the United States authorities, and that the detained alien and his companions had engaged a lawyer to handle the case. The refund was secured.

Case 3993.—An Italian came to Boston from Colorado leaving in a Colorado bank a deposit of $190. He wrote to the bank for the withdrawal of his savings. He was informed that he had only $90 deposited to his credit. The Bureau straightened out the difficulty, due to the misspelling of the applicant's name at one deposit, and the man was able to obtain his entire deposit.

Case 4082.—An Italian subscribed for a $50 Liberty Loan Bond through an agent taking subscriptions for a reputable bank. He paid $25 in weekly payments. He later forwarded the $25 balance due on the bond in a registered letter to the agent through whom he had subscribed. He did not receive his bond and could not locate the agent. The Bureau assisted the man in obtaining his bond from the company for which the agent was acting.

Case 4088.—A Syrian asked assistance in locating his missing cousin who had enlisted in the army. The Bureau traced the enlisted man through various cantonments in this country and overseas, and found that he had returned wounded and had been sent to an insane hospital at Washington. As his insanity was due to shell shock, and in lucid intervals he could find consolation in the visits of his friends, an arrangement for the transfer from the Washington Hospital to one in Boston was made.

Case 4214.—A Russian girl was brought here by well-to-do people of her own race as a maid. During six months' residence she had been allowed out but two or three times, was forced to work from 5 in the morning until 11 o'clock at night, and had received no wages. Although but seventeen years of age, and therefore subject to the compulsory education law, she was allowed no opportunity to learn English. The wages due were secured for her; she was taken from this unsuitable family and placed in the care of a society for girls which has placed her in a supervised home and assisted her in learning English.

Case 5206.—Five Poles were sent by a labor agency in Boston to work in New Hampshire as cordwood cutters. On arrival they found the character and conditions of employment were not as represented. After working one and one-half days they started to leave camp. They were stopped by an agent of the company and summoned to the office of the sheriff, where they were told that they must reimburse the company for their transportation and board. None of the men had any ready money. One Pole had a bank book with deposits amounting to several hundred dollars, which he showed to the sheriff and agent of the company. On seeing this they insisted that he deliver his bank book, with an assignment of $100 for payment not only of his own indebtedness and that of his four friends, but also for three other laborers who were unknown to him and for whom he was unwilling to assume responsibility. He objected to this, but was told that he and his companions would otherwise be sent to a farm where they would have to work for a month without pay. Although the net indebtedness for himself and his four friends amounted to but $35, the sum of $100 was deducted from the bank book. The Bureau secured a refund of all but the net indebtedness, and also the return of the bank book.

B. CALIFORNIA: A STATE BUREAU OF COMPLAINTS FOR IMMIGRANTS[1]

The Commission had determined from the very outset to make all of its work of a practical nature, based upon facts, not theories. Consequently it was decided not to theorize concerning the problems and difficulties met with by newly arrived immigrants, but to find out from the immigrants themselves what these facts and problems were. It would be obviously unwise to attempt to render direct aid to immigrants or to propose remedial legislation until the actual needs were thus ascertained. Therefore, in order to accomplish these results, a complaint bureau was organized. The purpose was to receive complaints from immigrants in trouble and aid them in securing justice, to carry on independent investigations, and to standardize the general problems and needs as a basis for remedial legislation and general relief measures.

Furthermore, the recorded experiences of the Bureau of Immigration of New York state and of other state immigration departments, disclosed the need for a specially equipped department in the handling and disposition of current complaints of immigrants. The preliminary surveys of the Commission had likewise shown that aliens within this state encounter serious difficulties in securing even a hearing when they have been exploited or actually defrauded, and the active work of the complaint department during the last eight months has demonstrated that such a department exercises a much broader and more human function than the mere collection of statistics for future use. Pressing and immediate needs, which have been unheeded for years, have received attention. Confidence in our government and in its institutions has been instilled into the justly suspicious immigrants; an ambition to become active, participating units in that government has been aroused; assimilation and adaptation have been encouraged instead of retarded and discouraged. . . . .

[1] Extract from *First Annual Report of the Commission of Immigration and Housing of California* (1914), pp. 52–70.

Organization.—During the first four months after its organization the Commission was so unexpectedly involved in the investigation of the Wheatland case and the inception of labor camp inspection that little was done toward getting into actual and personal contact with immigrants. Investigations disclosed a few cases where American exploiters had made capital of the ignorance and of the helplessness of newly arrived immigrants, and only a few straggling complainants found their way to the office of the Commission as a result of announcements in the foreign press. Years of unsympathetic treatment by public officials, of innumerable experiences where confidence had been misplaced and solicitous "American friends" and "immigrant protective societies" had turned out to be professional exploiters, had given rise to widespread distrust of all offers of advice and of assistance.

It soon became obvious, therefore, that a definite, organized effort would have to be made to inspire confidence and get in close touch with the immigrant and his peculiar problems. To this end, in April, 1914, posters containing the following announcement, printed in twelve different languages, were put up in conspicuous places throughout San Francisco, particularly in the "foreign quarters":

TO IMMIGRANTS

The State of California Commission of Immigration and Housing is created to protect and aid immigrants in California.

Immigrants who feel that they have been wronged or defrauded, or who wish information, are asked to come in person or write to the office of the State Commission, Underwood Building, 525 Market street, San Francisco.

The Commission will furnish information and will aid all in obtaining justice. We speak and write all languages.

The city of San Francisco was well placarded with these posters by April 24, 1914, and the record of the Complaint Bureau really dates from that time. This more or less impressive offer of assistance by the state, conspicuously displayed in their familiar haunts, reassured many disheartened immigrants who had been the almost helpless victims of fraud and deceit.

All complainants who came to the office were given a full and careful hearing, even when their complaints were seemingly of a trifling nature. An interpreter was employed who was proficient in the languages of the complainants from the larger immigrant colonies, and arrangements were made for the occasional services of interpreters for the rarer languages. Each complaint was carefully taken down in writing and submitted to the attorney of the Commission, who was in direct charge of the Complaint Bureau. The attorney then showed the investigators how to check up on the facts of the complainant's allegations and how to examine into the entire matter. If the charges proved to be entirely without foundation, the attorney would cross-examine the complainant and his witnesses to make sure the case had been properly reported. If no new evidence was thus discovered the complaint was dismissed, after a careful explanation to the complainant through the interpreter.

But if the complainant's charges were substantiated in the slightest degree by the investigation, the defendant[1] was either called upon or summoned to the office of the Commission and asked to give his version of the case. Further investigation was then made of any new facts brought out by the defendant. If the total evidence then showed that a crime had been committed by the defendant, prosecution was instituted and conducted by the Commission's attorney, who appeared in such criminal cases as special prosecutor for the state. If no crime was involved, but the defendant was shown to be civilly liable, the parties were brought before the attorney for an informal hearing, and every effort was made to bring about an amicable settlement or adjustment. If such a case could not be settled out of court, the complainant was advised of his rights and urged to employ an attorney to file suit against the defendant. This procedure was, of course, necessary, as the Commission, or its attorney, could not represent an individual in a civil suit. Our experience goes far in showing the need of a strong, well organized legal protection society. . . . .

If a defendant was shown to be morally liable, although not legally so, an even greater effort was made to effect a settlement or, at least, a compromise.

Two investigators and an interpreter, besides the Commission's attorney, have been regularly employed in handling complaints in San Francisco.

Branch offices.—When the Complaint Bureau, as organized in San Francisco, had proved to be an effective means for handling this important and pressing phase of the Commission's work, it was necessary that branch complaint offices be maintained elsewhere, so that the Commission might perform its proper functions as a state organization. Accordingly, offices were opened in Los Angeles and Sacramento with full time, salaried agents in charge, and the gratuitous services of residents, whose private offices were used, were secured in San Diego, Riverside, San Bernardino, Ventura, Santa Barbara, and San Luis Obispo. These agencies were established during July and August, 1914. The "To Immigrants" posters were placed in conspicuous positions in the districts about these cities, with the address of the local office stamped prominently thereon in red ink.

It also became necessary to open a branch complaint office in the foreign quarter in San Francisco as many immigrants who were loath to go to a distant office building were not being reached; consequently an office was opened on Columbus avenue in November and excellent results have been obtained.

[1] The person or corporation against whom a complaint is lodged is designated as the "defendant" in the records for the sake of brevity and clearness, though he is not a defendant in the legal or technical sense.

Summary of complaint records.—The fact that 2,224 complaints were filed with the Commission between April 24, 1914, and January 11, 1915, demonstrates the need of a complaint bureau. Practically all these complaints were based on justifiable grounds and very few were of a trivial nature. Numerous cases were successfully prosecuted or settled where the complainants had had established rights for months and even years, but had been unable to put the facts before the proper authorities or get action, because no one understood their language or had the patience to assist them, and because also of the terrifying and confusing paths of "red tape" and jurisdictional procedure, which even native born Americans lament.

Although no strictly judicial powers were vested in the Commission, section 10 of the creating act gave it "power to hold hearings for the purpose of investigation and inquiry, and for the purpose of reaching an amicable settlement of controversies existing between persons, firms and corporations" coming within the terms of the act. Through the exercise of this power, amicable adjustments of a majority of the complaints were obtained. Not only was justice secured for the individuals in such cases, but the informality and simplicity of the hearings had the broader and more far reaching effect of reassuring the wronged immigrants of the strength and fairness of our governmental institutions, and the further effect of creating in the minds of the American citizens involved a new viewpoint of respect for and a feeling of responsibility toward these potential citizens. . . . .

The Commission has instituted 11 criminal prosecutions, and appeared therein through its attorney, who acted as special prosecutor. These prosecutions have resulted in 9 convictions, only one of these being reversed by higher courts. One appeal is now pending, and five other cases are now awaiting trial. Evidence is now being collected in six cases in which arrests will be made and prosecutions begun within the next month.

This cooperation in criminal cases with the various district attorneys has resulted in bringing some criminals to justice who otherwise would have escaped prosecution, owing to the fact that the immigrant complainants were either too ignorant to know where to turn for aid in starting a prosecution, or too timorous to venture into strange and impressive buildings to search among numerous offices for the proper authorities, especially when they knew that only too often they would find no sympathetic hearing of their "foreign lingo" if they did finally find the proper office. This work has also impressed prosecuting authorities and other officials with the peculiar difficulties and problems of immigrants, and thus many of the old bulwarks of helplessness and prejudice, behind which those who preyed on immigrants safely hid, are broken down. . . . .

Need of legal aid societies, etc.—Great difficulty in disposing of complaints where no amicable adjustment could be reached, was encountered in those cases which could not be referred to public officials. The machinery for law enforcement where public officials can intervene was usually found to be adequate, but there is a deplorable lack of private organizations to which needy immigrants can be referred when public officials are without power to render aid. Particularly is there a great need for legal aid societies or public defenders and public prosecutors to handle civil cases in court for immigrants (as well as for needy citizens). In such cases the Commission had to avoid sending complainants to any particular attorneys, as the state can not assume such responsibility or subject itself to the possible criticism of showing favoritism. Yet it is an established fact that the immigrant usually falls into the clutches of unscrupulous attorneys who have their offices in or near the foreign colonies. The office of the public defender in the city of Los Angeles cooperated with the Commission in taking over the civil cases, but elsewhere there is no such official, or legal aid societies, and the Commission could only refer complainants generally to private attorneys and do what it could with propriety to keep them out of the hands of "shysters." The Commission has now started a movement for the organization of legal aid societies in San Francisco and in Sacramento.

There was found to be an equally great lack of reliable and efficient agencies to which destitute immigrants who can not find work could be referred for aid. Most of these complainants had at some time or other been defrauded or deceived by private employment agencies, and would not go to them even if the Commission had been willing to take the chance of recommending any; moreover, the majority of such complainants had no money with which to pay fees to an employment agency. The obvious remedy seems to be a system of free state labor exchanges, or employment offices. The evidence collected by the Complaint Bureau in this connection strongly influenced the Commission in recommending a state labor exchange as the first step toward the solution of the unemployment problem. Furthermore, in several cities the Commission found that there are no organized or associated charities to which destitute resident immigrants can be referred even for charity relief. This makes an acute problem, especially in the city of Sacramento. Obviously, it is a problem in which destitute resident citizens are concerned as well as immigrants. Since the Governor has designated this Commission to represent the state during the present winter in an endeavor to secure uniform action by the cities in furnishing relief to the unemployed, the Commission has an opportunity to encourage and aid in the organization of associated charities, and it is to be hoped that some of this temporary work will have a lasting effect.

Causes of complaints.—The nature and causes of complaints have been so varied that they can be set out effectively only in tabular form. But it is important that attention be called particularly to the more common and most serious frauds and abuses.

There were 193 complaints of fraud and deceit in the sale of land. While not numerically the greatest, this is probably the most serious cause of complaint. People are generally agreed that the economic assimilation of our immigrants can best be expedited by encouraging the "back to the land" movement and discouraging congestion in the cities. Yet practically all of these complaints of immigrants who had invested their savings in land were well founded, and they not only lost their meager capital but were discouraged from making further efforts to leave the cities and enter upon agricultural pursuits. News of such land frauds spreads like wildfire among immigrants, not only in the East but even in Europe. The good name of the state is endangered and the native born, as well as immigrants, are sufferers. The Commission has sought to offset these past abuses by giving widespread publicity to its prosecutions of several fraudulent land dealers. More stringent land fraud laws have also been proposed, and the creation of a land information bureau urged by the Commission.

There were approximately 260 complaints involving crimes and frauds of a criminal nature. These complaints indicate how the ignorance and helplessness of immigrants furnish food for the nourishing of criminals in our communities.

The 22 cases of fraud of attorneys-at-law, all of which were justified and of a serious nature, show how little the helpless immigrant can rely on even sworn officers of our courts. Likewise, the 6 complaints of fraud on the part of official interpreters emphasize the helplessness of the immigrant. As a result of these complaints, which were found to be based on facts, the Commission has recommended that official interpreters be put under high bond and placed under civil service.

The 31 complaints concerning "quack" doctors and illegal medical practice show what an easy prey the immigrant is for these leeches upon society. As a result of publicity obtained in this connection, the Commission started and aided in a movement to eliminate "quack" medical advertising, and evidence was furnished the State Board of Medical Examiners which led to the conviction of some of the illegal practitioners.

The 163 cases of general business frauds illustrate the difficulties the immigrant encounters in endeavoring to become more than a wage-earner and to acquire an independent business of his own. This sort of fraud discourages assimilation almost as much as does land fraud. . . . .

The 9 cases of contributing to the delinquency of minors, together with the 6 cases of white slavery charges, evidence the fact that the usually friendless and trusting immigrant girls are easy victims of the adroit exploiters of the underworld. Though the number of cases in this connection is seemingly small, it is really surprisingly large in view of the fact that these cases were reported voluntarily and to ferret them out no effort was made. The Commission plans to make a more positive effort and take the initiative in protecting immigrant women, if it is granted a sufficient appropriation.

The 186 cases where assistance in obtaining employment was requested indicate the difficulty immigrants have in becoming productive units who are not familiar with our language or with our labor markets. This emphasizes again the need of free labor exchanges, already alluded to, as does the record of 170 complaints concerning employment agency frauds. Independent inspections of private employment agencies in connection with the unemployment investigation disclosed many further instances of fraud.

The 326 cases where information and advice were requested show the important part the Commission can play in aiding immigrants to become useful citizens.

The 25 complaints concerning fraud on the part of insurance companies, most of which were justified, are typical in that they represent the result of the practice of many companies, in all kinds of business, of employing notoriously unscrupulous agents, who exploit the credulity of immigrants.

The 10 complaints of misrepresentation and fraud in the sale and refund of transportation tickets are prophetic of the abuses in this connection that will have to be guarded against when there is more direct immigrant travel to and from California through the Panama Canal.

That employers make a practice of holding back the wages of immigrant laborers is evidenced by the 287 wage claim cases. Only a few of these claims were without foundation. Owing to the fact that the Commission has given wide publicity in foreign languages to its Complaint Bureau, many of these cases were filed, brought to the attention of the Commissioner of the Bureau of Labor Statistics, and settled, where otherwise the immigrants would have been worn out by delay and would have left their claims uncollected, not knowing of the aid rendered by the Labor Bureau in this connection. All wage claim cases have been referred to the Bureau of Labor Statistics and the Commission has cooperated in collecting evidence and in furnishing translations and interpreters when necessary. . . . .

ILLUSTRATIVE CASES

Fake attorneys.—(I) A Greek, long resident in San Francisco, advertised as an attorney in many of the foreign papers. As a matter of fact, he was not an attorney, but many immigrants of all nationalities went to him with their legal and business troubles. He drew up many bills of sale, contracts, partnership agreements, and other legal papers which proved to be utterly worthless from a legal standpoint. Whenever a case had to go to court he employed cheap "shyster" lawyers to appear for him and charged his ignorant clients stupendous fees. The Commission of Immigration collected evidence concerning this man, its attorney prosecuted him under the Penal Code provision in regard to falsely advertising as an attorney, and he was sentenced to six months in the county jail.

II) In a case almost identical with the one above, a foreign-born resident of San Francisco acted as a sort of police court "runner" for a firm of lawyers, and likewise advertised himself as a lawyer on placards in cheap restaurants and hotels. This man was an attorney in his own country, but had never been admitted to practice here. Numerous immigrants were "fleeced" by this man, and by means of threats that he could send them to prison on account of laws peculiar to the United States if they did not pay his exorbitant demands for fees for trifling services, he has extorted literally thousands of dollars from the foreign colony of San Francisco. The Commission prosecuted this man, but was unable to convict him, because of certain legal technicalities. However, his "practice" was discontinued as a result of the publicity given to the case.

Insurance frauds.—(I) An Italian who had been in this country only a few months and spoke little or no English, was prevailed upon by a suave agent to take out a combined life and sick benefit policy in a supposedly reliable insurance company. He was told that this would fully protect his wife and three little children, to whom he was passionately devoted. There were many long paragraphs in fine print on the policy, but the American agent, through the Italian's ten-year-old daughter, who had learned English at school, explained that these were meaningless things required by law and that the policy covered any sickness or death from any cause. When the insured man became seriously ill of pleurisy, a kindly Italian doctor reported the fact to the insurance company; the company doctor called and made a cursory examination, saying not a word. The next day a formal notice was sent to the sick man that his policy was forfeited because he had refused to allow an examination for tuberculosis, and a part of the fine printed matter covering such an instance was quoted. To the bedridden man this message was meaningless, and the little family was too distressed and helpless to do anything. Three months later the man recovered sufficiently to come to the office of the Commission. He swore he had not refused to be examined by the company doctor. He went with a Commission interpreter to the company's office and offered to permit any examination. The general manager informed the interpreter that "our doctor's word is final, and though the defense is technical it is just!" The man suffered a relapse; the Commission had to call in the Associated Charities to support the family. The Immigration Commission appealed to the company to pay something, and before a reply was received the man suddenly died. Then it was found that the policy covered only violent, accidental deaths. However, $90 was really due under the sick benefit clause, and the Commission urged the widow to put the case in the hands of an attorney who volunteered his services. But an agent of the company called the day after the funeral and prevailed upon the distracted and penniless widow to take $10 as settlement in full, and she dropped the case.

II) An Armenian was approached by an agent of an accident insurance company, but declined to purchase accident insurance, saying he wanted to insure against fire. The agent thereupon sold this Armenian a policy which he represented furnished fire protection. It turned out to be an accident policy after all, as the Armenian discovered when he had already paid a $5 premium. The company claimed it was not bound by the acts of its agents, but after some argument $3.75 was refunded the victim of the misrepresentation, the remainder being kept as a premium to cover the risk during the period the policy had been in existence and the few days still left to run.

Fraudulent checks.—A little immigrant woman was persuaded to cash a $50 check for a young man of supposedly good family, who had ingratiated himself in her esteem. The check was returned unpaid, with the statement that the man had never opened an account in the bank. The affair dragged on for weeks with repeated promises to pay, and finally the man disappeared. The case was brought to the attention of the Immigration Commission. With the aid of the police the culprit was located and arrested for the statutory offense of cashing a check without sufficient funds, whereupon a prompt settlement was made by his relatives, and the case dismissed. In two other cases where fraudulent checks have been passed on immigrants, the Commission has brought criminal actions. Suspended sentences were given when the money was refunded.

General business frauds.—(I) A salesman of an automatic piano company induced two Greek boys to install one of his pianos in their restaurant. He explained that the deal was to be "at no cost" to them, for the piano was to be paid for by the nickels collected in its box. The Greeks, however, were persuaded to sign an innocent appearing document for the protection of the company as owner. In reality they bound themselves in this document to pay $850 for the piano. So far did the agent press this alleged obligation that an attachment was actually levied on the restaurant. But through the efforts of the Commission the matter was brought to the attention of the company's officers, a new agreement according to the terms of the original understanding was drawn up, and the Greeks released from their predicament. Four similar cases with such companies were settled in the same manner.

II) The defendant in another case used the simple and yet effective scheme of selling a half interest in his cleaning establishment. He had a little cubby hole of an office, run so it was more "establishment" than "cleaning." The complainant, however, was an easy going immigrant from Northern Europe, and was easily "stuffed" with stories of vacuum cleaners and lucrative incomes. He paid $50 cash for a partnership interest, and bound himself to pay $100 in installments. The profits from which the installments were to be met were not forthcoming, however, as none of the much talked of customers appeared, and the defendant was at the point of seeing his little game culminate successfully in the "freezing out" of the new man, when the Commission stepped in. The swindler was arrested on a charge of petit larceny by trick and device, and when haled before the court he offered to restore $40 to the victim of the hoax. The latter accepted this offer, as it meant more to him than the imprisonment of the defendant, and, as he refused to testify, the case was dismissed.

"Quack" doctors.—To the Commission's already lengthy list of complaints against "quack" doctors, a Sacramento Greek added three. He stated that these irresponsible and unlicensed physicians, two Chinese and one American, were advertising widely their herbs and extraordinary cures for all diseases, venereal and otherwise. These advertisements were printed in a Greek newspaper, in the Greek language. It is calculated that inestimable physical injury as well as monetary loss can be traced to these charlatans. As the California Board of Medical Examiners is conducting a strenuous campaign against all such "quacks," the matter was referred to it, and already one of the three has been convicted on the charge of practicing medicine without a license.

General aid and advice.—A Servian went to a rural post office to register and mail a letter to Belgrade. As it contained a draft, he was much disturbed to find, after some months, that it had not arrived. He was unable to explain his difficulty to the authorities, as he spoke no English. The Commission took the matter up with the local postmaster, obtained the necessary form for the Servian to fill out, and saw that he wrote in the necessary information. The difficulty has now been referred by the Immigration Commission to the Washington authorities, in the hope of hastening the investigation and shortening, as far as possible, the inevitable delay due to the war.

SECTION II

SOCIAL CASE RECORDS: PROTECTIVE WORK[1]
DIFFICULTIES IN REACHING FINAL DESTINATION

1. Anna Oleson
(The Train Journey from Ellis Island)

June 6, 1917.—Letter and inclosure received from the Norwegian American Line:

Superintendent Lydia Gardner
Immigrants' Protective League

MY DEAR MISS GARDNER: I send you enclosed a translation of a letter in Norwegian from Mr. Lars Anderson of Hillside, Iowa, who is a reputable man, and it appears to me that this letter shows very serious neglect on the part of the officials of the C. X. and Y. Road at Chesterton, Illinois, and I think you ought to go into this very strongly indeed. There is too much of that kind of neglect on the part of highly paid railroad employees.

Yours very truly,
O. PETERSEN

The inclosure follows [translation]:

HILLSIDE, IOWA
June 3

Mr. O. Petersen
15 Dearborn Street
Chicago, Illinois

DEAR SIR: I take the liberty of calling your attention to the "rotten" treatment which the emigrants received on the C. X. & Y. Railway enroute from Chicago to Hillside, Iowa. You will remember that I wrote to you last April and asked for information about Mr. Peter Anderson, who came over on S.S. "Kristianiafjord," and I received both letter and telegram from you concerning Peter Anderson, S.S. "Kristianiafjord." On April 17th, at 4 o'clock in the afternoon, he boarded the train and at 9 o'clock at night he was put off at Chesterton, where he had to stay all night. The agent did nothing for him—no sleep and nothing to eat. Finally, two days after he left Chicago he arrived at Hillside. However, what I now especially want to call to your attention is the case of a girl who came on "Kristiania-

[1] In these case records fictitious names have been substituted for real names in order to make it impossible to identify either the immigrants or any other persons mentioned in the records. See p. 298, n. 1. For a discussion of various aspects of what may be called "protective work" in behalf of immigrants, in addition to the various documents referred to in Section I, see Grace Abbott, *The Immigrant and the Community* (New York, 1917); S. P. Breckinridge, *New Homes for Old* (New York, 1921); K. H. Claghorn, *Immigrant's Day in Court* (New York, 1923); P. A. Speek, *A Stake in the Land* (New York, 1921); M. M. Davis, Jr., *Immigrant Health and the Community* (New York, 1921).

fjord" last trip; her name is Anna Oleson, from Stavanger; she also received ticket in New York over the C. X. & Y. to Hillside, Iowa, via Chicago. She came to Chicago Wednesday morning, May 31st; was put on a local train leaving at 4 o'clock and came to Chesterton at 9 o'clock; was "thrown" out there and had to spend two nights and a day without sleep and with little to eat. The agent did nothing for her. When the trains came she went to the conductor with her ticket, but was not paid any attention to. At the station there were three young men who constantly kept an eye on her; one of them spoke broken Norwegian; they laid all kind of plans to get her to go with them. The agent saw it but did not interfere. One of them took her handbag, and she had to follow them to a hotel, where she was taken into a room; she understood something was up, as one of them tried to bar the exit; she managed to get by, however, and went back to the station. They followed at her heels, and one tried to persuade her to go back to Chicago with him. In the handbag she had between 26 and 30 dollars which they stole from her. Anybody can imagine how terrible it would be to meet with such misfortune—no money, nothing to eat. When she finally got on the train some kind people took pity on her and bought fruit for her. On June 2nd, at 8 o'clock in the evening, she came to Hillside, Iowa. From sheer nervousness she can hardly sleep and her feet are so sore that it is difficult to walk. As you, Mr. Petersen, have always shown kindness to all—which fact I myself experienced in 1914 when I purchased a ticket from you—we would ask you to be kind enough to take up this matter and try to hold the Company responsible for the loss and for the "rotten" treatment. This is not a singular case, but something similar has happened for seven or eight years. If they had kept the passengers in Chicago until 10 o'clock at night, only one change of train would have been necessary. If they had had tickets over Illinois Central they would have been here Thursday morning at 5 o'clock. What is your opinion, Mr. Petersen, about sending in a claim for one hundred to one hundred fifty dollars to the Company? If you could obtain more it would be well for the girl, and on account of your being agent for the Norwegian American Line you might be able to get more from them than we can. We shall be grateful for any assistance you may render us.

Yours very truly,

LARS ANDERSON

June 8, 1917.—Letter written to the President of the C. X. & Y. Railroad as follows:

MY DEAR SIR:

I am inclosing a statement of the very serious complaints against the C. X. and Y. Railroad which came to us in this morning's mail. Is it too much to hope that this matter will receive your personal attention and that some plans will at once be made absolutely to prevent the recurrence of such complaints in the future?

Sincerely yours,

LYDIA GARDNER

Letter also sent to the Secretary of Labor containing the following statement:

Inclosed is a complaint which came to us in this morning's mail from Hillside, Iowa. It is typical of what I have been trying for many years to convince the Department in Washington is the result of bad routing of immigrants from Ellis Island and the total lack of interest on the part of the United States as to what happens to the immigrant after his admission. I am taking this up with the C. X. and Y. Railroad but I know that the federal government is the only agency that can prevent such occurrences so I am forwarding it to you in the hope that you will be able to secure some permanent improvement.

June 15, 1917.—The following extract is from a letter to the Commissioner of Immigration at Ellis Island:

Do you feel that authority must be given by Congress before you can take charge of the routing of immigrants to inland points? It would seem to me that inasmuch as the railroad bureau is maintained with the assent of the Immigration Bureau and not by Act of Congress, it would make the continuance of the arrangement dependent upon the Bureau's treating the immigrant fairly in selling him his railway ticket by the most direct route.

June 19, 1917.—Mr. A. B. North, representing the Passenger Department of C. X. and Y. Railroad, called at the office. He reports that the matter has been taken up with the Immigration Agent at the Union Depot. He thinks the first mistake was made there and that the railroad will hold them responsible for starting immigrants on train that makes connection in the future. Investigation in Chesterton has not been completed and he will report on that later. They are grateful to us for reporting matter and hope we will call Mr. North whenever we have any complaint.

[The case record contains more than a score of letters from railroad officials, from representatives of the Immigration Service, and others. A few of the more significant letters are given below. No reference will be made to the others.]

July 21, 1917.—Extract from letter to the President of the railroad as follows:

Your Mr. North called on me on Tuesday of this week and told me of the result of your investigation of the complaint which came to us from Hillside, Iowa, and which we forwarded to you. I was very glad to hear from him that the Immigrant Agent at the Union Station has been instructed to hold all immigrants for through connections. Failure to do this, was, of course, where the first mistake was made by the C. X. and Y. If, on the complaint indicated, there was a more direct route by which the girl could have been sent to Hillside, the first mistake was made by the railroad clearing office at Ellis Island. Mr. North tells me further that the investigation made by the C. X. and Y. shows that the girl was not insulted or mistreated by anyone in the employ of the railroad. I did not think the complaint indicated that she was, but I did think it indicated that the agent at Chesterton was indifferent as to what happened to her and that his indifference and carelessness were the main cause of the annoyance and loss she suffered there. I am sure you understand the reason why this complaint was sent you—namely, that others might not suffer similar discomforts and financial losses. Mr. North tells me that he thinks it has accomplished this and that if the agents have not felt it a part of their duty to give some special attention to the protection of the immigrant in the past, they will in the future.

600   IMMIGRATION: DOCUMENTS AND CASE RECORDS

August 8, 1917.—Letter received from the United States Bureau of Immigration:

DEAR MADAM:

In further reference to your letters of June 8 and July 15, concerning the method by which an immigrant girl named Anna Oleson was sent to her destination in Hillside, Iowa. An investigation of this matter has been made by the C. X. and Y. Railway, and it does not appear that the assertion of improper routing has been sustained. The girl was ticketed from New York via the Pennsylvania Railroad, which is certainly a direct and convenient route. It seems that an immigrant agent of the C. X. and Y. Railway made a mistake in placing this girl upon a train which left Chicago at 4 P.M., whereas it would have been more desirable to have her placed on a train leaving Chicago at 10:30 P.M., thus avoiding the necessity of a layover at Chesterton. The railway employee certainly erred in this matter, but it cannot be reasonably said that such an error relates back to the issuance of the ticket at Ellis Island. It also appears that the night station agent at Chesterton was remiss in his duty and failed to place the girl upon the train by which she should have been sent forward in the first place. Without attempting in the slightest degree to justify or excuse the remissness of the railway employees west of Chicago, it appears difficult to conceive how an occasional instance of misconduct could be prevented, unless an employee of the Government was detailed to accompany each individual alien to his or her final destination. Such a plan would be obviously impracticable, and would require an enormous expenditure of public funds. As soon as the volume of immigration justifies the opening and operation of the Chicago station,[1] it will probably be possible to minimize the liability of errors in so far as the transhipment in Chicago is concerned. If in the present instance the young woman was occasioned any additional expense because of the error which took place, the Bureau would be glad to have you obtain the particulars as to the object and amount of such expenditure, so that reimbursement may be accomplished if possible.

Very truly yours,

―――――, *Acting Commissioner-General*

August 16, 1917.—A letter of inquiry concerning the actual loss sustained by Anna Oleson brought the following reply:

Mr. D. Petersen
15 Dearborn Street
Chicago, Illinois

DEAR MR. PETERSEN: Received yours of August 11th as well as inclosure of copy of letter from United States Department of Labor, Bureau of Immigration. I shall be glad to inform you what Anna Oleson was robbed of—in money she had $26, which was taken from her in Chesterton the last day she was there so tired and discouraged after the long journey which would tell on the strength of the strongest—first to spend 36 hours from New York and to be held back 38 hours in Chesterton. Anna thinks she should be entitled to the $26 because if she had not been held back, she would not have been so unfortunate—and she insists that the C. X. and Y.

[1] [See above, Doc. 1, p. 472.]

owes her the above sum. This is not the only incident that I know of—but a great many have happened in the last six years. Immigrants with tickets to Hillside have been sent to Pender and from there by freight to Hillside. This is not the way to handle young girls either. I can inform you that the C. X. and Y. had a man here four weeks ago to examine Anna. He had the statement from Chesterton and he thought she was plainly entitled to the $26 and had no doubt but that that would be paid her. We have heard nothing so we are grateful for the information from you. Hope you will take it up with the railroad.

LARS ANDERSON

August 23, 1917.—The following letter sent to Washington to the Acting Commissioner-General of Immigration:

DEAR SIR:

In further reference to the case of Anna Oleson and your letter of August 5th, I should like to report that the girl feels very strongly that the money that she lost or that was stolen from her, $26, should be refunded to her by the Railroad because if she had not been detained unnecessarily in Chesterton, she would not have lost that sum. She will be very grateful indeed if you will take this matter up with the Railroad. I still consider this a case of incorrect routing because, although she was properly routed to Chicago via the Pennsylvania, she was improperly routed from Chicago to her final destination. If she had been sent by the Illinois Central from Chicago to Hillside, she would have arrived there more easily and promptly. Thanking you for your investigation in this matter, I am,

Sincerely yours,

LYDIA GARDNER

[The record for the next few months contains numerous other letters, but the matter was finally closed as the letter below indicates.]

December 20, 1917.—The following letter received from Washington:

Miss Lydia Gardner, Director
Immigrants' Protective League

DEAR MADAM: In reference to correspondence which has been going on for the past several months in regard to $26 lost by an alien named Anna Oleson, I take pleasure in advising you that the Bureau has finally succeeded in obtaining a settlement from the C. X. and Y. Railway Company, and there is transmitted herewith a draft of that Company in the amount of $26 the same being indorsed in blank. To complete the file in the case, will you kindly transmit this check to Anna Oleson and forward your receipt for attachment to the other papers in the case.

Very truly yours,

————, *Acting Commissioner-General of Immigration*

[Letter to girl transmitting railroad check and receipt and acknowledgment from Anna Oleson are omitted.]

2. Allegra Salvatore
(*Wrong Destination*)

July 19, 1917.—At 5:30 P.M., when J. H. [Magyar visitor] was closing the office an Italian woman came upstairs with bundles from some immigrant train. She handed over her address and a note from H. J. Feldt, Immigrant Agent at the Union Station, as follows:

Emigrant Protective League:

This Italian lady carries a ticket to Carson, Iowa, via C. X. and Y., but her address is not written clear enough as to justify me to send her there. Will you please take care.

Very truly yours,

H. J. FELDT, *Emigrant Agent*

J. H. looked at address carefully, it seems to be "Carson Lía," but might be Carson, Iowa, may be Carson, Louisiana, or possibly Carson, Ohio. *Later.*—Telephoned V. L. [Italian visitor]. She talked with woman over telephone. Finally made woman understand she must stay over night in Chicago and that J. H. will find her a place to stay. V. L. will see her in morning. Woman's name is Allegra Salvatore, age twenty-seven years, ex S.S. "Verdi," destined to her sister.

J. H. went with Allegra Salvatore to Y.W.C.A. They could not take the woman and advised Travellers' Aid Home. Woman was so tired and her bundles so heavy, I took her to a rooming-house near our office on Wabash Avenue, where some Italian people are living. We met by accident a United States immigration inspector as we were going down Wabash Avenue. Inspector explained that the woman was brought at 5 P.M. by a Parmalee bus to the United States Immigration Office, and he sent her over to us. If our office had been closed, woman would have been stranded on Michigan Avenue.

July 20, 1917.—V. L. [Italian visitor] called at rooming-house for Allegra. Talked with her and discovered her sister had lived in New Orleans and still lived near there. Woman bought steamship and railroad ticket in Palermo to join her sister in Carson. At Ellis Island she was given railroad ticket to Carson, Iowa. Immigrant agent in Chicago fortunately happened to look at her original address as well as the railroad ticket. He apparently thought a mistake had been made and sent her on to us. Girl has only 60 lire (about $9). *Later.*—Telegram sent to Allegra's brother-in-law, Giovanni Alfio, Box 30, Carson, Louisiana, as follows: "Allegra Salvatore here without railroad ticket. Wire thirty dollars." *Later.*—Took Allegra to Travellers' Aid Home to stay until tomorrow.

July 21, 1917.—Reply from brother-in-law as follows: "Call on General Agent J. O. Heart of Kansas City Southern Railway for ticket for Allegra Salvatore." *Later.*—Arrangements made to start Allegra for Carson from Union Station at 6 P.M. She must change at Kansas City. Allegra left ticket for us to secure refund on. Gave receipt for ticket. Gave Allegra letter to station matron, Kansas City, Missouri, as follows:

> The bearer of this note, Allegra Salvatore, is destined to her brother-in-law, John Alfio, Box 30, Carson, Louisiana. She is to leave on the Kansas City and Southern Railroad at 1 P.M. arriving in Carson 3:46 P.M., Sunday. Her relatives have been notified of the time of her arrival. Will you please see that she is placed on board the proper train.

Later.—Letter to officials at Union Station commending the work of the Immigrant Agent in refusing to send woman to Carson, Iowa, and letter also sent to the Commissioner of Immigration at Ellis Island as follows:

MY DEAR SIR:

> May I ask you to look into the following case which has come into our hands? On July 19, an Italian woman by the name of Allegra Salvatore arrived in Chicago on the B. & O. with a railroad ticket over the C.X. & Y. to Carson, Iowa. She arrived at Ellis Island on the S.S. "Verdi." The address which she held might have been Carson, Iowa, but seems to have been more clearly Carson, Louisiana. The Immigrant Agent at the Union Depot, having recently had some difficulty over a mistake he had made in an immigrant case, was particularly alert and refused to send the woman on to Carson, Iowa, and brought her to us. As soon as our Italian visitor talked with her she discovered that the town she was going to was near New Orleans so we telegraphed the relatives in Carson, Louisiana, and the following day received transportation from Chicago to that place. This mistake was made, I take it, by the railroad office at Ellis Island. I am sure you will agree with me that in case of doubtful addresses such as this, the woman should have been held until some reply had been received from her relatives. Had she been stranded in Carson, Iowa, you can understand how very difficult her position would have been.
>
> Sincerely yours,
LYDIA GARDNER

August 3, 1917.—Reply from Ellis Island, containing the following:

> This is to acknowledge receipt of your letter of July 21 with reference to the case of alien Allegra Salvatore. The records of this office show that this woman, who arrived on the S.S. "Giuseppe Verdi," July 17, was manifested as going to her sister, Vincenza Alfio, Box 30, Carson, Iowa, to which point she had prepaid railroad transportation No. 1618. I have seen this railroad order. The destination Carson, Iowa, written out in full, is plainly indicated thereon. It is regretted that this alien should have been sent to Carson, Iowa, when as a matter of fact, her destination was Carson, Louisiana, but clearly the error is neither the fault of this office nor the railroad officials at Ellis Island. I may say for your information that where there are any cases of doubtful addresses the aliens are always temporarily detained until it can be ascertained definitely where they wish to go.

[The remaining part of the record contains correspondence regarding the refund of $9.62 on girl's railroad ticket and letters from girl announcing her safe arrival, receipt for money, etc.]

3. Take Jonika
(Stranded en Route)

January 2.—Take Jonika, a Roumanian man, brought to the office by officer at Dearborn Station. He arrived on an immigrant train without any money. J. H. [Magyar visitor] spoke with man, who explained that he was on his way to join relatives in Burlington, Iowa, but he had only money to buy ticket to Chicago. He thought he would stay here until he could earn money to go on. He asked if we would telegraph his brother. He believes his brother will send money for him to go on from Chicago. If not, he would like us to help him get work in Chicago for a long-enough time to earn money to go on to Burlington. Brother's name and address, Pernyes Jonika, P.O. Box 211, Burlington, Iowa. Arrangements made for man to stay at League boarding-house until brother had been heard from. *Later.*—Telegram sent as requested.

January 4.—Telegram returned. The brother Pernyes no longer keeps a postal box as formerly, and no other address is available.

January 6.—J. H. [Magyar visitor] took man to Roumanian colony; found a place, 445 Fullerton Avenue, where he may stay with a Roumanian family until news of his brother can be found. His country people think they can find work for him.

January 11.—Photograph taken of Take Jonika and advertisement for brother put in Roumanian paper.

January 16.—Letter and money received from Pernyes Jonika to cover railroad fare of man to Burlington. Pernyes saw the advertisement in the paper yesterday. Man left on afternoon train.

4. Raisa and Maria Pavlik
(Lost Tickets and Refund)

May 1, 1914.—Two Croatian girls Raisa Pavlik, age seventeen, and Maria Pavlik, age nineteen, brought to Immigrants' Protective League office by representative of Travellers' Aid, from LaSalle Street Station, where they were found without tickets or money. [Interviewed by J. L., a Slavic visitor.] Maria explained that they were cousins travelling to California from Ellis Island to join John Pavlik, father of Raisa, and that they had lost their tickets to San Francisco. The girls arrived on the Cunard S.S. "Pannonia," from Trieste, second cabin, April 24. At Buffalo, where they changed trains, Maria dropped her handbag, which contained their tickets and most of their money. A man picked it up and got away with it before they could make anyone understand what they had lost. The girls had, however, some money in their lunch basket. They said nobody could understand them in Buffalo. They decided to go on to some other large town in the hope of finding a Croatian colony or Croatian interpreter and offered part of their money for tickets and were given tickets to Toledo. There they got off the train and tried to find a Croatian interpreter who could send word to their uncle. They said they were walking all around trying to find Croatian interpreter. Then they spent all their money and got tickets to Chicago and now have not one cent in pocket. They wish to telegraph John Pavlik, the father of Raisa; she has his address in notebook as Oakdale, California. The girls bought their railroad tickets as well as steamship tickets in Fiume for 643 kronen, second-class steamer and third-class railroad. *Later.*—The following night letter sent to John Pavlik, Oakdale, California, P.O. Box 715: "Raisa and Maria Pavlik stranded in Chicago—money and tickets to Oakdale, California, stolen in Buffalo, while changing trains. Wire enough money for tickets and expenses for them to go on.—IMMIGRANTS' PROTECTIVE LEAGUE."

[Three days later John Pavlik, of Oakdale, California, telegraphed $150 to the League and the girls were sent on at once.[1] A telegram was sent at the same time to the Associated Charities of San Francisco asking to have the girls met and transferred from the train to the Oakdale boat. A few days later a letter was sent to Ellis Island asking for a description of the railway tickets issued to the two girls. However, it appeared that the two girls had been second-class passengers and had been admitted at the steamship pier so that there was no record of their tickets at Ellis Island.

A long series of letters followed to the Cunard Steamship Company in New York, the Royal Hungarian Steam Navigation Company in Fiume, Hungary, to obtain the numbers of the railway tickets. Later there were letters to various railroad officials to find out whether a refund could be secured on the unused portion of the tickets. The record closes with the following letter, dated August 23, 1915:]

Emigrants' Protective League

GENTLEMEN: Your favor of 9th inst. at hand. We acknowledge receipt of your two checks for Raisa and Maria Pavlik for forty-six ($46) each refund, for which we thank you many times.

Yours respectfully,

OAKDALE, CALIFORNIA   JOHN PAVLIK

[1] Another immigrant girl who was sent West by a different route at this time had an experience so unpleasant that complaint was made to the passenger traffic manager of the railway. The following reply from the railway indicates the cause of the complaint:

DEAR MADAM:

I am in receipt of your favor of the 21st inst., with reference to an unaccompanied immigrant girl enroute to California who was placed in smoker on our train leaving Chicago Thursday night.

Emigrant, or third class tickets, are good for passage in chair cars and coaches, as well as smokers. Usually parties of immigrants traveling together are put in the smoker because it seems better to do so rather than to place them with their eatables and bundles with the better class of passengers using chair cars or coaches where smoking is not permitted.

If in cases of this kind the representative of your League who goes to the train would call attention of your desires to our Depot Passenger Agent I am sure that arrangements could promptly be made to place them in accommodations that would be entirely satisfactory in every way. In any event I will instruct Mr. Adams, our Depot Passenger Agent, to watch the situation and arrange so there will be no cases of this kind in the future. [Letter signed by the passenger traffic manager.]

5. Paul Swanson
(Arrival at Wrong Station)

April 21, 1916.—Letter received from Mr. Herman Olson, of the Norwegian American Line, inclosing a complaint from an agent of the line in the southwestern part of Chicago about the treatment of a passenger he had booked.

[Inclosure:]
Norwegian American Line
Chicago, Illinois

GENTLEMEN: Our passenger, Paul Swanson, prepaid ticket No. C 3121, arrived at the Terminal Station in the middle of last night. He was not let off at Kensington as specified on his ticket, but was carried all the way down town instead. Three other emigrants on the same train were let off at Kensington, but not a word was said to our passenger. It appears that no attention was paid to the instructions on his ticket, either by your office or by your agent at New York, otherwise this mistake could never have happened. The relatives of the passenger were at the Kensington station to meet him, but as he was not let off, they took for granted that he was taken all the way down town. When he arrived at the Terminal Station the conductor took up his check and told him to get off. One of those cabmen, I call them grafters, came and told him to follow him, took his satchel and brought him out to Kensington, when he claimed his bill was $10.00. The cabman's name is Mr. Dennis O'Brien, 26 East 24th Street, the number of the cab was 4275. Seldom has such a thing happened, during my twenty-five years of business as steamship agent, and I am very much dissatisfied with this act, furthermore, the relatives of said passenger are very angry that such an expense was imposed upon them, which I consider unwarrantable, and the passenger was not protected in any way. I believe this should be investigated, and we are justified in asking where the error has been made.

Yours truly,

HENRY NELSON, *Agent*

Later.—Telephoned agent and also Mr. Olson, who wrote letter to us, to say we would be glad to take up the matter with the City Vehicle Department. Told him it was our practice to have drivers who overcharged immigrants fined or suspended or to ask for revocation of license. Mr. Olson will come in when he has seen the man again.

[The record contains a number of other letters and entries, but these may be briefly summarized: (1) The League reported the complaint to the city inspector of vehicles; (2) a refund for the passenger was secured from the cab-driver; (3) the license of the cab-driver was temporarily revoked, (4) the Norwegian American Line could get no "satisfaction" from the railroad company.]

6. Maria Kowal
(A Ruthenian Woman Ill en Route to Oregon)

[The following letters state the case of a Ruthenian woman and child sent on by the League to Portland, Oregon:]

SOCIAL CASE RECORDS

1. Letter to the Director of Immigrants' Protective League, dated May 11, from C. Swanson, a steamship ticket agent in Portland, Oregon:

DEAR MADAM:

Mrs. Maria Kowal and child left New York about April 14 for Portland [description of routing omitted]. As she did not arrive here in a reasonable time, her husband wired the immigrant authorities at New York, who advised him that she had left New York via [routing described] for Portland; and from that time on he haunted my office almost incessantly for some trace of his folks, and at last in self-defense I was obliged to begin telegraphing New York, Chicago, St. Paul, and any place I thought I could get information concerning them. Yesterday he reported at my office with a telegram from your League, signed by R. Brinova, stating that the wife had arrived sick and they were taken to the hospital in Chicago on April 17 and released on May 6, leaving for Portland on that date. These people arrived here early this morning on a delayed train. Will you kindly advise me at your early convenience if it would not have been possible for someone connected with your institution to have notified her husband of their whereabouts before May 6, as he was in total ignorance of same and very much worried over their disappearance. Any information will be thankfully received.

Yours truly,

C. SWANSON

2. Letter sent by Director of the Immigrants' Protective League to the station master of the Chicago Central Station, dated May 16, with a copy of the letter received from Portland:

DEAR SIR:

I am inclosing a copy of a letter that is self-explanatory. You will find upon inquiry that this case was reported to us on the morning of May 6, when we were asked to go and bring in an immigrant mother and child from the County Hospital and see that they reached the depot in safety. We had had no notice of the case before that time or we should have been only too glad to communicate with the father and husband. I am calling your attention to this because I hope that in the future any cases of this sort will be reported to us in the first instance so that proper care may be given to them while in this city, and the relatives who are expecting them duly notified. I am quite sure that you did not want to cause the husband and father all this anxiety and that you would have been very glad to have us correspond with him as the woman herself was unable to write. In such cases our foreign visitors are able and willing to render efficient service.

Please believe how much we shall appreciate your co-operation in such cases.

Sincerely yours,

LYDIA GARDNER

3. The station master's reply, dated May 18:

DEAR MADAM:

Yours of May 16th received and must say I am very sorry this case turned out the way it did. I was at Depot at time and everything was done in our power for the Ladys comfort but we was handy caped as I could not find any one that could speak the Ladys language so I got her to the Hospital soon as I possibly could. We notified a young man from the X Society and he said he had a brother over their and that he would go over to Hospital and find out all about her and notify all concerned. We seen him afterwards and he said he could not find her but was going over again and he would attend to her as we did not hear anything more suppose the Society or the Hospital had attended to her want. In the future will be only too glad to notify your office. Hoping this will be satisfactory,

Respectfully,

CHARLES DENNIS

IMMIGRANT GIRLS TRAVELING ALONE WHO FAILED TO REACH DESTINATION

[Upon the organization of the Immigrants' Protective League in Chicago an effort was made to visit all newly arrived immigrant girls who had come to Chicago unaccompanied. It was hoped in this way to find out whether or not they were living under satisfactory conditions and whether they were in need of help. Arrangements were made with the Ellis Island authorities to have a transcript made from the "manifest" lists of the names of alien women traveling alone and destined to Chicago. This transcript gives the name, nationality, age, etc., of the girl and the address to which she is going.

In a number of cases the foreign-speaking workers who made these visits found the girls had never arrived although relatives were expecting them and were in many cases worried over their failure to arrive.[1] The

[1] Letters were sometimes sent to the names on the manifest when the German or Scandinavian names or the Chicago addresses indicated that the relatives were of a class not likely to need assistance. The following reply to one of these letters describes the difficulties faced by girls arriving at one of the large Chicago stations before the war:

Miss Lydia Gardner

DEAR MADAM: Your inquiry concerning Miss Nanna Johnson at hand. We appreciate this very much and wish to say frankly to you that there is nothing easier in the world than for the express and police attendance at X Station to lose every girl that comes into their hand, if they have a mind to do so. It looks to me as if they were in league to rob the poor immigrants of their money. This poor girl had to pay one robber expressman $3.00 for taking her about twenty-five blocks, no baggage but a valise. They all seem to work to get every one out of the station as fast as possible and shuff them onto the express people so as to make as much out of them as possible while their friends go through the station searching for them in vain trying to find them. We are indeed glad you wrote us and thankful that this expressman took her home, although he had a drink on the way with others and could, of course, have taken the girl away from us, we being none the wiser. However, she is safe. Thanking you again, we Sister and Uncle wish to remain,

Yours truly,

JOHN E. JOHNSON

facts about some of these cases are briefly given in the following letters of inquiry to Ellis Island to confirm the fact of the girl's arrival and departure for Chicago, and the official replies to these letters.]

7. Emelia Anderson

[A visitor of the League called at 136 Worth Avenue on February 8 to ask if Emelia Anderson, whose name appeared on the "manifest" list, had arrived safely. The visitor learned that the girl had never arrived, and that the aunt who expected her had heard nothing from her and was greatly distressed over her non-arrival and wished her landing verified. The following letter was received in reply to the inquiry sent to Ellis Island:]

MADAM:

In reply to a letter addressed to this office from your League, making inquiry as to the whereabouts of one Emelia Anderson, an immigrant girl who arrived at this port, December 3, and going to Mrs. Sophie Olson, 136 Worth Avenue, Chicago, Illinois, I have to say that the girl in question arrived on date mentioned, was duly admitted, and your office notified. Beyond passing a successful examination and leaving for her destination, we have no further knowledge of the girl. I hope she will not fall into evil hands.

Respectfully,

HENRY GAHAN

8. Maryana Pajakiewicz and Theresa Olshefski

[The names of these two Polish girls appeared on the manifest list as going to a cousin, Josef Pajakiewicz, 3400 West Street. The visitor who called on May 7 found that the girls had never arrived, nor had any word been received from them. The cousin and his wife were greatly excited over the failure of the girls to arrive and very anxious to have their arrival in New York confirmed. The following letter from Ellis Island in reply to the League's inquiry gives all the facts that were ever obtained about them:]

DEAR MADAM:

Referring further to the case of Maryana Pajakiewicz and Theresa Olshefski, ex S.S. "Yorck," April 1, I have to state that the following is quoted from the reply of the agent of the Immigrant Clearing House at Ellis Island to my request for an investigation as to the non-arrival of the aliens at their destination: "I have to report my investigation determined aliens named held North German Lloyd S.S. Company's orders for rail transportation to Chicago, which were exchanged at this agency on April 1st for immigrant tickets to that point via Delaware, Lackawanna and Western and Nickel Plate Roads. Inquiry made of roads en route elicits the information that tickets furnished aliens are in the collections of both, which indicates that they were used through to destination."

Respectfully,

HENRY JOSEPH, *Commissioner*

9. Rozalia Kazewski

[Four weeks after Rozalia Kazewski, a Polish girl, aged seventeen, who was coming to her married sister in Chicago, should have arrived, a visitor of the Immigrants' Protective League called at the address given on the "manifest" list and found that the girl had never arrived and that the sister was greatly worried and anxious to know what had happened. She could not believe that the girl had really landed in New York and had left Ellis Island for Chicago four weeks earlier. The following letter, dated May 2, is the reply to a letter of inquiry sent by the League to Ellis Island:]

MADAM:

Acknowledgment is made of your letter under date of April 14 reporting that the alien Rozalia Kazewski, aged seventeen, Polish, who arrived at this port on the S.S. "Haverford" March 4, destined to her brother-in-law, Nicholas Sopol, 2000 South End Place, Chicago, had not arrived. Inquiry has been made here and ascertained that the ticket for this alien was issued March 5 over the Grand Trunk Road and that the ticket was used to Chicago, which would show that the alien reached Chicago in due time. Should you have further information respecting this case should be pleased to be advised in the matter.

Respectfully,

HENRY JOSEPH, *Acting Commissioner*

10. Maryana Kucynski

[The following letters state the case of Maryana Kucynski. The record shows that on June 10 a Polish-speaking visitor called at the address given on the manifest card and received the information given in the letter to Ellis Island.]

The Acting Commissioner
Ellis Island, New York

MY DEAR SIR: Can you tell me anything about a Slovak girl by the name of Maryana Kucynski, who was supposed to have sailed for this country March 9, on the "Kronprinzessin Cecilie." Her aunt here has been unable to find her, and her mother writes that she knows nothing about her. Some friends of the aunt who have arrived say that they saw her at Ellis Island. The girl is sixteen years of age and should have come to Stanley Kucynski, 128 Port Street. We shall be glad to hear anything at all about this girl.

Yours sincerely,

LYDIA GARDNER

MADAM:

I am in receipt of your letter of the 8th inst., relative to the non-arrival of Maryana Kucynski at her destination in your city, and in reply have to advise you that our records show that said alien arrived on the S.S. "Kronprinzessin Cecilie" March 17, had ticket and $13 in her possession, and was discharged on primary inspection to proceed to her uncle Stanley Kucynski, 128 Port Street, Chicago, Illinois.

Respectfully,

CHARLES ABEL, *Acting Commissioner*

SOCIAL CASE RECORDS 611

11. Rozalia Michaelis and Marya Kopek

[The names of these girls were received on the manifest sheet, and the addresses given were visited. The father of Rozalia, a Polish girl, had heard nothing from his daughter and was afraid she had been deported. Marya's address was that of her brother, Jan Kopek, 909 Black Avenue. The brother could not be found and neighbors reported that he had gone a few weeks ago with his family to work on a farm in Michigan. No one knew whether the sister had arrived and gone with him or not. A letter was written to the brother, whose address was obtained in the neighborhood, inquiring about his sister. In reply, he said he had heard nothing about her arrival and begged the League to help find her if she had really arrived. The following letters give the facts:]

July 12.—Letter to the Commissioner of Immigration, Ellis Island:

Rozalia Michaelis, who arrived on S.S. "Georgia," April 6, and was destined to her father, Stanley Michaelis, 112 Eighth Street, has never arrived, and the father thinks she was deported and is anxious to know the cause of deportation. Marya Kopek, who came on the S.S. "Poland," arriving April 4, and was coming to her brother Jan Kopek, 909 Black Avenue, has never reached her brother. He, with his family, has gone to live on a farm in Lyons, Michigan, and thinks in this way the girl failed to connect with him. I wonder if the girl was admitted?

Sincerely yours,

LYDIA GARDNER

July 17.—Reply from Ellis Island:

MADAM:

Replying to yours of July 12, I have to advise you that the records of this office show that Rozalia Michaelis, aged seventeen, arrived by S.S. "Georgia" April 16. She was found to be insane and was deported April 22 by S.S. "Barbarossa," aliens so afflicted being, under the Immigration Law, excluded from admission. Marya Kopek, aged twenty-two, arrived by S.S. "Poland," April 4. She was admitted to go to her brother, Jan Kopek, 909 Black Avenue, Chicago, Illinois, upon the arrival of said steamer.

Respectfully,

HENRY JOSEPH, *Commissioner*

12. Marya Piotowski
(*Tracing a "Lost" Polish Girl*)

February 10, 1914.—Ivan Piotowski in the office to ask help in tracing his lost sister, Marya Piotowski. Marya sailed from Libau about the 20th or 22d of December, 1913, and has not been heard of since that time. She had probably two addresses on the manifest: Ivan Piotowski, 357 Ashland Street, a brother, and Alexander Potocki, 700 Ashland Street, a cousin. Ivan said, "Three weeks ago my parents sent word to me and to Alexander asking us about Marya. They wrote to us Marya left home with

Mr. and Mrs. Grabo, but they were returned from Libau on account of trouble of their eyes. Marya was left alone in Libau." The brother thinks she was going to sail on a boat landing in Philadelphia. *Later.*—The following letter of inquiry was sent to the Commissioner of Immigration at Philadelphia:

Will you kindly go over the "manifests" for the latter part of December and the month of January to verify the landing of Marya Piotowski, a twenty-year-old Polish girl? This girl was supposed to have sailed from Libau about December 20th or 22d, 1913. The girl had two addresses, one of her brother, Ivan Piotowski, 357 Ashland Street, and the other of a cousin, Alexander Potocki, 700 Ashland Street. Her parents have heard nothing from her, and the people here have heard nothing. They believe that she arrived at Philadelphia.

February 19, 1914.—The following reply from Philadelphia received:

Replying to your request dated February 10, 1914, for verification of landing of Marya Piotowski, a Polish girl, I beg to state that this office has been unable to verify the same. The following are the records which have been examined: all arrivals from December 1st to date.

February 20, 1914.—Letter written (in Polish) to Ivan Piotowski, transmitting reply from Philadelphia and suggesting that he try to get in touch with the people with whom his sister travelled.

March 12, 1914.—Brother in office to say that they are unable to find anyone who can give them information of what has happened to Marya and they wish to know what to do. Told them we would try to find out if and when she left Libau. *Later.*—Letter written to the Commissioner of Immigration at Libau, Russia, as follows:

DEAR SIR:

The relatives of Marya Piotowski living in Chicago have come to our office saying that the girl has failed to reach her destination. Marya expected to sail from Libau about December 20 or 22 in the company of Mr. and Mrs. Grabo, who were turned back on account of eye trouble. Marya was allowed to proceed alone. She had the address of her brother, Ivan Piotowski, 357 Ashland Street, and of her cousin, Alexander Potocki, 700 Ashland Street, Chicago. She has not arrived at either of these addresses, and her relatives are much worried. Would it be possible for you to send us the name of the steamer on which she left and the line? We shall be very grateful for this information.

Very truly yours,

IMMIGRANTS' PROTECTIVE LEAGUE

April 23, 1914.—Visited relatives and told them we had had no reply from Libau. They have heard nothing. *Later.*—A second letter of inquiry sent to Commissioner of Immigration, Libau.

May 28, 1914.—The following reply received from Libau and transmitted to Ivan Piotowski [translation from German]:

LIBAU COMMITTEE OF THE JEWISH COLONISATION SOCIETY
LIBAU, 14 April 1914

Immigrants' Protective League

RESPECTED GENTLEMEN: In reply to your inquiry of 12 March, we hasten to reply that in Libau the post of a Commissioner of Immigration does not exist and your letter has therefore been brought to us. As regards the Piotowski girl we have found that she sailed on the S.S. "Kursk" of the Russian-American Line on 24 December and that she had given as her destination not Chicago but Wilmington, Delaware, where she gave the name of an uncle John Piotowski (500 Poplar St.). Without doubt the young woman is now in Wilmington, Delaware, with her uncle. We can give no further information about her.

Yours respectfully,

SAMUEL BAUM, *Secretary*

[The girl was later located in Wilmington.]

13. Mathild "Moreik"
(Tracing a "Lost" Magyar Girl)

April 13, 1921.—Agent from H. Grossman and Company, steamship agents in Joliet, Illinois, in office [Immigrants' Commission]. A Magyar girl by the name of Mathild Moreik, aged eighteen years, who arrived on the S.S. "Rotterdam" April first and left New York April fourth via Grand Trunk, destined to her brother-in-law, Joseph Vesely, 15 Missouri Avenue, Joliet, has not arrived. Agent left photograph of the girl, which her brother-in-law had left with him. *Later.*—Looked up the list of immigrant arrivals of April sixth at Dearborn Street Station. Valerie Morik, a Magyar, 47 Throop Street, was on train. *Later.*—J. H. [Magyar visitor] visited 47 Throop Street. No such number. Inquired in the neighborhood. Mr. Boris at 17 Throop Street knows a number of Magyars. He says Mrs. Fleischer, at 500 Racine Avenue, keeps in touch with the Magyar families. Called on Mrs. Fleischer, not at home. Called in the evening, was told that Mrs. Fleischer had gone to a "movie."

April 14, 1921.—Visited 500 Racine Avenue. Mrs. Fleischer not at home. A neighbor said that woman will be at home at noon. *Later.*—Telephoned H. Grossman and Company, Joliet, to verify information about girl's name, age, etc. *Later.*—Sent telegram to Commissioner of Immigration as follows: "Mathild Moreik, steamship Rotterdam reported to have left Ellis Island on Lehigh Valley and Grand Trunk April fourth not arrived. Please wire description of railroad ticket."

April 15, 1921.—Telegram received from Commissioner at Ellis Island as follows: "Ellis Island records show ticket issued Mathild Moreik form seven two nine number one naught eight naught two seven Lehigh Valley and Grand Trunk April fourth." *Later.*—Went to Union Depot to find out if girl's ticket appears in conductor's collections. Was directed to the Chicago Chief Agent, Mr. Sharp, 200 Washington Street, Room 900. Found Mr. Sharp. He wired to Port Huron, Detroit, to the agent of the Lehigh

Valley to find out if girl's ticket appears in conductor's collections. Mr. Sharp will notify us as soon as an answer reaches him. *Later.*—Took paragraph about girl's disappearance and photograph to newspapers. The morning papers will publish.

April 16, 1921.—Station master from Grand Trunk called. He said Port Huron wired they know nothing of ticket, and New York wired that collection of tickets showed her ticket had been collected between New York and Buffalo. He said he would let us know Monday of further developments. *Later.*—Newspaper item in morning papers as follows:

Magyar Girl Lost in New York as She Quits Boat: Joseph Vesely of 15 Missouri Avenue, Joliet, yesterday appealed to the Illinois Commission of Immigration to search for his niece, Mathild Moreic, a Magyar girl, who disappeared last week in New York. She is supposed to have reached Ellis Island on April 1 on the steamship "Rotterdam" but failed to arrive in Joliet April 4 as expected although she had been provided with transportation. Officials of the Immigration Commission have wired Ellis Island for particulars.

April 18, 1921.—Man from Grand Trunk called. Conductor's collection shows ticket was collected to Chicago between Buffalo and Chicago. That is all they are able to do. *Later.*—Telephoned Joliet. Girl has not arrived, and no clue to her. She would travel to Joliet by Rock Island Railroad. *Later.*—Telephoned Parmalee Transfer Company. Impossible for their driver to give any information. They thought perhaps Immigrant Agent at LaSalle Street Station might be able to help. *Later.*—Telephoned Travellers' Aid. They saw our paragraph in the newspapers. Thus far they have heard or seen nothing of the girl, but they will question Travellers' Aid representative at LaSalle and Dearborn Street stations once more. *Later.*—Took copy of girl's picture, etc., to Detective Bureau, 179 N. LaSalle Street.

April 20, 1921.—Visited Dearborn Station again, examined record of immigrant arrivals of April 6 once more. Marta Boreic, a Magyar woman with a child, arrived destined 1900 Lincoln Avenue. Also Anna Brantigann, Magyar, 819 Park Street. *Later.*—Called at 1900 Lincoln Avenue. No such number. Inquired in neighborhood and was told at 2000 Lincoln Avenue that Marta Boreic and child arrived and that she was taken to the relative who moved out about three months ago. Woman will know address tomorrow.

April 21, 1921.—Obtained address of Marta Boreic, who lives with her brother-in-law at 202 Central Park Avenue. Visited there. Woman arrived with a Croatian group, and they were always together with their own people. Woman knows nothing about the Magyar girl. *Later.*—Visited Anna Brantigann, 819 Park Street. Found nobody at home. A neighbor said that the girl started to work this morning. The sister with whom she lives has gone out with the children to visit a friend. *Later.*—

Visited and talked to Mrs. Smietana, a sister-in-law of Anna. Mr. Smietana is a half-brother of Anna. They bought a prepaid ticket from Memel. Ticket was prepaid from Danzig to Chicago and cost $178.54. Number was not given in receipt.

April 22, 1921.—J. H. [Magyar visitor for Commission] went to Joliet. Visited Mr. and Mrs. Vesely. Name of the lost girl is Mathild Majiec. Girl came from Szeged, Hungary, and was coming to her half-sister, Mrs. Joseph Vesely. They are living at 15 Missouri Street, Joliet, Illinois. They came to the United States in 1912. They have two small children, and own a very nice bungalow, very well furnished. Man is working as railroad car builder.

The girl Mathild is an orphan, born February 14, 1902, self-supporting now at housework. Mr. Vesely sent at the request of the girl a prepaid ticket in November, 1920, through the steamship agents H. Grossman and Company. He says he paid $160 but receipt shows only $155.35 and at the same time they sent the girl 10,000 crowns, for which they paid $35 (they should cost only $18). Girl wrote a letter in January that she just arrived from some other town where she was working and the ticket and the money were received by some woman relation with whom the girl stays. Read a letter dated February 26. This letter reports to the relatives that she received a Hungarian passport but on account of her minor age she had some difficulties. When she went to Budapest to the American Consul, they kept all the documents and gave her a number and advised her to call again personally March 25, when the American visa will be given. Letter says, "and so I am planning to leave April 15 on the steamer Rotterdam. I am short of money because the American Consul wants $10—furthermore the Holland Consul, the German Consul and the Austrian Consul must be paid, besides I have to show before I sail $25 in cash." Letter dated March 9 says, "I am not feeling very well. I am going to Budapest the 25th [it means March] and I will write you and probably I will leave with the steamer April 15." Explained that girl could not have arrived at Ellis Island but must be on the way or still in Hungary.

Talked to the agent, Mr. Grossman, who said that the people were always inquiring about the girl, and he asked about the passenger at the Holland-American Line. They sent a message stating that the girl was admitted April 4, giving at the same time the exact ticket number. Some confusion must have taken place probably in Budapest at the American Consulate or by the steamship company.

April 23, 1921.—Letter written to Commissioner of Immigration, Ellis Island, containing the following:

Since we wired you about Mathild Moreik, steamship "Rotterdam," we have secured evidence that leads us to think that the girl, who is reported missing, has not really left Hungary. The correct name of the girl is Mathild Majiec. She is going to her brother-in-law, Joseph Vesely, Joliet, Illinois.

Will you please let us know what the manifest sheet of the steamship "Rotterdam," April 1, shows as the destination for Mathild Moreik? It may be possible in that way to clear up the situation.

April 30, 1921.—Letter from Commissioner of Immigration, Ellis Island, contains the following:

Replying to your letter of the 23d inst., I have to inform you that we do not find the name of Mathild Moreik under the third-cabin passengers arriving here on the steamer "Rotterdam." The nearest name found is that of Marta Boreic, ex steamer "Rotterdam," who was admitted April 4 to proceed to her sister Anna Laszlo, 1900 Lincoln Avenue, Chicago. On the list which the Holland American Line agent had the name appeared as Mathild Moreik. The mistake in name was probably made in the prepaid number of the ticket, causing confusion in the telegram the Company sent.

May 5, 1921.—Letter to Mrs. Vesely returning letters and pictures of girl by registered mail and saying:

We are sure from what we have heard from Ellis Island that your sister-in-law, Mathild Majiec, did not come on the "Rotterdam." The confusion in the Holland-American list and also at Ellis Island arose because there was another Magyar girl on the steamship by the name of Marta Boreic. As you perhaps know, we were told that your relative's name was Mathild Moreik, and we telegraphed to Ellis Island under that name. Marta Boreic is living with her sister, Anna Laszlo, 202 Central Park Avenue. We inclose the picture which Mr. Grossman left with us when he asked us to institute a search for her and also the letters which you gave to our visitor.

LOST BAGGAGE CASES

[Immigrants not infrequently arrive at their final destination to find that their baggage has been lost. The services of an organization like the Immigrants' Commission or the Immigrants' Protective League are needed to trace the lost articles. While the lost baggage is often not intrinsically valuable, the articles always seem very precious to the people who have lost them. The letters of inquiry indicate the method of retrieving baggage and the kind of articles brought to this country by the peasant people of the steerage.

The records as a whole are not copied, and letters in reply to the inquiries are also omitted as unnecessary since in all these cases the lost baggage was secured and restored to the owners except in the last two cases as indicated.][1]

[1] The following letters from a Polish woman who arrived December 8 without her baggage which she described as containing "one featherbed, two pillows, two shawls, skirts and other clothing and other household goods" are also of interest. This baggage in spite of a long correspondence was never found. The letters are translations from the Polish.

1. Letter dated April 8:

DEAR MADAM:

Writing this letter to you I am very anxious to get a reply from you to the last letter you wrote to Rotterdam. In case if you got a reply from the Company that there is no trace of it or at least you think you cannot do anything in regard

SOCIAL CASE RECORDS 617

14. Sofia Zichi

To the Baggage Agent, Steamship Line
Boston, Massachusetts

DEAR SIR: Sofia Zichi, who arrived on the S.S. "Cracow" at Boston on December 6th, has received only her checked baggage consisting of a trunk and a bale, and not her hand baggage.

Sofia Zichi describes this lost baggage as follows: one-half bale covered with linen cloth, grey with light blue corners buttoned together and with a yellow strap and contains one large pillow and four small pillows and two comforters, one grey and one pink on one side and red on the other; a light yellow basket about one yard long and about half a yard high, with a round lock, containing white linen and cotton underwear and dresses for a baby and a small child. The basket that is locked contains clothing for

---

to it, I would be pleased to hear even this from you, for you know I cannot forgive the Company my baggage; for one thing it is worth too much to be forgiven and for another I cannot afford to buy all those things that it bears inside, and it is worth over $300.

And if you cannot do anything please be so kind and notify me about it as soon as you possibly can and trusting to hear from you that you will send a reply in regard to the matter, I remain,

Very respectfully yours,

GISALA ZAPOLA

2. Letter dated May 10:

DEAR MADAM:

Awaiting your reply, and hoping that you received an answer from New York, I would be very glad to hear from you about my baggage. Thinking over it I sometimes have to cry on account of the delay of it since December. Please be so kind and let me know something at least about it, if you received any reply about it or not that is either from New York or from Rotterdam, from which the reply should come. As soon as you hear anything about the baggage, please let me know it as early as possible for I cannot wait any longer. Oh dear, I have to do something at least. Oh, yes. Please be so kind and send me the addresses from Halifax that is from the Company where they generally keep the baggages of the people coming from Europe. I suppose it was written with red ink from the steamship agent, Mr. Skala, and if you think you can do something in regard to it please let me hear from you, for I am getting more sick on account of it. Hoping that you will let me hear something in regard to it, I remain,

Yours very respectfully,

GISALA ZAPOLA

3. Letter dated May 26:

DEAR MADAM:

Replying to your favor of the 25 inst., I am thanking you very much for the letter you wrote to me, telling me about your reply from Rotterdam. With this reply I was very much rejoiced, and filled with happiness all the day long. Oh! I hope and trust that you will get a reply from New York and that you will be so kind to write me again telling me that my baggage is on its way on its journey home to me again. Oh! that would be my greatest joy for me, and then would I more heartily thank you than ever, and recommend you to all the immigrants not only from Europe and other countries but the whole world. Hoping that you really will get a reply from New York and that the few words I say will become true, I remain,

Very respectfully yours,

GISALA ZAPOLA

children initialed in red *SZ* and the baby clothing has a ruffle round the neck of the dress which has a scalloping of red embroidery. There was also a bundle of linen, women's, and initialed in red—*SZ*. The basket that is not locked and which is described as a hand basket is not quite as high as the other one and contains wine and some lunch, cheese and a teapot.

Very truly yours,

IMMIGRANTS' PROTECTIVE LEAGUE

15. Valeria Rezka

To the Baggage Agent, Cunard Line
Boston, Massachusetts

DEAR SIR: Valeria Rezka, a Russian woman, ex S.S. "Franconia," which arrived about July 29, 1913, has not received all her baggage. She holds Continental Checked Baggage check No. 233. She tells us that the missing piece is a large wooden box painted brown. The box contained among other things 14 towels, 1 sheet, 2 white tablecloths, 2 pink pillow-slips, 2 white waists, 3 children's dresses, 2 men's suits, 1 picture, 3 pieces of cheese, and 25 Russian books. Will you have the baggage traced and forwarded, sending the check to us? We will notify passenger. We are inclosing her original check.

Very truly yours,

IMMIGRANTS' PROTECTIVE LEAGUE

16. Domenica Levitzka

To the Commissioner of Immigration
Quebec, Ontario, Canada

DEAR SIR: May we ask you to refer this case to the proper steamship company or to the agency in Quebec handling such cases? Domenica Levitzka, a Polish woman, who arrived at Quebec on May 21 on the S.S. "Michigan," lost her baggage. The baggage consisted of a sack, containing one brown blanket, one large feather quilt, four large pillows, one small pillow, four suits of underwear, and one bed spread. She held a receipt for her baggage; but she gave it to a Mr. Latzko, an agent in this city, 725 Fourth Street, who endeavored to get her baggage for her, but he was not successful and the woman has turned to us. She lives at 481 Rush Street. If the baggage is found, we ask that the checks be turned over to us.

Very truly yours,

IMMIGRANTS' PROTECTIVE LEAGUE

[After correspondence extending over a period of a year and a half, a letter containing the following practically closed the case:]

Our agent, Mr. Latzko, states that no receipt for baggage was ever given to him by the passenger. Every possible search and inquiry for the missing bundle were made but nothing to fill the shortage was located. In the tracer form filled by this passenger statement is made that the missing package accompanied the passenger all the way and was in her own care while on board the steamer. It was therefore lost through her own neglect in not attending to the proper checking of it on arrival at the port of landing and although very sorry for her loss no claim can be entertained by this Company.

17. The Grunbergs' Baggage Case

[The Grunbergs' baggage case began August 26, 1913, with a request for advice about a deportation situation. A young Roumanian Jew, Simon Grunberg, apparently quite well-to-do from his account of his work and his brother's work, came to the office to ask for advice. He had brought over his father, mother, and sister, who were all at Ellis Island under detention. He had received a telegram that his sister had been excluded because of insanity. He thought perhaps one of his parents could be admitted and the other could return with the sister. He asked advice about whether it would be well for him to go to New York to see if they wished to be separated, and also to see his sister before she was sent back. He was advised to do this, and was given a letter of introduction to a social agency in New York that would help him at Ellis Island.

Upon his return from New York he reported that the parents did not want to be separated and decided that both would return with the excluded daughter. All were deported on the S.S. "Germania," December 13, 1913. The son, Simon Grunberg, came to the office early in 1914 to report that his parents had arrived at Bucharest but that they had not received back their own baggage. They had traveled from Bucharest to New York with a family by the name of Wolfson, their baggage looked very much alike, and the Wolfson baggage had arrived at Bucharest. The Grunberg family would not accept the Wolfson baggage and told the agent to send it to America. Then began a long correspondence. The Wolfson family, who were located in the town of Lakeville, Indiana, were using the Grunberg baggage and refused to give it up until their own arrived. This was delayed in arrival owing to a new error in shipment, and when it did arrive another controversy began as to whether the charges, $11.65, were to be paid by the Grunbergs, the Wolfsons, or the steamship company. The following letter refers to the situation and describes the baggage:]

May 7, 1914

Baggage Department, German-American Line
New York

DEAR SIRS: After considerable correspondence with the Wolfson family, they refuse to pay any further charges on the baggage. The Grunbergs are willing to pay the charges and have deposited $11.65 with us. They are very anxious to know that all their goods will be packed by the Wolfsons. The following is a list of articles:

- 1 large brass pan and cover
- 1 brass water can
- 1 brass strainer with ears
- 1 man's fur coat
- 1 lady's fur coat
- 2 pairs ratine curtains
- 1 wool skirt
- 1 lady's wrapper
- 1 summer blouse
- 1 white summer skirt
- 6 pewter tablespoons
- 6 pewter teaspoons
- 6 pewter forks
- 7 fancy bedspreads
- 1 feather bed
- 7 pillows

3 quilts
5 white pillow covers
5 pillow covers colored
2 colored mattress covers
1 pair pewter candlesticks
5 brass candlesticks
1 Persian lamb cap
3 men's shirts (white)
2 suits men's underwear
1 Turkish coffee grinder
2 salt and pepper holders, crystal
1 nickel lamp
1 large woolen shawl
1 large brass tray

2 ladies' aprons
7 good towels
1 table cover, white
1 pewter soup spoon
2 pair of house slippers
3 large Jewish books
1 Talis and book cover containing valuable papers
3 embroidered handkerchiefs
4 pair stockings
1 pair gloves
Several photographs
2 mortars and 2 pestles

We have no representative in Lakeville who can supervise the packing. As soon as it is done, we shall send to you a check to cover charges of forwarding. Thanking you for your co-operation in the matter, we are,

Very truly yours,

IMMIGRANTS' PROTECTIVE LEAGUE

[Finally July 3, 1914, the baggage went forward to the German-American Line in New York. However, the baggage reached Antwerp and was held there during the period of the war. After the Armistice, the baggage question was reopened. Simon Grunberg reported that he had received word through the Red Cross in Paris that his mother and a brother in Roumania had died. He wished to have the baggage returned to the United States. The following letter from the German-American Line completes the history of the vicissitudes of this piece of immigrant baggage:]

May 20, 1919

Immigrants' Protective League

DEAR SIRS: Referring to the Grunberg-Wolfson baggage our last letter to you on this subject was June 21, 1915, in answer to yours of 19th June, 1915. We have now been advised from our Antwerp Office relative to this piece of baggage which we shipped in July, 1914, to family of Grunberg at Bucharest, the piece of baggage did not leave Antwerp as the war came on and all traffic of this kind was suspended, when the Germans came to Antwerp they seized the Grunberg baggage along with about five hundred other pieces, so it looks as if any claim is filed it will have to be filed with the German Government. Now that we have ascertained what became of this baggage we find we are still short the charges of $11.65 which was to be deposited with you by the sons of the Grunberg family. Kindly give this matter your attention. We beg to remain,

Yours truly,

GERMAN-AMERICAN LINE, *Baggage Department*

FINDING EMPLOYMENT

18. Steve Blaha, Tony Arnescu, and Jan Ombroz
(*A "Harvesting Laborers" Advertisement*)

July 1, 1914.—Three Roumanian men, aged thirty-six, fifty, and forty-eight years, in the office. They have no money, no friends, and speak almost no English. They look sick and miserable, shoes and clothes in dreadful condition. They need everything. They will wait for Mr. H. *Later.*— J. H. [Magyar visitor who could also speak their language] spoke with these men. They were living in Cleveland and had no work. The Hungarian newspaper *Szabadsag* (*Liberty*), 702 Huron Road, Cleveland, published an advertisement of an employment agent in Cleveland who wanted "harvesting laborers" to be sent to Kansas. Many immigrant working people went to the agent, and they paid $17.89 each to go to Topeka, Kansas. On June 16, there were 99 men (Roumanians, Hungarians, and Slovaks) who left Cleveland. When they arrived in Topeka, these people found no work, and after one day's waiting everyone started his way in different directions. These three with nineteen other men tried to walk back to Cleveland, begging on the way all the time. Every day the company lost some friend who could not walk longer and was left sick without protection on the roads. Only these three Roumanians reached Chicago and they are in a miserable situation, exhausted to the limit. The men want to be helped to go on to Cleveland. Tried to persuade them to stay in Chicago.

[Certain other details are omitted here since they are incorporated in the letter below. Arrangements were made to have the men stay at Plymouth House (League boarding-house and headquarters) until a decision should be reached.]

July 2, 1914.—The following letter sent to the head of the Immigration Section of Public Welfare Department, Cleveland, Ohio:

My dear Mr. Wood:

Last night three Roumanians by the name of Steve Blaha, Tony Arnescu, and Jan Ombroz reached Chicago in an exhausted condition. They told the following story: On June 16th they left Cleveland with ninety-six other men who were principally Roumanians, Hungarians, and Slovaks, on the New York and St. Louis Railroad via Chicago for Topeka, Kansas. They reached Topeka, expecting to do harvest work. They found there was none there. The men say that of the ninety-nine, fifty had the extra $4.50 which was necessary to take them to the place where work was available, and twenty-two of the others started to walk back to Cleveland. Some of them were unable to keep up, but these three Roumanians say that they finally reached Chicago, walking all the way. The men paid the employment agent $18 for their railroad fare and were sent out by Emil Beclin, 80 Euclid Avenue, representing the firm of Ackerman and Jones in Cleveland. They had his card and the inclosed card and several envelopes addressed to *Szabadsag*, 702 Huron Road, Cleveland. I am not at all sure that the $18 that these men paid was in the nature of an employment agent's fee or that they were promised definite work. The men, of course, expected that the guides who were sent out with them by the agent would actually secure them work. They stayed two nights and one day about the station in Topeka; and then as there was no work available, they started out as I have described. It is an illustration of the way in which men who are unable to speak English and are therefore quite helpless are unable to adapt themselves to the kind of situation they met in Kansas, and although there was work in other parts of Kansas, they were unable to get to it unless personally conducted. The agent went off with the group of fifty men who were able to pay $4.50 to go farther, and these others were left stranded there. I should be very glad if you would let us know if you find out anything at all about these men. We are trying to persuade the men to stay on here as there seems to be no particular reason for their going on to Cleveland inasmuch as they have no relatives or friends there.

Sincerely yours,

LYDIA GARDNER, Superintendent

Later.—Men determined to walk on to Cleveland. No work found for them. Men taken to the Austro-Hungarian Consulate. Consul gave each man $2. J. H. got them shoes and some other necessaries.

July 8, 1914.—Men started to walk on to Cleveland via Gary.

19. Ivan Orliniecky
(Employment-Agency Refund)

April 24, 1915.—Ivan Orliniecky, a Russian Pole, aged thirty-two, married, wife and two children in Chicago, in office with employment agency complaint. Man brought with him to A. F. [the Polish visitor] a letter from the Chicago office of *Dziennik Narodowy* [national Polish daily]. Letter was as follows:

DEAR MADAM:

Please look into the matter of the bearer of this writing. He claims that Mr. Martzin, inspector in office of Superintendent of Private Employment Agencies, told him that nothing can be done, so far as his office is concerned.

Yours very truly,

JAN POLACEK

The man's story was that he paid $15 to the International Industrial Bureau and was promised a job in a wagon factory, where he was to earn 22 cents per hour. After a few days' work man discovered he was paid only 16½ cents per hour. Mr. Martzin told man he would get only part of the refund. Telephoned office of Mr. Day [i.e., office of State Supervisor of Private Employment Agencies]. He says all the various cases against Mrs. Flower [Manager of the International Industrial Bureau] are to be heard May 8. [Cross-references to other League cases against Mrs. Flower's agency omitted here. Notification about a hearing, etc., omitted.]

May 8, 1915.—A. F. visited Mrs. Flower's employment office. Mr. Day [State Supervisor] and one inspector, Mr. White, there. Mr. Orliniecky made the statement that the agent promised him work for 22 cents an hour and when he started they paid only 16½ cents so it was not satisfactory to him and he left the place. Man was working only six days. Mrs. Flower refunded $10. Our other League cases settled at this hearing as follows:

1. *Stef Maly, 607 South Maxwell Street.*—He paid on March 3, 1915, $15 fee. He worked three weeks, piece work, was not able to get more than 50 cents a day. Agent had said he would earn not less than $6 a week. After long argument Mrs. Flower paid back to the man $5.

2. *Jan Ivanoff.*—He had paid $7 fee on April 12, was discharged after four days. Agent gave him after a while a new receipt, and paid back $5.

3. *Joe Oster, 607 Maxwell Street.*—He paid $15 fee, March 3, was sent to few places without result. Agent paid back $10.

4. *Sam Christofer.*—He had paid $12 fee, worked fifteen days, was laid off. He got back $5.

5. *Harry Davos.*—He had paid $14, worked eight days, laid off. He got back $8.

6. *Mike Cesky, 1301 Union Avenue.*—He had paid $30 fee April 12. Receipt was given by agency on the legal form. Mrs. Flower claims this was not a fee but was money loaned to her. Mr. Day ordered Mrs. Flower and the man to come to his office on May 10.

7. *Nick Novak, 1301 Union Avenue.*—He paid $30, April 13. Agent denies this and showed in his record only $20. Receipt shows plainly $30. In the record are some corrections. This case had already been heard by Mr. Day; and he tried to settle it, but Nick was not satisfied with the offer of $10. He will call at our office and will take the case to the court.

It was announced that further hearing would be held Monday, May 10, at 12 noon in office of agency. All interested persons to be notified to come.

20. Peter Ganos, Seven Other Greek Men, and an Employment Agency

June 16, 1915.—Complaint made by eight Greek men [names and addresses omitted] living near Hull-House against the Immigrant Employment Agency, 800 Canal Street. The men told the following story to A. V. [Greek visitor]: They paid $40 ($5.00 each) to the employment agent two weeks ago and were promised jobs on the following day. The next day they went to the office, and the agent said, "No work." The next day they went again, and the next day they went, and they were always told there was no work. They asked then for their money back. They have gone to the agent many times, and he will give them no money and no work. Now, Peter Ganos himself and three of the other men have got jobs through a friend and are leaving for Davenport, Iowa, tomorrow. Men left receipts in office and asked that Mr. X., manager of a Greek coffee house on Halsted Street, be notified if claim were settled. *Later.*—Telephoned Mr. Day [State Supervisor of Private Employment Agencies], and he will investigate.

[The remaining portion of this case record is omitted. Court action was finally necessary in this case, which was not heard in court until after several of the men had left town. Each of the claims was, however, finally paid and the refund sent on to the men.]

21. Andrew Michaliuk
(Buying Jobs for Friends)

May 16, 1916.—Andrew Michaliuk, Russian, in office, sent by the United Charities with an employment agency complaint. Interviewed by R. B. [Russian visitor]. Man has been in this country four years, is married, and has two children.

[The details of the interview with Mr. Michaliuk are omitted here because they are conveniently summarized in the letter below.]

R. B. telephoned the State Supervisor of Private Employment Agencies and asked for Mr. Orlikowski. He will be there tomorrow morning between nine and ten o'clock. Told Mr. Michaliuk to go to the state officer tomorrow at this time and gave him a letter to Mr. Orlikowski:

Supervisor of Private Employment Agencies
Chicago, Illinois

ATTENTION, MR. ORLIKOWSKI: Andrew Michaliuk, 60 Bryant Street, tells us that he went with a friend of his, Gregory Pikowski, to the Bloom Employment Office in August, 1914. Mr. Bloom asked for $25 to get a job for Mr. Pikowski, and Mr. Michaliuk paid this because Mr. Pikowski had not the money. Later, when no job was secured, Mr. Michaliuk asked him to return the $25, which he did not do. His excuse was that Mr. Pikowski drank, and he could not get a job for him on that account. In about a month, Mr. Michaliuk took to the Bloom office another man, Peter Valczuk. Mr. Bloom promised a job but again charged $25, and Mr. Michaliuk gave him another $25. No job was given this man either. Mr. Michaliuk has tried several times to get his money back. Later, he says, Mr. Bloom changed the receipt from two separate ones in the names of the two applicants to this one receipt in the name of Andrew Michaliuk. We hope you will be able to help this man.

Yours very truly,

R. B._____

(For the Immigrants' Protective League)

May 18, 1916.—Mr. Orlikowski telephoned that he went with Mr. Michaliuk to Mr. Bloom. Mr. Bloom explained that the $50 had not been an employment agency fee but had been a loan by Mr. Michaliuk when Mr. Bloom was in trouble and needed money. He (Bloom) was willing to give Mr. Michaliuk a note, but Mr. Michaliuk refused to accept it and demanded instead a job receipt. Mr. Bloom will pay $10 a week for next five weeks, and Mr. Orlikowski will see that the money is paid each Saturday. Mr. Orlikowski is convinced that the Bloom story is a true one. *Later.*—Mr.

Michaliuk in office. He said he paid the $50 for work for the two men. He did not know Mr. Bloom, and why would he loan him his money? He can bring in the two men if necessary. *Later.*—Telephoned Mr. Orlikowski, but he was not in. He will telephone tomorrow.

May 19, 1916.—Mr. Orlikowski telephoned. Told him that man still insisted it was for employment that he paid. *Later.*—Mr. Orlikowski telephoned. He again telephoned Mr. Bloom, and Mr. Bloom will now pay the $50 on Wednesday at 4 P.M. Mr. Orlikowski will be there to see that it is done. Told him we will notify Andrew Michaliuk.

May 20, 1916.—Mr. Michaliuk and Peter Valczuk (the man for whom Michaliuk paid the $25 for work) in office. Mr. Valczuk says that one year and eight months ago Mr. Michaliuk paid the money to Mr. Bloom for Peter to get work. He did not get work—not one day. Told Mr. Michaliuk to go to Mr. Bloom next Wednesday. Mr. Michaliuk spoke about Russia; he does not want to return, says if he will get good work he will stay always in America.

May 24, 1916.—Mr. Michaliuk in office. He went to Mr. Bloom's agency yesterday at 4 P.M. Mr. Bloom said they have no money and Mrs. Bloom had gone to get some; man should call tomorrow. Mr. Orlikowski was not there. Tried to get Mr. Orlikowski by telephone. He will not be in until tomorrow.

May 26, 1916.—Letter written to Mr. Orlikowski, asking if the office cannot collect the money, explaining that Mr. Bloom had failed to pay and that since Andrew Michaliuk had a job, it was hard for him to lose his work and go to Bloom's and get nothing.

May 29, 1916.—Mr. Day [Supervisor of Private Agencies] telephoned, saying that Mr. Bloom was in a tight place. He had just telephoned Mr. Bloom and arranged to have him mail a money order Tuesday for $25 and another on Thursday for $25. Mr. Day will then mail the orders to Mr. Michaliuk. Another drawback to collection is the fact that the claim is so old.

June 1, 1916.—Mr. Day telephoned that Mr. Bloom had sent him a money order for $15 and says he will send more on Saturday or Monday. Mr. Day will mail this order to Mr. Michaliuk and ask him to send in his receipt.

June 2, 1916.—Letter from man [translation from the Russian]:

DEAR GENTLEMEN:

With this letter I am asking you not to refuse me to let me know if you have received from Mr. Bloom the $50 payable to Piotr Valtchuk. He said that he has sent $25 already and that the balance he will send in a week. If you will collect all the money from him, you can have $10 commission.

Respectfully personal,
ANDREW MICHALIUK

June 3, 1916.—Andrew Michaliuk in office. He received $15. Man thanks the League very much. He has sent $1 in a letter to pay the League for help given. Thanked him but said we would not charge for such work. Mr. Michaliuk will take receipt to Mr. Day's office. Gave man Mr. Day's letter and his receipt. *Later.*—Telephoned Mr. Day. Told him we did not believe that the money was a loan. He will collect balance as fast as possible. Told him Mr. Michaliuk would bring the receipt in Tuesday.

June 14, 1916.—Letter from Andrew Michaliuk [translation from the Russian]:

DEAR LADY:

I am asking you not to refuse my earnest request. It is already six weeks that I am trying to collect $50, but I have collected only $15, and the inspector has promised that I will have all my money in five weeks. I am not sorry about anything but that my earnest request is not fulfilled. My grandfather lived 99 years, my father is 56 years old, I am 30 years old, and we all were truthful and the man Bloom, the agent, has given me pain in that way that I have given him the money to get work but not that I have loaned him the money. Now I am left as a crook, and I want to bring him to court for slander and for insulting my pride. Goodbye, I send you one dollar.

Respectfully yours,

ANDREW MICHALIUK

June 30, 1916.—Russian letter received from Andrew Michaliuk [translation]:

DEAR LADY:

Please be so kind and do not leave my case without attention. Please telephone and ask the inspector if the money was sent to me. They have promised that I will receive $15 June 26th and the rest in two weeks. It is now the 29th and I have not heard anything or received anything. I am very impatient. Please answer at once.

Respectfully yours,

ANDREW MICHALIUK

July 14, 1916.—Postcard received from Mr. Michaliuk [translation]:

DEAR LADY:

I have not received any money and probably will not receive any until I bring them to court, and they will continue to cheat and my $35 will be lost.

Respectfully yours,

ANDREW MICHALIUK

Later.—R. B. telephoned Mr. Day. He says that Mr. Bloom had tried to borrow money but failed. He has now been told that if he does not bring it by Tuesday, the office will get out a warrant for him. Mr. Day goes to a convention in Buffalo next week, but he is leaving instructions for "collection or arrest."

July 18, 1916.—Mr. Michaliuk in office. Telephoned Mr. Day's office. No money collected. No one who knew about it in office.

July 20, 1916.—Telephoned Mr. Orlikowski. Another $10 collected. He wanted to know Michaliuk's address. He will send the $10 to him today, and Mr. Bloom will bring the other $25 tomorrow. Mr. Orlikowski will notify us when last payment is made.

August 7, 1916.—Balance of $25 was paid through Mr. Day's office to Mr. Michaliuk today.

22. The Employment-Agency Case of Alexander Mercu and Eight Other Roumanians and Boghoa Narhigian and Twenty-one Other Armenians

May 15, 1914.—Nine Roumanian laborers in office (no Chicago address). Someone, "a countryman," told them to come. Waited for Mr. H— [Magyar visitor] to come in. *Later.*—J. H. spoke with these people. These nine Roumanians are all recently arrived in United States. First they stopped in Indiana Harbor with some countryman, Joseph Balaxil. They got no jobs there, and May 8, 1914, they came on to Chicago to look for work. Next day the men were all walking on Canal Street in the labor agencies neighborhood when a man took them into an employment office where the man said laborers were wanted. The boss there offered all the Roumanian men steady track work during the summer in Ottawa, Illinois. These were the terms: their wages would be $1.75 for ten hours' daily work; the employer would furnish the men with lodging and with a stove. Each man should pay $12 to the boss (employment agent) in the office, $10 each for the job and the railroad fare of $2 to Ottawa. Men have card of employment agent, "Silver Employment Agency," 10 West Canal Street. Sunday, May 10, the group left Chicago on the night train, and with them went twenty-two Armenian men, also laborers, and two other men who were guides or interpreters from the employment office. They arrived in Ottawa early in the morning, May 11, and they could not get any work; they waited there until Thursday, but they did not get any work. One of the guides left the people, the other stayed with the men and all together they came back to Chicago; the men pooled what they had and paid their railroad fares back (each $1.62). *Later.*—J. H. took the nine men to office of Mr. Day, the Chief State Employment Inspector. Gave Mr. Day the facts, and complaint filed. There is already another complaint filed against the Silver Employment Agency, 10 West Canal Street. Mr. Day made some investigations by telephoning. The agent claims "that on Monday and Tuesday it was raining—that it was impossible to start work." Agent also claimed that these men refused to work in separate groups. The Roumanians deny this and say that they "would go anywhere and do all kinds of work." Receipts of these men left with Mr. Day, who wrote letters to investigate to the J. Appel Construction Camp, Ottawa, Illinois, and also to their foreman, Mr. Henry White, North Street, Ottawa, Illinois.

May 16, 1914.—Twenty-two Armenians came to the office this morning and wished also to complain about Mr. Silver. [Names of men and addresses omitted.] J. H. spoke with these men who have also a claim against the Silver agency. This Armenian group came back last night to Chicago. Each Armenian paid $12 to the employment agent and asks now for the return of this money. Telephoned Mr. Boghosian (Armenian Society) and asked if he could help us in this case. He will come to the office. *Later.*— Mr. Boghosian came and took his men to Mr. Day's office.

May 18, 1914.—Notice from Mr. Day's office to have both groups of men (Armenians and Roumanians) in his office on May 20. [Record of telephoning and sending notices omitted.]

May 20, 1914.—J. H. attended hearing with men. [Same facts stated again.] Agent Silver refused to make refund. We will take out warrant against him. The inspector's office has four other complaints now against this man. [Record of warrants taken out by the Roumanians omitted.] Hearing to be May 25 at DesPlaines Police Station.

May 25, 1914.—Attended DesPlaines Street Police Court. Hearing changed. Case is now taken to Criminal Court. Hearing set there for May 29. Men very impatient; they can get no work in city and want to "ship out." They have no money. Austrian Consul's office gave $2.50 and J. H. gave 25 cents to each of the Roumanians.

May 29, 1914.—J. H. attended with Miss Gardner [League Superintendent] the case in Criminal Court before Judge X. Attorney Y., who had been appointed special counsel for Mr. Day, agreed with the attorney for Silver in asking that case be postponed. Attorney Michael for Silver asked change of venue. Miss Gardner explained difficulties of delay. Men are all construction laborers and must "ship out" to get work and cannot stay in city waiting for this trial. Attorney Y. said he would see the Chief Justice and have case set at once. Miss Gardner again objected to delay. Judge agreed to reasons for objections.

June 1, 1914.—Telephoned Mr. Day. Attorney Y. at court all day and unable to see the Chief Justice.

June 2, 1914.—Nine Roumanians in office. They have all secured work through Green Employment Agency for farm work in Idaho and are to leave at 3 P.M. They cannot stay around with no work, waiting for trial. Telephoned Mr. Day's office and spoke with Mr. Brown. He said he would see their attorney, Mr. Y., at once and let us know before 11 o'clock what had been done. Alexander Mercu will wait in office to hear about case. *Later.* —Mr. Brown, employment office, reported that case had been set for June 10. He is sorry Roumanians are leaving town, but he thinks agent will probably settle with Roumanians. He says the Armenians are the best witnesses anyway, and they will probably remain until trial. The attorney, Mr. Y., "thinks" he did everything possible to secure earlier date. Told Mr. Mercu and other Roumanians to get the address in Idaho to which they are going and leave it with us. *Later.*—Roumanians report they were mistaken and that they are going to Iowa, not Idaho; address for Roumanians will be Box 33, Chestnut, Iowa.

June 3, 1914.—Three Armenians in office. Most of the group have already secured work and have shipped out. Three have remained as witnesses. They are living at 900 Green Avenue. Informed them of the trial on June 10.

June 5, 1914.—Letter received from Chestnut, Iowa, from the Roumanians [translation from the Roumanian]:

We wish to inform you that we, all of us, are now located on the Milwaukee line working about a steam shovel—all of us—Alexander Mercu and five others—and be so kind, Sir, as to send the money to us and deduct for your own effort whatever amount you desire; then send the balance to us, and we will divide it as we are all working together and all from one village. Be so kind as to give this letter to a Roumanian to read and be so kind as to send the money as we have great need as we have not even the means to buy food as we have not a cent and will not receive pay to the end of the month. We salute you with much esteem.

June 10, 1914.—J. H. went to Criminal Court for Silver case. The trial was not held. Attorney Michael, representing Silver, made a proposition to settle, promising that he will persuade Mr. Silver to repay all the money to the laborers. Mr. Day and his attorney, Mr. Y., were satisfied, and we have to wait again two weeks. Roumanians are still working in Chestnut, Iowa. Armenians will leave their receipts and one man in Chicago as a witness; all others to start to work somewhere within next few days.

June 12, 1914.—Another letter received from the Roumanians [translation from the Roumanian]:

Sir:

We beg you, we named [six names are listed], the six of us are in Chestnut, Iowa, and we are working here at the railroad line with a pay of $1.50 a day, and if you have straightened out the affair between us and the agent we beg you to write us soon and if you have received the money from the agent then we beg you to send it to us at this address: Box 33, Chestnut, Iowa. We beg you to answer us as soon as possible. May the good God repay you with long life, good health, many good years. We beg you to answer soon.

June 29, 1914.—Telephoned Mr. Day. He said they were waiting for settlement by bondsmen. Advised writing bonding company.

June 30, 1914.—Wrote Surety Bonding Company as follows:

We understand that your company has signed bonds for an employment agent named Silver against whom the State Employment Agency Inspector has a complaint. The complainants in the case, namely, nine Roumanian men and twenty-two Armenians, are very anxious to know when they can obtain their money. We shall be very grateful if you will give this matter your attention and advise us when the refund is ready for them.

July 3, 1914.—Letter received from Alex Mercu [translation from the Roumanian]:

HONORABLE SIR:

We have received your letter and with great pleasure have learned everything written in it by yourself. We are very happy to know we are to receive the money and therefore we beg you to send it to this address: Alex Mercu, P.O. Box 33, Chestnut, Iowa.

And we who are to receive the money are [six names are listed here]. And we beg you very courteously to send the money because we are very distressed on account of money as we haven't even a bad penny; and from home we receive letters to send money continually, and we have no money. We beg you to send us it. · All of us salute you.

Later.—Letter received from Surety Bonding Company as follows:

Replying to your letter of June 30th relative to the Silver Employment Agency, I beg to state that, as you probably are aware, the bond in question on which we are surety is a regular statutory form of bond and our total liability is limited to $500. The claims of those who have suffered through Silver's defalcations amount to over $1,500. Thus you see if an adjustment could be made with us the claimants would only get about 30 per cent of their money back. Both the State Employment Agent and ourselves are hoping that Silver will raise sufficient money so that these people can be paid in full. Our investigator and the people of the state office believe that Silver can raise some money. It therefore would seem advisable to me to allow Silver further time in which to do so. Another bad feature is that many of these people are ignorant and would not understand that they are only entitled to a percentage on the amount of the money that they paid Silver. Unless a settlement can work out as we are hoping for, I can see no other way than for the Surety Bonding Company to pay this $500 into Court, join all the parties and get a court order for the distribution. It is regrettable that the penal sum of bonds of this character is so small.

July 11, 1914.—Roumanian letters received from two other Roumanian complainants asking if they will get back their $12. Letters acknowledged by J. H.

July 27, 1914.—Telephoned Mr. Day. He had case in court Saturday. Judge Z. gave agency thirty days' continuance.

August 22, 1914.—J. H. in court. Judge Z. is now moved to another court. Chief Justice on a vacation. Case continued until September 16. Representative of the American Colonization Society present with the Armenian man who swore out the warrant.

September 17, 1914.—J. H. in court. Case of Armenians, under warrant issued to Boghoa Narhigian, heard in Judge X.'s court. Attorney Y. represented Armenians; Attorney Michael represented Agent Silver. Mr. Narhigian and two other Armenians testified that all the men were in Mr. Silver's office May 6, each paying him $12 for positions in Ottawa. Receipts, however, were dated May 9 and were issued by interpreter who sat at desk with Mr. Silver, who received the money. Silver testified that he received no money, that he was in Ottawa May 7, 8, 10, 19, contracting for the work and that any money collected had been taken by the interpreter, who did not pay it to Silver. Mr. Silver claimed he had attempted to have interpreter arrested but police would not take him to the station. A letter was produced written in Chicago and dated during time Silver claimed to have been in Ottawa. Silver first stated the signature was his, then denied it. The judge was ready to find Silver guilty and fine him $25 and costs. Attorney Michael asked for new trial. Motion for new trial will be heard September 25. Other cases against Silver to be heard September 21. Alexander Mercu, Roumanian, not in town. His case must be "nolle prossed."

[Details are now given of a new case. A Greek, Sam Gannas, and thirty other men paid $6 each to the Silver agency for jobs fourteen miles out on the Chicago and Milwaukee Railroad. None of the men got any jobs, and they asked help in getting their money back; case referred to Mr. Day; men to take out warrant.]

November 11, 1914.—Three Roumanians in office, have just come to Chicago and intend leaving as soon as possible. Telephoned Mr. Day. He said his office is collecting all claims and would divide the bond ($500) equally among the people holding receipts against Silver. He thinks Silver's father would probably pay something if Silver could be put in jail. Receipts against him amount to approximately $1,500.

February 12, 1915.—Letter received from Notary Public and Manager of Foreign Department, Indiana Harbor Bank, about the Roumanians:

Nine men who were mistreated by some employment agencies in Chicago some time ago last summer requested me to write and ask you to be so kind and inform me about their condition and if there is any hope for them to receive some certain part of the money that they paid the employment agencies as you have record of their complaint, according to their statement.

February 13, 1915.—H. C. [Assistant Superintendent of the League] went to Mr. Day's office. Mr. Day not in; spoke with Inspector Brown. The case now has a different sort of complication. The claims against Silver now total $1,662, and the bond is $500. One claimant, John Salvatore, 61 Milwaukee Avenue, who has a $260 claim, has filed suit in Municipal Court for recovery of the $260, which, of course, would leave only $240 to be divided among the others whose claims are $1,402. The case came up Thursday, and Inspector Brown was in court to ask for a continuance. Salvatore was represented by Attorney Andrew Spiros. He was very angry about Mr. Brown's interference, saying he was not a party to the suit. The judge finally agreed to a continuance until Wednesday. Mr. Brown wrote to the Roumanians and all others who have claims to come in. Only one Roumanian appeared. Mr. Brown met one of the Armenians on the street and told him to notify the others. For this reason he did not consider it necessary to notify us. Mr. Brown explained that the reason his office had not filed suit, and thus allowed this one claimant to get his claim in ahead, was that he was very anxious to convict Silver on the confidence game charge, and he felt that if some settlement had been made even at 30 cents on the dollar it would weaken the case when it came to trial. He also wanted to hold the interest of the complainants; thought that if the men got some kind of settlement the office would then lose them as witnesses in confidence game charge.

[Following this interview, the League made a new and vigorous attempt to push the case against Silver and to secure a distribution of the money from the Surety Company. The record contains numerous entries of interviews with lawyers, the state's attorney, the attorney for the state inspector, and the Legal Aid Society, hearings in court, a trip to Indiana Harbor to secure assignments of claims from the Roumanians so that the League could represent them in the matter of the bond, etc. On February 19, 1915, a new claimant appeared, a Greek man by the name of Peter Papigos. This man said he had a contract to take a gang out on May 1. On April 22, 1914, he paid Silver $100 as deposit, which money he was to have refunded when he came in later. He also paid $500; $300 on April 23 and $200 on April 24, as fees for men. When May 1 came and no jobs materialized, the Greek said he could not wait, and Mr. Silver paid back the $500, which Papigos returned to the men. Mr. Silver had then signed an agreement to pay the $100 in thirty days, that is, about June 1. He was in the League office on February 19 and had received nothing up to that time.

On March 10, 1915, there was a hearing in the Criminal Court in the case of the *People* v. *Silver* ("confidence game"), but new delays were devised by the defendant's attorney and the case was again postponed. In June the League again pressed the state inspector's office to get the case heard. The inspector reported that there was a chance of getting Mr. Silver to plead guilty, under an arrangement by which he was to repay his creditors; but nothing came of this plan.

The case dragged on for several years longer. In 1918 a settlement was finally made and then the case record shows numerous attempts made to find the men to whom the money was due. Registered letters, special delivery letters, returned letters are recorded. In December, 1918, Peter Papigos, who was located, was paid $60.94, a pro rata payment on his claim. In 1919 the League reported to the court that $113.60 was still being held in the bank for men who could not be located. The court directed that the money be held, and a later report made. Finally, in January, 1920, permission was given to pay the whole of the sums owing to the men who could be found since there appeared to be no hope at all that the others who would have shared in the pro rata distribution could ever be found. The last entry on the record is January 8, 1920.]

OTHER EMPLOYMENT CASES

23. The Wage Claim of Frank Capek and Seven Other Bohemian Immigrant Workers against the Beck Construction Company

[This case begins with a complaint made by Frank Capek about wages due to him and other Bohemians for railroad work. His story to B. P. (the Bohemian visitor) is summarized in the letter below.]

May 14, 1914.—Letter written to the Wisconsin Industrial Commission:

The Secretary, the Industrial Commission
Madison, Wisconsin

DEAR SIR: Is it within your power to assist in the following case: On February 21st, Frank Capek, Steve Horak, Vaclav Comensky, Frank Laski, Vaclav Frie, Frank Malacka and Vaclav Malacka, and Bohumil Cermak went to work excavating for the Chicago, Milwaukee and St. Paul near Merrill, Wisconsin. They were sent out from Chicago by the Union Agency of this city on February 19th. The work is being done by the Henry Beck Construction Company and the man who supervised the work at Merrill was J. E. Davis, Badger Hotel, Merrill. The employment agency receipt shows that the men were to receive seventeen cents per yard and were to board themselves. Five days after they started to work the men were required to sign a contract before the rubber boots which they needed were given them. The contract is in English. One of the men speaks some English but cannot read or write it. The others are recent immigrants and can speak no English. The contract provides that they are to receive no pay until the work between station 658 approx. and 681 approx. is completed and that this will be done by June 1st. The payment provided in the contract is as follows:

Common excavation, per cubic yard......(0.17) seventeen cents
Loose rock excavation, per cubic yard....(0.28) twenty-eight cents
Solid rock excavation, per cubic yard.....(0.60) sixty cents
Overhaul, beyond 600 feet free haul, per cubic yard 100 feet (0.003/4) three-fourths of one cent
Grubbing, per square rod (0.60) sixty cents

Food and supplies were brought to the camp by Mr. Davis and were charged against the men. They hold statements showing that $317.53 worth of supplies was furnished them. This includes $7.50 for oats which was fed the company horse, and $3.50 for lumber which was used in building the bridge across which the food was brought. The last five weeks, the food which they ordered was not brought and, at the last, they had only potatoes and flour. When Frank Capek, who speaks English, complained of this, the men were discharged, May 7th, and Mr. Davis refused to pay them anything. The men do not know how much is due them as they were given no kind of receipts or checks showing the amount excavated and the kind of excavation which would determine the rate of payment. They say that it was all hard work through rock or frozen ground. They say that they excavated about 1,650 feet and that about 400 feet were left to be done. In addition, when they began work they built a stable working on Sundays and were promised $2.00 a day for this. Another Sunday they worked carrying rails, for which they were promised the same wages.

When the men were dismissed without payment, Frank Capek went to the sheriff and was sent by the sheriff's wife to a lawyer in Merrill by the name of Jones. This lawyer undertook to act for them but the men say that after talking with Mr. Davis the lawyer said he was going to act for Mr. Davis instead. The men are entirely without money and have no way of securing what is due them unless some assistance is given them. I shall be very grateful for any suggestions you can make.

Very sincerely yours,

LYDIA GARDNER

(*For the Immigrants' Protective League*)

May 25, 1914.—Letter received from Mr. Stone, a representative of the Industrial Commission, containing the following:

I have taken the case up with a young lawyer in Merrill, whom I know, and have asked him to follow it up. I hardly think that it is within the power of our Industrial Commission to do anything in this matter. What the men need is a lawyer, and I think that I can get the young lawyer in Merrill to take up the case. I shall write you again as soon as I hear from him.

June 3, 1914.—Letter received from Mr. Stone of the Industrial Commission, inclosing reply from lawyer in Merrill and saying the matter has been referred to the Chicago Milwaukee and St. Paul Railroad. The reply from the lawyer in Merrill was as follows:

Your communication of May 25th at hand, and in compliance with your request I have investigated this matter in so far as the same can be investigated, with but very meager results. Davis tells me that the men really have nothing coming for the reason that they were very unsteady in their working hours. That they would get off on a week's tear, and they drew supplies and clothing sufficient to offset their earnings. There have been a number of lawsuits growing out of the contract in question, and the workingmen have fared ill in every case. Not that I believe the allegations of the contractors; I have no doubt in my own mind but that these men have some valid cause of action. It is practically impossible however to do anything in the matter, much as I would like to help them out. There is no possibility of any adjustment without suit, and I am not in a position to bring suit against them as the men are now scattered, and even if they were here, I would hesitate to bring suit because of the disastrous results in the past as I have mentioned. If there is anything which I can do for you further I would be glad to do so.

Later.—The following letter sent to Mr. Stone, Wisconsin Industrial Commission:

Thank you very much for sending me the letter from the lawyer in Merrill. I can appreciate the difficulty in which he is placed if he expects to make a go of it in that town. I am inclosing the bills which the men hold for the supplies which were furnished them during the time that they were at work. As you can see, the amounts do not at all equal what the men should receive in the way of wages. There is, for example, no meat, or practically no meat, charged against them and the supplies are all very costly. Will you please return these receipts after you have looked them over?

June 10, 1914.—Letter from Wisconsin Industrial Commission saying the matter has been referred to Mr. A. G. Everett, assistant chief engineer of the Chicago Milwaukee and St. Paul Railroad Company. *Later.*—Letter written to Mr. Everett:

DEAR SIR:

I have just received word from Mr. Stone of the Wisconsin State Industrial Commission that he has referred to you our letter asking for an investigation of the complaint of eight Bohemian workmen who were employed on the Chicago, Milwaukee and St. Paul tracks near Merrill, Wisconsin, by Henry Beck Construction Company. We have the receipts and bills for food furnished the men and I shall be glad to submit them to you if you desire to see them.

Yours very truly,

LYDIA GARDNER

June 13, 1914.—Letter received from Mr. A. G. Everett:

Referring to your letter of June 10th in regard to the eight Bohemian workmen who were employed on this road under the Henry Beck Construction Company at Merrill: I would be very glad to have you send me the receipts and bills furnished the men. The complaint furnished by your office is so far at variance from the statement made by the contractor in regard to this matter, I have been obliged to send one of my own men on the ground to investigate further.

Later.—Reply to Mr. Everett's letter sent containing the following:

I am inclosing the receipts and contract of the eight Bohemian workmen employed by the Henry Beck Construction Company at Merrill. The men did not receive checks of any kind indicating either the time or the amount of excavating that they had done, so they are unable to furnish any evidence as to the amount that they should have received. We were much impressed with the apparent truthfulness of the men and their story and are very grateful for the investigation which you are undertaking. Will you kindly return the receipts and contract after you have looked them over?

Sincerely yours,

LYDIA GARDNER

July 1, 1914.—The following letter with four inclosures received from the office of the chief engineer of the Chicago Milwaukee and St. Paul Railroad:

Miss Lydia Gardner
Immigrants' Protective League
Chicago, Illinois

DEAR MADAM: Referring to your letter of June 13th, I am returning you herewith the contract between the Henry Beck Construction Company and Frank Capek *et al.* Also copies of their bills which you referred to me some time ago, and a copy of the reports of our Assistant and Resident Engineers on the work on which Capek was working, copy of report of the Beck Construction Company and my report to the Wisconsin Industrial Commission.

Yours truly,

A. G. EVERETT

Inclosure No. 1, copy of report by the railroad's assistant engineer on the work:

MILWAUKEE, WIS., June 13, 1914

Mr. A. G. Everett, Asst. Chief Engineer
Chicago, Illinois

DEAR SIR: In regard to the complaint made by the industrial Commission of Wisconsin on account of mistreatment of laborers on the New Wood River Extension, this complaint refers to Frank Capek gang which was doing work between station 648 and the New Wood River. It appears that the contractor had some trouble with these men on account of them not pursuing the work as vigorously as it seemed they should. The climax of the trouble was reached when they claimed that they could not get food supplies to their camps. At the time in question, the roads into the camps were practically impassable and the supplies were left a short distance east of Capek's camp and on the opposite side of the river. It has been the practice of the contractor to deliver the supplies to each camp, charging the station gangs pro rata for the cost. As the contractor was unable to deliver the supplies to the camp, he left them a short distance away and told Capek that he would pay him if he would go and get the supplies and bring them in himself. This he declined to do and on May 8th the entire gang left the work. Most of the men of this crew could speak and understand English; all of Mr. Jackson's men will attest to that fact.

I presume there had been more or less dissatisfaction, as the work was difficult and this crew did not understand station work very well and that the matter of getting the supplies to the camp was merely the culmination of this dissatisfaction. The crew left the work, simply throwing down their tools and walked off and did not come to Mr. Jackson for their estimate. They had never had an estimate for the work done. On May 9th Mr. Jackson measured up the work and sent an estimate by request to the general contractor so that he could make a settlement with this crew. It is not our practice to give estimates to the general contractor for station work, but to give estimates to the station men themselves and let them take them to the contractors. The estimate which Mr. Jackson gave the Beck Construction Company was as follows:

Grubbing...............	106 square rods
Earth..................	483 cubic yards
Loose rock.............	1,235 cubic yards
Solid rock.............	508 cubic yards
Overhaul...............	9,350 cubic yards

He retained 126 cubic yards on account of the work not being finished, i.e., the slopes were not taken down, ditching was not done, etc. I think this estimate was handled correctly.

The Beck Construction Company did not ask particularly for the total amount of yardage moved, for if they had, it would have been increased by 126 cubic yards; they merely asked for the estimate.

I haven't any idea that the Beck Construction Company misrepresented anything to these laborers. The misunderstanding rests in the fact that they undoubtedly thought they would make at least day wages on this subcontract. I am of the opinion that the laborers on this line have received very good treatment at the hands of the general contractors.

O. H. HENRY, *Assistant Engineer*

Inclosure No. 2, report of the resident engineer of the railroad:

Referring to Capek Estimate Station 662-25–678-73, I gave the Beck Construction Company an estimate as follows:

Grubbing	106	square rods
Earth	483	cubic yards
Loose rock	1,235	cubic yards
Solid rock	508	cubic yards
	2,226	
Overhaul	9,350	cubic yards

Work actually done by Capek's gang was as follows:

Grubbing	106	square rods
Earth	517	cubic yards
Loose rock	1,294	cubic yards
Solid rock	541	cubic yards
	2,352	
Overhaul	9,350	cubic yards

The classification was the same as for the April estimate. The difference of 126 cubic yards was held back on account of finishing left undone—sloping and ditching of cuts.

Yours truly,

R. W. JACKSON, *Resident Engineer*

Inclosure No. 3, copy of the report of the Beck Construction Company to the assistant chief engineer of the railroad:

DEAR SIR:

We have yours of June 4th, enclosing copies of letters from the Industrial Commission of Wisconsin, regarding the claim of Frank Capek *et al.*, to the effect that they have not been paid for labor on our work at Merrill.

Beg to advise you that it appears that these men have grossly misrepresented their case to their representative, for as a matter of fact these men left this work indebted to this company, in support of which we are handing you herewith a statement of their account showing a balance overdrawn of $110.06.

In regard to the statement that these men could not speak or understand English, beg to advise you that this is not a fact as Mr. Beck and the writer as well as Mr. Davis has spoken to nearly all of them in English, and they replied in English, and as to the matter of the contract being in English and not understood by them, beg to advise you that in every case where we employ station men, the contract is fully explained to them before it is signed, and all of these men signed the contract after such an explanation had been made to them, and all their signatures are in English. We do not understand the logic of their assertion to the effect that they were required to sign the contract before they received rubber boots which they needed. In the first place rubber boots on this work were not necessary, although it is possible that they have reference to rubber overshoes as they took this work in the winter time. However, it certainly is not expected that we would furnish supplies of this nature before any contract was entered into, whereby we would have at least some possible assurance that these parties would start to work.

We certainly must deny their statement to the effect that for the last five weeks they were there the food which they ordered was not brought in. They had received promptly up to that time all the groceries and supplies that they had ordered, with the exception of one order that was left within one-half mile of their camp on the afternoon of the day before they left the camp; the reason for this being that the roads were so absolutely impassable that the groceries could not reach their camp that night. It would have been possible for them, however, to have gone where the groceries were and carried them to camp, but this they positively refused to do, even though Mr. Beck advised them that he would pay them at the rate of $2.00 per day for doing so.

You will also note that they claim that they had only potatoes and flour on hand at their camp. Beg to advise you, however, that the following groceries were found in their camp at the time they left, which was in addition to the bill of groceries that was within one-half mile of their camp:

3 lbs. Tea	3 Doz. cans milk
85 lbs. Sugar	100 lbs. Flour
¼ Can lard	5 lbs. Kraut
3 Pieces bacon	15 lbs. Dried apples
5 lbs. Raisins	5 Bushels potatoes
20 lbs. Oleomargarine	3 Packages cornstarch

In regard to the statement to the effect that these men were discharged on May 7th, beg to advise that this is not a true statement, as Mr. Beck, Mr. Davis and the writer were at their camp the afternoon of May 7th and found them all at the camp idle. We again came to their camp on the morning of May 8th and still found them idle, they claiming that the reason they were not working was that they had no food. This, notwithstanding the fact that there was the above-mentioned supplies of groceries in the camp and the additional supply that was within one-half mile of their camp, which they refused to go after, even though Mr. Beck had agreed to pay them wages for doing so. It was only on the morning of May 7th that they used up their last supply of eggs and in the supply that was within one-half mile of the camp, there was an additional supply of eggs. They were, however, informed by Mr. Beck that he was very anxious that they should go ahead with their work and complete it, as it would be very difficult to interest a new gang for the comparatively small amount of work, remaining undone, but that of course if they would not work, that we could no longer be put to the expense of boarding them and they would have to leave camp, which we think you will recognize as being a fully justified action.

In connection with this work, you understand that we furnished to these men rails, cars, bolts, spikes and rail splices free, delivered to them on the right of way, and in all cases the bolts, spikes and straps are to a very large extent lost; also the expense of getting this equipment to the work is extremely high, in this case the expense amounting to about $300. In the case of small tools such as shovels, picks, bars, etc., it is understood that they are to be given credit for all tools of this character that they return when the work is completed. You will notice in the statement that they have been given credit for the supply of feed, explosives and groceries on hand, amounting to $88.23. You will also note in the statement of their account that they have been furnished quite a considerable amount of clothing and tobacco.

We regret very much that you should be annoyed by a matter of this kind that cannot always be avoided and we trust that the foregoing will be sufficient to enable you to fully satisfy the Commission that no hardship has been by us imposed upon these men.

Very truly yours,

MILES MCCARTHY

(*For the James Beck Construction Co.*)

Inclosure No. 4, copy of letter to Wisconsin Industrial Commission from the office of the chief engineer of the Chicago Milwaukee and St. Paul Railroad:

OFFICE OF CHIEF ENGINEER, CHICAGO
June 27, 1914

Industrial Commission of Wisconsin
Madison, Wisconsin

GENTLEMEN: Referring to your letter of June 1st in regard to the treatment of laborers by the Henry Beck Construction Company who are working for this company near Merrill, Wisconsin: This matter has been investigated by our men, and I hand you herewith a copy of their report, also a copy of the letter received from the Beck Construction Company.

It appears that some of the statements made by these laborers are in error. It is customary among the railroad contractors to sublet small pieces of work to gangs of men and furnish them the necessary supplies for prosecuting the work, and when the work is completed settle with them on the basis of the engineer's estimates.

It is the custom of the Engineering Department on this road to furnish the estimate to the gang upon application to the resident engineer. The spokesman, or foreman of the gang, takes the estimate furnished by the engineer and goes with it to the nearest headquarters of the contractor and makes his settlement for the work performed. Testimony of both our engineers and of the Beck Construction Company goes to show that these men involved in this dispute could talk English, and a part of them, at least, could write as the Beck Construction Company state that certain members of the gang signed the contract. When the men decided that they did not care to complete the amount of work that they had contracted to do, instead of applying to the engineer for a statement of the various quantities handled, they left the work without notifying our engineer, consequently they left the work without an estimate, which estimate they could have had upon application. The work in question is being carried on through an uninhabited country with no roads to speak of except such trails as the contractors made to haul in their supplies. When the spring weather came on, such roads as were in use were in a very bad condition and the hauling of supplies was a very difficult proposition. It was necessary for our own engineers to pack a greater part of their supplies in on their backs. However, this station gang refused to do this which, under the existing circumstances, shows that they were not anxious to co-operate with the contractor in his difficulties. My personal opinion is that they are not entitled to a great deal of sympathy.

You will please note attached estimate of the work performed by this gang, signed by Mr. R. W. Jackson, the resident engineer, who is authorized to make such estimates. The classification of earth and rock is similar to that furnished to other gangs working in this vicinity and I have every reason to believe is ample.

You will please note that the resident engineer states that he held back 126 yards when he found that the gang had left the work. I wish to say in explanation that this is a customary thing to do as the gang leaving the work does not, and did not in this case, clean up the odds and ends of the work the same as they would have, had the work been entirely completed.

This 126 yards is used as a bonus for the next gang that is placed on the work. Had they stayed with the job until it was accepted by the engineer they would have received payment for the entire amount.

Yours truly,

A. G. EVERETT, *Assistant Chief Engineer*

July 1, 1914.—Letter written to Mr. Everett:

MY DEAR MR. EVERETT:

I have read very carefully your report to the Wisconsin Industrial Commission as well as the reports of your Assistant Engineer Mr. Henry and of Mr. McCarthy of the Beck Construction Company and have found nothing in them that convinces me that these Bohemians understood the contract they were signing. Frank Capek, who acted as foreman or leader of the gang, spoke English after a fashion and has had several years' experience in railroad work. He is, however, unable to read and write English and absolutely unable to understand the language of this contract were it read to him. As to the other men—three of them, if I remember correctly, speak a few words of English—the others cannot even do this. The extraordinary suggestion which is made in the reports that because the men *signed the contract in English* they must have known English shows that the contractor is apparently ignorant of the fact that the Bohemians use the same alphabet as we do and did not therefore sign their names in English any more than in Polish, French, Italian or any one of the other languages in which the Latin script is used.

Two of the men, Frank Malacka and Vaclav Malacka, while newcomers and therefore ignorant of English, are well educated and very good witnesses. We have sent them to farm work so they are not available at the present moment. They and the other men, I believe, did understand the *rates of payment* for the excavation as they are given in the contract but regarded this as "piecework" substitute for day wages. They had, however, no conception of what was involved in their being designated as "subcontractors" and would have little difficulty in convincing a jury of this fact.

Aside from the question of whether the contract could not be repudiated because of the method by which it was secured there are parts of Mr. McCarthy's statements that the men would question, for example: (1) the charge of $655.44 for groceries, tobacco, clothing, and horse-feed—their slips total a little more than $300 for these items; (2) why are they given no credit for camp buildings, utensils, blankets, tools, and tool supplies which were all left behind them; and (3) if it was impossible for the contractors to reach the camp with the last supply of provisions why was it assumed that it was possible for the men to get to the place where the food was left?

As I review the whole statement, it reads to me much like some we have had from the South where the longer the men worked the more they got into debt to the company for which they were working. These men were doing what the engineer and the contractor describe as difficult work. As payment for three months of this hard work, they received, according to the contractor's statement, $11.69 worth of clothing and very poor board —for example, only $3.00 worth of meat of any sort for eight men during the month of April. When they left, according to the company's method of figuring the supplies that were furnished them, they were in the company's debt $110.06. It does not seem to me that this will appeal to you as in any sense reasonable, and I trust that you will agree that the Immigrants' Protective League will have to advise them not to accept this accounting.

Sincerely yours,

LYDIA GARDNER

July 2, 1914.—Letter from the Wisconsin Industrial Commission inclosing copies of letters sent by Mr. Everett to the Industrial Commission (already received, see above). The letter concludes with the following sentence: "It seems to me that the Assistant Chief Engineer has heard only the employer's side of the question, and it might be well for you to call on him in the Railway Exchange Building and explain the men's side to him. If we can be of any further assistance in this matter, please do not hesitate to call upon us." *Later.*—Letter of acknowledgment to Wisconsin Industrial Commission, inclosing copy of letter sent to Mr. Everett on July 1.

July 3, 1914.—The following letter received (addressed to the Bohemian visitor of the League) [translated from the Bohemian]:

Please tell me kindly how our case is getting on regarding the money. I would have written you sooner but I had no permanent place. Now I am working on harvest and I shall be here one week and a half. I beg you to notify me about my case as soon as possible.

FRANK CAPEK

DEWITT, NEBRASKA
CARE OF L. KLAUS

[The record for July, August, and September is not copied. The matter was taken up with an experienced attorney, Mr. C. P. Black, who was a member of the League. He promptly offered to take the case for a nominal contingent fee. It was then necessary to get in touch with the eight men who were to be plaintiffs in the case. They had all "shipped out" to casual jobs of various kinds in the western states. They were all notified to come to the Immigrants' Protective League office immediately they returned to Chicago.]

November 23, 1914.—The two Malacka brothers came into the office. They have been working all summer on farms in Iowa, have good clothes and $150 in cash. They are very eager to "get justice" from the construction company. They promised to stay in town until the law suit is started and will help to find the other men.

November 27, 1914.—Frank Capek came in with the Malacka brothers. Telephoned Mr. Black. He will see them Monday, November 30. B. P. [Bohemian visitor of the League] is to accompany the men.

[The record beyond this point deals with the preparation and prosecution of the case and was largely in Mr. Black's hands. On January 15, 1915, the case of *Capek et al.* v. *Beck Construction Company* was filed in the Municipal Court of Chicago, case No. 524499. Hearings were held as follows: January 22; February 16, 18, and 20; March 8, 9, 12, 15, 19, 30; April 7, 8, 9, 12, 13, 14. On April 14 the jury found against the Construction Company and assessed damages at $325 and costs in favor of the men. The attorney for the defendant made a motion for a new trial. Hearing on this motion set for April 27, 1915, later postponed to May 1, postponed to May 8, postponed to May 14, postponed to May 18. On May 18, 1915, the motion for a new trial was overruled and the verdict of the jury for $325 and costs was sustained. The Construction Company then appealed the case, and it went to the Appellate Court. Neither the League, the attorney for the men, nor the men themselves wished to pay additional expenses made necessary by the appeal, i.e., court costs plus the cost of filing printed briefs. It was finally decided to furnish the money for court costs and typewritten briefs and to ask the court to allow the filing of typewritten briefs. If the court would not allow typewritten briefs, the attorney would do what he could by arguing it orally upon the hearing. The expenses for this case came to $53.58 for "filing suit," "appearance fee," and stenographic charges.]

November 19, 1915.—The following letter was sent to Judge X. of the Appellate Court by the Immigrants' Protective League in support of the attorney's request for permission to reduce expenses for the men by filing typewritten instead of printed briefs:

MY DEAR JUDGE X.:

I am taking the liberty of writing to you with regard to the appeal in the case of *Capek et al.* v. *Beck Construction Company.* We have been interested in helping the plaintiffs, Frank Capek and seven other Bohemian laborers, to push their claims since the circumstances in this case may be said to be typical of the kinds of exploitation from which many of our applicants suffer. The expense involved in the collection of a wage claim like this makes it seem that the merits of controversies of this sort can largely be decided by a court. We have got the money together for the court costs up to this point, but it will be quite impossible to pay for printed briefs. Mr. Black, our attorney, tells me that you said you could not hear a motion to file typewritten briefs until the men's appearance was filed. I understand now that this motion has been denied and I am writing to know if there may not be some way of modifying this decision. I understand that there are precedents for the filing of typewritten briefs, and I am sure you wish these men to have the opportunity to be heard on their claim, not only because you want justice to be done to these individual men but also because of the increase in industrial unrest which a situation like this creates. We shall be very grateful if you can find it possible to waive the requirement of a printed brief in this case.

Yours very sincerely,

LYDIA GARDNER, *Superintendent*
Immigrants' Protective League

SOCIAL CASE RECORDS 643

November 21, 1915.—Reply from Judge X. as follows:

Miss Lydia Gardner, Director
Immigrants' Protective League

MY DEAR MISS GARDNER: In answer to yours of the 19th in re *Capek* v. *Beck Construction Company*, No. 57221: The rules of court require that all briefs be printed, but I am informed by those oldest in service that typewritten briefs have never been allowed, although there are innumerable cases before us in which the lack of funds is as great as in the case you speak of. In other words, there are no special circumstances in this case different from those in many other cases, which call for an exception to our rules.

As your Mr. Black was informed, it is not absolutely necessary that a brief be filed. The case for the plaintiffs may be argued orally to the court and the merits of the controversy fully presented in this way. Many attorneys are of the opinion that oral argument has an advantage over the printed brief.

Yours very truly,

A. E. X.

April 11, 1916.—The following letter received from Mr. Black:

MY DEAR MISS GARDNER:

I am pleased to inform you that the Appellate Court has today handed down an opinion affirming the decision of the Municipal Court in the case of *Capek* v. *Beck Construction Company* in our favor. The defendant has twenty days within which to file a petition for re-hearing and when that is disposed of we ought to get our money.

Very truly yours,

CHARLES P. BLACK

April 12, 1916.—A copy of the opinion of the court in the Capek case received from Mr. Black as follows:

FRANK CAPEK ET AL., *Defendants in Error*
v.
HENRY BECK CONSTRUCTION CO., *Plaintiffs in Error*

To Municipal Court of Chicago

MR. PRESIDING JUSTICE X. delivered the opinion of the court.

Plaintiffs, eight in number, brought suit for the value of their services as laborers, while employed by the defendant. Upon trial, the jury returned a verdict against defendant for $325.00, upon which judgment was entered. Defendant seeks to have this judgment reversed. No briefs have been filed or arguments made in this court on behalf of plaintiffs.

The defendant is engaged in general railroad contracting. At the time in question, it was engaged in grading the right of way of the Chicago, Milwaukee and St. Paul Railway Company in Wisconsin. Through an employment agency in Chicago, plaintiffs were sent to the place of this work. Before commencing work, these laborers were asked to sign a contract, which apparently was signed by each of them. This contract is now interposed as a defense. We have inspected the original contract as it appears in the record. It fills the page of legal cap and is typewritten in half-space. There are also interlineations and insertions made with pen and ink in various places. It has been difficult for this court to understand parts of it, or even to read all of some of its provisions. In its general scheme, it seems to be an attempt to fix upon each of the laborers, the character of the subcontractor with conditions, that he should receive no pay for his work until the engineers of the Railway Company should, in writing, approve the work of all of the so-called sub-contractors. It also contemplates that from the laborers' pay should be deducted, rent of cars, truck and tools, and these must be returned in as good condition, as when furnished, and if not, the laborers were to be charged for their full value. There is also a provision written with pen and ink, which is not wholly legible, but it seems to obligate the laborers to assume the cost of constructing a camp and open roads, and other work done before they arrived at this place.

These laborers were born in foreign countries, most, if not all, in Bohemia. They had been in this country only a short time, and worked as hand laborers at track work. They were ignorant of English. Some of them testified that when the contract was presented, they were told that it was a receipt for rubber boots, which were given them. None of them understood what, in effect, they were signing.

From these facts, with other circumstances, the jury were at liberty to conclude that signing of the contract was procured by fraud. From the verdict, it was evident that the jury were of that opinion, and with this conclusion, this court, without hesitation, is in accord, and the mere statement of the facts, impels to this conclusion. A contract procured by fraud, in fact, is invalid, and therefore falls from the case.

Objections were made to the ruling of the court upon the introduction of testimony and to the instructions to the jury, but errors in this respect, if any, are not of sufficient importance to require a reversal. The points offered by counsel for defendant do not persuade us.

Plaintiffs were entitled to recover a reasonable value for their services as laborers. The evidence justifies the amount returned by the verdict. The judgment is right, and is affirmed.

AFFIRMED

April 29, 1916.—Judgment and costs paid $353.65.

[During the month of May various efforts were made to find the eight men who were to receive the money.]

May 5, 1916.—Advertisements were placed in three Bohemian papers, giving the names of eight men and asking them to come to the office of the League for their money.

May 6, 1916.—One man (Horak) came in reply to the advertisement. He does not know where the others are. Mr. Horak signed a receipt for his money. He will try to find out where the men are.

June 1, 1916.—Letter received from a friend of one of the men. This friend had evidently seen the advertisement. [Translation from Bohemian. Address is to Bohemian visitor of the League.]

DORCHESTER, NEBRASKA
May 29, 1916

DEAR MRS. P—:

I have spoken last time with Mr. Malacka in August past year, when he was just going to South Dakota, town of Taboc.

Yours truly,

VACLAV COMENSKY

July 15, 1916.—The following letter received [translation from Bohemian]:

Miss P—:

I beg you very much to tell me what the matter with C Visconsin Meril. I got a job here probably for one month. Having no penny I am not able to send you a postage stamp. I should like to know if we shall get anything.—Frank Laski, Ashland, Box 532, Neb., that's my address.

September 9, 1916.—Frank Capek came to the office to ask if case had been settled yet. He walked all the way from Minneapolis to Chicago because he said he would never give anything to the railroad. B. P. sent him to Mr. Black for his money.

October 12, 1916.—Letter in Bohemian addressed to B. P. [Bohemian visitor of the League] received [translation]:

Dear Mrs. P—:

Please accept my most cordial regards and also these few lines. I am in South Dakota now, working at a butcher store. I have quite a good place here. Dear Mrs. P—, I should like to know the court decision in our case; you know, I am one of those eight who has the case with the railway company. You are the only person who can give me any information about it. If we got some money please send me it. I thank you very much. I should rather like money, because I am going to be married and you can imagine then that I need money as salt and also for my brother to whom I owe some.

Yours truly,
Vaclav Malacka

Telephoned Mr. Black to send check.

November 1, 1916.—Letter from Vaclav Malacka: "Thanks for all the Immigrants' Protective League has done for us."

[The men were gradually located. One of them, however, was not found until January, 1920. Bohumil Cermak had enlisted after the United States entered the war and had gone to Detroit after his discharge and had a "steady job" in Detroit. His check, the last of the eight, was mailed to him January 24, 1920.]

24. Twenty-five Bulgarian Laborers in Mississippi

[The following letters give an account of the shipment of some immigrant Bulgarians for construction work in the South. The League did not succeed in helping them.]

1. Letter from Mr. Masureff, a Bulgarian living in Granite City, Illinois, to the Superintendent of the Immigrants' Protective League:

100 Main Street
Granite City, Illinois
November 11

My dear Miss Gardner:

I do not know if your League can help me much in a case I want to present to you, but I will present it to you so that you can at least take note of it.

Some twenty-five Bulgarians were sent by one of our merchants (K. Areff) and a labor agent from St. Louis to Mr. Davis Howell at Algoma, Mississippi, to work for him on ties for railroad tracks. They went about June and worked for three months. Made 7,570 ties at the rate of 14 cents apiece. They received no pay for their work, and for this they left the work. All they got was food and lodging in a camp. They had tools and kitchen ware, which they were compelled by threatening with revolvers to leave all there, and came back penniless. The men are dependent, as the merchant who sent them from up here did not allow them go out from Granite City to work but while seeing them to have gone to the station he went with a policeman and after taking their money from the ticket agent for what they owed him turned them back into his quarters to live. I wish you could suggest me what can be done for taking what is coming to the men, if you can get some advice for the case.

Can we reach and compel the contractor to pay or can we hold the merchant or the labor agent responsible and make them stand good for the claimed wages? Does the merchant have any right to keep the men here, not allowing them to go and look for work or even go to work outside of Granite City? If you can suggest anything I will be very much obliged to you.

Yours truly,
P. D. Masureff

2. Letter, dated November 13, to Honorable Edward Fisher, Labor Commissioner, Springfield, Illinois, from the Superintendent of the Immigrants' Protective League:

My dear Mr. Fisher:

We have had a complaint about a Mr. K. Areff, of Granite City, Illinois. Our report is that he sent twenty-five Bulgarians, acting through a labor agent in St. Louis, to work for Mr. Davis Howell at Algoma, Mississippi, making railroad ties. They made 7,570 for which they were to be paid 14 cents apiece. These men were not paid, but returned to Granite City, and, according to our report, are being held by Mr. Areff and not allowed to work for whomever they please or to leave Granite City. Evidently, Mr. Areff paid their fare over, and they are indebted to him. I do not know whether Mr. Areff is a licensed employment agent or not. If not, it might be easy for you to do something for these men. Will you please let me know what, if anything, can be done? Thanking you very much for the help, which I am sure you will give us, if possible, I am,

Sincerely yours,

LYDIA GARDNER

3. Letter, dated November 13, to Davis Howell, Algoma, Mississippi, from the Superintendent of the Immigrants' Protective League:

MY DEAR SIR:

The complaint has been made to us that twenty-five Bulgarians sent to work for you by a Mr. K. Areff, of Granite City, made 7,570 ties for which they were to be paid 14 cents apiece, and received no pay; and that their kitchen ware and tools were taken from them, and they came home penniless. Mr. Areff, I believe, acted through a St. Louis labor agency, and you may perhaps be able to trace the men by that means. I hope there has been no difficulty of this sort; but if there has, I feel sure that you will want these men to be paid. I shall be much obliged to you if you will furnish us any information about this whole matter.

Sincerely yours,

LYDIA GARDNER

(For the Immigrants' Protective League)

4. Letter, dated November 14, from the Illinois Commissioner of Labor to the Superintendent of the Immigrants' Protective League:

MY DEAR MISS GARDNER:

I am in receipt of your letter of the 13th inst. referring to complaint against a Mr. K. Areff, of Granite City, Illinois, who it is charged had sent twenty-five Bulgarians to Algoma, Mississippi, where they were to be employed in making railroad ties; that they received no compensation for their labor and returned to Granite City and are now held by Mr. Areff, who is not a licensed employment agent. I have referred your communication to Mr. Henry Dell, Superintendent of the Illinois Free Employment Office of East St. Louis, Illinois, with instructions that he thoroughly investigate the complaint in this case. On receipt of a statement of the facts, we will be able to advise you what action this department can take.

Yours very truly,

EDWARD FISHER

5. Letter of inquiry dated November 16, from the Superintendent of the East St. Louis Branch of the Illinois Employment Office saying:

As I wish to start an investigation of this report at once, I would be pleased to have the name of your informant so I can call on him, or her, as a clue to begin on.

Very respectfully,

HENRY DELL

6. A letter dated November 17, giving the East St. Louis Superintendent the name and address of Mr. P. D. Masureff, the Bulgarian gentleman of Granite City, Illinois, is omitted.

648   IMMIGRATION: DOCUMENTS AND CASE RECORDS

7. Letter dated November 25, from the Illinois Commissioner of Labor to the Superintendent of the Immigrants' Protective League:

MY DEAR MISS GARDNER:

Referring further to my letter of November 14, you are advised that I am in receipt of a report from our agent at East St. Louis, regarding the complaint made in the interest of twenty-five Bulgarians who were sent from Granite City, Illinois, about the middle of last June, to Algoma, Mississippi, or some point near there, will say, there seems to be some doubt as to the persons or corporation hiring these people and they are unable to explain for whom they were working. Upon their return to Granite City, some of them were detained by Mr. K. Areff, one of their countrymen, until they settled with him for rent and board. That part of the obligation has evidently been discharged as the parties have all left Granite City. Mr. Dell, upon investigation, believes that a Mr. William B. Brown, Labor Agent, Arlington Block, St. Louis, Missouri, procured the services of these men and believes that, if he can be forced to tell where they were sent to, the employer can be located and forced to pay the money alleged to be due these men as wages. There seems to be some complication as to the time of work, some stating that it was eight weeks and others that it was two weeks; that the employer at the time when they quit work stated that there was nothing due them as wages as all that they had earned was due on account of transportation and board.

I will communicate with Mr. Brown at the address given and request him to advise this office on whose account those men were employed. Mr. Areff, one of their countrymen, who advanced them money to settle the claim of Mr. Brown, did prevent five of these men from leaving Granite City and, in fact, had their transportation cancelled and tried to get the money paid by them for railroad fares from the agent. The agent refused to turn over to him the money advanced on account of such transportation. The amount he holds on that account is $21.86, which amount he is ready to turn over when authorized to do so by the proper authority. Mr. Dell also advises that the attention of the Department of Immigration at Washington, D.C., has been advised of the matter and that an investigation is under way by it. On receipt of the report from Mr. Brown, if one is received, will advise you of the same. There appears to be nothing in Mr. Dell's report that would justify this department in taking any action. The liability is in an adjoining state. Mr. Brown is presumably the responsible agent in this matter and should be prosecuted if the statement made can be confirmed, under the laws of Missouri or by the Federal Department of Immigration.

Yours very truly,

EDWARD FISHER

8. Letter, dated November 25, from the Superintendent of East St. Louis Branch of the Illinois Employment Offices to the Immigrants' Protective League:

MY DEAR MISS GARDNER:

I have completed the investigation of the report concerning K. Areff and the twenty-five Bulgarian laborers of Granite City, Illinois, and made a written report of same to Mr. Fisher, who no doubt will advise you of the results. Thanking you for your favor of the 17th inst., I beg to remain,

Yours very respectfully,

HENRY DELL

9. Letter, dated November 30, from the Illinois Commissioner of Labor to the Superintendent of the Immigrants' Protective League:

MY DEAR MISS GARDNER:

In further answer to my letter of the 25th inst. I enclose herewith a copy of a letter received this morning from William B. Brown, which is self-explanatory. I have furnished the Labor Commissioner of Missouri with this letter. It is his duty, if the complaint in this case can be sustained, to prosecute the employment agency through which these men were engaged. I understand that the laws regulating private employment agencies of Missouri are fashioned somewhat along the lines of our own.

Yours very truly,

EDWARD FISHER

Inclosure (copy):

Commissioner of Labor
Springfield, Illinois

DEAR SIR: In reply to yours of the 27th in regard to the twenty-five Bulgarians sent to Mississippi about the 12th of June, I beg to inform you that these men were hired by the Scott Labor Agency of St. Louis, for the Algoma Tie Company of Algoma, Mississippi, to make railroad ties for that company and were to work piecework. I do not remember how much they were to receive per tie but each man signed an agreement, stating that they were experienced tie-makers and that they were to go to Algoma, Mississippi, and work piecework for the said company and that they were to reimburse the company for transportation and tools that the Algoma Tie Company were to advance for them. This agreement was signed in presence of K. Areff, clerk, and Steve Mickleson, the interpreter who went with these men at their request and at their expense. K. Areff paid a small amount of the fee cash and balance by time check, payable after 19 days, providing the work and quarters were satisfactory to those men. This check K. Areff no doubt has on file cancelled. I cannot say what arrangement Mr. Areff made with these men but think he took their notes. The Algoma Tie Company have a copy of this agreement and the men also have a copy of it.

Yours very truly,

WILLIAM B. BROWN

10. Letter dated December 1, from Mr. Masureff, the Bulgarian gentleman in Granite City to the Superintendent of the Immigrants' Protective League:

DEAR MISS GARDNER:

Enclosed I sent you a list of names of thirty-seven men who have been overcharged by the agent whose card I have also enclosed herewith. The figures against each name show first the amount collected when the men were sent to work; the second figures the amount collected on the first pay day, after which the men were discharged from the work; the last figures show the total amount collected. The men were told and agreed to pay ten dollars apiece as agency fee, and you see that some have paid eleven, others twelve, sixteen, etc. I wrote to the state agent in East St. Louis who referred the matter to the Commissioner, and the latter wrote to me as the men, the agent and the work are under different states he could do nothing and suggests we could see the Railroad Company for the money overpaid to the agent by their officer. I do not hope we could get any of these moneys back and send it to you for information.

Yours truly,

P. D. MASUREFF

11. Letter, dated December 4, from Miss Mary Russell, Director of the South Road Settlement, St. Louis, Missouri, to the Director of the Immigrants' Protective League:

MY DEAR MISS GARDNER:

I thank you for your letter of December fourth and also for the letters you inclosed with regard to the Bulgarians who have suffered through a St. Louis Employment Agency. I assure you that I shall take up this matter immediately and shall let you know if there are any indications of satisfactory results.

Very sincerely yours,

MARY RUSSELL

25. Joseph Toney
(Difficulties of a Chiccgo Laborer Sent to a Wisconsin "Job")

March 29, 1921.—Miss Richards, Superintendent, Memorial Lodging House, telephoned that Joe Toney, who has been working most satisfactorily as their janitor since May, 1920, has been arrested by the United States immigration authorities, is now in the county jail, and is to be deported on April 8. Joe is an Austrian Pole, age twenty-three. Miss Richards gave these facts: Joe Toney was sent by some Chicago Employment Agent to Wisconsin to work sometime in 1918. After a week he was discharged and refused wages because the foreman claimed he hadn't even earned his fare up there. The man was penniless and did not know how to get back to Chicago. Finally he borrowed a hand car to take him to the next town, where he hoped to get work. He did not know much about running hand cars and left a switch open. No accident happened fortunately. Later Toney was arrested and sentenced to three years in Green Bay, Wisconsin, jail. He did not serve all his sentence but was paroled to the Chicago Parole Association in May, 1920, was to pay one-fourth his wages as a "bond." He went last week to see how long he would be expected to make these payments. He was sent to Mr. Hendrichs (United States immigration officer). The latter placed him under arrest and is having him deported. Miss Richards says Joe has been a most excellent employee, is very intelligent and has been learning a good deal about engineering in his odd time. There is an engineering firm in the neighborhood that is going to take him on just as soon as his parole expires and he can change his job. Miss Richards thinks it is most unjust that he should be sent back to Europe. He is a quiet, law-abiding fellow of good habits.

March 30, 1921.—Visited Chicago Parole Association for Assisting Discharged Prisoners. Mr. Emory [Superintendent] is out of town but will be back March 31. Their record shows Joe Toney paroled May 25, 1920, and Mr. Emory made parole officer by the United States Immigration Department. Joe Toney served 32 months in Green Bay, Wisconsin, jail, for "larceny of a hand car." Record also contains following data: *habits:* "good"; *mental condition:* "fair"; *physical condition:* "good"; *early environment:* "fair." He paid $10 per month up to December. This money was apparently toward a bond for the immigration authorities.

March 31, 1921.—Visited Chicago Parole Association. Mr. Emory said Joe had been most satisfactory in his work and is meeting all requirements as to reports, etc. He thinks Joe was very badly treated by the employment agency and the Wisconsin employers. Mr. Emory does not think Joe ought to be deported. He says Joe's behavior in prison was exemplary. Joe considers Warden X. one of his best friends and writes to him frequently. Joe buys all the brooms he uses at the lodging house from the prison. Mr. Emory will be glad to do what he can to prevent deportation. Mr. Emory also feels sure that Mr. Hendrichs, United States Inspector-in-Charge, would be glad to have Joe allowed to remain if the Immigration Law allowed him to use his own discretion. Joe has been on parole only until conditions in Europe made deportation feasible. He maintains he has been in this country for years but cannot give definite facts. He claims to have relatives in Pittsburgh who can give desired information. Their names and possible addresses given to Mr. Hendrichs, who has evidently found them useless. Mr. Emory will write at once to Board of Control, Wisconsin, and ask Secretary to push the matter of a pardon with the Governor. He will also write the Governor in the matter. He will see Mr. Hendrichs to ask for extension of time.

Later.—Called at the Cook County Jail but could not talk satisfactorily to Joseph Toney because unable to talk to him through the double screen. The assistant jailer said that special permission could be granted tomorrow morning after 9 A.M. to see him in the bundle cage.

April 1, 1921.—Visited Joseph. He says if he could go to Pittsburgh, Pennsylvania, he would get his papers showing that he arrived in December either 1911 or 1912. He thinks it was in 1911. He has a brother, Andrew Toneicki, in Donora, Pennsylvania, who has his passport. He thinks his brother could be reached by sending a letter there as he has a post-office box. He works in the steel mills in Donora. His two cousins, Joe and Mike Tomm, are also in Donora, Pennsylvania. Man begs us to help him.

April 2, 1921.—Spoke with Mr. Hendrichs, Immigration Inspector, about the case. When Toney was discharged May, 1920, he was paroled to the Chicago Parole Association until it could be learned when he came to the United States. Immigration Department succeeded in finding that he came in September, 1912, S.S. "Vaterland," under name of Joseph Toneicki. He was destined to brother Andrew Toneicki, Donora, Pennsylvania, so he arrived almost five years before being sent to prison.

Mr. Hendrichs advised writing Commissioner of Immigration, Washington, for a stay of deportation until a pardon can be secured.

April 4, 1921.—Telephoned Mr. Emory. He wrote Friday to the Governor of Wisconsin for a pardon but he has not heard anything yet. On Saturday Mr. Emory wired to Secretary of Labor and received reply Saturday afternoon from Assistant Secretary. He sees no reason why deportion should be stayed. Also Mr. Sargent, a director of the Association, leaves for Washington tonight and is to take a message to Commissioner of Immigration, asking clemency.

April 9, 1921.—Telephoned Mr. Emory. An eleventh-hour "stay" was granted by Washington. From what Mr. Emory has heard unofficially he believes the Governor of Wisconsin will be willing to grant man a pardon.

April 13, 1921.—Mr. Emory telephoned. The Governor of Wisconsin has granted man a pardon but nothing further has been heard from Washington. He is confident, however, that Washington will rescind the order of deportation or put the man on parole for one year. He will let us know if any other difficulties arise.

July 15, 1922.—L. G. saw Miss Richards, who gave further report about Joe Toney. He has had a very good job as a mechanic in a garage for nearly a year and is going to evening technical school. He wants to learn to be an engineer. Miss Richards thinks he will succeed. He is a hard worker and saves his money. She says he comes to see them at the "House" often.

RECENT IMMIGRANTS ON FARMS

26. Vlas Deniches
(A Russian on a Wisconsin Farm)

February 17, 1915.—Vlas Deniches brought to office by Russian friend, Mr. A. Maroff, 935 West Place. Man wants work. Interviewed by R. B. [Russian visitor]. Man also wants help to find out about money he sent to Russia which his wife did not receive. Man lived in Montreal. He sent 20 rubles to his wife, Jevdakeja Deniches, at Shilovo, P.O. Zolotoe, Saratovsky, Russia. The money was sent June 21, 1914, through Canadian Express Company in Montreal. His wife wrote that she did not get the money. Man sent receipt to his wife; the latter went with it to post office. She was told that money was not there. Since man came to Chicago, he wrote to Canadian Express Company, complaining about it in Russian. Answer was received in English.

Mr. Deniches asked somebody in Wolta's bank, through whom he now sends money home, to translate it into English and was told it would cost him 50 cents. The man is out of work and cannot afford to pay. He was advised by friends to come to the League. Man wants any kind of work. He was a farmer at home; worked in foundry here. He has a wife and four children in Europe.

SOCIAL CASE RECORDS 653

February 19, 1915.—R. B. wrote Canadian Express Company:

On June 21, 1914, Vlas Deniches sent through the Montreal office of the Canadian Express Company to Jevdakeja Deniches, his wife, at Shilovo, P.O. Zolotoe, station Zolotoe, Saratovsky gubernia, Russia, the sum of $10.40 and holds your receipt, No. 2205695, for same. His wife has written him repeatedly that she had been unable to get the money. Will you kindly have it traced and advise us?

February 23, 1914.—Miss E—[Employment Supervisor] asks if Russian man could be sent to Wisconsin. [Place described in following letter:]

ALBERTA, WISCONSIN
February 22, 1915

The Immigrant Employment Agency
Chicago, Illinois

DEAR SIR: Will you please send me one farm hand. He must be a good milker. I want him to begin work March 1, at $25 per month, board and washing. He can come any day before March 1. I still have the last man you sent out, and he is a good one. Have him come to Alberta, Wisconsin, and I will meet him.

Very truly yours,
OSCAR FREITAG

February 27, 1915.—Man came in to inquire about his money order. He also asked again for some kind of work. R. B. spoke to him about Mr. Freitag of Alberta, Wisconsin. Vlas is willing to go on farm. He was a farmer at home and says he is a good milker and can take care of animals and is strong and able to do hard work on farm. Telephoned to Union Station; train leaves afternoons at 2:00.

[Telegram to Mr. Freitag and reply accepting Vlas and letter to Vlas omitted.]

February 28, 1915.—Vlas came with his bag and baggage. He also brought with him Alexander Speransky, his Russian landlord, to whom Vlas owes $4.60 for board. Vlas says that as soon as he gets his pay at the end of the month, he will send to R. B. [visitor] $5.00. Out of this she is to pay Alexander $4.60, and 40 cents he would like to give the League to cover the expense which we had getting him the job and tracing his money. His friends took man to station. R. B. gave him a letter to Mr. Freitag. Also sent a telegram to Mr. Freitag. Told him Mr. Freitag will pay him $25 per month.

[The remaining portion of the record is summarized in the following letters:]

March 5, 1915.—Letter from Vlas Deniches [translation from Russian]:

How do you do, honorable lady, from me Vlas Deniches, whom you sent out February 28. I thank you very much—the boss is very good, so is his wife and the man who works for them. Am very much satisfied, thank you very much. Lady, I am asking you about my money. Have you received any word from Montreal? You have sent me to one man, but he did not want to keep me. He kept me only one day and did not pay me for that day. His man and my present boss's man gave me together $5 to go back to Chicago. My present boss found out why they gave me the $5 so he said that as there is no work in Chicago, I better stay with him.

VLAS DENICHES

March 23, 1915.—Letter from William Merritt, Alberta, Wisconsin, with $5 from Vlas Deniches:

DEAR MADAM:

This man is working for me at the present time as Mr. Freitag was going to send him back to the city Monday morning. I will keep him for a while as long as I can as he did not have any money to go back to the city. Mr. Frietag and I have dissolved partnership, and I will run this farm myself as we own this place. I will do the best I can for this poor fellow.

Yours respectfully,
WILLIAM MERRITT

March 24, 1915.—Letter from Vlas Deniches [translation from Russian]:

I, Vlas Deniches, am sending this to you, Lady. I send you $5, please give it to Alexander, the man who was with me in your office. Pay him $4.60 for my board and room. You take the rest as I promised you before I left. And, please notify me. Also let me know about the $10 which I sent to Russia and which my wife did not get. And now, Lady, I am sending my best regards to you and wish you health. I am very much satisfied with you. If you will find the $10 I would like to thank you and count you among those who protect and help all people and I shall tell to the newspapers about you and how you were good to all people so that everybody should know you as a protector and people will wonder at your goodness and maybe I shall reward you with something, which you should choose. When you write to me mention the kind of present you would like, and now goodbye.

VLAS DENICHES

May 1, 1915.—Letter from Vlas Deniches:

How do you do Immigrants' Protective League. I Vlas Deniches am asking about my $10 which you should get from Montreal—if you get the $10 from Montreal. Did you get the receipt? Please let me know.

VLAS DENICHES

May 3, 1915.—Letter to William Merritt:

DEAR SIR:

We are sending you herewith a receipt which we received from the man to whom Vlas Deniches owed board. We appreciate very much the interest you are taking in the man and hope that you will be able to keep him permanently.

Very truly yours,
IMMIGRANTS' PROTECTIVE LEAGUE

May 6, 1915.—Letter from Vlas Deniches [translation from Russian]:

How do you do, Solicitress of the American Office. I sent June 21, 1914, $10 to Russia, and in Russia they did not receive the money yet. Please find out what about these dollars. If they come back send them to me.

VLAS DENICHES

[The money was finally traced by the Express Company, and notice received May 26.]

27. Vincent and Lucija Kleinaitis
(A Lithuanian Family in the Beetfields)

September 1, 1916.—Vincent Kleinaitis, Lithuanian man, in office, complains about treatment on farm in Michigan. *Later.*—Interviewed by J. H. Man says he is staying temporarily at 425 Maple Avenue, back of saloon. His wife, Lucija, and three children, Katie fourteen, Annie twelve, Vladja eight, are in Lincoln, Michigan, where he went with them in May to work a piece of land for a sugar beet company. Man is forty-eight years old and has been ten years in the United States. I remember I interpreted contract when man signed with beet company. Vincent Kleinaitis and family signed on April 30 in the United States Employment Office an agreement for hand labor on beets. Man was told that he will get 26 acres of land to work and that the beets were already planted. He says that when he went to Lincoln, May 4, he had no work for one month. The beets were not planted until May 28. Man had to wait for two weeks until they came up. Man worked only 18 acres because the land was so bad the beets would not grow on the other 8 acres.

While Mr. Kleinaitis was working, a farmer, Mr. John Schwartz, was the actual boss, but man says he made a contract with the sugar company and not with John Schwartz. Mr. John Schwartz paid Mr. Kleinaitis on August 26, and when he paid him told him that he could go home, that the rest of the work Mr. Schwartz will do himself, and that man has to pay his own way back. Mr. Kleinaitis got $8 for each of the 18 acres, total $144. Mr. Kleinaitis wants to finish his work. He did the hardest work on it, and now Mr. Schwartz wants to harvest and to get the "good pay." Man spent for board $120 and he earned $144. The fare to Chicago to make this complaint, $9.30—spent $130 in all. Thus he has not even earned enough to bring his family home again to Chicago. Man says he got job through advertisement for sugar-beet workers in "Naujienas" (Lithuanian newspaper). Man was anxious to get farm work.

[There is a cross-reference also under this date to the following correspondence in June, 1916, regarding conditions in Michigan:]

LINCOLN, X. COUNTY, MICHIGAN
June 7, 1916

Immigrants' Protective League
Chicago, Illinois
Miss Lydia Gardner, Secretary

DEAR MADAM: About six weeks ago the Lincoln Sugar Company of Lincoln, Michigan, brought into this vicinity some Hungarian families for the purpose of having them work in the beet fields of this neighborhood.

Now the rainy weather that has prevailed here for the last six or seven weeks has hindered the farmers from getting any of their crops sowed, those people who came to work have been without any kind of employment, and many of them are without the means to buy food, and the merchants will not give them credit, and conditions are becoming serious with some of them.

One of these families presented me with one of your cards and asked me to write you, and ask if you could do anything to relieve the situation, or do anything to compel the Sugar Company to advance to those who are destitute, some means on which they could live until they can get work to support themselves.

They say the Sugar Company guaranteed them plenty of work even before the beets were ready to be taken care of, so they would be able to take care of themselves, but such is not the case.

Some of these people would go back to Chicago at once if they had the means to buy transportation.

Hoping to hear from you soon, I remain,

Yours very truly,

CHARLES HENRY
Justice of the Peace

[Letter is also signed by Frank Furmanck, Frank Temesvar, Josef Darcsi.]

CHICAGO, ILLINOIS
June 10, 1916

Mr. Charles Henry, Justice of the Peace
Lincoln, X. County, Michigan

MY DEAR SIR: We have written the Lincoln Sugar Company with regard to the state of the sugar beet workers in Lincoln, and we believe they will take action to fulfill their agreements with these people at once. We have also written the people in Hungarian, asking for further information and offering further assistance. We appreciate greatly your assistance in this matter.

Yours very sincerely,

HELEN CROTHERS
(*For the Immigrants' Protective League*)

CHICAGO, ILLINOIS
June 10, 1916

Mr. F. King
Lincoln Sugar Company
Lincoln, Michigan

MY DEAR MR. KING: I am inclosing a copy of a letter received by us yesterday morning. As we understand the arrangements your company has made with these laborers, credit was promised them until crops were ready for work. And we understand that this year work was promised even before the beet crops were ready. We trust that if a mistake has been made you will take steps to correct it and we are sure you will see that these people do not suffer any longer.

We can probably get firms in Chicago to advance transportation to bring these laborers back to Chicago because laborers are in great demand here now, but we should be sorry to have to do this since the moving of families back to town so soon will be a great disappointment to all of them. We hope to hear from you regarding this situation and we shall trust you can better the situation.

Yours very sincerely,

HELEN CROTHERS
(*For the Immigrants' Protective League*)

September 2, 1916.—Letter to Lincoln Sugar Company from H. Crothers [Assistant Superintendent of the League] as follows:

We have just received a complaint growing out of one of the contracts signed for work in the Michigan beetfields, and we would be glad to have such facts as you can give us about the matter. The contract, signed April 30, 1916, was between John Schwartz, William Schwartz, and W. E. Ringer, of Lincoln, Michigan, and Vincent Kleinaitis. The contract was carefully explained to Mr. Kleinaitis by one of our representatives, who witnessed the signing of the contract, and everything was clearly understood by all the parties to the agreement. Mr. Kleinaitis now reports to us that on August 26, when he was paid for the first three parts of the work, he was dismissed without cause. He, of course, wishes to complete the harvesting in accordance with the contract as that is the most profitable part of the work. May we ask for an immediate adjustment of this matter, as Mr. Kleinaitis has left his family in Lincoln and has come back to Chicago to ask our help in the matter?

September 8, 1916.—Letter written to Mr. King, of Lincoln, who represented the company when contracts were signed:

We had a complaint last week from Vincent Kleinaitis, a Lithuanian, who went to work in the beetfields last spring. The terms of the contract he signed here in Chicago concerning the work were apparently not kept by the farmers, and Mr. Kleinaitis seems to have been discharged without cause. He wishes to return and finish the work in accordance with the contract. We wrote to the Lincoln Sugar Company and hope that the matter has been called to your attention as you were here in Chicago at the time the agreements were made. We will be glad to know the result of your investigation as soon as it is made.

September 11, 1916.—Telegraphed Lincoln Sugar Company: "Situation in Lincoln growing serious for Kleinaitis family and others. Please hasten investigation requested by our letter."

September 12, 1916.—Reply from Lincoln Sugar Company as follows:

In reply to your letter of the second and wire of the eleventh regarding Kleinaitis trouble at Lincoln, our labor agent, Mr. King, is at present out of the city, and we are therefore obliged to refer this matter to the manager of our Washington plant, whom we have instructed to give it his prompt personal attention.

September 13, 1916.—Letter from Mr. Green, of the United Charities Stock Yards District:

We are sending you a copy of a letter one of our visitors received from Annie Kleinaitis, Lincoln, Michigan. We know of no way in which we could help these people, but are wondering if something could be done by your organization, if it is deemed advisable by you.

[Copy of letter from Annie Kleinaitis:]

DEAR SIR:

How are you getting along? We are working beets in Michigan. The company sent us by the farmers here for beets. We have worked first, second and third work but they would not let us work the last. Now we have no money to come back to Chicago or to buy food. The farmers are going to work the last work themselves. The agent that sent us here lives 1140½ South Michigan Avenue [address of Immigrants' Protective League]. His name is Mr. J. H——. Could you go to the office and help us? We cannot go to school here because we have none.

Yours sincerely,
ANNIE KLEINAITIS

LINCOLN, MICHIGAN, ROUTE 3

Later.—Letter to United Charities as follows:

We have your letter of September 12 with regard to the Kleinaitis family in Lincoln, Michigan. We have already taken the matter up with the Lincoln Sugar Company and have had one reply stating that the matter is under investigation. If we do not get a favorable report we are planning to send a representative to Lincoln to see that the matter is adjusted. The people were not sent out through our office but through the employment department of the United States Immigration Service at 845 South Wabash Avenue. One of our workers, Mr. J. H——, however, was asked to do some interpreting. He read the contracts to the men, and he and they had every reason to believe that the conditions were to be satisfactory at Lincoln. We are grateful for your letter, and we shall be glad to report to you the final outcome.

September 15, 1916.—J. H. [League visitor] left 9 A.M. for Washington and Lincoln, Michigan. He will try to find families he knows there. *Later.* —Letter received from Lincoln Sugar Company:

Your favor of September 2 addressed to the Lincoln Sugar Company at Washington, concerning a contract between Vincent Kleinaitis, John Schwartz, William Schwartz, and W. E. Ringer, at Lincoln, Michigan, has been referred to me. The crop of sugar beets grown by the above farmers has been abandoned and will not be harvested. This section has been visited by an unusual and severe drought, and in some places the crop has been entirely ruined. The contract referred to above takes care of this condition of things, and there has been no attempt on the part of the farmers or the Sugar Company to treat Mr. Kleinaitis unfairly. It has been very unfortunate and we are very sorry that conditions have been so unfavorable for our crop, but it is a matter entirely beyond our control.

Report of J. H. [League visitor] of visit to the sugar beet workers in Michigan:

I left Chicago September 15, stopped in Grand Rapids, reached Washington in the evening. There was no connection to Lincoln, Michigan, until Monday morning, so I spent Sunday looking around the city. The Lincoln Sugar Company, Washington Sugar Company, and Northern Sugar Company are interested in this vicinity. Walking four or six miles from Washington, I met the first stranded beet workers:

Ignatz Woloski.—R.F.D. No. 1, Washington, Michigan. Polish family —man, wife, and three children, aged fourteen, twelve, three—came three years ago through some agent from Chicago and contracted first with the Northern Sugar Company. They always worked hard, hoping for better conditions. They moved for the winter to the city but could never make enough for their living. In the spring again Woloski tried to contract with the Washington Sugar Company. Family was taken in May 20 to farmer M. P. Deer, where they had work on 17 acres of beets and 8 acres of chicory. The weather was bad in May and June so the weeding work started on June 20. Woloski was anxious to make use of the warm weather, called some relatives for help, and worked 30 acres. The second hoeing was the first week in August. Farmer paid the man for 30 acres' weeding and two hoeings $150 and told him to leave his place because the beets are poor and he will finish the work himself. Five grown people (man, wife and three relatives) earned for six weeks hard work $150. Family was forced to move and are living not far away in a deserted farm without any money, trying to earn here and there a little bit.

Felix Schlensievski.—Eastville near Washington. Polish, wife sick, rheumatism, unable to leave bed, eight children, four girls and four boys, seventeen, fifteen, thirteen, twelve, ten, eight, four, three months. Signed contract on April 27 with farmers W. A. Bridge and Henry on Washington Sugar Company blank for 22 acres beets and 14 acres of chicory. Family moved from Washington on April 9, was paid for some spring work. About 6th of July they started on the beet work but only 10½ acres beets and 7½ acres chicory were given them. Farmer Bridge paid them for weeding $38; Farmer Henry paid them for weeding $52 and for hoeing $23, a total of $113. During July the whole family was very busy; they tried to do the best they could. The farmer took advantage of the older children and gave them extra work without compensation; and when the father was unable to take care of the beets himself, he objected, and they started to quarrel and the whole family was forced to leave the place. All moved about two miles away, rented there an empty building, and are suffering:

Monday.—Families found in Lincoln, Michigan:

Kleinaitis family.—Route No. 3, near Lincoln, Michigan. Met wife and older daughter on the way to town and returned to their home with them. The farm belongs to John Schwartz, who signed the contract with the family through the Lincoln Sugar Company in the United States Immigration Office on April 30. Mother, two girls of fifteen and twelve, and a boy of nine are in this farm house four miles from the town. Mr. Kleinaitis went to Chicago three weeks ago, leaving the family with a few dollars only. Kleinaitis contracted with William Schwartz for 5 acres, John Schwartz 10¾ acres, W. E. Ringer, 3¾ acres William Schwartz refused to let him work on his 5 acres. John Schwartz paid for weeding and two hoeings $86. Ringer for first hoeing, $19.50—in all $105.50. Nobody called after our letter was sent to the Lincoln Sugar Company to see and speak with the people. They were waiting day after day. I telephoned to Mr. John Schwartz and succeeded in reaching him only after a second telephone call and asked him for his opinion. He told me that it is not worth while to take care of the beets. He will not give work to the Kleinaitis family, and he had nothing to do with them; if the Lincoln Sugar Company brought the people to Lincoln they will have to send them bac

There is absolutely no chance to earn money near the Kleinaitis place, and butcher and grocery store refuse to give credit to them. Farmer Schwartz urged the people to leave the house; he will close it as soon as possible. He is willing to help the family transfer the furniture to the Lincoln Station; this would be all the help he will give.

John Karel.—Slovak from Chicago. This family came to Lincoln on May 5 through Employment Agent Jones from Chicago. They contracted 13½ acres with farmer Simon Smith. Karel has wife and three small children; they live in an old dirty shanty in one room. He earned since May 5 on the beets $95.15 and on side work in the neighborhood $27—total $122.15. The beet crop is poor; farmers did not decide just now if they will need his help in October, but the family will stay and hope that they will get work for few more days. They will have enough to get back to Chicago and will return this fall.

Josef Jung.—German from Hungary, wife, and thirteen-year-old boy came from Detroit with other families to the Lincoln Sugar Company farmers. Jung is in his third place during this summer; on the former places they sent him away because the crop was poor. He supports the family helping around the station, loading coal, etc., and earned for two weeks $11 in this way. Jung will try to save enough for the moving expenses to Detroit.

Following families left Lincoln in July and August:

Frank Capek, wife, three children to Chicago, received money from friends, owes the butcher $18.87.

George Furbish, wife and one child left for Chicago, owes butcher $10.24.

Joe Kraus, wife and five children left for Chicago, relatives paid the fare, owes $1.80.

Frank Dombroski and wife left for Cleveland, owes butcher $5.12.

Anton Maguroff, wife and child, fare was paid by the former employer to Chicago, owes the butcher $2.97.

Josef Andreyoff, wife, sister, and four children left for Chicago with the last payment made by farmer.

Frank Furmanck, Frank Temesvar, Josef Darcsi and others.—These Hungarians who made complaints to us on June 7 through the Justice of Peace earned their railroad fare, working on the Bay City Western Railroad tracks and moved with their families to Chicago and Detroit in July.

September 22, 1916.—Letter written to Lincoln Sugar Company by H. Crothers [Assistant Superintendent of the League]:

We have had a reply from the manager of your Washington plant in reply to our request for an investigation of the difficulties of the Kleinaitis family at Lincoln, Michigan. We understand that no personal investigation of the matter was made as we had hoped would be the case from your letter of September 11. The family was sent out with others through the Employment Department of the United States Immigration Service, 845 South Wabash Avenue, and they had every reason to believe that conditions were to be satisfactory at Lincoln. Even though there is no legal responsibility, we wonder if the company may not feel a moral responsibility for these unfortunate people. We encouraged these workers to go to Lincoln because the company seemed to be back of the contract. It seems to us very hard that these workers should have to suffer as they are doing as a result of the drought. The Kleinaitis family is stranded and suffering at Lincoln. We are asking the County Agent to return them to Chicago, but it seems very hard that after a whole summer's work the family should have to ask public charity. Mr. Kleinaitis himself is in Chicago, having come here to try to get the matter straightened out, and Mrs. Kleinaitis and the children are in Lincoln alone.

Later.—Telephoned Mr. Roberts, United States Employment Office. He will look into the matter.

September 26, 1916.—Wrote County Agent of Lake County, Michigan, as follows:

We wish to report to you for return to Chicago the family of Vincent Kleinaitis, namely, his wife Lucija and his three children, Katie, Annie, and Vladja. They are on the farm of John and William Schwartz, route 3, Lincoln, Michigan. The Kleinaitis family went to Lincoln in May, 1916, to work in the beetfields. There was no harvesting for them to do because of the crop failure, and the family are stranded there. Mr. Kleinaitis came back to Chicago to see if he could get the matter adjusted and is now unable to send for his wife and children. Mr. Charles Henry, Justice of the Peace at Lincoln, can give you the full details of the matter. All the arrangements for their going to Michigan were made by Mr. Kleinaitis through the Lincoln Sugar Company, who sent an agent to Chicago to get workers for the beet-fields. It seems a great pity that the workers should have to bear the brunt of the failure of the crop in this way, and we trust that you will make a special effort to get the Kleinaitis family off as soon as possible as they are apparently suffering a good deal. They have their furniture with them, and the farmer, Mr. John Schwartz, has promised to get it to the train for them.

Later.—Letter received from United States Employment Service, inclosing the following letter from the Sugar Company:

United States Department of Labor
845 South Wabash Avenue
Chicago, Illinois
Attention of Mr. Roberts

DEAR SIR: Your communication with regard to one of our beet workers is at hand. I only need to say that the conditions during the early summer were anything but of an encouraging character, and not only were our beet workers inconvenienced, but everybody who had anything to do in securing a crop of sugar beets as well. It is true, as you say, that Mr. Kleinaitis was unable to fulfill his part of the contract because of these conditions. However, there was no reason for him to leave Michigan on account of not finding any work. We would have gladly given him all the necessary acreage which he and his family would have been able to work. Now, I would suggest that you tell this man to return to Michigan, and I will see to it that he will get all the beets to harvest that he can possibly do. There is good money in harvesting beets. We are paying at the rate of $10 an acre, and Mr. Kleinaitis and his family should be able to take out at least an acre and a half of beets each day, which would net them in the neighborhood of $8 or $9 for a day's work. We aim to do the fair thing by all of our people; but when some of them go into hysterics, it is almost impossible for anyone to satisfy them. Trusting that these few lines of explanation are satisfactory, I remain,

Yours very truly,
F. J. KING

September 28, 1916.—Telephoned Mr. Roberts, United States Employment Service, that we were very much dissatisfied with the attitude of the Sugar Company, that if there was work, the company ought to get these people in touch with it. Mr. Roberts did write and ask the company to send the Kleinaitis family back and intimated that whether or not they helped them get beet workers again depended on how they treated this family. *Later.*—Letter from Lincoln Sugar Company as follows:

I have been away from this office for the past month and find on my return home that there seems to be some misunderstanding with regard to the Kleinaitis family. I am informed that Mr. King, our manager in the Lincoln district, has made a reply to your first inquiry and he certainly knows what he is talking about, being thoroughly conversant with the situation. I need not go into details and would simply say that the past season has been a very trying one on the workmen and also the farmer and the Sugar Company. We have done the best we knew how in order to satisfy all our people, under these particular conditions. Of course, you understand that where there are so many people as we have, it is utterly impossible to satisfy them all. Mr. Kleinaitis should never have left here as he did. While it is true the farmer for whom he worked failed in his crop, our people were ready to give him work elsewhere and even now if he would return here, we would be perfectly willing to give him a fair chance and assist him in every possible way. Of course if he insists in pursuing his own course regardless of our interests, we will not be able to satisfy his desires. If you will have the kindness to tell him to return here immediately within the next few days we will pay his fare to point of destination. This is the best that we can do.

September 29, 1916.—Letter received from County Agent, of Lake County, Michigan, as follows:

DEAR MADAM:

Your letter of 22d and 26th received. I wish to state that the County Agent has no authority in Michigan to use the general public money, but I have mailed your letter of the 22d to the Superintendent of the Poor, Mr. Paul McPherson, P.O. address, Argyle. I think I will probably be able to meet Mr. McPherson at the County Fair today, and I will talk the matter over with him. Very likely he will want to know if Mr. Vincent Kleinaitis is working and in good health; it is generally considered that a man in good health can take care of his family. The taxpayers in Lake County were in no way to blame for what the Lincoln Sugar Company agent did, but I believe Mr. McPherson will give the Kleinaitis family prompt attention. I remain,

Yours very truly,

T. R. WHITE

Later.—Postcard received from family from Lincoln as follows:

You have fooled us, we did not get any tickets from the company Monday. We have nothing to eat. We are all packed up now and are ready. Send us tickets please.

ANNIE KLEINAITIS

LINCOLN, MICHIGAN, ROUTE NO. 3

Later.—Visited 30 Union Street to see Mr. Kleinaitis. Man is working on the South Side, address not known by brother with whom I spoke. Mr. Kleinaitis will have money tomorrow to bring home the family. Told him to send Mr. Kleinaitis surely tomorrow to our office; we will advise him how to send the money. Brother gave me letter Mr. Kleinaitis received from one of the little girls:

DEAR FATHER:

How are you getting along? Why don't you write us a letter? Was you in the office already? Mr. John Schwartz came here and said why don't we move out, and he said he is the boss on the beets, not Mr. Zuesziak. But the Polish man lives here yet. But they all wait for an answer from you.

ANNIE KLEINAITIS

LINCOLN, MICHIGAN, ROUTE NO. 3

[The remaining portion of the record deals with the sending of the money on the following day and the details about the homecoming of the wife and children. The family arrived on October 4; and on October 12 Annie and her mother came to the League office in great distress about their furniture, which they had left packed in a car ready to be shipped. Annie had prepared the following list of articles and their value:

One patent machine box, 4 big boxes of clothes, 1 clothes basket, 3 tubs of mantles, 1 dish box, 3 peaces of chairs in a box, 3 peaces of the stove, 10 peaces of the beds, 1 sewing machine, 1 big table, 1 tool table, 1 bag, 1 book satchel, 1 barrel, 1 ironing board. 33 peaces in all. Furniture, 3 beds, $60; 8 pillows, $32; 2 feather beds, $50; 1 stove, $35; 1 table, $6.00; 6 chairs, $10; sewing machine, $35; 3 blankets, $21; dishes, $20. Clothes, dresses, $39, 12 years old girl; dresses, $50, 16 years old girl; underware $50, everyone's; summer coat, $5.00, 12 years old girl; winter coat, $10, 12 years old girl; fall coat, $5.00, 12 years old girl; winter coat, $15, 16 years old girl; summer coat, $7.00, 16 years old girl; fall coat, $7.00, 16 years old girl; winter coat, $8.00, 9 years old boy; summer coat, $3.00, 9 years old boy; fall coat, $3.00, 9 years old boy; 2 jackets, $10, mother's; 1 overcoat, $20, mother's; other overcoat, $25, mother's; collar and muff, $30, mother's; raincoat, $7, father's; 3 tubs, $7.50. 5 hundred $75.00 and 55 ($575.55).

The following letter explains this final difficulty of the Kleinaitis family in Lincoln:]

Mr. Charles Henry, Justice of the Peace
Lincoln, Lake County, Michigan

DEAR SIR: May we ask for your assistance with the affairs of one of the families who went to the sugar beetfields from Chicago. We have appreciated your interest in these families previously. The family of Vincent Kleinaitis, who were sent out by the United States Employment Bureau to work on the farm of John Schwartz at Lincoln, left there October 2, to return to Chicago after many hardships. On that day their furniture was taken to the station by John Schwartz and given into the hands of the station master, who said in the presence of Mr. Schwartz that the furniture would be forwarded to Chicago the following day, C.O.D. He did not instruct Mrs. Kleinaitis to bill the furniture, and she, of course, did not know about doing this. The furniture was placed in an empty car. Now, the general freight agent writes us that the freight charges will have to be paid and a release signed before the furniture will be sent. Mr. Kleinaitis cannot send the charges today but will have the money within the next few days, that is, about the time the furniture arrives, if it is sent now. Mr. Kleinaitis was doing temporary work which was finished October 14. He expects to start work again today. Would you be willing to see the station master at Lincoln, find out the present condition of the furniture after the delay, and ascertain whether the furniture can be sent C.O.D. because of the fact that the agent originally agreed to do so? The family is so anxious to have the furniture that there can be no doubt that they will pay the charges out of Mr. Kleinaitis' next pay envelope. At any rate, we will be glad to know the exact status of the matter and what can be done. If the furniture is not in a safe place will you kindly do what is possible to protect it. We are inclosing a list that Mr. Kleinaitis has given us, saying what the thirty-three pieces are that were left at the station. We are exceedingly sorry to trouble you, and we shall greatly appreciate your co-operation. We are,

Very truly yours,

HELEN CROTHERS, *Assistant Superintendent*
Immigrants' Protective League

28. Andrei Ivanov
(*A Russian Immigrant on a Kansas Farm*)

[This case record begins with an application for employment in December, 1915, made by a Russian man, Andrei Ivanov, who had come to this country early in 1915 and was anxious to bring over his wife and two children. A Slavic visitor of the League, referred to as A. F., thought that he had probably deserted from the Russian army. Andrei Ivanov had been a farmer in Russia and said he would like very much to get work on a farm here if he knew how to go about it. The employment department of the League finally arranged to send Andrei to a Kansas farmer, Mr. Field, to whom the League had sent a farm hand the preceding year. Mr. Field had asked for a German or a Danish man but finally agreed to accept a Russian instead. The Russian visitor of the League found that Andrei was rather reluctant to leave Chicago because he felt that it would be easier to make arrangements with the steamship company for the tickets for his family if he stayed in Chicago. The visitor told Andrei that he might write to her in Russian if he needed any help about bringing over his family.]

March 10, 1916.—Letter received from Mr. H. H. Field, Thornhill, Kansas:

Immigrants' Protective League
Chicago, Illinois

GENTLEMEN: Andrei Ivanov is still living with us. He has turned out to be an excellent man; good habits and more than ordinary ability. He is very much distressed about his family. I promised to send for his family as soon as I think it is safe to let them come. He thinks it is safe for them to come at any time, by way of Yokohama, sailing from there to Seattle. On receipt of this letter, if it is not asking too much, I wish you would ask the Russian Consul if he thinks it would be advisable for them to attempt to come to the United States at this time. He may be able to give us some suggestions as to the best way to come. It has occurred to me that it would not be safe for them to come on anything but an American boat. It has been my idea that they might get out through Norway and get over to Liverpool and take an American boat from that point to New York. With kind personal regards, I am,

Yours very truly,

H. H. FIELD

March 11, 1916.—Letter in Russian sent to Andrei Ivanov by A. F., and letter also written to Mr. Field by the Superintendent. [Extract from letter to Mr. Field follows:]

We do not seem to have any record of what part of Russia Andrei Ivanov comes from, but it would seem to me that it would be very much better if he would plan to have his wife come by way of the Norwegian or Swedish Line. Like the American boats, they are neutral boats and therefore not subject to attack, and they are, of course, much more accessible from Russia. In order for his wife to leave Russia, however, she must have her passport and permit, as well as her husband's passport. Miss F— has written to Mr. Ivanov in Russian with regard to this, and he will perhaps speak to you about it. The Yokohama route would be a very expensive one for his wife to take.

March 13, 1916.—Russian letter from Andrei Ivanov to A. F. [The letter is written very illegibly, showing clearly that Andrei Ivanov was an almost illiterate peasant. Translation follows:]

FOR THE RUSSIAN MISS F—:

I, Andrei Ivanov, am writing to you, and I thank you many times for your good attitude toward me. I have been very glad to receive a letter from you and read it 5 times over—it was as if it was sent from my home. I can see from this letter that you care for the welfare of my family. I consider it my first duty to thank you for the position you gave me. From my whole soul, "a Russian thank you." I am very much satisfied with everything, I cannot find or remember one thing with which I should not be satisfied. My boss Field is a good boss to me and his daughter and sister are very good, with a word they are good people. What concerns the food, there is nothing to say—it is very good—what they eat themselves they give also to me. As far as my work is concerned, it is housework—they have 2 cows, chickens, 7 pigs, a calf. The 6th of March one cow calved happily, and I am glad about it. Now 2 calves I have. The whole family is very good, but I do not know how he (my boss) is satisfied with me. He surely wrote you about it. I am trying hard. I will try to my last day. I can see that my boss wants to do much good for me. I see he can appreciate my work. Of course, the term that you have set for me till April 1 is soon over, but it seems that I will remain here; although they did not say anything but I see this from his words and because he is trying to get over my family here, but he says I should wait, because they may perish in the sea. He said, "You wait and see. I will arrange everything." He more than once wrote to the Russian Consul, and it seems just recently he did so again. We went with him on the road and I said, "Mr. Field, write to the Russian Consul." [The answer of Mr. Field is given in Russian letters and English words and is not clear.] I went with him in his office and I understand that he dictated to the lady who sent me here. I myself crossed the Japan sea from Oskogamo to Seattle. Sixteen days I traveled only across Russia.

It is a longer way through Siberia to China, it took 18 days on the machine,[1] and from Seattle to Chicago it took 3 days. It cost 898 rubles. My family is in Kazan 800 verst from Moscow not far from Samara and Nishni-Novgorod. If it is possible the Consul should direct my family to come through Japan. I want to ask you, lady, if you could not get a cheap railroad ticket from Seattle for my family—the girl is 12 years of age and the boy 10—what tickets will they have to buy on the steamer as well as on the railroad? As far as the "passport" is concerned I made out a separate one for my wife for one year in May, 1915. My passport I have with me. They say that you have to get an affidavit from the Russian Consul in order to be able to pass the borders. Mr. Field asked advice from his wife—she and the daughter left for a warmer climate as they do in our country in Russia—they went South and they are there already a month. He went also to see them, and a second time in March. When he came he said that he consulted the Russian Consul regarding my family but that they are afraid to take them over because the "Germans" may drown them. Then regarding my English I am getting used and talk better than when I came here but this is necessary in order to prepare yourself for the citizen's examination.

March 17, 1916.—Letter from Mr. Field giving name and address of Andrei's wife in Russia.

March 19, 1916.—Letter from Andrei Ivanov [translation] as follows:

In the first place I thank you for your letter. Dear Miss F—, you will pardon me that I trouble you so much and take your time. I forgot to tell you that from the March the 7, I dont get the papers any more. You know that I am getting $15 a month and I received wages three times already and soon I will get the fourth pay. The first time Mr. Field took six dollars out of my wages for the railroad ticket. You told me that until the first of April I am to receive $15 and then I will get a different wage, but so I do not say anything because I think Mr. Field ought to know himself about it. I think it is perhaps not profitable for Mr. Field to pay me more, and for me it is worse not to have any work at all. I work from 6 A.M., until 7 P.M., and I never try to keep away from work. . . . .

But when my family comes I will have to arrange for definite hours of work. Mr. Field asked me to write a letter to my family. I think he wanted to send it through you. My dear Miss F—, I am very much worried about my family, because the children are not my own but my sister-in-law died and I did not adopt them legally. Now the children cannot get a passport and will not be able to come via Petrograd and will have to come via Japan. On the Japan boundaries there is a possibility to give to the officer a few rubles and he will let the children through. Or in case of trouble she can stop at Tchun-Tchien[?], where there is a hotel kept by a Japanese who talks a splendid Russian and he will take her over the boundary to Dairen and from there she can easily get a steamer to Seattle and this will cost her $95 and this will take her 18 or 19 days. But via Japan will in general take much more time and cost more money than via Petrograd to New York. I decided not to send steamship tickets but money; let my wife come anyway possible. Please write them both addresses and the address for the cable so that I should know when she will leave Petrograd and take the steamer, also the name of the steamer, if she should have to come via Japan—she should cable when she is leaving for Manchuria. I read in the papers, that if

[1] I.e., a train. The Russian peasant calls a train a machine.

I should declare here before the Russian Consul that the children are mine, they would be able to pass the boundaries without difficulties—would you kindly inquire about this and if it should be true do not send my letter to my wife but return it to me?

March 22, 1916.—A. F. visited Russian Consulate, spoke with Mr. X. They will send blank to be signed, etc. Russian letter received from Andrei Ivanov follows [translation]:

THE LADY, MISS F—:

I have the honor to tell you that I wrote a letter to my family and my boss took it and will send it to you. As to the children, I wrote that they are not mine, but my wife's sister's children. Both of their parents died and now the children cannot get a passport. If they will get it they should go via Petrograd, if they should not get a passport then they will have to come via Japan. This is what I wrote my wife; if you wish you can read the letter. A friend owes me some money and I told him to pay it to my wife. The little girl is 13 years, but I wrote them to say that she is 12, because Mr. Field explained to me that at 12 years of age you will need only half a ticket. Write in English and Russian letters that the girl is 12 years old and the boy 10 so that they will be able to show it in the office of the steamship. I wrote two addresses for you on an envelope, you can rewrite it from there. One is for my wife in Pomerach and the second to her brother if she moved from Pomerach. If there is anything to add to the letter do it but please write, so that they will be able to read.

March 23, 1916.—Visited the Russian Consulate and got blank. This blank Andrei Ivanov is to send back to have it signed by Russian Consul. Then this blank must be sent to his wife. This blank will permit her to get a foreign passport for herself and the two children of her sister she wishes to bring here. The Consul does not think she will have trouble in entering the children on her passport. The Consul advises them to come by the Russian Line. He thinks it is the safest and the cheapest way of getting them here. A. F. sent blank with information both as to Russian-American Line and Scandinavian Line.

March 25, 1916.—Letter received from Mr. Field:

Immigrants' Protective League
Chicago, Illinois

MY DEAR FRIENDS: I am sending you a letter that has been addressed by Andrew Ivanov to his wife in Russia. You are probably able to read the Russian language. I suggested to him that I had better send it to you so that you could have it properly addressed. He is very much distressed about his family and is very anxious to have them come to America. He has been telling me that he thinks it best for them to come by way of Yokohama. After receiving your letter I took the letter to a Russian who lives here and speaks the English language, and told him that you advised that she come by way of Petrograd. He still insists that he thinks the better way for them to come is by way of Yokohama. He has a boy that is ten years old and one girl of twelve. He thinks that the two children can come on half-fare tickets. In a former letter, you told me that Andrew was a deserter from the Russian Army. If this is true, he has no passport. He seems to think that they will be able to leave the country without a passport. When you answer this letter, won't you please give me the address of Mrs. Anna A. Ivanov? Write it in English. I am sending the letter that he has written and if you will kindly address it to her in Russian, you will confer a favor.

Yours very truly,
H. H. FIELD

March 29, 1916.—Letter from Andrei Ivanov with letter for his wife. [Translation of letter to visitor follows:]

MISS F—:

I beg to send an additional letter to my wife. I sent you a letter this morning, March 27, and afterward received a letter from home. I sent the letter through my brother—and he writes that one letter he received January the 28th and the second he does not write when he received, but my wife does not write anything whether she lives at "Pomerach" or whether she moved. Better send letter to brother's address.

Later.—Russian letter received from Andrei as follows [translation]:

MISS F—:

I inform you that your letter with the blank I received and signed my name and the rest I will have to ask you to fill out. The name of my wife is Anna [gives address] the children are orphans, the children of my sister-in-law Serafina Andreivna [gives her address]. The children lived with me five years. The girl's name is Eudokia, the boy's Alexander, the girl is twelve and the boy ten. Please write for all three of them the addresses in Russian and English. The address of my wife is Kazan, Russia. She was living there and wanted to remain there, but something happened and she moved. Maybe it is possible to write on the envelope that in case they don't find her they should try to look her up in the city directory—or send the letter to my brother's address and write the address in English. As to my job I must tell you the following: I have not been such a slave in Russia as I am here—like a boy I have to run errands and the cook should boss me. I promised you to do whatever I am told to so that you should not have trouble on account of me. I knew that in America I will have to work hard for a time, but now when my wife will come here I do not care to be a hired laborer. It seems that Mr. Field guessed my thought, and he said to a Russian merchant here that he will bring over my family and then he will build a house for me and give me some land for a garden and a pasture and also pigs and chickens, and a cow, but Mr. Field told the merchant not to tell it to me. But this is true because there is a large open piece of land near the river, and they brought already bricks. I will start to build on Friday. That is the reason why I think I will remain here after my family comes, but of course I could yet change my mind and come to Chicago, and I hope whenever I should ask you for help you would not leave me without it. March 25, I received a fourth time my wages, $15. Now, it is necessary I should be able to learn English. Please arrange it so that you or I shall know when they will take the steamer and the name of the steamer. P.S.: Please if there are some expenses pay it for me and I will send you the money. I do not want you to spend your money for me. In regard to my boss, Mr. Field, I want to say as follows: I think he will be of great help to me, and I think I must have patience.

March 30, 1916.—Russian letter sent to Andrei Ivanov asking if he is sure he is quite willing to have his family come on Russian-American Line. Explained that League does not wish to advise him either way. It is for him to decide. Letter also sent to Mr. Field explaining Andrei Ivanov's letter.

April 3, 1916.—Letter from Mr. Field as follows:

My dear Miss F—:

I am in receipt of your letter of March 30th, inclosed with letter to Andy. As requested, I am giving you my full address: Henry Field, 101 High Avenue, East, Thornhill, Fremont County, Kansas, U.S.A. Andy has inclosed a little note written in Russian that I presume is for you. With kind regards, I am,

Yours very truly,

H. H. Field

Letter from Andrei Ivanov as follows [translation]:

Dear Lady:

I received your letter and the letter for Mr. Field I delivered to him. In regard to the coming of my family I entirely depend on you. You know better what to do. I am satisfied they should come on the Russian-American Line. This is much cheaper and takes less time than to come through Japan. I think if she will have an affidavit from the Consul she will be able to get a passport from the [Russian] Government. Send letter to the address I wrote to you. I beg you to do as you think better. In the telegram write as little words as possible because a word costs from three to five rubles.

Sincerely yours,

Ivanov

April 9, 1916.—A. F. sent registered letter and Consulate blank to man's wife in Kazan, Russia, in care of Feodor Batuchkin. Mr. Batuchkin is a friend, who will turn blank over to Mr. Ivanov's wife. Her present address is uncertain. Letter written to Mr. Ivanov that everything he asked for had been done for him.

April 18, 1916.—Check for $1.55 and letter from Mr. Field as follows:

Immigrants' Protective League
Chicago, Illinois

Dear Friends: Andrew Ivanov says that you advanced $1.55 for him to the Russian Consul at Chicago. I have not been able to learn from Andy what the advancement was for. As near as I can get it, it was for stamps for some purpose. He has requested me to send you a draft for the above amount. I inclose draft on the First National Bank of Chicago for $1.55. Won't you please send Andy a receipt, written in the Russian language for the above amount. I desire to thank you very kindly for using such excellent judgment in sending us a man. Andrew is a bright, intelligent man, good disposition and perfectly responsible; he has complete access to the house and goes all over the house.

He is gradually getting the language. Won't you please let me know if this is the correct amount that you have advanced for Andy to the Russian Consul? With kind regards, I am,

Yours truly,

H. H. FIELD

[Letter and receipt sent.]

April 27, 1916.—Russian letter from Andrei Ivanov as follows [translation]:

MISS F—:

Wish you happy holidays and thank you for all the trouble you took in sending all the papers to my family. Would you please find out on what steamer they are coming and who is going to receive them in New York. If they will pass Chicago would you kindly meet them and send them on. April 25, my wages were raised to $20. You were right saying that Mr. Field will give me a raise himself, but I expected more than $5. Boys that work with me get .25 an hour and I work 13 hours a day and get .66 a day—this hurts me. I went to some Jews—they talk Russian—and told them that I expected $25 because that is what I was told in Chicago. They will tell this to my boss. [Letter also tells how he is fixing up the garden and house for his family.]

April 28, 1916.—A. F. sent Russian letter to A. Ivanov telling him it was too soon to plan anything yet about meeting his wife.

May 7, 1916.—Russian letter from Andrei Ivanov as follows [translation]:

MISS F—:

We are again out of luck. It seems that the Petrograd Harbor is closed. For Heaven's sake find out if this is so. I've nothing more to say.

May 8, 1916.—Russian letter from Andrei Ivanov as follows [translation]:

Read in the newspaper that Japan would interfere in Mexico, therefore there will be war between the United States and Japan and my family cannot come then. Please to find out how they could come then.

[Letter written by A. F. in Russian, telling man to be calm and work hard—not to worry. His family will get here in time.]

Later.—Visited office of Russian-American Line. The Russian government closed the Archangel port for military purposes. No private transportation of any sort until the month of June. There is no sailing list now. *Later.*—Wrote Andrei Ivanov, in Russian, about it. Also sent him a Scandinavian-American Line sailing list.

May 10, 1916.—Letter from Andrei Ivanov as follows[translation from Russian]:

MISS F—:

Thank you for information. We have no luck. The newspaper *Russkoye Slovo* writes that port Archangel is closed by England and that the whole Russia is under English control—poor Russia! But there is nothing we can do. I thought Archangel was closed only for war vessels, but did not know that it was closed also for passengers. Please give me an advice what to do. What about your new plan? We do not know how she can come from Petrograd to Christiania on the train or on a steamer and how much it costs and how much it costs from Christiania to New York, probably not less than $60 from Christiania to New York and no less than $20 from Petrograd to Christiania. The trouble is that this line has only four steamers and they leave Christiania twice a month and if she would not come exactly in time she may have to wait very long. . . . . I think she received the papers, if not she will surely have them by May 1. I had a letter from my wife May the 3rd.[1] She writes that if she would get her papers in first days in May she should be able to travel together with a teacher, who is also coming over and who has been here before. She writes also that it would be impossible to buy ½ a ticket for the girl because she has grown and is a whole head taller than my wife. Thus if we will have them come via Petrograd it may be very expensive. [He also writes that he wants to cable but is afraid that a few words would not make clear to his wife what she is to do and many words will be too expensive. Asks advice. He is working and his house will be ready June the first.]

May 15, 1916.—Russian letter written to Andrei Ivanov by A. F. Advised him to have his wife wait for the Russian boats and then I told him there is surely someone there who can advise, perhaps the Russian teacher who was planning to go to America.

June 1, 1916.—Letters from and to Andrei. He asked League to find Mr. E. Gourei, a Lithuanian, and to ask him for 100 rubles which Gourei borrowed from Ivanov. [When he went to Kansas he left 100 rubles and some things with boarding-house proprietor on this Lithuanian's recommendation.]

June 6, 1916.—Letter received from Andrei Ivanov as follows [translation from Russian]:

Miss F—:

May I inform you that I received a letter from Mr. Gourei, Chicago. He writes he is surprised to receive a letter from the lady who sent me to Kansas, but she wrote English and he could not understand. I answered Gourei the story of how I left this money. Please for a time don't write to him, I will try to remind him. I wrote to you and asked to find out if it is true that Russia closed the Petrograd Harbor. I am sorry that I did not have them come to Japan. If I would not have written her at all she probably would have gone to Japan herself, now she does not know what to do. Today I am sending a letter to my wife and advise her to come by Japan if she cannot come by Archangel or Petrograd. This letter she will receive in thirty-five or thirty-seven days. Then she will be able to arrive September 10th. The most important thing is the children should not miss school. Fate plays tricks on men, but we cannot help it.

June 13, 1916.—Russian letter received from Andrei Iavnov as follows [translation]:

Miss F—:

Thank you very much for your card you sent me. I had a letter from home. All are well, but mother died—she was eighty-five years old. She

---

[1] Date is by the Russian calendar.

was living with us. May 16, received a letter from you, and May 17 I decided to send following cable to my wife: "You can go to Petrograd." This would amount to $3.64. I think this would be easy for them to understand. I decided to cable because I think she herself would not decide to do so because we did not write her about it. It will cost more, but what can we do? They are impatiently waiting to come to America. I prepared for them some things. I planted 11 different vegetables in the garden. They are fixing the house, and on June 1 it will be ready. I wrote you that my wages are now $20, and I praise my employer and his family, but in some ways I am disappointed. The employer's wife is not very good. She is spiteful, and the cooks leave each after the other. She treats me bad, and it is hard to please her. Now I will wait for a cable. As soon as I will receive it, I will promptly write to you.

[Record contains several other entries between June 13 and July 10, largely discussions with steamship company and letters to and from Andrei about final arrangements for his family, sending money for them to Ellis Island, meeting them when they came through Chicago, etc. On July 25 a Russian letter was received from Andrei. He thanks Miss F— for her letter and asks her to excuse him for not writing—he was busy with his family. They went to Archangel and were lucky to get on a steamer which took them in fourteen days to New York. Mr. Field was nice to them, painted the walls in his house, and sent his automobile to meet the family; they had supper ready for the family. The family brought with them news from Russia about the rise of prices and he gives prices in detail. Three months later a letter was received from Mr. Field as follows:

DEAR FRIENDS:

Andrew Ivanov is getting along the nicest kind. His family came some time ago from Russia. We have built him a nice little cottage. His children are in school. He is drawing good wages and seems to be perfectly contented. He is a most excellent man. The next time I am in Chicago, I intend to come down to see you. With kind personal regards, I remain,

Yours very truly,

H. H. FIELD

Early in January, 1917, another Russian letter was received from Andrei Ivanov in which he sent regards to Miss F— from him and his family. Mr. Field still pays him $25 a month but gives him milk, coal, potatoes, etc., and often makes presents to the family. The children go to school and the address on the envelope is written by his little girl. He asks Miss F— if she will go to the Russian Consul and find out whether it is true that all the men rejected from military service in Russia of first degree have to come and report to the Consul. He read about this in the papers but has no money to go and see the Consul. He was rejected because he was wounded, but he came to America without having a foreign passport, and he wonders what they are going to do to him when he returns to Russia. He gives the name of the military division to which he formerly belonged. (Correspondence with the Russian Consul is omitted.)]

February 13, 1917.—Letter received from Andrei Ivanov, in which he thanks Miss F— for the trouble she took going to the Consul and asks her if she can not find in a second-hand store in Chicago a *balalaika*—a Russian musical instrument. His boy had one at home in Russia, but in the town in which they are living there is no such instrument. He also wants another Russian instrument, *guoli*, for his little girl. He suggests maybe Miss F— could get some instruments on the instalment plan as he could pay not more than $3 to $5 a month. He would also like to have a victrola with Russian records. He asks if she could find another musical instrument, he does not know the name of it, but he draws the picture of it. If she should see it he would like to buy it. He says his wages are not sufficient to meet expenditures. In the papers he read that it is possible to live on 35 cents a day but they spend 50 cents and they cannot help it.

[The League visitor would not undertake the purchase of the musical instruments and merely sent him the catalogue of a mail-order house. There are a few other letters but the correspondence gradually ceased.]

29. Choma Lutnicki

(A Russian Laborer in Tennessee)

November 3, 1914.—Choma Lutnicki, no address, Russian boy, age eighteen, just arrived in Chicago without money or friends. He was found wandering on streets and brought to League office and left here by a Polish man. *Later.*—A. F. [Slavic visitor] spoke with boy in Russian. He says he came to the United States to friends in Homestead, Pennsylvania, in July, 1914. Friends went back to Russia soon after. Boy secured work in foundry. As soon as foundry closed, the boy and two friends, Vlas Solovazx and Jan Maros, went over to Pittsburgh, each paid $2 to labor agent who sent them out to the woods. They got through with this work and then came to Chicago. Each paid $16 railroad fare. The boy had $60 with him. The friends thought the boy too "green" to have so much money with him, took the money and kept it for him. They also "took care" of his suit case. When they arrived in Chicago they got separated somehow while getting off the train, the boy does not know whether accidentally or intentionally, and he has never seen them since. The boy wandered out of the station and met a Polish man, who brought him to the League. Boy will wait to see about getting work. *Later.*—Sent boy out with address of Mr. X (employment agent) to try to get work. *Later.*—Boy back late in the afternoon, said agent told him he could send him on farm, if the boy paid him $1.60 for railroad fare. A. F. gave boy $2. Advised him not to go to farm until inquiries are made, as some men have complained that agents sent them out on farms but they must come back, as there was no work there. Sent boy to 100 West Street (in Russian Colony) to stay for few days.

November 6, 1914.—Boy came back, said the Russians could not do anything for him, as they are themselves without employment. Put boy over night at Salvation Army Hotel, paid 15 cents.

[After interview with Miss E— (visitor in charge of employment work of the League) it was arranged to send Choma to a farmer, Mr. George Leeder, address Rahway, Wisconsin, who wanted a farm hand. A Russian man had been placed with Mr. Leeder the preceding year and had stayed most of the year with him. Letters and telegrams to Mr. Leeder are omitted as letters refer also to other workers. Choma left on November 7 for Rahway.]

December 15, 1914.—Choma came in office, just came back from Rahway. He says he could not last much longer without food. He says he had to work every day in the week and every minute of the day, did not have time to write a letter to the League, as he wanted to do so badly. But he did not mind work, if they only gave him enough to eat. He asked for only dry bread and plenty of it, but they gave him only a small portion of everything at meal times. He was beginning to feel very weak, was afraid to get sick and decided to quit. Full amount due him was $20.35, but they bought for the boy all the clothing needed and deducted cost. He received $9.25. He insisted on Mr. Leeder giving an itemized account, which Choma brought. [Account attached to record showed overalls, gloves, jacket, underwear, shaving outfit, etc.]

[Choma was again referred to Miss E—, who had a letter from Mr. Volta, a Russian farmer, Portland, Tennessee, asking for worker for a whole year, if possible; if not, for a month. Arrangements were finally made to send Choma to Tennessee and he left December 19.]

December 20, 1914.—Letter received from Mr. Leeder, Rahway, Wisconsin:

IMMIGRANTS' PROTECTIVE LEAGUE:

I am writing to tell you Choma Lutnicki, who we got from your office stopped work 13th of this mounth and he came here the seventh of November and began to work the eight he worke 1 mounth and 5 days and we gave him $20.35 he said you sent him here for $30 dollars when we wrote to you for a man we said we would pay $20 to a man that could milk some and handle horses he could not do enny kind of farm work and was very slow and very lazy in learning he hardly earned his board we do not think he was truthful or honest we bought the necessary working clothes as you told us to out of his first salary but he did not want us to keep the money for them out of his wages he thought we give them to him he was the worst one I have ever settled with and I have kept men for the last 16 years. We had another boy from your office Peter Zabriske I think this is the way he spelled his name he stayed here 11 mounths and was a good worker and learned easily we paid him $17 the first mounth $20 for the winter mounths and $28 for summer mounths. I thought I would just let you know what this boy Choma Lutnicki is.

Yours very truly,
GEORGE LEEDER

December 26, 1914.—Russian letter received from Choma [translation]:

December 23, 1913

I hasten to let you know, "Pani," I do not know your name, that, praised be God, I came to the farm and am working, only I do not work on the farm. I sleep and eat on the farm, but work in the woods, cutting down trees. It is good to work for farmers, and their food is good, only the pay is small. I will not earn enough for a steamship ticket until fall, as I think I must go back to Russia this coming fall to do my service in the army. In case you find work for me with better pay, please write to me. Without your advice I will do nothing. I will not leave this place and will not go anywhere. Am very grateful for all you did for me; you have saved me from life's sufferings and bitter tears. I greet you and wish that God should bless you with the best. And now goodbye.

January 21, 1915.—Russian letter received from Choma [translation]:

In the first lines of my letter I hasten to notify you, dear "Pani," I do not know your name nor your father's name, that I am well and alive and in health which I wish also to you. May God give you all the best in this world. When my boss found out that I do not want to stay a whole year he was very angry and said if you do not want to stay a whole year I will pay you now only $10 a month, so please, Pani, be so kind and advise me what to do. Didn't you tell me that I will work 1 or 2 months at $10 per month and then he will pay me $15. And the boss does not want me to go back to Russia at all. So I said that young years could be spent in America and here we must be healthy and that I have lost my strength not by working hard but through worry and trouble. I was born unlucky and have to spend my young years in worry and unrest. I am locked on a farm like a nightingale in a cage, the nightingale is at least with his mate singing songs, but I am alone, have no voice to sing and no mate. I greet you and wish you the best in the world and beg you to write and advise me what to do; the boss would like I should work 5 years, not only 1 year, and I should not go home, so I told him if you will teach me English, read, and write, and speak, I will stay here, and he said there are no schools here.

Respectfully,

Choma Lutnicki

January 27, 1915.—Russian letter to Choma from A. F. [translation]:

I received your letter and am very sorry that you feel so lonely. As for your going back to Russia, I would like to tell you that you should not worry now about that. You should work and try to learn English. You want to go back in the fall. That is many months yet and you have plenty of time to earn a lot of money. First, comes spring, then summer, and then fall, so you see what amount of money you will have, if you decide to go back in the fall. I advise you to stay in that place and work and do not think so much of going back. I hope that everything will be all right. When you write to me my name is ———.

[Some follow-up letters brought no replies. There is no further record of Choma or his Russian employer.]

"LAWYERS" AND NOTARIES

30. Domenica Mareska
(Industrial Insurance; Incompetent Legal Advice)

October 17, 1920.—Mr. "Tony" Vanas, in the office [Immigrants' Commission] and complains of the mishandling of the insurance money left by his friend Frank Mareska, who was killed on December 18, 1918, in the works of the International Plough Company, Chicago. Mr. Vanas gave the following facts: Frank Mareska came to the United States in 1913, leaving in Nedanovice (Slovakia) his wife, Domenica, and five children. Owing to the war, he could never bring them to America. After Frank was killed, Mr. Vanas found a savings bank book with record of deposits of about $300 (Joseph's West Side Bank), and this Mr. Vanas deposited with Judge Bryan (Probate Judge). Mr. Vanas also wrote to the widow, Domenica Mareska, in Slovakia and secured from her power of attorney to collect whatever might be owing as compensation or insurance to her husband from the company. In the meantime an attorney had been appointed by the Judge to look after the widow's interests, and this attorney undertook to collect compensation from the company for his death. Then in 1920, Vanas, who was very impatient over the delays, engaged another attorney, Jacob Olshefsky, a lawyer living at 320 Milwaukee Street. Mr. Olshefsky is an old resident of the neighborhood and recently graduated from a law school. Vanas agreed to pay Olshefsky as an attorney's fee one-third of any money he collected. In June, 1920, Olshefsky reported to Mr. Vanas the settlement of the case against the company for $2,256 and on that day he sent to Domenica Mareska $500 (20,000 kronen). Later, on August 21, he again sent Domenica Mareska $500 (27,000 kronen at the then rate of exchange). Mr. Vanas received $25 and paid $15 to the priest and $10 for some other expenses. The attorney, according to Mr. Vanas, has not accounted for the remaining $1,231 and has refused many times to clear up the matter and make a final accounting. Mr. Vanas now feels that he should not have promised the lawyer so large a fee.

But if the 33⅓ per cent ($752) is a legal fee, then $479 is still due to Domenica Mareska. Mr. Vanas wishes the Commission to investigate the whole matter and to look after the "$300 in the bank book" and another "$700 cash money which belonged to the killed man and was taken by someone."

Mr. Vanas left Jacob Olshefsky's card. Apparently Olshefsky has no downtown office but uses his home as an office. The only address on the card is 320 Milwaukee Street.

Mr. Vanas also left at the office a letter which he received from Domenica, the widow of Frank Mareska after she received the first 20,000 crowns [translation from the Slovak]:

Praised be Jesus Christ and celebrated name of St. Virgin Maria. My good friend Anton Vanas, I salute you many times, and I thank you very much for your merciful kindness. I don't know how to thank you for your goodness and love. My children, my dear mother, and I, we shall pray the Lord to give you good health, divine Saint's blessing, and after your death a great pleasure in the heavenly glory; and meeting us all with our Frank in heavenly kingdom in joy and happiness forever and ever.

My dear friend Anton Vanas, I received 20,000 crowns, and God reward you for your goodness. But I got our Czecho-Slovak money, not the American, and I am informing you about it. Don't misunderstand me, but my husband had in the family where he lived the trunk with clothes, watch, and money. I beg you with my sore heart, if you can send it me with some one who is going to our country. I salute you sincerely and even your loved wife and all your family and also this officer who was a guardian to my children at the court. It is not such a big help these few crowns, but I can clothe my children a little better now. My dear Anton Vanas, it was a true trouble for my mother how to pay debts and living for our orphans whom she takes care of. She is sixty-six years of age this good old woman. I write it with a weak trembling hand.

My dear defender of my little children, I beg you if you can get still more for us, then do so, but do not inconvenience yourself financially or otherwise, but I trust you, that you present the case truthfully and precisely. I beg you to answer me, my sweet friend of my orphans. I have a daughter, seventeen years of age, and she is telling me that she would be pleased to go to America, if it does not cost so much. But it does cost a lot. I salute you and I thank you, my Anton Vanas. Let the Holy Mother reward you and St. Joseph help you during the day and the night and in your last hour of your life and to see our Lord after death. Amen.

[Several entries omitted relating to attempts made by the Bohemian visitor of the Commission (Miss Spacek) to see Mr. Olshefsky.]

December 8, 1920.—Report by R. Spacek. Last evening I found Mr. Olshefsky at home. He says that the case was given to John Patrick, a lawyer, by the Public Administrator before he (Olshefsky) handled the case. The case was also before the Industrial Board for almost two years but was dismissed. Frank Mareska was killed in a fight with a fellow-workman. The man claimed that he struck Mareska in self-defense. The company therefore was not liable. However, Mareska had insurance in the company's "Employes' Benefit Association" and insurance was collected to the amount of $2,252.57. Mr. Olshefsky would account for less than $2,000 of this as follows:

Attorney's fees as per agreement	$ 752.00
Paid Mr. Vanas for service	25.00
Sent to widow	1,000.00
Paid John Patrick as attorney's fee	150.00
Public administrator to be paid	67.58

John Patrick is in the Pacific Building and the Public Administrator has his office in the Pacific Building. Questioned about Mr. Mareska's so-called "cash money" of $700, Mr. Olshefsky said that Mareska lived with a man named Karen, and there is a suspicion that this man took the money, as the trunk was found open when the adminstrator came. This man moved out of the state some time ago. Though there is the suspicion that this man took the money, they cannot prove it. Mr. Olshefsky says that the case is ready to be closed, but he cannot make Vanas go to the court to witness to the heirship.

December 9, 1920.—Tony Vanas in office. He says he does not trust Olshefsky and thinks that more insurance was paid. He says he never saw the check. He also thinks that one-third to be paid to the lawyer is too much as no court action was necessary. Mr. Vanas paid all expenses, carfare, etc. *Later.*—Letter written to International Plough Company as follows:

A. C. Armstrong, Supt. International Plough Company
Chicago, Illinois

MY DEAR MR. ARMSTRONG: We have been asked by Mr. Anton Vanas, 415 Milwaukee Street, to help him in the following matter. A friend of his, Frank Mareska, was formerly employed by you at your plant on Milwaukee Street; we are unable to tell in what department he worked or what his check number was. This man died on December 18, 1918, his death being due to injuries inflicted on him by a fellow-employee, named Joseph. Anton Vanas was given power of attorney by Mr. Mareska's wife, whom he had known in Czecho-Slovakia, to settle the affairs of her husband. For this purpose he engaged a Polish lawyer. Now he brings accusation of misappropriation of funds against this lawyer, and wants our assistance in securing justice for the man's wife and children, who are still in Europe. Before we go any farther into the situation we should greatly appreciate a report from you on the case. What amount of death-benefit was paid to this man's estate, and when? Did the claim involve a lawsuit? If not, was there in your opinion any need for the services of a lawyer? We should be very much obliged to you for information on the above points.

Very truly yours,

LYDIA GARDNER, *Secretary*
Immigrants' Commission

December 13, 1920.—Reply received from the International Plough Company as follows:

GENTLEMEN:

Replying to yours of December 9th would state that under a proper Power of Attorney given by Domenica Mareska under date of April 2, 1920, appointing Jacob Olshefsky of Chicago her Attorney in Fact, this Association in June 11, 1920, paid to Mr. Olshefsky, as Attorney in Fact, the sum of $2,252.77, as death-benefit due under Frank Mareska's membership [in our Employes' Benefit Association]. The settlement of this claim did not involve any suit at Law, and was made in accordance with the usual practice of this Association. We know nothing of Anton Vanas, or any Power of Attorney given by beneficiary to Tony Vanas to represent her, other than as mentioned in your letter.

Yours truly,

A. C. ARMSTRONG

December 15, 1920.—R. S. visited the Public Administrator. Mr. Patrick was appointed by them to handle a compensation suit[1] against the International Plough Company. It was hoped they might recover $4,000 in that way instead of the $2,250 benefit. Mr. Patrick's fee represents work done by him on that case, and the administrator says it is far from exorbitant. The $67.58 is half the fee regularly charged by the Public Administrator for work like this. They knew nothing about Mr. Olshefsky except that he was attorney *de facto*. They think his charge outrageous and think a disbarment suit should be brought. The Public Administrator will do nothing about it, however. The Public Administrator has $357 of the Mareska estate (the man's bank book and wages and refund on a Liberty Bond. This money he must turn over to Alien Property Custodian). The Public Administrator gets 6 per cent for handling the estate. *Later.*— R. S. visited the Industrial Board. Talked with Mr. Hayward about whether there should be "workman's compensation" for Frank Mareska's widow. Mr. Hayward says the case was filed but was dismissed in the spring of 1920, as there was no proof of the company's responsibility for the man's death. Mr. Hayward had no dealings in the matter with Olshefsky. Mr. Patrick was the attorney. According to Mr. Hayward he is thoroughly reliable and honest. *Later.*—Visited Mr. Patrick. He was paid $150 for his services. Of this he had to pay $55 for the services of an interpreter, witnesses, etc. (He showed check stub in proof.) Mr. Olshefsky told him he was to receive $300 for his services and as Mr. Patrick had done all the work in the case (Olshefsky did nothing but collect the money), Olshefsky agreed to share.

December 17, 1920.—Telephoned Mr. Olshefsky, who is now employed by the Chicago Banking Company. He will come to office of the Immigrants' Commission, Saturday noon. *Later.*—Letter sent to Mr. Sargent, vice-president of the Chicago Banking Company and an old member and friend of the Immigrants' Protective League and Immigrants' Commission:

MY DEAR MR. SARGENT:

We have had under investigation an alleged exploitation case in connection with the settlement of an estate left by a Czecho-Slovak and have just discovered that the man concerned is an employee of the Chicago Banking Company. Knowing your interest in such cases, I am therefore writing you with reference to it. The facts as we have found them are as follows: In December of 1918 Frank Mareska was killed while at work for the International Plough Company. He left a widow and five minor children in Czecho-Slovakia. He was a member of the Plough Company's Benefit Association and left some money and property. The Public Administrator at first undertook to administer the estate he left. A compensation claim against the Plough Company was filed with the Industrial Board, the Public Administrator delegating a lawyer, John Patrick, to do the work connected with such a suit. A friend of the deceased, Mr. Anton Vanas, arranged

---

[1] [That is, a claim before the Industrial Board of Illinois under the Workmen's Compensation Law.]

with Jacob Olshefsky to act as the man's attorney and secured a power of attorney from the widow authorizing him to act as Attorney in Fact and to retain one-third of the estate collected. In April Mr. Olshefsky, acting under this authority, asked that the suit before the Industrial Board be dismissed. As it was then clear that responsibility on the part of the International Plough Company could not be established, Mr. Patrick did this.

Mr. Olshefsky collected the insurance from the International Plough Company. This was paid on presentation of his power of attorney without any suit. Mr. Olshefsky accounts for the money he collected ($2,252.77) as follows:

Sent to the widow	$1,000.00
Fee for Mr. Olshefsky as per agreement	752.00
To Mr. Vanas for services rendered	25.00
Fee for Mr. Patrick	150.00
Fee for the Public Administrator	67.58

The remaining $258.00 he did not account for. Our investigation indicates that Mr. Olshefsky did very little work in this case, and that his fee is exorbitant. Under what representations the widow signed the Power of Attorney I do not know, but she certainly cannot have understood the nature of the contract she entered into. I shall be very grateful if you will let me have your opinion of the case.

Very truly yours,

LYDIA GARDNER, *Secretary*

January 7, 1921.—Reply received from Mr. Sargent. He has had a statement from Mr. Olshefsky which he would like to discuss with the secretary of the Commission. Appointment made for January 12. *Later.*—Submitted report to International Plough Company.

January 19, 1921.—The following letter received from the Welfare Worker of the International Plough Company:

MY DEAR MISS GARDNER:

I am returning your file with regard to Frank Mareska. In going over our Industrial Accident Department file, there are letters from two other attorneys besides Mr. Olshefsky and Mr. Patrick. One of them (of the firm of Jones and Hay) says they were retained by Mr. Nyka, who was a friend and relative of the family; the other attorney, Joseph Leon, 201 Milwaukee Street, was retained by Tony Vanas. Our file shows a record of a visit from Mr. Olshefsky to the Employes' Benefit Association on March 8. During the course of this visit, Mr. Olshefsky was told of the appointment of Mr. Patrick by the Public Administrator to handle the case. The $2,252.77 was paid to Olshefsky through another attorney by the name of Mayer on June 11, 1920. This morning I talked to Mr. Farr in our Industrial Accident Department. He says there is very little to do, but for Mr. Vanas to go in and establish proof of heirship in the Probate Court so the will can be settled. He called my attention to the fact that in Mr. Olshefsky's report to you, on how the money had been expended, he does not take into account at all the $317 which he claims to have paid Mayer. Mr. Farr thought it might be a good thing to pursue Mr. Olshefsky for a more accurate account of receipts and expenditures in the settlement of Mr. Mareska's estate.

Yours very truly,

MARY S. WILLIAMS

Later.—Talked with Miss Williams, who reports that she has discussed the Mareska case with Mr. Harvard, head of the Compensation Department, and also with Mr. Hall, of the Employes' Benefit Association. Mr. Harvard thinks the charge is outrageous. The man's relatives and friends knew the money was at the Plough Company to be had whenever power of attorney was filed—$33\frac{1}{3}$ per cent fee might be reckoned on balance of estate in connection with the collection of which he had done some work. He regards the collection of a fee of $33\frac{1}{3}$ per cent on the Benefit an outrageous charge, no matter what was signed in the way of a contract.

January 12, 1921.—Saw Mr. Sargent of the Chicago Trust Company. He has had a report from Jacob Olshefsky but says he is not satisfied with it. He thinks we should have him come to the office of the Immigrants' Commission and make a settlement. Mr. Sargent looked up Olshefsky in the bar directory, and he is not there. Olshefsky is getting about $35–$40 a week in their employ. They could dismiss him, in fact he is only on a temporary basis and is not likely to be kept permanently, but Mr. Sargent thinks dismissal not so effective as the other method. He asks us to tell Mr. Olshefsky that he (Mr. Sargent) stands by us in the demands we make. Told Mr. Sargent we certainly did not want the man dismissed, but we did feel that he had been guilty of unprofessional conduct and that some way ought to be found to compel him to make restitution to the widow. *Later.*—The following letter sent to Mr. Olshefsky:

DEAR SIR:

Mr. Sargent has referred to us the explanation which was submitted to him of your conduct of the Mareska case, and I have also talked with him about the matter. Will you please come to this office on Saturday, January 15, at 12 o'clock in order that I may discuss this matter with you.

Yours very truly,
LYDIA GARDNER, *Secretary*
Immigrants' Commission

January 15, 1921.—Jacob Olshefsky did not come.

January 18, 1921.—Telephoned Chicago Banking Company. Mr. Olshefsky is no longer employed there. He left last week.

[Several entries are omitted here relating to proof of heirship, etc.]

February 21, 1921.—Saw Judge Bryan of the Probate Court. The "Death Benefit" was executed in favor of Mrs. Mareska; it does not come under the jurisdiction of the Probate Court (should have been paid to her directly by International Plough Company. Judge Bryan does not see why any power of attorney was necessary). Unfortunately Judge Bryan cannot make Olshefsky disgorge. He thinks that Olshefsky has behaved very badly. I asked Judge Bryan if the Public Administrator and Mr. Patrick had a right to have their fees paid out of the insurance with which they really had nothing to do. He seemed to think not. Judge Bryan has seen Mr. Olshefsky. The latter is uncomfortable but stubborn. He claims he is holding the $200 (balance) at the order of the Public Administrator, who wants to make sure the Mareska estate is large enough to settle claims of Public Administrator for fees, service, etc., against it. Judge Bryan advised taking the matter up with Mr. Bird, "Grievance Committee," Chicago Bar Association. *Later.*—Saw Mr. Bird. He agrees with the Immigrants' Commission in our opinion of Jacob Olshefsky. He will present the facts to his Committee and he is sure they will do all they can to make him do the right thing. He thinks they may be able to induce Olshefsky to part with some of the money, and it may be possible to disbar him. Must have a typewritten statement from us. *Later.*—Statement of case sent to Chairman of Grievance Committee.

March 2, 1921.—Letter received from Grievance Committee, acknowledging our letter. [The reply said:]

A rule has been entered against Mr. Olshefsky, requiring him to answer the complaint. As soon as the answer comes in, you will be forwarded a copy of the same and you will be advised of the further action of the Committee.

March 11, 1921.—Letter from Secretary of Committee on Grievances, Chicago Bar Association, saying that the complaint against Jacob Olshefsky has been set for hearing on March 16, 1921, at the Bar Association rooms at 3 o'clock and saying "the Committee wishes you to be present with such witnesses as you may wish to produce."

March 14, 1921.—Notified Mr. Vanas to call at the office of the Immigrants' Commission Wednesday, March 16, at 2 P.M. *Later.*—Saw Mr. Bird, Secretary of Committee on Grievances, and asked him about having other witnesses present. This was unnecessary, he said. The hearings are usually quite informal and our statements and correspondence with the Plough Company will be sufficient for their record.

March 16, 1921.—Attended hearing with Miss Spacek, and Mr. Vanas. The "Grievance Committee" consisted of Mr. Bird and one other man, the third member will read the record. Mr. Olshefsky made a very poor appearance, evidently he is thoroughly incompetent and inexperienced and is now willing to do whatever the Committee suggests. The Chairman of the Committee said "it was a crime that widow had not got even one half" —"never heard of taking one-third of gross rather than net receipts." Contract which Mr. Olshefsky submitted does not cover insurance but a contemplated damage suit. The Chairman of the Committee was evidently impressed by Mr. Olshefsky's apparent poverty and general ineffectiveness. He will summon the other lawyers, Patrick and Mr. Mayer, and see then what can be done. He asked that copy of Mr. Olshefsky's statement to Mr. Sargent be submitted. *Later.*—Letter written to Mr. Bird:

My dear Mr. Bird:

In accordance with your request I am sending for your files the statement which Mr. Olshefsky filed with Mr. Sargent, who is Vice-President of the Chicago Banking Company and who has been interested in the work of the Immigrants' Commission. I meant to say yesterday that I feel sure Mr. Olshefsky was not dismissed by the company as a result of this case. When I first talked to Mr. Sargent about it he said that the easy thing to do was to dismiss him but that seemed to him to get us nowhere and I immediately replied that I certainly did not want him dismissed. Mr. Olshefsky was, however, a comparatively recent employee in the Department and not one of the most efficient, and I think that the reason given him, a reduction in the Department staff, was undoubtedly correct. Certainly when I saw Mr. Sargent after the receipt of this reply, although Mr. Sargent was not at all satisfied with it and thought the man should be made to refund a part of the money, his dismissal was not contemplated.

Yours very truly,

Lydia Gardner

March 21, 1921.—Letter received from Chicago Bar Association. The Grievance Committee will meet again March 30, same hour and place.

March 30, 1921.—Hearing before Bar Association Grievance Committee. Mr. Mayer, the attorney who helped Olshefsky, was heard and told about the same story. He is brighter and more experienced—caught the drift of Mr. Bird's opinion and of the other Committee member (not the same attorney who attended previous hearing) and said he was not relying on the contract which he knew did not cover the insurance but on the work performed. The other member of the Committee suggested 6 to 10 per cent was the amount that was usually allowed. He said it should be left to Immigrants' Commission to settle; both Olshefsky and Mayer agreed to leave question to the Secretary of Commission. The suggestion was made that the Secretary of the Immigrants' Commission appear at court at time of hearing. Judge Bryan could probably make Patrick and Mayer pay back money they required Olshefsky to pay—not entitled to anything from the insurance money. Also suggested we hurry up settlement with Alien Property Custodian. Olshefsky gave me last letter from him and we promised to write and to write them about fee also.

March 31, 1921.—Letter written to Alien Property Custodian, Bureau of Trusts, Washington, D.C.:

My dear Sir:

We are interested in the settlement of the estate of Frank Mareska. I understand from the lawyer who collected the insurance from the International Plough Company that final payments are being deferred pending word from you. Frank Mareska was a member of the Employes' Benefit Association of the Plough Company, and his wife, Domenica, who, together with her five children, is in Czecho-Slovakia (Nedanovice, Com. Nyitra, Czecho-Slovakia) is the beneficiary. The amount of the insurance was $2,252.77. My understanding is that collections are not made on insurance of the fraternal type. As the family is in very great need, I hope that a decision may be promptly reached.

Yours very truly,
LYDIA GARDNER

Letter also written to Mr. Olshefsky as follows:

MY DEAR MR. OLSHEFSKY:

Inclosed is a letter from the Alien Property Custodian which you left with me yesterday. I have written him in accordance with the suggestion made and hope that a prompt decision will be rendered. On a re-reading of the record and after a conversation with the representative of the Plough Company I have come to the conclusion that it will be fair to allow for the attorney's fees the most liberal amount suggested by the Grievance Committee of the Bar Association; that is, 10 per cent.

Yours very truly
LYDIA GARDNER

[Mr. Olshefsky's "Defense," a typewritten document of six pages, is not included in this record. His "Defense" showed that he had spent a great deal of time on the case and while this time had not been spent efficiently or profitably it seemed just to give him the larger amount.]

April 1, 1921.—Mr. Olshefsky called up to say that he had received our letter. If payment was made as per our suggestion it would have to all go to Mr. Mayer. He wanted to come in and talk it over and said he would come Monday morning.

April 7, 1921.—Mr. Olshefsky and Mr. Mayer came in to discuss. I went over it all again. Both men argued that they must be allowed $400, $200 each, as a fair settlement. I said I could not consider that and suggested $300, which would give them $150 each. Mr. Mayer wanted to bargain further. I refused. They agreed then to accept $300. They will be here tomorrow with $652.39 to send the widow. This includes $201 balance of insurance money plus $452.39, which they pay back out of their fee. I also said I would be glad to attend hearing in probate court. *Later.* —Letter received from Alien Property Custodian. Extract from letter:

Under date of March 2, 1921, we wrote to Jacob Olshefsky, attorney at law, Chicago, explaining to him the steps necessary to be taken on behalf of the supposed enemy before the Government's interest in this estate could be released by the Attorney General. We have received one or two letters from Mr. Olshefsky but no card appeared thereon, and we had no street address and had to address him at Chicago, Illinois. Our first letter reached him apparently because we received a prompt reply but our letter to him above mentioned was returned by the postal authorities on March 15, 1921, undelivered. The Alien Property Custodian has not demanded the proceeds of the insurance held in the International Plough Company Employes' Benefit Association but the enemy interests have been demanded of the Public Administrator of Cook County, who is administering upon this estate. If you can give us the street address of Mr. Olshefsky we will be pleased to redirect our letter to him to the end that such steps may be taken as may result in enabling this estate to be closed upon the records of this office.

April 8, 1921.—Letter written to Alien Property Custodian, sending Mr. Olshefsky's address. *Later.*—Mr. Olshefsky in the office. Showed him letter from Alien Property Custodian. Then went with him to the bank, where he bought 45,304.80 crowns for the $652.39 payable to Mrs. Mareska. He will send it special delivery. We parted amicably. Mr. Olshefsky said he was sorry it had happened, etc., etc. His friend, Mr. Mayer, had refunded $7 less than his share. *Later.*—Letter written in Slovak to Mrs. Mareska about sending the money and the relation of the Immigrants' Commission to the case. Explained about the bank book, Liberty Bond, etc., with Public Administrator and Alien Property Custodian. Letter also written to Mr. Vanas.

June 20, 1921.—Letter received from Mrs. Mareska, dated May 29, 1921, Nedanovice [translation from the Slovak]:

Honored unknown Firm:

Receive our hearty greetings and good luck. We are giving you knowledge that we received 45,071 crowns. It did not come as much as you were writing to us as they deducted for expenses at the Ziouvstenska Banka, Prague. We received in words forty-five thousand and 71 crowns. What you are telling us that there is money with the public administrator I do not know anything about it. If you find out about it please attend to it as best you can. Now once more I send you hearty greetings and thank you for all your troubles.

Yours truly,

Domenica Mareska, *Widow*

[The remaining portion of the case record deals with efforts made to obtain a final settlement of the Mareska estate from the public administrator and the alien property custodian, correspondence with Czecho-Slovak Consulate and Legation regarding the necessary proofs of Czecho-Slovak citizenship of the heirs, etc.]

31. Martzen and Vassey Rubnik
(Complaint against a "Lawyer")

September 16.—Letter received from Juvenile Protective Association about a Mr. Kruk, apparently interpreter or "shyster" lawyer at West Street Police Station. Kruk has been involved in the case of a man named Martzen Rubnik, who was charged with having two wives. [Extract from letter follows:]

I am sending you a copy of the report made to me by Mr. B—, one of our Juvenile Protective officers. I remember that you were studying the treatment of immigrants in the police stations and lower courts and thought this would be of interest to you. If there is anything we can do to assist in this matter, please let us know.

[Copy of inclosed report:]

Rubnik is now locked up at West Street Station. His wife has only been in this country two years. She arrested her husband on day she arrived and found him married to another woman. After he was released on bail, his second wife arrested him. He only married this second wife six weeks after birth of child. He married his first wife eight years ago. Neighbors and friends of first wife said he admitted marriage to first wife; he denied marriage to second wife, although they claimed he secured a marriage license at the County Building. First wife does not even know the street where second wife lives. Case shows the crookedness of the hangers-on at the West Street Court. Kruk, who acts as interpreter and major domo for the shyster lawyers and other parasites, handled the case for Rubnik. When first wife arrested him, Kruk went to second wife and secured $60 from her to bail Rubnik out with. After he was bailed, second wife arrested him; and then Kruk came to first wife, who took pity on the man, and secured $20 from her for a bondsman. After he was let out on bond for a day, the bondsmen surrendered him; and he was put behind the bars again. When this was done, Kruk went again to second wife and got $70 from her— all the money she had, which he said would again go for a bond and for an attorney. Not satisfied with the money he secured, he again went to first wife and told her that if she gave him $75 he would have him freed. Something should be done in this matter by the Juvenile Protective Association in co-operation with other organizations. The Immigrants' Protective League should take a hand as both women in the case are immigrants.

Later.—Letter acknowledged. Case referred to N. R. [Russian visitor] for investigation.

September 17.—N. R. visited Bureau of Personal Service [a Jewish welfare bureau near West Street]. Miss X. knows Kruk and suspects him of being dishonest but cannot prove it. She does not know his address and has only seen him about the West Street Station. She does not know Martzen Rubnik, case of man with two wives in which Kruk was implicated. Bureau thinks this is not a Jewish case but will be glad to co-operate if such is found to be true. *Later.*—Also visited West Street Station and spoke with officer-in-charge; he said book of records was at City Hall to be checked by Assistant Chief of Police. He did not remember Rubnik, but will look him up when book comes back the last of the week.

September 20.—Telephoned West Street Station, book of reports still at office of Assistant Chief of Police. Officer who knew Rubnik case said Rubnik's address and that of his first wife was 56 West Street. Address of second wife, Clinton and Eighth streets. *Later.*—Visited 56 West Street. No one who lives there now or in three adjoining stores or in any part of that house knew anyone by name of Rubnik. Landlord of 56 West Street, living across the street, does not know Rubnik. Visited Clinton and Eighth streets. No one about the corner knew of Rubnik.

September 30.—N. R. visited West Police Station. Office gave name and address of Mr. Rubnik's second wife as Melania Berg, 54 South Eighth Street. Child, Mary, daughter of woman and Mr. Rubnik, died September

28, three weeks old. Mr. Rubnik is now released, paroled for one year, living with his first wife at 61 Bryant Street. Officer thinks Bureau of Personal Service handled case. Kruk is a Russian Jew who maintains an office at 94 East Halsted Street under name of Albert Kruk, lawyer. *Later.*— Called at 54 South Eighth Street. Melania Berg has just moved out. New address given as 340 Jefferson Street. Visited 340 Jefferson. No woman answering the description there. People said she had moved again to northwest corner Barber and Jefferson, second house from Jefferson on Barber, third floor back. Works in Kaplan's store, lives alone, and comes home after 6 o'clock.

October 3.—Visited Kaplan's store on corner of Eighth and Halsted. Mrs. Berg not there. Called at Bureau of Personal Service again. They could find no record of Rubnik but will search further. They said Mr. Kruk's office was 94 East Halsted Street. Mr. Kruk has not been about the West Street Station longer than a year. Social workers in the Bureau say they have known him to be very generous in cases of several poor women whose cases he has handled. They say the influences about the West Street Station are likely to lead to the corruption of lawyers there. *Later.*— Name of Vassey Rubnik found on "manifest list"[1] just received from Ellis Island. Address on "manifest" that of brother; Michael Jeromin, 25 West Street. *Later.*—Visited 25 West Street. Mrs. Rubnik not at home. Left card of League. A neighbor said Mrs. Rubnik came over to join her husband whom she had not seen for eight years and found he was living with another woman, Melania Berg. She had him arrested with the woman and charged with adultery. Man and woman were both paroled for a year, with the alternative of the Bridewell if they broke parole. Mr. Rubnik went back to live with his real wife and promised to pay $2 per week to support child of second "wife," Melania Berg.

October 4.—The original Mrs. Rubnik in office. She says her husband has run away with second wife. She says Mike Rubnik, 92 Light Street, Milwaukee, knows where he is. This wife's name is Vassey Rubnik, and she is living at 61 Bryant Street. *Later.*—N. R. visited West Street Station. Police know that Mr. Rubnik has broken parole. They are willing to send an officer to Milwaukee to bring him back but would do nothing about it unless someone in particular brings the case up again. Officer on the case will call League officer. Mr. William Henry, telephone Kedzie 835, is the detective. Visited Mrs. Rubnik, 61 Bryant Street. She has three Russian men boarding with her. She is anxious to bring her husband back and make him support her and also pay back the money she borrowed for his bond. Each of the three boarders says he contributed toward the bond—Peter Olanchek, $70; Alexander Jalchow, $40; Vincent Lasky, $24. Mr. Olanchek will get the address of the lawyer who "fixed it up" for Mrs. Rubnik when

[1] See p. 608.

Mr. Rubnik was arrested. The men want their money back that Mrs. Rubnik "advanced" to the lawyer.

Mrs. Rubnik arrived in the United States September 5 of this year. She had a letter while in Russia from a friend here telling her that Mr. Rubnik had "married" a second wife, Melania Berg. This latter woman also had a husband in the old country. Previous to running away with Mr. Rubnik, Melania Berg lived with her brother and his wife at 13 Liberty Street, third floor, front. *Later.*—Mr. Henry, officer from West Street Station, in our office, says detective will bring man back and hold him for prosecution by State's Attorney. Gave officer address of Mr. Rubnik in Milwaukee.

October 5.—Mrs. Rubnik and two boarders in the office. She says that at the time of Mr. Rubnik's arrest, she gave a lawyer, Jacob Stein, 808 Ashland Avenue, $105, which she borrowed, to handle the case. She also gave Mr. Kruk, 94 East Halsted Street, $9 for interpreting. Mr. Kruk visited Mrs. Rubnik yesterday, asked for $25 to handle the case again. Policeman has evidently told Mr. Kruk that Mr. Rubnik was to be brought back to Chicago.

October 6.—Mr. Kruk in the office. He said he had seen a man "taking his number" and was afraid the League would put story about his "graft" in the paper. He said the first Mrs. Rubnik had never given him any money. Some friends of hers had given him $9 for interpreting for her at time of Mr. Rubnik's arrest and for going bail for Mrs. Rubnik's brother, who fought with policeman. The second "wife" had given him $60 for securing bail for Mr. Rubnik, when the first wife had him arrested. Of that $60 Mr. Kruk kept $35, gave another lawyer $10, gave second wife $15 back because she had no money for food. He said Mrs. Rubnik, the first wife, had given another lawyer, Jacob Stein, 808 Ashland Avenue, $110 for dealing with the case. That, however, was against Mr. Kruk's advice to her. He says he "advised her to go to the Legal Aid Society."

October 8.—N. R. visited West Street Station. Mr. Rubnik has been brought back from Racine and locked up at West Station to await reinstatement of charge of adultery. The case will be brought up at West Street Court, October 10. Saw Mr. Rubnik. He is much frightened and now accuses his first wife of immoral relations with boarders. He does not want to go back to her.

October 10.—Attended hearing at West Street Station. Mr. Rubnik was given one year in House of Correction. Mrs. Rubnik's story now is that she paid to Mr. Kruk for interpreting $9 and to a Mr. Stein for taking the case $35. For promising to get Mr. Rubnik free without having to pay for support of Melania's child (who has since died) she paid Mr. Stein an additional $75. He promised that he would return this money ($75) if Mr. Rubnik had to pay same. Mr. Rubnik agreed to pay $2 per week. Mr. Stein did not return the $75. Mr. Kruk also took $75 from Melania

Berg, the second wife. Of this, $60 was for bail for Mr. Rubnik at time of first arrest; $15 for bail at second arrest. He also took $9 from Mrs. Rubnik for bail of her brother.

October 12.—Officer M— telephoned that Melania Berg has been found in Chicago. She was arrested on old charge of adultery and breaking parole. Case came up in Chicago Avenue Court. The witnesses were not present and case was continued until October 14 at 2 P.M. Officer requests that N. R. [representative of the League] bring the witnesses in at that time.

October 31.—Interviewed Attorney Jacob Stein. He finally returned $30 to be given to Mrs. Rubnik.

[*October 31–December 1.*—Various entries omitted relating to the finding of proper work for the first Mrs. Rubnik.]

December 13.—Letter written to Superintendent of Juvenile Protective Association, Chicago:

You will remember that you wrote us some time ago regarding the case of Martzen Rubnik, who was arrested and confined at West Street Station on a charge of adultery. The interpreter Mr. Kruk, you also informed us, had collected several high fees from both women concerned. Upon investigation, we found that Mr. Rubnik had been paroled for a year to live with his real wife, Vassey Rubnik, whose name appeared later reported on the ship's "manifest list" we received from New York. Mr. Rubnik broke parole and ran away with the second woman to Milwaukee. We notified the police, and the man and the woman were brought back to West Street Station and each sentenced to a year in the Bridewell. We found work for Mrs. Rubnik, the real wife, and are keeping in touch with her. We took up the matter of the large fee paid to Mr. Kruk and found that the largest charge was made by a lawyer, Mr. Stein, with whom Mr. Kruk works. Mr. Stein refused to acknowledge that there had been an overcharge, but we succeeded in securing a refund of $30 for Mrs. Rubnik.

We send this by way of report and wish to thank you for calling our attention to the matter. We are glad to be informed of cases of this nature. We have reason to think that the immigrant is frequently the victim of the corruption we believe to exist in some of the police stations, but evidence is difficult to secure.

[The remaining portion of the case is omitted. It covers various visits to and from the first Mrs. Rubnik about her various jobs and her future plans. She at first thought she "never wanted her husband back," and asked help in securing a divorce. She was advised to have a talk with her husband in the Bridewell, and was given a letter to the Legal Aid Society. When last visited on the tenth of November, 1914, she and her husband were living together, apparently on good terms. Mrs. Rubnik said her husband was working regularly, had paid the money owed to the boarders, and she also reported that her husband now "treats her very well." When last heard from, April 4, 1915, she had called at the office to ask help in collecting some money owed from a boarder who needed a "job." Work was found for the boarder.]

32. Jan Piotowski and Others
(Notary-Public Complaint)

December 29, 1913.—Jan Piotowski, a Polish man, in the office. He wishes to recover money paid to a "lawyer" (probably a notary public), Mr. Kalenin, who has done nothing for him. A. F. [Slavic visitor] spoke with man. Mr. Piotowski says that he had been in the United States (and Chicago) three years when his wife, Maria, came to America last fourth of July. When she arrived, she was pregnant. The baby was born after a few months. The father of the child is a man whose name is Ignace Przzych; he is still in Europe. Mr. Piotowski went to this "lawyer," Mr. Kalenin, and paid him $20. Mr. Kalenin promised to take care of this case. Mr. Piotowski says this was a few months ago and to this time the lawyer has done nothing. Mr. Kalenin has a downtown office and a West Side office.

January 16, 1914.—A. F. went to see Mr. Kalenin. He was not in his office. He is in his office in the morning. He is probably not a lawyer, only a notary.

January 21, 1914.—A. F. went second time to Mr. Kalenin's office. Mr. Kalenin was there. He said that he wrote to Galicia September 2 but no answer has he had to this time. Asked if he thinks the woman will get something, and he answered that he depends on the lawyer in Austria. He does not wish to give name of lawyer in Austria to the League.

January 30, 1914.—A. F. visited Mrs. Piotowski and spoke with her in Polish. Mrs. Piotowski said at the time when her husband went to Mr. Kalenin she went with him and two other men. Mr. Kalenin promised to get the money from Ignace Przzych from Galicia. He did not give any receipt for the twenty dollars. They have a professional card which reads:

E. KALENIN

*Notarial and Information Office in Foreign Matters
Real Estate and Colonization
Court Interpreter, German and All Slavic Languages*

CHICAGO OFFICES: 108 South Street, Suite 1400   Telephone Main 25

February 16, 1914.—A. M. [Assistant Superintendent] visited Mr. Kalenin, who said that he had given the case to the court in Austria, and he did not know when it would come up. There is no one in Austria handling the case. He thinks we misunderstood about lawyer in Austria. Mr. Kalenin is either very uncertain about what he has done or has done nothing. *Later.*—A. M. visited the Austrian Consul. He knows a lot about Kalenin, and he will give the case to a lawyer who has other cases in which Kalenin figures. Kalenin is not an attorney, merely a notary.

SOCIAL CASE RECORDS

[Several entries are omitted here. The consul's attorney, Mr. Frank Jung, was very slow to act, and several interviews between Mr. Jung and a League representative are omitted.]

April 18, 1914.—Telephoned Mr. Jung. He has now eight or ten cases against Mr. Kalenin. Consul is sending complaints to Mr. Jung. Several are clearly cases of misrepresentation. Several Polish people can testify that Mr. Kalenin stated to them that he was the Consul. Mr. Jung is waiting for one other man who has case against Mr. Kalenin to come to his office. He will then get out a warrant for Mr. Kalenin, on charge of misrepresentation, at Clark Street Police Station. He had hoped to have Mr. Kalenin in jail over Sunday. If the other witness does not come to his office today, he will get out warrant in day or two anyway. He will notify League about time of hearing.

May 28, 1914.—Telephoned Mr. Jung. He has repeatedly notified Mr. Piotowski to come to his office but he has not come. He is notifying him again. *Later.*—Telephoned Consulate. Mr. S. will take up matter with Mr. Jung.

June 18, 1914.—Telephoned Consulate (Mr. S). He will see lawyer (Mr. Jung) again. Lawyer had said he had written Immigrants' Protective League.

June 20, 1914.—Mr. S. of the Austro-Hungarian Consulate telephoned. He has another complaint against law office of E. Kalenin, 108 South Street. Complainant is Michael Filicek, a Slovak. Man lives at 64 West Street. Mr. S. wishes League would visit. He will come in to see us some time this week about the whole situation. *Later.*—A. H. [Slovak-speaking visitor] visited Michael Filicek. This man says he went November 20, 1913, to Kalenin and asked him to write to his country for a register of landed properties. Filicek paid in advance $15 to Kalenin, who cannot show that he has done anything in this matter. Filicek wishes some advice or help to get back the amount paid to Kalenin's office.

June 24, 1914.—Mr. S. from Consulate in office. He is not satisfied. The lawyer, Mr. Jung, will apparently not do anything. Kalenin denies all charges. Told Mr. S. if he did not object we would refer cases to Legal Aid Society. Mr. S. agreed that this should be done. *Later.*—Letter written to Superintendent of Legal Aid Society, stating facts in the two cases.

July 31, 1914.—Reply from Legal Aid Society as follows:

We have taken up the case of Maria Piotowski and also of Michael Filicek, both of which were reported against Mr. Kalenin, but we are not yet in a position to report this matter to you fully. These things are rather delicate and have to be handled slowly.

August 3, 1914.—Letter from Legal Aid Society as follows:

Since we heard from you with regard to the claim of Michael Filicek against Mr. Kalenin, the latter has sent a representative to this office who states that he would like very much to have the number of the ticket given from their office to Mr. Filicek when he called. Every person calling upon Mr. Kalenin is given a number which he is to retain so that his case may be located in their file. So far they have been unable to find a record of Mr. Filicek. We would write to Mr. Filicek directly but fear he would be unable to understand just what information we require. We would therefore appreciate the courtesy if you would be kind enough to obtain this information for us.

August 5, 1914.—Wrote Legal Aid as follows:

Replying to your letter of August 3 in the claim of Michael Filicek against Mr. Kalenin, we beg to state that Mr. Filicek left with us a card given him by Mr. Kalenin. It contains a stamped number, 7146, and also a number in pencil, 3495. We trust this is the desired information.

August 24, 1914.—Wrote Legal Aid, asking for a report.

August 28, 1914.—Letter from Legal Aid as follows:

We received your letter inquiring about the case of Maria Piotowski and Michael Filicek. Mr. Kalenin sent his representative over here and explained that they had taken up the matter of the Piotowskis and found that when the man was brought into court he swore that he was not the father of the child and Mr. Kalenin has the papers in regard to the matter. We sent for these people, but they have not come in. We shall be glad to take further steps if this is not the truth. In the Filicek case they (Kalenin) told us that they had been given not only a wrong first name but also the incorrect name of town and county. Mr. Filicek rectified this, and they are now working on the case. We have sent for him twice, but he has not come in.

October 13, 1914.—Letter received from Legal Aid Society as follows:

We should like to know whether Maria Piotowski and Mr. Filicek ever succeeded in bringing their matters to satisfactory conclusions with Mr. Kalenin. We have no address for them and consequently can only reach them through your organization. If they have not received satisfaction we should like to go on with the matter while it is still fresh in the minds of all of us.

October 15, 1914.—Letter written to Legal Aid Society as follows:

We have received your letter of October 13, concerning the case of Maria Piotowski and Michael Filicek against the notary Kalenin. We are very anxious to have the case pushed and will make every effort to get the information from Mr. Piotowski and Mr. Filicek that is necessary for the settlement of the case. We do not, however, understand the contents of your letter of August 28, which reads as follows:

"Mr. Kalenin sent his representative over here and explained that they had taken up the matter of the Piotowskis and found that when the man was brought into court he swore that he was not the father of the child and Mr. Kalenin has the papers in regard to the matter."

Consequently we are at a loss to know just what to ask the Piotowskis. If you will let us know just what is needed we will get that information, or if it would be more satisfactory to you we will arrange, if possible, to bring them to your office for an interview. Our visitor, Mr. H—, is to have an interview with Mr. Filicek today, and we will report regarding that at once.

October 16, 1914.—J. H. visited Michael Filicek last evening. He recapitulated his case with Kalenin. On November, 1913, Filicek went with his old mother to Kalenin and told him the following: Anna Martinjak Filicek née Rurbek (the mother), Michael Filicek, Maria Filicek, and John Filicek (children) have in possession some properties in Trencsenrako, Comitat Trenscen, Hungary. Land register office in Csacza, Comitat Trenscen. The family has no relatives left in old country, will never return, and for that reason they want to sell this real estate. He needed for this purpose the official register of his landed properties and asked Kalenin to furnish the documents. He paid Kalenin in advance $15 and was given Kalenin's business card with the number 3495. "First I visited him on January 9, 1914; he told me that no answer came up to date. I visited again few times at last in June or July when the Legal Aid write me a letter. Kalenin had by every occasion some excuse, since today we are waiting. Kalenin has with two other Slovak men the same kind of troubles, and posed before the people like General Consul Secretary."

[Names of other Slovaks omitted. They were old cases at the Consulate. Other details given in interview omitted as they are repeated in letter below.]

October 19, 1914.—Letter to Legal Aid Society:

In your letter of August 28 with regard to the case of Michael Filicek, you mentioned that Mr. Kalenin claimed that Filicek had not only given a wrong first name to him but also the incorrect name of town and county, and that nothing could be done until Filicek rectified these mistakes, which he already did.

We have asked Mr. Filicek about this, and from his statement it seems that this is merely another of Kalenin's excuses for delay, and this happens to be one excuse he has not used with Filicek. That is, Mr. Kalenin has never asked for any correction of names or addresses. [Names and addresses of members of the family, all of whom are now in Chicago, are given as above.] We hope that this information will be of some value. Please let us know if there is anything further we can do in the case.

October 21, 1914.—Visited Mrs. Piotowski, who said that three months ago Mr. Kalenin wrote a letter saying that Mr. Przzych showed in a court in Galicia that he is not the father of the child. Mrs. Piotowski is now quite convinced of the impossibility of getting any money from the child's father in Galicia, but thinks Mr. Kalenin ought to refund the money she paid to him. He did nothing in the case, and he promised to get the money for her.

October 22, 1914.—Letter received from Legal Aid as follows:

In regard to the matter of Maria Piotowski the facts as we know them are as follows: Mrs. Piotowski came to this country pregnant she claimed by a man by the name of Przzych who was still in Europe. Mr. Kalenin undertook to prosecute this man in Europe. This must have been done through some agency over there. He claims that when the case was in court the man swore he was not the father of the child and Mrs. Piotowski's charges were denied. He also claims that the papers in reference to the matter are all in his office. If Mrs. Piotowski still persists in her statements, we would advise that you arrange for some time preferably the first thing in the morning, when she can call at this office with one of your interpreters and talk with one of our domestic interviewers. We feel that in this way we will be able to get facts from her by which we will be enabled to give Mr. Kalenin's papers intelligent consideration. The same thing would apply to Filicek.

October 28, 1914.—Telephoned Legal Aid Society. Suggested that Mrs. Piotowski would have nothing to add to information and that Mr. Kalenin's papers should be examined. Legal Aid Society will arrange to have a representative go to his office with our Mr. H—.

November 6, 1914.—Telephoned Legal Aid Society. They state that Mr. Kalenin has moved, and his address is unknown to them. Their Miss Brown saw Mr. S., of the Austrian Consulate, who is anxious to have Kalenin prosecuted and will try to get his new address through the post office, since he is getting a good deal of mail still and having it forwarded. They will let us know when they hear.

April 28, 1915.—Michael Filicek and his mother in the office. Telephoned Legal Aid and spoke with Miss Brown. Nothing can be done about recovering the $15; but if Kalenin has any of Filicek's papers they might be recovered, since he left all his papers with a girl with whom he was living immorally. The Legal Aid may be able to locate her. Mr. Filicek says that Kalenin has none of his papers. Told him to come in Sunday and our Mr. H—, who is a Hungarian, will write letter to Hungary for him. The Austrian Consul had sent Mr. Filicek here today.

May 1, 1915.—Mr. S. [Austrian Consulate] telephoned that they have a new claim against Kalenin, but they have not the new address of Kalenin. The new claimant is Peter Markewicz, address 900 West Street.

May 7, 1915.—J. H. visited Peter Markewicz. The man was out working. The woman said that a few years ago her husband gave to Mr. Kalenin $10 as he promised to sell a farm for $1,000, which they have in Europe. For a long time the man went to Mr. Kalenin's office every week asking about sale of the farm and Mr. Kalenin constantly told the man that next week he will tell him the result of the sale. The man works all the time, but the woman thinks he will come to the League on Sunday if they send him a postcard asking him to come.

May 9, 1915.—Peter Markewicz in office. He had an interest of one-sixth part of his parents' estate in Zediele, Post Dovra near Limanova, Galicia. When father and mother died, the children were young and the oldest brother, Josef, took possession of the whole farm and home. Peter Markewicz went to Kalenin about six years ago and paid $10 to him for expenses and signed also an affidavit. Since this time the man visited Kalenin many times. Kalenin promised and asked always for money, but he did not get any more from the man. It seems Kalenin did not do in this case anything or he may have collected long ago the money coming to Peter—so Peter said. The case is already four years old and very complicated; in the meantime two or more other sisters and brothers died and changed the situation. The only way to know something about this case is to write to the authorities to Zediele, Galicia (now in the war zone). The property was 20 (*morgen*) acres and two houses valued about $3,500. Told the man we will try to find out about the case and will notify him. Answer cannot be expected for several months.

[The remaining portion of the case is omitted since no further facts are given about the activities of Mr. Kalenin. There are many other entries on the record, for the Hungarian visitor of the League wrote to Hungary for the information needed about the different properties there. After a fruitless appeal to the state's attorney, the League gave up all hope of securing any refunds or having Mr. Kalenin prosecuted.]

PURCHASE OF STEAMSHIP TICKETS AND FOREIGN EXCHANGE

33. Kasimir Pulaski
(A Returned Immigrant's Non-receipt of Money)

January 27, 1914.—Victor Orloff, a Polish man, in office. He wants advice about how to help his friend Kasimir Pulaski, a Polish immigrant, who has gone home to Galicia. Mr. Orloff has a letter from Kasimir complaining about the non-receipt of money. The facts given by Mr. Orloff are: On June 5, 1913, Kasimir, who was about to return to Poland, took $100 which he had saved (500 crowns) to a steamship agent, Mr. Samuels, 100 Ashland Avenue, and asked to have the money sent to his address in Galicia. After Kasimir had been some time back in Poland he wrote to the friend (Victor Orloff) asking him to find out from the steamship agent what happened to the money. Mr. Orloff had interviewed Mr. Samuels and had been told that the money had been sent June 27, 1913, but had been returned on account of wrong address. Mr. Samuels said that on December 28, 1913, when he received the correct address, the money was sent at once. He said it must have been received about January 15, 1914.

January 29, 1914.—Letter written in Polish to Kasimir Pulaski in Galicia, asking if he has received the money that Mr. Samuels claims to have sent.

March 14, 1914.—Letter received from Kasimir Pulaski dated February 24, 1914, Dobrowa, Galicia [translation from the Polish]:

HONORABLE SOCIETY:

In answer to your letter January 29, 1914, I am letting you know that the money amounting to 500 crowns sent through Jacob Samuels, residing 100 Ashland Avenue, Chicago, on the fifth of June, 1913, which money had to be sent to my address and which I haven't received as yet. I am very happy to hear that you will try to help me in the case and I beg very much that you will help me and I beg hard you will get my money which would be of very great use to me here at home. I am thanking you for your interest in my case and I remain,

Yours very truly,

KASIMIR PULASKI

March 15, 1914.—Interviewed Mr. White, the attorney for the Legal Aid Society. He thought money could be collected by suit if necessary. He will take the matter up with the bank and try to collect first without suit. If money is found to have been unlawfully withheld he will try to collect interest also. If proof of the payment is not shown, he will write the man for power of attorney and sue the bank. He will inform us of developments.

March 24, 1914.—The following extract is from a letter received from the Legal Aid Society:

We have a letter from Jacob Samuels, assuring us that he has attempted many times to send the foreign money to Kasimir Pulaski, but it has been returned each time. He, however, sent a draft on February 14, which was not returned. Therefore we have every reason to believe that Mr. Pulaski has received his money. If, however, this is not the case, we shall be very glad to go on with the matter.

April 28, 1914.—Letter received from Kasimir Pulaski, with inclosure [translation from Polish]:

DEAR MADAM:

I am very much obliged to you that you look after my matter. I send at once the receipt which I get from Samuels leaving 500 crowns in his office, June 5, 1913, and which I didn't get yet. He gave me two of the same receipts, one of them I sent to my friend Victor Orloff, 328 Erie. You can call for it if you need it. I send you a letter from Samuels which I received March 2, 1914, with a check. I was in a bank ten times but Samuels did not send money at all. If you wish to have a check which Samuels sent to me March 2, 1914, let me know, I will send at once.

KASIMIR PULASKI

[Translation from Polish of letter to Kasimir Pulaski from Jacob Samuels, March 16, 1914:]

CHICAGO, ILLINOIS
February 14, 1914

DEAR SIR:

After a long search and sending the money back and forth I am able today to state the results. Your 500 crowns I received back today and at once am sending to you also again a draft for this amount in bank in town Dobrowa. This check you have to send to the bank or you have to go there yourself. Because the check has to be certified through the bank in New York and Prague then will take about fourteen days until you will be able to get the money. I also advise you to wait fourteen days after you will get my letter and then go to the bank, otherwise your trip would be in vain. I am very sorry that the thing took so long, but I learned about it not very long ago, because Mr. Hornja is not in my office any more. Please do not be angry. The money will come to the bank surely.

May 4, 1914.—Polish letter received from Galicia [translation]:

HONORABLE MADAM:

Today I received your letter where you are asking me if I received the 500 crowns through Jacob Samuels, 100 Ashland Avenue, in June, 1913. Second of March I received from him a registered letter including a check for 500 crowns. I was told in the letter after two weeks to take the check to city Dobrowa that the *Kasa oszezednosci* of the city of Dobrowa will pay me the money. I was many times in the city but am always told that the bank does not know anything about the money that they did not get any order. I wish to know why he sent me the check and did not notify the bank.

Please go to Jacob Samuels and ask him why he did not notify the bank to pay me the money.

KASIMIR PULASKI

June 2, 1914.—Legal Aid Society telephoned. Mr. Samuels is ready to cash draft here if original draft sent to Austria can be produced showing it has not been paid. He says he has a dishonest foreign representative. Legal Aid Society wishes us to write for draft. *Later.*—Letter written to Mr. Pulaski to send draft over.

July 17, 1914.—Letter received from Mr. Pulaski, inclosing draft of Jacob Samuels.

[Letter to Legal Aid Society inclosing the draft and several other letters from and to Legal Aid Society omitted.]

August 14, 1914.—Legal Aid Society telephoned. They have some other cases against Jacob Samuels, which probably will be heard in September, date not fixed. This Pulaski case will be difficult to collect on, perhaps impossible. A civil suit is hardly advisable because Mr. Samuels has no property, and a criminal suit requires as evidence the testimony of main witness. In this case man is in Europe, and depositions or affidavits are not legal testimony.

September 2, 1914.—The following letter from Kasimir Pulaski [translation from the Polish]:

DOBROWA
August 14, 1914

DEAR MADAM:

I would like to find out what happened with my 500 crowns which Samuels, 100 Ashland Avenue, was supposed to send June 5, 1913. Since I had sent to you receipt in a registered letter I did not hear any word from you. I need the money very badly.

Respectfully,
KASIMIR PULASKI

September 3, 1914.—Telephoned Legal Aid Society. Status the same as on August 14, nothing has happened. *Later.*—Letter written in Polish to Kasimir Pulaski about status of case. Legal Aid Society holds out very little hope of ever collecting.

[A later entry in the record notes that Samuels had failed and absconded.]

34. Paul Nicholayev
(Purchase of Steamship Tickets)

February 13, 1913.—A Ruthenian man, Paul Nicholayev, called at the office with steamship ticket complaint. R. B. [Russian visitor] spoke with man, who reports that in December, 1912, he bought steamship tickets for relatives from Isaac Kantor, a Polish Jew, 600 Milwaukee Avenue, and paid $122. Mr. Nicholayev says he has been many times, asking for the tickets, but cannot get them from the agent, who has always some different subterfuge. The last answer was that he (Kantor) had sent the money to New York to the Polish-American Line. Now Mr. Nicholayev finds that Kantor has often such troubles with his customers. A neighbor, Theodor Kotik, also bought from Kantor for $62 a ticket for Helena Kotik on the Polish-American Line, S.S. "Cracow," and has not yet the ticket. R. B. told him to see Mr. Kantor again and to report to us and to bring in neighbor if tickets are not furnished in a short time. *Later.*—R. B. called at office of Polish-American Line and spoke with Mr. X. He said Mr. Kantor had applied for their agency several times and had been refused. Neither Mr. Kantor nor the agency in Germany with whom he deals can sell tickets on the Polish-American. Mr. X. says people prefer the Polish-American Line because steerage conditions are better. Agents like Kantor promise to send by the Polish-American and then send by one of the German lines. Mr. X. called up Kantor, who promised to bring the $122 down to the Polish-American office.

February 15, 1913.—Mr. Nicholayev came in to say that Mr. Kantor took money to Polish-American Line. Mr. Nicholayev paid $40 which was still due (Kantor had not collected right amount) and also sent $10 to his relative.

February 25, 1913.—Theodor Kotik, another Ruthenian who had trouble with Isaac Kantor, in office, sent by Paul Nicholayev. R. B. took him to Polish-American office. Mr. X. telephoned Mr. Kantor who promised to bring this man's money down also. Polish-American Line expects to prosecute Mr. Kantor and wants to know of any other cases.

February 26, 1913.—Mr. Nicholayev visited. No one at home. Left word for him to let us know of any other cases.

March 24, 1913.—Letter to Polish-American Line, inquiring whether any action had been taken against Isaac Kantor.

March 26, 1913.—Reply from Polish-American Line stating that Mr. Kantor never had represented their line and asking that the American-Atlantic Conference, 100 LaSalle Street, be consulted for any further information about Mr. Kantor.

March 27, 1913.—R. B. called at office of A. H. Burg, Secretary, American-Atlantic Conference. He said Polish-American Line had referred case to them. He has written Mr. Kantor several letters asking for an explanation of failure to get tickets or refund money. No response. American-Atlantic Conference has, however, photograph of receipts of money received from Mr. Nicholayev signed by Kantor, saying tickets were to be issued over Polish-American Line via Rotterdam to Chicago. It looks clearly like misrepresentation and confidence game. If such is proved, Kantor can be prosecuted. He cannot, however, be prosecuted under any law regulating steamship agents, for Illinois has no such law. Mr. Kantor is not agent for Polish-American Line. He is, however, for two other lines. Mr. Burg thinks those two lines will certainly drop Kantor if they have not already. He will notify them of the case and will also see Polish-American Line. He will bring matter up at next meeting of Conference, April 15, and give it careful consideration.

[The remaining portion of the case record is omitted. The Polish-American line did not prosecute because they thought it useless since there was no satisfactory law regulating steamship agencies. Mr. Kantor was, however, dropped by the two other lines which he had represented. The Legal Aid Society reported that they saw a notice in the paper to the effect that Kantor was arrested and in jail on charge of embezzlement. They found that the case was called in the Chicago Avenue Police Station but was dismissed because plaintiff did not appear. They found, however, that several other cases of embezzlement are pending against Mr. Kantor. Reports of further efforts to prosecute Mr. Kantor are omitted since they are dealt with also in the following case. In the meantime the tickets for the Nicholayev family were sent and arrived safely.]

35. Ignace Prystalski and Others
(Issue of Worthless Steamship Tickets)

July 10, 1913.—Telegram received from New York State Bureau of Immigration: "*Immigrants' Protective League, Chicago:* Ignace Prystalski, wife, and two others stranded in New York purchased steamship tickets for Austria from Isaac Kantor, 600 Milwaukee Avenue, Chicago, July third, on Bryde Line. Steamers not running. Tickets no good. Can you investigate quickly and wire? Thanks.—NEW YORK STATE BUREAU OF INDUSTRIES AND IMMIGRATION." *Later.*—Night letter sent to New York as follows: "*New York State Industries and Immigration, New York City:* Many serious complaints against Isaac Kantor. Under heavy bonds. Cases in police courts now. Has been discharged by all reputable steamship lines. Cannot secure agency again. Kindly send details of case Ignace Prystalski and others.—IMMIGRANTS' PROTECTIVE LEAGUE."

[A letter was received July 14 from New York giving details of Prystalski case and inclosing various documents. Among the documents sent were four steamship tickets. These tickets were the regular printed steamship tickets of the "Bryde" Line, Newport News to Rotterdam, bearing the printed legend "A. B. Smith, Inc., New York, Chicago, Newport News, General Passenger Agent, Chicago, 1 East LaSalle Street." Tickets marked Chicago to Cracow, via Rotterdam on S.S. "Potsdam," July 8, 1913, and issued to four passengers: Ignace Prystalski and his wife, Paul Czarkowski, Wladimir Suleika. Price of each ticket $41.40—total $165.60. When they arrived in New York they found that the S.S. "Potsdam" was a Holland-American Line steamer and that the Bryde Line steamships sailed from Newport News, but their tickets were not valid on the Bryde Line, for Kantor had no authority to issue tickets on this line. The passengers were referred to New York Bureau of Industries and Immigration and finally bought new tickets and went on to Europe. A deposition was inclosed with statements by A. B. Smith to the effect that the corporation of Smith and Company closed their Chicago office in December, 1912, and that Isaac Kantor had never been an agent of the Bryde Line and that the tickets issued by the said Isaac Kantor were forgeries. There was another deposition made by Henry Meyer, who closed up the accounts of Smith and Company's office in Chicago. This deponent stated that Smith and Company had never represented the Holland American Line to which the steamer "Potsdam" belonged and that the Bryde Line had never sailed from New York. He also stated that the Bryde Line had only one sailing from Newport News, on September 3, 1912, the "Noruega," and that to his knowledge this was the only steamer which sailed and carried passengers direct to Holland. The case record also contains the following entry: "The Bryde Line in Chicago is now represented by a Mr. Glasgow. Telephoned Mr. Glasgow, arranged for interview tomorrow."]

July 17, 1913.—Saw Mr. Glasgow. He says whole issue of tickets is fraudulent. He had appointment with Mr. Kantor for Saturday at 12 o'clock. Kantor did not come. He had promised to refund price of tickets. Mr. Glasgow said he would telegraph New York. Kantor promised to call at Mr. Glasgow's office and Mr. Glasgow will telephone us later as soon as he has had an interview. Left tickets with Mr. Glasgow, who gave receipt.

July 19, 1913.—Letter received from Mr. Glasgow inclosing the following copy:

Mr. Isaac Kantor
600 Milwaukee Avenue
Chicago, Illinois

DEAR SIR: After my telephone conversation yesterday morning, I have been looking for you to keep your promise and make a refund of the money you are holding for the Bryde Line tickets. From information which I have received, I believe the matter is a very serious one and I should judge it would be to your interest to make a settlement immediately. The tickets are in my possession. I telephoned your office two or three times yesterday and only got evasive answers; the last one being that you were not expected back until 7:00 or 8:00 o'clock in the evening which, of course, was long past the time I could possibly call you and even then there was no certainty as to whether I could see you.

J. M. GLASGOW

August 4, 1913.—Telephoned Mr. Glasgow. He has made various attempts to see Mr. Kantor but Kantor has eluded him. Mr. Kantor evidently thinks that since the people have returned to Europe there can be no prosecution. Mr. Glasgow will send over Bryde receipts. *Later.*—Letter sent to Legal Aid Society asking their assistance.

August 11, 1913.—Letter received from and reply sent New York Bureau:

MY DEAR MR. JONES:

Replying to your letter of August 9th regarding the claim of Ignace Prystalski against Isaac Kantor of this city we would say that the case has finally been placed in the hands of the Legal Aid Society. First, at your suggestion we took up the matter with Mr. Glasgow, local agent of the Bryde Line, who made some effort to extract the money from Mr. Kantor. At one time Mr. Kantor promised to refund the money if the original tickets were presented. These we placed in the hands of Mr. Glasgow. Mr. Kantor eluded him and the money could not be extracted. The Legal Aid Society advises us that the matter is receiving their most careful attention. As you are already advised, Mr. Kantor is held under $5,000 bonds. The Legal Aid Society states that all of their cases against him have been brought to the attention of the State's Attorney who has promised his assistance. The prospects in the other cases of obtaining the money from Kantor, however, are meager in the opinion of the Legal Aid Society. In this case since the steamship company and the general agent are in a measure behind the issue of the tickets the Legal Aid Society hopes for a favorable settlement. The matter is difficult to handle because the claimants have sailed from this country. The Legal Aid Society has promised to do all that is possible.

Yours very sincerely,

EMMA KENNETH, *Acting Superintendent Immigrants' Protective League*

December 23, 1913.—Telephoned Legal Aid Society asking status of case. Society thinks there is slight hope for recovering. Isaac Kantor has no money. His lawyer has been reporting that he has gone to Europe to raise the money and promises to repay everything. [Later it was discovered that Kantor had not been in Europe at all but in Airdale, Wisconsin, carrying on the same kind of fraudulent business there.]

May 5, 1914.—Legal Aid Society telephoned. Mr. Kantor's lawyer again is asking for how much Legal Aid Society will settle all cases against Kantor. Kantor is really in Europe now, he says, and wishes to return to America but is afraid to come back until matters are cleared. Mr. Suleika and Mr. Czarkowski have returned from Europe and will appear as witnesses if Kantor is prosecuted.

June 8, 1914.—Telephoned State's Attorney. Mr. Kantor is still in Europe.

June 22, 1914.—Isaac Kantor caught and in jail. He has been held to Grand Jury.

July 28, 1914.—Telephoned Legal Aid Society. Isaac Kantor is still in jail and unable to raise bail. His former lawyer, Goldberg, has withdrawn his services. Kantor failed to raise the money he expected in Austria, where he formerly operated a steamship agent business. His case will be heard in the Criminal Court. Five cases will be heard against him:

No. *5880.*—Confidence game; plaintiff, Paul Czarkowski.
No. *5889.*—Embezzlement game; plaintiff, John Tuka.
No. *5960.*—Confidence game; plaintiff, Wladimir Suleika.
No. *5961.*—Confidence game; plaintiff, Kasimir Zukowski.
No. *5991.*—Larceny game; plaintiff, Mary Jakoba.

Case of Ignace Prystalski not filed in Criminal Court as main witnesses are in Europe. It is useless to file in Civil Court as judgment if awarded could not be collected.

August 12, 1914.—Case of Wladimir Suleika, No. 5960, called for criminal jury trial. Attorney Goldberg again represented Isaac Kantor. Mr. Suleika told the following story: He bought ticket of Kantor issued via S.S. "Potsdam," July 6, 1913. He went to New York with Czarkowski and Ignace Prystalski and wife. He had paid $57 to Kantor. He cannot read, and he wore a button given by Kantor. He was taken to an Immigration Home, which cared for passengers, and stayed there several days. Then he learned that the tickets would not be honored and had been fraudulently issued. He bought a new ticket in New York and went on to Europe and has only recently returned. He works in a large tailoring firm. Mr. Kantor's attorney has a plan that Kantor shall plead guilty, and the attorney will then ask to have him placed under bond of $5,000 on probation for one year with instructions to repay the outstanding debts of $3,000. He claims Kantor has already repaid a part of the claims against him. He had several witnesses to testify that small sums were repaid. The alternative if debts are not paid would be a penitentiary sentence.

August 13, 1914.—Case of Wladimir Suleika against Isaac Kantor continued. Mr. Glasgow, agent of the Bryde Line, present. Judge and State's Attorney considered release on one-year probation the best sentence. Mr. Kantor plead guilty. A bond of $5,000 was signed by John Bolaski, 810 South Street. Mr. Kantor will repay the amount due the creditors on the criminal charges. All charges made larceny. Kantor will engage in real estate business and will live at 1850 Larrabee. He will report monthly to Mr. Walter Jones, adult probation officer, and will be sent to the penitentiary any time he fails in payments.

August 20, 1914.—Mr. Suleika reports that Ignace Prystalski and wife have also returned from Poland. A. F. [Polish visitor] visited Mr. Prystalski and talked with him about complaint versus Kantor. Mr. Prystalski paid Kantor $82.80 for fraudulent tickets. He cannot leave his work in the morning to come to court. Told him that we will make some other arrangement. Later arranged that Mrs. Prystalski, who was with her husband at the time he paid Kantor for the tickets, will sign the warrant.

August 26, 1914.—Discussed case with State's Attorney. He thinks it is a strong case. He advised warrant at Police Station for confidence game. We must swear out warrant between nine and twelve in the morning before judge at West Chicago Avenue Station. The warrant will be served from North Avenue Station.

September 15, 1914.—Mrs. Prystalski was taken to West Chicago Police Station, signed warrant against Isaac Kantor.

[*September 16–October 29, 1914.*—Several entries omitted regarding preparation of case and preliminary hearing at which the statement was made that Isaac Kantor had repaid $125 since he had been on probation, but it developed that the only evidence of this was Kantor's own statement made to the probation officer, who seemed to have confidence in Kantor. One representative of the State's Attorney's office said he did not favor doing anything with the case then. He said if Kantor did not fulfil the conditions of probation within a year he would go to the penitentiary—enough to put him there for forty years. Mr. Glasgow testified that tickets were fraudulent and that Mr. Kantor was not an agent for the line. The judge asked Mr. Kantor if he had paid the money to the steamship company, and Mr. Kantor said "yes." Mr. Glasgow said he would be willing to pay the full amount of the ticket if Kantor could produce a receipt. The attorney, Goldberg, said that Mr. Kantor had never been notified that the A. B. Smith and Company, Inc., had closed its offices as agents of the Bryde Line, and that he had been given blocks of tickets by the company. Mr. Glasgow explained that the tickets had been sold on the steamer "Potsdam," which belonged to the Holland-American Line which A. B. Smith and Company never represented, and that the Bryde Line never sailed from New York but from Newport News. Case continued one week to allow Kantor to bring in receipt. Other details are given of the preparation of further evidence. Then the case was called and continued again to allow the judge who had been hearing it and who was away to finish it.]

October 29, 1914.—Isaac Kantor and his lawyer, Goldberg, in office to offer a settlement. Mr. Kantor was looking very jaunty in new clothes and gloves. Mr. Goldberg said that they had to get rid of this case. Kantor made a plea for his wife and children. He says he has a very lucrative job with a well-established real estate company and that if we will let him alone he can repay everything. He has been afraid to pay any money back until he could pay all, for that would bring the whole group of creditors about his ears. He had hoped to get money from Europe to repay but the war prevented this. Attorney Goldberg said that we had no case, that it was the business of the steamship company to notify the agents that their office had closed. He knows of three people who have never been notified. He knows of two people who have blocks of tickets now, series of 5. Kantor has some signed by the A. B. Smith Co., of the sale of tickets in the same series as the tickets we hold but he admits that he has no receipt for the latter. He said that his office was rifled at the time he was arrested and he has not been able to find receipts, papers, or anything since. The offer they make is as follows: If we will drop case they will pay $25 on the 15th of November and $25 every fifteen days after that time. When we were asked what guarantee we would have, Mr. Goldberg said, "my guarantee." Immigrants' Protective League refused this offer. Mr. Goldberg said that he and Kantor were entitled to leniency from the League since "they had the case beaten" in the Criminal Court but Kantor consented to plead guilty in order to get probation and make restitution. Our reply was we must refuse offer without court order.

November 10, 1914.—Mr. Goldberg telephoned and offered to pay half the money in court on Wednesday and have the case continued thirty days, when he will pay the balance. If this agreement is not kept we can then go on with the prosecution. Told him we would decide in open court hearing.

November 11, 1914.—Case heard. We accepted the plan and received $40 in court and the case was continued to December 11. Interviewed Mr. Jones, probation officer, who said that he had lost all confidence in Kantor. He thinks Kantor has no intention of repaying and suspects that he is concealing money that he has. Mr. Jones says probation is hopeless for a person like Kantor, an old-time swindler. Mr. Kantor's attorney tried to make Mr. Jones believe that Kantor had paid $350 to a Polish lawyer named Komenski. Kantor claims that this lawyer has kept the money himself.

December 11, 1914.—Case called. Isaac Kantor paid balance on one case and case was dismissed. Other claims are to be paid in instalments.

February 15, 1915.—Talked to Mr. Jones, who reports that Mr. Kantor has made no payments yet. *Later.*—Saw Mr. Goldberg and told him that we did not think that Kantor was acting in good faith as he had made no further payments. Mr. Goldberg said that Mr. Kantor offered $250 to the probation officer, but he refused to take it because Kantor did not have the list of persons to whom it should be paid. He is to settle with the largest creditor by the transfer of some property.

[The record continues through to February 2, 1916, with the League keeping in touch with the Probation Department, which collected small instalments of money from time to time. When money came in, the question was to locate the man to whom it should be paid and, if the man first on the list could not be found, to pay to the next. The League found it difficult to keep in touch with the discouraged creditors and to keep track of their changes of address. Advertisements were placed at one time in three Polish papers in an effort to locate one creditor for whom something had been paid.]

February 2, 1916.—Isaac Kantor has been arrested and is in jail for forgery. The bank in the case is doing the prosecuting. Kantor probably will be sent to the penitentiary at last.

April 27, 1916.—Mr. Jones, Probation Department, telephoned that Kantor is out on bond. He thinks Kantor still has some money in reserve somewhere.

July 8, 1916.—Isaac Kantor's case was heard in court, violation of probation charged, various technicalities raised and case postponed.

October 4, 1916.—Miss F—[Polish visitor of the League] reports that pressure is being brought to bear on State's Attorney's office to allow the cases to be dismissed—chiefly because Mr. Kantor is a Pole.

October 5, 1916.—Telephoned State's Attorney's office. They would like a written statement from the League, telling what we know about Kantor. *Later.*—Letter written to Mr. John Anderson, Assistant State's Attorney:

DEAR MR. ANDERSON:

We are herewith enclosing a short summary of Isaac Kantor's history as we know it. We feel that it would be a great pity if he were allowed to escape from the jurisdiction of the court now, with this record behind him. We know that such a step would cause great indignation if it were made public not only among the Poles who have been victimized or who have known of his widespread frauds but among people in general who now have fresh in their minds the exploitation of immigrant groups on the West Side by the recent failure of certain immigrant banks. For just as the Russians have as a nationality suffered from the failure of Simon and Koburg, so the Poles and Ruthenians have been exploited mercilessly by Kantor. The fact that he is a Pole, therefore, he has no right to use in his favor. It is small wonder that the witnesses against him get discouraged and are willing to let the prosecution go, in view of the long delay in getting the cases against him into court and the apparent immunity from punishment which he enjoys, for he has tried every kind of fraud and has never been punished. Leniency, we feel, is futile in this case, for Kantor is not reformable and continues his career in spite of leniency. Moreover, if he agrees to pay his creditors of one group, he does more crooked business to make the payments. If the cases now pending against him actually come to trial, we will be willing to try to line up the witnesses so that they will see it through.

Very truly yours,

LYDIA GARDNER, *Superintendent*

Immigrants' Protective League

October 6, 1916.—The following statement taken to Mr. Anderson:

In July, 1913, Isaac Kantor was running a combination steamship-company-agency-bank-real-estate office at 600 Milwaukee Avenue. On the tenth of that month it was reported to us by the New York State Bureau of Industries and Immigration that a Ruthenian family was stranded in New York with fraudulent steamship tickets sold by this man, Isaac Kantor. Investigation showed that the tickets had been issued on the Bryde Line, a Gulf to Norway Line, on a Holland-American Line steamer—the whole issue a fraud. We got possession of four of these tickets but undoubtedly there were others issued. At this time other claims of all kinds began to pour in to the police against Kantor but he disappeared. It was given out by his attorney that he had gone to Europe to raise some money with which to pay his creditors, on some property he had there. It later developed that he was in Airdale, Wisconsin, carrying on the same frauds on the Poles there.

When Isaac Kantor was finally arrested in June, 1914, and indicted, five cases were selected to be heard against him, three charging "confidence game," one embezzlement, and one larceny—all later changed to larceny, I think. None of these cases had been reported directly to us, but all were handled by the Legal Aid Society. Mr. Kantor plead guilty and was placed on probation—all cases but one were stricken off with leave to reinstate, with the understanding that if he violated probation, he was to be sent immediately to the penitentiary. At this time and later the Assistant State's Attorney said: "If Kantor does not fulfill the conditions of probation within the year, he will go to prison—we have enough to send him up for forty years." The probation officer thinks that it was a mistake to put Mr. Kantor on probation as "he is a swindler of too long standing, and I have no faith that he will repay his creditors." The cases of a certain Ignace Prystalski and his wife, originally reported to us from New York as the victims of fraudulent steamship tickets were not included at the time the other cases were heard as the witnesses had gone on to Europe, so when they returned in August, 1914, we decided to bring these complaints against him also and the case was heard October 22, 1914. At that time the League was willing to try leniency and to allow the case to be dismissed after Kantor had paid the full amount of the claim in cash. Since Kantor was on probation and under a sort of suspension of sentence, we did not gather any further material, and the new claims as they came in went from the police station to the probation department. We understand, however, that in January, 1916, Kantor was again in jail with a whole new series of frauds against him and that one charge was forgery and was being pushed by the bank involved. On July 8, 1916, the charge of violation of probation was disposed of in court. A motion to quash the warrant was granted wholly on a technicality, thus the slight restraint of probation was removed. The fact that Mr. Goldberg still defends Mr. Kantor, although he protests violently each time that he is through with him, leads us to believe that Mr. Kantor has some money tucked away which ought to be going to his creditors. Officer Jones of the Adult Probation Department could give you further details about Mr. Kantor's career.

Later.—Mr. Anderson telephoned to say that he will not allow the case to be dismissed. He will telephone League if he needs us when the cases are coming up. E. K. went to East Chicago Avenue Station to see Mr. Jones. He will go over to Criminal Court, look the records up, and see Mr. Anderson.

[Other hearings, technicalities, postponements follow. The last entry in the record, which is given below, shows that the case was finally given up as hopeless:]

June 3, 1917.—Miss F— [Polish visitor] sent to inquire status of Kantor case. She reports that she called on State's Attorney Anderson and asked him about case. He sent her to clerk's office. Case No. 8303-4 called last October, 1916, by Judge Z. and can come up again in a month or two.

36. Michael Dobinski
(Transmitting Money)

July 11, 1913.—The following letter received from the New York Bureau of Immigration:

Miss Lydia Gardner
Immigrants' Protective League
Chicago, Illinois

MY DEAR MISS GARDNER: With further reference to the activities of Mr. Isaac Kantor, steamship agent of your city, I beg to attach herewith an excerpt of a report filed by one of our investigators recently relative to this agent's treatment of one Michael Dobinski, his wife, and two children, who arrived in this city from Chicago on June 11. Mr. Dobinski returned to Chicago as Mr. Friedman, of the Ocean Travelers Transfer Company, refused to cash Mr. Kantor's personal check for $280. I have thus far been unable to learn Mr. Dobinski's Chicago address, but if he is not already one of the complainants, kindly advise me and I shall have a search made through the office of the North German Lloyd Line.

Very truly yours,
HENRY JOSEPH, *Acting Chief Investigator*

Excerpt from New York investigator's *Report*, which was attached to the preceding letter:

On Wednesday, June 11, Michael Dobinski with wife and two children arrived in this city from Chicago. They were passengers who purchased tickets of Isaac Kantor in Chicago and were advised by the latter to go to the Ocean Travelers Transfer Company, where the $280 would be paid upon presentation of letter and check from Mr. Kantor. The following telegram was received by the Ocean Travelers Transfer Company on said day: "Meet tonight Wabash Railroad Michael Dobinski family, understand that Barbarossa won't sail so please keep family till George Washington sailing Saturday and tranfer ticket accordingly, for expenses am telegraphing you $15. Dobinski is holding my check for $280, which was not cashed by him. To cover this check, I am mailing you draft today which please pay to Dobinski and return my check.—ISAAC KANTOR." Mr. Friedman said check for $15 arrived on same day through the Western Union. Mr. Friedman waited for Kantor's draft until Friday morning at ten; meantime the passenger became restless, since he could not get cash or an European check for his domestic check. He was told by Friedman that his check would be no good in Europe. Then Friedman wired to Kantor, Friday, 10 A.M., saying draft not received yet, passenger very impatient, unless money received by telegram the family will return to Chicago. On Friday at about 5 P.M. Friedman received a telegram from Kantor, "Am unable to wire money. Induce man to sail. Will send you the draft positively Monday. Please wire whether man will sail." Friedman did not answer this telegram but gave it to the passenger, who returned with his family to Chicago.

July 14, 1913.—Letter from New York acknowledged and Bureau requested to send Michael Dobinski's Chicago address, if found. [The address was not found, but later the League's Polish visitor said she believed she had heard something about this man and thought she knew his friends on North Centre Street. She promised to investigate.]

July 19, 1913.—[Michael Dobinski's friends located by Polish visitor, who made the following report:]

Michael Dobinski was going to Galicia and wished to take with him $282 in money which he had been saving for a long time. Isaac Kantor said he would change the money to Austrian money for him. He gave Dobinski a check which he was to exchange in New York. When he got to New York he could not exchange the check as Kantor had said and he was told it would be no good to him in Europe. Kantor telegraphed him to go on to Europe and he would send money there but Dobinski would not do this. He returned to Chicago and demanded that Kantor should pay him the money. He could not get all the $280 at once, but he got the money little by little, sometimes he received $10, sometimes $30, sometimes only $2. Also when he went to New York the first time he had bought his ticket to Galicia in Kantor's office and had paid for a ticket to his home in Galicia, but in the steamship office in New York he was told the ticket was only to Bremen. When he came back to Chicago, he was here nearly one month collecting his money from Kantor. Finally it was all paid and he returned to New York and went to Europe.

July 23, 1913.—Letter with report of Dobinski's return to Europe sent to New York Bureau of Immigration.

37. Jan Witkowski
(Attempted Purchase of Steamship Ticket)

November 3, 1913.—Jan Witkowski, Polish, 210 Hoyne Avenue, in office. He was sent by Rachman (Banker and Steamship Agent) to complain that a steamship ticket ordered to be sent to his wife in Poland has never arrived. The ticket was ordered through Rachman from the Canadian Blue Line Company but has not been sent. Man sent $143.50 through Rachman's office for the steamship ticket. He says that he has been inquiring about the ticket every day. Mr. Rachman claims that he has written to the company several times with no result. Mr. Rachman himself sent man to the League. Mr. Witkowski says the money was all paid March 25, 1913. Rachman claims that Canadian Blue Line sent ticket April 15, 1913. Mrs. Witkowski stated in her letter written October 10, 1913, that she had not received the ticket. Mr. Witkowski would like to have the ticket cancelled and buy one from another agent and another line. Mr. Witkowski left letter from his wife as evidence that the ticket had not been received [translation from the Polish]:

LAKOCIN
October 10, 1913

DEAR HUSBAND AND FATHER:

We greet you all together with the following old Polish words, "Be God our Lord and Christ praised," and you will answer, "always and forever." Your letter found us in good health, which I and the children also wish you from all our hearts. Now, dear husband, you write me that you have already sent the steamship tickets and three hundred rubles, but I received only 20 and about more I do not know until now. Do not think, honored husband, that I am making fun of you. Sometimes you may think and say that I do not want to come to you. I have been honoring you from the day of our marriage, and I was true to you and I want to be to my grave. I only wish I could go to you sooner, dear husband. Now, dear husband, I want to ask you one thing. As soon as you get this letter write me accurately through which post office you sent the money and the steamship ticket; whether through the German or through our own. If you have sent it through the German, then I will try as hard as I can to get the money. But please write me through which company you sent the tickets. As soon as you will write, I will know what to do. I will write to the company that prepares all the papers for travelling. I will try to do it myself, but if you have taken any steps, dear husband, please let me know at once as I want to come as soon as possible because there is nothing good here. I have very much trouble with the children, and I have to work so hard that every muscle aches and yet I cannot be with you, dear husband. We are well, dear husband, and we greet you and wish you good health and all the blessings from God in this far away world and I wish from all my heart that I may go over to you as soon as possible. Please answer at once. Goodbye.

November 4, 1913.—Visited the Canadian Blue Line Company and talked with a clerk who promised to write the European agent about the case. He was not willing to show the books with the date when Witkowski's ticket was sent out.

November 6, 1913.—Telephoned Canadian Blue Line office for date when ticket was sent. Spoke with Mr. Green. Office record shows it was sent April 15. They see no reason why it has not reached destination. They have written general office Montreal for explanation and will inform League when answer arrives. Answer is expected middle of the week.

November 10, 1913.—Letter to Mr. Witkowski (in Polish), telling him of the company's promise to investigate.

November 21, 1913.—Letter written to Mr. Green, Canadian Blue Line Company, Chicago:

DEAR SIR:

On November 6, we telephoned your office regarding a ticket purchased by Jan Witkowski on April 15 from your agent Rachman for which purchaser holds receipt No. 128329, which has failed to reach the passenger for whom it was purchased. We were told by the person in your office that the matter would be taken up with the Montreal Agent, and that we would be advised as soon as you had a reply. May we ask whether you have had a reply from Montreal?

Yours very truly,
IMMIGRANTS' PROTECTIVE LEAGUE

November 24, 1913.—Reply from the Canadian Blue Line Company as follows:

Immigrants' Protective League
Chicago, Illinois

GENTLEMEN: *Re* prepaid 128329 Witkowski. In reply to your letter November 21, beg to advise that we have cabled our European Office requesting them to arrange immediate forwarding of above prepaid.

Yours very truly,

HENRY WOOD, *General Agent*

December 22, 1913.—Telephoned the Canadian Blue Line Company. They have received no information.

January 15, 1914.—Wrote to Mr. Witkowski (in Polish), asking if he has received any further information from the company or from his wife.

January 17, 1914.—Mr. Witkowski in the office. He is terribly discouraged. He has not had any notice from the company. His wife has not yet received the ticket.

January 22, 1914.—The following letter sent to the Canadian Blue Line Company:

Mr. Henry Wood
Canadian Blue Line Company

DEAR SIR: *Re* Prepaid 128329 Witkowski. Mr. Witkowski has again told us that his ticket purchased March 25, 1913, from your agent Rachman has not been received. On November 22 you wrote us that you were cabling your European office requesting them to arrange immediate forwarding of above prepaid. As you know, it is now nearly a year since this ticket was purchased. Will you kindly advise us at once what your intentions are in the matter.

Very truly yours,

IMMIGRANTS' PROTECTIVE LEAGUE

January 24, 1914.—Reply from Canadian Blue Line as follows:
Immigrants' Protective League

GENTLEMEN: *Re* prepaid 128329 Witkowski. Replying to your letter January 22, we regret exceedingly to delay in arranging forwarding of above prepaid but for your information wish to state that on January 3 our Montreal Office advised us that they had again requested our London Office to arrange immediate forwarding of above prepaid and as you can readily understand it requires nearly a month's time before the quickest possible reply can be received from Europe. We are today again writing them in this connection and hope to be able to advise your sailing date in the very near future.

Yours very truly,

HENRY WOOD, *General Agent*

January 28, 1914.—Visited the Canadian Blue Line office. They admit that there is no excuse for the delay but say that they are unable to get a reply to their letters asking why the ticket has not been forwarded. Canadian Blue Line Company advise that they will make a refund and not deduct the 10 per cent. This will require from six to eight weeks. The Canadian Blue Line has written the London office to advise them reason of delay and expect to have a reply about February 15. *Later.*—Wrote to Mr. Witkowski to call at the Settlement on February 3 [when Polish visitor of the League kept an office hour there].

February 3, 1914.—Mr. Witkowski came to Settlement yesterday evening. Told him of company's reply. He is much discouraged and cannot understand why he has such bad experience.

February 27, 1914.—Telephoned Canadian Blue Line. Still no explanation from Montreal or London office. Another letter sent to agent of Canadian Blue Line in Montreal asking for an immediate refund.

March 25, 1914.—Telephoned Canadian Blue Line. They have copy of letter from London Office, to Antwerp, asking the interior office to send the people forward. *Later.*—Wrote Polish letter to Mr. Witkowski telling him of conversation with Canadian Blue Line Company.

April 13, 1914.—The following letter received from Canadian Blue Line office [Polish translation sent to Jan Witkowski]:

We are in receipt of the following letter from our Montreal office: "Vienna has repeatedly notified this passenger and received no reply. Mr. Carmichael advises me that the purchaser should himself write to the passenger enquiring why she does not travel or if she had not received advice of ticket for some concealed reason or other over which we have no control then she the passenger should communicate with Vienna office." This is for your information and trust you will do the needful as per above.

June 24, 1914.—Called on Mr. Witkowski at 210 Hoyne Avenue. Man is not there, moved to Moss Street. Landlady said his wife is supposed to arrive this month, promised to notify League about woman's arrival.

August 24, 1914.—Polish letter written to Mr. Witkowski asking if his wife arrived.

September 2, 1914.—Letter received from Mr. Witkowski [translated from Polish]:

DEAR MISS F—:

You wish to know if my wife arrived. She did not and did not let us know what happened there. If you know something about her please let me know. When I get any news, I will notify you.

Respectfully,

J. WITKOWSKI

October 6, 1914.—Mr. Witkowski in office. He says he does not know anything about his wife. He wrote several letters but did not get any reply. He also states he sent $52.25 to his wife in Europe on July 29 through Rachman's office. Man would like to know if the above sum was sent out, as he has since heard that Rachman has been arrested for doing crooked business.

June 23, 1915.—The following letter received from Mr. Witkowski [translation from Polish]:

HONORED MADAM:

I am writing a few words to find out about the steamship ticket. I am wondering if it will get lost, because you told me it will not get lost. Please madam answer me as soon as possible, because I am worrying very much. I want to write to my wife and have her come here. Please, Miss F—, answer at once.

Respectfully,
JAN WITKOWSKI

June 24, 1915.—The following letter sent to the Canadian Blue Line agent:

Jan Witkowski, the purchaser of prepaid ticket No. 128329, is anxious to know whether the passenger on this ticket might travel at the present time. The passenger is in Austria and would probably come through your Vienna office if that is in operation at the present time. Will you kindly let us hear from you in the matter.

June 29, 1915.—Reply from Canadian Blue Line office as follows:

Prepaid 128329—Witkowski. Referring to your letter June 24th in connection with above: For your information beg to advise that at the present time we have no sailings from the continent and I shall appreciate it, if you will kindly advise me whether the purchaser wishes this ticket held open or cancelled.

[The remaining portion of the record deals with the matter of the refund. The man called at the League office one Sunday morning in despair over the whole situation and said there was nothing to do but have the ticket cancelled. On December 7, 1915, the steamship company refunded $112.55.]

38. Filiat Halaban
(Steamship-Ticket Refund)

July 7, 1913.—Filiat Halaban, Russian man, in office from South Chicago. R. B. [Russian visitor] spoke with man. He has been cheated of a steamship ticket by Peter Gold [Russian ticket agent and banker who was suspected of exploiting immigrants and who failed and later absconded]. Mr. Halaban bought a ticket from Gold on March 3, 1913. Gold was to send the ticket by cable to man's brother-in-law [name and address of brother-in-law given]. On May 19 Mr. Halaban received a letter from his brother-in-law asking why his ticket does not arrive. Mr. Halaban then went to Gold and asked why his ticket was not sent to Russia, and Gold answered that it was sent the next day after it was bought. Mr. Halaban has never yet heard from Russia that ticket has arrived. He wants League to get his money back from Gold or find out why his ticket is not sent. Ticket was bought from Gold's South Chicago office, but Mr. Halaban has spoken with Gold himself in main office.

R. B. telephoned Gold's bank, spoke with Mr. Gold. He will report back by telephone not later than tomorrow morning. He must first interview the South Chicago agent. Told Mr. Halaban to come in tomorrow afternoon and maybe we can tell him something. He will bring receipt for ticket.

[Mr. Halaban left the following letter from Russia, showing that ticket had not been received. The letter is given in full as an interesting example of a peasant's letter (translation from the Russian).]

June 5, 1913

How Do You Do, Our dear son Filiat?

We are greeting and bowing low, the father Dmitri Andreivitch, and more low bows from the mother Ninila Nickolievna, who sends you motherly blessings for all your life. Also bows from thy truthful and loving wife, Proskovja Halaban, and also greetings from your children Kornusha, Andrusha, Ania, and Vanija. Also very low bows from your aunt and kisses many times, also bows from Uncle Efil Andreivitch, who sends fatherly blessings for all your life. Also greets you your unforgetting brother Petrov and Domicilla sends greetings and bows low. And I am notifying you that we now live at home; that we will live all summer at home and you can send the letters to me here. We plan to build a house, and in the winter we will go to live in it.

I am delivering the herring from Astrakhan,[1] and father expects to go soon and get the calves. He and Domicilla plan to take the old garden for themselves and from the new garden he will take a half for himself and give the other half to Maxim, and the garden which was next to yours he wants to give to you. They want to divide the farm between Uncle Ivan and Uncle Timosha, but they will think it over because it is the idea of their parent and our grandfather. And the other house they want to divide between us and Maxim. Domicilla has built herself a house on the old place I think where the kitchen was.

Your parents, Dmitri and Ninila, and your wife and children ask that you send us money to purchase flour. We are buying ten pounds of flour at once. You can understand how long ten pounds can last for us. Please send the money, you know well that we have no place to get it. You have left your family on your old father's shoulders and on his sick wife and please try to help us as soon as possible. Your children are asking this, and your brother is also asking you not to forget your parents and children.

All of them are lamenting for sorrow, and they are constantly weeping, and the mother-in-law and uncle also because there is not enough flour. When I came, I was a witness of this, and they took from me money for one *pud* (40 pounds) of flour. So please don't forget them, and do not listen to any talk that is going on here. I tell you the truth. Your money they received on Palm Sunday. From this money they bought first some flour; 5 rubles they gave to Isaac and 5 rubles to Teofim, 1 ruble for the barn, 1 ruble for shirts, 1 ruble for fuel, 7 rubles for medical treatment, and for the rest of the money 10 pounds of wheat, a shirt and *portianky*[2] and a pair of shoes for every child.

And again we inform you that Poronja is sick, and there is no money to spend on her treatment. Your ticket your brother-in-law did not get, and he felt very much insulted; and he said he does not want to give you

---

[1] [A city on the Volga River, where they catch herring. Every spring the wholesalers go down to buy herring in Astrakhan.]

[2] [A piece of coarse linen worn instead of stockings.]

the *deciatina*[1] of land because you fooled him with the ticket. He says, "you never sent it and if you did you look for it now." Your letter your brother-in-law received the 5th June on Trinity holiday.

Poronja was sick for three weeks after Easter, in the hospital. She is not better even now, but she is home. Her disease is a disease of the liver; they say it can be cured, but we have no money. If she is to be cured, you ought to send her money before it is too late. If you send money for her cure, send it soon, and then we will plan to go to Saratoff in the Alexander Hospital. If you send money, try to send it soon before it is too late.

Your Vanija has grown so fast. He running runs; and when he is asked where his father is, he points to the picture. He constantly looks at the picture and says, "Daddy, Daddy, you never come to me and do not send a present."

July 8, 1913.—Mr. Gold telephoned. He says that Mr. Halaban is mistaken; the agent will be at League office Thursday morning. He will explain it all right and ticket was long ago sent. *Later.*—Filiat in office and brought his receipt. R. B. saw receipt for $68, dated March 3.

July 11, 1913.—Mr. Gold himself in office. He says South Chicago agent came in and ordered ticket for man in May. Agent told Mr. Gold that ticket had been ordered and first instalment paid by Mr. Halaban on March 3, but when agent came to office in May a balance of $6.50 was still unpaid on ticket of $68. Agent sent ticket May 10, and ticket must be in Russia now all right. R. B. told Mr. Gold that we have seen receipt for $68 on March 3. Mr. Gold will send original receipt, which he will get from agent. He is sure people have ticket by this time. *Later.*—Letter received from Filiat Halaban as follows [translation]:

I notified the Immigration Office that I had received a letter from Russia. In the letter it was said about the steamship ticket that they have not received it yet and have not heard anything about it. Please be so kind and try to get the money back. Respectfully, FILIAT HALABAN. Please answer me what the agent will say.

July 15, 1913.—Mr. Gold in office. He says that the clerk who made the mistake in South Chicago will soon be discharged. Mr. Gold claims that same clerk has made other mistakes and is hurting his business. Ticket was, however, not sent by cable. It was stamped so "by mistake." It should have reached man, however, first of July. *Later.*—Sent a letter in Russian, explaining things to Mr. Halaban.

July 24, 1913.—Letter from Filiat Halaban as follows [translation from the Russian]:

Immigrants' Bureau
The Lady-in-Charge, R. B.:

I am letting you know that I have received a letter from your office in which you write your conversation with Gold about the steamship ticket sent to Russia the 12th. For that it is too late. I have sent it not this month

[1] [Measure of land, equal to 2,400 square feet.]

but on March 10. This is a bad mistake, a mistake of four months. I am notifying you that I have received a letter from Russia. And from the same person that I have sent the steamship ticket to. He writes me that the ticket is not there and that he does not want to wait, because he will receive it very late. Because of the delay of this he does not want to decide to go to America. He does not want to come here. I have received the letter about it that was written in Russia the date thirteenth of July of this year. I am asking you about it because I want to get the whole amount from Peter Gold. Because of their mistake I do not need the steamship ticket any more. Please do defend us when you go to Gold; he has cheated many immigrants. Please answer.—FILIAT HALABAN. Please let me know if I should appear to you personally or by letter.

[The remaining part of the record deals with the refunding of the ticket money, which required several months, and also deals with a wage claim Halaban had against a former employer. On December 1, 1913, when he called at the League office to receive the check for wages which had been collected, he reported the steamship money had also been refunded.]

39. Strophin Trepoff
(Steamship-Ticket Complaint)

July 21, 1913.—Strophin Trepoff, Russian, Box 407, River Park, in office, wants to speak to Miss B— [Russian visitor]. *Later.*—R. B. spoke with man. May 12, 1913, he paid $72.30 for a steamship ticket to Stein and Company, River Park branch office. On July 19 he received a letter from his wife which made him feel very bad. His wife said she received a letter from him in which she learned that he had sent a steamship ticket but the ticket did not arrive. Only the letter with an affidavit and some little money he was also sending arrived. Mr. Trepoff wants to have the money ($51.00) back. His wife wrote the letter July third. Man is twenty-five years old. Wife's name is Maria Trepoff. He has been eleven months in the United States and is working with the River Park Fence Company. He earns $18 a week.

Mr. Trepoff's cousin, Feodor Filinov (same address), was with him when he paid the money and Feodor paid also for tickets for his wife and child. For the tickets Feodor paid $76.00. He also has had letter from his wife, and the same thing has happened. The letter and affidavit and the money he sent arrived, but the tickets did not arrive. He would like to have the League get his money back because he thinks now Stein and Company swindle the immigrants who buy tickets there. Mr. Trepoff will send letter from his wife as evidence to prove to Mr. Stein that the tickets did not arrive. *Later.*—Telephoned Mr. Stein, main office. Mr. Stein says he will himself visit River Park agency and will report at once to us about the two men.

July 22, 1913.—Letter received from Mr. Trepoff as follows [translation from Russian]:

How Do You Do, Honorable Ladies:

I, Strophin Trepoff, send you these letters from my wife and the envelopes. And we ask you to get the money from him as quick as possible and send it through another office, because through this office nobody is honest with an immigrant. I did not pay him all the money, this was because of his swindling; thus get the money from him as fast as possible. Goodbye.

Sincerely yours,

STROPHIN TREPOFF

[The following letters were inclosed; translation from Russian:]

The year 1913, the day June 21. In the first lines of my letter I hurry to inform you my dear husband, Strophin Trepoff, that I send you my conjugal respect and love. I bow low and wish you the best health from the Good Lord and everything best in the world. And I, Maria Maslovna, kiss you Strophin Trepoff, countless times.

We received your letter May 22, from which it appeared that you sent a steamship ticket and a certificate and money. The certificate I received the twenty-second of May together with the letter, and the money we received on the the third day of Trinity. The second letter we also received together with the money and you write us how to come, but the steamship ticket is still not here. Why? Did you send it on or not? If you sent the steamship ticket, then as soon as you get this letter start to look for it. But maybe you did not send it? You are surely making fun of me. You are turning me into ridicule before the people. Everybody asks when I am leaving, and I have nothing that I can answer. All other husbands send their wives money and presents and you did not even send me a little present. Perhaps I am not worth a present, you don't do anything to make me feel happy. You sent me great joy with your letter in which you wrote that you will take me to America, but it turned out to be false. Up to this time there is still no ticket. As soon as you get this letter, hurry to look for the tickets. And so goodbye.

Your loving wife,

MARIA MASLOVNA

[Translation from the Russian:]

The year 1913, the day July 3. How do you do, my dear husband, Strophin Trepoff. I am writing to you, your wife, Maria Maslovna. When you get this letter, hurry to look for the ticket and send it to us. We waited for this ticket and waited but neither did I receive it nor Marja Ivanova [i.e., wife of Feodor Filinov]. We all three were going to come to you. Marja is now with us—she does not want to wait but wants to go. Why does Feodor not send her a letter? It is not good to act in such a way. I remain living in good health and wish the same to you.

Your loving wife,

MARIA MASLOVNA

July 23, 1913.—Telephoned Mr. Stein. He will positively report to us in two days.

July 25, 1913.—Mr. Stein in office. He claims he has a very poor agent in River Park office. The tickets have not been sent, but he wants the men to let him keep the money, and he will send the tickets at once. He said a refund on steamship tickets means a deduction of 10 per cent. Told him this deduction could not be made when the mistake was in their office. There is a record of the payment of $49 by Mr. Trepoff and of $69 by Feodor Filinov. Upon presentation of receipts in River Park he will refund every cent.

July 26, 1913.—Russian letter written to Mr. Trepoff, asking him to come to office or write to us to tell us whether he wishes the tickets sent or the money paid.

August 4, 1913.—Russian letter, asking Mr. Trepoff to let us know when he will be at home and Mr. H— [another visitor] will come to see him.

August 6, 1913.—Russian letter from Mr. Trepoff. He has been to the River Park office, but they will refund only part of the money. He has paid $51, and they will refund to him only $32.77. Also his cousin has paid $76, and they will refund to him only $48.85. R. B. telephoned Mr. Stein. He will come to the office tomorrow at 12:30.

August 8, 1913.—Mr. Stein in office. He says Mr. Trepoff bought a ticket for $72.30 and his agent deducted 10 per cent ($7.23) for refund commission. Also $11 was paid to the Russian Consul for a passport and affidavit. This cannot be refunded. The man paid on the ticket $40 and $11 for the passport and he claims therefore he can refund only $32.77. The same with Filinov. Told him we believe he must refund whole amount. Mr. Stein very angry and says League is helping the immigrant to cheat the agency.

August 12, 1913.—J. H. visited Russian consulate. Mr. X. says that usually every immigrant has to have a passport to leave Russia and the charge for this is 18 rubles or $9. The passport is needed for identification at the Russian port Libau but very often it is easy for their people to cross the border without any passport, especially single men. Affidavits they do not need except of course when they are detained at United States ports. Affidavits are not sent to the Russian government before passports are issued. Mr. Stein is plainly cheating these men. *Later.*—Letter written to Mr. Stein:

DEAR SIR:

Upon further consideration of the matter of affidavits made in the cases of Strophin Trepoff and Feodor Filinov, we find that we evidently misunderstood you in your statements of yesterday. We understood you to say that affidavits are necessary, signed by the consul before passports can be issued by the Russian government. Upon inquiry of the consul, we are informed that this is not at all necessary. Affidavits are made only in cases where difficulty in admission is expected. As the tickets have never been sent, and the passengers have never travelled, the affidavits have of course never been needed.

When you called July 28 you remember you agreed to refund all the money paid, without reduction. We still feel that the matter cannot be satisfactorily settled until this is done. You admit that to your agent may be laid the whole blame for delay and trouble. We shall send a representative with Mr. Trepoff to your River Park office, August 20, at 12 o'clock and we shall expect to have refunds made covering the entire amounts due to these men. We shall be obliged to you if you will give instructions to your agent that will facilitate the matter of these refunds. We remain,

Very truly yours,

EMMA KENNETH, *Acting Superintendent Immigrants' Protective League*

August 15, 1913.—Russian letter sent to Mr. Trepoff, telling him that Mr. H— will go to the River Park office of Mr. Stein on August 20 and asking Mr. Trepoff and Mr. Filinov to meet him there.

August 20, 1913.—J. H. went to River Park. Mr. Trepoff was waiting at the office of Stein and Company. From River Park we were sent back to 100 Halsted Street to the main office of Mr. Stein. At first Mr. Stein refused to give the money to Mr. Trepoff because he said the money had really been paid by Mr. Filinov, who was not there. Then he wished also to deduct the refunds and passports, but this we would not permit him to do. Finally he gave the money to me as representing the League and asked for a receipt from me and this I gave him. The full amount paid, $76 by Mr. Filinov for ticket and passport and $40 by Mr. Trepoff and $11 for passport, was returned, $127 in all.

[These records were used with some others when Mr. Stein was brought into court later when other cases came into the League and Mr. Stein finally claimed to have no money to refund.]

IMMIGRANT GIRLS IN CHICAGO

40. Lucja Krajulis
(An Unmarried Lithuanian Mother)

October 5.—Lucja Krajulis, Lithuanian girl, age twenty, in office, wishes to see Mrs. K. [Lithuanian visitor]. Girl has no address, wishes Mrs. K. to find her a place to stay. She is sent to League by Reverend Zimintaitis [Lithuanian minister]. Girl will wait till Mrs. K. comes in. *Later.*—A. K. spoke with girl. She has a baby about six weeks old and would like to get work where she could keep her baby with her. It seems that Lucja was pregnant when she came to this country last March. The father of her child is a soldier in the army in Russia. He could not marry Lucja, but he borrowed the money for her to go to Pittsburgh to some country people there. Lucja did not want to stay in her old home if she was not to be married. In Pittsburgh these people did not want her to stay any longer after a few months with them, and they wrote to some people in Chicago who could take care of her. She came to Chicago a few weeks ago. When she arrived as far as Englewood she got off the train. She does not remember what time it was. Some one was trying to talk to her, but she could not understand anything but Lithuanian. There was an ambulance called from St. ———'s Hospital, where she was taken, and after an hour the child was born. She says her baby is a very nice boy. His name is Frank. She left all her belongings in the station. Girl can not read or write. She had in her pocket book address of people she was sent to from Pittsburgh. People at hospital sent for this Lithuanian woman, Mrs. Yerkes, 400 Wood Street.

Lucja looks well and strong. Her baby is with Mrs. Yerkes. Baby has no clothes, and Lucja has no clothes, but she says she does not need any clothes for herself, only for the baby. Spoke with Miss Gardner [League Superintendent] about her. Miss Gardner thinks she can get outfit for baby from Miss E. M. Griffin. A. K. telephoned Reverend Zimintaitis. He does not know anything about the girl, but thinks she is peasant girl who has had misfortune and will be all right if we can help her while she gets work. Mrs. Yerkes thinks girl is all right, but Mrs. Yerkes has a very small house and cannot keep girl. *Later.*—Arranged for Lucja and baby to go to Beulah Home until we can find what we should do with her. Reverend Zimintaitis thinks Mrs. Yerkes can take her to the Beulah Home. Gave her letter to Mrs. Watson, matron.

[Several other entries on record during the following week relate to the finding of a position for Lucja as wet-nurse. There are a few other entries, but not many. She was a competent girl and learned English quickly and was soon able to take care of herself and her child.]

41. Anastazia Pastrozna
(A Russian Rooming-House Case)

June 26, 1915.—Western "Home for Girls" telephoned, asking if visitor from League would come to Home to see Russian girl, Anastazia Pastrozna, who has been there several weeks. Girl is unmarried and has a baby. She came to "Home" from County Hospital. Promised that Mrs. Z. [Russian visitor] will call some time today. *Later.*—M. Z. visited "Home," and spoke with Anastazia. She has very nice baby girl. Baby was born in March in Cook County Hospital. Anastazia has been in America for over a year. She was boarding with some Russian people (Mr. and Mrs. Trusz, 600 West Street), where also boarded seven Russian men. One of these boarders, Pavel Stornieczik, was very much liked by Anastazia, and they were very good friends. He was father of her baby. But he went suddenly away when he found out about Anastazia's trouble. The girl had no place to stay. Mrs. Trusz could not keep her any more, but Mrs. Trusz had a friend, a Russian lady, Mrs. Korolup (1000 East River Street), and Mrs. Korolup said Anastazia could stay with her for a few weeks and they would find the man, Pavel Stornieczik. Man was never found, and baby was born in Cook County Hospital. Then after two weeks in Hospital she was placed in this Home. The girl said Mrs. Korolup had a letter from Pavel, asking how Anastazia was, and he said he was coming back to Chicago to see her and maybe marry her. Mrs. Korolup has letter, but she read it to Anastazia. Anastazia would like to find place for housework so she can take care of her baby. Girl is twenty years old; cannot read or write in Russian; has learned to speak some English at the "Home."

Later.—M. Z. visited Mrs. Korolup, 1000 East River Street. Mrs. Korolup has nice clean home; her husband works in the Ashland factory. She thinks Anastazia a very nice girl; takes very good care of her baby. She helped Mrs. Korolup with housework and knows something about how to work; she tries hard. It was very hard for girl living with so many boarders at Mrs. Trusz's. Mrs. Korolup gave address of Pavel Stornieczik, 100 Union Street, Pittsburgh; he wrote her he will come back but she does not think he will marry Anastazia. He is a better-educated man. He has cousin or brother, married man, who works with Chicago Electric Works, Peter Stornieczik. Mrs. Korolup could not give Peter's address but she gave M. Z. letter she received from Pavel Stornieczik [translation from the Russian]:

A letter from Pittsburgh written by Pavel, and I am in a hurry to inform you that I am in good health and am sending regards to you, Michael, and your wife, Elena, and wish God shall give you happiness in your present life and my regard and love for my dear and unforgotten Anastazia. (To Anastazia), I wish you the best and ask you don't scold me and don't worry. I would not leave you; as soon as I will settle down I will take you to me and we will get married and live together. What I did was not good, but this does not matter, everything will be all right, only don't be angry with me. I will write to you again in a few days. I sent you a letter before, but the address must have been wrong and you probably did not receive it. I am still without work.

Mike and Elena, please when you receive this letter, let Anastazia read it. My address is Pavel Stornieczik, 100 Union Street, Pittsburgh, Pennsylvania. P.S.—And I beg you Anastazia send me soon an answer. I will wait for it impatiently. Have nothing more to write and wish you to remain in good health as I am.

July 2, 1915.—M. Z. wrote Russian letter to Pavel Stornieczik, asking him if he will return and marry Anastazia.

[Record contains here some inquiries about a place for Anastazia. Nothing suitable was found for a Russian girl who could speak very little English and who had a baby to take care of, and she remained at the Home. Record also contains report of visits made to see the girl at the Home. On August 13 she went to work on a farm. Mrs. X (Superintendent of Home) had found place for her near Highville, Illinois. On September 21, when Mrs. Z. visited the "Home for Girls" to ask how Anastazia was getting along, Mrs. X said she received letter from the farm that Anastazia did not want to stay there any longer. They were anxious to keep her, however, and asked if someone could come to talk to Anastazia in Russian to explain that it was much better for her baby to stay because everybody liked the baby. She stayed finally until the following spring.]

April 27, 1916.—Telephoned Home for Girls. Mrs. X said Anastazia came back from Highville a few weeks ago. She stayed only a few days in the Home. She went to see a sister or friend on West Side and did not return, although she told them when she left she was coming back.

May 12, 1916.—M. Z. visited Mrs. Korolup to ask what happened to Anastazia. Mrs. Korolup said Anastazia is living with Pavel Stornieczik, who came back to Chicago. They are not married. Anastazia's address is 130 West Brown Street, front basement. *Later.*—M. Z. visited Anastazia and asked her why she is living with Pavel when he has not married her. Anastazia felt very bad. She said while she was away at the farm she got a Russian letter. She could not read it. She knew it came from Pavel. She came back to Chicago. She showed letter to M. Z. The letter was very much torn, but in it the man said he had written to her many times, and he never got any answers. He was coming back to Chicago to get her and take her with him to Pittsburgh. Anastazia went to see Russian friends. They read her the letter, and they told her Pavel was back with his brother. Anastazia stayed with friends till she found him. Then they got this flat because she is afraid to go to Pittsburgh. She said she would like to marry Pavel. She would like M. Z. to talk to him and tell him he should marry her. She says he is very good to her. He has good job at some electric works (probably Chicago Electric). She would like M. Z. to come at six o'clock when he comes home. M. Z. saw baby, very nice. Flat is very clean but furniture very little and very poor.

May 19, 1916.—M. Z. went in evening to see Pavel Stornieczik. Found him home. Told him that in America he cannot live this way. He said he is willing to marry Anastazia in two weeks when he gets another pay [i.e., next payment of wages]. He has no money now, paid rent last week. Asked Pavel if he would marry girl if League would loan him $5 to pay for marriage license. He would be glad to do this. Anastazia will be very thankful if we will help her. Told him I will write him Russian letter if we will help.

May 23, 1916.—M. Z. visited. Found they were already married. Pavel borrowed money. M. Z. saw certificate. Anastazia does not want to be married in church because she has not the clothes. Anastazia is very happy. They are moving to 500 Eastern Road. Pavel's brother has loaned them $50 to buy the furniture from a Russian woman who is leaving Chicago and who is living at this place, first floor rear, 500 Eastern Road. Spoke with Anastazia that she must try to go to class at Eastern Settlement, where she will learn something. She will be glad to go. *Later.*—Letter written to Eastern Settlement, asking them to visit Mrs. Stornieczik and to get her in mothers' class.

42. Nina Talpiniuk
(Assisting a Croatian Girl)

June 5.—Nina Talpiniuk, Croatian girl, sent by A. K. [Slavic visitor of League in charge of work at Dearborn Station] in a cab to 1100 Westover Street. She returned in the afternoon to the office [of the League]. She was crying because she found Jakub Dubiac, man she came to marry, had wedded last week. Girl would not stay with man's sister and wants League to find work for her. Girl had our card from the station and came back to us. A. K. asked girl if Jakub sent her ticket. She said he bought her ticket but long time ago. She was kept one week at Ellis Island and telegraphed Jakub. His sister, Mrs. Anastazia Kris, 1100 Westover Street, sent affidavit to Ellis Island; and when this arrived, Nina was released.

Nina was born in Russia and came with her parents to Croatia, where she met Jakub Dubiac and was engaged to him four years ago. Jakub went to America, and two years ago he sent Nina a steamship ticket. Nina was working with a family for six years, and the lady tried to persuade Nina to stay with her and send the passage back. Nina could not decide what to do, because the family was very good to her and she liked them all very much. Finally about a year ago she left but had hard time to come to this country. First she was detained for a week in Agram, then in Paris, and finally at the port because she did not have a pass from Russia. It took long time before the important pass from Russia came and girl could sail. Then in New York she was detained again at Ellis Island. The affidavit was furnished by Jakub's sister, who, to prevent the girl's deportation, promised that Jakub would marry her. At that time Mrs. Kris did not know surely that her brother was ready to marry another girl because he thought Nina did not care for him.

A. K. told girl we will find her place in a few days, and she can stay at Plymouth House[1] until that time.

June 6.—Nina sent to work in X Hospital. She will earn five dollars and board and room. She is satisfied to begin there and will go to evening class (English) at Ashland Settlement.

June 13.—Petroff's bank telephoned and asked what we have done with Nina Talpiniuk. Mrs. Kris is very much excited, not knowing where the girl is. A. K. telephoned Mrs. Kris and told her where Nina is working.

June 14.—Mrs. Kris telephoned that she went to hospital and brought Nina home to live with her. She will find her work sometime with Croatian people.

July 11.—A. K. visited Mrs. Kris, sister of Jakub Dubiac and asked, about Nina Talpiniuk. She is doing housework for Mrs. Voss on Douglas

[1] [A house maintained by the League where stranded immigrants could be kept overnight in emergencies.]

Boulevard near Marshall; has a very good place. Mrs. Kris is a very nice woman. She was sorry about her brother that he did not marry Nina. Nina is doing very well and likes her place.

INDUSTRIAL ACCIDENTS AND WORKMEN'S COMPENSATION

43. John Jalchow
(Settlement without Controversy, Indiana Law)

March 15, 1916.—John Jalchow, Russian man, in office, to see Miss B [Russian visitor]. R. B. spoke with man. He is twenty-two, was working for the Gary Wrought Iron Company in Gary, Indiana (Chicago office, 12 Michigan Avenue). He was employed from December 23, 1915, to January 13, 1916, three weeks, on the punch presswork. He claims the machine was out of order when he worked on January 13, and he was injured and lost three middle fingers on the left hand. Man was cared for by the company in a Gary hospital for one week and afterwards treated by the factory surgeon, Dr. C. A. Allen. Mr. Jalchow was advised to call at the Life Insurance Building, Chicago, Room 720, to see Mr. Fox. He visited this place, and they offered him $346.20; but he refused to accept this amount because he thinks perhaps he has a right to ask for more compensation. Told man to call here in a few days until we have time to find out about the compensation.

March 16, 1916.—H. C. [Assistant Superintendent] telephoned Gary Wrought Iron Company, Chicago office. They are insured by the General Indemnity Company, 1 Dearborn Street. *Later.*—Telephoned Mr. Fox, General Indemnity Company. He will not talk the matter over by telephone. He asks us to come in with man. Told him when man comes in, we will send a Russian visitor with him.

[In the meantime Miss C. looked up the Indiana Compensation Law and made certain notes for the Russian visitor.]

March 20, 1916.—John Jalchow in office. R. B. went with John Jalchow to the General Indemnity Company, 1 Dearborn Street. We spoke there with Mr. Fox. He wanted more details from the man's past, but Jalchow cannot give the places where he was employed during the three years in the United States. The Insurance Company handles the accident cases differently in every state. The present case is figured on the state law of Indiana with $345 compensation. This means 60 weeks at $5.75; 55 per cent of his weekly wages. The money can be paid out only in weekly instalments, and Jalchow must give a reliable address where he can be identified when every payment is made, until the sixty weeks are over. The money since the accident is deposited in the National Savings Bank.

Mr. Fox promised to ask the Indianapolis main office for Jalchow's documents. He asks us to come back again on March 23.

March 22, 1916.—John Jalchow back in office. R. B. got the following statement about the man's occupation in the United States: He arrived on November 16, 1913, was three months without work; then he worked in the spring four months (1914) on an Indiana farm (earned $40). He came back in May, 1914, to Chicago and was employed at the Belmont Twine Mills from June, 1914, to August, 1915. He was then without work one-and-a-half months. He worked again for the Western Broom Manufactory, 22 North Street, three weeks. He went about December 20 to Gary, Indiana, and worked for the Gary Wrought Iron Company from December, 1915, to January 13, 1916.

March 23, 1916.—R. B. went with John Jalchow to the Insurance Company. They have not received the papers from Indianapolis and will let us know when they arrive. Man would like to get work on a farm.

[Entries during April relate to placing man on a farm near Chicago.]

June 7, 1916.—Jalchow came back from farm of Mr. Brown near Glencoe. He did not like it because he received for labor job $2.00 and paid for board 85 cents a day. He worked only in good weather, and had no chance to earn money other times. His wages were always reduced. He will come back June 9, and R. B. will go with him to the Insurance Company.

June 9, 1916.—H. C. [Acting Superintendent] went to Insurance Company with John Jalchow and Miss B [Russian visitor]. He receives 60 weeks' part wages in lieu of all other compensation. Under the Indiana law it must be paid weekly—the company deposits the whole amount with the Indiana Trust Company and they send a check to him weekly. He has to sign twice and bank the check like any other check. He must also keep company informed of address. Mr. Fox suggested that our address be used. He wanted a letter giving him authority to fill out blanks, signed by Jalchow. *Later.*—Sent this letter.

[The remaining portions of the record are omitted. The record is a long one, covering the sixty weeks during which compensation was made, the opening of a savings account in a good downtown bank, the discovery that he had later opened an account for himself in a West Side Russian "immigrant" bank, and the loss of $120 there when the banker absconded. The record also contains entries about his enrolment in evening school and later about an arrangement for attending the day school for adult foreigners (maintained by the Board of Education) during a period of unemployment when he worked evenings to earn his meals and attended school in the day time. There was no controversy, however, at any time about the compensation matter. There is also a record about changing from one job to another because the first job kept him at work in the evening so that he could not attend evening school.]

44. Andrey Valeskii
(Workmen's Compensation under the Wisconsin Law)

February 12, 1918.—Andrey Valeskii, Russian, from Wisconsin, wants help about injury to his head. He has wife and three children in Russia; is thirty-nine years old; is five years in the United States. He will wait to see some visitor who can speak Russian. *Later.*—R. B. [Russian visitor] spoke with Andrey Valeskii. He worked one month for Wisconsin Brass Company, Fairfax, Wisconsin. He roomed at the company's boarding house. On January 13, while at work feeding the machine, a piece of brass broke off and struck him in the forehead. He was unconscious and was taken to the company's hospital and stayed there six days. He was not quite well and asked to be sent to Chicago to his friends as he was afraid he would die and wanted to be with his people. Man did not get any money. He has not signed anything. He has not heard from company since. Man is not able to work. He gets dizzy spells and headaches. He has a big scar on his face. He has no lawyer and wants League to take up his case. He was sent here by some Russian friends. Told him we will write to company and find out about things. He will come back again in one week.

February 14, 1918.—Letter written to Wisconsin Brass Company, Fairfax, Wisconsin:

GENTLEMEN:

We write to ask a report on the case of Andrey Valeskii, a Russian, now living at 259 Morgan Street, Chicago. He was employed by you and on January 13, while at work, was injured. He writes to ask what compensation you will offer. After hearing from you we shall be glad to explain to Mr. Valeskii what you have said.

Very truly yours,

MARY CANTEY, *Acting Superintendent*

February 16, 1918.—Letter received from the Wisconsin Brass Company as follows:

DEAR MADAM:

Re injury to Andrew Valesky. In response to your letter of February 14, regarding an injury to Andrew Valesky, we are glad to give you the following facts in this regard: The Wisconsin Brass Company is, of course, subject to the Workmen's Compensation Act of the State of Wisconsin, and all compensation paid for injuries at this plant is subject to the terms of the law and to the supervision of the Industrial Commission of the state. The injury to Andrew Valesky occurred on January 14, 1918, and the disability resulting, in accordance with our physician's report and certificate, of which we are in possession, should have terminated on Monday, February 4. According to the terms of the law, in addition to all reasonable medical and hospital expenses, compensation shall consist of 65 per cent of the injured man's wages up to a maximum wage of $15.00 per week to cover the period of disability, with the exception that compensation is not payable for the first seven days of disability, unless the total period is greater than 28 days. In the case of Valesky, therefore, compensation is due according to the following tabulation: daily wages, $3.00; average weekly, $15.00 maximum, and 65 per cent equals $9.75 divided by 6 equals $1.63 daily compensation. From January 21 noon to February 2, inclusive, equals 11½ days at $1.63 per day equals $18.74 compensation.

Compensation	$18.74
Hospital	3.20
Doctor	17.50
Total	$39.44

We have already paid the hospital and doctor bills connected with this case. Compensation in accordance with the law as outlined in the above tabulation was offered to this man, but he refused it, stating that he was going to Chicago and would not settle the case for less than $100. It should be stated in connection with this case that this company is obliged under present labor conditions to operate a boarding-house and commissariat for out-of-town men of the status of Valesky, and that this man also owes us for board and lodging in the amount of $7.75, covering nine days' board and lodging from January 21 to 29, inclusive, which amount of course we would deduct from the compensation paid to him. It seems to us that this man is without knowledge of the terms of the Wisconsin law and has in some way obtained the idea that he can secure a much larger sum of money for his injury than the law contemplates. We are perfectly willing to make a settlement with him on the above basis at any time, but are required by the Industrial Commission to obtain a receipt from the party to whom any payment is made, which is transmitted to Madison for record. Many foreign workmen seem to have the idea that in asking for this receipt, we are asking for a waiver of all claims upon the company, which is not the case.

Yours very truly,

CHARLES HARPER, *Superintendent*
Wisconsin Brass Company
Fairfax Branch

February 18, 1918.—Andrey Valeskii in office. R. B. explained letter and asked him to go to Western Free Dispensary. Miss Cantey [Acting Superintendent] gave him a note to Mrs. Mary Hendricks, Superintendent, as follows:

MY DEAR MRS. HENDRICKS:

The bearer of this is Andrey Valeskii, 259 Morgan Street, second floor, rear. He is a Russian, thirty-nine years of age. This man was injured in the Wisconsin Brass Company, Fairfax, Wisconsin. He states that he is not able to work at present, and we are anxious to have a diagnosis of his condition in order to be able to advise him with regard to the matter of compensation.

Yours very truly,

MARY CANTEY

March 9, 1918.—Letter from Western Free Dispensary:

MY DEAR MISS CANTEY:

Andrey Valeskii came to our Surgical Clinic, February 19, 1918, and an X-ray picture of his skull was advised. He returned the following morning and the picture was made. On February 25 he came again to Clinic but did not wait to see the doctor. No diagnosis can be made until the examination is completed.

Very truly yours,

MARY HENDRICKS

March 11, 1918.—Wrote Andrey Valeskii. [Letter returned later.]

April 8, 1918.—Andrey Valeskii in office. Man does not work, is sick. Nobody at Dispensary had told man to stay for an examination. Sent man to Western Free Dispensary again. Gave him letter to Mrs. Hendricks.

November 19, 1918.—Andrey Valeskii in office. He says he works but gets dizzy. Man was unable to work for six months. He says he did not come sooner because he could not find our office [League office had been moved]. He will bring certificate from a private doctor. Man started to work in June, 1918, but could not do hard work. Man will bring two witnesses to prove that he could not work. He now lives at 123 Morgan Street.

November 20, 1918.—Andrey Valeskii in office. He has a certificate from a Dr. Klein. He also brought affidavits signed by two witnesses who said he had not been able to work. R. B. spoke with man and told him to go back to Western Free Dispensary and wait for examination, as Dr. Klein's certificate would not do.

[The certificate contained the following statement:] "To whom it may concern: This will certify that I have on this date examined Andrey Valeskii and that he had a big scar on left side of cheek $2\frac{1}{2}$ inches in length, leaving a permanent disfigurement."

November 21, 1918.—Andrey Valeskii in office. He has been to Western Free Dispensary, and they told him that Immigrants' Protective League should write them for report. Man was not examined. *Later.*—Wrote Western Free Dispensary as follows:

MY DEAR MRS. HENDRICKS:

Will you be good enough to send us a report on the condition of Andrey Valeskii, now living at 123 Morgan Street. This man was at your surgical clinic February 19, 1918, and also on November 20 or 21, 1918. We shall be grateful for a report on this case.

Very truly yours,

MARY CANTEY

November 23, 1918.—Letter from Western Free Dispensary as follows:

Mr. Valeskii came to our Surgical Clinic November 20. His difficulty seems to be no longer due to the accident which he had last February. The X-ray picture taken was negative. The doctor who saw him on Wednesday suggests that he come to our Neurology Clinic, which is held every morning at nine o'clock. We have no further report to make.

Later.—Russian letter sent to Andrey Valeskii, explaining that he must attend clinic.

December 2, 1918.—Andrey Valeskii in office. He wants to know what to do about his case. Man says his head does not pain at all. He did not go back to Dispensary. He wants to go to a private doctor. He asked us to send him to a good doctor. R. B. finally suggested Dr. Martzen. Letter written to Dr. Martzen [a good Russian doctor]:

DEAR SIR:

The bearer of this note is Andrey Valeskii, a Russian, thirty-nine years of age, now living at 123 Morgan Street, Chicago. In January, 1918, while working for the Wisconsin Brass Company, Fairfax, he was injured by having a piece of brass fall and strike him in the forehead. He was taken to the company hospital and stayed there six days. He states that ever since this accident he has "dizzy spells," headache, and is at times unconscious. He came to us in February, then changed his address, and, as we moved a little later, we lost sight of him. He returned a few days ago, saying that he was still not well and had not been able to work for six months after the accident. We referred him to the Western Free Dispensary on February 19, 1918, and they had an X-ray picture of his skull. He did not keep up his attendance at the dispensary but returned there recently and they wrote on November 22 that the X-ray picture was negative and that "his difficulty seems to be no longer due to the accident which he had last February." The man wishes to claim compensation, but it is necessary to have a letter from a physician, stating his present condition. Will you kindly make an examination and give the man a letter which we can use with his employers or for the industrial board? Kindly let him know what your charges will be for these services. We shall be grateful to you for your interest in the case.

Very truly yours,

MARY CANTEY

December 12, 1918.—Man in office. Brought certificate from Dr. Martzen to R. B. Man says doctor said he should pay $10 for examination. He can't pay the $10 at once, but as soon as he can earn something, he will bring the money. Man was very well satisfied with the doctor. Man is willing to pay even $20 because the doctor told him exactly how he feels and felt. *Later.*—Wrote Dr. Martzen, inquiring result of examination.

December 14, 1918.—Reply received from Dr. Martzen:

MY DEAR MISS CANTEY:

In accordance with your request I have just made a physical examination of Andrey Valeskii, a Russian, thirty-nine years old, living at 123 Morgan Street. I can best state my position in this matter and serve your interests by detailing to you the results of my examination and the conclusions drawn therefrom. Man examined is well built and well nourished. He is entirely oriented as to time and place—information obtained through an interpreter. He has a proper insight as to his present and past state, memory is good, and he relates his story apparently connectedly and relevantly. The examination of his head is negative as to scars, swellings, or depressions. Almost concealed by the left eyebrow is a scar not adhered to the subjacent tissue, but apparently painful when touched. Eyes negative as to pupillary reaction and movements of eye muscles. Almost half an inch below the left zygoma and on a line running parallel to it is a scar about one and one-half inches, somewhat painful to touch and not adherent. There is no asymmetry of the two halves of the face and no twitchings. His teeth are in a very poor condition. Faucal reflexes present. Neck, negative; chest, negative; abdomen, negative; abdominal reflexes present and equal on the two sides. Now as to the extremities: There is a suggestion of anaesthesia to the pain sense of the skin of the left fingers, wrist and forearm up as far as the middle of the left forearm, with apparently a wasting of the group of muscles between the left thumb and index finger. Left ring finger is partially amputated. As to the lower extremities. He stands and walks well, no swaying or staggering, no stiffness or feebleness—reflexes all normal. Conclusion: It is my opinion—negative X-ray notwithstanding—that the pain the man is suffering today and his incapacitation for work are the results of his injuries alleged by him to have been received January, 1918, while at work in the Wisconsin Brass Company. It is also my opinion that it is altogether uncertain just when the man will be altogether well.

NOTE.—Not one of my conclusions has been translated to this man, Andrey Valeskii, so that he is in total ignorance of my findings. My charge for the examination of Andrey Valeskii is $10.00.

Respectfully yours,

MORRIS MARTZEN, M.D.

December 16, 1918.—Telephoned Dr. Martzen several times. Finally reached him. He says that the seizures which Valeskii describes and the pain in his face were sufficient reasons to explain his not working. Mr. Valeskii impressed him as being sincere and truthful in his statements. He was obliged to use an interpreter as the doctor does not speak Russian very well.

December 17, 1918.—Wrote Wisconsin Brass Company as follows:

Re Andrey Valeskii, 123 Morgan Street, Chicago. You will recall that in February we wrote you concerning the injury of Andrey Valeskii. We are inclosing two affidavits which state that the man has not been able to work for the last six months. He has been examined by a doctor who says that the seizures which Valeskii speaks of and the pain in his head are sufficient reasons for his not being able to work. He is very anxious to receive compensation. Will you kindly let us know what you intend to do about this case and we will inform Mr. Valeskii.

December 19, 1918.—Letter received from Wisconsin Brass Company:

Subject: *In re* Andrew Valeskii, 123 Morgan Street, Chicago. In referring to our records of this injury case, I find that in our previous letter to your organization, dated February 15, 1918, it was stated that compensation due under the laws of Wisconsin had been made up for this man to cover eleven and one-half days' disability, amounting to $18.74, which payment was subject to a bill for board and lodging to the amount of $7.75, owing to the company. I do not find that this money has ever been paid over to him and at any time the man will give you an order for the same we will be glad to forward it in your charge. It is apparent from your letter of the seventeenth, together with the inclosures, that there is a possibility of further compensation being due this man beyond the statement outlined in our letter of February 15. As stated in that letter, the man received proper medical attention at the time, and we are in possession of the doctor's certificate made after examination stating that the man should be able to return to work on February 4. It was in accordance with this physician's certificate that we terminated payment of compensation for disability. It now appears that you have two affidavits that the man has not worked in six months; also, apparently the report from the doctor that if Valeskii has seizures such as he claims these pains in his head are sufficient reason for his not being able to work. These facts we are not disposed to dispute. However, we would hardly like paying further compensation merely on evidence that the man has seizures of some kind and that they prevent him from working. The real question, of course, is what connection have these seizures with the fact of the injury while in this company's employ? If it is possible to obtain authoritative medical proof that the man's present condition is the result of the injury received in our employ we would, of course, be liable for further payments, and we would have no disposition to dispute the matter. Until such evidence is forthcoming, we feel we should rely upon the physician's certificate in our possession. If you find it possible to supply conclusive evidence of this nature to us, we will consider it at once in accordance with our duties under the Compensation Act of Wisconsin. However, we are inclined to feel under the circumstances the wise course to pursue would be to have your organization, as this man's representative, make a formal application upon the Industrial Commission of Wisconsin to determine the facts in this case and make award accordingly. In that case both parties will be fully protected, and we can assure you that we will make no effort to obstruct in any way this man's right to obtain a hearing before the commission, or to obtain an award which will square with such facts as investigation shall prove to hold in this case.

Yours very truly,

CHARLES HARPER, *Superintendent*

Later.—Letter written to Industrial Commission:

Industrial Commission of Wisconsin
Madison, Wisconsin

GENTLEMEN: *Re* Andrey Valeskii. We are writing in behalf of the above man, who is a Russian, thirty-nine years old, who cannot read nor write in English and who understands very little spoken English. He was employed by the Wisconsin Brass Company, Fairfax, and while at work on January 13, 1918, was injured by a piece of brass striking him and knocking him unconscious. He was treated by the company doctor in their hospital; but thinking that he was going to die and wishing to be among friends, he came to Chicago and asked us to ask for his compensation. We wrote to the Brass Company and as the man was still ill, referred him to the Western Free Dispensary. The man moved, our office also was moved, and we lost track of him. He says that he did not know how to find the new office. He did come back however, on November 19, and reported that he had tried to go to work in June, 1918, but was not physically able to hold his position. We are inclosing copies of the affidavits of two witnesses and of a letter from a private doctor. In a telephone communication the doctor told me that he believed the man was telling a straight story, and he thought that the seizures and pain were serious enough to prevent his working. The man is married, with a wife and children in Europe; he is uneducated and speaks very little English, and it is therefore particularly important that he should be assisted in the presentation of his case. The Wisconsin Brass Company suggested our writing to you and we are therefore filing a claim in his name for compensation. Kindly let us know how the man must proceed. Is it necessary for him to have a lawyer and will there be any expense for him?

Very truly yours,
MARY CANTEY

December 21, 1918.—Andrey Valeskii in office. He was sick. Probably had a cold. He was working last at an oil shop, Fifteenth Street, for two and a half days. Man says he does not work steadily because he has pains as soon as he bends his head. Man still lives at 123 Morgan Street, first flat. Man has no money. Gave him $2.00. He is sick, will repay when he can work. Man said he could not yet pay doctor but that he will pay after a while.

December 30, 1918.—Letter from Industrial Commission of Wisconsin:

Immigrants' Protective League
Chicago, Illinois

Re Andrey Valeskii vs. *The Wisconsin Brass Company.* We have your letter of December 19. Our records show a report from the employer, stating that this man was injured January 14, 1918; that he was putting the end of the bars into a shear to be cut off, but he did not put the bar in far enough, causing the shear plate to tip the bar up and strike him in his cheek; that he sustained a deep cut on the left cheek and a bruise over his left eye; at the time of the accident the man was earning $18.00 per week. Supplementary reports show that the man was offered compensation in compliance with the law, which he refused to accept, and that they have heard nothing from him since February 14, 1918. It is our suggestion that you write directly to the Wisconsin Brass Company, at Fairfax, Wisconsin, and make a demand upon them for the compensation due this man. If you are unable to agree with them upon the length of time he has been disabled because of the injury, it will be necessary that an application for the adjustment of the claim be filed with the Commission. We are inclosing blank forms of application. In the event that an application is filed, a copy of the same will be served on the Brass Company; they will make an answer to the application, one copy of which will be filed with the Commission and one served on the applicant. The case will then be set for hearing at Fairfax and both parties given an opportunity to appear before the Commission and present the facts before a decision is made. We are sending a copy of this letter to the Wisconsin Brass Company. It is our suggestion that you furnish them with copies of the affidavits which you inclosed in your letter of the nineteenth.

Yours very truly,
E. C. HOPKINS, *Chief Examiner*
Industrial Commission

Later.—Wrote Wisconsin Brass Company:

Re Andrey Valeskii. Complying with your suggestion, we wrote to the Industrial Commission, who now suggest that we write to you and inclose the statement of the doctor, which we are doing. When we wrote on December 17, we inclosed the affidavits stating that the man had not worked steadily since the accident. When speaking to the man, we explained to him that he must have a medical examination before the Industrial Commission would consider his case; and knowing that the statement of the Dispensary doctors cannot be used in court, we referred him to a private doctor. The man had asked, however, to be sent to a private doctor and is responsible for the charge of $10 which the doctor mentions. We simply gave him the name of a doctor who we thought was intelligent and honest. The man and his friends both repeat that he has these seizures. We shall wait to hear from you before referring the case again to the Industrial Commission.

January 2, 1919.—Long-distance call from Wisconsin Brass Company. They ask us to have Mr. Valeskii meet their representative on Friday, January 3, at the office of Dr. Alexander Smith, 125 Michigan Avenue, at one o'clock. *Later.*—Wrote Mr. Valeskii a Russian letter, special delivery, telling him to meet R. B. [Russian visitor] in our office at twelve o'clock tomorrow. *Later.*—Letter received from Wisconsin Brass Company, as follows:

Immigrants' Protective League
Chicago, Illinois

GENTLEMEN: Attention Miss Mary Cantey. Subject: *In re* Andrew Valesky, 123 Morgan Street. The report from Dr. Morris Martzen with regard to his examination of Andrew Valesky has received our earnest attention. Naturally, we would like to have this report confirmed by a physician of our own before accepting entire responsibility in this matter. Therefore, I am requesting our Mr. Mann, who is in charge of such matters at this plant, to call and see you at your office in Chicago whenever he is able to make arrangements with our physician for an interview and examination of Mr. Valesky. It is possible that by the time this letter reaches you Mr. Mann will have been in telephone communication with you. As soon as we can get confirmatory medical advice in this matter, we will be glad to make a proposition as to the settlement of the case in accordance with the terms of the law. You may expect to see Mr. Mann at your office within a day or two with regard to this matter.

Yours very truly,

CHARLES HARPER, *Superintendent*

January 3, 1919.—Andrey Valeskii in office at 10:15 A.M. R. B. spoke with him about his case. Man says he has no pains, but his head goes around. He does not see anything when he bends his head for a while, everything is black before him. The first place man worked after the injury was last summer for the same company at Fairfax. Man worked there six weeks but had to quit because his head was painful. Second place man worked was in September, 1918, at the time of registration, in an East Chicago factory. He worked there two weeks but left because of pain in his head. Third place man worked was at a rag shop at Blue Island Avenue and Fifteenth Street for two weeks. He started to work two weeks after he left East Chicago factory because he had to earn some money for food. His head was still painful. Fourth place he worked was in stockyards. He started to work there ten days after he left rag shop, but he worked in stockyards only one week. He had to leave because of pain in his head. Fifth place man worked was for three days the week before Christmas in an oil shop. He had to quit because of pain in his head. Man says he owes his brother $200 and his relatives about $100. Sent man to lunch. He will come back here at 2:30. *Later.*—R. B. went with man to Dr. Smith and interpreted. Dr. Smith examined man and said man is sick only from the thought. The injuries are not deep and could not cause his present condition. Man must keep clean and have good food and fresh air. Man has a goiter, but not one that must be taken out. He also has bad tonsils. If man would fight case in court, man could not prove his part. The gentleman who represented the Fairfax Company was quite nice. He thinks he could pay one-half wages for six months. Man was willing to settle the case for $100 at the time, shortly after injury occurred, but company thought the injuries to be very slight. The company representative wanted to know what Valeskii desires. Valeskii said he wants $400 so he can pay his debts and bring his family from Russia. He has not worked so he has no money for tickets. Fairfax Company representative will take the matter up with his people and let League know when settlement can be made. The representative was very nice and seemed to sympathize with the man. Mr. Valeskii seemed to be satisfied. Dr. Smith said Mr. Valeskii can not get anything if he should sue, and Dr. Smith advised him to take what the company would give him. Dr. Smith seemed to be honest and kind.

January 7, 1919.—Letter received from Fairfax Company:

I am inclosing herewith copy of a letter which I have today written to the Industrial Commission of Wisconsin with regard to the case of Andrew Valesky; also copy of a report given us by Dr. Smith after his examination of this man. The report of Dr. Martzen I believe you undoubtedly have on file. As soon as we hear from the Industrial Commission as to their advice for our future procedure, we will let you know.

[Copy of inclosure:]

Industrial Commission of Wisconsin
Madison, Wisconsin

GENTLEMEN: Attention of Mr. E. C. Hopkins, Chief Examiner. *Re Andrew Vulesky* vs. *Wisconsin Brass Company.* Please refer to your correspondence of December 26 with Miss Mary Cantey, Superintendent of the Immigrants' Protective League, Chicago, with reference to the claim of Andrew Valesky against the Company; also to the reports on this accident, the original of which was dated January 24, 1918, and the final report April 9, 1918. This case has proved a very puzzling one to us in the way of knowing what disposition to make of the claim upon this Company. We received from Miss Cantey on December 17, affidavits from the man's acquaintances stating that he had not worked steadily since the accident, and also the statement of Morris Martzen, M.D., that after examination he considered the man's present condition as due to result of injuries received at this plant. Upon receipt of this information a representative of this

Company had an interview with Miss Cantey and arranged for an independent examination by a physician in Chicago, Alexander Smith, M.D. We are inclosing for your information a copy of both physicians' reports of which we are in possession, from which you will readily see that the conclusions of the medical men as to the case do not agree. Dr. Hart, our own physician in Fairfax, who handled this case originally and who has read the reports from both physicians, substantiates Dr. Smith's conclusion that this man's physical condition, aside from any connection with the accident, may very possibly be the cause of his intermittent incapacitation. We desire to treat this man absolutely fairly and would be willing to submit the case to any medical authority acceptable to the Commission, paying the expenses of this final examination ourselves in order to clear up the case. Under the circumstances, we would prefer to have the Commission designate this umpire, if he may be so called, if they would care to handle the matter in this way. Otherwise, because of the conflicting testimony, we can hardly accede to this man's claim, and must advise Miss Cantey to make formal application to the Commission for judgment. Will you advise us in this matter?

Yours very truly,

CHARLES HARPER, *Superintendent*
Wisconsin Brass Company
Fairfax Branch

January 13, 1919.—Letter received from Industrial Commission, inclosing copy of letter to Wisconsin Brass Company, as follows:

INDUSTRIAL COMMISSION OF WISCONSIN
STATE CAPITOL, MADISON

The Wisconsin Brass Company
Fairfax, Wisconsin

DEAR SIRS: Attention of Mr. Harper. *In re* Andrew Valesky. We have your letter of January 7 and note that the report of your physician as to the condition of Mr. Valesky is different from that of the report of the physician who examined him for the Immigrants' Protective League. We note your willingness to have this claim disposed of by the Commission's selecting a disinterested surgeon to examine the man and making a decision upon his report and that you will pay the expenses of the injured man to Milwaukee in order that he may be examined by the physician to be selected by the Commission. We will send a copy of this letter to the Immigrants' Protective League, for the attention of Miss Cantey. If she agrees that the case may be disposed of in this manner, we will then select the physician to make the examination, and he will advise Miss Cantey when the injured man should report for the examination.

Yours very truly,

E. C. HOPKINS, *Chief Examiner*

Later.—Man in office. R. B. explained letter. He is willing to go to Milwaukee if his expenses are paid. Told him we would let him know date. Man said that he has had bad headache, cannot work. Wrote Industrial Commission.

January 22, 1919.—Letter received from Industrial Commission:

The Wisconsin Brass Company
Fairfax, Wisconsin

DEAR SIRS: Attention of Mr. Harper. *In re* Andrew Valesky. We are in receipt of a letter from the Immigrants' Protective League consenting to have the Commission select a disinterested surgeon to examine Mr. Valesky. We have accordingly selected Dr. S. H. Nikisch, of Milwaukee. He will write the Immigrants' Protective League when he is ready to have Mr. Valesky report at Milwaukee for the examination. It is our understanding that you will reimburse Mr. Valesky for the expense incident to the trip to Milwaukee and return, and that you will also pay Dr. Nikisch for making the examination. His bill will be sent to us, and we will then forward it to you. A copy of this letter is being sent to the Immigrants' Protective League.

Yours very truly,

E. C. HOPKINS, *Chief Examiner*

[Arrangements for examination, dates, etc., omitted.]

January 27, 1919.—Andrey Valeskii in office. His head has been so painful that he had to lie down for six days. Gave man ticket to Milwaukee and $3.75 for return ticket and food. Gave him letter to Dr. Nikisch as follows:

Dr. S. H. Nikisch
Milwaukee, Wisconsin

DEAR SIR: *Re Andrey Valeskii* vs. *Wisconsin Brass Company.* The bearer of this is Andrey Valeskii who was injured while working for the Wisconsin Brass Company in Fairfax in January, 1918. Mr. Valeskii has not been able to work since this accident. He has tried it and after two or three days is forced to give it up as he says he has a severe pain in his head. He has recently been sick in bed for six days with the same pain. The man has made a good impression on our Russian visitor. She thinks that he is an earnest, hard-working man and is sincere when he says that he is sick and unable to work. He has never been ill before. We are inclosing a copy of an examination made by a private physician in Chicago and presume that you have a copy of the one made by the company physician. We also forwarded two affidavits from men who had known Valeskii, stating that they knew that he had not been able to work and earn his living since he was injured. It is certainly a fact that since this injury the man has not worked, has suffered much pain, has been obliged to borrow money to live on and is no longer the hard-working, strong man that he was. Thanking you for your interest in this case, I am,

Very truly yours,

MARY CANTEY

January 30, 1919.—Valeskii in office. He went to Milwaukee Tuesday night. Dr. Nikisch examined man. Dr. Nikisch drove man around in an automobile looking for an interpreter. Dr. Nikisch said he will send a statement.

February 5, 1919.—Letter from Industrial Commission, inclosing copy of letter to Wisconsin Brass Company and a copy of letter from Dr. Nikisch.

[Copy of letter to Wisconsin Brass Company:]

We are inclosing a copy of the report of Dr. S. H. Nikisch. A copy of the report is also being sent to the Immigrants' Protective League. We will delay taking any further action in the case until we hear from you and the injured man or his representatives.

[Copy of letter from Dr. Nikisch to Industrial Commission of Wisconsin:]

GENTLEMEN:

Re Andrew Valesky vs. *Wisconsin Brass Company*. This patient presented himself for examination on Wednesday. It was impossible for me to talk to him, and I was forced to secure an interpreter to obtain a history. I learned that in January, 1918, the patient was hit over the forehead and the left side of the face by a piece of brass weighing about 200 pounds. He claims that he was unconscious nine hours and remained in the hospital at that time from three to four days. He was then sent home but later went back to the hospital again for several days. From his history there has been no paralysis at any time. Patient complains at the present time that he is unable to work on account of spells of dizziness and headaches, particularly when he works and is forced to bend. He says he has noises in the head and ringing in the ear, all of which keep him from work although when at rest he admits that he feels better. These symptoms are not continuous but are intermittent in their appearance. There has been no vomiting and indigestion disturbance at any time. I understand an X-ray of his head had been taken but I am in ignorance of its findings. Examination of this man shows the following condition: His mentality and memory are apparently normal. There are no depressions or elevations on his head suggestive of any fractures. There is a healed scar about one inch long, which is covered by the left eyebrow. This scar is freely movable and not adherent to the bone. He claims that it is somewhat painful, but I could not substantiate this by examination. There does not seem to be any involvement of the supra-orbital nerve. There is another scar about one and one-half inches long just below and parallel to the left cheek bone. This scar is also freely movable and apparently not painful. There is a slight twitching of the muscles around this scar, probably due to a slight irritation of the branch of the facial nerve. Examination of the eyes is negative as to pupillary reaction and muscular movements. There is no paralysis of any of the face muscles. Examination of the ears shows a definitely abnormal condition existing in the left ear, and I believe that this condition may be entirely responsible for many of his symptoms and certainly should be corrected. It consists of a large amount of hard, inspissated ear wax blocking up the entire external canal and pressing against the eardrum, causing a marked diminution of hearing in this ear. I tried to remove this wax, but the patient would not submit to it. Further examination of this patient's chest, abdomen, extremities, and reflexes were all negative. There are at least three possibilities that must be considered in this man's condition. Firstly, the ear condition described above, which I believe is mainly responsible for his present trouble, must be remedied to note whether or not the symptoms subside. Secondly, one must consider that this patient possibly sustained a skull fracture or a concussion of the brain without any paralytic symptoms. I have nothing definite to substantiate this theory except that he was unconscious, if this be true. Ordinarily the dizziness and headaches following concussions or fractures usually disappear within six months, but it is possible that such symptoms may last for a year or more. Thirdly, traumatic neurosis might account for symptoms such as described. There are no confirmatory symptoms to warrant one in concluding that this patient is suffering from a neurosis. I am of the opinion that this man should first of all be sent to a competent ear specialist to remedy his ear trouble and for a more thorough ear examination. If symptoms do not then abate, I would suggest putting him in a hospital for a week or more to keep him under observation.

Yours very truly,

S. H. NIKISCH

February 7, 1919.—Andrew Valeskii in office. R. B. persuaded man to have his ears examined and treated. Man is very pessimistic. He says he never has had any trouble with his ears, that the doctor at Milwaukee was a Jew and takes the company's side. Man is willing to go to the Dispensary. R. B. telephoned Western Free Dispensary. Miss Merritt will look after him and will report to us.

February 10, 1919.—Letter received from Western Free Dispensary, as follows:

MY DEAR MISS CANTEY:

Mr. Andrey Valeskii was examined in our Ear Clinic February 7. The doctor made a diagnosis of "impacted cerumen of the left ear" (hardened wax). He was given a prescription to use for his ear, which will soften and warm this wax, so that it can be easily removed. The doctor suggests that he come back in a week to see how he is getting along. We hope that this treatment will be satisfactory, and that he will soon be all right.

Very truly yours,

HELEN MERRITT
Social Service Department

February 12, 1919.—Letter from Wisconsin Brass Company:

Immigrants' Protective League
Chicago, Illinois

GENTLEMEN: Attention Mary Cantey, Superintendent. *In re* Andrew Valesky. Inclosed herewith you will find a copy of my last letter to the Industrial Commission of Wisconsin, commenting on the report of Dr. Nikisch as to his examination of Andrew Valesky. We will be glad to pay any expense which we have undertaken as soon as we get a bill therefor either from you direct, or through the Commission. However, as stated to the Commission, it seems to us that Dr. Nikisch's report is confirmatory of our own original impression, which was that the attacks which this man is undergoing have their rise in other conditions than the injury which he received at this plant. The matter, of course, is in safe hands if it is left with the Commission for adjustment, and we feel that this is the only correct course in the matter. That is to say, if you do not yet feel satisfied that this man has no claim upon this Company, then you should formally petition the Industrial Commission for an award. However, if you have any other opinion on the subject, we will be glad to give it due consideration.

Yours very truly,

CHARLES HARPER, *Superintendent*

The letter sent by the Wisconsin Brass Company to the Industrial Commission of Wisconsin was as follows:

Industrial Commission of Wisconsin
Madison, Wisconsin

GENTLEMEN: *In re* Andrew Valesky. The physician's report of examination on the above case made by Dr. S. H. Nikisch seems to us to leave this case in its previous condition. Our position is that we are perfectly willing to pay any sum of money which is justifiably due this man. On the other hand, we do not feel that our liability is sufficiently defined in this case to warrant an offer of settlement of any kind. We will be glad to settle any bills in connection with this examination, and presume this Company will receive them through the Industrial Commission in the near future.

CHARLES HARPER, *Superintendent*

February 13, 1919.—Letter written to Wisconsin Brass Company as follows:

GENTLEMEN:

Many thanks for your letter of February 11, concerning Andrey Valeskii. Following the directions of Dr. S. H. Nikisch we have persuaded the man to go to an ear clinic and he is now having treatments. We should like to see if these treatments and the removal of the wax affect any improvement in his general health and we therefore ask that you postpone your decision in this case until you hear from us again. We hope to write in the course of a week or ten days.

Very truly yours,

MARY CANTEY

Later.—Letter written to Industrial Commission as follows:

Industrial Commission of Wisconsin
Madison, Wisconsin

GENTLEMEN: *Re* Andrey Valeskii. We are inclosing a copy of our letter to the Wisconsin Brass Company, Fairfax. We feel that Dr. Nikisch's suggestion should be tried and with some difficulty we have persuaded the man to have his ears attended to.

IMMIGRANTS' PROTECTIVE LEAGUE

February 15, 1919.—Letter received from Wisconsin Industrial Commission:

In re Andrew Valesky vs. *Wisconsin Brass Company.* We are in receipt of a letter from the Wisconsin Brass Company, from which it appears that the Company is not satisfied with the report of Dr. Nikisch that the condition of Mr. Valesky is the result of the injury sustained while in the employ of the Brass Company. It seems very doubtful whether the condition of this man can be attributed to any injury sustained while in the employ of the Brass Company, and we feel that the Brass Company is justified in the position they are taking. It is apparent that there can be no final adjustment and determination of this man's claim without a hearing before the Commission. If you feel that he is entitled to the benefits of the Compensation Law, we suggest that you file a formal application to have the claim adjusted. We are inclosing blank forms. In the event that an application is filed, the case will be set for hearing, and both parties interested given an opportunity to present the facts in the case before a decision is made. We are sending a copy of this letter to the Wisconsin Brass Company.

E. C. HOPKINS, *Chief Examiner*

February 17, 1919.—Andrey Valeskii in office. Man says he was three times at the Dispensary. He got work at the Henry Brass Company, 9 Madison Street. Man could sit down while working. He worked three days but had to quit, had spells of dizziness. *Later.*—R. B. visited Henry Brass Company. Spoke to the man in the office and to the foreman. Foreman says that Valeskii did a boy's job. Foreman did not notice anything wrong. Valeskii just worked like any other man. Foreman thinks that Valeskii was not satisfied with his wages, that is why he quit, not saying anything. Valeskii has two days' pay coming to him, which he can get on Saturday.

February 19, 1919.—Letter written to Wisconsin Industrial Commission:

Industrial Commission of Wisconsin
Madison, Wisconsin

Gentlemen: *Re* Andrey Valeskii. We wish to report that, following the recommendation of Dr. Nikisch, Andrey Valeskii has been treated at the Western Free Dispensary, Chicago, and has had the wax removed from his ear. He states that he feels no better. He worked for three days at the Henry Brass Company, 9 Madison Street, Chicago. He said that he still felt dizzy and could not continue to work. We verified the fact that he had been at work. We realize that this is a difficult case. So far as we know, up to the time of the accident at the Wisconsin Brass Company, Valeskii was a hard-working, self-respecting workman. Since that time he has not been able to work and continues to say that he feels ill. His friends seem to be convinced that he is a genuinely sick man, and we have a letter from one doctor saying that the man is suffering pain and that his incapacity for work is the result of his injury alleged by him to have been received while at work in the Wisconsin Brass Company. The man's appearance is certainly not that of a vigorous, well person. We appreciate the difficulties of this situation and should be very glad if you would give us your advice as to what is the proper thing to do.

Very truly yours,

MARY CANTEY

February 26, 1919.—Letter received from Industrial Commission:

DEAR SIRS:

Attention of M. Cantey, *in re Andrew Valesky* vs. *Wisconsin Brass Company.* We have your letter of February 19 and suggest that in behalf of this man you file a formal application with the Commission for the adjustment of the claim. Blank forms of application are inclosed. In the event that the application is filed, the case will be set for hearing at Fairfax, and after all of the evidence is submitted by both parties the Commission will then make a decision.

Yours very truly,

INDUSTRIAL COMMISSION

March 3, 1919.—Russian letter written to Mr. Valeskii asking him to come to our office.

March 4, 1919.—Andrey Valeskii in office. He can't work. He says he is sick. Filled out application for adjustment claim. Told him to come to office tomorrow and R. B. will take him to another doctor.

March 5, 1919.—R. B. took man to North Dispensary and had him examined by Dr. Brown. Dr. Brown says man is sick. He has a kind of melancholy, depressed, no energy. Man may have had same condition when he was a boy, otherwise man is well physically. He is a sick man and needs care. It will take time until man will get well. The injury may have caused it or may not. The suggestion of getting compensation may change man's condition, and may not. Dr. Brown gave man a prescription. Doctor asked R. B. to bring man back in a week.

March 7, 1919.—Spoke to Miss Thomas of Society for Mental Hygiene about man. She said that she would interest one of the doctors in case if possible. *Later.*—Miss Thomas telephoned that Dr. X. would see Mr. Valeskii Tuesday, 9 A.M., in his office, 30 Michigan Avenue. Wrote Industrial Commission.

March 8, 1919.—Letter written to Wisconsin Industrial Commission:

Re Andrey Valeskii vs. Wisconsin Brass Company. We have received the copies of the application for the adjustment of claim and hoped to have had them filled out and returned to you before this. The delay, however, has been unavoidable, but we expect now to send them sometime next week. Kindly let us know if Mr. Valeskii will be summoned to appear before the Industrial Commission when his case is heard. If so we would be glad to furnish an interpreter if this meets with your approval.

March 10, 1919.—Special delivery letter [Russian] written to Mr. Valeskii telling him to be at our office at three o'clock Tuesday.

March 11, 1919.—Andrey Valeskii in office. Application blank for compensation filled out. Told him to wait at 30 Michigan Avenue for R. B. tomorrow morning. *Later.*—Summary of case prepared as follows:

Andrey Valeskii, 123 Morgan Street, Chicago, Illinois, a Russian, forty years of age, was employed by the Wisconsin Brass Company, Fairfax, Wisconsin. In January, 1918, he was injured by having a piece of brass fall and strike him in the forehead. He was made unconscious and was taken to the Company's hospital, and stayed there six days. Thinking that he was going to die, he left the hospital and came to Chicago, as he felt that he must see his friends. He stayed with these friends but could not work for about six months. During the summer of 1918, he worked six weeks for a contractor for the Wisconsin Brass Company, Fairfax, Wisconsin, but was forced to leave on account of the pain in his head. In September, 1918, he worked for two weeks at East Chicago, in a factory. He was not able to continue, but after two weeks, on account of his need, he was forced to try again. He worked in a rag shop at Blue Island and Fifteenth Street, Chicago, for two weeks. Again he was laid off. The next place was the stockyards, where he worked one week. He next worked in an oil shop, but felt ill and left. Man has friends who can testify to the fact that he attempted to work and was not able to continue. He constantly complained of the pain in his head, and thought that he would never get better and that the period of unconsciousness had permanently affected his mental and physical strength. From our knowledge of the case, it appears that this was a simple, uneducated man, hard working, and not expecting to be helped by others. This accident was the reason for changing his habits of life, caused him physical pain, and made necessary a readjustment which takes time and money. The man was in our office many times during the winter months. His expression showed great depression and loss of vigor. In March our visitor took him to see Dr. Brown, who prescribed for the man, and we have noticed an improvement since then. It should be recalled that the man was injured in January, 1918, and it was not until March, 1919, that he seemed able, in spite of many efforts to work, to pull himself together, and appear to be in a normal condition. The man has been forced to borrow from relatives and friends. He has gone through pain and humiliation, and we feel that these facts should be given due consideration.

March 12, 1919.—R. B. went with man to Dr. X. He could not find anything that he could state in a certificate. The certificate would only harm man. Dr. X. agreed with R. B. that Immigrants' Protective League should settle case as soon as possible. Man's mind is impressed by the accident. Case should be settled so man can be relieved.

March 13, 1919.—Letter received from Wisconsin Industrial Commission:

Attention Miss Cantey, *In re Andrew Valesky* vs. *Wisconsin Brass Company*. We wish to acknowledge receipt of your letter of March 8. If the application for the adjustment of the claim is filed with the Commission, we are required under the law to serve a copy of the application upon the employer. The employer is allowed ten days within which to file his answer to the application and serve a copy upon the applicant. The case will then be set for hearing, and without some agreement between the parties the case will be set for hearing at Fairfax. Possibly the Brass Company would consent to have the hearing held in Chicago; and, in fact, it might be less expensive to the Company to have the hearing held in Chicago, where the evidence of the examining physicians might be taken, than to bring the physicians to Fairfax to attend the hearing. After your application is filed, we suggest that you confer with the Brass Company regarding the place of hearing. The Commission is willing to hold the hearing at any place in order to accommodate the parties. When the applicant's testimony is taken, it will be necessary for him to supply an interpreter. We are sending a copy of this letter to the Wisconsin Brass Company.

Yours very truly,

E. C. HOPKINS, *Chief Examiner*

March 17, 1919.—Andrey Valeskii in office. He has letter from Industrial Commission saying that they have received his application and will let him know further. *Later.*—Letter written to Wisconsin Brass Company as follows:

GENTLEMEN:

At the request of Andrey Valeskii we have forwarded his application for adjustment of claim to the Industrial Commission of Wisconsin. We write to ask if you would be willing to have the hearing held in Chicago. If it were possible we would be very glad to have our Russian visitor act as interpreter as Mr. Valeskii is unable to state his own case in English. Miss Rachel Brinova, our visitor, has interpreted in many of the courts in Chicago, both County and Municipal, and for the United States Immigration Office as well as for many of the private agencies. Kindly let us know what you decide to do about this.

Yours very truly,

IMMIGRANTS' PROTECTIVE LEAGUE

March 18, 1919.—Mr. Valeskii in office. He brought copy of his medical statements.

March 20, 1919.—Letter received from Wisconsin Brass Company. *Later.*—Letter written to Wisconsin Industrial Commission as follows:

GENTLEMEN:

We have had a letter from the Wisconsin Brass Company, Fairfax, Wisconsin, saying that it would be agreeable for them to have the hearing on the case of Andrey Valeskii held in Chicago and they suggest that we notify you that it is our wish also.

IMMIGRANTS' PROTECTIVE LEAGUE

April 7, 1919.—Andrey Valeskii in office. He is anxious to know when case will come up. He is anxious to try working in the country. Told him that we would write to the Industrial Board. Spoke with Miss Shipman (Employment Division of the League). She thinks that it would be possible to get him farm work near Chicago. Will let him know. *Later.*—Letter written to Wisconsin Industrial Commission:

GENTLEMEN:

We write to ask if you can give us any idea as to when the Industrial Commission will hold the hearing in the case of *Andrew Valesky* vs. *The Wisconsin Brass Company*, Fairfax, Wisconsin. The man is still not working, and we are anxious that he should try to get work in the country but we do not think that any plan can be made until the case is settled. Kindly let us hear from you at your earliest convenience.

Very truly yours,

IMMIGRANTS' PROTECTIVE LEAGUE

May 7, 1919.—Andrey Valeskii in office. He was sick with a bad cold for a week. He was working at a rag shop. He wants to get work on a farm or on tracks. Told man to wait a little. *Later.*—Letter written to Industrial Commission as follows:

GENTLEMEN:

We regret having to write you again concerning Andrey Valeskii, but we do wish to know if there is anything that we can do to hasten the hearing before the Industrial Commission. The man is anxious to go to work on a farm, but he does not like to leave Chicago until after the hearing is held.

Yours very truly,

IMMIGRANTS' PROTECTIVE LEAGUE

May 10, 1919.—Received notice of hearing from Wisconsin Industrial Commission. Hearing to be at Fairfax Court House, May 21, at 2 P.M.
Later.—Russian letter sent to man telling him about arrangements to go to Fairfax with R. B.

May 22, 1919.—R. B. went with man to Fairfax yesterday. Case came up before the Industrial Board at the Fairfax Court House. After a long and quite exciting discussion, the arbitrator suggested that man should be paid one-half wages ($18 a week), $9 for six months, and $25 for the permanent injury. Man must start to work. Arbitrator and doctor agreed with R. B. that the man's case was a psychological one, and that he must get some satisfaction to save him. The arbitrator told the Wisconsin Brass representative that man can start a new suit in a year, if his condition does not improve. The Wisconsin Brass Company representative will call at Immigrants' Protective League with the papers to be signed by Mr. Valeskii and check. The letter asking the Brass Company to pay the expenses of Mr. Valeskii should be mailed to the Company, said the representative. Valeskii will put away $100 for tickets from Russia, and with the rest pay his debts. Man very happy. He is very grateful to the League.

[The statement given above is the Russian visitor's account of the hearing. The official "Findings and Award" of the Commission are given below:]

FINDINGS

That on January 14, 1918, the applicant and respondent were both subject to the provisions of Sections 2394–3 to 2394–31, inclusive, of the Wisconsin Statutes; that on said day while in the employ of the respondent performing services growing out of and incidental to his employment, the applicant sustained personal injuries; that the injuries so sustained were proximately caused by accident and not intentionally self-inflicted; that at the time of the accidental injury applicant was employed at a wage which entitles him to compensation at the maximum rate; that the respondent at the hearing admitted notice of the accidental injury; that the respondent furnished the applicant with the necessary medical, surgical and hospital treatment; that it was stipulated and agreed by the parties at the hearing, which said stipulation was reduced to writing, that the respondent, Wisconsin Brass Company, shall pay to the applicant the sum of Two Hundred Seventy-eight Dollars ($278) in full release of liability herein.

Now, therefore, upon the facts so found, the commission makes the following

AWARD

That within ten days from this date, the respondent, Wisconsin Brass Company, shall pay to the applicant, Andrew Valesky, the sum of Two Hundred Seventy-eight Dollars ($278) in full release of all liability herein.

[The remaining portion of the record deals with the final proceedings regarding payment of award (which was paid in a lump sum), opening a bank account for the man in a reputable bank, his new job, his plans for his wife and children, and so on. His physical condition slowly improved.]

45. Bozena Jez
(Injury in Box Factory—Legal Aid)

July 15, 1913.—A Moravian girl, aged twenty-one, Bozena Jez (20 Fir Street) in office to speak with B. P. [Bohemian visitor]. Bozena complains of an accident at work. She has been six months in the United States, a very nice-appearing girl, clean, neat, handsome. She was working at Poor's Box Factory, was fixing a cord when she lost her finger. She has not yet made settlement with the company. Her brother-in-law sent her to the office of *Spravedlnost* (Bohemian daily), and they sent her to the League. She is attended by company doctor. Doctor comes every second day. She is getting $5 per week compensation; earned $11 when working. Bozena wishes us to help her get compensation when she gets well. She is satisfied with $5 per week at present. Told her we will take her to Legal Aid Society and told her not to sign anything without consulting us. Girl left yellow receipt, which she had not yet signed. The "receipt" follows:

CHICAGO, ILLINOIS
July 14

Report No. 427.   *June 26, 1913.*   Bessie Jez. $5.00

Received of A. M. Poor and Company five dollars, being compensation payable in full under the Workmen's Compensation Act of Illinois for the period of six days from the seventh day of July to the twelfth day of July last, both dates inclusive, in consequence of an accident which occurred to me on or about the twenty-sixth day of June last, the nature of said accident being as follows: "Index finger on left hand cut off at first joint."

(Signature) ———

August 5.—Bozena came to the office for advice. The Poor Company offered her the fourth $5 and told her that was the last she could expect. B. P. went with Bozena to Legal Aid Society and translated for her. They will take up her case.

August 6.—Mr. Drava, Bozena's brother-in-law, called up and spoke with B. P. He said that the Poor Company now offer Bozena $115 and work and she wants to take it immediately and go to work. Told Mr. Drava to wait until the Legal Aid Society can be consulted. *Later.*—B. P. spoke to attorney at the Legal Aid. He advised Bozena to accept the $115 instead of going through the court.

August 8.—Visited Bozena. She has been at the court already but was told to bring a Bohemian-speaking man with her. The court wants her to be represented by some one.

August 9.—Went with Bozena to Poor's Factory. Spoke to the superintendent. He said they offered her a $100 and $15 (half of her earnings) under the Compensation Law. The company wants her to have the settlement go in a friendly way through the court, which they tried, but the judge wanted her to bring some man with her. They thought the alderman of the ward in which Bozena lives would be the proper man. B. P. promised to go to the office of Mr. Bartlett, the company's attorney, Monday morning, August 11.

August 11.—Went to Bozena's house, with her to the factory, where the appointment was made with Mr. Bartlett. Went with Bozena to Mr. Bartlett's law office and after a talk with him to the Superior Court before Judge X, who was not satisfied with the interpreter only but wanted a lawyer for Bozena's case. Called up the Legal Aid, who sent their lawyer, after which Bozena's case was settled. She received in presence of B. P. $115 at the Chicago Trust and Savings Bank.

August 25.—Bozena in the office. She was discharged from work after being abused by the forelady. She was earning only $4.00 per week. She wants to do housework. Sent her to Mrs. Taussig, 490 Vincennes Avenue, to do the second work. *Later.*—Found that Bozena did not go there.

October 16.—Wrote Bohemian letter to Bozena and asked her what she is doing now.

November 6.—The following letter received by Bohemian visitor [translation from Bohemian]:

HONORABLE MRS. P——:

Best greetings: I received your letter and wish you would forgive me for not answering your letter. Just these three weeks I was very busy and had very little time to write. Honorable lady, you are asking me what kind of work I have now. Since I stopped working in that shop, I had no work. The place you found me, I talked to my man about it, and he told me I should not go there and that we rather get married, so I thought it would be better for me to get married. Therefore I telephoned you the following day, but probably you were not at home at that time. Before you wrote me, a woman I know taught me finishing men's coats. I am very slow at it yet but if there is work I hope I will be able to help with few cents. I am only married this week and had many worries over this week. I looked for a rent and it was very hard to find a clean rent. In meantime I live only in a simple rent, pay $6, but the name of the street I do not know. It is near Eighteenth Street but in the rear. It would give me a great pleasure if you would come to see my household; later I write you a correct address. With hearty greetings and thanks for your letter,

I remain yours,

BOZENA JEZ-SLAVS

46. Nicolai Naumoff
(Hand Injured—Compensation by Agreement)

December 5, 1916.—Steve Niszkuc[1] brought his Russian friend, Nicolai Naumoff, to office. A. F. [Russian visitor] spoke with man. Nicolai has been working for Western Foundry Company. He worked six months for company. September 25, 1916, he injured two fingers (index and middle finger) on his right hand, was taken to the Company hospital, remained there

---

[1] A man who had already been helped by League.

only two days, preferred to go home, went to company doctor every day. Yesterday he was given check to go to work, but did not know what to do; came to office for advice. He took no compensation whatever because he did not want to sign. Nicolai is aged eighteen, has been three years in the United States, is living with Russian friends at 114 Peoria Street. Spoke with Miss Crothers [Assistant Superintendent] about man. She telephoned Western Foundry Company. They have two checks ready for Nicolai Naumoff now—one up to the fifteenth of November for $20.71, and another one made out for the period up to tomorrow when he starts work. He will be given suitable work. He signs receipts for these only. They have not yet considered the question of compensation for the injury of his fingers. A. F. explained to Nicolai in Russian. Told him we will let him know when to come back. *Later.*—Letter written to Superintendent, Claim Department, Western Foundry Company:

GENTLEMEN:

Referring to Nicolai Naumoff, concerning whom we telephoned you this morning, we beg to state that we explained to him the amounts that were now due him and just what he would have to sign in receiving the compensation. The man planned to go to your office this afternoon and get his checks and to start work Wednesday morning. We would be very grateful if you would notify us when the amount of compensation due him for the injury to his hand is decided upon as we have told him that we would explain that matter to him also.

Very truly yours,

HELEN CROTHERS

January 4, 1917.—Nicolai Naumoff in office. He went to the company, December 5, 1916. He has received checks for $18.25, $17.90, and $3.25. He started to work on December 6, 1916. He worked until January 3, 1917. The work he got first was not hard (scrap machine), but yesterday he was told to carry a big piece of wood. Nicolai refused because he could not move it, his right hand is not yet strong enough. The foreman told Nicolai if he cannot do it, he must go to the office. In the office Nicolai was told to leave. He was getting $2.53 a day. *Later.*—Gave Nicolai a letter to Mr. O'Brien [a friend of the League], O'Brien Mercantile Company, asking if he can give Nicolai some work. *Later.*—Wrote Western Foundry Company:

GENTLEMEN:

We wrote you on December 5, concerning compensation for Nicolai Naumoff, who was injured September 25, 1916. At that time you had not yet considered the question of compensation for the permanent injury which he sustained. We understand that the young man has now been laid off. He tells us that he has received to date $39.40. Will you kindly let us know what the compensation for the injury will be and when Mr Naumoff will receive it?

Very truly yours,

HELEN CROTHERS

January 18, 1917.—Nicolai Naumoff in office. He did not go to Mr. O'Brien because he got a job at the Western Furniture Factory. He tried to work but could not stay there. His hand troubled him when he worked the machine. He was afraid he would be hurt again. *Later.*—Mr. H. [another League visitor] went with Nicolai to the company physician, Dr. Brown, who examined the hand and told him (Nicolai) to call sometime again.

January 19, 1917.—Letter from Mr. Daniel, Company attorney, as follows:

Helen Crothers
Immigrants' Protective League
Chicago, Illinois

DEAR MADAM: Your letter under date of the fourth to the Western Foundry Company with reference to the Nicolai Naumoff case received. I do not quite understand your position. You state in your letter that the man has now been laid off. I did not know that there was anything in the Compensation Act of Illinois that would prevent an employer from discharging an employee during a time when he had no work for that employee to do. I am wondering if your intentions are to be helpful in fixing up this case or whether they are otherwise. An institution such as yours should help the employee, but it should not endeavor to get information from the employer unless it bona fidely intends to make an adjustment of the matter and not to turn it over to some lawyer who will use the information in the way of pushing litigation against the employer. Our giving you this information is with no other intention than of treating you absolutely fairly, and we want to be treated the same way and have you advise the injured employee who comes to you just what his rights are and then advise him to take it when it is offered to him. The writer never takes advantage of any employee under any circumstances, nor does his company. We are as careful about that as yourselves. Would be glad to have you suggest something definite as to what you want or as to what you would advise your client to do.

Yours truly,
R. B. DANIEL

January 22, 1917.—Letter to Mr. Daniel from Lydia Gardner [League Superintendent]:

R. B. Daniel, Esq.
220 Harris Building
Chicago, Illinois

MY DEAR MR. DANIEL: Your letter of January 17, in reply to our Miss Crothers' request for a statement of the terms the Western Foundry Company is offering in settlement of the claim of Nicolai Naumoff raises a question with regard to the League's motives and policies which I am very glad to answer. A good many non-English-speaking immigrants who are injured come to us for information as to whether what they have been offered is what they are entitled to under the law. If the company is operating under the Compensation Act, it is fairly simple in most cases. These injured persons, we have learned by experience, have so frequently not understood the offer made that we make it a rule to communicate directly with the company and learn exactly what has been offered. When this information is given us, we are able to explain to the men what the compensation law provides and what the company offers. If the offer is, in our opinion, what the law entitles the man to claim we advise him to accept it. If not, or if there is a reasonable doubt as to what he is entitled to under the law, we also advise him as to that fact. We are, of course, interested in the man's being able to make a settlement without the expense and delay incident to beginning suit before the Industrial Board or in court, but you will, I am sure, realize that this is not always possible. Some employers, as you know, make a practice of fighting every claim. I am glad to hear that you and the company you represent "never take advantage of any employee under any circumstances." But quite apart from any desire to take advantage of an employee there are, I am sure you would agree, cases where the interpretation of the law has not been passed on, and in such cases the obligations of the employer have not been settled and a request for a ruling on such a question is not charging the employer with bad faith in his dealings with his employees. In this particular instance, we are asking what, if any, offer the company was prepared to make at this time in the way of compensation for what appears to be a permanent injury to Nicolai Naumoff's hand. The fact that the man is no longer in the employ of the company has, as you say, no bearing on the amount of the claim to which he is entitled. It naturally makes him more anxious for a settlement. I hope you will feel that this is a frank statement of what we are trying to do. We should not like to seem to be asking for information that is in any sense confidential. We hope that you will be willing to give us your terms in order that we may explain them to the man. This was what you did in the claim of Steve Niszkuc, check Number 10820, and I do not understand why you should not do the same in this instance.

Sincerely yours,

LYDIA GARDNER

January 27, 1917.—Wrote Nicolai Naumoff to come to the office, Sunday or any other day.

January 28, 1917.—Letter from Mr. Daniel as follows:

Miss Lydia Gardner
Immigrants' Protective League
Chicago, Illinois

GENTLEMEN: I am in receipt of your letter under date of the 22d inst., with reference to the case of Nicolai Naumoff, and note carefully what you state. My objection is that after you have explained the situation to your clients, there does not seem to be any tendency on the part of the clients to accept either your explanation or my Company's offer. In the Steve Niszkuc case, check No. 10820, neither your explanation nor my offer to pay has been accepted by Niszkuc. What particular feature of the law is it which has not been interpreted in this Naumoff case? What is it that I can accomplish by going into a detailed explanation of what my Company is ready and willing to do in this case? If you can give me any assurance that your client will accept the proposition, I will be glad to explain it, and if it is not all that the law provides, I will be glad indeed to increase it to all the benefits which the law provides in this case. What does your client desire, and what do you recommend that he be paid? I shall be glad to hear from you and to co-operate with you if we can accomplish something.

Very truly yours,

R. B. DANIEL

February 5, 1917.—Nicolai was expected to call today; but only his friend Niszkuc called, who told us that Nicolai moved to Cicero.

March 3, 1917.—Nicolai in office. He wants to know about his case. He is working in the Screw Company. He earns $2.00 a day. He wants League to estimate the amount he should get for his injuries, and notify him when the case could be settled. *Later.*—Telephoned Mr. Daniel. He is out of town and will be back Wednesday or Thursday.

March 8, 1917.—Telephoned Mr. Daniel. He will see Mr. Naumoff. The best time is in the afternoon after four o'clock. So far as he knows, he will be in his office Monday afternoon at four. He wants to have Mr. Naumoff know definitely what he is to ask, and he will not talk to him if he asks for something unreasonable.

March 9, 1917.—Wrote Nicolai Naumoff a Russian letter to come Monday, March 12, at 3 o'clock to our office. Spoke with Miss Gardner, Superintendent. According to Compensation Act, if he lost use of two fingers he should get compensation of one-half wages for sixty-five weeks plus one week's wages while he was sick.

March 12, 1917.—A. F. took man to Mr. Daniel's office, 220 Harris Building. Mr. Daniel was very nice. He promised to take up the matter with the Industrial Board this week. Man will get one-half wages for sixty-five weeks. The amount will not be paid at once. Man said he will accept it. Mr. Daniel said that man can not get one-half wages for the ten weeks he was sick because he was not working for the company one year. One-half wages is $8.28. Total amount to be paid Nicolai $538.20. Mr. Daniel will do his best. He will telephone the company and ask them to take the man back to work. Man could not decide if he wants to work for the same company. He will think it over and notify us. Mr. Daniel will telephone us.

March 17, 1917.—Nicolai in office. He is going to work for the same foundry company. They promised to take him back to work.

March 27, 1917.—Letter from Mr. Daniel as follows:

Miss Lydia Gardner
Immigrants' Protective League
Chicago, Illinois

DEAR MADAM: Some days ago someone from your League came into this office with Nick Naumoff. At that time they desired to make some adjustment of the injury Naumoff had received to his first and second fingers. The writer looked at the fingers and from his best judgment of them, so far as a commercial purpose is concerned, he has lost the use of those two fingers, although he has considerable use of them for minor purposes. I have, therefore, agreed on the part of the Western Foundry Company to pay Naumoff for the loss of the use of those two fingers. A check is now made up in his favor covering all the payments due up to and including the fifteenth day of March, 1917. Other payments will be made twice a month, as we pay all our compensation at Cicero, until he has been paid 50 per cent of his average wages for a period of sixty-five weeks. This is in addition to what was paid him as in the way of compensation for disability. He has not, however, called for his check. Will you please ask him to do so if this is satisfactory to you. I am utterly unable to understand what further I can do in the case and hope that the settlement reached is satisfactory. If not, will be glad to have you advise me wherein my company has not complied with the law. Both Naumoff and the party representing your League when they were in the office appeared to be perfectly satisfied, and I am unable to understand why they do not call for the money.

Very truly yours,

R. B. DANIEL

March 27, 1917.—Letter to Mr. Daniel:

DEAR SIR:

When our representative and Nicolai Naumoff were in your office on March 12, concerning the adjustment of Naumoff's injury, they were satisfied with your agreement to pay Naumoff for the loss of the use of two fingers. Miss F, however, understood that you were to take the matter up first with the company and that you would telephone her here at the office as soon as the final arrangements had been made. Therefore, Mr. Naumoff was waiting for the message from you before he went to ask for his check. We are notifying him today to call for it immediately. We understand that he is working for the Western Foundry Company at present. We regret that there was this misunderstanding as we were also anxious to have the matter settled and considered that the statement reached was quite satisfactory.

Very truly yours,

HELEN CROTHERS

March 28, 1917.—Wrote Nicolai Naumoff Russian letter telling him what Mr. Daniel wrote. Told Mr. Naumoff to take the money and sign for it.

April 2, 1917.—Man in office. He is working for the Western Foundry Company since March 22, 1917, as a laborer. He is getting $2.53 a day. Man went to the company's office March 26. He was offered the six following checks: (1) $115.90; (2) $1.55; (3) $1.73; (4) $2.70; (5) $1.90; (6) $1.55. He was asked to sign but was afraid because he did not understand what was said on the slip. Told man to take some one who understands English to read the paper.

April 18, 1917.—A. F. wrote man in Russian, asking if he has received some money.

April 21, 1917.—Letter from Nicolai. He is working for the same company. He earns $2.70 a day. He received seven checks: $113.90;

$1.50; $1.73; $1.55; $1.90; $2.07; $18.97; equals $141.62. The rest he will receive twice a month.

April 27, 1917.—Nicolai in office. He wants to return to Russia and wants to get the balance of his money in a lump sum. He says he is determined to go. His family has left their old home and has gone to Siberia. Telephoned Industrial Board. It is easier to get lump sum if the employer consents. If employer does not consent it must be heard as a disputed case. Telephoned Mr. Daniel. He does not believe that Naumoff is really going to Russia—it is so old an excuse. After much discussion he finally said he would take it up with the company. Mr. Daniel wrote us yesterday about case. Told him letter had not come yet.

Wrote Mr. Daniel as follows:

DEAR MR. DANIEL:

Confirming our telephone conversation of this afternoon I beg to report that Nicolai Naumoff, who is receiving compensation from the Western Foundry Company on account of an injury received in September, 1916, desires to have the balance of his compensation paid in a lump sum. The young man plans to return to Russia in a short time and wishes to be able to take this money with him. You will undoubtedly appreciate the difficulty of sending the money to him regularly in Russia under present conditions. Mr. Naumoff is determined to return to Russia whether it is a reasonable plan for him or not, so the matter cannot be decided wholly on the basis of whether it is best for him to go. We realize that before the Russian Revolution this was a very common excuse used in trying to get compensation in a lump sum, but that this reason now assumes a different aspect because of the very general desire among the Russians in this country to return. In this particular case we feel convinced that the young man is planning to return to Russia, otherwise we would not bring this matter to your attention as we appreciate as well as you the desirability of an employee receiving compensation in weekly payments. We trust that you will agree to this request.

Very truly yours,

HELEN CROTHERS

May 2, 1917.—Letter from Mr. Daniel:

DEAR MADAM: Your letter under date of the twenty-seventh to the writer with reference to the case of Nicolai Naumoff received. I have presented this matter to the Western Foundry Company; and they are of the opinion that, in view of the facts in this case, we should not make a lump sum settlement but that we should continue the payments as provided by the Workmen's Compensation Act of this state until we have paid the money as provided therein. Aside from all the other facts in this case, it appears to me that in view of the one fact that this young man and a great many more of his countrymen who have come to this country have been given good employment and paid good wages by our industries here, and now that we are sorely in need of employees we are paying better wages than ever paid before, and the further fact that this country may find itself in trouble for its existence shortly, we do not believe that we should encourage or that anyone, for that matter, in this country should encourage persons who have been supported by this country and its industries for some time to return now to foreign countries, leaving us our own industrial battles as well as battles at arms to fight ourselves. We are sorry indeed we cannot accommodate you in this instance.

Very truly yours,
R. B. DANIEL

[The remaining portion of the record deals with the renewed efforts of Nicolai Naumoff to get his compensation in a lump sum so that he could return to Russia with a party of friends who were going. Mr. Daniel finally agreed to pay a lump sum if the man could give assurances that he really intended to go to Russia. But by that time (July 17, 1917) the Russian consul had received orders that no one could return to Russia until he had filed an application to return and had been "accepted in Russia." The case was really closed when the following letter was sent the attorney for the company by the Russian Consulate under date of July 24, 1917.]

GENTLEMEN:

Re Nicolai Naumoff vs. *Western Foundry Company*. I beg to acknowledge receipt of your esteemed favors of July 9 and 11, and to thank you for same. Mr. Naumoff is very anxious to return to Russia, and was willing to purchase his steamship ticket, provided the Company would advance the necessary money, simply to prove that he wishes to return. However, complications have arisen. A new rule has been established recently, according to which each Russian desiring to return to his native country must file application and photograph with this Consulate, which in turn must apply to the Russian Government in order to procure permission to visa the applicant's passport. This takes not less than two months. On July 13, 1917, Mr. Naumoff appeared at this Consulate and filed the necessary application and photograph, and steps are being taken to procure admission to visa his passport. Under the circumstances, you will see that there is nothing to be done at present. We will simply have to wait until the necessary permission is received, at which time I will let you know.

Yours very truly,
————, General Attorney for Consulate

47. Marie Macek and Three Children

(Mysterious Homicide—Illinois Industrial Board—Supreme Court)

October 17, 1917.—Last evening there called at the home of B. P.[1] Mrs. Marie Macek and friend, Mrs. Capek. Mrs. Macek is a widow with three children—Mamie aged seven, Josef three, and Bessie one. Her husband "Tony" (Antony) Macek was killed near the Great Western Railroad tracks at Sixty-third Street. He was on night duty. The coroner's jury thought he had been killed by someone who was his "enemy," but Mrs. Macek said "Tony had no enemy." He had been employed by the

---

[1] ["Case Record" was largely written by a Bohemian visitor referred to as B. P. and Mrs. P.]

railroad for four months and earned $65 a month. "Tony's boss" first said the company would give Mrs. Macek compensation. Later a representative of the company told her that they would "settle," but it is now two months ago and she wants to know if someone could not write for her to the company to find out if they would do anything for her. Mrs. Macek and her husband were born in Bohemia. He had been in America nine years and had his "first papers." She is living in a basement at 25 West Street. Her husband left $500 insurance in the X Company. She spent $200 for the funeral and is now living on the rest. She is twenty-eight years old, and Tony Macek was thirty when he was killed. Told her B. P. would speak with Miss Cantey [Acting Superintendent], who will probably send someone to see the company. Mrs. Macek will come again to B. P.'s house in a week.

October 19, 1917.—Letter to railroad company as follows:

Great Western Railroad
Claims Department
Chicago, Illinois

GENTLEMEN: We are interested in the case of Mrs. Marie Macek, 25 West Street, who is the widow of Antony Macek. Mrs. Macek states that her husband was killed on the Great Western tracks August 18 while on night duty. She is anxious to know what compensation she will receive from the company. Any information which you can give us will be appreciated. Thanking you, we are,

Very truly yours,
M. CANTEY

October 24, 1917.—Letter received from railroad company, saying that "the case of Antony Macek, who was shot and killed by some unknown person on August 17th" had been referred to Mr. George, the company's general claim agent, Detroit, Michigan.

November 1, 1917.—Mrs. Macek telephoned; asked what League had done in her case. B. P. told her she will be notified when League learns any news about her compensation. *Later.*—Mr. Skala (a neighbor) telephoned. He said Mrs. Macek signed something after her husband's death when the company agents came to her house and brought her husband's wages. Mr. Skala asks the League to find out what Mrs. Macek had signed and give her legal help, if necessary.

November 5, 1917.—Letter written to Mr. A. [an attorney who was a friend of the League] as follows:

We write to ask your advice about another one of our cases which may turn out to be a Workmen's Compensation case. If so, could you take care of the case? We do not want the woman to fall into the hands of a "shyster." The facts are these: Mrs. Marie Macek now living at 25 West Street, Chicago, tells us that her husband was killed on August 18, 1917, on the Great Western Line tracks at Sixty-third Street while on night duty. He had been in the employ of the Great Western four months and was shot while defending the property of the Great Western. A representative of the railroad company told the woman that they would do something for her, but up to now nothing has been done. Mrs. Macek says that she signed something after her husband's death when the company's agent came to her house and brought her husband's wages but she does not know what this paper was. On October 19, we wrote to the Claims Department of the Great Western Railroad and heard from them that they had referred the claim to Mr. George, Claim Agent, Detroit, Michigan. The number of their file is 3474-19. As we understand it the coroner's jury apparently thought the man had been killed as a result of a personal quarrel by an unknown enemy. Mrs. Macek tells us her husband had no enemy. She is a nice-appearing woman, and our Bohemian visitor, Mrs. P., thinks the man was undoubtedly a good, decent fellow who was probably killed at work. Mrs. Macek is twenty-eight years old and has three children of seven, three, and one. Thanking you for an early reply, I am,

Very truly yours,

MARY CANTEY

November 7, 1917.—Mr. A. telephoned. He will look up coroner's record. He would like to see Mrs. Macek and if there is any friend of her husband who knows about circumstances of his work or of his death would like to see him also. *Later.*—B. P. visited Mrs. Macek. Explained to her who Mr. A. is. She wants to know when she will get money from the company. She has very little money left, is getting worried. She will go with B. P. to see Mr. A. tomorrow. She says her husband worked alone; she does not know anyone at all who worked there. At the inquest there testified all railroad workers, engineer, detectives, brakemen—she did not know any.

November 8, 1917.—Mrs. Macek in office. B. P. took her to see Mr. A. He asked all kinds of questions. He will let us know in a few days, when he has time to look up a few things, what he thinks and what we shall do.

November 12, 1917.—Extract from note received from Mr. A.:

As regards the Macek case, I believe the widow ought to get full compensation. My examination of the records leads me to believe he was shot by a railroad detective who thought he was a tramp or thief trying to board the train. It is clear from position in which body was lying that he tried to board train and then fell back and down. Claim should be filed at once before Industrial Board of Illinois. The Company will probably attempt to call this an interstate case, but from my present examination of facts, I do not believe they can establish this. I am going to be out of town for a week and will try to take this up again as soon as I get back.

[*November 13–January 11, 1918.*—The record contains entries relating to the filing of the claim, interviews with attorney, etc., the hearing before the Industrial Board arbitrator, finally set for January 11, 1918. In the meantime Mrs. Macek had come to the end of her resources and had applied to a district office of the United Charities for help. The charity record shows that she first asked for help November 16, 1917, that she told the same story that she had already told to the League, and that the Charities "referred her to the County Agent and promised visit." No relief, however, was thought necessary at the time of the visit, and Mrs. Macek was told "to let visitor know if she was in need of assistance, either advice or material relief." On November 24 and on December 4, however, she did four hours' work in the Charities office and was given each time "$1 cash for work and also $1 for food." After that, she was given county supplies, clothing from a woman's club, and county coal. In January she asked "help with rent," but was told "to ask the landlady to wait until she got her compensation."

The compensation case moved slowly. On January 5, 1918, a letter from the attorney to the League explained that the case would be heard on January 11 and asked for name and address of witness whom Mrs. Macek was to find. The letter also said:

The Great Western called me up today and told me they would let me know in two or three days what they would do. I do not think they will offer to pay a satisfactory sum, and we must be prepared for trial. However, I will make no settlement without her approval and consent, and please explain to Mrs. Macek that I will advise her through you of any offer the Company makes.

The hearing before an arbitrator of the Industrial Board was held on January 11, 1918. The following extract from the testimony of one of the railroad witnesses before the arbitrator gives the most important facts known about the death of Antony Macek:]

My name is Eugene Hogan. I am assistant chief special agent for the Great Western Railway. Was so employed on the 17th of August last. I employed Antony Macek about three months before August 17th at $65 a month. I instructed him as to his duties. When he first started to work, he worked in the yards as a watchman; after that he got a job as train rider. He got a job as train rider about three or four weeks before he was killed. I gave him that job.

[From the cross-examination:]

I talked with Mr. Macek on the night before he was killed. . . . . That night I told him to go to Foray. I says, you go to Foray tonight and wait for 92, which is the fourth train. That was the day before the morning he was found dead. Macek had no regular hours. Some mornings they got back at 8:00, some mornings 9:00, and some mornings they got back at 3:00 or 4:00. He was supposed to work from 6 P.M until 6:00 the next morning. Until 11:35 or 12 o'clock when 92 was supposed to get out he was watching trains at Foray, watching the other trains passing at Foray. He was a special officer sworn in to make arrests. He watched the yards or trains. There are four sidetracks there. There may be one extra coming into the Belt and there may be five aside from the one going into the Belt, but I am not sure. The morning after he was killed I went down there. We were investigating his death. I did not go to see whether any of the cars on the sidings had been tampered with. Those cars are hay cars. There may be 20 to 40 cars at that time on the siding. Any one stealing brasses from any of those cars Macek would be supposed to arrest while he is watching down there in the yards, all about there, or if they were stealing other portions of the cars that thieves take, he would be supposed to arrest them, and at the time crippled cars or bad-order cars were being sent down there. Some of them would stay there a month or so. The tracks of the Great Western run north and south there and the Belt tracks intersect, running east and west. All trains from the city of Chicago going south stop north of the Belt tracks, that is compulsory and all trains coming north into Chicago would stop south of the tracks and that was generally known. A large number of hobos and trespassers, knowing that they had to stop there coming into Chicago, would be there to catch a ride, and I had given him instructions while he was watching there in the yards to apprehend and take suspicious characters that were loitering about there, and if they were in the draft age to demand a registration card from them. Macek would be supposed to prevent trespassers from riding the blind baggage into Chicago on any of those trains, suburban or manifest or anything else.

[The decision of the arbitrator after the hearing was that the widow was "not entitled to recover for the reason that deceased was engaged in interstate commerce when he met his death."

Mr. A. filed a petition for a review of the arbitrator's decision before the Industrial Board. In the meantime the company offered to settle for $1,000. Mr. A. reported this to Mrs. P., and asked her to explain to Mrs. Macek that he believed compensation of three times that amount could be secured if Mrs. Macek would wait. He also wished Mrs. P. to translate for him accounts published in the Bohemian newspapers of Antony Macek's death that he might have names of police officers, detectives, etc., who had investigated the case.

The League record contains report of interview between the Bohemian visitor and Mrs. Macek. "When all was explained to Mrs. Macek she said she would try to get on while the case was being tried and will let Mr. A. appeal case. She is willing to live this life of very hard work and charity for about one year if it is best for children. But she cannot live this way longer than one year. She is tired and worried." The case proved to be a vigorously contested one and dragged along for two years longer. On August 10, 1918, the Industrial Board found in favor of Mrs. Macek and their findings are summarized below:]

First.—That on August 17, 1917, Antony Macek, deceased, sustained an accidental injury arising out of and in the course of his employment, as the result of which he died on the 17th day of August, 1917.

Second.—That at the time of said injuries the parties hereto were operating under and subject to the terms and provisions of the Workmen's Compensation Act.

Third.—That at the time and immediately prior to said injury the deceased was not engaged in interstate commerce, nor was the work in which he was engaged an instrumentality of interstate commerce.

Fourth.—That the respondent had notice of said accident within thirty days thereafter, and that claim for compensation was made within the time fixed by statute.

Fifth.—That the compensation should be based upon average monthly earnings of $65.

Sixth.—That the deceased left surviving a widow and three minor children, the applicants herein, all of whom he was under legal obligation to support at the time of said injury.

It was therefore ordered that the applicants have and receive of and from the respondent the sum of thirty-two dollars and fifty cents per month for a period of ninety-six months commencing on the date of the injury as compensation on account of the death of Antony Macek. Bond for removal of this cause by respondent to the Circuit Court is hereby fixed at the sum of $3,700.

[The company then carried the case to the Circuit Court of Cook County, where the findings of the Industrial Board in favor of the widow were affirmed. The court found that the commission was right in fixing compensation at $32.50 a month and ordered payment of this sum with accrued instalments and interest. A new appeal was, however, taken by the company to the Supreme Court of Illinois, alleging (1) that such liability as arose out of the injury was defined by the federal Employers' Liability Act and (2) that the Illinois act was unconstitutional because applying automatically to the extra-hazardous occupations of carriage by land. But this court in October term, 1919, again affirmed the decision of the board. The company then applied for a rehearing of the case, but this was denied.

The following extracts from the opinion of the Illinois Supreme Court (291 Illinois 169) are of interest as summarizing the facts in this case and as setting forth the court's views on the Illinois compensation law:]

. . . . He was employed as a watchman and train rider, charged with the duty of guarding the property of plaintiff in error in its railroad yards at Foray, Illinois, and with the duty of riding its trains to guard merchandise carried by it. . . . .
The deceased was found dead about four o'clock in the morning of August 18, 1917. The body was lying four or five feet off the east-bound main track of plaintiff in error and a considerable distance south of the Belt Line tracks, which crossed the tracks of plaintiff in error approximately at right angles. . . . . There are several sidetracks near the point where the body was found, and upon these sidetracks were some cars loaded with merchandise and also some "bad order" cars. It was the duty of deceased to arrest anyone stealing journal brasses or merchandise from these cars and to otherwise protect his employer's property from trespassers. Some auto tires stolen from plaintiff in error had been discovered in the weeds and grass, and the officers of plaintiff in error had left these tires as a decoy, to see if the thieves would return for them. It is the contention of defendants in error that the deceased was shot by thieves returning for these tires or coming to steal other property of plaintiff in error. It is the contention of plaintiff in error that deceased had boarded interstate train No. 92, which was due to leave the yards about 11:30 o'clock and which it was the duty of deceased to ride to Valparaiso, Indiana, and that he was shot by someone on this train. The train crew all testified that they did not see deceased board the train or anywhere in the vicinity of the train. The train was required to stop north of the Belt Line crossing, and there was the place where the deceased was directed to board the train. His body was found south of the Belt Line crossing. Whether he was shot while guarding this

interstate train or while guarding the property of plaintiff in error stored in its yards was a question of fact to be determined from all the facts and circumstances in the record.

Some of the duties of the deceased had no connection with interstate commerce or its movement and transportation. Not every employee of an interstate carrier is engaged in interstate commerce. To be so engaged the work of the employee must constitute a real and substantial part of the interstate commerce in which the carrier is engaged. . . . . This is one of those cases where it is difficult, if not impossible, to determine just what deceased was doing when he was killed, and therefore it is a problem to determine under which act to proceed. There is evidence in the record to justify either conclusion. The injured employee or his personal representative must determine whether to proceed under the State Compensation law or the Federal Employers' Liability act. Here the surviving dependents chose to proceed under the State statute, and the defense is that they should have proceeded under the Federal statute. If the choice had been to proceed under the Federal statute the defense would in all probability have been the State statute. In such case we will not substitute our judgment for that of the Industrial Commission, when there is any evidence in the record which justifies its finding. . . . .

[On the question of constitutionality the court said among other things:]

The entire matter of liability for death caused by wrongful act, both within and without the relation of employer and employee, is a modern statutory innovation. The legislature may modify this right of action, extend it or limit it, or even abolish it altogether. . . . . The statute under consideration simply sets aside one body of rules to establish another system in its place. The employee or his personal representative is no longer able to recover as much as before in case of an injury growing out of the employer's negligence, but he is entitled to moderate compensation in all case of injury, and has a certain and speedy remedy without the difficulty and expense of establishing negligence or proving the amount of the damages. Instead of assuming the entire consequences of all ordinary risks of the occupation, he assumes the consequences, in excess of the scheduled compensation, of risks, ordinary and extraordinary. On the other hand, the employer is left without defense respecting the question of fault, but he is at the same time assured that the recovery is limited and that it goes directly to the relief of the designated beneficiary, and just as the employee's assumption of ordinary risks at common law presumably was taken into account in fixing the rate of wages, so the fixed responsibility of the employer and the modified assumption of risk by the employee under the new system presumably will be reflected in the wage scale. The act evidently is intended as a just settlement of a difficult problem affecting one of the most important of social relations, and it is to be judged in its entirety.

Much emphasis is laid upon the criticism that the act creates liability without fault. It must be remembered that the modern tendency is to compensate for loss of earning power. Such a loss stands to the employee as his capital in trade. It is a loss arising out of the business in which he is employed, and, however it may be charged up, is an expense of the operation just as truly as the cost of repairing broken machinery or any other expense that ordinarily is paid by the employer. On grounds of natural justice the business should bear this charge. The State by this kind of legislation relieves the employer from responsibility for damages measured by common law standards and payable in cases where he or those for whose conduct he is answerable are found to be at fault. It is not unreasonable for the State, in exchange, to require the employer to contribute a reasonable amount, according to a reasonable and definite scale, by way of compensation for the loss of earning power incurred in the common enterprise, irrespective of the question of negligence, instead of leaving the entire loss to rest where it may chance to fall—upon the injured employee or his dependents and indirectly upon the State. . . . .

[Unfortunately the remedy in this case was not what the court called "a certain and speedy remedy." Antony Macek was killed in August, 1917. It was more than three years later that the company finally began to pay compensation. In the meantime, the widow and children had led a wretched life of charity doles and overwork. Moreover, such compensation as was secured could not have been obtained without the assistance of an organization that could provide an attorney able enough to defeat the skilled railway counsel and generous enough to advance all the costs in the case and laboriously contest appeal after appeal with the prospect of no fee or, at most, a merely nominal one since the Compensation Law definitely limits the amount of the attorney's fee in such cases to a sum which is very small for a vigorously contested case.

In Mrs. Macek's case, the final award of the Industrial Commission was for compensation of $32.50 a month for 96 months.

The back payments were made in September, 1920, and monthly payments were begun. In the meantime Mrs. Macek had been supporting herself. On December 10, 1918, the Charities visited her for the "Goodfellows," an organization giving Christmas baskets, and the following final extracts from their record shows something of the hardships that the family suffered:

Mrs. Macek was home with the children. She said she worked nights and earns about $15 a week at Jones and Company. The home was clean but poorly furnished. Mrs. Macek stated it is pretty hard to have to work nights and be at home with the children in the day time. The children are all alone at night. She looks thin and careworn. Mrs. Macek said she can barely get along on her salary, and the reason she moved was that she was unable to pay her last two months' rent. Name given to the Goodfellow Department for Christmas.
December 20, 1918.—Visited. Mrs. Macek was home with the children. She said she is having a hard time getting along; that she works at Jones and Company, check Number 632, at night. She gets very little sleep. Mrs. Macek has been ill for the last couple of days and thinks it is due to the fact that she works in the Tin Shop at Jones' and that it makes her feel ill.

The Charities made no further visits and heard nothing more from Mrs. Macek until September, 1920, when a school nurse reported that the family "had no coal, no food, were getting County supplies." Mamie had been sent home from school for skin disease, apparently scabies, on the arms. Mrs. Macek had been working in a tailor shop but was laid off. She told the visitor that every tailor shop she visited was closed up; she had also tried to get work with a former employer for whom she did washing and cleaning but could get nothing. Just at this time, however, the compensation was finally paid, and Mrs. Macek moved without letting the landlord know her new address, and the Charities lost sight of her.]

48. Katherine Saurisaitis and Her Two Children
(Murder by Fellow-Workman—Illinois Industrial Board—Supreme Court)

[The Immigrants' Protective League first heard of Mrs. Saurisaitis and her two children when Mr. August Koshat, a roomer, called one evening, December 11, 1917, at the home of Mrs. J. (the Lithuanian visitor of the League). He explained that he had worked with Alexander Saurisaitis, the woman's husband, at the West Island Roundhouse, that they worked nights as boiler-washers in the roundhouse, and that Alexander had been shot on the evening of November 29, while he was working, by a fellow-worker by the name of Archer, whom he called a "Guinea" (i.e., an Italian. The man's real name was "Archieri" but had been anglicized to "Archer"). Alexander died later, December 5, at St. Y.'s Hospital. Mr. Koshat also explained that after his injury Alexander had first been taken "by the company" to the Avenue A. Hospital, but he was "untouched for two days." Then Mr. Koshat and Mrs. Saurisaitis took him to St. Y.'s Hospital, where "he was operated on and died, December 5, 1917." The "Guinea" had been arrested and was in jail. Mr. Koshat said "Alex was not fighting the 'Guinea,' Alex was a very quiet man." But the Italian worked as Alex's helper and "when the 'Guinea' left work early, Alex must tell this to the foreman." The Italian was angry and said he would "get even." Alex had then reported to the superintendent that he wanted a different helper because he was afraid to work any longer with Archer, but the superintendent would not listen to him. Alex then went back to work. The Italian had then attacked Alex, and Alex had been killed. Mr. Koshat asked, first, for help for the widow; and second, for information as to whether compensation could be collected from the railroad. Mr. Koshat had been told by various persons that if Alex was shot in a quarrel and not killed by an accident, he could get not one cent compensation. As regards the widow, she had two little babies and was "left with nothing." Alex had some money in the Halsted Bank (a well-known "immigrant bank" that had failed), but he had no insurance. He left nothing but his wages for nineteen days, still unpaid ($55 or $57), which Mrs. Saurisaitis wished the League to collect. Mr. Koshat had paid the funeral expenses, $365, and hospital bills, $72.60. Mr. Koshat reported that he was one of three boarders who paid $5 a month each for bed and preparation of food. They bought their own food, and she cooked for them and sometimes they gave her something.

Mr. Koshat was asked to bring Mrs. Saurisaitis to talk with the Lithuanian visitor on the following evening. In the meantime the visitor said she would try to find out what could be done.]

December 12, 1917.—Letter written to the United Charities stating facts already given and concluding:

We think that it would be wise to advise Mrs. Saurisaitis not to sign any quit claim to the railroad authorities. We hope to find out if there is any liability on the part of the West Island Railroad; but as Mrs. Saurisaitis is in need, we do not wish to delay reporting to you until we have this information.

Later.—Telephoned Industrial Board, spoke with Mr. Green. The West Island Railroad Company comes under the Illinois Compensation Act, only for those employees who are *not* engaged in Interstate Commerce. Mr. Green thinks that a boiler-washer in a roundhouse would be engaged in Interstate Commerce and would *not* come under the act. *Later.*—Letter to West Island Railroad as follows:

We are interested in the family of Mrs. Katherine Saurisaitis. Mrs. Saurisaitis is the widow of Alexander Saurisaitis, who was shot on November 29, 1917, and died December 5. He had been employed by you for ten years as a boiler-washer in your roundhouse. We write to ask whether you have made any plan for assisting the family and whether Mrs. Saurisaitis is entitled to any death benefit.

December 13, 1917.—Mrs. Saurisaitis at home of M. J. [Lithuanian visitor] last night with Mr. Koshat. Mrs. Saurisaitis is a very nice woman, eight years in the United States, husband seven years here, not a citizen. She has one brother, George Koshat, in the army at Fort Riley, Kansas. Another brother, Mike Koshat, does janitor work and also laborer's and earns $70 a month. And a brother of her husband's, August Saurisaitis, works for Surface Lines. Both are married and have a hard time getting on themselves. Her brother Mike says she can come to live with him, but she does not want to do this. She wants League to collect $55 or $57 due from company for husband's wages. They had $676 in Halsted Bank, all lost, but she hopes they may yet get something of this. Woman cried very much. She is a good tailoress and would like to go to work, but she has a baby six weeks old and another two years old and is nursing the baby. If she could get coal, she could get along with help from boarders and her brother until she can go to work.

December 14, 1917.—Mr. Koshat telephoned M. J. last evening. A visitor from the United Charities called and the Railroad Company has asked woman to come for her husband's wages.

December 16, 1917.—Letter received from West Island Railway Company as follows:

DEAR MADAM:

Your favor of the 13th instance with reference to the family of Alexander Saurisaitis, who was shot November 29, 1917, and died on December 5, 1917, is at hand, Mr. Saurisaitis, you state, having been employed by this Company as boiler-washer. There is no death-benefit. I am looking into the matter, however, and will be pleased to communicate further with you, after investigation is made.

Yours truly,

X. Y., *General Claim Agent*

[The Charities record throws no new light on the case and is not given here. It covers only the period December 13, 1917, to May 2, 1918. The Charities found Mrs. Saurisaitis able to manage with very little help. They sent her coal in an emergency and secured help[1] from the county agent for her. They asked the Red Cross to get the brother who was in the army to make an allotment, which he did not do, and they advised Mrs. Saurisaitis to live with her brother, Mike. This she refused to do. They also suggested that the League visitor have her take out citizenship papers and file application for a mother's pension at the Juvenile Court. The application for a pension was made on January 29, 1918, but on March 4, 1918, the court reported that she was Number 643, and as they "were investigating in the two hundreds," her case would not even be investigated for a long time.

In the meantime the Immigrants' Protective League had asked a lawyer, Mr. A., about the question of compensation. He said there were two problems involved: First, whether the man's death could be said to have arisen out of his employment. Second, whether or not he was engaged in interstate commerce as are many railroad employees and must then recover under the United States Compensation Act, or whether the widow could claim compensation under the Illinois Workmen's Compensation Act. Mr. A. asked to have Mr. Koshat, who was with Alex Saurisaitis when he was killed, come down to his office for an interview. Mr. A. then took charge of the widow's case and had her file a claim under the Illinois Workmen's Compensation Act. The facts, on the basis of which compensation was demanded, are stated in the following extracts from the lawyer's brief and argument:]

Our theory is that the death arose out of the employment:

1. The first boiler-washer, with some authority over his helper, but who cannot enforce obedience by discharging the helper, and whose only recourse is to report him to foreman, thereby runs an added hazard of assault. (Alexander Saurisaitis was first boiler-washer and the Italian his helper.)

2. The deceased, who was charged with the responsibility for the completion of the work by himself and his helper, ran an increased risk from assault, in having to report the subordinate, which would naturally provoke resentment and lead to attack.

[1] That is, outdoor relief in kind, chiefly groceries.

3. Danger of insubordination and assault is peculiar to, and incidental to, one in authority over another.

4. The altercation arose over the deceased's reporting the helper for quitting early, in the interest of the master and in the furtherance of the work and therefore, in fact, arose out of the employment. . . . .

8. That defendant was liable at common law for negligently ordering the deceased to resume work, promising him protection and negligently omitting it and in negligently retaining a dangerous employee in the service in the same roundhouse with knowledge that he had threatened to kill deceased; the assault then, with whatever consequences that might attend it, was in contemplation of the parties. . . . .[1]

[On February 20, 1918, an arbitrator for the Industrial Board heard the case, Mr. A., Mrs. Saurisaitis, and the Lithuanian interpreter of the League being present; and on March 8, the arbitrator decided in favor of the company. The attorney then took an appeal and on May 9 the case was heard by the Industrial Board. The case was late in coming up because the railroad wanted to bring in two new witnesses. The Board reversed the arbitrator's findings and awarded the widow compensation of $4,000. The company then took the case to the Circuit and later to the Supreme Court and both tribunals sustained the Board's award. The company then asked for a rehearing, but on June 5, 1919, the Supreme Court denied the petition for a rehearing of the case. The company then applied to the Supreme Court of the United States, for a writ of *certiorari*, but the application was denied in the October term, 1919, and the award finally went to the widow.

Approximately two years elapsed from the time the man was killed to the time when the payment of the award in monthly instalments began.

[1] The attorney's argument also contained the following statement regarding the general position of the workman and his family after the Workmen's Compensation Law had been substituted for the old common-law compensation:

"Under the compensation act the workman gave up the right to a jury trial, which, in practically all cases, was tantamount to a decision in his favor; he gave up also the right to unlimited damages for injuries, and, in case of death, he gave up big verdicts—from three to five times what he could recover under the compensation act. In return, he was given the certainty of payment of a smaller sum, wholly regardless of any fault, or blame or negligence on the part of the employer and regardless of any fellow servant rule or assumption of risk, regardless too, of whether the person inflicting the injury was acting in the course of his employment.

"It was an enlightened piece of legislation that regarded the workman as a soldier in the army of industry and held that the industry, and eventually the community as a whole, not the family of the workman alone, should bear the burden of the lives inevitably lost in the industry.

"Men, machines and beasts of burden are necessary and indispensable instruments the employer must use in the enterprise. Now, a master may use the utmost possible care in furnishing a physical machine, still the mechanism will go wrong and accidents will happen. That salutary piece of social legislation says that the family of the workman shall not alone bear the expense and risk of a death from

Moreover, Mrs. Saurisaitis undoubtedly would not have obtained this award without the assistance of an organization that provided her with an attorney who was willing to work on a difficult case, pay all the expenses of the various appeals, briefing, etc., for a merely nominal fee. In the meantime the widow had been overworking, her standard of living had greatly deteriorated, and she had moved in to live with her brother and was working nights from six to twelve o'clock and earning $7 a week. The little boy, now four years old, was reported not to be well, and the woman thought the basement flat which she shared with the family of her brother, the janitor, was not good for the children. The following extract from the decision of the Illinois Supreme Court[1] is of interest:]

The determination of the question whether an injury arose out of the employment in some cases presents one of the most difficult problems in connection with the act. . . . . This court has in several cases adopted the definition of the Supreme Court of Massachusetts in the *McNicol Case*, 215 Mass. 497, viz.: "It (the injury) arises out of the employment when there is apparent to the rational mind, upon consideration of all the circumstances, a causal connection between the condition under which the work is required to be performed and the resulting injury. Under this test, if the injury can be seen to have followed as a natural incident of the work and to have been contemplated by a reasonable person familiar with the whole situation, as a result of the exposure occasioned by the nature of the employment, then it arises out of the employment. . . . ." Saurisaitis was not the superior of Archer in the sense that he had authority to discharge him, but his (Saurisaitis') work was such that he could not perform it without the

the physical machine necessarily used in the business. It shall be charged to the industry and be borne by society ultimately. What difference, then, whether the death of the workman is caused by the physical machine, necessarily used in the prosecution of the enterprise, when it unexpectedly goes wrong, or whether the death is caused by the human machine, necessarily used in the prosecution of the work, when the human machine unexpectedly goes wrong. . . . .

"To the workman, is not the risk of the man going wrong, the man whom he must necessarily work with, as much a hazard of the employment as the risk of the machine going wrong, when he is required to work with a machine? And is not the risk of injury, from the master's tools of flesh and blood, as much an incident of the employment, as from the master's tools of iron and steel? And, is it not as important for society to safeguard the workmen's children (in this case there are two) from the dangers of destitution, when he is killed by the faulty human machine, as when he is killed by the faulty physical machine? . . . .

"The nature of the work deceased was performing prevented him from avoiding the injury. The accident therefore arose out of the employment.

"When the Italian appeared with the gun, the deceased was engaged in washing the engine boiler and was handling a large hose with a heavy metal nozzle under such heavy water pressure that he would be endangering the lives of others if he dropped it and he was unable, therefore, to escape and avoid injury."

[1] [288 Illinois 128–30. The names used here are the fictitious ones used elsewhere in this text.]

assistance of a helper. When the helper quit before the work was completed it was his duty to ask the foreman for help, which made it necessary for him to inform the foreman his helper had quit work. It was the performance of this duty that aroused the anger of Archer and caused him to quarrel and fight with Saurisaitis. It does not appear that Saurisaitis at any time was the aggressor or sought an altercation with Archer. The meeting of the two men at the storehouse the night of the shooting was accidental. Archer had learned that Saurisaitis had reported to the foreman that Archer had quit work Saturday night before quitting time and began abusing Saurisaitis and calling him an offensively vile name. They engaged in a fight, but Saurisaitis, who was the larger man, does not appear to have done anything more than throw Archer down and hold him until he pleaded to be allowed to get up. This Saurisaitis permitted him to do, and he then struck Saurisaitis on the jaw—a blow which a witness said "put him out." It was also testified Archer then said Saurisaitis had reported him and if he was discharged he would kill him. When Saurisaitis and his helper, Koshat, went with the foreman to the place where Archer was at work, Archer was the aggressor according to the testimony and sought to strike Koshat with a sledge hammer. It is not shown by the testimony that Saurisaitis then said or did anything. After Saurisaitis and Koshat had returned and were engaged in the duties of their employment Archer came to them with a revolver and began shooting at Koshat. When he ran away he then turned on and shot Saurisaitis, who was holding and directing the hose in washing out the boiler. The shooting was incidental to and arose out of the employment. It cannot be said, as a matter of law, that the injury was such a one as might happen to anyone and did not arise out of the employment. . . . . There was a causal connection between the conditions under which Saurisaitis was required to perform his work and the injury. It cannot be said that the proof does not tend to show that the shooting of Saurisaitis was caused by his report to the foreman that Archer had quit work. This the nature of his work required him to do, as he was obliged to ask the foreman for another helper. He was acting entirely in the line of his duties, and this brought upon him the murderous assault by Archer with a gun. That such an attack is an unusual and extraordinary result makes it none the less an incident of the employment. . . . .

49. Maryana Rusteika and Four Children
(Fraudulent Insurance—Workmen's Compensation)

[The Lithuanian visitor of the League first heard of Mrs. Rusteika in August, 1916. Some Lithuanian neighbors told the visitor that Mrs. Rusteika's husband had been killed by lightning and that she had four children and was having a very hard time. Neighbors also reported that the man had left $1,000 insurance and that the company for whom he had worked ten years had been kind to her. No investigation was made by the League. On November 13, 1916, a Lithuanian neighbor telephoned the League office that Mrs. Rusteika and children were destitute—no food, no clothes, no fire. The widow's address was given as 732 West Street, and the neighbor said it was a poor place, first floor rear, back of a barber shop. The League's Lithuanian visitor, Mrs. J., promptly visited Mrs. Rusteika, and the substance of her report is given below. The League telephoned the

United Charities, asking for an immediate visit; and later the following letter was written to Miss Green, a district superintendent of the United Charities, by one of the League's visitors:]

November 13, 1916

MY DEAR MISS GREEN:

We beg to submit the following facts in the case of Mrs. Maryana Rusteika, 732 West Street, for whom we asked emergency relief by telephone today: There are four children, Domenik age eight, Jakub age seven, Edward age four, and a baby boy born October 21, 1916. Jakub Rusteika, the father, was killed July 19, 1916, while in the employ of the American Tunnel Company, 958 Jackson Boulevard. Mr. Rusteika was switching trains at the foot of Thirteenth Street and the Lake Front. The company claims that he was killed by lightning and therefore refuses to pay compensation. The verdict of the jury in the coroner's inquest was that Mr. Rusteika had been killed by lightning, although men who worked with Mr. Rusteika have told his wife that his death was caused by an electric wire and not by lightning. Jakub Rusteika had worked for the company for ten years. Mrs. Rusteika was left without money and was pregnant at the time. The undertaker's bill was $170.70. For a while Mrs. Rusteika had credit at a grocery store where she had traded for a long time. Mr. Rusteika had an insurance policy with the Security Insurance Corporation for $1,000, but Mrs. Rusteika was advised at the time of her husband's death that she would get only $40 on this policy. She thinks because her husband had not paid long enough. Mrs. Rusteika applied to the Tunnel Company for assistance. On September 22 the company sent an investigator to her home and on the basis of this investigation gave her, during the first part of October, about $100, which Mrs. Rusteika used as follows: rent for three months, $24; grocery bill, $55; coal, $5.25. The balance she used for living expenses during the month. The company also sent some clothing for the children, but these things had to be burned as they were so soiled and ragged. The company also took up the matter of the insurance policy in an effort to make an adjustment with the Insurance Corporation and undertook to have the undertaker's bill reduced. They have her insurance papers.

At the time of Mrs. Rusteika's confinement, although she was registered with the Chicago Lying-in Dispensary, she was unable to reach them and sent for a doctor in the neighborhood. She also telephoned the company to send some money to her. They sent her, October 30, $50, which paid the doctor, the woman who took care of her at the time, and also the grocer. Mrs. Rusteika understood from the company's investigator that all this money was collected from her husband's fellow-workers in the tunnel. Mrs. Rusteika will undoubtedly be able to get a mother's pension, but we are asking you to take care of her until this investigation can be made and to refer the case to the court if you consider this the wisest plan. The woman has come to the end of her resources now. The family has always been self-supporting up to this time. Mrs. Rusteika is a Lithuanian and does not speak any English.

Yours very sincerely,

HELEN CROTHERS

November 17, 1916.—Telephoned United Charities (Miss Green). They visited yesterday. Their visitor reports family in clean and nicely furnished rooms. Woman said her husband was good to her, did not drink, worked ten years for the company. Woman has five brothers and four sisters in old country. Man has three brothers in old country and one here, but the one here is sickly and was once in the Illinois State Hospital for Insane. Mrs. Rusteika has a roomer, a countrywoman, Martha Gass, who is good to her and the children. Funeral bill is not paid. A Lithuanian neighbor, Mr. Vlass, has been looking after insurance but has apparently got nowhere. Mrs. Rusteika thinks Tunnel Company will give her something.

H. C. told Charities that we would ask a good attorney to look into the compensation matter and also into the Security Insurance Corporation. Man was killed by lightning and probably not entitled to compensation. Charities will look after other matters. Their visitor says that woman can buy on credit a few days longer.

November 24, 1916.—Miss Green of the United Charities telephoned that their Mrs. Down visited the man's company and interviewed Mr. Ware, Superintendent. Mr. Ware said he was much interested in welfare of family. The company's attorneys are looking up decisions to determine whether woman is entitled to compensation. If it is found that being struck by lightning comes under the hazards of industry, the company will promptly pay compensation. Mr. Ware said a similar case is now pending before the Illinois Industrial Board and will probably govern the decision in this case. Up to that time the company will support the family. They have already given woman $150, which is about what compensation would have been at rate of $37 a month. The company's investigator was informed by neighbor, Mr. Vlass, on August 8, 1916, that a society to which the man belonged had paid $200 for funeral expenses. Mr. Ware thought funeral bill excessive and gave statement of charges on bill: casket, $85; shroud, $15; hearse, $17; automobiles, $25; embalming, $10; candles, $7. He thought undertaker's bill should not be paid but should wait until undertaker is willing to reduce it. Mr. Ware also knew that man was insured in the Security Insurance Corporation for $1,000. The company's attorneys have looked into the insurance due from this corporation but prefer not to handle that matter and would like to turn it back to the United Charities or the Immigrants' Protective League. The Tunnel Company's investigator will visit and give relief until something is settled.

Told Miss Green that Miss Gardner, Superintendent of League, is going to talk over compensation question with a relative, Mr. A., who is a lawyer. Mrs. Rusteika probably ought to file claim with Illinois Industrial Board anyway.

November 28, 1916.—Miss Gardner talked with her relative, Mr. A., last night about workmen's compensation in case of accident from lightning. He will look up matter; says it is an interesting point. She also spoke with him about the insurance policy for $1,000. He will look up the Security Insurance Corporation. He would like to see the policy.

November 29, 1916.—Miss Gardner gave memorandum from Mr. A., who has looked up decisions:

As regards compensation from the Tunnel Company this is an interesting case. There have been no decisions directly affecting it in Illinois. But recovery can be made in cases of sunstroke, and this ought to be analogous. In Minnesota the courts allowed recovery in a case where an iceman was killed by lightning while seeking shelter under a tree during performance of his duties. There are various decisions in England under Workmen's Compensation Act there. I should be glad to tackle this, but I must talk with someone who knows where man worked and can give exact account of surroundings and circumstances under which he was killed.

The Security Insurance Corporation is quite a different matter, looks something like a "skin game," but we'll try to beat them on it. I will try to get to this next week or week after but must see the insurance policy.

Mrs. Rusteika's insurance papers to be sent to Mr. A. (This done.)

[The following extract is from the United Charities case record and is given to show how the family lived while the Insurance Corporation refused to pay and the compensation claim was hanging fire:]

December 2, 1916.—Mr. Mount, Claims Department, Tunnel Company, in office. Company is willing to give Mrs. Rusteika $50 as relief until legal decision is made. After consultation it was decided to use money in the following way:

December rent	$8.00
Children's shoes	6.50
One ton coal	5.25
Naturalization papers	1.00

The balance of money to be used for weekly pension of $6 for food and incidentals.

Mr. Mount asked interpreter to call with him. *Later.*—S. C.[1] visited with Mr. Mount, explained the new plan to Mrs. Rusteika. She was very unwilling at first, cannot live on $6 a week; company should take care of her and children until they are twenty years of age, etc. After a long talk she promised to make an attempt. She would like to move as there are a lot of bums who are in the alley during the night. Mr. Mount agreed to that and asked that United Charities approve the rooms. Mr. Mount expended $28.50.

[Between December 18, 1916, and January 5, 1917, the Immigrants' Protective League record contains various entries relating to the filing of claim before Industrial Board and interviewing of witnesses. Two legal problems were involved:

First, the liability of the Tunnel Company under the Illinois Workmen's Compensation Act. The question at issue was whether or not the man's death was an industrial accident, "an accident arising out of or in the course of the man's employment" or whether it was due to an "act of God," for which the company could not be held liable.

[1] Initials of visitor for the United Charities.

Second, the liability of the Security Insurance Corporation of Illinois, in which the man held a life insurance policy for $1,000. The following extract from a note, dated January 31, 1917, from the attorney, Mr. A., to the League states the insurance situation briefly:

In re Rusteika vs. *Security Insurance Corporation:* The insurance company filed an answer admitting it owed Mrs. Rusteika $40 on the policy but denied liability in excess of that. I sued for $1,150. The rules of court provide when any part is admitted to be due, you can have judgment for that amount and the suit then continued for the balance. Yesterday I appeared and took judgment for $40, and the suit will continue for the difference of $1,100. The insurance company paid an extra $6 to demand a jury trial, which would ordinarily mean that the case would not be reached for a year. Today I appeared and asked to have the case advanced and set down for immediate trial on the ground that Mrs. Rusteika was destitute. The attorney for the company very strenuously resisted this but the court was with me and set the case for February 26. The judge set it earlier, but the attorney begged so hard he put it off another week. I secured the insurance report from the secretary of state, which shows that this company collected about $32,000 in premiums last year and paid in benefits only $4,254.14 and the balance, about $28,889, went for officers' salaries, commissions, and fees paid to organizers; that is, it cost the company about $28,000 to collect and pay the $4,254 in disability benefits. It seems to be a cut-throat company organized for the benefit of the officers to exploit the immigrants. I wish when you give Mrs. Rusteika the check which I enclose you would caution her not to sign a release or talk about the case if they send someone around to interview her.

In the mean time the widow was finding it hard to live. The following entries from the United Charities record show something of her situation:

January 10, 1917.—Neighbor telephones asking coal. Promised visit.
January 11, 1917.—E. G. visited. Mrs. Rusteika is very much worried because of the baby's ill-health. Child has been sick for seven weeks and the county doctor and visiting nurse were in attendance. As the child did not improve Mrs. Rusteika took it to Dr. Sharp on January 6 and paid him $1.65 for treatment and medicine. Child cries constantly and is emaciated looking. Is nothing but skin and bone.

Mrs. Rusteika has had a hard time managing. The company gave her $6 for the last time on December 6. The roomer, Martha Gass, has loaned Mrs. Rusteika about $28. She, therefore, does not pay room rent but deducts the amount from the bill. Miss Gass came home while visitor was there and said that she is no relative. She is a fine-looking Lithuanian woman and is employed in a cake factory at $7 a week. It is difficult for her to assist Mrs. Rusteika all the time, but she felt sorry for her and loaned the money. She plans to take a position in a hotel as her present income is too small. Mrs. Rusteika had the last bucket of coal. As the range uses up too much coal she cooks on the gas range. Her rooms are in the rear of the barber shop and there is only one meter for both store and her rooms. Before Mr. Rusteika's death they paid the barber $1.50 a month for gas, but now Mrs. Rusteika pays only 75 cents a month no matter how much she uses.

Mr. Rusteika was a member of St. ——— Lodge, a small Society connected with St. ——— Church, which pays a death benefit of $200.

They gave Mrs. Rusteika $50 at the time of Mr. Rusteika's death but had not paid the balance because the undertaker stopped payment. Mrs. Rusteika could not explain this.

Gave Mrs. Rusteika $2 cash and promised to report case to the County Agent as she is unable to leave the baby for any length of time. She will borrow coal before the county coal comes. *Later.*—Telephoned Mr. Henry, County Agent. Reported case to him.

January 12, 1917.—E. G. visited. Mrs. Rusteika had no coal. County Agent had visited yesterday and left card to call on January 13 at office. Gave 30 cents for coal.

January 15, 1917.—E. G. visited neighbor, Mr. Vlass. Secured address of secretary of St. ——— Society. *Later.*—Visited secretary. He works and can be seen only in the evening.

January 19, 1917.—E. G. visited. Mrs. Rusteika did not get provisions from county as she could not carry them home. Did get coal. There was a man present when visitor called who Mrs. Rusteika said was a company spy. He comes often to inquire if she is taking any action against the Company and if she is getting help from some one. Baby is not better. Does not get milk from county. Asked if we could not help her get her naturalization papers. Gave $2 grocery order.

January 22, 1917.—E. G. visited Mr. Capek, secretary of the lodge, in the evening. Immediately after the death of a member of the lodge, the lodge gives family $50, but each of the members is supposed to pay $1 to the family and are given six months in which to make the payment. So far $116 has been collected. There are between 140 and 150 members. Mr. Jass, undertaker, reported to the president of the lodge that the funeral bill has not been paid and under their by-laws the funeral bill should be paid out of the insurance, but the money will not be turned over to the undertaker until agreement is made between undertaker and Mrs. Rusteika.

January 29, 1917.—E. G. visited. Baby is feeling better. Visiting nurse was there this morning and told Mrs. Rusteika not to nurse the baby and to take it to the Infant Welfare Station Thursday. Mrs. Rusteika says that almost every evening some man who works where Mr. Rusteika was killed comes to see her, trying to get some information as to the action she may be taking against the Company. She does not give them any satisfaction and says the city is giving her food. She also said that these visitors try to persuade her to let them bring some beer, but she will not allow liquor of any kind to be brought into the house. She says she is very tired of them, but being friends of the family for some time she hates to turn them away rudely. She said that one of these men had told some one that some members of the Company had said that if Mrs. Rusteika gets a good lawyer to fight her case she would be able to get something. Visitor told her that Mr. A. telephoned and said that probably the trial would take place this week and that he hoped she would get the $1,000 from the Insurance Company. The same woman is still living with her and helping her. She said the funeral bill she got amounted to about $177. Visitor asked to see bill, but Mrs. Rusteika could not find it; promised to have it next time. She said undertaker added $2 more because he had forgotten the first time to put in the cost of the shoes.

Returning to the case record of the Immigrants' Protective League the history of the attempts to collect compensation and insurance is continued.]

February 13, 1917.—M. J. attended case before the Industrial Board. United Charities visitor brought Mrs. Rusteika. The Tunnel Company's attorney asked for a postponement, as he was not quite prepared for the hearing. Mr. A. objected but finally agreed to postpone until Friday, February 16. When Mr. A. asked Mrs. Rusteika if her husband left any property, she said they had bought a lot near Western Avenue and Seventy-ninth Street, which cost $320, but only about half of this amount is paid; she would not like to give it up and thus lose the money they paid and the lot too. Moreover, she would like to have something to leave the children. United Charities did not know about this property.[1] Mr. A. says she can use property for bond, which may be needed. Mr. A. says there are expenses connected with the compensation case. He is getting an electrician to testify as an expert. Explained that woman was destitute. He said he would advance payment for electrician and court expenses for other case. He thinks we can win both, but insurance company will appeal if we get favorable decision in first court. He says they are both interesting cases. The insurance company has a very special kind of policy that no immigrant can understand, and the company is exploiting poor people who cannot understand what they are paying for. Company is organized not like an insurance company as its name indicates but as a sort of "fraternal

[1] [The later history of the real-estate transaction indicated that Mr. Rusteika had been exploited by a real-estate company as well as by the insurance company. On July 10, 1917, Mrs. Rusteika received a notice from the real-estate company stating that default had been made in the payment of $155.11 and interest $3.90. The notice concluded as follows: "You are further hereby notified that unless payment is made of the above-entitled amounts on or before August 1, 1917, we shall elect to forfeit and determine the said Articles of Agreement and shall retain all payments heretofore made in full satisfaction and in liquidation of damages sustained."

The secretary of the United Charities at once sent the notice to the attorney, and he replied as follows:]

DEAR MADAM:

Replying to your favor of the 16th inst. I think it would be improvident to make more payments on those lots for Mrs. Rusteika, even if she is to lose the payments made. I have not been out to see how the lots are situated or what the neighborhood there is like. In general, I know that where lots are sold like that on the instalment plan with cut-throat contracts, the purchaser generally pays about twice the market price. I have recorded the contract and have written the agent that he can only cut off the rights of the widow and children in the property by foreclosure. Recording the contract will interfere with their selling the property to anyone else and cloud the title. I think it will keep them from selling the property until Mrs. Rusteika's suits are settled. And if she is in a position then to pay out on them, I think they will be glad to make a deed for the balance due. I do not see that anything more can or should be done to further the real-estate speculation. I doubt whether it would be advisable to pay the balance even if she had the money to pay, but we can decide that when the time comes.

Very truly yours,

A. G. A.

lodge." This Mr. Rusteika did not know when he took out his policy. He and his wife thought this was straight insurance. Mr. A. said he believed insurance company could be made to "shell out."

February 16, 1917.—M. J. attended trial before Industrial Board. Charities visitor brought Mrs. Rusteika. Mr. A. had witnesses and electrician to testify for us. We will not get decision for a few days. Mr. A. remained to discuss matters further with company lawyer.

[The theory on which compensation was claimed by the lawyer was that the man's death arose out of conditions of his employment since he was tending an electric switch, and he was therefore in greater danger during an electric storm than an ordinary person would have been. Mr. A. claimed, therefore, that in his occupation Jakub Rusteika was exposed to a risk which was "appreciably and substantially beyond the ordinary normal risk which ordinary people run," that "extra danger from lightning arose out of his employment and brought his death under the Illinois Workmen's Compensation Act as an industrial accident." Mr. A. in his argument said:]

Where an accident is due to an agency beyond the control of the employer although the risk is one to which all are subject, yet if by reason of the employment, the workman is exposed to the risk of that injury for a longer time or if he must encounter the risk more often then the accident is one arising out of the employment. This doctrine has been firmly established by a series of cases where collectors, agents or "sandwich" men making rounds on bicycles or on foot are injured or killed by collisions with street cars (a risk to which all are exposed). But their employment subjects them to a more prolonged exposure to the dangers of the street. The ordinary person has "sense enough to come in when it rains," and these cases are direct authority for fixing a liability on respondent on the ground alone that his being required to work in the rain subjected him to a more prolonged exposure to risk of the elements even if the dangers of the location near the lake and the danger of handling the railroad switch are eliminated.[1]

[1] A further extract from the attorney's argument is of interest as indicating the points involved:

What right has this community to ask a man to incur the added risk of the elements in order that the waste of the city may be disposed of more cheaply, or what right has the community to ask his wife and children alone to bear the loss necessarily encountered from his exposure to the elements in order that excavations for the community's buildings may be more cheaply removed? What right has any industry to ask a man to incur an added risk by exposing himself to the elements in the prosecution of its work and he bear all the loss? This is not arguing fireside equities, nor an argument for the Legislature—it is advanced to justify a liberal interpretation of the law to include lightning hazards necessarily incurred in the work. The industry itself would have to bear the expense of the destruction of its engines or cranes by lightning, and we submit that the industry should bear the expense of the human machine just as necessarily employed in the prosecution of its business, when the human machine is destroyed by lightning from exposure to the elements in performing the business and work of the master during a rainstorm. It is conceded that Rusteika would be within the act if he negligently let the engine on the rails run him down, *a fortiori* he should recover where his death is due to the

[About a week later, the Industrial Board handed down a favorable decision, awarding the widow $3,500. However, the attorney explained that the company had fifteen days in which to file an appeal.

Later the Tunnel Company took an appeal.

In the meantime the insurance case came to trial and was decided in favor of the corporation. The attorney for the Immigrants' Protective League and for Mrs. Rusteika promptly took an appeal and assumed the expenses of appealing and of briefing the case,[1] since neither the League nor Mrs. Rusteika had any funds for carrying up the case. The facts in the case are interesting as illustrating difficulties encountered by immigrants in trying to provide for their families.

Although the man was insured for $1,000 the company offered to pay only $40, a sum actually less than the man had paid in premiums. As the attorney pointed out, the kind of policy under which such a settlement was offered was one that was clearly designed to mislead an immigrant workingman.

The policy contained, first, a general undertaking or covenant printed in large heavy type, which stated that Jakub Rusteika had "been regularly admitted as a member of the Security Insurance Corporation in Class X, a

invisible, the insiduous and sinister force that travels the rails, against which his prudence cannot protect him. . . . .

We think it appropriate and proper to explain that we exonerate the respondent from all fault or blame in the matter lest our references to the deceased's being required to work in rain might be misunderstood or misconstrued as intimating that respondent did not now have a proper regard for the safety of its employees. It is undoubtedly necessary in the reasonable prosecution of the work to keep the tunnel from being congested, but the fact that it is necessary for him to work in the rain makes the liability clearer under the act because it is a necessary accompaniment of the business—a necessary concomitant of the work as the English court puts it, which makes it an inevitable incident to the business. Nor do we contend that the result was contemplated by respondent any more than by the deceased and we make this concession advisedly for we know that some courts have said loosely that the accident must be in the contemplation of the parties. It can only mean legal not actual contemplation. It is immaterial whether the misadventure was foreseen as probable or contemplated as possible or otherwise apprehended either by the workman or employer—the question is, did it rise out of the employment? . . . .

It may be observed by the *Bulletin* of the Board that recovery may be had for injuries from cold and heat, where not due to the constitutional weakness or lack of resistance of the individual, and, while lightning is in the same category as the other elements, it does not present that doubtful feature. No man can withstand thunderbolts. It is not considered necessary to discuss those analogies.

[1] The expenses in such cases make it very difficult for poor plaintiffs to carry an action to a higher court. In these two cases the attorney advanced all expenses and took as a fee in the second case, in which he secured judgment for $3,500, a sum that was almost equivalent to the expenses he had paid in connection with the two cases. Thus, although the two cases involved a great deal of work not only in briefing but interviewing witnesses, court work, etc., the attorney received nothing for his services. A difficulty in such cases is, of course, that they can be handled successfully only by good lawyers, and the services of good lawyers, unfortunately, are difficult to secure when there is no prospect of a fee.

laborer by occupation," and upon the payment of $1.50 was to be entitled to the benefits specified. The corporation agreed to pay in the event of the death of the insured $1,000. The policy was marked at the top "Premium $1.50. Amount $1,000." Following this general undertaking or covenant, the policy contained a great deal of qualifying material in small type closely printed. It would have been absolutely impossible for an uneducated laborer, even if he read English, to understand the qualifying clauses. These clauses provided:

First.—Should the death of the member occur within two years from the date hereof, 10 per cent of the above amount shall be due in full payment of the claim; if after two years, 20 per cent; after three years, 30 per cent; after four years, 40 per cent; after five years, 50 per cent; after six years, 60 per cent; after seven years, 70 per cent; after eight years, 80 per cent; after nine years, 90 per cent; and after ten years, the full amount will be paid.

Second.—If the death of the member is caused from accident or from accidental injury, the benefit to be paid will be governed by the occupation, act or hazard in which the member is engaged at the time of injury, and the above benefit will be scaled as follows: Occupation, Class AA, o per cent; A, 10 per cent; B, 20 per cent; C, 30 per cent; D, 40 per cent; E, 50 per cent; F, X, and CC, 80 per cent, upon the surrender and cancellation of this certificate. One-half of the amount named as death benefit will be paid to the member for permanent total disability from old age, provided the member has attained the age of not less than 70 years, and has maintained this certificate in continuous force and effect for 20 years.

The following extracts from the attorney's brief and argument[1] explain the form of policy under which this immigrant laborer carried his insurance:

. . . . The general undertaking of the policy is to pay $1,000 upon assured's death, whether from sickness or accident, but the company insists the amount should be reduced from $1,000 to $40, under a subsequent clause (clause 2) because assured was accidently killed by a bolt of lightning. The insured had paid premiums for three years and three months at the rate of $18 per year. . . . . The company's liability under the policy is admitted and the extent of that liability under a proper construction of the contract, where death is due to lightning, is the principal question this court is called upon to decide. . . . . The evidence was documentary. Plaintiff ordered the policy and premium receipts in the sum of $58.50. . . . . The company introduced the application specifying benefits for deaths from sickness and accidental deaths. He is classified as a laborer in Class X. The amount in the blank for accidental death is not filled in. The amount for death from sickness is fixed at $1,000. It appears as follows:

"Class X. *Accidental death. Amt., $———. Death from sickness. Amt., $1,000."

The company offered in evidence a letter written by its president to plaintiff (*Abst.*, p. 19), which shows the construction and interpretation placed by defendant on the two clauses in controversy. It says the amount of $40 is arrived at as follows:

[1] In the Appellate Court of Illinois, First District, October term, 1917, *Brief. and Argument for Appellant*, by A. G. A., attorney for appellant, pp. 1-6, 22-33.

"Paragraph *First* on the face of your certificate states that the death benefit (death resulting from sickness) would be $200 which is 20 per cent of $1,000.

"Paragraph *Second* states that if death is caused by accident the amount payable will be scaled 80 per cent in Class X. Eighty per cent deduction from $200 leaves $40." . . . .

It will be observed that clause 2 which is relied on to reduce the amount applies where the cause of death is "governed by the occupation, act or hazard engaged in at the time of the injury" (not at the time of the issuance of the policy), which clearly implies a case, where the occupation at the time of the injury is not the same as at the time of the issuance of the policy, if a reduction is to be made. To insure a man as a laborer in Class X in the sum of $1,000 against death, and then to reduce the sum to $40 because he remains a laborer in Class X, is a ridiculous paradox. Did the defendant promise more in the insuring clause for the simple purpose of cutting it down in a subsequent clause?

Would the company insure a man as a laborer in Class X for $1,000 and then arbitrarily reduce it without cause, when there has been no change in the risk of hazard? The company knew he was a laborer in Class X, when it insured him, and promised $1,000. If it never intended to pay $1,000, under any circumstances, for the accidental death of a laborer in Class X, then why promise the $1,000 for his death, whether from natural or accidental causes? If the benefit is paid in all cases, whether there has been a change in employment or not, solely according to his occupation at the time of death, then why specify his class and occupation at the time of admitting him to membership, when his occupation at the time of admission has absolutely no bearing on the benefit to be paid? It is answered, to fix the premium. Precisely. Then, why reduce the benefit, when there has been no change in the occupation calling for higher premiums? . . . .

It will be observed that the insuring clause, appearing first and most prominently, contains an absolute, unconditional, unequivocal promise to pay $1,000 on death of assured, whether from sickness, accident, or Act of God, and that, too, as a laborer in Class X. After classifying him as a laborer in Class X, the policy provides:

"The (Security) Insurance Corporation hereby agrees on the death of said member, to pay to M. R. . . . . ($1,000) one thousand dollars payable as follows: . . . ."

The above language is distinguishable from other policies, where the amount may be reduced, in that it does not use the words, "Promises to pay *not to exceed* $1,000," nor is it followed by such words as "except" or "provided." It says this definite and fixed amount is "payable as follows," which can only refer to the time, manner or place of paying the sum absolutely promised, but not to the amount to be paid, for that is fixed conclusively and finally. That is, part of the $1,000 might be payable sooner as disability benefits, which by paragraph 9 of the policy are to be deducted from the death benefit on final settlement, but the amount of $1,000 is payable under the policy. . . . .

Practically to forfeit the insurance and allow merely a nominal sum, much less than the premiums paid, is certainly contrary to the general purpose and intent of the contract promising to pay a substantial sum. . . . .

No one would contemplate that a policy, which purports to insure against accidental death in the sum of $1,000, would be restricted to $40, because death was accidentally caused by lightning, especially when the policy is represented as a "Preferred Certificate." It is unthinkable that any sane man would pay $58.50 in premiums on a policy purporting to insure in the sum of $1,000 against death, if he understood that any accidental death, even by lightning, was to be governed by his employment and reduced to $40. Reductions must not be hidden in ambush, or concealed by camouflage.

It is unbelievable that any man would agree to pay $18 a year for forty or fifty years, understanding that, if killed by lightning, he could only recover $200. It is apparent the assured understood he had, what the policy purports to be, a "Preferred Certificate." The company having given the policy an attractive appearance by promising $1,000 absolutely upon death, will be held to those appearances. There are two parties to the contract. The company cannot place its own *ex parte* construction upon the policy. . . . .

The attorney's argument also set forth the general nature of the insurance company's business. The *Insurance Reports of Illinois for 1917*, Part II (p. 662), showed that the insurance corporation collected a total of $19,470, and out of this paid $5,887 to its members in benefits, while paying $13,934 in commissions, salaries, and other expenses. This was characterized by the attorney as:

. . . . A disreputable showing compared with other fraternal companies. For example, the Bohemian Slavonic Union, page 667, paid in benefits over $73,500, while paying only $4,743 in commissions, salaries and all other expenses. The Bohemian Slavonian Benefit Society (p. 666) organized seven years after defendant, paid during the year in death, sick and accident claims, over $315,000, while the salaries and other expenses were only $17,710. . . . .

Reports for previous years furnish further evidence that defendant is not a legitimate fraternal company, but exists for the benefit of its officers and employes and the exploitation of its members.

The case against the Insurance Company was lost, however. The final decision in this case may be found in 209 Ill. App. 147. This decision shows how the insurance contract was drawn, which provided that if the member died within two years from date of policy only 10 per cent of the amount would be due, if after two years 20 per cent, after three years 80 per cent, after four years all. Mr. Rusteika died after two years and would have been entitled to $200, but the policy also provided for a reduction of 80 per cent in case the insured was a laborer and met death by an accident. The court held therefore that nothing could be recovered except the $40 offered by the company.[1]

Meanwhile the widow found it hard to manage. The following extracts from the United Charities record show what her situation was:

February 21, 1917.—E. G. visited. Baby has been quite ill. Mrs. Rusteika wanted to take it to clinic at Infant Welfare Station February 19, but the weather was bad and she had to remain at home. Promised to go tomorrow. Children need shoes and underwear. Mr. Kevicz, a man

[1] See 209 Ill. App. 149.

wishing to marry Mrs. Rusteika, visits quite often. Mrs. Rusteika says that he is supposed to have a considerable amount of money but does not know how much he has. He earns $20 a week. Mrs. Rusteika says if she wins her suits against the Tunnel Company and insurance company, she does not think she will marry again, as she fears that a stepfather would not be too good to children. The children are very obedient and have had a good bringing up. Mrs. Rusteika is anxious to know how the trial is getting on, but as visitor had not heard from her attorney she could give no information. *Later.*—Miss Hugh, Infant Welfare Society, reports that the baby needs care but that Mrs. Rusteika does not bring it to the clinic. Mrs. Rusteika asks if United Charities could not make her a loan of $30, which she would return after she receives her money. She would like to pay her rent as landlord is threatening to evict her. She has no one to borrow money of except the woman staying with her, but she cannot get along on that. She would like to sell her property if possible. Mrs. Rusteika asks that we help her take out first papers so that she could apply for a pension if she loses the suit.

March 15, 1917.—Telephoned Mr. A. concerning the possibility of having Mrs. Rusteika sign a contract whereby she would agree to repay the United Charities money given to her previous to settlement of Industrial Board case. Mr. A. advised that this be done. Said Mrs. Rusteika could sign an agreement to that effect. Mr. A. advises Mrs. Rusteika apply for pension under Aid to Mothers Act in Juvenile Court. Thinks she would be entitled to this fund even though her suit is not settled.

March 27, 1917.—E. G. visited and had Mrs. Rusteika sign bond for appeal to the insurance suit, to mail to Mr. A. Mrs. Rusteika asks how soon United Charities will loan her money. Boys have practically no waists to wear. Mrs. Rusteika is unable to nurse baby and cannot afford to buy milk. Said she would go to Infant Welfare Society this week and see if she can get milk for baby. *Later.*—Telephoned Miss Ingram, Funds to Parents Department, Juvenile Court. As long as the case is in the hands of the Industrial Board, a settlement could be made and department would not consider taking Mrs. Rusteika's application for pension.

April 4, 1917.—Martha Gass, woman living with Mrs. Rusteika, telephoned that Mrs. Rusteika needs money and asks that we loan her some. *Later.*—E. G. visited Mr. Rusteika's brother, Domenik Rusteika. He was not at home. Neighbors said he is a bachelor and lives alone. He comes home from work about 6 o'clock.

April 5, 1917.—Mr. A. telephoned asking that superintendent serve as administratrix for estate. It is necessary to have one appointed even before definite settlement of appeal. Bond of $70 would be required. Asked that he take up matter with Immigrants' Protective League. *Later.*— E. G. visited. Talked over budget with Mrs. Rusteika and she feels that she will be able to manage on $3.25 per week for food. She is very much in need of stockings and blouses for the boys and clothes for the baby. She has had to tear up a bed sheet for clothes. Jack was refused shoes at the county agents. The woman who stays with Mrs. Rusteika helped a good deal, but cannot provide everything and often gets disgusted and threatens to leave. All the boys need trousers. Mrs. Rusteika also asks that United Charities loan her money for present month's rent; $4.00 on last month's was due March 23.

The Charities record contains numerous entries of other visits relating largely to treatment of baby as advised by Infant Welfare Society and to arrangements for summer outing for whole family. The Charities were supervising and largely supporting the family. The Immigrants' Protective League appeared only in connection with legal proceedings. Their secretary furnished bond as administratrix.

During the summer of 1917 the two cases were pending on appeal. There is no entry in the Immigrants' Protective League record except a discussion of summer-outing question with the Charities. The Charities record contains entries showing payment of weekly pension $3.15 regularly, rent $1 and an occasional purchase or gift of clothing, or ice tickets, correspondence about the gas bills with gas company and other minor matters. On September 1 there is the following entry:

Mrs. Rusteika telephones that children cannot begin school today as they have no shoes. Told her to get letter from priest or some teacher in school stating that children are in need of shoes, and to present letter to County Agent, who will give shoes. Mr. A., Mrs. Rusteika's attorney, has notified her that the trial with the Insurance Company will take place in October and the other before Christmas.

In October, the pension was raised to $4.40 a week, and woman was urged to find cheaper rooms. October 15 there is the following entry:

Neighbor telephones for Mrs. Rusteika that she has found rooms at No. 728 Twentieth Street for $9. *Later.*—Mr. A., attorney, telephoned that Mrs. Rusteika's case will come up on October 19 at 2 P.M. Told him we had not Lithuanian interpreter. He thinks it may not be necessary to have one. *Later.*—M. Z. visited rooms at 728 Twentieth Street and found Mrs. Rusteika had moved in this morning. She found the rooms October 14 and paid $1 down, which she borrowed from Martha Gass. The landlord at the other address pressed so for the rent that she moved out. Apparently got nervous and did not know that she was to wait for United Charities' approval before moving. Rooms are fair, but kitchen and kitchen bedrooms are not light. The agent, who was present, said he had rented the rooms for $8.50 but would reduce it to $8. Moving man just finished moving and was there asking $6 for the work, but said would accept $4, which Mrs. Rusteika thinks a reasonable charge. Martha Gass was visiting. Is working in the Indiana House. She would be willing to go down to court with Mrs. Rusteika if necessary on October 19, but would have to obtain permission from the superintendent.

During the autumn entries are much the same. On November 20 the following entry in the Charities record occurs:

M. Z. visited with A. K. (Lithuanian interpreter). Mrs. Rusteika is very anxious to hear the outcome of the suit. Told her we had not been able to reach Mr. A. by telephone and were waiting for an answer to our letter. Mrs. Rusteika seemed to be in a complaining mood. Complained of the rough treatment at the County Agent's office and that Infant Welfare nurse scolds her. Apparently does not follow instructions. Said however that she appreciated all that United Charities is doing for her. Domenik and Jacob need shoes. Told her to get a note from the priest and take it to the County Agent. Gave $4.40 pension. Gave coat, two dresses and a petticoat for the baby and two boys' waists.

On December 11, 1917, the decision of the Industrial Board in the case against, the Tunnel Company was affirmed, giving the woman $3,500. The Company had fifteen days in which to take an appeal. No appeal was taken. Arrangements were made for weekly payments instead of a lump-sum settlement. Mrs. Rusteika to receive $8.40 a week for eight years.

An entry in the United Charities record of January 11, 1918, is of interest:

M. Z. and A. K. visited Mrs. Rusteika, who was in a complaining mood —complained about everything. Is dissatisfied because she did not receive compensation and because it is to be paid in small amounts. Also said she cannot manage on the assistance she is receiving and is particularly dissatisfied because the County Agent refused to give milk tickets without a recommendation from the Infant Welfare Society. Visitors explained that she could not get this without going to the conference and urged her to go to next conference. Mrs. Rusteika said that maybe she would go. Visitors suggested that she go to cooking class at Gads Hill Center, but Mrs. Rusteika refused.

Mrs. Rusteika explained the absences from school of the children by saying it was difficult to prepare food for them when gas was frozen. They were home today for no good reason as Mrs. Rusteika can use the gas again.

She said stockings given the baby were too small. Visitor reminded her that she had received a great deal of clothing. She said it didn't fit anyway. Gave $4.40 pension. Mrs. Rusteika needs shoes.

Meanwhile Mrs. Rusteika continued to be dissatisfied because she did not get a lump-sum settlement. Charities and League thought weekly payments better for the children, and the attorney stood by their instructions and refused to change. Mrs. Rusteika threatened to get a new attorney. The following entries from the Charities record relate to this point:

January 24, 1918.—M. Z. visited Father Y., St. ——— Church. He thinks Mrs. Rusteika a good, trustworthy woman, and believes that if she is given enough to pay her debts, a weekly allowance will be by far the best plan for her. He thinks that most decidedly that she should go to work one or two days a week. He will be very glad to talk this over with her if she will come to him.

January 25, 1918.—M. Z. visited. Mrs. Rusteika seems to have changed completely. Said that if she gets enough to pay her debts she will be perfectly satisfied with her weekly payments, as she is planning to do a day's or two days' work a week as soon as the weather is warmer. Most of the $180 was borrowed from Martha Gass the last winter before regular allowance was given by United Charities. Part of this money was used to pay Dr. Sharp for medical services to the children. She thinks there is still some money due him. The rest was borrowed for food, clothing, and fuel. Mrs. Rusteika spoke in the highest terms of Mr. A. and said that she had no intention of changing lawyers. From time to time various men come there and try to get her to give them the case, but she pays no attention to them. Suggested that Mrs. Rusteika see Father Y.

Further efforts were made at different times by the woman and first by one friend and then by another to get a lump-sum settlement. The attorney, Mr. A., the League, and the United Charities, all stood firmly opposed to this plan, believing that the interests of the children could be protected only under the monthly payment plan.]

MISCELLANEOUS

50. Marciana Stender
(Unnecessary Arrest)

September 21, 1916.—Officer Bryan, Harrison Police Station Annex, telephoned. He wanted an interpreter right away for "Slavic" woman. He could not tell whether woman is Polish, Russian, Lithuanian, or what. It is impossible to understand her. She was arrested last Monday while running wildly on street. Officer stopped her. She acted in a very suspicious way and gave impression of being demented. Yesterday she was calmed down a little. Doctor is there now, examining woman, and they want interpreter. Told them we would send Mrs. J. *Later.*—M. J. went to the Annex. Woman is Lithuanian, name Marciana Stender, address 400 North Seventy-fifth Street. I spoke to woman in doctor's presence, he noticed that woman told her story in a straightforward manner and answered questions in a perfectly sane way. Woman's story: Her name is Marciana Stender; she is twenty-five years old and has a little girl four years. On Monday she and husband quarreled, with result that he left her. Mrs. Stender took child to her sister's house and herself ran to Police Station to report the desertion of her husband; she was very much excited. Before she had time to reach the station she was arrested. The doctor was very angry that she should be arrested.

Name of woman's brother-in-law is Kleofas Leskien. M. J. spoke with Mrs. Leskien, woman's sister, by telephone. Sister does not like to come alone to Annex. She will send her husband or Mrs. Stender's husband this afternoon. They have been very much frightened about Mrs. Stender. Her husband is looking everywhere for her. Her little girl cries always. M. J. told sister it was a mistake that officer arrested woman because he could not understand what the matter was. *Later.*—Telephoned Annex at 5 P.M. Woman is gone. Sister and brother-in-law came for her about three o'clock.

51. Christina Hensinger
(Unnecessary Commitment to Bridewell)

[The League first heard of Christina Hensinger, June 5, 1910, when a letter was received from the inspector-in-charge of the United States Immigration Service, Chicago, transmitting a report from one of his inspectors in the case of a recently arrived German-Austrian girl who had been reported by the authorities of the Bridewell as an alien to be deported. The letter was indorsed with the following memorandum by the inspector-in-charge: "Respectfully referred to Miss Gardner, Director of League for the Protection of Immigrants, Chicago, with the request that she advise whether she believes it is possible to assist this girl in any way.—(Signed) J. R. ROBERTS, *Inspector-in-Charge.*" The inspector's report which was transmitted was as follows:]

June 3, 1910

Inspector-in-Charge, Immigration Service
Chicago, Illinois

SIR: As per verbal instructions and information received from the Maxwell Street Police Station, I proceeded to the House of Correction, the so-called Bridewell, for the purpose of interviewing one Christina Hensinger, a German-Austrian girl, who is serving a ten-dollar fine at the above-stated institution under a charge of vagrancy. This girl has been unfortunate from the time of her landing. She came to this country with an aunt, and they had only been in this country a few days when the husband of this aunt was found dead by asphyxiation. As soon as the funeral was over, the aunt returned to Europe leaving this girl here to shift for herself. She tells me that she has a brother somewhere in the city of Chicago but that she does not know his address. She also says that she has an uncle by the name of Ernest living some place on Wentworth Avenue, this city. She stated that she had been working on a farm 180 miles from Chicago after her aunt left for Europe. She does not know the name of the man owning the farm or where the farm is situated. The girl is stout and well built, and I believe is able to earn her own living if given an opportunity. The lady in charge at the institution stated that she is clean in her habits. I would respectfully suggest that this case be brought to the attention of the League for the Protection of Immigrants with the suggestion that they find employment for the girl, if possible.

Respectfully,

R. E. HANNING
Immigrant Inspector

June 5, 1910.—Court records consulted. Name on court records Christina Hensinger, Case No. 11220. *Later.*—N. R. [visitor who spoke German] visited girl at Bridewell. In addition to facts in inspector's letter she says she has a friend living at 21 Locust Street, second floor, Mrs. Rebner. Christina says a woman named Gottlieb, wife of saloon-keeper at 313 Augusta Avenue, had her arrested; says she does not know why. She thinks the friend, Mrs. Rebner, has about six dollars of hers. Girl seems honest but stupid, is very unhappy and bewildered by what has happened, seems to have absolutely no idea why she is in prison.

June 6, 1910.—Visited Mrs. Gottlieb. Mrs. Gottlieb owns house to which Christina first came. She says girl was honest and clean when she arrived. After aunt returned to Hungary, girl went to country people on Locust Street, who found work for her. About three weeks ago, someone brought her back to Mrs. Gottlieb and left her. Girl was very dirty (verminous), and Mrs. Gottlieb was going to take her back to her friend, but girl got frightened and ran away. A policeman was in front of the house, and Mrs. Gottlieb thought he would take her to the Home for the Friendless.

June 7, 1910.—Visited Mrs. Rebner. She says she has not the girl's money. She refuses to have anything to do with her. Mrs. Rebner said policeman came to ask her if she would take the girl and she refused. Girl was verminous, had been working for people who were not clean. *Later.*—Telephoned to Bridewell to find out what judge sent her there. Information not given. *Later.*—N. R. visited Bridewell. Judge Henry, Englewood Branch, committed her. Officer Tim Hogan, ninth precinct, made the arrest.

June 8, 1910.—Went to Englewood court. Judge Henry not there. City attorney not there. Policeman at court said girl was so dirty and had no relatives to go to, that the Judge sent her to the Bridewell as this was the only way to clean her up. *Later.*—Telephoned Judge Henry. He says that he will see that the girl is released tomorrow.

June 9, 1910.—N. R. went to Bridewell. Judge Henry had arranged release. Christina eager to go to work. Took her to work for Mrs. Schulman, 12 Lake Street, Evanston. [Details of arrangement, telephoning, etc., to Mrs. Schulman omitted.]

June 15, 1910.—Letter written as follows:

The Chief Justice of the Municipal Court
Chicago, Illinois

DEAR SIR: May I call your attention to the disposition made of a German girl—Christina Hensinger—(Case No. 11220) at the Englewood Station by Judge Henry? Left alone in Chicago because of the sudden death of her foster uncle and the return of his wife, her only acquaintance refused to allow her to enter her house because the family for whom the girl had been working was dirty and her head was not clean in consequence. She was turned over to a policeman, brought before the court and fined $10 and costs for disorderly conduct because as the police said that was "the only way to clean her up." This the Home of the Friendless would have done for her without having a fine entered against her name or requiring her to be sent to the city's jail. Chicago also has an arrangement with the Women's Central Lodging House for the temporary care of homeless, women. The matron at the Bridewell said the girl was clean in her personal habits and a good worker. We were able to secure her release and find her a good place to work so that she is all right now, and I am calling your attention to her case only because I believe that Judge Henry and the other judges of the Municipal Court are anxious to avoid such mistakes as this and that they occur only because the resources of the city are not known. I wondered therefore if you might not think it possible to call the attention of the judges of your court to the fact that there are institutions in Chicago where friendless women and girls against whom there is no charge of any crime can always be cared for and that the organization which I represent would be glad at any time to assist in the adjustment of the difficulties of friendless men and women whose ignorance of our language makes their cases peculiarly difficult?

Cordially yours,

LYDIA GARDNER, *Director*

September 9, 1910.—Telephoned Mrs. Schulman. Girl getting along nicely.

September 12, 1910.—Letter received from Judge Henry:

Miss Lydia Gardner
Immigrants' Protective League

DEAR MADAM: Your letter of June 15, 1910, to the Chief Justice has recently been referred to me. I have read your letter with much interest as it contains information regarding the city's resources to care for the unfortunate which I did not know, and which is not generally known at police stations. At the time Christina Hensinger was before me at the Englewood Station she was in a pitiable condition and needed special care, and I was advised that the only place she could receive the same was the Bridewell, and consequently she was committed there for that purpose. At the time I felt that it was unfortunate that no other place seemed open to her to which I could send her. There are quite a number of similarly unfortunate cases that come before the Municipal Courts each year that excite the sympathy of a judge; each case has its own peculiar phases calling for special disposition. While I regret that it becomes necessary to send persons to prison, I feel, when it becomes the duty of a judge to do so, that in the Bridewell they are well cared for, and this fact mitigates the pang of the disagreeableness of a judge's duty. I have visited the Bridewell to learn for myself how persons are cared for, and was agreeably surprised to learn that they have a most excellent hospital for the care of the sick, injured and inebriate, and, also, that otherwise they are well treated and cared for. I am not fully informed, as yet, of the city's resources to care for the class of individuals you had in mind when you wrote your letter to the Chief Justice; but I do wish to assure you that I am ever interested in the unfortunate, and will esteem it as a cooperation upon your part with me in my work if you will advise me further regarding havens to which the unfortunate who have committed no wrong may be sent for help and treatment.

Sincerely yours,

RALPH HENRY

[From November 22, 1910, to January 9, 1915, the case record contains numerous entries. The German-speaking visitor of the League called to see Christina whenever an emergency arose. Thus she is taken to a tuberculosis clinic in November, 1910, for an examination, but she is found not to have tuberculosis. She was taken to open a bank account and in December, 1910, she had saved over $100. She began later to come to the League herself whenever she needed advice. She sent money to Hungary a number of times. She had an excellent work record and in September, 1912, she had $500 in the bank. In July, 1914, she sent some money to Hungary, which did not arrive, and she wanted it traced. The remaining portion of the record is of more interest.]

February 9, 1915.—Tina called at the office to ask advice regarding a man she wanted to marry. The man lives in West Virginia. She would like the League to find out if he is a good man. *Later.*—Letter written to the Secretary of Associated Charities:

C. D. Carr, Esq.
Associated Charities
Washington, West Virginia

MY DEAR MR. CARR: A girl whom we have known for the last four or five years and who has no relatives here in Chicago became acquainted with a man by the name of George G. Halpich, while he was here in Chicago last winter. He is now in Washington, West Virginia, living at the Hotel Virginia, Mountain Street, and working at 21 Hoopston. The girl wants to go down to marry him, but knows practically nothing about him; and while she wants to marry him, she feels very timid about it. She has about $500 saved; and as she is quite a little older than the man, I feel that probably we ought to make inquiries. The girl is an Austrian-German; the man is a Servian, who has lived here since he was a child. I promised the girl that inquiries could be made without revealing the fact that she was concerned in it. If you will be good enough to do this, I shall be very grateful indeed. If you think the man is an honest workingman, is there some place for the girl to stay until the marriage takes place, such as the Y.W.C.A.?

Sincerely yours,

LYDIA GARDNER

February 23, 1915.—Christina wishes to leave. No reply from Associated Charities. A telegram sent as follows: "Please wire today report Halpich. See letter February ninth. Girl insists upon leaving Wednesday morning." *Later.*—Reply from Associated Charities: "*Immigrants' Protective League:* Have girl wait for letter you will receive Thursday morning. Very important."

February 24, 1915.—Letter received as follows:

You will pardon our delay, I trust, in replying to your inquiry regarding George G. Halpich, which was overlooked until your wire this date was received. I immediately called on him at the address given and found him at a typewriter, smoking a cigarette, and had a conversation with him regarding his business, which evidently does not as yet amount to a great deal, in spite of his card, which I inclose. I left the office with the intention of wiring you that, to all outward appearances, Mr. Halpich was at least *unobjectionable*, and if he had arranged a marriage, I should not do anything to prevent it. However, I felt moved to return immediately to his office and, forgetting your caution to let him know nothing of why he was being questioned, I asked him plainly, although as tactfully as possible, regarding his approaching marriage with a Chicago girl. It is of course difficult to reproduce our conversation, since I am not gifted in that line, but the outcome of it all was the unmistakable fact that, as he himself said, he "was not crazy about getting married," and the further conclusion that the chances of incompatibility between him and whoever married him would be very great. In my opinion, to be brief, the union would be a grave mistake, and while I trust you will be more faithful than I to the confidence reposed in you, for I do not want to incur his enmity, I do not hesitate to advise the lady to go very slowly in the matter, if she is still determined to get married. If he is aware of her having the amount of money you name, it might be a good idea to have her *write him to send her the money for her traveling expenses*, and *note his reply*. I believe that would be sufficient to convince her whether his love were sufficient to stand the severer tests to which it would undoubtedly be put later on. I am not enough acquainted with the characteristics of the Servian and the Austrian peoples to form a reliable opinion regarding their union with one another in the bonds of matrimony, but from the little I have read concerning the cause and progress of the present struggle in these countries, it would appear a trifle dangerous, to say the least. I wish to disclaim any responsibility in this matter for the reason I have given above, and for that reason I would lay upon you the entire matter for adjustment; I hope you will be able to persuade the lady to write a few more letters before she comes to our city, especially the one suggested at the top of this page, and assure her that her friend will not be in any danger of leaving her for another at present, for I judge that making money is occupying more of his attention at present than any woman is doing, even his intended bride. Above all, do not show this letter to her. I did not show yours to him. Awaiting your further pleasure, I am,

Yours to command,
C. D. Carr

February 25, 1915.—Telegram to Miss Durfee, Y.W.C.A., asking her to meet Christina. Letter to Miss Durfee as follows:

This note will introduce Christina Hensinger, a German girl whom we have known for the last five years and who has no relatives here in Chicago. She has come to Washington to marry George G. Halpich. We hope that you will take an interest in the girl, that is, help her find a room before she is married and attend her wedding. Any advice that she may need in the matter we feel very sure you will give her. Thanking you for your cooperation in this matter, we are,

Very truly yours,

Immigrants' Protective League

Later.—Arrangements are completed for Christina to go to Washington, but she wishes to leave her bankbook with us. If she is satisfied with the man, she will send for it. She will look around before marriage and stay where Y.W.C.A. suggests.

March 3, 1915.—Letter written in German received and signed "Tina" [translation from German]:

Dear Friend:

I hope my letter finds you in good health; and I am yet in Washington, West Virginia, and I have not found out anything bad about him, it is all good with him, he is a good man and he is good to me and I have not found anything at all bad about him. I have no friend here, otherwise everything is good and he has promised me he is always good to me, "best regards from me, Tina." [This last in English.]

March 5, 1915.—Letter to Y.W.C.A. as follows:

Miss Mary C. Durfee, Y.W.C.A.
Washington, West Virginia

MY DEAR MISS DURFEE: May we ask for a report in the case of Christina Hensinger, the girl concerning whose arrival in Washington we telegraphed you on February 25th? We are anxious to know whether she has married Mr. Halpich, and if so, where they are living and how things are going with them.

Very truly yours,

LYDIA GARDNER

March 6, 1915.—A typewritten letter from Tina in English, even her signature typed, as follows:

Washington, w; va; march 4/ my dear miss Gardner you ack mi please to wirte to you and tell you how i gething along, im gething along allright and we are marid now and hi is very good to mi and i dont do no work yet and soon we gon to Be in ar onwe hom and im filling allright and please dont worry aBout mi everything com out good whit him and he promise mi hi be good to mi as long as we live and i like you to please do mi a favor sand mi Bank Book i like to have it whit mi best regarst from mi tina
mrs tina halpich rom 5 State Bldg washington w; va;

March 10, 1915.—Night letter sent to Miss Durfee, of the Y.W.C.A., as follows: "See Christina Hensinger Halpich personally privately. If she really wants bankbook that she left in our care to write letter own handwriting, German, upon receipt of which will forward book to you for delivery. Husband's office 5 State. Home address unknown. Suspect husband wants book without her consent.—IMMIGRANTS' PROTECTIVE LEAGUE."

March 11, 1915.—Telegram received from Miss Durfee advising the sending of the bankbook. Letter from Miss Durfee written before receipt of our message as follows:

MY DEAR MISS GARDNER:

Christina Hensinger arrived safely, and we brought her to the Y.W.C.A. I investigated as thoroughly as possible and found only favorable reports. This man is an interpreter, and his employers speak very well of him as do others for whom he has not worked. Christina was married the first of March. They have not begun housekeeping yet but expect to soon. George earns good wages, and Tina will not have to work outside her home. They are staying at a cheap hotel, patronized by foreigners. I'll be glad when they are somewhere else. But I believe everything is all right. Mountain Street is their present address. I'll let you know when they change their address and will be glad to assist you in any way possible at any time.

Very sincerely,

MARY C. DURFEE

March 12, 1915.—Letter to Tina:

MY DEAR TINA: We are inclosing herewith your bankbook which you left in our care February 25. We are sorry that there has been any delay in your receiving it, but you must realize that your letter asking for the book was typed so that we were not sure that it was really from you, and, since you had trusted the book to us, we felt that we had to be sure before we sent it. Will you please sign the inclosed receipt and mail it back to us? We shall see that your trunk gets off as soon as possible. We are very glad that everything is going well with you and will be glad to know about your new home when you start housekeeping.

Yours faithfully,
LYDIA GARDNER

[The record contains several other letters written by Tina in German to the League visitor or superintendent. In one of these she sends thanks for the bankbook and in a later one thanks for the trunk. A letter written more than a year later sends her new address and tells Miss Gardner that "everything goes good with me and my man is good to me." Later she writes in English. One letter tells of a small son and sends greetings to "all my friends."]

52. Marciana Ripalis
(Non-enforcement of Compulsory Education Law)

May 1.—Letter to the Superintendent of Schools,[1] Summerfield, Illinois, from Immigrants' Protective League:

DEAR SIR:

We have recently received from Ellis Island in accordance with our arrangements with the Federal Immigration Authorities the name and address of the following child under fourteen years of age who arrived with her parents destined to Summerfield. We shall be grateful if your Attendance Officer will send us on the inclosed postcard a report telling whether or not this child has been enrolled in school and is attending regularly.

Yours very sincerely,
LYDIA GARDNER, *Superintendent*

May 8.—The reply postcard with the name "Marciana Ripalis, age eleven, manifest address 157 West Street, corrected address 152 Monroe

---

[1] This was a form letter sent out to school authorities in all towns of Illinois given as the destination of immigrant children of compulsory school age admitted to the United States. The federal immigration authorities co-operated with the League by sending a list of children of school age admitted at Ellis Island and destined to Illinois. This case of Marciana Ripalis is typical of a large number of compulsory-education cases in the League files. See Abbott and Breckinridge, *Truancy and Non-attendance in the Chicago Schools*, chap. xviii, "The Special Problem of the Immigrant Child." See also *Report of the Massachusetts Commission on Immigration* (1914), chap. vi, "Education and the Immigrant."

Street, date of arrival, February 13," was found "not in school" when visited but "working and claims to be fourteen." The following note was added on the card by the attendance officer:

It will be well to look up record of Marciana Ripalis as the age on this card is three years younger than the age the mother now gives. She is reported as being employed in a home as a domestic.

(Signed) AUGUST STOLLE, *Truant Officer*

May 9.—Letter written to the truant officer at Summerfield:

MY DEAR MR. STOLLE:

We have noted your remarks regarding Marciana Ripalis, the Lithuanian girl living at the corrected address, 152 Monroe Street. We have referred again to the original records and find that she came in on the ship's manifest as eleven years of age, as before reported. It may be, of course, that she was in reality fourteen years at the time. Children are sometimes reported under age in order to secure the half-fare tickets. Once the statement as to age is made, however, we feel that the immigrant should be compelled to abide by the fact. The State Factory Inspector agrees with us that the manifest age should be considered the legal age and bases prosecution for violation of the child labor law on the parents' initial statement. We trust that you will take the matter up again with the child's parents and insist that the child be enrolled in school. Until some other documentary evidence of the child's age can be obtained we feel that she ought not to be denied the opportunity of learning English, which will so greatly benefit not only the child but her parents. We inclose a new blank for your convenience. Thanking you for your co-operation and hoping to hear that your efforts are successful, I am,

Sincerely yours,

LYDIA GARDNER, *Superintendent*

June 4.—Letter to Summerfield as follows:

DEAR SIR:

We should like very much to know the result of any further investigation regarding Marciana Ripalis, the Lithuanian girl regarding whom we wrote you last on May 9. You will remember that she appeared on the manifest list as being eleven years old and that you found her to be working. We shall greatly appreciate your co-operation in this matter.

Very truly yours,

LYDIA GARDNER

June 7.—Reply from Summerfield as follows:

In reply to your letter regarding Marciana Ripalis, I beg to submit the following: I can give you no further information than that contained in the blank as filled out and returned to you. The mother of the child is willing to swear that she is fourteen years of age. I am unable to speak the Lithuanian language and could not get very much information.

Respectfully,

AUGUST STOLLE, *Truant Officer*

[No further efforts were made by the League to get the child in school.]

53. Josef and Marya Novak
(*A Croatian Family in Trouble*)

April 25, 1914.—Josef Novak, age forty-four years, address 1000 Teal Street, in office. He was sent by the Austro-Hungarian consul to our office for B. P. [Bohemian visitor] to help in arranging for admission of his wife and four children from Ellis Island. Mr. Novak, a Croatian, is a laborer in the International Plough Works and has been earning $12 a week, but is out of work at present. He saved the money to bring over his wife and four children and has furnished a four-room flat on the instalment plan. April 6, when he was expecting his wife and children to arrive, he received a telegram from Ellis Island that youngest child was sick. (He had the telegram which was from the Acting Commissioner and said: "Jannina Novak, steamship La Touraine, seriously ill Ellis Island.") Soon after this he received also a letter from a Croatian Society in New York explaining that he must deposit $150 for treatment of child Jannina, who is sick, and then the mother and three other children can come to Chicago. He had only $30 when the letter came; but now he has borrowed from a Croatian friend the $150, which he wishes League to send to Ellis Island for him and to bring his wife and other children here. Mr. Novak left money for us to send if we think necessary. *Later.*—Sent night letter to Commissioner, Ellis Island, as follows: "Wire status case Marya Novak and children ex steamship La Touraine. If excluded, hereby appeal.—JOSEF NOVAK, CARE OF IMMIGRANTS' PROTECTIVE LEAGUE."

May 2, 1914.—Josef Novak in office with letter from Congressman Henry, saying "that the child Jannina has a fractured leg both bones. She is doing nicely, but it is impossible to say how soon she will be able to travel." A "Croatian friend" had written to Congressman Henry for Mr. Novak.

May 8, 1914.—Reply from Ellis Island, confirming order of $150 deposit for child before family will be allowed to proceed. *Later.*—Money order for $150 transmitted for Josef Novak to the Acting Commissioner of Immigration, Ellis Island.

May 15, 1914.—Reply from Ellis Island containing the following:

Referring to your letter of the 8th instant forwarding money order for $150 from Mr. Josef Novak, I write to inform you that Marya Novak and three children were permitted to land today, to join the husband and father in Chicago. The child Jannina is still detained in the Ellis Island Hospital under treatment for fractured leg.

June 30, 1914.—"Follow-up" visit by B. P. [Bohemian visitor]. B. P. found family living in basement, rear house. The house conditions are bad at Novak's. Man is sick in bed with lung trouble; he attends the Eastern Dispensary, the only time he leaves bed. They do not have any furniture, there are no sheets on beds, other ways all is clean. Mr. Novak is out of work since March, 1914. The only supporter of the family is the fifteen-year-old son, who earns $3 per week, at Richards' Box Factory. Oldest daughter (eighteen years) just started to work at the Chicago Can Factory on Maxwell Street. She does not know how much she will earn. Mr. Novak received a letter from Congressman Henry that his little daughter now sick at the Ellis Island hospital must have her foot amputated and father's consent is necessary and his presence. Mr. Novak went to Mr. Henry and told him about his troubles and the situation. Mr. Novak was injured at the International Plough Company, April 18, 1913. He was two months in St. Luke's Hospital, did not work until October, when he got an easier job, worked again until March this year. Since that time he kept going and going to ask for work but did not get any. He has a piece of paper in his hand, he thought it was valuable, but it is a few lines from a manager of one department to a manager of another about chance of finding work for this man. *Later.*—Telephoned Eastern Dispensary. They think that Mr. Novak is too sick to stay at home. Dispensary urged the County Agent to send man to County Hospital today. They will notify us if this is done.

July 30, 1914.—Visited the Novaks. Mr. Novak is at home. He stayed in the County Hospital ten days only. The boy does not work because the shop where he worked burned down four weeks ago. The oldest daughter earns $6 per week. Her check number is 245. Asked Mr. Novak more about his injury. He worked at the International Plough Company as a molder, earning 20 cents per hour, worked 12 hours a day. April 18, 1913, he was injured through the fault of a boy who worked with him, who filled the dipper with the liquid metal to overflowing and spilled it on Mr. Novak's foot. Mr. Novak was two months in St. Luke's Hospital and was getting compensation $6 per week till July, but was not able to work until October, when he got different work, earning $1 less per day—fourth floor, bolts and nuts making. He worked until March, 1914, and lost the job. He could not secure any other work. Now he is sick. He gave his case about the time his family was detained to Mr. James, the brother of Alderman James, whom he asked for help while the child was sick and the family at Ellis Island. Mr. James has not done anything on his case yet. Mr. Novak had received following letter of July 24 from the medical officer, Ellis Island:

Your little girl is doing nicely and you will not know the child when you see her as she has grown so fat. It will probably be about four weeks before she will be able to leave the hospital, and we will let you know one week in advance so you can come for her.

July 31, 1914.—Wrote Miss Williams in charge of the Welfare Department, International Plough Company:

MY DEAR MISS WILLIAMS:

I wonder if you could not help us in the following case. Josef Novak, a Croatian, was employed by the International Plough Company at the North Side Works as a molder. On April 18, 1913, his foot was injured when the dipper was filled too full and the molten metal poured out on his foot. Mr. Novak was taken to St. Luke's Hospital and was paid $6 a week until July; but he was not able to go to work until October, when he was given other work by the company (on the fourth floor, making bolts and nuts) and was dismissed in March, 1914. We first knew the man when on the 25th of April he came to us. His family were then detained at Ellis Island; his little daughter had suffered a double fracture of the leg on the way over. The wife and other children were admitted, but his little girl is still there and will probably not be released for another month. Our visitor called to see the family recently and found that Josef Novak, the father and husband, is now sick with tuberculosis and under the care of the Eastern Dispensary. The sixteen-year-old son, Adelbert, is working at Richards Box Factory earning $3 per week; and the oldest girl, Anna, eighteen years old, is working for the Chicago Can Factory on Maxwell Street, earning $6 per week. The family are in quite desperate straits. The basement flat is clean, but they are without proper bedding, food, or clothes. The man thinks he has a claim against the Plough Company for the time that he was unemployed last summer, and he took the case to Mr. James. I have told him that I was sure the company would meet its obligations. I wonder if it would not be possible to put the girl at work in the coreroom so that she might earn more, and if some care for the father might not be provided. The family seem to have had a very hard complication of misfortunes just at the time of their arrival.

Sincerely yours,
Lydia Gardner

August 7, 1914.—Miss Williams [welfare worker, Plough Works] in office.[1] She says only claim for permanent injury is because one of the man's toes is stiff. She says company is willing to pay full amount for entire loss of toe under compensation law if money goes to man and not to lawyer. Mr. James refused to accept these terms. *Later.*—B. P. visited Novak's,

[1] [Early in June, 1914, the Novak family had been referred by a local church to the United Charities. The Charities had therefore already taken up the matter of compensation for the man's injury with the Plough Company. The position taken by the company had been stated in the following letters. A letter of inquiry brought the following reply from the company's welfare secretary, dated June 30, 1914:]

My dear Miss Smith:

In reply to your letter of June 29 asking for a written statement in regard to the case of Josef Novak, I have the following to report: I understand that the accident was in the nature of a burn on the right foot, and occurred on April 18, 1913. Mr. Novak received $102 compensation, in accordance with the Illinois law. He was cared for at St. Luke's Hospital. He returned to work October 13, 1913, in good condition, the foot being entirely healed; and he continued to work until March 19, 1914, when he was laid off with a number of others on account of the slack season. In regard to the kind of insurance which he carried, I suppose you refer to our Employes' Benefit Association. This insurance terminated with his employment. He made no application for a continuance, and could not have done so, as it is a rule with the Company that death benefits can be applied for only by employes who have been with us three years or longer. You will see, therefore, that everything has been done for Mr. Novak that is called for, not only by the Illinois law but by the rules of the Company. I am very sorry to hear that the family is

told man about the company's offer. Mr. Novak said he not only lost use of one toe but the whole foot. Could not get any satisfaction from him and told him to come to the Immigrants' Protective League to talk to Miss Gardner. He also said that Mr. James asked 3 per cent for his services.

August 11, 1914.—Letter from Miss Williams, International Plough Company:

DEAR MISS GARDNER:

After leaving you on Friday, I was thinking over the situation of the Novak family and suddenly realized that according to the record I gave you the man was laid off six months instead of four months. Knowing that he had received full compensation and that the amount was $102, I could not reconcile these contradictory conditions. I went to the Industrial Accident Department this morning as soon as I reached the office in order to get more complete information. Before I had an opportunity to ask any questions, Mr. Harvard told me that he had received a telephone message early this morning from a representative of the firm of James and James, stating that

in such a difficult situation. I wish that we could take care of everybody as we should like to, but when I was a worker with the Charities I had to let some cases go, and of course with such a large number of employes the Company must take care first of the employes who have been with them for some time. Mr. Novak sustained his injury almost immediately after coming in to the North Side Plant and is really a very recent employe. Trusting that this information will be helpful, I am,

Yours very cordially,

MARY S. WILLIAMS, *Welfare Secretary*
International Plough Company

[In reply to another letter from the Charities, the welfare secretary wrote again to the Charities as follows:]

MY DEAR MISS SMITH:

In reply to your letter of July 21, in regard to Josef Novak, I wish to say that I consider this distinctly a case for the Charities to care for, much as I should enjoy helping the family and directing the relief work myself.

Having been a Charity Superintendent for three years before coming into the International Plough Company, I know enough about industrial concerns to know that very few of them take care of the employes as the Plough Company does. But with thousands of employes, if we were to undertake to extend our relief work to recent short-time employes who contract illness after leaving our employ, we should indeed become a charitable institution ourselves.

Moreover, the fact that a man, a new employe, showed such bad judgment as to send abroad for his entire family in a time of industrial depression when he knew that even old-time employes were being laid off, certainly places no responsibility upon the Plough Company to take care of the family, which became dependent almost immediately upon its arrival.

As I have stated before, there are certain cases which the Plough Company should care for and which it will care for. There are others which are distinctly the responsibility of the state or the Charities; and the case of Josef Novak certainly falls within the latter group.

I hope that the family will be cared for with all the thoughtfulness that their pitiable condition calls for.

Very truly yours,

MARY S. WILLIAMS, *Welfare Secretary*
International Plough Company

they withdrew the suit. I told Mr. Harvard that your visitor had probably reached the man and advised him before their representative saw him. Now as to the term of unemployment and compensation: The records show that compensation was paid from April 25 to August 25, at which time the surgeon certified the man's ability to return to work on August 26. As you know, the surgeon's statement to this effect terminates the payment of compensation. The man would have been given work on August 26 if he had returned; but he did not return until September 18, from which time he worked irregularly until October 13, the date which I had understood originally to be the beginning of his re-employment. I do not know why he worked so irregularly between September 18 and October 13 as he gave no reason so far as the record shows. From October 13 until he was laid off on March 19, I think he worked without any loss of time whatever. As you will understand, he would not receive compensation after the doctor certified his ability to work. He, therefore, received no compensation between August 25 and October 13, during the time he was able to work. If he claims that he did not receive full compensation, I suppose he refers to the time between August 25 and September 18, when for some reason he did not return to work, although the doctor stated that he was able to do so. Now as to the settlement. Mr. Harvard will send our representative of the Industrial Accident Department at the North Side Works some time today, I think. As I understand it the payment will be something over $60. Trusting that this clears up the whole situation, I am,

Very cordially yours,

MARY S. WILLIAMS, *Welfare Worker*

August 12, 1914.—B. P. visited Novak's again. Mr. Novak in bed, coughing more than ever, is weak, cannot get up. He could not attend the dispensary last Saturday. He does not remember how long he was getting the compensation but agrees that he received something like $100. He worked irregularly because he was not well enough. The foreman sent him home. He could not begin to work before September 18 because the wound was open. He has not left the house since Saturday, has not spoken to Mr. James or heard from him. He does not want to accept any charity, does not believe the law would give him so little for so much pain. He thinks that the injury was the cause of all his present troubles. He brought a doctor's certificate issued last year by T. H. Wak, to whom Mr. Novak was sent by a lawyer, Mr. Gray. He did not pay for the advice to the lawyer but paid the doctor $2. Mr. Novak is very low, probably feels that he will not live long, has one wish more to see the little daughter home from Ellis Island. Begs League to write there to send the child home as soon as possible. Went to see Mrs. Harkness at the Eastern Dispensary. Mrs. H. said she would have Mr. Novak arrested if he were just a little better. He does not want to obey the nurse's orders, does not want to use the paper napkins, and does not want to stay in the hospital, where he was sent. He stayed at the County Hospital only three days. He is in third stage of tuberculosis. Eastern Dispensary will report Mr. Novak to Visiting Nurse Association tomorrow.

August 13, 1914.—B. P. wrote Mr. Vesely, of Slavonic Immigrant Aid Society, New York City, as follows:

We are very anxious to have a report on Jannina Novak, a little Croatian girl who is in the hospital at Ellis Island having fractured her leg on the steamship coming to America. The child came with her mother and sisters and brothers the later part of March, and in May the commissioner wrote us that she was still having treatment. The father is seriously ill with tuberculosis, in fact may die at any time. We should be very glad if the child could be released. Will you kindly learn how much longer she will have to stay, and let us hear from you?

August 28, 1914.—Letter from Mr. Vesely, of New York, about other matters in which he says:

Regarding the Novak child of whom you also send us an inquiry, I was unable to find anything definite. The doctors expect to take an X-ray of the leg in a few days, and then I may be able to find something more satisfactory. The trouble, so the physicians claim, is that the broken bone refuses to heal. Otherwise the child is, so far as I could see, in perfect physical condition.

September 1, 1914.—The Bohemian Settlement called up to say that Mr. Novak received the following telegram from the Commissioner at Ellis Island: "Child Jannina is in condition to be discharged—call immediately or make arrangements for transportation to Chicago by some competent person."

September 2, 1914.—B. P. talked with the Welfare Department of the International Plough Company again. Miss Williams thinks they will be willing to give Mr. Novak $70 that he may have the child brought from Ellis Island.

September 3, 1914.—Went to see Mr. Novak. They have moved to 191 West Street, third floor rear. Talked to man about the new offer, but he refused to accept. He says he wants half of his wages till he gets well, and he wants work. Mr. Novak borrowed the $150 deposit for Ellis Island from a poor friend, Jan Malej, on 10 per cent interest. Man demands his money back. Jannina already has railroad ticket as far as Chicago. *Later.*—Telegram to Slavonic Immigrant Society as follows: "Jannina Novak ready to leave hospital. Arrange her coming home with competent person.—IMMIGRANTS' PROTECTIVE LEAGUE." *Later.*—B. P. wrote to Mr. Vesely, explaining to him the unfortunate situation of Novak family.

September 4, 1914.—Telegram received from Slavonic Immigrant Society: "Authorities here insist upon father or mother coming in person for Jannina Novak."

[Several rather fruitless discussions with Mrs. Novak about the situation omitted.]

September 17, 1914.—Letter from Slavonic Immigrant Society, of New York, containing the following:

I saw some of the officials at Ellis Island yesterday and after explaining to them the condition in which the Novak family is at present, they appeared willing to discharge the child if some evidence is presented showing that the mother will be able to take care of the child and to let it not become a public charge. You probably know that the officials at Ellis Island have information regarding the father's condition and that he had applied for admission to a county hospital for tuberculous people and is therefore on the point of becoming a public charge. This together with the condition of the child has made the officials here at first rather unwilling to admit her without having some statement from the parents. You may have the mother make such statement in the form of an affidavit or write a letter to the Commissioner of Immigration. Then there is another question, how to get the child to Chicago. I understand that her leg is not yet healed—it may never heal completely—and she will therefore require special care on the journey. The immigration of Slavic people is practically at a standstill, and so it will be rather hard to find someone willing to take the child along to Chicago. I am willing to look around for some trustworthy person with whom the child could be sent; but doubt that, even if we find one, he or she will care to do this for nothing. Will you kindly explain this to the parents and have them make some arrangements regarding this matter.

September 19, 1914.—Letter received from Mrs. Novak. She would like to see B. P. but she cannot come to the office as her husband is too sick to leave.

September 21, 1914.—B. P. visited Novaks again. Mr. Novak is slowly growing worse. He does not hear, is delirious, and speaks about going to a hospital. Recognized me and spoke to me in Croatian. Anna, the oldest girl, is out of work. One of the immigration officials has been to see the family. *Later.*—B. P. visited International Plough Company and asked Miss Williams if she will try to secure work for Anna in the coreroom. She gave me a letter for Anna to give to the foreman. Asked whether Mr. Novak would get the $70 in case he dies. Miss Williams is willing to help with the funeral in case Mr. Novak dies. *Later.*—Visited United States Immigration Office and saw Mr. Roth, the Inspector, who was investigating the Novak case. He says they have been receiving county aid. He promised to notify the League before coming to a final decision in the matter. He also thinks that the mother with the help of three children who could work will be enabled to take care of Jannina and that Jannina will be sent to Chicago just as soon as the family troubles will be settled. Immigration authorities at Ellis Island sent the case to the Chicago office for investigation.[1] *Later.*—B. P. took the letter to Anna in the evening. Father still living but asleep. Visiting Nurse Association sent the nurse there in the

[1] [The visit of the immigration inspector is explained by the following letters. On July 30, 1914, the first letter had been written by the superintendent of

afternoon; also United Charities visitor has been there. County aid had been given to the family three times. St. Vincent de Paul Society have helped at different times.

[Mr. Novak died on the following day. The entries in the record regarding the funeral arrangements, undertaker, etc., are omitted. The family received $94 in insurance, for which they had been paying ten cents a week.]

September 24, 1914.—Mrs. Novak came to League with telegram from French Line sent from Ellis Island: "Joseph Novak call Ellis Island for child Jannina immediately. French Line." Mrs. Novak also has been at the United States Immigration Office. Advised her that we hope to find someone who will bring the child from New York.

---

the United Charities District Office to the commissioner of immigration, Ellis Island:]

DEAR SIR:

We understand that there is being held at Ellis Island a little two-year-old child named Jannina Novak (or Novick or Novach), the youngest child of Josef and Mary, of 1000 Teal Street, Chicago.

This child arrived in America from Croatia with her mother in March of 1914. The child has been held, I understand, on account of an injury to her foot; and her recovery was made known by your department to her parents in a letter received a few days ago.

When the child is fully recovered and able to be with her parents in Chicago, have you any plans for its removal to this city, and how would you suggest that it be brought about? When Mrs. Novak and the rest of the family arrived in America, they found the husband and father unemployed, and very soon after that he developed tuberculosis, and is now quite incapacitated and altogether destitute; in fact, the county of Cook is giving outdoor relief, and we are urging Mr. Novak's admission to our County Infirmary.

The eldest daughter, who emigrated in March, is the only member of the family now working, and no one speaks any English; hardly even could the father get along. Thanking you for an early reply, I am,

Very truly yours,

HELEN SMITH, *District Superintendent*

[The second letter was a reply sent to the United Charities by the commissioner at Ellis Island:]

Replying to your letter of the 30th ultimo, I have to state that the hospital authorities at Ellis Island are of the opinion that the child, Jannina Novak, ex S.S. "La Touraine," March 29, will be able to travel in about three weeks. When the mother was admitted May 13th last, she stated "either myself or my husband will come here when the child is able to travel." Appropriate notice will be sent to the family as soon as the child is discharged from the hospital. I regret to learn that in the meantime the husband and father has developed tuberculosis, is destitute, and may be admitted to your County Infirmary. Due note of this fact will be taken when the child's case is finally passed upon by the immigration authorities. I suggest that you write again stating how long Mr. Novak has been in this country. State the ship and date of arrival here, if possible.

October 6, 1914.—Miss Williams, Welfare Department, telephoned B. P. and said that Anna Novak was discharged because it was too soon after her father's death from tuberculosis. International Plough Company do not employ anybody in whose family there has been a recent death from tuberculosis. If no one else in the family is affected in two years, they might apply again. Miss Williams also said that Mrs. Novak's lawyer wrote to the company making absurd demands. The company will have a talk with him and notify the League about the results.

October 7, 1914.—Visited Mrs. Novak. Jannina is at home. Mrs. Novak went to New York for her. Mrs. Novak bought her railroad ticket at the Maly Bank, where they helped her to be met in New York by their agent. Slavonic Immigrant Aid representative helped Mrs. Novak to get Jannina, and the bond, $150, was returned to Mrs. Novak. Mrs. Novak paid the borrowed money back right after she returned from New York.

Physician at the Ellis Island hospital told Mrs. Novak to take Jannina to a hospital, where her leg could be put in plaster. Mrs. Novak went at once to County Hospital but was told there it was not necessary.

[The later history of the Novak family need not be told in detail. The mother went to work in the stockyards, the son kept in regular employment, and Jannina was placed in a home for crippled children, where she remained for several years. The family apparently were self-supporting. They made no further demands on the Charities, who visited Mrs. Novak again in 1919, when the director of the Crippled Children's Home reported that Mrs. Novak had been ill and in a hospital and ought not to go on working.]

54. Stefan Trimaitis
(Co-operative Assistance)

February 11, 1923.—Stefan Trimaitis, Lithuanian, address 1000 Halsted Street, in office to ask assistance in getting back $200, lent by him to George Ciulis, 15 Henry Avenue, Northampton, Massachusetts, on December 21, 1921. He has a note written by and signed by George V. Ciulis. Mr. Trimaitis has tried to collect the money several times, but Mr. Ciulis pays no attention to letters. Once he wrote and said to send the note back and then he will send the money. Mr. Trimaitis states that George Ciulis owns real estate at 5 Barrow Street and 15 Henry Avenue and is well able to repay with interest. Mr. Trimaitis was on a vacation in the East at the time when he loaned the money. He helped Mr. Ciulis to start in the grocery business. Mr. Trimaitis is a barber, owns his own shop, and has a family—wife and four months' old baby.

February 12, 1923.—Registered letter, inclosing the note, to Director of the Massachusetts Division of Immigration and Americanization, State House, Boston, Massachusetts:

DEAR MADAM:

Could you refer the inclosed note to some correspondent in Northampton, Massachusetts? The case is that of a Lithuanian, Stefan Trimaitis, 1000 Halsted Street, who loaned money to a friend in Northampton and is unable to recover it. The friend is George Ciulis, 15 Henry Avenue. Mr. Trimaitis loaned him $200 on December 21, 1921. He has tried to collect the money several times since but unsuccessfully. As Mr. Ciulis is well to do, Mr. Trimaitis feels that there is no reason for the delay. Mr. Ciulis owns real estate at the Henry Avenue address and also at 5 Barrow Street. We inclose the only receipt or note that Mr. Trimaitis obtained in return for his money. He tells us that Mr. Ciulis once wrote that if he would send this receipt he would send the money. Mr. Trimaitis is unwilling to take such a chance. Possibly, however, if your correspondent in Northampton has this receipt, he can arrange the matter right then and there. We do not know if the loan calls for interest; we have no one in the office at present who can read Lithuanian. Possibly this sort of request is really outside of your field. If so, and if you know of no one in Northampton to whom you can refer it, will you let us know and will you return the receipt to us?

Very truly yours,

ALICE MARION, *Superintendent Immigrants' Protective League*

February 21, 1923.—Letter from Massachusetts Division of Immigration:

DEAR MADAM:

Re Stefan Trimaitis, 1000 Halsted Street. We are referring your letter of February 12 to our Branch Secretary, Mr. Henry A. Lewis, who will most likely communicate directly with you.

Very truly yours,

DIVISION OF IMMIGRATION AND AMERICANIZATION

March 9, 1923.—Letter from Massachusetts Division of Immigration:

MY DEAR MADAM:

Re Stefan Trimaitis, 1000 Halsted Street. Our director has referred to me your communication of February 12, with reference to the claim of Mr. Trimaitis against one George Ciulis, of Northampton. I am awaiting a favorable opportunity to make a trip to Northampton on several matters which are pending in our office and at the same time I have this matter to investigate for you. The weather of the past month has been so severe that I have not found it possible. I will advise you definitely as soon as I have taken the matter up with Mr. Ciulis as to what he is willing to do in this matter.

Very truly yours,

HENRY A. LEWIS, *Branch Secretary*

March 30, 1923.—Letter from Massachusetts Division of Immigration:

Yesterday the writer called upon Mr. George Ciulis of 15 Henry Avenue, Northampton, with reference to the loan of Mr. Trimaitis, about which you had written our director on February 12. Mr. Ciulis acknowledged his indebtedness to Mr. Trimaitis without any question and stated that he was perfectly willing to make the return of the principal, $200, without interest at any time. He claimed that the arrangements as to interest were made at the time of securing the loan, and that this money was paid to Mr. Trimaitis at that time.

I found Mr. Ciulis to be, so far as I could judge, a rather fine type of man who has felt rather grieved at the conduct of Mr. Trimaitis in having enticed his daughter, who is only sixteen years of age and who is a cousin of Mr. Trimaitis, to leave her home and to accompany him first to Philadelphia and then later to Chicago. The parents have never had any evidence of their marriage, or never had any word from the daughter since her leaving home except a request that this loan be returned to Mr. Trimaitis, this request coming some six months after her having left home. The translation which we had made of the memorandum signed by Mr. Ciulis would indicate that the note was to be paid on demand with interest, no rate of interest being mentioned. For that reason I hesitated about accepting the $200 at the time I called yesterday. If you can advise me whether this arrangement is satisfactory to Mr. Trimaitis, on my next trip to Northampton I shall be very glad to make the collection and to have a draft sent him in care of your office.

Very truly yours,

HENRY A. LEWIS

Later.—Letter written to Mr. Trimaitis, asking him to come to the office.

April 2, 1923.—Mr. Trimaitis in office. He says he married his cousin about a year ago. Promised to visit.

April 9, 1923.—Visited 1000 Halsted Street. Mrs. Trimaitis at home. She showed marriage license issued April 6, 1922, Chicago License Bureau. However, there was no marriage ceremony after license was obtained. They thought the license was all that was necessary. She thinks that license clerk told them so, says they both answered many questions. Mrs. Trimaitis certainly is honest and thought she was married. She says they will go tomorrow or as soon as her husband can go to have ceremony performed. They have a six months' old son—big, handsome baby. Mr. Trimaitis is part owner of barber shop, is evidently doing well. They have a nice flat, three rooms, clean and comfortable. Mrs. Trimaitis says she has written her family many times, but they pay no attention to her letters.

April 10, 1923.—Mr. and Mrs. Trimaitis in office with their new marriage certificate. Ceremony just performed at City Hall by judge.

Later.—Letter written to Massachusetts Division of Immigration:

MY DEAR MR. LEWIS:

Thank you very much for your assistance in the Trimaitis case. On receipt of your letter, we investigated the charge brought against Mr. Trimaitis by Mr. Ciulis. It is true that he eloped with the young daughter of Mr. Ciulis; she was at the time about seventeen. They are now married; they applied for a license last April. Through a misunderstanding, they were under the impression that a license was all that was necessary but when they found that they were mistaken, they promptly had the marriage ceremony performed by one of our Municipal Court judges. We have just seen the marriage certificate. They have a very attractive little boy of about six months.

Mr. Trimaitis is part owner of a barber shop at 1000 Halsted Street, and he and his family live in a three-room flat back of the shop. His wife keeps the place looking very clean and nice. We believe them to be really happy.

Mrs. Trimaitis tells us that she wrote three times to her parents to tell them where she was and about her marriage. She never had any reply, and the letters were never returned to her unclaimed. She feels that her father is not at all interested in her and her affairs. Mr. Trimaitis also wrote several times, but his letters were unanswered. Not till they sent a registered letter with a request for the $200 which they had loaned the father and which they themselves needed did they hear from her family.

Both Mr. and Mrs. Trimaitis say that Mr. Ciulis is making a false statement when he says that the interest was paid at the time the loan was made. Neither at that time nor any time since has Mr. Trimaitis received one penny from the father-in-law either for interest or for principal. If you can get Mr. Ciulis, who is said to be a well-to-do man, to pay the interest, please do so. Mr. Trimaitis says the rate arranged for was 6 per cent. However, they need their money and would rather compromise on the question of interest than to stick out for the whole amount and thereby delay payment still further.

We feel that Mr. Trimaitis will be satisfied with whatever arrangement you make in the case. If it were not for your help, he would have to retain a lawyer and that would cost him considerably more than the interest amounts to. It will be quite satisfactory to him to have you send him a draft for the money in our care.

Very truly yours,

ALICE MARION

May 3, 1923.—Letter received from Massachusetts Division of Immigration and Americanization:

DEAR MISS MARION:

I am inclosing my personal check for two hundred sixteen dollars ($216) covering the amount of the note of Mr. Ciulis with interest for one year and four months from December 21, 1921, to April of 1923. It was with difficulty that I could get Mr. Ciulis to pay the interest on this note as he still feels quite bitter toward Mr. Trimaitis because of taking his daughter. He further says that the letters his daughter speaks of sending never reached him, but it is true that he received several notes from his son-in-law which he ignored, and then he received a note from his daughter in which she offers no explanation of her conduct but merely requests that he return to them the money loaned as they were in need of it.

I feel that both the father and mother would be very glad to hear from the daughter if she would write them in the proper spirit, and the fact that she is properly married and now has a little son will help greatly in time to overcome the feeling that they have had both against her and her husband.

There was a slight expense connected with the collection of this check involved in two trips to Northampton, $2.24, which I feel Mr. Trimaitis should return to me as on the occasion of my visits I had no other business in Northampton at that time.

Very truly yours,

HENRY A. LEWIS

[The remaining entries on the record are omitted since they are summarized in the following letter:]

May 6, 1923.—Letter to Massachusetts Division of Immigration:

MY DEAR MR. LEWIS:

Thank you very much for your efficient assistance in the Trimaitis case. We inclose two receipts—one for your files and one for Mr. Ciulis, if you think he should have one. We also inclose a check for $2.24. Mr. Trimaitis was most willing to reimburse you; in fact, he would have been most willing to share with either you or us; he tried to press a fee upon us.

He has promised that he will have his wife write her mother at once and will have her send a picture of the baby. He wishes us to express his gratitude to you for your efforts in his behalf.

Very truly yours,

ALICE MARION

SUBJECT INDEX

"Ability to earn a living" defined, 254
Admission, 63, 95, 352
Admission, exclusion, and expulsion of aliens, Part II, 95–460
Agriculture, immigrants in, 55, 532, 546, 652, 655, 664, 673
Americanization, 464, 550, 566, 585; *see also* Education
Anarchist Act of 1918–20, Alien, 231
Anarchist deportations, 289
Anarchists, 216; philosophic, 280
Angel Island, 467
Armenians, 243, 530, 594, 627
Assassination, advocacy of, 284
Assimilation, 209, 464, 545, 547, 563
Assisted immigration, 37, 116, 117, 185, 201, 205, 266
Assyrian case records, 451, 454
Austria, emigration regulations and protection, 59, 63, 64
Austrian cases, 309, 408, 480, 780

Baggage cases, 616
Banks and bankers, immigrant, 209, 498, 582, 705, 724, 760; *see also* Money sent abroad, Steamship tickets
Barlin v. *Rodgers*, 258
Beetfields, Lithuanian family in the, 655
Belgium: examination system, 73; immigration legislation, 71
Bilingual schools, 563, 564
Blind girl, case record of, 427
Boarding-houses, emigrant, 77, 140
Boards of special inquiry, 206, 209, 224, 225, 253, 305, 314, 315, 318, 339
Bohemian cases, 340, 538, 633, 752
Bond, admission on, 219, 229, 352
Bonding system, 98, 126, 134
Boston immigration station, 467
Boston Municipal Court, 522
Botis v. *Davies et al.*, 264
British emigrant-carrying trade, 1850, 37
British passengers laws and regulations, 3, 14, 17, 21, 24, 26, 33, 38, 39, 40, 71
British paupers, *see* Paupers imported
Bulgarian cases, 484, 646

Cab-driver exploitation, 606
"Cable Act," 451
California Commission of Immigration and Housing, 489, 536, 587
Camps, labor, *see* Labor camps
Canada, immigrants to, 17, 18, 20, 21, 31, 33, 38
Canadian Border, immigration along, 184
Canfora v. *Williams*, 256
Canneries, 488
Capitation tax, federal, *see* Head tax
Case records, social, *see* Social case records
Cases, immigration: court decisions, *see* Immigration cases
Castle Garden, 174, 183, 324, 326
Causes of immigration, 116, 124, 201, 232, 233, 235
Chicago immigration station, 468, 472
Cholera epidemics and emigrant ships, 20, 42, 47
Christmas Order, 1921, 455
Church of the Holy Trinity v. *United States*, 262
Citizenship, 339, 451; class work, 569, 576; *see also* Naturalization
Civil courts, 525
Cleveland, Grover, veto of literacy test bill, 198
"Coffin ships," 4, 29
Colonial steerage laws, 3, 6
Colyer v. *Skeffington*, 288
Commutation: money, 98, 126, 145, 164; system, N.Y., declared unconstitutional, 168
Complaints, state bureau of, for immigrants, California, 587
Compulsory continuation school law, Illinois, 553
Compulsory education law, non-enforcement of, 787
Congestion of immigrants in cities, 543
Congress, power of, over immigration, 4, 28, 119, 156, 159, 160, 170, 171, 179; *see also* Federal control and Federal immigration laws
Construction camps, housing, and systems of living, 475, 633

804 IMMIGRATION: DOCUMENTS AND CASE RECORDS

Contagious-disease cases, 230, 300, 307, 309, 310, 319, 332, 386, 399, 452; *see also* Cholera, Ship fever
Contract-labor cases: court decisions, 262, 264, 268
Contract-labor legislation, 99, 185, 195, 205, 216, 218; typical cases, 188
Control stations, 73, 74, 86
Convicts, importation of, 128, 157, 184; prevention of, 102, 127, 182
Court decisions in immigration cases, 100, Part II, Section III, 252–97
Courts, immigrant and the, 521, 583, 633, 780
Crime involving moral turpitude defined, 261
Criminals, immigration of, 178, 204, 208, 540
Croatian case records, 405, 604, 722, 789
Czecho-Slovak case record, 339; *see also* Bohemian and Moravian
Czechoslovakia, emigration regulations, 59, 63, 64

Debarred aliens, *see* Exclusion
Deportation, 98, 160, 162, 225, 228, 284, 319, 355, 402, 406, 452
Destitute immigrants, 16, 27, 134, 591; necessity of public care for, 136
Detention, 298, 339; abroad, 363, 399, 447; contagious disease, 307, 309, 386; curable disease, 303; excess quota, 397; of mother of illegitimate child, 375, 384; of pregnant girl, 377, 382; possible permanent injury, 313; when deportation impossible, 273, 406
Diamond v. *Uhl*, 284
Disease contracted on shipboard, 3, 4, 6, 8, 14, 17, 20, 21, 23, 28, 34, 40, 57; *see also* Cholera, Fever ships
Diseased aliens, immigration of, 202; *see also* Contagious diseases
Distribution of immigrants, artificial, 546
Domestic immigration problems, Part III, 461–800
Domiciled alien, 230, 270, 386

Education, immigrant, 464; adult in Illinois, 549, in Massachusetts, 567, in New York, 572, in Passaic, N.J., 556; all-day schools for adults, 551, 577; education for immigrant women, 551, 573, 579; financing immigrant education, 560, 565; state aid for immigrant education in Massachusetts, 560, 566, in New York, 561, 573; *see also* Bilingual schools, Evening schools, Factory classes, Illiteracy, Parochial schools
Ellis Island, 244, 466; *see also* Social case records
Emigrant protective societies, *see* Protective societies
"Emigrant ships," 3, Part I, Section I, 6–58; horrors of, 3, 7, 9; mortality on, 3, 4, 6, 7, 13, 14, 17, 25, 28, 30, 33, 37, 38, 42, 44, 48, 54; *see also* Overcrowding
Employment, finding, 474, 621
Employment agencies, 474; in Chicago, 481; in New Jersey, 478; regulation of, 209
Employment-agency cases, 621–49
Employment-agency frauds, 592
Employment exchanges, public, 64, 65
English paupers, *see* Paupers, imported
European countries, emigration regulations of, 59
Evening schools, 550, 557, 567, 572
Examination systems at foreign ports, 72
Excluded classes under the Act of 1917, 216
Exclusion (social case records), 299, 300, 310, 332, 340, 341, 342, 346, 347, 348, 350, 392, 395
Exploitation, 29, 88, 209, 463, 468, 591; by passenger brokers, 15, 38; employment agencies, 476, 592, 621; in factories, 583; land purchase, 533, 536, 591; moral exploitation of girls, 468, 592; *see also* Notaries public, Transmission of savings
Expulsion cases: court decisions, 275, 288; social case records, 400, 405, 408, 420

Factories, exploitation in, 583
Factory classes, 551, 567, 570
"Fair hearing," what constitutes a, 275
Famine year of 1847, 4, 31
Farms, recent immigrants on, 652, 655, 664, 673; *see also* Agriculture
Federal control over admission of immigrants, 99; argument against, 164
Federal immigration laws, 3, 28, 38, 45, 50, 53, 71, 80; Act of 1917,

SUBJECT INDEX

100, 215; provisions, administration, and reasons for enactment, 1882–1922, Part II, Section II, 181–251; see also Passenger acts of Congress

Feeble-minded, exclusion and expulsion of, 299, 420

"Fever-ships," 29, 42

Finding employment cases, 621, 622, 623, 624, 627

Finnish case, 528

Food on shipboard, 6, 7, 8, 10, 12, 13, 14, 18, 19, 20, 21, 24, 26, 29, 30, 35, 36, 38, 39, 40, 41, 43, 52, 85, 90

Foreign exchange, see Money sent abroad

Fraud, see Exploitation

Frauds upon immigrants after arrival at port of N.Y., 130

Fugitive from justice excluded, 340

Gegiow v. Uhl, 216, 254

German cases, 341, 350, 382, 402, 470, 473, 608, 780

German Emigration Society of New York, 157

German Society of New York, 144

German Society of Philadelphia, 11

Germany: convicts from, 127, 129; emigrants from, 6, 7, 10, 11, 14, 39, 42, 55, 144, see also German cases; emigration regulations and examination, 60, 65, 69, 73; paupers from, see Paupers, imported

Girls, immigrant, 5, 30, 62, 298, 300, 310, 319, 340, 342, 344, 345, 346, 347, 348, 350, 355, 363, 365, 368, 395, 397, 400, 420, 427, 447, 451, 528, 597, 604, 718, 719, 722, 744, 780; housing of, 526; protection of, on arrival at interior points, 468; traveling alone who failed to reach destination, 472, 608

Great Britain: convicts from, 184; emigration regulations, 62, see also British passenger laws; immigrant cases, 262, 268, 280; immigrants from, 24; paupers from, see Paupers, imported

Greece, emigration regulations and examination, 60, 61, 62, 63, 65, 74

Greek cases, 261, 264, 275, 406, 527, 593, 595, 596, 623

Greeks, 530

Grosse Isle, 20, 21, 31

Head tax: federal, 177, 179, 210, 215; state, 98, 139, 147, 151, 177, 179

Henderson et al. v. Mayor of New York, 168, 177

Home teacher, 579

Hop pickers, 489

Hospital treatment of contagious-disease cases, 230, 302, 307, 309, 319

Hospitals, emigrant, 134, 136, 172

Housing conditions: immigrant girl, 526; immigrant lodger, 526; in cities, 543; in construction camps, 475; non-family groups of men, 529

Hungarians, 420, 483, 535; see also Magyar

Hungary, emigration regulations and protection, 60, 61, 63, 66, 74

Illegal entry, 355, 460

Illinois, educational need of immigrants in, 549

Illinois Immigrants' Commission, x, 100, 298, 464, 549, 597, 616

Illiteracy, social case records of, 367, 368, 372; see also Literacy test

Illiterate minors, 553

Immigrant banks and bankers, see Banks and bankers, immigrant

Immigrant fund, 181

Immigrant trains, 446, 468, 470

Immigrants' Commission of Illinois, see Illinois Immigrants' Commission

Immigrants' Protective League of Chicago, x, 100, 298, 464, 468, 481, 597, 608, 616

Immigration cases, court decisions, 252

Immigration law, legal problems of, 252

Immigration laws, see Legislation

Immigration situation, pre-war, 539

Immigration stations, 466

Immorality charges, social case records of, 400, 408

Induced immigration, 201, 205

Industrial accidents, 486, 723; see also Workmen's compensation

Industrial insurance case, 676

Information: Division of, 209, 471, 547; office, national, 64

Inspection: of emigrants in Europe, 71, 72; line inspection at Ellis Island, 244; see also Medical inspection

Inspectors, government, to be on all ships carrying immigrants, 5, 35, 37, 93, 208

Insurance frauds, 593, 594, 765
International Emigration Commission, 69, 79
International Labour Office Reports, 59, 63, 69, 79, 82
Interpreters, 463, 466, 476, 481, 521
Introductory notes, 3, 97, 463
Irish cases, 404, 473
Irish exodus, 4, 31
Irish "fever-ships," 29
Irish immigrants, 4, 10, 17, 19, 20, 21, 31, 33, 34, 37, 39; *see also* Irish cases
Italian cases, 252, 256, 284, 307, 397, 527, 539, 585, 586, 594, 602
Italian Emigration Law, 82
Italians: in agriculture, 546; in labor camps, 485
Italy, emigration regulations and examination, 5, 60, 61, 63, 66, 73, 75, 235

Jewish cases, 299, 319, 342, 355, 363, 365, 367, 368, 427, 452, 484, 527, 619
Jews as farmers, 546
Journey of the immigrant, Part I, 3–93; before 1882, 6–58; in the twentieth century, 59–93; end of, 466; of immigrant girls, 468, 608; to Chicago, 468; to point of final destination, 463, 597, 602
Jugo-Slav case records, 303, 386, 392, 395; *see also* Croatian, Serbian

Labor, methods of securing immigrant, 474; *see also* Employment agencies
Labor agencies, *see* Employment agencies
Labor camps: housing and sanitation, 463, 485, 487, 490; inspection in California, 489; *see also* Construction camps
Land: companies, 533; fraud cases, 533, 536, 591; purchasing by immigrants, 532; transport of emigrants, 69
Laws, *see* Legislation
Lawyers, 524, 592, 593, 676, 685, 759, 764, 773
Legal aid societies, need of, 590
Legislation, *see* Contract-labor legislation; Court decisions; Federal immigration laws; Immigration law; National legislation; Passenger acts; State laws; Steerage legislation
Lewis v. Frick, 270

Line inspection at Ellis Island, 244
"Literacy test," ix, 99, 192, 217; veto messages, 198, 211, 213; *see also* Illiteracy
Lithuanian cases, 375, 444, 527, 529, 585, 655, 718, 760, 765, 780, 787, 797
Liverpool, 29, 38, 76
Lodger, immigrant, 401, 526, 719
Lost-baggage cases, 616
Lost-girl cases, 472, 608
Lumber camps, peonage in, 496

Magyar case, 613; *see also* Hungarians
Manifests, 221, 468, 608
Maryland legislation, 108
Massachusetts Bureau of Immigration, 580
Massachusetts Commission on Immigration, 521, 526, 563
Massachusetts Division of Immigration, 797
Massachusetts: colonial steerage act of 1751, 6; deportation from, 160; Passenger Act of 1837, 147, 154; Pauper laws, 105, 108, 149
Matthews, ex parte, 273
Medical inspections and examinations, 67, 74, 77, 80, 85, 202, 244
Mental examination of arriving aliens, 223, 244
Mentally defective, immigration of, 205; *see also* Feeble-minded
Military-service regulations, European, 59
Mining communities and camps of Illinois, 555
Minors: European emigration regulations concerning, 61; illiterate, in Illinois, 553
Misstatement to inspector, 344
Money sent abroad, 463, 510, 513, 540, 582, 695, 707
Moral dangers, 30, 36, 50, 86, 468, 526, 531; *see also* "White Slavers"
Moral turpitude, crime involving, 261, 342
Moravian case record, 744

National Conference of Immigration, Land, and Labor Officials, 536
National legislation, 79, 176
Naturalization, 209, 230, 333, 451; *see also* Citizenship

SUBJECT INDEX 807

Naturalization classes, 552, 569, 578
"Near East" cases, 352, 451, 454
Netherlands, 80
"New immigration," 197, 233, 239, 539, 542, 544, 547
New Jersey Commission of Immigration, 478, 514, 532
New York City v. *Miln*, 118, 152, 168
New York State: immigrants in, 134, 164, 176, 182; laws, 104, 106, 140, evasion of, 122; U.S. Supreme Court decisions relating to N.Y. laws, 118, 151
New York State Bureau of Immigration, 699, 707
New York State Commission of Immigration, 485
New York State Emigration Commissioners, 4, 42, 98, 140, 144, 164, 172, 177, 182
New York State Legislature, 4, 28, 42
Non-family groups of men, 346, 529
Norris v. *City of Boston*, 147, 154
Norway, emigration regulations, 60
Norwegian cases, *see* Scandinavian
Notaries, public, 463, 514, 676, 690

Ocean voyage in the eighteenth century, 7; *see also* Steerage
"Old immigration," 196, 232, 539, 542
Overcrowding on emigrant ships, 8, 10, 14, 15, 17, 20, 28, 29, 43, 53, 54, 56; *see also* Space required for steerage passengers

Parochial schools, 563
Passaic, N.J., adult education in, 556
Passenger acts, of Congress, 3, 45, 51; of 1882, 53, 56
Passenger acts, state, *see* State passenger acts
Passenger acts and regulations, British, *see* British passenger laws
Passenger brokers, 15, 26, 38, 134
Passenger cases, 98, 147, 151, 168
Passports, 65, 204, 235, 355, 365, 444, 451, 452
Paupers, foreign: admission of, under state laws, 110; burden of, in Massachusetts, 112; "retransportation" of, 157, 162; treatment of, under state laws, 104, 147, 154, 155
Paupers, imported, 127, 128, 147, 154, 157, 178, 182, 206; from England, 21, 110, 111, 112, 113, 117, 118, 184; from Germany, 114, 115, 116, 127, 142, 157; from Ireland, 116, 117, 183
Pauperism, 178, 542
Pennsylvania, legislation, 9, 102
Peonage in relation to immigration, 492; in New England, 495; in the South, 493
Percentage plan, 237; *see also* Quota
Philadelphia, 9, 11
"Philosophic anarchist," 280
Physical defect, 75, 256, 258, 406, 427
Physical examination of arriving aliens, 223, 244
Physician, ship, 28, 29, 44, 45, 71; *see also* Surgeon
Poland, protection of emigrants, 67
Police-control station, Hungary, 74
Polish cases, 298, 300, 332, 344, 345, 347, 399, 469, 470, 471, 473, 485, 527, 529, 586, 609, 610, 611, 616, 618, 622, 650, 690, 695, 708
Polish farmers, 546
Poor laws, 97, 104, 147
Ports of entry, 463, 466
Postal savings banks, 498
Post-office, use in transmitting savings to Europe, 510, 513
Prentis v. *Stathakos*, 261
Prostitutes and prostitution, 208, 216, 220, 270, 373, 400, 408; *see also* "White slavers"
Protection of immigrants: before departure (European), 63; legislation for, 3, 140; on the journey, 3; through a state bureau, 580, 587; *see also* Protective work
Protective societies, 26, 68, 69, 130
Protective work for immigrants, social case records, Part III, Section II, 597-800; *see also* Protection
Public charge, likely to become, 216, 252, 402
Public-charge affidavit, 301
Public defenders, need of, 591
Public health and immigration, 541; *see also* Cholera, Contagious disease

"Quack" doctors, 592, 596
Quarantine Law, United States, 71, 72, 73, 120

"Quota" legislation, ix, 100; Act of 1921-22, 240; criticism of, 242; operation (social case records), 392, 395, 397, 399, 454; quota system recommended, 232

Railroad work, 474, 483, 646; see also Construction camps
Real estate companies, 533, 771
"Redemptioners," 3, 10, 11
Roumanian case records, 372, 384, 604, 621, 627
Russian cases, 254, 270, 346, 348, 377, 400, 447, 471, 528, 586, 618, 624, 652, 664, 673, 685, 712, 715, 719, 723, 725, 745
Ruthenian case records, 607, 698, 699

Savings, 463, 510
Scandinavian case records, 313, 597, 606, 608, 609
Schools, see Bilingual, Evening, Parochial schools; see also Education
Scotch immigrants, 17, 19, 39, 130
Serbs, Croats, and Slovenes, emigration regulations and protection, 61, 63, 68
Servian case, 596; see Jugo-Slav
Ship fever, 8, 17, 20, 22, 23, 28, 29, 34, 40, 42, 135, 167, 172, 173
Shipowners, 14, 18, 38, 46, 55, 57, 134, 177, 181
Ships, emigrant, see Emigrant ships
Shipwrecks, 25, 40
Sickness and Mortality on Board Emigrant ships, Select Committee on, 40
Slovak case records, 310, 610, 676
Smith v. Turner, 151
Social case records, ix, 100, 464, Part II, Section IV, 298-460; Part III, Section II, 597-800
South Carolina, legislation, 103
Space required for steerage passengers, 6, 8, 17, 22, 35, 45, 57, 81; see also Overcrowding on emigrant ships
Spain, emigration regulations, 63
Special inquiry, boards of, see Boards of special inquiry
State immigration bureaus, 464; see also Massachusetts and New York bureaus
State immigration commissions, 464; see also California, Illinois, Massachusetts, New Jersey, New York commissions
State laws: admission of immigrants under, 1788-1882, 97; Part II, Section I, 102-80; 1820-33, 106; evasion of, 122
State passenger acts, 97, 106; first U.S. Supreme Court decision relating to, 118
States, power of, over immigration, 159
Steamship companies, care of emigrants before embarkation, 76, 202; see also Passenger agents and brokers; Shipowners
Steamship-ticket agents, frauds of, 132, 202, 699; see also Passenger agents and brokers
Steamship-ticket purchase, 695, 698, 708, 712
Steerage conditions, 3, 4, 51, 91, 92, 208; attempted regulation of, 1751-1882, 6; in 1873, 48; in 1921, 79; congressional inquiry into, 5, 82, 86; failure of attempts at regulation of, 13-26; older-type steerage, 82
Steerage "horrors," 3, 4; see also Steerage conditions
Steerage, experience of an Englishman in the, 36; of United States investigators, in the steerage, 82, 86
Steerage regulations, 3, 5, 40, 79, 93
Stowaway, 342
Surgeon's certificate of physical defect, 256, 258
Surgeons, ship, 23, 25, 35, 37; see also Physician, ship
Sweden, emigration regulations and protection, 61, 69
Swedish cases, see Scandinavian
Swiss convicts, 128, 184
Swiss immigrants, 14, 539
Swiss regulations, 63
Syrian cases, 352, 586

Taft, President, veto message on literacy test, 211
Tapscott Poor House and Hospital, 136
Third class on steamships, 91
Trachoma, 71, 247, 301, 310, 332, 452
Transport companies, 26
Transportation of immigrants, 3, 4, 26; see also Journey of the immigrant
Turks, 530
Turner v. Williams, 280

SUBJECT INDEX 809

U.S. Bureau of Education, 556, 560
U.S. Bureau of Immigration, Advisory Committee on the Welfare of Immigrants, 466
U.S. court decisions, 100, 118, 252–97
U.S. Immigration Commission, 5, 81, 82, 92, 201, 474, 492, 498, 510, 539
U.S. v. *International Silver Company*, 268
Unmarried man and woman traveling together, 382
Unmarried mother, 528, 718, 719
Unskilled workmen, 195, 210, 475, 481, 540

Wage claims, 581, 585, 593, **633**
Wallis v. *U.S. ex rel. Mannara*, 252
War, deportation stopped by, 323, 406, 408
Ward's Island, 133, 172
Welfare work for immigrants, 466
Wheatland case, 489
"White slavers," 470, 592
Whitfield et al. v. *Hanges et al.*, 275
Wilson, President, veto messages on literacy test, 213
Wisconsin Board of Immigration, 56
Workmen's compensation cases, 585, 723, 725, 745, 752, 760, 789

PRINTED IN THE U.S.A.

428

Augsburg College
George Sverdrup Library
Minneapolis, Minnesota 55404